Compressive Imaging: Structure, Sampling, Learning

Accurate, robust and fast image reconstruction is a critical task in many scientific, industrial and medical applications. Over the last decade, image reconstruction has been revolutionized by the rise of compressive imaging. It has fundamentally changed the way modern image reconstruction is performed. This in-depth treatment of the subject commences with a practical introduction to compressive imaging, supplemented with examples and downloadable code, intended for readers without extensive background in the subject. Next, it introduces core topics in compressive imaging – including compressed sensing, wavelets and optimization – in a concise yet rigorous way, before providing a detailed treatment of the mathematics of compressive imaging. The final part is devoted to the most recent trends in compressive imaging: deep learning and neural networks. This highly timely component provides, for the first time, a readable overview of these nascent topics. With an eye to the next decade of imaging research, and using both empirical and mathematical insights, it examines the potential benefits and the pitfalls of these latest approaches.

Ben Adcock is Associate Professor of Mathematics at Simon Fraser University. He received the CAIMS/PIMS Early Career Award (2017), an Alfred P. Sloan Research Fellowship (2015) and a Leslie Fox Prize in Numerical Analysis (2011). He has published 15 conference proceedings, two book chapters and over 50 peer-reviewed journal articles. His work has been published in outlets such as *SIAM Review* and *Proceedings of the National Academy of Sciences*, and featured on the cover of *SIAM News*.

Anders C. Hansen is Reader in Mathematics at the University of Cambridge and Professor of Mathematics at the University of Oslo. He received the Leverhulme Prize in Mathematics and Statistics (2017), the 2018 IMA Prize in Mathematics and Applications and the Whitehead Prize (2019). He has had papers published in outlets such as the *Journal of the American Mathematical Society* and *Proceedings of the National Academy of Sciences*, and featured on the cover of *Physical Review Letters* and *SIAM News*.

Compressive Imaging: Structure, Sampling, Learning

BEN ADCOCK
Simon Fraser University

ANDERS C. HANSEN
University of Cambridge

with contributions by
VEGARD ANTUN

CAMBRIDGE
UNIVERSITY PRESS

CAMBRIDGE
UNIVERSITY PRESS

University Printing House, Cambridge CB2 8BS, United Kingdom

One Liberty Plaza, 20th Floor, New York, NY 10006, USA

477 Williamstown Road, Port Melbourne, VIC 3207, Australia

314–321, 3rd Floor, Plot 3, Splendor Forum, Jasola District Centre, New Delhi – 110025, India

103 Penang Road, #05-06/07, Visioncrest Commercial, Singapore 238467

Cambridge University Press is part of the University of Cambridge.

It furthers the University's mission by disseminating knowledge in the pursuit of education, learning, and research at the highest international levels of excellence.

www.cambridge.org
Information on this title: www.cambridge.org/9781108421614
DOI: 10.1017/9781108377447

First published 2021

Printed in Singapore by Markono Print Media Pte Ltd

A catalogue record for this publication is available from the British Library.

ISBN 978-1-108-42161-4 Hardback

For

Tina

Gyda, Anna and Christian

Contents

Preface

The objective of *compressive imaging* is to develop algorithms for image reconstruction that exploit the low-dimensional structure inherent to natural images to achieve higher-quality reconstructions from fewer measurements. This structure has been used in *image compression* since the 1990s. But it was not until the 2000s, which saw the advent of the related field of *compressed sensing* – introduced in the work of Candès, Romberg & Tao and Donoho – that it began to be exploited in the context of image reconstruction. Nowadays, compressive imaging is a large and vibrant subject, spanning mathematics, computer science, engineering and physics. It has fundamentally altered how images are reconstructed in a variety of real-world settings. Classical linear reconstruction techniques have in many cases been replaced by sophisticated nonlinear reconstruction procedures based on convex, or sometimes even nonconvex, optimization problems. Practical applications include Magnetic Resonance Imaging (MRI), X-ray Computed Tomography (X-ray CT), electron or fluorescence microscopy, seismic imaging and various optical imaging modalities, to name but a few. The field continues to evolve at a rapid rate, with the most recent trend being the introduction of tools from machine learning, such as deep learning, as means to achieve even further performance gains.

Objectives of this Book

This book is about compressive imaging and its mathematical underpinnings. It is aimed at graduate students, postdoctoral fellows and faculty in mathematics, computer science, engineering and physics who want to learn about modern image reconstruction techniques. Its goal is to span the gap between theory and practice, giving the reader both an overview of the main themes of compressive imaging and an in-depth mathematical analysis. A consistent theme of the book is the insight such mathematical analysis brings, both in designing methods in the first place and then enhancing their practical performance.

The book consists of 22 chapters, plus appendices containing various prerequisite materials. It is divided into five parts. Part I is a practical guide to compressive imaging, supported by many numerical examples and downloadable code. It is intended for readers without extensive background in the subject. Part II systematically introduces the main mathematical tools of compressive imaging, including conventional compressed sensing, convex optimization and wavelets. Parts III and IV are devoted to compressed sensing theory and its application to image reconstruction, respectively. Finally, Part V considers the most recent trends in compressive imaging, namely, deep learning and neural networks. It provides an overview of this nascent topic and includes both mathematical and empirical insights.

This book contains many numerical examples. A companion software library, *CIlib*, has been developed by Vegard Antun (University of Oslo). It contains a broad set of functions and tools for experimenting with various compressive imaging techniques. It is available at

`https://github.com/vegarant/cilib`

or through the book's website:

`www.compressiveimagingbook.com`

This library also includes code for reproducing most of the figures in the book.

Acknowledgements

Many people have contributed substantially to this book. First and foremost, we owe a great debt of gratitude to Vegard Antun. He has produced all the figures in the book and developed the aforementioned software library. He also provided vital input into many parts of this project. Suffice to say, without Vegard this would be a far worse book!

We also gratefully acknowledge the contributions of our (current and former) students and postdocs who have assisted with this project. They have proofread large parts of the manuscript, providing useful suggestions and pointing out both typos and more serious errors. They have also shown great patience during the final stages of its preparation as other projects suffered inevitable delays. They are (in alphabetical order): Edvard Aksnes, Anyi Bao, Alex Bastounis, Randall Bergman, Simone Brugiapaglia, Juan M. Cardenas, Il-Yong Chun, Matthew Colbrook, Nick Dexter, Einar Gabbassov, Milana Gataric, Nina Gottschling, Alex Jones, Matthew King-Roskamp, Chen Li, Zhen Ning David Liu, Mathias Lohne, Kristian Monsen Haug, Sebastian Moraga, Max Neyra-Nesterenko, Clarice Poon, Francesco Renna, Mohsen Seifi, Yi Sui, Laura Thesing and Qinghong Xu.

Many colleagues have also contributed to this book, through collaborating with us, discussing and answering our many questions, and proofreading parts of the manuscript. This long list includes (in alphabetical order): Simon Arridge, Richard Baraniuk, Stephen Becker, Claire Boyer, Robert Calderbank, Emmanuel Candès, Antonin Chambolle, Felipe Cucker, Ingrid Daubechies, Mike Davies, Ron DeVore, David Donoho, Yonina Eldar, Jalal Fadili, Alhussein Fawzi, Hamza Fawzi, Omar Fawzi, Jeffrey Fessler, Simon Foucart, Michael Friedlander, Pascal Frossard, Anne Gelb, Rémi Gribonval, Karlheinz Gröchenig, David Gross, Nick Higham, Bamdad Hosseini, Arieh Iserles, Mark Iwen, Laurent Jacques, Jakob Sauer Jørgensen, Felix Krahmer, Richard Kueng, Gitta Kutyniok, Bradley Lucier, Jackie Ma, Dustin Mixon, Mohsen Moosavi-Dezfooli, Amirafshar Moshtaghpour, Adrian Nachman, Arkadi Nemirovski, Nilima Nigam, Ozan Öktem, Hooman Owhadi, Gabriel Peyré, Yaniv Plan, Rodrigo Platte, Bogdan Roman, Justin Romberg, Øyvind Ryan, Rayan Saab, Carola Schönlieb, Thomas Strohmer, Andrew Stuart, Joel

Tropp, Michael Unser, Mihaela van der Schaar, Martin Vetterli, Verner Vlačić, Felix Voigtlaender, Michael Wakin, Rachel Ward, Clayton Webster, Pierre Weiss and Ozgur Yilmaz. We extend our thanks to all of them and to anyone whose name we have accidentally left off this list.

Several images were provided to the authors for use in the numerical experiments. We thank Elizabeth Sawchuk (and Bear) for the 'dog' image, Vegard Antun for the 'klubbe' and 'kopp' images, Andy Ellison for the 'pomegranate' image and GE Electric Healthcare for the 'brain' image. See Fig. 2.2. We also thank Dr. Cynthia McCollough, the Mayo Clinic, the American Association of Physicists in Medicine and the National Institute of Biomedical Imaging and Bioengineering for allowing the use of their data in the experiments shown in Figs 20.4 and 20.10. Table 18.1 and Figs 18.5 and 18.8 are from [359]. We thank the authors, Seyed-Mohsen Moosavi-Dezfooli, Alhussein Fawzi, Omar Fawzi and Pascal Frossard, for allowing us to reproduce them. The deep learning experiments in Chapters 19 and 20 were first produced in [36]. We thank the authors of [253, 278, 427, 512, 527] for sharing their code, data and network weights, and thereby allowing us to reproduce their networks and experiments. We also thank Kristian Monsen Haug for his assistance with Fig. 21.1.

Both authors would like to acknowledge their respective institutions for their support: Purdue University, Simon Fraser University, University of Cambridge and University of Oslo. BA also wishes to thank the Isaac Newton Institute for several productive visits. BA acknowledges support from an Alfred P. Sloan Research Fellowship, NSERC (the Natural Sciences and Engineering Research Council of Canada) through grant 611675, NSF (the National Science Foundation) through grant DMS-1318894, PIMS (the Pacific Institute for the Mathematical Sciences) through the Collaborative Research Group 'High-dimensional Data Analysis' and SFU's Big Data Initiative through the 'Next Big Question Fund'. ACH acknowledges support from a Royal Society University Research Fellowship, EPSRC (the Engineering and Physical Sciences Research Council) through grant EP/L003457/1 and the 2017 Leverhulme Prize. We also acknowledge Cambridge University Press and, in particular, our editor David Tranah, who has been an invaluable source of guidance while writing this manuscript. Lastly, we thank our respective families for their continued love and support throughout this project.

Burnaby, BC, Canada | Ben Adcock
Cambridge, UK | Anders C. Hansen
August 2020

1 Introduction

Images are everywhere. Whether on a social media page, a doctor's desk to aid diagnosis or a scientist's computer screen to help study a chemical, physical or biological process, the modern world is awash with digital images.

All images are produced by acquiring measurements using a physical device. The list of different acquisition devices is long and varied. It includes simple devices found in most homes, such as digital cameras; specialist medical imaging equipment found in hospitals, such as a Magnetic Resonance Imaging (MRI) or X-ray Computed Tomography (CT) scanner; or scientific devices, such as electron microscopes, found in laboratories.

The concern of this book is the task of image *reconstruction*. This is the algorithmic process of converting the raw data (the measurements) into the final image seen by the end user. The overarching aim of image reconstruction is to achieve the four following, and competing, objectives:

> **Objective #1 (accuracy):** to produce the highest-quality images.

Accuracy is of course paramount. High-quality images are desirable in virtually all applications. However, in direct competition with this is:

> **Objective #2 (sampling):** to use as few measurements as possible.

Acquiring more measurements usually comes at a cost. It could mean an additional outlay of time, power, monetary expense or risk, depending on the application at hand. Reducing the number of measurements is often the primary goal of image reconstruction. For example, in MRI, taking more measurements involves a longer scan time, which can be unpleasant and challenging for the patient – especially in paediatric MRI. It also makes the measurements acquired more susceptible to corruptions due, for instance, to patient motion. In X-ray CT, the number of measurements loosely corresponds to the amount of radiation to which the patient is exposed. Acquiring fewer measurements per scan opens the door for more frequent scans, which in turn allows for more effective treatment monitoring.

> **Objective #3 (stability):** to ensure that errors in the measurements or in the numerical computation do not significantly impact the quality of the recovered image.

All imaging systems introduce error in the measurements, due to noise, corruptions or modelling assumptions. There are also round-off errors in the numerical computations performed by image reconstruction algorithms. It is vital that reconstruction algorithms be robust to such perturbations, so that small errors do not have a deleterious effect on the output image.

Objective #4 (efficiency): to recover the image in reasonable computing time without significant computing power and memory.

In many applications, images need to be reconstructed rapidly. After all, a doctor does not want to wait a long time for an image to be generated after a scan has concluded. In other imaging systems, notably portable systems, computing resources may be severely limited. Since modern images are often comprised of tens of millions of pixels, practical image reconstruction algorithms must have the ability to scale to large problem sizes without suffering a blow-up in computing time or memory requirements.

1.1 Imaging and Inverse Problems

Mathematically, the simplest way to model an image reconstruction problem is as the following discrete, linear inverse problem:

$$\text{Given the measurements } y = Ax + e, \text{ recover } x. \tag{1.1}$$

Here $y \in \mathbb{C}^m$ is the vector of *measurements* produced by the sensing device, $A \in \mathbb{C}^{m \times N}$ is the *measurement matrix* representing the acquisition process, $e \in \mathbb{C}^m$ is a vector of measurement noise and $x \in \mathbb{C}^N$ is the (vectorized version of the) unknown image to be recovered. The integer m is the number of measurements, and N is the number of pixels in the image. Designing an image reconstruction procedure means constructing a *reconstruction map*

$$\mathrm{R} \colon \mathbb{C}^m \to \mathbb{C}^N, \tag{1.2}$$

that takes input y and outputs an approximation $\mathrm{R}(y)$ to the true image x.

It is important to note that (1.1) is derived through mathematical modelling of the sensing device, a process which usually involves a series of assumptions. While a finite-dimensional, linear model such as (1.1) may be appealing in its simplicity, it may result in *mismatch* between the model and the true physics, which in turn may lead to additional errors in the reconstruction. One common error of this type arises from *discretization*: the conversion of a continuous problem into a discrete one such as (1.1). To avoid subsequent errors in the reconstruction, it may be beneficial to consider an infinite-dimensional model:

$$\text{Given the measurements } y = \mathcal{A}f + e, \text{ recover } f. \tag{1.3}$$

Here $f \colon [0,1]^d \to \mathbb{C}$ is a function representing the image, $\mathcal{A}$ is a linear operator representing the acquisition process, $y \in \mathbb{C}^m$ is the vector of measurements and $e \in \mathbb{C}^m$ is measurement noise, as before. Of course, there may well be other modelling issues beyond discretization. The sensing process could be nonlinear, for example, in which case (1.3) will still result in model mismatch.

1.2 What is Compressive Imaging?

For the sake of simplicity, consider the discrete problem (1.1). If $m = N$ and A is invertible, then reconstructing x is, in principle, straightforward. In the absence of noise, we simply solve the linear system $Ax = y$. However, this situation is rare in practice. Because of Objective #2, it is often the case that the number of measurements m is much smaller than the problem size N. This renders the linear system highly *underdetermined*, making *exact* recovery of x from y generally impossible.

The classical way to *approximately* recover x is to apply a left inverse of A to y: for example, its pseudoinverse $A^{\dagger}$. This is a simple, linear recovery procedure (the map $\mathrm{R}: y \mapsto A^{\dagger}y$ is a linear map) that is often computationally efficient and robust. It also has a simple interpretation: the computed image $\hat{x} = A^{\dagger}y$ has the smallest ℓ^2-norm amongst all those that fit measurements. Unfortunately, this process generally leads to low-quality reconstructions. Figure 1.1(c) illustrates this phenomenon for a synthetic MRI experiment involving the classical Shepp–Logan phantom. The recovered image is a poor reconstruction of the original image. As we observe, it exhibits substantial *artefacts*.

What to do? The way forward is to realize that images are not just arbitrary arrays of pixels: they have characteristic features such as edges and textures. Mathematically, this means that natural images can be modelled as objects in low-dimensional, nonlinear spaces embedded in the high-dimensional vector space $\mathbb{C}^N$. This on its own is by no means a new concept. It lies at the heart of modern lossy image compression standards such as JPEG-2000 and MPEG. Yet it was not until the mid-2000s that researchers began to develop mathematical tools for exploiting such structure in the context of solving image reconstruction problems such as (1.1). This has led to a topic in its own right, termed *compressed sensing* (also known as *compressive sensing*, *compressed sampling* or *compressive sampling*), with applications not only in imaging but also many other problems in computational science and engineering.

This brings us to the topic of this book.

> This book is about *compressive imaging*: the development, analysis and application of sampling strategies and (nonlinear) reconstruction procedures that exploit the low-dimensional structure of images to achieve substantially better image recovery than with classical techniques.

The growth of compressive imaging has wrought a profound change on practical image reconstruction over the past decade. In many applications, not least MRI, classical linear recovery procedures have been replaced by a new generation of techniques.

It is not hard to see why. Figure 1.1(d) shows what happens when the procedure used in Fig. 1.1(c) is replaced by a compressive imaging procedure based on compressed sensing. Both procedures use exactly the same data, and in particular, the same number of measurements. Yet the compressed sensing recovery is significantly better. It has none of the artefacts that plagued the classical reconstruction and appears to reconstruct the image perfectly – at least to the human eye.

The purpose of this book is to explain how compressive imaging makes this possible. It aims to describe how Fig. 1.1(d) was computed, why it offers such a significant

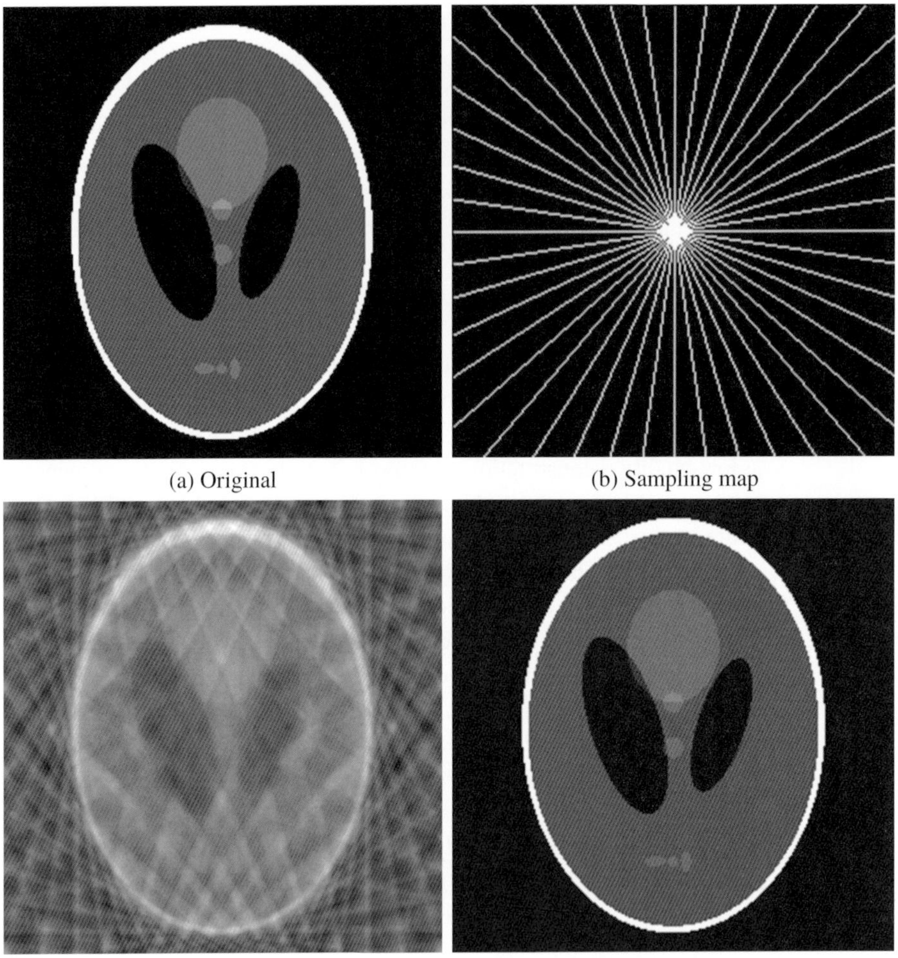

(a) Original
(b) Sampling map
(c) Classical recovery
(d) Compressed sensing recovery

Figure 1.1 Reconstruction of the Shepp–Logan phantom image from discrete Fourier measurements. (a) Original image of size $256 \times 256 = 65,536$. (b) Sampling map in frequency space with $m = 5481$. Each white dot represents a frequency sampled. (c) Classical reconstruction using the zero-padded inverse DFT (this is equivalent to $A^{\dagger}$). (d) Compressed sensing reconstruction using TV minimization.

improvement over Fig. 1.1(c) and how performance, in the sense of Objectives #1–#4, can be even further improved.

Key Point #1. Image reconstruction has been revolutionized in the last decade by the emergence of compressive imaging in tandem with compressed sensing.

Remark 1.1 Figure 1.1 has an important historical context. It replicates an experiment performed by Candès, Romberg & Tao in their seminal 2006 paper that introduced compressed sensing in tandem with the work of Donoho. The impact that this dramatic proof-of-concept experiment had on the imaging community is hard to overstate.

1.3 Terminology

In the remainder of this chapter, we discuss some of the main themes arising in this book. But, first, a word on terminology. Compressive imaging and compressed sensing are not synonymous. The latter is a mathematical theory for exploiting low-dimensional structures in abstract problems of the form (1.1), i.e. where x need not be an image and A need not arise from an imaging device. Unsurprisingly, the former deals exclusively with imaging. However, compressive imaging arguably owes its existence to the latter, imaging being both a primary motivation for much of compressed sensing research (see Remark 1.1) and one of the areas where it has been most successfully applied.

Yet compressive imaging is also not limited to compressed sensing techniques. Nowadays, it is beginning to see the increasing use of tools from machine learning, such as neural networks and deep learning. Part V of this book considers these approaches. Although closely related, they are not compressed sensing approaches per se.

Compressive imaging can also be seen as a subset of the larger, and rather older, field of *computational imaging*. Here the general goal is to enhance image quality through the design of better reconstruction algorithms and the availability of more powerful computing resources, rather than through hardware improvements in the sensor itself – the latter being ever increasingly harder to achieve due to physical limits.

1.4 Imaging Modalities

In order to exhibit some of the main aspects of the book, we now describe some of the different sampling processes that arise in typical imaging problems.

1.4.1 Integral Transforms

Measurements of an image are often acquired by sampling with an integral transform. The Fourier transform is an important example of this process. If f is a function representing a continuous image, then its Fourier transform is defined by

$$\mathcal{F} f(\omega) = \int_{\mathbb{R}^d} f(x) \mathrm{e}^{-\mathrm{i}\omega \cdot x} \, \mathrm{d}x, \qquad \omega \in \mathbb{R}^d.$$

In *Fourier imaging* the (noiseless) measurements $y \in \mathbb{C}^m$ correspond to samples

$$\{\mathcal{F} f(2\pi\omega) : \omega \in \Omega\}$$

of $\mathcal{F} f$ at a set of m frequencies $\Omega = \{\omega_1, \ldots, \omega_m\} \subset \mathbb{R}^d$. MRI is an important example of Fourier imaging.

The Radon transform is another key integral transform found in imaging. It models the acquisition process in *tomographic* modalities such as X-ray CT. Here the measurements correspond to line integrals through the object being scanned.

It is important to note that the integral transform in a given problem is generally fixed. The acquisition process in MRI is modelled by the Fourier transform; in CT it is modelled by the Radon transform. Neither can be easily changed. However, there may be substantial freedom to choose the samples themselves, i.e. the set of frequencies Ω in Fourier imaging. Hence a key challenge in imaging with integral transforms is to understand how the choice of Ω affects the recovery of f, and then to use this insight to design sets Ω that lead to the highest-quality reconstructions.

Key Point #2. Many imaging modalities involve sampling via an integral transform. An important challenge is determining values at which the integral transform should be sampled so as to produce the best reconstructions.

Since this is also an inherently infinite-dimensional problem, a second challenge is to devise suitable discretizations to render the problem amenable to computations.

1.4.2 Binary Sampling

Binary sampling occurs when an image is measured by taking inner products with a function or vector that takes values in $\{+1, -1\}$. In the discrete setting (1.1), a single, noiseless measurement of the image $x = (x_j)_{j=1}^N \in \mathbb{C}^N$ takes the form

$$\langle x, a \rangle = \sum_{j=1}^{N} x_j a_j, \qquad a = (a_j)_{j=1}^N \in \{-1, +1\}^N. \tag{1.4}$$

After repeating this process m times, one obtains a collection of measurements

$$\langle x, a_1 \rangle, \ldots, \langle x, a_m \rangle,$$

and a binary measurement matrix $A \in \{+1, -1\}^{m \times N}$ in which the ith row is the ith binary measurement vector $a_i \in \{-1, 1\}^N$.

Binary sampling arises in many *optical imaging* applications. Examples include lensless imaging and the so-called single-pixel camera, as well as fluorescence microscopy and numerous others. Usually in these applications a mask is placed in front of the object to be imaged. This selectively illuminates and obscures different pixels, thus effecting a binary measurement of the image. Because of this setup, there is often significant freedom to *design* the measurement vectors $a_1, \ldots, a_m$ to maximize the quality of the reconstructed images.

Key Point #3. Many optical imaging modalities involve binary sampling. This often affords significantly more flexibility than imaging with integral transforms in terms of the choice of measurements. In the discrete setting, choosing which measurements to acquire is equivalent to choosing the whole binary measurement matrix A.

1.4.3 Sampling with Orthonormal Vectors

Many discrete imaging problems can be cast as sampling an image $x \in \mathbb{C}^N$ by taking inner products with respect to an orthonormal basis $\{u_i\}_{i=1}^N \subset \mathbb{C}^N$. If $\Omega = \{i_1, \ldots, i_m\} \subseteq \{1, \ldots, N\}$ is a set of size $|\Omega| = m$, then the noiseless measurements in this case take the form

$$y = (y_j)_{j=1}^m, \qquad y_j = \langle x, u_{i_j} \rangle. \tag{1.5}$$

Let $U = (u_1 | \cdots | u_N) \in \mathbb{C}^{N \times N}$ be the matrix whose ith column is the ith vector u_i. This matrix is unitary, $U^*U = I$, since $\{u_i\}_{i=1}^N$ is an orthonormal basis. The measurement matrix A corresponding to (1.5) is known as a *subsampled unitary matrix*. It is constructed by selecting the rows of U^* corresponding to the indices in Ω.

Sampling with orthonormal vectors arises in standard discrete formulations of Fourier imaging problems, in which case $U^* = F$ is the *Fourier matrix*. This type of discretization is highly convenient. Matrix–vector multiplications with F are equivalent to *Discrete Fourier Transforms (DFTs)*, which can be implemented efficiently with *Fast Fourier Transforms (FFTs)*. Sampling with orthonormal vectors is also useful in binary imaging. In this case, $U^* = H$ might be chosen as the *Hadamard* matrix – the binary analogue of the Fourier matrix F – which can be implemented efficiently via the *Discrete Walsh–Hadamard Transform (DHT)* and its associated fast transform.

As with integral transforms, a key issue when sampling with orthonormal vectors is how to choose the sampling vectors, or equivalently, the index set Ω. A secondary issue is how well this discrete setup models the true acquisition process, and what effect any possible model mismatch may have on the resulting reconstruction.

1.5 Conventional Compressed Sensing

Since it lies at the heart of compressive imaging, in this section we briefly depart from the world of imaging to introduce some of the main facets of standard compressed sensing theory. A more thorough treatment is given in Chapter 5.

1.5.1 Sparsity and Compressibility

As noted, compressed sensing aims to solve the reconstruction problem (1.1) in an abstract sense, where $x \in \mathbb{C}^N$ is a vector and $A \in \mathbb{C}^{m \times N}$ is a matrix, neither of which may be strictly related to an imaging problem.

Standard compressed sensing is based on the *sparsity model*. Specifically, we assume that there is a fixed orthonormal basis $\{\phi_i\}_{i=1}^N \subset \mathbb{C}^N$ such that

$$x = \sum_{i=1}^{N} d_i \phi_i, \tag{1.6}$$

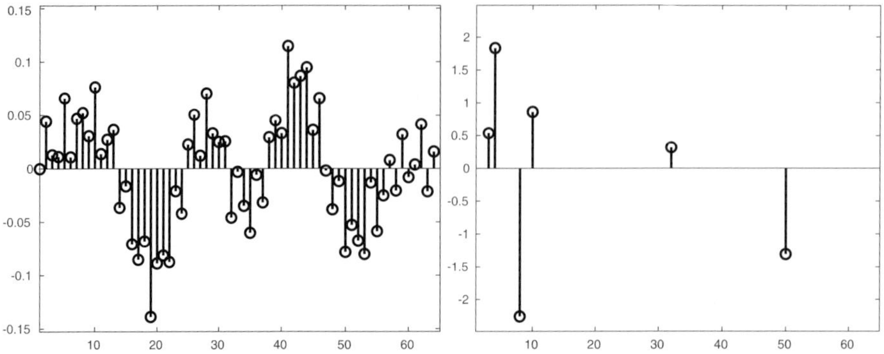

Figure 1.2 Left: Discrete signal $x \in \mathbb{R}^{64}$. Right: The 6-sparse vector of coefficients $d = \Phi^* x \in \mathbb{R}^{64}$, where Φ is a DCT.

where the vector of *coefficients* $d = (d_i)_{i=1}^N$ has only s nonzero entries for some number $s \ll N$. This number is known as the *sparsity* of d, and d is said to be *s-sparse*. The vector x is said to have an *s-sparse representation* in the basis $\{\phi_i\}_{i=1}^N$.

Observe that the set of s-sparse vectors does not constitute a subspace of $\mathbb{C}^N$. Adding two s-sparse vectors produces a vector that may be at most $2s$-sparse. In fact, this set is a union of s-dimensional subspaces of $\mathbb{C}^N$. Sparsity is therefore a type of nonlinear, low-dimensional structure.

Let $\Phi = (\phi_1 | \cdots | \phi_N) \in \mathbb{C}^{N \times N}$ be the unitary matrix corresponding to the basis $\{\phi_i\}_{i=1}^N$. Then (1.6) is equivalent to the expression $x = \Phi d$. Since Φ is unitary we also have $d = \Phi^* x$. We commonly refer to $\{\phi_i\}_{i=1}^N$ as the *sparsity basis* and Φ as the *sparsifying transform*. The latter highlights the fact that applying Φ^* to x yields the sparse vector d.

Note that Φ could be the identity matrix, in which case the vector x is itself s-sparse. This is relatively uncommon in imaging applications. Typical examples in imaging include the *Discrete Cosine Transform (DCT)* and *Discrete Wavelet Transform (DWT)*. Figure 1.2 illustrates a vector that is 6-sparse with respect to the DCT sparsifying transform.

Unfortunately, real-world objects such as images are never exactly sparse. However, they are typically *compressible*, or *approximately sparse*. This means that their coefficients $d = \Phi^* x$ can be accurately approximated by an s-sparse vector for some $s \ll N$. Figure 1.3 demonstrates this property when the DWT is applied to a natural image. In this case, 95% of its coefficients can be discarded, and the resulting sparse image is indistinguishable from the original – at least to the human eye.

Key Point #4. Conventional compressed sensing concerns the recovery of vectors that are approximately sparse in a fixed orthogonal sparsifying transform.

Remark 1.2 Sparsity and compressibility predate compressed sensing. Notably, they lie at the heart of modern lossy image compression algorithms such as JPEG-2000 and MPEG. In lossy compression, the coefficients $d = \Phi^* x$ of an image x are first computed by applying Φ^*, then all but the largest s (in absolute value) are set to zero. This yields an s-sparse vector $\tilde{d}$ that can be stored more efficiently. The number s can be viewed as the

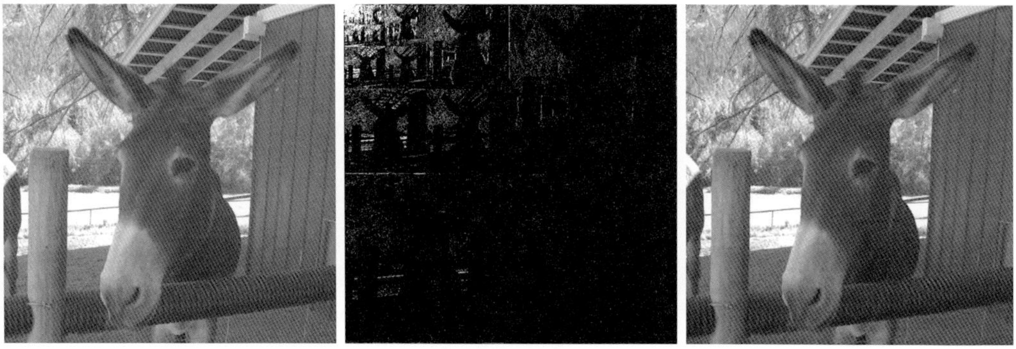

(a) Original (b) Wavelet coefficients (c) Compressed

Figure 1.3 (a) Original image x. (b) Its wavelet coefficients $d = \Phi^* x$. Light values correspond to large coefficients and dark values to small coefficients. (c) Compressed image $\tilde{x} = \Phi \tilde{d}$, where 95% of the wavelet coefficients have been set to zero.

compression factor: if s is small, storing the s coefficients and their locations requires significantly less memory than storing the full array of N coefficients. When the image is needed, one simply applies Φ to $\tilde{d}$ to obtain an approximation $\tilde{x} = \Phi \tilde{d}$ to x. Figure 1.3 shows an example of this process.

1.5.2 Recovery

Suppose x is compressible in a fixed sparsifying transform Φ. We now aim to use this information to recover accurately (Objective #1) and stably (Objective #3) from its noisy measurements

$$y = Ax + e. \tag{1.7}$$

Clearly, we lose all hope of high-quality recovery if the noise e is too large. Hence we now assume that e is bounded, and that its energy

$$\|e\|_{\ell^2} \leq \eta, \tag{1.8}$$

for some known and small $\eta \geq 0$. Note that other noise models are also possible – for instance, assuming that e follows some specific distribution – but (1.8) is typically most common in compressed sensing.

Consider (1.7). The question is how to exploit the compressibility of x in order to effect a good reconstruction. While numerous approaches have been proposed, arguably the most popular involves solving a convex optimization problem that minimizes the ℓ^1-norm of the coefficients $\Phi^* x$. A common example is *Quadratically Constrained Basis Pursuit (QCBP)*. This takes the form

$$\min_{z \in \mathbb{C}^N} \|\Phi^* z\|_{\ell^1} \text{ subject to } \|Az - y\|_{\ell^2} \leq \eta. \tag{1.9}$$

In other words, it finds a vector $\hat{x}$ for which the coefficients $\Phi^* \hat{x}$ have the smallest ℓ^1-norm amongst all vectors that fit the measurements up to the noise bound η. The choice of the ℓ^1-norm here is crucial. For reasons that are discussed in more detail in Chapter 5, the ℓ^1-norm *promotes* sparsity of x in the sparsifying transform Φ. It also renders the QCBP problem convex, thus making it amenable to efficient algorithms.

However, (1.9) is by no means the only possible approach, even within the realm of convex optimization-based approaches. Another common choice is the *Least Absolute Shrinkage and Selection Operator (LASSO)*. This is the unconstrained problem

$$\min_{z \in \mathbb{C}^N} \lambda \|\Phi^* z\|_{\ell^1} + \|Az - y\|_{\ell^2}^2. \tag{1.10}$$

Here, the term $\|Az - y\|_{\ell^2}^2$ promotes good fitting of the data and the term $\|\Phi^* z\|_{\ell^1}$ promotes sparsity. These two terms are balanced via a positive parameter $\lambda > 0$, the optimal choice of which, unsurprisingly, depends on the sparsity s and the noise level η. Note that (1.10) is the so-called *unconstrained* LASSO; we often write U-LASSO for clarity. We discuss the constrained version, the C-LASSO, in Chapter 6.

1.5.3 Stable and Accurate Recovery

Having chosen a sparsifying transform and recovery procedure, we now return to Objectives #1 and #2, as well as #3. These can be posed as the following question. How many measurements, and of what type, are sufficient for accurate and stable recovery of x through, for instance, the QCBP problem (1.9)? This is, in essence, the main question compressed sensing theory seeks to answer.

It does this by devising conditions on the measurement matrix A which are sufficient for recovery. There are various different conditions, several others of which we review in Chapter 5, but arguably the most well known is the *Restricted Isometry Property (RIP)*. A matrix $A \in \mathbb{C}^{m \times N}$ satisfies the RIP of order s if there is a constant $0 < \delta < 1$ such that

$$(1 - \delta)\|x\|_{\ell^2}^2 \leq \|Ax\|_{\ell^2}^2 \leq (1 + \delta)\|x\|_{\ell^2}^2,$$

for every s-sparse vector x. In other words, the *energy* of an s-sparse vector is approximately preserved via the measurement process $x \mapsto Ax$.

As we see in Chapter 5, the RIP is sufficient for stable and accurate recovery. An important result in compressed sensing states the following. Suppose the product $A\Phi \in \mathbb{C}^{m \times N}$ has the RIP of order $2s$ for sufficiently small constant δ. Then for all measurements of the form $y = Ax + e$ with $\|e\|_{\ell^2} \leq \eta$, every minimizer $\hat{x}$ of (1.9) satisfies the error bound

$$\|\hat{x} - x\|_{\ell^2} \lesssim CS_s(x, \eta), \qquad CS_s(x, \eta) = \frac{\sigma_s(\Phi^* x)_{\ell^1}}{\sqrt{s}} + \eta. \tag{1.11}$$

Here $\sigma_s(\cdot)_{\ell^1}$ is the *ℓ^1-norm best s-term approximation error*, defined by

$$\sigma_s(d)_{\ell^1} = \min\{\|z - d\|_{\ell^1} : z \text{ is } s\text{-sparse}\}.$$

In other words, $\sigma_s(\Phi^* x)_{\ell^1}$ measures how compressible x is in the sparsity basis Φ. Note that $\sigma_s(\Phi^* x)_{\ell^1} = 0$ if x happens to be exactly s-sparse in Φ.

We refer to (1.11) as a compressed sensing *error bound*, and the statement 'the RIP implies (1.11)' as a *recovery guarantee*. Crucially, it asserts accurate and stable recovery of x via QCBP. Accuracy is measured in terms of the best s-term approximation error $\sigma_s(\Phi^* x)_{\ell^1}$ and stability in terms of the noise bound η. In the idealized case where x is exactly s-sparse in Φ and the measurements are noiseless (i.e. $\eta = 0$), the bound (1.11) asserts that x is recovered *exactly*.

1.5.4 Measurement Matrices

The previous result leads naturally to the question of finding matrices that satisfy the RIP. Identifying explicit classes of matrices that have this property is a focal point of compressed sensing theory.

A *Gaussian random matrix* is a matrix whose entries are independent, normal random variables with mean zero and variance one. Such matrices have a prominent place in the compressed sensing canon, due to their particularly elegant theoretical properties. A celebrated result is that if Φ is any unitary matrix and $A = m^{-1/2}\tilde{A}$, where $\tilde{A}$ is a Gaussian random matrix, then $A\Phi$ satisfies the RIP with high probability, provided

$$m \gtrsim s \cdot \log(\mathrm{e}N/s). \tag{1.12}$$

The same result also holds if $\tilde{A}$ is replaced by a *Bernoulli random matrix* – that is, a matrix whose entries are independent random variables taking the values $+1$ and -1 with equal probability.

This result exemplifies the substantial potential of compressed sensing. It states that there are choices of measurements for which, according to (1.12), *all* vectors that are approximately s-sparse in a fixed, but arbitrary orthonormal sparsifying transform can be recovered using a number of measurements that scales linearly in s, and logarithmically in the ambient dimension N. Since $s \ll N$ in practice (recall Fig. 1.3), this represents a substantial saving over what one might classically think was needed, namely $m = N$, which of course is necessary for invertibility of A. In fact, (1.12) is *optimal* up to the constant: it is impossible, regardless of the type of matrix A and the reconstruction procedure used, to recover s-sparse vectors stably from asymptotically fewer than $s \cdot \log(\mathrm{e}N/s)$ measurements.

Key Point #5. Gaussian or Bernoulli random matrices are theoretically optimal for stable recovery of s-sparse vectors, regardless of orthonormal sparsity basis.

However, while theoretically elegant, these matrices are generally impractical for imaging problems. They are dense and unstructured, thus computationally infeasible at large scale (recall Objective #4). Perhaps surprisingly, they also offer relatively poor performance in practical imaging problems, despite being theoretically optimal for the recovery of sparse vectors. We will explain this seeming contradiction in §1.6.

Remark 1.3 Randomness is a crucial component in constructing matrices that satisfy the RIP. All constructions we see in this book involve some form of randomness, although typically less than in the case of the Gaussian random matrix, wherein each entry is an independent random variable. Despite significant research, practical constructions of deterministic matrices satisfying the RIP have remained elusive.

1.5.5 Algorithms for Compressed Sensing

We are now nearly ready to return to the problem of image reconstruction. However, before we do so, the reader will have noticed that there is one ingredient lacking. The QCBP or LASSO problem (1.9) or (1.10) defines a reconstruction map $\mathrm{R}: \mathbb{C}^m \to \mathbb{C}^N$, $y \mapsto \hat{x}$, where $\hat{x}$ is a minimizer of the corresponding problem.[1] This is not an algorithm. To actually compute $\mathrm{R}(y)$ for a given y, we need methods that solve these optimization problems up to some tolerance in finitely many arithmetic operations. Moreover, the resulting algorithms should be efficient and scalable to large problems (Objective #4). This is the topic of Chapter 7.

Interestingly, but also surprisingly, problems such as (1.9) are generally *uncomputable*. For certain classes of inputs (A, y), no algorithm can compute a minimizer of (1.9) to arbitrary accuracy in finitely many arithmetic operations. This is in stark contrast to many classical image reconstruction techniques.

Is compressed sensing therefore doomed to failure? Is it merely an elegant theoretical idea that fails to translate to the murky world of real computations? Fortunately, the answer is no. But the reason is rather subtle. While minimizers are not computable to arbitrary accuracy, they are computable to the accuracy needed – namely, the error term $CS_s(x, \eta)$ in (1.11). Moreover, this accuracy can be achieved with efficient first-order optimization algorithms capable of handling large-scale imaging problems. Chapter 8 considers this issue.

Key Point #6. Compressed sensing succeeds in practice because minimizers of problems such as QCBP, while generally uncomputable to arbitrary accuracy, are computable up to the accuracy needed. Moreover, this can be done efficiently.

1.6 Imaging with Compressed Sensing

We are now ready to make an initial foray into the application of compressed sensing to imaging. We do this through a series of examples.

1.6.1 Binary Imaging

Consider a discrete binary imaging problem. As described in §1.4.2, this can be modelled by the equation $y = Ax$, where $A \in \{+1, -1\}^{m \times N}$ is a binary matrix that can often be chosen arbitrarily (Key Point #3). Computational concerns aside, conventional compressed sensing suggests that we should take A as a Bernoulli random matrix. After all, this is optimal for the recovery of s-sparse vectors (Key Point #5). Figure 1.4(a) shows the recovery of an image from these measurements. So-called DB4 wavelets are used as the sparsifying transform (these are introduced formally in Chapter 9; see Remark 9.17 therein). The reconstruction is based on the QCBP problem (1.9).

[1] Such a minimizer may not be unique. Hence R is generally a multivalued map. Fortunately, this technicality does not cause an issue, since the error bound (1.11) is guaranteed to hold for *all* minimizers.

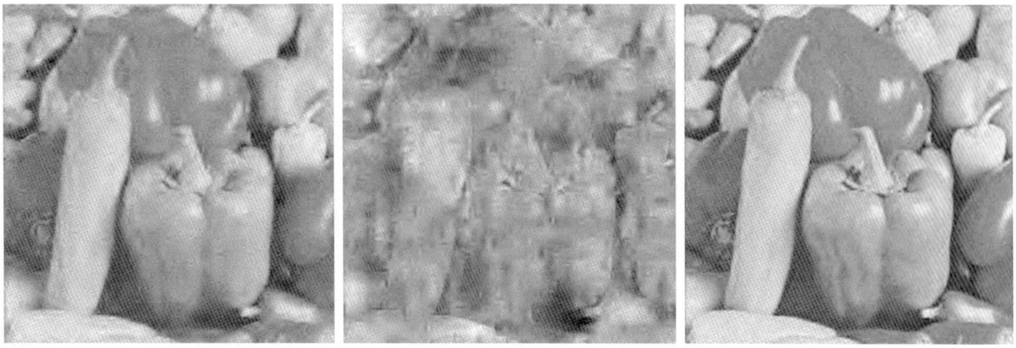

(a) Bernoulli (b) Walsh, uniform random (c) Walsh, variable density

Figure 1.4 Reconstructions from 20% measurements for a 256×256 image (i.e. $m = 0.2 \times 256^2 = 13,107$). (a) Random Bernoulli measurements. (b) Walsh measurements with uniform random sampling. (c) Walsh measurements with variable-density sampling. Figure 1.5 shows the sampling patterns used in (b) and (c).

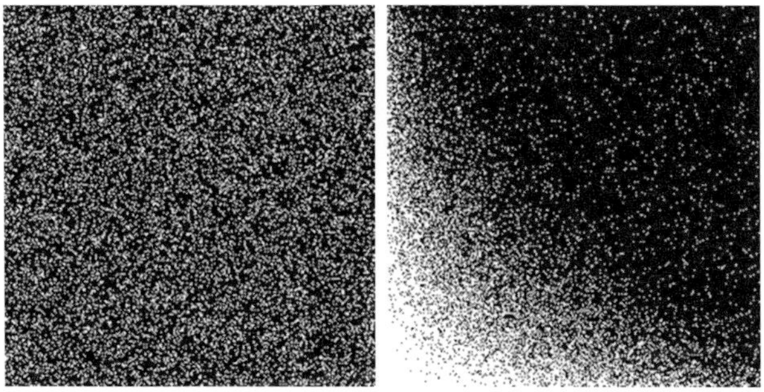

Uniform random Variable density

Figure 1.5 The Walsh sampling strategies used in Fig. 1.4(b,c). Each white dot represents a (Walsh) frequency sampled. The zero frequency is located in the bottom left corner.

On the other hand, suppose we consider the approach discussed in §1.4.3 and form A by selecting m rows of the $N \times N$ Hadamard matrix H. Because it has an associated fast transform, this is a better candidate for large-scale problems. This begs the question: which rows should we choose? Given our previous statement about randomness (Remark 1.3), a natural first choice is to select m rows uniformly at random – a strategy known as *uniform random sampling*. Figure 1.4(b) shows the reconstruction that results from these measurements. Unfortunately, the recovery quality is terrible!

Uniform random sampling is clearly a poor *sampling strategy* for Walsh measurements. Is there a better choice? It turns out that there is. The Walsh–Hadamard transform is a binary analogue of the Fourier transform. Therefore, much like with the Fourier matrix, the rows of the Hadamard matrix correspond to certain (Walsh) frequencies. Images tend to have more energy at low frequencies. Hence it makes sense to sample the low frequencies more densely and the high frequencies less densely. This is known as a *variable-density* sampling strategy. In Fig. 1.4(c) we do exactly that, with the strategy used being shown in Fig. 1.5. The improvement over uniform random sampling is dramatic. While the reconstruction shown in Fig. 1.4(b) is heavily polluted by artefacts, the reconstruction in Fig. 1.4(c) accurately recovers all the key image features.

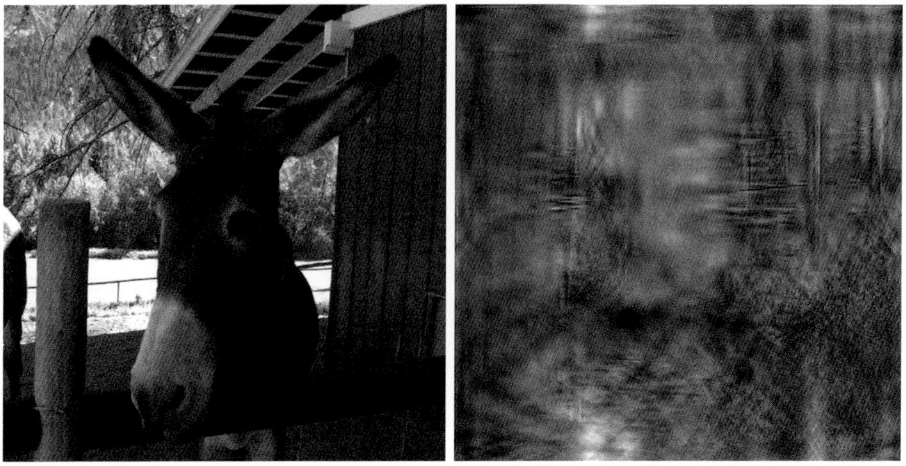

Figure 1.6 Left: A 768×768 image x which is s-sparse in the DB4 wavelet basis with $s = 58,982$. Right: The image $\tilde{x} = \Phi P \Phi^* x$ formed after a random permutation P of its wavelet coefficients $d = \Phi^* x$. Note that $\tilde{x}$ is exactly s-sparse in the DB4 wavelet basis but it is a highly nonphysical image.

1.6.2 Images and Structured Sparsity

But this is not all. The variable-density Walsh sampling scheme used in Fig. 1.4(c) also gives a significantly better reconstruction than the Bernoulli measurement matrix that was used in Fig. 1.4(a).

What has happened? Sampling with a Bernoulli random matrix is optimal for sparse recovery, yet it has been handsomely beaten in this example. This is no accident, and the reason can be traced to the underlying assumption: sparsity. Sparsity in a wavelet basis is just one model for natural images. And like all models, it is imperfect. While most natural images have approximately sparse wavelet coefficients, the converse is not true. As can be seen quite dramatically in Fig. 1.6, many (in fact, most) sparse vectors of wavelet coefficients do not correspond to natural images.

In fact, wavelet coefficients of natural images possess additional *local* sparsity structure. This can already be seen in Fig. 1.3(b), where the majority of the large coefficients tend to cluster in the upper-left corner of the matrix, with progressively fewer large coefficients as one transitions to the bottom right. As we explain later, this corresponds to moving from the *coarsest* to the *finest* wavelet *scales*.

> **Key Point #7.** Natural images are approximately sparse in wavelet bases. However, they also possess additional local sparsity structure across their wavelet scales.

So how does this relate to Fig. 1.4? Mathematically, this means that natural images are a subset of the set of vectors with s-sparse wavelet coefficients. While a Bernoulli random matrix is optimal for recovering s-sparse vectors, it ceases to be optimal over this subclass. It is essentially too conservative: its ability to recover *every* sparse vector means it is incapable of recovering those with additional structure more efficiently.

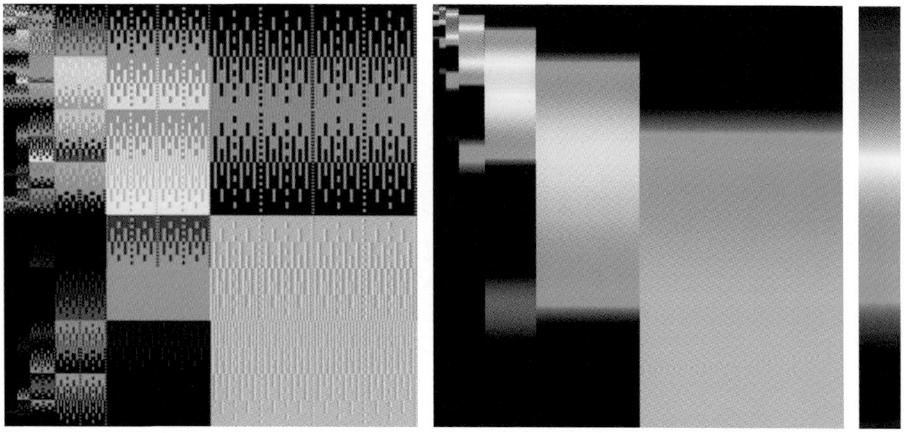

(a) Hadamard (b) Fourier

Figure 1.7 The absolute values of the matrix (a) $H\Phi$, where H is the Hadamard matrix, and (b) $F\Phi$, where F is the Fourier matrix. In both cases, Φ corresponds to the DB4 wavelet basis. The approximate block diagonality means that wavelets at a fixed scale (a single block of columns) are approximately concentrated in a band of Walsh or Fourier frequencies (a single block of rows).

Conversely, Walsh sampling is capable of exploiting this local structure. Wavelets at different scales are essentially compactly supported in *dyadic* regions of (Walsh) frequency space. Hence the sampling strategy can be designed to efficiently target the underlying sparsity structure of the wavelet coefficients.

This can be understood a little better by examining the entries of the matrix $H\Phi$. Here H is the Hadamard matrix and Φ is the DWT matrix, and therefore the (i, j)th entry of $H\Phi$ corresponds to the ith Walsh frequency of the jth wavelet. Figure 1.7(a) plots $H\Phi$. As is clear, this matrix has a distinct block structure. The column blocks correspond to the wavelet scales, going from coarsest (left) to finest (right). The row blocks correspond to the dyadic regions of frequency space, going from lowest (top) to highest (bottom).

Evidencing the (essential) compact support of wavelets in frequency space, the diagonal blocks of this matrix contain the largest values, with the entries in the off-diagonal blocks being much smaller in magnitude. Understanding this behaviour in a precise mathematical way leads to Walsh sampling strategies such as that used in Fig. 1.4(c) that are capable of exploiting local sparsity structure. How, exactly, this is done is the focal point of Chapters 15 and 16.

Key Point #8. The local sparsity structure of natural images can be efficiently captured by variable-density Walsh sampling schemes. For a suitably chosen scheme, this significantly outperforms random Bernoulli sampling.

1.6.3 Fourier Imaging

Now consider Fourier imaging. For simplicity, we assume the discrete model based on §1.4.3, where the measurements of the image $x \in \mathbb{C}^N$ correspond to rows of the Fourier

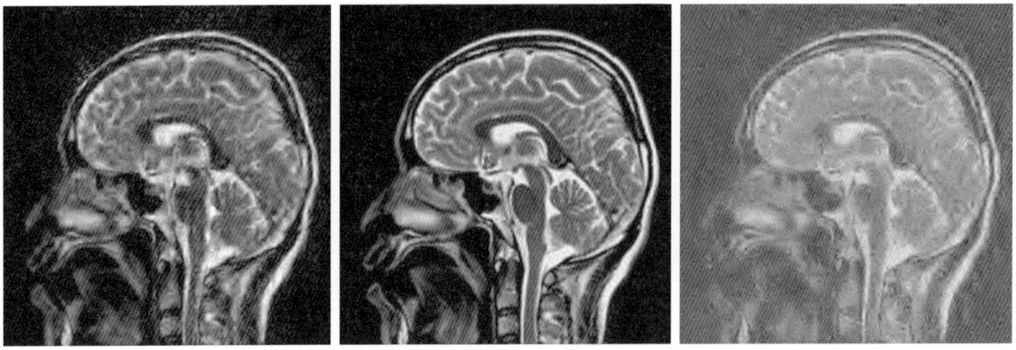

Figure 1.8 Reconstructions from 20% measurements for a 256×256 image. (a) Fourier measurements with radial sampling. (b) Fourier measurements with tuned variable-density sampling. (c) Gaussian random measurements.

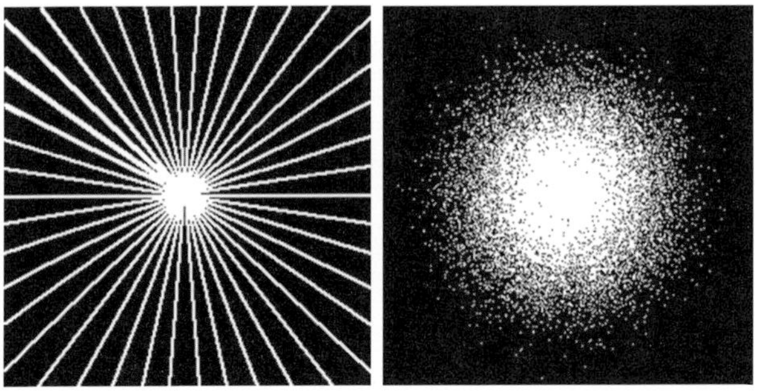

Figure 1.9 The Fourier sampling strategies used in Fig. 1.8(a,b). Each white dot represents a frequency sampled. The zero frequency is located in the centre.

matrix F. A similar story occurs in this case. Wavelets are essentially concentrated in Fourier frequency space, a fact which can again be visualized by plotting the matrix $F\Phi$. This is shown in Fig. 1.7(b). There is a similar dyadic structure to the Walsh case, which once more suggests the use of a variable-density sampling scheme taking more measurements at low frequencies and fewer at high frequencies.

A key question, which we now examine a little further, is which variable-density strategy gives the best reconstruction. In Fig. 1.8(a,b), we compare radial sampling – a standard sampling strategy in modalities such as MRI – with a variable-density scheme that has been tuned to give good performance. The schemes themselves are shown in Fig. 1.9. While both strategies qualitatively do the right thing – namely, they take more measurements at low frequencies and fewer at high frequencies – it is clear that the latter offers a significant improvement. A key topic in this book is explaining why this scheme performs better, and indeed, how it was designed in the first place. This is the aim of Chapters 15 and 16.

Figure 1.8 also compares Fourier sampling with a Gaussian random measurement matrix. This approach is not feasible in most Fourier imaging modalities – as discussed, the integral transform governing the sampling is usually fixed. Even if it were, though, doing so would still not be desirable. Like with Bernoulli measurements, Gaussian measurements do not target the local sparsity structure, and correspondingly yield significantly inferior reconstructions.

> **Key Point #9.** The benefit of compressed sensing in Fourier imaging lies not only with the fact that images are approximately sparse, but that they possess additional sparsity structure that can be exploited by carefully designed Fourier sampling strategies.

Fourier imaging modalities such as MRI have been some of the key beneficiaries of compressed sensing. This success is often attributed to sparsity. But this is not the full story. Had it been the case, we would have expected similar reconstructions in Fig. 1.8(b,c). In fact, the reason for this success is the following serendipity: the integral transform that arises in such modalities just happens to be the right one for efficiently exploiting the local sparsity structure inherent to natural images.

1.6.4 Beyond Wavelets: Total Variation and X-lets

Up to this point we have focused on wavelet sparsifying transforms. Another widely used strategy in compressive imaging involves taking $\Phi = \nabla$ to be the discrete gradient operator. This leads to the *Total Variation (TV) minimization* problem

$$\min_{z \in \mathbb{C}^N} \|z\|_{TV} \text{ subject to } \|Az - y\|_{\ell^2} \leq \eta,$$

where $\|\cdot\|_{TV} = \|\nabla \cdot\|_{\ell^1}$ is the TV semi-norm. Images have approximately sparse gradients, with large gradients corresponding to edges, and minimizing the ℓ^1-norm of the gradient promotes this structure. Yet gradient sparsity is also highly structured, since edges form piecewise smooth curves. Unsurprisingly, variable-density Walsh or Fourier sampling are also well suited to efficiently exploiting this local sparsity structure. Chapter 17 considers TV minimization in depth.

Other alternatives to wavelets are the various 'X-let' families – curvelets, shearlets and suchlike. These are generalizations of wavelets that aim to more efficiently capture geometric properties of images to produce higher-quality reconstructions. Images also possess similar local sparsity in such transforms, which once more is exploitable by the use of variable-density Walsh or Fourier sampling.

Figure 1.10 compares several of these transforms for Walsh sampling on a high-resolution image. Notice they all recover the image well. Yet the shearlet reconstruction exhibits fewer artefacts than both the wavelet and TV reconstructions.

1.7 Neural Networks and Deep Learning for Compressive Imaging

As noted in Key Point #1, compressed sensing ushered in a revolution in image reconstruction that led to the development of compressive imaging. Parts II–IV of this book are devoted to this topic, and in particular, the key issues raised in the previous sections. Yet, arguably, a second revolution is now taking place. Looking to push performance even further, compressive imaging strategies based on neural networks and deep learning

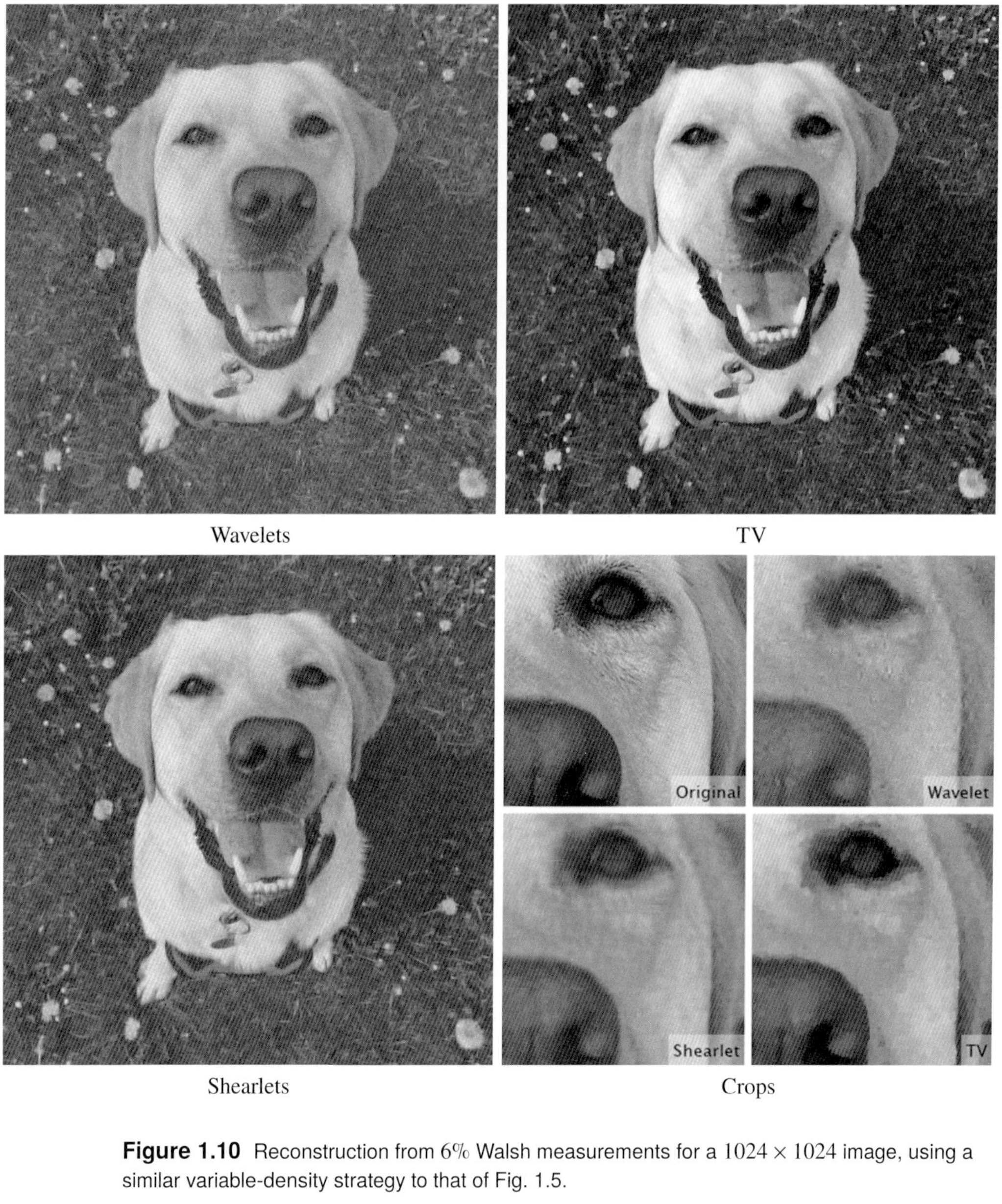

Figure 1.10 Reconstruction from 6% Walsh measurements for a 1024×1024 image, using a similar variable-density strategy to that of Fig. 1.5.

have begun to emerge in the last several years. As the reader is no doubt aware, deep learning has been used with tremendous effect in computer vision tasks such as image classification and recognition. It is therefore unsurprising that it has begun to percolate into the domain of image reconstruction. The aim of Part V of this book is to give an overview of this nascent topic and its relation to compressed sensing techniques.

1.7.1 From Model-Based to Data-Driven

Compressed sensing is primarily a *model-based* approach. The image model (i.e. structured sparsity in a fixed sparsifying transform) and reconstruction procedure (e.g. solving QCBP or LASSO) are both carefully designed in advance. However, in many imaging applications one has access to large databases of training images. This raises the following question: why not *learn* the reconstruction procedure instead of crafting it from a fixed model? Such approaches are often referred to as *data-driven*.

This is by no means a new idea. In the well-established field of *dictionary learning*, rather than using a fixed transform such as wavelets, one seeks to compute a better sparsifying transform Φ from the training data. In essence, an image model specific to the problem is learned *explicitly* from the data. This can then be incorporated into the QCBP or LASSO optimization problem to give a new recovery map based on the learned Φ. We discuss dictionary learning briefly in Chapter 4.

In some senses, the goal of deep learning is to go even further. Rather than just learning a better sparsifying transform, one instead seeks to learn the whole reconstruction map $\mathrm{R} \colon \mathbb{C}^m \to \mathbb{C}^N$. In other words, an image model is now *implicitly* learned in the process of learning R. The key idea is to choose R as a *neural network*.

1.7.2 Deep Learning for Image Reconstruction

We now describe a standard setup. Consider a *training set*

$$\Theta = \{(y_i, x_i)\}_{i=1}^K \subset \mathbb{C}^m \times \mathbb{C}^N, \qquad y_i = Ax_i,$$

where the x_i are the images and the y_i their respective measurements. Let $\mathcal{N}$ denote a family of neural networks $\mathrm{N} \colon \mathbb{C}^m \to \mathbb{C}^N$. We forgo a formal definition for now (see Chapter 18) and simply remark that a neural network is a mapping formed by alternately composing affine maps with an elementwise nonlinear function, known as an *activation* function. Why do this? Again, we shall not discuss the details now. But the effectiveness of deep learning on computer vision tasks strongly suggests that neural networks are capable of encoding complex image structures. Hence this is a seemingly good choice for the related problem of image reconstruction.

Having fixed $\mathcal{N}$, our task is to find a suitable reconstruction map $\mathrm{N} \in \mathcal{N}$. This is usually done by solving an optimization problem that minimizes a so-called *cost* (or *loss*) function over the training data. A simple example is the ℓ^2-loss, in which case this problem takes the form

$$\min_{\mathrm{N} \in \mathcal{N}} \frac{1}{K} \sum_{i=1}^{K} \|\mathrm{N}(y_i) - x_i\|_{\ell^2}^2. \tag{1.13}$$

The reconstruction map $\widehat{\mathrm{N}}$ is taken as a minimizer of (1.13). Solving (1.13) is known as *training* the network.

So far, all seems straightforward. However, behind this simple description lie many complexities. For one, there is the question of how to choose the class of neural networks $\mathcal{N}$. This is often termed *choosing the architecture*. Neural networks come in all sorts of flavours – feedforward, recurrent, fully connected, convolutional and so forth – and so there are countless ways to select $\mathcal{N}$. Quite unlike the case of model-based approaches, there is little theoretical guidance on which choice will work best in practice. Second, the optimization problem (1.13) – as well as the many variations that it, too, can have – is large-scale and nonconvex. It requires specialized techniques such as *backpropagation* and *stochastic gradients* to compute approximate minimizers.

Yet neither issue is a barrier to progress. There are heuristic principles for designing neural network architectures which work well in practice. Computations are also being made increasingly more manageable because of the development of specialized software and hardware (e.g., GPUs). Training neural networks for image reconstruction is becoming ever more feasible for practical problems.

1.7.3 The Accuracy–Stability Barrier

In Chapters 18 and 19 we present an overview of neural networks and deep learning, with a focus on the above questions. After this, we turn our attention to the following question. Supposing one has fixed an architecture and successfully trained a neural network, how good is this as a reconstruction map? In particular, is it stable, how accurate is it, and does it outperform state-of-the-art model-based techniques based on compressed sensing?

We shall see that some trained neural networks can indeed offer very high accuracy for certain image reconstruction tasks. Yet there is reason for concern. It is well known that trained neural networks for image classification problems are highly unstable, which makes them vulnerable to so-called *adversarial attacks*. A small perturbation of an image of a 'cat', often imperceptible to the human eye, can cause it to be mislabelled as a 'dog' by the network. Adversarial attacks and how to combat them is now an active area of research within the computer vision field.

A similar phenomenon also occurs in image reconstruction. Deep learning for compressive imaging has a tendency to produce networks that are unstable and highly susceptible to small perturbations in their input (the measurements y). Specifically, if R is a trained neural network reconstruction map, $x \in \mathbb{C}^N$ is a fixed image and $y = Ax \in \mathbb{C}^m$ its measurements, it is possible to find perturbations $r \in \mathbb{C}^N$ for which

$$\|\mathrm{R}(y + Ar) - \mathrm{R}(y)\|_{\ell^2} \gg 1, \qquad \|r\|_{\ell^2} \ll 1. \tag{1.14}$$

Figure 1.11 shows a typical instance of this phenomenon. The network recovers the image extremely well from the unperturbed measurements y. But the reconstruction from the perturbed measurements $y + Ar$ is badly affected by artefacts, even though the perturbed image $x + r$ is nearly indistinguishable from the original image x. As we explain in Chapter 20, this is not a rare event. Many trained networks are susceptible to perturbations, including, in some cases, completely random perturbations.

Much of Chapter 20 explores the theoretical reasons why this instability phenomenon occurs. The general idea is that the training procedure (1.13) can encourage the reconstruction map to *over-perform*, which forces it to become unstable. Specifically, the training procedure can lead to a neural network $\widehat{\mathrm{N}}$ that is able to reconstruct two distinct images x and x' (e.g. two elements of the training set) whose difference $x - x'$ lies

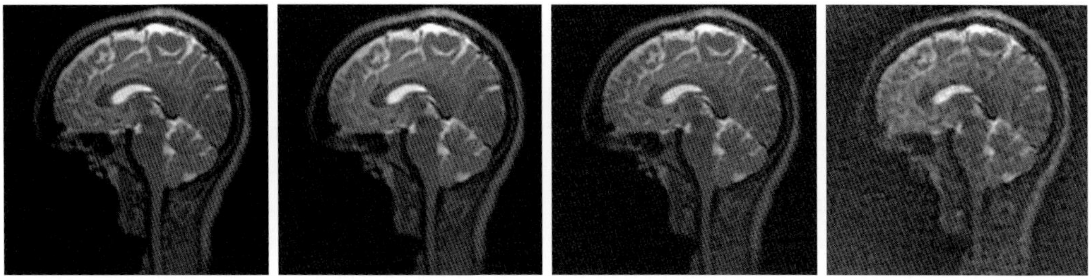

(a) $|x|$ (b) $\mathrm{R}(Ax)$ (c) $|x+r|$ (d) $\mathrm{R}(A(x+r))$

Figure 1.11 Reconstruction of a (complex-valued) image x via a deep learning strategy from Fourier measurements. For full details of this experiment, see Fig. 20.2. (a) Original image (absolute value is shown). (b) Reconstruction via the trained neural network reconstruction map R from unperturbed measurements $y = Ax$. (c) Perturbed image $x + r$ (absolute value is shown). (d) Reconstruction from perturbed measurements $y + Ar$. The perturbation is designed to ensure (1.14), i.e. to cause a significant effect on the output while being small in magnitude.

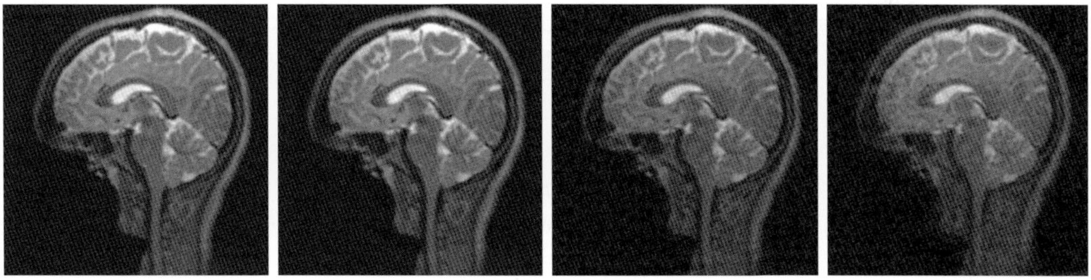

(a) $|x|$ (b) $\mathrm{R}(Ax)$ (c) $|x+r|$ (d) $\mathrm{R}(A(x+r))$

Figure 1.12 Reconstruction of the same image as in Fig. 1.11 from the same measurements using a stable neural network R. For full details of this experiment, see Fig. 21.1. (a) Original image (absolute value is shown). (b) Reconstruction from unperturbed measurements $y = Ax$. (c) Perturbed image $x + r$ (absolute value is shown). (d) Reconstruction from perturbed measurements $y + Ar$. The perturbation is designed to destabilize the network to the maximum extent possible, as in (1.14).

close to the null space of the measurement matrix A. In other words, $\widehat{\mathrm{N}}$ can reconstruct features that it has no right to recover from the measurements it sees. This lack of *kernel awareness* necessarily results in instabilities.

> **Key Point #10.** Current deep learning strategies for compressive imaging are prone to instabilities, with certain small perturbations in the measurements leading to severe image artefacts. This arises because of the training procedure, which can cause the resulting network to over-perform.

1.7.4 Stable and Accurate Neural Networks for Compressive Imaging

This situation is rather unsatisfactory. While neural networks have produced stunning results in various imaging tasks, their use in compressive imaging appears hampered by issues of instability. There is also an uncertainty surrounding their accuracy. Trained neural networks can sometimes produce very good reconstructions, yet there is little theoretical understanding as to when they do so and why.

All this raises the question: can stable and accurate neural networks be computed for compressive imaging problems? This book concludes by answering this question in the affirmative. Neural networks with the same accuracy and stability guarantees as compressed sensing are indeed computable. This is the objective of Chapter 21. To achieve this, one needs to develop a fundamental link between compressed sensing, optimization algorithms for problems such as QCBP and LASSO and neural networks. This is done through *unravelling*, the principle that a finite number of iterations of a standard optimization method for solving, for example, the QCBP problem (1.9) can be viewed as a neural network. Hence, by carefully choosing the number of iterations, one may assert the existence of a neural network with accuracy and stability matching that of compressed sensing. Through some further analysis, using similar ideas to those behind Key Point #6, one deduces that such a network can also be computed.

Key Point #11. While current training procedures can readily lead to instabilities, neural networks for compressive imaging that match the stability and accuracy of compressed sensing are computable.

To illustrate this, in Fig. 1.12 we show the same experiment as in Fig. 1.11, except using a stable neural network that was constructed in this way. The perturbation is once again computed with a view to causing a worst-case effect on the output. Yet because the network is stable, it does not lead to significant artefacts in the reconstruction. Note that this network also recovers the image from the unperturbed measurements with similar accuracy to the unstable network of Fig. 1.11.

1.7.5 Outlook

This book therefore ends on a positive note. Image reconstruction was first upended by the advent of compressed sensing. It now seems set to undergo a similar process through the introduction of neural networks and deep learning. These promising developments, however, come with pitfalls insofar as accuracy (Objective #1) and stability (Objective #3) are concerned. However, they certainly have substantial potential. As Key Point #11 makes clear, neural networks can at the very least perform as well as the current state-of-the-art. The questions of whether or not deep learning can do better, how it can do so, and by how much, are tantalizing ones on which to end this book.

1.8 Overview and Highlights

The aim of this book is to develop compressive imaging and the mathematics that underlies it. It is divided into five parts.

In Part I we cover the essentials of compressive imaging. We explain how popular imaging modalities can be formulated as linear inverse problems of the form (1.1) and

(1.3), and then how to apply compressed sensing techniques to them (Chapters 2 and 3). We also discuss sampling strategies and various methods for enhancing performance (Chapter 4). This part focuses on Key Points #1, #2, #3, #8 and #9.

Part II introduces the mathematics of compressive imaging via compressed sensing. We provide an overview of standard compressed sensing theory (Chapters 5 and 6), optimization for compressed sensing (Chapters 7 and 8), and wavelets and sparse approximation (Chapters 9 and 10). This part focuses on Key Points #4, #5, #6 and #7.

Next, in Part III, we develop a general compressed sensing framework that goes beyond that of Chapters 5 and 6 and, crucially, incorporates local sparsity structure (Chapters 11–13). This part of the book develops the tools needed in Part IV. We also consider the issue of discretization and develop so-called *infinite-dimensional compressed sensing* (Chapter 14) for overcoming the standard discretization errors in Fourier imaging.

In Part IV we use the techniques developed in Part III to examine the application of compressed sensing to imaging. In Chapters 15 and 16, we address the key question raised in §1.6: given the freedom, which (Fourier or Walsh) frequencies should one acquire? These chapters focus on wavelet sparsity. In Chapter 17 we consider gradient sparsity and TV minimization for imaging. This part focuses on Key Points #7, #8 and #9.

Finally, in Part V we address neural networks and deep learning. We first give a short introduction to the subject (Chapter 18), including an overview of its use in image classification. Next, we develop deep learning for compressive imaging (Chapter 19). We then conclude with two chapters examining accuracy and stability. Chapter 20 investigates how and why existing approaches tend to be unstable. On the other hand, Chapter 21 shows that neural networks that are as stable and accurate as compressed sensing are indeed computable. This part focuses on Key Points #10 and #11.

1.9 Disclaimers

1.9.1 What this Book Is and What it Is Not

Imaging is a vast topic. There are many interesting aspects of it that cannot be included in a single text. The guiding principle behind this book is to be both relevant to practice *and* mathematically rigorous, wherever possible. It aims to strike a delicate balance between methods that admit theory and those that are used in practice. Fortunately, these two sets have a large intersection! Moreover, many, if not most of the techniques used in practice are close cousins of those that can be theoretically analysed. This is arguably one of the most exciting aspects of compressed sensing research. This book therefore assumes the reader is interested not only in methods for compressive imaging, but also *how* and *why* they work. For readers only interested in finding an off-the-shelf, state-of-the-art reconstruction algorithm, this is not the best place to look. Having said that, in Chapter 4 we do give some recommendations for a good all-round compressive imaging strategy.

1.9.2 Areas Not Covered

This book is about image reconstruction from *indirect* measurements. A related problem is image *restoration*, in which one directly samples a corrupted version of the image itself. *Denoising*, *deblurring* and *inpainting* are examples of image restoration problems. While these are important image processing tasks, they are outside the scope of this book.

The underlying inverse problem encountered in this book is either well-posed (e.g. the Fourier transform) or only mildly ill-posed (e.g. the Radon transform). Sparsity appears frequently in ill-posed inverse problems as a regularization tool, wherein it is often termed *sparse regularization*. This topic is similar, but not the same as compressed sensing. Generally speaking, compressed sensing is concerned with issues around sampling and the number of measurements needed to achieve good recovery. In sparse regularization, by contrast, the main concern is often with the nature and quality of the solutions obtained from a sparsity-promoting regularization procedure.

This book takes a deterministic approach to image reconstruction in inverse problems (with the caveat that the sampling strategies are themselves random). Statistical methodologies such as Bayesian inverse problems have their place in compressive imaging – especially with the latest innovations in deep learning – but they are outside our scope.

1.9.3 Topics Not Covered

Within compressive imaging, we have tended to exclude, or only lightly touch upon methods that lack theory. For example, much of the book focuses on wavelets or TV minimization. We spend more time on the former, not because we advocate for it strongly over the latter, but because compressed sensing theory for wavelets is more comprehensive. We recommend the practitioner try both.

We have also omitted in-depth descriptions of curvelets and shearlets, as well as generalizations of TV such as *Total Generalized Variation (TGV)*. The compressed sensing theory for these approaches is generally less mature than that for wavelets and TV, although one might expect an eventual theory to be qualitatively similar, at least when it comes to the issue of sampling and sparsity structure. We also largely avoid more sophisticated reconstruction procedures, including learned strategies and nonconvex approaches. In Chapter 4 we briefly overview these and other techniques for boosting practical performance. We also do not treat structured sparsity models such as *wavelet trees*. While interesting, it is arguably the case that such models have not found widespread use in compressive imaging.

In terms of imaging modalities, after Part I we largely ignore tomographic imaging via the Radon transform. This is primarily because this problem has so far resisted substantial mathematical analysis from the compressed sensing perspective. We also focus on static, single-image recovery problems. Compressed sensing techniques have been applied to many *dynamic* imaging problems. Arguably, though, the particularities of dynamic compressive imaging are sufficiently manifold for it to be worthy of a book in its own right. For this reason, we also do not discuss *low-rank matrix recovery*. While closely related to compressed sensing, its use in imaging has predominantly been in dynamic imaging scenarios. We mainly treat standard, but ubiquitous, imaging models which can be recast as linear inverse problems of the form (1.1) or (1.3). We do not address nonlinear sampling operators. In particular, the *phase retrieval* problem, while it arises in some common imaging modalities, is outside the scope of this book. We also do not address calibration in any depth. While this is an important challenge in many practical imaging systems, it is also one that is often very specific to the modality.

Learning some part of the imaging process is an important topic in compressive imaging. As noted, a common approach is dictionary learning. Optimization parameters, sampling strategies and various other components of the imaging pipeline can also be learned. While much can and has been written about these 'classical' approaches to learning, we have chosen to forgo this. We have instead focused Part V of the book on the most contemporary approaches to learning in compressive imaging, namely, deep learning. Some discussion on dictionary learning is included in Chapter 4.

Note that many of the topics mentioned above are discussed in a little more detail in the Notes section of subsequent chapters, along with references for further reading.

Finally, we remark that we generally do not concern ourselves with constants in this book. Theoretically obtaining explicit constants in compressed sensing is a challenge, and one that arguably sheds little light on the underlying principles. We use the notation $\lesssim$ and $\gtrsim$ quite liberally throughout.

1.10 Reading this Book

We encourage everyone to read Part I to get a taste of compressive imaging. Readers familiar with conventional compressed sensing, optimization and wavelets may wish to skip elements of Part II. After Chapter 11, the remainder of Part III contains the main technical mathematics in the book. Part IV – specifically, Chapters 15 and 17 – answers one of the book's main questions: how should one sample? These chapters are intended to be read without necessarily having read Part III in detail. Finally, we recommend Part V to anyone who is interested in the latest innovations in compressive imaging.

1.10.1 Examples and Code

Aiming to make this book a practical guide for compressive imaging, we have included many numerical examples. A companion software library, *CIlib*, is available online:

`https://github.com/vegarant/cilib`

It is also accessible through the book's website

`www.compressiveimagingbook.com`

This library contains a broad set of functions and tools for compressive imaging, as well as code that reproduces many of the figures in the book. We encourage the reader to investigate this library. The website also contains further information about the experimental setup and software packages used.

1.10.2 Notes

Each subsequent chapter of this book concludes with a Notes section (or sections). These contain additional information, discussion and suggestions for further reading.

1.10.3 Prerequisites

In closing this chapter, we remark that this book assumes a level of mathematical background of a typical early-stage graduate student, but little specialist knowledge. The Appendices, while not comprehensive, contain some additional background material. The Notes sections at the ends of the chapters also give additional information and references.

Part I

The Essentials of Compressive Imaging

Summary of Part I

In Part I of this book we give a readable introduction to compressive imaging. We commence in Chapter 2 by formalizing a number of key concepts. We define continuous and discrete images and then introduce three transforms that arise frequently in imaging applications. These are the Fourier, Radon and Walsh transforms that were already seen briefly in Chapter 1. Since the Walsh transform is far less well known than the other two, we devote some additional time to it. We explain how each transform leads to a continuous reconstruction problem of the form (1.3), and then discuss how it can be discretized to yield a discrete reconstruction problem of the form (1.1).

Chapter 3 presents a practical and nontechnical guide to setting up and solving basic compressive imaging problems. To do this, we introduce a pipeline with six key stages: *Identify a mathematical model*, *Choose a discretization*, *Choose an image model*, *Determine which measurements to acquire*, *Choose a recovery procedure*, and *Find an algorithm to perform the computations*. For each stage, we list a series of key considerations to be taken into account. In the second half of the chapter, we illustrate this pipeline in the context of three examples: MRI, X-ray CT and optical imaging. In particular, we explain why the inverse problems in MRI and X-ray CT can be modelled by the Fourier and Radon transforms, respectively (Key Point #2) and why optical imaging can be set up as a binary sampling problem (Key Point #3). We also look briefly at compressed sensing recovery of image sequences using the *joint sparsity* model.

Chapter 4 is all about improving compressive imaging performance. Our first topic is perhaps the most important: how does one best design the sampling strategy? Recall Key Points #8 and #9. We introduce four principles for effective sampling strategy design and illustrate them with numerical examples. Next, we look at discretization and the artefacts it may cause, as well as the insidious *inverse crime*. Focusing on the setting of compressed sensing, we then consider ways to enhance performance by using different sparsifying transforms and recovery procedures. We briefly look at curvelets, shearlets, Total Generalized Variation (TGV) and combinations thereof, before introducing so-called *reweighted ℓ^1-minimization* techniques. Next, looking towards Part V, we discuss *dictionary learning*. We conclude this chapter with some practical advice for getting good performance in compressive imaging. In particular, we list (with caveats) our recommendations for the sampling strategy, and in the case of compressed sensing, the sparsifying transform(s) and recovery procedure for good all-round performance.

2 Images, Transforms and Sampling

We commence this chapter with a short introduction to images in §2.1. We define continuous and discrete images, and the relation between the two. Next, in §2.2, §2.3 and §2.4 we introduce the Fourier, Radon and Walsh transforms, respectively. We first formulate each transform in the continuous setting, before addressing its discretization. For the first and third, we also discuss the relation to the Discrete Fourier and Discrete Walsh–Hadamard Transforms (DFT and DHT), respectively.

Much of this chapter serves to fix concepts and notation that will be used throughout the rest of the book. In doing so, we will assume a number of standard mathematical concepts. Further details are given in the Appendices.

2.1 Images

We consider *continuous* and *discrete* images. A *continuous* image is a function $f\colon [0,1]^d \to \mathbb{C}$. We allow f to be complex-valued, since it is relevant for some applications and mathematically no more difficult to treat. Depending on the application, the values f can take may be restricted. For instance, in the real case, f may be nonnegative ($f(x) \geq 0$), nonnegative and bounded ($0 \leq f(x) \leq T$ for some T), or even binary ($f(x) \in \{0,1\}$). We shall not discuss such considerations in any detail.

Typically, d is equal to one, two or three. We somewhat euphemistically refer to a function $f\colon [0,1] \to \mathbb{C}$ as an image, even though it is one-dimensional. Where needed, we will also consider f as a function over the whole of $\mathbb{R}^d$ that takes the value zero outside $[0,1]^d$.

This setup applies to *greyscale* images, which are our primary focus. Colour images can be represented as vector-valued functions; for example, $f\colon [0,1]^d \to \mathbb{R}^3$ in the case of an RGB (Red, Green, Blue) image.

A *discrete* image is a d-dimensional array of numbers:

$$X = (X_{i_1,\ldots,i_d})_{i_1,\ldots,i_d=1}^{N} \in \mathbb{C}^{N\times\cdots\times N}. \tag{2.1}$$

For simplicity, we consider only square arrays. We refer to N as the *resolution* of the image. Often, it will be convenient to reshape X into a vector. We do this in the standard way via *lexicographical ordering*. Formally, this is the bijection $\varsigma\colon \{1,\ldots,N^d\} \to \{1,\ldots,N\}^d$ whose inverse is given by

$$\varsigma^{-1}(i) = N^{d-1}(i_1 - 1) + N^{d-2}(i_2 - 1) + \cdots + i_d, \qquad i = (i_1,\ldots,i_d). \tag{2.2}$$

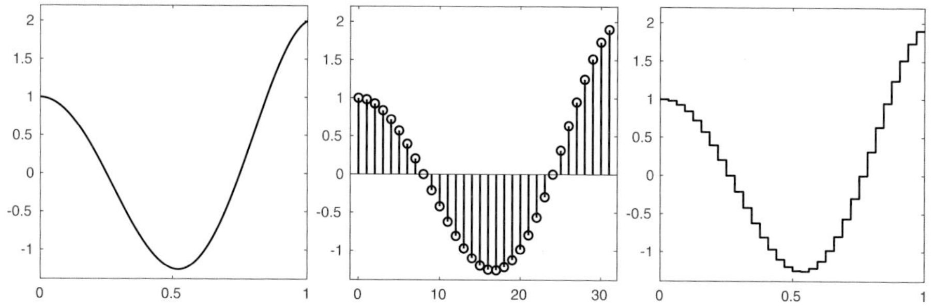

Figure 2.1 Left: A one-dimensional continuous image f. Middle: Its discretization $x \in \mathbb{C}^N$ at resolution $N = 32$. Right: The continuous image g given by (2.4).

Given X of the form (2.1), we define its *vectorization*

$$\operatorname{vec}(X) = x = (x_i)_{i=1}^{N^d} \in \mathbb{C}^{N^d}, \qquad x_i = X_{\varsigma(i)}. \tag{2.3}$$

Likewise, given $x \in \mathbb{C}^{N^d}$, we write $X = \operatorname{vec}^{-1}(x) \in \mathbb{C}^{N\times\cdots\times N}$ for its corresponding *anti-vectorization*.

A discrete image X can be converted to a continuous image g by

$$g = \sum_{j=1}^{N^d} x_j \chi_j, \qquad x = \operatorname{vec}(X). \tag{2.4}$$

We assume throughout that $\{\chi_j\}_{j=1}^{N^d}$ is the *pixel basis*. To be precise, if $\varsigma(j) = (i_1, \ldots, i_d)$, then χ_j is the indicator function of the corresponding cell

$$[(i_1 - 1)/N, i_1/N) \times \cdots \times [(i_d - 1)/N, i_d/N) \subset [0, 1]^d.$$

Conversely, a continuous image f can be *discretized*, giving a discrete image X, by sampling it on the corresponding equispaced grid of points:

$$X_{i_1,\ldots,i_d} = f((i_1 - 1)/N, \ldots, (i_d - 1)/N), \quad i_1, \ldots, i_d \in \{1, \ldots, N\}. \tag{2.5}$$

Throughout, we refer to X as the *discretization of f at resolution N*. Figure 2.1 gives an illustration of this process for $d = 1$.

There are other ways to convert between continuous and discrete images. For instance, one may replace the pixel basis by a smoother, but still local basis, or take local averages in (2.5) instead of pointwise samples. Different procedures lead to somewhat different *discretization errors*. However, for our purposes it will be sufficient to keep in mind that all discretizations commit errors, without worrying unduly about their specific nature.

2.1.1 Test Images

We use a number of different test images throughout this book to examine the various reconstruction procedures. These are shown in Fig. 2.2. The first two, 'SL phantom' and 'GLPU phantom', are synthetic brain images used to benchmark methods for MRI

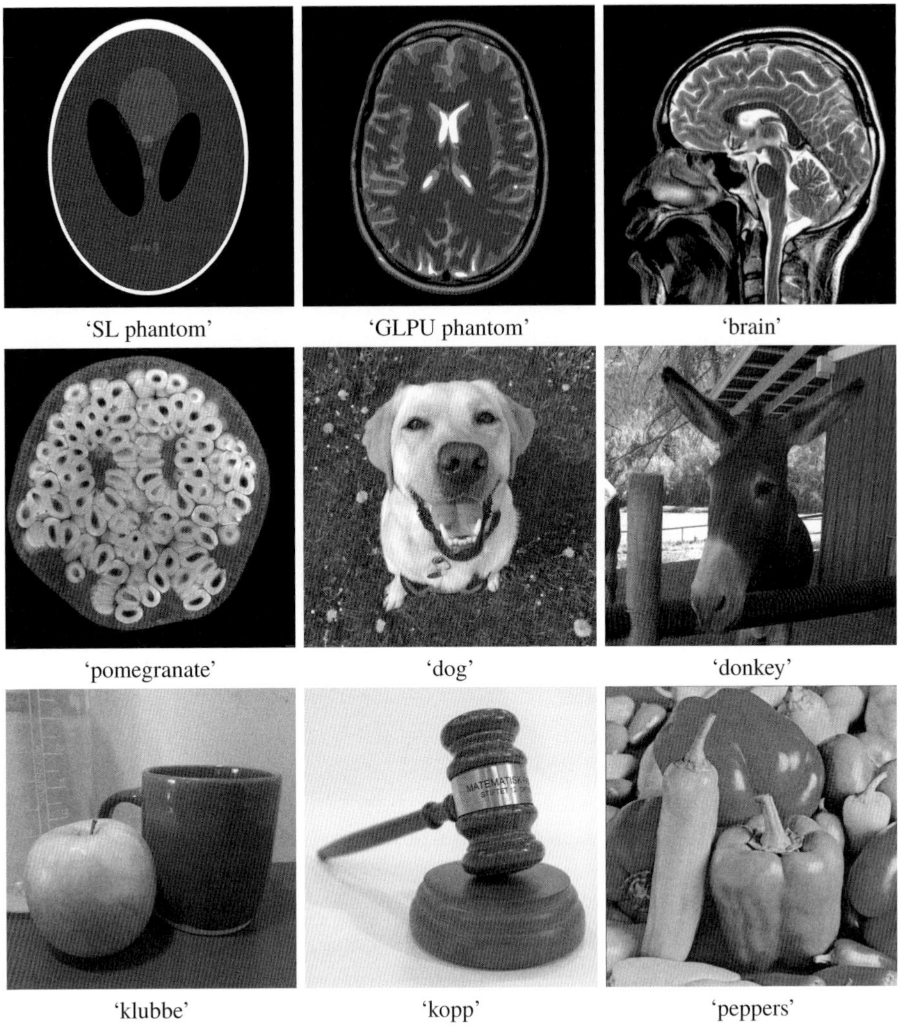

Figure 2.2 Test images. The original 'dog' image was provided by courtesy of Elizabeth Sawchuk, the 'kopp' and 'klubbe' images courtesy of Vegard Antun, the 'pomegranate' image courtesy of Andy Ellison, Boston University Medical School, and the 'brain' image courtesy of General Electric Healthcare. See the Notes section for more information about these and the other test images.

or X-ray CT reconstruction. The former is the famous *Shepp–Logan phantom* image, ubiquitous in imaging literature. They are both continuous images. The third and fourth, 'brain' and 'pomegranate', are discrete images obtained from actual MRI scans. The remaining images are natural images, also discrete, which will be used primarily to test reconstructions from binary measurements.

2.1.2 Assessing Image Quality

The quality of a recovered image can be assessed in many different ways. In this book, we use either a simple visual comparison (informally known as the 'eyeball metric') or the *Peak Signal-to-Noise Ratio (PSNR)*. PSNR is defined as

$$\mathrm{PSNR} = 20 \cdot \log_{10}\left(\frac{\mathrm{MAX}_X}{\sqrt{\mathrm{MSE}}}\right), \tag{2.6}$$

where MSE is the *Mean Squared Error*:

$$\mathrm{MSE} = \frac{1}{N^d} \sum_{i_1,\ldots,i_d=1}^{N} |X_{i_1,\ldots,i_d} - \widehat{X}_{i_1,\ldots,i_d}|^2.$$

Here X is the true image (often called the *ground truth*), $\widehat{X}$ is its reconstruction and MAX_X is the maximum possible pixel value of the image. Often, $\mathrm{MAX}_X = 255$. Pixel values are commonly represented as unsigned 8-bit integers, and hence they belong to the range $\{0, \ldots, 255\}$. PSNR is usually stated in decibel (dB) units, with a higher PSNR meaning better image quality. Typically, for good visual quality one wants the PSNR to be at least 30dB.

While PSNR is a widely used measure of image quality, it does have several limitations. It can be highly affected by, for instance, small rotations or shifts, even though such an operation barely changes the visual quality of the image. It also does not distinguish between different types of artefacts. Blurry artefacts, which are often more visually appealing, can easily carry the same PSNR as less visually appealing noisy artefacts. The design of more advanced image quality metrics is a subject in itself, and one we will not consider. The Notes section contains several references for the interested reader.

2.2 Sampling with the Fourier Transform

Having discussed images, we now move on to sampling and our first of three transforms, the Fourier transform. In this section, we make use of material in Appendix E.

2.2.1 The Fourier Reconstruction Problem

As noted in Chapter 1, a key problem in imaging is to recover a continuous image f from samples of its Fourier transform $\{\mathcal{F} f(2\pi\omega) : \omega \in \Omega\}$, where $\Omega \subset \mathbb{Z}^d$ is some finite index set. In the absence of noise, this is a problem of the form (1.3). Specifically:

$$\text{Given the data } \{\mathcal{F} f(2\pi\omega) : \omega \in \Omega\}, \text{ recover } f. \tag{2.7}$$

This is an infinite-dimensional inverse problem, which needs to be discretized in order to be solved numerically. We describe a standard discretization below.

2.2.2 Fourier Orderings

Before doing so, we need a short discussion on orderings. Let $\{\upsilon_\omega\}_{\omega\in\mathbb{Z}^d}$ denote the d-dimensional Fourier basis (E.3), and observe that $\mathcal{F}f(2\pi\omega) = \langle f, \upsilon_\omega\rangle_{L^2}$. The Fourier basis is naturally indexed over $\mathbb{Z}^d$. However, to convert (2.7) into a standard discrete inverse problem of the form (1.1), it is useful to reindex it over $\mathbb{N}$. We write $\{\upsilon_i\}_{i=1}^{\infty}$ for the corresponding basis, and note that such reindexing is permitted since the Fourier series (E.4) of f converges unconditionally. To distinguish between the two indexings, we refer to $\omega \in \mathbb{Z}^d$ as the *frequency* and $i \in \mathbb{N}$ as the *index*.

It is useful to formalize, at least partially, how such reindexing is performed. When $d = 1$, we do this via the bijection

$$\varrho \colon \mathbb{N} \to \mathbb{Z},\ i \mapsto (-1)^i \lfloor i/2 \rfloor. \tag{2.8}$$

Note that this bijection satisfies

$$\varrho(\{2L+1,\ldots,2M\}) = \{-M+1,\ldots,-L\} \cup \{L+1,\ldots,M\}, \tag{2.9}$$

for all $0 \le L < M$. In particular, for even N,

$$\varrho(\{1,\ldots,N\}) = \{-N/2+1,\ldots,N/2\}. \tag{2.10}$$

In other words, it gives a correspondence between the *first* N indices $i = 1,\ldots,N$ and the *lowest* N frequencies $\omega = -N/2+1,\ldots,N/2$.

When $d \ge 2$, there are many different ways to define a bijection $\varrho = \varrho^{(d)} \colon \mathbb{N} \to \mathbb{Z}^d$. Often, we do not worry about writing down the bijection explicitly as we did for the $d = 1$ case in (2.8). We do, however, assume that such a bijection takes the form

$$\varrho^{(d)}(i) = (\varrho(\varsigma(i)_1),\ldots,\varrho(\varsigma(i)_d)), \quad i \in \mathbb{N}, \tag{2.11}$$

where ϱ denotes the one-dimensional bijection (2.8), ς is an arbitrary bijection $\mathbb{N} \to \mathbb{N}^d$ and $\varsigma(i)_k$ is the kth component of $\varsigma(i)$.

2.2.3 Discrete Fourier Measurements and the Fourier Matrix

Let $f \colon [0,1] \to \mathbb{C}$. Then

$$\mathcal{F}f(2\pi\omega) = \int_0^1 f(x)\mathrm{e}^{-2\pi\mathrm{i}\omega x}\,\mathrm{d}x \approx \frac{1}{N}\sum_{j=1}^{N} x_j \mathrm{e}^{-2\pi\mathrm{i}\omega(j-1)/N}, \tag{2.12}$$

where $x_j = f((j-1)/N)$ and $x = (x_j)_{j=1}^N$ is the discretization of f at resolution N. Assume that N is even. Restricting ω to the values $\{-N/2+1,\ldots,N/2\}$, the expression (2.12) gives an approximation to $\mathcal{F}f$ at the lowest N frequencies. Using the bijection (2.8), and noting (2.10), we can write this as

$$(\langle f, \upsilon_{\varrho(i)}\rangle)_{i=1}^N \approx \frac{1}{N} F x. \tag{2.13}$$

Here the matrix $F \in \mathbb{C}^{N\times N}$ is defined as follows:

Definition 2.1 (Fourier matrix) The one-dimensional *Fourier matrix* is the matrix $F = F^{(1)} \in \mathbb{C}^{N\times N}$ with entries

$$F_{ij} = \exp(-2\pi \mathrm{i} \varrho(i)(j-1)/N), \quad i, j = 1, \ldots, N.$$

For $d \geq 2$, the d-dimensional Fourier matrix is given by

$$F^{(d)} = F^{(1)} \otimes \cdots \otimes F^{(1)} \in \mathbb{C}^{N^d \times N^d},$$

where $\otimes$ denotes the Kronecker product.

When clear, we simply write F for the d-dimensional Fourier matrix. Note that $N^{-d}F^*F = I$; that is, the Fourier matrix is unitary up to the scaling $1/\sqrt{N^d}$. As we discuss in Remark 2.2, F is closely related, although not identical, to the matrix of the *Discrete Fourier Transform (DFT)*.

Much as in the one-dimensional case (2.13), the d-dimensional Fourier matrix gives an approximation to the lowest N^d frequencies of a d-dimensional continuous image $f\colon [0,1]^d \to \mathbb{C}$. Let ς be the lexicographical ordering (2.2) and $\varrho = \varrho^{(d)} \colon \{1, \ldots, N^d\} \to \{-N/2+1, \ldots, N/2\}^d$ be the bijection defined by

$$\varrho^{(d)}(i) = (\varrho(\varsigma(i)_1), \ldots, \varrho(\varsigma(i)_d)), \quad i = 1, \ldots, N^d, \tag{2.14}$$

where ϱ is as in (2.8) and $\varsigma(i)_k$ denotes the kth component of $\varsigma(i)$. Let X be the discretization of f at resolution N and $x = \mathrm{vec}(X) \in \mathbb{C}^{N^d}$. Then

$$\begin{aligned}
\langle f, \upsilon_{\varrho(i)} \rangle &= \int_{[0,1]^d} f(x) \mathrm{e}^{-2\pi \mathrm{i} \varrho(i)\cdot x} \,\mathrm{d}x \\
&\approx N^{-d} \sum_{j=1}^{N^d} f\left(\frac{\varsigma(j)_1 - 1}{N}, \ldots, \frac{\varsigma(j)_d - 1}{N} \right) \exp\left(-2\pi \mathrm{i} \sum_{k=1}^{d} \frac{\varrho(\varsigma(i)_k)(\varsigma(j)_k - 1)}{N} \right) \\
&= N^{-d} \sum_{j=1}^{N^d} x_j \prod_{k=1}^{d} F^{(1)}_{\varsigma(i)_k, \varsigma(j)_k} = N^{-d} \sum_{j=1}^{N^d} F^{(d)}_{ij} x_j.
\end{aligned}$$

Here in the last step we used (A.21). This gives

$$\frac{1}{N^d} F x \approx \left(\langle f, \upsilon_{\varrho(i)} \rangle \right)_{i=1}^{N^d}.$$

In other words, $N^{-d}Fx$ is an approximation to the Fourier transform $\mathcal{F} f(2\pi\omega)$ at the lowest N^d frequencies $\omega \in \{-N/2+1, \ldots, N/2\}^d$.

Remark 2.2 The form of the Fourier matrix used in Definition 2.1 is convenient for several reasons. First, it arises directly in the discretization of the Fourier integral (2.12). Second, the ordering of its rows is useful for the mathematical analysis performed in later chapters. However, it is somewhat unconventional, and therefore worth explaining how it relates to the DFT $\mathcal{F} \colon \mathbb{C}^N \to \mathbb{C}^N$ (Definition E.1). The connection is as follows. For any $x \in \mathbb{C}^N$,

$$Fx = Q\mathcal{F}(Dx),$$

where $D \in \mathbb{C}^{N \times N}$ is the diagonal matrix with diagonal entries

$$D_{jj} = \exp(2\pi \mathrm{i}(N/2 - 1)(j - 1)/N), \quad j = 1, \dots, N,$$

and $Q \in \mathbb{R}^{N \times N}$ is the permutation matrix with

$$Q_{ij} = \delta_{\varrho(i)+N/2-j}, \quad i, j = 1, \dots, N.$$

Hence Fx is the DFT of a phase-shifted version of x, followed by a permutation to account for the different indexing of frequency space. As a result, the matrix–vector multiplications $x \mapsto Fx$ and $y \mapsto F^*y$ can be implemented efficiently, in $\mathcal{O}(N \log(N))$ arithmetic operations, using the *Fast Fourier Transform (FFT)*. A similar relation, which we will not discuss explicitly, also holds in two or more dimensions.

2.2.4 The Discrete Fourier Reconstruction Problem

Consider the problem (2.7) and let N be such that $\Omega \subseteq \{-N/2 + 1, \dots, N/2\}^d$. In other words, the maximal frequency sampled is at most $N/2$. Let $P \in \mathbb{R}^{m \times N^d}$ be the *row selector* matrix that picks the rows of the d-dimensional Fourier matrix F corresponding to the values

$$\{\varrho^{-1}(\omega) : \omega \in \Omega\} \subseteq \{1, \dots, N^d\},$$

where ϱ is as in (2.14), and write $A = PF \in \mathbb{C}^{m \times N^d}$. We now arrive at the following discrete counterpart of the problem (2.7):

$$\text{Given the data } y = Ax, \text{ recover } x. \tag{2.15}$$

Since Ω usually corresponds to a subset of the N^d lowest frequencies, we refer to the matrix A as a *subsampled Fourier matrix*. Because of Remark 2.2, matrix–vector multiplications with A and A^* can be performed efficiently.

It is worth stressing that (2.7) and (2.15) are related, but distinct problems. The former involves measurements of the continuous Fourier transform of a continuous image f, while the latter involves measurements of the discrete Fourier transform of its discretization $X = \mathrm{vec}^{-1}(x)$. The corresponding *discretization error* and its effect will be discussed further in the next chapters.

2.3 Sampling with the Radon Transform

While the Fourier transform arises in many imaging modalities, arguably even more modalities are based on the so-called *Radon transform*. This transform and its variants underlie *tomographic* imaging, which is found widely in applications. We now give a short introduction to this transform.

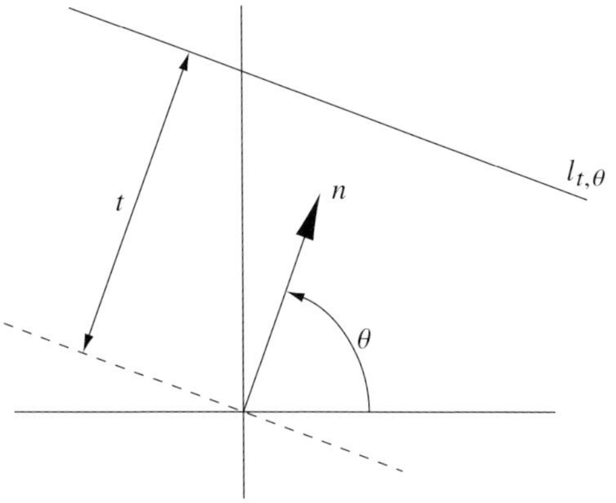

Figure 2.3 The parametrization (t, θ) of lines in the plane.

2.3.1 Definition

The Radon transform is an operator taking a function $f\colon \mathbb{R}^2 \to \mathbb{C}$ to the set of values corresponding to its integrals along arbitrary lines in the plane. In order to define it, we first need a parametrization of such lines. Every line in the plane can be expressed in terms of an angle $0 \le \theta < 2\pi$ measured counterclockwise from the x-axis that defines a normal vector $n = (\cos(\theta), \sin(\theta))$, and a perpendicular displacement $t \in \mathbb{R}$ from the origin. This is shown in Fig. 2.3. Given $(t, \theta) \in \mathbb{R} \times [0, 2\pi)$ we write $l_{t,\theta}$ for the corresponding line. Note that $l_{-t,\theta} = l_{t,\theta+\pi}$, meaning this parametrization is not one-to-one. To enforce uniqueness we may, for instance, consider angles $\theta \in [0, \pi)$ only.

Definition 2.3 (Radon transform) The *Radon transform* $\mathcal{R}f$ of $f\colon \mathbb{R}^2 \to \mathbb{R}$ is

$$\mathcal{R}f(t,\theta) = \int_{l_{t,\theta}} f \,\mathrm{d}s = \int_{-\infty}^{\infty} f(t\cos(\theta) - s\sin(\theta), t\sin(\theta) + s\cos(\theta))\,\mathrm{d}s,$$

for $t \in \mathbb{R}$ and $0 \le \theta < \pi$, where, in the first integral, $\mathrm{d}s$ is the arclength measure along the line $l_{t,\theta}$.

Note that $\mathcal{R}f$ need not be defined for arbitrary f and arbitrary (t, θ). We shall not discuss *existence* conditions in any depth, except to say that $\mathcal{R}f$ is defined everywhere when, for example, f is piecewise continuous and compactly supported. This is a suitable model for the images in this book. Observe that the Radon transform is linear, i.e. $\mathcal{R}(af + bg) = a\mathcal{R}(f) + b\mathcal{R}(g)$ whenever the corresponding transforms are defined.

2.3.2 The Radon Reconstruction Problem

Similar to the Fourier transform, the image reconstruction problem from Radon measurements takes the following form:

$$\text{Given the data } \{\mathcal{R}f(t,\theta) : (t,\theta) \in \Theta\}, \text{ recover } f. \tag{2.16}$$

Here $\Theta \subset \mathbb{R} \times [0, \pi)$ corresponds to a finite subset of lines in the plane.

This problem also requires discretization – an issue we pursue in a moment. First, however, we develop the intimate relationship between the Radon and Fourier transforms, the so-called *Fourier-slice* theorem.

2.3.3 The Fourier-Slice Theorem

The Fourier-slice (also *projection-slice* or *central-slice*) theorem states (under mild conditions on $f\colon \mathbb{R}^2 \to \mathbb{C}$) that the one-dimensional Fourier transform of $\mathcal{R}f(t,\theta)$ with respect to the displacement t is equal to the two-dimensional Fourier transform of f expressed in polar coordinates. Specifically,

$$\mathcal{F}_1\mathcal{R}f(\omega,\theta) = \mathcal{F}f(\omega\cos(\theta), \omega\sin(\theta)), \quad \omega \in \mathbb{R},\ \theta \in [0, 2\pi), \tag{2.17}$$

where $\mathcal{F}$ denotes the two-dimensional Fourier transform and $\mathcal{F}_1$ is the one-dimensional Fourier transform with respect to the first component.

From the perspective of measurements, the Fourier-slice theorem means that sampling the Radon transform of f at a fixed angle and a full set of displacements $t \in \mathbb{R}$, i.e. acquiring the data

$$\{\mathcal{R}f(t,\theta) : t \in \mathbb{R}\}, \tag{2.18}$$

is equivalent to sampling the Fourier transform of f along the *radial line* with angle θ, i.e. the data

$$\{\mathcal{F}f(\omega\cos(\theta), \omega\sin(\theta)) : \omega \in \mathbb{R}\}.$$

Note that (2.18), or more precisely, the function $g_\theta(t) = \mathcal{R}f(t,\theta)$, is often referred to as the *Radon projection* of f at angle θ. Hence, acquiring the Radon projection is equivalent to sampling the Fourier transform of f along the corresponding radial line. More generally, acquiring k Radon projections of f at k distinct angles is equivalent to sampling $\mathcal{F}f$ along the corresponding k radial lines.

2.3.4 Filtered Back-Projection

While not strictly connected to the question of discretization, since it follows naturally from the Fourier-slice theorem, we now briefly discuss the matter of inversion of the Radon transform.

The Fourier transform is invertible and its inverse has a simple expression. By contrast, inverting the Radon transform is a more delicate affair. The so-called *filtered back-projection* formula gives an explicit expression for a certain left inverse of $\mathcal{R}$. In order to state this, we first introduce the back-projection operator:

Definition 2.4 (Back-projection) Let $g = g(t,\theta)$ be a function on $\mathbb{R} \times [0,\pi)$. The *back-projection* of g, $\mathcal{B}g$, is

$$\mathcal{B}g(x) = \frac{1}{\pi}\int_0^\pi g(x_1\cos(\theta) + x_2\sin(\theta), \theta)\,\mathrm{d}\theta, \qquad \forall x = (x_1, x_2) \in \mathbb{R}^2.$$

Suppose that $g = \mathcal{R}f$ is the Radon transform of some function f. Then the back-projection $\mathcal{B}g(x)$ at a point x simply averages the value of the line integrals of f over all lines $l_{t,\theta}$ passing through the point x.

It is tempting to think that back-projection might invert the Radon transform. Unfortunately, applying $\mathcal{B}$ to the Radon transform $\mathcal{R}f$ of a function f does not return f itself, but rather a blurred version of it. We will illustrate this later in Fig. 3.7. To obtain an inversion formula, one first needs to filter $\mathcal{R}f$ in a suitable way before applying $\mathcal{B}$. This leads to the well-known *filtered back-projection* formula:

$$f = \frac{1}{2}\mathcal{B}\left(\mathcal{F}_1^{-1}\left(|\omega|\mathcal{F}_1\left(\mathcal{R}f\right)(\omega,\theta)\right)\right). \tag{2.19}$$

Observe that if the factor $|\omega|$ were omitted, the right-hand side would be precisely $\mathcal{B}\mathcal{R}f$, and therefore not equal to f. This factor provides the filtering needed – specifically, suppressing low frequencies and amplifying high frequencies – to counteract the blurring effect of the back-projection operator $\mathcal{B}$.

2.3.5 The Discrete Radon Reconstruction Problem 1: Radial Fourier Sampling

There are several ways to discretize the Radon transform. The first way is to use the Fourier-slice theorem followed by the Fourier discretization of §2.2.3 to obtain discrete Fourier measurements along radial lines. This approach assumes that the set of samples

$$\Theta = \{(t,\theta_i) : t \in \mathbb{R}, i = 1,\dots,k\}$$

consists of a finite set of angles $0 \leq \theta_1 < \cdots < \theta_k < \pi$ and all possible displacements $t \in \mathbb{R}$. That is, one acquires the full Radon projections of f at each angle θ_i. The Fourier-slice theorem then gives that (2.16) is equivalent to the Fourier reconstruction problem (2.7) with

$$\Omega' = \{(\omega\cos(\theta_i), \omega\sin(\theta_i)) : \omega \in \mathbb{R},\ i = 1,\dots,k\}.$$

To convert this to a discrete problem, we fix a resolution N and then approximate Ω' by a finite index set of integer frequencies $\Omega \subseteq \{-N/2+1,\dots,N/2\}^2$. This can be done, for instance, by replacing each point $(\omega\cos(\theta_i), \omega\sin(\theta_i)) \in \Omega' \cap (-N/2, N/2]^2$ with its nearest integer neighbour, a process known as *nearest-neighbour gridding* (also known as *regridding*). Having done this, the discrete analogue of (2.16) is then simply the discrete Fourier reconstruction problem (2.15) with the index set Ω.

This discretization procedure commits several errors. There is the error due to discretizing the continuous Fourier transform as in §2.2.3. There is also the error due to gridding. Moreover, in order to set up the discrete problem, one needs to take the one-dimensional Fourier transform $\mathcal{F}_1$ of the projection $\mathcal{R}f(\cdot,\theta)$. In fact, one usually cannot acquire $\mathcal{R}f(t,\theta)$ at all displacements $t \in \mathbb{R}$ in practice. Instead, the displacements are sampled on a finite, but sufficiently fine grid, and then the continuous Fourier transform $\mathcal{F}_1$ is replaced by a DFT. This, however, gives rise to another source of error.

2.3.6 The Discrete Radon Reconstruction Problem 2: Algebraic Formulation

Discretization errors aside, another issue with this approach is that it requires one to acquire the full Radon projection at each angle. As we explain in Chapter 3 in the context of X-Ray CT, this may not be desirable or even possible in practice.

We now describe a simpler and more flexible discretization procedure. Suppose that the measurements correspond to an arbitrary set of lines

$$\Theta = \{(t_i, \theta_i) : i = 1, \dots, m\} \subset \mathbb{R} \times [0, \pi).$$

We cannot appeal to the Fourier-slice theorem in this case. Instead, we discretize simply by replacing f with its discretization $x \in \mathbb{C}^{N^2}$ at resolution N. This gives

$$\mathcal{R}f(t_i, \theta_i) \approx \sum_{j=1}^{N^2} x_i \mathcal{R}(\chi_j)(t_i, \theta_i),$$

where $\{\chi_j\}$ is the pixel basis (see §2.1). Hence we may replace (2.16) with the discrete problem

$$\text{Given the data } y = Ax, \text{ recover } x, \tag{2.20}$$

where $A \in \mathbb{R}^{m \times N^2}$ is the matrix with (i, j)th entry $\mathcal{R}(\chi_j)(t_i, \theta_i)$. Note that these entries are straightforward to compute since $\{\chi_j\}$ is the pixel basis.

This discretization is not only simpler and more flexible than the previous approach, it also commits only one discretization error, instead of three. A downside is that FFTs cannot be used for the matrix–vector multiplications. Yet, the matrix A is usually sparse, since the vast majority of pixels do not intersect a given line. Hence sparse matrix tools can be employed to accelerate computations.

2.4 Binary Sampling with the Walsh Transform

We now introduce our final transform of this chapter, the *Walsh* (or *Walsh–Hadamard*) transform. This is a binary analogue of the Fourier transform, and shares many of its properties. Additional details on this transform and proofs of the results stated in this section can be found in Appendix F.

2.4.1 Walsh Functions

The derivation of the Walsh transform begins with the definition of the so-called *Walsh functions*. These are based on dyadic representations of numbers:

Definition 2.5 The *dyadic expansion* of $x \in [0, 1)$ is the series

$$x = \sum_{i=1}^{\infty} x_i 2^{-i}, \tag{2.21}$$

where $(x_i)_{i \in \mathbb{N}} \in \{0, 1\}^{\mathbb{N}}$. The sequence $(x_i)_{i \in \mathbb{N}}$ is denoted $\dot{x}$.

The dyadic expansion defines a mapping between the set of binary sequences $\{0,1\}^{\mathbb{N}}$ and the interval $[0,1)$. This map is not one-to-one. Indeed, a dyadic rational $x = k/2^j$ can be represented either by a finite expansion, or by an infinite expansion where $x_i = 1$ for all $i > j$. This problem is easily remedied, however, by simply choosing the finite expansion instead of the infinite expansion whenever the possibility arises. This yields a one-to-one correspondence between $[0,1)$ and the subset G of $\{0,1\}^{\mathbb{N}}$, defined by

$$G = \left\{ \dot{x} = (x_i)_{i \in \mathbb{N}} \in \{0,1\}^{\mathbb{N}} : x_i = 0 \text{ infinitely often} \right\}.$$

We write $g\colon [0,1) \to G$ for the corresponding bijection. Observe that every $\dot{x} \in \{0,1\}^{\mathbb{N}} \backslash G$ has $x_i = 0$ for only finitely many i, i.e. $x_i = 1$ for all $i > j$ for some j.

Similarly, but more straightforwardly, we define the dyadic expansion of a nonnegative integer $n \in \mathbb{N}_0$ as

$$n = \sum_{i=1}^{\infty} n_i 2^{i-1}, \tag{2.22}$$

where $(n_i)_{i \in \mathbb{N}} \in \{0,1\}^{\mathbb{N}}$. This gives a one-to-one mapping $\mathbb{N}_0 \to H \subset \{0,1\}^{\mathbb{N}}$, where H is the set of binary sequences with only finitely many nonzero terms.

Definition 2.6 (Walsh functions, Paley ordering) The *Paley-ordered Walsh functions* are defined by

$$\upsilon_n(x) = \upsilon_n^P(x) = (-1)^{\sum_{i=1}^{\infty} n_i x_i}, \quad x \in [0,1),\ n \in \mathbb{N}_0, \tag{2.23}$$

where $(x_i)_{i \in \mathbb{N}} \in G$ and $(n_i)_{i \in \mathbb{N}} \in H$ are the dyadic expansions of x and n, respectively.

Figure 2.4 plots the first 16 Walsh functions. Observe that each function takes values in $\{+1,-1\}$ and has finitely many sign changes in $[0,1)$. The pattern that these sign changes take is described further in Lemma F.1.

2.4.2 The Walsh Basis and Transform

As shown in Theorem F.7, the Walsh functions $\{\upsilon_n\}_{n \in \mathbb{N}_0}$ form an orthonormal basis of $L^2([0,1))$. Hence, we may write every $f \in L^2([0,1))$ as

$$f = \sum_{n=0}^{\infty} \mathcal{H} f(n) \upsilon_n,$$

where $\mathcal{H} f(n) = \langle f, \upsilon_n \rangle_{L^2}$ are the *(Paley-ordered) Walsh coefficients* of f. We refer to the operator

$$\mathcal{H} : L^2([0,1)) \to \ell^2(\mathbb{N}_0),\ f \mapsto (\langle f, \upsilon_n \rangle_{L^2})_{n=0}^{\infty} \tag{2.24}$$

as the (Paley-ordered) *Walsh* transform (also known as the *Walsh–Hadamard* transform).

We can extend the Walsh basis to higher dimensions via tensor products. Specifically, we define the system $\{\upsilon_n\}_{n \in \mathbb{N}_0^d}$, where υ_n is the d-fold tensor product

$$\upsilon_n = \upsilon_{n_1} \otimes \cdots \otimes \upsilon_{n_d}, \qquad n = (n_1, \ldots, n_d) \in \mathbb{N}_0^d, \tag{2.25}$$

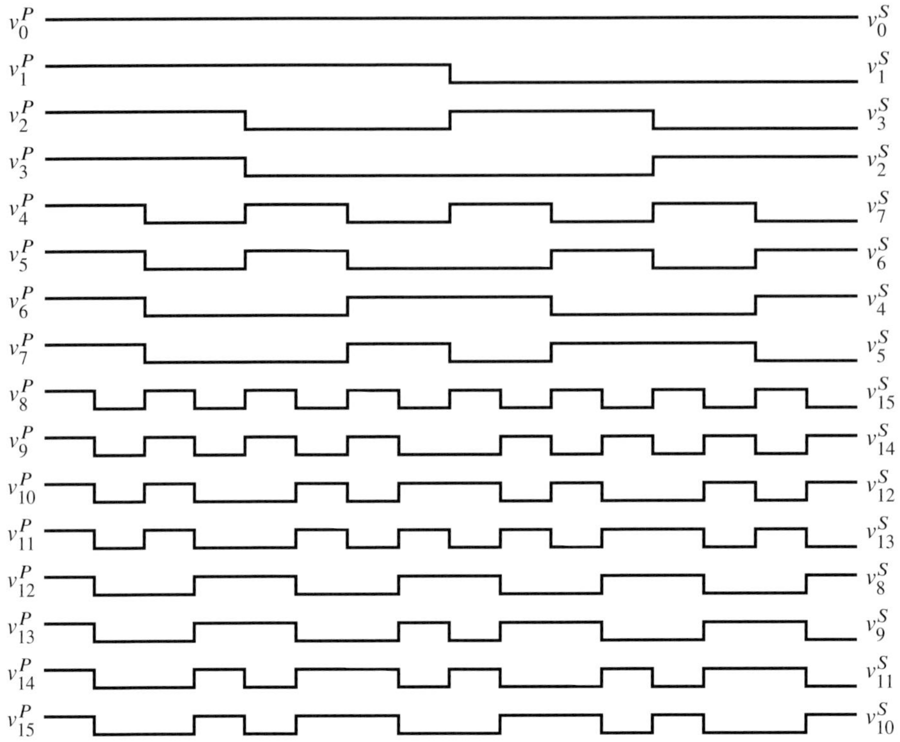

Figure 2.4 The first 16 Walsh functions with the Paley (v_n^P) or sequency (v_n^S) orderings.

of the univariate Walsh functions. This is an orthonormal basis of $L^2([0,1)^d)$ by construction. The d-dimensional Walsh transform $\mathcal{H}: L^2([0,1)^d) \to \ell^2(\mathbb{N}_0^d)$ is defined in the obvious manner.

2.4.3 The Sequency Ordering

The Paley ordering is convenient for establishing many of the theoretical properties of the Walsh functions. However, as shown in Fig. 2.4, it has the disadvantage that the number of sign changes of the nth Walsh function is generally not equal to n. The number of sign changes is known as the *sequency* of the Walsh function, a property that can be thought of as its frequency. Fortunately, this issue can be remedied by switching to the so-called *sequency* ordering:

Definition 2.7 (Walsh functions, sequency ordering) The *sequency-ordered Walsh functions* are defined by

$$v_n(x) = v_n^S(x) = (-1)^{\sum_{i=1}^{\infty}(n_i+n_{i+1})x_i}, \quad x \in [0,1),\ n \in \mathbb{N}_0,$$

where $(x_i)_{i\in\mathbb{N}} \in G$ and $(n_i)_{i\in\mathbb{N}} \in H$ are the dyadic expansions of x and n, respectively.

It will come as little surprise to the reader to learn that the sequency-ordered Walsh functions are ordered with increasing sequency. Specifically, for each n, $\upsilon_n = \upsilon_n^S$ has precisely n sign changes in $[0,1)$. See Fig. 2.4. Since sequency is analogous to frequency, we commonly refer to the index $n \in \mathbb{N}_0$ of the sequency-ordered Walsh function as the *Walsh frequency*. In particular, figures in this book showing Walsh sampling schemes (see Fig. 1.5, as well as other examples in Chapters 3 and 4) are always done with respect to this ordering.

Figure 2.4 describes the relation between the first 16 Paley- and sequency-ordered Walsh functions. As shown in Lemma F.8, in the general case one has

$$\upsilon_n^S = \upsilon_{h(n)}^P, \quad n \in \mathbb{N}_0,$$

where $h(n) \in \mathbb{N}_0$ is known as the *Gray code* of $n \in \mathbb{N}_0$. Lemma F.9 also shows that

$$\{\upsilon_n^P : 2^j \leq n < 2^{j+1}\} = \{\upsilon_n^S : 2^j \leq n < 2^{j+1}\}. \tag{2.26}$$

In particular, the first 2^r Paley-ordered Walsh functions coincide with the first 2^r sequency-ordered Walsh functions, and in general, switching between the two orderings has no effect on the *dyadic* structure of the Walsh basis.

2.4.4 The Hadamard Matrix and the Discrete Walsh–Hadamard Transform

Let $N = 2^r$ and $x = (x_j)_{j=1}^N \in \mathbb{C}^N$ be the discretization of a continuous, one-dimensional image $f\colon [0,1] \to \mathbb{C}$ at resolution N. As in §2.2.3, we can approximate the continuous Walsh transform of f by

$$\mathcal{H}f(n) \approx \frac{1}{N} \sum_{j=1}^{N} x_j \upsilon_n((j-1)/N).$$

Hence the lowest N Walsh frequencies can be approximated by

$$(\mathcal{H}f(n))_{n=0}^{N-1} \approx \frac{1}{N} Hx,$$

where $H \in \mathbb{R}^{N \times N}$ is the following matrix:

Definition 2.8 (Hadamard matrix) For $N = 2^r$, the one-dimensional *Paley- or sequency-ordered Hadamard matrix* is the matrix $H = H^{(1)} \in \mathbb{R}^{N \times N}$ with entries

$$H_{m+1,n+1} = \upsilon_m(n/N), \quad m, n = 0, \ldots, N-1,$$

where υ_m are the Paley- or sequency-ordered Walsh functions. For $d \geq 2$, the d-dimensional Hadamard matrix is given by

$$H^{(d)} = H^{(1)} \otimes \cdots \otimes H^{(1)} \in \mathbb{R}^{N^d \times N^d}.$$

As before, we write H for $H^{(d)}$ whenever the meaning in clear. The matrix H has entries in $\{-1,+1\}$. It is also symmetric, $H = H^\top$, and unitary up to a constant with $N^{-d} H^\top H = I$ (see Proposition F.10). As in one dimension, if $f\colon [0,1]^d \to \mathbb{C}$ and

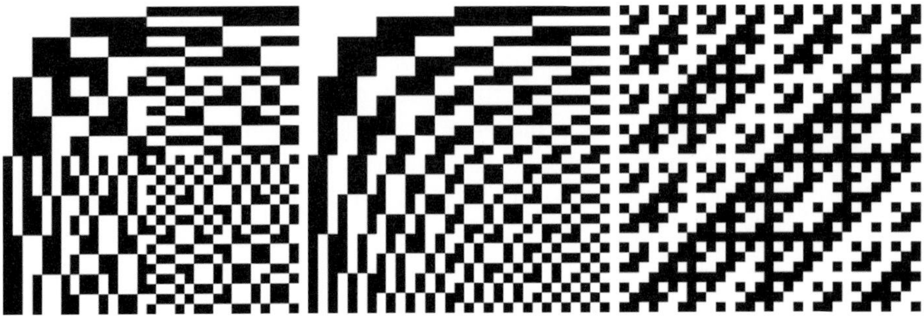

Figure 2.5 The 32×32 Hadamard matrix H with the Paley, sequency and ordinary orderings. White corresponds to a value of $+1$ and black to a value of -1.

$x \in \mathbb{C}^{N^d}$ is its discretization at resolution N, then $N^{-d}Hx$ is an approximation to the lowest N^d Walsh frequencies of f. Specifically,

$$\frac{1}{N^d} Hx \approx \left(\mathcal{H}f(\varrho^{-1}(i))\right)_{i=1}^{N^d},$$

where $\varrho = \varrho^{(d)} : \{1, \ldots, N^d\} \to \{0, \ldots, N-1\}^d$ is the bijection defined by

$$\varrho^{(d)}(i) = (\varsigma(i)_1 - 1, \ldots, \varsigma(i)_d - 1), \quad i = 1, \ldots, N^d, \tag{2.27}$$

and ς is as in (2.2).

Much like the discrete Fourier transform, the Hadamard matrix gives rise to a discrete transform $\mathcal{H} : \mathbb{C}^{N^d} \to \mathbb{C}^{N^d}$, the *Discrete Walsh–Hadamard Transform (DHT)*. It and its inverse are given by

$$\mathcal{H}(x) = Hx, \qquad \mathcal{H}^{-1}(y) = N^{-d}Hy, \qquad x, y \in \mathbb{C}^{N^d}. \tag{2.28}$$

Note that we use the letter 'H' here (rather than 'W') to avoid confusion with the Discrete Wavelet Transform (DWT) introduced in Chapter 9.

Finally, we remark that the Paley- and sequency-ordered Hadamard matrices are related to a third type of Hadamard matrix that is often found in the literature:

Definition 2.9 (Ordinary Hadamard matrix) Let $N = 2^r$. The *ordinary Hadamard matrix* $H = H_r \in \mathbb{R}^{N \times N}$ is defined by

$$H_1 = \begin{pmatrix} 1 & 1 \\ 1 & -1 \end{pmatrix}, \qquad H_r = H_{r-1} \otimes H_1 = \begin{pmatrix} H_{r-1} & H_{r-1} \\ H_{r-1} & -H_{r-1} \end{pmatrix}.$$

The ordinary Hadamard matrix is simply a reordering of the rows of of the Paley- or sequency-ordered Hadamard matrix (Proposition F.11). These three forms of the Hadamard matrix are shown in Fig. 2.5.

A motivation for introducing the ordinary Hadamard matrix is because it easily admits a fast transform. Its dyadic structure means that matrix–vector multiplications can be computed efficiently using a divide-and-conquer approach. This approach is described in §F.5. Much like the FFT, it involves only $\mathcal{O}(N \log(N))$ arithmetic operations. This means the DHT (with respect to either the Paley or sequency ordering) can also be implemented in $\mathcal{O}(N\log(N))$ time, since the Paley- or sequency-ordered Hadamard matrices are simply row permutations of the ordinary Hadamard matrix. We refer to the resulting procedure as the *Fast Walsh–Hadamard Transform (FHT)*.

2.4.5 The Continuous and Discrete Walsh Reconstruction Problems

Let $\Omega \subset \mathbb{N}_0^d$ be a finite set of Walsh frequencies (recall that this means we are considering the sequency ordering) and $f : [0,1]^d \to \mathbb{C}$ be a continuous d-dimensional image. The continuous Walsh reconstruction problem is

$$\text{Given the data } \{\mathcal{H}f(n) : n \in \Omega\}, \text{ recover } f.$$

To derive the discrete problem, let N be such that $\Omega \subseteq \{0,\ldots,N-1\}^d$ and $P \in \mathbb{R}^{m\times N^d}$ be the row selector matrix that picks out the rows of the sequency-ordered Hadamard matrix $H \in \mathbb{R}^{N^d\times N^d}$ corresponding to the values

$$\{\varrho^{-1}(n) : n \in \Omega\} \subseteq \{1,\ldots,N^d\},$$

where ϱ is as in (2.27). If $x \in \mathbb{C}^{N^d}$ is the discretization of f at resolution N, then the corresponding discrete reconstruction problem is simply

$$\text{Given the data } y = Ax, \text{ recover } x,$$

where $A = PH \in \mathbb{R}^{m\times N^d}$ is the corresponding *subsampled Hadamard matrix.*

Notes

The introduction to images given in §2.1 is brief, but sufficient for the remainder of this book. For a significantly more in-depth treatment, see for example [50]. See [50,273,491] for further discussion on the limitations of MSE and PSNR for assessing image quality.

The Shepp–Logan phantom ('SL phantom' in Fig. 2.2) is a famous test image in medical imaging, introduced in 1974 by Shepp and Logan [437]. It is a continuous, piecewise constant image defined as a sum of ten ellipses. In particular, its continuous Fourier and Radon transforms can be calculated exactly. Unfortunately, the SL phantom is rather too simple a test image in many cases. This motivated the development of the second image in Fig. 2.2, the 'GLPU phantom', introduced by Guerquin-Kern, Lejeune, Pruessmann & Unser [245]. Like the SL phantom it is a continuous, piecewise constant image with an analytic expression for its Fourier transform. Discretized versions of both images can, of course, be generated at any resolution. The 'brain' image is a 512×512 image obtained from an actual MRI scan. The resolution is limited by the scanner, and the object being scanned (a human brain). The 'pomegranate' image is a 2048×2048 image from an MRI scan of a pomegranate fruit, the higher resolution being possible in this case because the object is not a living subject.

The 'peppers' image is also a standard test image in image processing. It can be found in a database maintained by the University of Southern California's Signal and

Image Processing Institute [1]. The original image is colour, and of size 512×512. The 'donkey' image is from the authors' collection and is of size 768×768.

Our cursory treatment of the Radon transform hardly does it justice. Whole books have been devoted to its mathematical properties and practical implementation. We have based §2.3 on [198, 204, 305, 370]. Derivations of the Fourier-slice theorem (2.17) and filtered back-projection formula (2.19) can be found in these sources. What makes the Radon transform challenging and interesting, both theoretically and computationally, is the question of its inversion. Filtered back-projection (2.19) is just one possible *left inverse*. However, there are many others. This stems from the fact that the range of the Radon transform is not the whole space. In contrast, the Fourier transform has a unique inverse on $L^2(\mathbb{R})$.

Discretization of the filtered back-projection formula, as described in §2.3.5, is the standard means to numerically invert the Radon transform in the classical setting – that is, where there is 'sufficient' data. For an in-depth treatment, see [198, Chpt. 10] and [370, Chpt. 5]. By and large, this remains the standard algorithm for commercial X-ray CT scanners [386] (see also the Notes section of Chapter 3). The other approach described in §2.3.6 is related to the so-called *Algebraic Reconstruction Technique (ART)*. It ignores properties of the Radon transform such as the Fourier-slice theorem and simply discretizes the continuous image. Classically, when the number of measurements m exceeds the number of degrees of freedom N^d this has been solved as an overdetermined (and possibly also regularized) least-squares problem. Fast solvers use iterative algorithms such as Kaczmarz's method. See [198, 370]. As we note in §3.3, this type of discretization is often preferred when applying compressed sensing techniques.

Walsh series were introduced by Walsh in 1923 [485]. They are far less well known than their famous Fourier cousin, and used far less widely in practice. Historically, Walsh series have found applications in coding theory and image and signal processing. Our treatment here and in Appendix F covers only the basic properties, which will be sufficient for the remainder of this book. We have based these sections on [54, 224, 232], all of which contain far greater detail. The various orderings of the Walsh basis are sometimes given different names in the literature. The sequency ordering is often referred to as the *Walsh–Kaczmarz* ordering [54, p. 17], and the Paley ordering as the *natural*, *normal* or *dyadic* ordering. Typically, the Paley ordering is preferred for theory, whereas the sequency ordering is favoured in practice, due to its analogy with frequency.

3 A Short Guide to Compressive Imaging

In this chapter, we first introduce a general pipeline for compressive imaging (§3.1). We discuss the six stages of this process, along with a series of key considerations. As we explain, these considerations are heavily dependent on the problem being considered. We therefore devote the remainder of the chapter to exploring them in the context of various examples. We begin in §3.2 with MRI. MRI has been one of the main beneficiaries of compressed sensing, which makes it a natural starting point. In §3.3 we consider our second example, X-ray CT, before considering our third example, optical imaging, in §3.4. Finally, in §3.5 we discuss the recovery of image sequences and its application to so-called *parallel* MRI.

3.1 The Six Stages of the Compressive Imaging Pipeline

These are as follows:

1. Identify a mathematical model. First, we formulate the reconstruction problem as a linear inverse problem. In the continuous setting, this is

$$y = \mathcal{A} f + e, \tag{3.1}$$

where $y \in \mathbb{C}^m$ is a vector of measurements, $e \in \mathbb{C}^m$ is a vector of measurement noise, $\mathcal{A}$ is the linear operator representing the acquisition process and $f : [0, 1]^d \to \mathbb{C}$ is the unknown (continuous) image. The operator $\mathcal{A}$ is determined by the physical sensing apparatus, and substantial effort may be required to describe it mathematically. In the discrete setting, we simply have a (vectorized) image $x \in \mathbb{C}^N$ and a matrix $A \in \mathbb{C}^{m \times N}$.

Considerations
(i) How accurate a model is $\mathcal{A}$ (or A)? What is the tradeoff between a better model, accuracy of the reconstruction and computational efficiency?
(ii) In particular, is the acquisition process truly linear? If not, how should one deal with the nonlinearities?
(iii) What is an appropriate noise model for the problem, and how does this affect the choice of recovery procedure?

This derivation of $\mathcal{A}$ is not the focus of this book. We will briefly describe how this is done in MRI and X-ray CT (see §3.2 and §3.3, respectively). After that, we simply assume that this is an exact model for the problem. As we explain subsequently, MRI and X-ray CT can be modelled as linear inverse problems in most circumstances. We do not discuss in detail how nonlinearities arise in these or other inverse problems, nor how to deal with them. Similarly, we usually assume that the noise e is Gaussian, thus motivating the use of ℓ^2-norm data-fitting terms. Later, we note some instances where this assumption may not be reasonable.

2. Choose a discretization. If the inverse problem is already in a discrete form, which it may be in certain cases, this step can be skipped. However, in general, a discretization of (3.1) is needed to obtain a finite-dimensional problem

$$y = Ax + e, \tag{3.2}$$

amenable to computations.

Considerations
(iv) How should such a discretization be performed?
(v) How does the choice of discretization affect accuracy and efficiency?

Discretization was already discussed in Chapter 2. As observed, this induces an error which may cause significant artefacts in the recovered images. These artefacts can sometimes be mitigated by increasing the resolution (i.e. increasing N). Yet this, at the very least, increases the computational cost. Other discretization strategies may be needed in practice to avoid such artefacts.

3. Choose an image model. In the case of data-driven approaches such as deep learning (see §1.7), this step may be skipped since an image model is learned (either explicitly or implicitly) from the training data. Conversely, in model-based approaches such as compressed sensing, this step corresponds to choosing a sparsifying transform.

Considerations
(vi) What is a good sparsifying transform for the images under consideration?
(vii) Does this transform yield additional structure beyond sparsity?
(viii) How does the choice of sparsifying transform influence the choice of (a) the measurements and (b) the recovery procedure?

Standard sparsifying transforms in imaging are orthonormal wavelet transforms or the discrete gradient operator, with the latter leading to Total Variation (TV) minimization. These transforms are developed in depth later in this book, along with the necessary mathematics to fully understand considerations (vi)–(viii) in these cases. More exotic choices, including curvelets, shearlets, higher-order gradients or combinations of several different sparsifying transforms, are discussed in Chapter 4.

It is important to stress that compressed sensing involves the design of the sparsifying transform *and* the measurements. The tradeoff is often crucial. A well-designed sparsifying transform (i.e. one leading to very sparse representations) may perform poorly when combined with the wrong type of measurements.

4. Determine which measurements to acquire. The next step is to select the measurements. In some cases, it may be possible to identify a good sampling strategy – from the point of view of getting the highest-quality reconstruction – by mathematical analysis of the problem. As discussed in §1.5 for example, random Gaussian measurements are optimal for the recovery of sparse vectors. Yet, as noted in §1.4, one may not have the freedom to perform this type of sampling, since physical constraints in the sensing apparatus often place limitations on the type of measurements allowed.

Considerations
(ix) What types of measurements are allowed – for example, are they Fourier measurements, binary measurements or some other type?
(x) What is a good sampling strategy within the constraints identified in (ix)? In model-based strategies such as compressed sensing, how does this depend on the choice of sparsifying transform, the sparsity structure and the recovery procedure?
(xi) Can this sampling strategy be realized in practice? If not, what is a good sampling strategy within the physical constraints?

These considerations are discussed later in the context of the various examples.

5. Choose a recovery procedure. The penultimate step is to specify a *reconstruction map* (also termed a *decoder*) $\mathrm{R}: \mathbb{C}^m \to \mathbb{C}^N$ that takes the measurements y as an input and gives (an approximation to) x as the output. In the case of model-based strategies, this mapping should be designed to promote the chosen image model (e.g. sparsity in a wavelet transform). However, in all cases it must also have an efficient computational implementation (see next).

In the context of compressed sensing, a standard option, already discussed in Chapter 1, involves solving the Quadratically Constrained Basis Pursuit (QCBP) problem

$$\min_{z \in \mathbb{C}^N} \|\Phi^* z\|_{\ell^1} \text{ subject to } \|Az - y\|_{\ell^2} \leq \eta. \tag{3.3}$$

Here $\Phi \in \mathbb{C}^{N \times M}$, $M \geq N$, is the matrix of the sparsifying transform. Note that $M = N$ for orthonormal sparsifying transforms such as wavelets, however $M > N$ for choices such as curvelets and shearlets. See §4.5. Problem (3.3) is commonly referred to as the *analysis* problem, since it promotes sparsity of the coefficients $\Phi^* x$ in the sparsifying transform. An alternative is the *synthesis* problem

$$\min_{z \in \mathbb{C}^M} \|z\|_{\ell^1} \text{ subject to } \|A\Phi z - y\|_{\ell^2} \leq \eta, \tag{3.4}$$

which promotes a sparse representation of x, i.e. $x = \Phi d$ with d approximately sparse. Note that if $\hat{d} \in \mathbb{C}^M$ is a minimizer of this problem, then the approximation to x is given by $\hat{x} = \Phi \hat{d}$. As we discussed in §5.4.3, the problems (3.3) and (3.4) are equivalent when Φ is unitary, but differ in general. This aside, one may also prefer an unconstrained optimization problem such as the analysis LASSO

$$\min_{z \in \mathbb{C}^N} \lambda \|\Phi^* z\|_{\ell^1} + \|Az - y\|^2_{\ell^2}, \tag{3.5}$$

or its analogous synthesis formulation.

Considerations
(xii) How does the choice of recovery procedure influence accuracy and stability? How does this depend on the image model and the measurements?
(xiii) How should the parameters of the recovery procedure be chosen?

The compressed sensing component of this book is primarily focused on variants of the QCBP and LASSO problems – these are by far the most popular choices in practice. Yet, the performance of an optimization-based approach is typically quite dependent on good choices of the optimization parameter or parameters (i.e. η in (3.3) and λ in (3.5)). *Parameter tuning* is an important task for maximizing image quality, and by no means straightforward. In practice, it may depend on the type of image, the scaling of the data, the subsampling rate m/N, the sparsifying transform and the sampling scheme. We shall not discuss empirical parameter tuning strategies in any detail (see Chapter 4 for some further information). We do, however, identify theoretically optimal parameter choices for the QCBP and LASSO decoders, plus several others, in Chapter 6. In the context of deep learning, carefully setting the parameters in the procedure used to train the reconstruction map is also crucial. See Chapter 18 for further details.

6. Find an algorithm to perform the computations. The next, and final, stage is to find an algorithm to perform the necessary computations. In compressed sensing, this generally means finding an algorithm to compute (approximate) minimizers of the QCBP or LASSO optimization problems. Conversely, in deep learning, this means finding an algorithm that implements the training procedure that learns the reconstruction map R.

Considerations
(xiv) Can the necessary computations be performed efficiently?
(xv) Are there standard software packages for doing this?
(xvi) If not, how can one design an efficient algorithm?

We discuss these considerations further in the case of deep learning in Part V. In compressed sensing, generally speaking, concerns over (xiv) boil down to two factors: first, whether the algorithm needs to form A or Φ explicitly, or whether it only needs to perform matrix–vector multiplications with A, Φ and their adjoints; second, whether A and Φ have fast transforms that perform these operations efficiently.

Obviously, an affirmative answer to (xv) is desirable. Most software packages typically only implement some of the standard recovery procedures. For instance, many packages solve the synthesis problem (3.4), but not the analysis problem (3.3). When software is not available, designing a good algorithm from scratch requires additional effort, as does choosing the parameters that inevitably come with it (e.g. stepsizes, tolerances for stopping criteria). We consider optimization methods for compressive imaging further in Chapter 7.

Remark 3.1 Most of the compressed sensing examples in this book use basic recovery procedures involving QCBP or LASSO with wavelets or TV. Fortunately, there are many good software implementations of these problems. This allows us to focus on the major concerns of this book, namely, sampling and structure, rather than the challenges of

Table 3.1 The software packages and algorithms used in this book, unless otherwise stated. SPGL1 and NESTA are software packages. FISTA is an optimization algorithm which is described in Chapter 7.

Package/algorithm	Problem solved	Primary use
SPGL1	QCBP synthesis	Wavelets
NESTA	QCBP synthesis/analysis	TV
FISTA	LASSO synthesis	Wavelets

solving these problems in the first place. After experimentation, we settled on the three packages described in Table 3.1, which will be used henceforth unless stated otherwise. Note that FISTA is not a package per se, but an algorithm. It is discussed in Chapter 7. However, its implementation is fairly straightforward.

As mentioned in §1.10.1, further information about these packages (e.g. tolerances, parameters, etc.) can be found on the associated website. In the Notes section we also mention several other packages for the interested reader.

3.2 First Example: MRI

We now describe this pipeline in the context of several examples. We focus on the case of compressed sensing, reserving a discussion of deep learning for Part V. We begin in this section with (single-coil) MRI.

3.2.1 The Mathematical Model

MRI is based on rather subtle quantum mechanical phenomena. Providing the full derivation that leads to the so-called *image equation* would require a whole chapter, if not more. Hence, we limit ourselves to a rather short summary and refer to the Notes section for appropriate references. MRI is inherently a three-dimensional problem. Hence we base this derivation on a three-dimensional example. However, with certain modifications, similar ideas apply in two dimensions as well.

In most medical MRI applications one seeks to image the *spin density function*, that is, the distribution of spins arising from hydrogen protons in water molecules. Human tissue consists largely of water, and hence MRI is useful for imaging internal organs. The spin density function is usually denoted by

$$\rho\colon [0,1]^d \to [0,\infty),$$

where, in this discussion, the dimension $d = 3$.

A typical MRI setup consists of the following three key magnetic fields:

(a) The *static (time-independent)* field B_0. This field is parallel to the z-axis and induced by the main magnet in the scanner. Here we consider a coordinate system so that a three-dimensional vector is described as $(x, y, z) \in \mathbb{R}^3$ and the z-axis is parallel to the patient lying in the scanner. See Fig. 3.1.

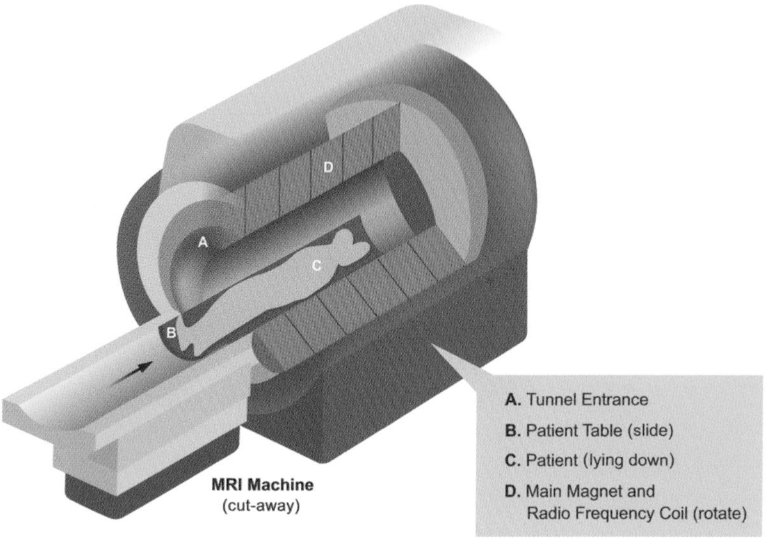

Figure 3.1 A cut-away of an MRI scanner showing the main magnet that creates the field B_0. Credit: Graphic_BKK1979/iStock/Getty Images Plus (detail).

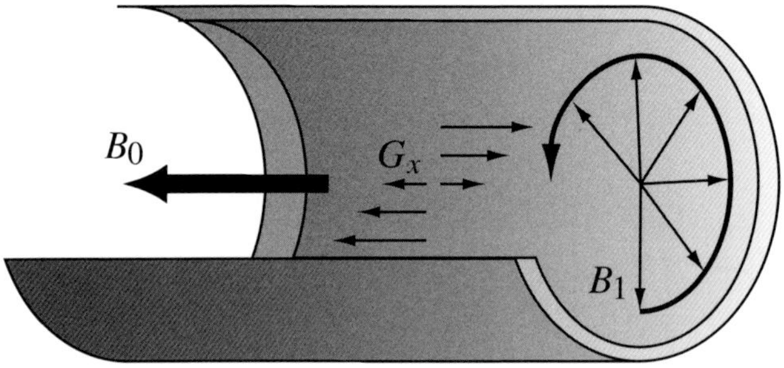

Figure 3.2 The magnetic fields B_0, B_1 and B_G. To simplify, only the G_x component of B_G is shown.

(b) The *Radio Frequency (RF)* field B_1. This is transverse to the z-axis and possibly time dependent.

(c) The *gradient* field B_G. This is parallel to the z-axis and potentially time dependent. It takes the form $B_G(r,t) = (0,0,G_x(t)x+G_y(t)y+G_z(t)z) = (0,0,G(t)\cdot r)$, where $G\colon [0,T] \to \mathbb{R}^3$ and $r = (x,y,z)$.

The total magnetic field, shown in Fig. 3.2, is the sum of these three fields:

$$B(r,t) = B_0(r) + B_G(r,t) + B_1(r,t).$$

The *magnetization* $M\colon [0,\infty) \times \mathbb{R}^3 \to \mathbb{R}^3$ induced by this field is governed by the *Bloch equation*:

$$\frac{\mathrm{d}M}{\mathrm{d}t} = \gamma M \times B - \frac{M^{\perp}}{T_2} + \frac{M_0 - M^{\parallel}}{T_1}. \tag{3.6}$$

Here $M^{\perp}$ is the component of M perpendicular to the z-axis, $M^{\parallel}$ is the component parallel to the z-axis, $M_0 = \mu\rho B_0$ is the equilibrium magnetization and μ is a constant.

The terms γ, T_1 and T_2 are constants depending on the particular material and tissue being scanned.

Making suitable assumptions, one can use (3.6) to show that the signal measured at the so-called *receiver coil* at time t is

$$S(\omega(t)) = \kappa e^{-\frac{t}{T_2}} \int_{\mathbb{R}^3} \rho(r) \mathrm{e}^{-2\pi \mathrm{i} \omega(t) \cdot r} \, \mathrm{d}r, \tag{3.7}$$

where

$$\omega(t) = \nu \int_0^t G(s) \, \mathrm{d}s, \tag{3.8}$$

and κ and ν are constants. Assuming the total acquisition time is small, we may neglect the exponential decay term to yield (up to a constant)

$$S(\omega(t)) = \mathcal{F}\rho(2\pi\omega(t)), \tag{3.9}$$

where the right-hand side is the Fourier transform of ρ. This is referred to as the *image equation*. It is a continuous mathematical model for the MRI acquisition process. The gradient field G is designed so that $\omega(t)$ traverses a piecewise continuous trajectory in frequency space, and (3.7) is usually sampled at fixed time intervals. The result is a finite set of Fourier measurements of ρ along the given trajectory.

While a full discussion is outside our scope, a few remarks on considerations (i)–(iii) are in order. With regards to (i) and (ii), neglecting the exponential decay factor e^{-t/T_2} in (3.7) is potentially an issue for the accuracy of the model. This depends on T_2 and the scanning time. As for (iii), it is standard in MRI to assume Gaussian noise that is independent of the frequency location. As higher-frequency measurements are generally smaller in amplitude, the corresponding samples are likely to be relatively more sensitive to noise. This problem is further augmented by the fact that high-frequency measurements may require longer scanning time, making the presence of the exponential decay factor e^{-t/T_2} an even more delicate issue.

3.2.2 Discretization

We have now seen that the MRI problem can be modelled as sampling the Fourier transform $\mathcal{F} f$ of the unknown image f (for consistency we now revert to writing f for the image). Hence we may use the strategy described in §2.2.3 to discretize it. Here f is replaced by its discretization $x \in \mathbb{C}^{N^d}$ on a grid of resolution N, and $\mathcal{F}$ is replaced by the d-dimensional Fourier matrix F. Let

$$\Omega \subseteq \{-N/2+1, \ldots, N/2\}^d, \qquad |\Omega| = m$$

be the subset of k-space values (assumed to be integer) that are measured by the receiver coil. Then we can model the MRI problem as the discrete Fourier reconstruction problem

$$y = Ax + e, \qquad A = PF, \tag{3.10}$$

where $P \in \mathbb{C}^{m \times N^d}$ is the row selector matrix introduced in §2.2.3 and $e \in \mathbb{C}^m$ is the measurement noise.

This discretization is convenient for computations, since it is amenable to FFTs. On the other hand, it may lead to artefacts, due to the mismatch between the data (continuous Fourier measurements of a function) and the model (discrete Fourier measurements of a vector). These artefacts are known as *Gibbs phenomena* (or ringing), and appear as wave-like oscillations near the edges of the image. Figure 3.3 shows these artefacts.

It is important to note that these artefacts are a result of subsampling the full set of frequencies $\{-N/2+1,\ldots,N/2\}^d$. Indeed, suppose that $m = N^d$, so all N^d lowest Fourier frequencies are sampled. Then, ignoring noise, the problem (3.10) becomes the $N^d \times N^d$ linear system

$$y = Fx, \tag{3.11}$$

where y contains the values $\mathcal{F}f(2\pi\omega)$, $\omega \in \{-N/2+1,\ldots,N/2\}^d$. Let

$$f_N = \sum_{\omega \in \{-N/2+1,\ldots,N/2\}^d} \langle f, \upsilon_\omega \rangle \upsilon_\omega = \sum_{\omega \in \{-N/2+1,\ldots,N/2\}^d} \mathcal{F}f(2\pi\omega)\upsilon_\omega$$

be the truncated Fourier series of f. It follows from the definition of F that the entries of $x = F^{-1}y$ are (up to the constant factor N^{-d}) exactly equal to the grid values of f_N:

$$\{f_N((i_1-1)/N,\ldots,(i_d-1)/N) : i_1,\ldots,i_d = 1,\ldots,N\}.$$

In other words, the reconstruction x obtained from this discrete model is nothing more than the discretization at resolution N of the truncated Fourier series f_N of the original image f. Since f typically has edges (i.e. discontinuities), it is poorly approximated by its truncated Fourier series f_N, the latter being a finite sum of the smooth complex exponentials υ_ω. The result, as seen in Fig. 3.3, is the Gibbs phenomenon.

In Chapter 14 we introduce an alternative discretization that avoids the Gibbs phenomenon in the standard discretization (3.10). This is based on so-called *infinite-dimensional compressed sensing*.

3.2.3 Sparsifying Transforms and Recovery Procedure

Putting this issue aside and continuing with the discrete model (3.10), the next step is to select a sparsifying transform Φ. Standard choices in MRI are orthonormal wavelet or discrete gradient transforms. In Fig. 3.4 we show two compressed sensing reconstructions based on these transforms. As expected, both procedures recover the image well, certainly better than the classical zero-padded inverse DFT reconstruction (recall §1.2). Yet the recovery is not perfect. As can be seen in the cropped images, they each introduce some sort of unphysical artefacts. One sees the characteristic blocky artefacts caused by wavelets, while the TV transform leads to a more 'cartoon-like' image. We consider several other choices for Φ in §4.5.

To compute these reconstructions, we solved the QCBP analysis problem (3.4), with A as in (3.10), $y = Ax + e$ where x is the exact image, and e having i.i.d. Gaussian entries with mean zero and variance σ^2. We set the parameter η in (3.4) as $\eta^2 = \mathbb{E}\|e\|_{\ell^2}^2 = m\sigma^2$. Justification for this choice is given in Chapter 6.

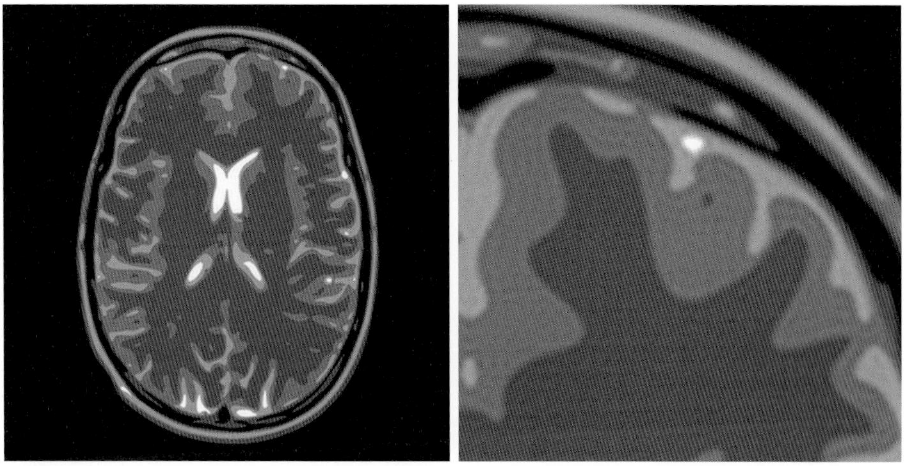

Figure 3.3 The Fourier series approximation f_N of the GLPU phantom image (see Fig. 2.2) with $N = 256$ shows Gibbs artefacts. Left: Full image. Right: Crop.

Note that the data for this experiment was simulated with the discrete model (that is, using the Fourier matrix F), rather than the continuous model. We therefore committed the *inverse crime* – a topic that will be discussed further in §4.4.

3.2.4 The Choice of Measurements

A primary concern in MRI is either to reduce the acquisition time while retaining image quality, or to improve image quality without lengthening the acquisition time.

Roughly speaking, the length of the acquisition is proportional to the number of measurements taken. Hence, it is critical to design Ω so as to maximize the reconstruction quality from a given measurement budget. As raised in consideration (x), optimizing Ω is often a nontrivial affair: it depends on the sparsifying transform, the sparsity structure and the recovery procedure. We shall discuss sampling strategy design in more depth in Chapter 4. However, let us first briefly illustrate how the choice of Ω can have a dramatic effect on the reconstruction.

In Fig. 3.5 we consider three choices for Ω: *uniform random sampling*, *half–half sampling* and *Gaussian multilevel sampling*. These are defined in §4.1. This figure shows Ω in each case and the reconstruction obtained from the corresponding measurements. As we see, despite all three sampling patterns using exactly the same total number of measurements, the quality of the reconstruction is highly dependent on the distribution of the samples. The first patten gives a meaningless reconstruction. The second yields a significantly improved reconstruction but still with some noticeable artefacts. The third gives the best reconstruction. The reasons behind this will be elaborated on in §4.2.

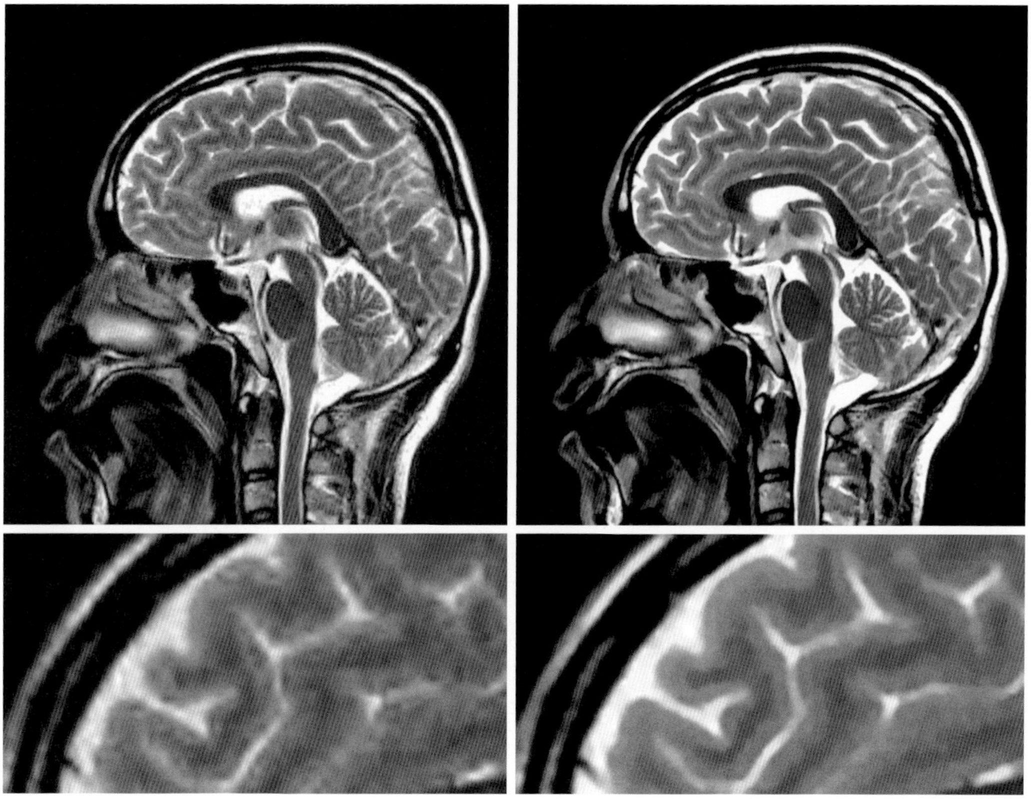

Figure 3.4 Reconstructions of the 512×512 brain image (see Fig. 2.2) from 15% discrete Fourier measurements (i.e. $m = 0.15 \times 512^2 = 39,321$) with different sparsifying transforms. Gaussian noise with standard deviation $\sigma = 0.001$ was added to the measurements, and the reconstructions were computed by solving (3.4) (left) or (3.3) (right) with $\eta = \sqrt{m}\sigma$. The sampling strategy is a Gaussian multilevel strategy based on the ℓ^2-ball with $a = 1$, $r_0 = 2$ and $r = 50$ (see §4.1.3). Top row: Full images. Bottom row: Crops.

3.2.5 Practical Considerations

In a two-dimensional MR acquisition, the sampling patterns used in Fig. 3.5 are typically infeasible. An MR scanner acquires k-space data continuously along piecewise smooth curves, whereas all these sampling patterns select individual frequencies. Designing a practical sampling strategy is unfortunately not a simple matter of fitting a smooth curve through these points. Such a pattern could easily exceed the maximum allowable scanner gradients, rendering it infeasible. Further complicating matters, the acquisition time in MRI is related to the length and geometry of the curves to be traversed, and not just the number of measurements acquired. An alternative, and arguably more straightforward, approach is to tune a standard MRI sampling trajectory, such as radial, spiral or Cartesian

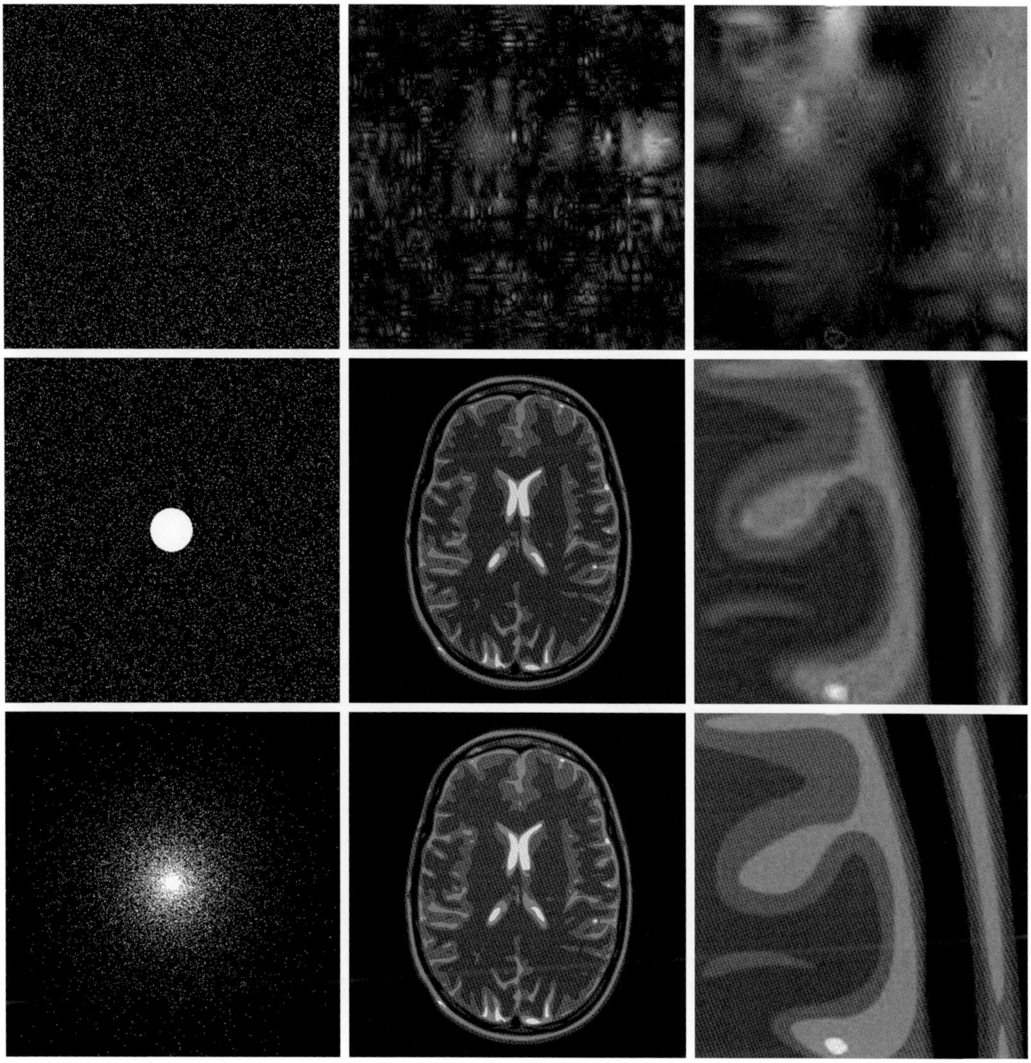

Sampling map Reconstruction Crop

Figure 3.5 Recovery of the discrete 2048×2048 GLPU phantom from 5% discrete Fourier measurements. First row: Uniform random sampling. Second row: Half–half sampling based on a circle with $(m_1, m_2) = (m/4, 3m/4)$. Third row: Gaussian multilevel sampling based on the ℓ^2-ball with $a = 1$, $r_0 = 2$ and $r = 100$. The reconstructions were computed by solving (3.4) with a DB4 wavelet sparsifying transform. The left column shows the sampling map used. Each white dot represents a frequency sampled. The zero frequency is located in the centre.

(see §4.1), to mimic a good performing sampling strategy, such as the Gaussian multilevel pattern of Fig. 3.5.

On the other hand, the sampling strategies introduced above are implementable in three-dimensional MR acquisitions. In this case, each point in the sampling pattern represents a line of frequency values in the third k-space dimension, which is fully sampled. Other sampling strategies which subsample in all three k-space dimensions are also possible, however – for example, three-dimensional spiral sampling.

A sampling trajectory in MRI will not take measurements at exactly integer frequencies. In order to use the above discretization, one can replace the true frequencies with their nearest integer values (nearest-neighbour gridding). However, this process – already mentioned in §2.3.5 in the context of Radon sampling – introduces an additional mismatch between the model and the data, which may further deteriorate the reconstruction quality. An alternative is to use better gridding strategies. Another is to work directly with the noninteger frequencies by employing *nonuniform FFTs*.

Finally, we remark that the maximal frequency N (the resolution of the discrete problem) is related to the strength of the magnetic fields. This is itself limited by the strength of the magnet and by patient considerations. As a result, arbitrarily high resolutions cannot be achieved in practical, and especially clinical, settings. Hence sampling strategies and recovery procedures much be capable of performing well at realistic resolutions.

3.3 Second Example: X-ray CT

We now move on to our second example, X-ray CT.

3.3.1 The Mathematical Model

X-ray CT and other forms of tomographic imaging are based on the principle that different materials – for instance, bone, muscle, grey matter – absorb particles at different rates when a beam (e.g. an X-ray) is passed through them. A CT image is a two-dimensional slice of an object showing the different absorption rates of the various materials in the slice.

The absorption rate, or *attenuation coefficient* as it is often known, cannot be measured directly. Indirect measurements are collected instead. This is done by passing a narrow beam (or beams) of X-rays through the medium at a given angle and displacement. The input intensity of the beam is known, and its output intensity is measured by a detector placed on the opposite side of the medium. The ratio of output intensity to input intensity (clearly less than one, since some photons will have been absorbed or scattered) gives a measure of the average absorption of the medium along the direction of the beam.

Clearly the measurement from a single beam is insufficient on its own to recover the attenuation coefficient throughout the slice. Hence the orientation of the beam is changed, and the process repeated at each new orientation. The result is a set of measurements at a sequence of angles and displacements. By varying the orientation in a systematic way, one aims to collect enough measurements to allow for reconstruction of the attenuation coefficient over the whole slice.

Unlike in MRI, a mathematical model for X-ray CT can be derived from simple physics. Consider a single X-ray beam passing through a medium. Let l be the corresponding line in the plane and $s \in \mathbb{R}$ be its arclength variable. Suppose that I_0 is the initial intensity of the beam at $s = a$ and I_1 is its output intensity (the measured value) at $s = b$. Let $I(s)$ be its intensity at an arbitrary point s between a and b, and $\mu(s)$ be the attenuation coefficient of the medium at s. *Beer's Law* states that the relative change in intensity ΔI when passing a small distance along the beam from s to $s + \Delta s$ is given by

$$\frac{\Delta I}{I(s)} = -\mu(s)\Delta s.$$

Letting $\Delta s \to 0$, this gives the ordinary differential equation

$$\frac{\mathrm{d}I}{\mathrm{d}s} = -\mu(s)I(s).$$

Integrating this equation along the line from the input (where the intensity is I_0) to the output (where the intensity is I_1), we obtain

$$I_1 = I_0 \exp\left(-\int_a^b \mu(s)\,\mathrm{d}s\right) \quad \Leftrightarrow \quad \int_a^b \mu(s)\,\mathrm{d}s = \log\left(\frac{I_0}{I_1}\right).$$

It is reasonable to assume the absorption rate outside the medium is zero. Hence this is equivalent to

$$\int_l \mu\,\mathrm{d}s = \log\left(\frac{I_0}{I_1}\right),$$

where the left-hand side is the integral of μ along the line l. Therefore a single X-ray CT measurement can be modelled as one evaluation of the Radon transform $\mathcal{R}\mu$ of the attenuation coefficient μ. As a result, the overall X-ray CT reconstruction problem can be modelled as the Radon reconstruction problem (2.16).

3.3.2 Practical Considerations

The above model makes several assumptions. First, there is no refraction or diffraction of the beam. This is reasonable in X-ray CT since X-rays have high energies. Second, the beam is infinitely thin. In practice, a thin beam is created through a process known as *collimation*, and in X-ray CT this is often not a significant issue. Third, the X-rays are *monochromatic*: the photons in the beam have the same energy level. This assumption is unrealistic in medical and laboratory X-ray CT scanners. But without it the inverse problem becomes nonlinear and significantly more difficult to solve. In contrast with the previous two, this third assumption can lead to a particular type of artefact in the reconstructed images, known as *beam hardening*.

Since X-ray CT involves high-intensity beams, it is common to model the noise as Gaussian. This assumption may fail, however, in the low-dose setting or in other tomographic modalities.

3.3.3 Measurements

Unlike in MRI, scan times in X-ray CT are typically fast. The primary motivation for reducing the number of measurements in X-ray CT is to reduce the radiation dosage to which a patient is exposed.

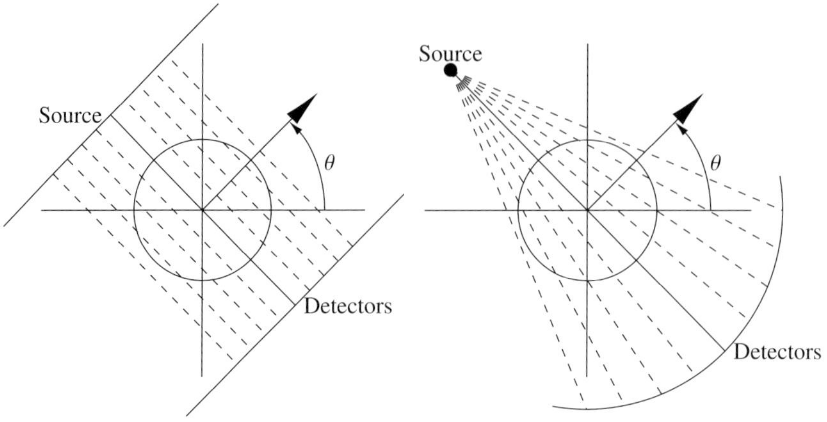

Figure 3.6 Typical geometries in X-ray CT. Left: Parallel beam. Right: Fan beam.

As seen above, selecting measurements in X-ray CT is equivalent to choosing a set of m lines, or equivalently, in the parametrization introduced in §2.3, angles and displacements. This choice is constrained by the geometry of the scanning apparatus.

There are several standard geometries used in practice. In the *parallel beam* geometry, for each choice of angle θ, a large number of beams are sent through the object in parallel and measured on the other side by a strip of detectors. This is shown in Fig. 3.6. This means that the full Radon projection $\mathcal{R}f(\cdot, \theta)$ is acquired at each chosen angle. The angle is then varied, and the process repeated. On the other hand, in *fan beam* geometry, X-rays are sent from a single source in a fan pattern. These are measured on the other side of the object by a circular arc of detectors, giving a collection of Radon measurements along the corresponding set of lines. The apparatus is then rotated, each time giving a different set of Radon measurements. An example of this is also shown in Fig. 3.6.

Parallel beam geometries are appealing because of the Fourier-slice theorem (see §2.3.3). However, fan beam geometries are often preferred in practice as they allow for faster scanning. Both of these geometries can be used in a slice-by-slice manner to image a three-dimensional object. But it is also possible to scan in a fully three-dimensional way, for example using so-called *cone beam* or *spiral beam* geometries.

> In contrast with MRI, there is generally far less scope to change the measurements acquired in X-ray CT. Measurements are largely dictated by the scanner geometry.

For instance, in parallel beam geometry one may decrease the number of angles, thus reducing the number of lines along which the Fourier transform is sampled. But this is nowhere near as flexible as changing the whole k-space trajectory, as is possible in MRI. For this reason, we spend no more time in this book on the design of Radon measurements.

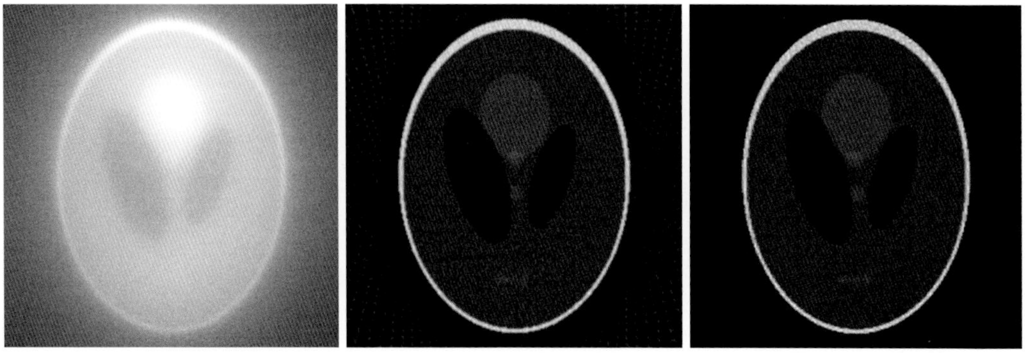

(a) Back-projection (b) Filtered back-projection (c) Compressed sensing

Figure 3.7 Reconstruction of the discretized 256×256 SL phantom (see Fig. 2.2) from discrete Radon measurements taken at 50 equally spaced angles. (a) Zero-padded back-projection. (b) Zero-padded filtered back-projection. (c) Compressed sensing using DB2 wavelets and the LASSO problem (3.5) with $\lambda = \sigma$ and $\sigma = 0.001$.

3.3.4 Discretization and Experiment

The two main options for discretizing the continuous Radon reconstruction problem were described in §2.3.5 and §2.3.6. Discretization via the Fourier-slice theorem (§2.3.5), leading to the equivalent problem of sampling the Fourier transform along radial lines, is possible in the case of parallel beam geometries. For other geometries, especially when the data is subsampled, it is more convenient to use the algebraic discretization (§2.3.6). As noted, this discretization commits several errors, which may cause artefacts in the recovered image. We defer a discussion of this topic to §4.4.

For now, let us simply illustrate the benefits of compressed sensing for X-ray CT reconstruction over classical filtered back-projection (see §2.3.4). This is shown in Fig. 3.7. Filtered back-projection gives a poor reconstruction with noticeable artefacts, due to the undersampling of the angles. In order to perform filtered back-projection, the measurements at the 'missing' angles are set to zero (so-called *zero padding*).

Conversely, compressed sensing gives a greatly improved reconstruction. In this case, it uses wavelets and solves the LASSO problem (3.5). The LASSO parameter λ was taken to be $\lambda = \sigma$, where σ^2 is the noise variance. Justification for this choice is provided in Chapter 6. However, to illustrate this empirically in Fig. 3.8 we plot the reconstruction PSNR versus the ratio λ/σ for several different values of σ. Observe that the choice $\lambda = \sigma$ attains amongst the highest PSNR in all cases, whereas too large or too small a λ leads to a noticeable drop in PSNR.

For completeness, Fig. 3.7 also illustrates the characteristic blurring encountered when using simple back-projection. This was previously mentioned in §2.3.4.

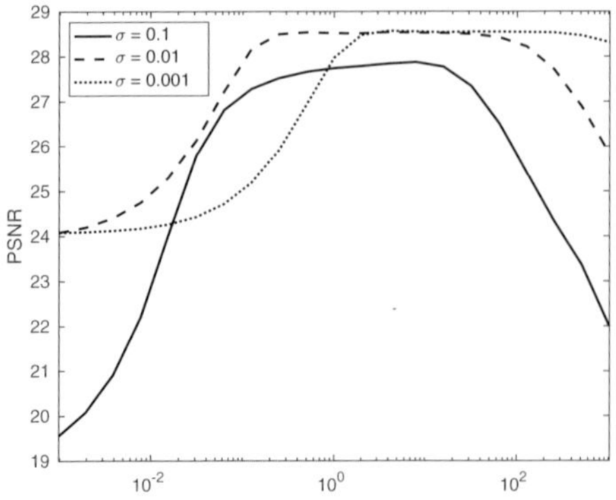

Figure 3.8 The PSNR versus the normalized LASSO parameter λ/σ for the compressed sensing reconstruction of Fig. 3.7 with several different values of σ.

3.4 Third Example: Optical Imaging

We now consider optical imaging. Unlike MRI and X-ray CT, optical imaging encompasses a range of imaging modalities with the common property that the samples are measurements of the light intensity of a source in some given spectral band (visible light, ultraviolet, infrared, etc.). The principal benefits compressive imaging may convey in optical imaging include reduction in the sensor cost, acquisition time, power or device size, with the specific type and amount of benefit depending on the application at hand.

3.4.1 Single-Pixel Imaging

A standard digital camera consists of an array of photon detectors, each of which measures the intensity of the corresponding image pixel. Detectors in the visible spectrum are inexpensive, allowing high-resolution digital cameras to be cheaply manufactured. On the other hand, sensors for other parts of the spectrum, such as *Short-Wave Infrared infrared (SWIR)* sensors, are far more expensive. The *single-pixel camera* is an empirical demonstration of how compressive imaging tools can be used to replace a full array of photon detectors with as little as one detector.

Figure 3.9 shows a typical setup. Light from the object is first focused by a lens onto a *Digital Micromirror Device (DMD)*. The DMD is an array of mirrors, each of which can be rapidly switched from the ‘off’ to the ‘on’ position. The reflected light from the DMD is next focused onto a single photon detector. This has the effect of integrating (summing) the light from the DMD. Assuming a discrete mathematical model and ignoring effects such as diffraction, the measurement at the detector can be considered as a weighted sum

$$\sum_{j=1}^{N} b_j x_j, \qquad b_j \in \{0, 1\} \tag{3.12}$$

of the discrete image $x = (x_i)_{i=1}^{N}$. In other words, a binary measurement of x, where the value of b_j is determined by whether the corresponding mirror is in the ‘off’ or the ‘on’ position.

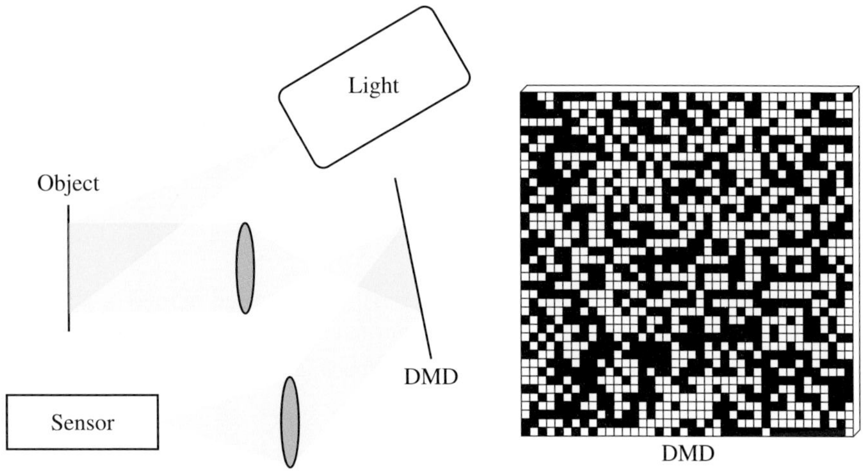

Figure 3.9 Left: A typical single-pixel camera setup. Right: The DMD showing a selection of mirrors in the 'on' (white) and 'off' (black) positions.

After this value is collected, the configuration of the DMD is changed and a new measurement is taken. Repeating this process for m distinct configurations of the DMD, we obtain the following linear measurement model:

$$w = Bx, \qquad B \in \{0, 1\}^{m \times N}. \tag{3.13}$$

It is generally preferable for the measurement matrix to have ± 1 entries. This can be achieved as follows. First, if not already included in the set of measurements, one takes an additional measurement corresponding to the total image intensity $\mu = \sum_{i=1}^{N} x_i$ by setting $b_j = 1$ in (3.12). Next, given B and w in (3.13) one defines

$$A = 2B - \mathbb{I}_{m \times N}, \qquad y = 2w - \mu \mathbb{I}_{m \times 1},$$

where $\mathbb{I}_{m \times n} \in \mathbb{R}^{m \times n}$ is the matrix of ones. This gives the linear system

$$y = Ax,$$

where the measurement matrix $A \in \{+1, -1\}^{m \times N}$.

Remark 3.2 The standard single-pixel camera arrangement (Fig. 3.9) involves several lenses. This limits its ability to be miniaturized, prohibiting its use in certain modalities, for instance, surveillance or endoscopy. In *lensless imaging*, these lenses are dispensed with. The overall principle, however, is similar. A rapidly switching micromirror array produces binary measurements, leading to a measurement model similar to (3.13).

3.4.2 Binary Measurement Design

Unlike both MRI and X-ray CT, this setup places very few constraints on the measurement matrix A, beside the imposition that it has ± 1 entries. As discussed in Chapter 1, there is significant scope to *design* the measurements to enhance the recovery quality. We now give further consideration to this issue.

We observed in §1.6 that a Bernoulli random matrix, while theoretically optimal for recovering sparse vectors, is computationally infeasible at higher resolutions. A standard approach in binary imaging is to try to mimic a Bernoulli random matrix using a matrix that has a fast transform. In a *scrambled orthogonal transform* one randomly subsamples the rows of the Hadamard matrix $H \in \mathbb{R}^{N \times N}$ (see §2.4.4), and then randomizes the columns. This gives the measurement matrix

$$A = PHQ, \tag{3.14}$$

where $P \in \mathbb{C}^{m \times N}$ is a row selector matrix that selects m rows of H uniformly at random. The matrix $Q \in \mathbb{C}^{N \times N}$ is either a random permutation matrix, or a random diagonal matrix with ± 1 entries. Another approach is *random convolution*. Here, one sets

$$A = PC, \tag{3.15}$$

where $C \in \mathbb{C}^{N \times N}$ is a circulant matrix generated by a random binary vector and P once more selects m rows uniformly at random. Note that both matrices (3.14) and (3.15) have efficient implementations.

However, by seeking to mimic a Bernoulli random matrix, these matrices do not exploit the structure of wavelet coefficients of natural images. By contrast, as was already seen in Chapter 1.6, a (nonscrambled) Walsh–Hadamard transform can exploit variations in sparsity from coarse to fine wavelet scales, and therefore deliver higher-quality reconstructions. In Fig. 3.10 we illustrate this difference for the same image as was used in Fig. 1.4. As is clearly seen, the reconstructions based on Walsh measurements significantly outperform those based on (3.14) and (3.15).

Much as was already shown in the case of Fourier sampling (Fig. 3.5), this experiment also demonstrates how the choice of sampling strategy for Walsh sampling (that is, the set of Walsh frequencies used) influences the reconstruction quality. The corresponding sampling maps are shown in Fig. 3.11. As we observe, the two schemes which sample in a variable-density fashion significantly outperform the simple half–half strategy.

Figure 3.12 shows a higher-resolution experiment on the same image considered in Fig. 1.10. Note that the computational efficiency of the measurement matrices (3.14) and (3.15) is critical in making such an experiment possible in the first place: Bernoulli measurements are computationally infeasible at this resolution. Yet the effect seen previously at lower resolution – namely, better performance from the variable-density Walsh strategy – is now even more pronounced. The underlying reason for this *resolution dependence* phenomenon is discussed further in §4.3.

3.4.3 Practical Considerations

In high-photon settings, measurement noise is reasonably modelled as Gaussian. However, certain modalities such as fluorescence microscopy involve low photon counts. Higher photon counts require longer acquisition times, higher laser power or more fluorescent dye. The latter two may destroy the sample being imaged. In the low-photon setting, the noise is better described by a Poisson process, leading to potential complications in how best to perform the reconstruction.

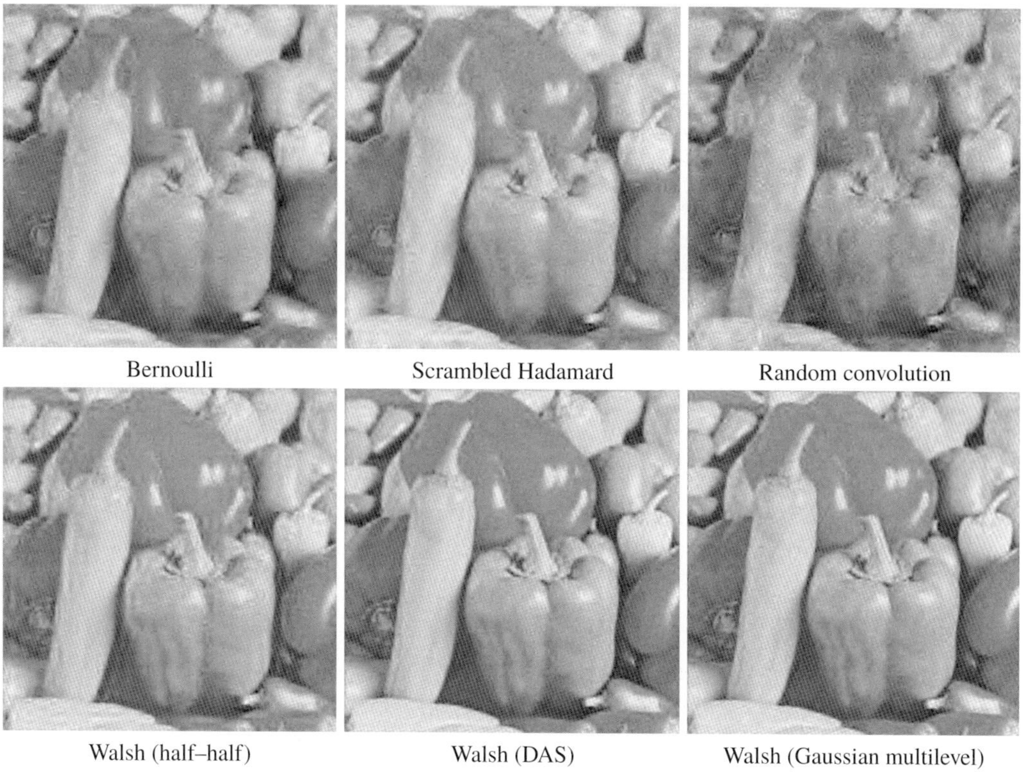

Figure 3.10 Recovery of the 256×256 peppers image from 20% measurements. The reconstruction uses DB4 wavelets and solves (3.4). The top row considers sampling with a Bernoulli random matrix, a scrambled Hadamard matrix (3.14) and a random convolution matrix (3.15). The bottom row considers (nonscrambled) Walsh measurements using three different sampling strategies, with the corresponding sampling maps shown in Fig. 3.11.

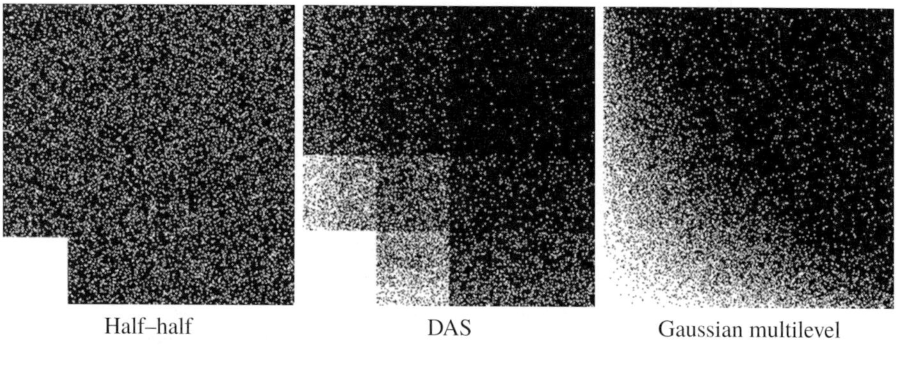

Figure 3.11 The sampling maps used in the second row of Fig. 3.10. The half–half scheme uses $(m_1, m_2) = (m/4, 3m/4)$ and uniform random sampling. The Gaussian multilevel scheme uses $r = 50$, $r_0 = 2$, $a = 2$ and is based on the $\ell^{1/2}$-ball. See §4.1 for the definition of these schemes. The DAS scheme is defined in Chapter 15. It uses the SL phantom as reference image and threshold parameter $\epsilon = 1$ (see §15.3.5).

Scrambled Hadamard | Random convolution | Variable-density Walsh

Figure 3.12 Recovery of the 1024×1024 dog image from 6% measurements. The reconstruction uses DB4 wavelets and solves (3.4). The variable-density Walsh strategy uses a Gaussian multilevel sampling map based on the $\ell^{1/2}$-ball, as in Fig. 3.10.

The sequential measurement collection process in the single-pixel camera can also lead to issues. Even with a DMD that can rapidly change its state, the acquisition time may be longer than with a classical sensor array. It may therefore be difficult to achieve high temporal resolution of moving sources. Moreover, shortening the acquisition time by increasing the speed of the DMD may lower the photon count, thus increasing the potential for Poisson noise.

In a similar vein, nonbinary measurements can be acquired by a single-pixel camera by switching the DMD k times, where k is the bit length of the entries of B, and summing the k measured values. However, this comes at the cost of a longer acquisition time.

If sensor cost is not the primary constraint, one alternative is to use a sensor array similar to in a classical digital camera (although the number of sensors need not be equal to the number of pixels in the image) in combination with a so-called *coded aperture*. There are several practical implementations of so-called *compressed coded aperture imagers*. This setup typically constrains the sensing matrix to have a circulant (or block circulant) structure.

Depending on the modality, it may also be important to use a continuous mathematical model, and take into account effects such as refraction and blurring. Calibration can then become an issue, since the refraction or blurring operator may be unknown in advance.

3.5 Recovery of Image Sequences

Up to this point, we have considered the recovery of a single image x. However, in some applications, the objective is to reconstruct a sequence of images from measurements. We now briefly discuss this problem.

We ignore application-specific modelling issues and assume that the problem has the following finite-dimensional model:

$$y^{(i)} = A^{(i)}x^{(i)} + e^{(i)}, \qquad i = 1, \ldots, M. \tag{3.16}$$

Here $x^{(i)} \in \mathbb{C}^N$ is the ith image, $A^{(i)} \in \mathbb{C}^{m_i \times N}$ is the measurement matrix for the ith image, $y^{(i)} \in \mathbb{C}^{m_i}$ are the corresponding measurements and $e^{(i)} \in \mathbb{C}^{m_i}$ is noise. Often in practice the measurement matrices are equal, i.e.

$$A^{(1)} = \cdots = A^{(M)} = A \in \mathbb{C}^{m \times N}. \tag{3.17}$$

Naïvely, one could recover the image sequence by reconstructing each image separately using a single-image reconstruction procedure. However, image sequences are typically not just individually sparse (in, say, a wavelet transform), but also highly correlated. They may have edges at the same spatial locations, for instance, meaning their large wavelet coefficients occur at similar indices. It is therefore beneficial to exploit this additional structure in the recovery procedure.

3.5.1 Joint Sparsity and $\ell^{2,1}$-Minimization

One way to do this is as follows. First observe that (3.16) is, assuming (3.17), equivalent to the matrix recovery problem

$$Y = AX + E,$$

where

$$Y = \left(y^{(1)}|\cdots|y^{(M)}\right) \in \mathbb{C}^{m \times M},$$
$$X = \left(x^{(1)}|\cdots|x^{(M)}\right) \in \mathbb{C}^{N \times M},$$
$$E = \left(e^{(1)}|\cdots|e^{(M)}\right) \in \mathbb{C}^{m \times M}.$$

To recover X, and therefore the $x^{(i)}$, we solve the $\ell^{2,1}$*-minimization problem*

$$\min_{Z \in \mathbb{C}^{N \times M}} \|Z\|_{\ell^{2,1}} \text{ subject to } \|AZ - Y\|_F \leq \eta. \tag{3.18}$$

Here $\|\cdot\|_F$ is the Frobenius norm (A.13), $\|\cdot\|_{\ell^{2,1}}$ is the $\ell^{2,1}$-norm (A.14) and η is chosen so that $\|E\|_F \leq \eta$. The problem (3.18) is convex and amenable to efficient algorithms.

Much as the ℓ^1-norm promotes standard sparsity, the $\ell^{2,1}$-norm promotes so-called *joint sparsity*. A collection of vectors $\{x^{(1)}, \ldots, x^{(M)}\} \subseteq \mathbb{C}^N$ is *s-joint sparse* if each vector is s-sparse and the *support sets* $\text{supp}(x^{(i)})$ overlap:

$$\left|\text{supp}(x^{(1)}) \cup \cdots \cup \text{supp}(x^{(M)})\right| \leq s.$$

Here $\text{supp}(x) = \{i : x_i \neq 0\}$ for $x = (x_i)_{i=1}^N \in \mathbb{C}^N$. Put another way,

$$\{x^{(1)}, \ldots, x^{(M)}\} \text{ is } s\text{-joint sparse} \quad \Longleftrightarrow \quad X \text{ has at most } s \text{ nonzero rows.}$$

This equivalence makes it apparent why the $\ell^{2,1}$-norm promotes joint sparsity. The term $\|X\|_{\ell^{2,1}}$ is nothing more than the ℓ^1-norm of the vector

$$\left(\|x_{(i)}\|_{\ell^2}\right)_{i=1}^N,$$

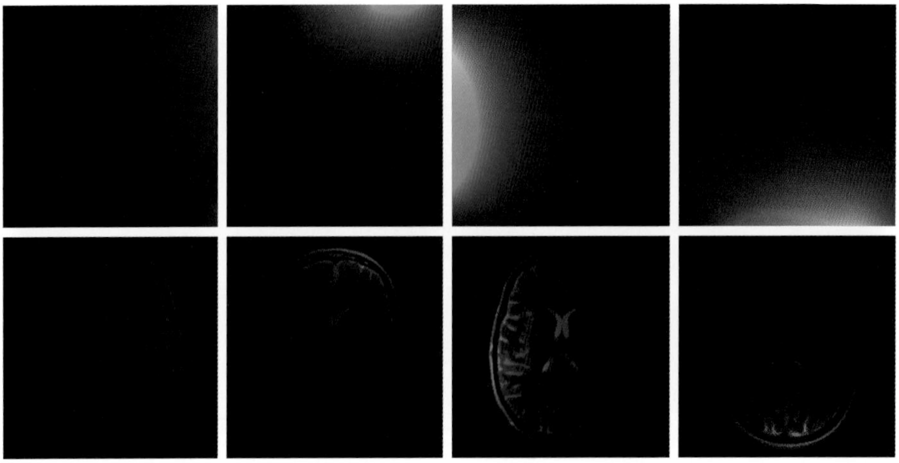

Figure 3.13 Complex sensitivity profiles $s^{(c)}$ (top), where $S^{(c)} = \mathrm{diag}(s^{(c)})$, and coil images $x^{(c)} = S^{(c)}x$ (bottom) for the GLPU phantom. The phase is colour coded.

where $x_{(i)} \in \mathbb{C}^M$ is the ith row of X. Minimizing the ℓ^1-norm promotes sparsity of this vector, which is equivalent to X having a small number of nonzero rows, and thus equivalent to joint sparsity.

3.5.2 Application to Parallel MRI

The mathematical model described in §3.2 applies to so-called *single-coil* MRI. The development of *parallel-coil* MR scanners in the 1990s was one of the most significant advances in MRI's history. Parallel MRI is now the standard in most modern scanners.

In parallel MRI, multiple receiver coils simultaneously acquire Fourier measurements of an image. Assuming a discrete model as in §3.2.2, the measurements in the cth coil can be expressed as

$$y^{(c)} = AS^{(c)}x + e^{(c)} \in \mathbb{C}^m, \quad c = 1, \ldots, C.$$

Here $e^{(c)}$ is noise and $A = PF \in \mathbb{C}^{m \times N}$ is the subsampled Fourier matrix as in (3.10). The matrix $S^{(c)}$ is diagonal, and is known as the *sensitivity profile* of the coil. It has the effect of attenuating the image away from the coil. In particular, the *coil image* $x^{(c)} = S^{(c)}x$ has entries whose magnitudes get progressively smaller away from the physical location of the coil. A typical example of this effect is shown in Fig. 3.13.

While their entries may differ, the coil images $x^{(c)}$ have common edges. Hence, they are approximately joint sparse under a wavelet or discrete gradient transform. Let Φ be such a transform. To recover the $x^{(c)}$ we consider the $\ell^{2,1}$-minimization problem

$$\min_{Z \in \mathbb{C}^{N \times C}} \|\Phi^* Z\|_{\ell^{2,1}} \text{ subject to } \|AZ - Y\|_F \leq \eta,$$

where $Y = (y^{(1)}|\cdots|y^{(C)})$. Let $\widehat{X} = (\widehat{x}^{(1)}|\cdots|\widehat{x}^{(C)})$ be a minimizer of this problem. Then $\widehat{x}^{(c)}$ is the reconstruction of the cth coil image $x^{(c)}$.

Our interest generally lies not with the coil images $x^{(c)}$ themselves, but rather with the overall image x. This can be recovered from the $\hat{x}^{(c)}$ via a *sum-of-squares* procedure. Specifically, given coil images $\hat{x}^{(c)}$ we reconstruct x as $\hat{x} = (\hat{x}_i)_{i=1}^N$, where

$$\hat{x}_i = \left(\sum_{c=1}^{C} |\hat{x}_i^{(c)}|^2 \right)^{1/2}, \qquad i = 1, \ldots, N. \tag{3.19}$$

3.5.3 Practical Considerations and Alternatives

An advantage of this approach is that it requires no knowledge of the sensitivity profiles $S^{(c)}$. Unfortunately, the sum-of-squares step (3.19) can introduce additional inhomogeneity artefacts to the recovered image. It implicitly assumes *homogeneity* of the sensitivity profiles, i.e. $\sum_{c=1}^{C} |S_{ii}^{(c)}|^2 \approx 1$ for all i, an assumption which may fail to hold in practice.

Other methods for parallel MRI reconstruction seek to reconstruct the image x directly, without first recovering the coil images $x^{(c)}$. For example, in *CS SENSE (Compressed Sensing Sensitivity Encoding)* one solves

$$\min_{z \in \mathbb{C}^N} \|\Phi^* z\|_{\ell^1} \text{ subject to } \|\tilde{A}z - \tilde{y}\|_{\ell^2} \leq \eta, \tag{3.20}$$

where

$$\tilde{A} = \begin{pmatrix} AS^{(1)} \\ \vdots \\ AS^{(C)} \end{pmatrix}, \qquad \tilde{y} = \begin{pmatrix} y^{(1)} \\ \vdots \\ y^{(C)} \end{pmatrix}.$$

Unfortunately, this requires knowledge of the sensitivity profiles. These need to be calibrated, a task usually carried out during a *calibration prescan*. Performing this step increases the overall acquisition time, and if the $S^{(c)}$ are not well estimated, the reconstruction of the overall image x can be relatively poor.

CS SENSE does not exploit joint sparsity. There are also methods that seek to incorporate this additional structure. For example, one can replace the ℓ^1-norm in (3.20) by the functional

$$g(z) = \left\| \left(\Phi^* S^{(1)} z | \cdots | \Phi^* S^{(C)} z \right) \right\|_{\ell^{2,1}}. \tag{3.21}$$

This functional exploits the joint sparsity of the coil images without having to recover them explicitly. Like CS SENSE, it also requires knowledge of the sensitivity profiles.

Finally, there are also *calibrationless* methods. These seek to overcome the need for the calibration prescan by jointly estimating the sensitivity profiles $S^{(c)}$ at the same time as the image x is reconstructed. This is often done through an alternating iterative procedure, for example, so-called *JSENSE (Joint Image Reconstruction and Sensitivity Estimation in SENSE)* and its many variants.

3.5.4 Group Sparsity

We close this section by returning briefly to the concept of joint sparsity. It transpires that this is a special case of a more general property known as *group sparsity* (or *block sparsity*). Group sparsity is particularly useful in applications where the nonzero entries of a vector tend to occur in clusters, rather than individually.

In group sparsity, the set $\{1, \ldots, N\}$ is divided into n (possibly overlapping) groups G_i, $i = 1, \ldots, n$. Consider a vector $x \in \mathbb{C}^N$ and let

$$x^{(i)} = \left(x_j\right)_{j \in G_i}$$

be the vector formed from the entries of x lying in the ith group G_i. We say that x is *s-group sparse* if at most s of these vectors are nonzero:

$$|\{i : x^{(i)} \neq 0\}| \leq s.$$

Note that the vectors $x^{(i)}$ need not be sparse themselves. On the other hand, if $G_i = \{i\}$ for all i, then one recovers the standard sparsity setting.

In the case of joint sparsity, let $\{x^{(1)}, \ldots, x^{(M)}\}$ be a sequence of vectors in $\mathbb{C}^N$, and define the concatenated vector

$$x = \begin{pmatrix} x^{(1)} \\ \vdots \\ x^{(M)} \end{pmatrix} \in \mathbb{C}^{MN},$$

as well as the (nonoverlapping) groups

$$G_i = \{i, N + i, 2N + i, \ldots, (M - 1)N + i\}, \quad i = 1, \ldots, N.$$

It follows that x is s-group sparse with respect to these groups if and only if $\{x^{(1)}, \ldots, x^{(M)}\}$ is s-joint sparse.

Similar to joint sparsity, group sparsity can be promoted by minimizing the *group ℓ^1-norm*. This is defined by

$$\|x\|_{\ell^1_g} = \sum_{i=1}^{n} \|x^{(i)}\|_{\ell^2}. \tag{3.22}$$

It is a norm, hence the corresponding minimization problem

$$\min_{z \in \mathbb{C}^N} \|z\|_{\ell^1_g} \text{ subject to } \|Az - y\|_{\ell^2} \leq \eta$$

is convex. For joint sparsity, this is equivalent (up to changes in A and y) to the $\ell^{2,1}$-minimization problem (3.18).

Notes

We discuss the methods underlying the packages listed in Table 3.1 in more detail in Chapter 7. As mentioned, choosing a good optimization solver is crucial for good performance. Many packages were rapidly developed in the initial years following the introduction of compressed sensing in 2006. We mention in passing l1-magic [119] (one of the earliest packages for compressed sensing), l1_ls [291], GSPR [209], SpaRSA

[506], FPC [252], FPC-AS [494], YALL1 [513] and split-Bregman [229], to name but a few. For comparisons of these methods against the packages listed in Table 3.1, see [60]. There are also other approaches to compressed sensing-based compressive imaging that do not explicitly solve optimization problems. An example is the class of *approximate message passing* techniques [182], which includes methods such as *TurboAMP* [446].

MRI was one of the original motivations for compressed sensing. As noted in §1.2, Candès, Romberg & Tao presented experiments in their seminal paper [121] showing the recovery of the SL phantom from radial Fourier measurements. We reproduced this experiment in Fig. 1.1. Significant developments followed quickly with the work of Lustig, Donoho, Pauly and others [314, 335, 336, 337]. These gave the first practical demonstrations of the benefits of compressed sensing in MRI. Since then, a wealth of literature has been produced on this topic. It is fair to say that MRI has been one of the true success stories of compressed sensing. FDA approval for the use of compressed sensing in MRI was received in 2017. Siemens, Philips (*Compressed SENSE*) and GE (*HyperSense*) have all introduced commercial MR scanners based on compressed sensing principles [411].

A review of the various clinical applications of compressed sensing in MRI has been presented in [276]. In this work, the authors highlight the various different sparsifying transforms, sampling patterns and reconstruction algorithms used in practice (stages 3–6 of the pipeline). It is interesting to note that there is no consensus in the clinical literature on how best to sample – a topic we discuss further in the next chapter and a major focus of this book. This work also considers the issue of parameter selection for optimization problems (consideration (xiv)), and its impact on image quality.

As noted in §3.2.5, sampling trajectories in two-dimensional MRI scans must traverse piecewise smooth curves. Some standard trajectories are presented in §4.1.4. A number of works have considered how to design novel piecewise smooth sampling trajectories for two-dimensional MRI using compressed sensing theory. See [71, 92, 93, 136] and references therein. For three-dimensional compressed sensing MRI, the technique discussed previously based on two-dimensional subsampling with full sampling in the third k-space direction was introduced in [336].

In Chapter 1 we compared structured Fourier measurements versus unstructured random Gaussian measurements (see §1.6). There have been some attempts to render MRI measurements more unstructured, so as to better mimic Gaussian measurements [251, 399, 401]. This can be achieved, for example, by modulating the image before sampling its Fourier transform. In view of Fig. 1.8 (see also Key Point #6 from Chapter 1), this approach may be of limited effectiveness in practice. The modulation step is also time-consuming, thus potentially defeating the purpose of using compressed sensing in MRI in the first place.

See [326,354,382] for an in-depth treatment of the physics of MRI and its mathematical modelling. Figure 3.2 is based on [335, Fig. 2.1]. See, for example, [354] for descriptions of the Gibbs phenomenon and gridding strategies. For more on nonuniform FFTs and reconstructions from nonuniform Fourier data, see [13, 207, 296, 396] and references therein. As noted, noise in MRI is often modelled as Gaussian [340]. For more on nonlinear models in MRI, see [178, 205] and references therein.

Fourier measurements are not limited to MRI. They occur in several other modalities, including the closely related Nuclear Magnetic Resonance (NMR), as well as Helium Atom Scattering (HAS) and radio interferometry. For applications of compressed sensing to these modalities, see [267, 289], [279] and [495], respectively. In other imaging modalities such as X-ray crystallography, the acquisition process involves sampling the square-magnitude of the Fourier transform $|\mathcal{F} f(\omega)|^2$. This leads to the nonlinear (and challenging) *phase retrieval* problem. Inspired by the developments in compressed sensing, this problem has received renewed attention over the last decade. New methods such as *PhaseLift* [115, 122] recast the problem as semidefinite programming, leading to better reconstructions over classical approaches. See also [117, 230, 274, 430, 484].

We refer to [198, 204, 305] for further information on CT and its various mathematical models (including nonlinear models). In particular, [198] provides an in-depth discussion of modelling assumptions and artefacts, including beam hardening, as well as the various different geometries (parallel, fan, cone, etc.) used in practice. For more on noise in low-dose CT, see, for example, [218].

It is often the case in practice that the CT scanner can only acquire projections at a limited range of angles within $[0, \pi)$. The *limited-angle* tomography problem is ill-posed, raising the prospect of artefacts in reconstruction [305, Chpt. 7], [370, Chpt. 6], [366, Chpt. 9]. This is a significant practical challenge. It is perhaps not surprising that sparsity-exploiting techniques such as TV minimization were used in CT some time prior to the advent of compressed sensing [238, 283]. See, for instance, [171] from 1998. See [366, Chpt. 9], [98, 217] and references therein for recent progress. Philosophically, limited-angle tomography and compressed sensing for CT are somewhat different. The former deals with the situation where certain angles cannot be measured, whereas the CT setup most reminiscent of compressed sensing assumes all angles can be measured, but then seeks to reduce the total number used. The terms *limited data* and *sparse data* are sometimes used to contrast these two settings.

The works [386, 439, 440] were among the earliest to apply compressed sensing to CT, and influential in popularizing its use. In particular, [439], which appeared in 2006, proposed compressed sensing using TV minimization based on an algebraic discretization. For the reasons mentioned previously, approaches based on algebraic discretizations have so far proved more popular than Fourier slice-based approaches.

It is arguably the case that compressed sensing has not been adopted as widely in commercial X-ray CT as it has been in MRI. Reasons for this have been discussed in [386] and, more recently, [238]. Amongst them, as noted in §3.3.3, is the fact that there is significantly less flexibility in X-ray CT to design measurements so as to enhance performance. Outside of medical applications, commercial implementations of TV minimization for X-ray microtomography applications in materials science have been developed, for example, by Zeiss [442].

The theory of compressed sensing for Fourier imaging, which is a key part of this book, is far more developed than that for Radon imaging. Empirical studies examining the tradeoff between sparsity and the number of Radon measurements have been performed on simulated data in [281, 282, 283] and real data in [280]. These studies compute *phase transitions* – a well-known concept in compressed sensing [183] – and indicate a possible linear relation between gradient sparsity and the number of Radon projections. Some theoretical analysis can be found in the work of Petra, Schnörr and others. See [172,388] and references therein.

We note in passing that the model derived in §3.3.1 for X-ray CT applies to many other tomographic imaging modalities. See, for instance, [305, Chpt. 3] and [370, Chpt. 3]. For the application of compressed sensing techniques to electron tomography, see [319].

The development of the original single-pixel camera at Rice University in 2006 launched optical imaging as a promising area of application of compressed sensing techniques [186]. Lensless compressive imaging was introduced in [269]. See [81] for a recent overview, as well as [43] for a practical implementation (so-called *Flatcam*). A similar setup to the single-pixel camera was introduced to fluorescence microscopy in [453]. Beyond this and the other modalities mentioned, there are various other implementations of compressed sensing in optical imaging systems. These include spectral imaging [38], light-field imaging [351], ghost imaging [288], STORM [528], holography [95] and many more.

Random convolutions (also known as *partial random circulant* matrices) and scrambled orthogonal transforms are standard techniques in compressed sensing. See, for instance, [419] and [177], respectively. The idea of designing a measurement matrix to capture the coarse image scales more efficiently was used by Romberg in his seminal paper on compressive imaging [418]. Specifically, he used DCT measurements for the coarse scales and noiselet measurements to recover the fine scales (noiselets [156] are orthonormal bases that are optimally incoherent with wavelets). Neither set of measurements is binary. The half–half sampling strategy for the Walsh transform – based on the same principle of acquiring the coarse scales more efficiently – was used in [453] in application to fluorescence microscopy. Variable-density Walsh sampling was considered in [21, 416, 490]. The observation that this outperforms standard binary measurement matrices, including Bernoulli random matrices, was shown in [416].

As noted in §3.4.3, transferring compressed sensing theory into practical optical imaging architectures is not straightforward. It involves modality-specific tradeoffs such as acquisition time versus number of sensors and (potentially Poisson) noise, lenses versus miniaturization, and so forth. Another potential consideration is computational time. This is a concern in real-time imaging, for instance. For this reason, it is perhaps unsurprising that compressed sensing has percolated somewhat less far into commercial optical imaging than it has in MRI. We shall not discuss these issues further, but instead refer the reader to [225,496,497]. For further information on compressed coded aperture imaging, see [38, 347, 348] and references therein. For background on optical imaging and physics, see [94].

The recovery of image sequences is a type of *Multiple Measurement Vector (MMV)* problem. For an introduction to both this and group/block sparsity, see [167, 187, 196, 478] and references therein. Beyond parallel MRI, other applications involving image sequences are hyperspectral imaging, multi-echo MRI, diffusion tensor imaging and dynamic imaging, to name but a few.

The origins of parallel MRI date back to the 1980s. However, it was not popularized until the late 1990s [313]. Amongst its benefits over single-coil MRI is scan time acceleration, since the data is acquired simultaneously by multiple sensors. The challenge is the more difficult measurement model, involving the sensitivity profiles, rather than simple Fourier measurements in single-coil MRI [473]. More detailed introductions to parallel MRI can be found in [313,473].

Early uses of joint sparsity in parallel MRI were considered in [343,367,492]. This is sometimes referred to as *CaLM (Calibration-Less Multi-coil)* [343]. For further information on CS SENSE, see [245,330,507]. Note that CS SENSE is an extension of classical *SENSE* (*SENSitivity Encoding*) that incorporates compressed sensing techniques. SENSE was introduced in 1999 by Pruessmann, Weiger, Scheidigger & Boesiger [397]. The functional (3.21) was introduced in [147].

The handful of methods discussed in §3.5.2 represent a small subset of a myriad of different procedures for both classical and compressed sensing parallel MRI. See [74,313] for an overview of classical techniques and, for instance, [147,342,411,473] for a selection of various different compressed sensing techniques. JSENSE was introduced in [519]. Other methods for calibrationless parallel MRI such as [438] use low-rank matrix techniques. For further information, see [438,473].

Finally, we reiterate that this book considers only static imaging scenarios. Compressed sensing techniques have been applied to numerous dynamic imaging problems, including, for instance, dynamic MRI. While there are challenges – e.g. computational time for real-time imaging, balancing spatiotemporal resolution in single-pixel imaging, and so forth – there are also significant potential benefits. Video sequences possess temporal sparsity in addition to spatial sparsity, which opens the door to a multitude of different techniques for leveraging this additional structure. Note that task-specific measurement design can help mitigate some of these challenges, for instance, the *STOne* (*Sum To One*) transform for real-time video imaging [231]. For further information, see [49,231] and references therein.

4 Techniques for Enhancing Performance

In this chapter, we consider techniques for improving compressive imaging performance. We begin with the topic of sampling. As noted in the previous chapter, in both Fourier and Walsh imaging the choice of frequencies used has a critical effect on the reconstruction quality. In §4.1 we introduce a series of different sampling schemes, and then in §4.2 we describe four key principles for designing effective sampling strategies. In §4.3 we investigate the issue of resolution. We show that compressive imaging, when done properly, becomes increasingly beneficial as the resolution increases. Discretization and the inverse crime are considered in §4.4. Focusing on the case of compressed sensing, we then discuss the choice of sparsifying transform in §4.5, and after that we consider iterative reweighting techniques in §4.6. In §4.7 we consider dictionary learning, before concluding this chapter in §4.8 with some take-home advice.

4.1 Sampling Strategies

We first consider Fourier sampling. In this case, the set Ω of frequencies sampled is a subset of $\{-N/2+1,\ldots,N/2\}^d$, where N is the resolution. The set Ω is variously referred to as a *sampling scheme*, *sampling map*, *sampling pattern* or *sampling strategy*. We use all four terms interchangeably.

4.1.1 Single-Density Schemes

Since randomness is important for compressed sensing, the majority of the schemes introduced below involve some kind of random sampling. Our first class of schemes, so-called *single-density schemes*, simply draw frequencies randomly and independently from a fixed probability distribution:

Definition 4.1 (Uniform random sampling) A d-dimensional *uniform random sampling scheme of order m* is a subset of frequencies $\Omega = \{\omega_1,\ldots,\omega_m\} \subseteq \{-N/2+1,\ldots,N/2\}^d$ where the ω_i are chosen i.i.d. and uniformly from $\{-N/2+1,\ldots,N/2\}^d$.

Remark 4.2 This scheme, as well as those discussed subsequently, draws samples with replacement. Repeats are therefore possible. When this occurs, Ω is no longer a set but an *indexed family*. However, since it is conventional to do so, we will continue to use the term ‘set’ throughout.

Remark 4.3 Repeats are generally undesirable, since they constitute a waste of the measurement budget m. Practically, they can be avoided simply by sampling without replacement. However, subsequent theory, which relies on independence, no longer applies. In §11.4.3 we introduce the *Bernoulli model* to counter this problem. This model maintains independence while avoiding repeats. The downside is that the total number of samples is now itself a random variable, equal to m only in expectation.

Definition 4.4 (Variable-density and power-law sampling) Let $\pi = \{\pi_\omega\}$ be a probability distribution on $\{-N/2+1, \ldots, N/2\}^d$. A d-dimensional *variable-density sampling scheme of order* m is a subset of frequencies $\Omega = \{\omega_1, \ldots, \omega_m\} \subseteq \{-N/2+1, \ldots, N/2\}^d$ where the ω_i are chosen i.i.d. according to π. A variable-density sampling scheme is a *power-law* sampling scheme if π_ω behaves like a power of $|\omega|$ for large $|\omega|$.

Typical examples of power-law sampling schemes are the one-dimensional *inverse linear law*

$$\pi_\omega = \frac{C_N}{\max\{1, |\omega|\}}, \qquad \omega \in \{-N/2+1, \ldots, N/2\} \tag{4.1}$$

and the two-dimensional *inverse square law*

$$\pi_\omega = \frac{C_N}{\max\{1, |\omega_1|^2 + |\omega_2|^2\}}, \qquad \omega = (\omega_1, \omega_2) \in \{-N/2+1, \ldots, N/2\}^2. \tag{4.2}$$

In both cases the normalization constant C_N satisfies $C_N \asymp 1/\log(N)$ as $N \to \infty$. These particular schemes arise naturally in compressed sensing theory for imaging. See Chapters 11, 15 and 17. More generally, one may also consider the schemes

$$\pi_\omega = \frac{C_{N,\alpha}}{(\max\{1, |\omega|\})^\alpha}, \qquad \omega \in \{-N/2+1, \ldots, N/2\} \tag{4.3}$$

and

$$\pi_\omega = \frac{C_{N,\alpha}}{(\max\{1, |\omega_1|^2 + |\omega_2|^2\})^\alpha}, \qquad \omega = (\omega_1, \omega_2) \in \{-N/2+1, \ldots, N/2\}^2, \tag{4.4}$$

for some parameter $\alpha \in \mathbb{R}$. We note in passing that the two-dimensional schemes (4.4) are radially symmetric, or as we shall more often say, *isotropic*.

4.1.2 Half–Half Schemes

The above schemes are *fully* random. We now consider schemes that are *semi-random* in the sense that some of the samples are chosen deterministically, with the remainder being chosen randomly. As we will discuss later, doing so is crucial for ensuring high reconstruction quality: in practice, certain frequencies (unsurprisingly, the low frequencies) should always be sampled.

Definition 4.5 (Half–half sampling) A d-dimensional *half–half sampling scheme* of order (m_1, m_2) is a subset $\Omega = \Omega_1 \cup \Omega_2 \subseteq \{-N/2+1, \ldots, N/2\}^d$ of $m = m_1 + m_2$ frequencies, where Ω_1 consists of the lowest m_1 frequencies and Ω_2 consists of m_2 frequencies chosen i.i.d. according to some probability distribution on $\{-N/2+1, \ldots, N/2\}^d \backslash \Omega_1$.

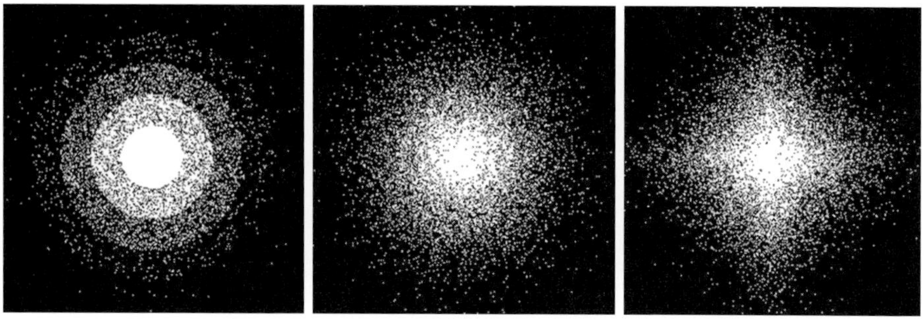

(a) (b) (c)

Figure 4.1 (a) Gaussian multilevel sampling with $a = 2$, $r_0 = 0$ and $r = 7$. (b) The same except with $r = 50$. (c) Gaussian multilevel sampling with $a = 2$, $r_0 = 0$ and $r = 50$ based on the ℓ^p-ball with $p = 1$. Each white dot represents a frequency sampled. The zero frequency is in the centre.

When $d > 1$ there is some ambiguity as to what constitutes the 'lowest m_1' frequencies. Typically, Ω_1 is chosen either as a square or circular region around the zero frequency. The particular choice will always be clear from the context.

4.1.3 Multilevel Sampling Schemes

Half–half schemes refine single-density schemes by ensuring that the low frequencies are always sampled. Yet their performance may still be limited due to the abrupt change from deterministic to random sampling. A more sophisticated approach is the following:

Definition 4.6 (Multilevel random sampling) Let $\mathcal{B} = \{B_k\}_{k=1}^r$ be a partition of $\{-N/2+1, \ldots, N/2\}^d$. A d-dimensional $(\mathbf{m}, \mathcal{B})$-*multilevel random sampling scheme* is a subset $\Omega = \Omega_1 \cup \cdots \cup \Omega_r$ of $m = m_1 + \cdots + m_r$ frequencies, where, for each k, the following holds. If $m_k < |B_k|$ then Ω_k consists of m_k frequencies chosen independently and uniformly at random from B_k, and if $m_k = |B_k|$ then $\Omega_k = B_k$.

A typical example of a multilevel scheme is the following:

Definition 4.7 (Gaussian multilevel sampling) A *Gaussian multilevel sampling scheme* with r levels and parameters $a > 0$ and $0 \leq r_0 \leq r$ is a multilevel random sampling scheme where $B_1, \ldots, B_{r-1}$ are concentric, circular annuli of fixed width, and the sampling fractions $p_k = m_k/|B_k|$ are given by $p_k = 1$ for $k = 1, \ldots, r_0$ and

$$p_k = \exp\left(-\left(\frac{b(k-r_0)}{r-r_0}\right)^a\right), \qquad k = r_0 + 1, \ldots, r.$$

Here b is a normalization constant which ensures that $m_1 + \cdots + m_r = m$.

See Fig. 4.1(a,b) for several examples of this approach. Observe that this is an isotropic sampling scheme. One may create potentially *anisotropic* versions by replacing the circular regions (ℓ^2-balls) with, for example, squares (ℓ^∞-balls), diamonds (ℓ^1-balls) or more generally, ℓ^p-balls. See Fig. 4.1(c) for an example.

There are two other types of multilevel sampling schemes that we consider in this book besides the Gaussian scheme. These are the *Dyadic Isotropic Sampling (DIS)* and *Dyadic Anisotropic Sampling (DAS)* schemes, respectively. They are defined formally in Chapter 15, but have been used already in several of the figures in the previous chapters. As we see in Chapter 15, they play a key role in compressed sensing theory for imaging.

4.1.4 Some Two-Dimensional MRI Sampling Schemes

As noted in §3.2.5, in two-dimensional MRI one is constrained to sample along piecewise smooth curves. We now introduce several standard sampling strategies for this modality:

Definition 4.8 (Cartesian sampling) A two-dimensional *(horizontal) Cartesian sampling scheme* with l lines is a set

$$\Omega = \{(\omega_1, \omega_2) : -N/2 < \omega_1 \leq N/2,\ \omega_2 \in \Omega'\},$$

where $\Omega' \subseteq \{-N/2 + 1, \dots, N/2\}$ with $|\Omega'| = l$.

This scheme, which is sometimes referred to as *random phase encoding*, fully samples the horizontal k-space direction while subsampling the vertical direction. A vertical Cartesian sampling scheme can be defined analogously. The values in Ω' are generally chosen according to some variable-density scheme. See Fig. 4.2(a) for an example.

Definition 4.9 (Radial sampling) A two-dimensional *radial sampling scheme* with l lines is a set of points $\Omega \subset \{-N/2 + 1, \dots, N/2\}^2$ consisting of the nearest integer neighbours to l equi-angular radial lines in $\mathbb{R}^2$.

See Fig. 4.2(b). In practical MRI, radial sampling takes Fourier measurements at frequencies (sampled at some constant rate) lying exactly on the prescribed radial lines in k-space. These will not generally be integer-valued. Definition 4.9 is therefore an idealization of the type of sampling done in practice. As noted in §3.2.5, the measurement mismatch stemming from the nearest-neighbour gridding inherent to this definition may cause additional artefacts in the recovered image.

Definition 4.10 (Spiral sampling) A two-dimensional *spiral sampling scheme* with parameters $a, b > 0$ is the set of points Ω consisting of the nearest integer neighbours to the parametric spiral curve

$$\left\{(\exp(bt^a)\cos(t), \exp(bt^a)\sin(t)) : 0 \leq t \leq (\log(N/2)/b)^{1/a}\right\}.$$

See Fig. 4.2(c). As before, this is an idealization of true spiral sampling in MRI.

4.1.5 Sampling Schemes for Walsh Sampling

Most of the schemes considered so far can also be defined in the case of Walsh sampling. We do this simply by considering the nonnegative frequencies only, changing Ω from

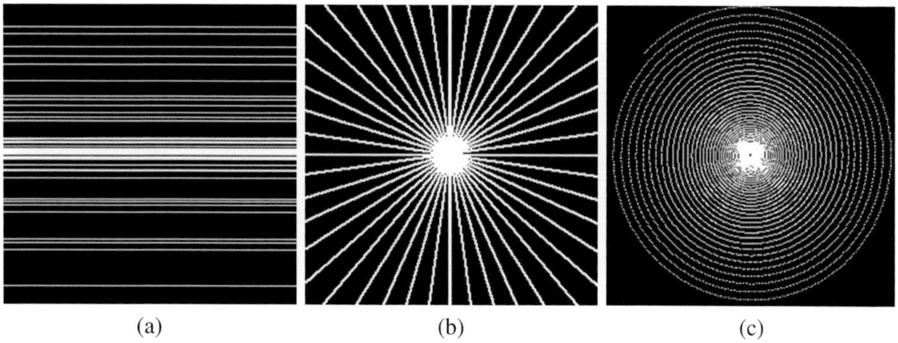

Figure 4.2 (a) Horizontal Cartesian sampling with lines chosen randomly from the distribution $\pi_\omega \propto 1/\max\{1, |\omega|\}$. (b) Radial sampling. (c) Spiral sampling.

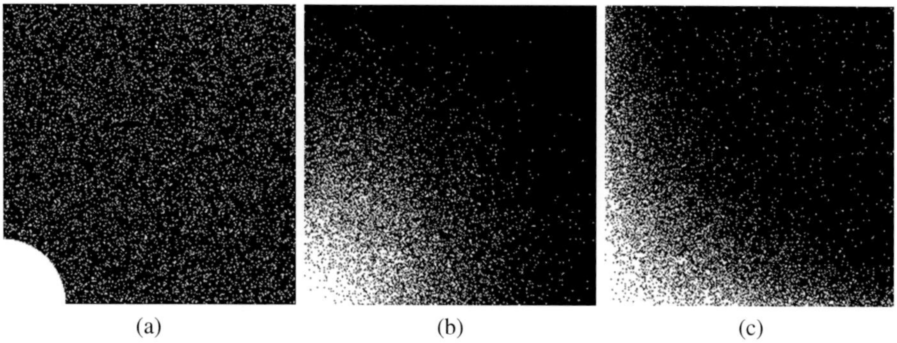

Figure 4.3 (a) Half–half Walsh sampling with $(m_1, m_2) = (m/4, 3m/4)$ and uniform random sampling in the subsampled region. (b) Gaussian multilevel sampling with $a = 2$, $r_0 = 0$ and $r = 50$ based on the ℓ^2-ball. (c) The same except based on the $\ell^{1/2}$-ball. Each white dot is a frequency sampled. The zero frequency is located in the bottom left corner.

a subset of $\{-N/2+1, \ldots, N/2\}^d$ to a subset of $\{0, \ldots, N-1\}^d$. For example, the one-dimensional inverse linear law scheme $\pi = \{\pi_n\}$ is given by

$$\pi_n = \frac{C_N}{\max\{1, n\}}, \quad n \in \{0, \ldots, N-1\} \tag{4.5}$$

in this case and the two-dimensional inverse square law is given by

$$\pi_n = \frac{C_N}{\max\{1, n_1^2 + n_2^2\}}, \quad n = (n_1, n_2) \in \{0, \ldots, N-1\}^2. \tag{4.6}$$

Figure 4.3 illustrates several other Walsh sampling schemes. At this moment, we remind the reader that whenever Walsh sampling schemes are defined or shown graphically, the Walsh basis is assumed to be ordered according to the sequency ordering (see §2.4.3).

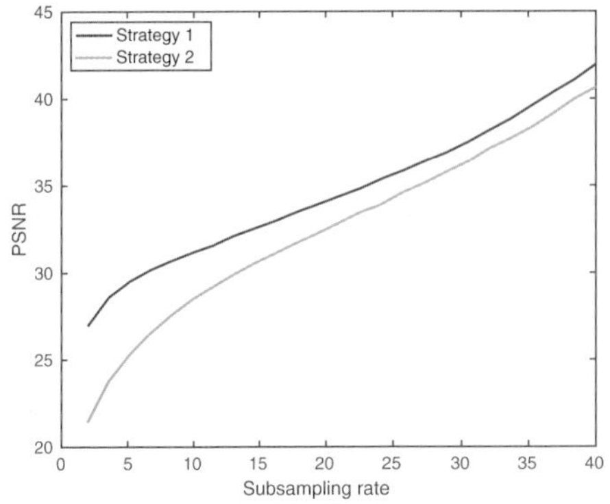

Figure 4.4 PSNR versus subsampling rate for Fourier sampling applied to the discrete 512×512 GLPU phantom (see Fig. 2.2) using two different sampling strategies. These are the Gaussian multilevel scheme with $a = 1$, $r_0 = 2$ and $r = 50$ (strategy 1) and the half–half scheme of order $(m/4, 3m/4)$ (strategy 2). Both schemes are based on the ℓ^2-ball. The subsampling rate is equal to the percentage of measurements taken from the full set of 512^2 measurements. The reconstructions were computed by solving (3.4) with DB4 wavelets.

4.2 How to Design a Sampling Strategy

We now discuss the following question: given a budget of m measurements, how should one best sample? We answer this question by introducing four principles for sampling strategy design. The mathematical basis for these principles is presented in Chapter 15.

Principle #1. Fully sample the low frequencies.

This is intuitive. In an extreme case, if the sampling scheme happens to miss the zero frequency, the recovered image will typically have the wrong mean value. More generally, low frequencies are often vital to sample. They correspond to global image features such as textures, and also carry the majority of the image's energy. This is precisely the motivation behind the half–half schemes.

Principle #2. Outside the region of full sampling, subsample in a smoothly decreasing manner.

This principle is also intuitive. The Fourier transform of an image decreases smoothly with increasing frequency, so it is natural to mimic this behaviour with a smoothlydecaying subsampling rate. This is the motivation behind the Gaussian multilevel schemes. Figure 4.4 demonstrates this principle. The half–half scheme switches abruptly from full sampling to random subsampling. Conversely, the Gaussian multilevel scheme with $r \gg 1$ levels creates a smoothly decreasing sampling density outside the fully sampled region, leading to better image recovery.

Principle #3. The optimal sampling strategy depends on the image, the resolution N, the number of measurements m and the recovery procedure.

The dependence on the image is completely natural. After all, recovering an image with many fine details will require more high-frequency samples than one with only coarse features. The dependence on the number of measurements also makes intuitive sense. When m is small the measurement budget may best be spent recovering the energy of the image, which is usually found at the low frequencies. But as m increases, the fine details become increasingly important to capture, thus requiring more high-frequency measurements. We discuss the dependence on the resolution N in the next section.

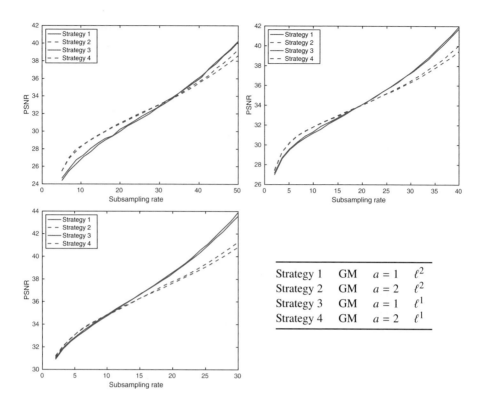

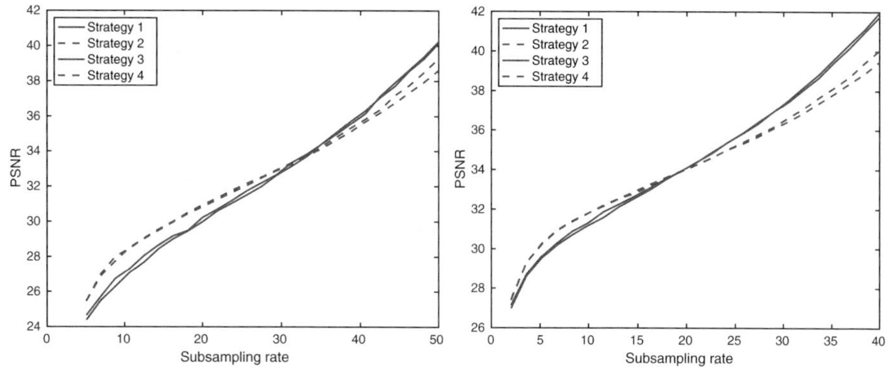

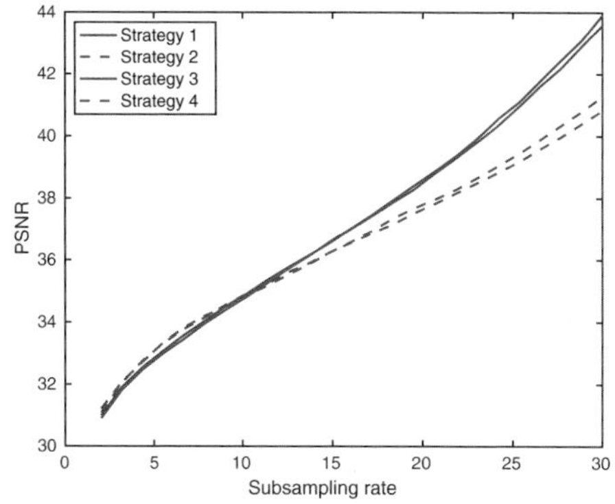

Strategy 1	GM	$a = 1$	ℓ^2
Strategy 2	GM	$a = 2$	ℓ^2
Strategy 3	GM	$a = 1$	ℓ^1
Strategy 4	GM	$a = 2$	ℓ^1

Figure 4.5 PSNR versus subsampling rate for Fourier sampling applied to the discretized GLPU phantom of size 256×256 (top left), 512×512 (top right) and 1024×1024 (bottom) using Gaussian multilevel (GM) sampling strategies based on the ℓ^1- or ℓ^2-ball. The values $r_0 = 2$ and $r = 50$ were used throughout. Typical sampling maps are shown in Fig. 4.6. The reconstructions were computed by solving (3.4) with DB4 wavelets.

Figures 4.5 and 4.7 illustrate Principle #3 for Fourier and Walsh sampling, respectively. In both cases the Gaussian multilevel scheme with parameter $a = 2$ is better for smaller m (lower subsampling rate), while the choice $a = 1$ is better for larger m. This makes sense. Larger a means faster decay of the Gaussian, which corresponds to fewer samples at higher frequencies. See also Figs 4.6 and 4.8. In further accordance with this principle, we also observe that the transition point between $a = 2$ being better and $a = 1$ being better changes with the image resolution.

Principle #4. The optimal sampling strategy may be anisotropic.

This principle is harder to explain. Generally speaking, it depends on the recovery procedure used. In the case of compressed sensing with a wavelet sparsifying transform, it arises because of the behaviour of wavelets in frequency space. In Chapter 15 we support this principle with mathematical theory. A notable consequence of this theory is that anisotropy is generally more important in the case of Walsh sampling than it is in Fourier sampling. In Fig. 4.7 we demonstrate this effect. Observe that the anisotropic DAS scheme, an example of which is shown in Fig. 4.8, gives the best performance.

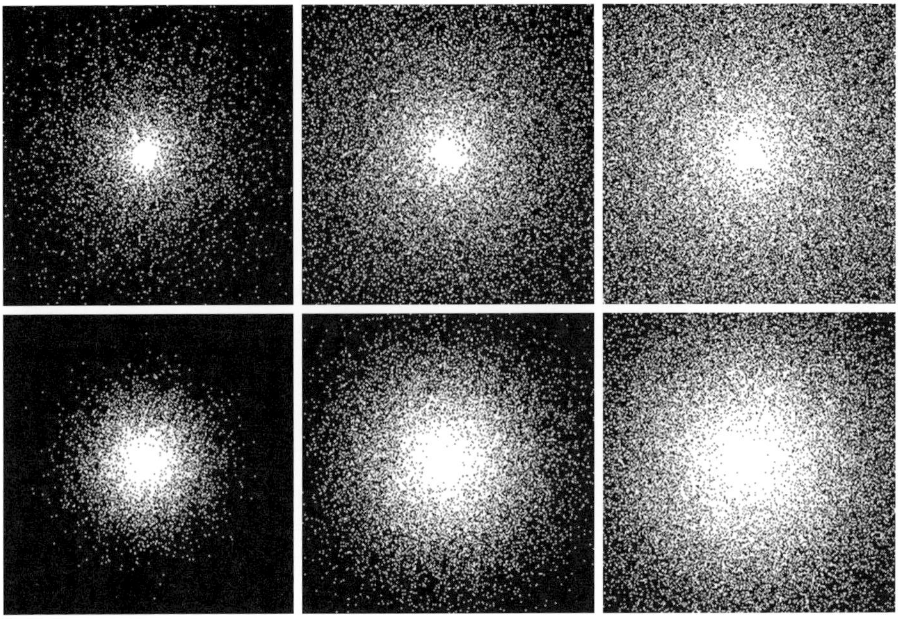

Figure 4.6 The sampling maps produced by strategy 1 (top row) and strategy 2 (bottom row) in Fig. 4.5 at resolution 256×256 for different subsampling percentages.

4.3 Resolution Enhancement

We now discuss resolution and its effect on compressive imaging performance.

> Compressive imaging techniques are generally more beneficial for imaging at higher resolutions than at lower resolutions.

Before discussing the reasons behind this statement, we first demonstrate it numerically in the context of compressed sensing. In Fig. 4.9 we use the same sampling strategy Ω – in particular, keeping the subsampling percentage fixed at 5% – and we vary the resolution from 256×256 to 2048×2048. In other words, we vary the range of k-space from which the m Fourier measurements are drawn. Figure 4.9 shows the result of this experiment on the pomegranate test image (see Fig. 2.2). As discussed in the Notes section of Chapter 2, the reason for using a nonliving subject is that it allows higher resolutions to be achieved by the MRI scanner.

This figure also shows each reconstructed image magnified by a factor equal to the change in the resolution. At the lowest resolution 256×256 the reconstruction exhibits clear artefacts. On the other hand, at the highest resolution 2048×2048 the magnified reconstruction is nearly indistinguishable from the true image. If resolution were irrelevant to the experiment, one would expect to see similar artefacts in the magnified 2048×2048 reconstruction as one sees in the unmagnified 256×256 reconstruction. Yet this does not occur. This demonstrates the improvement gained by moving to higher resolutions.

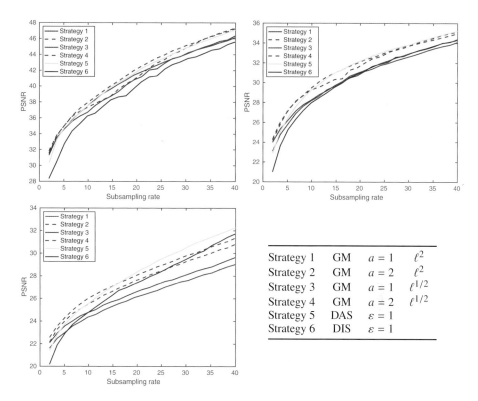

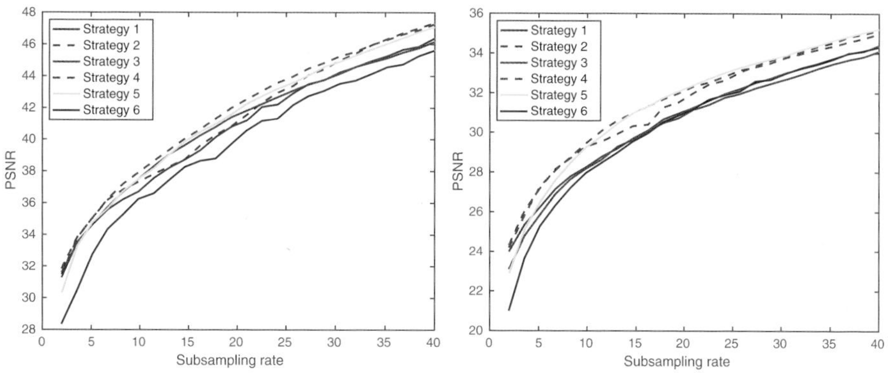

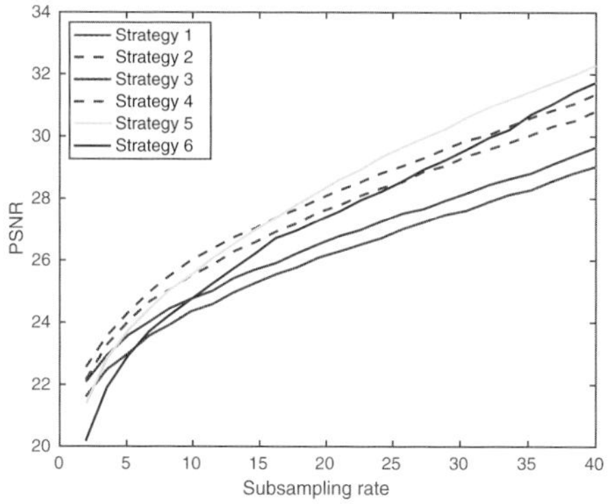

Strategy 1	GM	$a = 1$	ℓ^2
Strategy 2	GM	$a = 2$	ℓ^2
Strategy 3	GM	$a = 1$	$\ell^{1/2}$
Strategy 4	GM	$a = 2$	$\ell^{1/2}$
Strategy 5	DAS	$\varepsilon = 1$	
Strategy 6	DIS	$\varepsilon = 1$	

Figure 4.7 PSNR versus subsampling rate for Walsh sampling for the kopp (top left), peppers (top right) and dog (bottom left) images at resolution 512×512; see Fig. 2.2 for the originals. Strategies 1–4 are Gaussian multilevel (GM) sampling schemes based on different unit balls. The values $r_0 = 2$ and $r = 50$ were used in all cases. Strategies 5 and 6 are the DIS and DAS schemes, respectively. These are defined in Chapter 15. Both use the SL phantom as reference image along with threshold parameter $\epsilon = 1$ (see §15.3.5). Example sampling maps are shown in Fig. 4.8. All reconstructions were computed by solving (3.4) with DB4 wavelets.

Next, in Fig. 4.10 we vary the sampling strategy and the resolution, but now keep the total number of measurements m fixed. The image to recover is identical to the GLPU phantom, except that a small detail has been added. The first approach, shown in Fig. 4.10(a), fully samples the lowest 512×512 k-space values and recovers an approximation at resolution 512×512 to the true image by solving (3.11). This is a classical MRI procedure: fully sample all k-space values up to some maximal frequency, then apply an inverse DFT to the data. Next, we take the same amount of samples $m = 512^2$ and sample the lowest 512×512 frequencies from the first 2048×2048 k-space values. Figure 4.10(b) shows the corresponding reconstruction, obtained by zero padding the missing Fourier data and applying an inverse DFT of size 2048×2048. Although slightly better than the first reconstruction, the detail is still obscured.

This inability to recover the detail is unsurprising, since the sampling scheme contains no high frequencies. In Figs 4.10(c,d) we change the sampling pattern to a Gaussian multilevel scheme. This uses the same total number of measurements, but spreads them

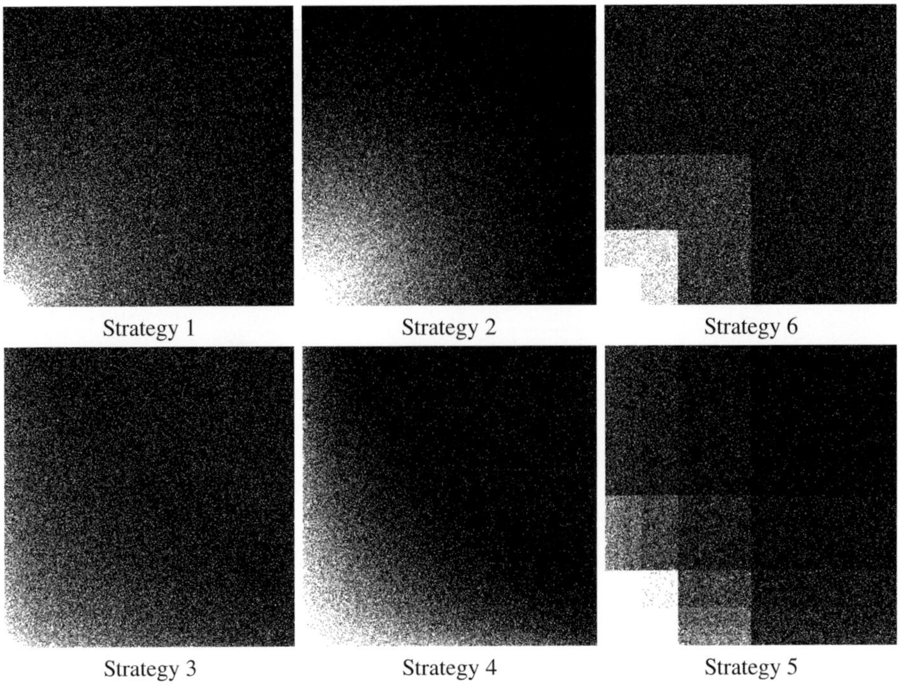

Figure 4.8 The sampling maps used in Fig. 4.7 with sampling percentage equal to 15%.

out across the full k-space. Figure 4.10(c) applies a zero-padded inverse DFT as before. This gives a better result than either of the previous two reconstructions, but the detail remains largely obscured. Finally, in Fig. 4.10(d) we replace the inverse DFT with a compressed sensing reconstruction. The detail is now clearly recovered.

This experiment shows the benefit of compressive imaging at higher resolutions over classical approaches. By distributing the measurements over the full range and using a sparsity-promoting reconstruction, one obtains a far higher-quality image. In particular, fine details, corresponding to higher-frequency measurements, are revealed. Note that this is a result of both the sampling strategy *and* the recovery procedure; simple zero padding followed by an inverse DFT obscures the fine details, even when the same high-frequency samples are used.

To summarize, the performance of compressive imaging with the right type of sampling strategy is generally better at higher resolutions. We loosely term this behaviour *resolution dependence*. Why does this occur? For compressed sensing there is a full mathematical explanation, which we defer until Chapter 15. But, informally, it follows directly from the phenomena noted in Chapter 1. Specifically, the local sparsity structure of images – namely, their tendency to be sparser at fine wavelet scales than at coarser ones (Key Point #8) – and the ability of structured sampling operators such as Fourier or Walsh sampling to exploit this structure (Key Point #9).

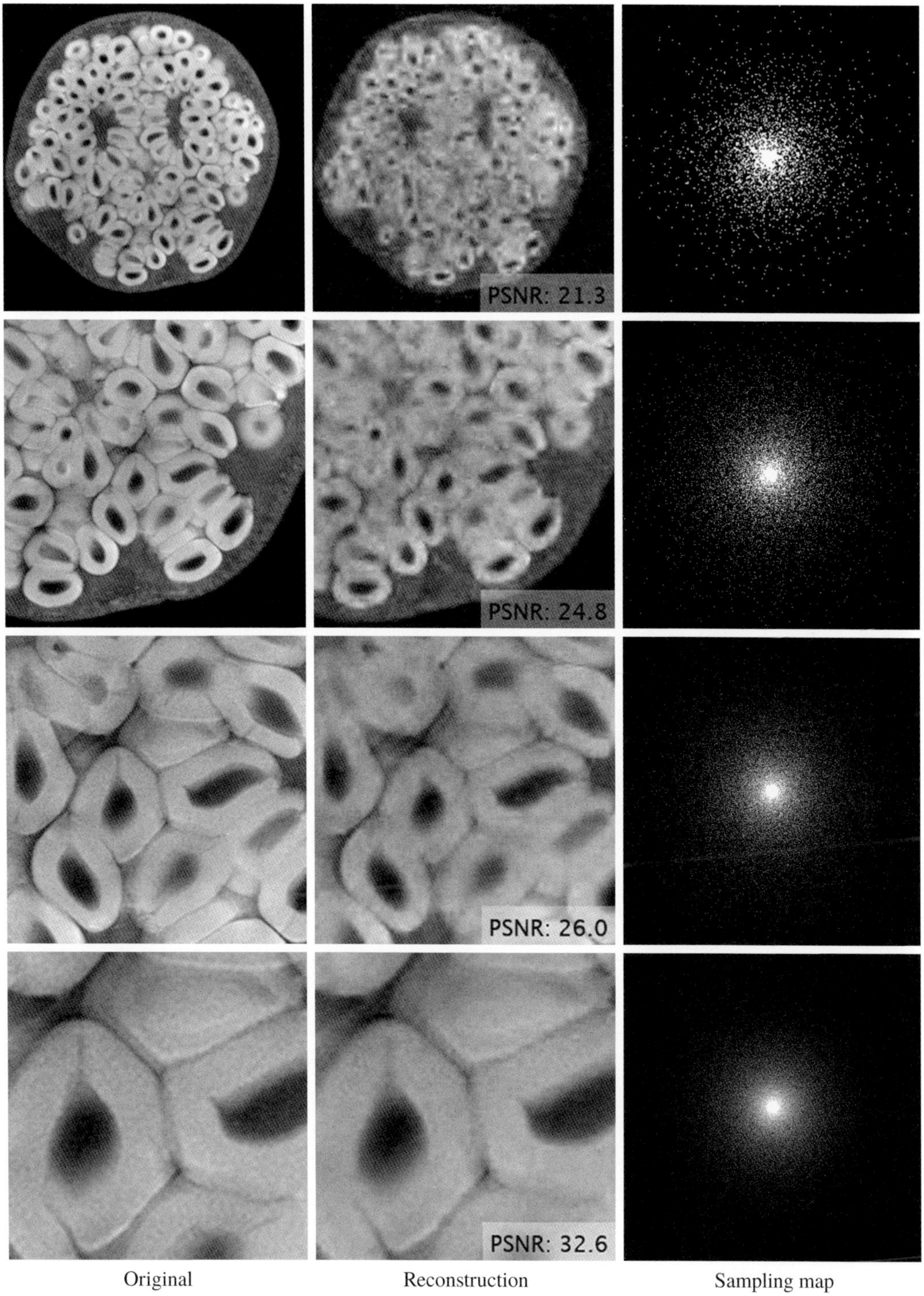

Figure 4.9 Recovery from 5% Fourier samples with the same sampling strategy at resolutions 256×256, 512×512, 1024×1024 and 2048×2048 (top to bottom). A Gaussian multilevel strategy based on the ℓ^2-ball is used with $a = 1$, $r_0 = 2$ and $r = 100$. The reconstructions were computed by solving (3.4) with DB4 wavelets. The top row shows the full image and its reconstruction. Subsequent rows show two, four and eight times magnification, respectively.

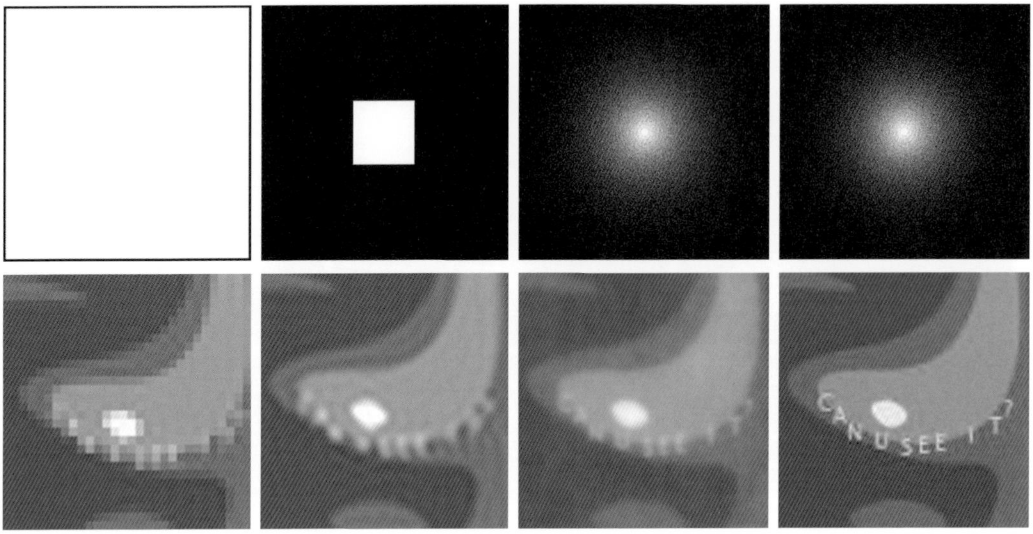

(a) IDFT (b) Zero-padded IDFT (c) Zero-padded IDFT (d) Compressed sensing

Figure 4.10 (a) Full sampling at 512×512 resolution with inverse DFT (IDFT) reconstruction. (b) Sampling the lowest 512×512 frequencies at resolution 2048×2048, followed by zero-padded inverse DFT reconstruction. (c) Sampling $m = 512^2$ measurements at resolution 2048×2048 taken according to a Gaussian multilevel scheme, followed by zero-padded IDFT reconstruction. (d) The same sampling scheme as in (c), but instead followed by (3.4) using DB4 wavelets. Top row: Sampling strategies. Bottom row: Crops of the recovered images showing the reconstruction of the inserted detail.

4.4 Discretization, Model Mismatch and the Inverse Crime

We now discuss discretization, a topic that has already been mentioned several times in previous chapters. We make two main points. The first, which is the following, should come as little surprise to the reader:

Poor discretization may destroy any benefits of compressive imaging.

A far more insidious issue, however, is the *inverse crime*. As discussed in Chapter 3, discretization of a continuous inverse problem $y = \mathcal{A}f + e$ eventually results in a finite inverse problem of the form $y = Ax + e$. The matrix A is used in the recovery procedure – for instance, when solving the optimization problem (3.4). In order to benchmark a new recovery procedure it is, of course, far more convenient to test it on simulated data than real data obtained from an actual device. Real data may not be available, and even when it is, it may be improperly formatted or otherwise difficult to work with. The inverse crime pertains to the situation where data is simulated using the discrete model A, rather than the 'true' model $\mathcal{A}$. This means that the simulated measurements $y' = Ax$, where x is the image to be recovered, now contain none of the discretization error made when passing from $\mathcal{A}$ to A. In the case of Fourier measurements, this usually means simulating the Fourier data of an image f by applying the DFT to its discretized version x (at some

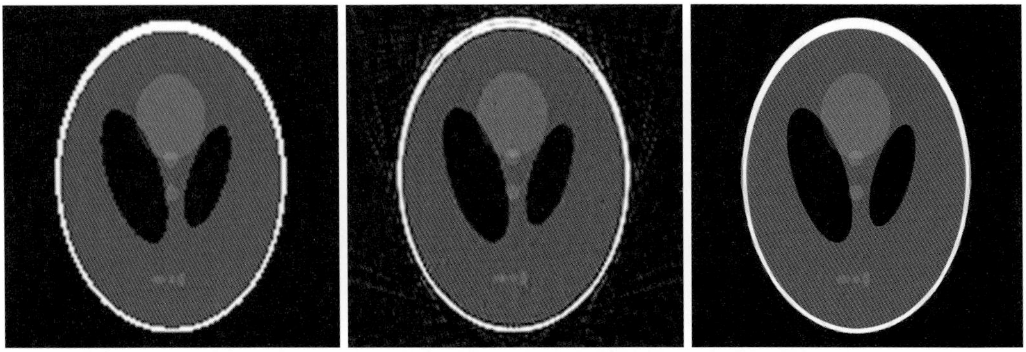

(a) Discrete, 128×128 (b) Continuous, 128×128 (c) Continuous, 512×512

Figure 4.11 Reconstruction of the SL phantom image from 50 equally spaced angles using TV minimization. (a) Discrete Radon measurements at resolution 128×128. (b) Continuous Radon measurements at resolution 128×128. (c) Continuous Radon measurements at resolution 512×512.

resolution), rather than applying the true continuous Fourier transform to f. We commit this crime multiple times throughout this book.

The inverse crime means that a recovery procedure benchmarked on simulated data can perform surprisingly badly when applied to real data. In other words, testing a procedure solely on simulated data may give an artificially inflated impression of its real-world performance. This leads us to the second point:

> When possible, avoid the inverse crime when simulating the data. In general, be wary that good performance on simulated data may not imply the same for real data.

We discuss the inverse crime and how to avoid it in the context of MRI (Fourier sampling) in Chapter 14. For now, let us consider X-ray CT. Figure 4.11 shows the recovery of the SL phantom from continuous Radon measurements. In Fig. 4.11(a) the inverse crime is committed by simulating the measurements as $y = Ax$, where A is the discrete measurement matrix corresponding to resolution 128×128. Since the gradient of the discrete SL phantom is exactly sparse, it is recovered exactly. However, Fig. 4.11(b) shows that this is purely a consequence of committing the inverse crime. Here the measurements y are simulated using the continuous Radon transform of the infinite resolution phantom. As is evident, the discretization error between the continuous measurements y and the discrete model $y = Ax$ leads to a far worse recovery.

In principle, mitigating the discretization error in this example is quite straightforward. We simply increase the resolution used in the reconstruction. In Fig. 4.11(c) , we choose A to be the discrete measurement matrix at resolution 512×512 instead of 128×128. This reduces the discretization error, leading to a substantially improved recovery.

This simple approach is not without its downsides. First, the optimization problem is larger, and hence it takes longer to solve. Second, the gradient of the 512×512 SL phantom is less sparse (in absolute terms) than that of the 128×128 phantom. Therefore, in principle, there might not be enough measurements to recover the higher-resolution image. In practice, a balance may need to be struck between the discretization error and the compressed sensing (sparse recovery) error. We shall not discuss this issue further.

4.5 Sparsifying Transforms

Having covered issues related to sampling for compressive imaging in general, we now switch focus and consider ways to improve the performance of compressed sensing specifically. In this section, we consider the choice of sparsifying transform.

Thus far, we have considered two particular sparsifying transforms: orthonormal wavelets and TV. Both lead to significantly better reconstructions over classical techniques. Yet, as seen in §3.2.3, the reconstructions are not perfect. This motivates the search for more sophisticated sparsifying transforms so as to further improve performance.

4.5.1 X-let Transforms

'X-let' transforms are extensions of wavelets that have a similar multiscale structure. The general aim of X-lets is to more efficiently capture geometric image features such as edges. Two prominent examples are *curvelets* and *shearlets*, which are discussed in a little more detail in §9.11.

Unlike wavelets, X-let transforms are typically nonorthogonal and *redundant* (also known as *overcomplete*). The discrete sparsifying transform $\Phi \in \mathbb{C}^{N \times M}$ is a fat matrix ($M \geq N$) and its columns $\{\phi_i\}$, while they span $\mathbb{C}^N$, are neither orthogonal nor even linearly independent. In particular, every vector $x \in \mathbb{C}^N$ can be represented in infinitely many different ways as a linear combination of the ϕ_i. Redundant X-let transforms are examples of *frames*. That is, they satisfy

$$A\|x\|_{\ell^2}^2 \leq \sum_{i=1}^{M} |\langle x, \phi_i \rangle|^2 \leq B\|x\|_{\ell^2}^2, \quad \forall x \in \mathbb{C}^N, \tag{4.7}$$

for constants $B \geq A > 0$ (the *frame bounds*). Often they are also *tight frames*, in which case (4.7) holds with $A = B$.

A consequence of this redundancy is that the QCBP analysis problem (3.3) is no longer equivalent to the QCBP synthesis problem (3.4). The two problems may give quite different results in practice. Analysis (3.3) is often preferred over synthesis (3.4), although this is by no means a consensus. As was previously observed, blackbox optimization solvers may only solve one type of problem.

We now illustrate the potential benefits of using X-let transforms. In Fig. 4.12 we perform the same experiment as in Fig. 3.4 but using curvelet and shearlet transforms instead. The synthesis problem (3.4) is solved in each case. As we see, both give more visually appealing recoveries over wavelets and TV. Yet the reader may also notice that they too lead to characteristic artefacts, which are stripe-like in nature.

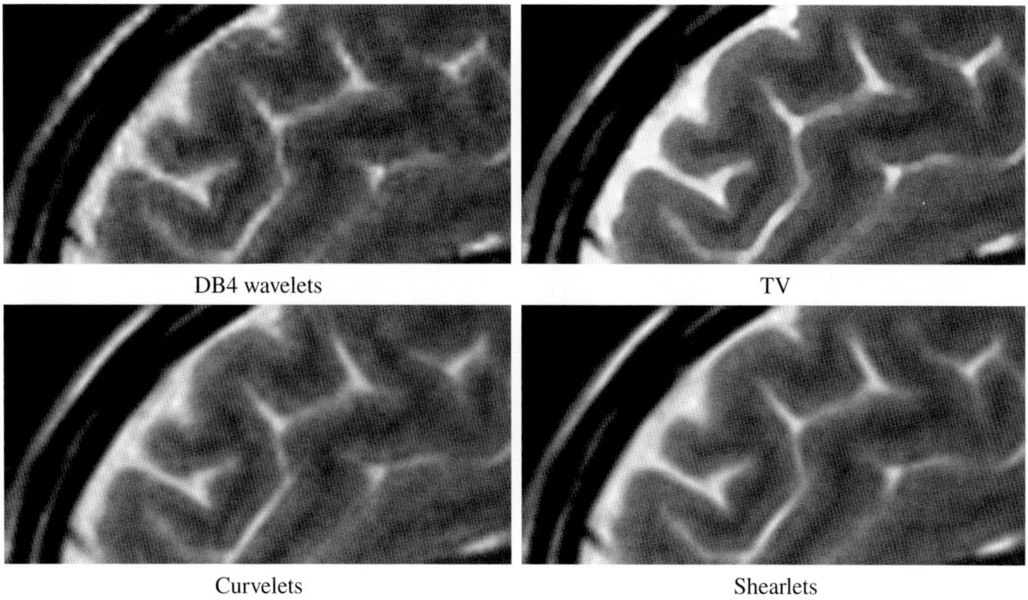

Figure 4.12 Reconstructions from discrete Fourier measurements with different sparsifying transforms. The setup is the same as in Fig. 3.4.

4.5.2 TGV

The second approach involves generalizations of TV. TV minimization suffers from the well-known *staircasing effect* in which smooth, but nonflat regions of an image tend to be recovered as piecewise constant 'staircases'. Extensions of TV attempt to mitigate this problem by penalizing higher-order derivatives. There are many possible ways to do this, but amongst the more popular is second-order *Total Generalized Variation (TGV)*. TGV seeks to minimize a combination of the first and second derivatives. In one dimension, it is defined as

$$\mathrm{TGV}^2_{\alpha}(x) = \inf_{v \in \mathbb{C}^N} \alpha_1 \|\nabla x - v\|_{\ell^1} + \alpha_0 \|\nabla v\|_{\ell^1}, \quad x \in \mathbb{C}^N,$$

where $\alpha = (\alpha_0, \alpha_1)$ are parameters that are used to balance the contributions of the two terms. In two dimensions, it is defined as

$$\mathrm{TGV}^2_{\alpha}(X) = \inf_{V \in \mathbb{C}^{2N \times N}} \alpha_1 \|\nabla X - V\|_{\ell^1_*} + \alpha_0 \|\mathcal{E}(V)\|_{\ell^1_*}, \quad X \in \mathbb{C}^{N \times N}, \tag{4.8}$$

where $\alpha = (\alpha_0, \alpha_1)$ are parameters,

$$\nabla X = \begin{pmatrix} \nabla_1 X \\ \nabla_2 X \end{pmatrix}$$

and $\mathcal{E}$ is the symmetrized derivative operator

$$\mathcal{E}(V) = \begin{pmatrix} \nabla_1' V_1 & \frac{1}{2}\left(\nabla_2' V_1 + \nabla_1' V_2\right) \\ \frac{1}{2}\left(\nabla_2' V_1 + \nabla_1' V_2\right) & \nabla_2' V_2 \end{pmatrix}, \qquad V = \begin{pmatrix} V_1 \\ V_2 \end{pmatrix}.$$

Here ∇_1 and ∇_2 are the vertical and horizontal discrete partial derivative operators defined by forwards differences and ∇_1', ∇_2' are the same except defined by backwards differences. The first norm in (4.8) is defined as

$$\|V\|_{\ell^1_*} = \sum_{i,j=1}^{N} \sqrt{|(V_1)_{ij}|^2 + |(V_2)_{ij}|^2}, \qquad V = \begin{pmatrix} V_1 \\ V_2 \end{pmatrix}$$

and, if $\mathcal{E}(V) = \begin{pmatrix} \mathcal{E}_{11}(V) & \mathcal{E}_{12}(V) \\ \mathcal{E}_{21}(V) & \mathcal{E}_{22}(V) \end{pmatrix}$, the second is defined as

$$\|\mathcal{E}(V)\|_{\ell^1_*} = \sum_{i,j=1}^{N} \sqrt{|(\mathcal{E}_{11}(V))_{ij}|^2 + |(\mathcal{E}_{12}(V))_{ij}|^2 + |(\mathcal{E}_{21}(V))_{ij}|^2 + |(\mathcal{E}_{22}(V))_{ij}|^2}.$$

4.5.3 Combinations of Sparsifying Transforms

While it is perfectly possible to use a single X-let or TGV transform, better performance can often be obtained by combining several different sparsifying transforms. This is sometimes known as *composite* ℓ^1-minimization. For example, if Φ is a wavelet transform, one might consider the *wavelets+TV* (analysis) problem

$$\min_{z \in \mathbb{C}^N} \lambda_1 \|\Phi^* z\|_{\ell^1} + \lambda_2 \|z\|_{TV} \text{ subject to } \|Az - y\|_{\ell^2} \leq \eta. \tag{4.9}$$

Curvelets+TV or shearlets+TGV, or other combinations, can be defined in the obvious manner. We present several examples of this approach in the next section. Note that one can also formulate this as a mixed optimization problem by treating the X-let transform in a synthesis fashion as opposed to an analysis fashion.

Unsurprisingly, getting the right balance of parameters in (4.9) is usually crucial to achieving a performance boost over simply wavelets ($\lambda_2 = 0$) or TV ($\lambda_1 = 0$) alone.

4.6 Iterative Reweighting

We now introduce another powerful method for improving compressed sensing performance. This is the idea of *reweighting*. Consider the QCBP problem

$$\min_{z \in \mathbb{C}^N} \|z\|_{\ell^1} \text{ subject to } \|Az - y\|_{\ell^2} \leq \eta. \tag{4.10}$$

Weighting refers to the process of replacing the ℓ^1-norm by a weighted ℓ^1-norm, leading to the *weighted QCBP* problem

$$\min_{z \in \mathbb{C}^N} \|z\|_{\ell^1_w} \text{ subject to } \|Az - y\|_{\ell^2} \leq \eta. \tag{4.11}$$

Here $\|z\|_{\ell^1_w} = \sum_{i=1}^N w_i |z_i|$ is the weighted ℓ^1-norm, and $w = (w_i)_{i=1}^N$ is a vector of positive weights. The question is: which weights should one choose? Suppose that x is

---

Algorithm 4.1: Iteratively reweighted ℓ^1-minimization

---

input: measurements y, measurement matrix A, parameter $\varepsilon > 0$, initial weights $w_i = 1, i = 1, \ldots, N$

output: reconstruction $\hat{x}$

for $l = 1, 2, \ldots$ **do**

  Compute a minimizer $\hat{x}^{(l)}$ of (4.11).

  Update the weights using (4.13).

end

---

s-sparse and its support $\mathrm{supp}(x) = \{i : x_i \neq 0\}$ was known. Then a natural choice is

$$w_i = \begin{cases} \frac{1}{|x_i|} & x_i \neq 0 \\ \infty & x_i = 0 \end{cases}, \quad i = 1, \ldots, N. \tag{4.12}$$

In this case, any minimizer of (4.11) must recover the support of x correctly, and under some mild assumptions on A will recover x as well, at least up to the noise level η.

Such *support information* is usually not available in practice. The idea of *iterative reweighting* is to solve a sequence of weighted ℓ^1-minimization problems where the weights are iteratively updated based on previous support estimates. Specifically, if $\hat{x}^{(l)}$ is the estimate for x at step l, then the new weights are defined as

$$w_i = \frac{1}{|\hat{x}_i^{(l)}| + \varepsilon}, \quad i = 1, \ldots, N, \tag{4.13}$$

where $\varepsilon > 0$ is a small parameter. If $\hat{x}^{(l)}$ estimates the true vector x reasonably well, then these weights should mimic the behaviour of the weights (4.12) and therefore promote an even better reconstruction $\hat{x}^{(l+1)}$ in the next weighted QCBP solve. This procedure is described in Algorithm 4.1.

Iterative reweighting can also be combined with multiple sparsifying transforms. The principle is quite straightforward. Consider the following problem, which is a mild generalization of (4.9):

$$\min_{z \in \mathbb{C}^N} \sum_{j=1}^{k} \lambda_j \|(\Phi^{(j)})^* z\|_{\ell^1} \text{ subject to } \|Az - y\|_{\ell^2} \leq \eta.$$

Here each $\Phi^{(j)}$ is a different sparsifying transform. The idea is to apply iterative reweighting to each term in the sum, while also simultaneously updating the λ_js. This is described in Algorithm 4.2. Note that the λ_j update can be achieved in a number of different ways. One possibility is to update each λ_j according to how sparse the current estimate $\hat{x}^{(l)}$ is in the corresponding transform $\Phi^{(j)}$. This can be done by setting

$$\lambda_j = \frac{N_j}{\|(\Phi^{(j)})^* \hat{x}^{(l)}\|_{\ell^1} + \varepsilon}, \quad j = 1, \ldots, k, \tag{4.14}$$

where N_j is the number of columns of the matrix $\Phi^{(j)}$. On the other hand, X-lets have a multiscale structure. Hence there is a natural division of an X-let sparsifying transform

Algorithm 4.2: Iteratively reweighted composite ℓ^1-minimization

input: measurements y, measurement matrix A, parameter $\varepsilon > 0$, initial weights $w_i^{(j)} = 1$ and parameters $\lambda_j = 1, i = 1, \dots, N, j = 1, \dots, k$

output: reconstruction $\hat{x}$

for $l = 1, 2, \dots$ **do**

Let $\|\cdot\|_{(j)}$ denote the weighted ℓ^1-norm with weights $w^{(j)}$. Compute a minimizer $\hat{x}^{(l)}$ of

$$\min_{z \in \mathbb{C}^N} \sum_{j=1}^{k} \lambda_j \|(\Phi^{(j)})^* z\|_{(j)} \text{ subject to } \|Az - y\|_{\ell^2} \leq \eta. \tag{4.16}$$

Update the weights:

$$w_i^{(j)} = \frac{1}{|((\Phi^{(j)})^* \hat{x}^{(l)})_i| + \varepsilon}, \quad i = 1, \dots, N, \ j = 1, \dots, k.$$

Update the parameters $\lambda_j, j = 1, \dots, N$.

end

as $\Phi = \left(\Phi^{(1)} | \dots | \Phi^{(r)}\right)$, where $\Phi^{(j)}$ represents the X-lets at scale j. If this splitting is used in the above reweighting scheme, then one may wish to update the λ_js as

$$\lambda_j = \|(\Phi^{(j)})^* \hat{x}^{(l)}\|_{\ell^\infty}. \tag{4.15}$$

This approach takes into account the difference in magnitudes of the X-let coefficients of an image at different scales.

Remark 4.11 It is rather more common in practice to consider a LASSO-type formulation instead of the QCBP problem (4.16). In this case, the optimization problem takes the form

$$\min_{z \in \mathbb{C}^N} \sum_{j=1}^{k} \lambda_j \|(\Phi^{(j)})^* z\|_{(j)} + \mu \|Az - y\|_{\ell^2}^2,$$

where $\mu > 0$ is a parameter. This parameter may either be fixed, or iteratively updated in a suitable manner. The rest of the reweighting procedure is unchanged.

In view of consideration (xiii) of the previous chapter, it is worth stressing that reweighted procedures are necessarily slower than non-reweighted procedures, since they involve multiple solves of a problem such as (4.16). Computational efficiency is traded for potentially higher accuracy.

Nonetheless, we now demonstrate their effectiveness on a Fourier imaging problem. In Fig. 4.13 we apply the reweighting procedure using the weighted LASSO formulation

$$\min_{z \in \mathbb{C}^N} \sum_{j=1}^{k} \lambda_j \|(\Phi^{(j)})^* z\|_{(j)} + \mathrm{TGV}_\alpha^2(z) + \frac{\mu}{2} \|Az - y\|_{\ell^2}^2. \tag{4.17}$$

Here $\Phi^{(j)}$ are the scales of a shearlet system and $\|\cdot\|_{(j)}$ is, as in Algorithm 4.2, the weighted ℓ^1-norm used in the reweighting procedure. We have also added an (unweighted) TGV penalty, with its associated parameters $\alpha = (\alpha_0, \alpha_1)$. The parameters α and μ are fixed, as is the parameter ε in the reweighting scheme.

In Fig. 4.13 this recovery is compared to that of LASSO using DB4 wavelets and the ℓ^1-norm (i.e. no reweighting) for two different sampling strategies, Cartesian (Definition 4.8) and Gaussian multilevel (Definition 4.7). As expected, the reweighting scheme gives a better recovery in both cases. However, it is notable that the improvement is far more significant in the case of Cartesian sampling. This is to be expected. Cartesian sampling is a fairly poor sampling strategy, whereas the multilevel scheme was designed according to the principles laid out in §4.2 to maximize the recovery performance. It should come as little surprise that when the sampling scheme is optimized, there is less scope to further boost the recovery performance by changing the reconstruction procedure. This leads us to an important point with which to conclude this section:

> If the measurements are poor and cannot be changed, more effort should be put into designing a better recovery procedure.

4.7 Learning: Incorporating Training Data

As discussed in §1.7, a limitation of compressed sensing is that it is model based: a suitable sampling strategy, sparsifying transformation, optimization procedure and regularization parameter (or parameters) need to be chosen beforehand. The idea of data-driven approaches is to (implicitly or explicitly) learn some of these components. This is often done using training data. Since such data is readily available in many imaging modalities, learning some part of the imaging pipeline is a very natural, and potentially very powerful, idea. Part V of this book discusses the most recent learning approaches based on deep learning. But first, we discuss what is arguably the most well-established type of learning for compressive imaging, so-called *dictionary learning*.

4.7.1 Dictionary Learning

Dictionary learning is the process of learning a sparsifying transform $\Phi \in \mathbb{C}^{N \times M}$ (the *dictionary*) as opposed to working with a fixed transform such as X-lets. This can either be done prior to the image recovery process by using training data or it can be done jointly with it, typically without training data. The latter is sometimes referred to as *blind* compressed sensing.

Consider the first approach. Given a training set of images $\{x_i\}_{i=1}^K \subset \mathbb{C}^N$, the search for a dictionary $\Phi \in \mathbb{C}^{N \times M}$ is usually posed as an optimization problem. A typical synthesis formulation takes the form

$$\min_{\substack{z_i \in \mathbb{C}^M \\ \Phi \in \mathbb{C}^{N \times M}}} \sum_{i=1}^{K} \left(\|x_i - \Phi z_i\|_{\ell^2}^2 + \lambda \|z_i\|_{\ell^1} \right) \text{ subject to } \Phi \in \mathcal{D}. \tag{4.18}$$

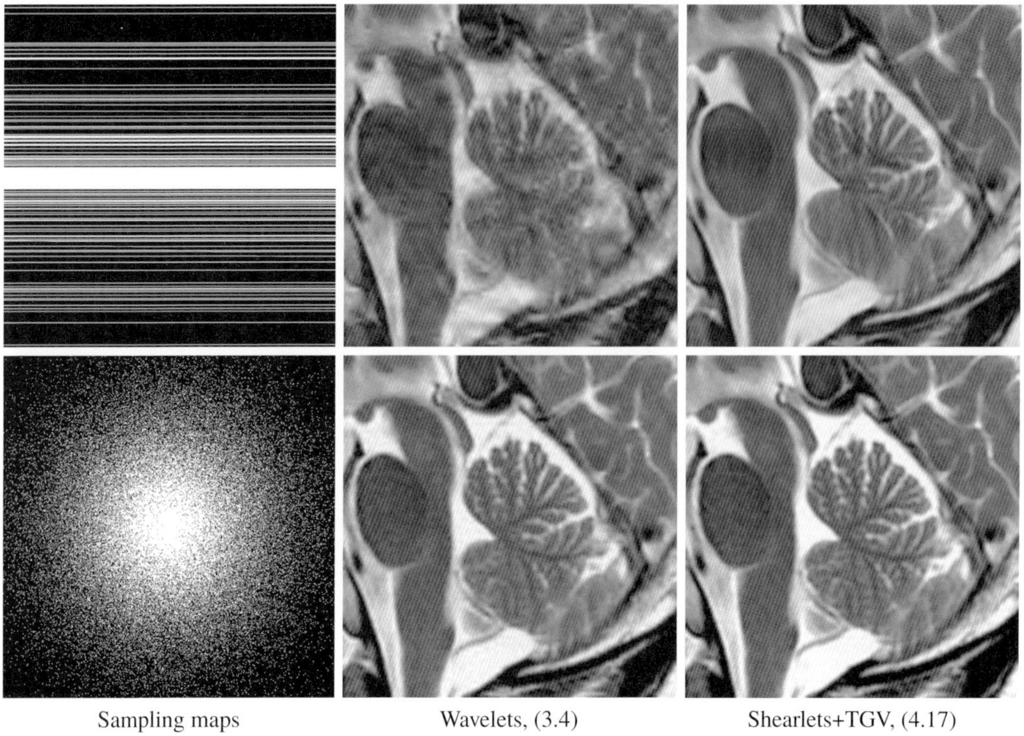

Figure 4.13 Recovery of the 512×512 brain image from 25% Fourier measurements. Left: Sampling maps. Middle: Recovery using DB4 wavelets and solving (3.4). Right: Recovery via the iterative reweighting scheme based on (4.17) using shearlets and TGV. The parameters are $\alpha = (1, 1)$, $\mu = 10^4$ and $\varepsilon = 10^{-5}$. The middle and right columns show a crop of the recovered image. The Cartesian sampling scheme (top) selects the vertical frequencies randomly and independently according to the inverse linear law $\pi_\omega \propto \frac{1}{\max\{1, |\omega|\}}$. The Gaussian multilevel scheme (bottom) has parameters $a = 2$, $r_0 = 2$ and $r = 50$.

Here $\mathcal{D} \subseteq \mathbb{C}^{N\times M}$ is a nonempty and closed constraint set which restricts the type of dictionaries allowed. A typical constraint is that the columns of Φ be normalized to either exactly one, or less than or equal to one. This helps avoid scale ambiguity in the learning process. When Φ is fixed, the minimization subproblem over the z_is is known as *sparse coding*, with the computed z_is being the *sparse codes* for the images x_i. The two terms in the LASSO-type objective function in (4.18) promote fitting of the true images $x_i \approx \Phi z_i$ and sparsity of the codes z_i in the given dictionary Φ.

Numerically, (4.18) can be solved via *alternating minimization*. This is described in Algorithm 4.3. Here one alternates between updating the sparse codes $\{z_i\}$ and the dictionary Φ. Since it is a convex problem, the sparse coding step can be solved using standard convex optimization procedures, as described in Chapter 7. The dictionary update can be tackled in several different ways depending on the constraint set $\mathcal{D}$. Standard methods include *Method of Optimal Directions (MOD)*, *projected gradient descent* and the well-known *K-SVD* algorithm.

Algorithm 4.3: Alternating minimization for (4.18)

input: images $x_1, \ldots, x_K$, initial dictionary $\Phi^{(0)}$, parameter $\lambda > 0$
output: dictionary $\widehat{\Phi}$, sparse codes $\hat{z}_1, \ldots, \hat{z}_K$

for $j = 0, 1, \ldots$ **do**
  for $i = 1, \ldots, K$ **do**
    Compute $z_i^{(j+1)} \in \underset{z_i \in \mathbb{C}^M}{\operatorname{argmin}} \|x_i - \Phi^{(j)} z_i\|_{\ell^2}^2 + \lambda \|z_i\|_{\ell^1}$ (sparse coding).
  end
  Compute $\Phi^{(j+1)} \in \underset{\Phi \in \mathcal{D}}{\operatorname{argmin}} \sum_{i=1}^K \|x_i - \Phi z_i^{(j+1)}\|_{\ell^2}^2$ (dictionary update).
end

4.7.2 Patch-Based Learning

Unfortunately, this process can be computationally demanding for large-scale problems. To reduce the computational burden, one can restrict the class of dictionaries $\mathcal{D}$. One way to do this is to allow only convolutional dictionaries, a process known as *convolutional* dictionary learning. Another approach is to consider *patch-based* dictionaries. Let $x \in \mathbb{C}^N$ be an image, and consider a collection of K (possibly overlapping) patches each consisting of L pixels. Let $P_i(x) \in \mathbb{C}^L$ denote the ith patch of x. Then a synthesis-type dictionary learning procedure can be defined as

$$\min_{\substack{z_i \in \mathbb{C}^M \\ \Phi \in \mathbb{C}^{L \times M}}} \sum_{i=1}^K \left(\|P_i(x) - \Phi z_i\|_{\ell^2}^2 + \lambda \|z_i\|_{\ell^1} \right) \text{ subject to } \Phi \in \mathcal{D}, \tag{4.19}$$

where $\mathcal{D} \subseteq \mathbb{C}^{L \times M}$. The premise of patch-based dictionary learning is that natural images tend to exhibit some nonlocal features, meaning that patches that are not necessarily close to each other can contain similar information. Observe that this procedure can be applied either to a single image (as above) or a collection of images (as before).

4.7.3 Patch-based Learning for Image Reconstruction

The patch-based approach also transfers naturally over to image reconstruction problems. Let $y = Ax + e$ be noisy measurements of an unknown image x. Then to recover x from y one replaces (4.19) with the optimization problem

$$\min_{\substack{z_i \in \mathbb{C}^M \\ \Phi \in \mathbb{C}^{L \times M} \\ x \in \mathbb{C}^N}} \|y - Ax\|_{\ell^2}^2 + \mu \sum_{i=1}^K \left(\|P_i(x) - \Phi z_i\|_{\ell^2}^2 + \lambda \|z_i\|_{\ell^1} \right) \text{ subject to } \Phi \in \mathcal{D}, \tag{4.20}$$

where $\mu > 0$ is a parameter. In other words, one seeks to simultaneously recover the image x, the dictionary Φ and the sparse codes $\{z_i\}$ for the patches. Numerically, this can be solved by alternating minimization over the three sets of variables x, Φ and $\{z_i\}$. The updates for Φ and $\{z_i\}$ are the same as before. The x update is performed as

Algorithm 4.4: Alternating minimization for (4.20)

input: measurements y, measurement matrix A, patch operators $P_1, \dots, P_K$, initial dictionary $\Phi^{(0)}$ and sparse codes $z_1^{(0)}, \dots, z_K^{(0)}$, parameters $\lambda, \mu > 0$

output: image $\hat{x}$, dictionary $\widehat{\Phi}$, sparse codes $\hat{z}_1, \dots, \hat{z}_K$

for $j = 0, 1, \dots$ **do**
  Compute $x^{(j+1)}$ via (4.21) (image update).
  for $i = 1, \dots, K$ **do**
    Compute $z_i^{(j+1)} \in \underset{z_i}{\operatorname{argmin}} \|P_i(x^{(j+1)}) - \Phi^{(j)} z_i\|_{\ell^2}^2 + \lambda \|z_i\|_{\ell^1}$ (sparse coding).
  end
  Compute $\Phi^{(j+1)} \in \underset{\Phi \in \mathcal{D}}{\operatorname{argmin}} \sum_{i=1}^{K} \|P_i(x^{(j+1)}) - \Phi z_i^{(j+1)}\|_{\ell^2}^2$ (dictionary update).
end

follows. Let $z_i^{(j)}$ and $\Phi^{(j)}$ be the sparse codes and dictionary obtained at the jth step. Then minimizing (4.20) over the variable x only is equivalent to

$$\min_{x \in \mathbb{C}^N} \|y - Ax\|_{\ell^2}^2 + \mu \sum_{i=1}^{K} \|P_i(x) - \Phi^{(j)} z_i^{(j)}\|_{\ell^2}^2.$$

This is a simple least-squares problem. If the patches form a partition of unity, i.e. $\sum_{i=1}^{K} P_i^* P_i = I$, then it has the explicit solution

$$x^{(j+1)} = (A^*A + \mu I)^{-1} \left(A^* y + \mu \sum_{i=1}^{K} P_i^* \Phi^{(j)} z_i^{(j)} \right). \tag{4.21}$$

The full procedure for solving (4.20) is described in Algorithm 4.4.

4.7.4 Challenges

We end this section by noting several drawbacks of dictionary learning. As already mentioned, it is often computationally intensive. There is also no guarantee that the alternating minimization procedure converges to a (local) minimum of the optimization problem. Moreover, dictionary learning usually involves a number of parameters. In (4.20), for instance, these include the optimization parameters λ and μ, the size of the patches L and the number of patches K. Carefully tuning each parameter is an important step towards getting good performance – one that is usually more critical than in purely model-based approaches.

4.8 An All-Round Model-Based Compressive Imaging Strategy

This concludes Part I of the book. We have gone from a basic understanding of sparsity, ℓ^1-minimization and how to take measurements to sophisticated sampling strategies and reconstruction algorithms, with the latter employing iterative reweighting, shearlets and TGV. Under the right conditions, each one can give a significant performance boost.

What strategy should one use for compressive imaging in practice? This is of course a matter of opinion! And speaking from a purely objective perspective, there is also no one-size-fits-all solution: it will depend crucially on the modality, as well as other constraints such as computational time. Nevertheless, we conclude with two general recommendations:

The sampling strategy. In Fourier imaging or binary imaging with Walsh sampling, we recommend a Gaussian multilevel scheme. The parameters r, r_0 and a should be tuned based on the image, resolution, sampling percentage and sparsifying transform. Typical values are given in the various experiments conducted in this chapter. While this strategy may not provide the absolute best performance on a single problem, we have found it to be a consistent all-rounder.

The recovery procedure. In terms of model-based procedures, we recommend a combination of wavelets/shearlets with TV/TGV, along with an iterative reweighting procedure such as that described in §4.6. As observed, the gains from this procedure may not be significant, especially at lower resolutions or when the sampling strategy has been highly tuned. But, as we saw in §4.6, when the measurements are relatively poor, having a good recovery procedure becomes all the more important. Of course, if computational time is a major constraint, reweighting may be undesirable, and a simple strategy such as QCBP with wavelets or TV should be considered instead.

Notes on Other Techniques for Enhancing Performance

In this chapter, we covered a number of techniques for boosting performance. There are many other strategies, some of which are modality dependent. We now list several of these other approaches:

Prior information. Quite often in imaging applications one has additional *prior* information (also known as *side* information). This may, for example, come from an image collected during an earlier acquisition, from previous frames in a sequential acquisition, or from a different imaging modality [363]. Such a prior could be exploited via weighted ℓ^1-minimization, by choosing large weights off the anticipated support and small weights on it [216]. Another option is to add an additional penalty term to the optimization problem [363], for example, replacing the standard QCBP problem (4.10) by

$$\min_{z \in \mathbb{C}^N} \|z\|_{\ell^1} + \beta f(z - x_0) \text{ subject to } \|Az - y\|_{\ell^2} \leq \eta, \tag{4.22}$$

where x_0 is the reference image and $f : \mathbb{C}^N \to [0, \infty)$ is some function measuring the similarity between z and x_0. Typical examples are $f(\cdot) = \|\cdot\|_{\ell^1}$ and $f(\cdot) = \|\cdot\|_{\ell^2}^2$. This approach was introduced in [138] in the context of dynamic CT imaging.

Nonconvex penalties. In principle, sparsity can be more effectively promoted by replacing the ℓ^1-norm with a nonconvex penalty. A typical choice in imaging is the ℓ^p-norm for some $0 < p < 1$. There are many other possibilities (see e.g. [332, 464, 504, 518] and references therein). The drawback is a more challenging, nonconvex optimization problem, for which global minima cannot generally be computed. Yet, in some cases, even local minima can give better reconstructions than ℓ^1-minimization [135].

Structured image models. Sparsity in a fixed transform is a standard image model. There are other more refined models. So-called *sparsity in levels* will play a key role in Parts III and IV of this book. We have also previously seen joint sparsity in the context of image sequences. Another is the so-called *wavelet tree* model [48, 262, 263, 446] (see also the Notes section of Chapter 5). A challenge is that a sophisticated model can be more difficult to exploit with a (computationally realizable) reconstruction procedure.

In some applications it may also be possible to exploit the *low-rankness* of the object to be recovered. So-called *low-rank matrix recovery* is closely related to compressed sensing. A low-rank matrix has only a small number of nonzero singular values, which is analogous to sparsity, and this structure can be promoted by nuclear norm minimization, which is analogous to ℓ^1-minimization. Low-rank models are particularly useful in video-imaging applications such as dynamic MRI. It is also possible to combine sparse and low-rank models, much as how sparsity in different sparsifying transforms was combined in (4.9). See [168, 342, 411, 412, 483] and references therein.

Optimization parameter tuning. As noted, tuning the optimization parameters – for instance, the LASSO parameter λ or the weights in a weighted ℓ^1-norm penalty – is often critical to enhancing performance. This is a large topic in its own right. Classical protocols such as *Morozov's discrepancy principle*, *cross-validation* and *L-curve* (plus many more) seek to estimate the parameter empirically, while techniques such as *bilevel optimization* strive to learn it from training data. See, for instance, [448, Chpt. 7], [42, §4.3] and references therein, as well as [276, 403] for applications in MRI. While largely outside the scope of this book, in Chapter 6 we discuss so-called *a priori* parameter selection rules in the compressed sensing setting (see Remark 6.1 therein).

Refine the model. Referring back to the first stage of the pipeline introduced in Chapter 3, if performance remains poor due to model mismatch then refining the mathematical model may be needed. This could involve better noise modelling (e.g. Poisson rather than Gaussian), or using a nonlinear model for the acquisition process. This is obviously highly dependent on the modality.

Calibration. Sensor calibration is needed in most imaging systems. Poor calibration can spoil any benefits that a compressive imaging strategy may convey [225]; see also §3.5.3. It can cause errors in the assembled measurement matrix (a form of model mismatch), leading to worse recovery. There are many different strategies to improve calibration; generally, these are quite dependent on the modality. One option is to design measurement matrices that allow for easier better calibration [43]. Others involve estimating the calibration parameters at the same time as the image is reconstructed (so-called *blind calibration*) [329], generally by solving a nonconvex optimization problem, or using low-rank matrix recovery techniques [438].

Notes

Power-law sampling was employed in MRI by Lustig and colleagues [334–336], both for fully two-dimensional subsampling, as in (4.4), and as the one-dimensional density for the subsampled k-space direction in two-dimensional Cartesian sampling (Definition 4.8). The inverse square law was used in [302]. We discuss this scheme further in Chapters 11, 15 and 17. Such strategies are essentially independent of the types of images being recovered. Various approaches for tuning the sampling strategy according to the image class have been considered. See, for example, [490], which uses statistical representations of wavelet coefficients of natural images, [293] and [47].

The importance of fully sampling low frequencies has long been acknowledged [336]. Partial theoretical justifications were given in [415] and [136]. A more comprehensive theoretical explanation in terms of wavelet approximation theory has been given in [7]; see also the Notes section of Chapter 16. We note in passing that full sampling of the low frequencies can be beneficial for other reasons, for instance, estimating phase variations in MRI, or calibrating the sensitivity profiles in parallel MRI (recall §3.5.2).

In MRI it is sometimes desirable that the frequencies selected in the subsampled regions of k-space are not too close to each other. This can be achieved via so-called *Poisson disc* sampling [479].

See the Notes section of Chapter 11 for more information on multilevel random sampling. The Gaussian multilevel sampling scheme was introduced in [416]. This work also documented the resolution-enhancing properties of compressed sensing for imaging. We have based §4.3 on it.

The inverse crime, a term first coined by Colton & Kress in [157], is a well-known phenomenon in inverse problems. See [366], as well as [245] and [137] for discussions related to MRI and ECG, respectively. For further information on discretization and its effect on compressed sensing in X-ray CT, see [386].

For information on curvelets and shearlets or TV, see the Notes sections of Chapters 9 and 10 and Chapter 17, respectively. TGV was introduced in [96]; this work also discusses the staircasing effect, as well as other higher-order TV schemes. For applications of TGV in MRI, see [75, 292].

In §4.5 we considered the analysis and synthesis problems. These are fundamentally different, both from a theoretical and computational standpoint. See [194, 368] for more information. As noted, analysis is often preferred in practice, however, there is by no means a general consensus. With the exception of [433], there are few empirical comparisons in the literature. Analysis may also be preferable from a computational standpoint, since the optimization problem (3.3), which is formulated in the image space $\mathbb{C}^N$, is often several times smaller than (3.4), which is formulated in the coefficient space $\mathbb{C}^M$. It may also be preferred since it allows one to more straightforwardly include a nonnegativity constraint $z \geq 0$. This constraint is used commonly in X-ray CT reconstruction, since CT images tend to be nonnegative.

Combining wavelets and TV minimization as in (4.9) is common practice in MRI. This dates back to the seminal work of Lustig, Donoho & Pauly [336]. While the details are not publicly available, it is believed that this is used for the compressed sensing implementations in several commercial MR scanners [411].

Iteratively reweighted ℓ^1-minimization was introduced by Candès, Wakin & Boyd [126]. The procedure can be interpreted as a type of *Majorization–Minimization (MM)* algorithm for solving the nonconvex log-sum penalty problem

$$\min_{z \in \mathbb{C}^N} \sum_{i=1}^{N} \log(|z_i| + \varepsilon) \text{ subject to } Az = y. \tag{4.23}$$

In the language of §5.4, the unit ball of this penalty function is even more 'spiky' than the ℓ^1-ball. Hence it is expected to better promote sparse solutions. The reweighting strategies (4.14) and (4.15) were introduced in [28] and [338], respectively. The strategy (4.14) can also be interpreted as an MM algorithm for a certain log-sum penalty. Outside of these applications, weights are also used to compensate for a poor measurement matrix, for instance, a matrix with differently scaled columns. This occurs notably in sparse approximation of high-dimensional functions [10, 143, 408].

For overviews of learning in inverse problems, see [42, 411]. A dictionary learning procedure for MRI was first proposed by Ravishankar & Bresler [410]. Dictionary learning is a vast topic that we have only very lightly touched upon. In particular, we presented only synthesis formulations – analysis formulations are also possible – and omitted a discussion on convolutional dictionary learning methods. See [148, 500] for more on the latter. We have based §4.7 primarily on [448, Chpt. 10]. See also [389] and [206] and references therein. For more information on sparse representations and dictionary learning in general, see [192] and [188]. For an overview of recent progress in dictionary learning for MRI, see [206, 493] and references therein.

Learning the dictionary is one way of using training data. There are other possibilities. As noted, one may use training data to learn the parameters of the regularization procedure. Another possibility is to learn the sampling pattern in modalities such as MRI. See [47, 237, 409].

Part II

Compressed Sensing, Optimization and Wavelets

Summary of Part II

In Part II of this book we formally develop the main mathematical techniques for compressive imaging via compressed sensing.

Expanding on §1.5, Chapter 5 presents an introduction to conventional compressed sensing. By this, we mean the standard theory pertaining to the recovery of a sparse or compressible vector $x \in \mathbb{C}^N$ from noisy linear measurements $y = Ax + e$ (Key Point #4). After introducing the main concepts, we next focus on *recovery guarantees*: that is, conditions on m (the number of measurements) and s (the sparsity) that ensure accurate and stable recovery via the QCBP minimization problem (1.9). We introduce the main tools for proving so-called *uniform* recovery guarantees, including the *robust Null Space Property (rNSP)* and the *Restricted Isometry Property (RIP)*. We also discuss optimality of Gaussian and Bernoulli random matrices (Key Point #5). We then consider so-called *nonuniform* recovery guarantees, and the *dual certificate* approach for proving them.

In Chapter 6 we take a closer look at several variants of QCBP. These are related to the famous *Least Absolute Shrinkage and Selection Operator (LASSO)*. Specifically, we consider *Constrained LASSO (C-LASSO)*, *Unconstrained LASSO (U-LASSO)*, which was already seen in (1.10), and the *Square-Root LASSO (SR-LASSO)*. The main results of this chapter show uniform and nonuniform recovery guarantees for these decoders under exactly the same conditions as described in the previous chapter for QCBP. We then use these guarantees to define *a priori* parameter choices for each decoder. An interesting conclusion of this chapter is that the SR-LASSO decoder enjoys a theoretical benefit over the others, in that its optimal parameter regime is completely independent of the noise level. It is therefore well suited to *noise-blind* recovery problems.

Chapters 7 and 8 consider algorithms for solving these optimization problems. In Chapter 7, after a short discussion on the flavours of optimization for imaging, we present a succinct overview of modern, first-order methods for imaging problems. In particular, we derive three main algorithms: *ISTA/FISTA* for solving U-LASSO, the *primal–dual iteration* for both QCBP and SR-LASSO and *NESTA* for QCBP.

The focus of Chapter 8 is the seeming paradox, already touched upon in §1.5.5, that problems such as QCBP are generally uncomputable. While standard optimization theory asserts that the minimum value of the objective function of, say, QCBP, can be computed to arbitrary accuracy via any number of methods, it transpires that it is generally impossible to compute a minimizer to arbitrary accuracy. This is a significant concern for compressed sensing, since our interest lies with the minimizer (i.e. the recovered image) and not the minimum value. Chapter 8 develops this topic in detail.

Serendipitously, as we see therein, whenever the measurement matrix A has the rNSP – that is, exact minimizers are guaranteed to be accurate and stable – the algorithms derived in Chapter 7 give approximate minimizers with the same accuracy and stability, up to constants. In other words, compressed sensing works in practice because the optimization problems we wish to solve (e.g. QCBP where A has the rNSP) are also computable up to the accuracy we require (Key Point #6).

Finally, Chapters 9 and 10 are devoted to wavelets. Wavelets, along with TV, are an important class of sparsifying transforms for compressive imaging. Chapter 9 first describes the derivation of an orthonormal wavelet basis of $L^2(\mathbb{R})$ from a so-called *MultiResolution Analysis (MRA)*, and then gives the construction of compactly supported wavelets. This culminates in the famous *Daubechies wavelets*, which are used throughout this book. We also introduce the so-called *Discrete Wavelet Transform (DWT)* for fast wavelet computations. We end by briefly discussing curvelets and shearlets.

In Chapter 9 we explain somewhat heuristically why wavelets are effective sparsifying transforms (Key Point #7). In Chapter 10 we examine this in the more formal setting of nonlinear approximation theory. For piecewise smooth functions (a suitable model for one-dimensional images), we show that the best s-term approximation error in a wavelet basis decays asymptotically faster than the linear s-term error. As we discuss, these rates explain why wavelet coefficients are compressible, and hence why wavelets (as well as other X-let transforms) are a natural fit for compressive imaging via compressed sensing.

5 An Introduction to Conventional Compressed Sensing

After some necessary notation, we begin this chapter in §5.2 by defining sparsity, best s-term approximation and compressibility. Next, in §5.3 we introduce several common types of measurement matrices in compressed sensing, including Gaussian/Bernoulli random matrices and so-called *randomly subsampled unitary matrices*. In §5.4 we discuss reconstruction maps (also termed *decoders*), explain why ℓ^1-minimization promotes sparsity and then reintroduce QCBP. In §5.5–5.7 we turn our attention to recovery guarantees. Mathematical techniques for uniform recovery are presented in §5.6, including various null space properties and the RIP. We also present uniform recovery guarantees for several of the classes of matrices introduced in §5.3. Nonuniform recovery techniques based on so-called *dual certificates* are introduced in §5.7 and illustrated in the case of randomly subsampled unitary matrices. Finally, we close this chapter in §5.8 with a brief discussion of oracle estimators; a topic which provides a useful yardstick for the measurement conditions developed in subsequent chapters.

In this chapter we consider the standard discrete problem $y = Ax + e$, where the unknown $x \in \mathbb{C}^N$ is a vector. Extensions to the infinite-dimensional case are considered in Chapter 14. We also make heavy use of standard linear algebra. Relevant background material can be found in Appendix A.

A word of caution: this chapter is a short, and inevitably incomplete, overview of standard compressed sensing theory. It focuses on the fundamental concepts needed in subsequent chapters, but in doing so leaves out many topics of independent interest. The Notes section provides some additional information and also lists several resources which give more thorough treatments of the subject.

5.1 Projections

We first require some notation. Let $\{e_i\}_{i=1}^N$ be the canonical basis of $\mathbb{C}^N$ and $\Lambda \subseteq \{1, \ldots, N\}$. We write $P_\Lambda \in \mathbb{C}^{N \times N}$ for the matrix of the orthogonal projection with range $\mathrm{span}\{e_i : i \in \Lambda\}$. Hence, if $x = (x_i)_{i=1}^N \in \mathbb{C}^N$ then

$$(P_\Lambda x)_j = \begin{cases} x_j & j \in \Lambda, \\ 0 & \text{otherwise}. \end{cases} \tag{5.1}$$

More generally, if $U \in \mathbb{C}^{N \times M}$ then $P_\Lambda U$ is an $N \times M$ matrix whose ith row is equal to the ith row of U whenever $i \in \Lambda$ and equal to zero otherwise. On the other hand, if

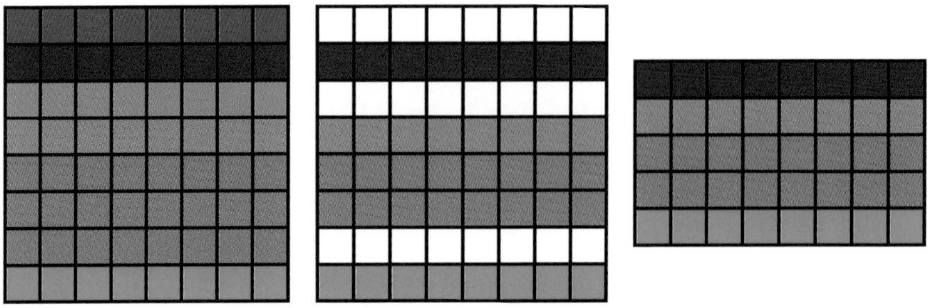

Figure 5.1 Left: 8×8 matrix U. Middle: 8×8 matrix corresponding to $P_\Lambda U$, where $\Lambda = \{2, 4, 5, 6, 8\}$. Right: 5×8 matrix corresponding to $P_\Lambda U$.

$V \in \mathbb{C}^{M \times N}$ and $V P_\Lambda$ is the $M \times N$ matrix whose jth column is equal to the jth column of V whenever $j \in \Lambda$ and zero otherwise.

Note that $P_\Lambda x$ is isomorphic to a vector in $\mathbb{C}^{|\Lambda|}$. On occasion, we shall slightly abuse notation and write $P_\Lambda x$ for this vector. Similarly, if $U \in \mathbb{C}^{N \times M}$ and $V \in \mathbb{C}^{M \times N}$ then we shall on occasion consider $P_\Lambda U$ as a $|\Lambda| \times M$ matrix and $V P_\Lambda$ as an $M \times |\Lambda|$ matrix. This distinction is illustrated in Fig. 5.1. The precise meaning will be clear from the context.

We also write $P^\perp$ for the orthogonal complement of an orthogonal projection $P : \mathbb{C}^N \to \mathbb{C}^N$. In particular, $P_\Lambda^\perp = P_{\Lambda^c}$, where $\Lambda^c = \{1, \ldots, N\} \backslash \Lambda$ is the set complement of Λ.

5.2 Sparsity and Compressibility

Let $x = (x_i)_{i=1}^N \in \mathbb{C}^N$. The *support* of x is the set

$$\mathrm{supp}(x) = \{i : x_i \neq 0\} \subseteq \{1, \ldots, N\}.$$

Definition 5.1 (Sparsity) A vector $x \in \mathbb{C}^N$ is *s-sparse* for some $1 \leq s \leq N$ if

$$\|x\|_{\ell^0} := |\mathrm{supp}(x)| \leq s. \tag{5.2}$$

The set of s-sparse vectors is denoted by Σ_s.

A few remarks are in order. First, it has become customary to refer to $\|\cdot\|_{\ell^0}$ as the ℓ^0-'norm', even though it is not a norm. We use this convention throughout.

Second, note that while s may be known (or estimated), $\mathrm{supp}(x)$ is typically unknown in practice. In the case of wavelet coefficients, for instance, it is related to the locations of the edges of an image, which are usually unknown.

Third, while not a subspace itself, the set of sparse vectors Σ_s can be expressed as a union of subspaces. One has

$$\Sigma_s = \bigcup_{\Delta \in D_s} E_\Delta, \tag{5.3}$$

where E_Δ is the subspace

$$E_\Delta = \left\{x \in \mathbb{C}^N : \mathrm{supp}(x) \subseteq \Delta\right\} = P_\Delta\left(\mathbb{C}^N\right), \tag{5.4}$$

and

$$D_s = \{\Delta : \Delta \subseteq \{1, \ldots, N\}, \ |\Delta| = s\}. \tag{5.5}$$

Hence Σ_s is a union over all s-dimensional subspaces corresponding to a fixed support set Δ of cardinality s. The number of such subspaces is

$$|D_s| = \binom{N}{s} = \frac{N!}{s!(N-s)!}.$$

Remark 5.2 The tendency of this number to be extremely large for even moderate values of s and N means that recovery algorithms based on exhaustively searching over all subspaces E_Δ, $\Delta \in D_s$ are typically impractical. See the Notes section.

As observed in §1.5, it is rare to encounter exactly sparse vectors. More generally, we consider vectors that are well approximated by sparse vectors. This motivates the following:

Definition 5.3 (Best s-term approximation) Let $x \in \mathbb{C}^N$ and $0 < p \leq \infty$. The ℓ^p-norm *best s-term approximation error* of x is

$$\sigma_s(x)_{\ell^p} = \min\{\|x - z\|_{\ell^p} : z \in \Sigma_s\}. \tag{5.6}$$

Loosely speaking, we say that x is *compressible* if $\sigma_s(x)_{\ell^p}$ decreases rapidly with increasing s (more formal definitions are also possible – see the Notes section). Suppose that $\pi : \{1, \ldots, N\} \to \{1, \ldots, N\}$ is a bijection which rearranges the elements of x in nonincreasing order of their absolute values. That is,

$$|x_{\pi(1)}| \geq |x_{\pi(2)}| \geq \cdots \geq |x_{\pi(N)}|.$$

Then it is easily seen that $\sigma_s(x)_{\ell^p}$ is equal to the ℓ^p-norm of the $(N - s)$ smallest entries of x in absolute value:

$$\sigma_s(x)_{\ell^p} = \left(\sum_{i=s+1}^{N} |x_{\pi(i)}|^p \right)^{1/p}. \tag{5.7}$$

In particular, compressibility is equivalent to rapid decay of the sorted coefficients $x_{\pi(i)}$.

As discussed in §1.5, natural images are typically not sparse (or compressible) themselves. Rather, their coefficients in some orthonormal basis are sparse (or compressible). Let $\{\phi_i\}_{i=1}^N$ be an orthonormal basis of $\mathbb{C}^N$. Then any $x \in \mathbb{C}^N$ has the expansion

$$x = \sum_{i=1}^{N} d_i \phi_i,$$

with *coefficients* $d = (d_i)_{i=1}^N \in \mathbb{C}^N$ given by

$$d_i = \langle x, \phi_i \rangle, \quad i = 1, \ldots, N.$$

In finite dimensions, orthonormal bases are equivalent to unitary matrices. Given the orthonormal basis $\{\phi_i\}_{i=1}^N$, we let

$$\Phi = (\phi_1 | \cdots | \phi_N) \in \mathbb{C}^{N \times N}$$

be the matrix whose columns are the basis vectors. Notice that

$$\Phi^*\Phi = \Phi\Phi^* = I,$$

and therefore Φ is unitary. In particular, one has the relations

$$x = \Phi d, \qquad d = \Phi^* x.$$

As noted previously, we refer to $\{\phi_i\}_{i=1}^N$ as a *sparsity basis* and Φ as a *sparsifying transform*. The operators $x \mapsto d = \Phi^* x$ and $d \mapsto x = \Phi d$ are known as the *analysis* and *synthesis* operators, respectively. The former *analyses* x by taking inner products with respect to the sparsity basis. The latter *synthesizes* x from its coefficients d.

5.3 Measurements and Measurement Matrices

Let $x \in \mathbb{C}^N$ be the vector we seek to recover. We consider measurements

$$y = Ax + e, \tag{5.8}$$

where $A \in \mathbb{C}^{m \times N}$ is the *measurement matrix* and $e \in \mathbb{C}^m$ is a vector of noise. In this chapter we will assume that the noise is adversarial (it follows no known distribution) and ℓ^2-bounded. That is,

$$\|e\|_{\ell^2} \leq \eta, \tag{5.9}$$

for some finite and known number $\eta > 0$. The assumption that η is known is quite strong, and may fail to hold in practice. In Chapter 6 we discuss compressed sensing in the absence of such a condition.

As observed in Remark 1.3, constructing deterministic measurement matrices that give stable recovery under optimal or near-optimal measurement conditions (that is, requiring a number of measurements m scaling linearly in s and polylogarithmically in N) has proved elusive. However, this can be achieved using certain random constructions. We now discuss several popular classes of random measurement matrices.

5.3.1 Gaussian and Bernoulli Random Matrices

Definition 5.4 (Gaussian/Bernoulli random matrix) A matrix $A \in \mathbb{R}^{m \times N}$ is a *Gaussian random matrix* if its entries are independent normal random variables with mean zero and variance one. It is a *Bernoulli random matrix* if its entries are independent Rademacher random variables; that is, random variables taking the values $+1$ and -1 with equal probability.

Since they are 'maximally random' these matrices are both the easiest to analyse from a compressed sensing perspective and give the best measurement conditions. See §5.6.3. However, as discussed in Chapter 1, they are of limited use in imaging applications.

5.3.2 Randomly Subsampled Unitary Matrices

A more practical family of measurement matrices arises by randomly selecting rows of a fixed unitary matrix $U \in \mathbb{C}^{N \times N}$.

Definition 5.5 A *randomly subsampled unitary matrix* is a matrix

$$A = \sqrt{\frac{N}{m}} P_\Omega U \in \mathbb{C}^{m \times N}, \tag{5.10}$$

where Ω is a subset of $\{1, \ldots, N\}$ of cardinality $|\Omega| = m$ that is chosen uniformly at random from the set of all $\binom{N}{m}$ possible such subsets.

Notice that in (5.10) we view $P_\Omega U$ as the $m \times N$ matrix whose rows are equal to the rows of U with indices in Ω (see §5.1). In practice, as discussed in previous chapters, U is often taken as a Fourier (Definition 2.1) or Hadamard (Definition 2.8) matrix.

Since subsampled unitary matrices are 'less' random than Gaussian or Bernoulli random matrices, their mathematical analysis is significantly more involved. In fact, the construction (5.10) is particularly difficult to analyse since the rows of A are not even independent. To overcome this issue, it is common to consider the following closely related construction instead.

Definition 5.6 A *randomly subsampled unitary matrix* is a matrix

$$A = \sqrt{\frac{N}{m}} P_\Omega U \in \mathbb{C}^{m \times N}, \tag{5.11}$$

where $\Omega = \{i_1, \ldots, i_m\}$ and the i_js are chosen randomly and independently from the set $\{1, \ldots, N\}$.

This yields a measurement matrix with independent rows. But as noted in Remark 4.2, there is now a possibility for repeats (we reiterate that Ω is not a set in this case but an indexed family). In §11.4.3 we consider how to remedy this issue.

Remark 5.7 A word on normalization. Notice that $\mathbb{E}(A^*A) = I$, where $\mathbb{E}$ denotes expectation, whenever A is constructed according to either Definition 5.5 or 5.6. For example, in the case of the latter, we can write P_Ω as $P_\Omega = \sum_{j=1}^{m} e_{i_j} e_{i_j}^*$ and use the fact that the i_j are chosen randomly from $\{1, \ldots, N\}$ to deduce that

$$\mathbb{E}(A^*A) = \frac{N}{m} \mathbb{E}\left(U^* \sum_{j=1}^{m} e_{i_j} e_{i_j}^* U \right) = NU^* \left(\sum_{i=1}^{N} \frac{1}{N} e_i e_i^* \right) U = U^* I U = U^* U = I.$$

This normalization is natural. It implies that $\mathbb{E}\|Ax\|_{\ell^2}^2 = \|x\|_{\ell^2}^2$ for fixed x, thus making A energy preserving in expectation.

Conversely, for a Gaussian or Bernoulli random matrix one has $\mathbb{E}(A^*A) = mI$. Indeed, by independence one has

$$\mathbb{E}((A^*A)_{ij}) = \sum_{k=1}^{m} \mathbb{E}\left(A_{ik} A_{kj}\right) = 0, \quad i \neq j,$$

and, since the entries of A have variance one,

$$\mathbb{E}((A^*A)_{ii}) = \sum_{k=1}^{m} \mathbb{E}\left((A_{ik})^2\right) = m.$$

For this reason, we will typically renormalize these matrices by the factor $1/\sqrt{m}$ in later use.

5.3.3 The Coherence of a Matrix

As observed in §1.5, Gaussian or Bernoulli random matrices are essentially optimal measurement matrices for stable recovery of sparse vectors. We discuss this point in more detail in Remark 5.23 below. The same cannot be said, however, for an arbitrary subsampled unitary matrix. For instance, suppose that $U = I$ is the identity matrix. Then random sampling with U equates to measuring m randomly chosen entries of x directly. This is a poor acquisition protocol: in general, $m = N$ measurements would be required to ensure recovery of every s-sparse vector, regardless of the size of s.

The problem with this choice of U is that both the vector x and its transformed vector $z = Ux$ are 'concentrated', in the sense that they are both sparse. Clearly, a good acquisition protocol should produce a transformed vector z that is 'spread out' whenever the original vector x is sparse, so that a random selection of m entries of z should (with high probability) contain sufficient information to recover x. Mathematically, this spreading can be quantified via the so-called *coherence* of U.

Definition 5.8 (Coherence of a matrix) The *coherence* of an $N \times M$ matrix $U = (U_{ij})_{i,j=1}^{N,M}$ is

$$\mu(U) = N \max_{i,j} |U_{ij}|^2.$$

Observe that if U is an isometry, i.e. $U^*U = I$, then $1 \leq \mu(U) \leq N$. This follows directly from the fact that such a matrix has orthonormal columns

$$\sum_{i=1}^{N} |U_{ij}|^2 = 1, \quad \forall j = 1, \ldots, M.$$

Accordingly, and somewhat informally, we say that U is *incoherent* if $\mu(U) \approx 1$ and *coherent* if $\mu(U) \approx N$. Note that the identity matrix $U = I$ satisfies $\mu(I) = N$ and is therefore *maximally* coherent. The mass of such a matrix is highly concentrated along its diagonal. Conversely, the mass of the normalized Fourier matrix $U = N^{-1/2}F$ (Definition 2.1) is equally spread across its entries with $|U_{ij}| = N^{-1/2}$ for each i and j. Hence $\mu(U) = 1$, making the Fourier matrix maximally incoherent.

Figure 5.2 shows how a typical incoherent matrix spreads out a sparse vector. Mathematically, this can be quantified by the following *discrete uncertainty principle*.

Proposition 5.9 (Discrete uncertainty principle) *Let $U \in \mathbb{C}^{N \times N}$ be unitary. Then*

$$\|x\|_{\ell^0} + \|Ux\|_{\ell^0} \geq 2\sqrt{N/\mu(U)}, \qquad \forall x \in \mathbb{C}^N.$$

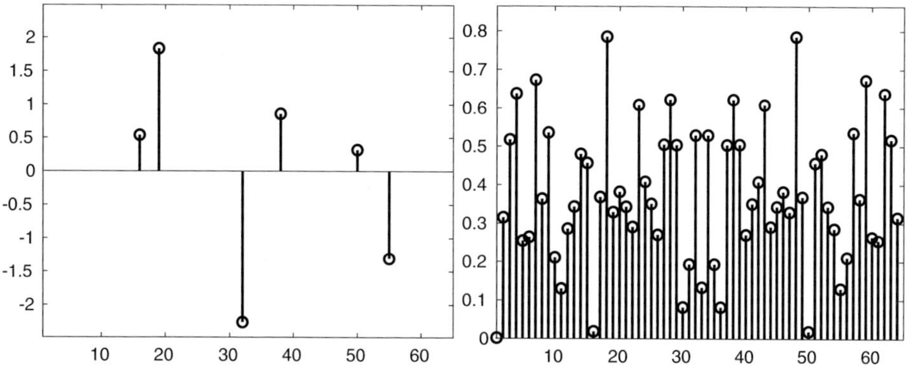

Figure 5.2 Sparsity and incoherence. Left: A 6-sparse vector x. Right: The absolute values of its (normalized) discrete Fourier transform $y = N^{-1/2}Fx$.

Proof Write $z = Ux$. Then

$$|z_i| = \left| \sum_{i=1}^{N} u_{ij} x_j \right| \leq \|x\|_{\ell^1} \sqrt{\mu(U)/N}, \qquad i = 1, \ldots, N,$$

and therefore

$$\|z\|_{\ell^1} = \sum_{i \in \operatorname{supp}(z)} |z_i| \leq \|z\|_{\ell^0} \|x\|_{\ell^1} \sqrt{\mu(U)/N}.$$

Note that $\mu(U) = \mu(U^*)$ and $x = U^* z$ since U is unitary. Therefore, by the same arguments, we have

$$\|x\|_{\ell^1} \leq \|x\|_{\ell^0} \|z\|_{\ell^1} \sqrt{\mu(U)/N}.$$

Multiplying this and the previous inequality and dividing by $\|z\|_{\ell^1} \|x\|_{\ell^1}$ gives

$$1 \leq \|x\|_{\ell^0} \|z\|_{\ell^0} \mu(U)/N,$$

which implies that

$$\sqrt{N/\mu(U)} \leq \sqrt{\|x\|_{\ell^0} \|z\|_{\ell^0}} \leq \frac{1}{2} \left(\|x\|_{\ell^0} + \|z\|_{\ell^0} \right),$$

as required. □

Note that in the final step of this proof we have used *Young's inequality*:

$$ab \leq \sigma a^2 + \frac{b^2}{4\sigma}, \qquad \forall a, b \geq 0, \sigma > 0. \tag{5.12}$$

We use this inequality several more times in subsequent chapters.

Later, in §5.7.1, we shall see that coherence plays a key role in (in fact, determines) the measurement condition for recovery from subsampled unitary matrices. In particular, for an incoherent U, the measurement condition is almost as good as that for Gaussian or Bernoulli random matrices.

5.4 ℓ^1-Minimization

We now turn our attention to the recovery of a compressible vector $x \in \mathbb{C}^N$ from its measurements (5.8). For this, we require a *reconstruction map* $\mathrm{R}: \mathbb{C}^m \to \mathbb{C}^N$ that takes $y = Ax + e$ as its input and gives a reconstruction $\hat{x} = \mathrm{R}(y)$ of x as its output. We shall also on occasion refer to R as a *decoder*, with the mapping $x \mapsto y = Ax + e$ that produces the measurements being the *encoder*.

5.4.1 Sparsity and Exact Recovery

Suppose first that $x \in \Sigma_s$ is exactly s-sparse and the measurements are noiseless, i.e. $y = Ax$. In this case, it is reasonable to ask whether or not x can be recovered *exactly* from its measurements y.

Consider the linear system

$$Az = y, \qquad y = Ax. \tag{5.13}$$

When $m < N$ this system is underdetermined and therefore has infinitely many solutions. Our goal is to find the solution that coincides with x. Since x is sparse, a rational way to proceed is by searching for the sparsest solution of (5.13). This is equivalent to minimizing the ℓ^0-norm, or in other words, solving the optimization problem

$$\min_{z \in \mathbb{C}^N} \|z\|_{\ell^0} \text{ subject to } Az = Ax. \tag{5.14}$$

Proposition 5.10 *Let $1 \leq s \leq N$, $A \in \mathbb{C}^{m \times N}$ and $x \in \mathbb{C}^N$ with $\|x\|_{\ell^0} = s$. Then the following are equivalent:*

(a) x is the unique s-sparse solution of the linear system (5.13), i.e. $\{z \in \Sigma_s : Az = Ax\} = \{x\}$;

(b) x is the unique minimizer of the optimization problem (5.14).

Proof The case (b) $\Rightarrow$ (a) is clear. Consider the case (a) $\Rightarrow$ (b). Let $\hat{x}$ be a minimizer of (5.14). Since x is feasible for (5.14), we have $\|\hat{x}\|_{\ell^0} \leq \|x\|_{\ell^0} = s$. Hence $\hat{x}$ is s-sparse and therefore by (a), $\hat{x} = x$. This gives (b). □

This proposition justifies formulating the optimization problem (5.14). Indeed, if x is the *only* s-sparse solution to (5.13), a property we clearly need if we are to have any hope of recovering it exactly, then it is the unique solution of (5.14). Provided we can solve (5.14), we can find x.

However, this is not a practical approach. The problem (5.14) is nonconvex and combinatorial in nature. Computing a minimizer turns out to be NP-hard (intuitively, this can be understood by recalling Remark 5.2). This renders (5.14) unusable for practical purposes.

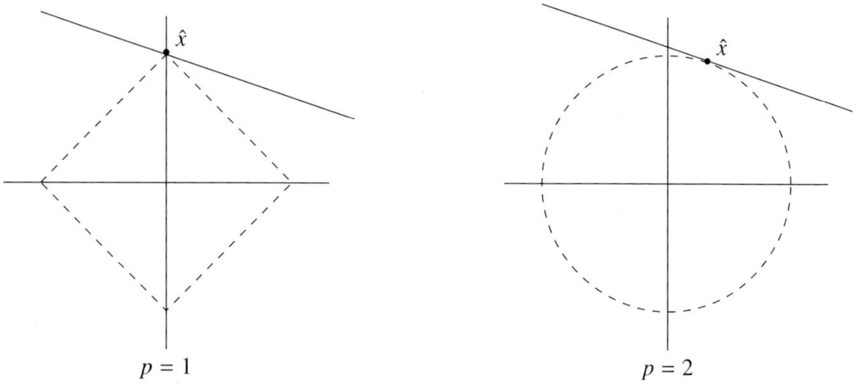

Figure 5.3 The ℓ^1-norm promotes sparsity. The solid line is the feasible set $\{z : Az = Ax\}$. The Dashed shape is an ℓ^1- (left) or ℓ^2- (right) ball, with the intersection point $\hat{x}$ being the minimal ℓ^1-norm (left) or ℓ^2-norm (right) solution. The ℓ^1-norm solution is generically sparse, whereas the ℓ^2-norm solution is generically nonsparse.

5.4.2 Convex Relaxation and Basis Pursuit

To obtain a practical decoder, one can pursue a familiar idea from optimization: namely, *relax* the problem. Replacing the ℓ^0-norm with the ℓ^1-norm yields the well-known *Basis Pursuit (BP)* problem, which is the convex ℓ^1-minimization problem

$$\min_{z \in \mathbb{C}^N} \|z\|_{\ell^1} \text{ subject to } Az = y. \tag{5.15}$$

Why choose the ℓ^1-norm? First, the ℓ^1-norm can be interpreted as the *convex relaxation* of the ℓ^0-norm (see §D.4). It is, in a formal sense, the 'closest' convex function to $\|\cdot\|_{\ell^0}$. It can also be motivated geometrically, as shown by Fig. 5.3. The ℓ^1-ball is 'spiky', meaning that solutions of (5.13) with minimal ℓ^1-norm should, in all but pathological cases, be sparse. Hence if x is the unique s-sparse solution to (5.13), BP should find it. Note that this is not the case for the ℓ^2-norm minimization problem

$$\min_{z \in \mathbb{C}^N} \|z\|_{\ell^2} \text{ subject to } Az = Ax.$$

As illustrated in Fig. 5.3, solutions of this problem tend not to be sparse.

5.4.3 Quadratically Constrained Basis Pursuit

Now consider the general case, where x is not sparse but compressible with respect to an orthonormal sparsifying transform Φ, and where the measurements $y = Ax + e$ are noisy, with noise e satisfying (5.9). As discussed in previous chapters, in this case we replace (5.15) with the Quadratically Constrained Basis Pursuit (QCBP) problem

$$\min_{z \in \mathbb{C}^N} \|\Phi^* z\|_{\ell^1} \text{ subject to } \|Az - y\|_{\ell^2} \leq \eta. \tag{5.16}$$

Note that this reduces to the BP problem when $\eta = 0$.

Formally, as observed in §3.1, (5.16) is the QCBP *analysis* problem. One may also consider the QCBP *synthesis* problem

$$\min_{z \in \mathbb{C}^N} \|z\|_{\ell^1} \text{ subject to } \|A\Phi z - y\|_{\ell^2} \leq \eta. \tag{5.17}$$

The problem (5.16) produces an approximation $\hat{x} \in \mathbb{C}^N$ to x. Conversely, (5.17) produces an approximation $\check{d} \in \mathbb{C}^N$ to its coefficients $d = \Phi^* x$, which then results in an approximation $\check{x} = \Phi \check{d}$ to x after an application of Φ. Since Φ is unitary, these problems are equivalent. It is straightforward to show that a vector $\hat{x} \in \mathbb{C}^N$ is a minimizer of (5.16) if and only if the vector $\hat{d} = \Phi^* \hat{x} \in \mathbb{C}^N$ is a minimizer of (5.17).

In view of this equivalence, going forwards we may without loss of generality consider QCBP problems of the form

$$\min_{z \in \mathbb{C}^N} \|z\|_{\ell^1} \text{ subject to } \|Az - y\|_{\ell^2} \leq \eta, \tag{5.18}$$

with the understanding that the matrix A incorporates both the measurement matrix *and* the sparsifying transform Φ, and that minimizers of this problem are approximations to the coefficients of a given signal or image with respect to Φ.

Remark 5.11 In general, the problem (5.18) will have multiple minimizers. This means that the reconstruction map R it defines is multivalued. It is typical to denote a multivalued map by double arrows. In this case, we write

$$\mathrm{R}\colon \mathbb{C}^m \rightrightarrows \mathbb{C}^N,$$

where, for $y \in \mathbb{C}^m$, $\mathrm{R}(y)$ is the set of minimizers

$$\begin{aligned} \mathrm{R}(y) &= \underset{z \in \mathbb{C}^N}{\operatorname{argmin}} \|z\|_{\ell^1} \text{ subject to } \|Az - y\|_{\ell^2} \leq \eta \\ &\equiv \left\{ \hat{x} \in \mathbb{C}^N : \|\hat{x}\|_{\ell^1} = \min_{z \in \mathbb{C}^N} \|z\|_{\ell^1} \text{ subject to } \|Az - y\|_{\ell^2} \leq \eta \right\}. \end{aligned}$$

When considering the accuracy and stability of such a map R, we will demand that *all* minimizers $\hat{x}$ satisfy the same guaranteed error bound. Hence, when we come to the question of algorithms for implementing this reconstruction map in Chapter 7, we only need to ensure that the algorithm produces an output that is close to *a* minimizer, i.e. a single, but otherwise arbitrary element of $\mathrm{R}(y)$.

5.5 Recovery Guarantees in Compressed Sensing

Having formulated the compressed sensing problem, we now turn our attention to *recovery guarantees*, i.e. conditions involving A (in particular m), s and N which ensure accurate and stable recovery via the QCBP decoder (5.18). As discussed, effective measurement matrices for compressed sensing are random in some sense. This means that subsequent recovery guarantees are probabilistic in nature. They arise in two flavours, known respectively as *uniform* and *nonuniform* recovery. A uniform recovery guarantee asserts that a single draw of the matrix A is (with high probability) sufficient for recovery of *all* sparse vectors x. Theorem 5.22 is an example of such a guarantee. On the other hand, a nonuniform guarantee asserts that a single draw of A is sufficient for recovery of a *fixed* sparse vector x. See Theorem 5.30 for an example of this type of guarantee.

Uniform recovery guarantees are stronger than nonuniform guarantees. A uniform guarantee means that the same measurement matrix A can be used to recover arbitrarily-many s-sparse vectors. Conversely, a nonuniform guarantee means that the measurement matrix needs to be redrawn each time a new vector needs to be recovered. As such, uniform guarantees are often associated with somewhat worse measurement conditions. Nonuniform guarantees, being weaker, tend to give measurement conditions that are closer to optimal.

It should come as little surprise that the tools used to prove uniform guarantees are quite different to those used to prove nonuniform guarantees. In the next two sections we briefly review both sets of tools. In each case, we give examples of recovery guarantees for one or more of the types of measurement matrices introduced in §5.3.

5.6 Techniques for Uniform Recovery

5.6.1 Null Space Properties

Definition 5.12 (Null space property) A matrix $A \in \mathbb{C}^{m\times N}$ satisfies the *Null Space Property (NSP)* of order $1 \leq s \leq N$ if

$$\|P_\Delta x\|_{\ell^1} < \|P_\Delta^\perp x\|_{\ell^1}, \tag{5.19}$$

for all $x \in \mathrm{Ker}(A)\backslash\{0\}$ and $\Delta \in D_s$, where $\mathrm{Ker}(A)$ is the null space of A and D_s is as in (5.5).

Note that (5.19) is equivalent to

$$\|x\|_{\ell^1} < 2\|P_\Delta^\perp x\|_{\ell^1}, \quad \forall x \in \mathrm{Ker}(A)\backslash\{0\},\ \Delta \in D_s, \tag{5.20}$$

which is obtained by adding $\|P_\Delta^\perp x\|_{\ell^1}$ to both sides, and

$$2\|P_\Delta x\|_{\ell^1} < \|x\|_{\ell^1}, \quad \forall x \in \mathrm{Ker}(A)\backslash\{0\},\ \Delta \in D_s,$$

which is obtained by adding $\|P_\Delta x\|_{\ell^1}$ to both sides. It is also straightforward to see that the NSP holds whenever (5.19) holds with Δ being the index set of the largest s entries of x in absolute value. Hence, by (5.20), the NSP is equivalent to the condition

$$\|x\|_{\ell^1} < 2\sigma_s(x)_{\ell^1}, \quad \forall x \in \mathrm{Ker}(A)\backslash\{0\},$$

where $\sigma_s(x)_{\ell^1}$ is as in (5.6). In particular, this means that vectors in the null space of A cannot be approximately sparse when A has the NSP. Intuitively, this seems like a necessary condition for successful recovery. The next result shows that the NSP in fact characterizes exact recovery via BP:

Theorem 5.13 *A matrix $A \in \mathbb{C}^{m \times N}$ satisfies the NSP of order s if and only if every s-sparse vector $x \in \mathbb{C}^N$ is the unique solution of the BP problem*

$$\min_{z \in \mathbb{C}^N} \|z\|_{\ell^1} \text{ subject to } Az = Ax. \tag{5.21}$$

Proof Suppose first that A satisfies the NSP of order s. Let x be s-sparse and $\Delta = \mathrm{supp}(x)$ be the support of x. Suppose that $z \neq x$ satisfies $Az = Ax$ and let $v := z - x \in \mathrm{Ker}(A)\backslash\{0\}$. Then

$$\|x\|_{\ell^1} \leq \|x - P_\Delta z\|_{\ell^1} + \|P_\Delta z\|_{\ell^1} = \|P_\Delta v\|_{\ell^1} + \|P_\Delta z\|_{\ell^1},$$

and the NSP gives

$$\|x\|_{\ell^1} < \|P_\Delta^\perp v\|_{\ell^1} + \|P_\Delta z\|_{\ell^1} = \|P_\Delta^\perp z\|_{\ell^1} + \|P_\Delta z\|_{\ell^1} = \|z\|_{\ell^1}.$$

Since z was arbitrary, it follows that x is the unique solution of (5.21), as required.

We now prove the converse. Let $\Delta \in D_s$ and $v \in \mathrm{Ker}(A)\backslash\{0\}$. Then, by assumption, $P_\Delta v$ is the unique minimizer of (5.21) with $x = P_\Delta v$. Since $Av = 0$, we have $A(-P_\Delta^\perp v) = AP_\Delta v$ and therefore $z = -P_\Delta^\perp v$ is feasible for (5.21). We deduce that $\|P_\Delta v\|_{\ell^1} < \|P_\Delta^\perp v\|_{\ell^1}$. Since Δ and v were arbitrary, we conclude that A has the NSP. □

We next consider accurate and stable recovery. For this, we introduce the following variation of the NSP:

Definition 5.14 (Robust null space property) A matrix $A \in \mathbb{C}^{m \times N}$ satisfies the *robust Null Space Property (rNSP)* of order $1 \leq s \leq N$ with constants $0 < \rho < 1$ and $\gamma > 0$ if

$$\|P_\Delta x\|_{\ell^2} \leq \frac{\rho}{\sqrt{s}} \|P_\Delta^\perp x\|_{\ell^1} + \gamma \|Ax\|_{\ell^2}, \tag{5.22}$$

for all $x \in \mathbb{C}^N$ and $\Delta \in D_s$.

Note that the rNSP implies the NSP, since $\|P_\Delta v\|_{\ell^1} \leq \sqrt{s}\|P_\Delta v\|_{\ell^2}$ by the Cauchy–Schwarz inequality and therefore

$$\|P_\Delta v\|_{\ell^1} \leq \rho \|P_\Delta^\perp v\|_{\ell^2} + \gamma\sqrt{s}\|Av\|_{\ell^2} < \|P_\Delta^\perp v\|_{\ell^2}, \quad \forall v \in \mathrm{Ker}(A)\backslash\{0\}.$$

But the rNSP also applies to arbitrary vectors, not just those in the null space. As a result, it implies two important bounds on the distance between arbitrary vectors x and z:

Lemma 5.15 (rNSP implies ℓ^1-distance bound) *Suppose that A has the rNSP of order s with constants $0 < \rho < 1$ and $\gamma > 0$. Let $x, z \in \mathbb{C}^N$. Then*

$$\|z - x\|_{\ell^1} \leq \frac{1+\rho}{1-\rho}\left(2\sigma_s(x)_{\ell^1} + \|z\|_{\ell^1} - \|x\|_{\ell^1}\right) + \frac{2\gamma}{1-\rho}\sqrt{s}\|A(z-x)\|_{\ell^2}.$$

Lemma 5.16 (rNSP implies ℓ^2-distance bound) *Suppose that A has the rNSP of order s with constants $0 < \rho < 1$ and $\gamma > 0$. Let $x, z \in \mathbb{C}^N$. Then*

$$\|z - x\|_{\ell^2} \leq \left(\frac{3\rho+1}{2}\right)\frac{\|z-x\|_{\ell^1}}{\sqrt{s}} + \frac{3\gamma}{2}\|A(z-x)\|_{\ell^2},$$

and therefore

$$\|z-x\|_{\ell^2} \leq \frac{(3\rho+1)(\rho+1)}{2(1-\rho)} \left(\frac{2\sigma_s(x)_{\ell^1} + \|z\|_{\ell^1} - \|x\|_{\ell^1}}{\sqrt{s}} \right) + \frac{(3\rho+5)\gamma}{2(1-\rho)} \|A(z-x)\|_{\ell^2}.$$

Lemmas 5.15 and 5.16 are simplified versions of Lemmas 13.6 and 13.7. Hence their proofs are omitted. We note, however, that the second inequality in Lemma 5.16 follows immediately by combining the first inequality with Lemma 5.15.

Using these lemmas, we can now show that the rNSP is sufficient for accurate and stable recovery via QCBP:

Theorem 5.17 (rNSP implies accurate and stable recovery for QCBP) *Suppose that* $A \in \mathbb{C}^{m\times N}$ *has the rNSP of order s with constants* $0 < \rho < 1$ *and* $\gamma > 0$*. Let* $x \in \mathbb{C}^N$*,* $y = Ax + e \in \mathbb{C}^m$ *and* $\eta \geq \|e\|_{\ell^2}$*. Then every minimizer* $\hat{x} \in \mathbb{C}^N$ *of the QCBP problem (5.18) satisfies*

$$\|\hat{x}-x\|_{\ell^1} \leq C_1\sigma_s(x)_{\ell^1} + C_2\sqrt{s}\eta, \qquad \|\hat{x}-x\|_{\ell^2} \leq C_3\frac{\sigma_s(x)_{\ell^1}}{\sqrt{s}} + C_4\eta, \tag{5.23}$$

where the constants $C_1, C_2, C_3, C_4 > 0$ *are given by*

$$C_1 = 2\left(\frac{1+\rho}{1-\rho}\right), \quad C_2 = \frac{4\gamma}{1-\rho}, \quad C_3 = \frac{(3\rho+1)(\rho+1)}{(1-\rho)}, \quad C_4 = \frac{(3\rho+5)\gamma}{(1-\rho)}.$$

Proof We first apply Lemma 5.15 with $z = \hat{x}$. Since $\hat{x}$ is a solution of (5.18) we have $\|x\|_{\ell^1} \geq \|\hat{x}\|_{\ell^1}$. Moreover,

$$\|A(\hat{x}-x)\|_{\ell^2} \leq \|A\hat{x}-y\|_{\ell^2} + \|Ax-y\|_{\ell^2} \leq 2\eta,$$

since x and $\hat{x}$ are both feasible for (5.18). Hence we obtain

$$\|\hat{x}-x\|_{\ell^1} \leq \frac{2(1+\rho)}{(1-\rho)}\sigma_s(x)_{\ell^1} + \frac{4\gamma}{1-\rho}\sqrt{s}\eta,$$

which gives the first bound. For the second, we simply use Lemma 5.16 instead. □

We refer to (5.23) as a compressed sensing *error bound*. It asserts stable and accurate recovery of x, with stability being measured by the noise bound η and accuracy measured by $\sigma_s(x)_{\ell^1}$. The reader may wonder why the term $\sigma_s(x)_{\ell^1}/\sqrt{s}$ appears in the ℓ^2-norm bound rather than $\sigma_s(x)_{\ell^2}$. We discuss the reason behind this later in Remark 5.23. Note that when x is exactly s-sparse and $\eta = 0$ (in particular, the measurements are noiseless), this result implies that x is recovered exactly by the BP problem (5.15), as expected.

Of the two estimates in Theorem 5.17, generally the ℓ^2-norm error bound is the more important in practice. In subsequent chapters we typically forgo the ℓ^1-norm bound. As we discuss in the Notes section, it is also possible to prove bounds in the ℓ^p-norm for arbitrary $1 \leq p \leq 2$.

5.6.2 The Restricted Isometry Property

It is generally difficult to show that a measurement matrix has the rNSP directly. Instead, one normally seeks to show that A satisfies a related condition, known as the restricted isometry property. As we see in Lemma 5.20 below, this is a sufficient condition for the rNSP.

Definition 5.18 (Restricted isometry property) Let $1 \leq s \leq N$. The sth *Restricted Isometry Constant (RIC)* δ_s of a matrix $A \in \mathbb{C}^{m \times N}$ is the smallest $\delta \geq 0$ such that

$$(1 - \delta)\|x\|_{\ell^2}^2 \leq \|Ax\|_{\ell^2}^2 \leq (1 + \delta)\|x\|_{\ell^2}^2, \quad \forall x \in \Sigma_s. \tag{5.24}$$

If $0 < \delta_s < 1$ then the matrix A is said to have the *Restricted Isometry Property (RIP)* of order s.

The following lemma provides a useful characterization of the RIC δ_s:

Lemma 5.19 *The sth RIC δ_s of a matrix $A \in \mathbb{C}^{m \times N}$ satisfies*

$$\delta_s = \sup_{\Delta \in D_s} \|P_\Delta A^* A P_\Delta - P_\Delta\|_{\ell^2}.$$

Proof Notice that (5.24) is equivalent to

$$\left| \|Ax\|_{\ell^2}^2 - \|x\|_{\ell^2}^2 \right| \leq \delta \|x\|_{\ell^2}^2, \quad \forall x \in \Sigma_s,$$

and therefore

$$\delta_s = \sup_{\substack{x \in \Sigma_s \\ x \neq 0}} \left\{ \frac{\left| \|Ax\|_{\ell^2}^2 - \|x\|_{\ell^2}^2 \right|}{\|x\|_{\ell^2}^2} \right\} = \sup_{\Delta \in D_s} \sup_{\substack{\mathrm{supp}(x) \subseteq \Delta \\ x \neq 0}} \left\{ \frac{\left| \|Ax\|_{\ell^2}^2 - \|x\|_{\ell^2}^2 \right|}{\|x\|_{\ell^2}^2} \right\}.$$

Consider $\Delta \in D_s$ and x with $\mathrm{supp}(x) \subseteq \Delta$. Then, using the fact that P_Δ is a projection,

$$\begin{aligned} \left| \|Ax\|_{\ell^2}^2 - \|x\|_{\ell^2}^2 \right| &= \left| \|AP_\Delta x\|_{\ell^2}^2 - \|P_\Delta x\|_{\ell^2}^2 \right| \\ &= |\langle AP_\Delta x, AP_\Delta x \rangle - \langle P_\Delta x, P_\Delta x \rangle| \\ &= |\langle (P_\Delta A^* A P_\Delta - P_\Delta) x, x \rangle| . \end{aligned}$$

The matrix $P_\Delta A^* A P_\Delta - P_\Delta$ is self-adjoint. Therefore (A.16) gives

$$\sup_{\substack{\mathrm{supp}(x) \subseteq \Delta \\ x \neq 0}} \left\{ \frac{\left| \|Ax\|_{\ell^2}^2 - \|x\|_{\ell^2}^2 \right|}{\|x\|_{\ell^2}^2} \right\} = \|P_\Delta A^* A P_\Delta - P_\Delta\|_{\ell^2}.$$

The result now follows immediately. □

As mentioned in §5.1, AP_Δ is equivalent to the $m \times s$ matrix formed from the columns of A with indices in Δ. The term $\|P_\Delta A^* A P_\Delta - P_\Delta\|_{\ell^2}$ measures how far this matrix is from being an isometry. Hence δ_s quantifies how far an *arbitrary* submatrix consisting of s columns of A is from being an isometry.

We now show that the RIP is a sufficient condition for the rNSP.

Lemma 5.20 (RIP implies rNSP) *Suppose that $A \in \mathbb{C}^{m \times N}$ satisfies the RIP of order $2s$ with constant*

$$\delta_{2s} < \sqrt{2} - 1.$$

Then A satisfies the rNSP of order s with constants

$$\rho = \frac{\sqrt{2}\delta_{2s}}{1 - \delta_{2s}}, \qquad \gamma = \frac{\sqrt{1 + \delta_{2s}}}{1 - \delta_{2s}}.$$

Proof Let $x \in \mathbb{C}^N$ and $\Delta = \Delta_0 \in D_s$ be the index set of the largest s entries of x in absolute value. Note that it suffices to establish (5.22) for this index set only.

To do this, we first construct a partition $\Delta_1, \Delta_2, \ldots$ of $\Delta^c = \{1, \ldots, N\} \backslash \Delta$. We let Δ_1 be the index set of the largest s entries of $P^{\perp}_{\Delta_0} x$ in absolute value, Δ_2 be the index set of the largest s entries of $P^{\perp}_{\Delta_0 \cup \Delta_1} x$ in absolute value, and so forth (it does not matter that the last set may have strictly less than s entries). Next we observe that

$$\|P_\Delta x\|^2_{\ell^2} \leq \|P_{\Delta_0 \cup \Delta_1} x\|^2_{\ell^2} \leq \frac{1}{1 - \delta_{2s}} \|A P_{\Delta_0 \cup \Delta_1} x\|^2_{\ell^2}, \tag{5.25}$$

since A has the RIP of order $2s$. Hence expanding according to the partition, we get

$$\begin{aligned} \|A P_{\Delta_0 \cup \Delta_1} x\|^2_{\ell^2} &= \langle A P_{\Delta_0 \cup \Delta_1} x, Ax \rangle - \sum_{i \geq 2} \langle A P_{\Delta_0 \cup \Delta_1} x, A P_{\Delta_i} x \rangle \\ &\leq \sqrt{1 + \delta_{2s}} \|P_{\Delta_0 \cup \Delta_1} x\|_{\ell^2} \|Ax\|_{\ell^2} + \sum_{i \geq 2} |\langle A P_{\Delta_0 \cup \Delta_1} x, A P_{\Delta_i} x \rangle| . \end{aligned} \tag{5.26}$$

Here, in the second step, we used the Cauchy–Schwarz inequality and the RIP once more. Consider the second term. Note that

$$|\langle A P_{\Delta_0 \cup \Delta_1} x, A P_{\Delta_i} x \rangle| \leq |\langle A P_{\Delta_0} x, A P_{\Delta_i} x \rangle| + |\langle A P_{\Delta_1} x, A P_{\Delta_i} x \rangle|$$

and, since the sets Δ_j and Δ_i are disjoint for $j = 0, 1$ and $i \geq 2$,

$$\begin{aligned} \left|\langle A P_{\Delta_j} x, A P_{\Delta_i} x \rangle\right| &= \left|\langle A^* A P_{\Delta_j} x, P_{\Delta_i} x \rangle\right| \\ &= \left|\langle (A^* A - I) P_{\Delta_j} x, P_{\Delta_i} x \rangle\right| \\ &= \left|\langle (P_\Lambda A^* A P_\Lambda - P_\Lambda) P_{\Delta_j} x, P_{\Delta_i} x \rangle\right| \\ &\leq \|P_\Lambda A^* A P_\Lambda - P_\Lambda\|_{\ell^2} \|P_{\Delta_j} x\|_{\ell^2} \|P_{\Delta_i} x\|_{\ell^2}, \end{aligned} \tag{5.27}$$

where $\Lambda = \Delta_j \cup \Delta_i$. Since $\Lambda \in D_{2s}$, Lemma 5.19 now gives that

$$\left|\langle A P_{\Delta_j} x, A P_{\Delta_i} x \rangle\right| \leq \delta_{2s} \|P_{\Delta_j} x\|_{\ell^2} \|P_{\Delta_i} x\|_{\ell^2},$$

and therefore

$$|\langle A P_{\Delta_0 \cup \Delta_1} x, A P_{\Delta_i} x \rangle| \leq \delta_{2s} \left(\|P_{\Delta_0} x\|_{\ell^2} + \|P_{\Delta_1} x\|_{\ell^2} \right) \|P_{\Delta_i} x\|_{\ell^2}.$$

Notice that

$$\left(\|P_{\Delta_0} x\|_{\ell^2} + \|P_{\Delta_1} x\|_{\ell^2} \right)^2 \leq 2 \left(\|P_{\Delta_0} x\|^2_{\ell^2} + \|P_{\Delta_1} x\|^2_{\ell^2} \right) = 2 \|P_{\Delta_0 \cup \Delta_1} x\|^2_{\ell^2},$$

since Δ_0 and Δ_1 are disjoint. Therefore, it follows that

$$|\langle A P_{\Delta_0 \cup \Delta_1} x, A P_{\Delta_i} x \rangle| \leq \sqrt{2} \delta_{2s} \|P_{\Delta_0 \cup \Delta_1} x\|_{\ell^2} \|P_{\Delta_i} x\|_{\ell^2}.$$

Substituting this into (5.26) and returning to (5.25) we obtain

$$\|P_{\Delta_0 \cup \Delta_1} x\|_{\ell^2} \leq \frac{\sqrt{1 + \delta_{2s}}}{1 - \delta_{2s}} \|Ax\|_{\ell^2} + \frac{\sqrt{2} \delta_{2s}}{1 - \delta_{2s}} \sum_{i \geq 2} \|P_{\Delta_i} x\|_{\ell^2}. \tag{5.28}$$

We now consider the second term. By definition of the Δ_i, we have

$$\|P_{\Delta_i} x\|_{\ell^2} \leq \sqrt{s} \max_{j \in \Delta_i} |x_j| \leq \sqrt{s} \min_{j \in \Delta_{i-1}} |x_j| \leq \sqrt{s} \left(\frac{\sum_{j \in \Delta_{i-1}} |x_j|}{s} \right) = \frac{\|P_{\Delta_{i-1}} x\|_{\ell^1}}{\sqrt{s}}.$$

Since the Δ_i form a partition of Δ^c, this gives

$$\sum_{i\geq 2} \|P_{\Delta_i} x\|_{\ell^2} \leq \frac{1}{\sqrt{s}} \sum_{i\geq 2} \|P_{\Delta_{i-1}} x\|_{\ell^1} = \frac{1}{\sqrt{s}} \|P^{\perp}_{\Delta} x\|_{\ell^1}.$$

Substituting this into (5.28) we finally obtain

$$\begin{aligned} \|P_{\Delta} x\|_{\ell^2} \leq \|P_{\Delta_0 \cup \Delta_1} x\|_{\ell^2} &\leq \frac{\sqrt{1+\delta_{2s}}}{1-\delta_{2s}} \|Ax\|_{\ell^2} + \frac{\sqrt{2}\delta_{2s}}{1-\delta_{2s}} \frac{\|P^{\perp}_{\Delta} x\|_{\ell^1}}{\sqrt{s}} \\ &= \gamma \|Ax\|_{\ell^2} + \rho \frac{\|P^{\perp}_{\Delta} x\|_{\ell^1}}{\sqrt{s}}. \end{aligned}$$

To complete the proof we observe that $\rho < 1$ if and only if $\delta_{2s} < \sqrt{2} - 1$. □

Combining this with Theorem 5.17, we immediately deduce the following:

Theorem 5.21 (RIP implies accurate and stable recovery for QCBP) *Suppose that $A \in \mathbb{C}^{m\times N}$ has the RIP of order $2s$ with constant*

$$\delta_{2s} < \sqrt{2} - 1. \tag{5.29}$$

Let $x \in \mathbb{C}^N$, $y = Ax + e \in \mathbb{C}^m$ and $\eta \geq \|e\|_{\ell^2}$. Then every minimizer $\hat{x} \in \mathbb{C}^N$ of the QCBP problem (5.18) satisfies

$$\|\hat{x} - x\|_{\ell^1} \leq C_1 \sigma_s(x)_{\ell^1} + C_2 \sqrt{s}\eta, \qquad \|\hat{x} - x\|_{\ell^2} \leq C_3 \frac{\sigma_s(x)_{\ell^1}}{\sqrt{s}} + C_4 \eta,$$

where the constants C_1, C_2, C_3, C_4 depend on δ_{2s} only.

This result means that the issue of accurate and stable recovery reduces to that of establishing when the RIP holds for a particular class of measurement matrices. This will be a focal point of Chapter 13.

5.6.3 Uniform Recovery with Gaussian and Bernoulli Random Matrices

We now turn our attention to uniform recovery for the various measurements matrices introduced in §5.3. We commence with Gaussian and Bernoulli random matrices (Definition 5.4). For this, we now also define the error term

$$\mathcal{CS}_s(x,\eta) = \frac{\sigma_s(x)_{\ell^1}}{\sqrt{s}} + \eta. \tag{5.30}$$

Theorem 5.22 *Let $0 < \varepsilon < 1$, $1 \leq s \leq N$ and $A = \frac{1}{\sqrt{m}} \tilde{A}$, where $\tilde{A} \in \mathbb{R}^{m\times N}$ is a Gaussian or Bernoulli random matrix. Suppose that*

$$m \gtrsim s \cdot \log(\mathrm{e}N/s) + \log(2\varepsilon^{-1}). \tag{5.31}$$

Then the following holds with probability at least $1 - \varepsilon$. For all $x \in \mathbb{C}^N$ and $y = Ax + e \in \mathbb{C}^m$, every minimizer $\hat{x} \in \mathbb{C}^N$ of (5.18) with parameter $\eta \geq \|e\|_{\ell^2}$ satisfies

$$\|x - \hat{x}\|_{\ell^1} \lesssim \sqrt{s} \cdot \mathcal{CS}_s(x,\eta), \qquad \|x - \hat{x}\|_{\ell^2} \lesssim \mathcal{CS}_s(x,\eta). \tag{5.32}$$

Stable and accurate recovery in this result are measured in terms of the quantity $\mathcal{CS}_s(x, \eta)$. Of primary importance, however, is the *measurement condition* (5.31). It asserts that recovery succeeds, provided the number of measurements scales linearly with s, up to log factors in N/s and the failure probability ε.

Remark 5.23 In the noise-free scenario, where η may be taken as $\eta = 0$, Theorem 5.22 gives the error bounds

$$\|x - \hat{x}\|_{\ell^1} \lesssim \sigma_s(x)_{\ell^1}, \qquad \|x - \hat{x}\|_{\ell^2} \lesssim \sigma_s(x)_{\ell^1}/\sqrt{s}.$$

These properties are referred to respectively as ℓ^1*-instance optimality* and *mixed* (ℓ^2, ℓ^1)*-instance optimality* of the BP decoder. In general, if an arbitrary decoder R is ℓ^1-instance optimal or mixed (ℓ^2, ℓ^1)-instance optimal then the number of measurements necessarily satisfies $m \gtrsim s \cdot \log(eN/s)$ regardless of their type. Hence BP in tandem with random Gaussian or Bernoulli encoding is effectively an optimal compressed sensing procedure. Conversely, it can be shown that an error bound of the form

$$\|x - \hat{x}\|_{\ell^2} \lesssim \sigma_s(x)_{\ell^2},$$

uniformly for all $x \in \mathbb{C}^N$, can only be attained with $m \gtrsim N$ measurements. Hence, one cannot achieve ℓ^2-instance optimality, regardless of the encoder and decoder pair, without taking a significantly larger number of measurements. See the Notes section for further information.

The proof of Theorem 5.22 follows by showing that the measurement matrix A has the RIP. This is based on a so-called *concentration inequality*:

Lemma 5.24 *Suppose that $A \in \mathbb{R}^{m \times N}$ is a random matrix drawn according to a distribution for which the concentration inequality*

$$\mathbb{P}\left(\left|\|Ax\|_{\ell^2}^2 - \|x\|_{\ell^2}^2\right| \geq t\|x\|_{\ell^2}^2\right) \leq 2\exp\left(-cmt^2\right) \tag{5.33}$$

holds for all $x \in \mathbb{R}^N$ and $0 < t < 1$, where $c > 0$ is a constant. Let $0 < \delta, \varepsilon < 1$. If

$$m \gtrsim c^{-1} \cdot \delta^{-2} \cdot \left(s \cdot \log(eN/s) + \log(2\varepsilon^{-1})\right),$$

then, with probability at least $1 - \varepsilon$, A satisfies the RIP of order s with $\delta_s \leq \delta$.

We shall not prove this result. The next lemma, which we will also not prove, asserts that both Gaussian and Bernoulli random matrices satisfy the concentration inequality.

Lemma 5.25 *Let $\tilde{A} \in \mathbb{R}^{m \times N}$ be a Gaussian or Bernoulli random matrix. Then the matrix $A = \frac{1}{\sqrt{m}}\tilde{A}$ satisfies the concentration inequality (5.33) for all $x \in \mathbb{R}^N$ and $0 < t < 1$, and some constant $c > 0$.*

Proof of Theorem 5.22 Lemmas 5.24 and 5.25 and the condition on m (5.31) imply that A has the RIP of order $2s$ with constant $\delta_{2s} \leq 1/4 < \sqrt{2} - 1$. The result now follows immediately from Theorem 5.21. □

Remark 5.26 Theorem 5.22 considers the case where the object to recover x is itself compressible. Now suppose that x is compressible in a unitary sparsifying transform

Φ. Recall from §5.4.3 that the effective measurement matrix is given by $\bar{A} = A\Phi$ in this case, where A is the (scaled) Gaussian or Bernoulli random matrix. Since unitary matrices preserve the ℓ^2-norm, $\bar{A}$ also satisfies the concentration inequality (5.33). Thus, Lemma 5.25 gives that $\bar{A}$ satisfies the RIP under the same measurement condition (5.31), which implies the error bounds

$$\|d - \hat{d}\|_{\ell^2} \lesssim CS_s(d, \eta), \qquad \|d - \hat{d}\|_{\ell^1} \lesssim \sqrt{s} \cdot CS_s(d, \eta),$$

where $d = \Phi^* x$ are the coefficients of x, $\hat{d}$ is any solution of (5.17) and $CS_s(d, \eta)$ is as in (5.30). Since Φ is unitary, the former also gives the bound

$$\|x - \hat{x}\|_{\ell^2} \lesssim CS_s(d, \eta),$$

where $\hat{x} = \Phi\hat{d}$ is the reconstruction of x. Hence x is recovered stably and accurately, with the latter measured by the best s-term approximation error $\sigma_s(d)_{\ell^1}$ of its coefficients d.

The fact that the measurement condition is unchanged when the sparsity occurs in an arbitrary unitary transform is an extremely powerful property of Gaussian or Bernoulli random matrices. It is known as *universality*. An interesting consequence of it is that the sparsifying transform used in the decoder need not be specified at the encoding phase.

5.6.4 Uniform Recovery with Randomly Subsampled Unitary Matrices

We now consider randomly subsampled unitary matrices:

Theorem 5.27 *Let $0 < \varepsilon < 1$, $N \geq s \geq 2$, $U \in \mathbb{C}^{N \times N}$ be unitary and $A \in \mathbb{C}^{m \times N}$ be a randomly subsampled unitary matrix based on U (in the sense of Definition 5.6). Suppose that*

$$m \gtrsim s \cdot \mu(U) \cdot \left(\log(\mu(U)s) \cdot \log^2(s) \cdot \log(N) + \log(\varepsilon^{-1})\right), \tag{5.34}$$

where $\mu(U)$ is as in Definition 5.8. Then the following holds with probability at least $1 - \varepsilon$. For all $x \in \mathbb{C}^N$ and $y = Ax + e \in \mathbb{C}^m$, every minimizer $\hat{x} \in \mathbb{C}^N$ of (5.18) with parameter $\eta \geq \|e\|_{\ell^2}$ satisfies

$$\|x - \hat{x}\|_{\ell^1} \lesssim \sqrt{s} \cdot CS_s(x, \eta), \qquad \|x - \hat{x}\|_{\ell^2} \lesssim CS_s(x, \eta).$$

Here $CS_s(x, \eta)$ is as in (5.30).

The measurement condition (5.34) depends on the coherence U, in general accordance with the discussion in §5.3.3. If U is incoherent, as is the case for the (normalized) Fourier matrix, it is linear in s, up to the log factors. Conversely, when U is coherent, the number of measurements implied by (5.34) may in fact exceed N.

Note that (5.34), or more precisely, the condition

$$m \gtrsim \delta^{-2} \cdot s \cdot \mu(U) \cdot \left(\log(\mu(U)s) \cdot \log^2(s) \cdot \log(N) + \log(\varepsilon^{-1})\right) \tag{5.35}$$

is a sufficient condition for A to have the RIP of order s with constant $\delta_s \leq \delta$. Armed with this fact, the rest of this theorem follows immediately from Theorem 5.21. The main challenge is proving that (5.35) implies the RIP for A. This is significantly more involved than establishing the RIP for Gaussian or Bernoulli random matrices. Its proof follows from a substantially more general result established later (see §13.4.2).

Remark 5.28 Unlike Gaussian or Bernoulli random matrices (see Remark 5.26), subsampled unitary matrices are highly nonuniversal. As an extreme demonstration of this fact, let $\tilde{A} = \sqrt{N/m} P_\Omega U$ be a subsampled unitary matrix and $\Phi = U^*$ be a sparsifying transform. Then the matrix $A = \tilde{A}\Phi = \sqrt{N/m} P_\Omega I$ is a subsampled identity matrix. This is the poor encoder discussed in §5.3.3. Thus, while $\tilde{A}$ will recover vectors that are sparse in the canonical basis well (whenever U is incoherent), it will fail to recover vectors that are sparse in the particular transform $\Phi = U^*$. Nor is this an isolated case. In general there will be many unitary sparsifying transforms for which $U\Phi$ is coherent.

5.7 Techniques for Nonuniform Recovery

The reader will have noticed that the log factor in Theorem 5.27, which is roughly $\log^3(s)\log(N)$ for incoherent U, is significantly larger than that of Theorem 5.22. Amongst its various uses, nonuniform recovery provides a means for obtaining smaller log factors in the former case. The key idea involves showing that recovery via QCBP is implied by the existence of a suitable *dual certificate*. This is the subject of the next result.

For convenience, we now define the sign of a complex number $z \in \mathbb{C}$ as

$$\text{sign}(z) = \frac{z}{|z|}, \quad z \in \mathbb{C}\backslash\{0\}, \qquad \text{sign}(0) = 0, \tag{5.36}$$

and the sign of a vector $z = (z_i)_{i=1}^N \in \mathbb{C}^N$ as $\text{sign}(z) = (\text{sign}(z_i))_{i=1}^N \in \mathbb{C}^N$.

Theorem 5.29 (Dual certificate implies recovery for QCBP) *Let $x \in \mathbb{C}^N$, $\Delta \subseteq \{1, \ldots, N\}$, $|\Delta| = s$ and $A \in \mathbb{C}^{m \times N}$. Suppose that*

(i) $\|P_\Delta A^* A P_\Delta - P_\Delta\|_{\ell^2} \leq \alpha$,
(ii) $\max_{i \notin \Delta} \|P_\Delta A^* A e_i\|_{\ell^2} \leq \beta$,

and that there is a vector $\rho \in \mathbb{C}^N$ of the form $\rho = A^*\xi$ for some $\xi \in \mathbb{C}^m$ such that

(iii) $\|P_\Delta \rho - \text{sign}(P_\Delta x)\|_{\ell^2} \leq \gamma$,
(iv) $\|P_\Delta^\perp \rho\|_{\ell^\infty} \leq \theta$,
(v) $\|\xi\|_{\ell^2} \leq \nu\sqrt{s}$,

for constants $0 \leq \alpha, \theta < 1$ and $\beta, \gamma, \nu \geq 0$ satisfying $\frac{\beta\gamma}{(1-\alpha)(1-\theta)} < 1$. Then, for all $y = Ax + e \in \mathbb{C}^m$, every minimizer $\hat{x} \in \mathbb{C}^N$ of (5.18) with parameter $\eta \geq \|e\|_{\ell^2}$ satisfies

$$\|\hat{x} - x\|_{\ell^2} \leq 2C_1\|x - P_\Delta x\|_{\ell^1} + 2C_2\sqrt{s}\eta, \tag{5.37}$$

where C_1 and C_2 depend on α, β, γ, θ and ν only and are given explicitly by (6.14).

The vector ρ is referred to as an *(inexact) dual certificate* (also *dual vector*). We defer the proof of this result to §6.4. Note that it is a nonuniform guarantee in the sense that it ensures recovery of a *fixed* vector x up to an error depending on a *fixed* support set Δ. In practice (for instance in the next result), this set is usually taken as the index set of the largest s entries of x in absolute value, so that $\|x - P_\Delta x\|_{\ell^1} = \sigma_s(x)_{\ell^1}$. Observe that in this case, the error bound resulting from (5.37) is worse by a factor of $\sqrt{s}$ than that obtained from a uniform recovery guarantee (see Theorem 5.21, for example) – this is symptomatic of the dual certificate approach. See the Notes section for further details.

5.7.1 Nonuniform Recovery with Subsampled Unitary Matrices

To illustrate this result, we consider subsampled unitary matrices once more:

Theorem 5.30 *Let $0 < \varepsilon < 1$, $N \geq s \geq 2$, $x \in \mathbb{C}^N$, $U \in \mathbb{C}^{N \times N}$ be unitary and $A \in \mathbb{C}^{m \times N}$ be a randomly subsampled unitary matrix based on U (in the sense of Definition 5.6). Suppose that*

$$m \gtrsim s \cdot \mu(U) \cdot (\log(N/\varepsilon) + \log(s) \cdot \log(s/\varepsilon)),$$

where $\mu(U)$ is as in Definition 5.8. Then the following holds with probability at least $1 - \varepsilon$. For all $y = Ax + e \in \mathbb{C}^m$, every minimizer $\hat{x} \in \mathbb{C}^N$ of (5.18) with parameter $\eta \geq \|e\|_{\ell^2}$ satisfies

$$\|\hat{x} - x\|_{\ell^2} \lesssim \sigma_s(x)_{\ell^1} + \sqrt{s}\eta.$$

Like Theorem 5.27, this result is a special case of a more general theorem proved later. See §12.3 for its proof.

5.7.2 Coherence Determines the Sampling Rate for Sparse Vectors

We have now seen that both the uniform and nonuniform recovery guarantees for subsampled unitary matrices have measurement conditions dependent on the coherence $\mu(U)$ times the sparsity s. In general, this cannot be improved. Indeed, it is generically impossible to recover arbitrary s-sparse vectors from fewer than

$$m \gtrsim \mu(U) \cdot s \tag{5.38}$$

measurements. Coherence therefore *determines* the sampling rate for sparse recovery.

To see why, suppose for simplicity that $L \in \mathbb{N}$ is an integer that divides N and consider the unitary matrix

$$U = \sqrt{\frac{L}{N}} \begin{pmatrix} F & 0 & \cdots & 0 \\ 0 & F & \cdots & 0 \\ \vdots & \vdots & \ddots & \vdots \\ 0 & 0 & \cdots & F \end{pmatrix},$$

where $F \in \mathbb{C}^{N/L \times N/L}$ is the Fourier matrix. Then

$$\mu(U) = L \max_{i,j} |F_{ij}|^2 = L.$$

Now let $x \in \mathbb{C}^N$ be an s-sparse vector and suppose that

$$\Delta = \operatorname{supp}(x) \subseteq \{(l-1)N/L + 1, \ldots, lN/L\},$$

for some $l = 1, \dots, L$. Then, since U is block diagonal, exact recovery of x from measurements $y = P_\Omega Ax$ is only possible if the matrix $P_{\Omega_l} F P_{\Delta_l}$ is injective, where $\Omega_l \subseteq \{1, \dots, N/L\}$ is the index set corresponding to the entries of Ω in the range $lN/L < i \leq lN/L$ and likewise for Δ_l. Notice that $|\Delta_l| = s$ by assumption. Hence for injectivity we must have $|\Omega_l| \geq |\Delta_l| = s$. However, x and, in particular, $1 \leq l \leq L$ were arbitrary. Therefore, we need $|\Omega| = |\Omega_1| + \cdots + |\Omega_L| \geq L \cdot s$ measurements to ensure recovery of an arbitrary s-sparse vector. Thus $m \geq L \cdot s = \mu(U) \cdot s$, which gives (5.38).

Note that this result makes no assumption on Ω; in particular, Ω need not be chosen randomly as in Definition 5.5 or 5.6. For random Ω, a more involved argument allows one to establish a stronger version of (5.38) that also includes a factor $\log(N)$. See the Notes section for further details.

5.8 Oracle Estimators

As discussed, standard compressed sensing considers the recovery of a sparse (or compressible) vector x where the support set Δ of the largest s entries of x is *a priori* unknown. When we consider structured sparsity models in Part III, it is informative to consider the scenario where Δ is provided by some oracle. This is usually not practical: as noted, in the case of wavelets it roughly corresponds to knowing the locations of the edges of an image. However, it gives some insight into the best achievable recovery guarantees; a consideration which will be of importance therein.

To this end, suppose that x is a sparse vector with known support $\Delta = \mathrm{supp}(x)$. To recover x from the noisy measurements $y = Ax + e$, we restrict A to the columns indexed by Δ and consider the $m \times |\Delta|$ linear system

$$y = AP_\Delta z$$

(recall from §5.1 that AP_Δ is equivalent to an $m \times |\Delta|$ matrix). This system will generally not have a solution when $e \neq 0$. Hence we consider the least-squares fit

$$\min_{z \in \mathbb{C}^{|\Delta|}} \|AP_\Delta z - y\|_{\ell^2}. \tag{5.39}$$

The solution of this problem is a vector in $\mathbb{C}^{|\Delta|}$. We let $\hat{x} \in \mathbb{C}^N$ be the vector formed by zero padding it outside Δ and refer to $\hat{x}$ as the *oracle estimator* for x.

Proposition 5.31 *Let $0 < \delta < 1$, $A \in \mathbb{C}^{m \times N}$ and $\Delta \subseteq \{1, \dots, N\}$ with*

$$\|P_\Delta A^* A P_\Delta - P_\Delta\|_{\ell^2} \leq \delta. \tag{5.40}$$

Suppose that $x \in \mathbb{C}^N$ with $\mathrm{supp}(x) \subseteq \Delta$ and $y = Ax + e \in \mathbb{C}^m$. Then the solution of (5.39) is unique, and the corresponding vector $\hat{x} \in \mathbb{C}^N$ satisfies

$$\|\hat{x} - x\|_{\ell^2} \leq \frac{1}{\sqrt{1-\delta}} \|e\|_{\ell^2}.$$

Proof In this proof we use standard properties of least-squares problems and pseudo-inverses (see §A.7). Lemma A.2 implies that $AP_\Delta \in \mathbb{C}^{m \times |\Delta|}$ is full rank and $\sigma_{\min}(AP_\Delta) \geq$

$\sqrt{1-\delta}$. In particular, (5.39) has a unique solution, and this is given by $(AP_\Delta)^\dagger y$, where $\dagger$ denotes the pseudoinverse. Observe that $x = P_\Delta x = (AP_\Delta)^\dagger AP_\Delta x$. Hence

$$\|\hat{x} - x\|_{\ell^2} = \|(AP_\Delta)^\dagger (AP_\Delta x - y)\|_{\ell^2} \leq \|(AP_\Delta)^\dagger\|_{\ell^2}\|e\|_{\ell^2} \leq \|e\|_{\ell^2}/\sqrt{1-\delta},$$

where in the last step we use the fact that $\|(AP_\Delta)^\dagger\|_{\ell^2} = 1/\sigma_{\min}(AP_\Delta)$. □

This result has several interpretations. First, notice that the RIP of order s guarantees (5.40) for every Δ of cardinality $|\Delta| = s$. Hence the RIP ensures stable recovery of the oracle least-squares estimator for any such Δ. Second, in the context of nonuniform recovery, notice that (5.40) is equivalent to condition (i) of Theorem 5.29. Therefore, measurement conditions which ensure nonuniform recovery for QCBP will also ensure stable recovery via the oracle least-squares estimator for fixed Δ. However, in both the uniform and nonuniform settings it may be (and sometimes is) the case that (5.40) holds under a rather weaker measurement condition than that which ensures the RIP or the nonuniform recovery conditions of Theorem 5.29. The oracle least-squares estimator is therefore an important yardstick against which we can compare compressed sensing measurement conditions, especially for the structured sparsity models considered later.

Notes

Compressed sensing as a field first developed in 2006 with the works of Candès, Romberg & Tao [121] and Donoho [179]. For overviews of the subject, see [108, 125, 195, 212, 451, 483]. A comprehensive treatment of the mathematics of compressed sensing is given in the book of Foucart & Rauhut [214].

Compressibility of a vector x is often informally defined as rapid decay of $\sigma_s(x)_{\ell^p}$ as s increases (this is somewhat meaningless in the finite-dimensional setting, since $\sigma_s(x)_{\ell^p} = 0$ when $s = N$). *Stechkin's inequality* shows that

$$\sigma_s(x)_{\ell^p} \leq \frac{1}{s^{1/q-1/p}}\|x\|_{\ell^q},$$

for every $p > q > 0$ and $x \in \mathbb{C}^N$. See, for instance, [214, Prop. 2.3]. Hence vectors with small ℓ^q-(quasi)-norms are compressible in this sense. In a more concrete setting, it is a signature result of nonlinear approximation theory that piecewise smooth functions are compressible in wavelet bases. See Chapter 10 for details.

The terms *encoder* and *decoder* were popularized in the work of Cohen, Dahmen & DeVore [151]. They also introduced the notions of instance optimality referred to in Remark 5.23. See also [214, Chpt. 11]. In the compressed sensing literature, the terms 'stable' and 'robust' are sometimes used instead of 'accurate' and 'stable'.

This book is primarily concerned with decoders for compressed sensing that involve solving optimization problems. These are arguably the most popular in imaging. We note, however, that there are many other approaches for sparse recovery. These include greedy algorithms such as *Orthogonal Matching Pursuit (OMP)* and *Compressive Sampling Matching Pursuit (CoSaMP)* [371], iterative algorithms such as *Iterative Hard Thresholding (IHT)* [78, 79] and message-passing algorithms [182], including, as previously mentioned, TurboAMP [446], as well as many others. See [214] for further information on greedy and iterative algorithms.

The NSP and RIP are ubiquitous in compressed sensing. For historical information, see [214, Chpt. 4 & 6]. The term *robust Null Space Property* was also introduced in [214]. Note that Definition 5.14 is formally the ℓ^2-norm rNSP. It can also be defined in terms of other ℓ^p-norms. Alternatives to the RIP include the *Restricted Eigenvalue Condition (REC)* [69] and *Robust Width Property (RWP)* [104].

Remark 5.2 hints at the impracticability of exhaustive search procedures for sparse recovery; for instance, as a means to solve the ℓ^0-minimization problem (5.14). This problem, as noted, is NP-hard to solve [369] (see also [214, Chpt. 2]). Similarly, computing the RIC δ_s or the best constants in the NSP is also NP-hard [461].

Theorem 5.21 is a standard result. It can also be shown that

$$\|\hat{x} - x\|_{\ell^p} \le C_1 s^{1/p-1} \sigma_s(x)_{\ell^1} + C_2 s^{1/p-1/2} \eta, \qquad 1 \le p \le 2.$$

See [214, Chpt. 4]. The cases $p = 1, 2$ in Theorem 5.21 are arguably the most useful.

The bound (5.29) in Theorem 5.21 is due to Candès [109]. This is part of a long line of work on sufficient conditions on RICs to ensure accurate and stable recovery via ℓ^1-minimization. See [214, Chpt. 6] for an overview. This investigation was closed by Cai & Zhang in [106], who showed that the condition $\delta_{ts} < \sqrt{1 - 1/t}, t \ge 4/3$ is both necessary and sufficient for recovery. See also [465]. In particular, for $t = 2$ the sharp bound is $\delta_{2s} < 1/\sqrt{2}$. Throughout this book, the various measurement conditions to ensure the RIP with constant $\delta_s \le \delta$ involve a factor of the form δ^{-2} (see e.g. Lemma 5.24). Since for the majority of this book optimal constants (or even optimal log factors) in such measurement conditions are unknown, we opted to present the simpler, but nonsharp bound $\delta_{2s} < \sqrt{2} - 1$ instead.

Theorem 5.22 is a well-known result in the compressed sensing literature. It can easily be extended to so-called *subgaussian* random matrices, which include both Gaussian and Bernoulli matrices as special cases. We refer to [214, Chpt. 9] for further details. Lemmas 5.24 and 5.25 are presented as Theorem 9.11 and Lemma 9.8 therein.

As noted, a substantially more general version of Theorem 5.27 will be proved in Chapter 13. For discussion on this theorem, see the Notes section of that chapter.

Nonuniform recovery via dual certificates was shown by Fuchs [219] and Tropp [467], and used by Candès, Romberg & Tao in their seminal work [121]. These works are based on a so-called *exact* dual certificate $\rho = A^* \xi \in \mathbb{C}^N$, which satisfies

$$P_\Delta \rho = \operatorname{sign}(P_\Delta x), \qquad \|P_\Delta^\perp \rho\|_{\ell^\infty} < 1.$$

The dual vector of Theorem 12.17 is referred to as an *inexact* dual certificate, and is typically easier to construct in practice. See, for instance, the 'golfing scheme' construction in §12.8 of Chapter 12.

Theorem 5.29 gives error bounds of the form (5.37) which are weaker than those obtained via the RIP by a factor of $\sqrt{s}$ (see Theorem 5.21). Candès & Plan have shown how to overcome this using a technical argument known as the *weak RIP* [118].

Prior to the advent of compressed sensing, the concept of *mutual coherence* of a sampling basis Ψ (e.g. the Fourier matrix) and sparsity basis Φ (e.g. a discrete wavelet basis) was considered in a series of works on discrete uncertainty principles, signal recovery and sparse representation [180, 181, 193]. See also [192] and references therein. In our notation, the mutual coherence is equal to the matrix coherence $\mu(U)$ (Definition 5.8), where $U = \Psi^* \Phi$. The discussion in §5.7.2 stems from [121] and [118]. These works also consider the case of random Ω.

The coherence of a unitary matrix U is distinct from the *cross-coherence* of a measurement matrix A. This is defined as

$$\mu = \max_{i \neq j} \frac{|\langle a_i, a_j \rangle|}{\|a_i\|_{\ell^2} \|a_j\|_{\ell^2}}, \qquad A = (a_1 | \cdots | a_N). \tag{5.41}$$

It is quite a common tool in compressed sensing theory, and unlike the RIP or NSP has the benefit of being easy to compute. However, it yields measurement conditions that are at best quadratic in the sparsity s – the so-called *quadratic bottleneck*. See [214, Chpt. 5]. For this reason, we consider this concept no further.

In this chapter we have assumed that $x \in \mathbb{C}^N$ is either sparse or sparse in a unitary transform $\Phi \in \mathbb{C}^{N \times N}$. In practice, as noted in §4.5, it may be preferable to use a *redundant* transform $\Phi \in \mathbb{C}^{N \times M}$, where $M \geq N$. A recovery guarantee for the corresponding QCBP analysis problem (5.16) can be derived under the assumption that A obeys the so-called *D-RIP*, introduced in [114] (in our notation, D is equal to the matrix Φ). That is,

$$(1 - \delta)\|x\|_{\ell^2} \leq \|Ax\|_{\ell^2} \leq (1 + \delta)\|x\|_{\ell^2}, \quad \forall x \in \Phi(\Sigma_s). \tag{5.42}$$

When the columns of Φ form a tight frame (that is, (4.7) holds with $A = B$), a sufficient condition $\delta_{2s} < 0.08$ for accurate and stable recovery up to $\sigma_s(\Phi^* x)_{\ell^1}$ was proved in [114], and improved to the s optimal condition $\delta_{2s} < 1/\sqrt{2}$ in [523]. For possibly nontight frames, uniform guarantees based on a suitable version of the rNSP can be found in [213,284]. Nonuniform recovery results are given in [285]. Note that a Gaussian random matrix has the D-RIP with high probability provided $m \gtrsim s \log(eM/s)$ [114], precisely as in the case of a unitary transform Φ (see §5.6.3). Measurement conditions for randomly subsampled unitary matrices, under an additional *localization* condition on the frame, were proved in [300].

However, it has been shown that analysis sparsity (i.e. $\Phi^* x$ being s-sparse, or approximately s-sparse) does not always fully determine the recovery performance of (5.16). In particular, the *structure* of the vector x plays a role, and not just its total sparsity. Notions such as *cosparsity* [368] (and generalizations thereof) have been introduced to seek to understand the role of structure. See also [226] and references therein.

Although they are generalizations of standard sparsity, both joint and group sparsity (see §3.5) could well be classed as 'conventional' compressed sensing tools. There are extensions of uniform and nonuniform recovery techniques for these problems. For a small selection of the many results in the literature, see [29, 139, 167, 170, 197, 240, 270, 312, 469], as well as many further references therein.

In turn, classical, joint or group sparsity are special cases of so-called *structured sparsity* models. Here, the signal model is typically assumed to consist of a union of low-dimensional subspaces. See [48, 87, 167, 187, 465] and references therein.

6 The LASSO and its Cousins

The focus of the previous chapter was the QCBP decoder. In this chapter, we consider a different family of decoders, introduced in §6.1, based on the well-known Least Absolute Shrinkage and Selection Operator (LASSO). We investigate these decoders from the compressed sensing perspective by establishing (uniform and nonuniform) recovery guarantees of a similar flavour to those shown in the previous chapter for QCBP. Our main results are summarized in §6.2, with the uniform and nonuniform recovery guarantees presented formally in §6.3 and §6.4, respectively.

This chapter demonstrates that the same conditions introduced previously for the QCBP decoder (rNSP, existence of dual certificates) are also sufficient for accurate and stable recovery with these LASSO-based decoders. Such analysis also shows how the parameter value for each decoder affects the corresponding recovery guarantee. This can then be used to identify optimal, *a priori* parameter regimes, typically depending on the sparsity and the noise level. These regimes are summarized in Table 6.1. In particular, this analysis demonstrates the theoretical benefit of the so-called *Square-Root LASSO (SR-LASSO)* decoder in the context of noise-blind problems. Unlike the others, its admits an optimal parameter choice that is independent of the noise level.

6.1 Definitions

We commence by defining the four decoders compared in this chapter. The first is the familiar QCBP decoder

$$\min_{z \in \mathbb{C}^N} \|z\|_{\ell^1} \text{ subject to } \|Az - y\|_{\ell^2} \leq \eta. \tag{6.1}$$

Next, we consider another decoder that was also discussed in previous chapters, the *Unconstrained LASSO (U-LASSO)*. It is defined by

$$\min_{z \in \mathbb{C}^N} \lambda \|z\|_{\ell^1} + \|Az - y\|_{\ell^2}^2, \tag{6.2}$$

where $\lambda > 0$ is a parameter. It is closely related to our third decoder, the *Constrained LASSO (C-LASSO)*, which is defined by

$$\min_{z \in \mathbb{C}^N} \|Az - y\|_{\ell^2} \text{ subject to } \|z\|_{\ell^1} \leq \tau, \tag{6.3}$$

for a parameter $\tau > 0$. Our fourth and final decoder is a modification of (6.2) in which the data fidelity term $\|Az - y\|_{\ell^2}$ is not squared. This is known as the *Square-Root LASSO*

Table 6.1 Conditions on the parameter for each of the decoders (6.1)–(6.4) to ensure an error bound of the form (6.5) or (6.6) subject to the assumptions in Theorem 5.17 or 5.29, respectively. The term ζ is given by $\zeta = \sigma_s(x)_{\ell^1}/\sqrt{s}$ or $\zeta = \|x - P_\Delta x\|_{\ell^2}/\sqrt{s}$ in the case of (6.5) or (6.6), respectively. The values of c_1 and c_2 affect the constants D_1, D_2, D_3, D_4 in (6.5) and (6.6). For the SR-LASSO, the minimum value $c_* > 0$ depends on the constants ρ and γ of the rNSP in the case of (6.5) or the constants α, β, γ, θ and ν of the dual certificate in the case of (6.6).

Decoder	Parameter	Notes
QCBP	$\eta = c_1\|e\|_{\ell^2} + c_2\zeta$	$c_1 \geq 1, c_2 \geq 0$
U-LASSO	$\lambda = (c_1\|e\|_{\ell^2} + c_2\zeta)/\sqrt{s}$	$c_1 > 0, c_2 \geq 0$
C-LASSO	$\tau = \|x\|_{\ell^1} + \sqrt{s}(c_1\|e\|_{\ell^2} + c_2\zeta)$	$c_1, c_2 \geq 0$
SR-LASSO	$\lambda = \|e\|_{\ell^2}/(\sqrt{s}(c_1\|e\|_{\ell^2} + c_2\zeta))$	$c_1 \geq c_*, c_2 \geq 0$

(SR-LASSO) decoder:

$$\min_{z\in\mathbb{C}^N} \lambda\|z\|_{\ell^1} + \|Az - y\|_{\ell^2}. \tag{6.4}$$

The Notes section contains some background information on these decoders. Algorithms for solving some of these optimization problems are discussed in Chapter 7.

6.2 Summary

In the previous chapter, we derived two main recovery guarantees for QCBP: uniform recovery via the rNSP (Theorem 5.17) and nonuniform recovery via dual certificates (Theorem 5.29). In this chapter we provide sufficient conditions on their respective parameters so that the decoders (6.1)–(6.4) exhibit similar recovery guarantees. Specifically, under the rNSP we show that any minimizer $\hat{x}$ of (6.1)–(6.4) satisfies

$$\|\hat{x} - x\|_{\ell^2} \leq D_1 \frac{\sigma_s(x)_{\ell^1}}{\sqrt{s}} + D_2\|e\|_{\ell^2}, \tag{6.5}$$

for constants $D_1, D_2 > 0$ (similar to Theorem 5.17, it is also possible to prove an ℓ^1-norm error bound in this case, but for simplicity we shall not do this) and subject to conditions (i)–(v) of Theorem 5.17 we show that

$$\|\hat{x} - x\|_{\ell^2} \leq D_3\|x - P_\Delta x\|_{\ell^1} + D_4\sqrt{s}\|e\|_{\ell^2}, \tag{6.6}$$

for constants $D_3, D_4 > 0$. Note that these guarantees are essentially the same as those shown previously for QCBP, except that the factor η has now been replaced by the true noise level $\|e\|_{\ell^2}$.

6.2.1 Parameter Regimes

The parameter regimes that ensure (6.5) and (6.6) for each decoder are summarized in Table 6.1. We now discuss these results.

An interesting component of this analysis is that the same parameter regimes apply for both the uniform and the nonuniform guarantees. Now suppose for convenience that

$\zeta = 0$, i.e. x is exactly s-sparse. Then, in the case of the U-LASSO we see that the hard parameter constraint of QCBP, i.e. $\eta \geq \|e\|_{\ell^2}$, has been replaced by a less stringent condition on λ, requiring it to scale like $c_1\|e\|_{\ell^2}/\sqrt{s}$ for *any* positive constant c_1 (whose value affects the constants in (6.5) and (6.6)). However, removing the hard constraint of QCBP, while desirable, comes at the price of having to know both the noise level $\|e\|_{\ell^2}$ *and* the sparsity s, at least up to a constant.

C-LASSO, on the other hand, is arguably worse than both U-LASSO and QCBP. There is both a hard constraint $\tau \geq \|x\|_{\ell^1}$, which ensures that x is feasible for (6.3), and a soft constraint $\tau \leq \|x\|_{\ell^1} + c_1\sqrt{s}\|e\|_{\ell^2}$. This constraint involves not only the noise level, but also the sparsity s and the ℓ^1-norm of x.

SR-LASSO, however, is more appealing, since the parameter λ can be chosen as $1/(c_1\sqrt{s})$ (this holds automatically if $\zeta = 0$ or, in general, if c_2 is taken as $c_2 = 0$). This is independent of the noise level $\|e\|_{\ell^2}$ and depends on the sparsity s only. We conclude:

> The SR-LASSO has the desirable theoretical property that there is an optimal parameter choice for it that is independent of the noise level. It is therefore well suited to *noise-blind* recovery problems, i.e. those where the $\|e\|_{\ell^2}$ is unknown.

A potential drawback is that c_1 cannot be arbitrary, since it must be no smaller than a constant c_* depending on, for instance, the constants in the rNSP. However, this may not be of great significance in practice nor, as discussed below, in theory.

The regimes identified in Table 6.1 are examined computationally in Fig. 6.1. This figure shows the recovery error as a function of the parameter for each of the decoders, using several different noise levels σ. These results are in good agreement with the table. For QCBP and U-LASSO, the smallest error occurs when the parameter is close to σ. On the other hand, for SR-LASSO the best error occurs at a value of λ that is independent of σ, and for C-LASSO the best error occurs when τ is close to $\|x\|_{\ell^1}$ (normalized to one in this experiment). The C-LASSO error is also sharply peaked. This again agrees with the table, since the width of the optimal parameter regime is proportional to σ in the case of an exactly sparse vector.

Remark 6.1 These parameter regimes identified in Table 6.1 correspond to explicit parameter selection rules depending on s and/or $\|e\|_{\ell^2}$ and ζ. These are known as *a priori* rules, in contrast to the strategies mentioned in the Notes sections of Chapter 4 which seek to estimate the optimal parameter empirically.

6.2.2 Parameter Choice for the SR-LASSO

These results highlight the desirable properties of the SR-LASSO. There remains, however, a potential downside in that the parameter regime identified in Table 6.1 still depends on the sparsity s. Fortunately, this can be mitigated. We shall see later that the constants D_2 and D_4 in (6.5)–(6.6) scale linearly with c_1 when $\lambda = 1/(c_1\sqrt{s})$. Hence the naïve choice $\lambda = 1/\sqrt{m}$ would give a worst-case noise term of the form $\sqrt{m/s}\|e\|_{\ell^2}$. The factor $\sqrt{m/s}$ is often not too large in practice. Furthermore, it can be avoided altogether if a measurement condition for A is known. A typical result of this flavour is the following:

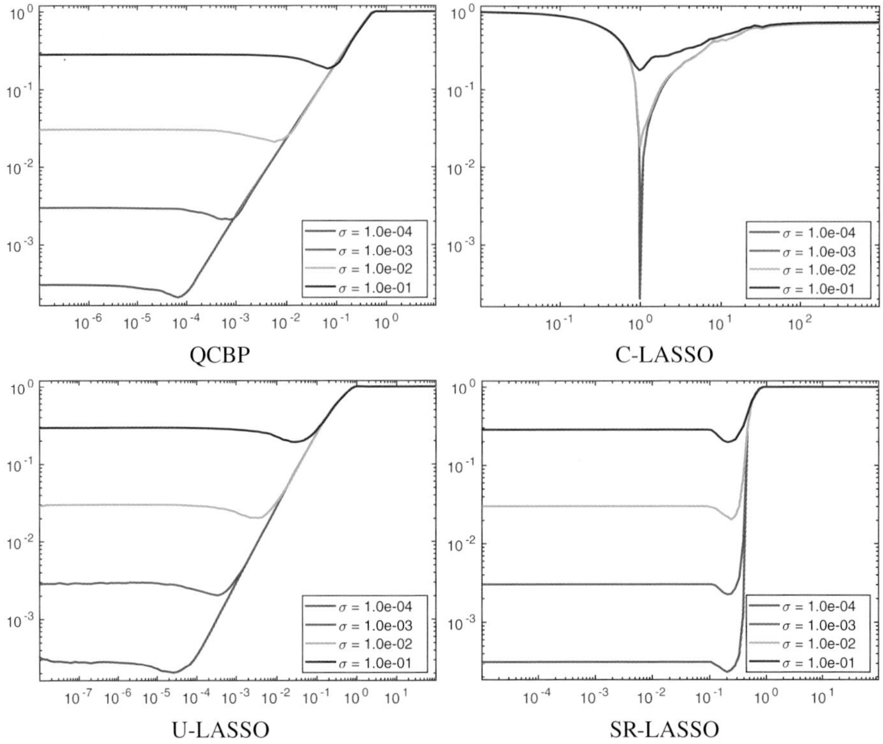

Figure 6.1 Error versus parameter values for the recovery of $s = 5$ sparse vectors of length $N = 64$ from $m = 32$ noisy random Gaussian measurements with different noise levels σ. For each value of the parameter, a random s-sparse vector x, random $m \times N$ matrix $A = m^{-1/2}\tilde{A}$, where $\tilde{A}$ is a Gaussian random matrix, and random noise vector e were drawn, and the recovery error $\|x - \hat{x}\|_{\ell^2}/\|x\|_{\ell^2}$ computed. This process was repeated for $T = 50$ trials. The median error is displayed. The random s-sparse vector x was constructed by first selecting a support set of size s uniformly and randomly, and then choosing its nonzero entries independently from the unit normal distribution. The vector was then normalized so that it had unit ℓ^1-norm (this was done on account of the C-LASSO decoder). The noise vector e was computed as $e = \sigma z/\|z\|_{\ell^2}$, where $z \in \mathbb{R}^m$ has independent entries drawn from the unit normal distribution.

Theorem 6.2 *There exist numerical constants $c_1, c_2 > 0$ such that the following holds. Let $1 \leq m \leq N$ and $A = \frac{1}{\sqrt{m}}\tilde{A}$, where $\tilde{A} \in \mathbb{C}^{m\times N}$ is a Gaussian or Bernoulli random matrix. Then, with probability at least $1 - 2\exp(-m/c_1)$, for all $x \in \mathbb{C}^N$ and $y = Ax + e \in \mathbb{C}^m$, every minimizer $\hat{x} \in \mathbb{C}^N$ of (6.2) with*

$$\lambda = \frac{\|e\|_{\ell^2}}{\sqrt{m/\log(\mathrm{e}N/m)}}, \tag{6.7}$$

or (6.4) with

$$\lambda = \frac{1}{3\sqrt{m/(c_2\log(\mathrm{e}N/m))}}, \tag{6.8}$$

satisfies

$$\|x - \hat{x}\|_{\ell^2} \lesssim \frac{\sigma_s(x)_{\ell^1}}{\sqrt{s}} + \nu \|e\|_{\ell^2}, \tag{6.9}$$

where $\nu = \sqrt{\frac{m}{s \log(eN/m)}}$. *This holds for all* $1 \leq s \leq m/(c_2 \log(eN/m))$.

Note that s now only appears in the error bound (6.9), and not in the parameter λ. Since $\nu \lesssim 1$ when $s \asymp m/\log(eN/m)$ this gives a recovery guarantee for Gaussian measurements analogous to that of the QCBP decoder (Theorem 5.22), while requiring no knowledge of the noise level $\|e\|_{\ell^2}$ in the SR-LASSO case (6.8). Much as for QCBP in §5.6.4, a similar theorem could also be proved for randomly subsampled unitary matrices.

6.3 Uniform Recovery Guarantees

In this and the next section we present the formal recovery guarantees, after which the parameter regimes identified in Table 6.1 follow immediately from the corresponding error bounds. We commence in this section with uniform recovery via the rNSP (Definition 5.14). For convenience, given constants $0 < \rho < 1$ and $\gamma > 0$ we now let

$$C_1 = \frac{(3\rho + 1)(\rho + 1)}{2(1 - \rho)}, \qquad C_2 = \frac{(3\rho + 5)\gamma}{2(1 - \rho)}. \tag{6.10}$$

The following three results are modifications of Theorem 5.17 for (6.2)–(6.4).

Theorem 6.3 (rNSP implies accurate and stable recovery for C-LASSO) *Suppose that* $A \in \mathbb{C}^{m \times N}$ *has the rNSP of order* s *with constants* $0 < \rho < 1$ *and* $\gamma > 0$. *Let* $x \in \mathbb{C}^N$, $y = Ax + e \in \mathbb{C}^m$ *and* $\tau \geq \|x\|_{\ell^1}$. *Then every minimizer* $\hat{x}$ *of (6.3) satisfies*

$$\|\hat{x} - x\|_{\ell^2} \leq 2C_1 \frac{\sigma_s(x)_{\ell^1}}{\sqrt{s}} + C_1 \frac{(\tau - \|x\|_{\ell^1})}{\sqrt{s}} + 2C_2 \|e\|_{\ell^2}, \tag{6.11}$$

where C_1 *and* C_2 *are as in (6.10).*

Proof Lemma 5.16 gives

$$\|\hat{x} - x\|_{\ell^2} \leq 2C_1 \frac{\sigma_s(x)_{\ell^1}}{\sqrt{s}} + \frac{C_1}{\sqrt{s}} (\|\hat{x}\|_{\ell^1} - \|x\|_{\ell^1}) + C_2 \|A(\hat{x} - x)\|_{\ell^2}. \tag{6.12}$$

Note that $\|\hat{x}\|_{\ell^1} \leq \tau$ and $\|x\|_{\ell^1} \leq \tau$ by assumption. Since $\hat{x}$ is a minimizer, we get

$$\|A(\hat{x} - x)\|_{\ell^2} \leq \|Ax - y\|_{\ell^2} + \|A\hat{x} - y\|_{\ell^2} \leq 2\|Ax - y\|_{\ell^2} = 2\|e\|_{\ell^2},$$

which gives the result. □

Theorem 6.4 (rNSP implies accurate and stable recovery for U-LASSO) *Suppose that* $A \in \mathbb{C}^{m \times N}$ *has the rNSP of order* s *with constants* $0 < \rho < 1$ *and* $\gamma > 0$. *Let* $x \in \mathbb{C}^N$, $y = Ax + e \in \mathbb{C}^m$ *and* $\lambda > 0$. *Then every minimizer* $\hat{x}$ *of (6.2) satisfies*

$$\|\hat{x} - x\|_{\ell^2} \leq 2C_1 \frac{\sigma_s(x)_{\ell^1}}{\sqrt{s}} + C_1 \frac{\|e\|_{\ell^2}^2}{\lambda \sqrt{s}} + \frac{C_2^2}{4C_1} \lambda \sqrt{s} + C_2 \|e\|_{\ell^2},$$

where C_1 *and* C_2 *are as in (6.10).*

Proof Using Lemma 5.16 and the bound $\|A(\hat{x} - x)\|_{\ell^2} \leq \|A\hat{x} - y\|_{\ell^2} + \|e\|_{\ell^2}$, we get

$$\|\hat{x} - x\|_{\ell^2} \leq 2C_1 \frac{\sigma_s(x)_{\ell^1}}{\sqrt{s}} + \frac{C_1}{\sqrt{s}} \left(\|\hat{x}\|_{\ell^1} - \|x\|_{\ell^1}\right) + C_2\|A\hat{x} - y\|_{\ell^2} + C_2\|e\|_{\ell^2}.$$

We now apply Young's inequality (5.12) to the term $\|A\hat{x} - y\|_{\ell^2}$ with parameters

$$\sigma = \frac{C_1}{C_2}, \quad a = \frac{\|A\hat{x} - y\|_{\ell^2}}{\sqrt{\lambda\sqrt{s}}}, \quad b = \sqrt{\lambda\sqrt{s}},$$

to obtain

$$\|\hat{x} - x\|_{\ell^2} \leq 2C_1 \frac{\sigma_s(x)_{\ell^1}}{\sqrt{s}} + \frac{C_1}{\sqrt{s}} \left(\|\hat{x}\|_{\ell^1} + \frac{\|A\hat{x} - y\|^2_{\ell^2}}{\lambda} - \|x\|_{\ell^1}\right) + \frac{C_2^2}{4C_1}\lambda\sqrt{s} + C_2\|e\|_{\ell^2}.$$

Since $\hat{x}$ is a minimizer, we have

$$\lambda\|\hat{x}\|_{\ell^1} + \|A\hat{x} - y\|^2_{\ell^1} \leq \lambda\|x\|_{\ell^1} + \|Ax - y\|^2_{\ell^2} = \lambda\|x\|_{\ell^1} + \|e\|^2_{\ell^2},$$

and therefore

$$\|\hat{x} - x\|_{\ell^2} \leq 2C_1 \frac{\sigma_s(x)_{\ell^1}}{\sqrt{s}} + \frac{C_1}{\sqrt{s}\lambda}\|e\|^2_{\ell^2} + \frac{C_2^2}{4C_1}\lambda\sqrt{s} + C_2\|e\|_{\ell^2},$$

as required. □

Theorem 6.5 (rNSP implies accurate and stable recovery for SR-LASSO) *Suppose that $A \in \mathbb{C}^{m\times N}$ has the rNSP of order s with constants $0 < \rho < 1$ and $\gamma > 0$. Let $x \in \mathbb{C}^N$, $y = Ax + e \in \mathbb{C}^m$ and*

$$\lambda \leq \frac{C_1}{C_2\sqrt{s}}.$$

Then every minimizer $\hat{x}$ of (6.4) satisfies

$$\|\hat{x} - x\|_{\ell^2} \leq 2C_1 \frac{\sigma_s(x)_{\ell^1}}{\sqrt{s}} + \left(\frac{C_1}{\sqrt{s}\lambda} + C_2\right)\|e\|_{\ell^2},$$

where C_1 and C_2 are as in (6.10).

Proof By Lemma 5.16 we have

$$\|\hat{x} - x\|_{\ell^2} \leq 2C_1 \frac{\sigma_s(x)_{\ell^1}}{\sqrt{s}} + \frac{C_1}{\sqrt{s}} \left(\|\hat{x}\|_{\ell^1} - \|x\|_{\ell^1}\right) + C_2\left(\|A\hat{x} - y\|_{\ell^2} + \|e\|_{\ell^2}\right).$$

The condition on λ gives

$$\|\hat{x} - x\|_{\ell^2} \leq 2C_1 \frac{\sigma_s(x)_{\ell^1}}{\sqrt{s}} + \frac{C_1}{\sqrt{s}\lambda} \left(\lambda\|\hat{x}\|_{\ell^1} + \|A\hat{x} - y\|_{\ell^2} - \lambda\|x\|_{\ell^1}\right) + C_2\|e\|_{\ell^2}.$$

We now use the fact that $\hat{x}$ is a minimizer to deduce that

$$\|\hat{x} - x\|_{\ell^2} \leq 2C_1 \frac{\sigma_s(x)_{\ell^1}}{\sqrt{s}} + \frac{C_1}{\sqrt{s}\lambda}\|Ax - y\|_{\ell^2} + C_2\|e\|_{\ell^2}.$$

Since $\|Ax - y\|_{\ell^2} = \|e\|_{\ell^2}$ this gives the result. □

To conclude this section, we now also give the proof of Theorem 6.2.

Proof of Theorem 6.2 Lemmas 5.24 and 5.25 assert that A has the RIP of order $2s$ and constant $\delta_{2s} \leq 1/4$ provided

$$m \geq c \cdot \left(2s \cdot \log(eN/(2s)) + \log(2\varepsilon^{-1})\right), \tag{6.13}$$

for some numerical constant $c > 0$. We now show that this holds with ε chosen as $\varepsilon = 2\exp(-m/c_1)$. First, observe that

$$\begin{aligned} m \geq c_2 s \log(eN/m) &= c_2 s \log(eN/(2s)) + c_2 s \log(2s/m) \\ &= c_2 s \log(eN/(2s)) + c_2 m \left(2s/m \log(2s/m)\right)/2, \end{aligned}$$

by assumption on m. The function $t \mapsto t\log(t)$ is decreasing on $(0, 1/e)$. Notice also that $m \geq c_2 s$ by assumption, and therefore $2s/m \leq 2/c_2 \leq 1/e$ provided $c_2 \geq 2e$. Supposing that this holds, we then have

$$m \geq c_2 s \log(eN/(2s)) + c_2 m(2/c_2 \log(2/c_2))/2 = c_2 s \log(eN/(2s)) + m\log(2/c_2),$$

which, after rearranging, gives

$$m \geq \frac{c_2}{\log(ec_2/2)} s \log(eN/(2s)).$$

Since $m = c_1 \log(2\varepsilon^{-1})$ we deduce that

$$m \geq \frac{c_2}{2\log(ec_2/2)} s \log(eN/(2s)) + \frac{c_1}{2}\log(2\varepsilon^{-1}).$$

Therefore (6.13) holds for all sufficiently large c_1 and c_2, as required.

We now complete the proof. Since A has the RIP of order $2s$ with constant $\delta_{2s} \leq 1/4$, Lemma 5.20 implies that A has the rNSP of order s with constants $\rho = \sqrt{2}/3$ and $\gamma = 2\sqrt{5}/3$. For the U-LASSO the result now follows immediately from Theorem 6.4, (6.7) and the fact that $\nu \gtrsim 1$. For the SR-LASSO, we use Theorem 6.5. In order to do this, we first need to check that the value of λ given in (6.8) satisfies $\lambda \leq C_1/(C_2\sqrt{s})$, where C_1 and C_2 are as in (6.10) for the given values of ρ and γ. Observe that

$$\frac{C_1}{C_2} = \frac{5 + 4\sqrt{2}}{2\sqrt{5}(5 + \sqrt{2})} > \frac{1}{3} \geq \lambda\sqrt{s}.$$

Hence the result for SR-LASSO now follows as well. □

6.4 Nonuniform Recovery Guarantees

We now consider nonuniform recovery. As we show, the existence of a dual certificate satisfying the conditions of Theorem 5.29 (which applies to QCBP) is also sufficient for recovery with the other three decoders. Since it was not done in Chapter 5, in this section we also give the proof of Theorem 5.29.

Theorem 6.6 (Dual certificate implies recovery) *Let $x \in \mathbb{C}^N$, $\Delta \subseteq \{1, \ldots, N\}$, $|\Delta| = s$ and $A \in \mathbb{C}^{m \times N}$ be such that conditions (i)–(v) of Theorem 5.29 hold. Then the following holds for all $y = Ax + e \in \mathbb{C}^m$:*

(a) *If* $\tau \geq \|x\|_{\ell^1}$, *every minimizer* $\hat{x}$ *of the C-LASSO problem (6.3) satisfies*

$$\|\hat{x} - x\|_{\ell^2} \leq 2C_1\|x - P_\Delta x\|_{\ell^1} + C_1\left(\tau - \|x\|_{\ell^1}\right) + 2C_2\sqrt{s}\|e\|_{\ell^2}.$$

(b) *If* $\lambda > 0$, *every minimizer* $\hat{x}$ *of the U-LASSO problem (6.2) satisfies*

$$\|\hat{x} - x\|_{\ell^2} \leq 2C_1\|x - P_\Delta x\|_{\ell^1} + C_1\frac{\|e\|_{\ell^2}^2}{\lambda} + \frac{C_2^2}{4C_1}\lambda s + C_2\sqrt{s}\|e\|_{\ell^2}.$$

(c) *If* $\lambda \leq \frac{C_1}{C_2\sqrt{s}}$ *every minimizer* $\hat{x}$ *of the SR-LASSO problem (6.4) satisfies*

$$\|\hat{x} - x\|_{\ell^2} \leq 2C_1\|x - P_\Delta x\|_{\ell^1} + \left(\frac{C_1}{\lambda} + C_2\sqrt{s}\right)\|e\|_{\ell^2}.$$

Here C_1 *and* C_2 *depend on* α, β, γ, θ *and* ν *only and are given explicitly by (6.14).*

Both this and Theorem 5.29 are consequences of the following lemma:

Lemma 6.7 (Dual certificate implies ℓ^2-distance bound) *Let* $x \in \mathbb{C}^N$, $\Delta \subseteq \{1,\ldots,N\}$, $|\Delta| = s$ *and* $A \in \mathbb{C}^{m\times N}$ *be such that conditions (i)–(v) of Theorem 5.29 hold. Then*

$$\|z - x\|_{\ell^2} \leq 2C_1\|x - P_\Delta x\|_{\ell^1} + C_1\left(\|z\|_{\ell^1} - \|x\|_{\ell^1}\right) + C_2\sqrt{s}\|A(z-x)\|_{\ell^2},$$

for all $z \in \mathbb{C}^N$, *where*

$$\begin{aligned}
C_1 &= \frac{1}{1-\theta} + \left(1 + \frac{\gamma}{1-\theta}\right)\left(1 - \frac{\beta\gamma}{(1-\alpha)(1-\theta)}\right)^{-1}\frac{\beta}{(1-\alpha)(1-\theta)},\\
C_2' &= \left(1 + \frac{\gamma}{1-\theta}\right)\left(1 - \frac{\beta\gamma}{(1-\alpha)(1-\theta)}\right)^{-1}\frac{\sqrt{1+\alpha}}{1-\alpha},\\
C_2 &= C_1\nu + C_2'.
\end{aligned} \tag{6.14}$$

We remark in passing that this result also holds with the term $C_2\sqrt{s}$ replaced by the slightly smaller factor $C_1\nu\sqrt{s} + C_2'$.

Proof Let $v = z - x$. The idea is to split v into $v = P_\Delta v + P_\Delta^\perp v$ and estimate the two terms separately. Consider $P_\Delta v$. Using Lemma A.2, we note that condition (i) implies that $P_\Delta A^* A P_\Delta$, when considered as an $|\Delta| \times |\Delta|$ matrix, is invertible with

$$\|(P_\Delta A^* A P_\Delta)^{-1}\|_{\ell^2} \leq \frac{1}{1-\alpha}.$$

By (A.15) we also have

$$\|P_\Delta A^*\|_{\ell^2}^2 = \|AP_\Delta\|_{\ell^2}^2 = \|P_\Delta A^* A P_\Delta\|_{\ell^2} \leq 1 + \alpha.$$

Therefore

$$\begin{aligned}
\|P_\Delta v\|_{\ell^2} &\leq \|(P_\Delta A^* A P_\Delta)^{-1}\|_{\ell^2}\|P_\Delta A^* A P_\Delta v\|_{\ell^2}\\
&\leq \frac{1}{1-\alpha}\left(\|P_\Delta A^* A v\|_{\ell^2} + \|P_\Delta A^* A P_\Delta^\perp v\|_{\ell^2}\right)\\
&\leq \frac{\sqrt{1+\alpha}}{1-\alpha}\|Av\|_{\ell^2} + \frac{1}{1-\alpha}\|P_\Delta A^* A P_\Delta^\perp v\|_{\ell^2}.
\end{aligned}$$

We estimate the second term using condition (ii):

$$\|P_\Delta A^* A P_\Delta^\perp v\|_{\ell^2} \leq \sum_{i \notin \Delta} |v_i| \|P_\Delta A^* A e_i\|_{\ell^2} \leq \beta \|P_\Delta^\perp v\|_{\ell^1}.$$

This gives

$$\|P_\Delta v\|_{\ell^2} \leq \frac{\sqrt{1+\alpha}}{1-\alpha}\|Av\|_{\ell^2} + \frac{\beta}{1-\alpha}\|P_\Delta^\perp v\|_{\ell^1}. \tag{6.15}$$

We now focus on estimating $\|P_\Delta^\perp v\|_{\ell^1}$. Observe that

$$\begin{aligned}
\|z\|_{\ell^1} = \|P_\Delta z\|_{\ell^1} + \|P_\Delta^\perp z\|_{\ell^1} &\geq \operatorname{Re}\langle P_\Delta z, \operatorname{sign}(P_\Delta x)\rangle + \|P_\Delta^\perp v\|_{\ell^1} - \|P_\Delta^\perp x\|_{\ell^1} \\
&= \operatorname{Re}\langle P_\Delta v, \operatorname{sign}(P_\Delta x)\rangle + \|P_\Delta x\|_{\ell^1} + \|P_\Delta^\perp v\|_{\ell^1} - \|P_\Delta^\perp x\|_{\ell^1} \\
&= \operatorname{Re}\langle P_\Delta v, \operatorname{sign}(P_\Delta x)\rangle + \|x\|_{\ell^1} + \|P_\Delta^\perp v\|_{\ell^1} - 2\|P_\Delta^\perp x\|_{\ell^1},
\end{aligned}$$

and therefore

$$\|P_\Delta^\perp v\|_{\ell^1} \leq |\langle P_\Delta v, \operatorname{sign}(P_\Delta x)\rangle| + 2\|P_\Delta^\perp x\|_{\ell^1} + \|z\|_{\ell^1} - \|x\|_{\ell^1}. \tag{6.16}$$

We next estimate $|\langle P_\Delta v, \operatorname{sign}(P_\Delta x)\rangle|$. We have

$$\begin{aligned}
|\langle P_\Delta v, \operatorname{sign}(P_\Delta x)\rangle| &\leq |\langle P_\Delta v, (\operatorname{sign}(P_\Delta x) - P_\Delta \rho)\rangle| + |\langle P_\Delta v, P_\Delta \rho\rangle| \\
&\leq |\langle P_\Delta v, (\operatorname{sign}(P_\Delta x) - P_\Delta \rho)\rangle| + |\langle v, \rho\rangle| + |\langle P_\Delta^\perp v, P_\Delta^\perp \rho\rangle|.
\end{aligned}$$

Note that $|\langle P_\Delta v, (\operatorname{sign}(P_\Delta x) - P_\Delta \rho)\rangle| \leq \gamma \|P_\Delta v\|_{\ell^2}$ by (iii). Also $\langle v, \rho\rangle = \langle v, A^*\xi\rangle = \langle Av, \xi\rangle$ and therefore (v) gives

$$|\langle v, \rho\rangle| \leq \nu\sqrt{s}\|Av\|_{\ell^2}.$$

Furthermore, by (iv) we have

$$|\langle P_\Delta^\perp v, P_\Delta^\perp \rho\rangle| \leq \|P_\Delta^\perp v\|_{\ell^1}\|P_\Delta^\perp \rho\|_{\ell^\infty} \leq \theta\|P_\Delta^\perp v\|_{\ell^1}.$$

Combining these estimates, we get

$$|\langle P_\Delta v, \operatorname{sign}(P_\Delta x)\rangle| \leq \gamma\|P_\Delta v\|_{\ell^2} + \nu\sqrt{s}\|Av\|_{\ell^2} + \theta\|P_\Delta^\perp v\|_{\ell^1},$$

and substituting this into (6.16) and rearranging, we obtain

$$(1-\theta)\|P_\Delta^\perp v\|_{\ell^1} \leq \gamma\|P_\Delta v\|_{\ell^2} + \nu\sqrt{s}\|Av\|_{\ell^2} + 2\|P_\Delta^\perp x\|_{\ell^1} + \|z\|_{\ell^1} - \|x\|_{\ell^1}. \tag{6.17}$$

We now apply (6.15) to get

$$\begin{aligned}
\|P_\Delta v\|_{\ell^2} &\leq \frac{\sqrt{1+\alpha}}{1-\alpha}\|Av\|_{\ell^2} \\
&\quad + \frac{\beta}{(1-\alpha)(1-\theta)}\left(\gamma\|P_\Delta v\|_{\ell^2} + \nu\sqrt{s}\|Av\|_{\ell^2} + 2\|P_\Delta^\perp x\|_{\ell^1} + \|z\|_{\ell^1} - \|x\|_{\ell^1}\right),
\end{aligned}$$

which implies that

$$\begin{aligned}
\|P_\Delta v\|_{\ell^2} \leq \left(1 - \frac{\beta\gamma}{(1-\alpha)(1-\theta)}\right)^{-1} &\left[\frac{1}{1-\alpha}\left(\sqrt{1+\alpha} + \frac{\beta}{1-\theta}\nu\sqrt{s}\right)\|Av\|_{\ell^2}\right. \\
&\left. + \frac{\beta}{(1-\alpha)(1-\theta)}\left(2\|P_\Delta^\perp x\|_{\ell^1} + \|z\|_{\ell^1} - \|x\|_{\ell^1}\right)\right].
\end{aligned} \tag{6.18}$$

Note that $\|P_\Delta^\perp v\|_{\ell^2} \leq \|P_\Delta^\perp v\|_{\ell^1}$. Hence (6.17) gives

$$\begin{aligned}\|v\|_{\ell^2} &\leq \|P_\Delta v\|_{\ell^2} + \|P_\Delta^\perp v\|_{\ell^1} \\ &\leq \left(1 + \frac{\gamma}{1-\theta}\right)\|P_\Delta v\|_{\ell^2} + \frac{1}{1-\theta}\left(\nu\sqrt{s}\|Av\|_{\ell^2} + 2\|P_\Delta^\perp x\|_{\ell^1} + \|z\|_{\ell^1} - \|x\|_{\ell^1}\right).\end{aligned}$$

Combining this with the estimate (6.18) for $\|P_\Delta v\|_{\ell^2}$, we deduce that

$$\|z - x\|_{\ell^2} \leq 2C_1\|x - P_\Delta x\|_{\ell^1} + C_1\left(\|z\|_{\ell^1} - \|x\|_{\ell^1}\right) + \left(C_2' + C_1\nu\sqrt{s}\right)\|A(z-x)\|_{\ell^2}.$$

The result now follows from the fact that $C_2' + C_1\nu\sqrt{s} \leq (C_2' + C_1\nu)\sqrt{s} = C_2\sqrt{s}$. □

Proof of Theorem 5.29 Let $\hat{x}$ be a minimizer of (5.18). Then $\|\hat{x}\|_{\ell^1} \leq \|x\|_{\ell^1}$ and

$$\|A(\hat{x} - x)\|_{\ell^2} \leq \|A\hat{x} - y\|_{\ell^2} + \|Ax - y\|_{\ell^2} \leq 2\eta.$$

We now apply Lemma 6.7 with $z = \hat{x}$. □

Proof of Theorem 6.6 We first consider part (a). Let $\hat{x}$ be any minimizer of (6.2). Then Lemma 6.7 with $z = \hat{x}$ gives

$$\begin{aligned}\|\hat{x} - x\|_{\ell^2} \leq{}& 2C_1\|x - P_\Delta x\|_{\ell^1} + C_1\left(\|\hat{x}\|_{\ell^1} - \|x\|_{\ell^1}\right) \\ &+ C_2\sqrt{s}\left(\|A\hat{x} - y\|_{\ell^2} + \|e\|_{\ell^2}\right).\end{aligned} \tag{6.19}$$

Recall that $\|\hat{x}\|_{\ell^1} \leq \tau$ and $\|x\|_{\ell^1} \leq \tau$ by assumption, and therefore $\|A\hat{x} - y\|_{\ell^2} \leq \|Ax - y\|_{\ell^2} = \|e\|_{\ell^2}$. Part (a) now follows immediately.

Now consider (b). The bound (6.19) and Young's inequality give

$$\begin{aligned}\|\hat{x} - x\|_{\ell^2} \leq{}& 2C_1\|x - P_\Delta x\|_{\ell^1} + C_1\left(\|\hat{x}\|_{\ell^1} + \|A\hat{x} - y\|_{\ell^2}^2/\lambda - \|x\|_{\ell^1}\right) \\ &+ \frac{C_2^2}{4C_1}\lambda s + C_2\sqrt{s}\|e\|_{\ell^2}.\end{aligned}$$

The result now follows after recalling that $\hat{x}$ is a minimizer, since this implies that $\|\hat{x}\|_{\ell^1} + \|A\hat{x} - y\|_{\ell^2}^2/\lambda - \|x\|_{\ell^1} \leq \|Ax - y\|_{\ell^2}^2/\lambda$.

Now consider (c). We once more apply Lemma 6.7 with $z = \hat{x}$, where $\hat{x}$ is a minimizer of (6.4), to get

$$\|\hat{x} - x\|_{\ell^2} \leq 2C_1\|x - P_\Delta x\|_{\ell^1} + C_1\left(\|\hat{x}\|_{\ell^1} - \|x\|_{\ell^1}\right) + C_2\sqrt{s}\left(\|A\hat{x} - y\|_{\ell^2} + \|e\|_{\ell^2}\right).$$

The condition on λ implies that $C_2\sqrt{s} \leq C_1/\lambda$. Therefore, using the fact that $\hat{x}$ is a minimizer, we obtain

$$\begin{aligned}\|\hat{x} - x\|_{\ell^2} &\leq 2C_1\|x - P_\Delta x\|_{\ell^1} + C_1\left(\|\hat{x}\|_{\ell^1} + \|A\hat{x} - y\|_{\ell^2}/\lambda - \|x\|_{\ell^1}\right) + C_2\sqrt{s}\|e\|_{\ell^2} \\ &\leq 2C_1\|x - P_\Delta x\|_{\ell^1} + \left(C_1/\lambda + C_2\sqrt{s}\right)\|e\|_{\ell^2}.\end{aligned}$$

This completes the proof. □

Having established both the uniform and nonuniform recovery guarantees, we conclude by noting that the parameter regimes listed in Table 6.1 now follow immediately from the corresponding error bounds. This is done simply by matching terms, so as to ensure the overall error bound takes the form (6.5) or (6.6). In particular, this demonstrates our earlier observation that both sets of guarantees yield the same parameter regimes.

Notes

The LASSO is an extremely widely used technique in statistics [258], where it was originally introduced in its constrained form (6.3) by Tibshirani [460]. The unconstrained formulation (6.2) is identical to so-called *basis pursuit denoising*, introduced by Chen, Donoho and Saunders for computing sparse representations of signals in redundant dictionaries [140].

The constrained and unconstrained LASSO are related in the following sense. If $\hat{x}$ is a minimizer of, say, C-LASSO then there exists a $\lambda \geq 0$ such that $\hat{x}$ is also a minimizer of U-LASSO. Conversely, if $\hat{x}$ is a minimizer of U-LASSO then there exists a $\tau \geq 0$ such that it is a minimizer of C-LASSO. The same statement also holds for QCBP, subject to feasibility. See, for example, [214, Thm. B.28].

These equivalences can be exploited algorithmically. They are used, for example, by the solver in the SPGL1 package (see the Notes section of Chapter 7). However, they should be taken with some caution. First, the corresponding parameters are typically non-explicit and dependent on $\hat{x}$. Hence explicitly switching between problems is usually not possible. Second, they say nothing about the sets of minimizers of each problem. Therefore, a separate compressed sensing analysis ensuring that *all* minimizers are sufficiently close to x is required for each problem.

The SR-LASSO is far less well known than its famous cousin. It was introduced in [62] to avoid the estimation of the noise level in the standard LASSO (as seen in Table 6.1). For further information, see [45, 63, 100] and [475, Chpt. 3]. Its application to compressed sensing was first proposed in [4].

There is a large literature on the analysis of the LASSO. See [391, Chpts. 2 & 3], [258, 476] and references therein. From the compressed sensing perspective, an early analysis of the U-LASSO based on the cross-coherence (5.41) was presented by Tropp [468]. From a statistical perspective, analysis based on the REC was considered in [69] and the so-called *compability* condition in [476]. See the latter and [258, Chpt. 11] for an overview of various different conditions used in the literature. In [118], Candès & Plan analysed the U-LASSO using the weak RIP. The simultaneous analysis of the constrained, unconstrained and SR-LASSO via the rNSP as shown in this chapter is based on [4].

The parameter regimes derived in this chapter are similar to existing results. A difference is that we consider adversarial, but ℓ^2-bounded noise as is most common in compressed sensing. Hence, for instance, the optimal U-LASSO parameter scales like $\|e\|_{\ell^2}/\sqrt{s}$ in the sparse case. Conversely, it is usually more common in the statistical literature to assume that e is white noise with standard deviation $\sigma/\sqrt{m}$, in which case a suitable scaling is $\sigma\sqrt{\log(N)/m}$ [118]. Another common scaling found in the literature is $\lambda \asymp \|A^* e\|_{\ell^\infty}/m$ [258, Chpt. 11]. The fact that the C-LASSO solution admits the usual compressed sensing-type guarantee for a range of τ (rather than simply $\tau = \|x\|_{\ell^1}$ [258, Thm. 11.1]) appears to be novel.

The parameter regimes identified in Table 6.1 and shown in Fig. 6.1 are non-asymptotic. For a precise *asymptotic* analysis (in the sense $N \to \infty$), see [67]. In particular, this work establishes a certain asymptotic instability of the C-LASSO to the parameter choice. In the pre-asymptotic regime, evidence of this is seen empirically in Fig. 6.1 by the presence of the sharp peak around $\tau = \|x\|_{\ell^1}$.

An alternative to the decoders discussed in this chapter is the *Dantzig selector*, introduced by Candès & Tao [124] in the context of model selection in statistics. This solves the problem

$$\min_{z \in \mathbb{C}^N} \|z\|_{\ell^1} \text{ subject to } \|A^*(Az - y)\|_{\ell^\infty} \leq \tau, \tag{6.20}$$

for suitable τ depending on the noise level. Analyses in terms of the RIP, restricted eigenvalue condition and weak RIP were presented in [124], [69] and [118], respectively. See also [214, Ex. 4.11] for an analysis based on a variation of the rNSP.

The decoders introduced in this chapter were motivated in part by the desire to avoid the condition $\eta \geq \|e\|_{\ell^2}$ in the recovery guarantees for QCBP. One may ask what happens in the case of QCBP when this condition is violated. An immediate concern is that the optimization problem (6.1) may be infeasible in this regime. However, whenever its feasibility set is nonempty (for instance, if A is full rank) then, subject to the rNSP, it can be shown that

$$\|\hat{x} - x\|_{\ell^2} \leq C_1 \frac{\sigma_s(x)_{\ell^1}}{\sqrt{s}} + C_2\eta + C_3 Q_s(A)_{\ell^1} \max\left\{\|e\|_{\ell^2} - \eta, 0\right\}, \tag{6.21}$$

regardless of the choice of $\eta \geq 0$ [97]. Here,

$$Q_s(A)_{\ell^1} = \sup_{\substack{e \in \mathbb{C}^m \\ e \neq 0}} \inf_{\substack{z \in \mathbb{C}^N \\ Az = e}} \frac{\|z\|_{\ell^1}}{\sqrt{s}\|e\|_{\ell^2}}$$

is the so-called *ℓ^1-quotient*. This is related to the *quotient property* [502], see also [173, 213] and [214, Chpt. 11]. The estimate (6.21) generalizes Theorem 5.17. Notice that the effect of violating the condition $\eta \geq \|e\|_{\ell^2}$ is captured by the third term, which is proportional to the quotient multiplied by $\|e\|_{\ell^2} - \eta$. Hence the effect lessens as η approaches $\|e\|_{\ell^2}$. Conversely, since (6.21) remains valid for $\eta = 0$, this result also gives a recovery guarantee for the BP decoder (5.15) with noisy measurements.

To use (6.21), it is necessary to estimate $Q_s(A)_{\ell^1}$. For a Gaussian random matrix, it can be shown that $Q_{s^*}(A)_{\ell^1} \lesssim 1$ with high probability for $s_* = m/\log(eN/m)$ and $m \leq N/2$ [97, Lem. 30]. Such a matrix also has the rNSP for every $s \leq cs_*$, for some numerical constant c. In other words, QCBP admits accurate and stable recovery for Gaussian random matrices even when the condition $\eta \geq \|e\|_{\ell^2}$ is violated (in particular, when $\eta = 0$). Unfortunately, it is not known whether such simple estimates hold for more general classes of random matrices. See [97] for further discussion.

The decoders considered in this chapter assume small-norm noise. It practice, it is sometimes the case that the data y contains a small number of highly corrupted entries. This could be, for instance, due to failures of the sensing device, or effects such as signal clipping. This is known as the *compressed sensing with sparse corruptions* problem. Precisely, one has $y = Ax + u + e$, where x is the approximately s-sparse signal, u is a k-sparse vector representing the corruptions and e is bounded noise, i.e. $\|e\|_{\ell^2} \leq \eta$. For recovery, it is natural to promote sparsity in both x and u, for instance, by solving the *augmented QCBP* problem

$$\min_{\substack{z \in \mathbb{C}^N \\ w \in \mathbb{C}^m}} \lambda \|z\|_{\ell^1} + \|w\|_{\ell^1} \text{ subject to } \|Az + w - y\|_{\ell^2} \leq \eta.$$

See, for instance, [315, 323, 381, 452, 505]. Compressed sensing recovery guarantees have been shown for this model. In particular, when A is a Gaussian random matrix, an RIP-type analysis shown in [323] gives that

$$\|\hat{x} - x\|_{\ell^2} \lesssim \frac{\sigma_s(x)_{\ell^1}}{\sqrt{s}} + \eta, \tag{6.22}$$

with high probability, provided $\lambda \asymp \sqrt{k/s}$, $m \gtrsim s \cdot \log(eN/s)$ and $k \leq cm$ for some numerical constant $0 < c < 1$. Hence, somewhat remarkably, a constant fraction of unknown corruptions can be successfully overcome. Unfortunately, such a strong guarantee does not hold for other measurement matrices (e.g. subsampled unitary matrices) [5], unless the corruptions are assumed to be random in a suitable sense [323].

Note that when $\eta = 0$ the problem (6.22), after eliminating the auxiliary variable w, reduces to the *LAD–LASSO* problem

$$\min_{z \in \mathbb{C}^N} \lambda \|z\|_{\ell^1} + \|Az - y\|_{\ell^1}.$$

The *Least Absolute Deviations (LAD)* is a classical tool in statistics [73]. The LAD–LASSO has been considered in, for instance, [221, 222, 487, 509, 510]. Compressed sensing analysis via the rNSP has been presented in [4].

7 Optimization for Compressed Sensing

In Chapters 5 and 6 we saw that decoders based on the QCBP, U-LASSO or SR-LASSO optimization problems give accurate and stable recovery of approximately sparse vectors (from now on, we no longer consider the C-LASSO problem due to the parameter sensitivity issue discussed in Chapter 6). Yet, these decoders are not *algorithms*, since they involve exact minimizers of the corresponding problems. The purpose of this chapter is to develop practical methods for solving these optimization problems.

We commence with a short overview of several features of optimization for imaging in §7.1 and §7.2. We then focus on three main approaches: *forward–backward splitting* (§7.4), which leads to *ISTA* and *FISTA* for solving the U-LASSO problem, the *primal–dual iteration* (§7.5) and *Nesterov's method* (§7.6), which leads to *NESTA* for solving QCBP. These approaches represent two different methodologies for handling nonsmooth objective functions, such as those found in optimization problems for compressed sensing. The first two split the problem into smaller subproblems which can be solved more easily, while the third uses controlled smoothing of the objective function.

Several remarks are in order. First, this chapter only touches upon the substantial topic of optimization methods for large-scale problems – a more comprehensive treatment of this subject would warrant a book in its own right. In the Notes section we list references for the interested reader. Second, our focus is on modern, *first-order* methods, since these are most practical for the problems that commonly arise in imaging. Third, our presentation is purposefully informal in places, so as to not get derailed by technical issues. Fourth, this chapter is about methods. The developments needed to design efficient software, e.g. parameter selection and stopping criteria, are outside its scope.

Finally, we note that this chapter relies heavily on material from Appendix D. The reader may wish to review this material first.

7.1 Minimizers, Not Minimum Values

We commence this chapter with an important remark. Consider the optimization problem

$$\min_{x \in \mathbb{R}^N} f(x), \tag{7.1}$$

where $f: \mathbb{R}^N \to \mathbb{R}$ is a convex objective function. Much of classical optimization focuses on accurately computing the minimum value $\hat{f} = f(\hat{x})$ of f (here $\hat{x}$ denotes a minimizer). Standard analysis of optimization algorithms, some of which we will see later, generally provides error bounds on $f(\tilde{x}) - f(\hat{x})$, where $\tilde{x}$ is the computed candidate minimizer. Yet in compressed sensing, our main concern is how well $\tilde{x}$ approximates a true minimizer $\hat{x}$. After all, our aim is to accurately recover the unknown image. These, however, are fundamentally different problems. As we shall see next, closeness of the objective function does not necessarily imply closeness of $\tilde{x}$ to a minimizer $\hat{x}$. That is to say, in general

$$f(\tilde{x}) - f(\hat{x}) \leq \zeta \quad \not\Rightarrow \quad \|\tilde{x} - \hat{x}\|_{\ell^2} \leq C\zeta, \quad \forall \zeta > 0, \tag{7.2}$$

for any constant $C > 0$.

7.1.1 A Benign Looking, but Challenging Linear Program

We now show this via a simple example. Consider the problem

$$\min_{x \in \mathbb{R}^2} x_1 + x_2 \text{ subject to } x_1 + (1-\delta)x_2 = 1, \; x_1, x_2 \geq 0, \tag{7.3}$$

where δ is a parameter. This is a type of linear programming problem (see Remark 7.1). When $\delta \neq 0$ it has the unique minimizer

$$\hat{x} = \begin{pmatrix} 1 \\ 0 \end{pmatrix}, \quad \delta > 0, \qquad \hat{x} = \begin{pmatrix} 0 \\ \frac{1}{1-\delta} \end{pmatrix}, \quad \delta < 0, \tag{7.4}$$

and when $\delta = 0$ it has infinitely many minimizers, given by

$$\hat{x} = \begin{pmatrix} t \\ 1-t \end{pmatrix}, \quad 0 \leq t \leq 1.$$

The optimal value of the objective function is $\min\{\frac{1}{1-\delta}, 1\}$.

Remark 7.1 A *linear programming problem* is a problem of the form

$$\min_{z \in \mathbb{R}^N} c^\top z \text{ subject to } Az = b, \; z \geq 0, \tag{7.5}$$

where $c \in \mathbb{R}^N$, $A \in \mathbb{R}^{m \times N}$ and $b \in \mathbb{R}^m$ are given. The constraint $z \geq 0$ means that each component of z is nonnegative.

Even though it appears very simple, computing minimizers of (7.3) proves to be a challenge for standard algorithms. To illustrate, we consider Matlab's `linprog` command – a well-established and reliable optimization algorithm for linear programs. This general-purpose algorithm offers three different solvers: 'dual-simplex' (the default), 'interior-point' and 'interior-point-legacy'. Given the input $A \in \mathbb{R}^{m \times N}$, $c \in \mathbb{R}^N$ and $b \in \mathbb{R}^m$, `linprog` strives to compute a minimizer of the linear program (7.5) (other forms of linear programs can also be considered, but this suffices for our purposes). Besides a minimizer, `linprog` also computes an additional output, `EXITFLAG`. This is an integer corresponding to a reason for why the algorithm halted. The possible values and reasons are listed in Table 7.1. Note that +1 indicates convergence to a minimizer, with all other values indicating some form of failure.

Table 7.1 Possible values for the `EXITFLAG` output of `linprog` and the corresponding reason why the algorithm halted.

+3	The solution is feasible with respect to the relative `ConstraintTolerance` tolerance, but is not feasible with respect to the absolute tolerance.
+1	Function converged to a solution `x`.
0	Number of iterations exceeded `options.MaxIterations` or solution time in seconds exceeded `options.MaxTime`.
−2	No feasible point was found.
−3	Problem is unbounded.
−4	`NaN` value was encountered during execution of the algorithm.
−5	Both primal and dual problems are infeasible.
−7	Search direction became too small. No further progress could be made.
−9	Solver lost feasibility.

Table 7.2 The output of `linprog` applied to (7.3) for the three algorithms 'dual-simplex', 'interior-point' and 'interior-point-legacy'. The table shows $\|\hat{x} - \tilde{x}\|_{\ell^2}$ (Min. err), $f(\tilde{x}) - f(\hat{x})$ (Obj. err) and the value of `EXITFLAG` (Fl.), where $\hat{x}$ is the true minimizer (7.4), $\tilde{x}$ is the computed minimizer and $f(x) = x_1 + x_2$ is the objective function. Note that machine epsilon is 2^{-52}.

	Dual-simplex			Interior-point			Interior-point-legacy		
δ	Obj. err.	Min. err.	Fl.	Obj. err.	Min. err.	Fl.	Obj. err.	Min. err.	Fl.
2^{-1}	0	0	1	0	0	1	2.7e-12	6.0e-12	1
2^{-15}	0	0	1	0	0	1	6.4e-10	3.0e-05	1
2^{-20}	0	0	1	0	0	1	4.7e-13	7.0e-07	1
2^{-24}	0	0	1	0	0	1	3.3e-15	7.1e-08	1
2^{-26}	1.5e-08	1.4e+00	1	1.5e-08	1.4e+00	1	1.3e-09	1.2e-01	1
2^{-28}	3.7e-09	1.4e+00	1	3.7e-09	1.4e+00	1	1.2e-09	4.6e-01	1
2^{-30}	9.3e-10	1.4e+00	1	9.3e-10	1.4e+00	1	4.7e-10	7.1e-01	1

In Table 7.2 we apply the three `linprog` algorithms (with default settings) to the problem (7.3) with different values of δ. The results are eyebrow raising! Not only does `linprog` completely fail to compute a minimizer accurately, it also fails to recognize that the computed minimizer is incorrect. In all cases, `EXITFLAG` returns a value +1, indicating a successful termination.

7.1.2 Inexact Input and Paradoxical Issues when Computing Minimizers

This phenomenon can be traced to a fundamental issue at the heart of scientific computing: namely, algorithms work with *inexact* inputs. Real numbers can only be represented approximately on a computer as finite strings of binary digits. Thus, an algorithm for solving the linear program (7.5) does not generally have access to the true inputs A, c and b, but rather approximations $A' \approx A$, $c' \approx c$ and $b' \approx b$. Note that this is not just an issue for irrational input numbers. Numbers are represented in base-2 in standard hardware, hence even the base-10 rational 0.1 will end up being approximated. Further complicating matters, computers also commit round-off errors when performing the standard arithmetic operations (addition, subtraction, multiplication and division) on which all algorithms are based.[1]

It transpires that this phenomenon is not a failure of `linprog`. In fact:

> No algorithm can generally succeed in solving problems such as (7.5) down to an arbitrary accuracy when given inexact input.

The precise statement to this effect, Theorem 8.18, is presented in the next chapter, since it requires a series of formal definitions. We note, however, that this result holds even when the input can be made arbitrarily accurate – in a floating point architecture, for example, this can be done by decreasing machine epsilon. It also holds even when the arithmetic operations that constitute the algorithm are performed exactly.

This is a negative result. It immediately raises the following question:

> Is it possible to compute approximate minimizers of the standard convex optimization problems used in compressed sensing, and if so, why?

This is the focus of Chapter 8. Fortunately, as noted in §1.5.5, the answer is yes! Compressed sensing problems form a sufficiently nice subclass of inputs, where properties such as the rNSP imply computability of approximate minimizers down to the accuracy that is needed in practice – namely, the standard compressed sensing error bound.

7.2 Flavours of Optimization for Compressive Imaging

Although the reader may be justifiably concerned, we now put this issue aside and devote the remainder of this chapter to introducing various algorithms for solving the convex optimization problems arising in compressed sensing. In order to initiate this study, we first make a series of remarks.

7.2.1 Reformulations

As discussed in Chapter 5, in the absence of noise the simplest optimization problem for compressed sensing is Basis Pursuit (BP). Over the reals, this takes the form

$$\min_{z \in \mathbb{R}^N} \|z\|_{\ell^1} \text{ subject to } Az = y, \tag{7.6}$$

where $A \in \mathbb{R}^{m \times N}$ and $y \in \mathbb{R}^m$.

The BP problem can be recast as a linear programming problem. Given $z = (z_i)_{i=1}^N$, we first define the slack variables $z_i^+ = \max\{z_i, 0\}$ and $z_i^- = \max\{-z_i, 0\}$ so that $z_i = z_i^+ - z_i^-$, and then set

$$\tilde{z} = \begin{pmatrix} z^+ \\ z^- \end{pmatrix} \in \mathbb{R}^{2N}.$$

[1] In fact, the input to `linprog` in Table 7.2 is exact since δ is purposefully chosen as a power of two. Hence, the error in the output is caused solely by the round-off error in the computation. However, round-off errors can often be modelled by considering the same algorithm applied with exact operations to an inexact input. Thus, we consider the setting of inexact input in what follows.

Next, we let $\tilde{A} \in \mathbb{R}^{m \times 2N} = (A| - A)$ be the horizontal concatenation of the matrices A and $-A$. It now follows immediately that (7.6) is equivalent to

$$\min_{\tilde{z} \in \mathbb{R}^{2N}} \sum_{i=1}^{2N} \tilde{z}_i \text{ subject to } \tilde{A}\tilde{z} = y, \; \tilde{z} \geq 0, \tag{7.7}$$

which is a linear program of the form (7.5).

What about QCBP? Consider the QCBP problem over the complex numbers

$$\min_{z \in \mathbb{C}^N} \|z\|_{\ell^1} \text{ subject to } \|Az - y\|_{\ell^2} \leq \eta,$$

where $A \in \mathbb{C}^{m \times N}$, $y \in \mathbb{C}^m$ and $\eta \geq 0$. This cannot be converted into a linear program as with BP. But it turns out that it can be recast in a similar way into a related problem, known as a *convex quadratic program*. We omit the details.

Linear and convex quadratic programs are fundamental classes of problems in convex optimization. One of its great achievements has been the development of effective algorithms for solving these problems, the so-called *interior point* methods. These methods offer high accuracy, in the sense of rapid convergence of the objective function to the true minimum value. Nowadays, they are used in many standard software packages, including Matlab's `linprog`.

So why not simply convert BP or QCBP to a linear or convex quadratic program, and use interior point methods? The reason is that imaging problems are typically large scale, often involving millions of variables. Interior point methods, which require both gradients *and* Hessians of the objective function (the latter being an $N \times N$ matrix), generally have too high a computational cost and require too much memory to be practical for such problems.

7.2.2 First-Order Methods

Instead, we consider so-called *first-order* methods. These methods use only the gradient (or subgradient) of the objective function, and while they generally converge more slowly than interior point methods, they typically have a lower computational cost per iteration. For problems such as QCBP, the main cost is performing several matrix–vector multiplications with A and A^*, i.e. $x \mapsto Ax$ and $y \mapsto A^*y$. As discussed in Part I, these operations can often be done efficiently in imaging via fast transforms. Hence, each iteration can be computed cheaply. In addition, high accuracy is simply not needed in many imaging problems: after all, the eyeball metric certainly cannot tell the difference between three digits of accuracy and six. Thus, the slower convergence of such methods is often tolerable in practice.

7.2.3 Real Variables

Many imaging problems involve real-valued images. Yet some, notably MRI, involve complex-valued images. In this chapter we will generally consider real-valued optimization problems, such as the real QCBP problem

$$\min_{z \in \mathbb{R}^N} \|z\|_{\ell^1} \text{ subject to } \|Az - y\|_{\ell^2} \leq \eta, \qquad A \in \mathbb{R}^{m \times N},\ y \in \mathbb{R}^m. \tag{7.8}$$

This is primarily to keep the presentation straightforward. Most of what we say extends to the complex case, for instance the complex QCBP problem

$$\min_{z \in \mathbb{C}^N} \|z\|_{\ell^1} \text{ subject to } \|Az - y\|_{\ell^2} \leq \eta, \qquad A \in \mathbb{C}^{m \times N},\ y \in \mathbb{C}^m. \tag{7.9}$$

This can be achieved by defining new variables $u = \mathrm{Re}\,(z)$ and $v = \mathrm{Im}\,(z)$ and replacing (7.9) with the equivalent real-valued problem

$$\min_{u,v \in \mathbb{R}^N} \sum_{i=1}^{N} \sqrt{u_i^2 + v_i^2} \text{ subject to } \left\| \begin{pmatrix} \mathrm{Re}\,(A) & -\mathrm{Im}\,(A) \\ \mathrm{Im}\,(A) & \mathrm{Re}\,(A) \end{pmatrix} \begin{pmatrix} u \\ v \end{pmatrix} - \begin{pmatrix} \mathrm{Re}\,(y) \\ \mathrm{Im}\,(y) \end{pmatrix} \right\|_{\ell^2} \leq \eta.$$

This problem is amenable to the methods we present in subsequent sections. Wherever appropriate in what follows, we also comment on the extension of the methods derived to problems involving complex variables.

7.3 Gradient Descent

The remainder of this chapter develops first-order methods for solving convex optimization problems of the form (7.1).

We commence with the most straightforward setting, where $f : \mathbb{R}^N \to \mathbb{R}$ is a differentiable and convex function. In this case, the most elementary way to compute solutions of (7.1) is via *gradient descent* (also known as *steepest descent*). Here, given an initial point $x_0 \in \mathbb{R}^N$, one generates the sequence

$$x_{n+1} = x_n - \tau \nabla f(x_n), \qquad n = 0, 1, \ldots, \tag{7.10}$$

where $\tau > 0$ is a fixed *stepsize*. This iteration has a simple interpretation. At each step, we simply move in the direction $-\nabla f(x_n)$ along which f is most rapidly decreasing.

As with any iterative algorithm, we are interested in the behaviour of the iterates x_n as $n \to \infty$. For this, we first make the following additional assumption on f:

Definition 7.2 A continuously differentiable function $f : D \to \mathbb{R}$ over a domain $D \subseteq \mathbb{R}^N$ has *Lipschitz continuous* gradient if

$$\|\nabla f(x) - \nabla f(y)\|_{\ell^2} \leq L\|x - y\|_{\ell^2}, \qquad \forall x, y \in D, \tag{7.11}$$

for some $L > 0$. The smallest constant L such that (7.11) holds is known as the *Lipschitz constant*.

Suppose that f satisfies this property. Then a standard result asserts that the sequence $\{x_n\}$ generated by (7.10) converges to a minimizer $\hat{x}$ provided the stepsize τ satisfies $\tau < 2/L$. One also has the following rate of convergence for the objective function:

$$f(x_n) - f(\hat{x}) = O(1/n), \qquad n \to \infty.$$

It transpires that this rate is not optimal. The idea behind *acceleration* is to modify the gradient descent step (7.10) so that it depends on more than one previous iterate, in combination with varying the stepsize τ from iteration to iteration. The former is often referred to as incorporating *memory* into the update step. It helps achieve faster convergence by avoiding the well-known *zigzag* phenomenon in the standard gradient descent. Nesterov's method, introduced in §7.6, is an example of an *accelerated gradient* scheme. Under suitable conditions, Nesterov's method (as well as other accelerated gradient schemes) achieve the convergence rate

$$f(x_n) - f(\hat{x}) = \mathcal{O}(1/n^2), \qquad n \to \infty,$$

which is optimal for first-order methods (see the Notes section).

7.4 Forward–Backward Splitting

Gradient descent is limited by the requirement that f be differentiable. This is, of course, not valid for ℓ^1-minimization problems. A potential way to overcome this issue is to replace $\nabla f(x_n)$ by a suitable element of the subdifferential $\partial f(x_n)$ (see §D.2). This gives a so-called *subgradient descent* method. Unfortunately, this iteration usually converges very slowly, with the error in the objective function decreasing like $\mathcal{O}(1/\sqrt{n})$ as $n \to \infty$. Fortunately, many problems are amenable to a better approach based on *splitting*.

7.4.1 Derivation

Many optimization problems – for instance, the U-LASSO problem – take the form

$$\min_{x \in \mathbb{R}^N} f(x) + g(x), \tag{7.12}$$

where $g \colon \mathbb{R}^N \to (-\infty, \infty]$ is convex, lower semicontinuous and proper (see §D.1) and $f \colon \mathbb{R}^N \to \mathbb{R}$ is convex and continuously differentiable with Lipschitz continuous gradient. The idea of splitting methods is to perform gradient steps in the differentiable function f and *proximal gradient* steps in the nondifferentiable function g.

Suppose for the moment that $g = \delta_C$ is the indicator function (see (D.3)) of some nonempty, closed and convex set C. Then (7.12) is equivalent to the constrained minimization problem

$$\min_{x \in C} f(x). \tag{7.13}$$

This problem can be solved by a simple modification of gradient descent, which then leads to a way to tackle the general problem (7.12). To see how to do this, consider the gradient descent update step (7.10). This can be rewritten as the minimization problem

$$x_{n+1} = \operatorname*{argmin}_{x \in \mathbb{R}^N} \left\{ f(x_n) + \langle \nabla f(x_n), x - x_n \rangle + \frac{1}{2\tau} \|x - x_n\|^2_{\ell^2} \right\}.$$

The first term is a local linear approximation of f around $x = x_n$, and the second term is a *proximity* term, which encourages the x_{n+1} to not deviate too far from x_n.

This formulation immediately suggests a way to solve (7.13). We simply replace the minimization over $\mathbb{R}^N$ by a minimization over C, to get

$$x_{n+1} = \underset{x \in C}{\operatorname{argmin}} \left\{ f(x_n) + \langle \nabla f(x_n), x - x_n \rangle + \frac{1}{2\tau} \|x - x_n\|_{\ell^2}^2 \right\}.$$

After performing several manipulations, we observe that this can be written as

$$x_{n+1} = \underset{x \in C}{\operatorname{argmin}} \frac{1}{2} \|x - (x_n - \tau \nabla f(x_n))\|_{\ell^2}^2. \tag{7.14}$$

The right-hand side is precisely the *projection* proj_C onto C (see (D.6)) of $x_n - \tau \nabla f(x_n)$. Therefore, we get the iteration

$$x_{n+1} = \operatorname{proj}_C(x_n - \tau \nabla f(x_n)), \qquad n = 0, 1, \ldots. \tag{7.15}$$

This is known as the *projected gradient* method.

Now, observe that we can write (7.14) as

$$x_{n+1} = \underset{x \in \mathbb{R}^N}{\operatorname{argmin}} \left\{ \delta_C(x) + f(x_n) + \langle \nabla f(x_n), x - x_n \rangle + \frac{1}{2\tau} \|x - x_n\|_{\ell^2}^2 \right\}.$$

This provides a means to tackle the general problem (7.12). We simply replace δ_C by the function g, and then perform the same manipulations to get

$$\begin{aligned} x_{n+1} &= \underset{x \in \mathbb{R}^N}{\operatorname{argmin}} \left\{ g(x) + f(x_n) + \langle \nabla f(x_n), x - x_n \rangle + \frac{1}{2\tau} \|x - x_n\|_{\ell^2}^2 \right\} \\ &= \underset{x \in \mathbb{R}^N}{\operatorname{argmin}} \left\{ \tau g(x) + \frac{1}{2} \|x - (x_n - \tau \nabla f(x_n))\|_{\ell^2}^2 \right\}. \end{aligned}$$

The final expression is precisely the *proximal map* of the function τg (see §D.5). This gives rise to the new scheme

$$x_{n+1} = \operatorname{prox}_{\tau g}(x_n - \tau \nabla f(x_n)), \qquad n = 0, 1, \ldots, \tag{7.16}$$

known as the *forward–backward* iteration. Under suitable conditions, it produces iterates for which the error in the objective function behaves like $\mathcal{O}(1/n)$, exactly as with gradient descent for smooth objective functions.

We remark that while this scheme does not require g to be differentiable, it does require g to be *simple* in the sense that its proximal map should be easy to evaluate. Fortunately this is the case for problems such as U-LASSO, as we show in §7.4.2.

Before that, a word on terminology. The update $x_n \mapsto x_n - \tau \nabla f(x_n)$ is referred to as a *forward* (or, to use the language of numerical analysis, *explicit*) gradient step in f. Similarly, an application of $\operatorname{prox}_{\tau g}$ can be viewed as a *backward* (or *implicit*) proximal gradient step in g. This can be seen by noting (see (D.17)) that $\operatorname{prox}_{\tau g}$ is equal to the resolvent $(I + \tau \partial g)^{-1}$ of $\tau \partial g$. We therefore interpret the forward–backward scheme (7.16) as a forward gradient step in f followed by a backward (proximal) gradient step in g.

Note that when $g = 0$, (7.16) is precisely gradient descent (7.10) for minimizing f. On the other hand, when $f = 0$, in which case $x_{n+1} = \operatorname{prox}_{\tau g}(x_n)$, (7.16) is known as the *proximal point* algorithm.

Remark 7.3 One may also develop forward–backward splitting as a fixed-point iteration.[2] Recall from §D.3 that $\hat{x}$ is a minimizer of (7.12) if and only if

$$0 \in \partial(f+g)(\hat{x}) = \nabla f(\hat{x}) + \partial g(\hat{x}).$$

Multiplying both sides by τ, adding $\hat{x}$ and subtracting $\tau\nabla f(\hat{x})$ gives

$$\hat{x} - \tau\nabla f(\hat{x}) \in \hat{x} + \tau\partial g(\hat{x}).$$

But by (D.16) this is equivalent to the fixed-point equation

$$\hat{x} = \mathrm{prox}_{\tau g}\left(\hat{x} - \tau\nabla f(\hat{x})\right).$$

Hence (7.16) is precisely the fixed-point iteration applied to this equation.

7.4.2 ISTA and FISTA

As an example, consider the U-LASSO problem

$$\min_{x\in\mathbb{R}^N} \lambda\|x\|_{\ell^1} + \|Ax-y\|_{\ell^2}^2. \tag{7.17}$$

We now apply the forward–backward scheme to this problem using

$$f(x) = \|Ax-y\|_{\ell^2}^2, \qquad g(x) = \lambda\|x\|_{\ell^1}.$$

Observe that f is differentiable and $\nabla f(x) = 2A^\top(Ax-y)$ is Lipschitz continuous with constant $L = 2\|A\|_{\ell^2}^2$. In order to define the proximal map of g we now introduce the following function:

Definition 7.4 (Soft thresholding) The scalar *soft thresholding* (or *soft shrinkage*) operator $\mathcal{S}_\tau : \mathbb{R} \to \mathbb{R}$ is defined by

$$\mathcal{S}_\tau(x) = \begin{cases} \mathrm{sign}(x)(|x|-\tau) & |x| \geq \tau \\ 0 & \text{otherwise} \end{cases}, \qquad x \in \mathbb{R}. \tag{7.18}$$

The vector soft thresholding operator $\mathcal{S}_\tau : \mathbb{R}^N \to \mathbb{R}^N$ is defined as the componentwise application of its scalar counterpart, i.e.

$$(\mathcal{S}_\tau(x))_i = \begin{cases} \mathrm{sign}(x_i)(|x_i|-\tau) & |x_i| \geq \tau \\ 0 & \text{otherwise} \end{cases}, \qquad x = (x_i)_{i=1}^N.$$

Figure 7.1 illustrates this function in the scalar case. As shown in §D.5, the soft thresholding operator is precisely the proximal map for the ℓ^1-norm. Specifically,

$$\mathrm{prox}_{\lambda\|\cdot\|_{\ell^1}} = \mathcal{S}_\lambda.$$

Hence, substituting this and the expression for ∇f into (7.16), we now arrive at the forward–backward iteration for (7.17):

$$x_{n+1} = \mathcal{S}_{\lambda\tau}\left(x_n - 2\tau A^\top(Ax_n - y)\right), \qquad n = 0, 1, 2, \ldots.$$

[2] The *fixed-point iteration* for solving the fixed-point equation $x = h(x)$ is given by $x_{n+1} = h(x_n)$.

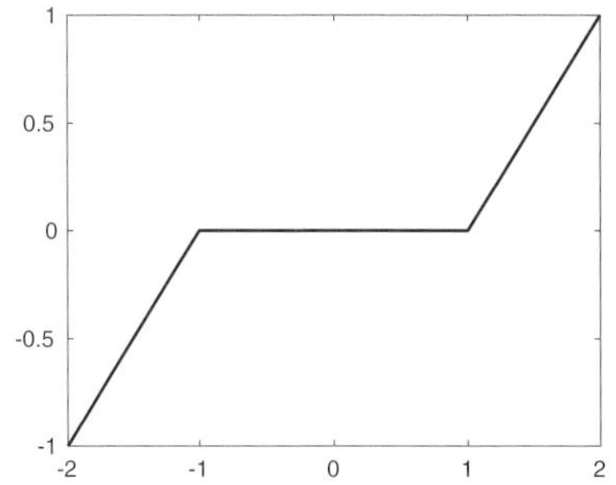

Figure 7.1 The scalar soft thresholding operator $\mathcal{S}_1$.

Algorithm 7.1: ISTA for the U-LASSO problem (7.17)

input: measurements y, measurement matrix A, parameter $\lambda > 0$, stepsize $\tau > 0$, initial point x_0

output: $\tilde{x}$, an approximate minimizer of (7.17)

for $n = 0, 1, \dots$ **do**

$\quad x_{n+1} = \mathcal{S}_{\lambda\tau}\left(x_n - 2\tau A^\top(Ax_n - y)\right)$

end

This is commonly known as the *Iterative Shrinkage-Thresholding Algorithm (ISTA)*. It is summarized in Algorithm 7.1.

The convergence of ISTA is well understood. For appropriate choices of τ, it achieves an $\mathcal{O}(1/n)$ convergence rate to the optimal value of the objective function. To attain an $\mathcal{O}(1/n^2)$ convergence rate, one can use a memory-exploiting acceleration procedure, much as with classical gradient descent. One such method is known as *Fast ISTA (FISTA)*, which is shown in Algorithm 7.2. We omit its derivation.

Remark 7.5 The update steps in ISTA and FISTA are extremely cheap to apply. They require just two matrix–vector multiplications per step, along with vector operations and soft thresholding. Specifically, the computational cost of one step of ISTA or FISTA is $2N_A + \mathcal{O}(N)$, where N_A is the maximum number of arithmetic operations required to calculate either $x \mapsto Ax$ or $y \mapsto A^\top y$. For instance, if A is a subsampled Fourier or Hadamard matrix, possibly combined with a discrete wavelet sparsifying transform, then $N_A = \mathcal{O}(N \log(N))$. This gives a total cost per iteration of $\mathcal{O}(N \log(N))$ operations.

Remark 7.6 Algorithms 7.1 and 7.2 easily generalize to the complex case, where $A \in \mathbb{C}^{m \times N}$ and $y \in \mathbb{C}^m$. One simply replaces $A^\top$ by A^* and the real soft thresholding operator by its complex version $\mathcal{S}_\tau : \mathbb{C} \to \mathbb{C}$. This is defined exactly as in (7.18) but with $\mathrm{sign}(z)$ now representing the complex sign function (5.36).

7.5 The Primal–Dual Iteration

While useful for solving problems such as U-LASSO, forward–backward splitting has the disadvantage that it requires f to be differentiable. This fails to be the case for

Algorithm 7.2: FISTA for the U-LASSO problem (7.17)

input: measurements y, measurement matrix A, parameter $\lambda > 0$, stepsize $\tau > 0$, initial point x_0

output: $\tilde{x}$, an approximate minimizer of (7.17)

Set $z_0 = x_0$, $t_0 = 1$

for $n = 0, 1, \dots$ **do**

$x_{n+1} = \mathcal{S}_{\lambda\tau}\left(z_n - 2\tau A^\top (Az_n - y)\right)$

$t_{n+1} = \frac{1+\sqrt{1+4t_n^2}}{2}$

$z_{n+1} = x_{n+1} + \left(\frac{t_n - 1}{t_{n+1}}\right)(x_{n+1} - x_n)$

end

the SR-LASSO problem, where $f(x) = \|Ax - y\|_{\ell^2}$, or indeed for QCBP, where f is the indicator function of the feasible set. The *primal–dual iteration*, also known as the *Chambolle–Pock algorithm*, is a rather general way to tackle problems where both terms in (7.12) may be nondifferentiable. We now describe this method. Alternative and related approaches such as ADMM are discussed briefly in the Notes section.

7.5.1 General Formulation

With problems such as these in mind, we now slightly generalize (7.12) and consider

$$\min_{x \in \mathbb{R}^N} f(Bx) + g(x), \tag{7.19}$$

where $B \in \mathbb{R}^{m \times N}$ is a matrix, $f \colon \mathbb{R}^m \to (-\infty, \infty]$ and $g \colon \mathbb{R}^m \to (-\infty, \infty]$ are convex, lower semicontinuous and proper. We term (7.19) the *primal* problem. As we see below, including B in (7.19) allows one to deal with the measurement matrix A in QCBP or SR-LASSO explicitly, which is often a more convenient way to proceed.

By the assumptions on f, we have $f^{**} = f$, where f^{**} is its biconjugate (see §D.4). Hence, we may write $f(Bx) = f^{**}(Bx) = \max_{\xi \in \mathbb{R}^m} \langle \xi, Bx \rangle - f^*(\xi)$ to give

$$\min_{x \in \mathbb{R}^N} f(Bx) + g(x) = \min_{x \in \mathbb{R}^N} \max_{\xi \in \mathbb{R}^m} \mathcal{L}(x, \xi), \tag{7.20}$$

where

$$\mathcal{L}(x, \xi) = \langle \xi, Bx \rangle - f^*(\xi) + g(x) \tag{7.21}$$

is the *Lagrangian*. This is referred to as the *saddle-point* formulation of the problem. Under mild assumptions on f and g, which are always satisfied for the problems in this book, one can interchange the maximization and minimization in (7.20), to yield

$$\min_{x \in \mathbb{R}^N} f(Bx) + g(x) = \max_{\xi \in \mathbb{R}^m} \min_{x \in \mathbb{R}^N} \mathcal{L}(x, \xi) = \max_{\xi \in \mathbb{R}^m} -f^*(\xi) - g^*(-B^\top \xi).$$

The problem

$$\max_{\xi \in \mathbb{R}^m} -f^*(\xi) - g^*(-B^\top \xi) \tag{7.22}$$

Algorithm 7.3: The primal–dual iteration for (7.20)

---

input: functions f, g, matrix B, stepsizes $\tau, \sigma > 0$, initial points (x_0, ξ_0)
output: $(\tilde{x}, \tilde{\xi})$, an approximate solution to (7.20)

for $n = 0, 1, \ldots$ **do**
  $x_{n+1} = \mathrm{prox}_{\tau g}(x_n - \tau B^\top \xi_n)$
  $\xi_{n+1} = \mathrm{prox}_{\sigma f^*}(\xi_n + \sigma B(2x_{n+1} - x_n))$
end

---

is known as the *(Fenchel–Rockafeller) dual* problem of (7.19). We say that $(\hat{x}, \hat{\xi})$ is a *primal–dual* optimal pair if $\hat{x}$ is a solution to the primal problem (7.19) and $\hat{\xi}$ is a solution to the dual problem (7.22). Under mild conditions, every primal–dual optimal pair is also a solution to the saddle-point problem (7.20).

With this in mind, the idea of a primal–dual method is to search for solutions of the saddle-point problem (7.20); it is a type of *saddle-point* method. It does so by alternating between minimizing the primal variable x and maximizing the dual variable ξ, performing a forward–backward step in each variable at every iteration. It is tempting at first to formulate the iteration as follows:

$$
\begin{aligned}
x_{n+1} &= \mathrm{prox}_{\tau g}(x_n - \tau B^\top \xi_n), \\
\xi_{n+1} &= \mathrm{prox}_{\sigma f^*}(\xi_n + \sigma B x_{n+1}),
\end{aligned}
\tag{7.23}
$$

where $\tau, \sigma > 0$ are stepsize parameters. Unfortunately, this iteration may not have desirable convergence properties. A remedy is to perform an *over-relaxation* in the ξ_n update, replacing (7.23) with

$$
\begin{aligned}
x_{n+1} &= \mathrm{prox}_{\tau g}(x_n - \tau B^\top \xi_n), \\
\xi_{n+1} &= \mathrm{prox}_{\sigma f^*}(\xi_n + \sigma B(2x_{n+1} - x_n)).
\end{aligned}
\tag{7.24}
$$

This is known as the *primal–dual* iteration. It is summarized in Algorithm 7.3.

Remark 7.7 Much like forward–backward splitting (see Remark 7.3), (7.24) also has a fixed-point interpretation. Observe that a saddle point $(\hat{x}, \hat{\xi})$ of the Lagrangian

$$
\mathcal{L}(x, \xi) = \langle \xi, Bx \rangle - f^*(\xi) + g(x)
$$

of (7.20) satisfies

$$
0 \in \partial g(\hat{x}) + B^\top \hat{\xi}, \qquad 0 \in \partial f^*(\hat{\xi}) - B\hat{x}.
$$

We now manipulate each equation as in Remark 7.3, to get

$$
\hat{x} - \tau B^\top \hat{\xi} \in \hat{x} + \tau \partial g(\hat{x}), \qquad \hat{\xi} + \sigma B\hat{x} \in \hat{\xi} + \sigma f^*(\hat{\xi}).
$$

Hence, by (D.16) this is equivalent to the fixed-point equation

$$
\begin{pmatrix} \hat{x} \\ \hat{\xi} \end{pmatrix} = \begin{pmatrix} \mathrm{prox}_{\tau g}(\hat{x} - \tau B^\top \hat{\xi}) \\ \mathrm{prox}_{\sigma f^*}(\hat{\xi} + \sigma B\hat{x}) \end{pmatrix}
$$

and (7.24) can be considered a type of fixed-point iteration for solving it.

7.5.2 Convergence of the Primal–Dual Iteration

Since it will be used in the next chapter, we now state a convergence result for the primal–dual iteration. The following result pertains to the so-called *ergodic* sequences $X_n = \frac{1}{n}\sum_{i=1}^{n} x_i$ and $\Xi_n = \frac{1}{n}\sum_{i=1}^{n} \xi_i$.

Theorem 7.8 *Let f, g be convex, lower semicontinuous functions, $B \in \mathbb{R}^{m\times N}$ and $\tau, \sigma > 0$ satisfy $(\tau\sigma)^{-1} \geq \|B\|_{\ell^2}^2$. Let $(x_0, \xi_0) \in \mathbb{R}^N \times \mathbb{R}^m$ be given and consider the sequence $\{(x_n, \xi_n)\}$ produced by Algorithm 7.3. Then for every $(x, \xi) \in \mathbb{R}^N \times \mathbb{R}^m$,*

$$\mathcal{L}(X_n, \xi) - \mathcal{L}(x, \Xi_n) \leq \frac{\tau^{-1}\|x - x_0\|_{\ell^2}^2 + \sigma^{-1}\|\xi - \xi_0\|_{\ell^2}^2}{n}, \tag{7.25}$$

where X_n and Ξ_n are the ergodic sequences and $\mathcal{L}$ is the Lagrangian

$$\mathcal{L}(x, \xi) = \langle \xi, Bx\rangle - f^*(\xi) + g(x).$$

To elaborate on the bound (7.25), consider the so-called *primal–dual gap*

$$\mathcal{G}(X_n, \Xi_n) = \sup_{(x,\xi)\in\mathbb{R}^N\times\mathbb{R}^m} \mathcal{L}(X_n, \xi) - \mathcal{L}(x, \Xi_n).$$

This quantity is equal to the value of the primal objective function at X_n minus the value of the dual objective function at Ξ_n. It is always nonnegative. Moreover, $\mathcal{G}(\hat{x}, \hat{\xi}) = 0$ for some primal–dual pair $(\hat{x}, \hat{\xi})$ if and only if $(\hat{x}, \hat{\xi})$ is a saddle point of the Lagrangian $\mathcal{L}$. Hence, the primal–dual gap $\mathcal{G}(X_n, \Xi_n)$ can be considered as a measure of the distance to optimality for the pair (X_n, Ξ_n).

Since its right-hand side is unbounded in $(x, \xi) \in \mathbb{R}^N \times \mathbb{R}^m$, it is clear that (7.25) does not give a bound for $\mathcal{G}(X_n, \Xi_n)$. However, it does provide a bound for the so-called *partial primal–dual gap* in certain cases. Given open sets $B_1 \subseteq \mathbb{R}^N$ and $B_2 \subseteq \mathbb{R}^m$, the partial primal–dual gap is defined as

$$\mathcal{G}_{B_1\times B_2}(X_n, \Xi_n) = \sup_{(x,\xi)\in B_1\times B_2} \mathcal{L}(X_n, \xi) - \mathcal{L}(x, \Xi_n).$$

If $B_1 \times B_2$ contains a saddle point, then $\mathcal{G}_{B_1\times B_2}(x, \xi) \geq 0$ with equality holding if and only if (x, ξ) is a saddle point. Hence $\mathcal{G}_{B_1\times B_2}(X_n, \Xi_n)$, like the full primal–dual gap, can also be viewed as a measure of the error in the iterate (X_n, Ξ_n). When B_1 and B_2 are bounded sets, Theorem 7.8 states that this partial gap behaves like $\mathcal{O}(1/n)$ as $n \to \infty$. Specifically, (7.25) gives

$$\mathcal{G}_{B_1\times B_2}(X_n, \Xi_n) \leq C/n, \qquad C = \tau^{-1} \sup_{x\in B_1} \|x - x_0\|_{\ell^2}^2 + \sigma^{-1} \sup_{\xi\in B_2} \|\xi - \xi_0\|_{\ell^2}^2.$$

Later, in Lemma 8.6 we see that (7.25) also gives a bound for the error in the objective function in the case of the SR-LASSO problem.

Remark 7.9 The primal–dual iteration can also be developed for a more general model problem of the form

$$\min_{x\in\mathbb{R}^N} f(Bx) + g(x) + h(x), \tag{7.26}$$

where h is assumed to be convex and differentiable with Lipschitz continuous gradient. The saddle-point formulation of this problem is

$$\max_{\xi \in \mathbb{R}^m} \min_{x \in \mathbb{R}^N} \mathcal{L}(x, \xi), \qquad \mathcal{L}(x, \xi) = \langle \xi, Bx \rangle - f^*(\xi) + g(x) + h(x),$$

and to solve it one replaces the x_n update in (7.24) with the following modified forward–backward step:

$$x_{n+1} = \mathrm{prox}_{\tau g}(x_n - (\tau B^\top \xi_n + \tau \nabla h(x_n))).$$

In particular, Theorem 7.8 holds whenever $(\tau^{-1} - L)\sigma^{-1} \geq \|B\|_{\ell^2}^2$, where L is the Lipschitz constant of h.

7.5.3 The Primal–Dual Iteration for QCBP and SR-LASSO

We now consider two applications of the primal–dual iteration. First, we consider the QCBP problem (7.8). This can be viewed as a particular case of (7.19) with

$$B = A, \qquad f(\cdot) = \delta_{\{z : \|z\|_{\ell^2} \leq \eta\}}(\cdot - y), \qquad g(\cdot) = \|\cdot\|_{\ell^1},$$

where $\delta_{\{z : \|z\|_{\ell^2} \leq \eta\}}$ is the indicator function of the set $\{z : \|z\|_{\ell^2} \leq \eta\}$, see (D.3). To derive the scheme, we need the proximal mappings of g and f^*. As noted previously,

$$\mathrm{prox}_{\tau g} = \mathcal{S}_\tau \tag{7.27}$$

is the soft thresholding operator. We next consider f. Although it is not strictly needed in order to find its proximal map, we first derive f^*. By Table D.1, we have

$$f^*(\xi) = \left(\delta_{\{z : \|z\|_{\ell^2} \leq \eta\}}(\cdot)\right)^* (\xi) + \langle y, \xi \rangle,$$

and a straightforward calculation involving the definition of the convex conjugate gives

$$f^*(\xi) = \eta \|\xi\|_{\ell^2} + \langle y, \xi \rangle.$$

Rather than using this expression, we shall instead use Moreau's identity (D.18) to compute the proximal map of f^*. This gives

$$\mathrm{prox}_{\sigma f^*}(\xi) = \xi - \sigma \mathrm{prox}_{f/\sigma}(\xi/\sigma).$$

By (D.13), we observe that the proximal map of f/σ is precisely

$$\mathrm{prox}_{f/\sigma}(\xi) = \mathrm{proj}_{\{z : \|z - y\|_{\ell^2} \leq \eta\}}(\xi) = \begin{cases} \xi & \|\xi - y\|_{\ell^2} \leq \eta \\ y + \frac{\eta}{\|\xi - y\|_{\ell^2}}(\xi - y) & \|\xi - y\|_{\ell^2} > \eta \end{cases}.$$

Here proj_C denotes the projection onto a convex set C, see (D.6). In the second step, we also used (D.7). Hence, $\mathrm{prox}_{\sigma f^*}$ is given by

$$\mathrm{prox}_{\sigma f^*}(\xi) = \begin{cases} 0 & \|\xi - \sigma y\|_{\ell^2} \leq \sigma\eta \\ \left(1 - \frac{\sigma\eta}{\|\xi - \sigma y\|_{\ell^2}}\right)(\xi - \sigma y) & \|\xi - \sigma y\|_{\ell^2} > \sigma\eta \end{cases}.$$

Combining this with the expression (7.27) now gives the primal–dual iteration for QCBP. This is shown in Algorithm 7.4.

Algorithm 7.4: The primal–dual iteration for the QCBP problem (7.8)

input: measurements y, measurement matrix A, parameter $\eta \geq 0$, stepsizes $\tau, \sigma > 0$, initial points (x_0, ξ_0)

output: $\tilde{x}$, an approximate minimizer of (7.8)

for $n = 0, 1, \dots$ **do**

$$x_{n+1} = \mathcal{S}_\tau(x_n - \tau A^\top \xi_n)$$
$$\zeta = \xi_n + \sigma A(2x_{n+1} - x_n) - \sigma y$$
$$\xi_{n+1} = \begin{cases} 0 & \|\zeta\|_{\ell^2} \leq \sigma\eta \\ \left(1 - \frac{\sigma\eta}{\|\zeta\|_{\ell^2}}\right)\zeta & \|\zeta\|_{\ell^2} > \sigma\eta \end{cases}$$

end

Next we apply the primal–dual iteration to the SR-LASSO problem

$$\min_{x \in \mathbb{R}^N} \lambda\|x\|_{\ell^1} + \|Ax - y\|_{\ell^2}. \tag{7.28}$$

We set

$$B = A, \quad f(\cdot) = \|\cdot - y\|_{\ell^2}, \quad g(\cdot) = \lambda\|\cdot\|_{\ell^1} \tag{7.29}$$

and, proceeding as before, we first calculate f^*. Table D.1 gives that

$$f^*(\xi) = (\|\cdot\|_{\ell^2})^*(\xi) + \langle y, \xi\rangle,$$

and since the dual norm of the ℓ^2-norm is the ℓ^2-norm, using (D.10) we obtain

$$f^*(\xi) = \delta_{\{z : \|z\|_{\ell^2} \leq 1\}}(\xi) + \langle y, \xi\rangle. \tag{7.30}$$

We now calculate the proximal mapping of σf^*. Simple algebraic manipulations give

$$\begin{aligned} \mathrm{prox}_{\sigma f^*}(\xi) = \underset{z : \|z\|_{\ell^2} \leq 1}{\operatorname{argmin}} \left\{\sigma\langle y, z\rangle + \frac{1}{2}\|z - \xi\|_{\ell^2}^2\right\} &= \underset{z : \|z\|_{\ell^2} \leq 1}{\operatorname{argmin}} \left\{\frac{1}{2}\|z - (\xi - \sigma y)\|_{\ell^2}^2\right\} \\ &= \mathrm{proj}_{\{z : \|z\|_{\ell^2} \leq 1\}}(\xi - \sigma y). \end{aligned}$$

Applying (D.7) once more, we deduce that

$$\mathrm{prox}_{\sigma f^*}(\xi) = \min\left\{1, \frac{1}{\|\xi - \sigma y\|_{\ell^2}}\right\}(\xi - \sigma y).$$

Finally, recalling that $\mathrm{prox}_{\tau g} = \mathcal{S}_{\tau\lambda}$, we obtain the primal–dual iteration for solving (7.28). This is shown in Algorithm 7.5.

Remark 7.10 As with ISTA/FISTA, the update steps in Algorithms 7.4 and 7.5 involve only two matrix–vector multiplications. Each step therefore requires $2N_A + \mathcal{O}(N)$ arithmetic operations, where N_A is as in Remark 7.5. Both algorithms also extend easily to the complex case in exactly the same way as described in Remark 7.6.

Remark 7.11 One can also derive a version of the primal–dual iteration for the U-LASSO problem. However, U-LASSO easily fits into the forward–backward iteration framework, yielding ISTA and its accelerated version FISTA. Generally speaking, if a problem fits into the forward–backward framework, it is often better to solve it that way.

Algorithm 7.5: The primal–dual iteration for the SR-LASSO problem (7.28)

input: measurements y, measurement matrix A, parameter $\lambda > 0$, stepsizes $\tau, \sigma > 0$, initial points (x_0, ξ_0)

output: $\tilde{x}$, an approximate minimizer of (7.28)

for $n = 0, 1, \ldots$ **do**

$x_{n+1} = \mathcal{S}_{\tau\lambda}(x_n - \tau A^\top \xi_n)$

$\zeta = \xi_n + \sigma A(2x_{n+1} - x_n) - \sigma y$

$\xi_{n+1} = \min\left\{1, \frac{1}{\|\zeta\|_{\ell^2}}\right\} \zeta$

end

7.6 Nesterov's Method and NESTA for QCBP

We conclude this chapter by introducing another algorithm for QCBP. This is based on an accelerated gradient method, known as *Nesterov's method*. This method was originally developed for smooth, constrained convex optimization problems, and later combined with *smoothing* techniques to solve certain nonsmooth problems. Its application to the QCBP problem yields the so-called *NESTA* algorithm.

7.6.1 Nesterov's Method

Consider the smooth, constrained convex optimization problem

$$\min_{x \in Q_p} f(x), \tag{7.31}$$

where $Q_p \subseteq \mathbb{R}^N$ is a closed, bounded and convex set and f is convex and continuously differentiable with Lipschitz gradient in some neighbourhood of Q_p. Here p denotes 'primal', for reasons that will become clear in a moment.

Nesterov's method makes use of a *proximity function* $p_p(x)$ for the set Q_p. A proximity function (also known as a *prox-function*) is a proper, lower semicontinuous and strongly convex function over Q_p that satisfies $\min_{x \in Q_p} p_p(x) = 0$. Such a function always exists. For example, $p_p(x) = \frac{1}{2}\|x - x_p\|_{\ell^2}^2$ for some $x_p \in Q_p$. In fact, for general p_p, if

$$x_p = \operatorname*{argmin}_{x \in Q_p} p_p(x)$$

is the so-called *prox-centre*, then property (d) of §D.3 implies that

$$p_p(x) \geq \frac{\sigma_p}{2}\|x - x_p\|_{\ell^2}^2, \quad x \in Q_p,$$

where $\sigma_p > 0$ is the strong convexity parameter of p_p.

Given p_p, Nesterov's method for (7.31) is now shown in Algorithm 7.6. We forgo the details of its derivation and simply observe that it is a type of accelerated gradient

---

Algorithm 7.6: Nesterov's method for (7.31)

---

input: function f, closed, convex set Q_p, proximity function p_p, Lipschitz constant L of f, strong convexity parameter $\sigma_p > 0$, sequences $\{\alpha_n\}_{n=0}^{\infty}$, $\{\tau_n\}_{n=0}^{\infty}$, initial point z_0

output: $\tilde{x}$, an approximate minimizer of (7.31), where $\tilde{x} = x_{n^*}$ for some n^*

for $n = 0, 1, \dots$ **do**

$x_n = \underset{x \in Q_p}{\operatorname{argmin}} \frac{L}{2} \|x - z_n\|_{\ell^2}^2 + \langle \nabla f(z_n), x - z_n \rangle$

$v_n = \underset{x \in Q_p}{\operatorname{argmin}} \frac{L}{\sigma_p} p_p(x) + \sum_{i=0}^{n} \alpha_i \langle \nabla f(z_i), x - z_i \rangle$

$z_{n+1} = \tau_n v_n + (1 - \tau_n) x_n$

end

---

method. To see this, we first note that if $\tau_n = 0$, then $z_{n+1} = x_n$ and the x_n update is

$$x_{n+1} = \underset{x \in Q_p}{\operatorname{argmin}} \frac{L}{2} \|x - x_n\|_{\ell^2}^2 + \langle \nabla f(x_n), x - x_n \rangle = \operatorname{proj}_{Q_p} \left(x_n - \frac{1}{L} \nabla f(x_n) \right).$$

In other words, the method reduces to the projected gradient method (7.15). The projected gradient method converges with rate $O(1/n)$, much like with classical gradient descent. To increase the convergence rate, Algorithm 7.6 performs two modifications. First, it introduces a sequence v_n which keeps the memory of the previously computed gradients via a weighted average. Second, it employs a proximity function to encourage the iterates v_n to not deviate too far from the prox-centre. Coupled with a suitable choice of parameters α_n and τ_n, for example

$$\alpha_n = \frac{n+1}{2}, \qquad \tau_n = \frac{2}{n+3}, \tag{7.32}$$

this gives an algorithm with an $O(1/n^2)$ convergence rate. In fact, one has the following:

Theorem 7.12 *Let $Q_p \subseteq \mathbb{R}^N$ be a closed, bounded and convex set and suppose that f is convex and differentiable with Lipschitz continuous gradient in some neighbourhood of Q_p. Then Nesterov's method (Algorithm 7.6) with α_n and τ_n as in (7.32) produces a sequence $\{x_n\}$ satisfying*

$$f(x_n) - f(\hat{x}) \leq \frac{4 L p_p(\hat{x})}{(n+1)^2 \sigma_p},$$

where $\hat{x}$ is a minimizer of (7.31) and L is the Lipschitz constant of f.

7.6.2 Smoothing

Nesterov's method can be extended to certain nonsmooth functions via smoothing. Here, we assume that the objective function f can be written as

$$f(x) = \max_{u \in Q_d} \langle u, Wx \rangle, \tag{7.33}$$

for some closed, bounded and convex set $Q_d \subseteq \mathbb{R}^M$, known as the *dual* feasible set, where $W \in \mathbb{R}^{M\times N}$ is a matrix with full column rank. Note that when we apply this to the QCBP problem (7.8), the matrix W will be taken as the identity matrix. Yet, including it in the general formulation (7.33) is useful, since it allows Nesterov's method to be easily extended to the QCBP analysis problem. This is discussed in §7.6.4. With (7.33) in hand, the idea now is to replace f in (7.31) by the smoother function

$$f_\mu(x) = \max_{u\in Q_d} \langle u, Wx\rangle - \mu p_d(u),$$

where $p_d(u)$ is a suitably chosen proximity function for Q_d and $\mu > 0$ is a smoothing parameter. Since p_d is strongly convex, this optimization problem has a unique solution. Hence f_μ is well defined. It is also convex and continuously differentiable with

$$\nabla f_\mu(x) = W^\top u_\mu(x), \qquad u_\mu(x) = \operatorname*{argmax}_{u\in Q_d} \langle u, Wx\rangle - \mu p_d(u),$$

and its gradient is Lipschitz continuous with Lipschitz constant

$$L = L_\mu = \frac{1}{\mu\sigma_d}\|W\|_{\ell^2}^2, \tag{7.34}$$

where σ_d is the strong convexity parameter for p_d. Therefore, we now replace (7.31) with the smoothed problem

$$\min_{x\in Q_p} f_\mu(x), \tag{7.35}$$

and then apply Algorithm 7.6 to (7.35). Note that the smoothing parameter μ is used to control the closeness of solutions of (7.35) to solutions of (7.31). We discuss this choice further in the context of compressed sensing in §8.3.

7.6.3 NESTA for QCBP

We now consider the QCBP problem (7.8). Throughout this section, we assume that $AA^\top = cI$ for some constant $c > 0$, in other words, the rows of A are orthogonal and have equal ℓ^2-norms. This is quite common in compressed sensing – it arises, for example, in the case of randomly subsampled unitary matrices (Definition 5.5).

To apply Nesterov's method with smoothing to (7.8), we let $Q_p = \{x : \|Ax - y\|_{\ell^2} \leq \eta\}$ and $f(x) = \|x\|_{\ell^1}$. Observe that f has the form (7.33): namely,

$$f(x) = \max_{u\in Q_d} \langle u, x\rangle, \qquad Q_d = \{u \in \mathbb{R}^N : \|u\|_{\ell^\infty} \leq 1\}, \tag{7.36}$$

where $M = N$ and $W = I$ in this case. We take the dual proximity function as $p_d(u) = \frac{1}{2}\|u\|_{\ell^2}^2$, in which case $\sigma_d = 1$. This gives

$$f_\mu(x) = \max_{u\in Q_d} \{\langle u, x\rangle - \mu p_d(u)\} = \sum_{i=1}^N \max_{|u_i|\leq 1} \left\{x_i u_i - \frac{\mu}{2}(u_i)^2\right\} = \sum_{i=1}^N |x_i|_\mu = \|x\|_{\ell^1,\mu},$$

where

$$|x|_\mu = \begin{cases} \frac{1}{2\mu}x^2 & |x| \leq \mu \\ |x| - \frac{\mu}{2} & |x| > \mu \end{cases}, \qquad x \in \mathbb{R}, \tag{7.37}$$

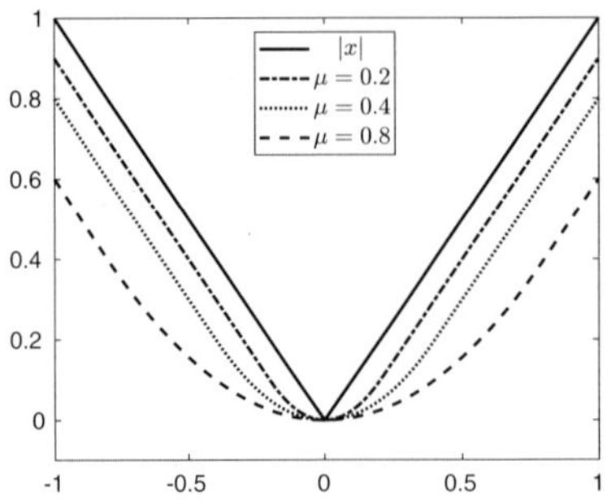

Figure 7.2 The Huber function $|x|_\mu$ for various $\mu > 0$ and the absolute value function $|x|$.

and

$$\|x\|_{\ell^1,\mu} = \sum_{i=1}^{N} |x_i|_\mu, \qquad x = (x_i)_{i=1}^N. \tag{7.38}$$

This function is known as the *Huber function*. It is convex and continuously differentiable by construction, and since $W = I$ and $\sigma_d = 1$ in this case, its Lipschitz constant (7.34) is given by

$$L = \mu^{-1}.$$

Its gradient can also be written explicitly as $\nabla\|x\|_{\ell^1,\mu} = \mathcal{T}_\mu(x)$, where $\mathcal{T}_\mu : \mathbb{R}^N \to \mathbb{R}^N$ is defined by

$$(\mathcal{T}_\mu(x))_i = \begin{cases} x_i/\mu & |x_i| \le \mu \\ \operatorname{sign}(x_i) & |x_i| > \mu \end{cases}, \qquad x = (x_i)_{i=1}^N \in \mathbb{R}^N. \tag{7.39}$$

Figure 7.2 plots the univariate Huber function. Here we see the smoothing behaviour in action. As μ increases, it smooths out the discontinuity in the absolute value function at zero, at the expense of approximating it less well away from zero.

Since (7.38) defines the smoothed objective function, Nesterov's method when applied to the QCBP problem produces a sequence $\{x_n\}_{n=0}^\infty$ of approximations to the *smoothed* QCBP problem

$$\min_{z \in \mathbb{R}^N} \|z\|_{\ell^1,\mu} \text{ subject to } \|Az - y\|_{\ell^2} \le \eta. \tag{7.40}$$

In order to derive the NESTA algorithm itself, we also need to choose the primal proximity function $p_p(x)$ to be used in Nesterov's method. To make the iterative updates efficient, we take

$$p_p(x) = \frac{1}{2}\|x - z_0\|_{\ell^2}^2,$$

where z_0 is the initial point of the algorithm. Note that $\sigma_p = 1$ in this case. Having done this, all that remains to obtain NESTA is to calculate the update formulae for x_n and v_n in Algorithm 7.6, where $f(x)$ is replaced by $f_\mu(x) = \|x\|_{\ell^1,\mu}$ and Q_p is as above. Since $\sigma_p = 1$, $L = \mu^{-1}$ and $\nabla f_\mu(x) = \mathcal{T}_\mu(x)$, where $\mathcal{T}_\mu$ is as in (7.39), the x_n update is

$$x_n = \operatorname*{argmin}_{x \in Q_p} \frac{1}{2\mu}\|x - z_n\|_{\ell^2}^2 + \langle \mathcal{T}_\mu(z_n), x - z_n \rangle, \tag{7.41}$$

Algorithm 7.7: NESTA for the smoothed QCBP problem (7.40)

---

input: measurements y, measurement matrix A with $AA^\top = cI$, parameter $\eta > 0$, smoothing parameter μ, sequences $\{\alpha_n\}_{n=0}^\infty$, $\{\tau_n\}_{n=0}^\infty$, initial point z_0

output: $\tilde{x}$, an approximate minimizer of (7.40), where $\tilde{x} = x_{n^*}$ for some n^*

for $n = 0, 1, \ldots$ **do**

Compute

$$\begin{aligned} q &= z_n - \mu \mathcal{T}_\mu(z_n), \\ \lambda &= \max\left\{0, \eta^{-1}\|y - Aq\|_{\ell^2} - 1\right\}, \\ x_n &= \left(I - \frac{\lambda}{(\lambda+1)c} A^\top A\right)\left(\frac{\lambda}{c} A^\top y + q\right). \end{aligned} \tag{7.44}$$

Compute

$$\begin{aligned} q &= z_0 - \mu \sum_{i=0}^{n} \alpha_i \mathcal{T}_\mu(z_i), \\ \lambda &= \max\left\{0, \eta^{-1}\|y - Aq\|_{\ell^2} - 1\right\}, \\ v_n &= \left(I - \frac{\lambda}{(\lambda+1)c} A^\top A\right)\left(\frac{\lambda}{c} A^\top y + q\right). \end{aligned} \tag{7.45}$$

Compute $z_{n+1} = \tau_n v_n + (1 - \tau_n) x_n$.

end

---

and, after some manipulations the v_n update is

$$v_n = \underset{x \in Q_p}{\operatorname{argmin}} \frac{1}{2\mu}\|x - z_0\|_{\ell^2}^2 + \left\langle \sum_{i=0}^{n} \alpha_i \mathcal{T}_\mu(z_i), x - z_0 \right\rangle. \tag{7.42}$$

Recalling the choice of Q_p, we observe that both these updates are of the form

$$\hat{x} = \underset{x : \|Ax - y\|_{\ell^2} \leq \eta}{\operatorname{argmin}} \left\{ \frac{1}{2\mu}\|x - v\|_{\ell^2}^2 + \langle u, x - v \rangle \right\},$$

for vectors u and v. When $AA^\top = cI$, it is a straightforward exercise using the KKT (Karush–Kuhn–Tucker) conditions to show that the solution to this problem is given by

$$\begin{aligned} q &= v - \mu u, \\ \lambda &= \max\left\{0, \eta^{-1}\|y - Aq\|_{\ell^2} - 1\right\}, \\ \hat{x} &= \left(I - \frac{\lambda}{(\lambda+1)c} A^\top A\right)\left(\frac{\lambda}{c} A^\top y + q\right). \end{aligned} \tag{7.43}$$

Substituting the values for u and v corresponding to (7.41) and (7.42), respectively, we now deduce the x_n and v_n updates. This yields NESTA for QCBP, which is summarized in Algorithm 7.7.

Remark 7.13 As written, each step of Algorithm 7.7 involves six matrix–vector multiplications, resulting in a total cost of $6N_A + \mathcal{O}(N)$ per iteration, where N_A is as in

Remark 7.5. Suppose that $A = \sqrt{c} P_\Omega U$ is a subsampled unitary transform in the sense of Definition 5.5. Then this can be reduced to just two matrix–vector multiplications involving U and $U^\top$, giving a total cost of $2N_U + O(N)$ per iteration. The idea is to make a change of variables and replace (7.40) by

$$\min_{z \in \mathbb{R}^N} \|U^\top z\|_{\ell^1,\mu} \text{ subject to } \|\sqrt{c} P_\Omega z - y\|_{\ell^2} \leq \eta.$$

Observe that $\nabla \|U^\top x\|_{\ell^1,\mu} = U \mathcal{T}_\mu (U^\top x)$, where $\mathcal{T}_\mu$ is as in (7.39). Hence the update step (7.44) becomes

$$\begin{aligned} q &= z_n - \mu U \mathcal{T}_\mu (U^\top z_n), \\ \lambda &= \max\left\{0, \eta^{-1} \left\| y - \sqrt{c} P_\Omega q \right\|_{\ell^2} - 1\right\}, \\ x_n &= \left(I - \frac{\lambda}{\lambda + 1} P_\Omega^\top P_\Omega\right)\left(\frac{\lambda}{\sqrt{c}} P_\Omega^\top y + q\right), \end{aligned} \tag{7.46}$$

and similarly for (7.45). Since P_Ω is just a restriction operator, the main computational cost is now just the two matrix–vector multiplications involving U and $U^\top$ to evaluate q, as opposed to the six evaluations of A and $A^\top$ in Algorithm 7.7.

7.6.4 NESTA for QCBP Analysis

As discussed in §4.5, in practical imaging one may wish to employ a redundant sparsifying transform $\Phi \in \mathbb{R}^{N \times M}$ via either a synthesis or an analysis formulation. The U-LASSO, QCBP and SR-LASSO synthesis problems can easily be solved with only minor modifications of existing algorithms, namely, replacing A by $A\Phi$. Analysis, however, presents more challenges. Forward–backward splitting is less well suited in this case, since $g(x) = \lambda \|\Phi^\top x\|_{\ell^1}$ is generally not simple: its proximal map typically has no explicit expression.

Conversely, NESTA can easily be extended to the QCBP analysis problem (3.3). To do so, we only need to modify the calculation of ∇f_μ in Algorithm 7.7, where $f_\mu(x) = \|\Phi^\top x\|_{\ell^1,\mu}$ is the smoothed analysis penalty. As in Remark 7.13, this is given by $\nabla f_\mu(x) = \Phi \mathcal{T}_\mu (\Phi^\top x)$. In particular, this means that NESTA for the analysis problem is computationally efficient. The resulting algorithm requires only two additional matrix–vector multiplications per step, one with Φ and the other with $\Phi^\top$, both of which are normally amenable to fast algorithms.

Notes on Other Methods

Optimization for imaging is a large topic that we have not attempted to fully survey in this chapter. For more comprehensive overviews, see, for example, [132], as well as [58, 102] and [448, Chpt. 7]. See also [56] for an in-depth treatment of first-order methods in optimization, and [88,158] for an overview of proximal algorithms. The focus of this chapter is on optimization methods for generic imaging problems, as opposed to a specific modality. For a recent overview of efficient optimization methods for MRI, see [206]. See also [102] for other imaging modalities including X-ray CT.

Rather than giving a broad survey, our focus in this chapter has been on a handful of techniques, specifically forward–backward splitting, the primal–dual iteration and Nesterov's method. In the next chapter, we theoretically examine why these methods perform well in the compressed sensing setting. Yet we emphasize that we are not suggesting that these are the only possible methods for efficient optimization in compressive imaging. To this end, we now mention several other popular approaches.

Douglas–Rachford (DR) splitting and *Alternating Descent Method of Multipliers (ADMM)* are two types of saddle-point methods. DR splitting was introduced by Douglas & Rachford [185]. See [132, 158, 297] and references therein. As shown in [132, Sec. 5.4], it can in fact be derived from the primal–dual iteration. We refer to [89], [56, Chpt. 15] and [199] for more information on ADMM.

DR splitting and ADMM are types of *variable-splitting* techniques. Another popular approach along these lines is the *split-Bregman* method, due to Goldstein & Osher [229], which is closely related to ADMM. The primal–dual iteration, DR splitting, ADMM and split-Bregman methods share many interesting connections. We refer to [132, 158, 199, 434, 524] for further information on the relations between them.

There are various other common methods for solving compressed sensing optimization problems. The SPGL1 package [477] that we use in our numerical experiments throughout this book solves QCBP via a sequence of C-LASSO problems (6.3). It exploits the underlying relation between the C-LASSO and QCBP parameters (see the Notes section of Chapter 6) and iteratively updates the C-LASSO parameter τ until a solution of QCBP is obtained. The C-LASSO problems are more straightforward to solve than the original QCBP problem. In SPGL1 they are solved using *spectral projected gradient* techniques [72].

In the *homotopy* [385] and *Least Angle Regression (LARS)* [190] methods, the idea is to follow the path of solutions of the U-LASSO with respect to the parameter λ to obtain a solution of BP or QCBP. Such methods tend to perform well on very sparse vectors. See also the *adaptive Inverse Scale Space (aISS)* method [101].

While we have largely not discussed interior-point and other second-order methods, since they generally require explicit matrices rather than matrix–vector multiplications, there are some works that apply interior-point methods in a matrix-free way that are therefore applicable to compressive imaging. See, for instance, [163, 215].

Finally, we mention *Iteratively Re-weighted Least Squares (IRLS)* [166]. This is another method for solving ℓ^1-minimization problems which proceeds by solving a sequence of weighted ℓ^2-minimization problems, with the weights being updated at each iteration. See [166] and [214, Sec. 15.3] for more information.

Notes

The intense study of interior-point methods for linear programming was initiated by Karmarkar's seminal work in 1984 [287]. For further information on these methods, including complexity analysis, we refer to [65], [383, Chpt. 14] and [90, Chpt. 11].

Forward–backward splitting, also referred to as the *proximal gradient* method, is an old technique in optimization. See [158], [132, Sec. 4], [56, Chpt. 10] and references therein. ISTA can be found in [165, 208]. Its accelerated version, FISTA was presented in [57]; see also [58]. FISTA belongs to a general class of accelerated algorithms due to Nesterov and various others. See, for example, [471] and [132, Sec. 4]. The paper [57] also defines a method, termed the *fast proximal gradient* method [58], which, like the standard proximal gradient method, applies to the general problem (7.12). For convergence analysis of these methods, see, for example [56, Chpt. 10].

See [378] (also [99]) for an in-depth discussion on complexity in optimization, including optimal rates of convergence. As noted earlier, $\mathcal{O}(1/n^2)$ is the 'optimal' rate, in a sense defined by Nemirovski and Yudin [375], achievable by a first-order method when minimizing a smooth, convex function. Gradient descent has rate $\mathcal{O}(1/n)$, and is therefore not optimal. An $\mathcal{O}(1/n^2)$ first-order scheme for smooth functions was proposed by Nesterov in 1983 [376]. FISTA can be viewed as an extension of this method to problems of the form (7.12) [57].

Our very brief discussion of duality theory in §7.5 hardly does justice to this important topic. We refer to [53, 90, 191, 414] for much more in-depth treatments.

The primal–dual iteration in its general form is due to Chambolle & Pock in [131], and stems from a previous work by Pock, Cremers, Bischof & Chambolle for minimizing the Mumford–Shah functional [392]. A similar approach, known as the *Primal–Dual Hybrid Gradient (PDHG)* method was also introduced around the same time by Esser, Zhang & Chan [200]. Our presentation is based on [132, Sec. 5].

The iteration (7.23) is a classical technique, sometimes known as the *Arrow–Hurwicz* method. Theorem 7.8 is [132, Thm. 5.1], which is based on [133]. The extended form described in Remark 7.9 is due to Condat [159]. Interestingly, the primal–dual iteration for (7.19) can also be viewed as a type of proximal point algorithm applied to certain monotone operators, and its extended version (7.26) as a type of forward–backward splitting [260] (see also [132]). This viewpoint helps explain the over-relaxation step made in the ξ_n update.

Note that if f^* or g happen to be strongly convex (see (D.2)), it is possible to accelerate the primal–dual iteration, yielding an $\mathcal{O}(1/n^2)$ convergence rate for the partial primal–dual gap. See, for example, [132] for further information on the primal–dual iteration, including the topics of acceleration and preconditioning.

Nesterov's method was introduced by Nesterov in 2005 [377], with the accelerated scheme tracing its origins back to Nesterov's $\mathcal{O}(1/n^2)$ scheme mentioned above. *Smoothing* – that is, the process of approximating a nonsmooth objective function by a smooth one – is a general concept in optimization. As seen through Nesterov's method, by solving the smoothed problem (with suitable smoothing parameter) using accelerated gradient methods, one can enhance the convergence rate from $\mathcal{O}(1/\sqrt{n})$ for general nonsmooth objective functions to $\mathcal{O}(1/n)$. See [378], [59], [56, Chpt. 10] and references therein for further information.

Note that the Huber function (7.38) can also be interpreted as the *Moreau envelope* (also known as the *Moreau–Yosida* regularization) of the function $f(x) = \|x\|_{\ell^1}$. This is a standard way to smooth a nonsmooth function [56, 88].

NESTA was introduced by Becker, Bobin & Candès in [60]. Our derivation of NESTA via Nesterov's method is based on this paper, although we have used slightly different notation to be consistent with the rest of the chapter. See [60, Sec. 3.2] for the derivation of the update rule (7.43). Theorem 7.12 is [377, Thm. 2]. Note that NESTA can also be applied when $AA^\top \neq cI$. See [61, Sec. 3.7] for further information.

This chapter considers a fixed choice of the NESTA smoothing parameter μ. As described in [60], this parameter can be iteratively updated to provide better practical performance. This is based on continuation techniques, which were previously used to accelerate forward–backward splitting [252]. For NESTA, this is motivated from the error estimate Theorem 7.12, which when applied to the smoothed QCBP problem reads

$$\|x_n\|_{\ell^1,\mu} - \|\hat{x}^{(\mu)}\|_{\ell^1,\mu} \leq \frac{2\|\hat{x}^{(\mu)} - z_0\|_{\ell^2}^2}{\mu n^2}$$

(see the proof of Theorem 8.9). Hence, a good initial guess z_0 and a large value of μ yields more rapid convergence of the modified objective function $f_\mu = \|\cdot\|_{\ell^1,\mu}$. Conversely, smaller μ ensures closeness of f_μ to the original objective function $f = \|\cdot\|_{\ell^1}$. The continuation approach repeatedly applies NESTA with a progressively smaller value of μ, using the output of the previous algorithmic instance as the initial guess for the next instance. The large initial values of μ promote fast initial convergence of the modified objective function, while the subsequent smaller values promote good approximation to the true objective function.

While §7.6.4 focused on NESTA, the primal–dual iteration can also be adapted to solve analysis problems. See [132]. See also [448, Chpt. 7] for a general discussion on optimization methods for analysis problems.

8 Analysis of Optimization Algorithms

Having introduced various optimization methods in the previous chapter, we now return to the question raised in §7.1 concerning the computability of minimizers of convex optimization problems. We develop this in several stages. First, in §8.1 we show how the rNSP ensures accuracy and stability of inexact minimizers for the QCBP and SR-LASSO problems. Next, we show how this implies error bounds for the iterates of several of the algorithms introduced in Chapter 7. Specifically, we prove bounds for the primal–dual iteration applied to the SR-LASSO problem (§8.2) and NESTA applied to QCBP (§8.3).

The rest of the chapter is devoted to computability. In §8.4 we introduce a formal model of computability, and then in §8.5 we present the previously touted result on the general impossibility of computing minimizers. This result states the following. For every $K > 1$ there is a class of *inputs* (matrices A and vectors y) where one cannot compute minimizers to K digits of accuracy, however, one can compute them to $K - 1$ or $K - 2$ digits of accuracy and, in the latter case, do so efficiently (i.e. in polynomial time). Finally, in §8.6 we return to QCBP and SR-LASSO. In each case, we show that an approximate minimizer can be computed up to an error proportional to the corresponding accuracy and stability bound for exact minimizers. Moreover, this can be done efficiently, with the computational cost scaling mildly with the problem size N. Unfortunately, the computational cost scales exponentially with the number of digits of accuracy K. To counter this, we show that there is an algorithm (based on *Nemirovski's surface-following method*) whose computational cost grows polynomially in K, at the expense of worse (but still polynomial) growth with respect to N.

8.1 The rNSP and Inexactness

Our main tool in this analysis is the rNSP (Definition 5.14). In this section, we show two important properties that follow directly from it, both of which are needed later. As in Chapter 6, we consider ℓ^2-norm error bounds only – bounds for the ℓ^1-norm error can also be shown – and, as in Chapter 7, we focus on the QCBP and SR-LASSO problems in the real case.

8.1.1 The rNSP Implies Accuracy of Approximation Solutions

The first property asserts closeness of inexact minimizers to exact minimizers. Recall from (7.2) that this is not guaranteed in general. However, we now show that when A has the rNSP, any vector that is approximately feasible and approximately minimizes the objective function of SR-LASSO or QCBP – for example, the nth step of an optimization algorithm – is also guaranteed to be close to an exact minimizer.

We first consider the SR-LASSO problem (7.28).

Definition 8.1 (μ-Suboptimality for SR-LASSO) A vector $\tilde{x} \in \mathbb{R}^N$ is *μ-suboptimal* for the problem (7.28) for some $\mu \geq 0$ if

$$\lambda \|\tilde{x}\|_{\ell^1} + \|A\tilde{x} - y\|_{\ell^2} \leq \mu + \min_{z \in \mathbb{R}^N} \{\lambda \|z\|_{\ell^1} + \|Az - y\|_{\ell^2}\}.$$

Lemma 8.2 *Suppose that $A \in \mathbb{R}^{m \times N}$ has the rNSP of order s with constants $0 < \rho < 1$ and $\gamma > 0$. Let $x \in \mathbb{R}^N$, $y = Ax + e \in \mathbb{R}^m$ and*

$$\lambda \leq \frac{C_1}{C_2\sqrt{s}},$$

where C_1 and C_2 are as in (6.10). Then every vector $\tilde{x} \in \mathbb{R}^N$ that is μ-suboptimal for (7.28) satisfies

$$\|\tilde{x} - x\|_{\ell^2} \leq 2C_1 \frac{\sigma_s(x)_{\ell^1}}{\sqrt{s}} + \frac{C_1}{\sqrt{s}\lambda}\mu + \left(\frac{C_1}{\sqrt{s}\lambda} + C_2\right) \|e\|_{\ell^2}.$$

Proof Lemma 5.16 and the condition on λ give

$$\begin{aligned} \|\tilde{x} - x\|_{\ell^2} &\leq C_1 \left(\frac{2\sigma_s(x)_{\ell^1} + \|\tilde{x}\|_{\ell^1} - \|x\|_{\ell^1}}{\sqrt{s}}\right) + C_2\|A\tilde{x} - y\|_{\ell^2} + C_2\|e\|_{\ell^2} \\ &\leq 2C_1 \frac{\sigma_s(x)_{\ell^1}}{\sqrt{s}} + \frac{C_1}{\sqrt{s}\lambda} (\lambda\|\tilde{x}\|_{\ell^1} + \|A\tilde{x} - y\|_{\ell^2} - \lambda\|x\|_{\ell^1}) + C_2\|e\|_{\ell^2}. \end{aligned}$$

Since $\tilde{x}$ is μ-suboptimal we have

$$\lambda\|\tilde{x}\|_{\ell^1} + \|A\tilde{x} - y\|_{\ell^2} \leq \mu + \lambda\|x\|_{\ell^1} + \|Ax - y\|_{\ell^2} = \mu + \lambda\|x\|_{\ell^1} + \|e\|_{\ell^2}.$$

Substituting this into the previous expression now gives the result. □

This seemingly innocuous lemma yields the key conclusion. To obtain successful compressed sensing recovery via an algorithm for solving SR-LASSO, we only need to ensure that it produces an output $\tilde{x}$ for which the objective function at $\tilde{x}$ is within some value μ of the minimum, with μ chosen proportional to the desired error bound.

Next, we consider the QCBP problem (7.8). Since an algorithm for QCBP may not produce feasible iterates, we now also require an approximate notion of feasibility.

Definition 8.3 (μ-Suboptimality and ν-feasibility for QCBP) A vector $\tilde{x} \in \mathbb{R}^N$ is *μ-suboptimal* for the problem (7.8) for some $\mu \geq 0$ if

$$\|\tilde{x}\|_{\ell^1} \leq \mu + \min_{z \in \mathbb{R}^N} \{\|z\|_{\ell^1} : \|Az - y\|_{\ell^2} \leq \eta\}.$$

It is *ν-feasible* for (7.8) for some $\nu \geq 0$ if

$$\|A\tilde{x} - y\|_{\ell^2} \leq \eta + \nu.$$

Lemma 8.4 *Suppose that $A \in \mathbb{R}^{m\times N}$ has the rNSP of order s with constants $0 < \rho < 1$ and $\gamma > 0$. Let $x \in \mathbb{R}^N$, $y = Ax + e \in \mathbb{R}^m$ and $\eta \geq \|e\|_{\ell^2}$. Then*

$$\|\tilde{x} - x\|_{\ell^2} \leq 2C_1 \frac{\sigma_s(x)_{\ell^1}}{\sqrt{s}} + C_1 \frac{\mu}{\sqrt{s}} + C_2 (2\eta + \nu),$$

for every vector $\tilde{x} \in \mathbb{R}^N$ that is μ-suboptimal and ν-feasible for (7.8), where C_1 and C_2 are as in (6.10).

Proof Observe that $\|\tilde{x}\|_{\ell^1} - \|x\|_{\ell^1} \leq \mu$ and $\|A(\tilde{x} - x)\|_{\ell^2} \leq 2\eta + \nu$. The result now follows from Lemma 5.16. □

Once more we have the same basic idea. In order to produce a desired error bound, an algorithm for QCBP need only ensure approximate feasibility and sufficient closeness of the objective function to the true minimum value.

8.1.2 The rNSP Implies Stability to Inexact Input

Keeping in mind the discussion in §7.1.2, we now briefly consider inexact input. This is discussed in detail later. As we see therein, inexactness in y can be easily addressed. Conversely, to tackle inexactness in the input matrix A, we require the following lemma:

Lemma 8.5 *Suppose that $A \in \mathbb{R}^{m\times N}$ has the rNSP of order s with constants $0 < \rho < 1$ and $\gamma > 0$. Let $A' \in \mathbb{R}^{m\times N}$ be such that $\|A - A'\|_{\ell^2} \leq \delta$, where*

$$0 \leq \delta < \frac{1-\rho}{\gamma(\sqrt{s}+1)}.$$

Then A' has the rNSP of order s with constants $0 < \rho' < 1$ and $\gamma' > 0$ given by

$$\rho' = \frac{\rho + \gamma\delta\sqrt{s}}{1-\gamma\delta}, \qquad \gamma' = \frac{\gamma}{1-\gamma\delta}.$$

Proof Let $x \in \mathbb{R}^N$ and $\Delta \in D_s$. Then, since A has the rNSP,

$$\begin{aligned}
\|P_\Delta x\|_{\ell^2} &\leq \frac{\rho}{\sqrt{s}} \|P_\Delta^\perp x\|_{\ell^1} + \gamma\|Ax\|_{\ell^2} \\
&\leq \frac{\rho}{\sqrt{s}} \|P_\Delta^\perp x\|_{\ell^1} + \gamma\|A'x\|_{\ell^2} + \gamma\delta\|x\|_{\ell^2} \\
&\leq \frac{\rho}{\sqrt{s}} \|P_\Delta^\perp x\|_{\ell^1} + \gamma\|A'x\|_{\ell^2} + \gamma\delta\|P_\Delta x\|_{\ell^2} + \gamma\delta\|P_\Delta^\perp x\|_{\ell^1}.
\end{aligned}$$

Hence

$$(1-\gamma\delta)\|P_\Delta x\|_{\ell^2} \leq \frac{\rho + \gamma\delta\sqrt{s}}{\sqrt{s}} \|P_\Delta^\perp x\|_{\ell^1} + \gamma\|A'x\|_{\ell^2}.$$

The result now follows immediately from the assumptions on δ. □

This lemma shows that every sufficiently small perturbation A' of a matrix A possessing the rNSP also has the rNSP. In particular, we can still expect stable and accurate recovery if the optimization problem is solved with A' in place of A. This observation will be crucial later.

8.2 Compressed Sensing Analysis of the Primal–Dual Iteration

We now move on to the analysis of the algorithms themselves subject to the rNSP. Our aim is to provide recovery guarantees that are identical to those given in Chapters 5 and 6 for exact minimizers, up to an additional term depending on the iteration number n.

We first consider the primal–dual iteration for the SR-LASSO problem (7.28). This was previously derived in §7.5.3. Our main tool is Theorem 7.8, which we apply with the values of B, f, and g given by (7.29). Recalling the expression (7.30) for f^* in this case, we first observe that the Lagrangian (7.21) of this problem takes the form

$$\mathcal{L}(x, \xi) = \langle \xi, Ax - y \rangle - \delta_{\{z : \|z\|_{\ell^2} \leq 1\}}(\xi) + \lambda \|x\|_{\ell^1}. \tag{8.1}$$

The following lemma shows that the error in the objective function evaluated at the ergodic sequence decays with rate $1/n$:

Lemma 8.6 *Let $A \in \mathbb{R}^{m \times N}$ and $y \in \mathbb{R}^m$ and consider Algorithm 7.5 applied to the SR-LASSO problem (7.28) with $\xi_0 = 0$, x_0 arbitrary and τ and σ such that $\tau\sigma\|A\|_{\ell^2}^2 \leq 1$. Then the ergodic sequence $X_n = \frac{1}{n}\sum_{i=1}^n x_i$ satisfies*

$$(\lambda\|X_n\|_{\ell^1} + \|AX_n - y\|_{\ell^2}) - (\lambda\|x\|_{\ell^1} + \|Ax - y\|_{\ell^2}) \leq \frac{\tau^{-1}\|x - x_0\|_{\ell^2}^2 + \sigma^{-1}}{n}, \quad \forall x \in \mathbb{R}^N.$$

Proof We apply Theorem 7.8. Observe first that the iterates ξ_n produced by Algorithm 7.5 satisfy $\|\xi_n\|_{\ell^2} \leq 1$. Hence, the ergodic sequence $\Xi_n = \frac{1}{n}\sum_{i=1}^n \xi_i$ satisfies $\|\Xi_n\|_{\ell^2} \leq 1$ as well. Suppose first that $AX_n - y \neq 0$ and set $\xi = \frac{AX_n - y}{\|AX_n - y\|_{\ell^2}}$. Then $\delta_{\{z : \|z\|_{\ell^2} \leq 1\}}(\xi) = \delta_{\{z : \|z\|_{\ell^2} \leq 1\}}(\Xi_n) = 0$ and therefore Theorem 7.8 and (8.1) give

$$\|AX_n - y\|_{\ell^2} + \lambda\|X_n\|_{\ell^1} - \langle \Xi_n, Ax - y \rangle - \lambda\|x\|_{\ell^1} \leq \frac{\tau^{-1}\|x - x_0\|_{\ell^2}^2 + \sigma^{-1}}{n}.$$

Clearly, the same inequality holds if $AX_n - y = 0$, since in that case we can simply let ξ be any unit vector. To obtain the result, we apply the Cauchy–Schwarz inequality to $\langle \Xi_n, Ax - y \rangle$ and recall that $\|\Xi_n\|_{\ell^2} \leq 1$. □

We now show that this implies an $O(1/n)$ error bound for recovering a vector x whenever the rNSP holds.

Theorem 8.7 (Primal–dual iteration, accuracy and stability for SR-LASSO) *Suppose that $A \in \mathbb{R}^{m \times N}$ has the rNSP of order s with constants $0 < \rho < 1$ and $\gamma > 0$, and let $x \in \mathbb{R}^N$ and $y = Ax + e \in \mathbb{R}^m$. Consider the SR-LASSO problem (7.28) with parameter λ satisfying*

$$\lambda \leq \frac{C_1}{C_2\sqrt{s}},$$

where C_1 and C_2 are as in (6.10), and suppose that Algorithm 7.5 is applied to this problem with $x_0 \in \mathbb{R}^N$, $\xi_0 = 0$ and τ and σ such that $\tau\sigma\|A\|_{\ell^2}^2 \leq 1$. Then the ergodic sequence $X_n = \frac{1}{n}\sum_{i=1}^n x_i$ satisfies

$$\|X_n - x\|_{\ell^2} \leq 2C_1 \frac{\sigma_s(x)_{\ell^1}}{\sqrt{s}} + \frac{C_1}{\sqrt{s}\lambda}\left(\frac{\tau^{-1}\|x - x_0\|_{\ell^2}^2 + \sigma^{-1}}{n}\right) + \left(\frac{C_1}{\sqrt{s}\lambda} + C_2\right)\|e\|_{\ell^2}.$$

In particular, if $\lambda = \frac{C_1}{C_2\sqrt{s}}$ and $D_1, D_2 > 0$ then

$$\|X_n - x\|_{\ell^2} \leq (2C_1 + D_1 C_2)\frac{\sigma_s(x)_{\ell^1}}{\sqrt{s}} + C_2(2 + D_2)\|e\|_{\ell^2},$$

whenever

$$n \geq \frac{\tau^{-1}\|x - x_0\|_{\ell^2}^2 + \sigma^{-1}}{D_1\sigma_s(x)_{\ell^1}/\sqrt{s} + D_2\|e\|_{\ell^2}}.$$

Proof Lemma 8.6 implies that X_n is μ-suboptimal (Definition 8.1) for (7.28), where

$$\mu = \frac{\tau^{-1}\|x - x_0\|_{\ell^2}^2 + \sigma^{-1}}{n}.$$

The first result now follows immediately from Lemma 8.2. For the second, we simply use the specific choice of λ and the bound for n. □

This result says the following. If $\tau = \sigma = \|A\|_{\ell^2}^{-1}$ (for example), then $\|X_n - x\|_{\ell^2}$ satisfies a standard compressed sensing error bound, i.e.

$$\|X_n - x\|_{\ell^2} \leq C \cdot \mathcal{CS}_s(x, e), \qquad \mathcal{CS}_s(x, e) = \frac{\sigma_s(x)_{\ell^1}}{\sqrt{s}} + \|e\|_{\ell^2}, \tag{8.2}$$

where $C > 0$ depends on ρ and γ only, provided the number of iterations

$$n \approx \frac{(\|x - x_0\|_{\ell^2}^2 + 1)\|A\|_{\ell^2}}{\mathcal{CS}_s(x, e)}. \tag{8.3}$$

In particular, n is inversely proportional to the error $\mathcal{CS}_s(x, e)$ one seeks to achieve, multiplied by the norm of A.

Remark 8.8 It is important to note that when A is a compressed sensing matrix, its ℓ^2-norm $\|A\|_{\ell^2}$ is typically not bounded by a constant independent of its dimensions. Indeed, suppose that A is a randomly subsampled unitary matrix in the sense of Definition 5.5. Then $\|A\|_{\ell^2} = \sqrt{N/m}$, since U is unitary. If A is a randomly subsampled unitary matrix in the sense of Definition 5.6, then $\|A\|_{\ell^2} \geq \sqrt{N/m}$ since in this case A may have repeated rows. Additionally, if $A = m^{-1/2}\tilde{A}$, where $\tilde{A}$ is a Gaussian random matrix, then $\|A\|_{\ell^2} \approx \sqrt{N/m}$ with high probability (this follows from standard estimates for the maximum singular value of a Gaussian random matrix).

In general, an upper bound for $\|A\|_{\ell^2}$ can be obtained whenever A has the RIP (Definition 5.18). Suppose that A satisfies the RIP of order s and let $\Delta_1 \cup \cdots \cup \Delta_r$ be a partition of $\{1, \ldots, N\}$ into index sets of size at most s. Note that this can be done with $r = \lceil N/s \rceil$ sets. Then by the RIP,

$$\|Ax\|_{\ell^2} \leq \sum_{k=1}^{r} \|AP_{\Delta_k} x\|_{\ell^2} \leq \sqrt{1+\delta} \sum_{k=1}^{r} \|P_{\Delta_k} x\|_{\ell^2} \leq \sqrt{2}\sqrt{r}\|x\|_{\ell^2}, \qquad \forall x \in \mathbb{R}^N.$$

We conclude that $\|A\|_{\ell^2} \leq \sqrt{2\lceil N/s \rceil}$ in this case.

In light of this remark, we typically expect the number of iterations (8.3) to be proportional to $\sqrt{N/s}$. In particular, if $\|x\|_{\ell^2} \leq 1$ and $x_0 = 0$, then this means that

$$n \approx \frac{\sqrt{N/s}}{\mathcal{CS}_s(x, e)}. \tag{8.4}$$

When combined with Remark 7.10, this estimate also yields a bound for the total computational cost of the algorithm. Assuming that A has a fast transform, i.e. $N_A = \mathcal{O}(N \log(N))$, the computational cost for recovering x accurately and stably via the primal–dual iteration (when A has the RIP) scales like

$$\frac{N^{3/2} \log(N)}{\sqrt{s} \cdot \mathcal{CS}_s(x, e)}.$$

In particular, if s is proportional to N (as is often reasonable in practice, although somewhat meaningless from the perspective of compressed sensing measurement conditions), this reduces to

$$\frac{N \log(N)}{\mathcal{CS}_s(x, e)}.$$

This is an appealing scaling with respect to N, albeit somewhat less appealing with respect to the error $\mathcal{CS}_s(x, e)$. We return to this matter in §8.6.

8.3 Compressed Sensing Analysis of NESTA

We now consider NESTA for solving QCBP. Our main result is the following:

Theorem 8.9 (NESTA, accuracy and stability for QCBP) *Let $\eta \geq 0$, $A \in \mathbb{R}^{m \times N}$ satisfy $AA^\top = cI$ for some $c > 0$, $x \in \mathbb{R}^N$, $y = Ax + e \in \mathbb{R}^m$ and $\eta \geq \|e\|_{\ell^2}$. Suppose that Algorithm 7.7 is applied to (7.8) with $\alpha_n = \frac{n+1}{2}$ and $\tau_n = \frac{2}{n+3}$. Then for $n \geq 1$, the nth iterate x_n is feasible for (7.8) and μ'-suboptimal (Definition 8.3), where*

$$\mu' = \frac{N\mu}{2} + \frac{2\|\hat{x}^{(\mu)} - z_0\|_{\ell^2}^2}{\mu n^2},$$

and $\hat{x}^{(\mu)}$ is any minimizer of (7.40). Furthermore, if A has the rNSP of order s with constants $0 < \rho < 1$ and $\gamma > 0$, then

$$\begin{aligned} \|x - x_n\|_{\ell^2} \leq{}& 2C_1 \frac{\sigma_s(x)_{\ell^1}}{\sqrt{s}} + 2C_2\eta + C_1 \frac{N\mu}{2\sqrt{s}} \\ &+ \frac{2C_1}{\mu n^2 \sqrt{s}} \left(2C_1 \frac{\sigma_s(x)_{\ell^1}}{\sqrt{s}} + C_1 \frac{N\mu}{2\sqrt{s}} + 2C_2\eta + \|x - z_0\|_{\ell^2} \right)^2, \end{aligned} \tag{8.5}$$

where C_1 and C_2 are as in (6.10).

Proof Recall that the iterate x_n in Nesterov's method (Algorithm 7.6) is chosen as an element of Q_p. Since NESTA corresponds to Nesterov's method with $Q_p = \{x : \|Ax - y\|_{\ell^2} \leq \eta\}$, feasibility of x_n follows immediately.

We now consider suboptimality. Recall from §7.6.3 that NESTA is Nesterov's method applied to (7.40) with $p_p(x) = \frac{1}{2}\|x - z_0\|_2^2$. Recall also that $\sigma_p = 1$ and $L = \mu^{-1}$ in this case. Hence Theorem 7.12 gives

$$\|x_n\|_{\ell^1,\mu} - \|\hat{x}^{(\mu)}\|_{\ell^1,\mu} \leq \frac{2\|\hat{x}^{(\mu)} - z_0\|_{\ell^2}^2}{\mu n^2}, \tag{8.6}$$

where $\hat{x}^{(\mu)}$ is any minimizer of (7.40). We now estimate $\|x_n\|_{\ell^1}$. Observe that the Huber function (7.37) satisfies

$$|z|_\mu \leq |z| \leq |z|_\mu + \mu/2,$$

and therefore $\|z\|_{\ell^1,\mu} = \sum_{i=1}^N |z_i|_\mu$ satisfies

$$\|z\|_{\ell^1,\mu} \leq \|z\|_{\ell^1} \leq \|z\|_{\ell^1,\mu} + N\mu/2, \quad \forall z \in \mathbb{R}^N. \tag{8.7}$$

Hence (8.6) gives

$$\|x_n\|_{\ell^1} \leq \|x_n\|_{\ell^1,\mu} + \frac{N\mu}{2} \leq \|\hat{x}^{(\mu)}\|_{\ell^1,\mu} + \frac{2\|\hat{x}^{(\mu)} - z_0\|_{\ell^2}^2}{\mu n^2} + \frac{N\mu}{2}.$$

Since $\hat{x}^{(\mu)}$ is a minimizer of (7.40) and any minimizer $\hat{x}$ of (7.8) is feasible for (7.40), it follows that $\|\hat{x}^{(\mu)}\|_{\ell^1,\mu} \leq \|\hat{x}\|_{\ell^1,\mu} \leq \|\hat{x}\|_{\ell^1}$. Substituting this into the previous bound now shows that x_n is μ'-suboptimal for (7.8), as required.

For the second result, we first apply Lemma 8.4 to obtain

$$\|x - x_n\|_{\ell^2} \leq 2C_1\frac{\sigma_s(x)_{\ell^1}}{\sqrt{s}} + \frac{C_1}{\sqrt{s}}\left(\frac{N\mu}{2} + \frac{2\|\hat{x}^{(\mu)} - z_0\|_{\ell^2}^2}{\mu n^2}\right) + 2C_2\eta. \tag{8.8}$$

We need to estimate $\|\hat{x}^{(\mu)} - z_0\|_{\ell^2}$. By Lemma 5.16 and the fact that both x and $\hat{x}^{(\mu)}$ are feasible for (7.8), we have

$$\|\hat{x}^{(\mu)} - x\|_{\ell^2} \leq 2C_1\frac{\sigma_s(x)_{\ell^1}}{\sqrt{s}} + \frac{C_1}{\sqrt{s}}\left(\|\hat{x}^{(\mu)}\|_{\ell^1} - \|x\|_{\ell^1}\right) + 2C_2\eta.$$

Using (8.7) and the fact that $\hat{x}^{(\mu)}$ is a minimizer of (7.40), we observe that

$$\|\hat{x}^{(\mu)}\|_{\ell^1} \leq \|\hat{x}^{(\mu)}\|_{\ell^1,\mu} + N\mu/2 \leq \|x\|_{\ell^1,\mu} + N\mu/2 \leq \|x\|_{\ell^1} + N\mu/2.$$

Hence

$$\begin{aligned}\|\hat{x}^{(\mu)} - z_0\|_{\ell^2} &\leq \|\hat{x}^{(\mu)} - x\|_{\ell^2} + \|x - z_0\|_{\ell^2} \\ &\leq 2C_1\frac{\sigma_s(x)_{\ell^1}}{\sqrt{s}} + C_1\frac{N\mu}{2\sqrt{s}} + 2C_2\eta + \|x - z_0\|_{\ell^2}.\end{aligned}$$

Combining this with (8.8) now gives (8.5). □

The bound (8.5) splits the error for NESTA into three groups of terms. The first two terms are the usual compressed sensing error bound for (7.8) under the rNSP. The next term, which depends on $N\mu/\sqrt{s}$, is the error incurred by solving the smoothed problem (7.40) instead of (7.8). The final term shows the effect of the iteration number n. This result therefore provides insight into how to set both the smoothing parameter μ and number of iterations n. To see this more clearly, let

$$\mathcal{CS}_s(x, \eta) = \frac{\sigma_s(x)_{\ell^1}}{\sqrt{s}} + \eta$$

be the standard compressed sensing error term for QCBP. Then we have the following:

Corollary 8.10 *Consider the setup of Theorem 8.9. Suppose that A has the rNSP of order s with constants* $0 < \rho < 1$ *and* $\gamma > 0$ *and let*

$$\mu = \frac{\sqrt{s} \cdot \mathcal{CS}_s(x, \eta)}{N}.$$

Then

$$\|x - x_n\|_{\ell^2} \leq C \cdot \mathcal{CS}_s(x, \eta),$$

where $C > 0$ *depends on* ρ *and* γ *only, provided*

$$n \geq \sqrt{\frac{N}{s}} \left(1 + \frac{\|x - z_0\|_{\ell^2}}{\mathcal{CS}_s(x, \eta)} \right). \tag{8.9}$$

Proof We consider (8.5). The condition on μ gives that the third term is equal to $C_1 \cdot \mathcal{CS}_s(x, \eta)/2$. Hence, the result follows, provided n is chosen so that

$$\frac{N}{sn^2 \cdot \mathcal{CS}_s(x, \eta)} \left(\mathcal{CS}_s(x, \eta) + \|x - z_0\|_{\ell^2} \right)^2 \leq \mathcal{CS}_s(x, \eta).$$

Rearranging, we get (8.9). □

Note that one could also set $\mu = c \cdot \mathcal{CS}_s(x, \eta)\sqrt{s}/N$ in the above for some constant $c > 0$, with corresponding changes in the error bound.

To explain this result, assume for simplicity that $\|x\|_{\ell^1} \leq 1$ and $\mathcal{CS}_s(x, \eta) \leq 1$. Then (8.9) states that a number of iterations

$$n \approx \frac{\sqrt{N/s}}{\mathcal{CS}_s(x, \eta)}$$

is sufficient to achieve an error proportional to $\mathcal{CS}_s(x, \eta)$, provided $\mu = \mathcal{CS}_s(x, \eta)\sqrt{s}/N$. Up to constants and replacing $\|e\|_{\ell^2}$ by η, this is identical to the scaling (8.4) for the primal–dual iteration applied to the SR-LASSO problem. By the same token, if $N_A = \mathcal{O}(N \log(N))$, then the total computational cost for NESTA also scales like

$$\frac{N^{3/2} \log(N)}{\sqrt{s} \cdot \mathcal{CS}_s(x, \eta)},$$

and, if s is proportional to N, like

$$\frac{N \log(N)}{\mathcal{CS}_s(x, \eta)}.$$

8.4 Computability and Complexity of Finding Minimizers

We now shift focus and consider computability and complexity of finding minimizers. The example in §7.1 highlights that this is a delicate matter in general. However, the analysis conducted in the previous sections suggests that compressed sensing problems may indeed be computable with reasonable complexity. In order to discuss these issues rigorously, we first need to define a formal model of computation. This is the topic of this section.

8.4.1 Algorithms and Oracles

The *input* to a convex optimization problem is the pair $(A, y) \in \mathbb{R}^{m\times N} \times \mathbb{R}^m$. We let $\mathcal{I} \subseteq \mathbb{R}^{m\times N} \times \mathbb{R}^m$ be a *class* of inputs and write ι for a generic element of $\mathcal{I}$. The class $\mathcal{I}$ may, for instance, correspond to matrices A satisfying the rNSP and measurements y of the form $y = Ax + e$, where x is approximately s-sparse and e is bounded.

As noted in §7.1, we generally cannot access the exact input $\iota = (A, y)$, only approximations to it. We assume that we can access approximations of ι to arbitrary precision and think of these input approximations as infinite sequences. To this end, we consider mappings of the form $\tilde{\iota}\colon \mathbb{N} \to \mathbb{R}^{m\times N} \times \mathbb{R}^m$ that satisfy

$$\|\tilde{\iota}(n) - \iota\| \leq 10^{-n}, \qquad \forall n \in \mathbb{N},$$

where $\|\iota\| = \max\{\|A\|_{\ell^2}, \|y\|_{\ell^2}\}$. Such a mapping is referred to as an *oracle* for the input ι. It is an unspecified 'subroutine' that, when called with an input integer $n \in \mathbb{N}$, returns an output approximating ι to n digits of (absolute) accuracy.

We also define a *class* of oracles for the input class $\mathcal{I}$. Typically, this is simply the set of all possible oracles for inputs $\iota \in \mathcal{I}$:

$$\overline{\mathcal{I}} = \bigcup_{\iota\in\mathcal{I}} \left\{\tilde{\iota}\colon \mathbb{N} \to \mathbb{R}^{m\times N} \times \mathbb{R}^m : \|\tilde{\iota}(n) - \iota\| \leq 10^{-n},\ \forall n \in \mathbb{N}\right\}. \tag{8.10}$$

However, in some situations, it may be unreasonable to consider all possible oracles. We therefore define an *oracle class* $\widetilde{\mathcal{I}}$ for $\mathcal{I}$ as any set that satisfies

(i) $\widetilde{\mathcal{I}} \subseteq \overline{\mathcal{I}}$, where $\overline{\mathcal{I}}$ is as in (8.10);
(ii) each $\iota \in \mathcal{I}$ has at least one oracle in $\widetilde{\mathcal{I}}$, i.e. there exists an $\tilde{\iota} \in \widetilde{\mathcal{I}}$ with $\lim_{n\to\infty} \tilde{\iota}(n) = \iota$.

What is important is that an algorithm that makes use of an oracle must work for *every* oracle from the oracle class, that is, every $\tilde{\iota} \in \widetilde{\mathcal{I}}$. For example, suppose we consider oracles for providing approximations to the number $\exp(x)$ for $x \in \mathbb{R}$. There are, of course, many different ways to compute an approximation to $\exp(x)$ to n digits of accuracy. All we require of an algorithm that relies on an oracle for $\exp(x)$ is that it must produce an output, regardless of the scheme used to generate the inexact input.

Remark 8.11 Generally speaking, we consider $\widetilde{\mathcal{I}} = \overline{\mathcal{I}}$ and demand that the algorithm works for all possible oracles. However, there are some situations that necessitate $\widetilde{\mathcal{I}} \subsetneq \overline{\mathcal{I}}$. For instance, consider a class of inputs consisting of upper triangular matrices. A generic oracle $\tilde{\iota} \in \overline{\mathcal{I}}$ will replace the zero entries below the diagonal with small nonzero values.

This is of course unnatural. It is far more natural to take $\widetilde{\mathcal{I}}$ as the class of oracles that approximate the upper triangular part of the matrix only, while leaving the subdiagonal zeros intact. Another example is when $\mathcal{I}$ is a class of circulant matrices. Here it would be natural to require that the oracles preserve the circulant structure.

We now formalize what we mean by an algorithm that takes inexact input.

Definition 8.12 (General algorithm) Let $\mathcal{I}$ be a class of inputs and $\widetilde{\mathcal{I}}$ be an oracle class for $\mathcal{I}$. A *general algorithm* is a mapping $\mathrm{A} \colon \widetilde{\mathcal{I}} \to \mathbb{R}^N$ that satisfies the following. For each $\tilde{\iota} \in \widetilde{\mathcal{I}}$:

(i) there exists a finite set $\Lambda_{\tilde{\iota}} \subset \mathbb{N}$;
(ii) $\mathrm{A}(\tilde{\iota})$ depends only on the values $\{\tilde{\iota}(n) : n \in \Lambda_{\tilde{\iota}}\}$;
(iii) if $\tilde{\iota}' \in \widetilde{\mathcal{I}}$ satisfies $\tilde{\iota}'(n) = \tilde{\iota}(n)$ for every $n \in \Lambda_{\tilde{\iota}}$ then $\Lambda_{\tilde{\iota}'} = \Lambda_{\tilde{\iota}}$ (and therefore $\mathrm{A}(\tilde{\iota}') = \mathrm{A}(\tilde{\iota})$).

Conditions (i)–(iii) are extremely weak. The first two state that A uses only finite information about the input. The third is simply a consistency condition: if A sees the same input, it must produce the same output. The reason for such a broad definition is as follows. There are many different ways to define an 'algorithm', and each of these lead to different, nonequivalent models of computation. However, in order to make a rigorous statement asserting the impossibility of computing minimizers, one's definition of an algorithm must encompass *all* models of computation. Definition 8.12 is sufficiently general so that every reasonable definition of an 'algorithm' will also be a general algorithm.

This definition suffices for nonexistence results. Conversely, for existence results, and in particular, statements about complexity, one needs to fix a model of computation. We follow the standard setup in the field of continuous optimization, where one assumes that the algorithm can perform exact arithmetic operations and comparisons of real numbers. In addition, we assume that the algorithm can extract radicals of positive real numbers. In order to make this rigorous, in particular in terms of complexity analysis, one needs a formal definition. The most natural approach is to use the *Blum–Shub–Smale (BSS) machine*. This approach permits an algorithm to take inputs from a field (typically $\mathbb{R}$ or $\mathbb{C}$), however, it also allows for adding extra 'oracles' or 'subroutines' such as computing the square root of a positive real number.[1] In what follows, we forgo a formal definition of BSS machines, and instead refer the reader to the Notes section for references.

Definition 8.13 (Arithmetic algorithm) Let $\mathcal{I}$ be a class of inputs and $\widetilde{\mathcal{I}}$ be an oracle class for $\mathcal{I}$. An *arithmetic algorithm* (with radicals) is a mapping $\mathrm{A} \colon \widetilde{\mathcal{I}} \times \mathbb{N} \to \mathbb{R}^N$ such that $\mathrm{A}(\cdot, k)$ is a general algorithm for each $k \in \mathbb{N}$, and there is a BSS machine such that for each $k \in \mathbb{N}$ and $\tilde{\iota} \in \widetilde{\mathcal{I}}$, the mapping $k \mapsto \mathrm{A}(\tilde{\iota}, k)$ is executable on this machine with a node (subroutine) for the operation $a \mapsto \sqrt{a}$, $a > 0$, and a node for any oracle $\tilde{\iota}$.

[1] Indeed, as Blum, Shub and Smale point out in their original paper: 'We focus on rings because their basic operations – addition, subtraction, and multiplication – are the basic arithmetic operations. Polynomials are built from these basic operations. Fields add division and rational functions to our repertoire, but also some complications. So for simplicity of exposition, we sometimes define concepts first for rings, modifying them later for fields. Later one could add "subroutines" or "oracle" nodes for other functions or operations.'

In short, an arithmetic algorithm can perform arithmetic operations with real numbers, comparisons of real numbers (is $a \leq b$ or $b \leq a$?) and execute a square root of a positive number. Note that the input k is typically used to denote some desired accuracy of the output. Since an arithmetic algorithm is intended to approximate the solution of a computational problem from an input $\tilde{\iota} \in \widetilde{\mathcal{I}}$, the quantity $\mathrm{A}(\tilde{\iota}, k)$ will usually provide an approximation to the exact solution to k digits of accuracy. We caution, however, that it may not always be possible to find an algorithm that will produce approximations to arbitrary accuracy; indeed, this is the main point of Theorem 8.18 below.

8.4.2 Error Analysis and Computational Cost

Consider, for example, the QCBP problem (7.8). Similar to Remark 5.11, we define the reconstruction map as the multivalued function $\mathrm{R}\colon \mathcal{I} \rightrightarrows \mathbb{R}^N$, where

$$\mathrm{R}(\iota) = \underset{z \in \mathbb{R}^N}{\operatorname{argmin}} \|z\|_{\ell^1} \text{ subject to } \|Az - y\|_{\ell^2} \leq \eta. \tag{8.11}$$

Let $\mathcal{I}$ be a class of inputs and $\widetilde{\mathcal{I}}$ be an oracle class for $\mathcal{I}$. We now formalize what we mean by the error of an algorithm for approximating $\mathrm{R}(\iota)$. Let $\tilde{\iota} \in \widetilde{\mathcal{I}}$ be any oracle for $\iota \in \mathcal{I}$. In the case of a general algorithm $\mathrm{A}\colon \widetilde{\mathcal{I}} \to \mathbb{R}^N$, we first define the distance

$$\operatorname{dist}(\mathrm{A}(\tilde{\iota}), \mathrm{R}(\iota)) := \inf_{\hat{x} \in \mathrm{R}(\iota)} \|\mathrm{A}(\tilde{\iota}) - \hat{x}\|_{\ell^2},$$

and in the case of an arithmetic algorithm $\mathrm{A}\colon \widetilde{\mathcal{I}} \times \mathbb{N} \to \mathbb{R}^N$, we define

$$\operatorname{dist}(\mathrm{A}(\tilde{\iota}, k), \mathrm{R}(\iota)) := \inf_{\hat{x} \in \mathrm{R}(\iota)} \|\mathrm{A}(\tilde{\iota}, k) - \hat{x}\|_{\ell^2}, \qquad k \in \mathbb{N}.$$

Next, since we demand that algorithms work for all oracles, we define the error by taking the supremum of these quantities over all oracles for an input ι.

Definition 8.14 (Error of an algorithm) Let $\mathcal{I}$ be a class of inputs and $\widetilde{\mathcal{I}}$ be an oracle class for $\mathcal{I}$. The *error* of a general algorithm $\mathrm{A}\colon \widetilde{\mathcal{I}} \to \mathbb{R}^N$ is

$$\operatorname{Error}(\mathrm{A}, \mathrm{R}, \iota) = \sup \left\{ \operatorname{dist}(\mathrm{A}(\tilde{\iota}), \mathrm{R}(\iota)) : \tilde{\iota} \in \widetilde{\mathcal{I}}, \lim_{n\to\infty} \tilde{\iota}(n) = \iota \right\}, \quad \iota \in \mathcal{I}.$$

The error of an arithmetic algorithm $\mathrm{A}\colon \widetilde{\mathcal{I}} \times \mathbb{N} \to \mathbb{R}^N$ is

$$\operatorname{Error}(\mathrm{A}, \mathrm{R}, \iota, k) = \sup \left\{ \operatorname{dist}(\mathrm{A}(\tilde{\iota}, k), \mathrm{R}(\iota)) : \tilde{\iota} \in \widetilde{\mathcal{I}}, \lim_{n\to\infty} \tilde{\iota}(n) = \iota \right\}, \quad \iota \in \mathcal{I},\ k \in \mathbb{N}.$$

A general or arithmetic algorithm *produces K correct digits (digits of accuracy)* over $\mathcal{I}$ for some $K \in \mathbb{N}$ if either

$$\operatorname{Error}(\mathrm{A}, \mathrm{R}, \iota) \leq 10^{-K}, \quad \forall \iota \in \mathcal{I}, \tag{8.12}$$

in the case of a general algorithm or

$$\operatorname{Error}(\mathrm{A}, \mathrm{R}, \iota, K) \leq 10^{-K}, \quad \forall \iota \in \mathcal{I}, \tag{8.13}$$

in the case of an arithmetic algorithm.

With this in hand, we now also define the computational cost of an arithmetic algorithm $\mathrm{A}\colon \widetilde{\mathcal{I}} \times \mathbb{N} \to \mathbb{R}^N$. Given an input $(\tilde{\iota}, k) \in \widetilde{\mathcal{I}} \times \mathbb{N}$, we first let $n = n_{\mathrm{A}}(\tilde{\iota}, k)$ be the number of arithmetic operations, comparisons and radicals used by $\mathrm{A}(\tilde{\iota}, k)$ plus the number $\max\{n : n \in \Lambda_{\tilde{\iota}}\}$, where $\Lambda_{\tilde{\iota}}$ is as in Definition 8.12. Then:

Definition 8.15 (Computational cost of an arithmetic algorithm) Let $\mathcal{I}$ be a class of inputs, $\widetilde{\mathcal{I}}$ be an oracle class for $\mathcal{I}$ and $\mathrm{A}\colon \widetilde{\mathcal{I}} \times \mathbb{N} \to \mathbb{R}^N$ be an arithmetic algorithm. The *computational cost* (or *runtime*) of A is

$$\mathrm{CompCost}(\mathrm{A}, \iota, k) = \sup \left\{ n_{\mathrm{A}}(\tilde{\iota}, k) : \tilde{\iota} \in \widetilde{\mathcal{I}}, \lim_{n \to \infty} \tilde{\iota}(n) = \iota \right\}, \qquad \iota \in \mathcal{I},\ k \in \mathbb{N}. \tag{8.14}$$

Note that this is equivalent to defining the computational cost as the runtime of a BSS machine using oracles for the inexact input as well as an extra node for executing the square root.

Remark 8.16 Notice that the error (8.12) or (8.13) and computational cost (8.14) depend on ι and not the oracle used. Motivated by this, we will sometimes, with slight abuse of notation, write $\mathrm{A}(\iota)$ or $\mathrm{A}(\iota, k)$ rather than $\mathrm{A}(\tilde{\iota})$ or $\mathrm{A}(\tilde{\iota}, k)$ for the output of a general or arithmetic algorithm with oracle $\tilde{\iota}$ for ι.

8.5 Impossibility of Computing Minimizers from Inexact Input

In this section, we present our main nonexistence result on computing minimizers of QCBP (we consider this problem only for simplicity). We also make statements about whether a computational problem is 'in P', i.e. *in polynomial time*. In order to do this, we now consider a class of inputs

$$\mathcal{I} = \bigcup_{i=1}^{\infty} \mathcal{I}_i, \tag{8.15}$$

where $\mathcal{I}_i \subseteq \mathbb{R}^{m_i \times N_i} \times \mathbb{R}^{m_i}$ is a set of inputs of fixed size and $m_i, N_i \to \infty$ as $i \to \infty$. To avoid unnecessary notation, we write R for the QCBP reconstruction map defined in (8.11), regardless of the dimensions of the input.

We are interested in approximating R for inputs $\iota \in \mathcal{I}$. Hence we consider a sequence of algorithms $\{\mathrm{A}_i\}_{i=1}^{\infty}$, where the A_i are either general algorithms (in the case of nonexistence results) or arithmetic algorithms (in the case of existence results) for the classes $\mathcal{I}_i$. In order to avoid unnecessary complications, we slightly abuse our terminology and refer to the sequence $\{\mathrm{A}_i\}_{i=1}^{\infty}$ as an *algorithm* even though it is formally a sequence of algorithms.

Definition 8.17 Let $\mathcal{I}$ be as in (8.15), $\widetilde{\mathcal{I}}$ be an oracle class for $\mathcal{I}$, R be the QCBP reconstruction map and $K \in \mathbb{N}$. The *problem of computing K digits for the input class $\mathcal{I}$ is in P* if there is a polynomial p and a sequence of arithmetic algorithms $\{\mathrm{A}_i\}_{i=1}^{\infty}$, $\mathrm{A}_i\colon \mathcal{I}_i \times \mathbb{N} \to \mathbb{R}^{N_i}$ that satisfy

$$\mathrm{Error}(\mathrm{A}_i, \mathrm{R}, \iota, k) \leq 10^{-K}, \qquad \forall \iota \in \mathcal{I}_i,$$

and, if $n_i = m_i + m_i N_i$ is the size of the input,

$$\mathrm{CompCost}(\mathrm{A}_i, \iota, k) \leq p(n_i), \qquad \forall \iota \in \mathcal{I}_i.$$

Moreover, there is one BSS machine that can execute all A_i on its input for any $i \in \mathbb{N}$.

We are now ready to present the main result of this section.

Theorem 8.18 (Impossibility of computing minimizers) *Let* R *be the QCBP reconstruction map (8.11) and $K > 2$ be an integer. Then there exists a class of inputs $\mathcal{I} = \mathcal{I}_K$ of the form* (8.15) *and an oracle class $\widetilde{\mathcal{I}}$ for $\mathcal{I}$ such that the following holds:*

(a) No algorithm (not even a general algorithm) can produce K correct digits for all inputs in $\mathcal{I}$.
(b) There is an arithmetic algorithm that can produce $K - 1$ correct digits for all inputs in $\mathcal{I}$. However, any such algorithm will require an arbitrarily long time to do so. Specifically, there is a subclass $\mathcal{I}' \subset \mathcal{I}$ of inputs with fixed dimensions m and N such that the following holds. For every $T > 0$ and algorithm A*, there is an input $\iota \in \mathcal{I}'$ such that either* $\mathrm{A}(\iota)$ *does not approximate* $\mathrm{R}(\iota)$ *correctly to $K - 1$ digits or the runtime of* A *on ι is greater than T.*
(c) The problem of producing $K - 2$ correct digits for $\mathcal{I}$ is in P.
(d) If one considers (a)–(b) only then $\mathcal{I}$ can be chosen with fixed dimensions $m < N$ and $N \geq 4$. Moreover, if one only considers (a) then K can be chosen to be one.

This states the following. For any desired accuracy, given in terms of the number of digits K, there is a class of QCBP problems for which no algorithm can produce an error of less than 10^{-K} for all problems in the class. Moreover, while an error less than 10^{1-K} can be achieved for all problems in this class, the computational cost of doing so can be arbitrarily large. On the other hand, an error less than 10^{2-K} can be achieved in polynomial time.

Theorem 8.18 helps explain the dramatic failure witnessed in Table 7.2. None of the algorithms used in Matlab's `linprog` command are able to compute an approximation that is accurate to a certain number of digits. Yet, this is exactly the phenomenon described in part (a). Hence, the failure seen in Table 7.2 is not due to poor design of algorithms, but rather a fundamental mathematical barrier in computation.

Remark 8.19 The reader may be tempted to think that Theorem 8.18 arises because the class of input $\mathcal{I}$ is very unpleasant, and therefore irrelevant to applications. This is not the case. It can be shown that the class of inputs can be bounded above and below (in norm) and is well conditioned in a suitable sense. Moreover, the matrices in these classes can also be made to satisfy the rNSP. These details, and indeed, the proof of Theorem 8.18, are outside the scope of this book. See the Notes section for further information.

8.6 Complexity Theory for Compressed Sensing Problems

To conclude this chapter, we now present several positive counterparts to Theorem 8.18. These demonstrate that compressed sensing problems, specifically those for which the input matrices satisfy the rNSP, are efficiently computable up to a certain accuracy. To do this, we use the tools developed in this and the previous chapter to show that precise, algorithmic instances of methods considered previously produce approximate minimizers with accuracy proportional to the standard compressed sensing error bounds.

8.6.1 The SR-LASSO via the Primal–Dual Iteration

We first consider SR-LASSO. As before, we let

$$CS_s(x,e) = \frac{\sigma_s(x)_{\ell^1}}{\sqrt{s}} + \|e\|_{\ell^2},$$

and define constants D_0, D_1, D_2 depending on the rNSP constants ρ and γ as

$$D_0 = 2\max\{D_1, D_2\}, \quad D_1 = \frac{(3+\rho)(3\rho+5)}{4(1-\rho)}, \quad D_2 = \frac{(13+3\rho)(\rho+1)}{4(1-\rho)\rho}\gamma. \tag{8.16}$$

We now have the following result:

Theorem 8.20 (Cost of computing inexact minimizers of SR-LASSO) *Let $1 \leq s, m \leq N$, $0 < \rho < 1$, $\gamma > 0$, $\alpha > 0$ and $\zeta_0 \geq 0$. Consider any class of inputs $\mathcal{I} \subseteq \mathbb{R}^{m\times N} \times \mathbb{R}^m$ such that every $\iota = (A, y) \in \mathcal{I}$ has the following properties:*

(i) $A \in \mathbb{R}^{m\times N}$ satisfies the rNSP of order s with constants ρ and γ;
(ii) $\|A\|_{\ell^2} \leq \alpha$;
(iii) $y = Ax + e$ for some $x \in \mathbb{R}^N$ and $e \in \mathbb{R}^m$ satisfying $CS_s(x,e) \leq \zeta_0$ and $\|x\|_{\ell^2} \leq 1$.

Let $\mathrm{R}\colon \mathcal{I} \rightrightarrows \mathbb{R}^N$ denote the reconstruction map of the SR-LASSO problem (7.28) with parameter $\lambda = C_1(C_2\sqrt{s})^{-1}$, where C_1 and C_2 are as in (6.10), and $\widetilde{\mathcal{I}}$ be any oracle class for $\mathcal{I}$. Then there exists an arithmetic algorithm A such that

$$\mathrm{Error}(\mathrm{A}, \mathrm{R}, \iota, k) \leq 10^{-k}, \quad \forall \iota \in \mathcal{I},$$

for all $k \in \mathbb{N}$ satisfying

$$10^{-k} > \zeta_1 = 4D_0\zeta_0. \tag{8.17}$$

Moreover,

$$\mathrm{CompCost}(\mathrm{A}, \iota, k) \leq \left\lceil \frac{4D_2\alpha}{10^{-k} - \zeta_1} \right\rceil (2N_A + cN) + M, \quad \forall \iota \in \mathcal{I}, \tag{8.18}$$

where $c > 0$ is a numerical constant,

$$M = \lceil |\log_{10}(\delta)| \rceil, \qquad \delta = \min\left\{ \frac{10^{-k}}{8D_2}, \frac{1-\rho}{\gamma(2\sqrt{s}+\rho+1)} \right\},$$

and N_A is the maximum number of arithmetic operations and comparisons required to perform the matrix–vector multiplications $x \mapsto A'x$ and $y \mapsto (A')^\top y$ for any $(A', y') = \tilde{\iota}(M)$ and $\tilde{\iota} \in \widetilde{\mathcal{I}}$. Specifically, this algorithm is defined by $\mathrm{A}(\iota, k) = X_n$, where $n = n(k)$, $X_n = \frac{1}{n}\sum_{i=1}^n x_i$ and x_i is the output of the ith step of the primal–dual iteration (Algorithm 7.5) with the values

- $(A', y') = \tilde{\iota}(M)$,
- $\lambda' = \frac{D_1}{D_2\sqrt{s}}$,
- $x_0 = 0$, $\xi_0 = 0$,
- $\tau = \sigma = 1/\alpha$,
- $n(k) = \left\lceil \frac{4D_2\alpha}{10^{-k}-\zeta_1} \right\rceil$.

Proof Lemma 8.5 implies that A' has the rNSP with constants ρ' and γ', where

$$\rho' = \frac{\rho + \gamma\delta\sqrt{s}}{1-\gamma\delta} \leq \frac{\rho+1}{2} = \rho'', \qquad \gamma' = \frac{\gamma}{1-\gamma\delta} \leq \frac{\rho+1}{2\rho}\gamma = \gamma''.$$

Here the inequalities follow from the definition of δ. Observe that

$$\frac{(3\rho''+1)(\rho''+1)}{2(1-\rho'')} = D_1, \qquad \frac{(3\rho''+5)\gamma''}{2(1-\rho'')} = D_2, \tag{8.19}$$

where D_1 and D_2 are as in (8.16). Also, we may write $y' = A'x + e'$, where $e' = y' - y + e + (A - A')x$. Hence Theorem 8.7, the choices for $x_0, \xi_0, \tau, \sigma, \lambda'$ and the fact that $\|x\|_{\ell^2} \leq 1$ give

$$\|X_n - x\|_{\ell^2} \leq 2D_1 \frac{\sigma_s(x)_{\ell^1}}{\sqrt{s}} + \frac{2D_2\alpha}{n} + 2D_2\|e'\|_{\ell^2}.$$

Notice that

$$\|e'\|_{\ell^2} \leq \|y' - y\|_{\ell^2} + \|A' - A\|_{\ell^2}\|x\|_{\ell^2} + \|e\|_{\ell^2} \leq 2\delta + \|e\|_{\ell^2}.$$

Hence

$$\begin{aligned} \|X_n - x\|_{\ell^2} &\leq 2D_1 \frac{\sigma_s(x)_{\ell^1}}{\sqrt{s}} + \frac{2D_2\alpha}{n} + 2D_2(\|e\|_{\ell^2} + 2\delta) \\ &\leq D_0\zeta_0 + 2D_2\left(2\delta + \alpha/n\right). \end{aligned} \tag{8.20}$$

Now, since A has the rNSP with constants ρ and γ, Theorem 6.5 and the value for λ give

$$\|x - \hat{x}\|_{\ell^2} \leq 2C_1 \frac{\sigma_s(x)_{\ell^1}}{\sqrt{s}} + 2C_2\|e\|_{\ell^2},$$

for all $\hat{x} \in \mathrm{R}(\iota)$, where C_1 and C_2 are as in (6.10). Notice that the constants (6.10) are increasing in ρ and γ. Since $\rho \leq \rho''$ and $\gamma \leq \gamma''$, (8.19) gives that $C_1 \leq D_1$ and $C_2 \leq D_2$. Therefore

$$\|x - \hat{x}\|_{\ell^2} \leq D_0\zeta_0.$$

Combining this with (8.20) and using the definition of n and δ, we obtain

$$\|X_n - \hat{x}\|_{\ell^2} \leq 2D_0\zeta_0 + 2D_2\left(2\delta + \alpha/n\right) \leq 10^{-k},$$

as required. Note that the estimate for computational cost follows immediately from Algorithm 7.5 and the definition of $n(k)$. □

8.6.2 QCBP via NESTA

Next we consider QCBP. As before, we define

$$\mathcal{CS}_s(x,\eta) = \frac{\sigma_s(x)_{\ell^1}}{\sqrt{s}} + \eta.$$

Theorem 8.21 (Cost of computing inexact minimizers of QCBP) *Let $1 \leq s, m \leq N$, $0 < \rho < 1, \gamma > 0, \alpha > 0, \eta \geq 0$ and $\zeta_0 \geq 0$. Consider any class of inputs $\mathcal{I} \subseteq \mathbb{R}^{m\times N} \times \mathbb{R}^m$ such that every $\iota = (A, y) \in \mathcal{I}$ has the following properties:*

(i) $A \in \mathbb{R}^{m \times N}$ *satisfies the rNSP of order s with constants* ρ *and* γ*;*

(ii) $AA^\top = \alpha^2 I$*;*

(iii) $y = Ax + e$ *for some* $x \in \mathbb{R}^N$ *and* $e \in \mathbb{R}^m$ *satisfying* $\|e\|_{\ell^2} \leq \eta$, $CS_s(x, \eta) \leq \zeta_0$ *and* $\|x\|_{\ell^2} \leq 1$.

Let $\mathrm{R}\colon \mathcal{I} \rightrightarrows \mathbb{R}^N$ *denote the reconstruction map of the QCBP problem (7.8) with parameter* η*. Consider any oracle class* $\widetilde{\mathcal{I}}$ *for* $\mathcal{I}$ *with the property that* $A'(A')^\top = \alpha^2 I$ *whenever* $(A', y') = \tilde{\iota}(m)$ *for some* $m \in \mathbb{N}$ *and* $\tilde{\iota} \in \widetilde{\mathcal{I}}$*. Then there exists an arithmetic algorithm* A *such that*

$$\mathrm{Error}(\mathrm{A}, \mathrm{R}, \iota, k) \leq 10^{-k}, \quad \forall \iota \in \mathcal{I},$$

for all $k \in \mathbb{N}$ *satisfying*

$$10^{-k} > \zeta_1 = 4D_0\zeta_0, \tag{8.21}$$

where D_0 *is as in (8.16). Moreover, if* D_1, D_2 *are also as in (8.16), then*

$$\mathrm{CompCost}(\mathrm{A}, \iota, k) \leq \left\lceil \frac{17D_1\sqrt{N}}{\sqrt{s}(10^{-k} - \zeta_1)} \right\rceil (6N_A + cN) + M, \quad \forall \iota \in \mathcal{I}, \tag{8.22}$$

where $c > 0$ *is a numerical constant,*

$$M = \lceil |\log_{10}(\delta)| \rceil, \qquad \delta = \min\left\{ \frac{10^{-k}}{8D_2}, \frac{1-\rho}{\gamma(2\sqrt{s} + \rho + 1)} \right\},$$

and N_A *is the maximum number of arithmetic operations and comparisons required to perform the matrix–vector multiplications* $x \mapsto A'x$ *and* $y \mapsto (A')^\top y$ *for any* $(A', y') = \tilde{\iota}(M)$ *and* $\tilde{\iota} \in \widetilde{\mathcal{I}}$*. Specifically, this algorithm is defined by* $\mathrm{A}(\iota, k) = x_n$*, where* $n = n(k)$ *and* x_n *is the output of the nth step of NESTA (Algorithm 7.7) with parameters*

- $(A', y') = \tilde{\iota}(M)$,
- $\eta' = \eta + 2\delta$,
- $z_0 = 0$,
- $\mu(k) = \frac{\sqrt{s}(10^{-k} - \zeta_1)}{17D_1 N}$,
- $n(k) = \left\lceil \frac{17D_1\sqrt{N}}{\sqrt{s}(10^{-k} - \zeta_1)} \right\rceil$.

Proof As in the proof of Theorem 8.20, we first note that A' has the rNSP with constants $\rho'' = \frac{\rho+1}{2}$ and $\gamma'' = \frac{\rho+1}{2\rho}\gamma$. We also have $y' = A'x + e'$, where $e' = y' - y + e + (A - A')x$ satisfies

$$\|e'\|_{\ell^2} \leq \delta + \|e\|_{\ell^2} + \delta\|x\|_{\ell^2} \leq 2\delta + \eta = \eta'. \tag{8.23}$$

Hence, we now apply Theorem 8.9 with A', y', η', ρ'' and γ'', to obtain

$$\begin{aligned}\|x - x_n\|_{\ell^2} &\leq 2D_1\frac{\sigma_s(x)_{\ell^1}}{\sqrt{s}} + 2D_2(\eta + 2\delta) + D_1\frac{N\mu}{2\sqrt{s}} \\ &\quad + \frac{2D_1}{\mu n^2\sqrt{s}}\left(2D_1\frac{\sigma_s(x)_{\ell^1}}{\sqrt{s}} + D_1\frac{N\mu}{2\sqrt{s}} + 2D_2(\eta + 2\delta) + \|x - z_0\|_{\ell^2}\right)^2,\end{aligned}$$

where D_1, D_2 are as in (8.16). Using the definitions of D_0 and δ and the facts that $z_0 = 0$, $\|x\|_{\ell^2} \leq 1$ and $CS_s(x, \eta) \leq \zeta_0$, we get

$$\|x - x_n\|_{\ell^2} \leq D_0\zeta_0 + \frac{10^{-k}}{2} + D_1\frac{N\mu}{2\sqrt{s}} + \frac{2D_1}{\mu n^2\sqrt{s}}\left(D_0\zeta_0 + \frac{10^{-k}}{2} + D_1\frac{N\mu}{2\sqrt{s}} + 1\right)^2.$$

Observe that

$$D_1\frac{N\mu}{2\sqrt{s}} = \frac{10^{-k} - \zeta_1}{34} < \frac{1}{34} < \frac{1}{4}.$$

Since $n(k) \geq \frac{1}{\sqrt{N\mu(k)}}$, we also have

$$\frac{2D_1}{\mu n^2\sqrt{s}} \leq \frac{2D_1 N\mu}{\sqrt{s}} = \frac{2(10^{-k} - \zeta_1)}{17}.$$

We may assume that $D_0\zeta_0 < 1/4$ (otherwise (8.21) does not hold for any k). Substituting this and the previous two expressions into the earlier bound and simplifying gives

$$\begin{aligned}\|x - x_n\|_{\ell^2} &\leq D_0\zeta_0 + \frac{10^{-k}}{2} + \frac{10^{-k} - \zeta_1}{34} + \frac{2(10^{-k} - \zeta_1)}{17}\left(\frac{1}{4} + \frac{1}{2} + \frac{1}{4} + 1\right)^2 \\ &= D_0\zeta_0 + \frac{10^{-k}}{2} + \frac{10^{-k} - \zeta_1}{2}.\end{aligned}$$

To complete the proof, we apply Theorem 5.17 to get, after noting that the constants therein are increasing in ρ and γ,

$$\|x - \hat{x}\|_{\ell^2} \leq D_0\zeta_0,$$

for all $\hat{x} \in \mathrm{R}(\iota)$. Thus, by the triangle inequality and the definition of ζ_1,

$$\|\hat{x} - x_n\|_{\ell^2} \leq 2C_0\zeta_0 + 10^{-k} - \zeta_1/2 = 10^{-k},$$

as required. The estimate for the computational cost follows immediately from Algorithm 7.7 and the definition of $n(k)$. □

8.6.3 Why Compressed Sensing is Successful

Theorems 8.20 and 8.21 provide a positive counterpart to Theorem 8.18. They assert that minimizers of SR-LASSO or QCBP can be computed not to arbitrary accuracy, but rather to a limiting accuracy ζ_1 (defined by (8.17) and (8.21), respectively) that is proportional to the standard compressed sensing error bound. This brings us to the main conclusion of this chapter.

> Compressed sensing succeeds not because minimizers of problems such as QCBP and SR-LASSO can be computed to arbitrary accuracy, but rather because they can be computed down to the accuracy needed: namely, the standard compressed sensing error bounds $CS_s(x, \eta)$ and $CS_s(x, e)$.

As is to be expected from Theorem 8.18 – recall from Remark 8.19 that the classes in this theorem can be made to satisfy the rNSP – the computational cost in either Theorem 8.20 or Theorem 8.21 blows up as the accuracy one seeks gets closer to the limiting value ζ_1. We do not claim that the value for ζ_1 is completely sharp. Nevertheless, these results capture the essence of the underlying computational limit.

8.6.4 Polynomial Cost in the Dimension, Potentially Exponential Cost in the Number of Digits

There is, however, one issue that warrants further investigation: the computational cost. Let K be the number of digits of accuracy desired, and assume for convenience that $10^{-K} \geq 2\zeta_1$ (this ensures that the denominator $10^{-K} - \zeta_1$ in the computational cost bounds (8.18) and (8.22) is not too small). As in §8.2, suppose that $\alpha \lesssim \sqrt{N/s}$ in the case of Theorem 8.20 and let $s \asymp N$ in both cases. Then Theorem 8.20 and Theorem 8.21 state that the computational cost of producing K correct digits behaves like

$$O(N^2 10^K),$$

for general classes of matrices, since $N_A = O\left(N^2\right)$ in general, or

$$O(N \log(N) 10^K),$$

whenever $\mathcal{I}$ is a class of matrices that have fast transforms (e.g. a class of subsampled Fourier matrices). In both cases, these computational cost bounds are polynomial in the number of inputs (note that the number of inputs is at most $m + mN \leq (N+1)N$). However, they are *exponential* in the number of digits of accuracy desired K.

The extent to which this exponential dependence is undesirable depends on the application. In imaging, as noted in §7.2.2, two to three digits often suffice. Imaging problems are often large scale, but amenable to fast transforms. Having an $N\log(N)$ cost in N is often more important than a potentially exponential cost in K. Moreover, the above estimates are only upper bounds – algorithms may perform better in practice than these worst-case estimates predict. On the other hand, other applications may involve smaller-scale problems, but demand higher accuracy. In this case, a worse scaling with respect to N may be tolerable, but a potentially exponential cost in K may not.

8.6.5 Nemirovski's Surface-Following Method: Polynomial Time in N and K

Fortunately, this exponential dependence in K can be provably overcome by using a different method. In the following theorem, we employ *Nemirovski's surface-following method* (a type of interior point method). This method uses only arithmetic operations, comparisons and square roots of positive real numbers, and thus it fits within the assumed model of computation. Using it, this theorem shows that there is an algorithm for solving QCBP that is provably polynomial in both N *and* K. The caveat is a worse rate of polynomial growth with respect to the former than in Theorem 8.21.

Theorem 8.22 *Let $1 \leq s, m \leq N$, $0 < \rho < 1$, $\gamma > 0$, $\alpha > 0$, $\eta \geq 0$ and $\zeta_0 \geq 0$. Consider a class of inputs $\mathcal{I} \subseteq \mathbb{R}^{m \times N} \times \mathbb{R}^m$ such that every $\iota = (A, y) \in \mathcal{I}$ has the following properties:*

(i) $A \in \mathbb{R}^{m \times N}$ *satisfies the rNSP of order* s *with constants* ρ *and* γ*;*

(ii) $\|A\|_{\ell^2} \leq \alpha$*;*

(iii) $y = Ax + e$ *for some* $x \in \mathbb{R}^N$ *and* $e \in \mathbb{R}^m$ *satisfying* $\|e\|_{\ell^2} \leq \eta$, $\mathcal{CS}_s(x, \eta) \leq \zeta_0$ *and* $\|x\|_{\ell^2} \leq 1$.

Let $\mathrm{R}\colon \mathcal{I} \rightrightarrows \mathbb{R}^N$ *denote the reconstruction map of the QCBP problem (7.8) with parameter* η *and* $\widetilde{\mathcal{I}}$ *be any oracle class for* $\mathcal{I}$*. Then there exists an arithmetic algorithm* A *such that*

$$\mathrm{Error}(\mathrm{A}, \mathrm{R}, \iota, k) \leq 10^{-k}, \quad \forall \iota \in \mathcal{I},$$

for all $k \in \mathbb{N}$ *satisfying*

$$10^{-k} > \zeta_1 = 4D_0\zeta_0,$$

where D_0 *is as in (8.16). Moreover, if* D_1, D_2 *are also as in (8.16), then*

$$\mathrm{CompCost}(\mathrm{A}, \iota, k) \leq cN^{7/2}\left(\log(2N) + \log\left(\frac{2(D_1 + D_2)(\alpha + \eta + 2)}{10^{-k} - \zeta_1}\right)\right) + M, \quad \forall \iota \in \mathcal{I},$$

where $c > 0$ *is a numerical constant and*

$$M = \lceil |\log_{10}(\delta)| \rceil, \qquad \delta = \min\left\{\frac{10^{-k}}{8D_2}, \frac{1-\rho}{\gamma(2\sqrt{s} + \rho + 1)}, 1\right\}.$$

This result is similar to Theorem 8.21, which also applies to QCBP, except for the computational cost bound. To see this, consider the setup of §8.6.4, where K is the number of digits desired, and suppose that $10^{-K} \geq 2\zeta_1$, $\alpha \lesssim \sqrt{N/s}$, $s \asymp N$ and $\eta \leq 1$. Then the computational cost of producing K correct digits via the algorithm of Theorem 8.22 behaves like

$$\mathcal{O}(N^{7/2}(\log(N) + K)).$$

In particular, the computational cost is linear in K, whereas the previous algorithms were exponential in K. On the other hand, as expected, the scaling with respect to N is worse, roughly $N^{7/2}$, as opposed to N^2, or even $N\log(N)$, for the previous algorithms.

Proof of Theorem 8.22 The proof is based on Nemirovski's surface-following method. We shall forgo a formal definition of this method, as well as an in-depth discussion of the key properties of it that we use in the proof. We refer to the Notes section for further information and references.

Let $\iota = (A, y) \in \mathcal{I}$ and write $y = Ax + e$, where $\|e\|_{\ell^2} \leq \eta$, $\mathcal{CS}_s(x, \eta) \leq \zeta_0$ and $\|x\|_{\ell^2} \leq 1$. Let $(A', y') = \tilde{\iota}(M)$, where $\tilde{\iota} \in \widetilde{\mathcal{I}}$ is any oracle for ι. As in the previous proofs, A' has the rNSP of order s with constants $\rho'' = \frac{\rho+1}{2}$ and $\gamma'' = \frac{\rho+1}{2\rho}\gamma$. Now, consider the following convex quadratic problem:

$$\begin{aligned} \min_{(z^+, z^-) \in \mathbb{R}^N \times \mathbb{R}^N} \quad \langle \mathbb{I}, z^+ \rangle + \langle \mathbb{I}, z^- \rangle \quad \text{s.t.} \quad & \|A'z^+ - A'z^- - y'\|_{\ell^2}^2 \leq (\eta')^2, \\ & z^+ \geq 0, \ z^- \geq 0, \\ & \|z^+\|_{\ell^2}^2 + \|z^-\|_{\ell^2}^2 \leq 1, \end{aligned} \tag{8.24}$$

where $\mathbb{I}$ is the vector of ones, $\eta' = 2\delta + \eta$ and the inequalities $z^+ \geq 0$ and $z^- \geq 0$ are understood elementwise. Write $x = x^+ - x^-$, where $x^+ \geq 0$ is the positive part of x and

$x^- \geq 0$ is the negative part. Then (8.23) implies that the point $(x^+, x^-) \in \mathbb{R}^N \times \mathbb{R}^N$ is feasible for (8.24).

Let $\delta' = \frac{10^{-k} - \zeta_1}{2(D_1 + D_2)}$. We now apply Nemirovski's surface-following method to find a $(\delta')^2$-solution $(\tilde{x}^+, \tilde{x}^-) \in \mathbb{R}^N \times \mathbb{R}^N$ to (8.24), i.e. a point such that

$$\begin{aligned} &\|\tilde{x}^+\|_{\ell^2}^2 + \|\tilde{x}^-\|_{\ell^2}^2 \leq 1, \\ &\|A'\tilde{x}^+ - A'\tilde{x}^- - y'\|_{\ell^2}^2 \leq (\eta')^2 + (\delta')^2, \\ &\tilde{x}^+ \geq -(\delta')^2, \ \tilde{x}^- \geq -(\delta')^2, \\ &\langle \mathbb{I}, \tilde{x}^+ \rangle + \langle \mathbb{I}, \tilde{x}^- \rangle \leq \langle \mathbb{I}, \check{x}^+ \rangle + \langle \mathbb{I}, \check{x}^- \rangle + (\delta')^2, \end{aligned}$$

where $(\check{x}^+, \check{x}^-)$ is a minimizer of (8.24). Define the output of the arithmetic algorithm as $\mathrm{A}(\iota, k) = \tilde{x} := \tilde{x}^+ - \tilde{x}^- \in \mathbb{R}^N$. Notice that $\delta' \leq 1$ since $k \geq 1$ and $D_1 \geq 15/4$. Therefore

$$\|\tilde{x}\|_{\ell^1} - \|x\|_{\ell^1} = (\langle \mathbb{I}, \tilde{x}^+ \rangle + \langle \mathbb{I}, \tilde{x}^- \rangle) - (\langle \mathbb{I}, x^+ \rangle + \langle \mathbb{I}, x^- \rangle) \leq (\delta')^2 \leq \delta',$$

and, by definition of δ,

$$\begin{aligned} \|A'(\tilde{x} - x)\|_{\ell^2} &\leq \|A'\tilde{x} - y'\|_{\ell^2} + \|Ax - y\|_{\ell^2} + \|(A' - A)x\|_{\ell^2} + \|y - y'\|_{\ell^2} \\ &\leq \sqrt{(\eta')^2 + (\delta')^2} + \eta + \delta + \delta \leq 2\eta + 4\delta + \delta'. \end{aligned}$$

Lemma 5.16 gives

$$\|x - \tilde{x}\|_{\ell^2} \leq 2D_1 \frac{\sigma_s(x)_{\ell^1}}{\sqrt{s}} + D_1 \frac{\|\tilde{x}\|_{\ell^1} - \|x\|_{\ell^1}}{\sqrt{s}} + D_2 \|A'(\tilde{x} - x)\|_{\ell^2},$$

where D_1, D_2 are as in (8.16). Hence

$$\|x - \tilde{x}\|_{\ell^2} \leq 2D_1 \frac{\sigma_s(x)_{\ell^1}}{\sqrt{s}} + D_1\delta' + D_2(2\eta + 4\delta + \delta') \leq D_0\zeta_0 + 4D_2\delta + (D_1 + D_2)\delta'.$$

Exactly as in the proof of Theorem 8.21, we also have $\|x - \hat{x}\|_{\ell^2} \leq D_0\zeta_0$ for all $\hat{x} \in \mathrm{R}(\iota)$. Hence, by the definition of δ, δ' and the condition on k,

$$\|\hat{x} - \tilde{x}\|_{\ell^2} \leq 2D_0\zeta_0 + 4D_2\delta + (D_1 + D_2)\delta' \leq 2D_0\zeta_0 + \frac{10^{-k}}{2} + \frac{10^{-k} - \zeta_1}{2} = 10^{-k},$$

as required. The computational cost of the algorithm is bounded by a constant multiple of the quantity

$$N^{7/2} \cdot \log\left(N\left(2 + V/(\delta')^2\right)\right), \tag{8.25}$$

where V is the *scale factor*, given by

$$V := \max\left\{1, \frac{1}{2}\|A'\|_{\ell^2}^2 + \|(A')^\top y'\|_{\ell^2} + \|y'\|_{\ell^2}^2\right\}.$$

Notice that $\|A'\|_{\ell^2} \leq \|A\|_{\ell^2} + \delta \leq \alpha + \delta$ and

$$\|y'\|_{\ell^2} \leq \|y\|_{\ell^2} + \delta \leq \|Ax\|_{\ell^2} + \|e\|_{\ell^2} + \delta \leq \alpha + \eta + \delta.$$

Since $\delta \leq 1$, we deduce that V can be bounded by

$$V \leq \frac{1}{2}(\alpha + 1)^2 + (\alpha + 1)(\alpha + \eta + 1) + (\alpha + \eta + 1)^2 \leq 4(\alpha + \eta + 1)^2.$$

Hence

$$\log\left(N\left(2+V/(\delta')^2\right)\right) \leq \log\left(4N\left(1+(\alpha+\eta+1)^2/(\delta')^2\right)\right)$$
$$\leq \log(4N) + 2\log\left(\frac{\alpha+\eta+2}{\delta'}\right),$$

where we use the fact that $\delta' \leq 1$ once more. Substituting the value of δ' now yields the result. □

Notes

There has been relatively little work that seeks to combine compressed sensing theory with optimization methods for compressed sensing problems. Definition 8.3 is based on Ben-Tal & Nemirovski [65, Sec. 1.3.1]. To the best of our knowledge, the analysis of the primal–dual iteration conducted in §8.2 is new. Analysis of NESTA in terms of the NSP was considered in [422], along with a restart procedure (similar in spirit to the continuation approach of [60]) that yields a faster, linear order of convergence. See [286,422,526] and references therein for related work in this direction. See also [166] and [214, Sec. 15.3] for related results for the IRLS method.

Complexity analysis in the fields of discrete and combinatorial optimization (see, for example, [244]) and continuous optimization (see, for example, [66, 379]) have traditionally been quite different.The former community primarily uses the *Turing model*, whereas the latter typically allows for arithmetic operations and comparisons with real numbers. In addition, certain elementary functions such as the square root are commonly assumed. The Turing model is well defined through the *Turing machine* [472]. The BSS machine, introduced by Blum, Shub & Smale in [77], is a natural choice for complexity analysis when considering computations with real numbers. Although the classical BSS machine only allows for arithmetic operations and comparisons, it is easy to add oracles or subroutines (such as computing a square root) to this framework. For more information on BSS machines, see [76] as well as [444]. See also [103] for further discussion on analysis of algorithms.

Since algorithms for optimization problems in compressed sensing are primarily of continuous optimization type, our analysis has been conducted in the BSS model. However, Theorem 8.18 holds in all models of computation, in particular, the Turing model. In that case the definition of 'in P' is the classical definition using a Turing machine. Given that the proofs of the existence results allow for arbitrary inexact input, all the convergence analysis in Theorems 8.20–8.22 also applies in the Turing model, as long as the square root is appropriately approximated. The complexity analysis is, however, different.

The idea of attaching oracles to a BSS machine, as we do in Definition 8.13, is an integrated part of the theory (just as it is for Turing machines). To be precise, when in Definition 8.13 we describe a BSS machine with a node for the oracle $\tilde{\iota}$, we mean that the same machine allows for different oracles $\tilde{\iota}$. This is similar to the concept of a Turing machine with an oracle tape, where it is the same machine, but the oracle tape can be replaced. The reason for this seemingly cumbersome way of rewriting the input as an oracle is that both Turing and BSS machines were typically meant to take a finite string of information. If one wants an infinite string as an input for a Turing machine, for example a computable irrational number represented in its digit expansion, this is usually put in an oracle tape, where the machine can make a query about the nth digit. It is exactly the same issue for a BSS machine: an infinite string of information is treated as an oracle, where one can, for example, make a query about the nth digit of a number.

It is somewhat idealized to let the square root be an allowed operation, since it will be approximated in any real-world algorithm. However, allowing square roots is a fairly common assumption and one that makes the various statements and proofs significantly simpler. Performing complexity analysis without allowing an exact square root can be very cumbersome. Thus, to keep the length of our analysis at a reasonable level, we have followed the standard tradition and allowed square roots. However, the results do not require exact computation of any other functions.

Theorem 8.18 was first shown in [52], see also [256]. Similar results also hold for U-LASSO, C-LASSO and, furthermore, linear programming (7.5). This may come as a surprise to the reader. One of the more celebrated results in complexity theory of optimization is the statement 'linear programming is in P' [220, 290, 316]. We caution, however, that this statement applies to exact input, whereas Theorem 8.18 deals with the setting of inexact input. See [52, 256] for further discussion.

For further information on Remark 8.19, see [52, 256]. As is also discussed therein, Theorem 8.18 extends to the more general class of *randomized* algorithms. In this case, statements analogous to (a) and (b) hold with a certain probability.

Theorems 8.20–8.22 are new. Nemirovski's surface-following method was introduced in the paper [374]. It is also described in detail in [64, Secs. 16.3.2 & 16.4.2]. The estimate for the computational cost of the surface-following method used in (8.25) in the proof of Theorem 8.22 can be found in [64, Sec. 16.4.2.6].

9 Wavelets

In this chapter, we introduce wavelets in a formal way. After a short motivating section (§9.1), we first present the general construction of orthogonal wavelets via a MultiResolution Analysis (MRA) (§9.2 and §9.3). We next discuss the various properties that one may wish a wavelet basis to possess in order for it to be effective at compressively representing piecewise smooth functions (§9.4). After that, we present the construction of the famous Daubechies wavelets (§9.5 and §9.6), including the frequently used DB4 wavelet. Next, in §9.7 we discuss strategies for constructing orthonormal wavelet bases on finite intervals. Up to this point, the wavelets constructed are one-dimensional. In §9.8 we extend these constructions to the two-dimensional setting. After summarizing the various constructions in §9.9, in §9.10 we consider discrete wavelet computations, in particular, the Discrete Wavelet Transform (DWT) and wavelet sparsifying transforms. Finally, we conclude in §9.11 with a brief discussion on generalizations of wavelets.

We make heavy use of orthonormal bases of Hilbert spaces and Fourier transforms and series in this chapter. Background material can be found in Appendices B and E.

9.1 Introduction

A wavelet is a function whose integer translations and dilations by factors of two generate an orthonormal basis of the Hilbert space $L^2(\mathbb{R})$.

Definition 9.1 (Orthonormal wavelet) An *orthonormal wavelet* is a function $\psi \in L^2(\mathbb{R})$ for which the set

$$\{\psi_{j,n} := 2^{j/2}\psi(2^j \cdot -n) : j, n \in \mathbb{Z}\} \tag{9.1}$$

is an orthonormal basis of $L^2(\mathbb{R})$.

9.1.1 The Haar Wavelet

The Haar wavelet is the classical example of an orthonormal wavelet:

Example 9.2 (The Haar wavelet) The Haar wavelet is the function

$$\psi(x) = \begin{cases} 1 & 0 \leq x < 1/2 \\ -1 & 1/2 \leq x < 1 \\ 0 & \text{otherwise} \end{cases}. \tag{9.2}$$

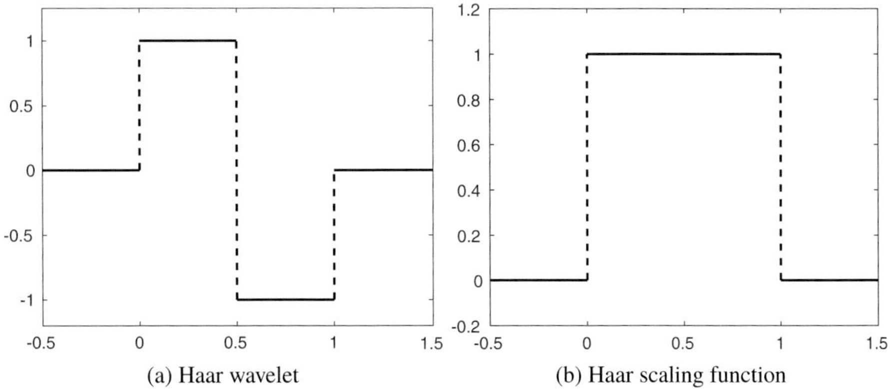

Figure 9.1 The Haar wavelet and its scaling function.

See Fig. 9.1(a). It is straightforward to show that $\{\psi_{j,n} : j, n \in \mathbb{Z}\}$ is an orthonormal system in $L^2(\mathbb{R})$. That it also forms a basis will be proved later (see Theorem 9.9 and Example 9.4).

Consider the Haar wavelet (9.2). By virtue of the fact that (9.1) is an orthonormal basis, every function $f \in L^2(\mathbb{R})$ can be expressed as

$$f = \sum_{j\in\mathbb{Z}} \sum_{n\in\mathbb{Z}} d_{j,n}\psi_{j,n}, \tag{9.3}$$

where $d_{j,n} = \langle f, \psi_{j,n}\rangle_{L^2}$ are the *wavelet coefficients* of f. For the purposes of sparse approximation using wavelets, we are interested in the extent to which these coefficients are compressible.

To examine this, we first notice that $\psi_{j,n}$ is a dilation of ψ by a factor of 2^j. For large j, the support of $\psi_{j,n}$ – namely the interval $[n/2^j, (n+1)/2^j)$ – is increasingly localized around the point $x = n/2^j$. Hence the coefficient $d_{j,n}$ carries *local* information about the behaviour of f around this point. If f is sufficiently smooth in a neighbourhood of $x = n/2^j$, then

$$\begin{aligned} d_{j,n} &= 2^{j/2} \int_{n/2^j}^{(n+1)/2^j} f(x)\psi(2^j x - n)\,\mathrm{d}x \\ &= 2^{-j/2} \int_0^1 f((z+n)/2^j)\psi(z)\,\mathrm{d}z \\ &\approx 2^{-j/2} \int_0^1 \left(f(n/2^j) + z/2^j f'(n/2^j)\right)\psi(z)\,\mathrm{d}z = -2^{-3j/2} f'(n/2^j)/4, \end{aligned}$$

since $\int_0^1 \psi(z)\,\mathrm{d}z = 0$ and $\int_0^1 z\psi(z)\,\mathrm{d}z = -1/4$. Hence $d_{j,n} = O(2^{-3j/2})$ as $j \to \infty$ whenever f is smooth within the support of $\psi_{j,n}$. On the other hand, one always has

$$|d_{j,n}| \le 2^{-j/2}\|f\|_{L^\infty}.$$

Therefore nonsmooth regions of f correspond to wavelet coefficients of magnitude $|d_{j,n}| = O(2^{-j/2})$ as $j \to \infty$.

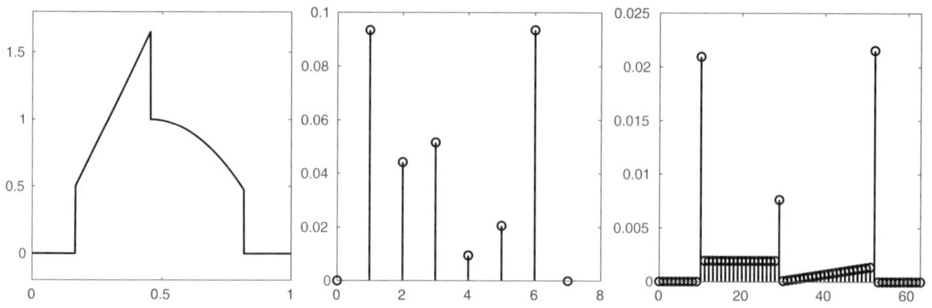

Figure 9.2 Piecewise smooth function (left), wavelet coefficients $|d_{j,n}|$ at scale $j = 3$ (middle), wavelet coefficients at scale $j = 6$ (right). The coefficients at fine scales are compressible, with only those coefficients corresponding to the three discontinuities of f being large.

This implies the following. Suppose that f is a piecewise smooth function with a finite number of discontinuities (this is a reasonable one-dimensional model for images). Then at a large – or, as we will say later, *fine* – scale $j \gg 1$ the majority of its Haar wavelet coefficients $\{d_{j,n}\}_{n\in\mathbb{Z}}$ are relatively small, with only those whose supports intersect the discontinuities of f being large. In other words, wavelet coefficients at fine scales are *compressible*. Figure 9.2 illustrates this property. At the coarse scale $j = 3$ the majority of the coefficients are relatively large, but at the fine scale $j = 6$ all the coefficients are small, except for those corresponding to the three discontinuities of the function.

9.1.2 The Haar Scaling Function

What about when j is negative? In this case, as $j \to -\infty$ the support of $\psi_{j,n}$ becomes increasingly wide, meaning that $d_{j,n}$ encompasses increasingly *global* features of f. This is undesirable for the purposes of compressibility. Fortunately, as we now demonstrate, the wavelets and corresponding coefficients at these scales can be conveniently reformulated into a new set of localized basis functions.

Associated with a wavelet ψ is a second function φ, known as the *scaling function*. In the case of (9.2), φ is the indicator function of the interval $[0, 1)$:

$$\varphi(x) = \begin{cases} 1 & 0 \leq x < 1 \\ 0 & \text{otherwise} \end{cases}. \tag{9.4}$$

See Fig. 9.1(b). As we show later, the integer translates $\{\varphi_{0,n} := \varphi(\cdot - n),\ n \in \mathbb{Z}\}$ of the scaling function φ span exactly the same space as the wavelets $\{\psi_{j,n} : j < 0,\ n \in \mathbb{Z}\}$ at negative scales. This therefore gives rise to a new orthonormal basis of $L^2(\mathbb{R})$:

$$\{\varphi_{0,n} : n \in \mathbb{Z}\} \cup \{\psi_{j,n} : j = 0, 1, 2, \ldots, n \in \mathbb{Z}\}. \tag{9.5}$$

Hence, we may now replace (9.3) with the expansion

$$f = \sum_{n\in\mathbb{Z}} c_{0,n}\varphi_{0,n} + \sum_{j\geq 0}\sum_{n\in\mathbb{Z}} d_{j,n}\psi_{j,n}, \tag{9.6}$$

where $c_{0,n} = \langle f, \varphi_{0,n} \rangle_{L^2}$ are the so-called *scaling coefficients* and, as before, $d_{j,n} = \langle f, \psi_{j,n} \rangle_{L^2}$ are its wavelet coefficients.

9.1.3 The Haar Wavelet Basis of $L^2([0, 1])$

Equation (9.6) describes the expansion of a function on the real line in terms of Haar wavelets and scaling functions. However, since images are compactly supported, we are primarily interested in functions that are supported on compact intervals, which we take to be $[0, 1]$ without loss of generality. For the Haar wavelet, it is elementary to construct an orthonormal basis of $L^2([0, 1])$. Since $\text{supp}(\varphi_{0,n}) = [n, n + 1)$ and $\text{supp}(\psi_{j,n}) = [n/2^j, (n + 1)/2^j)$, we simply replace the expansion (9.6) by

$$f = c_{0,0}\varphi_{0,0} + \sum_{j \geq 0} \sum_{n=0}^{2^j - 1} d_{j,n}\psi_{j,n},$$

for $f \in L^2([0, 1])$. The corresponding system

$$\{\varphi_{0,0}\} \cup \{\psi_{j,n} : n = 0, \ldots, 2^j - 1, \ j = 0, 1, 2, \ldots\} \tag{9.7}$$

then yields the orthonormal Haar wavelet basis of $L^2([0, 1])$.

As an aside, we caution the reader that the above procedure only works for the Haar wavelet. For other wavelets, constructing orthonormal bases on intervals will require additional effort (see §9.7).

9.1.4 Beyond Haar

To summarize, via the Haar wavelet (9.2) and scaling function (9.4) we have constructed orthonormal bases (9.5) and (9.7) of $L^2(\mathbb{R})$ and $L^2([0, 1])$, respectively in which the coefficients of a piecewise smooth function are increasingly compressible at fine scales ($j \gg 1$). This can also be extended to two dimensions (see §9.8), thus yielding a sparsifying transform suitable for representing two-dimensional piecewise smooth images.

Why then is there a need to go any further? Unfortunately, the Haar basis is rather limited. First, the $\mathcal{O}(2^{-3j/2})$ decay rate of the 'smooth' coefficients is not particularly fast in j, meaning the coefficients are not especially sparse at moderate scales. Second, any approximation to f using finitely many Haar wavelets is itself piecewise constant, which results in undesirable 'blocky' artefacts. Figure 9.3(b) illustrates this effect for a two-dimensional image.

With this in mind, the rest of this chapter is devoted to the construction of families of wavelets – in particular, the so-called *Daubechies wavelets* – that mitigate these issues. These wavelets possess more *vanishing moments* than the Haar wavelet, a property that results in faster decay of the 'smooth' coefficients, and higher orders of smoothness, which leads to less blocky artefacts. An illustration of this benefit is shown in Fig. 9.3(c), which uses the DB4 wavelet (see Remark 9.17). While the original image is not approximated perfectly, the smooth elliptical curves that define its edges are recovered more faithfully with this wavelet than they are when the Haar wavelet is used.

(a) Original (b) Haar (c) DB4

Figure 9.3 (a) Piecewise constant image. (b) Its approximation using Haar wavelets up to scale $j = 7$. (c) Its approximation using DB4 wavelets up to scale $j = 7$ (right). The figures shown are crops of the full images.

9.2 Multiresolution Analysis

The construction of more general wavelets typically begins with a so-called multiresolution analysis.

Definition 9.3 (Multiresolution analysis) A *MultiResolution Analysis (MRA)* is a sequence of closed subspaces V_j, $j \in \mathbb{Z}$, of $L^2(\mathbb{R})$ satisfying

(i) $V_j \subset V_{j+1}$ for all $j \in \mathbb{Z}$,
(ii) $f \in V_j$ if and only if $f(2\cdot) \in V_{j+1}$, for all $j \in \mathbb{Z}$,
(iii) $\bigcap_{j\in\mathbb{Z}} V_j = \{0\}$,
(iv) $\overline{\bigcup_{j\in\mathbb{Z}} V_j} = L^2(\mathbb{R})$,
(v) there exists a function $\varphi \in V_0$ such that $\{\varphi(\cdot - n) : n \in \mathbb{Z}\}$ is an orthonormal basis for V_0.

When it exists, the function φ is known as a *scaling function* of the MRA.

An MRA is a nested sequence of subspaces V_j that are *translation invariant* (this follows from property (v)) and generated by *dilations* (property (ii)). We often refer to the V_j as *multiresolution spaces*. Property (iv) asserts that every function $f \in L^2(\mathbb{R})$ can be approximated to arbitrary accuracy by its orthogonal projection onto V_j for large enough j, or, to use the terminology introduced earlier, sufficiently *fine resolution*. Dilation, i.e. moving from V_j to V_{j-1} (or V_{j+1}), provides a *coarser* (*finer*) approximation to f, in which fewer (more) details are recovered. This is demonstrated in Fig. 9.4(a,b). Observe that the approximation (orthogonal projection) in finer space V_6 gives a less blocky reconstruction of f than the approximation in the coarser space V_5. In particular, it nearly resolves the discontinuities of the function.

We also note that the set of functions $\{2^{j/2}\varphi(2^j \cdot -n) : n \in \mathbb{Z}\}$ is an orthonormal basis for the space V_j for every j. This follows from (ii) and (v). In particular, this means the

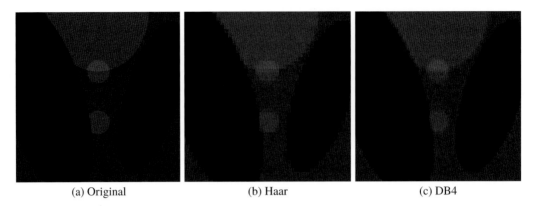

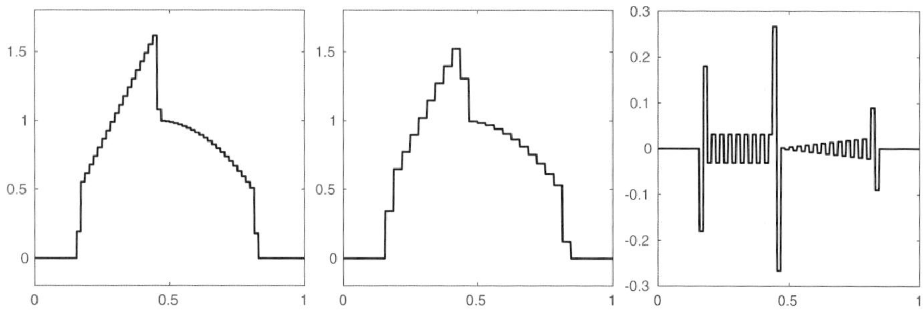

(a) V_6 (b) V_5 (c) W_5

Figure 9.4 Approximation in (a) V_6, (b) V_5 and (c) W_5 for the Haar wavelet. The approximation in (a) is the sum of the approximations in (b) and (c).

approximation of f from V_j, i.e. its orthogonal projection, has a simple mathematical expression as the expansion

$$2^j \sum_{n\in\mathbb{Z}} \langle f, \varphi(2^j \cdot -n)\rangle_{L^2} \varphi(2^j \cdot -n).$$

Example 9.4 (The MRA of the Haar wavelet) For each j, let V_j be the closed subspace of piecewise constant functions on an equispaced grid of size 2^{-j}:

$$V_j = \left\{ f \in L^2(\mathbb{R}) : f|_{[n/2^j,(n+1)/2^j)} = \text{constant},\ n \in \mathbb{Z} \right\}.$$

It is easily verified that this forms an MRA with the scaling function given by (9.4). As we explain in §9.3, this is precisely the MRA associated with the Haar wavelet.

We now state two results that are used later (we do not present their proofs – see the Notes section for details). The first demonstrates that the conditions of an MRA are not completely independent.

Theorem 9.5 *Properties (i), (ii) and (v) of Definition 9.3 imply property (iii).*

The second gives conditions under which property (iv) is implied by the behaviour of the Fourier transform $\mathcal{F}\varphi$ of the scaling function:

Theorem 9.6 *Let $\{V_j\}_{j\in\mathbb{Z}}$ be a sequence of closed subspaces satisfying (i), (ii) and (v). Suppose that $|\mathcal{F}\varphi|$ is continuous at $\omega = 0$. Then*

$$\mathcal{F}\varphi(0) \neq 0 \quad \Longleftrightarrow \quad \overline{\bigcup_{j\in\mathbb{Z}} V_j} = L^2(\mathbb{R}).$$

Moreover, if either holds then $|\mathcal{F}\varphi(0)| = 1$.

9.3 Wavelet Construction from an MRA

It is always possible to construct an orthonormal wavelet from an MRA. We now describe this construction.

First, let $W_0 \subset L^2(\mathbb{R})$ be the orthogonal complement of V_0 in V_1,

$$W_0 = \{f \in V_1 : f \perp g, \ \forall g \in V_0\},$$

so that $V_1 = V_0 \oplus W_0$. The space W_0 is closed by construction. Now dilate the elements of W_0 by 2^j to give the closed subspace

$$W_j = \left\{f(2^j \cdot) : f \in W_0\right\}$$

of V_{j+1}. Observe that W_j is in turn the orthogonal complement of V_j in V_{j+1}: that is, $V_{j+1} = V_j \oplus W_j$. Hence, for any $j_0 \leq j$,

$$V_{j+1} = V_{j_0} \oplus W_{j_0} \oplus W_{j_0+1} \oplus \cdots \oplus W_j. \tag{9.8}$$

Conditions (iii) and (iv) of Definition 9.3 therefore imply the following two decompositions of the space $L^2(\mathbb{R})$:

$$L^2(\mathbb{R}) = V_{j_0} \oplus W_{j_0} \oplus W_{j_0+1} \oplus \cdots, \qquad L^2(\mathbb{R}) = \bigoplus_{j=-\infty}^{\infty} W_j. \tag{9.9}$$

In particular, the second decomposition means that finding an orthonormal wavelet is equivalent to finding a function $\psi \in W_0$ for which the translates $\{\psi(\cdot - n) : n \in \mathbb{Z}\}$ form an orthonormal basis of W_0.

Before doing so, let us briefly comment on the spaces V_j and W_j. Recall that approximating a function $f \in L^2(\mathbb{R})$ in the space V_{j+1} recovers fine details that are lost when approximating it in the dilated space V_j. The wavelet space W_j satisfies $V_{j+1} = V_j \oplus W_j$. Therefore it (or, to be precise, the projection of f onto it) contains the information of the details that are lost when passing from V_{j+1} to V_j. An example of this is shown in Fig. 9.4. We observe that the projection onto W_5 contains the edge content that is present in the finer space V_6 but not in the coarser space V_5. Because of this properly, W_j is sometimes referred to as the *detail* space.

We now return to the derivation of the wavelet ψ. First, note that the dilated scaling function $\frac{1}{\sqrt{2}}\varphi(\cdot/2)$ is an element of $V_{-1} \subset V_0$. Hence, we may use condition (v) to write

$$\frac{1}{\sqrt{2}}\varphi\left(\frac{\cdot}{2}\right) = \sum_{n\in\mathbb{Z}} h_n \varphi(\cdot - n), \tag{9.10}$$

where, by orthogonality, the coefficients h_n are given by

$$h_n = \frac{1}{\sqrt{2}} \int_{-\infty}^{\infty} \varphi(x/2)\overline{\varphi(x-n)} \, \mathrm{d}x. \tag{9.11}$$

The sequence $h = (h_n)_{n\in\mathbb{Z}} \in \ell^2(\mathbb{Z})$ is referred to as the *filter* associated with the scaling function φ, and coefficients h_n are referred to as *filter coefficients* (these terms will be elaborated upon in §9.10). Applying the Fourier transform and using Table E.1, we get

$$\mathcal{F}\varphi(2\omega) = \frac{1}{\sqrt{2}}\mathcal{F}\varphi(\omega) \sum_{n\in\mathbb{Z}} h_n \mathrm{e}^{-\mathrm{i}n\omega} = \mathcal{F}\varphi(\omega) m_0(\omega), \tag{9.12}$$

where

$$m_0(\omega) = \frac{1}{\sqrt{2}} \sum_{n\in\mathbb{Z}} h_n \mathrm{e}^{-\mathrm{i}n\omega} \tag{9.13}$$

is the so-called *transfer function* of the filter h.[1] Note that m_0 is 2π-periodic.

Before proceeding further, we require the following property of m_0:

Lemma 9.7 *The function m_0 satisfies the partition-of-unity formula*

$$|m_0(\omega)|^2 + |m_0(\omega+\pi)|^2 = 1, \ a.e.\ \omega \in \mathbb{R}. \tag{9.14}$$

To prove this lemma we require the following result:

Lemma 9.8 *Let $g \in L^2(\mathbb{R})$. Then $\{g(\cdot - n) : n \in \mathbb{Z}\}$ is an orthonormal system if and only if*

$$\sum_{n\in\mathbb{Z}} |\mathcal{F}g(\omega + 2n\pi)|^2 = 1, \quad a.e.\ \omega \in \mathbb{R}.$$

Proof Plancherel's theorem (E.1) and standard properties of the Fourier transform (Table E.1) give that

$$\begin{aligned}
\int_{-\infty}^{\infty} g(x)\overline{g(x-n)}\,\mathrm{d}x &= \frac{1}{2\pi}\int_{-\infty}^{\infty} \mathcal{F}g(\omega)\overline{\mathcal{F}g(\omega)}\mathrm{e}^{\mathrm{i}n\omega}\,\mathrm{d}\omega \\
&= \frac{1}{2\pi}\sum_{k\in\mathbb{N}}\int_{2k\pi}^{2(k+1)\pi} |\mathcal{F}g(\omega)|^2\mathrm{e}^{\mathrm{i}n\omega}\,\mathrm{d}\omega \\
&= \frac{1}{2\pi}\int_0^{2\pi}\left(\sum_{k\in\mathbb{N}} |\mathcal{F}g(\omega+2k\pi)|^2\right)\mathrm{e}^{\mathrm{i}n\omega}\,\mathrm{d}\omega.
\end{aligned}$$

The final integral is the $-n$th Fourier coefficient of the 2π-periodic function

$$h(\omega) = \sum_{k\in\mathbb{N}} |\mathcal{F}g(\omega+2k\pi)|^2.$$

Hence $\{g(\cdot - n) : n \in \mathbb{Z}\}$ is an orthonormal system if and only if the nth Fourier coefficient of h is equal to one when $n = 0$ and zero otherwise. But this is equivalent to $\sum_{k\in\mathbb{Z}} |\mathcal{F}g(\omega+2k\pi)|^2 = 1$ a.e. $\omega \in \mathbb{R}$. Hence we get the result. □

Proof of Lemma 9.7 Condition (v) and Lemma 9.8 give that

$$\sum_{n\in\mathbb{Z}} |\mathcal{F}\varphi(2\omega + 2n\pi)|^2 = 1, \quad \text{a.e. } \omega \in \mathbb{R}.$$

Using (9.12) we obtain

$$1 = \sum_{n\in\mathbb{Z}} |\mathcal{F}\varphi(\omega+n\pi)|^2|m_0(\omega+n\pi)|^2, \quad \text{a.e. } \omega \in \mathbb{R}.$$

[1] Technically speaking, $\sqrt{2}m_0(\omega) = \sum_{n\in\mathbb{Z}} h_n \mathrm{e}^{-\mathrm{i}n\omega}$ is the transfer function of h (the sum is the Fourier transform of h). We include the factor $1/\sqrt{2}$ for convenience, and henceforth ignore this distinction.

We now split the sum over the even and odd integers and use the fact that m_0 is 2π-periodic to get

$$1 = |m_0(\omega)|^2 \sum_{n\in\mathbb{Z}} |\mathcal{F}\varphi(\omega + 2n\pi)|^2 + |m_0(\omega+\pi)|^2 \sum_{n\in\mathbb{Z}} |\mathcal{F}\varphi(\omega + (2n+1)\pi)|^2.$$

The result now follows by applying Lemma 9.8 once more. □

With this result in hand, we may now present the following theorem giving the construction of a wavelet ψ from an MRA:

Theorem 9.9 (Construction of a wavelet from an MRA) *Let $\{V_j\}_{j\in\mathbb{Z}}$ be an MRA with scaling function φ and corresponding transfer function m_0 given by (9.11) and (9.13). Let $\psi \in L^2(\mathbb{R})$ be the function with Fourier transform*

$$\mathcal{F}\psi(\omega) = -\mathrm{e}^{-\mathrm{i}\omega/2}\overline{m_0(\omega/2+\pi)}\mathcal{F}\varphi(\omega/2), \tag{9.15}$$

and define

$$W_0 = \overline{\operatorname{span}\{\psi_{0,n} : n \in \mathbb{Z}\}},$$

where $\psi_{0,n}(\cdot) = \psi(\cdot - n)$. Then

(a) $\psi \in V_1$,
(b) $\{\psi_{0,n} : n \in \mathbb{Z}\}$ is an orthonormal basis of W_0,
(c) W_0 is the orthogonal complement of V_0 in V_1, i.e. $V_0 \oplus W_0 = V_1$,
(d) ψ is an orthonormal wavelet.

Proof We first prove (a). Combining (9.13) with (9.15) gives

$$\mathcal{F}\psi(\omega) = -\mathcal{F}\varphi(\omega/2)\mathrm{e}^{-\mathrm{i}\omega/2}\sum_{n\in\mathbb{Z}}\frac{\overline{h_n}}{\sqrt{2}}\mathrm{e}^{\mathrm{i}n(\omega/2+\pi)} = \mathcal{F}\varphi(\omega/2)\sum_{n\in\mathbb{Z}}\frac{\overline{h_n}}{\sqrt{2}}(-1)^{n-1}\mathrm{e}^{\mathrm{i}(n-1)\omega/2}.$$

We now apply the inverse Fourier transform to obtain

$$\psi(x) = \sqrt{2}\sum_{n\in\mathbb{Z}}(-1)^{n-1}\overline{h_n}\varphi(2x+n-1).$$

Hence $\psi \in V_1$, as required.

For (b), we apply Lemma 9.8 to note that $\{\psi_{0,n} : n \in \mathbb{Z}\}$ is an orthonormal basis for W_0 if and only if

$$1 = \sum_{n\in\mathbb{Z}} |\mathcal{F}\psi(2\omega + 2n\pi)|^2, \quad \text{a.e. } \omega \in \mathbb{R}. \tag{9.16}$$

Using (9.15) and arguing as in the proof of Lemma 9.7, we have

$$\sum_{n\in\mathbb{Z}} |\mathcal{F}\psi(2\omega + 2n\pi)|^2 = |m_0(\omega)|^2 + |m_0(\omega+\pi)|^2.$$

Hence (9.16) follows from Lemma 9.7.

Now consider (c). We first show that $V_0 \perp W_0$. Since $\{\varphi_{0,n} : n \in \mathbb{Z}\}$ and $\{\psi_{0,n} : n \in \mathbb{Z}\}$ are orthonormal bases for each space, this is equivalent to the condition

$$\langle \psi, \varphi_{0,k}\rangle_{L^2} = 0, \quad \forall k \in \mathbb{Z}. \tag{9.17}$$

By Plancherel's theorem (E.1),

$$\begin{aligned}\langle\psi, \varphi_{0,k}\rangle_{L^2} &= \frac{1}{2\pi}\int_{-\infty}^{\infty} \mathcal{F}\psi(\omega)\overline{\mathcal{F}\varphi(\omega)}\mathrm{e}^{\mathrm{i}k\omega}\,\mathrm{d}\omega \\ &= \frac{1}{2\pi}\int_{0}^{2\pi}\left(\sum_{n\in\mathbb{Z}} \mathcal{F}\psi(\omega+2n\pi)\overline{\mathcal{F}\varphi(\omega+2n\pi)}\right)\mathrm{e}^{\mathrm{i}k\omega}\,\mathrm{d}\omega.\end{aligned}$$

Hence (9.17) holds if and only if

$$\sum_{n\in\mathbb{Z}} \mathcal{F}\psi(\omega+2n\pi)\overline{\mathcal{F}\varphi(\omega+2n\pi)} = 0, \qquad \text{a.e. } \omega\in\mathbb{R}.$$

For convenience, let $g(\omega) = \mathrm{e}^{-\mathrm{i}\omega}\overline{m_0(\omega+\pi)}$ and note that g is 2π-periodic. Then (9.12) and (9.15) give

$$\sum_{n\in\mathbb{Z}} \mathcal{F}\psi(2\omega+2n\pi)\overline{\mathcal{F}\varphi(2\omega+2n\pi)} = \sum_{n\in\mathbb{Z}} g(\omega+n\pi)\overline{m_0(\omega+n\pi)}|\mathcal{F}\varphi(\omega+n\pi)|^2.$$

We now split the sum into even and odd integers and apply Lemma 9.8 to get

$$\sum_{n\in\mathbb{Z}} \mathcal{F}\psi(2\omega+2n\pi)\overline{\mathcal{F}\varphi(2\omega+2n\pi)} = g(\omega)\overline{m_0(\omega)} + g(\omega+\pi)\overline{m_0(\omega+\pi)}.$$

The right-hand side is zero by definition of g. Hence (9.17) holds and therefore $V_0 \perp W_0$, as required.

It remains to show that $V_0 + W_0 = V_1$. This is equivalent to showing that for all $a \in \ell^2(\mathbb{Z})$ there exist $b, c \in \ell^2(\mathbb{Z})$ such that

$$2\sum_{n\in\mathbb{Z}} a_n\varphi(2x-n) = \sum_{n\in\mathbb{Z}} b_n\varphi(x-n) + \sum_{n\in\mathbb{Z}} c_n\psi(x-n). \tag{9.18}$$

Applying the Fourier transform gives

$$\sum_{n\in\mathbb{Z}} a_n\mathrm{e}^{-\mathrm{i}n\omega/2}\mathcal{F}\varphi(\omega/2) = \sum_{n\in\mathbb{Z}} b_n\mathrm{e}^{-\mathrm{i}n\omega}\mathcal{F}\varphi(\omega) + \sum_{n\in\mathbb{Z}} c_n\mathrm{e}^{-\mathrm{i}n\omega}\mathcal{F}\psi(\omega).$$

Let $A(\omega) = \sum_{n\in\mathbb{Z}} a_n\mathrm{e}^{-\mathrm{i}n\omega}$, $B(\omega) = \sum_{n\in\mathbb{Z}} b_n\mathrm{e}^{-\mathrm{i}n\omega}$ and $C(\omega) = \sum_{n\in\mathbb{Z}} c_n\mathrm{e}^{-\mathrm{i}n\omega}$. Using (9.12) and (9.15), we deduce that (9.18) holds if

$$A(\omega/2) = B(\omega)m_0(\omega/2) + C(\omega)g(\omega/2), \tag{9.19}$$

where g is as defined above. Hence $V_0 + W_0 = V_1$ if for every $A \in L^2(\mathbb{T})$, where $\mathbb{T} = \mathbb{R}/(2\pi\mathbb{Z})$ is the one-dimensional torus, we can find $B, C \in L^2(\mathbb{T})$ such that (9.19) holds. Given $A \in L^2(\mathbb{T})$, let

$$\begin{aligned}B(\omega) &= A(\omega/2)\overline{m_0(\omega/2)} + A(\omega/2+\pi)\overline{m_0(\omega/2+\pi)}, \\ C(\omega) &= A(\omega/2)\overline{g(\omega/2)} + A(\omega/2+\pi)\overline{g(\omega/2+\pi)}.\end{aligned}$$

Using the definition of g and Lemma 9.7, one easily verifies that (9.19) holds for these choices of B and C. This completes the proof of (c).

Finally, (d) follows immediately from (b) and (9.9). □

This theorem yields a construction of an orthonormal wavelet ψ from an arbitrary MRA in terms of the scaling function φ and function m_0. Note that ψ is defined in terms of its Fourier transform (9.15). But, as shown in the first stage of the proof, it can also be expressed directly in terms of φ and the filter coefficients h_n as

$$\psi(x) = \sqrt{2} \sum_{n \in \mathbb{Z}} (-1)^{n-1} \overline{h_n} \varphi(2x + n - 1). \tag{9.20}$$

Example 9.10 We illustrate this theorem for the Haar scaling function (9.4). In this case, one has

$$\frac{1}{\sqrt{2}} \varphi(x/2) = \frac{1}{\sqrt{2}} \begin{cases} 1 & 0 \leq x < 2 \\ 0 & \text{otherwise} \end{cases} = \frac{1}{\sqrt{2}} \varphi(x) + \frac{1}{\sqrt{2}} \varphi(x - 1).$$

Due to (9.10), we deduce that the filter coefficients h_n are given by $h_0 = h_1 = 1/\sqrt{2}$ and $h_n = 0$ otherwise. By (9.13), the corresponding transfer function is

$$m_0(\omega) = \frac{1}{2} \left(1 + \mathrm{e}^{-\mathrm{i}\omega} \right). \tag{9.21}$$

It is clear that this function satisfies (9.14). We now use (9.20) and the values of the filter coefficients to construct the wavelet. This gives

$$\psi(x) = -\varphi(2x - 1) + \varphi(2x) = \begin{cases} 1 & 0 \leq x < 1/2 \\ -1 & 1/2 \leq x < 1 \\ 0 & \text{otherwise} \end{cases},$$

which is precisely the Haar wavelet (Example 9.2).

9.4 Wavelet Design

Having shown the general procedure for constructing a wavelet from an MRA, we now ask the following question: what types of wavelets do we want to construct? In this section, we discuss three key properties that we wish for a wavelet to possess: vanishing moments, compact support and smoothness. Later, in §9.6, we will demonstrate the construction of wavelets with these properties.

9.4.1 Vanishing Moments

Definition 9.11 (Vanishing moments) A wavelet ψ has *p vanishing moments* if

$$\int_{-\infty}^{\infty} x^k \psi(x) \, \mathrm{d}x = 0, \quad k = 0, \ldots, p - 1.$$

The Haar wavelet has precisely $p = 1$ vanishing moments. As we saw in §9.1.1, this property implies that the wavelet coefficients $d_{j,n}$ supported in smooth regions of a piecewise regular function are $O(2^{-3j/2})$ as $j \to \infty$. In general, higher numbers of vanishing moments correspond to faster decay of such coefficients. This follows from the observation that

$$\langle f, \psi_{j,n} \rangle_{L^2} = \langle f - P, \psi_{j,n} \rangle_{L^2}, \tag{9.22}$$

for any polynomial P of degree less than p, for instance, a Taylor polynomial of f. Formalizing this argument, in Lemma 10.10 we show that these coefficients behave like $O(2^{-(p+1/2)j})$ for the Daubechies wavelet with p vanishing moments. Hence, the more vanishing moments, the more compressible the wavelet coefficients are at fine scales.

It is useful at this stage to develop several equivalent conditions for a wavelet to have p vanishing moments:

Proposition 9.12 *Let $\varphi \in L^2(\mathbb{R})$ be the scaling function of an MRA and $\psi \in L^2(\mathbb{R})$ the corresponding wavelet. Suppose that $|\varphi(x)| \lesssim (1+|x|)^{-p-2}$ and $|\psi(x)| \lesssim (1+|x|)^{-p-2}$. Then the following statements are equivalent:*

(a) ψ has p vanishing moments;
(b) $\mathcal{F}\psi(\omega)$ and its first $p-1$ derivatives are zero at $\omega = 0$;
(c) the function $m_0(\omega)$ and its first $p-1$ derivatives are zero at $\omega = \pi$.

Proof The decay conditions and the result stated in (9.23) below imply that $\mathcal{F}\varphi$ and $\mathcal{F}\psi$ are p times continuously differentiable. By Table E.1, we have

$$\mathcal{F}\psi^{(k)}(0) = \int_{-\infty}^{\infty} (-\mathrm{i}x)^k \psi(x)\,\mathrm{d}x,$$

for all $k \in \mathbb{N}_0$. Hence (a) and (b) are equivalent.

For (c), recall from (9.15) that $\mathcal{F}\psi(2\omega) = -\mathrm{e}^{-\mathrm{i}\omega}\overline{m_0(\omega+\pi)}\mathcal{F}\varphi(\omega)$. Since $\mathcal{F}\varphi(0) \neq 0$ by Theorem 9.6, differentiating this expression and setting $\omega = 0$ yields the desired equivalence between (b) and (c). □

A consequence of this result is that a wavelet must have at least one vanishing moment. Indeed, (9.12) and Theorem 9.6 give that $m_0(0) = 1$, and therefore $m_0(\pi) = 0$ by (9.14).

9.4.2 Compact Support

While vanishing moments are desirable, they are not enough on their own. We also want ψ to be compactly supported, with as small a support as possible, so that at fine scales the majority of the dilated wavelets do not intersect a discontinuity of f. The following result gives a characterization of compact support for a wavelet and scaling function:

Theorem 9.13 *Let $-\infty < N_1 \leq N_2 < \infty$ be integers. If the scaling function φ of an MRA has support in $[N_1, N_2]$ then the function m_0 is a trigonometric polynomial of the form $m_0(\omega) = \frac{1}{\sqrt{2}}\sum_{n=N_1}^{N_2} h_n \mathrm{e}^{-\mathrm{i}n\omega}$. The converse holds under the additional assumption that $m_0(0) = 1$. In either case, the corresponding wavelet ψ has support in $[(N_1 - N_2 + 1)/2, (N_2 - N_1 + 1)/2]$.*

Proof Suppose first that $\mathrm{supp}(\varphi) \subseteq [N_1, N_2]$. It follows immediately from (9.11) that $h_n \neq 0$ for only finitely many n. Now we use (9.10) to write

$$\frac{1}{\sqrt{2}}\varphi(x/2) = \sum_{n=n_1}^{n_2} h_n \varphi(x-n),$$

for some $n_1 \leq n_2$. The function on the left-hand side has support $[2N_1, 2N_2]$ and the function on the right-hand side has support contained in $[N_1 + n_1, N_2 + n_2]$. Equating terms we see that $n_1 = N_1$ and $n_2 = N_2$, as required. We omit the proof of the converse statement (see the Notes section).

For the final result, we recall (9.20). By assumption, the right-hand side has support contained in $[(N_1 - N_2 + 1)/2, (N_2 - N_1 + 1)/2]$, as required. □

To illustrate this result, consider the Haar wavelet. The scaling function (9.4) has support $\mathrm{supp}(\varphi) = [0, 1]$. Hence $N_1 = 0$ and $N_2 = 1$. In agreement with the theorem, the transfer function (9.21) takes the form $m_0(\omega) = \frac{1}{2}(1 + \mathrm{e}^{-\mathrm{i}\omega})$, and the Haar wavelet (9.2) has support in $[0, 1] = [(N_1 - N_2 + 1)/2, (N_2 - N_1 + 1)/2]$.

9.4.3 Smoothness

Smoothness of the wavelet ψ is less of a concern insofar as compressibility goes. However, it does impact the visual quality of an approximation, or equivalently the nature of the artefacts in a wavelet-based image reconstruction (recall Fig. 9.3).

It is useful to understand smoothness in terms of the Fourier transform. Let $\alpha = k + \beta$, where $k \in \mathbb{N}_0$ and $0 < \beta \leq 1$, and let $C^{\alpha}(\mathbb{R})$ be the set of bounded functions f that are k-times continuously differentiable and for which the kth derivative $f^{(k)}$ is Hölder continuous with exponent β, i.e.

$$|f^{(k)}(x) - f^{(k)}(y)| \leq C|x - y|^{\beta}, \quad \forall x, y \in \mathbb{R}.$$

The following result is well known:

$$\int_{-\infty}^{\infty} |\mathcal{F} f(\omega)|(1 + |\omega|)^{\alpha} \,\mathrm{d}\omega < \infty \quad \Longrightarrow \quad f \in C^{\alpha}(\mathbb{R}). \tag{9.23}$$

In particular, for $q > 0$ it implies the following:

$$|\mathcal{F}\psi(\omega)| \lesssim (1 + |\omega|)^{-1-q} \quad \Longrightarrow \quad \psi \in C^{\alpha}(\mathbb{R}),\ \forall \alpha < q. \tag{9.24}$$

That is to say, faster decay of the Fourier transform implies higher regularity.

Later, we determine such values of q for the Daubechies wavelets. While this allows us to estimate their smoothness via (9.24), it also has another important use. In Part IV we study Fourier imaging with wavelets. It comes as little surprise that the decay of the $\mathcal{F}\psi$ plays a key role in the analysis of the procedures developed therein.

9.5 Compactly Supported Wavelets

With the previous section in mind, we now seek to construct compactly supported wavelets with arbitrary numbers of vanishing moments. We do this by constructing a suitable transfer function m_0. Proposition 9.12 shows that m_0 and its first $p-1$ derivatives must vanish at $\omega = \pi$ for the wavelet ψ to have $p \geq 1$ vanishing moments. Moreover, Theorem 9.13 shows that compactness of the support of ψ is guaranteed whenever m_0 is a trigonometric polynomial, with the size of the support of ψ depending on the degree of m_0. Hence, we now attempt to design a function m_0 that satisfies these two criteria. However, we also require such an m_0 to be the transfer function of an MRA. The following result gives conditions for this to be the case:

Theorem 9.14 *Suppose that* $m_0(\omega) = \frac{1}{\sqrt{2}} \sum_{n=N_1}^{N_2} h_n e^{-in\omega}$ *satisfies*

(a) $|m_0(\omega)|^2 + |m_0(\omega + \pi)|^2 = 1, \ \forall \omega \in \mathbb{R}$,
(b) $m_0(0) = 1$,
(c) $m_0(\omega) \neq 0$ *for all* $|\omega| \leq \pi/2$.

Then the function φ *with Fourier transform*

$$\mathcal{F}\varphi(\omega) = \prod_{j=1}^{\infty} m_0(\omega/2^j), \qquad \omega \in \mathbb{R} \tag{9.25}$$

is well defined and in $L^2(\mathbb{R})$. *Moreover,* φ *has support in* $[N_1, N_2]$ *and is the scaling function of an MRA with transfer function* m_0. *The corresponding wavelet*

$$\psi(x) = \sqrt{2} \sum_{n=N_1}^{N_2} (-1)^{n-1} \overline{h_n} \varphi(2x + n - 1) \tag{9.26}$$

has support contained in $[(N_1 - N_2 + 1)/2, (N_2 - N_1 + 1)/2]$.

These conditions are not unreasonable. Lemma 9.7 shows that condition (a) is necessary for m_0 to define a transfer function of an MRA. Recall also that $\mathcal{F}\varphi(0) \neq 0$ for a scaling function φ of an MRA for which $|\mathcal{F}\varphi|$ is continuous at $\omega = 0$ (Theorem 9.6). When this occurs, (9.12) gives that $m_0(0) = 1$. Hence condition (b) is essentially necessary as well. Additionally, it can be shown that without (c) the translates $\varphi(\cdot - n)$ need not be orthogonal, in which case φ would fail to be a scaling function.

The construction (9.25) is also natural. Suppose that φ is the scaling function of an MRA with transfer function m_0. Then repeated application of (9.12) gives

$$\mathcal{F}\varphi(\omega) = \mathcal{F}\varphi(\omega/2^N) \prod_{j=1}^{N} m_0(\omega/2^j).$$

Since a scaling function of an MRA can be multiplied by a unit-norm complex number and still remain a scaling function, under the conditions of Theorem 9.6 one may allow $\mathcal{F}\varphi(0) = 1$. In other words, if the infinite product converges, any scaling function with $\mathcal{F}\varphi(0) = 1$ also satisfies $\mathcal{F}\varphi(\omega) = \prod_{j=1}^{\infty} m_0(\omega/2^j)$.

The proof of Theorem 9.14 relies on two lemmas, which we shall not prove.

Lemma 9.15 *Suppose that* m_0 *is a trigonometric polynomial satisfying (a) and (b) of Theorem 9.14 Then* $\Theta(\omega) = \prod_{j=1}^{\infty} m_0(\omega/2^j)$ *is a continuous function,* $\Theta \in L^2(\mathbb{R})$ *and* $\frac{1}{2\pi} \int_{-\infty}^{\infty} |\Theta(\omega)|^2 \, d\omega \leq 1$.

Lemma 9.16 *Suppose that* m_0 *is a trigonometric polynomial satisfying (a)–(c) of Theorem 9.14. If* φ *is the function defined by (9.25) then* $\{\varphi(\cdot - n) : n \in \mathbb{Z}\}$ *is an orthonormal system.*

Proof of Theorem 9.14 Lemma 9.15 guarantees the existence of $\varphi \in L^2(\mathbb{R})$, and Lemma 9.16 gives that the set $\{\varphi(\cdot - n) : n \in \mathbb{Z}\}$ is an orthonormal basis for $V_0 := \overline{\operatorname{span}\{\varphi(\cdot - n) : n \in \mathbb{Z}\}}$. We need to show that φ is the scaling function of an MRA. Define $V_j = \{f(2^j \cdot) : f \in V_0\}$. Conditions (ii) and (v) of Definition 9.3 automatically hold. By (9.25) we have

$$\mathcal{F}\varphi(2\omega) = m_0(\omega)\mathcal{F}\varphi(\omega),$$

and taking the inverse Fourier transform we deduce that $\frac{1}{2}\varphi(x/2) = \sum_{n=N_1}^{N_2} h_n\varphi(x-n) \in V_0$. Hence $V_{-1} \subset V_0$. This gives condition (i) of Definition 9.3. Theorem 9.5 now implies condition (iii). Finally, condition (iv) follows from Theorem 9.6 after noticing from Lemma 9.15 that $\mathcal{F}\varphi$ is continuous and $\mathcal{F}\varphi(0) = 1 \neq 0$. Hence φ is the scaling function of an MRA. To complete the proof, we use Theorem 9.13. □

9.6 Daubechies Wavelets

We are now in a position to complete one of the main tasks of this chapter, the construction of orthonormal wavelets with desirable properties (vanishing moments, compact support and smoothness). The main takeaway is the following:

> For each $p \geq 1$, the Daubechies wavelet with p vanishing moments (the *DBp wavelet*) has the smallest possible support of size $2p - 1$. The support of its scaling function is also of size $2p - 1$. The smoothness q (as in (9.24)) of the wavelet and scaling function increases roughly linearly as a function of p.

Remark 9.17 Here and elsewhere we use the customary shorthand 'DBp' to refer to the Daubechies wavelet with p vanishing moments. We also refer to p as the *order* of the Daubechies wavelet. In particular, DB1 is the Haar wavelet, although we continue to use the term 'Haar' in what follows. The DB4 wavelet with $p = 4$ vanishing moments is arguably the most commonly used Daubechies wavelet in practice. It can be seen in many of the examples throughout this book.

9.6.1 Derivation

The construction is based on applying Theorem 9.14 with $N_1 = 0$ and $N_2 = p+m-1$ for suitable m. Since we seek p vanishing moments, Proposition 9.12 states that the function m_0 of the corresponding MRA should take the form

$$m_0(\omega) = \frac{1}{\sqrt{2}} \sum_{n=0}^{p+m-1} h_n e^{-in\omega} = \left(\frac{1 + e^{-i\omega}}{2}\right)^p r_0(\omega), \tag{9.27}$$

for some trigonometric polynomial $r_0(\omega) = \sum_{n=0}^{m-1} b_n e^{-in\omega}$. Since we want the filter coefficients h_n to be real to make computations easier, we also assume that $b_n \in \mathbb{R}$. Let

$$M_0(\omega) = |m_0(\omega)|^2.$$

Then, in order to apply Theorem 9.14, we require M_0 to satisfy

(a) $M_0(\omega) + M_0(\omega + \pi) = 1, \forall \omega \in \mathbb{R}$,
(b) $M_0(0) = 1$,
(c) $M_0(\omega) > 0$, for all $|\omega| \leq \pi/2$.

Consider condition (a). Write

$$M_0(\omega) = \left(\cos^2(\omega/2)\right)^p R_0(\omega), \tag{9.28}$$

where $R_0(\omega) = |r_0(\omega)|^2$. Since r_0 is a trigonometric polynomial with real coefficients, R_0 is an even trigonometric polynomial with real coefficients. Hence it can be expressed as an algebraic polynomial in $\cos(\omega)$. Using the identity $\cos(\omega) = 1 - 2\sin^2(\omega/2)$, we now rewrite (9.28) as

$$M_0(\omega) = \left(\cos^2(\omega/2)\right)^p P(\sin^2(\omega/2)), \tag{9.29}$$

where $P(y)$ is an algebraic polynomial of degree $m - 1$ in the variable $y = \sin^2(\omega/2)$. Expressed in terms of P and y, condition (a) can now be restated as

$$(1 - y)^p P(y) + y^p P(1 - y) = 1, \quad \forall y \in \mathbb{R}. \tag{9.30}$$

Recall that our interest lies with finding a wavelet with the smallest possible support. To do this, we want to find the minimum-degree polynomial P that satisfies (9.30). This can be achieved via *Bezout's theorem*:

Theorem 9.18 (Bezout's theorem) *If p_1 and p_2 are two polynomials of degrees n_1 and n_2, respectively, that have no common zeros, then there exist unique polynomials q_1 and q_2 of degrees $n_2 - 1$ and $n_1 - 1$, respectively, such that*

$$p_1(y)q_1(y) + p_2(y)q_2(y) = 1.$$

Let $p_1(y) = (1 - y)^p$ and $p_2(y) = y^p$. Then this theorem gives that there are polynomials q_1 and q_2 of degree $p - 1$ for which

$$(1 - y)^p q_1(y) + y^p q_2(y) = 1, \quad \forall y \in \mathbb{R}.$$

By the symmetry $y \mapsto 1 - y$ and the uniqueness of q_1 and q_2, we must have $q_1(y) = q_2(1-y) = P(y)$. Hence, we deduce that (9.30), and therefore condition (a) above, holds with $m = p$. It is also straightforward to derive an explicit expression for the polynomial P. Rearranging (9.30) and taking Taylor expansions, we see that

$$P(y) = (1 - y)^{-p}(1 - y^p P(1 - y)) = \sum_{k=0}^{p-1} \binom{p + k - 1}{k} y^k + O\left(y^p\right).$$

Since $P(y)$ is a polynomial of degree $p - 1$, the $O\left(y^p\right)$ term vanishes. This gives

$$P(y) = \sum_{k=0}^{p-1} \binom{p + k - 1}{k} y^k. \tag{9.31}$$

Observe that $P(0) = 1$ and $P(y) > 0$ for all $y \geq 0$. Hence, not only does the corresponding function (9.29) satisfy condition (a), it also satisfies conditions (b) and (c).

This completes the construction of the functions R_0 and M_0. However, we still need to construct the transfer function m_0 and its filter coefficients h_n. To do this, we need to find a trigonometric polynomial r_0 with real coefficients that satisfies

$$|r_0(\omega)|^2 = R_0(\omega) = P(\sin^2(\omega/2)), \quad \forall \omega. \tag{9.32}$$

This is achieved through a procedure termed 'extracting the square root'. Define the new variable $z = e^{-i\omega}$ and write

$$r_0(\omega) = q(z) = c \prod_{n=0}^{p-1} (1 - a_n z), \tag{9.33}$$

where $c \in \mathbb{R}$ and $a_n \in \mathbb{C}$ are to be determined. Notice that $\overline{q(z)} = q(1/z)$ since r_0 has real coefficients. Since $\sin^2(\omega/2) = \frac{2-z-1/z}{4}$, we can therefore replace (9.32) with

$$c^2 \prod_{n=0}^{p-1} (1 - a_n z)(1 - a_n/z) = P\left(\frac{2 - z - 1/z}{4}\right), \quad \forall z.$$

By symmetry, the roots of this function occur in pairs $(z_n, 1/z_n)$. Out of any such pair of roots, one must lie within the unit disc $\{z \in \mathbb{C} : |z| \leq 1\}$. We now pick that one and set a_n equal to it (this is known as the *minimal phase* solution).

With this in hand, we have now found r_0 and m_0, and therefore completed the construction of the Daubechies wavelets for arbitrary p. Since $m = p$, Theorem 9.14 gives that the scaling function φ and wavelet ψ have supports contained in intervals of length $2p - 1$: namely, $[0, 2p - 1]$ and $[-p + 1, p]$, respectively. As it transpires, this is optimal.

Theorem 9.19 (Optimal support size) *Let ψ be an orthonormal wavelet with p vanishing moments. Then ψ has support of size at least $2p - 1$. Furthermore, for each p there exists an orthonormal wavelet (e.g. the Daubechies wavelet) with support equal to $[-p + 1, p]$. The support of the corresponding scaling function φ is $[0, 2p - 1]$.*

Remark 9.20 It is convenient in what follows to shift the scaling function φ guaranteed by Theorem 9.19 so that its support is also contained in $[-p + 1, p]$. Since the spaces V_j are shift-invariant, this has no effect whatsoever on the MRA or corresponding wavelet.

Notice that the above construction yields m_0 and the filter coefficients h_n, which in turn define the corresponding Daubechies wavelet and scaling function via (9.25) and (9.26). In all but the Haar case, the corresponding wavelet and scaling function do not have explicit expressions. Yet, as we will see in §9.10, it is actually the filter coefficients themselves that are the key to performing numerical computations with wavelets. These are typically reported in a table, as we have done in Table 9.1 for the values $p = 1, 2, 3, 4$. For concreteness, we also plot the first few Daubechies wavelets and scaling functions in Fig. 9.5. We omit the details of how these were actually computed (there are standard methods for doing this – see the Notes section).

We conclude this derivation with an example to illustrate the above procedure. It is easily verified that the Haar wavelet is the DB1 wavelet. Indeed, the function m_0, given by (9.21), has the correct form. We now construct the DB2 wavelet:

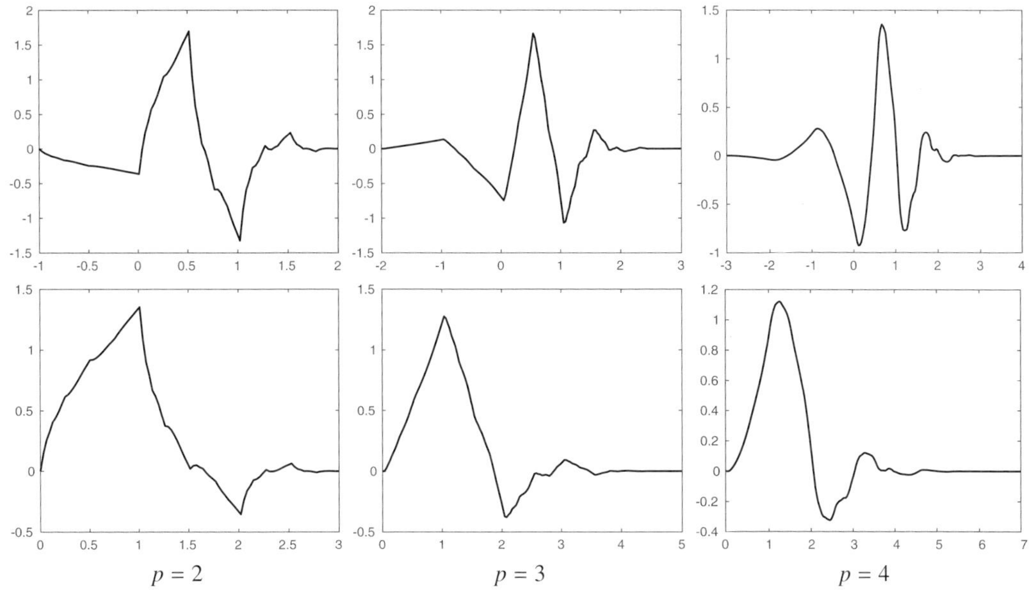

Figure 9.5 The Daubechies mother wavelet ψ (top) and scaling function φ (bottom).

Table 9.1 The filter coefficients h_n for the Daubechies wavelets.

n	$p = 1$	$p = 2$	$p = 3$	$p = 4$
0	+0.7071067814	+0.4829629131	+0.3326705530	+0.2303778133
1	+0.7071067814	+0.8365163037	+0.8068915093	+0.7148465706
2		+0.2241438680	+0.4598775021	+0.6308807679
3		−0.1294095226	−0.1350110200	−0.0279837694
4			−0.0854412739	−0.1870348117
5			+0.0352262919	+0.0308413818
6				+0.0328830117
7				−0.0105974018

Example 9.21 (The DB2 wavelet) Since $p = 2$, we write $r_0(\omega)$ as in (9.33) as $r_0(\omega) = q(z) = c(1 - az)$. We also note from (9.31) that $P(y) = 1 + 2y$ in this case. Hence we require a and c to satisfy

$$c^2(1 - az)(1 - a/z) = P\left(\frac{2 - z - z^{-1}}{4}\right) = 2 - \frac{1}{2z} - \frac{z}{2}.$$

The function on the right-hand side has roots at the reciprocal pair $z = 2 - \sqrt{3}$ and $z = 2 + \sqrt{3}$. Of these two roots, the former lies within the unit disc (it is the minimal phase solution). Therefore we set $a = 2 - \sqrt{3}$. After finding the corresponding value of c, this gives

$$q(z) = \frac{\sqrt{3} + 1}{2}\left(1 - (2 - \sqrt{3})z\right).$$

Table 9.2 The parameter q, given by (9.35), for the Daubechies wavelets.

p	1	2	3	4	5	6	7	8	9	10
q	0	0.339	0.636	0.913	1.177	1.432	1.682	1.927	2.168	2.406

We have now found r_0. To get m_0 we recall from (9.27) that

$$m_0(\omega) = \left(\frac{1 + e^{-i\omega}}{2}\right)^2 r_0(\omega) = \left(\frac{1+z}{2}\right)^2 \frac{\sqrt{3}+1}{2}(1 - (2 - \sqrt{3})z).$$

After expanding in powers of z and recalling that $z = e^{-i\omega}$, we conclude that

$$m_0(\omega) = \frac{1+\sqrt{3}}{8} + \frac{3+\sqrt{3}}{8}e^{-i\omega} + \frac{3-\sqrt{3}}{8}e^{-2i\omega} + \frac{1-\sqrt{3}}{8}e^{-3i\omega}.$$

This is a trigonometric polynomial of the required form. In particular, the resulting filter coefficients are given by

$$h_0 = \frac{1+\sqrt{3}}{4\sqrt{2}}, \quad h_1 = \frac{3+\sqrt{3}}{4\sqrt{2}}, \quad h_2 = \frac{3-\sqrt{3}}{4\sqrt{2}}, \quad h_3 = \frac{1-\sqrt{3}}{4\sqrt{2}},$$

which are precisely the values given in Table 9.1 for $p = 2$.

9.6.2 Smoothness of Daubechies Wavelets

To close this section, let us make several remarks concerning the smoothness of the Daubechies wavelets and the decay of their Fourier transforms. Recall from §9.4 that these are related in the sense that if

$$|\mathcal{F}\varphi(\omega)| \lesssim (1 + |\omega|)^{-1-q}, \tag{9.34}$$

then $\varphi \in C^\alpha(\mathbb{R})$ for every Hölder exponent $\alpha < q$. Note also that since ψ is a finite linear combination of translates of φ, it has precisely the same regularity as φ.

For the Daubechies wavelet of order p it can be shown that (9.34) holds with

$$q = p - 1 - \frac{\log|P(3/4)|}{2\log(2)}, \tag{9.35}$$

where P is the polynomial (9.31). Values for this expression are given in Table 9.2 for various p. Note that asymptotically one has

$$q = p - 1 - \frac{\log|P(3/4)|}{2\log(2)} = \left(1 - \frac{\log(3)}{2\log(2)}\right)p + O(\log(p)) \approx 0.2075p, \tag{9.36}$$

as $p \to \infty$. That is, regularity increases linearly with the number of vanishing moments, albeit at a rather slower rate.

Equations (9.35) and (9.36) give the exact decay rates of $\mathcal{F}\varphi$ and $\mathcal{F}\psi$. Unfortunately, they do not yield sharp Hölder exponents for the regularity of the wavelet and scaling function themselves. These can be found via different techniques which we shall not discuss (see the Notes section for references). The sharp values of α are reported in Table 9.3 for $p = 2, 3, 4$. It is interesting to note that the DB3 wavelet is actually continuously differentiable with $\alpha = 1.0878 > 1$, a fact which cannot be deduced from the value $q = 0.636 < 1$ given in Table 9.2.

Table 9.3 The largest value of α such that the Daubechies wavelet of order p belongs to C^{α}.

p	2	3	4
α	0.5500	1.0878	1.6179

9.7 Wavelets on Intervals

In many applications, the function to be approximated is defined on a finite interval, which may be taken to be $[0, 1]$ without loss of generality, rather than the whole real line. It is therefore important to construct wavelet bases for the space $L^2([0, 1])$. For the Haar wavelet, as seen in §9.1, this process is straightforward. Each Haar wavelet is either fully supported in $[0, 1]$ or fully supported outside $[0, 1]$. Hence an orthonormal basis of $L^2([0, 1])$ is constructed as in (9.7) simply by including only those Haar wavelets supported in $[0, 1]$.

Unfortunately, such a property is unique to the Haar wavelet. For higher-order wavelets, there are always wavelets whose supports intersect $[0, 1]$ but are not fully contained in it. To construct an orthonormal basis, these 'boundary' functions must be modified in a suitable way. We now discuss ways to do this.

9.7.1 Periodization

The most straightforward approach involves *periodizing* an existing orthonormal wavelet basis of $L^2(\mathbb{R})$. Define the periodizing operation

$$g(x) \mapsto g^{\mathrm{per}}(x) = \sum_{n \in \mathbb{Z}} g(x+n). \tag{9.37}$$

Notice that $g^{\mathrm{per}}(x)$ is a 1-periodic function. Given wavelets $\psi_{j,n}$ and scaling functions $\varphi_{j,n}$, let $\psi^{\mathrm{per}}_{j,n}$ and $\varphi^{\mathrm{per}}_{j,n}$ be their corresponding periodized versions, and define the periodized spaces

$$V^{\mathrm{per}}_j = \mathrm{span}\{\varphi^{\mathrm{per}}_{j,n} : n = 0, \ldots, 2^j - 1\}, \quad W^{\mathrm{per}}_j = \mathrm{span}\{\psi^{\mathrm{per}}_{j,n} : n = 0, \ldots, 2^j - 1\}.$$

Note that the maximal index $n = 2^j - 1$ is now finite, since $\varphi^{\mathrm{per}}_{j,n+2^j} = \varphi^{\mathrm{per}}_{j,n}$ and likewise for $\psi^{\mathrm{per}}_{j,n}$. These spaces and functions inherit all the properties of the original MRA construction on $L^2(\mathbb{R})$. The functions $\{\varphi^{\mathrm{per}}_{j,n}\}$ and $\{\psi^{\mathrm{per}}_{j,n}\}$ are orthonormal bases for V^{per}_j and W^{per}_j, respectively,

$$V^{\mathrm{per}}_j, W^{\mathrm{per}}_j \subset V^{\mathrm{per}}_{j+1}, \qquad V^{\mathrm{per}}_j \oplus W^{\mathrm{per}}_j = V^{\mathrm{per}}_{j+1}$$

and, given a *coarsest scale* $j_0 \geq 0$, we have the decomposition

$$V^{\mathrm{per}}_{j_0} \oplus W^{\mathrm{per}}_{j_0} \oplus W^{\mathrm{per}}_{j_0} \oplus \cdots = L^2([0, 1]).$$

In particular, this implies that

$$\{\varphi^{\mathrm{per}}_{j_0,n} : n = 0, \ldots, 2^{j_0} - 1\} \cup \{\psi^{\mathrm{per}}_{j,n} : n = 0, \ldots, 2^j - 1,\ j \geq j_0\}$$

is an orthonormal basis for $L^2([0,1])$, as required. Hence every function $f \in L^2([0,1])$ has the expansion

$$f = \sum_{n=0}^{2^{j_0}-1} c_{j_0,n} \varphi_{j_0,n}^{\text{per}} + \sum_{j \geq j_0} \sum_{n=0}^{2^j-1} d_{j,n} \psi_{j,n}^{\text{per}}, \tag{9.38}$$

where $c_{j_0,n} = \langle f, \varphi_{j_0,n}^{\text{per}} \rangle_{L^2}$ are the (periodized) scaling function coefficients of f and $d_{j,n} = \langle f, \psi_{j,n}^{\text{per}} \rangle_{L^2}$ are its (periodized) wavelet coefficients.

It is worth noting how the periodization operation modifies the wavelets at the boundary. Suppose that the original orthonormal wavelet for $L^2(\mathbb{R})$ has $p \geq 1$ vanishing moments and minimal support, i.e. it is of the type ensured by Theorem 9.19. Let $j_0 \geq 0$ if $p = 1$ or $j_0 \geq \log_2(2p)$ if $p \geq 2$ (this condition ensures that there is at least one wavelet at scale $j \geq j_0$ fully supported in $[0,1]$). Then

$$\text{supp}(\psi_{j,n}) = [(n-p+1)/2^j, (n+p)/2^j], \tag{9.39}$$

and therefore

$$\text{supp}(\psi_{j,n}) \subseteq [0,1] \quad \Longleftrightarrow \quad n = p-1, \ldots, 2^j - p,$$

and likewise for the scaling functions $\varphi_{j,n}$ (recall Remark 9.20). Hence, when considered over the interval $[0,1]$, we have

$$\psi_{j,n}^{\text{per}} = \psi_{j,n}, \quad \varphi_{j,n}^{\text{per}} = \varphi_{j,n}, \qquad n = p-1, \ldots, 2^j - p. \tag{9.40}$$

In other words, the majority of the wavelets and scaling functions at a given scale are unchanged, and only those whose supports intersect the boundary are modified. These modified wavelets, of which there are exactly $2(p-1)$ per scale, take the form

$$\begin{aligned} \psi_{j,n}^{\text{per}} &= \psi_{j,n} + \psi_{j,n+2^j}, \quad n = 0, \ldots, p-2, \\ \psi_{j,n}^{\text{per}} &= \psi_{j,n} + \psi_{j,n-2^j}, \quad n = 2^j - p + 1, \ldots, 2^j - 1, \end{aligned} \tag{9.41}$$

and likewise for $\varphi_{j,n}^{\text{per}}$. In particular, they are linear combinations of two wavelets (or scaling functions) at the same scale.

Figure 9.6 illustrates this process for the DB4 wavelet. The wavelet $\psi_{3,0}$ intersects the endpoint $x = 0$, and therefore, as specified by (9.41), its periodization $\psi_{3,0}^{\text{per}}$ is a linear combination of itself and the wavelet $\psi_{3,8}$. Note that at this scale, there is a total of $6 = 2(p-1)$ modified wavelets $\psi_{3,i}^{\text{per}}$, $i \in \{0,1,2,5,6,7\}$, with the rest being unchanged.

9.7.2 Boundary-Corrected Wavelets

While simple, periodization effectively treats a function $f\colon [0,1] \to \mathbb{C}$ as a periodic function on the real line with a discontinuity at the endpoint $x = 1$. This 'artificial' discontinuity results in additional large wavelet coefficients near the endpoint, thus reducing the compressibility of the wavelet decomposition at a given scale. Such behaviour is undesirable. So-called *boundary-corrected* (or *boundary-adapted*) wavelets are designed to overcome this issue.

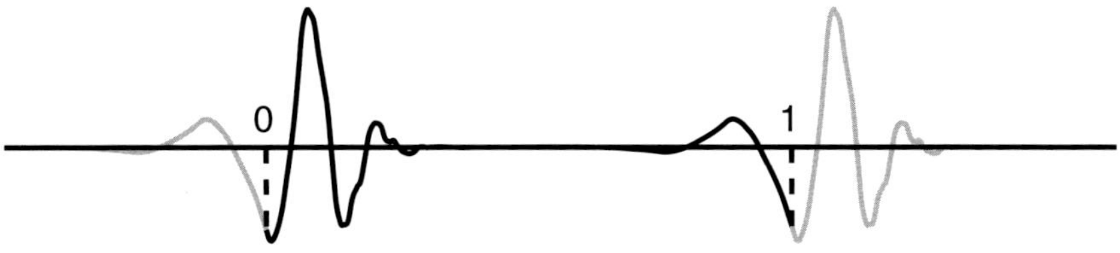

Figure 9.6 Periodization for the DB4 wavelet. Black line: the wavelet $\psi^{\text{per}}_{3,0} = \psi_{3,0} + \psi_{3,8}$. Grey lines: $\psi_{3,0}$ (left) and $\psi_{3,8}$ (right).

Their construction is based on modifying those wavelets that overlap the boundary by using certain linear combinations of scaling functions. More precisely, beginning with the DBp wavelet basis, this procedure constructs new wavelets and scaling functions as

$$\psi^{\text{int}}_{j,n}(x) = \begin{cases} 2^{j/2}\psi^{\text{left}}_n(2^j x) & 0 \le n < p \\ 2^{j/2}\psi(2^j x - n) & p \le n < 2^j - p \\ 2^{j/2}\psi^{\text{right}}_n(2^j x) & 2^j - p \le n < 2^j \end{cases}$$

and

$$\varphi^{\text{int}}_{j,n}(x) = \begin{cases} 2^{j/2}\varphi^{\text{left}}_n(2^j x) & 0 \le n < p \\ 2^{j/2}\varphi(2^j x - n) & p \le n < 2^j - p \\ 2^{j/2}\varphi^{\text{right}}_n(2^j x) & 2^j - p \le n < 2^j \end{cases},$$

where ψ^{left}_n, ψ^{right}_n, φ^{left}_n and φ^{right}_n are functions that modify the wavelets and scaling functions at the left and right endpoints, respectively. These functions are constructed by taking specific linear combinations of scaling functions. We omit the details of this construction. Much as before, the functions $\varphi^{\text{int}}_{j,n}$ and $\psi^{\text{int}}_{j,n}$ constitute orthonormal bases for the multiresolution and detail spaces

$$V^{\text{int}}_j = \text{span}\{\varphi^{\text{int}}_{j,n} : n = 0, \ldots, 2^j - 1\}, \quad W^{\text{int}}_j = \text{span}\{\psi^{\text{int}}_{j,n} : n = 0, \ldots, 2^j - 1\},$$

and these spaces satisfy $V^{\text{int}}_j \subset V^{\text{int}}_{j+1}$, $V^{\text{per}}_{j+1} = V^{\text{per}}_j \oplus W^{\text{int}}_j$ and

$$V^{\text{int}}_{j_0} \oplus W^{\text{int}}_{j_0} \oplus W^{\text{int}}_{j_0+1} \oplus \cdots = L^2([0,1]).$$

In particular, every $f \in L^2([0,1])$ has an expansion of the form (9.38), with the superscript 'per' replaced by 'int'.

Unlike periodization, this construction preserves vanishing moments. To be precise, the restriction of a polynomial $P(x)$ of degree less than p to $[0,1]$ belongs to V^{int}_j and is therefore orthogonal to the detail space W^{int}_j. Analogous to (9.22), one then has

$$d_{j,n} = \langle f, \psi^{\text{int}}_{j,n} \rangle_{L^2} = \langle f - P, \psi^{\text{int}}_{j,n} \rangle_{L^2}.$$

This implies fast decay of the wavelet coefficients in smooth regions of f, including, crucially, regions containing the endpoint $x = 0$ or $x = 1$.

9.8 Higher Dimensions

Thus far, we have constructed orthonormal wavelet bases for spaces of functions of one variable. We now consider the extension to spaces of functions of two or more variables.

9.8.1 Wavelet Bases of $L^2(\mathbb{R}^2)$

Every orthonormal wavelet basis $\{\psi_{j,n} : j, n \in \mathbb{Z}\}$ of $L^2(\mathbb{R})$ can be extended to an orthonormal basis of $L^2(\mathbb{R}^2)$ simply by taking tensor products of the basis elements:

$$\psi_{j_1,n_1} \otimes \psi_{j_2,n_2}, \qquad j_1, j_2, n_1, n_2 \in \mathbb{Z}. \tag{9.42}$$

However, this construction mixes wavelets at different scales; a behaviour which is often undesirable in practice. An alternative approach is to take tensor products of the one-dimensional MRA.

Let $\{V_j\}_{j\in\mathbb{Z}}$ be an MRA of $L^2(\mathbb{R})$ and define

$$V_j^{(2)} = V_j \otimes V_j = \overline{\text{span}\{f = g \otimes h : g, h \in V_j\}} \subset L^2(\mathbb{R}^2), \quad j \in \mathbb{Z}.$$

It is straightforward to show that the spaces $V_j^{(2)}$ form an MRA of $L^2(\mathbb{R}^2)$, known as a *separable* MRA. Indeed, one readily verifies that

(i) $V_j^{(2)} \subset V_{j+1}^{(2)}$,
(ii) $f \in V_j^{(2)}$ if and only if $f(2\cdot, 2\cdot) \in V_{j+1}^{(2)}$,
(iii) $\bigcap_{j\in\mathbb{Z}} V_j^{(2)} = \{0\}$,
(iv) $\overline{\bigcup_{j\in\mathbb{Z}} V_j^{(2)}} = L^2(\mathbb{R}^2)$,
(v) the set $\{\varphi_{0,n} := \varphi_{0,n_1} \otimes \varphi_{0,n_2} : n = (n_1, n_2) \in \mathbb{Z}^2\}$ is an orthonormal basis of $V_0^{(2)}$.

Much as in the one-dimensional case, we define the detail space $W_j^{(2)}$ as the orthogonal complement of $V_j^{(2)}$ in $V_{j+1}^{(2)}$. Properties (iii) and (iv) now immediately give that

$$L^2(\mathbb{R}^2) = V_{j_0}^{(2)} \oplus W_{j_0}^{(2)} \oplus W_{j_0+1}^{(2)} \oplus \cdots, \qquad L^2(\mathbb{R}^2) = \bigoplus_{j=-\infty}^{\infty} W_j^{(2)}, \tag{9.43}$$

for any $j_0 \in \mathbb{Z}$.

With this in hand, we next construct the orthonormal wavelet basis. First, observe that

$$\{\varphi_{j,n} = \varphi_{j,n_1} \otimes \varphi_{j,n_2} : n = (n_1, n_2) \in \mathbb{Z}^2\}$$

is an orthonormal basis of $V_j^{(2)}$ for every $j \in \mathbb{Z}$. This follows from properties (ii) and (v). Now consider the space $W_j^{(2)}$. Note that

$$\begin{aligned} V_{j+1}^{(2)} = V_{j+1} \otimes V_{j+1} &= (V_j \oplus W_j) \otimes (V_j \oplus W_j) \\ &= (V_j \otimes V_j) \oplus (W_j \otimes V_j) \oplus (V_j \otimes W_j) \oplus (W_j \otimes W_j) \\ &= V_j^{(2)} \oplus W_j^{(2)}. \end{aligned}$$

Hence $W_j^{(2)}$ is a direct sum of the three subspaces $W_j \otimes V_j$, $V_j \otimes W_j$ and $W_j \otimes W_j$.

The functions $\psi_{j,n_1} \otimes \varphi_{j,n_2}$, $\varphi_{j,n_1} \otimes \psi_{j,n_2}$ and $\psi_{j,n_1} \otimes \psi_{j,n_2}$ generate orthonormal bases for these spaces, respectively, which in turn leads to an orthonormal basis for $W_j^{(2)}$. However, since there are now three types of function in this basis, it is convenient to introduce some additional notation. Let

$$\psi_{j,n}^{(0)} = \varphi_{j,n}, \qquad \psi_{j,n}^{(1)} = \psi_{j,n} \tag{9.44}$$

denote the one-dimensional wavelet and scaling functions with dilation $j \in \mathbb{Z}$ and translation $n \in \mathbb{Z}$. Then we define

$$\psi_{j,n}^{(e)} = \psi_{j,n_1}^{(e_1)} \otimes \psi_{j,n_2}^{(e_2)}, \quad e = (e_1, e_2) \in \{0,1\}^2, \ j \in \mathbb{Z}, \ n = (n_1, n_2) \in \mathbb{Z}^2.$$

From the above arguments, orthonormal bases of $V_j^{(2)}$ and $W_j^{(2)}$ are given by

$$\left\{\psi_{j,n}^{(0,0)} : n = (n_1, n_2) \in \mathbb{Z}^2\right\}$$

and

$$\left\{\psi_{j,n}^{(e)} : e = (e_1, e_2) = \{0,1\}^2 \backslash \{0\}, n = (n_1, n_2) \in \mathbb{Z}^2\right\},$$

respectively. With this in hand, we now have all the ingredients we need. Using (9.43) we conclude that the set

$$\left\{\psi_{j,n}^{(e)} : e = (e_1, e_2) = \{0,1\}^2 \backslash \{0\}, j \in \mathbb{Z}, \ n = (n_1, n_2) \in \mathbb{Z}^2\right\}$$

is the corresponding orthonormal wavelet basis of $L^2(\mathbb{R}^2)$.

9.8.2 Wavelet Bases of $L^2([0,1]^2)$

Following §9.7, an orthonormal wavelet basis of $L^2([0,1]^2)$ can be similarly constructed by tensorizing the spaces V_j^{type}, where type denotes either the periodic (per) or boundary-corrected (int) wavelets. Let

$$V_j^{\text{type},(2)} = V_j^{\text{type}} \otimes V_j^{\text{type}} \subseteq L^2([0,1]^2)$$

and $W_j^{\text{type},(2)}$ be the orthogonal complement of $V_j^{\text{type},(2)}$ in $V_{j+1}^{\text{type},(2)}$, so that

$$L^2([0,1]^2) = V_{j_0}^{\text{type},(2)} \oplus W_{j_0}^{\text{type},(2)} \oplus W_{j_0+1}^{\text{type},(2)} \oplus \cdots$$

for any j_0. Now let

$$\psi_{j,n}^{\text{type},(e)} = \psi_{j,n_1}^{\text{type},(e_1)} \otimes \psi_{j,n_2}^{\text{type},(e_2)}, \quad e \in \{0,1\}^2, \ j \in \mathbb{Z}, \ n \in \mathbb{Z}^2.$$

Then

$$\left\{\psi_{j,n}^{\text{type},(0,0)} : n = (n_1, n_2), \ n_1, n_2 = 0, \ldots, 2^j - 1\right\}$$

is an orthonormal basis for $V_j^{\text{type},(2)}$,

$$\left\{\psi_{j,n}^{\text{type},(e)} : e \in \{0,1\}^2 \backslash \{0\}, \ n = (n_1, n_2), \ n_1, n_2 = 0, \ldots, 2^j - 1\right\}$$

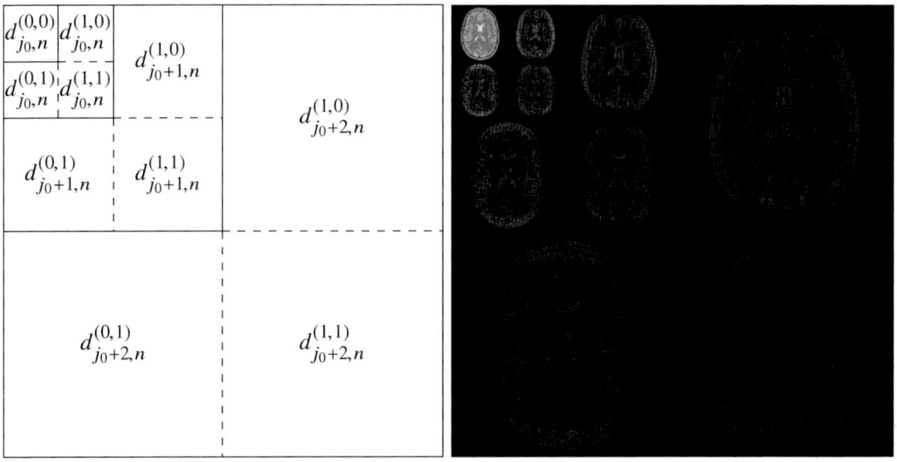

Figure 9.7 Left: Arrangement of the wavelet coefficients in two dimensions. Right: DB4 wavelet coefficients of an image from scale $j = j_0$ to $j = j_0 + 2$.

is an orthonormal basis for $W_j^{\text{type},(2)}$, and therefore

$$\bigcup_{\substack{j \geq j_0 \\ e \in \{0,1\}^2, e \neq 0, j > j_0}} \left\{ \psi_{j,n}^{\text{type},(e)} : n = (n_1, n_2),\ n_1, n_2 = 0, \ldots, 2^j - 1 \right\} \tag{9.45}$$

is an orthonormal wavelet basis of $L^2([0,1]^2)$ for any j_0. In particular, this implies the following two-dimensional analogue of (9.38). Every $f \in L^2([0,1]^2)$ has the expansion

$$f = \sum_{j \geq j_0} \sum_{\substack{e \in \{0,1\}^2, \\ e \neq 0, j > j_0}} \sum_{\substack{n=(n_1,n_2) \\ 0 \leq n_1, n_2 < 2^j}} d_{j,n}^{(e)} \psi_{j,n}^{\text{type},(e)}, \tag{9.46}$$

where $d_{j,n}^{(e)} = \langle f, \psi_{j,n}^{\text{type},(e)} \rangle_{L^2}$ are its corresponding coefficients.

In computations, it is customary to arrange the coefficients $d_{j,n}^{(e)}$ into a square array. This is shown in Fig. 9.7. The top left square, which is of size $2^{2(j_0+1)}$, corresponds to the coarsest scale $j = j_0$ in the decomposition (9.46). It is divided into four squares of size 2^{2j_0}, each corresponding to one of the four possible choices of $e \in \{0,1\}^2$. Next, each subsequent L-shaped region (of size 3×2^{2j}) contains the coefficients at scale $j > j_0$, and is divided into three squares of size 2^{2j} corresponding to the three possible choices of $e \in \{0,1\}^2 \backslash \{0\}$. Moving from the top left of this array to the bottom right equates to moving from the coarsest to the finest wavelet scale.

Remark 9.22 The extension to higher dimensions is analogous. If $d \geq 2$, one defines $V_j^{(d)} = V_j \otimes \cdots \otimes V_j$ and constructs $W_j^{(d)}$ as the orthogonal complement of $V_j^{(d)}$ in $V_{j+1}^{(d)}$. An orthonormal basis for $W_j^{(d)}$ is given by

$$\left\{ \psi_{j,n}^{(e)} : e = (e_1, \ldots, e_d) = \{0,1\}^d \backslash \{0\},\ j \in \mathbb{Z},\ n = (n_1, \ldots, n_2) \in \mathbb{Z}^d \right\},$$

where $\psi_{j,n}^{(e)} = \psi_{j,n_1}^{(e_1)} \otimes \cdots \otimes \psi_{j,n_d}^{(e_d)}$. In particular, in d dimensions, there are 2^d distinct types of wavelet functions at the coarsest scale $j = j_0$ and $2^d - 1$ distinct types of wavelet functions at each scale $j > j_0$.

9.9 Summary and Orderings

Let us sum up. Having first constructed the Daubechies wavelet bases of $L^2(\mathbb{R})$, we have now shown how to generate the corresponding bases on the unit interval $L^2([0,1])$ and unit square $L^2([0,1]^2)$. We now summarize this with the following definition:

Definition 9.23 (Daubechies wavelet basis of $L^2([0,1]^d)$, $d = 1,2$) The *periodized* or *boundary-corrected Daubechies wavelet basis* of $L^2([0,1])$ is the orthonormal wavelet basis constructed from the Daubechies wavelet basis of $L^2(\mathbb{R})$ via the approach of §9.7.1 or §9.7.2, respectively. The periodized or boundary-corrected Daubechies wavelet basis of $L^2([0,1]^2)$ is the orthonormal wavelet basis constructed as in §9.8.2 from the corresponding basis of $L^2([0,1])$.

This completes a key ingredient needed in subsequent parts of this book. Note that from now on we generally only consider the periodized basis, although much of what we say can be adapted to the boundary-corrected basis with additional effort.

Later in the book, it will often be convenient to index the basis functions over the natural numbers $\mathbb{N}$, rather than the multi-indexing used in the above constructions. In the one-dimensional case, this is straightforward. Let

$$\{\varphi^{\text{type}}_{j_0,n} : n = 0,\ldots,2^{j_0} - 1\} \cup \{\psi^{\text{type}}_{j,n} : n = 0,\ldots,2^j - 1,\ j \geq j_0\}$$

be the orthonormal basis of $L^2([0,1])$, with coarsest scale j_0. Then we define the basis $\{\phi_i\}_{i\in\mathbb{N}}$ indexed over $\mathbb{N}$ by

$$\phi_i = \begin{cases} \varphi^{\text{type}}_{j_0,i-1} & 1 \leq i \leq 2^{j_0} \\ \psi^{\text{type}}_{j,i-2^j-1} & 2^j < i \leq 2^{j+1},\ j \geq j_0 \end{cases},$$

and write $d = (d_i)_{i\in\mathbb{N}} \in \ell^2(\mathbb{N})$, $d_i = \langle f, \phi_i\rangle_{L^2}$, for the infinite vector of coefficients of a function $f \in L^2([0,1])$. Note that ordering the basis functions and coefficients in this way naturally divides $\mathbb{N}$ into *levels*; a property that will be of significance in later chapters. Defining

$$M_k = 2^{j_0+k-1}, \quad k = 1,2,\ldots, \tag{9.47}$$

we see that the first M_1 indices $\{1,\ldots,M_1\}$ correspond to the scaling functions $\varphi^{\text{type}}_{j_0,n}$, and for $k > 1$, the indices $\{M_{k-1}+1,\ldots,M_k\}$ in the kth level correspond to the wavelets $\psi^{\text{type}}_{j,n}$ at the scale $j = j_0 + k - 2$.

In two dimensions, let

$$\bigcup_{\substack{j\geq j_0 \\ e\in\{0,1\}^2, e\neq 0, j>j_0}} \left\{\psi^{\text{type},(e)}_{j,n} : n = (n_1,n_2),\ n_1,n_2 = 0,\ldots,2^j - 1\right\}$$

be the orthonormal basis of $L^2([0,1]^2)$ as in (9.45). We now also write this in the form

$\{\phi_i\}_{i\in\mathbb{N}}$, however, in this case we do not worry about how the ϕ_i are exactly defined. We just specify the corresponding levels. Let

$$M_k = 2^{2(j_0+k-1)}, \quad k = 1, 2, \dots. \tag{9.48}$$

Then the indices $\{1, \dots, M_1\}$ in the first level are assumed to contain the functions

$$\psi^{\text{type},(0,0)}_{j_0,n}, \quad n = (n_1, n_2),\ n_1, n_2 = 0, \dots, 2^{j_0} - 1,$$

and for $k > 1$ the indices $\{M_{k-1} + 1, \dots, M_k\}$ in the kth level correspond to the functions

$$\psi^{\text{type},(e)}_{j,n}, \quad e \in \{0,1\}^2\backslash\{0\},\ n = (n_1, n_2),\ n_1, n_2 = 0, \dots, 2^{j_0} - 1,$$

at scale $j = j_0 + k - 2$. In particular, if $d \in \ell^2(\mathbb{N})$ is the resulting infinite vector of coefficients of a function $f \in L^2([0,1]^2)$, the first M_1 entries correspond to the upper-left square in Fig. 9.7, and for $k > 1$, the entries d_i, $M_{k-1} < i \leq M_k$ correspond to the $(k-1)$th L-shaped region.

Remark 9.24 Generally speaking, the *intra-scale* orderings of a wavelet basis do not matter, since wavelets have characteristically *inter-scale* properties. This is the case throughout this book, and explains why we did not specify an intra-scale ordering above.

Remark 9.25 In the above constructions, the coarsest wavelet scale j_0 is a free parameter. We shall not consider the effect of the choice of j_0 on the wavelet basis. Unless otherwise stated, we henceforth assume that j_0 is chosen as small as possible, i.e.

$$j_0 = \begin{cases} 0 & p = 1 \\ \lceil \log_2(2p) \rceil & p \geq 2 \end{cases}, \tag{9.49}$$

where p is the order of the Daubechies wavelet.

9.10 Discrete Wavelet Computations

Having constructed orthonormal wavelet bases, we now discuss how to perform discrete computations with them. We consider the computation of the wavelet coefficients from function values, and its inverse operation, the evaluation of a function from its coefficients. For simplicity, we work exclusively in the one-dimensional setting in this section. The extension to higher dimensions is conceptually straightforward.

9.10.1 The Discrete Wavelet Transform

Suppose we want to approximate a function $f \in L^2(\mathbb{R})$ using a wavelet basis (we work on $\mathbb{R}$ for the moment, rather than $[0,1]$). Recall that the spaces V_j allow an approximation to a function at a certain scale, with more detail being present at finer scales (large j) than at coarse scales (small j). Hence we first fix a finite maximum scale $j = j_1$ and then approximate f by its orthogonal projection $P_{j_1} f$ onto V_{j_1}. This projection can be represented in terms of scaling functions as

$$P_{j_1} f = \sum_{n\in\mathbb{Z}} c_{j_1,n} \varphi_{j_1,n}, \qquad c_{j_1,n} = \langle f, \varphi_{j_1,n} \rangle_{L^2}, \tag{9.50}$$

but because of (9.8) it can also be represented as

$$P_{j_1} f = \sum_{n \in \mathbb{Z}} c_{j_0,n} \varphi_{j_0,n} + \sum_{j=j_0}^{j_1-1} \sum_{n \in \mathbb{Z}} d_{j,n} \psi_{j,n}, \qquad d_{j,n} = \langle f, \psi_{j,n} \rangle_{L^2}, \tag{9.51}$$

for any $j_0 < j_1$. The first expression (9.50) is convenient for synthesizing the approximation $P_{j_1} f$ on a grid of points (see later), while (9.51) is desirable because of the compressibility of the wavelet coefficients $d_{j,n}$. Hence, we now seek a (fast) algorithm for transforming between the two. We refer to this process as follows:

Definition 9.26 (Discrete wavelet transform) The *forwards Discrete Wavelet Transform (DWT)* between scales j_0 and j_1, where $j_0 < j_1$, is the mapping

$$\mathcal{W} \colon \{c_{j_1,n} : n \in \mathbb{Z}\} \mapsto \{c_{j_0,n} : n \in \mathbb{Z}\} \cup \{d_{j,n} : n \in \mathbb{Z},\ j_0 \le j < j_1\}.$$

Its inverse, the *inverse DWT*, is the mapping

$$\mathcal{W}^{-1} \colon \{c_{j_0,n} : n \in \mathbb{Z}\} \cup \{d_{j,n} : n \in \mathbb{Z},\ j_0 \le j < j_1\} \mapsto \{c_{j_1,n} : n \in \mathbb{Z}\}.$$

Note that $\mathcal{W}$ is a unitary operator (this follows from the fact that (9.50) and (9.51) are both expansions in orthonormal bases), and therefore $\mathcal{W}^{-1} = \mathcal{W}^*$.

9.10.2 Reconstruction and Decomposition Formulae

The forwards and inverse DWT are computed by successively applying formulae – known as *decomposition* and *reconstruction* formulae – that relate the coefficients $c_{j-1,n}$ and $d_{j-1,n}$ at a scale $j-1$ to the scaling coefficients $c_{j,n}$ at scale j. To state and prove these, we require some notation. First, if $z = (z_n)_{n\in\mathbb{Z}}$ is a sequence, we define the sequences $z' = (z'_n)_{n\in\mathbb{Z}}$ and $\tilde{z} = (\tilde{z}_n)_{n\in\mathbb{Z}}$ by

$$z'_n = \overline{z_{-n}}, \qquad \tilde{z}_n = \begin{cases} z_{n/2} & n \text{ even} \\ 0 & n \text{ odd} \end{cases}.$$

Second, given two sequences $x = (x_n)_{n\in\mathbb{Z}}$ and $z = (z_n)_{n\in\mathbb{Z}}$, we write $x \star z = ((x \star z)_n)_{n\in\mathbb{Z}}$ for their convolution, i.e.

$$(x \star z)_n = \sum_{k\in\mathbb{Z}} x_k z_{n-k} = \sum_{k\in\mathbb{Z}} x_{n-k} z_k, \qquad n \in \mathbb{Z}.$$

Finally, let $h = (h_n)_{n\in\mathbb{Z}}$ be the filter associated with the MRA – see (9.11). We now define a new filter $g = (g_n)_{n\in\mathbb{Z}}$ by $g_n = (-1)^n \overline{h_{1-n}}$. It follows immediately from (9.20) that

$$\frac{1}{\sqrt{2}} \psi\left(\frac{\cdot}{2}\right) = \sum_{n\in\mathbb{Z}} g_n \varphi(\cdot - n). \tag{9.52}$$

Hence the g_n are the coefficients of the representation of the wavelet $\psi_{-1,0} \in W_{-1}$ in V_0. Notice that the transfer function associated with g is

$$m_1(\omega) = \sqrt{2} \sum_{n\in\mathbb{Z}} g_n \mathrm{e}^{-\mathrm{i}n\omega} = -\sqrt{2}\mathrm{e}^{-\mathrm{i}\omega} \sum_n \overline{h_n} \mathrm{e}^{\mathrm{i}n(\omega+\pi)} = -\mathrm{e}^{-\mathrm{i}\omega} \overline{m_0(\omega+\pi)}. \tag{9.53}$$

Theorem 9.27 *The coefficient sequences* $c_{j-1} = (c_{j-1,n})_{n\in\mathbb{Z}}$, $d_{j-1} = (d_{j-1,n})_{n\in\mathbb{Z}}$ *and* $c_j = (c_{j,n})_{n\in\mathbb{Z}}$ *satisfy*

$$c_{j-1,n} = \left(c_j \star h'\right)_{2n}, \quad d_{j-1,n} = \left(c_j \star g'\right)_{2n}, \qquad \forall n \in \mathbb{Z} \tag{9.54}$$

and

$$c_{j,n} = \left(\widetilde{c_{j-1}} \star h + \widetilde{d_{j-1}} \star g\right)_n, \qquad \forall n \in \mathbb{Z}. \tag{9.55}$$

Proof For the first part of (9.54), we apply (9.10) with the argument $2^j x - 2n$ to get

$$2^{-1/2}\varphi(2^{j-1}x - n) = \sum_{k\in\mathbb{Z}} h_n \varphi(2^j x - 2n - k) = \sum_{k\in\mathbb{Z}} h_{k-2n}\varphi(2^j x - k).$$

Multiplying by $2^{j/2}$ yields

$$\varphi_{j-1,n} = \sum_{k\in\mathbb{Z}} h_{k-2n}\varphi_{j,k}, \tag{9.56}$$

and therefore

$$c_{j-1,n} = \langle f, \varphi_{j-1,n}\rangle_{L^2} = \sum_{k\in\mathbb{Z}} \overline{h_{k-2n}} \langle f, \varphi_{j,k}\rangle_{L^2} = \left(c_j \star h'\right)_{2n},$$

as required. For the other part, we use (9.52) and argue in the same way.

Now consider (9.55). Using (9.56) and the equivalent formula for $\psi_{j-1,n}$, we get

$$\langle \varphi_{j,n}, \varphi_{j-1,k}\rangle_{L^2} = \sum_{l\in\mathbb{Z}} \overline{h_{l-2k}} \langle \varphi_{j,n}, \varphi_{j,l}\rangle_{L^2} = \overline{h_{n-2k}},$$

$$\langle \varphi_{j,n}, \psi_{j-1,k}\rangle_{L^2} = \sum_{l\in\mathbb{Z}} \overline{g_{l-2k}} \langle \varphi_{j,n}, \varphi_{j,l}\rangle_{L^2} = \overline{g_{n-2k}}.$$

Since $\varphi_{j,n} \in V_j = W_{j-1} \oplus V_{j-1}$, it follows that

$$\varphi_{j,n} = \sum_{k\in\mathbb{Z}} \left(\overline{g_{n-2k}}\psi_{j-1,k} + \overline{h_{n-2k}}\varphi_{j-1,k}\right),$$

and therefore

$$c_{j,n} = \langle f, \varphi_{j,n}\rangle_{L^2} = \sum_{k\in\mathbb{Z}} \left(g_{n-2k} d_{j-1,k} + h_{n-2k} c_{j-1,k}\right) = \left(\widetilde{d_{j-1}} \star g + \widetilde{c_{j-1}} \star h\right)_n,$$

as required. □

This theorem is interpreted as follows. Decomposition, i.e. (9.54), corresponds to convolution of c_j with the filters h' and g', followed by downsampling by a factor of 2. On the other hand, reconstruction, which is given by (9.55), corresponds to interpolation (zero padding), convolution with the filters g and h, followed by linear combination.

Note that h, and therefore h', is a *low-pass* filter. Hence convolution with it removes high frequencies. Conversely, g' is a *high-pass* filter, meaning that convolution with it removes low frequencies.[2] To see why this is the case, notice that the transfer functions m_0 and m_1 satisfy

$$|m_0(\omega)|^2 + |m_1(\omega)|^2 = 1, \quad a.e.\ \omega \in \mathbb{R}$$

[2] A filter is *low pass* if its transfer function $m(\omega)$ is concentrated in the range $|\omega| \le \pi/2$, and *high pass* if $m(\omega)$ is concentrated in the range $\pi/2 < |\omega| \le \pi$.

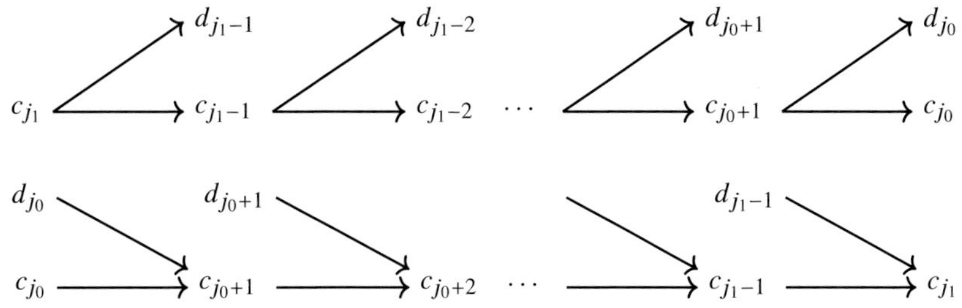

Figure 9.8 Implementation of the DWT (top row) and its inverse (bottom row) via cascades of decompositions (9.54) and reconstructions (9.55).

(this follows from Lemma 9.7 and (9.53)) and m_0 takes the value $m_0(0) = 1$ at $\omega = 0$ and vanishes along with its first $p-1$ derivatives at $\omega = \pi$. Hence $m_0(\omega)$ is concentrated in $|\omega| \leq \pi/2$, and therefore $m_1(\omega)$ is concentrated in $\pi/2 < |\omega| \leq \pi$.

9.10.3 Implementation of the DWT

With these formulae, the DWT $\mathcal{W}$ is implemented as a cascade of filtering and downsampling operations, moving progressively from $j = j_1$ down to $j = j_0$. Given the scaling function coefficients c_{j_1} at some fine scale j_1, it computes the wavelet coefficients d_j at all scales $j \leq j \leq j_1$, as well as the scaling function coefficients c_{j_0} at the coarsest scale j_0. Likewise, its inverse $\mathcal{W}^{-1}$ proceeds as a cascade of zero padding, filtering and linear combinations to recover the fine-scale scaling function coefficients c_{j_1} from the given coefficients. These processes are illustrated schematically in Fig. 9.8.

By definition, the forwards DWT produces the wavelet coefficients of a function given its scaling function coefficients $c_{j_1} = (c_{j_1,n})_{n\in\mathbb{Z}}$ at some fine scale. However, this input is generally unknown in practice. A typical *initialization* of the DWT involves simply replacing this input by the evaluations of f on an equispaced grid of size 2^{-j_1}:

$$\left(2^{-j_1/2} f(n/2^{j_1})\right)_{n\in\mathbb{Z}}.$$

Note that if φ has compact support, then $2^{j_1}\varphi(2^{j_1}x - n)$ is an approximation to the Dirac centred at $x = n/2^{j_1}$ for large j_1. Hence

$$c_{j_1,n} \approx 2^{-j_1/2} f(n/2^{j_1}), \tag{9.57}$$

under mild assumptions on f. This means that the forwards DWT is an approximate mapping from function values to wavelet coefficients (it *analyses* f), and therefore by definition, the inverse DWT is an approximate mapping between wavelet coefficients and function values (it *synthesizes* f).

This approach is standard. We remark, however, that the error it commits may affect the accuracy of certain numerical computations. Making the approximation (9.57) is commonly referred to as *committing the wavelet crime*.

9.10.4 Wavelets on Intervals and the Fast Wavelet Transform

Consider the periodized Daubechies wavelet basis introduced in §9.7. In this case, the DWT $\mathcal{W}$ is a linear mapping from $\mathbb{C}^N \to \mathbb{C}^N$, where $N = 2^{j_1}$. Hence it can be expressed as a unitary matrix W. Note that the decomposition and reconstruction formulae (9.54) and (9.55) are modified slightly in this setting, with the convolution $\star$ being replaced by a circular convolution due to the periodicity of the wavelet basis. The circular convolution of two vectors $x, z \in \mathbb{C}^N$ is given by (A.20).

Implementation of $\mathcal{W}$ is computationally efficient in this case, requiring less than $O(N\log(N))$ arithmetic operations for large N. To see this, we first recall that the filters h and g have $2p$ nonzero entries. Hence the convolutions in (9.54) require at most $4p$ arithmetic operations, and the vectors c_{j-1} and d_{j-1} (which have length 2^j) can be computed from c_j in at most $8p2^j$ arithmetic operations using the decomposition formula (9.54). Iterating this from $j = j_1$ down to $j = j_0$ as in Fig. 9.8, we deduce that computing the forwards DWT requires only $O(pN)$ operations. The same applies for the inverse DWT.

The DWT can also be computed efficiently in the case of the boundary-corrected wavelets. The procedure is rather more complicated, however, due to the more involved way in which the boundary wavelets are modified than in the periodized case. We forgo its description.

9.10.5 Discrete Wavelet Bases and Sparsifying Transforms

Recall from Chapter 5 that an orthonormal sparsifying transform is a unitary matrix $\Phi \in \mathbb{C}^{N\times N}$ which takes a vector $x \in \mathbb{C}^N$ and produces a sparse vector of coefficients $d = \Phi^* x \in \mathbb{C}^N$. We are now finally able to define exactly what we mean by a discrete wavelet sparsifying transform:

Definition 9.28 (Discrete wavelet sparsifying transform) A *discrete wavelet sparsifying transform* of $\mathbb{C}^N$ is a matrix $\Phi = W^*$, where W is the matrix of a DWT.

To understand why it is defined in this way, let $N = 2^r$ and $x \in \mathbb{C}^N$ be the discretization at resolution $N = 2^r$ of a continuous one-dimensional image $f : [0, 1] \to \mathbb{C}$, i.e.

$$x = (2^{-r/2} f(n/2^r))_{n=0}^{2^r-1}$$

(we normalize according to $2^{-r/2}$ for the sake of (9.57)). Then, ignoring the wavelet crime, the vector $d = Wx$ is precisely the vector containing the first N coefficients of f in its wavelet decomposition. In other words, W applied to x yields the compressible vector d, making $\Phi = W^*$ a sparsifying transform.

Recall that the columns of any orthonormal sparsifying transform form an orthonormal basis of $\mathbb{C}^N$, the so-called sparsity basis. Hence we also define the following:

Definition 9.29 (Discrete wavelet basis) A *discrete wavelet (sparsity) basis* of $\mathbb{C}^N$ is the orthonormal basis consisting of the rows of a DWT matrix W.

Remark 9.30 In the case of the Haar wavelet, but not in general, the corresponding discrete wavelet basis has a simple expression. It arises simply by sampling the continuous Haar wavelet basis of $L^2([0,1])$ on the equispaced grid $\{n/N\}_{n=0}^{N-1}$ and then renormalizing. In particular, choosing $j_0 = 0$ and letting $N = 2^r$, this basis is given by

$$\{\varphi\} \cup \{\psi_{j,n} : n = 0, \dots, 2^j - 1,\ j = 0, \dots, r-1\},$$

where $\varphi = \varphi_{0,0} = (\varphi_i)_{i=0}^{N-1}$ and $\psi_{j,n} = ((\psi_{j,n})_i)_{i=0}^{N-1}$ are now vectors containing the (normalized) sample values of the corresponding Haar scaling function and wavelets. Specifically,

$$\varphi_i = 2^{-r/2}, \quad i = 0, \dots, N-1,$$

and

$$(\psi_{j,n})_i = \begin{cases} 2^{\frac{j-r}{2}} & n2^{r-j} \leq i < (n+\frac{1}{2})2^{r-j} \\ -2^{\frac{j-r}{2}} & (n+\frac{1}{2})2^{r-j} \leq i < (n+1)2^{r-j} \\ 0 & \text{otherwise} \end{cases}, \quad i = 0, \dots, N-1,$$

respectively. If we also write $\varphi_{j,n} = ((\varphi_{j,n})_i)_{i=0}^{N-1}$ for the vector containing the discretized scaling functions for arbitrary j and n, then in the compact notation (9.44), we may write

$$(\psi_{j,n}^{(e)})_i = \begin{cases} 2^{\frac{j-r}{2}} & n2^{r-j} \leq i < (n+\frac{1}{2})2^{r-j} \\ (-1)^e 2^{\frac{j-r}{2}} & (n+\frac{1}{2})2^{r-j} \leq i < (n+1)2^{r-j} \\ 0 & \text{otherwise} \end{cases}, \tag{9.58}$$

for $i = 0, \dots, N-1$, where $e \in \{0,1\}$. We make extensive use of this basis in subsequent chapters to illustrate the various compressed sensing recovery guarantees.

9.11 Beyond Wavelets

This chapter has developed orthogonal wavelets as a means to efficiently approximate piecewise smooth functions in one dimension. It transpires that they are *optimal* for this task – a matter we discuss further in the next chapter. However, in two dimensions the situation becomes more complicated. Images possess geometric features such as edges, which can generally be modelled by piecewise regular curves. Wavelets are *isotropic*, meaning that a wavelet at scale j is supported in a square of side length $O(2^{-j})$. As shown in Fig. 9.9, this means that roughly $O(2^j)$ wavelets intersect an edge. This is a large number, and it causes the wavelet approximation to be asymptotically suboptimal.

There are various generalizations of orthogonal wavelets that aim to overcome this problem by better capturing the geometry. *Curvelets*, already used in Chapter 4, are multiscale systems generated by dilations, translations and *rotations*. They form tight frames as opposed to bases. Unlike with wavelets, the dilation is based on a *parabolic scaling* law, meaning the individual curvelets (the *atoms*) have width proportional to the square of their height. This *anisotropy* allows them to more efficiently capture edges. In fact, roughly $O(2^{j/2})$ curvelets are needed to capture a curve, a figure that is asymptotically much smaller than the number of wavelets needed to do so.

Figure 9.9 illustrates this principle. Wavelets at scale j are supported in squares of size roughly $2^{-j} \times 2^{-j}$, whereas curvelets are supported in rectangles of size roughly $2^{-j/2} \times$

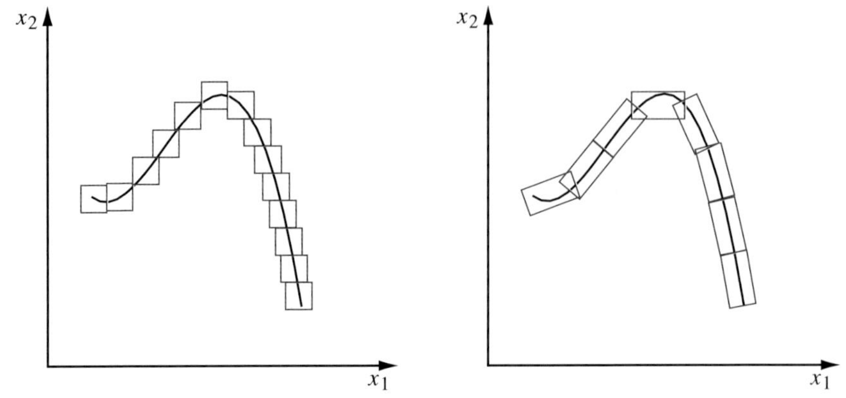

Figure 9.9 Left: wavelet approximation of an edge in two dimensions. Wavelets are supported in squares, meaning many wavelets intersect the edge. Right: curvelet approximation of the same edge. Curvelets are supported in rectangles whose width is the square of their height, meaning that far fewer curvelets intersect the edge.

2^{-j}. Intuitively, one therefore expects curvelets to provide better sparse approximations of piecewise smooth images. This turns out to be the case, as we discuss in §10.5.

In recent years, so-called *shearlets* have also been developed. These are similar in concept to curvelets, except that a shearlet system uses a shearing operation to generate an anisotropic multiscale system as opposed to a rotation. This has some advantages. In particular, it preserves the integer lattice $\mathbb{Z}^2$, a property which is useful for computations. Like curvelets, shearlets form a tight frame (in fact, they form a so-called *Parseval* frame).

We have already seen the significant practical benefits of using curvelets or shearlets instead of wavelets in Chapter 4. An in-depth description of these systems is outside the scope of this book. After a short follow-up discussion in §10.5, we do not consider them in any further detail. Additional information for the interested reader can be found in the references listed in the Notes section.

Notes

Wavelets and wavelet theory is a vast topic. In this chapter we have covered only the basics, consequently leaving out many interesting further topics. Our primary references have been [164, 264, 344, 450, 501]. We refer the reader to these sources and references therein for further historical context and additional information on the many applications of wavelets outside of compressive imaging.

In particular, we have not discussed continuous wavelet transforms, only orthonormal bases of wavelets, the latter being rather more relevant to compressed sensing. We have also not discussed nonorthogonal wavelets, e.g. biorthogonal (Riesz) wavelets or wavelet frames. Note that certain biorthogonal wavelets, namely the *Cohen–Daubechies–Feauveau (CDF)* wavelets [152], are used in JPEG-2000 compression. See [344] for further information. We have focused exclusively on compactly supported orthogonal wavelets, due to their application to imaging. Yet there are many other types of noncompactly supported wavelets, including the Lemarie, Meyer and Shannon wavelets, which are an important part of the wavelet literature.

Theorems 9.5 and 9.6 can be found in [264, Chpt. 2, Thms 1.6 & 1.7], for example. Theorem 9.9 is based on [164, Thm. 5.1.1]. In fact, a stronger version of Theorem 9.9 states that (a)–(d) hold if and only if

$$\mathcal{F}\psi(\omega) = \mathrm{e}^{-\mathrm{i}\omega/2}\nu(\omega)\overline{m_0(\omega/2+\pi)}\mathcal{F}\varphi(\omega/2),$$

for some 2π-periodic function ν satisfying $|\nu(\omega)| = 1$ a.e. $\omega \in [0, 2\pi)$. The choice of the phase factor $\nu(\omega) = -1$ in our result was to ensure the correct sign and support for the Haar wavelet in Example 9.10. Other choices are sometimes made in the literature, based on phase factors of the form $\nu(\omega) = \rho\mathrm{e}^{\mathrm{i}m\omega}$ with ρ and m constant. This corresponds to a shift and a phase change of ψ, and thus has no overall effect on the resulting wavelet basis. See [164, Sec. 5.1].

The results in §9.4 are based on [344, Sec. 7.2]. Note that [344, Thm. 7.4] gives a stronger version of Proposition 9.12 in which it is also shown that (a)–(c) are equivalent to a fourth condition:

(d) $q_k(x) = \sum_{n=-\infty}^{\infty} n^k\varphi(x-n)$ is a polynomial of degree k for $0 \leq k < p$.

That is, shifted versions of the scaling function can reproduce all polynomials of degrees up to $p-1$. This is known as the *Strang–Fix* condition [449], and was first introduced in the context of finite element methods.

The omitted part of the proof of Theorem 9.13 can be found in [264, Lem. 3.12], for instance, and Lemmas 9.15 and 9.16 in [264, Prop. 3.9, Lem. 3.12 and Thm. 3.13]. A proof of (9.23) can be found in [344, Thm. 6.1]. The derivation in §9.6 is based on [164, 264]. As noted, condition (c) of Theorem 9.14 is used to ensure an orthonormal wavelet basis. Without it, the resulting system $\{\psi_{j,n} : j, n \in \mathbb{Z}\}$ is a tight frame. We note also that (c) is sufficient but not necessary. Necessary and sufficient conditions are given in [164, Thm. 6.3.6]. Bezout's theorem (Theorem 9.18) can be found in [164, Thm. 6.1.1]. For further discussion on the construction and evaluation of the Daubechies wavelets, see [164, Chpt. 6] and [344, Chpt. 7]. For further information on the smoothness of the Daubechies wavelets – including proofs of (9.35) and (9.36), and the derivation of the optimal regularity parameters in Table 9.3 – see [164, Chpt. 7] and references therein.

Wavelets on intervals are discussed in [344, Sec. 7.5]. Boundary-corrected wavelets are due to Cohen, Daubechies & Vial [153]; see [37] for implementation details. We have not mentioned a third possible construction, known as *folding* – which is popular in image processing – since it pertains to biorthogonal, but not orthogonal, wavelets.

Curvelets were introduced by Candès & Donoho [111, 112, 113], based on an earlier X-let family known as *ridgelets* [110]. Shearlets were introduced in [247, 311]. For more information, see [308] and references therein. These are perhaps the two most well-known families of X-let transforms for images. Other examples include contourlets [176], directional wavelets [480], platelets [498], dual-tree complex wavelets [432] and bandlets [318, 346]. See also [308, 339, 448] for further discussion.

10 A Taste of Wavelet Approximation Theory

The previous chapter focused on the construction of wavelets and their implementation. In this chapter, we reconnect wavelets with the topic of sparsity, and specifically, elaborate in a precise mathematical sense why wavelets provide approximately sparse representations of certain functions. We do this by developing several results in wavelet approximation theory for classes of piecewise regular functions of one variable.

We commence in §10.1 by formalizing so-called *linear* and *nonlinear* (i.e. best s-term) approximation in abstract Hilbert spaces. Next, in §10.2, we present two results on linear and nonlinear approximation with wavelets, one for piecewise Hölder functions, the other for functions of bounded variation. These illustrate the benefit of best s-term wavelet approximation over linear approximation, a benefit that increases with the number of vanishing moments in the case of the former. This helps explain why wavelets are such effective tools for compression, and therefore, as we discuss in §10.3, compressed sensing. Proofs of these results are given in §10.4.

10.1 Linear and Nonlinear Approximation

Let $\mathbb{H}$ be a separable Hilbert space with inner product $\langle \cdot, \cdot \rangle$ and norm $\|\cdot\|$, and let $\{\phi_i : i \in \mathbb{N}\}$ be an orthonormal basis for $\mathbb{H}$. Let $f \in \mathbb{H}$ and consider its expansion

$$f = \sum_{i=1}^{\infty} \langle f, \phi_i \rangle \phi_i. \tag{10.1}$$

In *linear approximation*, our concern is approximating f from the subspace

$$\mathbb{H}_s = \operatorname{span}\{\phi_1, \ldots, \phi_s\},$$

spanned by the first s basis elements. We define the best linear approximation error as

$$\epsilon_s(f) = \inf_{g \in \mathbb{H}_s} \|f - g\|,$$

and recall that since $\mathbb{H}$ is a Hilbert space and $\{\phi_i\}$ is an orthonormal basis, the infimum (i.e. the best approximation) is unique and attained by the truncated expansion

$$f_s = \sum_{i=1}^{s} \langle f, \phi_i \rangle \phi_i.$$

Notice that the mapping $f \mapsto f_s$ is linear, hence the name *linear* approximation. Moreover, due to Parseval's identity the error satisfies

$$\epsilon_s(f) = \sqrt{\sum_{i>s} |\langle f, \phi_i \rangle|^2},$$

and therefore the rate of decrease of the error as $s \to \infty$ is directly related to the decay of the coefficients $|\langle f, \phi_i \rangle|$ as $i \to \infty$.

Nonlinear approximation, also known as *best s-term approximation*, concerns the approximation of f from the subset

$$\widetilde{\mathbb{H}}_s = \left\{ g = \sum_{i \in \Delta} d_i \phi_i,\ d_i \in \mathbb{C},\ \Delta \subset \mathbb{N},\ |\Delta| \leq s \right\} \subset \mathbb{H},$$

consisting of all finite linear combinations of at most s of the basis elements ϕ_i.[1] The corresponding best approximation error is

$$\sigma_s(f) = \inf_{g \in \widetilde{\mathbb{H}}_s} \|f - g\|. \tag{10.2}$$

Note that this generalizes best s-term approximation for vectors, a topic discussed previously in §5.2. Indeed, if $\mathbb{H} = \mathbb{C}^N$ (with the Euclidean inner product) and $f \in \mathbb{C}^N$ is expressed as $f = \sum_{i=1}^{N} d_i \phi_i$ for some orthonormal basis $\{\phi_i\}_{i=1}^{N}$ of $\mathbb{C}^N$, then $\sigma_s(f) = \sigma_s(d)_{\ell^2}$, where $\sigma_s(d)_{\ell^2}$ is as in Definition 5.3.

Much as for vectors, we obtain the infimum $\sigma_s(f)$ in general Hilbert spaces through a nonincreasing rearrangement. Let $\pi \colon \mathbb{N} \to \mathbb{N}$ be a bijection which rearranges the coefficients $\langle f, \phi_i \rangle$ into nonincreasing order of their absolute values:

$$|\langle f, \phi_{\pi(1)} \rangle| \geq |\langle f, \phi_{\pi(2)} \rangle| \geq \cdots .$$

Then the infimum in (10.2) is attained by the *best s-term approximation*

$$\tilde{f}_s = \sum_{i=1}^{s} \langle f, \phi_{\pi(i)} \rangle \phi_{\pi(i)},$$

and the error satisfies

$$\sigma_s(f) = \sqrt{\sum_{i>s} |\langle f, \phi_{\pi(i)} \rangle|^2}. \tag{10.3}$$

Hence the rate of decay of the error is related to the decay of the *sorted* coefficients $|\langle f, \phi_{\pi(i)} \rangle|$. This relationship is made precise by the following result:

Proposition 10.1 *Let $\alpha > 0$, $c_1 > 0$, $f \in \mathbb{H}$ and $\pi \colon \mathbb{N} \to \mathbb{N}$ be a nonincreasing rearrangement of the coefficients $\langle f, \phi_i \rangle$ in absolute value. Then*

$$|\langle f, \phi_{\pi(i)} \rangle| \leq c_1 i^{-\alpha - 1/2},\ \forall i > 1 \quad \Longrightarrow \quad \sigma_s(f) \leq c_1 c_2 s^{-\alpha},\ \forall s \geq 1,$$

[1] Technically speaking, nonlinear approximation also includes more general forms of approximation than best s-term approximation. However, we will continue to use the two terms interchangeably.

where the constant c_2 *depends on* α *only. Conversely,*

$$\sigma_s(f) \leq c_1 s^{-\alpha},\ \forall s \geq 1 \quad \Longrightarrow \quad |\langle f, \phi_{\pi(i)} \rangle| \leq c_1 c_3 i^{-\alpha-1/2}, \forall i > 1,$$

where the constant c_3 *depends on* α *only.*

Proof For the first result, we use (10.3) to get

$$(\sigma_s(f))^2 \leq c_1^2 \sum_{i>s} i^{-2\alpha-1} \leq c_1^2 \int_s^\infty z^{-2\alpha-1}\, dz = \frac{c_1^2 s^{-2\alpha}}{2\alpha},$$

as required. For the second, we note that $\sigma_{\lfloor s/2 \rfloor}(f) \leq c_3 c_1 s^{-\alpha}$ for all $s \geq 2$, where c_3 depends on α, and

$$(\sigma_{\lfloor s/2 \rfloor}(f))^2 \geq \sum_{i=\lfloor s/2 \rfloor+1}^{s} |\langle f, \phi_{\pi(i)} \rangle|^2 \geq \frac{s}{2} |\langle f, \phi_{\pi(s)} \rangle|^2.$$

The result now follows after a possible change of c_3. □

10.2 Linear and Nonlinear Wavelet Approximation Rates

The central tenet of wavelet approximation theory is that, for suitable classes of functions, the rate of decay of the reordered coefficients $\langle f, \phi_{\pi(i)} \rangle$ is much faster than that of the original coefficients $\langle f, \phi_i \rangle$. Hence, nonlinear approximation using wavelets is more effective than linear approximation.

To elaborate, we first consider wavelet approximation of piecewise smooth functions with finitely many discontinuities. We require several definitions. The first is the Hölder space, already used briefly in the previous chapter, but now formally defined:

Definition 10.2 (Hölder continuity) For $0 < \alpha \leq 1$, the Hölder semi-norm of index α of a continuous function f is

$$|f|_{C^\alpha([a,b])} = \sup_{\substack{x,y \in [a,b] \\ x \neq y}} \left\{ \frac{|f(x) - f(y)|}{|x-y|^\alpha} \right\}.$$

A function f is *α-Hölder continuous* if $|f|_{C^\alpha([a,b])} < \infty$.

Definition 10.3 (Hölder space) For $\alpha = k + \beta$, where $k \in \mathbb{N}_0$ and $0 < \beta \leq 1$, the *Hölder space* $C^\alpha([a,b])$ on a compact interval $[a,b]$ consists of those functions f which are k-times continuously differentiable on $[a,b]$ and for which the kth derivative is β-Hölder continuous. The space $C^\alpha([a,b])$ is a Banach space with norm

$$\|f\|_{C^\alpha([a,b])} = \sum_{j=0}^{k} \|f^{(j)}\|_{C([a,b])} + |f^{(k)}|_{C^\beta([a,b])},$$

where $\|g\|_{C([a,b])} = \sup_{x \in [a,b]} |g(x)|$.

Definition 10.4 (Piecewise Hölder space) For $\alpha > 0$ the space $PC^{\alpha}([a,b])$ consists of all functions that are discontinuous at (at most) a finite number of points in $[a,b]$ and are α-Hölder continuous in between any two consecutive discontinuities.

We define the norm of $f \in PC^{\alpha}([a,b])$ as the maximum of its C^{α}-norms over all subintervals of smoothness, and write $\|f\|_{PC^{\alpha}([a,b])}$, or $\|f\|_{PC^{\alpha}}$ when the domain of f is clear. This makes $PC^{\alpha}([a,b])$ a Banach space. For convenience, we also let

$$\mathcal{N}(f) = |\{\text{discontinuities of } f \text{ in } (a,b)\}| + 1, \qquad f \in PC^{\alpha}([a,b]).$$

We now consider linear and nonlinear wavelet approximation in $PC^{\alpha}([0,1])$:

Theorem 10.5 (Wavelet approximation in PC^{α}) *Suppose that $f \in PC^{\alpha}([0,1])$, where $\alpha = k+\beta \geq 1/2$ for $k \in \mathbb{N}_0$ and $0 < \beta \leq 1$. Consider the periodized Daubechies wavelet basis (Definition 9.23) of order $p > k$ with j_0 as in (9.49). Then there are constants $c_1, c_2, c_3 > 0$ depending on p and α only such that*

$$\epsilon_s(f) \leq c_1 \sqrt{\mathcal{N}(f)} \|f\|_{PC^{\alpha}} / \sqrt{s},$$

and, if $s/\log(s) \geq c_2 \mathcal{N}(f)$,

$$\sigma_s(f) \leq c_3 \|f\|_{PC^{\alpha}} / s^{\alpha}.$$

The above result applies to functions with only finitely many discontinuities. Functions with potentially infinitely many discontinuities can be modelled via the BV spaces:

Definition 10.6 (Bounded variation) The *total variation* of a function f on an interval $[a,b] \subset \mathbb{R}$ is

$$V(f;[a,b]) = \sup\left\{ \sum_{i=0}^{n-1} |f(x_{i+1}) - f(x_i)| : a = x_0 < x_1 < \cdots < x_{n-1} < x_n = b,\ n \in \mathbb{N} \right\}.$$

A function f is of *bounded variation* on $[a,b]$ if $V(f;[a,b]) < \infty$. The space of all functions of bounded variation on $[a,b]$ is denoted by $BV([a,b])$.

When the domain of f is clear, we also write $V(f)$. Note that $V(f) = \int_a^b |f'(x)| \,\mathrm{d}x$ whenever f' is Riemann integrable.

Theorem 10.7 (Wavelet approximation in BV) *Let $f \in BV([0,1])$ and consider the periodized Daubechies wavelet basis of order $p \geq 1$ with j_0 as in (9.49). Then there are constants $c_1, c_2 > 0$ depending on p only such that*

$$\epsilon_s(f) \leq c_1 V(f)/\sqrt{s}, \qquad \sigma_s(f) \leq c_2 V(f)/s.$$

10.3 Discussion

The main conclusion from these results is as follows:

> The power of wavelets as a compression tool stems from nonlinear approximation. For piecewise smooth functions, the best s-term approximation error decays asymptotically faster than the linear s-term error.

In fact, the rate $O(1/s)$ for the space $BV([0,1])$ is *optimal*, in the sense that no other approximation procedure (suitably defined) can achieve a better rate over this class.

10.3.1 Comparison with Fourier Approximation

It is worth contrasting this situation with that of Fourier approximation. Consider the Fourier basis $\{\upsilon_i\}_{i\in\mathbb{N}}$ of $L^2([0,1])$, ordered as in §2.2.2. For this basis, the linear and nonlinear approximation errors both behave like $O(s^{-1/2})$ for the BV and PC^α classes. To see why, one may consider the function $f(x) = \mathbb{I}_{[0,1/2]}(x)$. This function belongs to both classes and its Fourier coefficients satisfy

$$\int_0^1 f(x)\mathrm{e}^{-2\pi\mathrm{i}\omega x}\,\mathrm{d}x = \frac{1+(-1)^{\omega+1}}{2\omega\pi\mathrm{i}}, \qquad \omega \in \mathbb{Z}\backslash\{0\}.$$

Hence the unsorted coefficients $\langle f, v_i\rangle$ and the sorted coefficients $\langle f, v_{\pi(i)}\rangle$ both decay at the same rate $O(i^{-1})$. Proposition 10.1 now implies that nonlinear Fourier approximation conveys no benefit over linear Fourier approximation. The rate is also slower than the corresponding nonlinear approximation error rate achieved by wavelets. This is hardly surprising. The Fourier basis consists of global functions, meaning that local features such as discontinuities affect all the coefficients. Conversely, for wavelets only a small proportion of the coefficients 'see' the discontinuity.

10.3.2 Proof Technique

The proofs of Theorems 10.5 and 10.7 are presented in the next section. They are quite intuitive. In the nonlinear case, they proceed by making a judicious choice of s coefficients so as to approximate the given function at the desired rate. Specifically, for PC^α functions, we:

(i) choose all coefficients (roughly $s/2$ in total) in the coarsest $\log_2(s/2)$ scales,
(ii) select roughly $c\mathcal{N}(f)$ coefficients in each subsequent scale to capture the discontinuities of f,
(iii) continue up to a finest scale $j \approx (2\alpha+1)\log_2(s)$.

The reason for this is the following. As we noted in the previous chapter, coefficients corresponding to wavelets that are supported in a smooth region of f decay rapidly (due to the vanishing moments), and therefore only need to be chosen at the coarser scales. On the other hand, wavelets that cross a discontinuity of f correspond to much more slowly decaying coefficients, and therefore need to be chosen at both the coarse and fine scales. However, since only a small number of wavelets cross a discontinuity, they constitute only a relatively small number of the total coefficients. Moreover, beyond a certain finest scale, they too become insignificant.

10.3.3 Wavelets and Compressed Sensing

The procedure described above asserts that one can construct an s-term wavelet approximation that achieves the desired $O(s^{-\alpha})$ approximation rate for PC^{α} functions and uses s wavelet coefficients taken from the first $N \approx 2^{(2\alpha+1)\log_2(s)} = s^{2\alpha+1}$ possible coefficients (when ordered as in §9.9).

It is informative to relate this back to Chapter 5. Consider the vector in $\mathbb{C}^N$ consisting of the first N wavelet coefficients. The ratio $s/N = O(s^{-2\alpha})$ decays rapidly as $s \to \infty$, meaning that this vector is highly compressible for large N. Moreover, the indices of the coefficients selected in (ii) are unknown, since they depend on the unknown locations of discontinuities of f. This is, of course, the exact scenario compressed sensing aims to solve: namely, compressibility, with no *a priori* knowledge of where the large coefficients lie. In this sense, wavelets are an ideal fit for compressed sensing.

Remark 10.8 The above procedure also sheds light on the *local* sparsity structure of best s-term wavelet approximation. Proportionally more coefficients are taken at the coarse scales – in particular, all coefficients are chosen in the coarsest $\log_2(s/2)$ scales – relative to the size of the scale than at the fine scales, where only a constant number are chosen (recall that a scale consists of 2^j wavelets). As discussed in §1.6.2, this structure – which we term *asymptotic sparsity* in Chapter 11 – plays an important role in Fourier and Walsh sampling with wavelets for compressive imaging.

The reader may have noticed that the previous results consider the best s-term error measured in the L^2-norm, which by Parseval's identity is equivalent to the ℓ^2-norm of the coefficients. However, recovery guarantees in compressed sensing involve the ℓ^1-norm of the coefficients (see Chapter 5). We now give analogous results for this norm. As in §9.9 we let d denote the infinite vector of wavelet coefficients, which is now assumed to be in $\ell^1(\mathbb{N})$, and define

$$\sigma_s(f)_{\ell^1} = \sum_{i>s} |\langle f, \phi_{\pi(i)} \rangle| = \sigma_s(d)_{\ell^1}, \tag{10.4}$$

where $\sigma_s(d)_{\ell^1}$ is as in Definition 5.3, with $\mathbb{C}^N$ replaced by $\ell^1(\mathbb{N})$.

Theorem 10.9 *Suppose that $f \in PC^{\alpha}([0,1])$, where $\alpha = k + \beta > 1/2$ for $k \in \mathbb{N}_0$ and $0 < \beta \leq 1$. Consider the periodized Daubechies wavelet basis of order $p > k$ with j_0 as in (9.49). Then the wavelet coefficients of f belong to $\ell^1(\mathbb{N})$ and (10.4) satisfies*

$$\sigma_s(f)_{\ell^1} \leq c_1 \|f\|_{PC^{\alpha}} s^{1/2-\alpha},$$

for all $s/\log(s) \geq c_2 N(f)$, where $c_1, c_2 > 0$ depend on p and α only. Conversely, the wavelet coefficients are also in $\ell^1(\mathbb{N})$ whenever $p \geq 1$ and $f \in BV([0,1])$, and in this case (10.4) satisfies

$$\sigma_s(f)_{\ell^1} \leq c_3 V(f) s^{-1/2},$$

where $c_3 > 0$ depends on p only.

If $f \in PC^{\alpha}([0,1])$, for example, then this result gives that

$$\frac{\sigma_s(f)_{\ell^1}}{\sqrt{s}} \leq c_1 \|f\|_{PC^{\alpha}} s^{-\alpha}. \tag{10.5}$$

This is the same upper bound as shown in Theorem 10.5 for the best s-term approximation in the ℓ^2- (equivalently L^2-) norm. A similar statement applies for $f \in BV([0,1])$. To connect this with compressed sensing, we notice that the left-hand side of (10.5) is essentially the same term that arises in the uniform recovery guarantees shown in Chapter 5. Therefore, despite lacking ℓ^2-instance optimality (see Remark 5.23), one expects compressed sensing with wavelets to provide an optimal approximation (up to log factors) in the L^2-norm.

This, however, should be taken with a grain of salt. The setup in Chapter 5 is finite-dimensional (i.e. it pertains to finite vectors), whereas the wavelet approximation results shown above are infinite-dimensional (i.e. they pertain to functions). This incongruity can be overcome, but to do so we require techniques from infinite-dimensional compressed sensing (Chapter 14). The demonstration that compressed sensing with wavelets provides optimal approximation rates (up to log factors) is presented later in §16.2.

10.4 Proofs of the Approximation Results

Throughout this section, $c \geq 0$ is an arbitrary constant that depends on p and α only. It may take different values at different stages of the proofs.

We first require several facts about the periodization operation (9.37). Note if $f \in L^1(\mathbb{R})$ then $f^{\text{per}} \in L^1([0,1])$ and $\|f^{\text{per}}\|_{L^1([0,1])} \leq \|f\|_{L^1(\mathbb{R})}$. Next, let $f \in L^{\infty}([0,1])$ and $g \in L^1(\mathbb{R})$. Then

$$\langle f, g^{\text{per}} \rangle_{L^2([0,1])} = \langle f^{\text{ext}}, g \rangle_{L^2(\mathbb{R})}, \tag{10.6}$$

where f^{ext} is the periodic extension of f, i.e. $f^{\text{ext}}(x+n) = f(x)$ for $0 \leq x < 1$, $n \in \mathbb{Z}$. Note that $f^{\text{ext}} \in L^{\infty}(\mathbb{R})$ with $\|f^{\text{ext}}\|_{L^{\infty}(\mathbb{R})} = \|f\|_{L^{\infty}([0,1])}$.

Lemma 10.10 (Wavelet coefficients of PC^{α} functions) *Suppose that $f \in PC^{\alpha}([0,1])$, where $\alpha = k + \beta$ for $k \in \mathbb{N}_0$ and $0 < \beta \leq 1$. Consider the periodized Daubechies wavelet basis of order $p > k$ with j_0 as in (9.49). Then*

$$|\langle f, \psi^{\text{per}}_{j,n} \rangle_{L^2}| \leq c_1 \|f\|_{PC^{\alpha}} 2^{-(\alpha+1/2)j}$$

whenever the interval $[(n-p+1)/2^j, (n+p)/2^j] = \overline{\text{supp}(\psi_{j,n})}$ contains no discontinuities of f^{ext}, where f^{ext} is the periodic extension of f, and

$$|\langle f, \psi^{\text{per}}_{j,n} \rangle_{L^2}| \leq c_2 \|f\|_{PC^{\alpha}} 2^{-j/2}$$

otherwise. Here $c_1, c_2 > 0$ are constants depending on p and α only.

This lemma formalizes and extends an important property of wavelet coefficients that was discussed in §9.1 in the context of the Haar wavelet. Namely, at fine scales the wavelet coefficients supported in smooth regions of f are asymptotically smaller than those that intersect a discontinuity. We note that the use of periodized wavelets effectively increases the number of singularities, since the endpoint $x = +1$ (and its periodic copies) are also singularities of f^{ext}. However, since the function class is one of finitely many discontinuities, this has no effect on the asymptotic order of convergence.

Proof Notice that f^{ext} belongs to $PC^{\alpha}([a,b])$ for any finite subinterval $[a,b] \subset \mathbb{R}$ and satisfies $\|f^{\text{ext}}\|_{PC^{\alpha}([a,b])} \leq \|f\|_{PC^{\alpha}([0,1])}$. Let $I = [(n-p+1)/2^j, (n+p)/2^j] = \overline{\text{supp}(\psi_{j,n})}$. In the first case, $f^{\text{ext}} \in C^{\alpha}(I)$ and therefore Taylor's theorem implies that there exists a polynomial P of degree k such that

$$|f^{\text{ext}}(x) - P(x)| \leq c\|f^{\text{ext}}\|_{C^{\alpha}(I)}|x - n/2^j|^{\alpha}, \quad \forall x \in I. \tag{10.7}$$

Since the wavelet has $p > k$ vanishing moments, we obtain

$$\begin{aligned}\left|\langle f^{\text{ext}}, \psi_{j,n}\rangle_{L^2([0,1])}\right| &= \left|\langle f^{\text{ext}} - P, \psi_{j,n}\rangle_{L^2(\mathbb{R})}\right| \\ &\leq c2^{j/2}\|f\|_{PC^{\alpha}} \int_{(n-p+1)/2^j}^{(n+p)/2^j} |\psi(2^j x - n)||x - n/2^j|^{\alpha}\,\mathrm{d}x \\ &= c2^{-(\alpha+1/2)j}\|f\|_{PC^{\alpha}} \int_{-p+1}^{p} |\psi(x)|\,|x|^{\alpha}\,\mathrm{d}x.\end{aligned}$$

The first result now follows from (10.6). In the second case, note that

$$\begin{aligned}|\langle f, \psi^{\text{per}}_{j,n}\rangle_{L^2([0,1])}| = |\langle f^{\text{ext}}, \psi_{j,n}\rangle_{L^2(I)}| &\leq \|f^{\text{ext}}\|_{L^{\infty}(I)}\|\psi_{j,n}\|_{L^1(I)} \\ &\leq \|f\|_{PC^{\alpha}([0,1])}\|\psi_{j,n}\|_{L^1(\mathbb{R})}.\end{aligned}$$

Since ψ has unit L^2-norm and is supported on an interval of length $2p-1$, the Cauchy–Schwarz inequality gives $\|\psi_{j,n}\|_{L^1(\mathbb{R})} = \|\psi\|_{L^1(\mathbb{R})}/2^{j/2} \leq \sqrt{2p-1}/2^{j/2}$. This now implies the second result. □

Proof of Theorem 10.5 Consider the linear approximation error $\epsilon_s(f)$. Without loss of generality, we may assume that $s \geq 2^{j_0+1}$. Hence there exists a $j_1 \geq 1$ such that $2^{j_0+j_1} \leq s < 2^{j_0+j_1+1}$. Due to the ordering of the basis (see §9.9), the linear approximation of f of order s includes at least all the scaling function coefficients, as well as the wavelet coefficients at scales $j = j_0, \ldots, j_0 + j_1 - 1$. Therefore

$$(\epsilon_s(f))^2 \leq \sum_{j \geq j_0+j_1} \sum_{n=0}^{2^j-1} |\langle f, \psi^{\text{per}}_{j,n}\rangle_{L^2}|^2.$$

We use Lemma 10.10. Since f has $\mathcal{N}(f) - 1$ discontinuities the function f^{ext} has at most $c\mathcal{N}(f)$ discontinuities on the interval $[-p+1, p]$, and therefore there are at most $c\mathcal{N}(f)$ wavelets $\psi_{j,n}$ at a fixed scale j whose support contains a discontinuity of f^{ext}. Since there each scale contains 2^j wavelets, we deduce that

$$(\epsilon_s(f))^2 \leq c\|f\|^2_{PC^{\alpha}} \sum_{j \geq j_0+j_1} \left(\mathcal{N}(f)2^{-j} + 2^{-2\alpha j}\right) \leq c\|f\|^2_{PC^{\alpha}}\mathcal{N}(f)2^{-j_0-j_1}.$$

Here in the second step we also use the fact that $\alpha \geq 1/2$. Since $2^{-j_0-j_1} < 2/s$, the first result now follows.

Now consider the nonlinear approximation error $\sigma_s(f)$. Since this is the infimum over all s-term wavelet approximations to f, our strategy is to choose s wavelet coefficients in a suitable way so as to obtain the desired error decay rate. Let $s \geq 2^{j_0+1}$ and $\{I_j\}$ be a collection of index sets with $I_j \subseteq \{0, \ldots, 2^j - 1\}$ and

$$\left| \bigcup_{j \geq j_0} I_j \right| \leq s - 2^{j_0} \tag{10.8}$$

(the -2^{j_0} factor takes into account the scaling function coefficients). Then

$$(\sigma_s(f))^2 \leq \sum_{j=j_0}^{\infty} \sum_{\substack{0 \leq n < 2^j \\ n \notin I_j}} |\langle f, \psi^{\text{per}}_{j,n} \rangle_{L^2}|^2. \tag{10.9}$$

We now define the index sets. Let $1 \leq j_1 \leq j_2$ be numbers whose values will be chosen in a moment. Then, let

$$\begin{aligned} I_j &= \{0, \ldots, 2^j - 1\}, \quad j_0 \leq j < j_0 + j_1, \\ I_j &= \emptyset, \quad j \geq j_0 + j_2, \end{aligned} \tag{10.10}$$

and for $j_0 + j_1 \leq j < j_0 + j_2$ let I_j be the index set consisting of those values of n where the support of $\psi_{j,n}$ contains a discontinuity of f^{ext}. Recall that $|I_j| \leq c\mathcal{N}(f)$ from the first part of the proof. This gives

$$\left| \bigcup_{j \geq j_0} I_j \right| = \sum_{j=j_0}^{j_0+j_1-1} 2^j + \sum_{j=j_0+j_1}^{j_0+j_2-1} |I_j| \leq 2^{j_0+j_1} + c\mathcal{N}(f)(j_2 - j_1). \tag{10.11}$$

We now examine the error. From (10.9) and the definition of the I_j, we have

$$(\sigma_s(f))^2 \leq \sum_{j=j_0+j_1}^{j_0+j_2-1} \sum_{\substack{0 \leq n < 2^j \\ n \notin I_j}} |\langle f, \psi^{\text{per}}_{j,n} \rangle_{L^2}|^2 + (\epsilon_{\tilde{s}}(f))^2, \tag{10.12}$$

where $\tilde{s} = 2^{j_0+j_2}$. Using Lemma 10.10 and the first part of the theorem, we deduce that

$$\begin{aligned} (\sigma_s(f))^2 &\leq c\|f\|^2_{PC^\alpha} \left(\sum_{j=j_0+j_1}^{j_0+j_2-1} 2^{-2\alpha j} + \mathcal{N}(f) 2^{-j_0-j_2} \right) \\ &\leq c\|f\|^2_{PC^\alpha} \left(2^{-2\alpha(j_0+j_1)} + \mathcal{N}(f) 2^{-j_0-j_2} \right). \end{aligned}$$

Now suppose without loss of generality that $s \geq 2^{j_0+2}$. Set $j_1 = \lfloor \log_2(s/2) \rfloor - j_0 \geq 1$ so that $s/4 \leq 2^{j_0+j_1} \leq s/2$, and let $j_2 = \lfloor (2\alpha + 1) \log_2(s) \rfloor - j_0 \geq j_1$ so that $s^{2\alpha+1}/2 \leq 2^{j_0+j_2} \leq s^{2\alpha+1}$. This gives

$$(\sigma_s(f))^2 \leq c\|f\|^2_{PC^\alpha} s^{-2\alpha} \left(1 + \mathcal{N}(f) s^{-1} \right) \leq c\|f\|^2_{PC^\alpha} s^{-2\alpha},$$

where in the second step we use the fact that $s/\log(s) \geq c\mathcal{N}(f)$. It remains to verify that (10.8) holds for this choice of index sets. Substituting the values of j_2 and j_1 into (10.11) and recalling that $s/\log(s) \geq c\mathcal{N}(f)$, we deduce that

$$\left| \bigcup_{j \geq j_0} I_j \right| \leq s/2 + c\mathcal{N}(f)\log(s) \leq s.$$

Hence (10.8) holds and the proof is complete. □

We now turn our attention to functions of bounded variation. Unlike in the previous case (see Lemma 10.10), we cannot separate the wavelet coefficients of a function $f \in BV([0,1])$ into those with fast and slow decay. Nevertheless, the finite variation of f allows us to control the size of the coefficients at a fixed scale.

Lemma 10.11 (Wavelet coefficients of BV functions I) *Let $f \in BV([0,1])$ and consider the periodized Daubechies wavelet basis of order $p \geq 1$ with j_0 as in (9.49). Then*

$$\sum_{n=0}^{2^j-1} |\langle f, \psi^{\text{per}}_{j,n} \rangle_{L^2}| \leq cV(f)/2^{j/2}, \qquad j \geq j_0,$$

for some constant $c \geq 0$ depending on p only.

Proof Let g be the restriction of f^{ext} to $\text{supp}(\psi) = [-p+1, p]$. Observe that $g \in BV([-p+1,p])$ with total variation $V(g;[-p+1,p]) \leq cV(f;[0,1])$. By (10.6),

$$\sum_{n=0}^{2^j-1} \left|\langle f, \psi^{\text{per}}_{j,n} \rangle_{L^2}\right| = 2^{j/2} \sum_{n=0}^{2^j-1} \left| \int_{-p+1}^{p} g(t)\psi(2^j x - n)\,\mathrm{d}x \right|.$$

Let $\theta(x)$ be the antiderivative of $\psi(x)$, defined by $\theta(x) = \int_{-\infty}^{x} \psi(t)\,\mathrm{d}t$. Observe that θ is continuous and $\text{supp}(\theta) \subseteq [-p+1, p]$. The latter follows because ψ is supported in $[-p+1, p]$ and $\int_{-\infty}^{\infty} \psi(x)\,\mathrm{d}x = 0$. Hence, integrating by parts, we get[2]

$$\begin{aligned}
\sum_{n=0}^{2^j-1} \left|\langle f, \psi^{\text{per}}_{j,n} \rangle_{L^2}\right| &= 2^{-j/2} \sum_{n=0}^{2^j-1} \left| \int_{-p+1}^{p} g'(t)\theta(2^j x - n)\,\mathrm{d}x \right| \\
&\leq 2^{-j/2} \|\theta\|_{C([-p+1,p])} \sum_{n=0}^{2^j-1} \int_{\frac{-p+1+n}{2^j}}^{\frac{p+n}{2^j}} |g'(x)|\,\mathrm{d}x \\
&\leq 2^{-j/2} \|\theta\|_{C([-p+1,p])} \int_{-p+1}^{p} |g'(x)|\,\mathrm{d}x \\
&= 2^{-j/2} \|\theta\|_{C([-p+1,p])} V(g;[-p+1,p]),
\end{aligned}$$

from which the result now follows. □

Lemma 10.12 (Wavelet coefficients of BV functions II) *Let $f \in BV([0,1])$ and consider the periodized Daubechies wavelet basis of order $p \geq 1$ with j_0 as in (9.49). Let*

[2] This step is only valid when g is sufficiently regular. When it is not, one can use a standard limiting process, recalling that for each $g \in BV([a,b])$ there exists a sequence $g_k \in C^\infty([a,b])$ with $g_k \to g$ in $L^1([a,b])$ and $V(g_k;[a,b]) \to V(g;[a,b])$ (see, for example, [32, Thm. 3.9]).

$j \geq j_0$ and $\pi_j : \{1, \ldots, 2^j\} \to \{0, \ldots, 2^j - 1\}$ be a bijection which gives a nonincreasing rearrangement of the coefficients $d_{j,n} = \langle f, \psi_{j,n}^{\mathrm{per}} \rangle_{L^2}$ at scale j, that is,

$$|d_{j,\pi_j(1)}| \geq \cdots \geq |d_{j,\pi_j(n)}|.$$

Then there exists a constant $c > 0$ depending on p only such that

$$|d_{j,\pi_j(n)}| \leq cV(f)2^{-j/2}n^{-1}, \quad n = 1, \ldots, 2^j.$$

Proof We use Lemma 10.11. By this and the fact that π_j is a nonincreasing rearrangement, we have

$$cV(f)2^{-j/2} \geq \sum_{l=1}^{2^j} \left|d_{j,\pi_j(l)}\right| \geq \sum_{l=1}^{n} \left|d_{j,\pi_j(l)}\right| \geq n|d_{j,\pi_j(n)}|.$$

This gives the result. □

Proof of Theorem 10.7 As in the proof of Theorem 10.5, we may assume that $s \geq 2^{j_0+1}$ so that there exists a $j_1 \geq 1$ such that $2^{j_0+j_1} \leq s < 2^{j_0+j_1+1}$. Consider $\epsilon_s(f)$. Lemma 10.11 implies that

$$\begin{aligned}(\epsilon_s(f))^2 \leq \sum_{j \geq j_0+j_1} \sum_{n=0}^{2^j-1} |\langle f, \psi_{j,n}^{\mathrm{per}} \rangle_{L^2}|^2 &\leq \sum_{j \geq j_0+j_1} \left(\sum_{n=0}^{2^j-1} |\langle f, \psi_{j,n}^{\mathrm{per}} \rangle_{L^2}| \right)^2 \\ &\leq c(V(f))^2 \sum_{j \geq j_0+j_1} 2^{-j}.\end{aligned}$$

The sum is equal to $2^{-j_0-j_1+1}$. This gives the first result.

For the second result, we argue as in the proof of Theorem 10.5. Assuming the setup therein, let the index sets I_j be defined as in (10.10) for $j_0 \leq j < j_0 + j_1$ and $j \geq j_0 + j_2$. The values of j_1 and j_2 will again be chosen so that (10.8) holds for large enough s. For $j_0 + j_1 \leq j < j_0 + j_2$, let $s_j = \lfloor ds^{3/2}/2^{j/2} \rfloor$, where $d > 0$ is a constant that will be chosen later. We now define I_j to be the index set of the largest s_j coefficients at scale j in absolute value. Notice that

$$\left| \bigcup_{j \geq j_0} I_j \right| \leq \sum_{j=j_0}^{j_0+j_1-1} 2^j + \sum_{j \geq j_0+j_1} ds^{3/2} 2^{-j/2} \leq 2^{j_0+j_1} + ds^{3/2} \frac{2^{-(j_0+j_1)/2}}{1 - 1/\sqrt{2}}.$$

Now suppose without loss of generality that $s \geq 2^{j_0+3}$ and let $j_1 = \lfloor \log_2(s/2) \rfloor - j_0 \geq 1$. Then $s/4 \leq 2^{j_0+j_1} \leq s/2$, and therefore

$$\left| \bigcup_{j \geq j_0} I_j \right| \leq s/2 + ds^{3/2} \frac{2}{1 - 1/\sqrt{2}} s^{-1/2} = s\left(1/2 + 2\sqrt{2}d/(\sqrt{2} - 1)\right).$$

Choosing $d = 1/32 < (\sqrt{2} - 1)/(4\sqrt{2})$ implies that (10.8) holds for sufficiently large s, and hence the choice of index sets is valid.

It remains to estimate the right-hand side of (10.9) for this choice of index sets. Fix a scale $j \geq j_0 + j_1$ and let π_j and $d_{j,n}$ be as in Lemma 10.12. Then

$$\sum_{\substack{0 \leq n < 2^j \\ n \notin I_j}} |d_{j,n}|^2 = \sum_{n=s_j+1}^{2^j} |d_{j,\pi(n)}|^2 \leq c(V(f))^2 2^{-j} \sum_{n>s_j} n^{-2}$$
$$\leq c(V(f))^2 2^{-j}/s_j \leq c(V(f))^2 2^{-j/2} s^{-3/2}.$$

This holds provided $s_j \geq 1$, a fact that will be verified in a moment when we choose j_2. Assuming this, we now use (10.12) to obtain

$$(\sigma_s(f))^2 \leq c(V(f))^2 s^{-3/2} \sum_{j=j_0+j_1}^{j_0+j_2-1} 2^{-j/2} + (\epsilon_{\tilde{s}}(f))^2,$$

where $\tilde{s} = 2^{j_0+j_2}$. Using the first part of the theorem and the definition of j_1, we get

$$(\sigma_s(f))^2 \leq c(V(f))^2 \left(s^{-2} + 2^{-j_0-j_2}\right).$$

We now let $j_2 = 2\lfloor \log_2(s) \rfloor - j_0 \geq j_1$ to obtain $(\sigma_s(f))^2 \leq c(V(f))^2 s^{-2}$. Finally, observe that this choice of j_2 gives $s_j \geq ds^{3/2}/2^{(j_0+j_2)/2} - 1 \geq cs^{1/2} - 1$ and therefore $s_j \geq 1$ for all sufficiently large s. □

Proof of Theorem 10.9 Suppose that $f \in PC^\alpha([0,1])$. The arguments are similar to those used in the proof of Theorem 10.5. With the same choice of index sets I_j, we have

$$\sigma_s(f)_{\ell^1} \leq \sum_{j=j_0+j_1}^{j_0+j_2-1} \sum_{\substack{0 \leq n < 2^j \\ n \notin I_j}} |\langle f, \psi^{\text{per}}_{j,n} \rangle_{L^2}| + \sum_{j \geq j_0+j_2} \sum_{n=0}^{2^j-1} |\langle f, \psi^{\text{per}}_{j,n} \rangle_{L^2}|.$$

Lemma 10.10 and the fact that $\alpha > 1/2$ give

$$\sigma_s(f)_{\ell^1} \leq c\|f\|_{PC^\alpha} \left[\sum_{j=j_0+j_1}^{j_0+j_2-1} 2^{-(\alpha-1/2)j} + \sum_{j \geq j_0+j_2} \left(2^{-(\alpha-1/2)j} + \mathcal{N}(f) 2^{-j/2}\right) \right]$$
$$\leq c\|f\|_{PC^\alpha} \left[2^{-(\alpha-1/2)(j_0+j_1)} + \mathcal{N}(f) 2^{-(j_0+j_2)/2}\right].$$

We now use the same values for j_1 and j_2 as before and the fact that $s \geq c\mathcal{N}(f)$ to deduce the result.

Now suppose that $f \in BV([0,1])$. In this case, we let j_1 be such that $2^{j_0+j_1} \leq s < 2^{j_0+j_1+1}$ and obtain

$$\sigma_s(f)_{\ell^1} \leq \sum_{j \geq j_0+j_1} \sum_{n=0}^{2^j-1} |\langle f, \psi^{\text{per}}_{j,n} \rangle_{L^2}| \leq cV(f) \sum_{j \geq j_0+j_1} 2^{-j/2} \leq cV(f) s^{-1/2},$$

where the second step follows from Lemma 10.11. This gives the result. □

10.5 Higher Dimensions

The focus of this chapter has been one-dimensional piecewise smooth functions. Picking up where §9.11 left off, we now briefly discuss the two-dimensional case.

For bivariate functions of bounded variation, the best s-term wavelet approximation converges at the optimal rate $O(1/\sqrt{s})$. However, unlike in one dimension, this rate does not increase if more regularity is assumed. For example, the rate is unchanged if one considers the class of *cartoon-like* functions. These are functions that are C^2 except along a C^2 curve. As discussed in §9.11, the reason for this is the isotropy of two-dimensional wavelets, which means that it takes many wavelets to capture a discontinuity.

It transpires that the optimal rate for the class of cartoon-like functions is $O(1/s)$. Both curvelets and shearlets attain this rate up to a log factor. Their anisotropy allows them to capture the edge more efficiently, with the result being a best s-term approximation that converges at the rate $O((\log(s))^{3/2}/s)$.

Notes

See [174] for a thorough overview of nonlinear approximation theory, including a formal statement and proof that wavelets are an optimal nonlinear approximation scheme for $BV([0,1])$. We note in passing that linear and nonlinear approximation using wavelets are typically studied in Besov spaces. Following [344, Chpt. 9], we have used the piecewise Hölder and bounded variation spaces for their easy interpretability.

Our approximation results (Theorems 10.5 and 10.7) follow similar arguments to those of [344, Chpt. 9], except they are proved for the periodized Daubechies wavelets. They are unchanged (besides constants) if the boundary-corrected wavelets of §9.7.2 are used instead, as is done in [344]. The underlying reason for this, as shown, is that the periodic extension operation introduces only a finite number of additional discontinuities, and hence preserves the initial regularity (whether piecewise Lipschitz or bounded variation). We use the periodized wavelets since the proofs are somewhat simpler. In practice, as noted, boundary-corrected wavelets may be preferable because they avoid the introduction of these artificial discontinuities.

More fundamental differences between the boundary-corrected and periodized wavelets arise when considering Sobolev regularity. Periodized wavelets (of suitable smoothness) characterize the periodic Sobolev spaces $H^{\alpha}(\mathbb{T})$, where $\mathbb{T} = \mathbb{R}/\mathbb{Z}$ is the unit torus, whereas boundary-corrected wavelets characterize the nonperiodic Sobolev spaces $H^{\alpha}([0,1])$. However, there is no benefit of nonlinear approximation over linear approximation within these classes. This fact is unsurprising given that functions in such spaces cannot have local features such as edges. See [174] or [344] for further information.

Near-optimal approximation rates for piecewise C^2 functions using curvelets and shearlets were shown in [112, 113] and [248, 309], respectively. We remark that, unlike the one-dimensional case with wavelets, curvelets and shearlets both fail to yield optimal approximations for piecewise C^α functions when $\alpha \neq 2$. Bandlets [318, 346] lead to formally optimal schemes in these settings. For overviews of approximation theory of piecewise smooth functions in two or more dimensions, see [344, Chpt. 9] and [308].

Part III

Compressed Sensing with Local Structure

Summary of Part III

Conventional compressed sensing, as developed in Chapter 5, is based on global principles. Sparsity dictates that a vector has s nonzero components whose locations can be arbitrary. Conditions such as the RIP guarantee recovery of *every* s-sparse vector, regardless of the locations of its nonzero entries. In Key Points #8 and #9 of Chapter 1, we highlighted the fact that *local structure* in the sparsifying transform and sampling strategy play a key role in compressive imaging. Hence, there is a need for a framework for compressed sensing that incorporates such structure. In Part III we develop this framework.

Chapter 11 first provides a more thorough rationale as to why this framework is needed. Developing Fig. 1.6, we present an experiment that demonstrates the importance of local structure in Fourier imaging (Key Point #9). Next, this sparsity structure is formalized via the so-called *local sparsity in levels* model. In this model, rather than a single quantity s, one associates a collection of *local sparsities* $\mathbf{s} = (s_1, \ldots, s_r)$ to a vector $x \in \mathbb{C}^N$, with each s_k measuring the sparsity of x within a specific subset of its entries (a *level*). We then introduce a general notion of *sampling operators* in compressed sensing, based on drawing measurements randomly from (collections of) families of random vectors. This includes standard measurement matrices as special cases, but it also allows for much broader types of sampling, including those well suited to exploiting local sparsity structure. We also discuss ways to measure the quality of such a sampling operator, based on so-called *coherence* and *local coherence in levels*.

Formalizing the arguments given in §1.6, we next introduce a new class of measurement matrices, the so-called *multilevel subsampled unitary* matrices. Here the rows of a unitary matrix U are divided into r *sampling levels*, with a number m_k of measurements chosen randomly per level. We conclude this chapter by introducing the one-dimensional *discrete Fourier–Haar wavelet* problem (that is, discrete Fourier sampling with sparsity in the discrete Haar wavelet basis), in which case the sparsity levels correspond to the wavelet scales and the sampling levels correspond to dyadic bands in frequency space. This will be the main example used in the two chapters that follow.

Chapters 12 and 13 present recovery guarantees (of nonuniform and uniform type, respectively) for the sparsity in levels model. These extend the results shown in Chapter 5 for the sparse model. We use the discrete Fourier–Haar wavelet problem as our main example throughout, in which case the measurement condition takes the form

$$m_k \gtrsim \left(s_k + \sum_{l=1}^{k-1} s_l 2^{-(k-l)} + \sum_{l=k+1}^{r} s_l 2^{-3(l-k)} \right) \cdot L, \quad k = 1, \ldots, r, \qquad (\star)$$

where L is a log factor. Here s_k is the local sparsity of the Haar wavelet coefficients in the kth wavelet scale, and m_k in the number of measurements taken in the kth frequency band. Crucially, ($\star$) involves local quantities, not global ones. Moreover, the right-hand side is dominated by s_k, with its dependence on s_l decreasing exponentially in $|k - l|$. Hence, the number of measurements used in the kth frequency band is largely determined by the corresponding local sparsity s_k. This type of guarantee will play a key role in Part IV of this book, where we focus on sampling strategy design.

Finally, we conclude with Chapter 14, which develops *infinite-dimensional compressed sensing* in Hilbert spaces. Up to this point, we have considered the problem of recovering a vector $x \in \mathbb{C}^N$ from measurements $y = Ax + e$. Yet, as discussed in Part I, imaging modalities such as MRI are more faithfully modelled with integral transforms. This corresponds to an infinite-dimensional inverse problem of the form $y = \mathcal{A}f + e$, where f is a function. In Chapter 4 we observed that naïve discretizations of this problem can lead to significant errors, due to mismatch between the discrete model and the data. The main motivation for Chapter 14 stems from the desire to avoid such errors. We first show how to do this, and then present a series of recovery guarantees. Despite its name, this approach does indeed lead to a practical reconstruction procedure. As a secondary motivation, it transpires that this model is simply more convenient to work with when we come to analyse sampling strategies for compressive imaging in Chapters 15 and 16. As is often the case, working with continuous objects (i.e. integrals) turns out to be easier than working with discrete ones (i.e. sums).

11 From Global to Local

We begin this chapter in §11.1 by considering recovery from Fourier samples using wavelet sparsifying transforms. In §11.2, via an experiment known as the *flip test*, we demonstrate how local sparsity structure within the wavelet scales, and not just global sparsity, plays a key role in the quality of the recovered image. We then develop the promised framework. In §11.3 we introduce the local sparsity in levels model. Next, in §11.4 we introduce a general approach to sampling based on random sampling with *jointly isotropic collections*. We then introduce various notions of coherence in §11.5. Finally, in §11.6 we present the one-dimensional discrete Fourier–Haar wavelet problem.

11.1 The Fourier-Wavelets Problem

Recall from §2.2 that the discrete Fourier reconstruction problem involves recovering an image x from a subset of its Fourier measurements Fx, where F is the Fourier matrix (Definition 2.1). Let $A = PF$ be the corresponding measurement matrix, Φ be a discrete wavelet sparsifying transform (Definition 9.28) and suppose we compute a reconstruction $\hat{x}$ by solving the QCBP synthesis problem

$$\min_{z \in \mathbb{C}^N} \|z\|_{\ell^1} \text{ subject to } \|A\Phi z - y\|_{\ell^2} \leq \eta. \tag{11.1}$$

As usual (see §5.4.3), if $\hat{d}$ is a minimizer of this problem, we set $\hat{x} = \Phi\hat{d}$.

11.1.1 The Fourier-Wavelets Problem is Coherent

This is a standard compressed sensing problem. Since the scaled matrix $U = N^{-1/2}F\Phi$ is unitary, the measurement matrix A is an example of a subsampled unitary matrix. In §5.3.2 we discussed one option for subsampling the rows of such a matrix, namely, uniform random sampling. However, this is a poor choice. This was previously shown in Fig. 3.5 and we now highlight it once more in Fig. 11.1(a).

The underlying reason for this poor performance turns out to be quite simple. The Fourier-wavelet matrix U is *coherent* in the sense of Definition 5.8. In fact, its coherence $\mu(U) \asymp N$ as $N \to \infty$.[1] Therefore, both the corresponding uniform (Theorem 5.27) and

[1] This is easily seen if the wavelet used is the Haar wavelet. In this case, the column of Φ corresponding to the scaling function (which is constant) is equal to the row of F corresponding to the zeroth frequency.

(a) Uniform random (b) Gaussian multilevel

Figure 11.1 Recovery of the 256×256 klubbe image (see Fig. 2.2) from 20% Fourier measurements using DB4 wavelets. (a) Uniform random sampling (Definition 4.1). (b) Variable-density sampling using a Gaussian multilevel sampling strategy with $r = 50$, $a = 2$ and $r_0 = 1$ (Definition 4.7).

nonuniform (Theorem 5.30) recovery guarantees suggest poor performance in this case when $m \ll N$, which agrees with what we observe in practice.

11.1.2 The Fourier-Wavelets Problem has Local Structure

Yet, as was previously observed in §1.6, the matrix U has substantial local structure. This can be seen by plotting the absolute values of the matrix U, as we now do once more in Fig. 11.2. The matrix has a block structure, where the sizes of the block scale as powers of two. While it is globally coherent, the large values of U are limited to its upper left-hand corner, corresponding to the lowest Fourier frequencies and the coarsest wavelet scales (recall the orderings defined in §2.2 and §9.9, respectively). Regions of U corresponding to either high frequencies or fine-scale wavelets present smaller values, with the largest values occurring in the diagonal blocks.

As discussed in §1.6, this structure motivates the use of a variable-density sampling strategy. The lowest frequencies (where the coherence is higher) should be sampled more densely, with the higher frequencies (where the coherence is lower) being sampled less densely. The significant improvement that sampling in this way brings was previously demonstrated in Fig. 3.5. In Fig. 11.1(b) we show a second example of its effect.

Hence U has an entry, corresponding to the zeroth frequency of the scaling function, that is exactly one. This implies that $\mu(U) = N$. Similar arguments hold for higher-order wavelets.

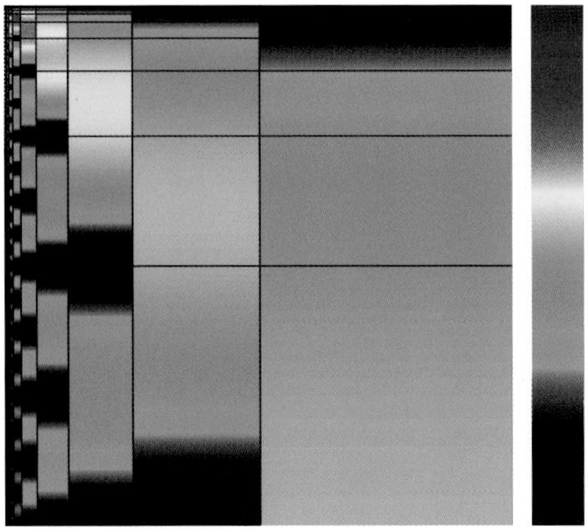

Figure 11.2 The absolute values of the matrix $F\Phi$ in one dimension, where F is the Fourier matrix and Φ is the matrix of the discrete Haar wavelet basis. The vertical and horizontal lines occur at powers of two, and denote the so-called sparsity and sampling levels that are defined later in §11.6.

11.1.3 The Frequency Concentration of Wavelets

Where does this local structure come from? The answer is actually quite straightforward: the behaviour of wavelets in frequency space. Consider the one-dimensional setting and let $\psi_{j,n}$ be the Daubechies wavelet of order p at scale j. Then it is a simple calculation to show that

$$|\mathcal{F}\psi_{j,n}(\omega)| = 2^{-j/2}|\mathcal{F}\psi(\omega/2^j)|.$$

Now, since ψ has p vanishing moments, Proposition 9.12 gives that $|\mathcal{F}\psi(\omega)| \lesssim |\omega|^p$ for small $|\omega|$. On the other hand, recall from §9.6.2 that $|\mathcal{F}\psi(\omega)| \lesssim (1+|\omega|)^{-1-q}$ for large $|\omega|$, where q is given by (9.35). We deduce that

$$|\mathcal{F}\psi_{j,n}(\omega)| \lesssim 2^{-j/2}\begin{cases} |\omega/2^j|^p & |\omega| \leq 2^j \\ |2^j/\omega|^{q+1} & |\omega| > 2^j \end{cases}.$$

In particular, for the Haar wavelet, in which case $p = 1$ and $q = 0$, we have

$$|\mathcal{F}\psi_{j,n}(\omega)| \lesssim 2^{-j/2}\begin{cases} |\omega/2^j| & |\omega| \leq 2^j \\ |2^j/\omega| & |\omega| > 2^j \end{cases}. \tag{11.2}$$

We conclude that $\mathcal{F}\psi_{j,n}$ is concentrated in a band of frequencies around $\omega = 2^j$ and becomes exponentially smaller in bands around $\omega = 2^l$ for $l \neq j$. Figure 11.3 illustrates this property. In §11.6 we formally define these frequency bands, but they can already be seen in Fig. 11.2 as the horizontal lines shown therein. The lth block of rows corresponds to frequencies in a band around $\omega = 2^l$. The vertical lines, on the other hand, correspond to the wavelet scales, with the jth block of columns containing the wavelets at scale j. Hence, (11.2) implies that diagonal blocks exhibit larger values, while off-diagonal blocks exhibit smaller values – exactly as is seen in Fig. 11.2.

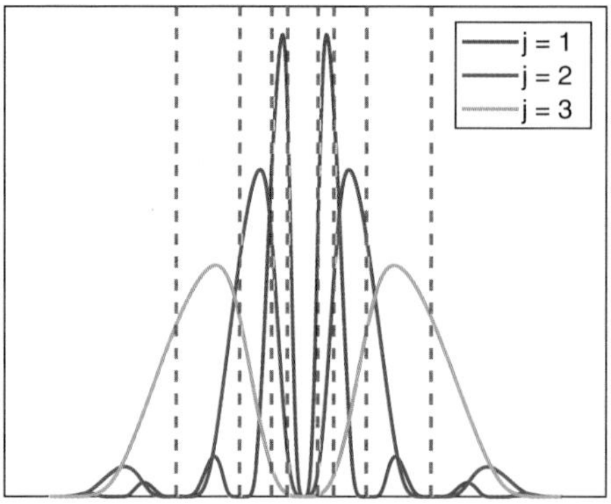

Figure 11.3 Frequency concentration of wavelets. The diagram shows $|\mathcal{F}\psi_{j,n}(2\pi\omega)|$ for $j = 1, 2, 3$ in the case of the DB4 wavelet. The vertical dashed lines indicate powers of two.

11.2 Structured Sparsity and the Flip Test

This discussion suggests that the global notion of coherence (Definition 5.8) should be replaced by a suitable local version to take into account the structure in the sampling operator. But what about the sparsifying transform? Does the local structure of the wavelet coefficients play a role as well, or is sparsity alone sufficient to account for the vastly improved reconstruction seen in Fig. 11.1(b)? We now discuss this question.

11.2.1 A Recovery Guarantee for Power-Law Sampling

Recalling §4.1, suppose we consider the family of power-law sampling schemes in two dimensions, where $\pi = \{\pi_\omega\}$ is given by

$$\pi_\omega = \frac{C_{N,\alpha}}{(\max\{1, |\omega_1|^2 + |\omega_2|^2\})^\alpha}, \qquad \omega = (\omega_1, \omega_2) \in \{-N/2+1, \ldots, N/2\}^2, \tag{11.3}$$

for $\alpha \in \mathbb{R}$. Note that we are not suggesting that these are the best strategies to use in practice (recall §4.8), but they are useful to demonstrate the following point. Given (11.3), a natural first question is how to set the parameter α. Standard compressed sensing theory in fact provides an answer. As we show in §12.5.2, the measurement condition for recovering an image that is approximately s-sparse in Haar wavelets from samples chosen randomly according to (11.3) takes the form

$$m \gtrsim s \cdot \widetilde{C}_{N,\alpha} \cdot L, \qquad \widetilde{C}_{N,\alpha} = \begin{cases} \log(N) & \alpha = 1 \\ N^{2|\alpha-1|} & \alpha \neq 1 \end{cases}, \tag{11.4}$$

where L is a log factor. Hence the answer is clear. Choose $\alpha = 1$, i.e. inverse square law sampling, otherwise the measurement condition depends algebraically on N.

But does this agree with practice? The answer is resoundingly no. Figure 11.4 gives an illustration of this point. The power-law schemes with $\alpha = 2$ and $\alpha = 3$ both lead to a meaningless recovery guarantee (11.4). Yet they significantly outperform the inverse square law scheme for this example. Nor is this a special case. As we show in Chapter 15, in most cases the best value of α does not correspond to the choice $\alpha = 1$.

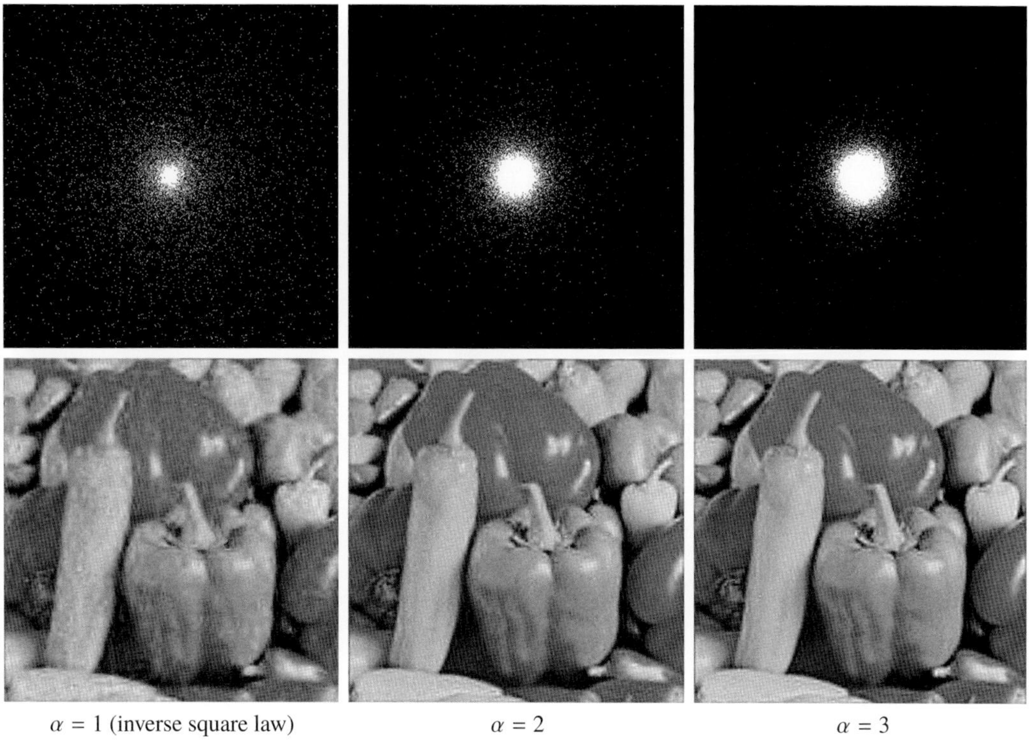

Figure 11.4 Reconstruction of the 512×512 peppers image using DB4 wavelets and 3% Fourier measurements taken according to the power-law density (11.3). Top row: Sampling maps. Bottom row: Reconstructed images.

11.2.2 The Flip Test

Although not clear at this point, the reason for this discrepancy is the sparsity structure. We defer the theoretical explanation of this effect to Chapter 15, once the necessary technical tools have been developed. Instead, we now empirically demonstrate the importance of such structure. We do this via an experiment termed the *flip test.*

Let $x \in \mathbb{C}^N$ be the (vectorized) image to recover, $A \in \mathbb{C}^{m \times N}$ be the measurement matrix, $d = \Phi^* x$ be the coefficients of x in some orthonormal sparsifying transform Φ and $Q \in \mathbb{C}^{N \times N}$ be a permutation matrix. The flip test is based on the following principle:

Sparsity is unchanged by permutations. If d is s-sparse, then so is $d' = Qd$.

Let $d' = Qd$ be the permuted coefficients of x, and define the corresponding *permuted image* $x' = \Phi d'$. Notice that

$$x' = Rx, \qquad R = \Phi Q \Phi^*.$$

Figure 11.5 shows this process for a random permutation Q. Observe that x' is s-sparse in the given sparsifying transform, but unlike x, it is a completely unphysical image.

The flip test now proceeds as follows:

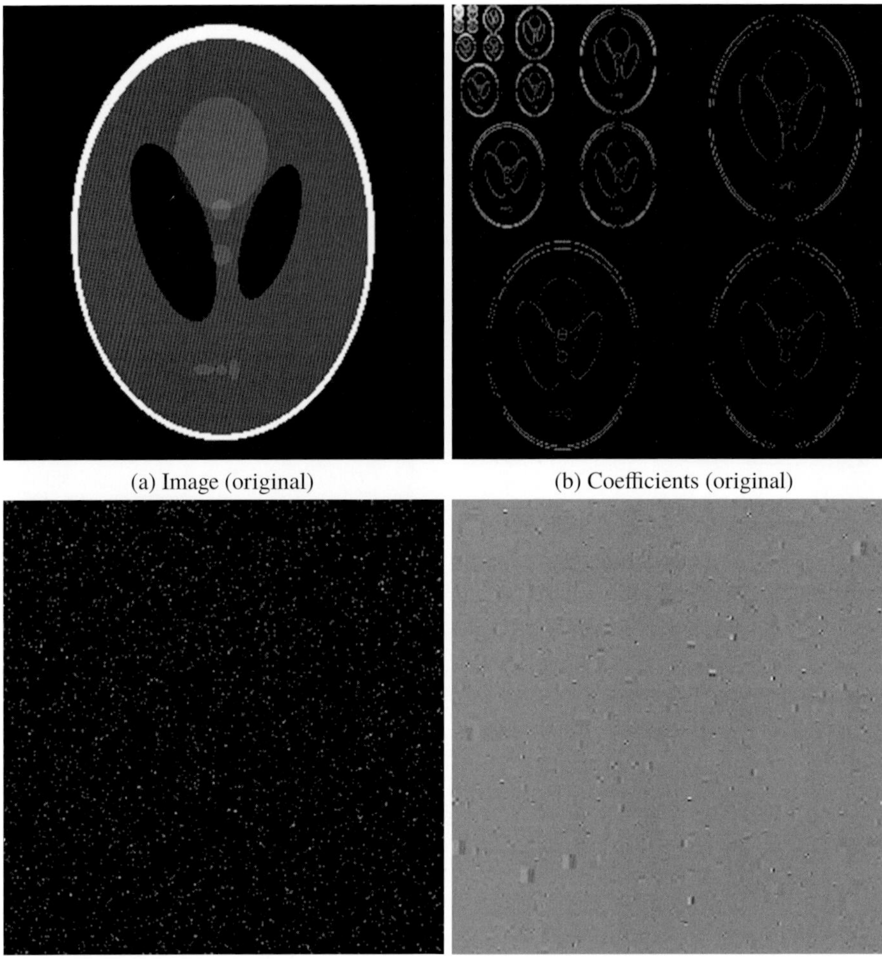

(a) Image (original) (b) Coefficients (original)

(c) Coefficients (permuted) (d) Image (permuted)

Figure 11.5 (a) Discrete 256×256 SL phantom image. (b) Haar wavelet coefficients d with sparsity $s = 3769$. (c) Randomly permuted coefficients $d' = Pd$ with sparsity $s = 3769$. (d) Permuted image $x' = \Phi d' = Rx$.

1. Generate measurements $y = Ax$ and compute a reconstruction $\hat{x}$ via (11.1).
2. Generate measurements $y' = Ax'$ of the flipped image x' and compute a reconstruction $\hat{x}'$ of x' via (11.1).
3. Reverse the flipping operation to get a reconstruction $\check{x} = R^{-1}\hat{x}'$ of x.

This produces two reconstructions $\hat{x}$ and $\check{x}$ of the image x. Since x and x' have the same sparsity, if sparsity alone determines the recovery quality then we expect $\hat{x}$ and $\check{x}$ to both recover x equally well. Yet Fig. 11.6 shows that this is not the case. The flipped recovery $\check{x}$ (based on a random permutation Q) gives significantly worse results than the unflipped

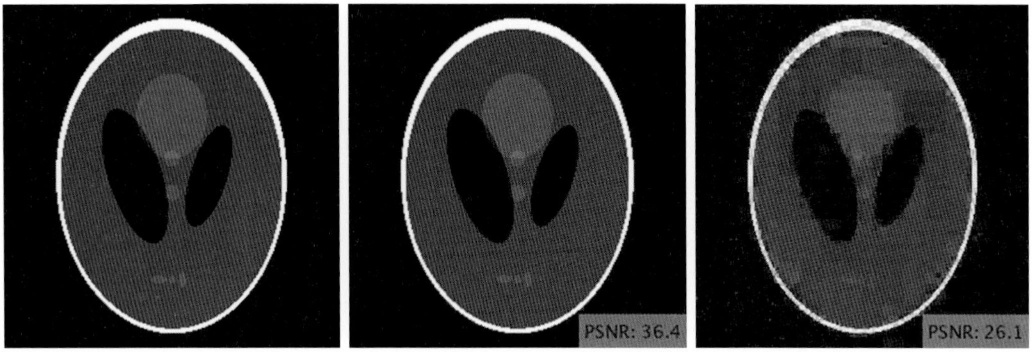

(a) Original (b) Unflipped reconstruction (c) Flipped reconstruction

Figure 11.6 The flip test for Fourier measurements. (a) Discrete 256×256 SL phantom image. (b) Unflipped reconstruction. (c) Flipped reconstruction based on a random permutation Q. The recovery was obtained from 20% Fourier measurements, taken according to a Gaussian multilevel scheme with $r = 50$, $a = 2$ and $r_0 = 1$, using Haar wavelets.

recovery $\hat{x}$. Furthermore, as we show in Fig. 11.7, this effect can be made even more dramatic by using adversarial, as opposed to random, permutations.

Note that these conclusions are in no way limited to the sampling pattern used nor the fact that the image is exactly sparse in the given sparsifying transform. Figure 11.8 shows the flip test on a compressible, but nonsparse image using DB4 wavelets and radial sampling. Once more, we see a similar result.

> The flip test demonstrates that the local sparsity structure of the wavelet coefficients of an image plays a key role in the reconstruction quality from Fourier measurements.

11.2.3 The Flip Test for Gaussian Random Matrices

It is informative to compare this situation to the case of Gaussian measurements. Figure 11.9 shows the results of the flip test when A is a Gaussian random matrix. In this case, the flipped and unflipped reconstructions are very similar, indicating that local sparsity structure plays little or no role in the recovery from such measurements via (11.1). This fact is further highlighted by plotting the absolute values of the $A\Phi$, as we do in Fig. 11.10. Unlike in the case of Fourier sampling (Fig. 11.2), there is no structure to the entries of $A\Phi$. It turns out that this matrix is *incoherent* according to the more general notion of coherence we define later, and therefore ideally suited to recovering sparse vectors but not those with additional local structure. Note that this phenomenon is unaltered if the sparsifying transform is changed; a fact which is unsurprising in view of the universality of Gaussian measurements (see Remark 5.26).

11.2.4 The Flip Test in Levels and Asymptotic Sparsity

Consider the Fourier-wavelets problem once more. Evidently, local sparsity structure plays an important role in the recovery. But what type of structure is this exactly? Since

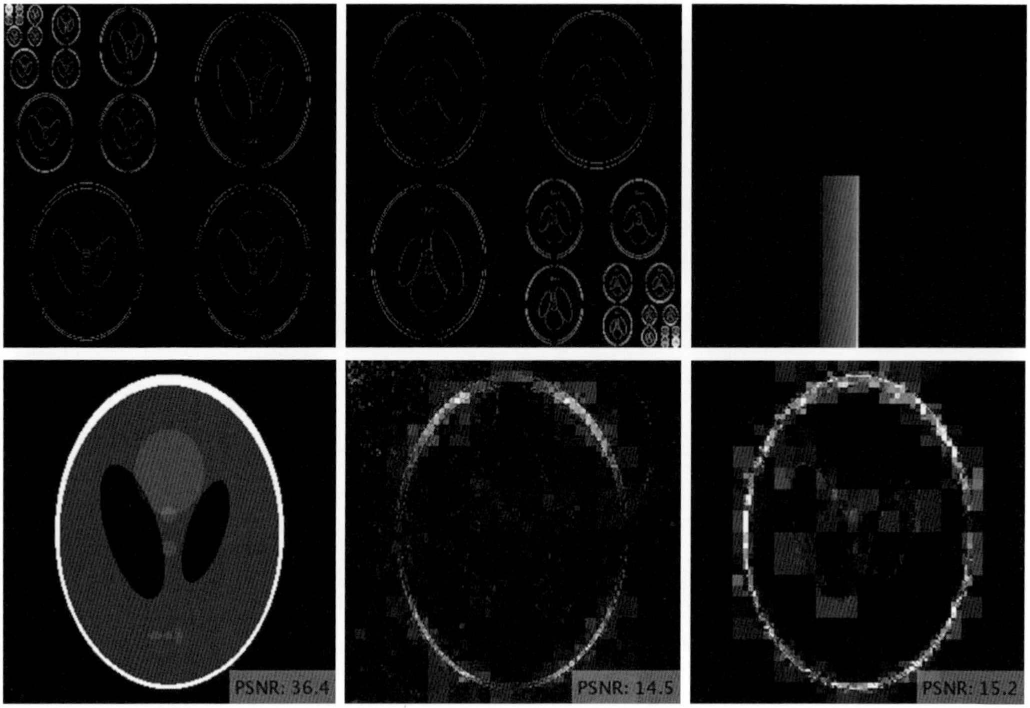

Unflipped Flipped Flipped

Figure 11.7 The same as Fig. 11.6 except using different permutations. Top row: (Flipped) wavelet coefficients. Bottom row: Reconstruction.

a wavelet basis is divided into dyadic scales, it is informative to consider a *local* version of the flip test where random permutations are performed within the scales only. An example of this is shown in Fig. 11.8(d).

The comparison with the original flip test in Fig. 11.8(c) is striking. Unlike global permutations, local permutations within scales have almost no effect on the reconstruction quality. We deduce that the characteristic property of wavelet coefficients that drives the good reconstruction quality via (11.1) in the Fourier-wavelets recovery problem is not their global sparsity, but their local sparsities within the individual scales.

Remark 11.1 Another conclusion of Fig. 11.8 is that *inter-scale* dependencies of wavelet coefficients – for instance, tree structures (see the Notes section) – have little bearing on the reconstruction quality obtained from (11.1).

This raises the question of how such local sparsities behave in practice. Figure 11.11 demonstrates this behaviour for a typical image. The main observation is that wavelet coefficients are *asymptotically sparse*: namely, they are relatively more sparse at fine scales than they are at coarse scales. This, of course, agrees with the discussion in Chapters 9 and 10, where it was argued that the large wavelet coefficients correspond to those intersecting the edges of the image and the small coefficients correspond to those located within smooth regions. Yet it is the fact that this behaviour aligns with the

(a) Sampling pattern (b) Unflipped

(c) Flipped (d) Flipped (in levels)

Figure 11.8 Flip test for the discrete 256×256 klubbe image using radial sampling (Definition 4.9) with 20% and DB4 wavelets. (a) Sampling pattern. (b) Unflipped reconstruction. (c) Flipped reconstruction. (d) Flipped reconstruction obtained from the flip test in levels (see §11.2.4).

asymptotic incoherence of the Fourier-wavelets matrix – namely, the property, as seen in Fig. 11.2, that the coherence decreases as either the Fourier frequency or wavelet scale increases – that underlies the good reconstruction quality in the Fourier-wavelets problem. We therefore conclude this section with the following:

The Fourier-wavelet recovery problem achieves high accuracy because the asymptotic sparsity of natural images aligns with the asymptotic incoherence of the Fourier-wavelets matrix. The flip test destroys the asymptotic sparsity structure, hence leading to worse recovery.

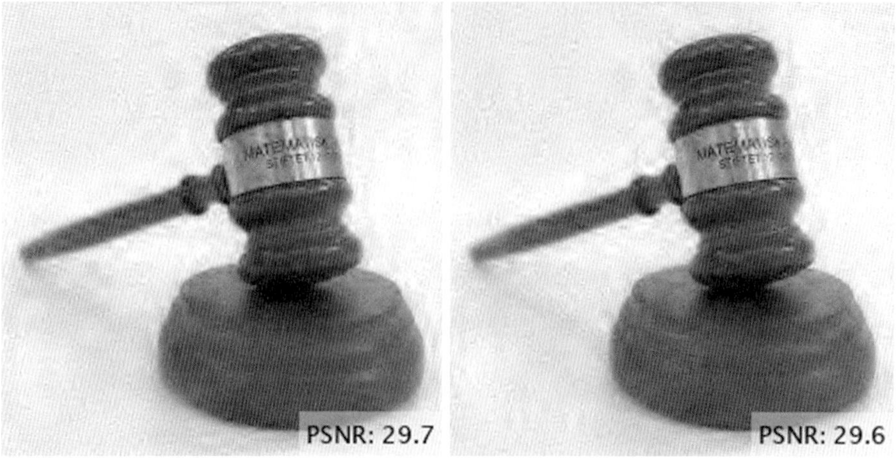

Unflipped Flipped

Figure 11.9 The flip test for Gaussian measurements applied to the 256×256 klubbe image with sampling percentage 20% and using DB4 wavelets.

Haar DB4

Figure 11.10 The absolute values of the matrix $A\Phi$, where A is a 128×256 Gaussian random matrix and Φ is a one-dimensional discrete wavelet sparsifying transform.

11.3 Local Sparsity in Levels

We have now seen that local properties of the sampling operator and sparsifying transform play a key role in compressive imaging with wavelets. It is also clear that the standard compressed sensing setup described in Chapter 5 is insufficient for understanding this phenomenon, since it is based on global notions such as sparsity and incoherence. Hence, in the remainder of this chapter we introduce a more general compressed sensing framework that is better adapted to this task.

We commence in this section by formalizing the local sparsity in levels model.

Definition 11.2 (Sparsity in levels) Let $1 \leq r \leq N$, $M_0 = 0$, $\mathbf{M} = (M_1, \ldots, M_r)$, where $1 \leq M_1 < \cdots < M_r = N$, and $\mathbf{s} = (s_1, \ldots, s_r)$, where $s_k \leq M_k - M_{k-1}$ for $k = 1, \ldots, r$. A vector $x \in \mathbb{C}^N$ is $(\mathbf{s}, \mathbf{M})$-*sparse in levels* if

$$|\mathrm{supp}(x) \cap \{M_{k-1} + 1, \ldots, M_k\}| \leq s_k, \quad k = 1, \ldots, r.$$

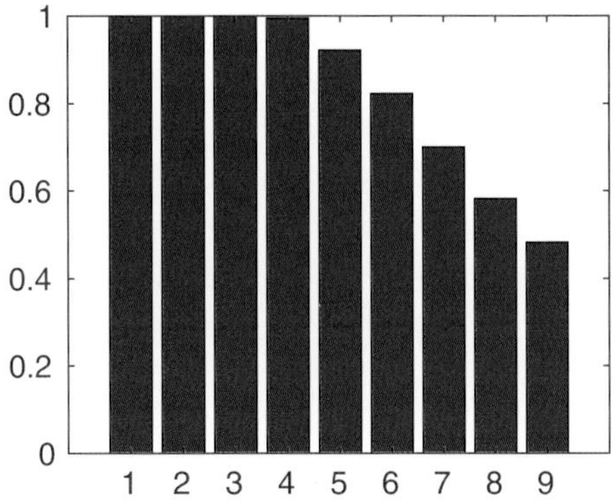

Figure 11.11 Fraction of Haar wavelet coefficients per scale exceeding a given threshold for the 512×512 klubbe image. The threshold is $\epsilon = 0.6$. Note that the range of the pixel values in this image (its dynamic range) is $[2, 255]$, which gives a scaled threshold $\epsilon/(255-2) = 2.37 \times 10^{-3}$.

The *total sparsity* of x is $s = s_1 + \cdots + s_r$ and the set of $(\mathbf{s}, \mathbf{M})$-sparse vectors is denoted by $\Sigma_{\mathbf{s},\mathbf{M}}$.

The vector $\mathbf{M}$ defines the r *sparsity levels*, and the vector $\mathbf{s}$ enumerates the *local sparsities* within them. Observe that when $r = 1$, sparsity in levels reduces to standard sparsity (Definition 5.1). While motivated by wavelets, we also note that Definition 11.2 is completely general. The sparsity levels $\mathbf{M}$ need not correspond to wavelet scales, although this is the main example we consider later. Outside of wavelets, several other uses for this model are mentioned in the Notes section.

Some additional notation is now useful. If $\Lambda = \{1, \ldots, M\}$ for some $M \in \mathbb{N}$ then rather than writing P_Λ for the orthogonal projection onto $\mathrm{span}\{e_i : i \in \Lambda\}$ we merely write P_M. Moreover, if $\Lambda = \{M_1 + 1, \ldots, M_2\}$ for $0 \leq M_1 < M_2 \leq N$ then we write

$$P_{M_2}^{M_1} = P_{\{M_1+1,\ldots,M_2\}} = P_{M_2} P_{M_1}^{\perp}.$$

With this, given levels $\mathbf{M}$ and a vector $x \in \mathbb{C}^N$, we also write

$$x = \sum_{k=1}^{r} x^{(k)}, \qquad x^{(k)} = P_{M_k}^{M_{k-1}} x.$$

Here $x^{(k)}$ is equal to the vector x in the kth level $\{M_{k-1} + 1, \ldots, M_k\}$ and zero elsewhere. Technically, $x^{(k)}$ is an element of $\mathbb{C}^N$. However, it may on occasion be convenient to view $x^{(k)}$ as an element of $\mathbb{C}^{M_k - M_{k-1}}$. This will be clear from the context. Note that if x is $(\mathbf{s}, \mathbf{M})$-sparse then

$$x^{(k)} \in \Sigma_{s_k} \cap P_{M_k}^{M_{k-1}}\left(\mathbb{C}^N\right), \qquad k = 1, \ldots, r,$$

where Σ_{s_k} is as in Definition 5.1. That is, $x^{(k)}$ is s_k-sparse with its nonzero entries constrained to lie in the kth level.

In a similar manner to (5.3), one may express the set of $(\mathbf{s}, \mathbf{M})$-sparse vectors $\Sigma_{\mathbf{s},\mathbf{M}}$ as the union

$$\Sigma_{\mathbf{s},\mathbf{M}} = \bigcup_{\Delta \in D_{\mathbf{s},\mathbf{M}}} E_\Delta,$$

where E_Δ is as in (5.4) and

$$D_{\mathbf{s},\mathbf{M}} = \{\Delta \subseteq \{1,\dots,N\} : |\Delta \cap \{M_{k-1}+1,\dots,M_k\}| = s_k,\ k=1,\dots,r\}. \tag{11.5}$$

A simple counting argument gives that

$$|D_{\mathbf{s},\mathbf{M}}| = \binom{M_1 - M_0}{s_1}\binom{M_2 - M_1}{s_2}\cdots\binom{M_r - M_{r-1}}{s_r}.$$

It is also informative to view $\Sigma_{\mathbf{s},\mathbf{M}}$ as a subset of sparse vectors with additional constraints on the locations of the nonzero entries. Indeed, one has

$$\Sigma_{\mathbf{s},\mathbf{M}} \subseteq \Sigma_s, \qquad s = s_1 + \cdots + s_r.$$

Conversely, given $1 \leq s \leq \min_{k=1,\dots,r}\{M_k - M_{k-1}\}$ one also has

$$\Sigma_s \subseteq \Sigma_{\mathbf{s},\mathbf{M}}, \qquad \mathbf{s} = (s, s, \dots, s).$$

Finally, we note that if the number of levels $r = 1$ then $\Sigma_{\mathbf{s},\mathbf{M}} = \Sigma_s$.

Analogously to Definition 5.3, we now also write

$$\sigma_{\mathbf{s},\mathbf{M}}(x)_{\ell^p} = \{\|x - z\|_{\ell^p} : z \in \Sigma_{\mathbf{s},\mathbf{M}}\}, \qquad x \in \mathbb{C}^N \tag{11.6}$$

for the error of the best approximation of $x \in \mathbb{C}^N$ by an $(\mathbf{s},\mathbf{M})$-sparse vector. Similar to (5.7), we have

$$\sigma_{\mathbf{s},\mathbf{M}}(x)_{\ell^p} = \left(\sum_{k=1}^{r}\left(\sigma_{s_k}(x^{(k)})_{\ell^p}\right)^p\right)^{1/p} = \left(\sum_{k=1}^{r}\sum_{i>s_k}|x^{(k)}_{\pi_k(i)}|^p\right)^{1/p}, \tag{11.7}$$

where π_k is a bijection which gives a nonincreasing rearrangement of the entries of $x^{(k)}$ in absolute value.

11.4 Sampling Operators

In Chapter 5 we saw two types of *global* measurement matrix constructions, Gaussian or Bernoulli random matrices and randomly subsampled unitary matrices. We now introduce a framework for sampling in compressed sensing that not only includes both of these as special cases, but also allows for local structure in the sampling operator.

11.4.1 Sampling with Jointly Isotropic Collections

This framework is based on random families of vectors in $\mathbb{C}^N$, realizations of which constitute the rows of the resulting measurement matrix. Let $\mathcal{A}$ be a distribution of vectors in $\mathbb{C}^N$, and write $a \sim \mathcal{A}$ if $a \in \mathbb{C}^N$ is drawn from this distribution. Note that $\mathcal{A}$ may not be the whole of $\mathbb{C}^N$, and may consist of only finitely many vectors. If $\mathcal{A}$ is finite, we let $|\mathcal{A}|$ denote its cardinality. If not, we write $|\mathcal{A}| = \infty$.

Definition 11.3 (Isotropy condition) The distribution $\mathcal{A}$ is *isotropic* if $\mathbb{E}(aa^*) = I$, where $I \in \mathbb{C}^{N\times N}$ is the identity matrix.

Note that an isotropic distribution preserves lengths and angles in expectation:

$$\mathbb{E}(x^* a a^* z) = x^* z, \quad \mathbb{E}|\langle a, x\rangle|^2 = \|x\|_{\ell^2}^2, \qquad \forall x, z \in \mathbb{C}^N. \tag{11.8}$$

For reasons explained below, it is also convenient to consider not only a single family, but also collections of families.

Definition 11.4 (Joint isotropy condition) Let $\mathcal{A}_1, \ldots, \mathcal{A}_m$ be independent families of random vectors on $\mathbb{C}^N$. The collection $C = \{\mathcal{A}_i\}_{i=1}^m$ is *jointly isotropic* if

$$\frac{1}{m} \sum_{i=1}^m \mathbb{E}_{\mathcal{A}_i}(a_i a_i^*) = I,$$

where $a_i \sim \mathcal{A}_i$ for $i = 1, \ldots, m$.

The factor $1/m$ is included here primarily for convenience. In particular, in the important case where each $\mathcal{A}_i$ is an independent copy of a single isotropic distribution $\mathcal{A}$ it ensures that the resulting collection $C = \{\mathcal{A}_i\}_{i=1}^m$ is jointly isotropic.

Let $C = \{\mathcal{A}_i\}_{i=1}^m$ be a jointly isotropic collection. We construct the measurement matrix $A \in \mathbb{C}^{m \times N}$ by randomly and independently drawing vectors from these distributions. Specifically, we let

$$A = \frac{1}{\sqrt{m}} \begin{pmatrix} a_1^* \\ \vdots \\ a_m^* \end{pmatrix} \in \mathbb{C}^{m \times N}, \tag{11.9}$$

where each vector a_i is an independent realization from its respective distribution $\mathcal{A}_i$. We refer to A as the *measurement matrix corresponding to* C. Observe that $\mathbb{E}(A^* A) = I$, which, as discussed in Remark 5.7, is the standard normalization in compressed sensing. Indeed, due to the joint isotropy condition (Definition 11.4), we have

$$\mathbb{E}(A^* A) = \frac{1}{m} \sum_{i=1}^m \mathbb{E}_{\mathcal{A}_i}(a_i a_i^*) = I.$$

11.4.2 Examples

The above model is simple, yet sufficiently general to cover many of the sampling operators found in practice. We now list several examples.

Example 11.5 (Randomly subsampled unitary matrices) Let $U \in \mathbb{C}^{N \times N}$ be a unitary matrix and $u_i = U^* e_i$ for $i = 1, \ldots, N$. Let $\mathcal{A}$ be the family of scaled vectors $\{\sqrt{N} u_i\}_{i=1}^N$ equipped with the uniform distribution, i.e. $a \sim \mathcal{A}$ if

$$\mathbb{P}\left(a = \sqrt{N} u_i\right) = \frac{1}{N}, \quad i = 1, \ldots, N.$$

Now define the collection $C = \{\mathcal{A}_i\}_{i=1}^m$, where the $\mathcal{A}_i$ are independent copies of $\mathcal{A}$. Observe that

$$\mathbb{E}_{\mathcal{A}}(a a^*) = \sum_{i=1}^N u_i u_i^* = \sum_{i=1}^N U^* e_i e_i^* U = U^* U = I.$$

Hence this family is isotropic. Sampling according to this collection is identical to the randomly subsampled unitary matrix construction of Definition 5.6.

Example 11.6 (Nonuniformly subsampled unitary matrices) A simple extension of the previous example allows the rows of U to be chosen with different probabilities. This is related to variable-density sampling (Definition 4.4) and therefore particularly relevant to compressive imaging. Let $0 < \pi_1, \ldots, \pi_N \leq 1$ with $\sum_{i=1}^{N} \pi_i = 1$. Given a unitary matrix $U \in \mathbb{C}^{N \times N}$ we consider a distribution $\mathcal{A}$ defined by $a \sim \mathcal{A}$ if

$$\mathbb{P}\left(a = \frac{1}{\sqrt{\pi_i}} u_i\right) = \pi_i, \quad i = 1, \ldots, N,$$

where $u_i = U^* e_i$ as before, and let $C = \{\mathcal{A}_i\}_{i=1}^{m}$ be the collection consisting of m independent copies of $\mathcal{A}$. In other words, the measurement vectors are rescaled rows of U selected randomly according to the probabilities π_i. Since

$$\mathbb{E}_{\mathcal{A}}(aa^*) = \sum_{i=1}^{N} \pi_i \frac{1}{\pi_i} u_i u_i^* = \sum_{i=1}^{N} U^* e_i e_i^* U = I,$$

this is also an isotropic family.

Example 11.7 (Subsampled semi-discrete Fourier transforms) As discussed in Chapters 3 and 4, in some applications of Fourier imaging the frequencies sampled do not lie on an integer grid. In the discrete setting, where the unknown is a vector $x \in \mathbb{C}^N$, this type of sampling can be modelled with the *semi-discrete* Fourier transform

$$\mathcal{F} : \mathbb{C}^N \to L^2([0,1]), \; x \mapsto \mathcal{F}(x)(\omega) = \sum_{i=1}^{N} x_i \exp(-2\pi \mathrm{i}(i-1)\omega).$$

This can also be viewed in the above framework. Let ω be a random variable that is uniformly distributed in $[0, 1]$ and define the vector $a = (a_i)_{i=1}^{N}$ as

$$a_i = \exp(-2\pi \mathrm{i}(i-1)\omega), \quad i = 1, \ldots, N.$$

Then the resulting family $\mathcal{A}$ is isotropic:

$$(\mathbb{E}_{\mathcal{A}}(aa^*))_{ij} = \int_0^1 \exp(2\pi \mathrm{i}(j-i)\omega) \, \mathrm{d}\omega = \delta_{ij}, \quad i, j = 1, \ldots, N.$$

Let $C = \{\mathcal{A}_i\}_{i=1}^{m}$ be the collection consisting of m independent copies of $\mathcal{A}$. Then the measurements $y = Ax$, where A is defined by (11.9), are now given by

$$y = \frac{1}{m} \left(\mathcal{F}(x)(\omega_i)\right)_{i=1}^{m},$$

where the frequencies $\omega_1, \ldots, \omega_m$ are chosen independently and uniformly from $[0, 1]$, as opposed to on an equispaced grid.

As in Example 11.6 one could also consider variable-density sampling within this context. For example, let $\nu(\omega)$ be a probability density function on $[0, 1]$ with $\nu(\omega) > 0$ almost everywhere and suppose that ω is distributed on $[0, 1]$ with density ν. Then we define the measurement vector $a \sim \mathcal{A}$ by

$$a_i = \frac{1}{\sqrt{\nu(\omega)}} \exp(-2\pi \mathrm{i}(i-1)\omega), \quad i = 1, \ldots, N.$$

The corresponding measurements y are proportional to the Fourier samples $\mathcal{F}(x)(\omega_i)$, $i = 1, \ldots, m$ taken at frequencies $\omega_1, \ldots, \omega_m$ drawn independently according to ν.

Example 11.8 (Gaussian and Bernoulli random matrices) A Gaussian random matrix (Definition 5.4) is a particular case of this framework, where $\mathcal{A}$ is the family of vectors whose entries are independent normal random variables with mean zero and variance one. This family is isotropic, and therefore the collection $C = \{\mathcal{A}_i\}_{i=1}^m$ consisting of independent copies of $\mathcal{A}$ is jointly isotropic. The same applies to Bernoulli random matrices.

All the previous examples are cases where the families $\mathcal{A}_i$ are independent copies of a single isotropic family $\mathcal{A}$. The advantage of allowing different families is that it gives more precise control over how measurements are taken. For instance:

Example 11.9 (Deterministic plus randomly subsampled unitary matrices) Suppose that $U \in \mathbb{C}^{N \times N}$ is a unitary matrix. Consider a sampling scheme that fully samples the first m_1 rows of U, and then randomly selects $m_2 = m - m_1$ rows from the remaining $N - m_1$ rows. In the context of Fourier or Walsh sampling, this is the half–half scheme introduced in Definition 4.5.

This setup can be realized in the above framework. For $i = 1, \ldots, m_1$, let $\mathcal{A}_i$ be the singleton family consisting of the vector $\sqrt{m} u_i$ drawn with probability 1. Next, let $\mathcal{A}_{m_1+1}, \ldots, \mathcal{A}_m$ be independent copies of a family $\mathcal{A}$ which consists of the scaled rows of U from index $m_1 + 1$ to N equipped with the uniform distribution. That is, $a \sim \mathcal{A}$ if

$$\mathbb{P}\left(a = \sqrt{\frac{(N-m_1)m}{m_2}} u_i\right) = \frac{1}{N - m_1}, \quad i = m_1 + 1, \ldots, N.$$

Note that $\mathcal{A}$ itself is not generally isotropic. However, the collection $C = \{\mathcal{A}_i\}_{i=1}^m$ is jointly isotropic. Indeed, we have

$$\begin{aligned}\frac{1}{m} \sum_{i=1}^m \mathbb{E}_{\mathcal{A}_i}(a_i a_i^*) &= \frac{1}{m}\left(\sum_{i=1}^{m_1} m u_i u_i^* + m_2 \sum_{i=m_1+1}^N \frac{(N-m_1)m}{m_2} \frac{1}{N-m_1} u_i u_i^*\right) \\ &= \sum_{i=1}^N u_i u_i^* = I.\end{aligned}$$

Remark 11.10 Recall from §5.4.3 that it is often convenient to combine the measurement matrix and sparsifying transform into a single matrix. This can easily be incorporated into the above framework. Let $x \in \mathbb{C}^N$ be the vector to recover and $d = \Phi^* x$ be its coefficients, where $\Phi \in \mathbb{C}^{N \times N}$ is the orthonormal sparsifying transform. Let $C = \{\mathcal{A}_i\}_{i=1}^m$ be a jointly isotropic collection, so that the measurements are

$$y = Ax = A\Phi d,$$

where A is the measurement matrix defined in (11.9). One now simply introduces the new families of vectors $\widetilde{\mathcal{A}}_i$ with $\tilde{a} \sim \widetilde{\mathcal{A}}_i$ if $\tilde{a} = \Phi^* a$ for $a \sim \mathcal{A}_i$. Notice that

$$y = \widetilde{A} d,$$

where $\widetilde{A} = A\Phi$ is the matrix defined by $\widetilde{\mathcal{A}}$. Since

$$\frac{1}{m}\sum_{i=1}^{m} \mathbb{E}_{\widetilde{\mathcal{A}}_i}\left(\tilde{a}_i \tilde{a}_i^*\right) = \Phi^* \left(\frac{1}{m}\sum_{i=1}^{m} \mathbb{E}_{\mathcal{A}_i}\left(a_i a_i^*\right)\right)\Phi = I \quad \Leftrightarrow \quad \frac{1}{m}\sum_{i=1}^{m} \mathbb{E}_{\mathcal{A}_i}\left(a_i a_i^*\right) = I,$$

we conclude that the collection $\widetilde{C} = \{\widetilde{\mathcal{A}}_i\}_{i=1}^m$ is jointly isotropic if and only if $C = \{\mathcal{A}_i\}_{i=1}^m$ is jointly isotropic.

11.4.3 Repeats and the Bernoulli Model

When a family $\mathcal{A}$ is finite, the model of drawing vectors independently from $\mathcal{A}$ allows the possibility for a vector, and therefore a measurement, to be repeated. As mentioned previously in Remark 4.3, this is a waste of the measurement budget m.

Remark 11.11 In particular, suppose we wish to ensure (in probability) that all rows of U are sampled in Example 11.5. Then we would need around $m \gtrsim N \log(N)$ measurements, due to the *coupon collector's effect*. Thus, logarithmically more measurements would end up being taken than if the N rows were just deterministically selected.

One alternative is to select rows without replacement. In the case of a randomly-subsampled unitary matrix, this is equivalent to Definition 5.5. However, as mentioned, the rows of A are no longer independent in this model; unfortunately, independence of the rows is an essential ingredient in all subsequent theoretical analysis.

A second alternative is the *Bernoulli model*. Here the ith row $u_i = U^* e_i, i = 1, \ldots, N$, is selected based on the outcome of an independent biased coin toss, with the probability of heads being $m\pi_i$ for some $0 \leq \pi_i \leq 1/m$, where $\sum_{i=1}^N \pi_i = 1$. Note that $\pi_i = 1/N$ if the rows are drawn with equal probability (analogous to Example 11.5), but the π_is can also be unequal (as in Example 11.6). This model successfully avoids repeated rows, with the price to pay being that the total number of measurements is now itself a random variable, equal to m in expectation only.

Conveniently, the Bernoulli model can also be recast into the framework of sampling from a jointly isotropic collection. Specifically, let $\mathcal{A}_i$ be the family consisting of the vector $\sqrt{N/(m\pi_i)}u_i$ and the zero vector, with $a_i \sim \mathcal{A}_i$ if

$$\mathbb{P}\left(a_i = \sqrt{\frac{N}{m\pi_i}} u_i\right) = m\pi_i, \qquad \mathbb{P}(a_i = 0) = 1 - m\pi_i.$$

Then the collection $C = \{\mathcal{A}_i\}_{i=1}^N$ is jointly isotropic, since

$$N^{-1}\sum_{i=1}^{N} \mathbb{E}_{\mathcal{A}_i}(a_i a_i^*) = N^{-1}\sum_{i=1}^{N} m\pi_i \frac{N}{m\pi_i} u_i u_i^* = U^* U = I.$$

Note that the resulting measurement matrix (11.9) is now $N \times N$ in this model. However, it only has $m' \approx m$ nonzero rows, where m' is the total number of heads, making it equivalent to an $m' \times N$ matrix.

11.4.4 Saturation

As discussed in Chapter 4, in Fourier or Walsh sampling it is important in practice to deterministically sample certain rows (e.g. those corresponding to low frequencies) and subsample the others. Typically, this deterministic sampling occurs in a band in frequency space. In this case, we henceforth refer to that band as being *saturated.*

Example 11.9 has already shown how such a scheme can be accommodated within the context of jointly isotropic families by choosing the corresponding $\mathcal{A}_i$s as singleton families. To this end, we now define the following:

Definition 11.12 (Saturation) A jointly isotropic collection $C = \{\mathcal{A}_i\}_{i=1}^m$ has *saturation* $0 \leq \widetilde{m} \leq m$ if precisely $\widetilde{m}$ of the families $\mathcal{A}_i$ consist of a single vector. If $\widetilde{m} = 0$ we say that C is *unsaturated.*

Recall that $|\mathcal{A}_i|$ denotes the cardinality of the family $\mathcal{A}_i$, with $|\mathcal{A}_i| = \infty > 1$ if $\mathcal{A}_i$ has infinite cardinality. Hence $\widetilde{m}$ can be expressed as

$$\widetilde{m} = |\{i : 1 \leq i \leq m,\ |\mathcal{A}_i| > 1\}|\,.$$

11.4.5 Multilevel Random Sampling

Consider the Fourier-wavelets problem, and specifically, Fig. 11.2. As discussed, the columns of $U = F\Phi$ are divided into sparsity levels corresponding to the wavelet scales, and the rows of U are divided into levels corresponding to bands in frequency space. Much as in Definition 4.6, we seek sampling strategies that allow for different amounts of sampling within each such level. Hence we now define the following:

Definition 11.13 (Multilevel random sampling) Let $N_0 = 0$, $\mathbf{N} = (N_1, \ldots, N_r)$, where $1 \leq N_1 < \cdots < N_r = N$, and $\mathbf{m} = (m_1, \ldots, m_r)$, where $m_k \leq N_k - N_{k-1}$ for $k = 1, \ldots, r$. An $(\mathbf{m}, \mathbf{N})$*-multilevel random sampling scheme* is a set $\Omega = \Omega_1 \cup \cdots \cup \Omega_r$ of $m = m_1 + \cdots + m_r$ indices, where for each k the following holds. If $m_k = N_k - N_{k-1}$ then $\Omega_k = \{N_{k-1}+1, \ldots, N_k\}$, otherwise Ω_k consists of m_k indices chosen independently and uniformly at random from the set $\{N_{k-1} + 1, \ldots, N_k\}$.

The vector $\mathbf{N}$ defines the r *sampling levels* and $\mathbf{m}$ the local number of measurements within them. Observe that Ω may contain repeated entries, due to the drawing model. Recall Remark 4.2. Note also that Definition 11.13 is completely general, since the levels $\mathbf{N}$ can be arbitrary (i.e. they need not be related to the Fourier-wavelets problem).

Our interest lies with using Ω to subsample the rows of a unitary matrix $U \in \mathbb{C}^{N \times N}$. Accordingly, we define:

Definition 11.14 (Multilevel subsampled unitary matrix) A matrix $A \in \mathbb{C}^{m \times N}$ is an $(\mathbf{m}, \mathbf{N})$*-multilevel subsampled unitary matrix* if $A = P_{\Omega} D U$ for a given unitary matrix

$U \in \mathbb{C}^{N\times N}$ and $(\mathbf{m},\mathbf{N})$-multilevel random sampling scheme Ω. Here D is a diagonal scaling matrix with entries

$$D_{ii} = \sqrt{\frac{N_k - N_{k-1}}{m_k}}, \qquad i = N_{k-1}+1,\ldots,N_k,\ k = 1,\ldots,r.$$

As we see in a moment, the scaling matrix D is natural. Note that when $r = 1$, this is precisely Definition 5.6.

Multilevel random sampling plays a crucial role later in this book, in particular, Part IV. As we show therein, it allows one to refine a sampling strategy in relation to a particular sparsity in levels model by tuning the r parameters $m_1,\ldots,m_r$ in accordance with the local sparsities $s_1,\ldots,s_r$. See also §11.6. Chapters 12 and 13 provide the theoretical tools needed in order to do this.

Levels for which $m_k = N_k - N_{k-1}$ are referred to as *saturated*. It is important to note that within such levels the sampling procedure is different. Rather than random, independent samples, we deterministically select all the rows in the level instead. The motivation for doing this comes from the coupon collector effect (Remark 11.11): had we insisted upon random sampling regardless of the value of m_k, it would have required $m_k \gtrsim (N_k - N_{k-1})\log(N_k - N_{k-1})$ to ensure saturation of the level with high probability. This is clearly wasteful. An alternative, as described in §11.4.3, is to use the Bernoulli model. While it is possible to do so, we will not consider this approach further.

Remark 11.15 Definition 11.13 is related to Definition 4.6. The latter considers an arbitrary partition $\mathcal{B} = \{B_k\}_{k=1}^r$ of d-dimensional frequency space $\{-N/2+1,\ldots,N/2\}^d$, whereas the former considers a partition of the indices $\{1,\ldots,N\}$ into sampling levels. Clearly, an $(\mathbf{m},\mathcal{B})$-multilevel random sampling scheme (in the sense of Definition 4.6) is equivalent to an $(\mathbf{m},\mathbf{N})$-multilevel random sampling scheme (in the sense of Definition 11.13) applied to the Fourier matrix F, after reindexing its rows so that the kth block B_k is associated with the kth level $\{N_{k-1}+1,\ldots,N_k\}$.

Importantly, a multilevel subsampled unitary matrix can also be viewed as sampling from a jointly isotropic collection $C = \{\mathcal{A}_i\}_{i=1}^m$. We now describe this construction. First, suppose that k is the index of an unsaturated level, i.e. $m_k < N_k - N_{k-1}$. Let $\mathcal{A}^{(k)}$ be the random family corresponding to the scaled rows $u_i = U^* e_i$ in this level equipped with the uniform distribution. That is, $a \sim \mathcal{A}^{(k)}$ if

$$\mathbb{P}\left(a = \sqrt{\frac{(N_k - N_{k-1})m}{m_k}}u_i\right) = \frac{1}{N_k - N_{k-1}}, \qquad i = N_{k-1}+1,\ldots,N_k.$$

We now let $\mathcal{A}_i$, $m_1+\cdots+m_{k-1} < i \leq m_1+\cdots+m_k$, be an independent copy of $\mathcal{A}^{(k)}$. Second, if k is the index of a saturated level, we let $\mathcal{A}_i$, $m_1+\cdots+m_{k-1} < i \leq m_1+\cdots+m_k$, be the singleton families equal to the rows of U in level k scaled by $\sqrt{m}$. This fully specifies the collection $C = \{\mathcal{A}_i\}_{i=1}^m$. To see that it is jointly isotropic, we note that

$$\begin{aligned}\frac{1}{m}\sum_{i=1}^{m}\mathbb{E}_{\mathcal{A}_i}(a_i a_i^*) &= \frac{1}{m}\sum_{\substack{k=1\\ m_k<N_k-N_{k-1}}}^{r} m_k \sum_{j=N_{k-1}+1}^{N_k}\frac{(N_k-N_{k-1})m}{m_k}\frac{1}{N_k-N_{k-1}}u_j u_j^*\\ &\quad+\frac{1}{m}\sum_{\substack{k=1\\ m_k=N_k-N_{k-1}}}^{r}\sum_{j=N_{k-1}+1}^{N_k} m u_j u_j^*\\ &=\sum_{k=1}^{r}\sum_{j=N_{k-1}+1}^{N_k} u_j u_j^* = U^*U = I.\end{aligned}$$

Finally, let A be the matrix (11.9) corresponding to C. Then it is straightforward to see that $A = P_\Omega D U$, where Ω is an $(\mathbf{m},\mathbf{N})$-multilevel random sampling scheme. In other words, A coincides exactly with the matrix of Definition 11.14.

11.5 Notions of Coherence and Recovery Guarantees

Having introduced local notions of sparsity and sampling, we now turn our attention to various notions of coherence – including local versions suitable to capture the structure seen in Fig. 11.2 – as well as the recovery guarantees they imply.

11.5.1 Coherence

The following two definitions generalize the coherence of a matrix (Definition 5.8) to the general class of sampling operators introduced in the previous section.

Definition 11.16 (Coherence of a family $\mathcal{A}$) The *coherence* $\mu(\mathcal{A})$ of the family $\mathcal{A}$ is the smallest constant such that

$$\|a\|_{\ell^\infty}^2 \leq \mu(\mathcal{A}), \tag{11.10}$$

almost surely for $a \sim \mathcal{A}$.

Observe that $\mu(\mathcal{A}) \geq 1$ for an isotropic family $\mathcal{A}$. Indeed, (11.8) gives

$$1 = e_i^*\mathbb{E}(aa^*)e_i = \mathbb{E}|\langle a, e_i\rangle|^2 \leq \mu(\mathcal{A}).$$

Accordingly, we say that $\mathcal{A}$ is *incoherent* if $\mu(\mathcal{A}) \approx 1$ and *coherent* if $\mu(\mathcal{A}) \gg 1$.

To see that Definition 11.16 is a generalization of Definition 5.8, consider the isotropic family $\mathcal{A}$ of Example 11.5 corresponding to a randomly subsampled unitary matrix U. In this case, $\mu(\mathcal{A})$ reduces to $\mu(U)$. Specifically,

$$\mu(\mathcal{A}) = N \max_{i=1,\ldots,N}\|u_i\|_{\ell^\infty}^2 = \mu(U). \tag{11.11}$$

Definition 11.17 (Coherence of a collection C) The *coherence* of an unsaturated collection $C = \{\mathcal{A}_i\}_{i=1}^m$ is

$$\mu(C) = \max_{i=1,\ldots,m}\mu(\mathcal{A}_i).$$

The coherence of a collection $C = \{\mathcal{A}_i\}_{i=1}^m$ with saturation $1 \leq \widetilde{m} \leq m$ (Definition 11.12) is the maximum over the unsaturated families:

$$\mu(C) = \max_{i:|\mathcal{A}_i|>1} \mu(\mathcal{A}_i).$$

Observe that the coherence of a saturated collection excludes the coherences of the singleton families. This expresses the idea that the quality of the deterministic samples (coherence being a measure of the quality of the samples) should not affect the number of random samples required for recovery. As for a single family, we also note that $\mu(C) \geq 1$ for an unsaturated jointly isotropic collection.

Recalling the discussion in §5.7.2, we observe that the coherence $\mu(C)$ determines the sampling rate for sparse vectors, in the sense that for each μ there exists a collection C with coherence $\mu(C) = \mu$ for which $m \gtrsim \mu \cdot s$ measurements are required for exact recovery regardless of the decoder user. Later, in Chapter 12, we show that

$$m \gtrsim s \cdot \mu(C) \cdot (\log(N/\varepsilon) + \log(s) \cdot \log(s/\varepsilon)) \tag{11.12}$$

measurements suffice for exact recovery of an s-sparse vector via BP (see Corollary 12.5). Hence, BP is an optimal decoder, up to log factors. We also show stable and accurate recovery via QCBP under a similar measurement condition.

Remark 11.18 Because of (11.11), for a randomly subsampled unitary matrix (Example 11.5) the measurement condition (11.12) reduces to the following condition, which was already stated in Theorem 5.30:

$$m \gtrsim s \cdot \mu(U) \cdot (\log(N/\varepsilon) + \log(s) \cdot \log(s/\varepsilon)) \,. \tag{11.13}$$

The same condition also applies when U is subsampled according to the Bernoulli model (see §11.4.3). Indeed, suppose that the drawing probabilities in this model are all equal, i.e. $\pi_i = 1/N$, corresponding to selecting each row with equal probability. Then, with $a_i \sim \mathcal{A}_i$ and $\mathcal{A}_i$ as in §11.4.3, one has

$$\|a_i\|_{\ell^\infty}^2 = \frac{N}{m\pi_i}\|u_i\|_{\ell^\infty}^2 \leq \frac{N}{m}\mu(U).$$

Therefore, the measurement condition (11.12) becomes

$$N \gtrsim s \cdot \frac{N}{m}\mu(U) \cdot (\log(N/\varepsilon) + \log(s) \cdot \log(s/\varepsilon))$$

(notice that m has been replaced by N on the left-hand side since C consists of N families in the Bernoulli model). After simplifying, we see that this is exactly the same as (11.13). The only caveat is that m is no longer equal to the number of measurements in this model. As discussed, the latter is a random variable with expected value m.

11.5.2 Local Coherence in Levels

Definitions 11.16 and 11.17 are global notions based on the ℓ^∞-norm of the sampling vectors. They are therefore suitable for the sparsity model. For the sparsity in levels model, we now introduce the following local notion:

Definition 11.19 (Local coherence of a family $\mathcal{A}$) Let $\mathbf{M} = (M_1, \ldots, M_r)$ be sparsity levels, where $1 \leq M_1 < \cdots < M_r = N$. For $l = 1, \ldots, r$, the lth *local coherence* $\mu_l(\mathcal{A}) = \mu_l(\mathcal{A}; \mathbf{M})$ of a family of random vectors $\mathcal{A}$ is the smallest constant such that

$$\|P_{M_l}^{M_{l-1}} a\|_{\ell^\infty}^2 \leq \mu_l(\mathcal{A}; \mathbf{M}),$$

almost surely for $a \sim \mathcal{A}$, where $M_0 = 0$.

We examine the connection between local coherence and reconstruction quality in detail in Chapters 12 and 13. In particular, we show that an $(\mathbf{s}, \mathbf{M})$-sparse vector is recovered exactly (we also show stable and accurate recovery) when sampling with a collection $C = \{\mathcal{A}_i\}_{i=1}^m$, provided

$$m \gtrsim \max_{i:|\mathcal{A}_i|>1} \left\{ \sum_{l=1}^{r} s_l \mu_l(\mathcal{A}_i) \right\} \cdot L, \tag{11.14}$$

where $L = r \cdot (\log(N/\varepsilon) + \log(rs) \cdot \log(rs/\varepsilon))$. See Corollary 12.7. This generalizes the measurement condition (11.12) for the sparse model. In fact, (11.12) is the particular case of (11.14) corresponding to $r = 1$ level. Crucially, though, when $r > 1$ the condition (11.14) relates local quantities (local sparsities and local coherences) rather than global ones (sparsity and coherence).

11.5.3 Multilevel Random Sampling and Local Coherences

It is worth specializing (11.14) to the case of multilevel subsampled unitary matrices (Definition 11.14). Suppose that U is unitary and consider an $(\mathbf{m}, \mathbf{N})$-multilevel random sampling scheme (Definition 11.13). It is convenient to represent U in block form

$$U = \begin{pmatrix} U^{(1,1)} & U^{(1,2)} & \cdots & U^{(1,r)} \\ U^{(2,1)} & U^{(2,2)} & \cdots & U^{(2,r)} \\ \vdots & \vdots & \ddots & \vdots \\ U^{(r,1)} & U^{(r,2)} & \cdots & U^{(r,r)} \end{pmatrix}, \tag{11.15}$$

where, for $k, l = 1, \ldots, r$, the matrix $U^{(k,l)}$ is the block of U defined by the kth sampling level and lth sparsity level:

$$U^{(k,l)} = P_{N_k}^{N_{k-1}} U P_{M_l}^{M_{l-1}} \in \mathbb{C}^{(N_k - N_{k-1}) \times (M_l - M_{l-1})}.$$

As was shown in §11.4.5, an $(\mathbf{m}, \mathbf{N})$-multilevel random sampling scheme applied to U is equivalent to a jointly isotropic collection based on the families $\mathcal{A}^{(1)}, \ldots, \mathcal{A}^{(r)}$, where $\mathcal{A}^{(k)}$ selects rows of U in the range $\{N_{k-1}+1, \ldots, N_k\}$ randomly and uniformly. Hence, for $a_k \sim \mathcal{A}^{(k)}$ we have

$$\|P_{M_l}^{M_{l-1}} a_k\|_{\ell^\infty}^2 \leq \frac{(N_k - N_{k-1})m}{m_k} \max_{N_{k-1} < i \leq N_k} \|P_{M_l}^{M_{l-1}} u_i\|_{\ell^\infty}^2 \leq \frac{m}{m_k} \mu\left(U^{(k,l)}\right),$$

where $\mu(U^{(k,l)})$ is the matrix coherence of $U^{(k,l)}$ (Definition 5.8). Therefore

$$\mu_l(\mathcal{A}^{(k)}) \leq \frac{m}{m_k} \mu\left(U^{(k,l)}\right) \tag{11.16}$$

is a multiple of the coherence of the (k,l)th block of U in the block form (11.15). Substituting this into (11.14) gives

$$m \gtrsim \max_{k: m_k < N_k - N_{k-1}} \left\{ \sum_{l=1}^{r} \frac{m}{m_k} s_l \mu\left(U^{(k,l)}\right) \right\} \cdot L,$$

where $L = r \cdot (\log(N/\varepsilon) + \log(rs) \cdot \log(rs/\varepsilon))$. In particular, this means that

$$m_k = \min \left\{ N_k - N_{k-1}, \left\lceil c \cdot \left(\sum_{l=1}^{r} s_l \mu\left(U^{(k,l)}\right) \right) \cdot L \right\rceil \right\}, \quad k = 1, \ldots, r \tag{11.17}$$

measurements suffice for the recovery of an $(\mathbf{s}, \mathbf{M})$-sparse vector, for some universal constant $c > 0$. As in (11.14), the key observation is that this condition relates purely local quantities (the m_ks, s_ks and local coherences), rather than global ones.

Remark 11.20 In subsequent chapters, we will typically just write

$$m_k \gtrsim \left(\sum_{l=1}^{r} s_l \mu\left(U^{(k,l)}\right) \right) \cdot L, \quad k = 1, \ldots, r$$

instead of the lengthier expression (11.17). This is with the understanding that $m_k = N_k - N_{k-1}$ whenever $c \left(\sum_{l=1}^{r} s_l \mu\left(U^{(k,l)}\right) \right) \cdot L \geq N_k - N_{k-1}$, where c is the constant implied by the $\gtrsim$ symbol.

11.6 The One-Dimensional Discrete Fourier–Haar Wavelet Problem

To conclude this discussion, we now introduce the main example that will be used in the next several chapters. This is the one-dimensional discrete Fourier–Haar wavelet problem, i.e. discrete Fourier sampling with sparsity (in levels) in the discrete Haar wavelet basis. Note that generalizations of this example to the two-dimensional case, other wavelets and to the Walsh transform will be developed in Part IV of this book. These generalizations address more practical imaging problems. Yet the one-dimensional, discrete Haar case will serve to illuminate the key features of the problem without the additional technicalities that these extensions require.

11.6.1 Setup

Let $N = 2^{r-1}$ for some $r \geq 2$ (henceforth it will be convenient to define N as 2^{r-1} instead of 2^r), $\Phi \in \mathbb{C}^{N \times N}$ be the discrete Haar wavelet sparsifying transform (see §9.10.5 and, specifically, Remark 9.30) and $F \in \mathbb{C}^{N \times N}$ be the Fourier matrix (Definition 2.1). Define

$$U = \frac{1}{\sqrt{N}} F \Phi. \tag{11.18}$$

Our first task is to describe appropriate sparsity levels and sampling levels for this problem. For the sparsity levels, we follow the approach of §9.9 and define $\mathbf{M} = (M_1, \ldots, M_r)$ according to the wavelet scales. Specifically, we let

$$M_k = 2^{k-1}, \quad k = 1, \ldots, r, \tag{11.19}$$

so that the first level $\{M_0+1, M_1\} = \{1\}$ contains the coefficient $\langle x, \psi^{(0)}_{0,0}\rangle$ corresponding to the discrete scaling function, and for $k = 2, \ldots, r$, the kth level $\{2^{k-2}+1, \ldots, 2^{k-1}\}$ contains the wavelet coefficients

$$\{\langle x, \psi^{(1)}_{k-2,n}\rangle : n = 0, \ldots, 2^{k-2}-1\},$$

at scale $k-2$. Here $\psi^{(e)}_{j,n}$ is as in (9.58).

We now define the sampling levels. The local coherence structure of Fig. 11.2 and the arguments given in §11.1.3 suggest that the rows of $U = F\Phi$ should be grouped into dyadic bands. We do this as follows. Let

$$\begin{aligned} &B_1 = \{0\}, \quad B_2 = \{1\}, \\ &B_{k+2} = \{-2^k+1, \ldots, -2^{k-1}\} \cup \{2^{k-1}+1, \ldots, 2^k\}, \quad k = 1, \ldots, r-2. \end{aligned} \tag{11.20}$$

Notice that these sets partition $\{-N/2+1, \ldots, N/2\}$ into r bands of size

$$|B_1| = |B_2| = 1, \qquad |B_{k+2}| = 2^k, \quad k = 1, \ldots, r-2.$$

Recall from §2.2.2 that the mapping ϱ defined in (2.8) reindexes the set $\{-N/2+1, \ldots, N/2\}$ over $\{1, \ldots, N\}$. Define the sampling levels

$$N_k = 2^{k-1}, \quad k = 1, \ldots, r. \tag{11.21}$$

Then, by (2.9),

$$\varrho(\{N_{k-1}+1, \ldots, N_k\}) = B_k, \quad k = 1, \ldots, r.$$

Hence, the kth sampling level $\{N_{k-1}+1, \ldots, N_k\}$, when defined in this way, corresponds precisely to the frequencies in the band B_k.

With the sampling and sparsity levels in hand, we have now determined the block structure (11.15) for the matrix U. This is exactly as was previously shown in Fig. 11.2. Observe that the entries of $U^{(k,l)}$ are the frequency values in band B_k of the wavelets at scale $l-2$. Specifically, we have

$$\left(U^{(k,1)}\right)_{i,1} = \frac{1}{\sqrt{N}} \left(F\psi^{(0)}_{0,0}\right)_{N_{k-1}+i}, \tag{11.22}$$

for $i = 1, \ldots, N_k - N_{k-1}$, and for $l = 2, \ldots, r$,

$$\left(U^{(k,l)}\right)_{i,n+1} = \frac{1}{\sqrt{N}} \left(F\psi^{(1)}_{l-2,n}\right)_{N_{k-1}+i}, \qquad n = 0, \ldots, 2^{l-2}-1. \tag{11.23}$$

11.6.2 Local Coherences and Recovery Guarantees

In §11.5.3 we gave a measurement condition (11.17) for a multilevel subsampled unitary matrix U in terms of its local coherences $\mu(U^{(k,l)})$. In Lemma 12.11 we will show that

$$\mu\left(U^{(k,l)}\right) \lesssim \begin{cases} 2^{-(k-l)} & l \le k \\ 2^{-3(l-k)} & l > k \end{cases}, \qquad k, l = 1, \ldots, r, \tag{11.24}$$

in the case of the discrete Fourier–Haar wavelet problem. This formalizes the informal arguments given in §11.1.3: the local coherences are order one on the diagonal blocks of U, and decrease exponentially as $|k-l|$ increases (recall Fig. 11.2). Taking (11.24) and substituting it into (11.17) also yields the measurement condition

$$m_k \gtrsim \left(s_k + \sum_{l=1}^{k-1} s_l 2^{-(k-l)} + \sum_{l=k+1}^{r} s_l 2^{-3(l-k)} \right) \cdot L, \qquad k = 1, \ldots, r, \tag{11.25}$$

where $L = \log(N) \cdot (\log(N/\varepsilon) + \log(\log(N)s) \cdot \log(\log(N)s/\varepsilon))$ (note that $r = \log_2(N) + 1$ in this case). By convention, the first sum vanishes when $k = 1$ and likewise for the second sum when $k = r$.

This guarantee, and its various generalizations, are discussed further in Part IV in the context of imaging, where they play a key role in the matter of sampling strategy design. But for now, we merely note that it implies that the number of samples m_k in the kth sampling level should be proportional to s_k, the corresponding local sparsity in the kth sparsity level, plus terms involving the other local sparsities s_l multiplied by exponentially decaying factors in $|k-l|$. Hence, the number of measurements used to recover the wavelets at scale k is primarily influenced by the local sparsity in that and the nearby levels. In particular, this explains the results of the flip test. Globally permuting the wavelet coefficients changes the s_ks, which can cause the situation to arise where there are no longer enough measurements m_k in some level to satisfy (11.25). The result, as seen, is worse recovery in the flipped case.

Notes

The systematic study of the Fourier-wavelets recovery problem in compressed sensing arguably began with the seminal work of Lustig, Donoho & Pauly on compressed sensing for MRI [336]; see also [335, 337]. They observed both poor recovery from uniform random sampling and the improvement offered by variable-density sampling (see Fig. 11.1). Intuitive arguments for variable-density sampling were given in terms of the energy of natural images concentrating at low frequencies, and the tendency of their wavelet coefficients to be sparser at fine scales than at coarse scales, i.e. asymptotic sparsity (see Fig. 11.11). While the local coherence of the Fourier-wavelet matrix was not investigated, the so-called *transformed point spread function* was studied in terms of *interference* between the wavelet and Fourier domains. This is similar to the cross-coherence (5.41). Variable-density sampling was empirically shown to yield smaller interference artefacts than uniform random sampling.

The flip test was introduced in [20] and the flip test in levels was first shown in [51]. See [21] for a flip test for discrete gradient sparsity. A similar experiment to the flip test in levels was previously performed by Choi & Baraniuk [144] to illustrate the limitations of the Besov space model for wavelet-based modelling of real-world images. For a discussion of tree structure and statistical persistence across scales of wavelet coefficients, see [144, 160].

The flip test shows the influence of the sparsity structure when reconstructing from Fourier, but not Gaussian, measurements with orthonormal wavelet sparsifying transforms. As remarked in the Notes section of Chapter 5, structured sparsity (albeit of a different nature) also plays a role when using redundant sparsifying transforms (see

§4.5) in combination with analysis ℓ^1-minimization (3.3). This occurs even with Gaussian measurements [226], unlike in the case of orthonormal sparsifying transforms.

Sparsity in levels was introduced in [20] (see also [21]), although the notion of breaking a sparse vector up into different regions and measuring the local sparsities can be found elsewhere in the literature. In particular, some of the early work in compressed sensing by Tsaig & Donoho [470] considers sampling and recovery of wavelet scales separately, allowing for different sparsities within them. In [418] Romberg considered what is now referred to as two-level sparsity in combination with DCT and noiselet measurements for the coarse and fine wavelet scales, respectively. Separate sensing of the wavelet scales was later considered in [120] in the context of Fourier sampling. The procedures [120, 470] are rather impractical, however, since they require direct sensing of individual wavelet scales. Wang & Arce [490] used a similar idea to design empirical Fourier sampling patterns based on certain statistical models for wavelet coefficients.

Besides wavelet sparsity, sparsity in levels can also be used to model sparse vectors whose nonzero entries are spread out. These are sometimes referred to as *sparse and distributed* or *sparse and balanced* vectors. They have found applications in parallel acquisition systems [146] and compressive radar [184]. Two-level sparsity also arises in the compressed sensing with sparse corruptions problem that was discussed in the Notes section of Chapter 6. As shown in [5, 323], measuring separately the sparsity s in the signal x and k in the corruption u allows for tighter recovery guarantees than a single sparsity measure of the augmented signal (the concatenation of x and u).

Sampling with isotropic families of vectors is due to Candès & Plan [118]. Randomly subsampled Fourier matrices were used in some of the earliest papers on compressed sensing [121], and randomly subsampled unitary matrices were considered in [120, 123] (see Example 11.5). Sampling with isotropic families is similar to, although more general than, the concept of *bounded orthonormal systems* [214, Chpt. 12]. A bounded orthonormal system is a set of orthonormal, complex-valued functions $\{\phi_1, \ldots, \phi_N\}$, defined on a set $\mathcal{D} \subseteq \mathbb{R}^d$ with a probability measure ν, that satisfy

$$\sup_{t \in \mathcal{D}} |\phi_j(t)| \leq K, \quad j = 1, \ldots, N,$$

for some constant $K < \infty$. Random sampling with a bounded orthonormal system corresponds to the measurement matrix $A = \frac{1}{\sqrt{m}}(\phi_j(t_i))_{i,j=1}^{m,N}$, where $t_1, \ldots, t_m$ are drawn i.i.d. according to ν. This is a special case of sampling with an isotropic family, in which $\mathcal{A}$ consists of the vectors $(\phi_j(t))_{j=1}^{N}$ with t distributed according to ν. Note that the coherence $\mu(\mathcal{A}) = K^2$ in this case.

Sampling with collections of jointly isotropic families was first presented in [6]. Multilevel subsampled unitary matrices were introduced rather earlier in [20].

For details of the coupon collector problem, see [364, Chpt. 3]. Saturation, introduced in §11.4.4, unifies several notions that have appeared previously; for instance, [418], the half–half scheme of [453] and the two-level scheme of [20].

The coherence $\mu(\mathcal{A})$ of an isotropic family $\mathcal{A}$ is from [118]. We note in passing that the stipulation that (11.10) holds almost surely may be too strong in practice. For example, it excludes Gaussian random matrices (Example 11.8). In [118] it was shown that one can relax this to a statement in probability. Specifically, let E be the event $\{\|a\|_{\ell^\infty}^2 \leq \mu\}$. Then one can take $\mu(\mathcal{A})$ to be the smallest number μ such that

$$\mathbb{E}\left(N^{-1}\|a\|_{\ell^2}^2 \mathbb{I}_{E^c}\right) \leq \frac{1}{20} N^{-3/2}, \qquad \mathbb{P}(E^c) \leq \frac{1}{mN}.$$

It is a simple exercise to show that with this definition the coherence of the family of Example 11.8 satisfies $\mu(\mathcal{A}) \lesssim \log(N)$.

Local coherence has its origins in [20]. Definition 11.19 is from [146]. The term *local coherence* has also been defined elsewhere as the maximum ℓ^∞-norm of the rows of a unitary matrix [301, 302, 407]. This motivates subsampling the rows of this matrix nonuniformly according to a probability distribution proportional to this local coherence. See also [400]. After scaling the rows corresponding to the probabilities (see Example 11.6), this is precisely the coherence $\mu(\mathcal{A})$ of the corresponding isotropic family $\mathcal{A}$. Note that this notion of coherence is local with respect to the matrix rows only. Unlike Definition 11.19, it does not consider variations across the matrix columns, which is important for the sparsity in levels model.

The one-dimensional discrete Fourier–Haar wavelet problem was developed formally in a compressed sensing context in [120], and later in [22]. Dividing frequency space into separate bands $B_1, \ldots, B_r$ related to the wavelet scales, as we did in §11.6, was introduced in [120].

Finally, we note that the model of sampling from a jointly isotropic collection of families of random vectors in $\mathbb{C}^N$ can easily be generalized to sampling from families of $\mathbb{C}^{N \times d_i}$ matrices. The idea of randomly drawing matrices rather than vectors was introduced by Boyer, Weiss & Bigot in [93] and referred to as *block sampling*. See also [6, 71, 91, 146]. It models more practical acquisition systems where only groups (or blocks) of measurements can be acquired, rather than individual measurements. This situation arises in applications such as MRI. As discussed in Chapters 3 and 4, frequencies in MRI are sampled along smooth curves in k-space, rather than individually. In this instance, each block of measurements corresponds to the frequencies sampled along one smooth curve.

12 Local Structure and Nonuniform Recovery

We now turn our attention to establishing recovery guarantees for the framework introduced in the previous chapter. The corresponding measurement conditions relate the number of measurements m (or $\mathbf{m} = (m_1, \ldots, m_r)$ in the context of multilevel random sampling) to parameters such as the sparsity s or local sparsities $\mathbf{s} = (s_1, \ldots, s_r)$. Following the discussion in §5.5, this chapter focuses on nonuniform recovery guarantees, while Chapter 13 considers uniform guarantees.

For the sparsity in levels model, it transpires that the measurement conditions we derive for QCBP fall some ways short of those for the oracle least-squares estimator based on prior knowledge of the support set Δ (recall §5.8). Fortunately, this can be overcome by using a variant of QCBP, wherein the ℓ^1-norm is replaced by a weighted ℓ^1-norm. This is introduced in §12.1. Note that this is quite different to the reweighting procedure discussed in §4.6. Next, in §12.2 we derive a completely local recovery guarantee, before applying it in §12.3 and §12.4 to the sparse and sparse in levels models respectively. In particular, for the sparse model, unweighted QCBP and any jointly isotropic collection $C = \{\mathcal{A}_i\}_{i=1}^m$ (Definition 11.4), we show the measurement condition

$$m \gtrsim s \cdot \mu(C) \cdot (\log(N/\varepsilon) + \log(s) \cdot \log(s/\varepsilon)),$$

where $\mu(C)$ is as in Definition 11.17. This implies Theorem 5.30. Next, for the sparse in levels model and weighted QCBP with suitable weights, we show that

$$m \gtrsim \max_{i:|\mathcal{A}_i|>1} \left\{ \sum_{l=1}^{r} s_l \mu_l(\mathcal{A}_i) \right\} \cdot L,$$

measurements suffice, where the $\mu_l(\mathcal{A}_i)$ are the local coherences (Definition 11.19) and L is a log factor. As we explain later in §12.6, this condition is comparable to that of the corresponding oracle estimator. In §12.5 we specialize this result to the discrete Fourier–Haar wavelet problem introduced in §11.6. This leads to the measurement condition

$$m_k \gtrsim \left(s_k + \sum_{l=1}^{k-1} s_l 2^{-(k-l)} + \sum_{l=k+1}^{r} s_l 2^{-3(l-k)} \right) \cdot L, \quad k = 1, \ldots, r.$$

For later use, in §12.5.2 we also discuss the Fourier–Haar wavelet problem in the context of the sparse model using power-law sampling (recall §11.2.1).

After discussing oracle estimators in §12.6 and giving proofs of the main results in §12.7 and §12.8, in the final section, §12.9, we briefly return to the unweighted QCBP decoder. We demonstrate that better measurement conditions are achievable under the assumption that the signs of the entries of the vector to be recovered are random.

12.1 Weighted ℓ^1-Minimization

Let $w = (w_i)_{i=1}^N \in \mathbb{R}^N$ be a vector of weights, where each $w_i > 0$ is strictly positive. The weighted ℓ^1_w-norm is defined as

$$\|z\|_{\ell^1_w} = \sum_{i=1}^N w_i |z_i|, \quad z = (z_i)_{i=1}^N \in \mathbb{C}^N.$$

We now consider the weighted QCBP problem

$$\min_{z \in \mathbb{C}^N} \|z\|_{\ell^1_w} \text{ subject to } \|Az - y\|_{\ell^2} \leq \eta. \tag{12.1}$$

We could, though, consider weighted versions of any of the decoders discussed in Chapter 6 instead. Our first recovery guarantee (Theorem 12.4) applies to general weight vectors w. However, when considering the sparse in levels model, we restrict our attention to weights that are constant on each level. Specifically, if $\mathbf{M} = (M_1, \ldots, M_r)$ are the sparsity levels then we consider weights of the form

$$w_{M_{l-1}+1} = \cdots = w_{M_l} = w^{(l)}, \qquad l = 1, \ldots, r, \tag{12.2}$$

where $w^{(1)}, \ldots, w^{(r)} > 0$. In accordance with $\mathbf{s}$ and $\mathbf{M}$, we write $\mathbf{w} = (w^{(1)}, \ldots, w^{(r)})$.

Remark 12.1 As discussed in §4.6, weights in the regularization term constitute a prior on anticipated support of the vector. A small weight w_i at index $i \in \{1, \ldots, N\}$ reflects a belief that the index i lies in the support of x. In this sense, it is not surprising that for the sparse in levels model the weights should take the form (12.2). This model constrains the sparse vector x to having specific local sparsities $\mathbf{s} = (s_1, \ldots, s_r)$, but within each level does not constrain the locations of the nonzero entries. The weights $\mathbf{w}$ are therefore used to exploit the inter-level, as opposed to intra-level, variations in the sparsity. In particular, we find later that an optimal choice of weights (in the sense that it gives the best measurement condition) takes the form

$$w^{(l)} = \sqrt{s/s_l}, \quad l = 1, \ldots, r. \tag{12.3}$$

The error bounds for the weighted decoder (12.1) with the sparse in levels model involve the best $(\mathbf{s}, \mathbf{M})$-term approximation error measured in the ℓ^1_w-norm. Generalizing (11.6), we now write

$$\sigma_{\mathbf{s},\mathbf{M}}(x)_{\ell^1_w} = \inf\left\{\|x - z\|_{\ell^1_w} : z \in \Sigma_{\mathbf{s},\mathbf{M}}\right\} \tag{12.4}$$

for this error. Similar to (11.7), if the weights are given by (12.2) then

$$\sigma_{\mathbf{s},\mathbf{M}}(x)_{\ell^1_w} = \sum_{l=1}^r w^{(l)} \sigma_{s_l}(x^{(l)})_{\ell^1},$$

where $x^{(l)} = P_{M_l}^{M_{l-1}} x$ is the restriction of x to the lth sparsity level and $\sigma_{s_l}(x)_{\ell^1}$ is the error of the best s_l-term approximation to $x^{(l)}$ in the unweighted ℓ^1-norm.

12.2 Local Recovery Guarantee

We now present our first recovery guarantee for (12.1). This result does not assume a *model* (e.g. the sparse or sparse in levels model) for the unknown vector $x \in \mathbb{C}^N$. It allows the approximate support set $\Delta \subseteq \{1, \ldots, N\}$ to be arbitrary and then relates the number of measurements m to intrinsic properties of the sampling operator and the set Δ – in particular, two local coherence quantities relative to Δ. For this reason, we refer to this result as a *local* recovery guarantee. Results for the sparse and sparse in levels models follow in §12.3 and §12.4, respectively by analysing these local coherences in the case when Δ corresponds to an s-sparse or $(\mathbf{s}, \mathbf{M})$-sparse support set.

Definition 12.2 Let $\Delta \subseteq \{1, \ldots, N\}$ and $C = \{\mathcal{A}_i\}_{i=1}^m$ be a jointly isotropic collection (Definition 11.4). The *first local coherence of C relative to Δ* is the smallest constant $\Pi(C, \Delta)$ such that

$$\|P_\Delta a_i\|_{\ell^2}^2 \leq \Pi(C, \Delta),$$

almost surely for $a_i \sim \mathcal{A}_i$ and for each $1 \leq i \leq m$ such that $|\mathcal{A}_i| > 1$.

Given weights $w = (w_i)_{i=1}^N$, we now also let

$$W = \operatorname{diag}(w_1, w_2, \ldots, w_N) \in \mathbb{C}^{N \times N}. \tag{12.5}$$

Definition 12.3 Let $w \in \mathbb{C}^N$ be a set of weights, $\Delta \subseteq \{1, \ldots, N\}$ and $C = \{\mathcal{A}_i\}_{i=1}^m$ be a jointly isotropic collection. The *second local coherence of C relative to Δ* with respect to the weights w is

$$\Gamma(C, \Delta, w) = \max\{\Gamma_1(C, \Delta, w), \Gamma_2(C, \Delta, w)\},$$

where $\Gamma_1(C, \Delta, w)$ and $\Gamma_2(C, \Delta, w)$ are the smallest constants such that

$$\|W^{-1} a_i\|_{\ell^\infty} \|W P_\Delta a_i\|_{\ell^1} \leq \Gamma_1(C, \Delta, w),$$

almost surely for $a_i \sim \mathcal{A}_i$ and each $1 \leq i \leq m$ such that $|\mathcal{A}_i| > 1$, and

$$\sup_{\substack{z \in \mathbb{C}^N \\ \|z\|_{\ell^\infty} = 1}} \max_{j=1,\ldots,N} \mathbb{E}\left(m^{-1} \sum_{i : |\mathcal{A}_i| > 1} |\langle e_j, W^{-1} a_i \rangle|^2 \, |\langle z, W P_\Delta a_i \rangle|^2 \right) \leq \Gamma_2(C, \Delta, w),$$

where $a_i \sim \mathcal{A}_i$ for $i = 1, \ldots, m$ and the expectation is taken over all the a_is.

Since C is jointly isotropic, $\|P_\Delta x\|_{\ell^2}^2 = m^{-1} \sum_{i=1}^m \mathbb{E}|\langle P_\Delta a_i, P_\Delta x \rangle|^2 \leq \|P_\Delta x\|_{\ell^2}^2 \Pi(C, \Delta)$, $\forall x \in \mathbb{C}^N$. Hence $\Pi(C, \Delta) \geq 1$. We also have

$$1 \leq \Pi(C, \Delta) \leq \Gamma_1(C, \Delta, w) \leq \Gamma(C, \Delta, w), \tag{12.6}$$

for all w. The reason for defining both $\Gamma(C, \Delta, w)$ and $\Pi(C, \Delta)$ will become clear later.

We now present the main result of this section. For this, we also define the *weighted cardinality* of a set $\Delta \subseteq \{1, \ldots, N\}$ to be

$$|\Delta|_w = \sum_{i \in \Delta} w_i^2. \tag{12.7}$$

Note that if $w_i = 1, \forall i$, then $|\Delta|_w = |\Delta|$ is just the cardinality of Δ.

Theorem 12.4 (Local nonuniform recovery guarantee) *Let $0 < \varepsilon < 1$, $N \geq 2$, $\Delta \subseteq \{1, \ldots, N\}$ with $|\Delta| \geq 2$, $x \in \mathbb{C}^N$, $C = \{\mathcal{A}_i\}_{i=1}^m$ be a jointly isotropic collection, $A \in \mathbb{C}^{m \times N}$ be as in (11.9) and $w = (w_i)_{i=1}^N$ be weights with $w_i \geq 1$, $\forall i$. Suppose that*

$$m \gtrsim \Pi(C, \Delta) \cdot \log(N/\varepsilon) + \Gamma(C, \Delta, w) \cdot \left(\log(N/\varepsilon) + \log(|\Delta|_w) \cdot \log(|\Delta|_w/\varepsilon)\right). \quad (12.8)$$

Then the following holds with probability at least $1 - \varepsilon$. For all $y = Ax + e \in \mathbb{C}^m$, every minimizer $\hat{x} \in \mathbb{C}^N$ of (12.1) with parameter $\eta \geq \|e\|_{\ell^2}$ satisfies

$$\|\hat{x} - x\|_{\ell^2} \lesssim \|x - P_\Delta x\|_{\ell^1_w} + \sqrt{|\Delta|_w}\eta. \quad (12.9)$$

We defer the proof of this theorem until §12.8. Observe that we require $w_i \geq 1$ for this result. This can always be ensured by a rescaling, since rescaling leaves the optimization problem (12.1) unchanged. The quantity $\Gamma(C, \Delta, w)$ is also unchanged by such a rescaling.

12.3 The Sparse Model

As noted above, Theorem 12.4 does not impose a signal model on the vector x. The set Δ, although fixed in advance of drawing the measurement matrix A, can be arbitrary. To obtain a recovery guarantee for the sparse model, we let Δ be the set of cardinality s corresponding to the largest s indices of x in absolute value and then estimate the local coherences $\Pi(C, \Delta)$ and $\Gamma(C, \Delta, w)$ in terms of s.

> In the sparse model, the measurement condition for unweighted QCBP is determined by the sparsity s and the coherence $\mu(C)$ of C (Definition 11.17).

Specifically, we have the following:

Corollary 12.5 (Sparse model, nonuniform recovery) *Let $0 < \varepsilon < 1$, $N \geq s \geq 2$, $x \in \mathbb{C}^N$, $C = \{\mathcal{A}_i\}_{i=1}^m$ be a jointly isotropic collection and $A \in \mathbb{C}^{m \times N}$ be as in (11.9). Suppose that*

$$m \gtrsim s \cdot \mu(C) \cdot (\log(N/\varepsilon) + \log(s) \cdot \log(s/\varepsilon)), \quad (12.10)$$

where $\mu(C)$ is the coherence of C. Then the following holds with probability at least $1 - \varepsilon$. For all $y = Ax + e \in \mathbb{C}^m$, every minimizer $\hat{x} \in \mathbb{C}^N$ of the unweighted QCBP problem (5.18) with parameter $\eta \geq \|e\|_{\ell^2}$ satisfies

$$\|\hat{x} - x\|_{\ell^2} \lesssim \sigma_s(x)_{\ell^1} + \sqrt{s}\eta, \quad (12.11)$$

where $\sigma_s(x)_{\ell^1}$ is the ℓ^1-norm best s-term approximation error (5.6).

Proof Let $\Delta \subseteq \{1, \ldots, N\}$, $|\Delta| = s$, be such that $\|x - P_\Delta x\|_{\ell^1} = \sigma_s(x)_{\ell^1}$. We apply Theorem 12.4 with this choice of Δ and with weights $w_i = 1$. Note that (12.9) gives the desired error bound. Hence it remains to estimate the local coherences in (12.8).

Suppose that $a_i \sim \mathcal{A}_i$. Then $\|a_i\|_{\ell^\infty} \|P_\Delta a_i\|_{\ell^1} \leq s\mu(\mathcal{A}_i)$ almost surely, where $\mu(\mathcal{A}_i)$ is as in Definition 11.16. Hence, using the definition of $\mu(C)$ and (12.6), we get

$$\Pi(C, \Delta) \leq \Gamma_1(C, \Delta, 1) \leq s\mu(C), \quad (12.12)$$

where 1 denotes the vector of ones. Next let $z \in \mathbb{C}^N$, $\|z\|_{\ell^\infty} = 1$, and $1 \le j \le N$. Then

$$\mathbb{E}\left(\sum_{i:|\mathcal{A}_i|>1} |\langle e_j, a_i \rangle|^2 |\langle z, P_\Delta a_i \rangle|^2 \right) \le \sum_{i=1}^{m} \mu(\mathcal{A}_i) \mathbb{E} |\langle P_\Delta z, a_i \rangle|^2$$
$$\le m\mu(C) \|P_\Delta z\|_{\ell^2}^2 \le m\mu(C)s.$$

Here, in the penultimate step we use the fact that C is jointly isotropic and therefore $\sum_{i=1}^{m} \mathbb{E}|\langle P_\Delta z, a_i \rangle|^2 = m\|P_\Delta z\|_{\ell^2}^2$. This gives $\Gamma_2(C, \Delta, 1) \le s\mu(C)$. We deduce that

$$\Gamma(C, \Delta, 1) = \max\{\Gamma_1(C, \Delta, 1), \Gamma_2(C, \Delta, 1)\} \le s\mu(C). \tag{12.13}$$

Hence (12.10) implies (12.8), and the result now follows from Theorem 12.4. □

As expected in light of Remark 12.1, no weights are required in this result. We note also that the proof of Theorem 5.30 now follows immediately.

Proof of Theorem 5.30 Recall from Example 11.5 that a randomly subsampled unitary matrix corresponds to sampling with a particular jointly isotropic collection C, where, as shown in (11.11), the coherence $\mu(C) = \mu(U)$. We now apply Corollary 12.5. □

12.4 The Sparse in Levels Model

We next consider the sparse in levels model with sparsity levels $\mathbf{M}$, local sparsities $\mathbf{s}$ and total sparsity $s = s_1 + \cdots + s_r$. For our first result we require one additional piece of notation. If $\mathcal{A}$ is a random family, $a \sim \mathcal{A}$ and $\Sigma_{\mathbf{s},\mathbf{M}}$ is as in Definition 11.2, then we let

$$\tau(\mathcal{A}) = \tau(\mathcal{A}; \mathbf{s}, \mathbf{M}) = \sup\left\{ m^{-1}\mathbb{E}|\langle z, a \rangle|^2 : \|z\|_{\ell^\infty} = 1,\ z \in \Sigma_{\mathbf{s},\mathbf{M}} \right\}. \tag{12.14}$$

Corollary 12.6 (Sparse in levels model, nonuniform recovery I) *Let $0 < \varepsilon < 1$, $N \ge s \ge 2$, $x \in \mathbb{C}^N$, $C = \{\mathcal{A}_i\}_{i=1}^m$ be a jointly isotropic collection and A be as in (11.9). Suppose that*

$$m \gtrsim \max_{i:|\mathcal{A}_i|>1} \left\{ \sum_{l=1}^{r} s_l \sqrt{\mu_l(\mathcal{A}_i; \mathbf{M}) \mu(\mathcal{A}_i)} \right\} \cdot L, \tag{12.15}$$

where $L = \log(N/\varepsilon) + \log(s) \cdot \log(s/\varepsilon)$, and

$$m \gtrsim \left(\sum_{i:|\mathcal{A}_i|>1} \mu_l(\mathcal{A}_i; \mathbf{M}) \tau(\mathcal{A}_i; \mathbf{s}, \mathbf{M}) \right) \cdot L, \qquad l = 1, \ldots, r, \tag{12.16}$$

where $\mu_l(\mathcal{A}_i; \mathbf{M})$ is the lth local coherence (Definition 11.19) and $\tau(\mathcal{A}_i; \mathbf{s}, \mathbf{M})$ is as in (12.14). Then the following holds with probability at least $1-\varepsilon$. For all $y = Ax + e \in \mathbb{C}^m$, every minimizer $\hat{x} \in \mathbb{C}^N$ of (5.17) with parameter $\eta \ge \|e\|_{\ell^2}$ satisfies

$$\|\hat{x} - x\|_{\ell^2} \lesssim \sigma_{\mathbf{s},\mathbf{M}}(x)_{\ell^1} + \sqrt{s}\eta, \tag{12.17}$$

where $\sigma_{\mathbf{s},\mathbf{M}}(x)_{\ell^1}$ is the ℓ^1-norm best $(\mathbf{s}, \mathbf{M})$-term approximation error (11.6).

Proof We use Theorem 12.4 with $\Delta \in D_{\mathbf{s},\mathbf{M}}$ chosen so that $\|x - P_\Delta x\|_{\ell^1} = \sigma_{\mathbf{s},\mathbf{M}}(x)_{\ell^1}$, where $D_{\mathbf{s},\mathbf{M}}$ is as in (11.5). As in the previous corollary, we need to estimate the local coherences relative to Δ. Write $\Delta = \Delta_1 \cup \cdots \cup \Delta_r$ with $\Delta_k \subseteq \{M_{k-1}+1, \ldots, M_k\}$, $|\Delta_k| = s_k$, and let $a_i \sim \mathcal{A}_i$. Then

$$\|P_\Delta a_i\|_{\ell^2}^2 = \sum_{l=1}^r \|P_{\Delta_l} a_i\|_{\ell^2}^2 \leq \sum_{l=1}^r s_l \|P_{M_l}^{M_{l-1}} a_i\|_{\ell^\infty}^2 \leq \sum_{l=1}^r s_l \mu_l(\mathcal{A}_i),$$

almost surely. Hence

$$\Pi(C, \Delta) \leq \max_{i:|\mathcal{A}_i|>1} \left\{ \sum_{l=1}^r s_l \mu_l(\mathcal{A}_i) \right\} \leq \max_{i:|\mathcal{A}_i|>1} \left\{ \sum_{l=1}^r s_l \sqrt{\mu_l(\mathcal{A}_i)\mu(\mathcal{A}_i)} \right\}. \tag{12.18}$$

Similarly,

$$\|a_i\|_{\ell^\infty} \|P_\Delta a_i\|_{\ell^1} \leq \sqrt{\mu(\mathcal{A}_i)} \sum_{l=1}^r \|P_{\Delta_l} a_i\|_{\ell^1} \leq \sqrt{\mu(\mathcal{A}_i)} \sum_{l=1}^r s_l \sqrt{\mu_l(\mathcal{A}_i)},$$

almost surely, and therefore

$$\Gamma_1(C, \Delta, 1) \leq \max_{i:|\mathcal{A}_i|>1} \left\{ \sum_{l=1}^r s_l \sqrt{\mu_l(\mathcal{A}_i)\mu(\mathcal{A}_i)} \right\}. \tag{12.19}$$

Finally, we consider $\Gamma_2(C, \Delta, 1)$. Let $z \in \mathbb{C}^N$ with $\|z\|_{\ell^\infty} = 1$ and $1 \leq j \leq N$. Let l be such that $M_{l-1} < j \leq M_l$. Then

$$\begin{aligned} \mathbb{E}\left(m^{-1} \sum_{i:|\mathcal{A}_i|>1} |\langle e_j, a_i \rangle|^2 |\langle z, P_\Delta a_i \rangle|^2 \right) &\leq m^{-1} \sum_{i:|\mathcal{A}_i|>1} \mu_l(\mathcal{A}_i) \mathbb{E}_{\mathcal{A}_i} |\langle P_\Delta z, a_i \rangle|^2 \\ &\leq \sum_{i:|\mathcal{A}_i|>1} \mu_l(\mathcal{A}_i) \tau(\mathcal{A}_i), \end{aligned}$$

and hence

$$\Gamma_2(C, \Delta, 1) \leq \max_{l=1,\ldots,r} \left\{ \sum_{i:|\mathcal{A}_i|>1} \mu_l(\mathcal{A}_i) \tau(\mathcal{A}_i) \right\}.$$

The result now follows from Theorem 12.4. □

Although this result produces an error bound (12.17) of the right form, i.e. involving the best $(\mathbf{s}, \mathbf{M})$-term approximation error $\sigma_{\mathbf{s},\mathbf{M}}(x)_{\ell^1}$, the second measurement condition (12.16) is quite opaque. In particular, it is not clear how large the $\tau(\mathcal{A}_i; \mathbf{s}, \mathbf{M})$s are in practice and whether or not they relate to the local coherences $\mu_l(\mathcal{A}_i; \mathbf{M})$ and local sparsities s_l. In §12.5, we provide estimates for these factors in the case of the Fourier–Haar wavelet problem. Fortunately, however, the incorporation of weights in the decoder allows us to avoid these factors altogether:

> In the sparse in levels model, the measurement condition for weighted QCBP (with suitable weights) is determined by the local sparsities s_l and coherences $\mu_l(\mathcal{A}_i; \mathbf{M})$.

Specifically, we have the following:

Corollary 12.7 (Sparse in levels model, nonuniform recovery II) *Let $0 < \varepsilon < 1$, $N \geq s \geq 2$, $x \in \mathbb{C}^N$, $C = \{\mathcal{A}_i\}_{i=1}^m$ be a jointly isotropic collection, A be as in (11.9), $w = (w_i)_{i=1}^N$ be weights of the form (12.2) where $w^{(l)} \geq 1$, $\forall l$, and $\mathbf{w} = (w^{(1)}, \ldots, w^{(r)})$. Suppose that*

$$m \gtrsim \left(\max_{i:|\mathcal{A}_i|>1} \left\{ \xi(\mathbf{s}, \mathbf{w}) \sum_{l=1}^{r} \frac{\mu_l(\mathcal{A}_i; \mathbf{M})}{(w^{(l)})^2} + \sum_{l=1}^{r} s_l \mu_l(\mathcal{A}_i; \mathbf{M}) \right\} \right) \cdot L, \tag{12.20}$$

where $L = \log(N/\varepsilon) + \log(\xi) \cdot \log(\xi/\varepsilon)$ and $\xi = \xi(\mathbf{s}, \mathbf{w}) = \sum_{k=1}^{r} (w^{(k)})^2 s_k$. Then the following holds with probability at least $1 - \varepsilon$. For all $y = Ax + e \in \mathbb{C}^m$, every minimizer $\hat{x} \in \mathbb{C}^N$ of (12.1) with parameter $\eta \geq \|e\|_{\ell^2}$ satisfies

$$\|\hat{x} - x\|_{\ell^2} \lesssim \sigma_{\mathbf{s},\mathbf{M}}(x)_{\ell^1_w} + \sqrt{\xi}\eta, \tag{12.21}$$

where $\sigma_{\mathbf{s},\mathbf{M}}(x)_{\ell^1_w}$ is the ℓ^1_w-norm best $(\mathbf{s}, \mathbf{M})$-term approximation error (12.4). In particular, if $\mathbf{w}$ is chosen as in (12.3) then (12.20) reduces to

$$m \gtrsim \max_{i:|\mathcal{A}_i|>1} \left\{ \sum_{l=1}^{r} s_l \mu_l(\mathcal{A}_i) \right\} \cdot L, \tag{12.22}$$

where $L = r \cdot (\log(N/\varepsilon) + \log(rs) \cdot \log(rs/\varepsilon))$.

Proof Let $\Delta \in D_{\mathbf{s},\mathbf{M}}$ be such that $\|x - P_\Delta x\|_{\ell^1_w} = \sigma_{\mathbf{s},\mathbf{M}}(x)_{\ell^1_w}$ and write $\Delta = \Delta_1 \cup \cdots \cup \Delta_r$ as before. If $a_i \sim \mathcal{A}_i$ then

$$\begin{aligned}
\|W^{-1} a_i\|_{\ell^\infty} \|W P_\Delta a_i\|_{\ell^1} &= \max_{k=1,\ldots,r} \left\{ \frac{\|P_{M_k}^{M_{k-1}} a_i\|_{\ell^\infty}}{w^{(k)}} \right\} \sum_{l=1}^{r} w^{(l)} \|P_{\Delta_l} a_i\|_{\ell^1} \\
&\leq \max_{k=1,\ldots,r} \left\{ \frac{\sqrt{\mu_k(\mathcal{A}_i)}}{w^{(k)}} \right\} \sum_{l=1}^{r} w^{(l)} s_l \sqrt{\mu_l(\mathcal{A}_i)} \\
&\leq \sqrt{\sum_{k=1}^{r} \frac{\mu_k(\mathcal{A}_i)}{(w^{(k)})^2}} \sqrt{\sum_{l=1}^{r} (w^{(l)})^2 s_l} \sqrt{\sum_{l=1}^{r} s_l \mu_l(\mathcal{A}_i)}.
\end{aligned}$$

Therefore

$$\Gamma_1(C, \Delta, w) \leq \max_{i:|\mathcal{A}_i|>1} \left\{ \sqrt{\xi} \sqrt{\sum_{k=1}^{r} \frac{\mu_k(\mathcal{A}_i)}{(w^{(k)})^2}} \sqrt{\sum_{l=1}^{r} s_l \mu_l(\mathcal{A}_i)} \right\}. \tag{12.23}$$

Now consider $\Gamma_2(C, \Delta, w)$. Let $z \in \mathbb{C}^N$ with $\|z\|_{\ell^\infty} = 1$ and $1 \le j \le N$. Then

$$\begin{aligned}
\mathbb{E}\left(m^{-1} \sum_{i:|\mathcal{A}_i|>1}^{m} |\langle e_j, W^{-1} a_i\rangle|^2 |\langle z, W P_\Delta a_i\rangle|^2\right)
&\le m^{-1} \max_{i:|\mathcal{A}_i|>1} \max_{k=1,\dots,r} \left\{\frac{\mu_k(\mathcal{A}_i)}{(w^{(k)})^2}\right\} \sum_{i=1}^{m} \mathbb{E}_{\mathcal{A}_i} |\langle P_\Delta W z, a_i\rangle|^2 \\
&= \max_{i:|\mathcal{A}_i|>1} \max_{k=1,\dots,r} \left\{\frac{\mu_k(\mathcal{A}_i)}{(w^{(k)})^2}\right\} \|W P_\Delta z\|_{\ell^2}^2 \\
&\le \max_{i:|\mathcal{A}_i|>1} \left\{\sum_{k=1}^{r} \frac{\mu_k(\mathcal{A}_i)}{(w^{(k)})^2}\right\} \left(\sum_{l=1}^{r} (w^{(l)})^2 s_l\right).
\end{aligned}$$

Hence

$$\Gamma_2(C, \Delta, w) \le \max_{i:|\mathcal{A}_i|>1} \left\{\xi \sum_{k=1}^{r} \frac{\mu_k(\mathcal{A}_i)}{(w^{(k)})^2}\right\}.$$

Young's inequality (5.12), (12.6), (12.23) and the definition of $\Gamma(C, \Delta, w)$ give

$$\Pi(C, \Delta) \le \Gamma(C, \Delta, w) \le \max_{i:|\mathcal{A}_i|>1} \left\{\xi \sum_{k=1}^{r} \frac{\mu_k(\mathcal{A}_i)}{(w^{(k)})^2} + \sum_{l=1}^{r} s_l \mu_l(\mathcal{A}_i)\right\}.$$

Applying Theorem 12.4 now yields the result. □

This result shows that (12.3) is generally a good choice of weights, since the measurement condition (12.20) now only involves the local coherences and sparsities. As we see later in §12.6, this condition is, up to the log factor, equivalent to that of the oracle estimator for the sparse in levels model.

In the next two results we specialize Corollaries 12.6 and 12.7 to the case of multilevel random sampling. Recall from §11.4.5 that such a measurement matrix arises from randomly sampling the rows of a unitary matrix $U \in \mathbb{C}^{N\times N}$ according to sampling levels $\mathbf{N} = (N_1, \dots, N_r)$ and local numbers of measurements $\mathbf{m} = (m_1, \dots, m_r)$. As in (11.15), we now also let

$$U^{(k,l)} = P_{N_k}^{N_{k-1}} U P_{M_l}^{M_{l-1}} \in \mathbb{C}^{(N_k - N_{k-1})\times(M_l - M_{l-1})} \tag{12.24}$$

denote the (k, l)th block of U.

Corollary 12.8 (Multilevel random sampling, nonuniform recovery I) *Let $0 < \varepsilon < 1$, $N \ge s \ge 2$, $x \in \mathbb{C}^N$, $U \in \mathbb{C}^{N\times N}$ be unitary and $A \in \mathbb{C}^{m\times N}$ be as in Definition 11.14. Suppose that*

$$m_k \gtrsim \left(\sum_{l=1}^{r} s_l \max_{j=1,\dots,r} \sqrt{\mu\left(U^{(k,l)}\right) \mu\left(U^{(k,j)}\right)}\right) \cdot L, \qquad k = 1, \dots, r \tag{12.25}$$

and

$$1 \gtrsim \sum_{\substack{k=1 \\ m_k < N_k - N_{k-1}}}^{r} \frac{\mu\left(U^{(k,l)}\right) \left(\sum_{j=1}^{r} \sqrt{s_j} \|U^{(k,j)}\|_{\ell^2}\right)^2}{m_k} \cdot L, \qquad l = 1, \dots, r, \tag{12.26}$$

where $L = \log(N/\varepsilon) + \log(s) \cdot \log(s/\varepsilon)$*. Then the following holds with probability at least* $1 - \varepsilon$*. For all* $y = Ax + e \in \mathbb{C}^m$*, every minimizer* $\hat{x} \in \mathbb{C}^N$ *of (5.17) with parameter* $\eta \geq \|e\|_{\ell^2}$ *satisfies*

$$\|\hat{x} - x\|_{\ell^2} \lesssim \sigma_{\mathbf{s},\mathbf{M}}(x)_{\ell^1} + \sqrt{s}\eta,$$

where $\sigma_{\mathbf{s},\mathbf{M}}(x)_{\ell^1}$ *is the* ℓ^1*-norm best* $(\mathbf{s}, \mathbf{M})$*-term approximation error (11.6).*

Proof We use Corollary 12.6. Recall from §11.4.5 that multilevel random sampling corresponds to sampling with a certain jointly isotropic collection C. We first estimate the local coherences for this collection. Let i be an index in the kth block of measurements. Then, in view of (11.16), we have

$$\mu_l(\mathcal{A}_i) = \mu_l(\mathcal{A}^{(k)}) \leq \frac{m}{m_k}\mu\left(U^{(k,l)}\right), \tag{12.27}$$

where $\mathcal{A}^{(k)}$ is as in §11.4.5. Note also that

$$\mu(\mathcal{A}_i) = \max_{j=1,\ldots,r} \mu_j(\mathcal{A}_i) \leq \frac{m}{m_k} \max_{j=1,\ldots,r} \mu\left(U^{(k,j)}\right), \tag{12.28}$$

and therefore (12.15) is implied by (12.25).

Next consider (12.14). By the definition of $\mathcal{A}^{(k)}$, we have

$$\tau(\mathcal{A}_i) = \tau(\mathcal{A}^{(k)}) = \sup\left\{\frac{1}{m_k}\sum_{i=N_{k-1}+1}^{N_k} |\langle u_i, z\rangle|^2 : \|z\|_{\ell^\infty} = 1,\ x \in \Sigma_{\mathbf{s},\mathbf{M}}\right\},$$

where $u_i = U^* e_i$. Observe that

$$\sqrt{\sum_{i=N_{k-1}}^{N_k} |\langle u_i, z\rangle|^2} = \|P_{N_k}^{N_{k-1}} U z\|_{\ell^2}$$
$$\leq \sum_{l=1}^{r} \|P_{N_k}^{N_{k-1}} U P_{M_l}^{M_{l-1}}\|_{\ell^2} \|P_{M_l}^{M_{l-1}} z\|_{\ell^2} \leq \sum_{l=1}^{r} \|U^{(k,l)}\|_{\ell^2}\sqrt{s_l},$$

for $z \in \Sigma_{\mathbf{s},\mathbf{M}}$ with $\|z\|_{\ell^\infty} = 1$. Hence

$$\tau(\mathcal{A}_i) = \tau(\mathcal{A}^{(k)}) \leq \frac{1}{m_k}\left(\sum_{l=1}^{r} \sqrt{s_l}\|U^{(k,l)}\|_{\ell^2}\right)^2. \tag{12.29}$$

This and (12.27) now imply that

$$\sum_{i:|\mathcal{A}_i|>1} \mu_l(\mathcal{A}_i)\tau(\mathcal{A}_i) \leq \sum_{k:m_k<N_k-N_{k-1}} m_k \frac{m}{m_k}\mu\left(U^{(k,l)}\right)\frac{1}{m_k}\left(\sum_{l=1}^{r}\sqrt{s_l}\|U^{(k,l)}\|_{\ell^2}\right)^2$$
$$= m \sum_{k:m_k<N_k-N_{k-1}} \frac{\mu\left(U^{(k,l)}\right)\left(\sum_{l=1}^{r}\sqrt{s_l}\|U^{(k,l)}\|_{\ell^2}\right)^2}{m_k}.$$

Hence (12.16) is implied by (12.26). □

As before, incorporating weights significantly simplifies matters. The following result shows that this leads to a sharper measurement condition, both without the second term (12.26) and with a simpler expression in place of (12.25).

Corollary 12.9 (Multilevel random sampling, nonuniform recovery II) *Let* $0 < \varepsilon < 1$, $N \geq s \geq 2$, $x \in \mathbb{C}^N$, $U \in \mathbb{C}^{N \times N}$ *be unitary,* $A \in \mathbb{C}^{m \times N}$ *be as in Definition 11.14 and* $w = (w_i)_{i=1}^N$ *be weights of the form (12.2) with the* $w^{(l)}$ *as in (12.3). Suppose that*

$$m_k \gtrsim \left(\sum_{l=1}^{r} s_l \mu \left(U^{(k,l)} \right) \right) \cdot L, \quad k = 1, \ldots, r, \tag{12.30}$$

where $L = r \cdot (\log(N/\varepsilon) + \log(rs) \cdot \log(rs/\varepsilon))$. *Then the following holds with probability at least* $1 - \varepsilon$. *For all* $y = Ax + e \in \mathbb{C}^m$, *every minimizer* $\hat{x} \in \mathbb{C}^N$ *of (12.1) with parameter* $\eta \geq \|e\|_{\ell^2}$ *satisfies*

$$\|\hat{x} - x\|_{\ell^2} \lesssim \sigma_{\mathbf{s},\mathbf{M}}(x)_{\ell^1_w} + \sqrt{rs}\eta,$$

where $\sigma_{\mathbf{s},\mathbf{M}}(x)_{\ell^1_w}$ *is the* ℓ^1_w*-norm best* $(\mathbf{s}, \mathbf{M})$*-term approximation error (12.4).*

Proof This follows immediately from Corollary 12.7 and (12.27). □

At this point, we repeat that for multilevel random sampling, conditions such as (12.25) and (12.30) are only meaningful when the right-hand side (including the constant c implied by the $\gtrsim$ symbol) is less than the size of the corresponding sampling level. Otherwise, we simply have $m_k = N_k - N_{k-1}$. See Remark 11.20.

12.5 The Fourier–Haar Wavelet Problem

We now apply these results to the one-dimensional discrete Fourier sampling problem with Haar wavelet sparsity that was previously introduced in §11.6. In this section, $U \in \mathbb{C}^{N \times N}$ is as in (11.18) and $N = 2^{r-1}$ for some $r \geq 2$.

12.5.1 Multilevel Random Sampling

We first consider sparsity in levels and multilevel random sampling.

Theorem 12.10 (Multilevel Fourier–Haar, nonuniform recovery) *Consider the one-dimensional Fourier–Haar wavelet problem with multilevel random sampling based on sampling levels* $\mathbf{N}$ *given by (11.21), and let the sparsity levels* $\mathbf{M}$ *be given by (11.19). Then conditions (12.25) and (12.26) of Corollary 12.8 are implied by*

$$m_k \gtrsim \left(s_k + \sum_{l=1}^{k-1} s_l 2^{-(k-l)/2} + \sum_{l=k+1}^{r} s_l 2^{-3(l-k)/2} \right) \cdot L, \quad k = 1, \ldots, r, \tag{12.31}$$

where $L = \log(N/\varepsilon) + \log(s) \cdot \log(s/\varepsilon)$, *and condition (12.30) of Corollary 12.9 is implied by*

$$m_k \gtrsim \left(s_k + \sum_{l=1}^{k-1} s_l 2^{-(k-l)} + \sum_{l=k+1}^{r} s_l 2^{-3(l-k)} \right) \cdot L, \quad k = 1, \ldots, r, \tag{12.32}$$

where $L = \log(N) \cdot (\log(N/\varepsilon) + \log(s \log(N)) \cdot \log(s \log(N)/\varepsilon))$.

As discussed in §11.6, the importance of these measurement conditions is that they relate the local measurements m_k to the local sparsities s_k plus exponentially decaying terms in the sparsities s_l with $l \neq k$. It is interesting to note that the unweighted QCBP decoder also admits a simple recovery guarantee (12.31) of this type – a fact which may be surprising in view of the general results for unweighted QCBP (Corollaries 12.6 and 12.8). However, log factors aside, the weighted QCBP decoder yields a sharper guarantee (12.32) with faster rates of exponential decrease.

The proof of Theorem 12.10 uses the following lemma, which is itself proved in §12.7:

Lemma 12.11 (Fourier–Haar local coherences) *Let U be as in (11.18) and $U^{(k,l)}$ be its (k,l)th block (12.24) according to the sampling and sparsity levels of Theorem 12.10. Then*

$$\mu\left(U^{(k,l)}\right) \lesssim \begin{cases} 2^{-(k-l)} & l \leq k \\ 2^{-3(l-k)} & l > k \end{cases}, \qquad k,l = 1,\ldots,r \tag{12.33}$$

and

$$\|U^{(k,l)}\|_{\ell^2} \lesssim \begin{cases} 2^{-(k-l)/2} & l \leq k \\ 2^{-(l-k)} & l > k \end{cases}, \qquad k,l = 1,\ldots,r. \tag{12.34}$$

Proof of Theorem 12.10 Recall that $r = \log_2(N)+1$. The second result, namely (12.32) implies (12.30), now follows immediately from Lemma 12.11.

Now consider the first result. Lemma 12.11 immediately gives that (12.31) implies (12.25). Now consider condition (12.26). Lemma 12.11 gives

$$\begin{aligned}\left(\sum_{j=1}^{r} \sqrt{s_j}\|U^{(k,j)}\|_{\ell^2}\right)^2 &\lesssim \left(\sum_{j=1}^{k} \sqrt{s_j}2^{-(k-j)/2} + \sum_{j=k+1}^{r} \sqrt{s_j}2^{-(j-k)}\right)^2 \\ &\leq \left(\sum_{j=1}^{r} 2^{-|k-j|/2}\right)\left(\sum_{j=1}^{k} s_j 2^{-(k-j)/2} + \sum_{j=k+1}^{r} s_j 2^{-3(j-k)/2}\right) \\ &\lesssim \sum_{j=1}^{k} s_j 2^{-(k-j)/2} + \sum_{j=k+1}^{r} s_j 2^{-3(j-k)/2}.\end{aligned}$$

Hence, using Lemma 12.11 once more, we get

$$\begin{aligned}&\sum_{\substack{k=1 \\ m_k < N_k - N_{k-1}}}^{r} \frac{\mu\left(U^{(k,l)}\right)\left(\sum_{j=1}^{r} \sqrt{s_j}\|U^{(k,j)}\|_{\ell^2}\right)^2}{m_k} \\ &\qquad \lesssim \sum_{\substack{k=1 \\ m_k < N_k - N_{k-1}}}^{r} \frac{2^{-|k-l|}}{m_k}\left(\sum_{j=1}^{k} s_j 2^{-(k-j)/2} + \sum_{j=k+1}^{r} s_j 2^{-3(j-k)/2}\right).\end{aligned}$$

Therefore (12.26) is also implied by (12.31). This completes the proof. □

12.5.2 Power-Law Sampling

We now consider the sparse model in the context of the Fourier–Haar wavelet problem, as was previously discussed in §11.2.1. In this section, we establish nonuniform recovery guarantees for power-law sampling (more general densities could also be studied in a similar manner).

Since it presents few additional difficulties and will be useful in Part IV, we now consider both the one- and two-dimensional cases. Hence, $U = N^{-d/2} F \Phi \in \mathbb{C}^{N^d \times N^d}$, where $d = 1, 2$ and F is the d-dimensional Fourier matrix (Definition 2.1) and Φ is the sparsifying transform corresponding to the d-dimensional discrete Haar wavelet basis. We consider power-law sampling with $\pi = \{\pi_\omega\}$ given by

$$\pi_\omega = \frac{C_{N,\alpha}}{(\max\{1, |\omega|\})^\alpha}, \quad \omega \in \{-N/2+1, \ldots, N/2\}, \tag{12.35}$$

when $d = 1$ and

$$\pi_\omega = \frac{C_{N,\alpha}}{(\max\{1, |\omega_1|^2 + |\omega_2|^2\})^\alpha}, \quad \omega = (\omega_1, \omega_2) \in \{-N/2+1, \ldots, N/2\}^2, \tag{12.36}$$

when $d = 2$. Here $\alpha \in \mathbb{R}$ is a parameter. As in §4.1, we write $\Omega \subseteq \{-N/2+1, \ldots, N/2\}^d$ for the corresponding sampling scheme, i.e. set of frequencies chosen according to either (12.35) or (12.36). Recall that $C_{N,\alpha}$ is a normalization constant that ensures that π is a probability distribution. It is straightforward to show that

$$C_{N,\alpha} \asymp \begin{cases} N^{d(\alpha-1)} & \alpha < 1 \\ (\log(N))^{-1} & \alpha = 1 \\ 1 & \alpha > 1 \end{cases}, \quad N \to \infty. \tag{12.37}$$

Note that in this and what follows we allow the constant implied by the symbols $\asymp$, $\lesssim$ and $\gtrsim$ to depend on α. We also define two further constants:

$$\widetilde{C}_{N,\alpha} = \begin{cases} \log(N) & \alpha = 1 \\ N^{d|\alpha-1|} & \alpha \neq 1 \end{cases}, \quad \bar{C}_{N,\alpha} = \begin{cases} N^{-d\alpha/2} & \alpha < 0 \\ 1 & 0 \leq \alpha < 1 \\ \sqrt{\log(N)} & \alpha = 1 \\ N^{d(\alpha-1)/2} & \alpha > 1 \end{cases}. \tag{12.38}$$

Our main result is the following:

Theorem 12.12 (Power-law Fourier–Haar, nonuniform recovery) *Consider the discrete Fourier–Haar wavelet problem in $d = 1$ or $d = 2$ dimensions. Let $0 < \varepsilon < 1$, $N^d \geq s \geq 2$, $x \in \mathbb{C}^{N^d}$, $\Omega \subseteq \{-N/2+1, \ldots, N/2\}^d$ be the sampling scheme corresponding to (12.35) ($d = 1$) or (12.36) ($d = 2$) for some $\alpha \in \mathbb{R}$, and let $A = (N^d/m)^{1/2} P_\Omega U \in \mathbb{C}^{m \times N^d}$ be the resulting measurement matrix. Suppose that*

$$m \gtrsim s \cdot \widetilde{C}_{N,\alpha} \cdot \log(N) \cdot (\log(N/\varepsilon) + \log(s) \cdot \log(s/\varepsilon)). \tag{12.39}$$

Then the following holds with probability at least $1 - \varepsilon$. For all $y = Ax + e \in \mathbb{C}^m$, every minimizer $\hat{x} \in \mathbb{C}^N$ of (5.18) with parameter $\eta \geq \|e\|_{\ell^2}$ satisfies

$$\|\hat{x} - x\|_{\ell^2} \lesssim \sigma_s(x)_{\ell^1} + \bar{C}_{N,\alpha} \sqrt{s} \eta,$$

where $\sigma_s(x)_{\ell^1}$ is the ℓ^1-norm best s-term approximation error (5.6). In particular, when $\alpha = 1$, the measurement condition (12.39) takes the form

$$m \gtrsim s \cdot \log^2(N) \cdot (\log(N/\varepsilon) + \log(s) \cdot \log(s/\varepsilon)) . \qquad (12.40)$$

This result confirms the claim made in §11.2.1. The best power-law scheme (for the sparse model) corresponds to the value $\alpha = 1$, since this yields a measurement condition (12.40) that is linear in s and logarithmic in N. This means inverse linear law sampling in one dimension and inverse square law sampling in two dimensions. Conversely, all other values of α lead to suboptimal measurement conditions that depend algebraically on N. We reiterate, however, that this does not generally agree with what one sees in practice (recall Fig. 11.4). We return to this matter in Chapter 15.

Remark 12.13 Since $\Omega \subseteq \{-N/2+1, \ldots, N/2\}^d$ the projection P_Ω should, technically speaking, be written as $P_{\varrho^{-1}(\Omega)}$, where $\varrho \colon \{1, \ldots, N^d\} \to \{-N/2+1, \ldots, N/2\}^d$ is the bijection defined in (2.14). To avoid unnecessary notation, we simply write P_Ω whenever this situation arises.

The proof of Theorem 12.12 is based on the following lemma:

Lemma 12.14 *Consider the discrete Fourier–Haar wavelet problem in $d = 1$ or $d = 2$ dimensions. Let $U = N^{-d/2} F \Phi \in \mathbb{C}^{N^d \times N^d}$ and $\mathcal{A}$ be the isotropic family with $a \sim \mathcal{A}$ if*

$$\mathbb{P}\left(a = U^* e_{\varrho^{-1}(\omega)}/\sqrt{\pi_\omega}\right) = \pi_\omega, \quad \omega \in \{-N/2+1, \ldots, N/2\}^d, \qquad (12.41)$$

where π corresponds to (12.35) ($d = 1$) or (12.36) ($d = 2$) for some $\alpha \in \mathbb{R}$ and ϱ is as in (2.14). Then the coherence

$$\mu(\mathcal{A}) \lesssim \widetilde{C}_{N,\alpha}.$$

See §12.7 for the proof of this lemma.

Remark 12.15 It is tempting to think that Theorem 12.12 follows immediately from Lemma 12.14 by applying Corollary 12.5 to the isotropic collection $C = \{\mathcal{A}_i\}_{i=1}^m$, where the $\mathcal{A}_i$ are independent copies of $\mathcal{A}$. However, there is a problem. The measurement matrix (11.9) of this collection is

$$A' = \frac{1}{\sqrt{m}} \begin{pmatrix} a_1^* \\ \vdots \\ a_m^* \end{pmatrix}, \qquad (12.42)$$

where $a_i \sim \mathcal{A}$ independently for each i. But these vectors correspond to rows of U that are scaled according to the probability distribution π (see (12.41)). Hence A' is not equal to the measurement matrix A of Theorem 12.12. Rather, one has

$$A' = DA, \qquad (12.43)$$

where D is a diagonal matrix, with its entries taking the form $(N^d \pi_\omega)^{-1/2}$ with ω corresponding to the frequencies sampled. The reason for not using A' directly in Theorem 12.12 is that it would enforce a weighted ℓ^2-norm bound on the noise. Indeed, suppose that $y = Ax + e$. Then $y' = A'x + e'$, where $y' = Dy$ and $e' = De$, and therefore

$\|e'\|_{\ell^2} \leq \eta$ if and only if $\|De\|_{\ell^2} \leq \eta$. In this weighted model, noise at higher frequencies is more or less heavily penalized depending on whether α is positive or negative. This is undesirable. It is for this reason that Theorem 12.12 is formulated in terms of A rather than A'. Since doing so causes several technical hurdles, we delay its proof until §12.8.5.

12.6 Comparison with Oracle Estimators

Thus far, we have determined a variety of different measurement conditions for nonuniform recovery with the weighted and unweighted QCBP decoders. We now consider the sharpness of these conditions. We do this by comparing them to measurement conditions that ensure recovery via the oracle least-squares estimator.

Recall from §5.8 that if the support set Δ is known, one may recover x via the least-squares fit (5.39). Proposition 5.31 asserts that this oracle estimator gives not only exact, but also stable recovery whenever the matrix AP_Δ satisfies $\|P_\Delta A^* A P_\Delta - P_\Delta\|_{\ell^2} \leq \delta$ for some $0 < \delta < 1$. As we show in Lemma 12.21, if $C = \{\mathcal{A}_i\}_{i=1}^m$ is a jointly isotropic collection and A is as in (11.9) then this property holds with probability $1 - \varepsilon$, provided

$$m \gtrsim \delta^{-2} \cdot \Pi(C, \Delta) \cdot \log(|\Delta|/\varepsilon). \tag{12.44}$$

We now compare this measurement condition to those presented in §12.2–§12.5.

A. The abstract case. Theorem 12.4 gives the measurement condition

$$m \gtrsim \Pi(C, \Delta) \cdot \log(N/\varepsilon) + \Gamma(C, \Delta, w) \cdot \left(\log(N/\varepsilon) + \log(|\Delta|_w) \cdot \log(|\Delta|_w/\varepsilon)\right)$$

for the weighted QCBP decoder. Log factors aside, this is in general more stringent than (12.44) due to the presence of the second factor $\Gamma(C, \Delta, w)$.

B. The sparse case. Now suppose that Δ is an arbitrary s-sparse support set. Then, using (12.12) we see that the oracle condition (12.44) is implied by

$$m \gtrsim s \cdot \mu(C) \cdot \log(s/\varepsilon). \tag{12.45}$$

Conversely, Corollary 12.5 asserts recovery via unweighted QCBP whenever

$$m \gtrsim s \cdot \mu(C) \cdot \left(\log(N/\varepsilon) + \log(s) \cdot \log(s/\varepsilon)\right).$$

Besides a somewhat larger log factor, this is identical to (12.45). This therefore reiterates a classical compressed sensing result that was already mentioned in §5.8:

QCBP achieves recovery of an arbitrary s-sparse vector from roughly the same number of measurements as is sufficient for the oracle estimator, but without having any prior knowledge of its support set.

C. The sparse in levels case. Suppose that Δ is an arbitrary $(\mathbf{s}, \mathbf{M})$-sparse support set. Then, using (12.18) to estimate $\Pi(C, \Delta)$, we deduce that (12.44) is implied by

$$m \gtrsim \max_{i:|\mathcal{A}_i|>1} \left\{ \sum_{l=1}^{r} s_l \mu_l(\mathcal{A}_i) \right\} \cdot \log(s/\varepsilon), \tag{12.46}$$

where $s = s_1 + \cdots + s_r$. Corollary 12.6 considers recovery via QCBP for this model. Observe that (12.46) is smaller than the first condition therein, namely (12.15), since $\mu_l(\mathcal{A}_i) \leq \mu(\mathcal{A}_i)$. Moreover, the second condition (12.16) is not required at all for the oracle estimator. On the other hand, Corollary 12.7 asserts recovery via weighted QCBP with weights as in (12.2) and (12.3) under the condition

$$m \gtrsim \max_{i:|\mathcal{A}_i|>1} \left\{ \sum_{l=1}^{r} s_l \mu_l(\mathcal{A}_i) \right\} \cdot r \cdot (\log(N/\varepsilon) + \log(rs) \cdot \log(rs/\varepsilon)) .$$

Up to r and the log terms, this is equivalent to (12.46). Hence:

Weighted QCBP (with suitable weights) achieves recovery of an arbitrary $(\mathbf{s}, \mathbf{M})$-sparse vector from roughly the same number of measurements as is sufficient for the oracle estimator, but without any prior knowledge of its support set.

D. The Fourier–Haar wavelet case. In this case, (12.27) and Lemma 12.11 give the condition

$$m_k \gtrsim \left(s_k + \sum_{l=1}^{k-1} s_l 2^{-(k-l)} + \sum_{l=k+1}^{r} s_l 2^{-3(l-k)} \right) \cdot \log(s/\varepsilon)$$

for the oracle estimator for each $k = 1, \ldots, r$. This is the same, up to log factors, as the condition (12.32) for weighted QCBP with weights as in (12.2)–(12.3). Conversely, for unweighted QCBP the corresponding estimate (12.31) is

$$m_k \gtrsim \left(s_k + \sum_{l=1}^{k-1} s_l 2^{-(k-l)/2} + \sum_{l=k+1}^{r} s_l 2^{-3(l-k)/2} \right) \cdot (\log(N/\varepsilon) + \log(s) \cdot \log(s/\varepsilon)) .$$

As noted, this exhibits worse exponential decay for $l \neq k$.

This discussion raises the following question: in the sparse in levels case, can unweighted QCBP succeed under a measurement condition that is closer to that of the oracle? We show in §12.9 that this is indeed the case, provided the entries of vector x satisfy an additional random sign assumption.

12.7 Coherences of the Discrete Fourier–Haar Matrix

We now give the proofs of Lemmas 12.11 and 12.14. These are based on the behaviour of the Fourier transform of the Haar wavelet, a topic which was already considered in §11.1.3. Yet there is a small technical issue, in that the discussion therein considered the continuous case, whereas we now consider the discrete Fourier transform of the discrete Haar wavelet. Hence some additional effort is required.

Lemma 12.16 *Let $N = 2^r$, $r \geq 1$, F be the Fourier matrix (Definition 2.1), $\psi^{(e)}_{j,n}$ denote the discrete Haar wavelet basis (9.58) and ϱ be as in (2.8). Then, for $j = 0, \ldots, r-1$,*

$n = 0, \dots, 2^j - 1$ and $e \in \{0, 1\}$ we have

$$(F\psi_{j,n}^{(e)})_{\varrho^{-1}(0)} = \begin{cases} 2^{\frac{r-j}{2}} & e = 0 \\ 0 & \text{otherwise} \end{cases}$$

and for $\omega \in \{-N/2 + 1, \dots, N/2\} \backslash \{0\}$,

$$(F\psi_{j,n}^{(e)})_{\varrho^{-1}(\omega)} = 2^{\frac{j-r}{2}} \mathrm{e}^{-2\pi \mathrm{i}\omega n/2^j} \left(1 + (-1)^e \mathrm{e}^{-2\pi \mathrm{i}\omega/2^{j+1}}\right) \left(\frac{1 - \mathrm{e}^{-2\pi \mathrm{i}\omega/2^{j+1}}}{1 - \mathrm{e}^{-2\pi \mathrm{i}\omega/2^r}}\right).$$

Moreover, for all $\omega \in \{-N/2 + 1, \dots, N/2\}$,

$$\frac{1}{\sqrt{N}} \left|(F\psi_{j,n}^{(e)})_{\varrho^{-1}(\omega)}\right| \lesssim \frac{1}{\sqrt{\max\{1, |\omega|\}}} \min \left\{ \left(\frac{2^j}{\max\{1, |\omega|\}}\right)^{1/2}, \left(\frac{\max\{1, |\omega|\}}{2^j}\right)^{1/2+e} \right\}.$$

We recall here that the rows of F are indexed over $\{1, \dots, N\}$, hence the use of the bijection ϱ.

Proof We proceed by direct calculation. We have

$$\begin{aligned}(F\psi_{j,n}^{(e)})_{\varrho^{-1}(\omega)} &= 2^{\frac{j-r}{2}} \sum_{n2^{r-j} < t \leq (n+1/2)2^{r-j}} \mathrm{e}^{-2\pi \mathrm{i}\omega(t-1)/N} \\ &\quad + (-1)^e 2^{\frac{j-r}{2}} \sum_{(n+1/2)2^{r-j} < t \leq (n+1)2^{r-j}} \mathrm{e}^{-2\pi \mathrm{i}\omega(t-1)/N} \\ &= 2^{\frac{j-r}{2}} \left(\mathrm{e}^{-2\pi \mathrm{i}\omega n 2^{r-j}/N} + (-1)^e \mathrm{e}^{-2\pi \mathrm{i}\omega(n+1/2)2^{r-j}/N}\right) \sum_{s=0}^{2^{r-j-1}-1} \mathrm{e}^{-2\pi \mathrm{i}\omega s/N}.\end{aligned}$$

The first two results now follow by evaluating the geometric sums and simplifying. Consider the third result. When $\omega = 0$ this follows immediately from the first result and the fact that $N = 2^r$. Hence we now assume that $\omega \neq 0$. By the second result, we have

$$\frac{1}{\sqrt{N}} \left|(F\psi_{j,n}^{(e)})_{\varrho^{-1}(\omega)}\right| \leq 2^{j/2-r+1} \frac{|\sin(\pi\omega/2^{j+1})|^{1+e}}{|\sin(\pi\omega/2^r)|}.$$

Suppose first that $1 \leq |\omega| < 2^j$. Then, since $|\sin(\pi z)| \leq \pi|z|$, $\forall z \in \mathbb{R}$, and $|\sin(\pi z)| \geq 2|z|$ for $|z| \leq 1/2$, we obtain

$$\frac{1}{\sqrt{N}} \left|(F\psi_{j,n}^{(e)})_{\varrho^{-1}(\omega)}\right| \lesssim 2^{j/2-r} \frac{(|\omega|/2^j)^{1+e}}{|\omega|/2^r} = \frac{1}{\sqrt{|\omega|}} \left(\frac{|\omega|}{2^j}\right)^{1/2+e}.$$

Conversely, if $2^j \leq |\omega| \leq 2^{r-1}$ then we use the bound $|\sin(\pi z)| \leq 1$, $\forall z \in \mathbb{R}$, for the numerator to get

$$\frac{1}{\sqrt{N}} \left|(F\psi_{j,n}^{(e)})_{\varrho^{-1}(\omega)}\right| \lesssim 2^{j/2-r} \frac{1}{|\omega|/2^r} = \frac{1}{\sqrt{|\omega|}} \left(\frac{2^j}{|\omega|}\right)^{1/2}.$$

This gives the third result for $\omega \neq 0$, and thus completes the proof. □

Proof of Lemma 12.11 The entries of the matrix $U^{(k,l)}$ are given by (11.22) for $l = 1$ and (11.23) otherwise. We use the previous lemma, with r replaced by $r - 1$ (since $N = 2^{r-1}$ in this case). Recall that $\varrho(\{N_{k-1} + 1, \dots, N_k\}) = B_k$, where B_k is as in (11.20), and let $\omega \in B_k$. If $l = 1$ then the previous lemma gives

$$\left| \left(U^{(k,1)} \right)_{\varrho^{-1}(\omega),1} \right| \lesssim 2^{-k} \leq 2^{-k/2} 2^{-(k-1)/2}.$$

Using Definition 5.8 and the fact that $|B_k| \leq 2^k$, we see that

$$\mu\left(U^{(k,1)}\right) = \max_{\omega \in B_k} \left\{ |B_k| \left| \left(U^{(k,1)} \right)_{\varrho^{-1}(\omega),n} \right|^2 \right\} \lesssim 2^{-(k-1)}, \quad k = 1, \dots, r,$$

which gives (12.33) for $l = 1$. Now suppose that $l = 2, \dots, r$. Then Lemma 12.16 gives

$$\left| \left(U^{(k,l)} \right)_{\varrho^{-1}(\omega),n} \right| \lesssim 2^{-k/2} \min\left\{ 2^{(l-k)/2}, 2^{3(k-l)/2} \right\}.$$

Therefore

$$\mu\left(U^{(k,l)}\right) = \max_{\substack{\omega \in B_k \\ 0 \leq n < 2^{l-2}}} \left\{ |B_k| \left| \left(U^{(k,l)} \right)_{\varrho^{-1}(\omega),n} \right|^2 \right\} \lesssim \min\left\{ 2^{(l-k)}, 2^{3(k-l)} \right\},$$

for $k = 1, \dots, r$, which gives (12.33) for $l = 2, \dots, r$ as well. We omit the proof of (12.34). See the Notes section for details. □

Proof of Lemma 12.14 We commence with the one-dimensional case. By definition, the coherence of $\mathcal{A}$ is

$$\mu(\mathcal{A}) = \max_{-N/2 < \omega \leq N/2} \left\{ \frac{\|U^* e_{\varrho^{-1}(\omega)}\|^2_{\ell^\infty}}{\pi_\omega} \right\}. \tag{12.47}$$

The definition of U and Lemma 12.16 give

$$\|U^* e_{\varrho^{-1}(\omega)}\|^2_{\ell^\infty} = \frac{1}{N} \max\left\{ \left|(F\psi^{(0)}_{0,0})_{\varrho^{-1}(\omega)}\right|^2, \max_{\substack{0 \leq j < r \\ 0 \leq k < 2^j}} \left|(F\psi^{(1)}_{j,k})_{\varrho^{-1}(\omega)}\right|^2 \right\} \lesssim \frac{1}{\max\{1, |\omega|\}}.$$

Hence, using (12.35) and (12.47), we get

$$\mu(\mathcal{A}) \lesssim \max_{-N/2 < \omega \leq N/2} \left\{ \frac{(\max\{1, |\omega|\})^{\alpha-1}}{C_{N,\alpha}} \right\} \lesssim (C_{N,\alpha})^{-1} \cdot \begin{cases} 1 & \alpha < 1 \\ N^{\alpha-1} & \alpha \geq 1 \end{cases}.$$

The result now follows from (12.37) and (12.38).

Now consider the two-dimensional case. Observe that

$$\mu(\mathcal{A}) = \max_{\substack{\omega = (\omega_1, \omega_2) \\ -N/2 < \omega_1, \omega_2 \leq N/2}} \left\{ \frac{\|U^* e_{\varrho^{-1}(\omega)}\|^2_{\ell^\infty}}{\pi_\omega} \right\}. \tag{12.48}$$

Using the Kronecker product structure of F, the fact that the wavelets are themselves tensor products and Lemma 12.16, we see that

$$\|U^* e_{\varrho^{-1}(\omega)}\|_{\ell^\infty} \lesssim \max_{j=0,\dots,r-1} \left\{ \min\left\{ \frac{2^{j/2}}{\max\{1, |\omega_1|\}}, \frac{1}{2^{j/2}} \right\} \min\left\{ \frac{2^{j/2}}{\max\{1, |\omega_2|\}}, \frac{1}{2^{j/2}} \right\} \right\}.$$

After splitting into different cases and simplifying, we deduce that

$$\|U^* e_{\varrho^{-1}(\omega)}\|_{\ell^\infty} \lesssim \frac{1}{\max\{1, \max\{|\omega_1|, |\omega_2|\}\}} \lesssim \frac{1}{\sqrt{\max\{1, |\omega_1|^2 + |\omega_2|^2\}}}.$$

Hence, by (12.36) and (12.48),

$$\mu(\mathcal{A}) \lesssim (C_{N,\alpha})^{-1} \cdot \begin{cases} 1 & \alpha < 1 \\ N^{2(\alpha-1)} & \alpha \geq 1 \end{cases}.$$

We now use (12.37) and (12.38) once more. □

12.8 Proof of Theorem 12.4

We now present the proof of the first result stated in this chapter, Theorem 12.4, on which the subsequent results in §12.3 and §12.4 were based. As discussed in §5.7, nonuniform recovery guarantees are generally established by constructing a suitable dual certificate. Our proof follows this approach. First, we use Theorem 5.29 (or, to be precise, a slightly generalized version, Theorem 12.17) to reduce the problem to ensuring conditions (i) and (ii) of the theorem, and constructing a dual certificate ρ satisfying conditions (iii)–(v). The remainder of the proof is probabilistic and leverages the randomness of A. First, using tools from random matrix theory, we establish conditions (i) and (ii) via two technical results, Lemmas 12.21 and 12.23, which are proved by bounding the deviation of (submatrices of) A^*A from its expectation $\mathbb{E}(A^*A)$. Recall that $\mathbb{E}(A^*A) = I$ since C is jointly isotropic. Then we construct the dual certificate. This is done via the so-called *golfing scheme*, which iteratively constructs a vector ρ to ensure that conditions (iii)–(v) hold with high probability after a certain number of iterations. Note that this construction requires two further technical lemmas, Lemmas 12.22 and 12.24, which provide deviation bounds for the multiplication of a vector by (submatrices of) A^*A.

12.8.1 Dual Certificate Implies Recovery

Since we consider weighted QCBP, we first need the following generalization of Theorem 5.29 that incorporates weights.

Theorem 12.17 (Dual certificate implies recovery for weighted QCBP) *Let $x \in \mathbb{C}^N$, $\Delta \subseteq \{1, \ldots, N\}$, $A \in \mathbb{C}^{m \times N}$ and $w \in \mathbb{C}^N$ be weights with $w_i \geq 1$, $\forall i$. Suppose that*

(i) $\|P_\Delta A^* A P_\Delta - P_\Delta\|_{\ell^2} \leq \alpha$,
(ii) $\max_{i \notin \Delta} \|P_\Delta A^* A W^{-1} e_i\|_{\ell^2} \leq \beta$,

and that there is a vector $\rho \in \mathbb{C}^N$ of the form $\rho = W^{-1} A^* \xi$ for some $\xi \in \mathbb{C}^m$, where W is as in (12.5)*, such that*

(iii) $\|W(P_\Delta \rho - \mathrm{sign}(P_\Delta x))\|_{\ell^2} \leq \gamma$,
(iv) $\|P_\Delta^\perp \rho\|_{\ell^\infty} \leq \theta$,
(v) $\|\xi\|_{\ell^2} \leq \nu \sqrt{|\Delta|_w}$,

for constants $0 \leq \alpha, \theta < 1$ *and* $\beta, \gamma, \nu \geq 0$ *satisfying* $\frac{\beta\gamma}{(1-\alpha)(1-\theta)} < 1$. *Then, for all* $y = Ax + e \in \mathbb{C}^m$, *every minimizer* $\hat{x} \in \mathbb{C}^N$ *of (12.1) with parameter* $\eta \geq \|e\|_{\ell^2}$ *satisfies*

$$\|\hat{x} - x\|_{\ell^2} \leq C_1 \|x - P_\Delta x\|_{\ell^1_w} + C_2 \sqrt{|\Delta|_w} \eta, \tag{12.49}$$

where the constants C_1 *and* C_2 *depend on* α, β, γ, θ *and* ν *only.*

Proof The proof is quite similar to Theorem 5.29, which was shown in §6.4. Hence we only sketch the main details. Let $v = \hat{x} - x$. Identical arguments give

$$\|P_\Delta v\|_{\ell^2} \leq \frac{\sqrt{1+\alpha}}{1-\alpha} \|Av\|_{\ell^2} + \frac{1}{1-\alpha} \|P_\Delta A^* A P_\Delta^\perp v\|_{\ell^2},$$

and since $\hat{x}$ and x are both feasible for (12.1), we have $\|Av\|_{\ell^2} \leq 2\eta$ and hence

$$\|P_\Delta v\|_{\ell^2} \leq \frac{2\sqrt{1+\alpha}}{1-\alpha} \eta + \frac{1}{1-\alpha} \|P_\Delta A^* A P_\Delta^\perp v\|_{\ell^2}.$$

The estimate for the second term is now modified slightly to include the weights w_i. Writing $v = W^{-1}(\sum_{i=1}^N w_i v_i e_i)$ and using (ii) gives

$$\|P_\Delta v\|_{\ell^2} \leq \frac{2\sqrt{1+\alpha}}{1-\alpha} \eta + \frac{\beta}{1-\alpha} \|P_\Delta^\perp v\|_{\ell^1_w}. \tag{12.50}$$

We now consider $\|P_\Delta^\perp v\|_{\ell^1_w}$. Arguing in a similar way and also using the fact that $\|x\|_{\ell^1_w} \geq \|\hat{x}\|_{\ell^1_w}$, we obtain

$$\|P_\Delta^\perp v\|_{\ell^1_w} \leq |\langle P_\Delta v, W \mathrm{sign}(P_\Delta x) \rangle| + 2\|P_\Delta^\perp x\|_{\ell^1_w}. \tag{12.51}$$

Following similar arguments once more, we deduce that

$$|\langle P_\Delta v, W \mathrm{sign}(P_\Delta x) \rangle| \leq \gamma \|P_\Delta v\|_{\ell^2} + 2\eta\nu\sqrt{|\Delta|_w} + \theta \|P_\Delta^\perp v\|_{\ell^1_w},$$

and therefore

$$(1-\theta)\|P_\Delta^\perp v\|_{\ell^1_w} \leq \gamma \|P_\Delta v\|_{\ell^2} + 2\eta\nu\sqrt{|\Delta|_w} + 2\|P_\Delta^\perp x\|_{\ell^1_w}. \tag{12.52}$$

Applying (12.50) and rearranging now yields

$$\|P_\Delta v\|_{\ell^2} \leq C_1 \|P_\Delta^\perp x\|_{\ell^1_w} + C_2 \sqrt{|\Delta|_w} \eta$$

for constants C_1 and C_2 depending on α, β, γ, θ and ν. After noting that $\|P_\Delta^\perp v\|_{\ell^2} \leq \|P_\Delta^\perp v\|_{\ell^1} \leq \|P_\Delta^\perp v\|_{\ell^1_w}$ (since the weights satisfy $w_i \geq 1$) and using (12.52), we get

$$\begin{aligned} \|v\|_{\ell^2} &\leq \|P_\Delta v\|_{\ell^2} + \|P_\Delta^\perp v\|_{\ell^1_w} \\ &\leq \left(1 + \frac{\gamma}{1-\theta}\right) \|P_\Delta v\|_{\ell^2} + \frac{2}{1-\theta} \eta\nu\sqrt{|\Delta|_w} + \frac{2}{1-\theta} \|P_\Delta^\perp x\|_{\ell^1_w} \\ &\leq C_1 \|P_\Delta^\perp x\|_{\ell^1_w} + C_2 \sqrt{|\Delta|_w} \eta, \end{aligned}$$

for possibly different constants C_1 and C_2. □

12.8.2 Bernstein's Inequalities

In order to prove the four technical lemmas, Lemmas 12.21–12.24, we require some standard tools from probability theory, namely, several versions of *Bernstein's inequality*. We commence with the standard Bernstein inequality for bounded random variables:

Theorem 12.18 *Let $X_1, \ldots, X_m$ be independent random variables satisfying $\mathbb{E}(X_i) = 0$ and $|X_i| \leq K$ almost surely for $i = 1, \ldots, m$. Let $\sigma > 0$ be such that $\sum_{i=1}^m \mathbb{E}|X_i|^2 \leq \sigma^2$. Then*

$$\mathbb{P}\left(\left|\sum_{i=1}^m X_i\right| \geq t\right) \leq 2\exp\left(-\frac{t^2/2}{\sigma^2 + Kt/3}\right), \qquad \forall t > 0.$$

Next, we require an extension of Bernstein's inequality for random vectors:

Theorem 12.19 *Let $X_1, \ldots, X_m$ be independent random vectors in $\mathbb{C}^n$ satisfying $\mathbb{E}(X_i) = 0$ and $\|X_i\|_{\ell^2} \leq K$ almost surely for $i = 1, \ldots, m$. Let $\sigma, \mu > 0$ be such that*

$$\sup\left\{\sum_{i=1}^m \mathbb{E}|\langle X_i, x\rangle|^2 : x \in \mathbb{C}^n, \|x\|_{\ell^2} = 1\right\} \leq \sigma^2, \qquad \mathbb{E}(Z) \leq \mu,$$

where $Z = \| \sum_{i=1}^m X_i\|_{\ell^2}$. Then

$$\mathbb{P}\left(|Z - \mathbb{E}(Z)| \geq t\right) \leq 3\exp\left(-\frac{t}{cK}\log\left(1 + \frac{Kt}{\sigma^2 + K\mu}\right)\right), \qquad \forall t > 0,$$

where $c > 0$ is the numerical constant of Theorem 13.33.

Finally, we consider sums of independent random matrices. The following result is sometimes known as the *matrix Bernstein inequality*:

Theorem 12.20 *Let $X_1, \ldots, X_m$ be independent, self-adjoint random matrices in $\mathbb{C}^{n\times n}$ satisfying $\mathbb{E}(X_i) = 0$ and $\|X_i\|_{\ell^2} \leq K$ almost surely for $i = 1, \ldots, m$. Let $\sigma > 0$ be such that*

$$\left\|\sum_{i=1}^m \mathbb{E}(X_i^2)\right\|_{\ell^2} \leq \sigma^2.$$

Then

$$\mathbb{P}\left(\left\|\sum_{i=1}^m X_i\right\|_{\ell^2} \geq t\right) \leq 2n\exp\left(-\frac{t^2/2}{\sigma^2 + Kt/3}\right), \qquad \forall t > 0.$$

Theorems 12.18 and 12.20 are standard; see the Notes section for further information. On the other hand, vector versions of Bernstein's inequality are typically formulated for identically distributed random vectors. Crucially for our purposes, Theorem 12.19 does not impose this condition on the X_i. We shall prove it in §13.5.5 via a version of Talagrand's theorem (Theorem 13.33).

12.8.3 Technical Lemmas

We now present the four technical lemmas. As mentioned, these all involve the deviation of certain quantities related to A^*A from their expected values. Recalling the definition of A (see (11.9)), we first observe that

$$A^*A - I = A^*A - \mathbb{E}(A^*A) = \frac{1}{m} \sum_{i:|\mathcal{A}_i|>1} \left(a_i a_i^* - \mathbb{E}(a_i a_i^*)\right), \tag{12.53}$$

with probability one (here and henceforth we drop the subscript $\mathcal{A}_i$ from $\mathbb{E}_{\mathcal{A}_i}(a_i a_i^*)$ as the distribution of a_i is always $\mathcal{A}_i$ in what follows). Note that in the second equality in (12.53), we used the fact that $a_i a_i^* = \mathbb{E}(a_i a_i^*)$ with probability one whenever $|\mathcal{A}_i| = 1$. Since the right-hand side of (12.53) is a sum of independent random matrices, each lemma is proved by using a suitable version of Bernstein's inequality.

Lemma 12.21 (Local isometry) *Let $0 < \varepsilon < 1$, $\delta > 0$, $\Delta \subseteq \{1, \ldots, N\}$, $C = \{\mathcal{A}_i\}_{i=1}^m$ be a jointly isotropic collection and A be as in (11.9). Then*

$$\|P_\Delta A^* A P_\Delta - P_\Delta\|_{\ell^2} < \delta,$$

with probability at least $1 - \varepsilon$, provided

$$m \geq \Pi(C, \Delta) \cdot (2\delta^{-2} + 4\delta^{-1}/3) \cdot \log(2|\Delta|/\varepsilon), \tag{12.54}$$

where $\Pi(C, \Delta)$ is as in Definition 12.2.

This lemma ensures that the matrix formed from the columns of A with indices in Δ is close to an isometry. It is similar in spirit to the RIP, although substantially weaker since it only holds for a single fixed Δ, as opposed to all $\Delta \in D_s$ (recall Lemma 5.19).

Proof Let $X_i = \frac{1}{m} P_\Delta \left(a_i a_i^* - \mathbb{E}(a_i a_i^*)\right) P_\Delta$. Then, by (12.53),

$$P_\Delta A^* A P_\Delta - P_\Delta = \sum_{i:|\mathcal{A}_i|>1} X_i.$$

The matrices X_i are independent with $\mathbb{E}(X_i) = 0$ and isomorphic to matrices of size $|\Delta| \times |\Delta|$. Hence the matrix Bernstein inequality (Theorem 12.20) gives

$$\mathbb{P}\left(\|P_\Delta A^* A P_\Delta - P_\Delta\|_{\ell^2} \geq \delta\right) \leq 2|\Delta| \exp\left(-\frac{\delta^2/2}{\sigma^2 + K\delta/3}\right), \tag{12.55}$$

where K and σ^2 are such that $\|X_i\|_{\ell^2} \leq K$ almost surely for each i, and

$$\left\| \sum_{i:|\mathcal{A}_i|>1} \mathbb{E}(X_i^2) \right\|_{\ell^2} \leq \sigma^2.$$

We now estimate these constants.

Let $x \in \mathbb{C}^N$, $\|x\|_{\ell^2} = 1$, be arbitrary. From the definition of $\Pi(C, \Delta)$, we get

$$|\langle X_i x, x\rangle| = m^{-1} \left| |\langle P_\Delta a_i, x\rangle|^2 - \mathbb{E}|\langle P_\Delta a_i, x\rangle|^2 \right| \leq 2\Pi(C, \Delta)/m.$$

Since X_i is self-adjoint and x was arbitrary, we deduce that

$$\|X_i\|_{\ell^2} = \sup_{\substack{x \in \mathbb{C}^N \\ \|x\|_{\ell^2}=1}} |\langle X_i x, x\rangle| \leq 2\Pi(C, \Delta)/m := K.$$

Next, observe that

$$\langle \mathbb{E}(X_i^2)x, x\rangle = m^{-2}\left(\mathbb{E}\left(\|P_\Delta a_i\|_{\ell^2}^2 |\langle P_\Delta a_i, x\rangle|^2\right) - \|\mathbb{E}(P_\Delta a_i a_i^* P_\Delta)x\|_{\ell^2}^2\right)$$
$$\leq m^{-2}\Pi(C,\Delta)\mathbb{E}|\langle a_i, P_\Delta x\rangle|^2.$$

Hence, since C is jointly isotropic,

$$\left\langle \sum_{i:|\mathcal{A}_i|>1} \mathbb{E}(X_i^2)x, x\right\rangle \leq m^{-2}\Pi(C,\Delta)\sum_{i=1}^{m}\mathbb{E}|\langle a_i, P_\Delta x\rangle|^2 = m^{-1}\Pi(C,\Delta)\|P_\Delta x\|_{\ell^2}^2.$$

Therefore, since $\sum_{i:|\mathcal{A}_i|>1}\mathbb{E}(X_i^2)$ is self-adjoint and nonnegative definite, we have

$$\left\|\sum_{i:|\mathcal{A}_i|>1}\mathbb{E}(X_i^2)\right\|_{\ell^2} = \sup_{\substack{x\in\mathbb{C}^N \\ \|x\|_{\ell^2}=1}} \left\langle \sum_{i:|\mathcal{A}_i|>1}\mathbb{E}(X_i^2)x, x\right\rangle \leq \Pi(C,\Delta)/m := \sigma^2.$$

Substituting these values into (12.55) gives

$$\mathbb{P}\left(\|P_\Delta A^*AP_\Delta - P_\Delta\|_{\ell^2} \geq \delta\right) \leq 2|\Delta|\exp\left(-\frac{m\delta^2}{\Pi(C,\Delta)(2+4\delta/3)}\right) \leq \varepsilon,$$

where in the last step we used (12.54). □

The previous lemma asks that A be an approximate isometry on Δ, and therefore approximately norm preserving for every vector supported on Δ, i.e. $\|AP_\Delta x\|_{\ell^2} \approx \|P_\Delta x\|_{\ell^2}$, $\forall x \in \mathbb{C}^N$. In the next lemma, we give conditions under which A approximately preserves the norm of a fixed vector supported on Δ. However, for technical reasons in the construction of the dual certificate, we now use the ℓ^∞-norm, rather than the ℓ^2-norm.

Lemma 12.22 (Low distortion) *Let $0 < \varepsilon < 1$, $\delta > 0$, $\Delta \subseteq \{1, \ldots, N\}$, $z \in \mathbb{C}^N$, $w \in \mathbb{C}^N$ be a vector of positive weights, $C = \{\mathcal{A}_i\}_{i=1}^m$ be a jointly isotropic collection and A be as in (11.9). Then*

$$\|W^{-1}(P_\Delta A^*AP_\Delta - P_\Delta)Wz\|_{\ell^\infty} < \delta\|z\|_{\ell^\infty},$$

with probability at least $1-\varepsilon$, provided

$$m \geq \left(\frac{4\sqrt{2}}{3}\Gamma_1(C,\Delta,w)\delta^{-1} + 4\Gamma_2(C,\Delta,w)\delta^{-2}\right)\cdot\log(4|\Delta|/\varepsilon), \tag{12.56}$$

where $\Gamma_1(C,\Delta,w)$ and $\Gamma_2(C,\Delta,w)$ are as in Definition 12.3.

Proof Without loss of generality, we assume that $\|z\|_{\ell^\infty} = 1$. Fix $j \in \Delta$. Then

$$\langle e_j, W^{-1}(P_\Delta A^*AP_\Delta - P_\Delta)Wz\rangle = \sum_{i:|\mathcal{A}_i|>1} X_i,$$

where the $X_i = m^{-1}\langle e_j, W^{-1}\left(a_i a_i^* - \mathbb{E}(a_i a_i^*)\right) P_\Delta W z\rangle$ are independent, complex-valued random variables. Note that $\mathbb{E}(X_i) = 0$. Hence, splitting each X_i into real and imaginary parts, using the union bound (C.1) and Bernstein's inequality (Theorem 12.18) gives

$$\begin{aligned}
&\mathbb{P}\left(\left|\langle e_j, W^{-1}(P_\Delta A^* A P_\Delta - P_\Delta)W z\rangle\right| \geq \delta\right) \\
&\leq \mathbb{P}\left(\left|\sum_{i:|\mathcal{A}_i|>1} \mathrm{Re}\,(X_i)\right| \geq \delta/\sqrt{2}\right) + \mathbb{P}\left(\left|\sum_{i:|\mathcal{A}_i|>1} \mathrm{Im}\,(X_i)\right| \geq \delta/\sqrt{2}\right) \\
&\leq 4\exp\left(-\frac{\delta^2/4}{\sigma^2 + K\delta/(3\sqrt{2})}\right), \qquad (12.57)
\end{aligned}$$

where K and σ^2 are such that $|X_i| \leq K$ almost surely for each i and $\sum_{i:|\mathcal{A}_i|>1} \mathbb{E}|X_i|^2 \leq \sigma^2$. We now estimate these terms. We have

$$|X_i| = m^{-1}\left|\langle e_j, W^{-1}a_i\rangle\langle W P_\Delta a_i, z\rangle - \mathbb{E}(\langle e_j, W^{-1}a_i\rangle\langle W P_\Delta a_i, z\rangle)\right|.$$

Observe that

$$\left|\langle e_j, W^{-1}a_i\rangle\langle W P_\Delta a_i, z\rangle\right| \leq \|W^{-1}a_i\|_{\ell^\infty}\|W P_\Delta a_i\|_{\ell^1}\|z\|_{\ell^\infty} \leq \Gamma_1(C, \Delta, w).$$

Here, in the second step we use the fact that $\|z\|_{\ell^\infty} = 1$. Hence

$$|X_i| \leq 2\Gamma_1(C, \Delta, w)/m := K.$$

Next, we observe that

$$\begin{aligned}
&\sum_{i:|\mathcal{A}_i|>1} \mathbb{E}|X_i|^2 \\
&\quad = m^{-2}\sum_{i:|\mathcal{A}_i|>1}\left(\mathbb{E}\left|\langle e_j, W^{-1}a_i\rangle\langle W P_\Delta a_i, z\rangle\right|^2 - \left|\mathbb{E}\left(\langle e_j, W^{-1}a_i\rangle\langle W P_\Delta a_i, z\rangle\right)\right|^2\right) \\
&\quad \leq m^{-2}\sum_{i:|\mathcal{A}_i|>1}\mathbb{E}\left|\langle e_j, W^{-1}a_i\rangle\langle W P_\Delta a_i, z\rangle\right|^2 \leq \Gamma_2(C, \Delta, w)/m := \sigma^2.
\end{aligned}$$

Substituting the expressions for K and σ^2 into (12.57) and using the union bound yields

$$\mathbb{P}\left(\|W^{-1}(P_\Delta A^* A P_\Delta - P_\Delta)W z\|_{\ell^\infty} \geq \delta\right) \leq 4|\Delta|\exp\left(-\frac{m\delta^2/4}{\Gamma_2(C, \Delta, w) + \frac{\sqrt{2}}{3}\delta\Gamma_1(C, \Delta, w)}\right).$$

Hence (12.56) gives $\mathbb{P}\left(\|W^{-1}(P_\Delta A^* A P_\Delta - P_\Delta)W z\|_{\ell^\infty} \geq \delta\right) \leq \varepsilon$, as required. □

Lemma 12.23 (Uniform off-support incoherence) *Let $0 < \varepsilon < 1$, $\delta > 0$, $N \geq 2$, $\Delta \subseteq \{1, \ldots, N\}$, $w \in \mathbb{C}^N$ be a vector of weights with $w_i \geq 1$, $\forall i$, $C = \{\mathcal{A}_i\}_{i=1}^m$ be a jointly isotropic collection and A be as in (11.9). Then*

$$\max_{j \notin \Delta}\|P_\Delta A^* A W^{-1} e_j\|_{\ell^2} < \delta,$$

with probability at least $1 - \varepsilon$, provided

$$m \geq \max\{30c, 6\} \cdot \left(\Pi(C, \Delta)\delta^{-2} + \Gamma_1(C, \Delta, w)\delta^{-1}\right) \cdot \log(N/\varepsilon), \qquad (12.58)$$

where $c > 0$ is as in Theorem 12.19 and $\Pi(C, \Delta)$ and $\Gamma_1(C, \Delta, w)$ are as in Definitions 12.2 and 12.3, respectively.

This lemma asserts that no vector supported outside Δ can correlate too well with a vector supported in Δ.

Proof Fix $j \notin \Delta$ and observe that $P_\Delta \mathbb{E}(A^*A)W^{-1}e_j = P_\Delta W^{-1}e_j = 0$. Therefore

$$Z = \left\|P_\Delta A^* A W^{-1} e_j\right\|_{\ell^2} = \left\|P_\Delta (A^*A - \mathbb{E}(A^*A))W^{-1}e_j\right\|_{\ell^2} = \left\|\sum_{i:|\mathcal{A}_i|>1} X_i\right\|_{\ell^2}, \tag{12.59}$$

where X_i are the random vectors $X_i = m^{-1} P_\Delta \left(a_i a_i^* - \mathbb{E}(a_i a_i^*)\right) W^{-1} e_j$. We wish to use the vector Bernstein inequality (Theorem 12.19). To this end, we first estimate the corresponding constants K, σ^2 and μ. First, observe that

$$\begin{aligned} \|P_\Delta a_i a_i^* W^{-1} e_j\|_{\ell^2} = \|P_\Delta a_i\|_{\ell^2} |\langle e_j, W^{-1} a_i\rangle| &\leq \|P_\Delta a_i\|_{\ell^1} \|W^{-1} a_i\|_{\ell^\infty} \\ &\leq \|W P_\Delta a_i\|_{\ell^1} \|W^{-1} a_i\|_{\ell^\infty} \\ &\leq \Gamma_1(C, \Delta, w). \end{aligned}$$

Here, in the penultimate step we use the fact that $w_i \geq 1$, $\forall i$. Hence

$$\|X_i\|_{\ell^2} = m^{-1} \|P_\Delta \left(a_i a_i^* - \mathbb{E}(a_i a_i^*)\right) W^{-1} e_j\|_{\ell^2} \leq 2\Gamma_1(C, \Delta, w)/m := K.$$

Now consider μ. By the Cauchy–Schwarz inequality for expectations (C.4),

$$\left(\mathbb{E}\left\|\sum_{i:|\mathcal{A}_i|>1} X_i\right\|_{\ell^2}\right)^2 \leq \mathbb{E}\left(\left\|\sum_{i:|\mathcal{A}_i|>1} X_i\right\|_{\ell^2}^2\right) = \sum_{\substack{i:|\mathcal{A}_i|>1 \\ k:|\mathcal{A}_k|>1}} \mathbb{E}(\langle X_i, X_k\rangle).$$

Since the X_i are independent and $\mathbb{E}(X_i) = 0$, we get

$$\left(\mathbb{E}\left\|\sum_{i:|\mathcal{A}_i|>1} X_i\right\|_{\ell^2}\right)^2 \leq \sum_{i:|\mathcal{A}_i|>1} \mathbb{E}\|X_i\|_{\ell^2}^2.$$

Also,

$$\begin{aligned} \sum_{i:|\mathcal{A}_i|>1} \mathbb{E}\|X_i\|_{\ell^2}^2 &= m^{-2} \sum_{i:|\mathcal{A}_i|>1} \left(\mathbb{E}\|P_\Delta a_i a_i^* W^{-1} e_j\|_{\ell^2}^2 - \|\mathbb{E}(P_\Delta a_i a_i^* W^{-1} e_j)\|_{\ell^2}^2\right) \\ &\leq m^{-2} \sum_{i:|\mathcal{A}_i|>1} \mathbb{E}\left(\|P_\Delta a_i\|_{\ell^2}^2 |\langle a_i, W^{-1} e_j\rangle|^2\right) \\ &\leq m^{-2} \Pi(C, \Delta) \sum_{i=1}^{m} \mathbb{E}|\langle a_i, W^{-1} e_j\rangle|^2 \\ &= m^{-1} \Pi(C, \Delta)/w_j, \end{aligned}$$

since C is jointly isotropic. Therefore, since $w_i \geq 1$, $\forall i$, we deduce that

$$\left(\mathbb{E}\left\|\sum_{i:|\mathcal{A}_i|>1} X_i\right\|_{\ell^2}\right)^2 \leq \sum_{i:|\mathcal{A}_i|>1} \mathbb{E}\|X_i\|_{\ell^2}^2 \leq \Pi(C, \Delta)/m. \tag{12.60}$$

The condition (12.58) and the facts that $N \geq 2$, $0 < \varepsilon < 1$ imply that

$$m \geq 6\Pi(C,\Delta)\delta^{-2}\log(2) \geq 4\Pi(C,\Delta)\delta^{-2}.$$

Therefore

$$\mathbb{E}(Z) = \mathbb{E}\left\| \sum_{i:|\mathcal{A}_i|>1} X_i \right\|_{\ell^2} \leq \sqrt{\Pi(C,\Delta)/m} \leq \delta/2 := \mu.$$

Finally, we consider σ^2. By (12.60), we have

$$\sup_{\substack{x\in\mathbb{C}^N \\ \|x\|_{\ell^2}=1}} \sum_{i:|\mathcal{A}_i|>1} \mathbb{E}|\langle X_i, x\rangle|^2 \leq \sum_{i:|\mathcal{A}_i|>1} \mathbb{E}\|X_i\|_{\ell^2}^2 \leq \Pi(C,\Delta)/m := \sigma^2.$$

With this in hand, we now use (12.59) and Theorem 12.19 with $t = \delta/2$ and the above values of K, σ^2 and μ to get

$$\begin{aligned}
&\mathbb{P}(\|P_\Delta A^* A W^{-1} e_j\|_{\ell^2} \geq \delta) \\
&\qquad = \mathbb{P}(Z \geq \delta) \\
&\qquad \leq \mathbb{P}(|Z - \mathbb{E}(Z)| \geq \delta/2) \\
&\qquad \leq 3\exp\left(-\frac{m\delta}{4c\Gamma_1(C,\Delta,w)} \log\left(1 + \frac{\delta\Gamma_1(C,\Delta,w)/\Pi(C,\Delta)}{1+\delta\Gamma_1(C,\Delta,w)/\Pi(C,\Delta)}\right)\right).
\end{aligned}$$

By the union bound, we see that

$$\mathbb{P}\left(\max_{j\notin\Delta} \|P_\Delta A^* A W^{-1} e_j\|_{\ell^2} \geq \delta\right) \leq \varepsilon,$$

provided

$$m \geq 4c \cdot \delta^{-1} \cdot \Gamma_1(C,\Delta,w) \cdot \left(\log\left(1 + \frac{\delta\Gamma_1(C,\Delta,w)/\Pi(C,\Delta)}{1+\delta\Gamma_1(C,\Delta,w)/\Pi(C,\Delta)}\right)\right)^{-1} \cdot \log(3N/\varepsilon). \tag{12.61}$$

The function $x \mapsto \log(1 + x/(1+x))$ is monotonically increasing on $[0,\infty)$ and satisfies $\log(1 + x/(1+x)) \geq \log(3/2)x$ for $0 \leq x \leq 1$ and $\log(1 + x/(1+x)) \geq \log(3/2)$ for $x > 1$. Hence

$$(\log(1 + x/(1+x)))^{-1} \leq \frac{1}{\log(3/2)\min\{x,1\}} \leq \frac{1}{\log(3/2)}(1/x + 1).$$

Therefore (12.61) is implied by

$$\begin{aligned}
m &\geq \frac{4c}{\log(3/2)} \cdot \delta^{-1} \cdot \Gamma_1(C,\Delta,w) \cdot \left(\frac{\Pi(C,\Delta)}{\delta\Gamma_1(C,\Delta,w)} + 1\right) \cdot \log(3N/\varepsilon) \\
&= \frac{4c}{\log(3/2)} \cdot \left(\Pi(C,\Delta)\delta^{-2} + \Gamma_1(C,\Delta,w)\delta^{-1}\right) \cdot \log(3N/\varepsilon).
\end{aligned}$$

Since $N/\varepsilon \geq 2$ by assumption, we have $\log(3N/\varepsilon) \leq (1 + \log(3)/\log(2))\log(N/\varepsilon)$. This implies that $4/\log(3/2)\log(3N/\varepsilon) \leq 30\log(N/\varepsilon)$. Hence the above condition on m is implied by (12.58), which completes the proof. □

Finally, we require a weaker (and slightly different) version of Lemma 12.23 valid for a single vector:

Lemma 12.24 (Off-support incoherence) *Let* $0 < \varepsilon < 1$, $\delta > 0$, $N \geq 2$, $\Delta \subseteq \{1, \ldots, N\}$, $w \in \mathbb{C}^N$ *be a vector of weights with* $w_i \geq 1$, $\forall i$, $z \in \mathbb{C}^N$, $C = \{\mathcal{A}_i\}_{i=1}^m$ *be a jointly isotropic collection and* A *be as in (11.9). Then*

$$\|P_\Delta^\perp W^{-1} A^* A P_\Delta W z\|_{\ell^\infty} < \delta \|z\|_{\ell^\infty},$$

with probability at least $1 - \varepsilon$, *provided*

$$m \geq \left(\frac{4\sqrt{2}}{3} \Gamma_1(C, \Delta, w) \delta^{-1} + 4\Gamma_2(C, \Delta, w) \delta^{-2} \right) \cdot \log(4N/\varepsilon), \tag{12.62}$$

where $\Gamma_1(C, \Delta, w)$ *and* $\Gamma_2(C, \Delta, w)$ *are as in Definition 12.3.*

Proof We assume that $\|z\|_{\ell^\infty} = 1$ without loss of generality. Fix $j \notin \Delta$. As in the proofs of the previous lemmas, observe that

$$\langle e_j, W^{-1} A^* A P_\Delta W z \rangle = \langle e_j, W^{-1} (A^* A - I) P_\Delta W z \rangle = \sum_{i : |\mathcal{A}_i| > 1} X_i,$$

where X_i are the random variables $X_i = m^{-1} \langle e_j, W^{-1} (a_i a_i^* - \mathbb{E}(a_i a_i^*)) W P_\Delta z \rangle$. Note that $\mathbb{E}(X_i) = 0$ and since

$$|\langle e_j, W^{-1} a_i a_i^* W P_\Delta z \rangle| \leq \|W^{-1} a_i\|_{\ell^\infty} \|P_\Delta W a_i\|_{\ell^1} \leq \Gamma_1(C, \Delta, w),$$

we also have

$$|X_i| \leq 2\Gamma_1(C, \Delta, w)/m := K.$$

Furthermore

$$\sum_{i : |\mathcal{A}_i| > 1} \mathbb{E}|X_i|^2 \leq m^{-2} \sum_{i : |\mathcal{A}_i| > 1} \mathbb{E}|\langle e_j, W^{-1} a_i \rangle|^2 |\langle a_i, W P_\Delta z \rangle|^2 \leq \Gamma_2(C, \Delta, w)/m := \sigma^2.$$

As in the proof of Lemma 12.22, we now separate into real and imaginary parts and apply Bernstein's inequality (Theorem 12.18) and the union bound to deduce that

$$\mathbb{P}\left(\|P_\Delta^\perp W^{-1} A^* A P_\Delta W z\|_{\ell^\infty} \geq \delta \right) \leq 4N \exp\left(- \frac{m\delta^2/4}{\Gamma_2(C, \Delta, w) + \frac{\sqrt{2}}{3} \delta \Gamma_1(C, \Delta, w)} \right).$$

The inequality (12.62) now yields $\mathbb{P}\left(\|P_\Delta^\perp W^{-1} A^* A P_\Delta W z\|_{\ell^\infty} \geq \delta \right) \leq \varepsilon$, as required. □

12.8.4 Construction of the Dual Certificate via the Golfing Scheme

We now construct a vector ρ so that Theorem 12.17 holds for appropriate parameters, which we somewhat arbitrarily take to be

$$\alpha = 1/4, \quad \beta = 1, \quad \gamma = 1/4, \quad \theta = 5/8, \quad \nu = 12. \tag{12.63}$$

Recall that $N \geq |\Delta| \geq 2$. Also, since $w_i \geq 1$, $\forall i$, we have $|\Delta|_w \geq |\Delta| \geq 2$ and therefore $\log(|\Delta|_w) \geq \log(|\Delta|) \geq \log(2) > 0$. We now define a series of quantities. First, for convenience, we set $s^* = |\Delta|_w \geq 2$. Next, we let

$$L = 3 + \left\lceil \log_2(\sqrt{s^*}) \right\rceil > 3. \tag{12.64}$$

Note that $m \geq 2L + 2$ by assumption, since $\Gamma(C, \Delta, w) \geq \Pi(C, \Delta) \geq 1$ (see (12.6)) and $|\Delta|_w \geq 2$. We also define

$$a_1 = a_2 = \frac{1}{2\sqrt{\log_2(\sqrt{s^*})}}, \qquad a_l = 1/2, \quad l = 3, \ldots, L, \tag{12.65}$$

$$b_1 = b_2 = \frac{1}{4}, \qquad b_l = \frac{\log_2(\sqrt{s^*})}{4}, \quad l = 3, \ldots, L \tag{12.66}$$

and, if $m^* := \lfloor m - L \rfloor \geq m - L - 1 \geq L + 1 > 1$,

$$m_1 = m_2 = \left\lceil \frac{1}{4} m^* \right\rceil, \qquad m_l = \left\lceil \frac{1}{2(L-2)} m^* \right\rceil, \quad l = 3, \ldots, L.$$

Observe that $\sum_{l=1}^{L} m_l \leq m^* + L \leq m$. Finally, for $l = 1, \ldots, L$, we let

$$A_l = \sqrt{\frac{m}{m_l}} P_{\Omega_l} A \in \mathbb{C}^{m \times N}, \qquad \Omega_l = \{m_1 + \ldots + m_{l-1} + 1, \ldots, m_1 + \ldots + m_l\} \tag{12.67}$$

(we remark that the m_l and Ω_l used here are unrelated to the m_k and Ω_k used in a multilevel random sampling scheme). Note that the m_l rows of A_l with indices in Ω_l are (up to the constant) equal to the corresponding rows of A, and the rest are zero. In particular, we may also consider A_l as an $m_l \times N$ matrix when needed.

The dual certificate is now constructed iteratively as follows. Let $\rho^{(0)} = 0$,

$$\rho^{(l)} = W^{-1}(A_l)^* A_l W \left(\operatorname{sign}(P_\Delta(x)) - P_\Delta \rho^{(l-1)}\right) + \rho^{(l-1)}, \qquad l = 1, \ldots, L$$

and set $\rho = \rho^{(L)}$. For convenience, we also define

$$v^{(l)} = W \left(\operatorname{sign}(P_\Delta x) - P_\Delta \rho^{(l)}\right), \qquad l = 0, \ldots, L,$$

so that

$$\rho^{(l)} = W^{-1}(A_l)^* A_l v^{(l-1)} + \rho^{(l-1)}, \tag{12.68}$$

as well as the following events:

$$\begin{aligned}
B_l: &\quad \|W^{-1}(P_\Delta - P_\Delta(A_l)^* A_l P_\Delta) v^{(l-1)}\|_{\ell^\infty} \leq a_l \|W^{-1} v^{(l-1)}\|_{\ell^\infty}, \qquad l = 1, \ldots, L, \\
C_l: &\quad \|P_\Delta^\perp W^{-1}(A_l)^* A_l P_\Delta v^{(l-1)}\|_{\ell^\infty} \leq b_l \|W^{-1} v^{(l-1)}\|_{\ell^\infty}, \qquad l = 1, \ldots, L, \\
D: &\quad \|P_\Delta A^* A P_\Delta - P_\Delta\|_{\ell^2} \leq 1/4, \\
E: &\quad \max_{i \notin \Delta} \|P_\Delta A^* A W^{-1} e_i\|_{\ell^2} \leq 1, \\
F: &\quad B_1 \cap \cdots \cap B_L \cap C_1 \cap \cdots \cap C_L \cap D \cap E.
\end{aligned}$$

In the proof below, we proceed in two steps: first, showing that event F implies conditions (i)–(v) of Theorem 12.17, and second, showing that event F holds with high probability. Before doing so, some intuition is useful. First, notice that

$$\begin{aligned}
v^{(l)} &= W \operatorname{sign}(P_\Delta x) - P_\Delta(A_l)^* A_l P_\Delta v^{(l-1)} - P_\Delta W \rho^{(l-1)} \\
&= \left(P_\Delta - P_\Delta(A_l)^* A_l P_\Delta\right) v^{(l-1)}.
\end{aligned} \tag{12.69}$$

By definition, the ℓ^2-norm of $\upsilon^{(l)}$ measures how far the vector $\rho^{(l)}$ at the lth iteration is from satisfying the condition (iii). However, (12.69) implies that this can be bounded via the event B_l, meaning that the iterates converge to a suitable dual vector which satisfies (iii) in an essentially geometric way. This is the idea behind the golfing scheme: namely, each iteration (shot) brings us closer to the desired condition (the hole, as it were). The challenge is to simultaneously enforce condition (iv). This is done via event C_l, since

$$P_{\Delta}^{\perp}\rho^{(l)} = P_{\Delta}^{\perp}W^{-1}(A_l)^* A_l P_{\Delta}\upsilon^{(l-1)} + P_{\Delta}^{\perp}\rho^{(l-1)}. \tag{12.70}$$

Finally, we note that events B_l, C_l, D and E are all equivalent to the statements in Lemmas 12.21–12.24 (for suitable parameter values). This allows us to estimate the probability that event F holds in the second step.

Proof of Theorem 12.4 Suppose first that event F occurs. Then events D and E give conditions (i) and (ii) of Theorem 12.17. Next consider (iii). Observe that (12.69) and the events B_l give

$$\|\upsilon^{(l)}\|_{\ell^2} \leq \sqrt{s^*}\|W^{-1}\upsilon^{(l)}\|_{\ell^\infty} \leq \sqrt{s^*}a_l\|W^{-1}\upsilon^{(l-1)}\|_{\ell^\infty} \leq \sqrt{s^*}\left(\prod_{j=1}^{l} a_j\right), \tag{12.71}$$

where in the last step we used the fact that $\|W^{-1}\upsilon^{(0)}\|_{\ell^\infty} = \|\mathrm{sign}(P_\Delta x)\|_{\ell^\infty} = 1$. Hence, by the choice of L and the a_l,

$$\|W(P_\Delta \rho - \mathrm{sign}(P_\Delta x))\|_{\ell^2} = \|\upsilon^{(L)}\|_{\ell^2} \leq \frac{\sqrt{s^*}}{2^L \log_2(\sqrt{s^*})} \leq \frac{1}{4},$$

since $s^* \geq 2$ and therefore $\log_2(\sqrt{s^*}) \geq 1/2$. This implies (iii). Now consider (iv). Using event C_l, (12.70) and (12.71) we have

$$\begin{aligned}
\|P_{\Delta}^{\perp}\rho^{(l)}\|_{\ell^\infty} &\leq \|P_{\Delta}^{\perp}W^{-1}(A_l)^* A_l P_{\Delta}\upsilon^{(l-1)}\|_{\ell^\infty} + \|P_{\Delta}^{\perp}\rho^{(l-1)}\|_{\ell^\infty} \\
&\leq b_l\|W^{-1}\upsilon^{(l-1)}\|_{\ell^\infty} + \|P_{\Delta}^{\perp}\rho^{(l-1)}\|_{\ell^\infty} \\
&\leq b_l \prod_{j=1}^{l-1} a_j + \|P_{\Delta}^{\perp}\rho^{(l-1)}\|_{\ell^\infty}.
\end{aligned}$$

Therefore, since $\rho^{(0)} = 0$, the values for a_l and b_l give

$$\|P_{\Delta}^{\perp}\rho\|_{\ell^\infty} = \|P_{\Delta}^{\perp}\rho^{(L)}\|_{\ell^\infty} \leq \sum_{l=1}^{L} b_l \prod_{j=1}^{l-1} a_j \leq \frac{1}{4}\left(1 + \frac{1}{2\sqrt{\log_2(\sqrt{s^*})}} + \frac{1}{4} + \frac{1}{8} + \cdots\right) \leq \frac{5}{8},$$

where again we use the fact that $\log_2(\sqrt{s^*}) \geq 1/2$. This implies that (iv) holds. Finally, consider (v). Define $\xi^{(0)} = 0$ and

$$\xi^{(l)} = \sqrt{\frac{m}{m_l}}A_l\upsilon^{(l-1)} + \xi^{(l-1)}.$$

Then by (12.67), we have

$$W^{-1}A^*\xi^{(l)} = \frac{m}{m_l}W^{-1}A^*P_{\Omega_l}A\upsilon^{(l-1)} + W^{-1}A^*\xi^{(l-1)} = W^{-1}(A_l)^*A_l\upsilon^{(l-1)} + W^{-1}A^*\xi^{(l-1)}.$$

Hence (12.68) and the fact that $W^{-1}A^*\xi^{(0)} = \rho^{(0)} = 0$ give $\rho^{(l)} = W^{-1}A^*\xi^{(l)}$ for all l. We therefore let $\xi = \xi^{(L)}$ so that $\rho = W^{-1}A^*\xi$. Now observe that

$$\|\xi^{(l)}\|_{\ell^2} \leq \sqrt{\frac{m}{m_l}}\|A_l v^{(l-1)}\|_{\ell^2} + \|\xi^{(l-1)}\|_{\ell^2} \tag{12.72}$$

and

$$\|A_l v^{(l-1)}\|_{\ell^2}^2 = \langle v^{(l-1)}, (A_l)^* A_l v^{(l-1)} \rangle = \langle v^{(l-1)}, v^{(l-1)} - v^{(l)} \rangle$$

by (12.69) and the fact that $v^{(l)}$ is always supported in Δ. Therefore

$$\|A_l v^{(l-1)}\|_{\ell^2}^2 \leq \|v^{(l-1)}\|_{\ell^2}^2 + \|v^{(l-1)}\|_{\ell^2}\|v^{(l)}\|_{\ell^2}.$$

An application of (12.71) now gives

$$\|A_l v^{(l-1)}\|_{\ell^2}^2 \leq s^* \left(a_l + 1\right)\left(\prod_{j=1}^{l-1} a_j\right)^2,$$

and we deduce that $\xi = \xi^{(L)}$ satisfies

$$\|\xi\|_{\ell^2} \leq \sqrt{s_*}\sqrt{m}\sum_{l=1}^{L}\sqrt{\frac{a_l + 1}{m_l}}\prod_{j=1}^{l-1} a_j.$$

Now observe that

$$\frac{a_l + 1}{m_l} \leq \frac{4}{m^*}\left(1 + \frac{1}{2\sqrt{\log_2(\sqrt{s^*})}}\right) \leq \frac{8}{m^*}, \qquad l = 1, 2$$

and

$$\frac{a_l + 1}{m_l} \leq \frac{3(L-2)}{m^*}, \qquad l = 3, \ldots, L.$$

Hence

$$\begin{aligned}
\|\xi\|_{\ell^2} &\leq \sqrt{s^*}\sqrt{m}\left(\sqrt{\frac{8}{m^*}}\left(1 + \frac{1}{2\sqrt{\log_2(\sqrt{s^*})}}\right) + \sqrt{\frac{3(L-2)}{m^*}}\sum_{l=3}^{L}\frac{1}{2^{l-1}\log_2(\sqrt{s^*})}\right) \\
&\leq \sqrt{\frac{s^* m}{m^*}}\left(4\sqrt{2} + \frac{\sqrt{3(\log_2(\sqrt{s^*}) + 2)}}{2\log_2(\sqrt{s^*})}\right) \\
&\leq \sqrt{\frac{s^* m}{m^*}}\left(4\sqrt{2} + 2\sqrt{2}\right) = 6\sqrt{2}\sqrt{\frac{s^* m}{m^*}}.
\end{aligned}$$

Here, in the penultimate step we used the fact that $\log_2(\sqrt{s^*}) \geq 1/2$ several times. Now recall that $m^* = \lfloor m - L \rfloor \geq m - L - 1 \geq L + 1$. Therefore $m/m^* \leq 2$. We deduce that $\|\xi\|_{\ell^2} \leq 12\sqrt{s^*}$ and therefore condition (v) holds.

To complete the proof, it remains to show that event F holds with probability at least $1 - \varepsilon$. By the union bound, we have

$$\mathbb{P}(F^c) \leq \sum_{l=1}^{L} \left(\mathbb{P}(B_l^c) + \mathbb{P}(C_l^c) \right) + \mathbb{P}(D^c) + \mathbb{P}(E^c).$$

Suppose that

$$\begin{aligned} &\mathbb{P}(B_l^c), \mathbb{P}(C_l^c) \leq \varepsilon/16, \qquad l = 1, 2, \\ &\mathbb{P}(B_l^c), \mathbb{P}(C_l^c) \leq \varepsilon/(8(L-2)), \qquad l = 3, \ldots, L, \\ &\mathbb{P}(D^c), \mathbb{P}(E^c) \leq \varepsilon/4. \end{aligned} \tag{12.73}$$

Then $\mathbb{P}(F^c) \leq \varepsilon$, as required. We now show that these bounds hold.

For the events B_l we apply Lemma 12.22 to the matrices A_l with the appropriate values of ε and δ. Recalling the definition of the m_l and after some algebra, this gives the condition

$$m \gtrsim \Gamma(C, \Delta, w) \cdot \log(|\Delta|_w) \cdot \log(|\Delta|_w/\varepsilon). \tag{12.74}$$

For the events C_l, we apply Lemma 12.24 to deduce, after some algebra, the condition

$$m \gtrsim \Gamma(C, \Delta, w) \cdot \log\left(N \log(|\Delta|_w)/\varepsilon\right). \tag{12.75}$$

Next, for the event D we use Lemma 12.21 to get the condition

$$m \gtrsim \Pi(C, \Delta) \cdot \log(|\Delta|/\varepsilon) \tag{12.76}$$

and for the event E we use Lemma 12.23 to obtain the condition

$$m \gtrsim (\Pi(C, \Delta) + \Gamma(C, \Delta, w)) \cdot \log(N/\varepsilon). \tag{12.77}$$

Finally, we note that (12.74)–(12.77) are all implied by the condition

$$m \gtrsim \Pi(C, \Delta) \cdot \log(N/\varepsilon) + \Gamma(C, \Delta, w) \cdot \left(\log(N/\varepsilon) + \log(|\Delta|_w) \cdot \log(|\Delta|_w/\varepsilon)\right).$$

Hence (12.73) holds and the proof is complete. □

12.8.5 Proof of Theorem 12.12

The reader will recall that we deferred the proof of this theorem because of the technical issue raised in Remark 12.15. We now present the proof.

Proof of Theorem 12.12 Let $\mathcal{A}$ be the isotropic family defined in Lemma 12.14, C the corresponding isotropic collection and A' the measurement matrix given by (12.42). Let $\Delta \subseteq \{1, \ldots, N^d\}$, $|\Delta| = s$ be such that $\|x - P_\Delta x\|_{\ell^1} = \sigma_s(x)_{\ell^1}$ and set the weights $w_i = 1$, $\forall i$. Using (12.12), (12.13) and Lemma 12.14, we first note that (12.8) holds for this choice of C, Δ and w due to the condition (12.39) on m. Hence, the proof of Theorem 12.4 gives that conditions (i)–(v) of Theorem 5.29 (which is merely the special case of Theorem 12.17 with weights $w_i = 1$) hold for A' with constants α, β, γ, θ and ν given by (12.63). Hence Lemma 6.7 with $z = \hat{x}$ gives

$$\|\hat{x} - x\|_{\ell^2} \lesssim \sigma_s(x)_{\ell^1} + \sqrt{s}\|A'(\hat{x} - x)\|_{\ell^2}.$$

Recalling (12.43) and the fact that $\hat{x}$ and x are both feasible, i.e. $\|A\hat{x} - y\|_{\ell^2} \leq \eta$ and $\|Ax - y\|_{\ell^2} \leq \eta$, we deduce that

$$\|\hat{x} - x\|_{\ell^2} \lesssim \sigma_s(x)_{\ell^1} + \sqrt{s}\|D\|_{\ell^2}\eta.$$

It remains to bound $\|D\|_{\ell^2}$. By definition, we have

$$\|D\|_{\ell^2} \leq \max_{\omega \in \{-N/2+1,\ldots,N/2\}^d} \left\{ 1/\sqrt{N^d \pi_\omega} \right\}.$$

Now, using (12.35) and (12.36), we see that

$$\|D\|_{\ell^2} \leq (N^d C_{N,\alpha})^{-1/2} \begin{cases} 1 & \alpha \leq 0 \\ N^{d\alpha/2} & \alpha > 0 \end{cases}.$$

Hence (12.37) gives that

$$\|D\|_{\ell^2} \lesssim \bar{C}_{N,\alpha}, \tag{12.78}$$

where $\bar{C}_{N,\alpha}$ is as in (12.38). This completes the proof. □

12.9 Improvements for Random Signal Models

As discussed in §12.6, the measurement conditions for unweighted QCBP are consistently worse for the sparse in levels model than for both the oracle estimator and weighted QCBP with suitable weights. Numerical results suggest that this is an artefact of the proofs: the practical performance of weighted and unweighted QCBP is generally quite similar. To shed some light on this discrepancy, in this section we show that unweighted QCBP does indeed admit better measurement conditions, comparable to those for weighted QCBP, provided x satisfies a *random sign* assumption.

Recall that a Rademacher random variable takes values $+1$ and -1 with equal probability. We say that a random variable is a *Steinhaus* random variable if it is uniformly distributed on the unit circle $\{z \in \mathbb{C} : |z| = 1\}$.

Definition 12.25 (Rademacher/Steinhaus sequence) A sequence $\epsilon = (\epsilon_1, \ldots, \epsilon_n)$ is a *Rademacher (Steinhaus) sequence* if the ϵ_i are independent Rademacher (Steinhaus) random variables.

With this in hand, we now state the main assumption for this section:

Assumption The vector $\mathrm{sign}(P_\Delta x)$ is a Rademacher or Steinhaus sequence.

Of course, this assumption is not generally valid in practice. Yet the additional randomness allows us to derive better recovery guarantees for unweighted QCBP than in the deterministic signs case.

12.9.1 Main Results

As in §12.6, we split into three cases, A, C and D (we omit case B since it pertains to the sparse model). For case A (the abstract case), we have the following:

Theorem 12.26 *Let* $0 < \varepsilon < 1$, $N \geq 2$, $\Delta \subseteq \{1, \ldots, N\}$ *with* $|\Delta| \geq 2$, $x \in \mathbb{C}^N$, $C = \{\mathcal{A}_i\}_{i=1}^m$ *be a jointly isotropic collection and* $A \in \mathbb{C}^{m \times N}$ *be as in (11.9). Suppose that* $\operatorname{sign}(P_\Delta x) \in \mathbb{C}^{|\Delta|}$ *is a Rademacher or Steinhaus sequence and*

$$m \gtrsim \left(\Pi(C, \Delta) \log(N/\varepsilon) + \Gamma_1(C, \Delta, 1)\sqrt{\log(N/\varepsilon)}\right) \cdot \log(N/\varepsilon). \tag{12.79}$$

Then the following holds with probability at least $1 - \varepsilon$. *For all* $y = Ax + e \in \mathbb{C}^m$, *every minimizer* $\hat{x} \in \mathbb{C}^N$ *of (5.18) with parameter* $\eta \geq \|e\|_{\ell^2}$ *satisfies*

$$\|\hat{x} - x\|_{\ell^2} \lesssim \|x - P_\Delta x\|_{\ell^1} + \sqrt{|\Delta|}\eta.$$

This result is analogous to Theorem 12.4. It shows that when the signs of $P_\Delta x$ are random, the second local coherence factor Γ_2 is no longer required. Furthermore, with an additional assumption one can also remove the term Γ_1:

Theorem 12.27 *Consider the setup of Theorem 12.26. Let* $\overline{\Pi} \geq \Pi(C, \Delta)$ *and* $\bar{\mu} \geq \mu(C)$ *be any upper bounds for* $\Pi(C, \Delta)$ *and* $\mu(C)$, *respectively. Then the following holds for every* $c > 0$:

(a) if $\overline{\Pi} \geq c\bar{\mu}$, *the (12.79) can be replaced by* $m \gtrsim \overline{\Pi} \cdot \left(\log(N/\varepsilon) + c^{-1} \log^2(N/\varepsilon)\right)$;

(b) if $\overline{\Pi} \geq c\bar{\mu} \log(N/\varepsilon)$, *then (12.79) can be replaced by* $m \gtrsim \overline{\Pi} \cdot (1 + c^{-1}) \cdot \log(N/\varepsilon)$.

This result removes Γ_1 and Γ_2 from the measurement conditions, thus rendering them similar to that of the oracle estimator (12.44), at the expense of an additional condition involving Π and μ. Note that incorporating the upper bounds $\overline{\Pi}$ and $\bar{\mu}$ in this result (as opposed to just Π and μ themselves) is beneficial, since the next two results then become straightforward consequences of it.

Conditions of the form $\overline{\Pi} \geq c\bar{\mu}$ or $\overline{\Pi} \geq c\bar{\mu} \log(N/\varepsilon)$ may at first sight appear strange. But in the sparse in levels model (case C of §12.6), they essentially reduce to bounds on the local sparsities. Specifically, we have the following:

Corollary 12.28 *Consider the setup of Corollary 12.6. Suppose that* $\operatorname{sign}(P_\Delta x) \in \mathbb{C}^{|\Delta|}$ *is a Rademacher or Steinhaus sequence, where* Δ *is such that* $\|x - P_\Delta x\|_{\ell^1} = \sigma_{\mathbf{s},\mathbf{M}}(x)_{\ell^1}$. *Then the following hold:*

(a) In general, conditions (12.15) and (12.16) can be replaced by

$$m \gtrsim \max_{i:|\mathcal{A}_i|>1} \left\{ \sum_{l=1}^r s_l \mu_l(\mathcal{A}_i) \right\} \cdot \log^2(N/\varepsilon)$$
$$+ \max_{i:|\mathcal{A}_i|>1} \left\{ \sum_{l=1}^r s_l \sqrt{\mu_l(\mathcal{A}_i)\mu(\mathcal{A}_i)} \right\} \cdot \log^{3/2}(N/\varepsilon).$$

(b) If $s_k \geq 1$, $k = 1, \ldots, r$, *then (12.15) and (12.16) can be replaced by*

$$m \gtrsim \max_{i:|\mathcal{A}_i|>1} \left\{ \sum_{l=1}^r s_l \mu_l(\mathcal{A}_i) \right\} \cdot \log^2(N/\varepsilon).$$

(c) If $s_k \geq c\log(N/\varepsilon)$, $k = 1, \ldots, r$, *for any* $c > 0$ *then (12.15) and (12.16) can be replaced by*

$$m \gtrsim \max_{i:|\mathcal{A}_i|>1} \left\{ \sum_{l=1}^{r} s_l \mu_l(\mathcal{A}_i) \right\} \cdot (1 + c^{-1}) \cdot \log(N/\varepsilon). \tag{12.80}$$

Recall that the measurement condition for the oracle estimator in the sparse in levels case is given by (12.46). Hence this result states that unweighted QCBP can attain nearly the same measurement condition, subject to a random signs assumption and some rather mild conditions on the local sparsities. In fact, (12.80) is almost identical to (12.46), except for the factor of N/ε in the log term instead of s/ε.

An interesting aspect of this result is that the measurement condition in (c) is better than that in (b), even though the sparsities s_k are potentially larger. This may at first sight seem counterintuitive. However, larger s_k effectively means more randomness, due to the assumption on $\mathrm{sign}(P_\Delta x)$. Therefore it is perhaps not surprising that the log factor can be reduced in case (c).

Finally, we consider case D (the Fourier–Haar wavelet case):

Corollary 12.29 *Consider the setup of Theorem 12.10. Suppose that* $\mathrm{sign}(P_\Delta x) \in \mathbb{C}^{|\Delta|}$ *is a Rademacher or Steinhaus sequence, where* Δ *is such that* $\|x - P_\Delta x\|_{\ell^1} = \sigma_{\mathbf{s},\mathbf{M}}(x)_{\ell^1}$. *Then the following hold:*

(a) If $s_k \geq 1$, $k = 1, \ldots, r$, *then (12.31) can be replaced by*

$$m_k \gtrsim \left(s_k + \sum_{l=1}^{k-1} s_l 2^{-(k-l)} + \sum_{l=k+1}^{r} s_l 2^{-3(l-k)} \right) \cdot \log^2(N/\varepsilon).$$

(b) If $s_k \geq c \cdot \log(N/\varepsilon)$, $k = 1, \ldots, r$, *for any* $c > 0$, *then (12.31) can be replaced by*

$$m_k \gtrsim \left(s_k + \sum_{l=1}^{k-1} s_l 2^{-(k-l)} + \sum_{l=k+1}^{r} s_l 2^{-3(l-k)} \right) \cdot (1 + c^{-1}) \cdot \log(N/\varepsilon).$$

The conclusion is again the same. The measurement condition for unweighted QCBP is similar to that of the oracle estimator, provided $P_\Delta x$ obeys the random sign assumption. As above, the log factor also improves whenever the s_k are not too small.

12.9.2 Proofs

We once again use Theorem 12.17. The main difference now is that (because of the random sign assumption) we can avoid the golfing scheme, and instead construct a dual certificate ρ so that condition (iii) of this theorem holds with $\gamma = 0$, i.e.

$$P_\Delta \rho = \mathrm{sign}(P_\Delta x), \quad \rho = A^* \xi.$$

Since we want condition (v) to hold with as small a constant ν as possible, we choose ξ as the minimal ℓ^2-norm solution of this equation. This is given in terms of the pseudoinverse of $P_\Delta A$ as

$$\xi = (P_\Delta A^*)^\dagger \mathrm{sign}(P_\Delta x).$$

Hence, after noting that $(B^*)^\dagger = (B^\dagger)^*$ for every matrix B, we obtain the dual certificate

$$\rho = A^*\xi = A^*\left((AP_\Delta)^\dagger\right)^* \operatorname{sign}(P_\Delta x). \tag{12.81}$$

Recall that $\operatorname{sign}(P_\Delta x) \in \mathbb{C}^{|\Delta|}$ is a Rademacher or Steinhaus sequence. For the proof of Theorem 12.26, we now also need the following version of *Hoeffding's inequality*:

Lemma 12.30 *Let $x \in \mathbb{C}^n$ and $(\epsilon_1, \ldots, \epsilon_n)$ be a Rademacher or Steinhaus sequence. Then*

$$\mathbb{P}\left(\left|\sum_{i=1}^n \epsilon_i x_i\right| \geq t\|x\|_{\ell^2}\right) \leq 2\exp(-t^2/2), \quad \forall t > 0.$$

See the Notes section for further information.

Proof of Theorem 12.26 We apply Theorem 12.17 with $w_i = 1$, $\forall i$, and parameters $\gamma = 0$, $\alpha = \theta = 1/2$, $\beta = 1$ and $\nu = \sqrt{2}$. Define the following events:

$$\begin{aligned}
B&: \quad \|P_\Delta A^* A P_\Delta - P_\Delta\|_{\ell^2} \leq 1/2, \\
C&: \quad \max_{i \notin \Delta} \|P_\Delta A^* A e_i\|_{\ell^2} \leq t := 1/\sqrt{32\log(6N/\varepsilon)}, \\
D&: \quad \max_{i \notin \Delta} \left|\langle (AP_\Delta)^\dagger A e_i, \operatorname{sign}(P_\Delta x)\rangle\right| \leq 1/2, \\
E&: \quad B \cap C \cap D.
\end{aligned}$$

As noted, condition (iii) holds with $\gamma = 0$ by construction. Event B implies that condition (i) holds with $\alpha = 1/2$ and event C implies that condition (ii) holds with $\beta = 1 \geq t$. Using (12.81), we observe that condition (iv) is equivalent to

$$\max_{i \notin \Delta} \left|\langle (AP_\Delta)^\dagger A e_i, \operatorname{sign}(P_\Delta x)\rangle\right| \leq 1/2.$$

Hence event D implies that condition (iv) holds with $\theta = 1/2$. Finally, if event B holds then, by Lemma A.2, we have

$$\|\xi\|_{\ell^2} \leq \|(AP_\Delta)^\dagger\|_{\ell^2} \|\operatorname{sign}(P_\Delta x)\|_{\ell^2} \leq \sqrt{2}\sqrt{s}.$$

Hence condition (v) holds with $\nu = \sqrt{2}$.

To complete the proof, it remains to show that event E occurs with probability at least $1 - \varepsilon$. First, we use the union bound to write

$$\mathbb{P}(E^c) \leq \mathbb{P}(B^c) + \mathbb{P}(C^c) + \mathbb{P}(D^c). \tag{12.82}$$

Suppose that events B and C occur and consider the third term. Lemma A.2 gives that AP_Δ is full rank, and therefore

$$\|(AP_\Delta)^\dagger A e_i\|_{\ell^2} \leq \|(P_\Delta A^* A P_\Delta)^{-1}\|_{\ell^2} \|(AP_\Delta)^* A e_i\|_{\ell^2} \leq 2\|(AP_\Delta)^* A e_i\|_{\ell^2}.$$

Hence

$$\max_{i \notin \Delta} \|(AP_\Delta)^\dagger A e_i\|_{\ell^2} \leq 2t,$$

by event C. Now let F denote the event $\max_{i \notin \Delta} \|(AP_\Delta)^\dagger A e_i\|_{\ell^2} \le 2t$ and observe that $\mathbb{P}(F^c) \le \mathbb{P}(B^c) + \mathbb{P}(C^c)$. Then (C.2) and the union bound give

$$\begin{aligned}\mathbb{P}(D^c) &= \mathbb{P}\left(\max_{i \notin \Delta} \left|\langle (AP_\Delta)^\dagger A e_i, \operatorname{sign}(P_\Delta x)\rangle\right| > 1/2\right) \\ &\le \mathbb{P}\left(\max_{i \notin \Delta} \left|\langle (AP_\Delta)^\dagger A e_i, \operatorname{sign}(P_\Delta x)\rangle\right| > \frac{1}{4t} \max_{i \notin \Delta} \|(AP_\Delta)^\dagger A e_i\|_{\ell^2} \,\middle|\, F\right) + \mathbb{P}\left(F^c\right) \\ &\le \sum_{i \notin \Delta} \mathbb{P}\left(\left|\langle (AP_\Delta)^\dagger A e_i, \operatorname{sign}(P_\Delta x)\rangle\right| > \frac{1}{4t} \max_{i \notin \Delta} \|(AP_\Delta)^\dagger A e_i\|_{\ell^2} \,\middle|\, F\right) + \mathbb{P}(F^c).\end{aligned}$$

Lemma 12.30, the definition of t and the fact that $\mathbb{P}(F^c) \le \mathbb{P}(B^c) + \mathbb{P}(C^c)$ now give

$$\mathbb{P}(D^c) \le 2N \exp(-1/(32t^2)) + \mathbb{P}(B^c) + \mathbb{P}(C^c) \le \varepsilon/3 + \mathbb{P}(B^c) + \mathbb{P}(C^c),$$

Hence (12.82) implies that

$$\mathbb{P}(E^c) \le \varepsilon/3 + 2\mathbb{P}(B^c) + 2\mathbb{P}(C^c).$$

It remains to bound the last two terms. Lemma 12.21 with $\delta = 1/2$ gives that $\mathbb{P}(B^c) \le \varepsilon/6$, provided m satisfies

$$m \gtrsim \Pi(C, \Delta) \cdot \log(12|\Delta|/\varepsilon).$$

Similarly, Lemma 12.23 with $w_i = 1$, $\forall i$, and $\delta = t$ gives that $\mathbb{P}(C^c) \le \varepsilon/6$, provided

$$m \gtrsim \left(\Pi(C, \Delta) \log(6N/\varepsilon) + \Gamma_1(C, \Delta, 1)\sqrt{\log(6N/\varepsilon)}\right) \cdot \log(6N/\varepsilon). \tag{12.83}$$

Both these conditions are implied by (12.79). Hence we get $\mathbb{P}(E^c) \le \varepsilon$ as required. □

To prove Theorem 12.27 we first require a slight modification of Lemma 12.23:

Lemma 12.31 *Let* $0 < \varepsilon < 1$, $\delta > 0$, $N \ge 2$, $\Delta \subseteq \{1, \ldots, N\}$, $C = \{\mathcal{A}_i\}_{i=1}^m$ *be a jointly isotropic collection and* A *be as in (11.9). Then*

$$\max_{j \notin \Delta} \|P_\Delta A^* A e_j\|_{\ell^2} < \delta,$$

with probability at least $1 - \varepsilon$, *provided*

$$m \ge 4\delta^{-2} \cdot \Pi(C, \Delta) + 30c \cdot \left(\mu(C)\delta^{-2} + \sqrt{\Pi(C, \Delta)\mu(C)}\delta^{-1}\right) \cdot \log(N/\varepsilon), \tag{12.84}$$

where $c > 0$ *is as in Theorem 12.19 and* $\mu(C)$ *and* $\Pi(C, \Delta)$ *are as in Definitions 11.16 and 12.2, respectively.*

Proof As in the proof of Lemma 12.23, we fix $j \notin \Delta$ and write $Z = \|P_\Delta A^* A e_j\|_{\ell^2} = \|\sum_{i:|\mathcal{A}_i|>1} X_i\|_{\ell^2}$, where X_i are the random vectors $X_i = m^{-1} P_\Delta \left(a_i a_i^* - \mathbb{E}(a_i a_i^*)\right) e_j$. We apply Theorem 12.19 once more, but with rather different values of K, μ and σ^2. First, observe that

$$\|P_\Delta a_i a_i^* e_j\|_{\ell^2} = \|P_\Delta a_i\|_{\ell^2} |\langle e_j, a_i\rangle| \le \sqrt{\mu(C)\Pi(C, \Delta)}.$$

Therefore, by identical arguments,

$$\|X_i\|_{\ell^2} \leq 2\sqrt{\mu(C)\Pi(C,\Delta)}/m := K.$$

We next estimate μ. Since $m \geq 4\delta^{-2} \cdot \Pi(C,\Delta)$, the same arguments as before give

$$\mathbb{E}(Z) = \mathbb{E}\left\|\sum_{i=1}^{m} X_i\right\|_{\ell^2} \leq \delta/2 := \mu.$$

Finally, we estimate σ^2:

$$\begin{aligned}\sup_{\substack{x\in\mathbb{C}^N\\ \|x\|_{\ell^2}=1}} \sum_{i:|\mathcal{A}_i|>1} \mathbb{E}|\langle X_i, x\rangle|^2 &\leq m^{-2} \sup_{\substack{x\in\mathbb{C}^N\\ \|x\|_{\ell^2}=1}} \sum_{i:|\mathcal{A}_i|>1} \mathbb{E}\left(|\langle P_\Delta a_i, x\rangle|^2 |\langle a_i, e_j\rangle|^2\right)\\ &\leq m^{-2} \sup_{\substack{x\in\mathbb{C}^N\\ \|x\|_{\ell^2}=1}} \sum_{i:|\mathcal{A}_i|>1} \mu(\mathcal{A}_i)\mathbb{E}|\langle a_i, P_\Delta x\rangle|^2\\ &\leq m^{-1}\mu(C) \sup_{\substack{x\in\mathbb{C}^N\\ \|x\|_{\ell^2}=1}} \|P_\Delta x\|_{\ell^2}^2 = \mu(C)/m := \sigma^2.\end{aligned}$$

Theorem 12.19 and the union bound now give

$$\begin{aligned}&\mathbb{P}\Big(\max_{j\notin\Delta}\|P_\Delta a_i a_i^* e_j\|_{\ell^2} \geq \delta\Big)\\ &\qquad\leq 3N\exp\left(-\frac{m\delta}{4c\sqrt{\mu(C)\Pi(C,\Delta)}}\log\left(1+\frac{\sqrt{\Pi(C,\Delta)/\mu(C)}\delta}{1+\sqrt{\Pi(C,\Delta)/\mu(C)}\delta}\right)\right).\end{aligned}$$

Using the same arguments as in the proof of Lemma 12.23, we deduce that

$$\mathbb{P}\left(\max_{j\notin\Delta} \|P_\Delta a_i a_i^* e_j\|_{\ell^2} \geq \delta\right) \leq \varepsilon,$$

provided

$$m \geq 30c \cdot \left(\mu(C)\delta^{-2} + \sqrt{\mu(C)\Pi(C,\Delta)}\delta^{-1}\right) \cdot \log(N/\varepsilon).$$

This gives the result. □

Proof of Theorem 12.27 We follow the same arguments as in the proof of Theorem 12.26. First, we observe that $\mathbb{P}(E^c) \leq \varepsilon/3 + 2\mathbb{P}(B^c) + 2\mathbb{P}(C^c)$, and that $\mathbb{P}(B^c) \leq \varepsilon/6$, provided

$$m \gtrsim \Pi(C,\Delta) \cdot \log(12|\Delta|/\varepsilon). \tag{12.85}$$

Next, rather than Lemma 12.21 we use Lemma 12.31 with $\delta = t$ to get that $\mathbb{P}(C^c) \leq \varepsilon/6$ if

$$\begin{aligned}m &\gtrsim \Pi(C,\Delta)\log(6N/\varepsilon)\\ &\quad + \left(\mu(C)\log(6N/\varepsilon) + \sqrt{\Pi(C,\Delta)\mu(C)}\sqrt{\log(6N/\varepsilon)}\right) \cdot \log(6N/\varepsilon),\end{aligned} \tag{12.86}$$

as opposed to (12.83). Since $\overline{\Pi}$ and $\bar{\mu}$ are upper bounds for Π and μ, respectively, (12.85) and (12.86) are both implied by the condition

$$m \gtrsim \overline{\Pi} \log(N/\varepsilon) + \bar{\mu} \log^2(N/\varepsilon) + \sqrt{\overline{\Pi}\bar{\mu}} \log^{3/2}(N/\varepsilon).$$

Using Young's inequality this reduces to

$$m \gtrsim \overline{\Pi} \log(N/\varepsilon) + \bar{\mu} \log^2(N/\varepsilon).$$

To complete the proof, we use the condition $\overline{\Pi} \geq c\bar{\mu}$ or $\overline{\Pi} \geq c\bar{\mu}\log(N/\varepsilon)$. □

Proof of Corollary 12.28 Part (a) follows immediately from Theorem 12.26, (12.18) and (12.19). For parts (b) and (c), we use Theorem 12.27. First, we note that

$$\Pi(C, \Delta) \leq \overline{\Pi} := \max_{i:|\mathcal{A}_i|>1} \left\{ \sum_{l=1}^{r} s_l \mu_l(\mathcal{A}_i) \right\},$$

from (12.18). Second, recall by definition that $\mu(C) = \max_{i:|\mathcal{A}_i|>1} \mu(\mathcal{A}_i) := \bar{\mu}$. Suppose that $s_k \geq 1$ and let $a_i \sim \mathcal{A}_i$. Then

$$\|a_i\|_{\ell^\infty}^2 = \max_{l=1,\dots,r} \|P_{M_l}^{M_{l-1}} a_i\|_{\ell^\infty}^2 \leq \max_{l=1,\dots,r} \{\mu_l(\mathcal{A}_i)\} \leq \sum_{l=1}^{r} s_l \mu_l(\mathcal{A}_i) \leq \overline{\Pi},$$

almost surely. Hence $\bar{\mu} \leq \overline{\Pi}$ and we see that part (b) follows from Theorem 12.27. Similarly, $\bar{\mu} \leq \overline{\Pi}/(c\log(N/\varepsilon))$ if $s_k \geq c\log(N/\varepsilon)$, $\forall k$. Hence part (c) also follows in the same way. □

Proof of Corollary 12.29 This follows immediately from Corollary 12.28 after using (12.27) and Lemma 12.11 to bound the local coherences $\mu_l(\mathcal{A}_i)$. □

Notes

The use of weights to exploit sparsity in levels – where the priors are the local sparsities $\mathbf{s}$ – was introduced in [465]. See also [3]. Local coherences relative to a set Δ (Definitions 12.2 and 12.3) were introduced in the unweighted case by Boyer, Bigot & Weiss [91]. They also considered more general block sampling (see the Notes section of Chapter 11). See [24] for the extension to the weighted case. A more general version of Theorem 12.4 was proved in [24], which slightly generalizes the results of [91, 146].

Corollary 12.5 is similar to a result first proved by Candès & Plan [118]. It extends their result to collections of families of random vectors, as opposed to a single isotropic family. As discussed further below, the result of [118] has a slightly different log factor. It takes the form

$$m \gtrsim \mu(\mathcal{A}) \cdot s \cdot (1 + \log(\varepsilon^{-1})) \cdot \log(N). \tag{12.87}$$

Also, as remarked in the Notes section of Chapter 5, [118] used the weak RIP to obtain a recovery guarantee in the nonsparse and noisy case for the unweighted LASSO decoder that is better than (12.11) by a factor of $1/\sqrt{s}$ (up to several log terms). Unfortunately, the weak RIP imposes a signal model, so cannot be used in the local recovery guarantee Theorem 12.4. In Chapter 13 we improve the error bound (12.11) using versions of the RIP (which also produces a uniform recovery guarantee) at the expense of a slightly worse log factor in the measurement condition.

Corollary 12.6 is an extension of a result of [20], which considered only multilevel random sampling. The quantity τ defined in (12.14) is related to the so-called *relative sparsities* of [20]. Specifically, if C corresponds to a multilevel random sampling scheme with families $\mathcal{A}^{(1)}, \ldots, \mathcal{A}^{(r)}$ as defined in §11.4.5, then $\tau(\mathcal{A}^{(k)}; \mathbf{s}, \mathbf{M})$ is (up to a factor of m) the kth relative sparsity of [20]. The idea is that the relative sparsities typically do not greatly exceed the local sparsities s_k. For the Fourier–Haar wavelet problem, this was demonstrated implicitly in the proof of Theorem 12.10 (recall also (12.29)).

For §12.5 we followed the approach of [22]. Somewhat weaker versions of Theorem 12.10 and Lemma 12.11 were first proved in [22]. See the proof of Lemma 4 in [22] for a proof of (12.34).

As mentioned in the Notes section of Chapter 5, nonuniform recovery via dual certificates was used by Candès, Romberg & Tao for randomly subsampled Fourier matrices [121]. The dual certificate construction given therein is specific to the Fourier transform, and does not extend to more general sampling operators. In [120], Candès & Romberg used a random sign assumption to prove a nonuniform recovery guarantee for randomly subsampled unitary matrices. See also [405]. We have used similar ideas in §12.9.

Bernstein inequalities are ubiquitous in compressed sensing. See [214, Chpts. 7 & 8] for an in-depth treatment. Theorems 12.18 and 12.20 are Corollaries 7.31 and 8.15 therein. As noted, Theorem 12.19 is a variation on the standard vector Bernstein inequality for identically distributed random vectors (see, for instance, [214, Cor. 8.45]).

The golfing scheme was a major breakthrough in compressed sensing theory. Introduced in the context of low-rank matrix recovery by Gross [243], it was adapted and extended to compressed sensing in [118] and [17]. We have used the nomenclature of [118] for the technical lemmas in §12.8. The setup used in §12.8 differs somewhat from those works, and was originally used in [20] for the unweighted QCBP decoder. Specifically, in §12.8 the events B_l and c_l use the ℓ^∞-norm throughout, whereas in the original golfing scheme the ℓ^2-norm was used on both sides of the inequality in b_l and for the right-hand side of the inequality in c_l. This requires rather different versions of Lemmas 12.22 and 12.24. The modified setup, however, is crucial in proving the local recovery guarantee Theorem 12.4, whereas the original golfing scheme only considers the sparse model. The weighted case was first considered in [2] in the context of function approximation. We have also simplified the golfing scheme used in [17, 20, 118] by avoiding an additional step where updates are rejected if B_l or C_l fail to occur (see [146]). This additional step is used in the case of the sparse model to obtain the rather different log factor in (12.87), as opposed to that of (12.10). It is not known whether Theorem 12.4 holds with a log factor similar to that of (12.87).

The results in §12.9 can be found in [6]. Hoeffding's inequality for Rademacher and Steinhaus sequences (Lemma 12.30) can be found, for example, in [214, Cor. 8.8 & 8.10]. As discussed above, our use of random signs is based on the approach of [120]. See also [405] and [214, Chpt. 12].

13 Local Structure and Uniform Recovery

We now focus on uniform recovery guarantees. As discussed in §5.5, the standard tools for establishing such guarantees are the robust Null Space Property (rNSP) and the Restricted Isometry Property (RIP). This chapter therefore has two components. First, in §13.2 we introduce generalizations of the rNSP and RIP for the sparse in levels model and then in §13.3 we show how these imply accurate and stable recovery. Second, in §13.4 and §13.5 we derive measurement conditions under which the various measurement matrices introduced in Chapter 11 satisfy this generalized RIP. Up to log factors, these are the same as the measurement conditions for nonuniform recovery seen in the previous chapter. Specifically, for the sparse model (Corollary 13.15) the measurement condition for sampling from an isotropic collection C is

$$m \gtrsim s \cdot \mu(C) \cdot \left(\log(\mu(C)s + 1) \cdot \log^2(s) \cdot \log(N) + \log(\varepsilon^{-1})\right).$$

Besides the log factor, this is identical to the nonuniform measurement condition (12.10). For the sparse in levels model we once more employ weights to improve the measurement condition. For weighted QCBP, with the same choice of weights as in Chapter 12, it is

$$m \gtrsim \max_{i:|\mathcal{A}_i|>1} \left\{ \sum_{l=1}^{r} s_l \mu_l(\mathcal{A}_i) \right\} \cdot L,$$

where L is a similar log factor (Theorem 13.14). Up to L, this is identical to the nonuniform condition (12.22). In particular, when specialized to the Fourier–Haar wavelet problem in §13.4.4, the measurement condition becomes

$$m_k \gtrsim \left(s_k + \sum_{l=1}^{k-1} s_l 2^{-(k-l)} + \sum_{l=k+1}^{r} s_l 2^{-3(l-k)} \right) \cdot L, \qquad k = 1, \ldots, r,$$

as in the nonuniform case (12.32). These conditions aside, we also extend the setup slightly in this chapter to allow the collection C to be nonisotropic. This is achieved via a further generalization of the RIP. This flexibility is useful in subsequent chapters – in particular, Chapter 14.

13.1 Decoders and Recovery Guarantees

Throughout this chapter, unless otherwise stated, $\mathbf{M} = (M_1, \ldots, M_r)$ are sparsity levels, $\mathbf{s} = (s_1, \ldots, s_r)$ are local sparsities and $s = s_1 + \cdots + s_r$ is the total sparsity. As in

Chapter 12, given noisy measurements $y = Ax + e$, we consider the weighted QCBP decoder

$$\min_{z \in \mathbb{C}^N} \|z\|_{\ell^1_w} \text{ subject to } \|Az - y\|_{\ell^2} \leq \eta, \tag{13.1}$$

with positive weights $w = (w_i)_{i=1}^N$ and parameter $\eta \geq \|e\|_{\ell^2}$. Given sparsity levels $\mathbf{M}$, we let $\mathbf{w} = (w^{(1)}, \dots, w^{(r)})$ and set the weights as

$$w_{M_{l-1}+1} = \cdots = w_{M_l} = w^{(l)} > 0, \qquad l = 1, \dots, r, \tag{13.2}$$

where $w^{(l)} > 0$, $\forall l$. Once more we find that the choice

$$w^{(l)} = \sqrt{s/s_l}, \qquad l = 1, \dots, r \tag{13.3}$$

yields the best measurement conditions.

In order to avoid lengthy theorem statements, we now also define the following:

Definition 13.1 (QCBP uniform recovery property) A matrix $A \in \mathbb{C}^{m \times N}$ has the (weighted) *QCBP uniform recovery property of order* $(\mathbf{s}, \mathbf{M})$ *with constant* $\tau > 0$ if the following holds. For all $x \in \mathbb{C}^N$ and $y = Ax + e \in \mathbb{C}^m$, every minimizer $\hat{x} \in \mathbb{C}^N$ of (13.1) with parameter $\eta \geq \|e\|_{\ell^2}$ and weights (13.2)–(13.3) satisfies

$$\|x - \hat{x}\|_{\ell^2} \lesssim r^{1/4} \left(\sigma_{\mathbf{s},\mathbf{M}}(x)_{\ell^1_w} / \sqrt{rs} + \tau\eta \right), \tag{13.4}$$

where $\sigma_{\mathbf{s},\mathbf{M}}(x)_{\ell^1_w}$ is as in (12.4).

The reason for the particular dependence on r will become apparent later. Note that if $r = 1$ – i.e. the sparsity model, in which case the weights $w_i = 1$, $\forall i$ – we simply say that A has the *QCBP uniform recovery property of order s with constant $\tau > 0$*. In this case, observe that (13.4) reduces to

$$\|x - \hat{x}\|_{\ell^2} \lesssim \sigma_s(x)_{\ell^1} / \sqrt{s} + \tau\eta,$$

where $\sigma_s(x)_{\ell^1}$ is as in (5.6).

Unlike in Chapter 12, we now also consider a weighted version of the SR-LASSO decoder that was previously introduced in Chapter 6. This takes the form

$$\min_{z \in \mathbb{C}^N} \lambda \|z\|_{\ell^1_w} + \|Az - y\|_{\ell^2}. \tag{13.5}$$

This decoder will be particularly useful in later chapters. Much like in Chapter 6, we show later that the parameter λ can be chosen in a way that is independent of the noise level $\|e\|_{\ell^2}$ and dependent on the total sparsity s only. As above, we also define the following:

Definition 13.2 (SR-LASSO uniform recovery property) A matrix $A \in \mathbb{C}^{m \times N}$ has the (weighted) *SR-LASSO uniform recovery property of order* $(\mathbf{s}, \mathbf{M})$ *with constant* $\tau > 0$ if the following holds. For all $x \in \mathbb{C}^N$ and $y = Ax + e \in \mathbb{C}^m$, every minimizer $\hat{x} \in \mathbb{C}^N$ of (13.5) with weights (13.2)–(13.3) and parameter $\lambda \leq \frac{1}{\tau\sqrt{rs}}$ satisfies

$$\|x - \hat{x}\|_{\ell^2} \lesssim r^{1/4} \left(\frac{\sigma_{\mathbf{s},\mathbf{M}}(x)_{\ell^1_w}}{\sqrt{rs}} + \frac{1}{\sqrt{rs}\lambda} \|e\|_{\ell^2} \right), \tag{13.6}$$

where $\sigma_{\mathbf{s},\mathbf{M}}(x)_{\ell^1_w}$ is as in (12.4).

13.2 Restricted Isometry and Robust Null Space Properties

Recall that standard compressed sensing matrices $A \in \mathbb{C}^{m\times N}$ are generally normalized so that $\mathbb{E}(A^*A) = I$. In particular, $\mathbb{E}\|Ax\|_2^2 = \|x\|_2^2$ for every $x \in \mathbb{C}^N$. The RIP (Definition 5.18) therefore demands that, for each $x \in \Sigma_s$, the random variable $\|Ax\|_{\ell^2}^2$ does not deviate too much from its expectation. In this chapter, we consider a more general setup in which $\mathbb{E}(A^*A)$ can be an arbitrary positive-definite matrix. Hence we write

$$\mathbb{E}(A^*A) = G^*G, \tag{13.7}$$

for some invertible matrix $G \in \mathbb{C}^{N\times N}$. Typically, G is taken to be the unique positive-definite square root of $\mathbb{E}(A^*A)$. As mentioned, the flexibility gained by allowing $\mathbb{E}(A^*A) \neq I$ will be useful in later chapters. Note that while this setup allows $\mathbb{E}(A^*A)$ to be arbitrary, we generally assume that it is not too badly behaved. As we see later, the various recovery guarantees depend on the norms of G and G^{-1}.

13.2.1 The G-adjusted Restricted Isometry Property (in Levels)

In view of (13.7), we first modify the classical RIP (Definition 5.18) as follows:

Definition 13.3 (G-adjusted restricted isometry property) Let $1 \leq s \leq N$ and $G \in \mathbb{C}^{N\times N}$ be invertible. The sth *G-adjusted Restricted Isometry Constant (G-RIC)* $\delta_{s,G}$ of a matrix $A \in \mathbb{C}^{m\times N}$ is the smallest $\delta \geq 0$ such that

$$(1-\delta)\|Gx\|_{\ell^2}^2 \leq \|Ax\|_{\ell^2}^2 \leq (1+\delta)\|Gx\|_{\ell^2}^2, \quad \forall x \in \Sigma_s. \tag{13.8}$$

If $0 < \delta_{s,G} < 1$ then the matrix A is said to have the *G-adjusted Restricted Isometry Property (G-RIP)* of order s.

Note that A having the G-RIP is generally not equivalent to the matrix AG^{-1} having the RIP. This is only true when $G(\Sigma_s) = \Sigma_s$, e.g. when G is diagonal.

Since this definition applies to the sparse model, we also need a further extension to the sparsity in levels model. This is straightforward, and is done simply by replacing the set Σ_s in (13.8) by the set $\Sigma_{\mathbf{s},\mathbf{M}}$.

Definition 13.4 (G-adjusted restricted isometry property in levels) Let $G \in \mathbb{C}^{N\times N}$ be invertible. The $(\mathbf{s},\mathbf{M})$th *G-adjusted Restricted Isometry Constant in Levels (G-RICL)* $\delta_{\mathbf{s},\mathbf{M},G}$ of a matrix $A \in \mathbb{C}^{m\times N}$ is the smallest $\delta \geq 0$ such that

$$(1-\delta)\|Gx\|_{\ell^2}^2 \leq \|Ax\|_{\ell^2}^2 \leq (1+\delta)\|Gx\|_{\ell^2}^2, \quad \forall x \in \Sigma_{\mathbf{s},\mathbf{M}}.$$

If $0 < \delta_{\mathbf{s},\mathbf{M},G} < 1$ then the matrix A is said to have the *G-adjusted Restricted Isometry Property in Levels (G-RIPL)* of order $(\mathbf{s},\mathbf{M})$.

Notice that Definition 13.3 is a special case of Definition 13.4 corresponding to $r = 1$. For convenience, if $G = I$ we refer to the G-RIPL and G-RICL as simply the RIPL and RICL, respectively.

13.2.2 The Weighted Robust Null Space Property (in Levels)

Recall from §5.5 that the standard RIP implies the rNSP (Lemma 5.20) and the rNSP in turn implies accurate and stable recovery for the unweighted QCBP decoder (Theorem 5.17). In the following definition we extend the rNSP to the weighted setting (since we now consider weighted QCBP) and to the sparse in levels model. Here we recall that $D_{\mathbf{s},\mathbf{M}}$ is the set of all possible support sets of an $(\mathbf{s},\mathbf{M})$-sparse vector (see (11.5)) and $|\Delta|_w$ is the weighted cardinality of Δ (see (12.7)).

Definition 13.5 (Robust null space property in levels) Let $w = (w_i)_{i=1}^N \in \mathbb{R}^N$ be positive weights. A matrix $A \in \mathbb{C}^{m \times N}$ has the weighted *robust Null Space Property in Levels (rNSPL)* of order $(\mathbf{s},\mathbf{M})$ with constants $0 < \rho < 1$ and $\gamma > 0$ if

$$\|P_\Delta x\|_{\ell^2} \leq \frac{\rho \|P_\Delta^\perp x\|_{\ell^1_w}}{\sqrt{|\Delta|_w}} + \gamma \|Ax\|_{\ell^2}, \tag{13.9}$$

for all $x \in \mathbb{C}^N$ and $\Delta \in D_{\mathbf{s},\mathbf{M}}$.

13.3 Stable and Accurate Recovery via the rNSPL and G-RIPL

As in the sparse case (see §5.6), we commence by showing that the weighted rNSPL implies both an ℓ^1_w-norm and an ℓ^2-norm distance bound. For simplicity, we now specialize our attention to weights w of the form (13.2). We write $\mathbf{w} = (w^{(1)}, \ldots, w^{(r)})$ as before. We also define the following two quantities:

$$\xi = \xi(\mathbf{s},\mathbf{w}) = \sum_{k=1}^{r} (w^{(k)})^2 s_k, \qquad \zeta = \zeta(\mathbf{s},\mathbf{w}) = \min_{k=1,\ldots,r} \{(w^{(k)})^2 s_k\}. \tag{13.10}$$

Note that the former is just the weighted cardinality $|\Delta|_w = \sum_{i \in \Delta} w_i^2$ of any $\Delta \in D_{\mathbf{s},\mathbf{M}}$ with respect to the weights (13.2).

13.3.1 The Weighted rNSPL Implies Distance Bounds

The following two lemmas extend Lemmas 5.15 and 5.16, respectively. Observe that the latter follow immediately by setting $r = 1$, since in this case $\xi = \zeta = s$.

Lemma 13.6 (rNSPL implies ℓ^1_w-distance bound) *Suppose that A has the weighted rNSPL of order $(\mathbf{s},\mathbf{M})$ with weights w of the form (13.2) and constants $0 < \rho < 1$ and $\gamma > 0$. Let $x, z \in \mathbb{C}^N$. Then*

$$\|z - x\|_{\ell^1_w} \leq \frac{1+\rho}{1-\rho} \left(2\sigma_{\mathbf{s},\mathbf{M}}(x)_{\ell^1_w} + \|z\|_{\ell^1_w} - \|x\|_{\ell^1_w} \right) + \frac{2\gamma}{1-\rho} \sqrt{\xi} \|A(z-x)\|_{\ell^2}.$$

Proof Let $v = z - x$ and $\Delta \in D_{\mathbf{s},\mathbf{M}}$ be such that $\|P_\Delta^\perp x\|_{\ell^1_w} = \sigma_{\mathbf{s},\mathbf{M}}(x)_{\ell^1_w}$. Then

$$\begin{aligned}\|x\|_{\ell^1_w} + \|P_\Delta^\perp v\|_{\ell^1_w} &\leq 2\|P_\Delta^\perp x\|_{\ell^1_w} + \|P_\Delta x\|_{\ell^1_w} + \|P_\Delta^\perp z\|_{\ell^1_w} \\ &= 2\|P_\Delta^\perp x\|_{\ell^1_w} + \|P_\Delta x\|_{\ell^1_w} + \|z\|_{\ell^1_w} - \|P_\Delta z\|_{\ell^1_w} \\ &\leq 2\sigma_{\mathbf{s},\mathbf{M}}(x)_{\ell^1_w} + \|P_\Delta v\|_{\ell^1_w} + \|z\|_{\ell^1_w},\end{aligned}$$

which implies that

$$\|P_\Delta^\perp v\|_{\ell^1_w} \leq 2\sigma_{\mathbf{s},\mathbf{M}}(x)_{\ell^1_w} + \|z\|_{\ell^1_w} - \|x\|_{\ell^1_w} + \|P_\Delta v\|_{\ell^1_w}. \tag{13.11}$$

Now consider $\|P_\Delta v\|_{\ell^1_w}$. Write $\Delta = \Delta_1 \cup \cdots \cup \Delta_r$, where $\Delta_k \subseteq \{M_{k-1}+1, \ldots, M_k\}$ and $|\Delta_k| = s_k$ for each k. Then

$$\begin{aligned}\|P_\Delta v\|_{\ell^1_w} = \sum_{k=1}^r w^{(k)} \|P_{\Delta_k} v\|_{\ell^1} &\leq \sum_{k=1}^r w^{(k)} \sqrt{s_k} \|P_{\Delta_k} v\|_{\ell^2} \\ &\leq \sqrt{\sum_{k=1}^r (w^{(k)})^2 s_k} \sqrt{\sum_{k=1}^r \|P_{\Delta_k} v\|_{\ell^2}^2},\end{aligned}$$

and therefore $\|P_\Delta v\|_{\ell^1_w} \leq \sqrt{\xi}\|P_\Delta v\|_{\ell^2}$. Hence the weighted rNSPL and the fact that $|\Delta|_w = \xi$ give

$$\|P_\Delta v\|_{\ell^1_w} \leq \sqrt{\xi}\|P_\Delta v\|_{\ell^2} \leq \rho \|P_\Delta^\perp v\|_{\ell^1_w} + \sqrt{\xi}\gamma \|Av\|_{\ell^2}.$$

Substituting this into (13.11) now yields

$$\|P_\Delta v\|_{\ell^1_w} \leq \rho \left(2\sigma_{\mathbf{s},\mathbf{M}}(x)_{\ell^1_w} + \|z\|_{\ell^1_w} - \|x\|_{\ell^1_w} + \|P_\Delta v\|_{\ell^1_w} \right) + \sqrt{\xi}\gamma\|Av\|_{\ell^2},$$

and after rearranging we obtain

$$\|P_\Delta v\|_{\ell^1_w} \leq \frac{\rho}{1-\rho} \left(2\sigma_{\mathbf{s},\mathbf{M}}(x)_{\ell^1_w} + \|z\|_{\ell^1_w} - \|x\|_{\ell^1_w} \right) + \frac{\gamma}{1-\rho}\sqrt{\xi}\|Av\|_{\ell^2}.$$

Therefore, using this and (13.11) once more, we deduce that

$$\begin{aligned}\|z - x\|_{\ell^1_w} &= \|P_\Delta v\|_{\ell^1_w} + \|P_\Delta^\perp v\|_{\ell^1_w} \\ &\leq 2\|P_\Delta v\|_{\ell^1_w} + \left(2\sigma_{\mathbf{s},\mathbf{M}}(x)_{\ell^1_w} + \|z\|_{\ell^1_w} - \|x\|_{\ell^1_w} \right) \\ &\leq \frac{1+\rho}{1-\rho} \left(2\sigma_{\mathbf{s},\mathbf{M}}(x)_{\ell^1_w} + \|z\|_{\ell^1_w} - \|x\|_{\ell^1_w} \right) + \frac{2\gamma}{1-\rho}\sqrt{\xi}\|A(z-x)\|_{\ell^2},\end{aligned}$$

which gives the result. □

Lemma 13.7 (rNSPL implies ℓ^2-distance bound) *Suppose that A has the weighted rNSPL of order $(\mathbf{s}, \mathbf{M})$ with weights w of the form (13.2) and constants $0 < \rho < 1$ and $\gamma > 0$. Let $x, z \in \mathbb{C}^N$. Then*

$$\|z - x\|_{\ell^2} \leq \left(\rho + (1+\rho)\frac{(\xi/\zeta)^{1/4}}{2} \right) \frac{\|z - x\|_{\ell^1_w}}{\sqrt{\xi}} + \left(1 + \frac{(\xi/\zeta)^{1/4}}{2} \right) \gamma \|A(z-x)\|_{\ell^2},$$

and therefore

$$\|z-x\|_{\ell^2} \leq \left(\rho + (1+\rho)\frac{(\xi/\zeta)^{1/4}}{2}\right)\left(\frac{1+\rho}{1-\rho}\right)\left(\frac{2\sigma_{\mathbf{s},\mathbf{M}}(x)_{\ell^1_w} + \|z\|_{\ell^1_w} - \|x\|_{\ell^1_w}}{\sqrt{\xi}}\right)$$
$$+ \left(\frac{1+\rho}{1-\rho} + \frac{3+\rho}{1-\rho}\frac{(\xi/\zeta)^{1/4}}{2}\right)\gamma\|A(z-x)\|_{\ell^2}.$$

Proof Let $v = z - x$ and $\Delta = \Delta_1 \cup \cdots \cup \Delta_r \in D_{\mathbf{s},\mathbf{M}}$, where $\Delta_k \subseteq \{M_{k-1}, \ldots, M_k\}$, $|\Delta_k| = s_k$ is the index set of the largest s_k entries of $P^{M_{k-1}}_{M_k} v$ in absolute value. Then

$$\|P_{\Delta_k} v\|_{\ell^2} = \sqrt{\sum_{i\in\Delta_k} |v_i|^2} \geq \sqrt{s_k}\min_{i\in\Delta_k}|v_i| \geq \sqrt{s_k} \max_{\substack{M_{k-1}<i\leq M_k \\ i\notin\Delta_k}} |v_i|, \quad k = 1, \ldots, r,$$

which gives

$$\begin{aligned}
\|P^{\perp}_{\Delta} v\|^2_{\ell^2} &= \sum_{k=1}^{r} \sum_{\substack{M_{k-1}<i\leq M_k \\ i\notin\Delta_k}} |v_i|^2 \leq \sum_{k=1}^{r} \max_{\substack{M_{k-1}<i\leq M_k \\ i\notin\Delta_k}} |v_i| \sum_{\substack{M_{k-1}<i\leq M_k \\ i\notin\Delta_k}} |v_i| \\
&\leq \sum_{k=1}^{r} \frac{\|P_{\Delta_k} v\|_{\ell^2}}{\sqrt{s_k}} \sum_{\substack{M_{k-1}<i\leq M_k \\ i\notin\Delta_k}} |v_i| \\
&\leq \max_{l=1,\ldots,r}\left\{\frac{\|P_{\Delta_l} v\|_{\ell^2}}{w^{(l)}\sqrt{s_l}}\right\} \sum_{k=1}^{r} w^{(k)} \sum_{\substack{M_{k-1}<i\leq M_k \\ i\notin\Delta_k}} |v_i| \\
&= \max_{l=1,\ldots,r}\left\{\frac{\|P_{\Delta_l} v\|_{\ell^2}}{w^{(l)}\sqrt{s_l}}\right\} \|P^{\perp}_{\Delta} v\|_{\ell^1_w}.
\end{aligned}$$

Since $\|P_{\Delta_l} v\|_{\ell^2} \leq \|P_{\Delta} v\|_{\ell^2}$ we deduce that

$$\|P^{\perp}_{\Delta} v\|_{\ell^2} \leq \sqrt{\frac{\|P_{\Delta} v\|_{\ell^2}\|P^{\perp}_{\Delta} v\|_{\ell^1_w}}{\min_{l=1,\ldots,r}\{w^{(l)}\sqrt{s_l}\}}} = \sqrt{\frac{\|P_{\Delta} v\|_{\ell^2}\|P^{\perp}_{\Delta} v\|_{\ell^1_w}}{\sqrt{\zeta(\mathbf{s},\mathbf{w})}}}.$$

Applying Young's inequality (5.12), we obtain

$$\|P^{\perp}_{\Delta} v\|_{\ell^2} \leq \frac{(\xi/\zeta)^{1/4}}{2}\frac{\|P^{\perp}_{\Delta} v\|_{\ell^1_w}}{\sqrt{\xi}} + \frac{(\xi/\zeta)^{1/4}}{2}\|P_{\Delta} v\|_{\ell^2}.$$

Hence

$$\|v\|_{\ell^2} \leq \|P_{\Delta} v\|_{\ell^2} + \|P^{\perp}_{\Delta} v\|_{\ell^2} \leq \left(1 + \frac{(\xi/\zeta)^{1/4}}{2}\right)\|P_{\Delta} v\|_{\ell^2} + \frac{(\xi/\zeta)^{1/4}}{2}\frac{\|P^{\perp}_{\Delta} v\|_{\ell^1_w}}{\sqrt{\xi}}.$$

We now use the weighted rNSPL to get

$$\|v\|_{\ell^2} \leq \left(\rho + (1+\rho)(\xi/\zeta)^{1/4}/2\right)\frac{\|P^{\perp}_{\Delta} v\|_{\ell^1_w}}{\sqrt{\xi}} + \left(1 + (\xi/\zeta)^{1/4}/2\right)\gamma\|Av\|_{\ell^2}.$$

To complete the proof of the first result, we use the inequality $\|P^{\perp}_{\Delta} v\|_{\ell^1_w} \leq \|v\|_{\ell^1_w}$. For the second result, we simply apply Lemma 13.6 to the term $\|v\|_{\ell^1_w} = \|z - x\|_{\ell^1_w}$. □

13.3.2 The G-RIPL Implies the Weighted rNSPL

Similar to Lemma 5.20, we next show that the G-RIPL implies the weighted rNSPL. For this, we recall that the condition number of an invertible matrix G is defined as

$$\kappa(G) = \|G\|_{\ell^2} \|G^{-1}\|_{\ell^2}. \tag{13.12}$$

Lemma 13.8 (G-RIPL implies rNSPL) *Let $G \in \mathbb{C}^{N\times N}$ be invertible, w be weights of the form (13.2), $0 < \rho < 1$ and $\xi(\mathbf{s}, \mathbf{w})$ be as in (13.10). Suppose that A has the G-RIPL of order $(\mathbf{t}, \mathbf{M})$ and constant $0 < \delta < 1$, where $\mathbf{t} = (t_1, \ldots, t_r)$ satisfies*

$$t_l = \min\left\{2\left\lceil\left(\frac{1+\delta}{1-\delta}\right)\frac{(\kappa(G))^2}{\rho^2}\frac{\xi(\mathbf{s},\mathbf{w})}{(w^{(l)})^2}\right\rceil, M_l - M_{l-1}\right\}, \quad l = 1, \ldots, r.$$

Then A has the weighted rNSPL of order $(\mathbf{s}, \mathbf{M})$ with constants ρ and $\gamma = \|G^{-1}\|_{\ell^2}/\sqrt{1-\delta}$.

Proof Let $\mathbf{s}^* = (s_1^*, \ldots, s_r^*)$ be defined by

$$s_l^* = \begin{cases} M_l - M_{l-1} & t_l = M_l - M_{l-1} \\ s_l & t_l < M_l - M_{l-1} \end{cases}, \qquad l = 1, \ldots, r.$$

We now show that A has the weighted rNSPL of order $(\mathbf{s}^*, \mathbf{M})$. This will imply the result, since $s_l^* \geq s_l$, $\forall l$, and it is straightforward to see that the weighted rNSPL of order $(\mathbf{s}, \mathbf{M})$ holds whenever it holds with order $(\mathbf{s}', \mathbf{M})$ for some $\mathbf{s}' = (s_1', \ldots, s_r')$ with $s_l' \geq s_l$, $\forall l$.

Let $x \in \mathbb{C}^N$ and $\Delta = \Delta_1 \cup \cdots \cup \Delta_r \in D_{\mathbf{s},\mathbf{M}}$, where Δ_l is the index set of the largest s_l^* values of $P_{M_l}^{M_{l-1}} x$ in absolute value. Notice that it suffices to establish the inequality (13.9) for this set only. For each $l = 1, \ldots, r$, we now generate subsets $\Lambda_{l,0}, \Lambda_{l,1}, \ldots$ as follows. First, if $t_l = M_l - M_{l-1}$ then we let $\Lambda_{l,0} = \{M_{l-1}+1, \ldots, M_l\}$ and $\Lambda_{l,1} = \Lambda_{l,2} = \cdots = \emptyset$. Next, if $t_l < M_l - M_{l-1}$ we define $t_l' = t_l/2$ (notice that this is also an integer) and let $\Lambda_{l,0}$ be the index set of the largest t_l' values of $P_{M_l}^{M_{l-1}} x$ in absolute value, $\Lambda_{l,1}$ be the index set of the next largest t_l' values and so forth until a partition of $\{M_{l-1}+1, \ldots, M_l\}$ into sets of size t_l' is obtained (it is of no consequence that the final set may be of size less than t_l'). Define $\Lambda_{l,i} = \emptyset$ for all other values of i. With this in hand, we also let

$$\Lambda_i = \Lambda_{1,i} \cup \cdots \cup \Lambda_{r,i}, \qquad i = 0, 1, \ldots.$$

Notice that the Λ_i form a partition of $\{1, \ldots, N\}$.

Next, observe that $\xi(\mathbf{s}, \mathbf{w})/(w^{(l)})^2 \geq s_l$ and $\left(\frac{1+\delta}{1-\delta}\right)\frac{(\kappa(G))^2}{\rho^2} > 1$. Hence $t_l' \geq s_l$ whenever $t_l < M_l - M_{l-1}$. Therefore $\Delta_k \subseteq \Lambda_{0,k}$, $k = 1, \ldots, r$, which implies that $\Delta \subseteq \Lambda_0 \subseteq \Lambda_0 \cup \Lambda_1$. Since $\Lambda_0 \cup \Lambda_1 \in D_{\mathbf{t},\mathbf{M}}$ the G-RIPL now gives

$$\|P_\Delta x\|_{\ell^2}^2 \leq \|P_{\Lambda_0\cup\Lambda_1} x\|_{\ell^2}^2 \leq \|G^{-1}\|_{\ell^2}^2 \|G P_{\Lambda_0\cup\Lambda_1} x\|_{\ell^2}^2 \leq \frac{\|G^{-1}\|_{\ell^2}^2}{1-\delta}\|A P_{\Lambda_0\cup\Lambda_1} x\|_{\ell^2}^2. \tag{13.13}$$

Expanding with respect to the Λ_i, we get

$$\|A P_{\Lambda_0\cup\Lambda_1} x\|_{\ell^2}^2 = \langle A P_{\Lambda_0\cup\Lambda_1} x, Ax\rangle - \sum_{i\geq 2}\langle A P_{\Lambda_0\cup\Lambda_1} x, A P_{\Lambda_i} x\rangle,$$

and therefore, using the Cauchy–Schwarz inequality and the G-RIPL once more,

$$\begin{aligned}\|AP_{\Lambda_0 \cup \Lambda_1} x\|_{\ell^2} &\leq \|Ax\|_{\ell^2} + \sum_{i \geq 2} \|AP_{\Lambda_i} x\|_{\ell^2} \\ &\leq \|Ax\|_{\ell^2} + \sqrt{1+\delta} \sum_{i \geq 2} \|GP_{\Lambda_i} x\|_{\ell^2} \\ &\leq \|Ax\|_{\ell^2} + \sqrt{1+\delta} \|G\|_{\ell^2} \sum_{i \geq 2} \|P_{\Lambda_i} x\|_{\ell^2}.\end{aligned} \tag{13.14}$$

Consider the final term. Recall that $\Lambda_{l,i} = \emptyset$ whenever $t_l = M_l - M_{l-1}$ and $i \geq 1$. Now suppose that $t_l < M_l - M_{l-1}$. Then $|\Lambda_{l,i}| \leq t'_l$ and therefore

$$\|P_{\Lambda_{l,i}} x\|^2_{\ell^2} \leq t'_l \max_{j \in \Lambda_{l,i}} |x_j|^2 \leq t'_l \min_{j \in \Lambda_{l,i-1}} |x_j|^2 \leq \frac{\|P_{\Lambda_{l,i-1}} x\|^2_{\ell^1}}{t'_l}.$$

Hence

$$\begin{aligned}\|P_{\Lambda_i} x\|^2_{\ell^2} = \sum_{l: t_l < M_l - M_{l-1}} \|P_{\Lambda_{l,i}} x\|^2_{\ell^2} &\leq \sum_{l: t_l < M_l - M_{l-1}} \frac{\|P_{\Lambda_{l,i-1}} x\|^2_{\ell^1}}{t'_l} \\ &\leq \frac{\sum_{l: t_l < M_l - M_{l-1}} (w^{(l)})^2 \|P_{\Lambda_{l,i-1}} x\|^2_{\ell^1}}{\min_{l: t_l < M_l - M_{l-1}} \{(w^{(l)})^2 t'_l\}} \\ &\leq \frac{\left(\sum_{l=1}^r w^{(l)} \|P_{\Lambda_{l,i-1}} x\|_{\ell^1}\right)^2}{\min_{l: t_l < M_l - M_{l-1}} \{(w^{(l)})^2 t'_l\}} \\ &= \frac{\|P_{\Lambda_{i-1}} x\|^2_{\ell^1_w}}{\min_{l: t_l < M_l - M_{l-1}} \{(w^{(l)})^2 t'_l\}}.\end{aligned}$$

Returning to (13.14), we deduce that

$$\begin{aligned}\|AP_{\Lambda_0 \cup \Lambda_1} x\|_{\ell^2} &\leq \|Ax\|_{\ell^2} + \frac{\sqrt{1+\delta}\|G\|_{\ell^2}}{\min_{l: t_l < M_l - M_{l-1}} \{w^{(l)} (t'_l)^{1/2}\}} \sum_{i \geq 2} \|P_{\Lambda_{i-1}} x\|_{\ell^1_w} \\ &= \|Ax\|_{\ell^2} + \frac{\sqrt{1+\delta}\|G\|_{\ell^2}}{\min_{l: t_l < M_l - M_{l-1}} \{w^{(l)} (t'_l)^{1/2}\}} \|P^{\perp}_{\Lambda_0} x\|_{\ell^1_w} \\ &\leq \|Ax\|_{\ell^2} + \frac{\sqrt{1+\delta}\|G\|_{\ell^2}}{\min_{l: t_l < M_l - M_{l-1}} \{w^{(l)} (t'_l)^{1/2}\}} \|P^{\perp}_{\Delta} x\|_{\ell^1_w}.\end{aligned}$$

Combining this with (13.13) and the definition of the t'_l, we obtain

$$\begin{aligned}\|P_\Delta x\|_{\ell^2} &\leq \frac{\sqrt{1+\delta}\|G\|_{\ell^2}\|G^{-1}\|_{\ell^2}}{\sqrt{1-\delta}\min_{l: t_l < M_l - M_{l-1}} \{w^{(l)} (t'_l)^{1/2}\}} \|P^{\perp}_{\Delta} x\|_{\ell^1_w} + \frac{\|G^{-1}\|_{\ell^2}}{\sqrt{1-\delta}} \|Ax\|_{\ell^2} \\ &\leq \rho \frac{\|P^{\perp}_{\Delta} x\|_{\ell^1_w}}{\sqrt{\xi}} + \frac{\|G^{-1}\|_{\ell^2}}{\sqrt{1-\delta}} \|Ax\|_{\ell^2}.\end{aligned}$$

This establishes (13.9) with $\gamma = \|G^{-1}\|_{\ell^2} / \sqrt{1-\delta}$, and thus completes the proof. □

13.3.3 The G-RIPL Implies Stable and Accurate Recovery

We now combine the previous three lemmas to show that the G-RIPL implies stable and accurate recovery (for succinctness, we do not state the corresponding result for the weighted rNSPL).

Theorem 13.9 (G-RIPL implies stable and accurate recovery) *Let $G \in \mathbb{C}^{N \times N}$ be invertible, $w = (w_i)_{i=1}^N$ be weights of the form (13.2), $\xi = \xi(\mathbf{s}, \mathbf{w})$ and $\zeta = \zeta(\mathbf{s}, \mathbf{w})$ be as in (13.10) and suppose that A has the G-RIPL of order $(\mathbf{t}, \mathbf{M})$ and constant $0 < \delta < 1$, where $\mathbf{t} = (t_1, \ldots, t_r)$ satisfies*

$$t_l = \min \left\{ 2 \left\lceil 4 \left(\frac{1+\delta}{1-\delta} \right) (\kappa(G))^2 \frac{\xi(\mathbf{s}, \mathbf{w})}{(w^{(l)})^2} \right\rceil, M_l - M_{l-1} \right\}, \quad l = 1, \ldots, r. \tag{13.15}$$

Let $x \in \mathbb{C}^N$ and $y = Ax + e \in \mathbb{C}^m$. Then the following hold:

(a) Suppose that $\eta \geq \|e\|_{\ell^2}$. Then every minimizer $\hat{x} \in \mathbb{C}^N$ of (13.1) satisfies

$$\|\hat{x} - x\|_{\ell^2} \leq 8(\xi/\zeta)^{1/4} \left(\frac{\sigma_{\mathbf{s},\mathbf{M}}(x)_{\ell^1_w}}{\sqrt{\xi}} + \frac{2\|G^{-1}\|_{\ell^2}}{\sqrt{1-\delta}} \eta \right).$$

(b) Suppose that $\lambda \leq \frac{\sqrt{1-\delta}}{2\|G^{-1}\|_{\ell^2}\sqrt{\xi}}$. Then every minimizer $\hat{x} \in \mathbb{C}^N$ of (13.5) satisfies

$$\|\hat{x} - x\|_{\ell^2} \leq 8(\xi/\zeta)^{1/4} \left(\frac{\sigma_{\mathbf{s},\mathbf{M}}(x)_{\ell^1_w}}{\sqrt{\xi}} + \left(\frac{1}{2\lambda\sqrt{\xi}} + \frac{\|G^{-1}\|_{\ell^2}}{\sqrt{1-\delta}} \right) \|e\|_{\ell^2} \right).$$

Proof Lemma 13.8 and the conditions on $\mathbf{t}$ imply that A has the weighted rNSPL of order $(\mathbf{s}, \mathbf{M})$ with constants $\rho = 1/2$ and $\gamma = \|G^{-1}\|_{\ell^2}/\sqrt{1-\delta}$. We now apply Lemma 13.7 with $z = \hat{x}$ to get

$$\begin{aligned} \|\hat{x} - x\|_{\ell^2} \leq & \left(\frac{3}{2} + \frac{9}{4}(\xi/\zeta)^{1/4} \right) \left(\frac{2\sigma_{\mathbf{s},\mathbf{M}}(x)_{\ell^1_w} + \|\hat{x}\|_{\ell^1_w} - \|x\|_{\ell^1_w}}{\sqrt{\xi}} \right) \\ & + \left(3 + \frac{7}{2}(\xi/\zeta)^{1/4} \right) \frac{\|G^{-1}\|_{\ell^2}}{\sqrt{1-\delta}} \|A(\hat{x} - x)\|_{\ell^2}. \end{aligned}$$

Since $\xi/\zeta \geq 1$, this simplifies to

$$\|\hat{x} - x\|_{\ell^2} \leq 4(\xi/\zeta)^{1/4} \left(\frac{2\sigma_{\mathbf{s},\mathbf{M}}(x)_{\ell^1_w} + \|\hat{x}\|_{\ell^1_w} - \|x\|_{\ell^1_w}}{\sqrt{\xi}} + \frac{2\|G^{-1}\|_{\ell^2}}{\sqrt{1-\delta}} \|A(\hat{x} - x)\|_{\ell^2} \right). \tag{13.16}$$

For (a), observe that $\|\hat{x}\|_{\ell^1_w} \leq \|x\|_{\ell^1_w}$, since $\hat{x}$ is a minimizer of (13.1), and

$$\|A(\hat{x} - x)\|_{\ell^2} \leq \|A\hat{x} - y\|_{\ell^2} + \|Ax - y\|_{\ell^2} \leq 2\eta,$$

since $\hat{x}$ and x are both feasible for (13.1). The result now follows immediately.

For (b), write $\|A(\hat{x} - x)\|_{\ell^2} \leq \|A\hat{x} - y\|_{\ell^2} + \|e\|_{\ell^2}$. Then (13.16) and the condition on λ give

$$\|\hat{x} - x\|_{\ell^2} \leq 4(\xi/\zeta)^{1/4}\left(\frac{2\sigma_{\mathbf{s},\mathbf{M}}(x)_{\ell^1_w}}{\sqrt{\xi}} + \frac{\lambda\|\hat{x}\|_{\ell^1_w} + \|A\hat{x} - y\|_{\ell^2} - \lambda\|x\|_{\ell^1_w}}{\lambda\sqrt{\xi}}\right.$$
$$\left. + \frac{2\|G^{-1}\|_{\ell^2}}{\sqrt{1-\delta}}\|e\|_{\ell^2}\right).$$

Since $\hat{x}$ is a minimizer of (13.5) we deduce that

$$\|\hat{x} - x\|_{\ell^2} \leq 4(\xi/\zeta)^{1/4}\left(\frac{2\sigma_{\mathbf{s},\mathbf{M}}(x)_{\ell^1_w}}{\sqrt{\xi}} + \frac{\|e\|_{\ell^2}}{\lambda\sqrt{\xi}} + \frac{2\|G^{-1}\|_{\ell^2}}{\sqrt{1-\delta}}\|e\|_{\ell^2}\right),$$

as required. □

Remark 13.10 It is worth comparing Theorem 13.9 to the corresponding result for the sparse model, Theorem 5.21. Let $r = 1$, $G = I$ and note that $w^{(1)} = 1$ in this case. Then Theorem 13.9 implies that a matrix that has the RIP of order

$$t = \min\left\{2\left\lceil 4\left(\frac{1+\delta}{1-\delta}\right)s\right\rceil, N\right\}, \tag{13.17}$$

for any $0 < \delta < 1$, yields stable and accurate recovery for unweighted QCBP. Note that the order of the RIP (being t) depends not only on s, but also on the RIC δ. This is rather different to Theorem 5.21, which asserts stable and accurate recovery subject to A having the RIP of order $2s$ with RIC $\delta_{2s} < \sqrt{2} - 1$.

This difference arises because we do not necessarily have $P_\Delta A^* A P_\Delta \approx P_\Delta$ when A has the G-RIPL. Hence, in the proof of Lemma 13.8 (a key result on which Theorem 13.9 relies) we cannot argue as we did in (5.27) in the proof of the corresponding result in the sparse case, Lemma 5.20. Instead, the idea pursued in the proof of Lemma 13.8 is to enlarge the support sets to sets of size t (or t_l in the levels case), and then use the relation between t and s (or s_l) to get the desired bound.

The key point, however, is that t (or t_l) scales linearly with s (or s_l). Since the various measurement conditions that assert the RIP (or G-RIPL) all depend linearly on t (or t_l), this approach does not lead to worse estimates besides, potentially, in the constants.

13.4 Measurement Conditions for Uniform Recovery

Having shown that it implies stable and accurate recovery, we next present measurement conditions under which the G-RIPL holds. As discussed, we also generalize the class of sampling operators to allow for the collections to be nonisotropic in a suitable sense. Extending Definition 11.4, we now consider the following:

Definition 13.11 (Nondegenerate collection) Let $\mathcal{A}_1, \ldots, \mathcal{A}_m$ be independent families of random vectors on $\mathbb{C}^N$. The collection $C = \{\mathcal{A}_i\}_{i=1}^m$ is *nondegenerate* if the matrix

$$\frac{1}{m}\sum_{i=1}^{m}\mathbb{E}(a_i a_i^*), \tag{13.18}$$

where $a_i \sim \mathcal{A}_i$ for each i, is positive definite. In this case, we write $G = G_C \in \mathbb{C}^{N\times N}$ for its unique positive-definite square root.

Recall that the matrix (13.18) is precisely $\mathbb{E}(A^*A)$ for A is as in (11.9). It is nonnegative definite by definition. As mentioned, we are interested in the case where it is both positive definite *and* reasonably well conditioned.

Given a nondegenerate collection $C = \{\mathcal{A}_i\}_{i=1}^m$, we write $\mu(C)$ for its coherence (as in Definition 11.17) and $\mu_l(\mathcal{A}_i;\mathbf{M})$ for the lth local coherence of the family $\mathcal{A}_i$ (as in Definition 11.19). We also define the following quantity:

$$\Xi = \Xi(C;\mathbf{s},\mathbf{M}) = \|G^{-1}\|_{\ell^2}^2 \cdot \max_{i:|\mathcal{A}_i|>1}\left\{\sum_{l=1}^r s_l\mu_l(\mathcal{A}_i;\mathbf{M})\right\}. \tag{13.19}$$

We now state the main result of this section.

Theorem 13.12 (Measurement condition for the G-RIPL) *Let $0 < \delta, \varepsilon < 1$, $N \geq s \geq 2$, $C = \{\mathcal{A}_i\}_{i=1}^m$ be a nondegenerate collection and A be as in (11.9). Suppose that*

$$m \gtrsim \delta^{-2} \cdot \Xi(C;\mathbf{s},\mathbf{M}) \cdot L, \tag{13.20}$$

where $\Xi(C;\mathbf{s},\mathbf{M})$ is as in (13.19), $G = G_C$ is as in Definition 13.11 and

$$L = r \cdot \log\left(2(\Xi(C;\mathbf{s},\mathbf{M}) + 1)\right) \cdot \log^2(s) \cdot \log(N) + \log(\varepsilon^{-1}). \tag{13.21}$$

Then, with probability at least $1-\varepsilon$, the matrix A has the G-RIPL of order $(\mathbf{s},\mathbf{M})$ with constant $\delta_{\mathbf{s},\mathbf{M}} \leq \delta$.

Since it requires significant work, we defer the proof of this result to §13.5.

Remark 13.13 The log factor (13.21) can be replaced by the slightly simpler factor

$$L' = r \cdot \log(2m) \cdot \log^2(s) \cdot \log(N) + \log(\varepsilon^{-1})$$

and a possibly different constant in (13.20). This follows by noticing that $L' \gtrsim 1$, and therefore any m that satisfies $m \gtrsim \delta^{-2} \cdot \Xi \cdot L'$ also satisfies $m \gtrsim \Xi$ and $m \geq 1$ (since it is an integer). Hence $\log(2m) \gtrsim \log(2(\Xi + 1))$ and therefore m satisfies (13.20) as well. We make a similar simplification in a number of the subsequent results. See the Notes section for some further discussion on the log factors in these results.

13.4.1 Uniform Recovery for the Sparse in Levels Model

Consider the sparse in levels model. Combining Theorem 13.12 with Theorem 13.9 we now deduce the following result. For this, we also recall Definitions 13.1 and 13.2.

Theorem 13.14 (Sparse in levels model, uniform recovery) *Let $0 < \varepsilon < 1$, $N \geq s \geq 2$, $C = \{\mathcal{A}_i\}_{i=1}^m$ be a nondegenerate collection and $A \in \mathbb{C}^{m\times N}$ be as in (11.9). Suppose that*

$$m \gtrsim (\kappa(G))^2 \cdot \Xi(C;\mathbf{s},\mathbf{M}) \cdot L,$$

where $\Xi(C; \mathbf{s}, \mathbf{M})$ *is as in (13.19),* $G = G_C$ *is as in Definition 13.11 and*

$$L = r^2 \cdot \log\left(2\left(r(\kappa(G))^2 \Xi(C; \mathbf{s}, \mathbf{M}) + 1\right)\right) \cdot \log^2(r(\kappa(G))^2 s) \cdot \log(N) + r \cdot \log(\varepsilon^{-1}).$$

Then, with probability at least $1 - \varepsilon$*, the matrix* A *has the QCBP uniform recovery property of order* $(\mathbf{s}, \mathbf{M})$ *with constant* $\tau = \|G^{-1}\|_{\ell^2}$ *and the SR-LASSO uniform recovery property of order* $(\mathbf{s}, \mathbf{M})$ *with constant* $\tau = 2\sqrt{2}\|G^{-1}\|_{\ell^2}$.

Proof Let $\mathbf{t} = (t_1, \ldots, t_r)$ be given by (13.15) with $\delta = 1/2$. With weights as in (13.3), observe that $\zeta(\mathbf{s}, \mathbf{w}) = s$, $\xi(\mathbf{s}, \mathbf{w}) = rs$ and

$$t_l \lesssim (\kappa(G))^2 \frac{\xi(\mathbf{s}, \mathbf{w})}{(w^{(l)})^2} = (\kappa(G))^2 r s_l, \quad l = 1, \ldots, r.$$

Hence

$$\Xi(C; \mathbf{t}, \mathbf{M}) = \|G^{-1}\|^2_{\ell^2} \cdot \max_{i:|\mathcal{A}_i|>1} \left\{ \sum_{l=1}^{r} t_l \mu_l(\mathcal{A}_i; \mathbf{M}) \right\} \lesssim r(\kappa(G))^2 \Xi(C; \mathbf{s}, \mathbf{M}),$$

and $t_1 + \cdots + t_r \lesssim r(\kappa(G))^2 s$. Theorem 13.12 now implies that A satisfies the G-RIPL of order $(\mathbf{t}, \mathbf{M})$. The result now follows from Theorem 13.9. □

Comparing this with the corresponding nonuniform recovery guarantee, Corollary 12.7, we conclude the following:

For the sparse in levels model, the same measurement condition, up to log factors, ensures both uniform and nonuniform recovery for weighted QCBP (with the same weights in both cases).

Recall from §12.6 that this measurement condition is also the same (up to r and the log factor) to that which is sufficient for the oracle estimator. As in the sparse case (recall §5.7), the error bound in the uniform recovery guarantee is also better than the corresponding bound in the nonuniform guarantee by a factor that is roughly equal to $\sqrt{s}$ (compare (13.4) with (12.21), for instance).

It is not surprising that the same choice of weights should work in both the nonuniform and uniform cases. To see why this choice is suitable for the latter, notice that the condition on t_l in Theorem 13.9 depends on $\xi(\mathbf{s}, \mathbf{w})/(w^{(l)})^2$. Hence, if the weights are given by (12.3) this reduces to just rs_l, which depends solely on the lth local sparsity s_l and, in particular, is independent of the other local sparsities s_k, $k \neq l$. On the other hand, Theorem 13.9 yields a poor measurement condition in the unweighted case. If $w^{(l)} = 1$, $\forall l$, then the condition on t_l depends on the total sparsity $s = s_1 + \cdots + s_r$, which is undesirable. This differs from the nonuniform setting of Chapter 12, in which measurement conditions for unweighted QCBP in terms of the local sparsities were indeed possible. But, as discussed therein, they are rather worse than those for the weighted case.

13.4.2 Uniform Recovery for the Sparse Model

We now consider the sparse model. Theorem 13.14 implies the following uniform recovery guarantee in this case:

Corollary 13.15 (Sparse model, uniform recovery) *Let* $0 < \varepsilon < 1$, $N \geq s \geq 2$, $C = \{\mathcal{A}_i\}_{i=1}^m$ *be a nondegenerate collection, and* A *be as in (11.9). Suppose that*

$$m \gtrsim \delta^{-2} \cdot \|G^{-1}\|_{\ell^2}^2 \cdot (\kappa(G))^2 \cdot \mu(C) \cdot s \cdot L,$$

where $\mu(C)$ *is as in Definition 11.17,* $G = G_C$ *is as in Definition 13.11 and*

$$L = \log\left(2\left(\|G^{-1}\|_{\ell^2}^2(\kappa(G))^2\mu(C)s + 1\right)\right) \cdot \log^2((\kappa(G))^2 s) \cdot \log(N) + \log(\varepsilon^{-1}).$$

Then, with probability at least $1 - \varepsilon$, A *has the G-RIP of order* s *with constant* $\delta_s \leq \delta$. *In particular, if*

$$m \gtrsim \|G^{-1}\|_{\ell^2}^2 \cdot (\kappa(G))^2 \cdot \mu(C) \cdot s \cdot L,$$

then, with probability at least $1 - \varepsilon$, A *has the QCBP uniform recovery property of order* s *with constant* $\tau = \|G^{-1}\|_{\ell^2}$ *and the SR-LASSO uniform recovery property of order* s *with constant* $\tau = 2\sqrt{2}\|G^{-1}\|_{\ell^2}$.

Proof This follows from Theorems 13.12 and 13.14 by setting $r = 1$ and noting that $\Xi(C, \mathbf{s}, \mathbf{M}) = \|G^{-1}\|_{\ell^2}^2 \mu(C)s$ in this case. □

Besides the larger log factor (see the Notes section) and the factors in G stemming from the more general sampling model (Definition 13.11 as opposed to Definition 11.4), this is the same as the nonuniform recovery guarantee Corollary 12.5. Hence:

> For the sparse model, the same measurement condition, up to log factors, ensures both uniform and nonuniform recovery for unweighted QCBP.

In particular, the number of measurements is determined by the sparsity s multiplied by the coherence $\mu(C)$. Note that this result also implies Theorem 5.27.

Proof of Theorem 5.27 Recall that a randomly subsampled unitary matrix is equivalent to sampling with the jointly isotropic collection C defined in Example 11.5. Since $\mu(C) = \mu(U) \geq 1$ in this case (see (11.11)) and $U^*U = I$, which implies that $G = I$, the result follows immediately from Corollary 13.15. □

Remark 13.16 Unsurprisingly, the various measurement conditions presented above are invariant to rescaling A. Indeed, suppose that the vectors a_i that define A are rescaled to ca_i, so that $A \mapsto cA$. Then $G \mapsto cG$, $\kappa(G)$ remains unchanged and $\|G^{-1}\|_{\ell^2} \mapsto \|G^{-1}\|_{\ell^2}/c$. But the various coherence factors, for instance $\mu(C)$ in the case of Corollary 13.15, are also scaled by c, i.e. $\mu(C) \mapsto c^2\mu(C)$. Therefore, the overall measurement conditions remain unchanged.

13.4.3 Multilevel Random Sampling

We now consider multilevel random sampling. Recall from §11.4.5 that this corresponds to sampling the rows of a unitary matrix $U \in \mathbb{C}^{N\times N}$ with sampling levels $\mathbf{N} = (N_1, \ldots, N_r)$ and local numbers of measurements $\mathbf{m} = (m_1, \ldots, m_r)$. In particular, the corresponding collection C is jointly isotropic, and therefore $G = I$. Specializing Theorem 13.14 to this case gives the following:

Corollary 13.17 (Multilevel random sampling, uniform recovery) *Let $0 < \varepsilon < 1$, $N \geq s \geq 2$, $U \in \mathbb{C}^{N\times N}$ be unitary and A be as in Definition 11.14. Suppose that*

$$m_k \gtrsim \left(\sum_{l=1}^{r} s_l \mu\left(U^{(k,l)}\right) \right) \cdot L, \qquad k = 1, \ldots, r, \tag{13.22}$$

where

$$L = r^2 \cdot \log(2m) \cdot \log^2(rs) \cdot \log(N) + r \cdot \log(\varepsilon^{-1}),$$

and $m = m_1 + \cdots + m_r$. Then, with probability at least $1 - \varepsilon$, A has the QCBP uniform recovery property of order $(\mathbf{s}, \mathbf{M})$ with constant $\tau = 1$ and the SR-LASSO uniform recovery property of order $(\mathbf{s}, \mathbf{M})$ with constant $\tau = 2\sqrt{2}$.

Proof Recall that $G = I$ in this case. Hence, Theorem 13.14, Remark 13.13 and the definition of Ξ imply that the result holds, provided

$$m \gtrsim \max_{i:|\mathcal{A}_i|>1} \left\{ \sum_{l=1}^{r} s_l \mu_l(\mathcal{A}_i; \mathbf{M}) \right\} \cdot \left(r^2 \cdot \log(2m) \cdot \log^2(rs) \cdot \log(N) + r \cdot \log(\varepsilon^{-1}) \right).$$

To get (13.22) we use (12.27) to estimate the local coherences $\mu_l(\mathcal{A}_i; \mathbf{M})$. □

This result is the uniform version of the nonuniform recovery guarantee Corollary 12.9. Note that the measurement condition is once more identical, up to the log factor.

13.4.4 The Fourier–Haar Wavelet Problem

To conclude this section, we consider the discrete Fourier–Haar wavelet problem. First, we consider the sparse in levels model and multilevel random sampling (see §11.6). For this, we have the following uniform version of Theorem 12.10:

Theorem 13.18 (Multilevel Fourier–Haar, uniform recovery) *Consider the one-dimensional Fourier–Haar wavelet problem with multilevel random sampling based on sampling levels $\mathbf{N}$ given by (11.21), and let the sparsity levels $\mathbf{M}$ be given by (11.19). Then condition (13.22) of Corollary 13.17 is implied by*

$$m_k \gtrsim \left(s_k + \sum_{l=1}^{k-1} s_l 2^{-(k-l)} + \sum_{l=k+1}^{r} s_l 2^{-3(l-k)} \right) \cdot L, \quad k = 1, \ldots, r,$$

where

$$L = \log^3(N) \cdot \log(2m) \cdot \log^2(\log(N)s) + \log(N) \cdot \log(\varepsilon^{-1}).$$

Proof This follows immediately from Corollary 13.17, Lemma 12.11 and the fact that $r = \log_2(N) + 1$ in this case. □

Recall that in §12.5.2 we proved a nonuniform recovery guarantee for the Fourier–Haar wavelet problem with the sparse model and using power-law sampling. We now prove the analogous uniform guarantee. As in §12.5.2, we consider both the one- and two-dimensional cases. We let $U = N^{-d/2} F\Phi \in \mathbb{C}^{N^d \times N^d}$ for $d = 1, 2$, where F is the d-dimensional Fourier matrix (Definition 2.1) and Φ is the d-dimensional discrete Haar wavelet sparsifying transform. For simplicity, we consider the QCBP decoder only.

Theorem 13.19 (Power-law Fourier–Haar, uniform recovery) *Consider the discrete Fourier–Haar wavelet problem in $d = 1$ or $d = 2$ dimensions. Let $0 < \varepsilon < 1$, $N^d \geq s \geq 2$ and $\Omega \subseteq \{-N/2+1, \ldots, N/2\}^d$ be the sampling scheme corresponding to (12.35) ($d = 1$) or (12.36) ($d = 2$) for some $\alpha \in \mathbb{R}$, and let $A = (N^d/m)^{1/2} P_\Omega U \in \mathbb{C}^{m \times N^d}$ be the resulting measurement matrix. Suppose that*

$$m \gtrsim s \cdot \widetilde{C}_{N,\alpha} \cdot \left(\log\left(s \cdot \widetilde{C}_{N,\alpha}\right) \cdot \log^2(s) \cdot \log(N) + \log(\varepsilon^{-1})\right), \tag{13.23}$$

where $\widetilde{C}_{N,\alpha}$ is as in (12.38). Then, with probability at least $1 - \varepsilon$, A has the QCBP uniform recovery property of order s with constant $\tau = \overline{C}_{N,\alpha}$, where $\overline{C}_{N,\alpha}$ is as in (12.38).

As we expect, the measurement condition (13.23) is identical up to log factors to that of the nonuniform case (12.39). In particular, the best choice of α (from the perspective of the sparse model) is once more $\alpha = 1$.

To prove Theorem 13.19, it is convenient to first formulate the following lemma:

Lemma 13.20 *Consider the discrete Fourier–Haar wavelet problem in $d = 1$ or $d = 2$ dimensions. Let $0 < \delta, \varepsilon < 1$, $N^d \geq s \geq 2$ and $\mathcal{A}$ be the isotropic family with $a \sim \mathcal{A}$ if*

$$\mathbb{P}\left(a = U^* e_{\varrho^{-1}(\omega)}/\sqrt{\pi_\omega}\right) = \pi_\omega, \quad \omega \in \{-N/2+1, \ldots, N/2\}^d,$$

where π corresponds to (12.35) ($d = 1$) or (12.36) ($d = 2$) for some $\alpha \in \mathbb{R}$ and ϱ is as in (2.14). Suppose that $A' \in \mathbb{C}^{m \times N^d}$ is the measurement matrix (11.9) corresponding to this family, and let

$$m \gtrsim \delta^{-2} \cdot s \cdot \widetilde{C}_{N,\alpha} \cdot \left(\log\left(s \cdot \widetilde{C}_{N,\alpha}\right) \cdot \log^2(s) \cdot \log(N) + \log(\varepsilon^{-1})\right),$$

where $\widetilde{C}_{N,\alpha}$ is as in (12.38). Then, with probability at least $1 - \varepsilon$, the matrix A' has the RIP of order s with constant $\delta_s \leq \delta$.

Proof This follows immediately from Lemma 12.14 and Corollary 13.15. □

Proof of Theorem 13.19 Let A' be as in the previous lemma. The condition (13.23) and Lemma 13.8 (with $r = 1$, $w_i = 1$, $\forall i$ and $\delta = \rho = 1/2$) imply that A' has the rNSP of order s with constant $\rho = 1/2$ and $\gamma \lesssim 1$.

Now let $x \in \mathbb{C}^{N^d}$ and $y = Ax + e \in \mathbb{C}^m$, where $\|e\|_{\ell^2} \leq \eta$. As in Remark 12.15, note that $A' = DA$ where D is diagonal. Using Lemma 13.7 with $z = \hat{x}$ and the fact that x and $\hat{x}$ are both feasible, we deduce that

$$\|\hat{x} - x\|_{\ell^2} \lesssim \frac{\sigma_s(x)_{\ell^1}}{\sqrt{s}} + \|A'(\hat{x} - x)\|_{\ell^2} \leq \frac{\sigma_s(x)_{\ell^1}}{\sqrt{s}} + 2\|D\|_{\ell^2}\eta.$$

We now use (12.78) to get the desired result. □

13.5 Proof of Theorem 13.12

The remainder of this chapter is devoted to the proof of Theorem 13.12. This is broken into several steps. First, in §13.5.1 we rewrite the G-RICL $\delta_{\mathbf{s},\mathbf{M},G}$ as a particular semi-norm of a sum of independent random matrices:

$$\delta_{\mathbf{s},\mathbf{M},G} = m^{-1} \left\| \sum_{i:|\mathcal{A}_i|>1} \left(a_i a_i^* - \mathbb{E}(a_i a_i^*) \right) \right\|_{\mathbf{s},\mathbf{M},G}. \tag{13.24}$$

Next, in §13.5.2 we introduce several tools that will be needed later, and then in §13.5.3 we estimate the expectation $\mathbb{E}(\delta_{\mathbf{s},\mathbf{M},G})$. This step is based on Dudley's inequality (Theorem 13.25) and uses Maurey's lemma (Lemma 13.30) to estimate the resulting covering numbers. Finally, in §13.5.4, we return to (13.24) and use a version of Talagrand's theorem (Theorem 13.33) to bound the deviation of $\delta_{\mathbf{s},\mathbf{M},G}$ from its expectation.

13.5.1 Setup

Let $C = \{\mathcal{A}_i\}_{i=1}^m$ and G as in Definition 13.11. Recall that $D_{\mathbf{s},\mathbf{M}}$, which was defined in (11.5), is the set of all possible support sets of an $(\mathbf{s}, \mathbf{M})$-sparse vector. For each $\Delta \in D_{\mathbf{s},\mathbf{M}}$ we write

$$B_{\Delta,G} = \{z \in \mathbb{C}^N : \|Gz\|_{\ell^2} \leq 1, \ \mathrm{supp}(z) \subseteq \Delta\},$$

and then let

$$B_{\mathbf{s},\mathbf{M},G} = \bigcup_{\Delta \in D_{\mathbf{s},\mathbf{M}}} B_{\Delta,G}. \tag{13.25}$$

Using this, we define a semi-norm $\|\!|\cdot|\!\|_{\mathbf{s},\mathbf{M},G}$ on $\mathbb{C}^{N \times N}$ as follows:

$$\|\!|V|\!\|_{\mathbf{s},\mathbf{M},G} = \sup_{x \in B_{\mathbf{s},\mathbf{M},G}} |\langle Vx, x\rangle|.$$

We now show that (13.24) holds. First, note that

$$\left| \|Ax\|_{\ell^2}^2 - \|Gx\|_{\ell^2}^2 \right| = |\langle (A^*A - G^*G)x, x\rangle| = |\langle (A^*A - \mathbb{E}(A^*A))x, x\rangle|, \quad x \in \mathbb{C}^N,$$

where in the second step we recall that $\mathbb{E}(A^*A) = G^*G$. Hence the G-RICL is given by

$$\delta_{\mathbf{s},\mathbf{M},G} = \sup_{x \in B_{\mathbf{s},\mathbf{M},G}} |\langle (A^*A - \mathbb{E}(A^*A))x, x\rangle| = \|\!|A^*A - \mathbb{E}(A^*A)|\!\|_{\mathbf{s},\mathbf{M},G}.$$

The expression (13.24) now follows from (12.53).

13.5.2 Covering Numbers, Rademacher Processes and Dudley's Inequality

Before estimating $\mathbb{E}(\delta_{\mathbf{s},\mathbf{M},G})$ we first require some additional tools, in particular, Dudley's inequality. See the Notes section for references.

Definition 13.21 (Covering) Let $(\mathbb{M}, d)$ be a metric space, K be a subset of $\mathbb{M}$ and $t > 0$. A *t-covering* of K is a subset $C \subseteq K$ such that

$$K \subseteq \bigcup_{x \in C} B(x,t), \qquad B(x,t) = \{z \in \mathbb{M} : d(x,z) \leq t\}.$$

The *covering number* $\mathcal{N}(K, d, t)$ is the minimum cardinality of a t-covering C of K.

Note that $\mathcal{N}(K, d, t)$ is sometimes referred to as the *internal* covering number since the centres C are elements of K. The following lemma lists some basic properties of covering numbers:

Lemma 13.22 *The covering number $\mathcal{N}(K, d, t)$ satisfies the following properties:*

(a) $\mathcal{N}(J \cup K, d, t) \leq \mathcal{N}(J, d, t) + \mathcal{N}(K, d, t)$,
(b) $\mathcal{N}(J, d, t) \leq \mathcal{N}(K, d, t/2)$ *whenever* $J \subseteq K$,
(c) $\mathcal{N}(K, ad, t) = \mathcal{N}(K, d, t/a)$ *for all* $a > 0$,
(d) if d' is another metric on $\mathbb{M}$ with $d'(x, y) \leq d(x, y)$, $\forall x, y \in \mathbb{M}$, then $\mathcal{N}(K, d', t) \leq \mathcal{N}(K, d, t)$,
(e) if d is induced by a norm then $\mathcal{N}(aK, d, t) = \mathcal{N}(K, d, t/a)$ *for all* $a > 0$.

Next, we give a result concerning the covering number of a subset of the unit ball in a normed space:

Lemma 13.23 *Let $\|\cdot\|$ be a norm on $\mathbb{R}^n$, K be a subset of the unit ball $\{x \in \mathbb{R}^n : \|x\| \leq 1\}$ and $t > 0$. Then*

$$\mathcal{N}(K, \|\cdot\|, t) \leq (1 + 2/t)^n.$$

In order to state Dudley's inequality, we now introduce stochastic processes.

Definition 13.24 (Stochastic process) A *stochastic process* $\{X_t : t \in T\}$ is a collection of random variables on a common probability space indexed by some set T. The process is *centred* if $\mathbb{E}(X_t) = 0$, $\forall t \in T$.

Note that a stochastic process induces a pseudometric[1] on the set T, defined by

$$d(s,t) = \sqrt{\mathbb{E}|X_s - X_t|^2}, \qquad s, t \in T.$$

In what follows, we consider *Rademacher* processes. These are centred stochastic processes of the form

$$X_t = \sum_{i=1}^{m} \epsilon_i f_i(t),$$

[1] A pseudometric d satisfies the same properties as a metric, except that the condition $d(x, y) = 0$ for two elements x and y need not imply that $x = y$.

where $(\epsilon_i)_{i=1}^m$ is a Rademacher sequence (Definition 12.25) and $f_i \colon T \to \mathbb{R}$ are real-valued functions. Note that for such a process, the pseudometric d is

$$d(s,t) = \sqrt{\sum_{i=1}^{m} (f_i(s) - f_i(t))^2}. \tag{13.26}$$

Finally, we are ready to state Dudley's inequality.

Theorem 13.25 (Dudley's inequality) *Let $\{X_t : t \in T\}$ be a Rademacher process with pseudometric (13.26) and define $\varpi = \sup_{t\in T} \sqrt{\mathbb{E}|X_t|^2}$. Then*

$$\mathbb{E} \sup_{t\in T} X_t \leq 4\sqrt{2} \int_0^{\varpi/2} \sqrt{\log(\mathcal{N}(T,d,z))}\, \mathrm{d}z,$$
$$\mathbb{E} \sup_{t\in T} |X_t| \leq 4\sqrt{2} \int_0^{\varpi/2} \sqrt{\log(2\mathcal{N}(T,d,z))}\, \mathrm{d}z.$$

13.5.3 Estimation of $\mathbb{E}(\delta_{\mathbf{s},\mathbf{M},G})$

The first step in estimating $\mathbb{E}(\delta_{\mathbf{s},\mathbf{M},G})$ uses a technique known as *symmetrization*.

Lemma 13.26 (Symmetrization) *Let $X_1, \ldots, X_m$ be independent random vectors in a finite-dimensional vector space $\mathbb{V}$ and $f \colon \mathbb{V} \to \mathbb{R}$ be a convex function. Then*

$$\mathbb{E} f\left(\sum_{i=1}^{m} (X_i - \mathbb{E}(X_i))\right) \leq \mathbb{E} f\left(2 \sum_{i=1}^{m} \epsilon_i X_i\right),$$

where $\epsilon = (\epsilon_1, \ldots, \epsilon_m)$ is a Rademacher sequence independent of the X_i.

Note that on the right-hand side the expectation is taken with respect to both the X_i and the ϵ_i. Applying this lemma to (13.24) with $f = |||\cdot|||_{\mathbf{s},\mathbf{M},G}$, we get

$$\mathbb{E}\left(\delta_{\mathbf{s},\mathbf{M},G}\right) \leq 2m^{-1} \mathbb{E} \left|\left|\left| \sum_{i:|\mathcal{A}_i|>1} \epsilon_i a_i a_i^* \right|\right|\right|_{\mathbf{s},\mathbf{M},G}. \tag{13.27}$$

Lemma 13.27 *Conditional on the a_is, we have*

$$\mathbb{E}_\epsilon \left|\left|\left| \sum_{i:|\mathcal{A}_i|>1} \epsilon_i a_i a_i^* \right|\right|\right|_{\mathbf{s},\mathbf{M},G} \lesssim R_p \|G^{-1}\|_{\ell^2} \int_0^{\chi/2} \sqrt{\log(2\mathcal{N}(B_{\mathbf{s},\mathbf{M}}, |||\cdot|||_{a,q}, t))}\, \mathrm{d}t,$$

for all $1 \leq p < \infty$, where $\mathbb{E}_\epsilon$ denotes expectation with respect to the Rademacher sequence $\epsilon = (\epsilon_i)$,

$$R_p = \sup_{x \in B_{\mathbf{s},\mathbf{M},G}} \left(\sum_{i:|\mathcal{A}_i|>1} |\langle a_i, x\rangle|^{2p} \right)^{\frac{1}{2p}}, \tag{13.28}$$

the constant χ is given by

$$\chi = \frac{m^{\frac{1}{2q}} \sqrt{\Xi}}{\|G^{-1}\|_{\ell^2}}, \tag{13.29}$$

$B_{\mathbf{s},\mathbf{M}} = B_{\mathbf{s},\mathbf{M},I}$ *for* $I \in \mathbb{C}^{N\times N}$ *the identity matrix,* $|||\cdot|||_{a,q}$ *is defined as*

$$|||x|||_{a,q} = \left(\sum_{i:|\mathcal{A}_i|>1} |\langle a_i, x\rangle|^{2q} \right)^{\frac{1}{2q}}, \qquad x \in \mathbb{C}^N,$$

and $1 < q \le \infty$ *satisfies* $1/p + 1/q = 1$.

Proof By definition

$$\mathbb{E}_\epsilon \left|\left|\left| \sum_{i:|\mathcal{A}_i|>1} \epsilon_i a_i a_i^* \right|\right|\right|_{\mathbf{s},\mathbf{M},G} = \mathbb{E}_\epsilon \sup_{x\in B_{\mathbf{s},\mathbf{M},G}} \left| \sum_{i:|\mathcal{A}_i|>1} \epsilon_i |\langle a_i, x\rangle|^2 \right|.$$

This is (the expected value of) the supremum of the absolute value of the Rademacher process $\{Z_x : x \in B_{\mathbf{s},\mathbf{M},G}\}$, where

$$Z_x = \sum_{i:|\mathcal{A}_i|>1} \epsilon_i |\langle a_i, x\rangle|^2, \qquad x \in B_{\mathbf{s},\mathbf{M},G}. \tag{13.30}$$

It has the corresponding pseudometric

$$d(x,z) = \left(\sum_{i:|\mathcal{A}_i|>1} \left(|\langle a_i, x\rangle|^2 - |\langle a_i, z\rangle|^2 \right)^2 \right)^{1/2}, \qquad x, z \in \mathbb{C}^N.$$

Hence Dudley's inequality (Theorem 13.25) gives

$$\mathbb{E}_\epsilon \left|\left|\left| \sum_{i:|\mathcal{A}_i|>1} \epsilon_i a_i a_i^* \right|\right|\right|_{\mathbf{s},\mathbf{M},G} \le 4\sqrt{2} \int_0^{\varpi/2} \sqrt{\log(2\mathcal{N}(B_{\mathbf{s},\mathbf{M},G}, d, t))}\, \mathrm{d}t, \tag{13.31}$$

where

$$\varpi = \sup_{x\in B_{\mathbf{s},\mathbf{M},G}} \sqrt{\mathbb{E}|Z_x|^2} = \sup_{x\in B_{\mathbf{s},\mathbf{M},G}} d(x,0). \tag{13.32}$$

We now bound this integral. First, using Hölder's inequality (A.3), we note that

$$\begin{aligned} d(x,z) &= \left(\sum_{i:|\mathcal{A}_i|>1} \left(|\langle a_i, x\rangle|^2 - |\langle a_i, z\rangle|^2 \right)^2 \right)^{1/2} \\ &= \left(\sum_{i:|\mathcal{A}_i|>1} (|\langle a_i, x\rangle| - |\langle a_i, z\rangle|)^2 (|\langle a_i, x\rangle| + |\langle a_i, z\rangle|)^2 \right)^{1/2} \\ &\le \left(\sum_{i:|\mathcal{A}_i|>1} (|\langle a_i, x\rangle| + |\langle a_i, z\rangle|)^{2p} \right)^{\frac{1}{2p}} \left(\sum_{i:|\mathcal{A}_i|>1} |\langle a_i, x - z\rangle|^{2q} \right)^{\frac{1}{2q}}, \end{aligned}$$

and therefore

$$d(x,z) \le 2R_p |||x - z|||_{a,q}. \tag{13.33}$$

Note that $\|x\|_{\ell^2} \leq \|G^{-1}\|_{\ell^2}$ for $x \in B_{\mathbf{s},\mathbf{M},G}$, and therefore $B_{\mathbf{s},\mathbf{M},G} \subseteq \|G^{-1}\|_{\ell^2} B_{\mathbf{s},\mathbf{M}}$. This, (13.33) and properties (b)–(e) of Lemma 13.22 give

$$\mathcal{N}(B_{\mathbf{s},\mathbf{M},G}, d, t) \leq \mathcal{N}\left(B_{\mathbf{s},\mathbf{M}}, |||\cdot|||_{a,q}, t/(4R_p\|G^{-1}\|_{\ell^2})\right). \tag{13.34}$$

We next estimate ϖ. To do this, we first bound $|||x|||_{a,q}$ for $x \in B_{\mathbf{s},\mathbf{M},G}$. For such an x, note that $|\langle a_i, x\rangle| = |\langle P_\Delta a_i, x\rangle| \leq \|P_\Delta a_i\|_{\ell^2}\|x\|_{\ell^2}$, where $\Delta = \mathrm{supp}(x) \in D_{\mathbf{s},\mathbf{M}}$. Using the definition (13.19) of Ξ, we see that

$$\|P_\Delta a_i\|_{\ell^2}^2 = \sum_{l=1}^{r} \|P_{\Delta_l} a_i\|_{\ell^2}^2 \leq \sum_{l=1}^{r} s_l \|P_{M_l}^{M_{l-1}} a_i\|_{\ell^\infty}^2 \leq \Xi/\|G^{-1}\|_{\ell^2}^2, \tag{13.35}$$

and therefore

$$|\langle a_i, x\rangle| \leq \sqrt{\Xi}\|x\|_{\ell^2}/\|G^{-1}\|_{\ell^2}, \quad \forall x \in B_{\mathbf{s},\mathbf{M},G}. \tag{13.36}$$

This gives

$$|||x|||_{a,q} = \left(\sum_{i:|\mathcal{A}_i|>1} |\langle a_i, x\rangle|^{2q}\right)^{\frac{1}{2q}} \leq \frac{m^{\frac{1}{2q}}\sqrt{\Xi}\|x\|_{\ell^2}}{\|G^{-1}\|_{\ell^2}} = \chi\|x\|_{\ell^2}. \tag{13.37}$$

Combining this with (13.33), (13.32) and the fact that $\|x\|_{\ell^2} \leq \|G^{-1}\|_{\ell^2}\|Gx\|_{\ell^2} \leq \|G^{-1}\|_{\ell^2}$ for $x \in B_{\mathbf{s},\mathbf{M},G}$ we now get

$$\varpi \leq 2R_p m^{\frac{1}{2q}}\sqrt{\Xi}.$$

To complete the result, we apply this bound and (13.34) to (13.31) and then make a change of variables in the integral. □

Our next task is to estimate the integral in the previous lemma. We do this by bounding the covering number separately for small and large values of t.

Lemma 13.28 (Small t bound) *For all $t > 0$, we have*

$$\sqrt{\log\left(2\mathcal{N}(B_{\mathbf{s},\mathbf{M}}, |||\cdot|||_{a,q}, t)\right)} \leq \sqrt{2s}\left(\sqrt{\log(2eN/s)} + \sqrt{\log(1 + 2\chi/t)}\right),$$

where χ is as in (13.29).

Proof Recalling (13.25) and property (a) of Lemma 13.22, we see that

$$\mathcal{N}(B_{\mathbf{s},\mathbf{M}}, |||\cdot|||_{a,q}, t) \leq \sum_{\Delta \in D_{\mathbf{s},\mathbf{M}}} \mathcal{N}(B_\Delta, |||\cdot|||_{a,q}, t), \tag{13.38}$$

where $B_\Delta = B_{\Delta,I}$. The bound (13.37) and properties (c) and (d) of Lemma 13.22 give

$$\mathcal{N}(B_\Delta, |||\cdot|||_{a,q}, t) \leq \mathcal{N}\left(B_\Delta, \|\cdot\|_{\ell^2}, t/\chi\right).$$

Since B_Δ is the unit ball of $(\mathbb{C}^{|\Delta|}, \|\cdot\|_{\ell^2})$, it is isometric to the unit ball of $(\mathbb{R}^{2|\Delta|}, \|\cdot\|_{\ell^2})$. Hence Lemma 13.23 implies that

$$\mathcal{N}(B_\Delta, |||\cdot|||_{a,q}, t) \leq (1 + 2\chi/t)^{2|\Delta|}.$$

Returning to (13.38), noting that $|\Delta| \leq s = s_1 + \cdots + s_r$ and

$$|D_{\mathbf{s},\mathbf{M}}| \leq \binom{N}{s} \leq \left(\frac{\mathrm{e}N}{s}\right)^s$$

(the second inequality is an elementary bound), we get

$$2\mathcal{N}(B_{\mathbf{s},\mathbf{M}}, |||\cdot|||_a, t) \leq 2\left(\frac{\mathrm{e}N}{s}\right)^s (1 + 2\chi/t)^{2s} \leq \left(\frac{2\mathrm{e}N}{s}\right)^{2s} (1 + 2\chi/t)^{2s}.$$

The result now follows by taking the logarithms of both sides and applying the bound $\sqrt{a+b} \leq \sqrt{a} + \sqrt{b}$, $a, b > 0$. □

Lemma 13.29 (Large t bound) *If χ is as in (13.29) and $0 < t \leq \chi/2$, we have*

$$\sqrt{\log(2\mathcal{N}(B_{\mathbf{s},\mathbf{M}}, |||\cdot|||_{a,q}, t))} \lesssim \chi\sqrt{rq\log(4N)}/t. \tag{13.39}$$

The proof of this result is based on *Maurey's lemma*:

Lemma 13.30 (Maurey's lemma) *Let $\mathbb{X}$ be a normed vector space with norm $\|\cdot\|$ and $U \subset \mathbb{X}$ be a finite set of size $|U| = M$. Suppose that, for every $L \in \mathbb{N}$ and $u_1, \ldots, u_L \in U$,*

$$\mathbb{E}_{\epsilon}\|\sum_{l=1}^{L} \epsilon_l u_l\| \leq C\sqrt{L},$$

where $\epsilon = (\epsilon_1, \ldots, \epsilon_L)$ is a Rademacher sequence. Then

$$\log(\mathcal{N}(\mathrm{conv}(U), \|\cdot\|, t)) \lesssim (C/t)^2 \log(M), \qquad \forall t > 0,$$

where $\mathrm{conv}(U)$ *denotes the convex hull of U.*

Here, we recall that $\mathrm{conv}(U)$ is the smallest convex set containing U. Equivalently, it is the set of all convex combinations of elements of U:

$$\mathrm{conv}(U) = \left\{\sum_{i=1}^{n} t_i u_i : n \geq 1,\ t_1, \ldots, t_n \geq 0,\ \sum_{i=1}^{n} t_i = 1,\ u_1, \ldots, u_n \in U\right\}.$$

We also make use of the following result, known as *Khintchine's inequality*:

Lemma 13.31 (Khintchine's inequality) *Let $x = (x_i)_{i=1}^n \in \mathbb{C}^n$ and $\epsilon = (\epsilon_1, \ldots, \epsilon_n)$ be a Rademacher sequence. Then*

$$\left(\mathbb{E}\left|\sum_{i=1}^{n} \epsilon_i x_i\right|^p\right)^{1/p} \leq 2^{3/(4p)}\mathrm{e}^{-1/2}\sqrt{p}\|x\|_{\ell^2}, \qquad \forall p > 0.$$

See the Notes section for details on these results.

Proof of Lemma 13.29 Since the right-hand side of (13.39) is $\gtrsim 1$ for all $0 < t \leq \chi/2$, we may ignore the factor of two on the left-hand side and simply consider $\log(\mathcal{N}(B_{\mathbf{s},\mathbf{M}}, |||\cdot|||_{a,q}, t))$. Let $w_i = (w_i)_{i=1}^N$ be the weights (13.2)–(13.3) and define a norm $\|\cdot\|^*_{\ell^1_w}$ on $\mathbb{C}^N$ by

$$\|z\|^*_{\ell^1_w} = \sum_{i=1}^{N} w_i (|\mathrm{Re}(z_i)| + |\mathrm{Im}(z_i)|), \qquad z \in \mathbb{C}^N.$$

If $x \in B_{\mathbf{s},\mathbf{M}}$, observe that

$$\|x\|^*_{\ell^1_w} = \sum_{l=1}^{r} \sqrt{s/s_l} \sum_{i=M_{l-1}}^{M_l} \sqrt{2}|x_i| \leq \sum_{l=1}^{r} \sqrt{2s} \sqrt{\sum_{i=M_{l-1}}^{M_l} |x_i|^2} \leq \sqrt{2rs}.$$

Hence $B_{\mathbf{s},\mathbf{M}}$ is a subset of the ball $\left\{x : \|x\|^*_{\ell^1_w} \leq \sqrt{rs}\right\} = \mathrm{conv}(U)$, where

$$U = \left\{\pm\sqrt{2rs_l}e_i, \pm\mathrm{i}\sqrt{2rs_l}e_i : i = M_{l-1}+1,\dots,M_l,\ l = 1,\dots,r\right\}.$$

Therefore, by part (b) of Lemma 13.22,

$$\mathcal{N}(B_{\mathbf{s},\mathbf{M}}, |||\cdot|||_{a,q}, t) \leq \mathcal{N}(\mathrm{conv}(U), |||\cdot|||_{a,q}, t/2). \tag{13.40}$$

We now seek to use Lemma 13.30. Note first that $|U| = 4N$. Next, let $u_1,\dots,u_L \in U$ and $\epsilon = (\epsilon_1,\dots,\epsilon_L)$ be a Rademacher sequence. Then, by Hölder's inequality (C.4),

$$\mathbb{E}_\epsilon \left|\left|\left|\sum_{l=1}^{L} \epsilon_l u_l\right|\right|\right|_{a,q} \leq \left(\mathbb{E}_\epsilon \left|\left|\left|\sum_{l=1}^{L} \epsilon_l u_l\right|\right|\right|_{a,q}^{2q}\right)^{\frac{1}{2q}} = \left(\sum_{i:|\mathcal{A}_i|>1} \mathbb{E}_\epsilon \left|\sum_{l=1}^{L} \epsilon_l \langle a_i, u_l\rangle\right|^{2q}\right)^{\frac{1}{2q}},$$

and therefore

$$\mathbb{E}_\epsilon \left|\left|\left|\sum_{l=1}^{L} \epsilon_l u_l\right|\right|\right|_{a,q} \leq 2^{3/(8q)}\mathrm{e}^{-1/2}\sqrt{2q}\left(\sum_{i:|\mathcal{A}_i|>1}\left(\sum_{l=1}^{L}|\langle a_i,u_l\rangle|^2\right)^q\right)^{\frac{1}{2q}},$$

by Khintchine's inequality (Lemma 13.31). Next, observe that

$$|\langle a_i, u_l\rangle| \leq \max_{k=1,\dots,r} \sqrt{2rs_k}\|P^{M_{k-1}}_{Mk} a_i\|_{\ell^\infty} \leq \sqrt{2r\Xi}/\|G^{-1}\|_{\ell^2}.$$

Hence

$$\mathbb{E}_\epsilon \left|\left|\left|\sum_{l=1}^{L} \epsilon_l u_l\right|\right|\right|_{a,q} \leq \sqrt{2}\mathrm{e}^{-1/2}\sqrt{2q}m^{\frac{1}{2q}}\sqrt{2r\Xi}\sqrt{L}/\|G^{-1}\|_{\ell^2} \leq C\sqrt{L},$$

where $C = 2\sqrt{rq}\chi$. We now use Lemma 13.30, (13.40) and the fact that $|U| = 4N$ to get

$$\log(\mathcal{N}(B_{\mathbf{s},\mathbf{M}}, |||\cdot|||_{a,q}, t)) \lesssim rq\chi^2 \log(4N)/t^2,$$

as required. □

With Lemmas 13.28 and 13.29 in hand we are now ready to give the main estimate for the expectation $\mathbb{E}(\delta_{\mathbf{s},\mathbf{M},G})$.

Lemma 13.32 (Bound for $\mathbb{E}(\delta_{\mathbf{s},\mathbf{M},G})$) *Let $0 < \delta < 1$ and suppose that*

$$m \gtrsim \delta^{-2}\cdot r\cdot \Xi \cdot \log(2(\Xi+1))\cdot \log^2(s)\cdot \log(N).$$

Then $\mathbb{E}\left(\delta_{\mathbf{s},\mathbf{M},G}\right) \leq \delta$.

Proof We first estimate the integral in Lemma 13.27. To do this, we split the range of integration into $(0,\tau)$ and $(\tau,\chi/2)$ for some $0<\tau<\chi/2$ to be determined. Then

$$\int_0^\tau \sqrt{\log\left(2\mathcal{N}(B_{\mathbf{s},\mathbf{M}}, |||\cdot|||_{a,q}, t)\right)}\,\mathrm{d}t \le \sqrt{2s}\sqrt{\log(2\mathrm{e}N/s)}\tau + \sqrt{2s}\int_0^\tau \sqrt{\log(1+2\chi/t)}\,\mathrm{d}t,$$

by Lemma 13.28. The second integral may be estimated by the Cauchy–Schwarz inequality and integrating by parts:

$$\begin{aligned}
\int_0^\tau \sqrt{\log(1+2\chi/t)}\,\mathrm{d}t &\le \sqrt{\tau\int_0^\tau \log(1+2\chi/t)\,\mathrm{d}t}\\
&= \sqrt{2\tau\chi\int_{2\chi/\tau}^\infty \log(1+u)/u^2\,\mathrm{d}u}\\
&= \sqrt{2\tau\chi\left(-\log(1+u)/u\Big|_{2\chi/\tau}^\infty + \int_{2\chi/\tau}^\infty 1/(u(u+1))\,\mathrm{d}u\right)}\\
&= \sqrt{2\tau\chi\left(-\log(1+u)/u\Big|_{2\chi/\tau}^\infty + \int_{2\chi/\tau}^\infty 1/u^2\,\mathrm{d}u\right)}\\
&\le \sqrt{2\tau\chi\left(\tau\log(1+2\chi/\tau)/(2\chi)+\tau/(2\chi)\right)}\\
&= \tau\sqrt{\log(\mathrm{e}(1+2\chi/\tau))}.
\end{aligned}$$

Hence

$$\int_0^\tau \sqrt{\log\left(2\mathcal{N}(B_{\mathbf{s},\mathbf{M}}, |||\cdot|||_{a,q}, t)\right)}\,\mathrm{d}t \le \sqrt{2s}\tau\left(\sqrt{\log(2\mathrm{e}N/s)}+\sqrt{\log(\mathrm{e}(1+2\chi/\tau))}\right).$$

Using Lemma 13.29 we also get

$$\int_\tau^{\chi/2} \sqrt{\log\left(2\mathcal{N}(B_{\mathbf{s},\mathbf{M}}, |||\cdot|||_{a}, t)\right)}\,\mathrm{d}t \lesssim \chi\sqrt{rq}\log(4N)\log(\chi/(2\tau)).$$

We now set $\tau=\chi/(2\sqrt{s})$ and recall that $N\ge s\ge 2$ to get

$$\int_0^{\chi/2} \sqrt{\log\left(2\mathcal{N}(B_{\mathbf{s},\mathbf{M}}, |||\cdot|||_{a,q}, t)\right)}\,\mathrm{d}t \lesssim \chi\sqrt{rq\log^2(s)\log(N)}.$$

Hence Lemma 13.27 gives

$$\mathbb{E}_\epsilon\left|\left|\left|\sum_{i:|\mathcal{A}_i|>1}\epsilon_i a_i a_i^*\right|\right|\right|_{\mathbf{s},\mathbf{M},G} \lesssim R_p\|G^{-1}\|_{\ell^2}\chi\sqrt{rq\log^2(s)\log(N)}.$$

Using this, (13.27), Fubini's theorem and the definition of χ we obtain

$$\mathbb{E}\left(\delta_{\mathbf{s},\mathbf{M},G}\right) \lesssim \frac{\sqrt{\Xi}\sqrt{rq\log^2(s)\log(N)}}{m^{1-\frac{1}{2q}}}\mathbb{E}(R_p). \tag{13.41}$$

Consider $\mathbb{E}(R_p)$. By (13.28), (13.36) and the fact that $\|x\|_{\ell^2} \leq \|G^{-1}\|_{\ell^2}$ for $x \in B_{\mathbf{s},\mathbf{M},G}$, we have

$$\mathbb{E}(R_p) \leq \Xi^{\frac{1}{2}-\frac{1}{2p}} m^{\frac{1}{2p}} \mathbb{E}\left(\sup_{x \in B_{\mathbf{s},\mathbf{M},G}} \left(m^{-1} \sum_{i:|\mathcal{A}_i|>1} |\langle a_i, x\rangle|^2 \right)^{\frac{1}{2p}} \right).$$

Applying Hölder's inequality (C.4), we obtain

$$\begin{aligned} \mathbb{E}(R_p) &\leq \Xi^{\frac{1}{2}-\frac{1}{2p}} m^{\frac{1}{2p}} \left(\mathbb{E}\left(\sup_{x \in B_{\mathbf{s},\mathbf{M},G}} m^{-1} \sum_{i:|\mathcal{A}_i|>1} |\langle a_i, x\rangle|^2 \right) \right)^{\frac{1}{2p}} \\ &= \Xi^{\frac{1}{2}-\frac{1}{2p}} m^{\frac{1}{2p}} \left(\mathbb{E}\left(m^{-1} \left\| \sum_{i:|\mathcal{A}_i|>1} a_i a_i^* \right\|_{\mathbf{s},\mathbf{M},G} \right) \right)^{\frac{1}{2p}}. \end{aligned} \tag{13.42}$$

Note that

$$\begin{aligned} & m^{-1} \left\| \sum_{i:|\mathcal{A}_i|>1} a_i a_i^* \right\|_{\mathbf{s},\mathbf{M},G} \\ & \quad \leq m^{-1} \left\| \sum_{i:|\mathcal{A}_i|>1} \left(a_i a_i^* - \mathbb{E}(a_i a_i^*) \right) \right\|_{\mathbf{s},\mathbf{M},G} + m^{-1} \left\| \sum_{i:|\mathcal{A}_i|>1} \mathbb{E}(a_i a_i^*) \right\|_{\mathbf{s},\mathbf{M},G}, \end{aligned}$$

and, by definition of C and $G = G_C$, we have

$$G^* G = m^{-1} \sum_{i=1}^{m} \mathbb{E}(a_i a_i^*) = m^{-1} \sum_{i:|\mathcal{A}_i|=1} \mathbb{E}(a_i a_i^*) + m^{-1} \sum_{i:|\mathcal{A}_i|>1} \mathbb{E}(a_i a_i^*).$$

Hence, since $m^{-1} \sum_{i:|\mathcal{A}_i|=1} \mathbb{E}(a_i a_i^*)$ is nonnegative definite, we see that

$$\left\langle x, \left(m^{-1} \sum_{i:|\mathcal{A}_i|>1} \mathbb{E}(a_i a_i^*) \right) x \right\rangle \leq \|Gx\|_{\ell^2}^2 \leq 1, \quad \forall x \in B_{\mathbf{s},\mathbf{M},G}.$$

Therefore, since the matrix on the left-hand side is also nonnegative definite, we have

$$m^{-1} \left\| \sum_{i:|\mathcal{A}_i|>1} \mathbb{E}(a_i a_i^*) \right\|_{\mathbf{s},\mathbf{M},G} \leq 1.$$

Combining this and (13.24) now yields

$$\mathbb{E}\left(m^{-1} \left\| \sum_{i:|\mathcal{A}_i|>1} a_i a_i^* \right\|_{\mathbf{s},\mathbf{M},G} \right) \leq \mathbb{E}(\delta_{\mathbf{s},\mathbf{M},G}) + 1.$$

With this in hand, we now return to (13.42) and use the fact that $p \geq 1$ to get

$$\mathbb{E}(R_p) \leq \Xi^{\frac{1}{2}-\frac{1}{2p}} m^{\frac{1}{2p}} \sqrt{\mathbb{E}(\delta_{\mathbf{s},\mathbf{M},G}) + 1}.$$

Therefore (13.41) gives

$$\mathbb{E}(\delta_{\mathbf{s},\mathbf{M},G}) \lesssim \frac{\Xi^{1-\frac{1}{2p}}\sqrt{rq\log^2(s)\log(N)}}{m^{1-\frac{1}{2q}-\frac{1}{2p}}}\sqrt{\mathbb{E}(\delta_{\mathbf{s},\mathbf{M},G})+1}$$
$$= \frac{\Xi^{1-\frac{1}{2p}}\sqrt{rq\log^2(s)\log(N)}}{\sqrt{m}}\sqrt{\mathbb{E}(\delta_{\mathbf{s},\mathbf{M},G})+1}.$$

It is now time to choose p. Set $p = 1 + 1/\log(\lambda)$, where $\lambda = 1 + \Xi$, and notice that this gives $q = 1 + \log(\lambda)$. Observe that

$$\lambda^{\frac{1}{2}-\frac{1}{2p}} \leq \lambda^{\frac{p-1}{2}} = \lambda^{\frac{1}{2\log(\lambda)}} = \sqrt{\mathrm{e}}.$$

Therefore, writing $\Xi^{1-\frac{1}{2p}} \leq \sqrt{\Xi}\lambda^{\frac{1}{2}-\frac{1}{2p}} \leq \sqrt{\Xi}\sqrt{\mathrm{e}}$, we get

$$\mathbb{E}(\delta_{\mathbf{s},\mathbf{M},G}) \leq D\sqrt{\mathbb{E}(\delta_{\mathbf{s},\mathbf{M},G})+1},$$

where

$$D = c\sqrt{\frac{\Xi r\log(2(\Xi+1))\log^2(s)\log(N)}{m}},$$

for some numerical constant $c > 0$. It follows after some algebra that $\mathbb{E}(\delta_{\mathbf{s},\mathbf{M},G}) \leq D + D^2$. Thus, $\mathbb{E}(\delta_{\mathbf{s},\mathbf{M},G}) \leq \delta$ provided $D \leq \delta/2$. This gives the result. □

13.5.4 Estimation of $\delta_{\mathbf{s},\mathbf{M},G}$

Having estimated its expectation, we are now able to provide the desired probabilistic bound for $\delta_{\mathbf{s},\mathbf{M},G}$ itself. We do this using the following powerful result, which is a version of Talagrand's theorem:

Theorem 13.33 *There exists a numerical constant $c > 0$ with the following property. Let $X_1, \ldots, X_m$ be independent random variables valued in a measurable space Ω, $\mathcal{F}$ be a countable class of real-valued, measurable functions on Ω such that $\mathbb{E}(f(X_i)) = 0$, $\forall f \in \mathcal{F}$ and $i = 1, \ldots, m$, and Z be the random variable $Z = \sup_{f\in\mathcal{F}} \sum_{i=1}^m f(X_i)$. Let K and σ be such that $\sup_{x\in\Omega} |f(x)| \leq K$, $\forall f \in \mathcal{F}$, and*

$$\sup_{f\in\mathcal{F}} \mathbb{E}\left(\sum_{i=1}^m f(X_i)^2\right) \leq \sigma^2.$$

Then

$$\mathbb{P}(|Z - \mathbb{E}(Z)| \geq t) \leq 3\exp\left(-\frac{t}{cK}\log\left(1 + \frac{Kt}{\sigma^2 + K\mathbb{E}(\overline{Z})}\right)\right),$$

where $\overline{Z} = \sup_{f\in\mathcal{F}} \left|\sum_{i=1}^m f(X_i)\right|$.

Proof of Theorem 13.12 We use Theorem 13.33. We first define the class $\mathcal{F}$. Observe that (13.24) gives

$$\delta_{\mathbf{s},\mathbf{M},G} = m^{-1} \left\| \sum_{i:|\mathcal{A}_i|>1} \left(a_i a_i^* - \mathbb{E}(a_i a_i^*) \right) \right\|_{\mathbf{s},\mathbf{M},G} = \left\| \sum_{i:|\mathcal{A}_i|>1} X_i \right\|_{\mathbf{s},\mathbf{M},G},$$

where $X_i = m^{-1} \left(a_i a_i^* - \mathbb{E}(a_i a_i^*) \right)$. Therefore, by self-adjointness,

$$\delta_{\mathbf{s},\mathbf{M},G} = \sup_{x \in B^*_{\mathbf{s},\mathbf{M},G}} \max \left\{ \left\langle \sum_{i:|\mathcal{A}_i|>1} X_i x, x \right\rangle, - \left\langle \sum_{i:|\mathcal{A}_i|>1} X_i x, x \right\rangle \right\},$$

where $B^*_{\mathbf{s},\mathbf{M},G}$ is a countable dense subset of $B_{\mathbf{s},\mathbf{M},G}$. Hence we may write

$$Z = \delta_{\mathbf{s},\mathbf{M},G} = \sup_{x \in B^*_{\mathbf{s},\mathbf{M},G}} \max \left\{ \sum_{i:|\mathcal{A}_i|>1} f_x^+(X_i), \sum_{i:|\mathcal{A}_i|>1} f_x^-(X_i) \right\}, \tag{13.43}$$

where $f_x^{\pm}(X) = \pm\langle Xx, x \rangle$. Notice that $\mathbb{E}(f_x^{\pm}(X_i)) = 0$. We now define the measurable space Ω. Let $x \in B_{\mathbf{s},\mathbf{M},G}$ and notice that $|\langle a_i, x \rangle| \leq \sqrt{\Xi}$. Therefore

$$|\langle X_i x, x \rangle| = m^{-1} \left| |\langle a_i, x \rangle|^2 - \mathbb{E}|\langle a_i, x \rangle|^2 \right| \leq 2\Xi/m := K.$$

Since x was arbitrary, this implies in particular that $|||X_i|||_{\mathbf{s},\mathbf{M},G} \leq K$. Hence we now define $\Omega = \{X \in \mathbb{C}^{N \times N} : X = X^*,\ |||X|||_{\mathbf{s},\mathbf{M},G} \leq K\}$. Next, we estimate σ^2. Let $x \in B^*_{\mathbf{s},\mathbf{M},G}$. Then

$$\begin{aligned} \mathbb{E}\left(\sum_{i:|\mathcal{A}_i|>1} (f_x^{\pm}(X_i))^2 \right) &\leq m^{-2} \sum_{i:|\mathcal{A}_i|>1} \mathbb{E}\left(|\langle a_i, x \rangle|^4 \right) \\ &\leq \Xi m^{-2} \sum_{i:|\mathcal{A}_i|>1} \mathbb{E}\left(|\langle a_i, x \rangle|^2 \right) \\ &= \Xi m^{-1} \|Gx\|_{\ell^2}^2 \\ &\leq \Xi/m := \sigma^2. \end{aligned}$$

Finally, observe that

$$\overline{Z} = \sup_{x \in B^*_{\mathbf{s},\mathbf{M},G}} \max \left\{ \left| \sum_{i:|\mathcal{A}_i|>1} f_x^+(X_i) \right|, \left| \sum_{i:|\mathcal{A}_i|>1} f_x^-(X_i) \right| \right\} = Z,$$

in this case. In particular, $\mathbb{E}(\overline{Z}) = \mathbb{E}(Z) = \mathbb{E}(\delta_{\mathbf{s},\mathbf{M},G})$.

We are now ready to use Theorem 13.33. First, observe from Lemma 13.32 that $\mathbb{E}\left(\delta_{\mathbf{s},\mathbf{M},G}\right) \leq \delta/2$, provided

$$m \gtrsim \delta^{-2} \cdot r \cdot \Xi \cdot \log(2(\Xi + 1)) \cdot \log^2(s) \cdot \log(N).$$

Since this holds by assumption, we may apply Theorem 13.33 with $t = \delta/2$, to get

$$\mathbb{P}\left(\delta_{\mathbf{s},\mathbf{M},G} \geq \delta\right) \leq 3 \exp\left(-\frac{\delta m}{4c\Xi} \log\left(1 + \frac{\delta}{1+\delta} \right) \right) \leq 3 \exp\left(-\frac{\log(3/2)\delta^2 m}{4c\Xi} \right).$$

Here, in the second step we used the fact that $\log(1 + \delta/(1 + \delta)) \geq \log(3/2)\delta$ for $0 < \delta < 1$. Hence, we deduce that $\mathbb{P}(\delta_{\mathbf{s},\mathbf{M},G} \geq \delta) \leq \varepsilon$, provided

$$m \gtrsim \delta^{-2} \cdot \Xi \cdot \log(3/\varepsilon).$$

Since $\log(3/\varepsilon) = \log(3) + \log(\varepsilon^{-1})$ and $r \cdot \log(2(\Xi + 1)) \cdot \log^2(s) \cdot \log(N) \geq \log^4(2) \gtrsim \log(3)$, this holds by assumption. Hence the proof is complete. □

13.5.5 Proof of Theorem 12.19

Finally, having now introduced Talagrand's theorem, we may also give a proof of the vector Bernstein inequality, Theorem 12.19.

Proof of Theorem 12.19 Let $\Omega = \{x \in \mathbb{C}^n : \|x\|_{\ell^2} \leq K\}$, Q be a countable subset of the unit ball $\{x \in \mathbb{C}^n : \|x\|_{\ell^2} = 1\}$ and define the functions $f_x(z) = \mathrm{Re}\,\langle z, x\rangle$. Notice that $\mathbb{E}(f_x(X_i)) = 0$ for all $x \in Q$, $i = 1, \ldots, m$ and $|f_x(z)| \leq K$ for all $x \in Q$, $z \in \Omega$. We also have

$$Z = \left\| \sum_{i=1}^{m} X_i \right\|_{\ell^2} = \sup_{x \in Q} \mathrm{Re} \left\langle \sum_{i=1}^{m} X_i, x \right\rangle = \sup_{x \in Q} \sum_{i=1}^{m} f_x(X_i).$$

Observe that $\overline{Z} = \sup_{x \in Q} \left| \sum_{i=1}^{m} f_x(X_i) \right| = Z$ in this case. In particular, $\mathbb{E}(\overline{Z}) \leq \mu$. Moreover,

$$\sup_{x \in Q} \mathbb{E}\left(\sum_{i=1}^{m} (f_x(X_i))^2 \right) \leq \sup_{x \in Q} \sum_{i=1}^{m} \mathbb{E}|\langle X_i, x\rangle|^2 \leq \sigma^2.$$

The result now follows immediately from Theorem 13.33. □

Notes

The G-RIP used in this chapter is not the same as the D-RIP (5.42). As discussed in the Notes section of Chapter 5, the D-RIP is used to study the QCBP analysis problem (3.3). Conversely, the G-RIP can be considered as a tool for the synthesis problem (3.4). Indeed, suppose that $A = \tilde{A}\Phi$, where Φ is a sparsifying transform and $\tilde{A}$ is a standard compressed sensing matrix with $\mathbb{E}(\tilde{A}^*\tilde{A}) = I$. Then the matrix A satisfies $\mathbb{E}(A^*A) = \Phi^*\Phi$. If, for instance, Φ corresponds to a Riesz basis, then $\Phi^*\Phi$ (the Gram matrix of the basis) is positive definite and well conditioned (this is not the case, however, when Φ is a frame). Hence, the results of this chapter apply. As mentioned in the Notes section of Chapter 9, biorthogonal wavelet bases are examples of Riesz bases that arise commonly in imaging.

Another application of the G-RIPL is the case where Fourier samples are not acquired on a Cartesian grid. The complex exponentials υ_ω defined in (E.3) only form an orthonormal basis when the frequencies $\omega \in \mathbb{Z}^d$. However, certain countable sets of non-Cartesian frequencies $\omega \in \mathbb{R}^d$ give rise to so-called *Fourier frames* (see [14] and references therein). The problem of randomly subsampling from a Fourier frame instead of the orthonormal Fourier basis can be studied within the G-RIPL framework.

See also [31]. Note that this approach, in which the measurement matrix is based on noninteger Fourier frequencies, avoids the gridding error discussed in Chapters 3 and 4, although the matrix–vector multiplications require more costly nonuniform FFTs.

In [118] the isotropy condition $\mathbb{E}(A^*A) = I$ was relaxed to a *near-isotropy* condition $\|\mathbb{E}(A^*A) - I\|_{\ell^2} \lesssim 1/\sqrt{N}$ in the context of nonuniform recovery. This chapter has removed this constraint in the case of uniform recovery, making the dependence on $\mathbb{E}(A^*A) = G^2$ explicit in the measurement condition and error bounds. As mentioned, such flexibility is useful in later chapters. Kueng & Gross [306] also consider sampling from nondegenerate (or, as referred to therein, *anisotropic*) families of random vectors. Their (nonuniform) recovery guarantees are of a similar flavour to those proved in this chapter. See also [31, 321] for related results.

The RIPL and rNSPL were introduced in [51] in the context of unweighted ℓ^1-minimization, with the extension to the weighted case given in [3]. Lemmas 13.6, 13.7 and 13.8 are extensions of classical results (Lemmas 5.15, 5.16 and 5.20) and were proved in [3]. Theorem 13.9 was originally proved in [51] for the unweighted case with $G = I$. This work gave error bounds for unweighted QCBP of the form

$$
\begin{aligned}
\|x - \hat{x}\|_{\ell^1} &\lesssim \sigma_{\mathbf{s},\mathbf{M}}(x)_{\ell^1} + \sqrt{s}\eta, \\
\|x - \hat{x}\|_{\ell^2} &\lesssim (r\lambda)^{1/4}\sigma_{\mathbf{s},\mathbf{M}}(x)_{\ell^1}/\sqrt{s} + (r\lambda)^{1/4}\eta,
\end{aligned}
\tag{13.44}
$$

provided A satisfies the rNSPL, where $\lambda = \lambda_{\mathbf{s},\mathbf{M}} = \max_{k=1,\dots,r} s_k / \min_{l=1,\dots,r} s_l$ is the *sparsity ratio*. These are special cases of Lemmas 13.6 and 13.7 with weights $w^{(k)} = 1$, $k = 1, \dots, r$. Note that $\xi/\zeta \leq r\lambda$ in this case. Interestingly, the dependence on $(r\lambda)^{1/4}$ in the ℓ^2-norm bound is sharp. Similar statements also apply when A satisfies the RIPL. In light of this, moving to weighted QCBP can be viewed as a way to remove the undesirable sparsity ratio factor λ in (13.44).

We have limited our discussion in this and other chapters to convex optimization approaches for the sparse in levels model. See [8, 9] for iterative and greedy algorithms for this model and their analysis via the RIPL.

Our proof of Theorem 13.12, which is based on Dudley's inequality, follows similar lines to [405, 408, 423], albeit with some significant extensions to incorporate the more general sensing model and the sparse in levels signal model. Note that the result for multilevel random sampling (Corollary 13.17) was first proved in [322]. We refer to [214, Chpts. 8 & 12] for further information and background on the techniques used, including covering numbers, the proofs of Lemma 13.23, Dudley's inequality (Theorem 13.25), symmetrization (Lemma 13.26) and Khintchine's inequality (Lemma 13.31). Maurey's lemma (Lemma 13.30) can be found in [299, Lem. 4.2]. We remark in passing that Dudley's inequality holds not only for Rademacher processes, but also for more general *subgaussian* processes. For more information on Talagrand's theorem and its various different forms, see [85, 320]. Theorem 13.33 can be found in [320, Cor. 7.8]. It is particularly useful for our purposes in that it allows for nonidentically distributed random variables. Note that if the a_i are identically distributed (i.e. the sampling operator corresponds to a single nondegenerate family, as opposed to a collection) then a simpler version of Talagrand's theorem can be used instead (e.g. [214, Thm. 8.42]).

Finally, let us make a few remarks on the log factors in the various measurement conditions. The special case of Corollary 13.15 (also Theorem 5.27) for randomly subsampled Fourier matrices was first proved in [123] with the measurement condition

$$m \gtrsim s \cdot \log^5(N) \cdot \log(\varepsilon^{-1}).$$

This commenced a long line of work on establishing sharper conditions under which randomly subsampled Fourier matrices (as well as related matrices) satisfy the RIP. Various improvements and extensions were obtained in, for example, [214, 405, 423], resulting in a condition of the form

$$m \gtrsim K^2 \cdot s \cdot \left(\log(m) \cdot \log^2(s) \cdot \log(N) + \log(\varepsilon^{-1})\right),$$

valid for random sampling with bounded orthonormal systems (see the Notes section of Chapter 11). Here K is the bound for the system ($K = 1$ in the case of the randomly subsampled Fourier matrices). This was further improved in [408] to

$$m \gtrsim K^2 \cdot s \cdot \left(\log(K^2 s) \cdot \log^2(s) \cdot \log(N) + \log(\varepsilon^{-1})\right). \tag{13.45}$$

Recall Remark 13.13. This particular improvement was obtained by using Hölder's inequality with a specific choice p. Such an approach was first employed in [33, 141]. We used the same idea in the proof of Lemma 13.32. Recall that random sampling with bounded orthonormal systems is a particular case of sampling with an isotropic family of vectors (in particular, $G = I$) with coherence $\mu(\mathcal{A}) = K^2$. Hence (13.45) is a special case of Corollary 13.15. More recently, in [143] – which is based on an approach of Bourgain [86], see also [259] – the bound (13.45) was further improved by one log factor, replacing $\log^2(s)$ with the term $\log(K^2 s \log(K^2 s))$.

Whether this log factor can be further reduced is a long-standing question, even in the special case of randomly subsampled Fourier matrices. It has been conjectured that such matrices possess the RIP with high probability for m scaling like $s \cdot \log(N)$. However, this remains an open problem. For this reason, uniform recovery guarantees for this and the other measurement matrices considered in this chapter all come with measurement conditions that exhibit larger log factors (and worse dependence on r in the levels case) than the corresponding nonuniform guarantees shown in Chapter 12.

14 Infinite-Dimensional Compressed Sensing

In this final chapter of Part III, we develop infinite-dimensional compressed sensing in Hilbert spaces. We first motivate this generalization by highlighting model mismatch and the inverse crime in the context of Fourier imaging in §14.1. In §14.2 we develop the sampling and reconstruction problem in Hilbert spaces. Next, in §14.3 we discuss a key issue, referred to as *bandwidth*, which arises naturally in infinite dimensions but not typically in finite dimensions. In §14.4 we discuss so-called *generalized sampling* as a tool to address it. We then develop infinite-dimensional compressed sensing in §14.5 and give uniform recovery guarantees for it in §14.6. These pertain to the (infinite-dimensional) sparse in levels model, multilevel random sampling and the weighted QCBP decoder. However, this decoder encounters an issue in infinite dimensions due to the additional error that arises when truncating the original infinite-dimensional problem. Fortunately, this can be overcome by switching to the weighted SR-LASSO. This is possible because of the favourable properties of this decoder with regard to its optimal parameter choice, as was shown previously in Chapters 6 and 13. We conclude in §14.7 by presenting uniform recovery guarantees for this decoder.

In this chapter, we make use of standard concepts in Hilbert spaces. See Appendix B for further information.

14.1 Motivations

Let $f\colon [0,1]^d \to \mathbb{C}$ be a continuous image. In Fourier imaging, recall from §2.2 that the corresponding reconstruction problem involves recovering f from its frequency values

$$y = \{\mathcal{F} f(2\pi\omega) : \omega \in \Omega\}, \tag{14.1}$$

for some $\Omega \subset \mathbb{Z}^d$. As discussed in §3.2.2, the typical discretization strategy simply replaces f by its discretization $x \in \mathbb{C}^{N^d}$ at resolution N and the continuous Fourier transform $\mathcal{F}$ by its discrete counterpart. This yields the discrete inverse problem

$$y = Ax, \qquad A = P_{\Omega} F \in \mathbb{C}^{m \times N^d}. \tag{14.2}$$

However, as was also discussed in §3.2.2, this discretization leads to unpleasant Gibbs artefacts, even in the non-subsampled case where $m = N^d$.

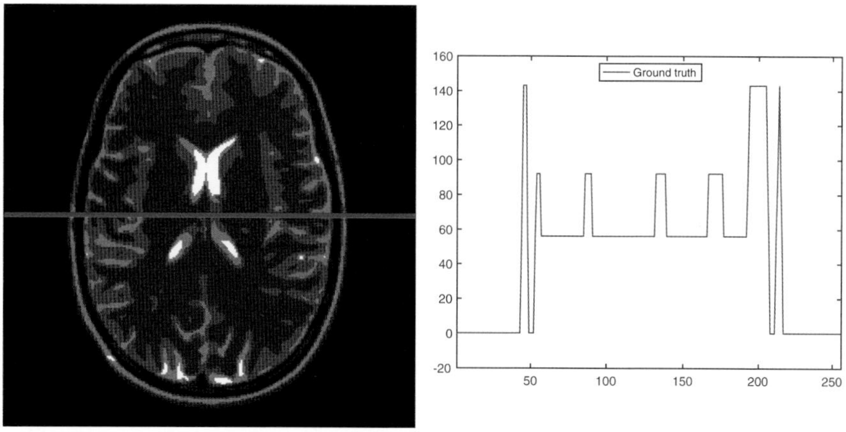

Figure 14.1 Ground truth discrete 256×256 GLPU phantom (left) and its horizontal cross-section (right). The cross-section is shown in blue in the left diagram.

In Fig. 14.2 we show a similar effect in the subsampled setting. The image to be recovered is the GLPU phantom, which is shown in Fig. 14.1. We conduct the following two experiments. First, we commit the inverse crime (see §4.4) by simulating the data via the DFT as $y = P_\Omega F x$, where x is the discretized 256×256 image. Second, we avoid the inverse crime by simulating the data as in (14.1) using the continuous Fourier transform of the original continuous image f. In both cases, the reconstruction is obtained by solving the finite-dimensional QCBP problem

$$\min_{z \in \mathbb{C}^{N^2}} \|\Phi^* z\|_{\ell^1} \text{ subject to } \|Az - y\|_{\ell^2} \leq \eta, \tag{14.3}$$

where A is as in (14.2) and $\Phi \in \mathbb{R}^{N^2 \times N^2}$ is the discrete Haar wavelet sparsifying transform.

Both approaches give roughly the same recovery for the lowest sampling percentage. This is to be expected. In this regime, the overall error is dominated by the compressed sensing error (i.e. the error in recovering the approximately sparse wavelet coefficients). However, as the sampling percentage increases, this error decreases and we witness the effect of the inverse crime. When the inverse crime is committed (see the top row of Fig. 14.2) we obtain an artificially high PSNR value, indicating more or less exact recovery of the discrete image. On the other hand, when the data is simulated according to the continuous model, the error stagnates at a PSNR value of around 32dB. The bottom row of Fig. 14.2 shows that Gibbs artefacts persist in this case, as one expects, due to the mismatch between the discrete reconstruction model and the continuous Fourier data.

To avoid these artefacts we need to change the discretization. We now do this by working directly with the infinite-dimensional model (i.e. the continuous Fourier transform) and by using orthonormal bases of the relevant Hilbert space. The result is what we term *infinite-dimensional compressed sensing*.

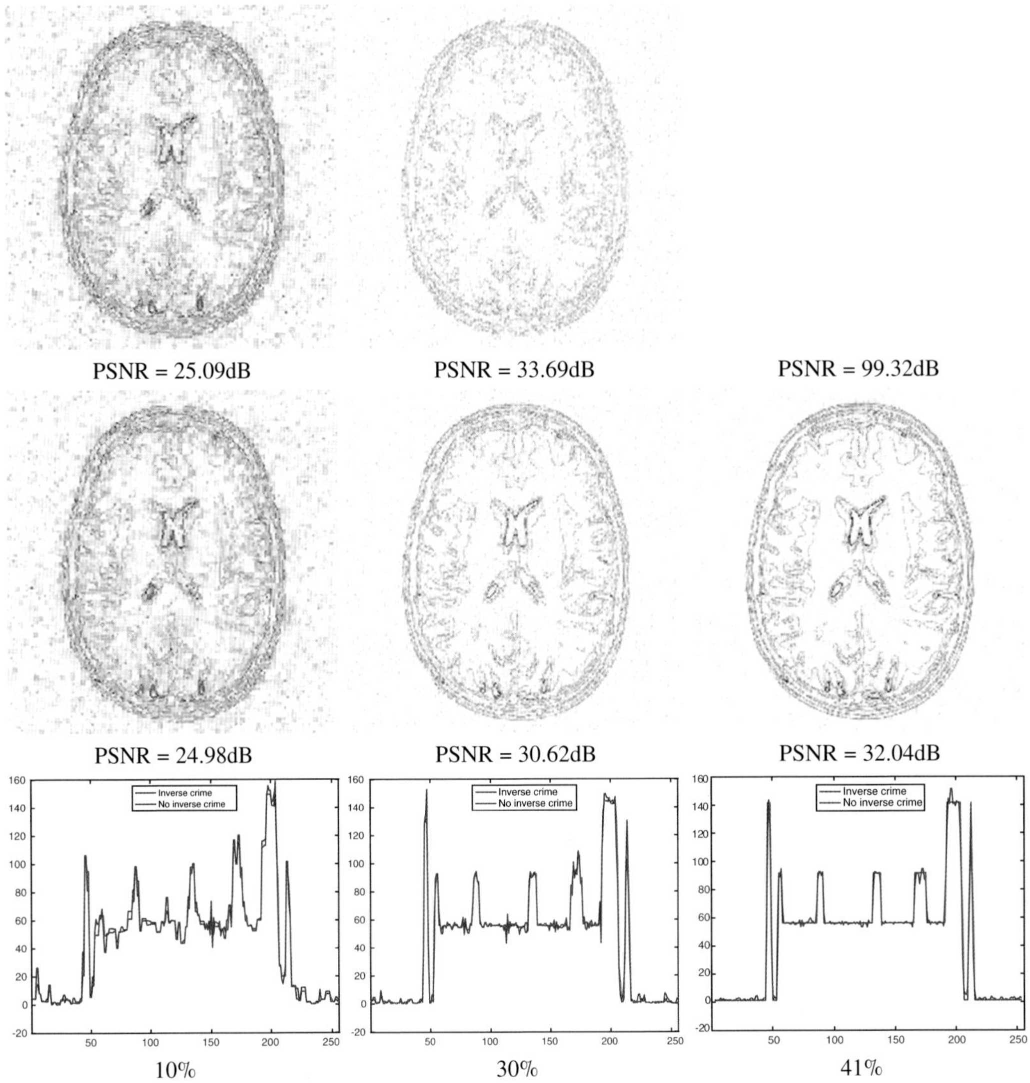

Figure 14.2 Haar wavelet reconstruction of the continuous GLPU phantom image. The first and second rows show the error maps $|\hat{x} - x|$, where $\hat{x}$ is the reconstructed image of resolution 256×256 and x is the ground truth image shown in Fig. 14.1. The colour has been inverted for visualization purposes. Top row: The measurements are generated as $y = P_\Omega F$, thus committing the inverse crime. Bottom row: The inverse crime is not committed. The measurements are generated using the Fourier transform of the true continuous image. In all experiments, the sampling map is the inverse square law (4.2). The bottom row gives the recovery of the horizontal cross-section shown in Fig. 14.1.

14.2 When Vectors Become Functions

Let $\mathbb{H}$ be a separable Hilbert space and $\Upsilon = \{\upsilon_i : i \in \mathbb{N}\}$ and $\Phi = \{\phi_j : j \in \mathbb{N}\}$ be two orthonormal bases of $\mathbb{H}$. We term these the *sampling* and *sparsity* bases, respectively.

For instance, $\{\upsilon_i\}$ could be the Fourier basis of $\mathbb{H} = L^2([0,1]^d)$, and $\{\phi_j\}$ a wavelet basis. As in the finite-dimensional setting (see §5.2), to each basis we can associate a synthesis operator

$$\mathcal{T}_\Upsilon : \ell^2(\mathbb{N}) \to \mathbb{H};\ x \mapsto \sum_{i\in\mathbb{N}} x_i \upsilon_i, \qquad \mathcal{T}_\Phi : \ell^2(\mathbb{N}) \to \mathbb{H};\ d \mapsto \sum_{j\in\mathbb{N}} d_j \phi_j. \tag{14.4}$$

These operators are unitary and their adjoints (which are equal to their inverses) are the corresponding analysis operators:

$$\mathcal{T}_\Upsilon^* : \mathbb{H} \to \ell^2(\mathbb{N}); f \mapsto (\langle f, \upsilon_i\rangle)_{i\in\mathbb{N}}, \qquad \mathcal{T}_\Phi^* : \mathbb{H} \to \ell^2(\mathbb{N}); f \mapsto \left(\langle f, \phi_j\rangle\right)_{j\in\mathbb{N}}.$$

See §B.6 for more information. Let $f \in \mathbb{H}$ be the element we wish to recover, and write

$$f = \sum_{j\in\mathbb{N}} d_j \phi_j = \mathcal{T}_\Phi d,$$

where $d = \mathcal{T}_\Phi^* f$ are the coefficients of f in the sparsity basis. Our goal is to approximate these coefficients, and therefore f, from a finite set of measurements chosen from the infinite collection of samples taken with respect to the sampling basis. We write

$$b = (\langle f, \upsilon_i\rangle)_{i\in\mathbb{N}} = \mathcal{T}_\Upsilon^* f \in \ell^2(\mathbb{N}),$$

for the infinite sequence of such samples.

It is useful to explicitly write down the relation between the coefficients $d = \mathcal{T}_\Phi^* f$ and samples $b = \mathcal{T}_\Upsilon^* f$. Let $\mathcal{U}$ be the unitary operator

$$\mathcal{U} : \ell^2(\mathbb{N}) \to \ell^2(\mathbb{N}),\ \mathcal{U} = \mathcal{T}_\Upsilon^* \mathcal{T}_\Phi.$$

Then, since $\mathcal{U} d = \mathcal{T}_\Upsilon^* \mathcal{T}_\Phi \mathcal{T}_\Phi^* f = \mathcal{T}_\Upsilon^* f$, we have

$$\mathcal{U} d = b.$$

Note that we may also view $\mathcal{U}$ as the infinite matrix with entries

$$U = \left(\langle \phi_j, \upsilon_i\rangle\right)_{i\in\mathbb{N}, j\in\mathbb{N}}. \tag{14.5}$$

From now on, we make no distinction between infinite matrices and bounded, linear operators on $\ell^2(\mathbb{N})$. For obvious reasons, we refer to U as the *change-of-basis* matrix between Φ and Υ. Written another way, the vector d can now be viewed as the solution of the infinite linear system of equations

$$U d = b. \tag{14.6}$$

14.3 Bandwidth

Of course, in practice we never have access to the whole infinite vector $b = (\langle f, \upsilon_i\rangle)_{i\in\mathbb{N}}$. Hence, we need to select m values from it in a suitable way. However, there is an important constraint to take into account first: namely, we can usually only choose these values from some fixed range of indices $1 \le i \le N$. In MRI for instance, this range is related to the maximum resolution of the scanner, which is itself limited by various physical constraints. See §3.2.5. Therefore, rather than (14.6) we now consider the semi-infinite linear system of equations

$$P_N U d = P_N b.$$

From now on, we refer to this N as the *sampling bandwidth*.

Remark 14.1 Here and henceforth, for a set $\Lambda \subset \mathbb{N}$, P_Λ is the orthogonal projection $P_\Lambda \colon \ell^2(\mathbb{N}) \to \ell^2(\mathbb{N})$ onto $\overline{\mathrm{span}\{e_j : j \in \Lambda\}}$, where $\{e_i\}_{i\in\mathbb{N}}$ is the canonical basis of $\ell^2(\mathbb{N})$. The only difference between this and previous chapters is that P_Λ is a mapping on $\ell^2(\mathbb{N})$ rather than $\mathbb{C}^N$. If P_Λ denotes an orthogonal projection we write $P_\Lambda^\perp = P_{\Lambda^c}$ for the complementary projection. As before, if Λ is finite we shall on occasion consider $P_\Lambda x$ as an element of $\mathbb{C}^{|\Lambda|}$. Similarly, if U is an infinite matrix we occasionally consider $P_\Lambda U$ as a $|\Lambda| \times \infty$ matrix (that is, a bounded operator $\ell^2(\mathbb{N}) \to \mathbb{C}^{|\Lambda|}$), UP_Λ as a $\infty \times |\Lambda|$ matrix (a bounded operator $\mathbb{C}^{|\Lambda|} \to \ell^2(\mathbb{N})$) and, for finite Δ, $P_\Lambda U P_\Delta$ as a $|\Lambda|\times|\Delta|$ matrix. As before, we write P_N when $\Lambda = \{1,\ldots,N\}$ and $P_{M_2}^{M_1}$ when $\Lambda = \{M_1+1,\ldots,M_2\}$.

A finite sampling bandwidth places a limitation on what we can expect to recover. For example, suppose that $\{\phi_j\}$ is an orthonormal basis of compactly supported wavelets and $\{\upsilon_i\}$ is the Fourier basis. As we have already seen, and will see again later, wavelets at scale j are essentially concentrated in frequency, with most of their energy being found in the band $\{\omega : 2^{j-1} \leq |\omega| \leq 2^j\}$. Hence, most of the energy of the wavelets at scale $j < \log_2(N)$ is contained within the finite sampling bandwidth, which, in this case, corresponds to the frequencies $\{-N/2+1,\ldots,N/2\}$. However, for scales $j > \log_2(N)$ most of the energy of the wavelets lies outside the sampling bandwidth. It is not surprising, and turns out to be the case, that wavelet coefficients at those scales cannot be recovered accurately and stably from Fourier measurements taken within this sampling bandwidth. Note that this situation does not change if the coefficients are sparse. If the nonzero coefficients correspond to wavelets whose energy is not captured by the sampling bandwidth, there is generally little hope of recovery.

This argument leads us to introduce a second parameter $M \leq N$, referred to as the *sparsity bandwidth*, from which we seek to recover coefficients in the sparsity basis. That is, given samples in the range $\{1,\ldots,N\}$ we now look to recover only those coefficients in the range $\{1,\ldots,M\}$.

This raises the question: how should N and M depend on each other? This is the concern of the next section.

14.4 Generalized Sampling

Let us put sparsity aside for the moment, and consider the following reconstruction problem: given *all* the measurements $b_i = \langle f, \upsilon_i \rangle$, $1 \leq i \leq N$, up to the sampling bandwidth N, recover *all* the coefficients d_j, $1 \leq j \leq M$, up to the sparsity bandwidth M. This is equivalent to solving the $N \times M$ linear system of equations

$$P_N U P_M d = P_N b \tag{14.7}$$

(note that we consider $P_N U P_M$ as an $N \times M$ matrix here). Clearly, we require $N \geq M$, otherwise there are more unknowns than equations. But, for reasons we explain below, we also cannot simply set $N = M$ in general.

Notice that (14.7) is generally an overdetermined system when $N > M$ and therefore may not have a solution. We now solve it approximately in a least-squares sense, by defining $\hat{d}$ as a minimizer of

$$\min_{z \in \mathbb{C}^M} \|P_N U P_M z - P_N b\|_{\ell^2}. \tag{14.8}$$

We refer to this procedure – that is, the process of recovering the first M coefficients in the sparsity basis from the first N coefficients in the sampling basis via (14.8) – as *generalized sampling*.

There is, of course, no guarantee that $\hat{d}$ will recover d exactly, and in practice it generally will not. Hence, it is important to understand how the error $\|\hat{d} - d\|_{\ell^2}$ behaves. Moreover, we also need to understand the stability of $\hat{d}$ to noise in the samples $P_N b$. As we show next, both of these depend on how large N is in comparison to M. To do this, we first introduce the following property:

Definition 14.2 (Balancing property) Let $U \colon \ell^2(\mathbb{N}) \to \ell^2(\mathbb{N})$ be unitary, $0 < \theta \leq 1$ and $N \geq M \geq 1$. Then U has the *balancing property* with constant θ if

$$\|P_M U^* P_N U P_M - P_M\|_{\ell^2} \leq 1 - \theta. \tag{14.9}$$

The balancing property measures how close the $N \times M$ matrix $P_N U P_M$ is to being an isometry. The following theorem asserts that it is sufficient for stable and accurate recovery via generalized sampling, with the latter being measured in terms of $\|P_M^{\perp} d\|_{\ell^2}$, i.e. the ℓ^2-norm of the coefficients not sought in the reconstruction.

Theorem 14.3 (Accuracy and stability of generalized sampling) *Let $U \colon \ell^2(\mathbb{N}) \to \ell^2(\mathbb{N})$ be unitary, $0 < \theta < 1$ and $N \geq M \geq 1$ be such that the balancing property holds with constant θ. Let $b = Ud + e$, where $e \in \ell^2(\mathbb{N})$. Then (14.8) has a unique solution $\hat{d}$, and that solution satisfies*

$$\|d - \hat{d}\|_{\ell^2} \leq (1 + 1/\sqrt{\theta})\|P_M^{\perp} d\|_{\ell^2} + \|e\|_{\ell^2}/\sqrt{\theta}. \tag{14.10}$$

Technically speaking, the solution of (14.8) is a vector in $\mathbb{C}^M$. Here and henceforth, we also write $\hat{d}$ for its extension by zero to $\ell^2(\mathbb{N})$, so that the term on the left-hand side of (14.10) is well defined.

Proof We use standard properties of least-squares problems (see §A.7). The balancing property and Lemma A.2 guarantee that the matrix $P_N U P_M \in \mathbb{C}^{N \times M}$ is full rank. Hence (14.8) has the unique solution

$$\hat{d} = (P_M U P_N)^{\dagger} P_M U^* P_N b,$$

where $\dagger$ denotes the pseudoinverse. Writing $b = Ud + e = UP_M d + (UP_M^{\perp} d + e)$ and using the properties of the pseudoinverse, we get

$$\hat{d} = P_M d + (P_M U P_N)^{\dagger} P_M U^* P_N \left(U P_M^{\perp} d + e \right).$$

Hence

$$\|P_M d - \hat{d}\|_{\ell^2} \leq \|(P_M U P_N)^\dagger\|_{\ell^2} \|P_M U^* P_N\|_{\ell^2} \|U P_M^\perp d + e\|_{\ell^2}$$
$$\leq \frac{1}{\sigma_{\min}(P_N U P_M)} \left(\|P_M^\perp d\|_{\ell^2} + \|e\|_{\ell^2} \right).$$

Here, we used the fact that $\|P_M U^* P_N\|_{\ell^2} \leq \|U\|_{\ell^2} = 1$ since P_M and P_N are orthogonal projections and U is unitary. The balancing property and Lemma A.2 give that $\sigma_{\min}(P_N U P_M) \geq \sqrt{\theta}$. Since

$$\|d - \hat{d}\|_{\ell^2} \leq \|P_M d - \hat{d}\|_{\ell^2} + \|P_M^\perp d\|_{\ell^2},$$

the result now follows. □

Theorem 14.3 begs the following question: when does the balancing property hold? To answer this, we first note that, for each fixed M, there always exists an N such that U has the balancing property. This follows straightforwardly from the fact that U is unitary. However, the matter of precisely how large N must be depends completely on the two orthonormal bases under consideration. For example, in the case of the one-dimensional Fourier-wavelets problem, this scaling is linear. The balancing property holds with constant θ whenever $N \geq c_\theta M$ for some constant $c_\theta \geq 1$ depending on θ (see Theorem 16.10). However, for other bases the scaling can be quadratic, i.e. $N \geq c_\theta M^2$, or higher. See the Notes section for further information.

But is this really important? After all, the balancing property was introduced to analyse just one method to approximate $P_M d$ from the samples $P_N b$, namely, the least-squares fit (14.8). Perhaps a different method could circumvent the aforementioned scalings. And moreover, our overall interest does not lie with the 'full' sampling problem (14.7), but rather with compressed sensing, where we can only access a subset of samples. One might hope that subsampling voids this issue.

In fact, the balancing property is a fundamental quantity to the problem. Under mild conditions, it dictates how many coefficients M can be stably recovered from N samples, regardless of the method used (see the Notes section). In other words, if it is violated, the recovery is guaranteed to be unstable. Regarding the second consideration, we remark that while subsampling might ameliorate this instability effect a little, it would eventually reappear as the sampling percentage was increased. This is counterintuitive, and of course, undesirable.

> In general, it is not possible to stably recover coefficients in the same range as that of the samples. For stable recovery to be possible, one first needs to ensure that the sampling bandwidth N and sparsity bandwidth M are chosen so that the balancing property holds for U.

Remark 14.4 We stress that this is an issue in infinite dimensions only. Let $\{\upsilon_i\}_{i=1}^N$ and $\{\phi_j\}_{j=1}^N$ be two orthonormal bases of $\mathbb{C}^N$. Then their change-of-basis matrix

$$U = \left(\langle \phi_j, \upsilon_i \rangle \right)_{i,j=1}^N \in \mathbb{C}^{N \times N}$$

is unitary, and therefore stably invertible. Conversely, in infinite dimensions, the truncated matrix $P_N U P_N$ is unitary if and only if the first N elements from each basis both span the same space, i.e. $\mathrm{span}(\{v_i\}_{i=1}^N) = \mathrm{span}(\{\phi_j\}_{j=1}^N)$. This is generally not the case. For example, if the sampling basis is the Fourier basis, then the former is a space of smooth trigonometric polynomials. But if the sparsity basis consists of Haar wavelets, then the latter is a space of piecewise constant functions. The balancing property in effect measures how well elements in the span of the truncated sparsity basis $\mathrm{span}(\{\phi_j\}_{j=1}^M)$ are approximated by elements in the span of the truncated sampling basis $\mathrm{span}(\{v_i\}_{i=1}^N)$.

14.5 Compressed Sensing in Infinite Dimensions

Generalized sampling and the balancing property explicate the relation between the sampling and sparsity bandwidths N and M. We are now ready to introduce infinite-dimensional compressed sensing. To this end, we now assume that the first M coefficients are also approximately sparse in levels (we now work with this model only), and then seek to recover them using m measurements chosen appropriately from the samples within the sampling bandwidth N.

Let $0 = M_0 < M_1 < M_2 < \cdots$ be a sequence determining the sparsity levels, and $\mathbf{M} = (M_1, \ldots, M_r)$ for some $r \geq 1$, where $M = M_r$. Let $\mathbf{s} = (s_1, \ldots, s_r)$ be the local sparsities within the levels, where $s_k \leq M_k - M_{k-1}$ for each k. We assume that the finite vector $P_M d$ is approximately $(\mathbf{s}, \mathbf{M})$-sparse. Next, let $0 = N_0 < N_1 < N_2 < \cdots$ be a sequence determining the sampling levels, and $\mathbf{N} = (N_1, \ldots, N_r)$, where $N = N_r$. Let $\mathbf{m} = (m_1, \ldots, m_r)$ where $m_k \leq N_k - N_{k-1}$ is the number of measurements taken in level k, and define $\Omega \subseteq \{1, \ldots, N\}$ as the corresponding $(\mathbf{m}, \mathbf{N})$-multilevel random sampling scheme (Definition 11.13). Similar to Definition 11.14, we let D be the infinite diagonal matrix with ith diagonal entry

$$D_{ii} = \begin{cases} \sqrt{\frac{N_k - N_{k-1}}{m_k}} & i = N_{k-1}+1, \ldots, N_k, \; k = 1, \ldots, r \\ 1 & i > N \end{cases} . \tag{14.11}$$

We now consider the noisy measurements

$$y = P_\Omega D U d + e \in \mathbb{C}^m,$$

of the unknown infinite vector d. Note that, up to the scaling D, these are noisy samples of the values $b_i = \langle f, v_i \rangle$, $i \in \Omega$.

The matrix $P_\Omega D U \in \mathbb{C}^{m \times \infty}$ is the semi-infinite matrix corresponding to the $(\mathbf{m}, \mathbf{N})$-multilevel sampling of the rows of U. Since our aim is to recover the first M coefficients $P_M d$, we now restrict this matrix to its first M columns, yielding

$$A = P_\Omega D U P_M \in \mathbb{C}^{m \times M}.$$

Note that this finite matrix arises simply by applying the $(\mathbf{m}, \mathbf{N})$-multilevel random sampling scheme to the matrix $P_N U P_M$. However, it is not a multilevel subsampled unitary matrix (Definition 11.14), since $P_N U P_M$ is generally nonsquare and nonunitary.

Nonetheless, we now have the ingredients we need to define the compressed sensing problem. To begin with, we consider the weighted QCBP decoder

$$\min_{z \in \mathbb{C}^M} \|z\|_{\ell^1_w} \text{ subject to } \|Az - y\|_{\ell^2} \leq \eta, \tag{14.12}$$

where $w = (w_i)_{i=1}^M$ is a sequence of positive weights. As in the finite-dimensional case, we assume that the weights w_i are constant on the sparsity levels, i.e.

$$w_i = w^{(k)}, \quad M_{k-1} < i \leq M_k, \quad k = 1, \ldots, r, \tag{14.13}$$

and take the form

$$w^{(k)} = \sqrt{s/s_k}, \quad k = 1, \ldots, r, \tag{14.14}$$

where s_k are the local sparsities. We also write $\mathbf{w} = (w^{(1)}, \ldots, w^{(r)})$.

So far, all seems straightforward. The problem (14.12) is a finite-dimensional convex optimization problem over $\mathbb{C}^M$, therefore (approximately) solvable. A minimizer $\hat{d} \in \mathbb{C}^M$ is an approximation to the first M coefficients $P_M d$, which in turn gives an approximation $\hat{f} = \sum_{i=1}^M \hat{d}_i \phi_i$ of the original element f we sought to recover. Seemingly, the only major difference between this and the finite-dimensional setting is that of bandwidth.

However, there is one other issue. Recall that for the QCBP decoder it is important that the true vector we seek to recover be feasible. Our goal in solving (14.12) is to recover $P_M d$. However, the measurements y are not noisy measurements of $P_M d$, but rather noisy measurements of d. Specifically,

$$y = P_\Omega D U d + e = P_\Omega D U P_M d + P_\Omega D U P_M^\perp d + e = A P_M d + P_\Omega D U P_M^\perp d + e.$$

Hence, feasibility of $P_M d$ is equivalent to the condition

$$\|P_\Omega D U P_M^\perp d + e\|_{\ell^2} \leq \eta. \tag{14.15}$$

In other words, to set the parameter η we need to know an *a priori* bound for both the noise e, e.g. $\|e\|_{\ell^2} \leq \eta/2$, *and* the term $P_\Omega D U P_M^\perp d$, e.g. $\|P_\Omega D U P_M^\perp d\|_{\ell^2} \leq \eta/2$. While the former may be reasonable, the latter is quite unrealistic since it depends on the expansion tail $P_M^\perp d$ of the unknown infinite vector d.

What to do? The answer, fortunately, is quite straightforward. In Chapter 6 we studied different decoders and their optimal parameter regimes, and in particular, we found the SR-LASSO decoder was particularly well suited to problems with unknown noise. This is exactly the situation that we now encounter. Hence, to overcome this issue we may now replace the weighted QCBP decoder (14.12) by the weighted SR-LASSO decoder

$$\min_{z \in \mathbb{C}^M} \lambda \|z\|_{\ell^1_w} + \|Az - y\|_{\ell^2}. \tag{14.16}$$

Much like in Chapters 6 and 13, we show later that the parameter λ in (14.16) can be chosen in a way that is completely independent of both the noise e and the expansion tail $P_M^\perp d$. We therefore conclude:

Ensuring feasibility in infinite-dimensional compressed sensing with (weighted) QCBP requires knowledge of the expansion tail, which is generally not available. This issue can be overcome by switching to the (weighted) SR-LASSO decoder.

14.6 Recovery Guarantees for Weighted QCBP

Before tackling this issue, we first give uniform recovery guarantees for weighted QCBP. Note that we do not present nonuniform guarantees, although they could also be derived in this setting (see the Notes section).

Given the weights $w_1, \ldots, w_M$ as in (14.13)–(14.14), we define the infinite weighting vector $w = (w_i)_{i=1}^{\infty} \in \ell^{\infty}(\mathbb{N})$ by letting $w_i = 1$ for $i > M$ (these values are arbitrary). We also define the weighted best $(\mathbf{s}, \mathbf{M})$-term approximation error as

$$\sigma_{\mathbf{s},\mathbf{M}}(x)_{\ell^1_w} = \min\left\{\|x - z\|_{\ell^1_w} : z \in \Sigma_{\mathbf{s},\mathbf{M}}\right\}, \qquad x \in \ell^1_w(\mathbb{N}).$$

Here $\Sigma_{\mathbf{s},\mathbf{M}}$ is the set of infinite sequences z that are $(\mathbf{s}, \mathbf{M})$-sparse:

$$\Sigma_{\mathbf{s},\mathbf{M}} = \left\{z : P_M^{\perp} z = 0,\ |\mathrm{supp}(z) \cap \{M_{k-1}+1, \ldots, M_k\}| \leq s_k,\ k = 1, \ldots, r\right\}.$$

Note that vectors in $\Sigma_{\mathbf{s},\mathbf{M}}$ are, by definition, zero outside their first M indices. In other words, they are isomorphic to $(\mathbf{s}, \mathbf{M})$-sparse vectors in $\mathbb{C}^M$. Finally, as in previous chapters, it is convenient to write U in block form as

$$U = \begin{pmatrix} U^{(1,1)} & U^{(1,2)} & \cdots \\ U^{(2,1)} & U^{(2,2)} & \cdots \\ \vdots & \vdots & \ddots \end{pmatrix},$$

where

$$U^{(k,l)} = P_{N_k}^{N_{k-1}} U P_{M_l}^{M_{l-1}} \in \mathbb{C}^{(N_k - N_{k-1}) \times (M_l - M_{l-1})}$$

corresponds to the kth sampling and lth sparsity level.

We now have the following uniform recovery guarantee. This generalizes the corresponding finite-dimensional result, Corollary 13.17, to infinite dimensions:

Theorem 14.5 (Infinite-dimensional compressed sensing with QCBP) *Let $0 < \varepsilon < 1$, $N \geq M \geq s \geq 2$, $U \colon \ell^2(\mathbb{N}) \to \ell^2(\mathbb{N})$ be unitary, Ω be an $(\mathbf{m}, \mathbf{N})$-multilevel sampling scheme, D be as in (14.11) and $\mathbf{M}$ and $\mathbf{s}$ be sparsity levels and local sparsities respectively. Suppose that*

(i) $N = N_r$ and $M = M_r$ are such that the balancing property (14.9) holds with constant $0 < \theta \leq 1$;

(ii) the m_k satisfy

$$m_k \gtrsim \theta^{-2} \cdot \left(\sum_{l=1}^{r} s_l \mu\left(U^{(k,l)}\right)\right) \cdot L, \quad k = 1, \ldots, r, \tag{14.17}$$

where $L = r^2 \cdot \log(2m) \cdot \log^2(rs/\theta) \cdot \log(M) + r \cdot \log(\varepsilon^{-1})$;

(iii) the weights $w = (w_i)_{i=1}^{\infty}$ are as in (14.13)–(14.14) for $i = 1, \ldots, M$.

Then the following holds with probability at least $1 - \varepsilon$. For all $d \in \ell^2(\mathbb{N})$ and $y =$

$P_\Omega DUd+e \in \mathbb{C}^m$, *every minimizer* $\hat{d}$ *of* (14.12) *with parameter* $\eta \geq \|P_\Omega DUP_M^\perp d + e\|_{\ell^2}$ *satisfies*

$$\|\hat{d} - d\|_{\ell^2} \lesssim \frac{\sigma_{\mathbf{s},\mathbf{M}}(P_M d)_{\ell^1_w}}{r^{1/4}\sqrt{s}} + \frac{r^{1/4}}{\sqrt{\theta}}\eta + \|P_M^\perp d\|_{\ell^2}. \tag{14.18}$$

As before, in (14.18) we consider $\hat{d}$ as an element of $\ell^1_w(\mathbb{N})$ which is zero outside its first M entries. Observe that the parameter θ arises both in the measurement condition and the noise term in (14.18). In particular, both terms get worse as θ gets smaller, i.e. as $P_N U P_M$ gets further from an isometry and therefore becomes less well behaved.

Proof We first claim that the matrix $A = P_\Omega DUP_M$ has the QCBP uniform recovery property (Definition 13.1) of order $(\mathbf{s}, \mathbf{M})$ with constant $\tau = 1/\sqrt{\theta}$. For this, recall that A is precisely the measurement matrix of the $(\mathbf{m}, \mathbf{N})$-multilevel random sampling scheme applied to $P_N U P_M$. The corresponding collection C (see §11.4.5) is nondegenerate (Definition 13.11), since the balancing property implies that the matrix $\mathbb{E}(A^*A) = P_M U^* P_N U P_M = G^*G \in \mathbb{C}^{M\times M}$ is positive definite. Also,

$$\|G^{-1}\|_{\ell^2} = 1/\sigma_{\min}(P_N U P_M) \leq 1/\sqrt{\theta},$$

and $\|G\|_{\ell^2} = \sigma_{\max}(P_N U P_M) = \|P_N U P_M\|_{\ell^2} \leq 1$ since U is unitary. Hence, the claim now follows from Theorem 13.14, Remark 13.13, the coherence estimates (12.27) and the assumed conditions on the m_k.

Next, observe that $y = P_\Omega DUx + e = AP_M x + e'$, where $e' = P_\Omega DUP_M^\perp x + e$ satisfies $\|e'\|_{\ell^2} \leq \eta$. Hence, the uniform recovery property gives

$$\|\hat{d} - P_M d\|_{\ell^2} \lesssim \frac{\sigma_{\mathbf{s},\mathbf{M}}(P_M d)_{\ell^1_w}}{r^{1/4}\sqrt{s}} + \frac{r^{1/4}}{\sqrt{\theta}}\eta.$$

To complete the proof, we simply use the triangle inequality. □

We remark in passing that the G-RIPL provides useful flexibility here over the RIPL, since $G^*G = \mathbb{E}(A^*A) = P_M U^* P_N U P_M \neq I$ in general. Indeed, $G = I$ would correspond to the balancing property holding with $\theta = 1$, which is generally not the case for any finite N and M. This was, in fact, the primary motivation for introducing the G-RIPL in Chapter 13.

14.7 Feasibility and the SR-LASSO

We now consider the feasibility issue (14.15). To this end, it is first useful to derive a bound for the tail $P_\Omega DUP_M^\perp d$:

Lemma 14.6 (Tail bound) *Let* U, D, Ω *and* $\mathbf{N}$ *be as in Theorem 14.5. Then*

$$\|P_\Omega DUP_M^\perp d\|_{\ell^2} \leq \left(\sum_{k=1}^{r} \mu\left(P_{N_k}^{N_{k-1}} U P_M^\perp\right)\right)^{1/2} \|P_M^\perp d\|_{\ell^1} < \infty,$$

for all $M \geq 0$. *Moreover, for every fixed* $\mathbf{N}$,

$$\sum_{k=1}^{r} \mu\left(P_{N_k}^{N_{k-1}} U P_M^\perp\right) \to 0, \qquad M \to \infty.$$

Proof By direct calculation

$$\|P_\Omega D U P_M^\perp d\|_{\ell^2}^2 \leq \sum_{k=1}^{r} \frac{N_k - N_{k-1}}{m_k} m_k \max_{N_{k-1} < i \leq N_k} |\langle u_i, P_M^\perp d\rangle|^2,$$

where $u_i = U^* e_i$. Observe that

$$|\langle u_i, P_M^\perp d\rangle|^2 = \left| \sum_{j>M} U_{ij} d_j \right|^2 \leq \max_{j>M} |U_{ij}|^2 \|P_M^\perp d\|_{\ell^1}^2.$$

Hence

$$\begin{aligned}\|P_\Omega D U P_M^\perp d\|_{\ell^2}^2 &\leq \sum_{k=1}^{r} (N_k - N_{k-1}) \max_{\substack{N_{k-1} < i \leq N_k \\ j>M}} |U_{ij}|^2 \|P_M^\perp d\|_{\ell^1}^2 \\ &= \sum_{k=1}^{r} \mu\left(P_{N_k}^{N_{k-1}} U P_M^\perp\right) \|P_M^\perp d\|_{\ell^1}^2,\end{aligned}$$

which gives the first result. For the second result, note first that $\|u_i\|_{\ell^2} = 1$ since U is unitary. In particular, $U_{ij} \to 0$ as $j \to \infty$ for fixed i. Hence $\mu(P_{N_k}^{N_k-1} U P_M^\perp) \to 0$ as $M \to \infty$ for each k, and this gives the result. □

Later, in Chapter 16, we will show that

$$\sum_{k=1}^{r} \mu\left(P_{N_k}^{N_{k-1}} U P_M^\perp\right) \leq c_p, \tag{14.19}$$

in the case of Fourier or Walsh sampling with wavelets for suitable choices of N and M (see §16.4.8). Here $p \geq 1$ is the number of vanishing moments of the (Daubechies) wavelet and $c_p > 0$ is a constant depending on p. Hence, given *a priori* knowledge of how the tail $\|P_M^\perp d\|_{\ell^1}$ decays as $M \to \infty$, one could in theory choose η to meet the feasibility condition $\|P_\Omega D U P_M^\perp d + e\|_{\ell^2} \leq \eta$.

However, this is hardly satisfactory. Such a tail bound may be unknown and, even if it were, the constant c_p in (14.19) depends on the wavelet used and may be difficult to estimate accurately. Fortunately, we now conclude this chapter by showing that this issue can be overcome by switching to the weighted SR-LASSO decoder (14.16):

Theorem 14.7 (Infinite-dimensional compressed sensing with SR-LASSO) *Let ε, N, M, s, U, Ω, D, $\mathbf{M}$ and $\mathbf{s}$ be as in Theorem 14.5 and suppose that (i)–(iii) of that result hold. Suppose also that $\lambda > 0$ satisfies*

$$\lambda \leq \frac{\sqrt{\theta}}{2\sqrt{2}} \frac{1}{\sqrt{rs}}. \tag{14.20}$$

Then the following holds with probability at least $1 - \varepsilon$. For all $d \in \ell^2(\mathbb{N})$ and $y = P_\Omega D U d + e \in \mathbb{C}^m$, every minimizer $\hat{d}$ of (14.16) satisfies

$$\|\hat{d} - d\|_{\ell^2} \lesssim \frac{\sigma_{\mathbf{s},\mathbf{M}}(P_M d)_{\ell^1_w}}{r^{1/4}\sqrt{s}} + \frac{r^{1/4}}{\sqrt{rs}\lambda}\left(\|e\|_{\ell^2} + \|P_\Omega D U P_M^\perp d\|_{\ell^2}\right) + \|P_M^\perp d\|_{\ell^2}. \tag{14.21}$$

Proof As in the proof of Theorem 14.5, the matrix $A = P_\Omega D U P_M$ has the SR-LASSO uniform recovery property (Definition 13.2) of order $(\mathbf{s}, \mathbf{M})$ with constant $\tau = 2\sqrt{2}/\sqrt{\theta}$. Since $y = AP_M d + e'$ with $e' = P_\Omega D U P_M^\perp d + e$, this gives

$$\|\hat{d} - P_M d\|_{\ell^2} \lesssim \frac{\sigma_{\mathbf{s},\mathbf{M}}(P_M d)_{\ell^1_w}}{r^{1/4}\sqrt{s}} + \frac{r^{1/4}}{\sqrt{rs}\lambda}\|e'\|_{\ell^2}.$$

We now write $\|e'\|_{\ell^2} \leq \|e\|_{\ell^2} + \|P_\Omega D U P_M^\perp d\|_{\ell^2}$, and then use the triangle inequality to bound $\|\hat{d} - d\|_{\ell^2}$. □

This theorem extends the results of Chapters 6 and 13 to the infinite-dimensional setting and shows how the weighted SR-LASSO overcomes the expansion tail issue, provided λ is chosen according to the total sparsity s. As we see, the additional term in the error bound is proportional to $\|P_\Omega D U P_M^\perp d\|_{\ell^2}$. This, as discussed above, can be bounded by a constant times $\|P_M^\perp d\|_{\ell^1}$ for the problems considered in later chapters.

Notes

There have been a variety of different approaches towards extending conventional compressed sensing from finite-dimensional to infinite-dimensional models. In [356, 357] a union of subspaces model was considered, see also [167] and [187]. Davenport & Wakin [169] considered recovery via discrete prolate spheroidal sequences (see [443] or [266]). Recovery of sparse trigonometric polynomials was considered in [404], and later adapted to sparse Legendre polynomial expansions [407] and spherical harmonic expansions [406]. This is part of a growing body of work on multivariate function approximation via compressed sensing. See, for instance, [2, 10] and references therein.

In this chapter we have mainly followed the framework of [17], which introduced compressed sensing in Hilbert spaces. The results proved therein are nonuniform. Uniform recovery guarantees, such as those given in this chapter, were introduced in [3] for weighted QCBP and [7] for the weighted SR-LASSO. The results of this chapter consider only orthonormal sampling and sparsity bases. For extensions to frames, see [31, 394].

In [398, 465, 466] a quite general framework for compressed sensing in (possibly nonseparable) Hilbert spaces was introduced, where the sparse or sparse in levels class was replaced by a generic low-dimensional model Σ. This work introduced extensions of the RIP for such classes, and showed how to design Gaussian-type encoding strategies that satisfy this RIP with a number of measurements depending linearly, up to a log factor, on a suitable notion of dimension. Convex decoders based on atomic norms were also introduced for this model. Beyond sparsity in levels and its applications, this work also applies to block sparsity as well as low-rank matrix recovery problems.

A different line of work in the infinite-dimensional setting considers the recovery of sparse *analog* signals. A typical problem of this form is to recover a measure μ that is a sparse linear combination of Diracs $\mu = d_1\delta_{x_1} + \cdots + d_s\delta_{x_s}$, where both the locations x_i and the coefficients d_i are unknown. Problems such as this arise in radar, astronomy, array processing, seismology and various other applications. Typically, the measurements are samples of the Fourier transform of μ, in which case the recovery problem is equivalent to *frequency estimation*. This is sometimes referred to as the *superresolution* problem [116] (since, often, only low frequencies are prescribed) or *off-the-grid* compressed sensing [455]. The term 'analog' reflects the fact that the locations x_i are not constrained to lie in a discrete grid, but rather a continuum. Discretizing this problem naïvely using a finite grid leads to a mismatch between the finite-dimensional model and the measurements, and much as with the Fourier imaging problem studied in this chapter, can lead to severe artefacts in the recovery [142]. Approaches such as [116, 455], which are based on certain convex relaxations, seek to avoid this by working directly in the continuum. More general analog frameworks have also been studied. See, for instance, [80, 189, 395] and references therein.

Generalized sampling was introduced in [15]; see also [16, 18]. It also has straightforward extensions to nonorthonormal systems such as Riesz bases or frames. Estimating the relationship between N and M such that the balancing property holds (the so-called *stable sampling rate*) was a major focus of these works. Note that it is provably linear for the Fourier-wavelets problem [19], but quadratic if the wavelet basis is replaced by an orthonormal polynomial basis [16]. This quadratic scaling is optimal: no method can stably recover polynomial coefficients from asymptotically fewer Fourier samples [23]. In general, the fundamentality of the balancing property for stable recovery in one space given samples in another was shown in [18].

As noted, the balancing property generally fails to hold when $N = M$. The matrix $P_N U P_N$, known as the *finite section* of U, is a widely studied object in computational spectral theory. See, for example, [83, 250, 254, 328]. Unfortunately, finite sections of unitary operators can behave wildly. So-called *uneven sections*, namely, matrices of the form $P_N U P_M$ with $N \geq M$, have been used in computational spectral theory to overcome this issue [255]. See also [241, 328]. In computational harmonic analysis, besides generalized sampling they have also been used to numerically compute the so-called *inverse frame* operator [127, 145, 447].

The feasibility issue for QCBP in infinite dimensions was first considered in [3, 17, 20]. There, an additional *data fidelity* parameter $K \geq M$ was introduced, leading to a matrix

$$A = P_\Omega D U P_K \in \mathbb{C}^{m \times K},$$

and a minimization problem over $\mathbb{C}^K$, as opposed to $\mathbb{C}^M$. Note that the sparsity bandwidth remains M: the parameter K is used solely to enforce feasibility. In particular, the relevant condition in Theorem 14.5 now becomes $\|P_\Omega D U P_K^\perp d + e\|_{\ell^2} \leq \eta$. For the Fourier-wavelets problem, this can be guaranteed whenever $\|e\|_{\ell^2} \leq \eta/2$ and

$$(N/K)^{p+1/2} \|d\|_{\ell^1} \leq c_p \eta.$$

Taking K sufficiently large ensures this condition holds, although exactly how large still depends on p and the unknown coefficients d, albeit only the norm $\|d\|_{\ell^1}$ rather than the tail $\|P_M^\perp d\|_{\ell^1}$. We refer to [3] for details. The SR-LASSO overcomes this issue without the need for such a K.

Finally, a word on computations. As discussed, the standard discretization (14.3) is attractive since matrix–vector multiplications with A and A^* can be performed in

$\mathcal{O}(N\log(N))$ operations via the DFT and DWT. The approach introduced in this chapter is in principle not quite as straightforward. For one, the entries of the matrix U are now inner products of functions. Yet, due to the intimate relationship between wavelets and the Fourier transform (see Chapter 9), fast matrix–vector multiplications with the corresponding measurement matrix A can still be performed in $\mathcal{O}(N\log(N))$ time. Algorithms for doing this have been developed in [223].

Part IV

Compressed Sensing for Imaging

Summary of Part IV

In Part IV we address one of the main question of this book: namely, how to use compressed sensing theory to guide the design and understand the performance of sampling strategies for compressive imaging (Key Points #7, #8 and #9 of Chapter 1).

Chapters 15 and 16 consider wavelet sparsifying transforms with either Fourier or Walsh sampling. In Chapter 15 we first introduce a series of sampling schemes in one and two dimensions that arise as a consequence of the theory developed in Part III. These are specific types of multilevel random sampling schemes (Definition 4.6), termed the *Dyadic Sampling (DS)* scheme in one dimension, and the *Dyadic Isotropic Sampling (DIS)* and *Dyadic Anisotropic Sampling (DAS)* schemes in two dimensions. The schemes sample randomly within dyadic bands in frequency space. We then present a series of measurement conditions for them. These conditions extend the previously presented result for the Fourier–Haar wavelet problem to higher-order wavelets and both one and two dimensions. A signature result is that, for Fourier sampling and the Daubechies wavelet of order p, the number of measurements in the kth dyadic band should scale like

$$m_k \gtrsim \left(s_k + \sum_{l=1}^{k-1} s_l 2^{-(2q+1)(k-l)} + \sum_{l=k+1}^{r} s_l 2^{-(2p+d)(l-k)} \right) \cdot L, \quad k = 1, \ldots, r, \qquad (\star)$$

for $d = 1, 2$, where $\mathbf{s} = (s_1, \ldots, s_r)$ are the local sparsities of the image with respect to the wavelet scales, q is the wavelet smoothness (see §9.6.2) and L is a log factor. Recall that $q \to \infty$ as $p \to \infty$. Hence, the higher the order, the less the influence of the s_l, $l \neq k$, on the measurement condition ($\star$). Up to the log factor, as p increases ($\star$) becomes progressively closer to the optimal condition $m_k \gtrsim s_k \cdot L$ for the sparse in levels model.

Besides introducing these schemes, in Chapter 15 we also examine why certain sampling patterns work well. The key point is the local sparsities s_k. We revisit and explain the four principles for sampling strategy design that were introduced in §4.2, and then develop a framework based on ($\star$) for understanding quite general classes of schemes. We illustrate this by returning to the case of power-law sampling (Definition 4.4), which was previously discussed in Chapters 11–13. The main point, shown clearly by ($\star$), is the need to adapt the sampling strategy to the *asymptotic* sparsity structure of the images under consideration. In particular, this substantially narrows the gap identified previously in §11.2.1 between theory and practice.

Chapter 16 contains the formal statements and proofs of the associated recovery guarantees. In the one-dimensional case, it also reconnects compressed sensing to best

s-term wavelet approximation, which was the topic of Chapter 11. In particular, it shows rigorously that compressed sensing with wavelets can achieve quasi-best s-term approximation of piecewise smooth functions from Fourier or Walsh samples.

Up to this point, our main focus has been on sparsity in wavelets. Chapter 17 returns to another important sparsifying transform considered earlier in this book: the discrete gradient operator. We commence by taking a look at different sampling schemes for TV minimization, before presenting a series of recovery guarantees. While not as refined as those for wavelet sparsity, these guarantees clearly illustrate the benefit of variable-density sampling in Fourier imaging over uniform random sampling. We also present a recovery guarantee for two-dimensional Walsh sampling with variable-density sampling.

15 Sampling Strategies for Compressive Imaging

We commence this chapter in §15.1 with an overview. Here, we first revisit the four principles of §4.2 and then, using the power laws as an example, we discuss sampling strategy design. In the next section, §15.2, we formally define the specific multilevel random sampling strategies for Fourier and Walsh sampling – the one-dimensional Dyadic Sampling (DS) and the two-dimensional Dyadic Isotropic Sampling (DIS) and Dyadic Anisotropic Sampling (DAS) schemes. In §15.3 we present the corresponding measurement conditions for these strategies. For reasons of length, formal statements of the recovery guarantees are deferred until Chapter 16, along with their proofs. Having introduced these schemes and their measurement conditions, in the final section, §15.4, we show how they can be used to address sampling strategy design for quite general classes of schemes.

15.1 Overview

In this chapter, we consider Daubechies wavelet sparsifying transforms. Let s_k, $k = 1, 2, \ldots$, denote the sparsity of an image in the kth wavelet scale. The DS, DIS and DAS schemes sample randomly within dyadic bands in (Walsh or Fourier) frequency space, and the various measurement conditions for these schemes take the form

$$m_k \gtrsim \left(s_k + \sum_{l=1}^{k-1} s_l 2^{-a(k-l)} + \sum_{l=k+1}^{r} s_l 2^{-b(k-l)} \right) \cdot L, \qquad k = 1, \ldots, r \tag{15.1}$$

(as before, we adopt the convention that the first sum vanishes when $k = 1$ and the second sum vanishes when $k = r$). Here m_k is the total number of measurements taken within the kth band, L is a log factor and $a, b > 0$ are constants depending on the wavelet order and whether the sampling is of Fourier or Walsh type. This condition generalizes that seen in Chapters 12 and 13 for the case of multilevel Fourier sampling with Haar wavelets.[1] As discussed therein, the key point is that the number of measurements in the kth level is dominated by the corresponding local sparsity s_k, with an exponentially small dependence on s_l as $|l - k|$ increases. Hence, as was previously predicted by the

[1] Technically, this is not a generalization. The problem considered in Chapters 12 and 13 is discrete Fourier sampling with the discrete Haar basis, whereas here and in Chapter 16 we consider the infinite-dimensional setup of Chapter 14. But we will see later that the continuous one-dimensional Fourier–Haar problem admits exactly the same measurement condition as the discrete problem considered previously.

flip test in Chapter 11, local properties of the image (namely its local sparsity in the corresponding scale) guide the local nature of the sampling strategy.

Remark 15.1 In this and the next chapter, we allow the constants implicit in the symbols $\lesssim$, $\gtrsim$ and $\asymp$ to depend on p, the order of the Daubechies wavelet under consideration. When it is useful to do so, we also make this dependence explicit, by writing $c_p > 0$ for a constant depending on p. When considering the power-law schemes (see §15.1.2), we also allow these constants to depend on the parameter α.

15.1.1 The Four Principles Revisited

In §4.2 we introduced four principles for sampling strategy design. The condition (15.1) now allows us to give them a theoretical footing.

Principle #1. Fully sample the low frequencies.

This is clear. Recall from §11.2 that wavelet coefficients of natural images are *asymptotically* sparse . Hence, when k is small, $s_k \approx N_k - N_{k-1}$, where $N_k - N_{k-1}$ is the size of the wavelet scale. The right-hand side of (15.1) exceeds the size of the sampling level (which, as we see later, is equal to the size of the wavelet scale) and we therefore simply take all samples in that level, i.e. $m_k = N_k - N_{k-1}$ (recall Remark 11.20). Note that, much as in the discrete Fourier–Haar case (see §11.6), the kth sampling band in any of the DS, DIS and DAS schemes corresponds to low frequencies when k is small and high frequencies when k is large.

Principle #2. Outside the region of full sampling, subsample in a smoothly decreasing manner.

This is implied by (15.1) and the asymptotic sparsity of the wavelet coefficients. As k increases, s_k decreases relative to the size of the scale, therefore the corresponding sampling density $m_k/(N_k - N_{k-1})$ also decreases.

Principle #3. The optimal sampling strategy depends on the image, the resolution N, the number of measurements m and the recovery procedure.

The image dependence follows directly from the local sparsities s_k. An image with more features will have relatively larger local sparsities s_k at fine scales ($k \gg 1$), thus requiring more measurements at high frequencies. Conversely, an image with fewer features will have relatively smaller local sparsities at fine scales.

To explain the dependence on the number of measurements, consider the following scenario. Suppose that we have a fixed budget of measurements m. Then, according to (15.1), we can recover s wavelet coefficients, where $s \approx m/L$. Given s, let $s_k = s_k(m)$ be the number of the s largest wavelet coefficients that come from the kth sparsity level. We now choose the local measurements m_k according to (15.1) using these values of s_k. The point is that, as the budget m changes, so do the $s_k = s_k(m)$ and therefore the sampling strategy. When m is small, we typically expect no wavelet coefficients at fine scale to be amongst the s largest. Hence the sampling scheme will simply densely sample the low frequencies. On the other hand, as m increases we start picking up more fine scale wavelet coefficients, thus requiring more high-frequency measurements.

The dependence on the recovery procedure (in this case, this just means the choice of sparsifying transform) is also straightforward to understand. Within the setting of wavelets, changing the wavelet order will generally result in a change in the local sparsities s_k. It will also typically alter the constants a and b in the measurement condition (15.1). Of course, Principle #3 does not just pertain to wavelet sparsifying transforms. In §17.6 we show that switching from wavelets to the discrete gradient operator also generally precipitates a change in the best sampling strategy.

Principle #4. The optimal sampling strategy may be anisotropic.

This principle is explained in more detail later. As we show, in two dimensions it is sometimes not possible to obtain a measurement condition of the form (15.1) with the DIS scheme, since it samples uniformly (i.e. isotropically) within the kth dyadic band. See Fig. 15.1(a). The underlying reason for this is the relatively slow decay of (typically lower-order) wavelets in (Fourier or Walsh) frequency space. Switching to nonuniform sampling within these bands solves this issue. In the DAS scheme, each band is further subdivided into subregions, with a different amount of uniform random sampling performed in each. See Fig. 15.1(b). Such anisotropic sampling overcomes the issue with the DIS scheme, and restores a measurement condition of the form (15.1).

Remark 15.2 In §4.3 we discussed the resolution dependence of compressive imaging. This, and, in particular, the effect seen in Fig. 4.9, can now also be explained in the wavelet setting. If the resolution N doubles, then asymptotic sparsity implies that the local sparsity at the new finest wavelet scale is smaller relative to the size of the scale than in those preceding it. Hence we require a smaller fraction of additional samples in the new sampling level than in the existing levels in order to capture the new scale.

15.1.2 Analysis and Design of Sampling Strategies

The DS, DIS and DAS schemes are specific types of multilevel random sampling schemes (in the sense of Definition 4.6) whose levels are directly related to the wavelet scales. As discussed in Chapter 4, in practice one may prefer a finer-graded sampling strategy, such as the Gaussian multilevel scheme, so as to allow for sampling in a more smoothly decreasing manner. Compare, for instance, Fig. 4.1 with Fig. 15.1. Nonetheless, the measurement conditions for the DS, DIS and DAS schemes can be used to understand the performance of other classes of sampling schemes in terms of the local sparsities s_k.

This is the topic of §15.4. As an example, we consider the class of power-law sampling schemes. Specifically, let $\pi = \{\pi_\omega\}$ be given by

$$\pi_\omega = \frac{C_{N,\alpha}}{(\max\{1, |\omega|\})^\alpha}, \quad \omega \in \{-N/2 + 1, \ldots, N/2\} \tag{15.2}$$

in one dimension and

$$\pi_\omega = \frac{C_{N,\alpha}}{(\max\{1, |\omega_1|^2 + |\omega_2|^2\})^\alpha}, \quad \omega = (\omega_1, \omega_2) \in \{-N/2 + 1, \ldots, N/2\}^2 \tag{15.3}$$

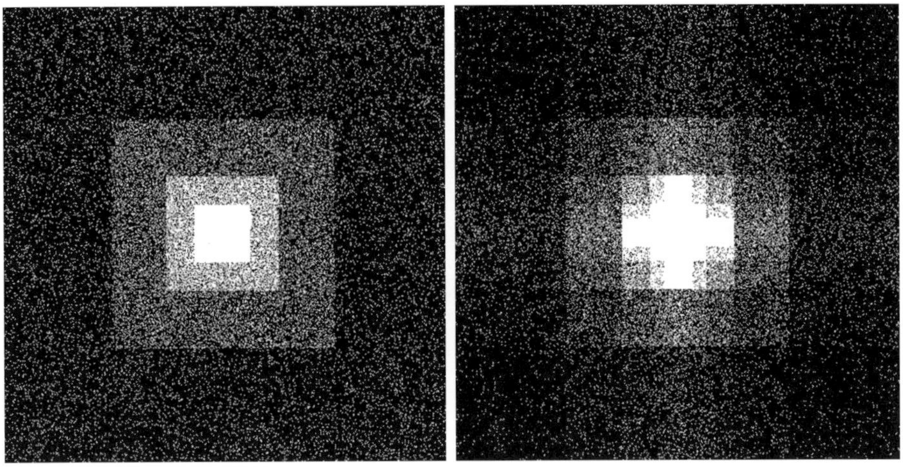

(a) DIS (b) DAS

Figure 15.1 Examples of the schemes for Fourier sampling. (a) DIS. (b) DAS.

in two dimensions, where $\alpha \in \mathbb{R}$ is a parameter. These schemes were discussed previously in Chapters 11–13. In Chapters 12 and 13, we showed that the value $\alpha = 1$ is optimal for the sparse model in the case of the discrete Fourier–Haar wavelet problem. However, this fact is misleading, since this value generally does not give the best performance on natural images – see §11.2, as well as Table 15.1.

Remark 15.3 Although we shall not prove it, the result that $\alpha = 1$ is optimal for the sparse model in the case of discrete Fourier–Haar wavelet problem generalizes. The schemes (15.2) or (15.3) with $\alpha = 1$ yield near-optimal measurement conditions of the form $m \gtrsim s \cdot L$ for *any* Daubechies wavelet basis with Fourier samples. In particular, the best sampling strategy for the sparse model is independent of the wavelet used. The same result also holds in the Walsh setting, upon replacing (15.2) or (15.3) with the analogous power-law schemes defined over the set of nonnegative Walsh frequencies.

On the other hand, in §15.4 we show how different values of α perform better depending on the behaviour of the local sparsities. To do this, we employ a variant of the measurement condition (15.1). Even though it does not pertain to a power-law sampling scheme itself, we use it to derive a relationship between α and the s_k under which the total number of measurements m in the power-law scheme scales like $s \cdot L$, where $s = s_1 + \cdots + s_r$ is the total sparsity. Specifically, for $d = 1, 2$ we show that

$$\alpha = 1 \quad \rightsquigarrow \quad s^*_k \lesssim 1/r, \; k = 1, \ldots, r,$$

where $s^*_k = s_k/s$ is the kth *unit local sparsity*, and for sufficiently high-order wavelets,

$$\alpha < 1 \quad \rightsquigarrow \quad s^*_k \lesssim 2^{d(1-\alpha)(k-r)}, \; k = 1, \ldots, r$$

and

$$\alpha > 1 \quad \rightsquigarrow \quad s^*_k \lesssim 2^{-d(\alpha-1)k}, \; k = 1, \ldots, r.$$

Table 15.1 The value of α that gives the highest PSNR reconstruction for a given test image (see Fig. 2.2), resolution and sampling percentage. The value of α is chosen from the set $\{0.50, 0.75, 1.00, 1.25, 1.50, 1.75, 2.00, 2.25, 2.50, 2.75, 3.00\}$. The corresponding PSNR values are given below each line of α values. DB4 wavelets are used as the sparsifying transform.

Image/Percentage	5%	10%	15%	20%	25%	30%	35%	40%
Dog (256 × 256)	3.00	3.00	3.00	3.00	2.50	2.75	2.50	2.25
	24.64	26.78	28.31	29.50	30.62	31.67	32.82	33.89
Dog (512 × 512)	2.50	3.00	3.00	2.75	2.50	2.25	2.25	2.25
	25.94	28.16	29.78	31.10	32.23	33.34	34.45	35.60
Brain (256 × 256)	2.75	2.75	3.00	2.50	2.25	2.25	2.25	1.75
	19.62	22.65	24.67	26.30	27.86	29.27	30.81	32.28
Brain (512 × 512)	3.00	2.50	2.75	2.75	2.50	2.25	2.00	2.25
	24.71	28.80	31.66	33.87	35.84	37.77	39.65	41.57
Peppers (256 × 256)	2.50	2.75	2.25	1.75	2.25	2.00	1.50	1.75
	26.73	30.17	32.17	33.91	35.69	37.39	39.04	40.72
Peppers (512 × 512)	2.50	1.75	1.50	1.50	1.25	1.00	1.00	1.25
	28.62	31.28	32.77	33.98	35.00	35.86	36.57	37.32
Kopp (256 × 256)	2.25	2.50	1.50	1.00	1.75	1.25	1.00	1.00
	32.58	35.37	37.65	39.73	41.48	44.27	45.99	47.36
Kopp (512 × 512)	2.50	1.25	1.50	1.00	1.25	1.00	1.25	1.25
	35.89	38.72	41.30	43.74	46.20	47.62	49.02	50.36

Here, the symbol $\rightsquigarrow$ indicates that a condition $m \gtrsim s \cdot L$ holds for the given α whenever the s^*_k satisfy the corresponding condition. In other words, the choice of α is associated with a particular growth or decay of the local sparsities. This is intuitive. If the local sparsities s^*_k are increasing, then one needs more high-frequency samples to capture the larger numbers of fine-scale wavelet coefficients. This suggests choosing a slower-decaying power law ($\alpha < 1$). Conversely, if the s^*_k are decreasing, one uses a more rapidly decaying power law ($\alpha > 1$) since there are fewer fine-scale coefficients. It is also not surprising that $\alpha = 1$ corresponds to constant local sparsities. After all, this is the value of α that leads to the best measurement condition for the sparse model.

This phenomenon is highlighted in Table 15.1. Here we compute the best value of α (in the sense that it yields the highest accuracy reconstruction) for a variety of different test images, resolutions and sampling percentages using Fourier sampling with DB4 wavelets. Of the four images, the dog image has the most fine-scale features. Accordingly, the best performance is obtained for larger values of α. Conversely, the kopp image is the most simple, hence smaller values of α give the best recovery.

It is also notable that the optimal value of α decreases in all cases as the sampling percentage increases. This again makes sense. As discussed, when the measurement budget is low, it is best spent capturing the coarse scales, since these carry most of the image's energy. Hence a larger value of α is preferred. Conversely, as the budget increases, there are enough measurements available to capture the fine scales, which necessitates higher frequencies and hence a smaller value of α.

15.2 The DS, DIS and DAS Schemes

In this section we introduce the DS, DIS and DAS schemes. As mentioned, we use the infinite-dimensional compressed sensing setup of Chapter 14. Hence we consider the Fourier and Walsh sampling bases and wavelet sparsity bases of $L^2([0,1])$ or $L^2([0,1]^2)$. The reason for doing this, as previously observed, is that it is easier to prove recovery guarantees in the infinite-dimensional setting. In particular, the various local coherence estimates – which are central to the measurement conditions developed in Chapter 14 – are easier to derive in the continuous case than in the discrete case, since they involve estimating integrals as opposed to sums. Chapter 16 addresses this task.

15.2.1 Partitions

Recall from Definition 4.6 that a multilevel random sampling scheme is characterized by a finite partition of the lowest N frequencies (or N^2 in the two-dimensional case) into different regions, within which the sampling is performed randomly and uniformly. We now introduce the partitions that define the schemes. Since we work in the infinite-dimensional setting, we first define countable partitions of the sets $\mathbb{Z}^d$ and $\mathbb{N}_0^d$. The former indexes the d-dimensional Fourier basis of $L^2([0,1]^d)$ (see (E.3)), while the latter indexes the Walsh basis (see (2.25)). Once we have these, a partition of the lowest N or N^2 frequencies is then obtained by taking a finite number of these sets.

Definition 15.4 (Dyadic partition, $d = 1$) The *dyadic partition* $\mathcal{B} = \{B_k\}_{k \in \mathbb{N}}$ of $\mathbb{N}_0$ of index $j_0 \in \mathbb{N}_0$ is

$$B_1 = [0, 2^{j_0}) \cap \mathbb{N}_0, \qquad B_k = [2^{j_0+k-2}, 2^{j_0+k-1}) \cap \mathbb{N}_0, \quad k = 2, 3, \ldots.$$

The dyadic partition of $\mathbb{Z}$ of index $j_0 \in \mathbb{N}_0$ is

$$\begin{aligned} B_1 &= (-2^{j_0-1}, 2^{j_0-1}] \cap \mathbb{Z}, \\ B_k &= \left((-2^{j_0+k-2}, -2^{j_0+k-3}] \cup (2^{j_0+k-3}, 2^{j_0+k-2}]\right) \cap \mathbb{Z}, \quad k = 2, 3, \ldots. \end{aligned}$$

Note that j_0 generally corresponds to the coarsest wavelet scale.

Definition 15.5 (Dyadic partitions, $d = 2$) The *dyadic anisotropic partition* $\mathcal{B}^{(2)} = \{B^{(2)}_{k_1,k_2}\}_{k_1,k_2 \in \mathbb{N}}$ of $\mathbb{N}_0^2$ or $\mathbb{Z}^2$ of index $j_0 \in \mathbb{N}_0$ is given by

$$B^{(2)}_{k_1,k_2} = B_{k_1} \times B_{k_2},$$

where $\{B_k\}_{k \in \mathbb{N}}$ is the dyadic partition of $\mathbb{N}_0$ or $\mathbb{Z}$, respectively. The *dyadic isotropic partition* $\overline{\mathcal{B}}^{(2)} = \{\overline{B}^{(2)}_k\}_{k \in \mathbb{N}}$ of $\mathbb{N}_0^2$ or $\mathbb{Z}^2$ of index $j_0 \in \mathbb{N}_0$ is

$$\overline{B}^{(2)}_k = \bigcup_{\max\{k_1,k_2\}=k} B^{(2)}_{k_1,k_2}.$$

The sets defining these partitions are illustrated in Fig. 15.2. The isotropic partition divides the plane into annular bands of width roughly 2^k, whereas the anisotropic

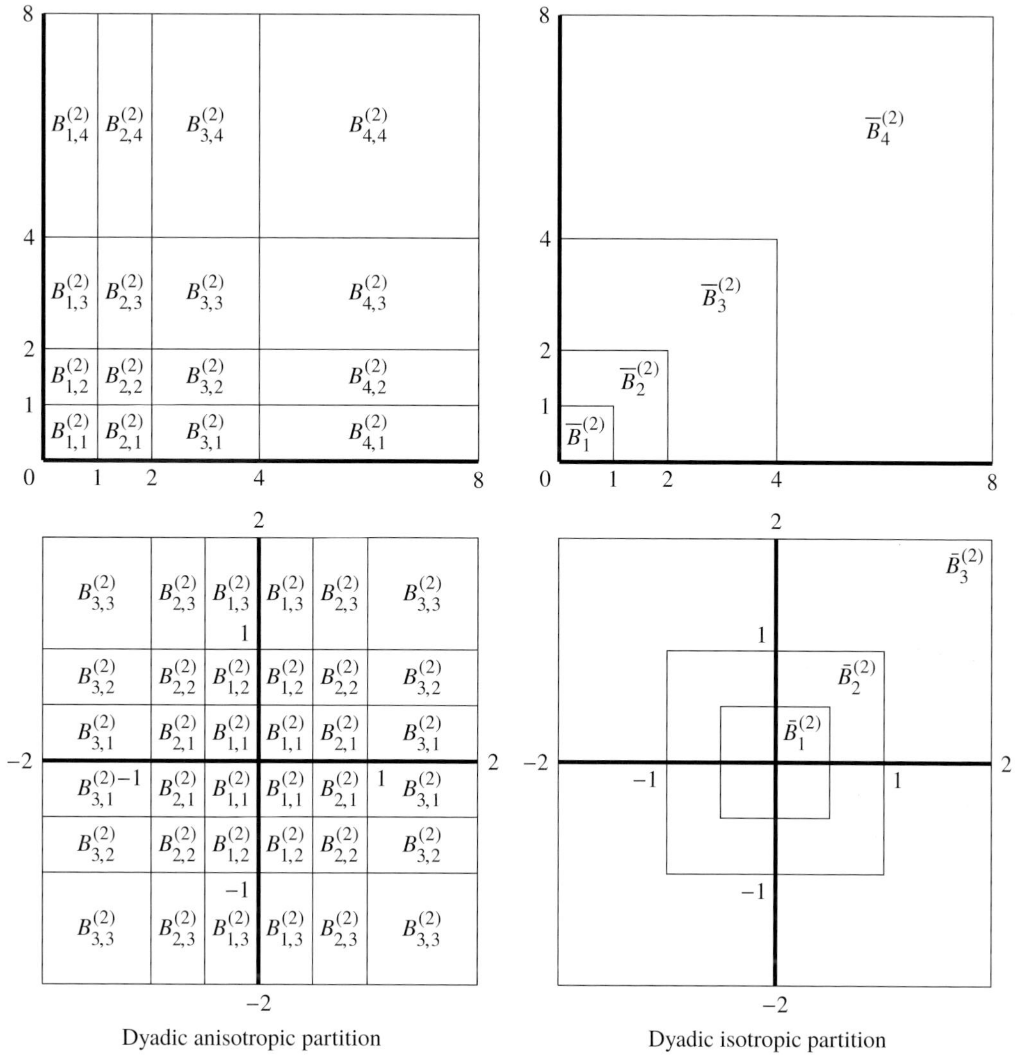

Figure 15.2 The sets that define the dyadic partitions of $\mathbb{N}_0^2$ (top row) and $\mathbb{Z}^2$ (bottom row) with index $j_0 = 0$.

partition divides the plane into (unions of four) rectangles with side lengths 2^{k_1} and 2^{k_2}.

Observe also that, for the dyadic partition of $\mathbb{Z}$, we have

$$B_1 \cup \cdots \cup B_r = \{-N/2 + 1, \ldots, N/2\}, \qquad N = 2^{j_0+r-1},$$

and, for the dyadic partition of $\mathbb{N}_0$, we have

$$B_1 \cup \cdots \cup B_r = \{0, \ldots, N-1\}, \qquad N = 2^{j_0+r-1}.$$

Hence the first r such sets in the partition correspond to the lowest N Fourier or Walsh frequencies. Similarly, for the dyadic isotropic partition

$$\overline{B}_1^{(2)} \cup \cdots \cup \overline{B}_r^{(2)} = \{-N/2+1, \ldots, N/2\}^2, \qquad N = 2^{j_0+r-1},$$

in the Fourier case, and likewise in the Walsh case. Whereas, for the dyadic anisotropic partition, we have

$$\bigcup_{k_1,k_2=1}^{r} B_{k_1,k_2}^{(2)} = \{-N/2+1, \ldots, N/2\}^2, \qquad N = 2^{j_0+r-1}.$$

Therefore, in the anisotropic case, we cover the lowest N frequencies using r^2 sets, as opposed to r in the other cases. This difference will be of consequence later.

15.2.2 Sampling Schemes

We are now ready to define the various multilevel sampling schemes. We commence with the one-dimensional case.

Definition 15.6 (DS scheme) Let $\mathcal{B} = \{B_k\}$ be the dyadic partition of $\mathbb{N}_0$ or $\mathbb{Z}$ and $\mathbf{m} = (m_1, \ldots, m_r)$ be such that $|m_k| \leq |B_k|$ for $k = 1, \ldots, r$. The *Dyadic Sampling (DS) scheme of order* $\mathbf{m}$ is the $(\mathbf{m}, \{B_k\}_{k=1}^r)$-multilevel random sampling scheme in the sense of Definition 4.6.

Next, we consider the two-dimensional case.

Definition 15.7 (DIS scheme) Let $\overline{\mathcal{B}}^{(2)} = \{\overline{B}_k^{(2)}\}$ be the dyadic isotropic partition of $\mathbb{N}_0^2$ or $\mathbb{Z}^2$ and $\mathbf{m} = (m_1, \ldots, m_r)$ be such that $|m_k| \leq |\overline{B}_k^{(2)}|$ for $k = 1, \ldots, r$. The *Dyadic Isotropic Sampling (DIS) scheme of order* $\mathbf{m}$ is the $(\mathbf{m}, \{\overline{B}_k^{(2)}\}_{k=1}^r)$-multilevel random sampling scheme in the sense of Definition 4.6.

An example of this sampling strategy is shown in Fig. 15.1(a).

Definition 15.8 (DAS scheme) Let $\mathcal{B}^{(2)} = \{B_{k_1,k_2}^{(2)}\}$ be the dyadic anisotropic partition of $\mathbb{N}_0^2$ or $\mathbb{Z}^2$ and $\mathbf{m} = (m_{k_1,k_2})_{k_1,k_2=1}^r$ be such that $|m_k| \leq |B_{k_1,k_2}^{(2)}|$ for $k_1, k_2 = 1, \ldots, r$. The *Dyadic Anisotropic Sampling (DAS) scheme of order* $\mathbf{m}$ is the $(\mathbf{m}, \{B_{k_1,k_2}^{(2)}\}_{k_1,k_2=1}^r)$-multilevel random sampling scheme in the sense of Definition 4.6.

Figure 15.1(b) gives an illustration of this scheme. Observe that is it anisotropic, unlike the isotropic scheme shown in Fig. 15.1(a). This property arises because the DAS scheme allows for different amounts of sampling in each dyadic rectangle $B_{k_1,k_2}^{(2)}$.

15.3 Summary of the Measurement Conditions

With the sampling schemes in place, we now move on to the measurement conditions. These are conditions on the m_k (or m_{k_1,k_2} in the case of the DAS scheme) that suffice for accurate and stable compressed sensing recovery. The formal recovery guarantees can be found in the corresponding theorems, which are stated and proved in Chapter 16. Throughout this section, L denotes a certain log factor, which we shall not specify here. We also recall Remark 15.1.

15.3.1 Sparsifying Transforms

We consider the periodized Daubechies wavelet basis of $L^2([0,1])$ or $L^2([0,1]^2)$ (Definition 9.23). We write $p \geq 1$ for the wavelet order and $q \geq 0$ for its smoothness (see §9.6.2). The coarsest scale j_0 is chosen as in (9.49) throughout. We also write s_k for the local sparsity in the kth wavelet scale. Note that this setup can be viewed within the abstract framework of Part III (this is important for the proofs in the next chapter). Suppose the wavelet basis is indexed over $\mathbb{N}$ in the way described in §9.9. Then s_k is precisely the local sparsity in the level $\{M_{k-1}+1, \ldots, M_k\}$, where M_k is given by (9.47) in the one-dimensional case or (9.48) in the two-dimensional case.

15.3.2 One Dimension

We commence with Fourier sampling in one dimension according to the DS scheme. The measurement condition is as follows:

1D Fourier sampling (Theorem 16.3)

$$m_k \gtrsim \left(s_k + \sum_{l=1}^{k-1} s_l 2^{-(2q+1)(k-l)} + \sum_{l=k+1}^{r} s_l 2^{-(2p+1)(l-k)} \right) \cdot L, \qquad k = 1, \ldots, r.$$

This extends the results given in Chapters 12 and 13 for the discrete Haar wavelet (recall from Chapter 9 that $p = 1$ and $q = 0$ for the Haar wavelet). In much the same manner, the number of measurements in the kth level is dominated by the corresponding sparsity s_k. On the other hand, as the wavelet order increases (which also implies a larger q, see §9.6) there is faster exponential decrease with respect to $|k-l|$. Hence the measurement condition becomes progressively closer to the optimal condition $m_k \gtrsim s_k \cdot L$. This occurs precisely for the reasons discussed in §11.1.3 – namely, the frequency concentration of Daubechies wavelets, which gets better as the order p increases. The arguments given therein are the essence of the proof.

At this point, we remind the reader that in this and all subsequent results below, the measurement condition is only meaningful when the right-hand side of the expression (including the constant implicit in the $\gtrsim$ symbol) is less than the size of the level $N_k - N_{k-1}$. If not, then $m_k = N_k - N_{k-1}$. See Remark 11.20.

1D Walsh sampling (Theorem 16.7) For $p \geq 3$,

$$m_k \gtrsim \left(s_k + \sum_{l=1}^{k-1} s_l 2^{-(k-l)} + \sum_{l=k+1}^{r} s_l 2^{-(l-k)} \right) \cdot L, \qquad k = 1, \ldots, r.$$

Unlike in Fourier sampling, the rate of exponential decrease in $|k-l|$ does not change with p in the case of Walsh sampling. This will have an important consequence when we consider the two-dimensional case later. This result also assumes the wavelet has $p \geq 3$ vanishing moments. When $p = 2$ the factor $2^{-(k-l)}$ in the first sum is replaced by the more slowly decaying term $2^{-(2\alpha-1)(k-l)}$, where $\alpha \approx 0.5500$ (see Theorem 16.7).

On the other hand, the case of Haar wavelets (i.e. $p = 1$) is rather different. The reason is that Haar wavelets can be expressed as finite linear combinations of Walsh functions and vice versa (Lemma F.6). This leads to the following simple condition:

1D Walsh sampling with Haar wavelets (Theorem 16.6)

$$m_k \gtrsim s_k \cdot L, \quad k = 1, \ldots, r.$$

Since m_k only depends on s_k, this condition is optimal up to the log term.

15.3.3 Two Dimensions

We commence with the DIS scheme.

Two-dimensional DIS Fourier sampling (Theorem 16.4)

$$m_k \gtrsim \left(s_k + \sum_{l=1}^{k-1} s_l 2^{-2q(k-l)} + \sum_{l=k+1}^{r} s_l 2^{-2(p+1)(l-k)} \right) \cdot L.$$

As in one dimension, this result shows that the number of measurements in the kth level is dominated by the local sparsity s_k with exponentially decaying dependence on the other local sparsities s_l, $l \neq k$. However, the exponents, which were previously $2q + 1$ and $2p+1$, are now $2q$ and $2p+2$, respectively. This causes a problem. The Haar wavelet has smoothness $q = 0$, and hence in this case the above condition becomes

$$m_k \gtrsim \left(s_1 + \cdots + s_k + \sum_{l=k+1}^{r} s_l 2^{-4(l-k)} \right) \cdot L. \tag{15.4}$$

In particular, in the rth level the number of samples $m_r \gtrsim s \cdot L$ scales like the total sparsity $s = s_1 + \cdots + s_r$. This is disappointing. The whole reason for introducing local sampling schemes was to enable us to exploit the local sparsity structure of the wavelet coefficients, as opposed to just their total sparsity.

This effect occurs because the levels in the DIS scheme, which correspond to the annular regions $\overline{B}_k^{(2)}$ (see Fig. 15.2), are too large to capture the local variations in the Haar wavelet in frequency space. The low smoothness of this wavelet means that its Fourier transform decays slowly for large $|\omega|$. Hence, coarse-scale Haar wavelets have relatively large Fourier transforms in the higher-frequency annular regions.

Fortunately, this issue can be overcome by transitioning to the DAS scheme. In order to state our recovery guarantee for this scheme, we first define the following quantity.

For $r \geq 2$, $\mathbf{s} = (s_1, \ldots, s_r)$ and $k_1, k_2 = 1, \ldots, r$, we let

$$\begin{aligned}\mathcal{M}(\mathbf{s}, k_1, k_2) &= \sum_{l=1}^{k_1} s_l 2^{-(2q+1)(k_1-l)-(2q+1)(k_2-l)} + \sum_{l=k_1+1}^{k_2} s_l 2^{-(l-k_1)-(2q+1)(k_2-l)} \\ &\quad + \sum_{l=k_2+1}^{r} s_l 2^{-(l-k_1)-(2p+1)(l-k_2)} \qquad 1 \leq k_1 \leq k_2 \leq r, \\ \mathcal{M}(\mathbf{s}, k_1, k_2) &= \sum_{l=1}^{k_2} s_l 2^{-(2q+1)(k_1-l)-(2q+1)(k_2-l)} + \sum_{l=k_2+1}^{k_1} s_l 2^{-(2q+1)(k_1-l)-(l-k_2)} \\ &\quad + \sum_{l=k_1+1}^{r} s_l 2^{-(2p+1)(l-k_1)-(l-k_2)}, \qquad 1 \leq k_2 \leq k_1 \leq r,\end{aligned}$$

with the convention that the second sum is zero when $k_1 = k_2$ and the third sum is zero when either $k_2 = r$ (first case) or $k_1 = r$ (second case). We now have the following:

> **2D DAS Fourier sampling (Theorem 16.5)**
>
> $$m_{k_1,k_2} \gtrsim \mathcal{M}(\mathbf{s}, k_1, k_2) \cdot L, \quad k_1, k_2 = 1, \ldots, r. \tag{15.5}$$

On its own, this condition is rather devoid of meaning. To gain some insight into what (15.5) actually implies about sampling, we now let

$$\overline{m}_k = \sum_{\substack{k_1,k_2=1 \\ \max\{k_1,k_2\}=k}}^{r} m_{k_1,k_2}, \qquad k = 1, \ldots, r \tag{15.6}$$

be the total number of measurements taken by the DAS scheme within the isotropic region $\overline{B}_k^{(2)}$ (recall Fig. 15.2). Then we have the following:

> **2D DAS Fourier sampling** If $m_{k_1,k_2} \lesssim \mathcal{M}(\mathbf{s}, k_1, k_2) \cdot L$ for $k_1, k_2 = 1, \ldots, r$, then
>
> $$\overline{m}_k \lesssim \left(s_k + \sum_{l=1}^{k-1} s_l 2^{-(2q+1)(k-l)} + \sum_{l=k+1}^{r} s_l 2^{-(2p+2)(l-k)} \right) \cdot L, \quad k = 1, \ldots, r.$$

See Proposition 15.9 below. Note that we have switched from $\gtrsim$ to $\lesssim$ here for obvious reasons. This result means that the number of samples $\overline{m}_k$ taken by the DAS scheme in each dyadic annular region obeys essentially the same estimate (in fact, it is slightly better for the terms $l > k$) as in the one-dimensional case. That is, it is dominated by the corresponding sparsity s_k, with exponentially decaying dependence on the s_l, $l \neq k$. This holds even for Haar wavelets, where $q = 0$. It therefore avoids the issue with the DIS scheme in that case. It is important to recall, however, that the sampling within $\overline{B}_k^{(2)}$ is *nonuniform*, unlike in the DIS scheme. Yet it is exactly by sampling in this manner that we overcome the previous issue.

We next consider Walsh sampling. Here, for any wavelet, sampling according to a DIS scheme would lead to a measurement condition depending on the total sparsity s, similar to in (15.4). This is unsurprising; after all, the one-dimensional measurement condition for Walsh sampling has factors of the form $2^{-|k-l|}$ regardless of the wavelet order. Fortunately, this issue is once more overcome by using the DAS scheme:

2D DAS Walsh sampling (Theorem 16.8) For $p \geq 3$,

$$m_{k_1,k_2} \gtrsim \left(\sum_{l=1}^{r} s_l 2^{-|k_1-l|-|k_2-l|} \right) \cdot L, \quad k_1, k_2 = 1, \ldots, r. \tag{15.7}$$

As in the Fourier case previously, sampling in this way ensures that the number of measurements taken in the whole isotropic region $\overline{B}_k^{(2)}$ satisfies a similar bound to the one-dimensional Walsh sampling case:

2D DAS Walsh sampling If $p \geq 3$ and $m_{k_1,k_2} \lesssim \left(\sum_{l=1}^{r} s_l 2^{-|k_1-l|-|k_2-l|} \right) \cdot L$ for $k_1, k_2 = 1, \ldots, r$, then

$$\overline{m}_k \lesssim \left(s_k + \sum_{l=1}^{k-1} s_l 2^{-(k-l)} + \sum_{l=k+1}^{r} s_l 2^{-2(l-k)} \right) \cdot L, \quad k = 1, \ldots, r.$$

This follows from Proposition 15.9 below after setting $p = q = 0$ in the definition of $\mathcal{M}(\mathbf{s}, k_1, k_2)$ (note that the right-hand side of (15.7) is precisely $\mathcal{M}(\mathbf{s}, k_1, k_2) \cdot L$ with $p = q = 0$).

Finally, we consider Haar wavelets with Walsh sampling. This is once more a special case. Unlike for higher-order wavelets, the DIS scheme can be employed in this setting and, as in one dimension, the recovery guarantee is optimal up to L:

2D DIS Walsh sampling with Haar wavelets (Theorem 16.6)

$$m_k \gtrsim s_k \cdot L, \quad k = 1, \ldots, r.$$

To conclude this section, we state and prove the following proposition, which was already used on several occasions:

Proposition 15.9 *Let $\overline{m}_k$ be as in (15.6). If $p, q \geq 0$, and*

$$m_{k_1,k_2} \lesssim \mathcal{M}(\mathbf{s}, k_1, k_2) \cdot L, \qquad k_1, k_2 = 1, \ldots, r,$$

then

$$\overline{m}_k \lesssim \left(s_k + \sum_{l=1}^{k-1} s_l 2^{-(2q+1)(k-l)} + \sum_{l=k+1}^{r} s_l 2^{-(2p+2)(l-k)} \right) \cdot L.$$

Proof It suffices to estimate the quantity

$$\sum_{k_1=1}^{k} \mathcal{M}(\mathbf{s}, k_1, k) + \sum_{k_2=1}^{k} \mathcal{M}(\mathbf{s}, k, k_2).$$

Consider the first sum. We have

$$\sum_{k_1=1}^{k} \mathcal{M}(\mathbf{s}, k_1, k) \leq \sum_{k_1=1}^{k} \sum_{l=1}^{k} s_l 2^{-|k_1-l|} 2^{-(2q+1)(k-l)} + \sum_{k_1=1}^{k} \sum_{l=k+1}^{r} s_l 2^{-(l-k_1)} 2^{-(2p+1)(l-k)}$$
$$\lesssim \sum_{l=1}^{k} s_l 2^{-(2q+1)(k-l)} + \sum_{l=k+1}^{r} s_l 2^{-(2p+2)(l-k)}.$$

It is readily checked that the same bound holds for the other sum $\sum_{k_2=1}^{k} \mathcal{M}(\mathbf{s}, k, k_2)$. The result now follows immediately. □

15.3.4 Sampling Anisotropy

As noted, the DAS scheme samples nonuniformly within the isotropic regions $\overline{B}_k^{(2)}$. For Fourier sampling, the level of nonuniformity depends on the wavelet order p. In Fig. 15.3 we illustrate this effect by plotting *sampling density*

$$\mathcal{M}^*(\mathbf{s}, k_1, k_2) = \frac{\mathcal{M}(\mathbf{s}, k_1, k_2)}{|B_{k_1,k_2}^{(2)}|}, \tag{15.8}$$

for typical values of the local sparsities $\mathbf{s}$. When $p = 1$, this density is significantly higher in those rectangles $B_{k_1,k_2}^{(2)}$ for which $k_1 \gg k_2$ or $k_2 \gg k_1$ than those with $k_1 \approx k_2$. This demonstrates the highly anisotropic nature of the scheme. Conversely, when $p = 4$ the densities are roughly equal across the region $\overline{B}_k^{(2)}$, indicating higher isotropy. This latter observation can be explained by noting that

$$\mathcal{M}(\mathbf{s}, k_1, k_2) \to s_{\max\{k_1,k_2\}} 2^{-|k_1-k_2|},$$

as $p \to \infty$ for fixed $\mathbf{s}$ (recall that $q \to \infty$ as $p \to \infty$). Hence

$$\mathcal{M}^*(\mathbf{s}, k_1, k_2) \asymp \frac{s_k}{|\overline{B}_k^{(2)}|}, \qquad k = \max\{k_1, k_2\}.$$

The right-hand side depends only on k and not k_1 and k_2 themselves, thus demonstrating isotropy in the large p limit. Hence, higher-order wavelets require less anisotropy, which results in increasingly similar DAS and DIS schemes. This effect is shown in Fig. 15.4, where several typical DAS and DIS schemes are compared.

We remark that this effect does not occur for Walsh sampling. Here, as shown in (15.7), the anisotropy of the sampling scheme persists even as the wavelet order increases.

15.3.5 Construction of DIS and DAS Schemes

In order to implement a DIS or DAS scheme in practice, one needs to specify the local sparsities $\mathbf{m}$. This can be done using the various measurement conditions. To conclude this section, we now explain this construction in the case of the DAS scheme (the DIS construction is analogous).

Let $m \geq 1$ be the total measurement budget. We first generate local sparsities $\mathbf{s}$ using a reference image. Specifically, given the wavelet order $p \geq 1$, we compute the wavelet coefficients of this image and then determine the number $s_k = s_k(\epsilon)$ of coefficients in

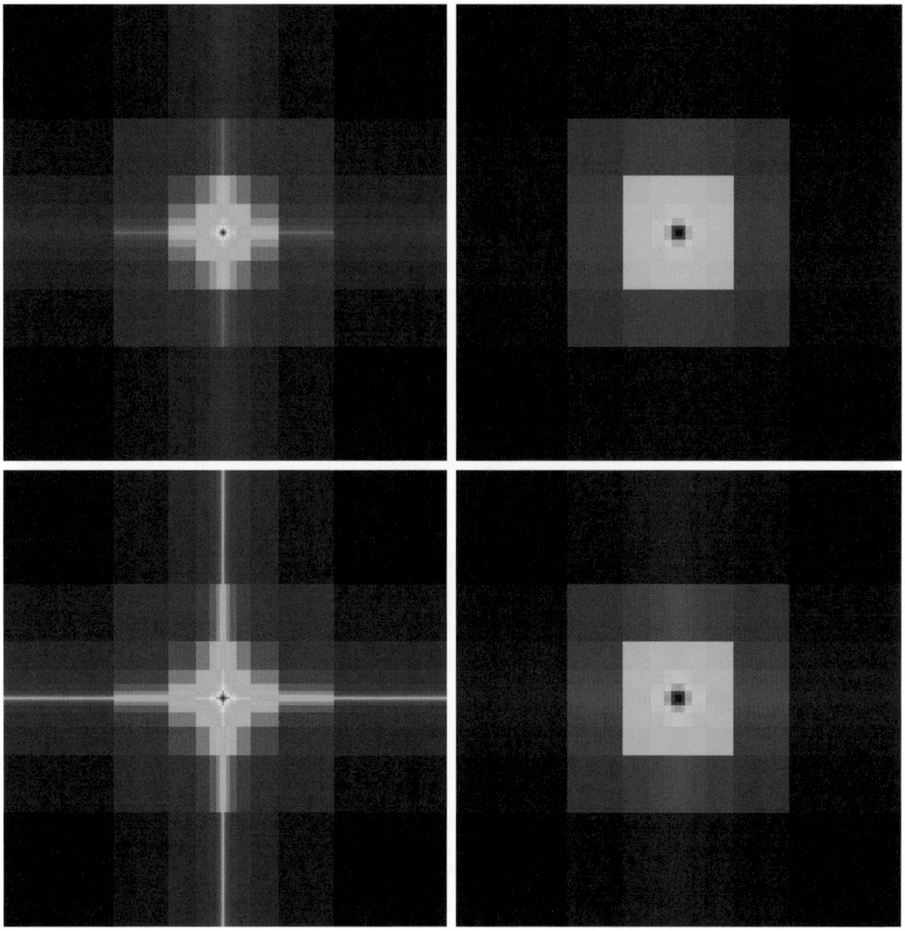

Figure 15.3 The sampling densities (15.8) for different wavelet orders p, normalized to $[0, 1]$ and shown within each of the regions $B^{(2)}_{k_1,k_2}$. The parameters used are $r = 10$ and $\mathbf{s} = (1, 1, \ldots, 1)$ (top) and $\mathbf{s} = (1, 1/2, \ldots, 1/2^{r-1})$ (bottom). Red corresponds to higher density and blue to lower density.

each scale that exceed a given threshold parameter ε. Now let $\mathcal{M}(\mathbf{s}, k_1, k_2)$ be as above. Then, ignoring the constants and log factor in the measurement condition, we now fit a constant $C > 0$ so that

$$m = \sum_{k_1,k_2=1}^{r} \min\left\{|B^{(2)}_{k_1,k_2}|, \lfloor C \cdot \mathcal{M}(\mathbf{s}, k_1, k_2)\rfloor\right\}.$$

Here $\{B^{(2)}_{k_1,k_2}\}$ is the dyadic anisotropic partition. Note that in the Walsh case, as discussed above, we use $\mathcal{M}(\mathbf{s}, k_1, k_2)$ with $p = q = 0$. Having found C, we then specify $\mathbf{m}$ by

$$m_{k_1,k_2} = \min\left\{|B^{(2)}_{k_1,k_2}|, \lfloor C \cdot \mathcal{M}(\mathbf{s}, k_1, k_2)\rfloor\right\}.$$

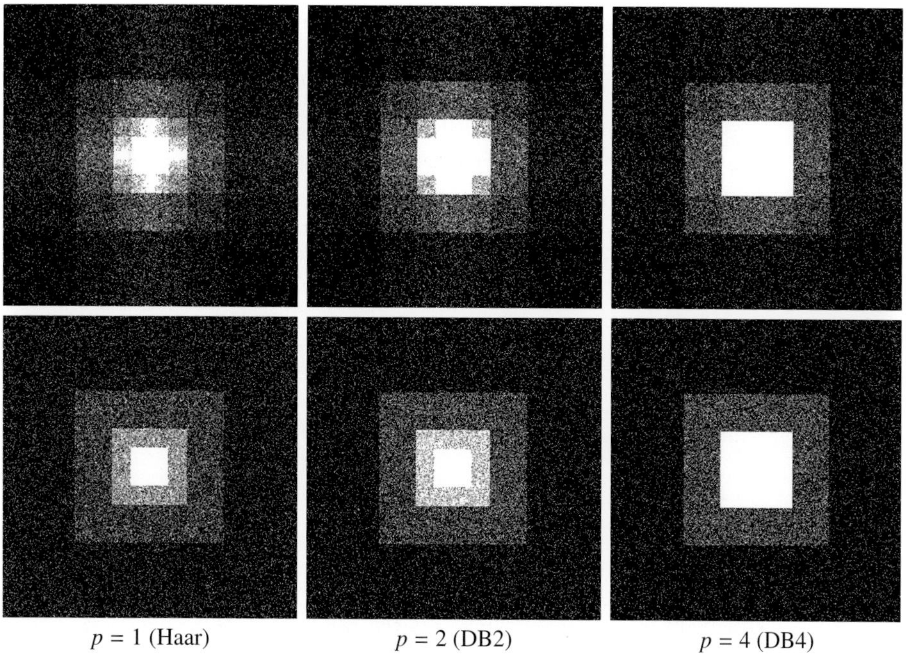

Figure 15.4 Typical Fourier DAS (top row) and DIS (bottom row) sampling patterns for 14% subsampling and different wavelet orders p (see §15.3.5).

Note that this approach requires a reference image and a threshold parameter. We have used the SL phantom with $\varepsilon = 1$ throughout this book. In particular, these were used to generate the schemes in Figs 15.1 and 15.4. Other images and parameters could also be used, particularly in the context of a specific application.

15.4 When and Why Do Certain Patterns Work Well?

Having developed the DS, DIS and DAS schemes, we conclude this chapter by showing how they can be adjusted in a minor way to help understand the performance of other classes of sampling schemes, for instance, the power-law schemes. The main idea is that the former schemes relate the local sparsities $\mathbf{s}$ to local numbers of measurements $\mathbf{m}$. Hence, any other sampling scheme can be examined by looking at how it samples locally within the sampling regions that define a DS, DIS or DAS scheme.

15.4.1 Variable Density Dyadic Sampling

Multilevel random sampling schemes sample randomly and uniformly within each partition element. It is now useful to generalize this approach slightly to allow variable-density sampling within each element.

Consider one-dimensional Fourier sampling with the dyadic partition $\{B_k\}$ of $\mathbb{Z}$. Let

$$p^{(k)} = \{p^{(k)}_\omega : \omega \in B_k\}, \quad k = 1, \ldots, r$$

be a discrete probability distribution on B_k with $p^{(k)}_\omega > 0$, $\forall \omega \in B_k$. The *Variable-Density Dyadic Sampling (VDDS)* scheme simply selects m_k frequencies within each B_k independently from $p^{(k)}$, rather than the uniform distribution as in the standard DS scheme (Definition 15.6). Let

$$P^{(k)} = |B_k| \min_{\omega \in B_k} \left\{ p^{(k)}_\omega \right\}. \tag{15.9}$$

Generalizing that of §15.3, a measurement condition for the VDDS scheme is

$$m_k \gtrsim \frac{1}{P^{(k)}} \left(s_k + \sum_{l=1}^{k-1} s_l 2^{-(2q+1)(k-l)} + \sum_{l=k+1}^{r} s_l 2^{-(2p+1)(l-k)} \right) \cdot L. \tag{15.10}$$

See Remark 16.24. In particular, and as expected, the measurement condition is the same (up to constants) as that for the DS scheme whenever $p^{(k)}$ is *quasi-uniform*, i.e. $P^{(k)} \asymp 1$.

The extension to two dimensions is straightforward. We let $p^{(k)}$ or $p^{(k_1,k_2)}$ be a discrete probability distribution on $\overline{B}^{(2)}_k$ or $B^{(2)}_{k_1,k_2}$ in the DIS or DAS case, respectively, giving the so-called *VDDIS* and *VDDAS* schemes. Define $P^{(k)}$ or $P^{(k_1,k_2)}$ in an analogous fashion to (15.9). Then, as in (15.10), to get the corresponding measurement condition, we simply divide the measurement condition given in §15.3 for the standard, uniform density DIS or DAS scheme by the appropriate factor $P^{(k)}$ or $P^{(k_1,k_2)}$.

15.4.2 Local Sparsities and Variable-Density Sampling

Consider the one-dimensional setting with a variable-density sampling scheme in the sense of Definition 4.4. Write $\pi = \{\pi_\omega\}$ for the corresponding probability distribution on $\{-N/2+1, \ldots, N/2\}$. We would like to analyse this scheme from the perspective of local sparsity. In order to do so, we first mimic it with a suitable VDDS scheme. This can be done by setting

$$p^{(k)}_\omega = \frac{\pi_\omega}{c^{(k)}}, \quad \omega \in B_k,$$

where the constant

$$c^{(k)} = \sum_{\omega \in B_k} \pi_\omega$$

ensures that $p^{(k)}$ is a probability distribution. Due to (15.10), the measurement condition for this VDDS scheme is

$$m_k \gtrsim \frac{c^{(k)}}{\Pi^{(k)}} \left(s_k + \sum_{l=1}^{k-1} s_l 2^{-(2q+1)(k-l)} + \sum_{l=k+1}^{r} s_l 2^{-(2p+1)(l-k)} \right) \cdot L, \tag{15.11}$$

for $k = 1, \ldots, r$, where for each k,

$$\Pi^{(k)} = |B_k| \min_{\omega \in B_k} \{\pi_\omega\}. \tag{15.12}$$

Now let us return to the original variable-density scheme defined by the probability distribution π. Let $\Omega = \{\omega_1, \dots, \omega_m\}$ be the m frequencies drawn independently according to π and

$$m_k^\pi = \mathbb{E}| \{i : \omega_i \in B_k\} | = mc^{(k)} \tag{15.13}$$

be the expected number of those ω_i that lie within the kth partition B_k. Putting full rigour aside, we notice that, in order to ensure recovery, the number m_k^π should be roughly m_k, where m_k is the number of samples taken by the equivalent VDDS scheme in the region B_k. Since $m_k^\pi = mc^{(k)}$, replacing m_k by m_k^π in (15.11) yields

$$m \gtrsim \frac{1}{\Pi^{(k)}} \left(s_k + \sum_{l=1}^{k-1} s_l 2^{-(2q+1)(k-l)} + \sum_{l=k+1}^{r} s_l 2^{-(2p+1)(l-k)} \right) \cdot L, \quad k = 1, \dots, r.$$

This condition is interpreted as follows. Given a fixed measurement budget m, it dictates how large the local sparsities $\mathbf{s} = (s_1, \dots, s_r)$ can be in order to ensure recovery via the VDS scheme π. To see this, and to gain further insight, let $\mathbf{s}^* = (s_1^*, \dots, s_r^*)$ be the *unit local sparsities*

$$s_k^* = s_k / s, \quad k = 1, \dots, r,$$

where $s = s_1 + \cdots + s_r$ is the total sparsity. Now suppose we want the total number of measurements m to be equal to $c \cdot s \cdot L$, where c is the constant implied in the $\gtrsim$ symbol above. Then the unit local sparsities should satisfy the following conditions:

$$s_k^* + \sum_{l=1}^{k-1} s_l^* 2^{-(2q+1)(k-l)} + \sum_{l=k+1}^{r} s_l^* 2^{-(2p+1)(l-k)} \leq \Pi^{(k)}, \quad k = 1, \dots, r. \tag{15.14}$$

Now, finally, we have what we wanted. For the variable-density scheme π, we have conditions on the local sparsities $\mathbf{s}^*$ given solely in terms of the $\Pi^{(k)}$ – quantities which are completely intrinsic to the scheme – that ensure recovery from $m \approx s \cdot L$ samples.

Remark 15.10 As noted, we forfeited some rigour in deriving (15.14). Specifically, we replaced the original variable-density sampling scheme π with the multilevel VDDS scheme and then replaced m_k in (15.11) by the expected value m_k^π from (15.13). We shall not address the matter of making such arguments rigorous.

15.4.3 Power Laws and Local Sparsities

Let us now illustrate how this condition sheds light on the power-law schemes (15.2). Here, we also recall Remark 15.1 once more.

Proposition 15.11 *Let $\pi = \{\pi_\omega\}$ be as in (15.2). If $\alpha = 1$ then condition (15.14) holds if and only if*

$$s_k^* \lesssim 1/r, \quad k = 1, \dots, r.$$

If $-2p < \alpha < 1$ then (15.14) holds if and only if

$$s_k^* \lesssim 2^{(1-\alpha)(k-r)}, \quad k = 1, \dots, r.$$

Finally, if $1 < \alpha < 2(q+1)$ *then (15.14) holds if and only if*

$$s_k^* \lesssim 2^{-(\alpha-1)k}, \quad k = 1, \ldots, r.$$

This result says the following. We may sample according to *any* power-law scheme and expect recovery using a total of $m \approx s \cdot L$ samples, provided the unit local sparsities s_k^* grow exponentially (in the case $\alpha < 1$) or decay exponentially (in the case $\alpha > 1$) in the correct way.

It may be surprising to observe that recovery is still possible even when $\alpha = 0$, which corresponds to uniform random sampling, or $\alpha < 0$ which corresponds to a bizarre strategy that samples higher frequencies more densely than lower ones. We noted in §11.1.1 that the Fourier-wavelets problem is globally coherent, which seemingly prohibits recovery. However, recovery is in fact possible, provided most of the wavelet coefficients are at fine scales, since fine scales are incoherent with Fourier measurements. Of course, wavelet coefficients of natural images (piecewise smooth functions) do not behave in this way, which is why such a scheme generally performs poorly in practice.

Proof of Proposition 15.11 Recall that N is roughly 2^r and the band B_k contains frequencies of magnitude roughly 2^k. Hence, using (12.37), we deduce that

$$\Pi^{(k)} \asymp \begin{cases} 2^{(1-\alpha)k} & \alpha > 1 \\ r^{-1} & \alpha = 1 \\ 2^{(1-\alpha)(k-r)} & \alpha < 1 \end{cases}.$$

Since the left-hand side of (15.14) is at least s_k^*, the 'only if' part of the proposition now follows immediately. Moreover, for $\alpha = 1$ the 'if' part is also immediate since

$$\sum_{l=1}^{k} 2^{-(2q+1)(k-l)} + \sum_{l=k+1}^{r} 2^{-(2p+1)(l-k)} \lesssim 1.$$

Suppose next that $-2p < \alpha < 1$ and let $t_k^* = 2^{(1-\alpha)(k-r)}$. Since these values are increasing, we have

$$\sum_{l=1}^{k} t_l^* 2^{-(2q+1)(k-l)} + \sum_{l=k+1}^{r} t_l^* 2^{-(2p+1)(l-k)} \lesssim t_k^* \left(1 + \sum_{l=k+1}^{r} 2^{-(\alpha+2p)(l-k)} \right) \lesssim t_k^*,$$

which gives the second result. Finally, let $1 < \alpha < 2(q+1)$ and $t_k^* = 2^{-(\alpha-1)k}$. Since these values are decreasing, we have

$$\sum_{l=1}^{k} t_l^* 2^{-(2q+1)(k-l)} + \sum_{l=k+1}^{r} t_l^* 2^{-(2p+1)(l-k)} \lesssim t_k^* \left(\sum_{l=1}^{k} 2^{-(2q+2-\alpha)(k-l)} + 1 \right) \lesssim t_k^*.$$

Hence we obtain the result in this case as well. □

15.4.4 The Two-Dimensional Case

In two dimensions, we proceed in a similar manner. Let $\pi = \{\pi_\omega\}$ be a probability distribution on $\{-N/2+1, \ldots, N/2\}^2$. Consider the isotropic setting (which of course makes sense for power-law schemes) and let

$$\overline{\Pi}^{(k)} = |\overline{B}_k^{(2)}| \min \left\{ \pi_\omega : \omega \in \overline{B}_k^{(2)} \right\}. \tag{15.15}$$

Then, after identical arguments we arrive at the following condition. If we want the total number of measurements m to be of order $s \cdot L$ for the variable-density scheme π, then the unit local sparsities should satisfy

$$s_k^* + \sum_{l=1}^{k-1} s_l^* 2^{-2q(k-l)} + \sum_{l=k+1}^{r} s_l^* 2^{-2(p+1)(l-k)} \lesssim \overline{\Pi}^{(k)}, \quad k = 1, \ldots, r. \tag{15.16}$$

Now consider the two-dimensional power-law schemes (15.3). For this, we have the following:

Proposition 15.12 *Suppose that $q > 0$ and let $\pi = \{\pi_\omega\}$ be as in (15.3). If $\alpha = 1$ then condition (15.16) holds if and only if*

$$s_k^* \lesssim 1/r, \quad k = 1, \ldots, r. \tag{15.17}$$

If $-p < \alpha < 1$ then (15.16) holds if and only if

$$s_k^* \lesssim 2^{2(1-\alpha)(k-r)}, \quad k = 1, \ldots, r.$$

Finally, if $1 < \alpha < q + 1$ then (15.16) holds if and only if

$$s_k^* \lesssim 2^{-2(\alpha-1)k}, \quad k = 1, \ldots, r.$$

Proof The proof is similar to that of Proposition 15.11. First, note that

$$\overline{\Pi}^{(k)} \asymp \begin{cases} 2^{2(1-\alpha)k} & \alpha > 1 \\ r^{-1} & \alpha = 1 \\ 2^{2(1-\alpha)(k-r)} & \alpha < 1 \end{cases}.$$

We now argue in the same manner. □

We therefore arrive at the same conclusion as before. Increasing local sparsities (i.e. images with more fine details) benefit from slower-decaying power-law sampling, and decreasing local sparsities (i.e. images with fewer fine details) benefit from faster-decaying power-law sampling. This agrees with the results shown in Table 15.1. Such insight significantly narrows the theoretical gap that was first identified in §11.2.1.

Notes

The DS, DIS and DAS sampling strategies are new, although earlier results for the one-dimensional Fourier case based on essentially the same approach were first developed in [20]. The main difference is the use of periodic wavelets here, whereas [20] used a wavelet basis on a larger interval to approximate functions in [0, 1]. The DS scheme for the one-dimensional Walsh case was developed in [3] for both periodic and boundary-corrected wavelets. The Walsh–Haar problem in one and two dimensions was investigated in detail in [362]. See also [361].

We have limited our discussion to the one- and two-dimensional cases. The extension to $d \geq 3$ dimensions is conceptually straightforward. It is interesting to note that in d dimensions, the measurement condition for the d-dimensional DIS scheme is

$$m_k \gtrsim \left(s_k + \sum_{l=1}^{k-1} s_l 2^{-(2q+2-d)(k-l)} + \sum_{l=k+1}^{r} s_l 2^{-(2p+d)(l-k)} \right) \cdot L.$$

Hence, the issue with low-order wavelets becomes even more acute in higher dimensions. However, this is fully resolved by moving to the d-dimensional DAS scheme, in which case the corresponding condition on the $\overline{m}_k$ becomes

$$\overline{m}_k \lesssim \left(s_k + \sum_{l=1}^{k-1} s_l 2^{-(2q+1)(k-l)} + \sum_{l=k+1}^{r} s_l 2^{-(2p+d)(l-k)} \right) \cdot L.$$

In particular, the exponent in the first term is $2q+1$ in any dimension, while the exponent in the second term actually improves with dimension (this was already seen previously in the $d = 2$ case).

In Remark 15.3 we noted that the power-law schemes with $\alpha = 1$ are sufficient for recovery of s-sparse vectors of wavelet coefficients in one or two dimensions, for any Daubechies wavelet. This can be shown by working in the infinite-dimensional setting and estimating the coherence of the corresponding isotropic family. The technical steps to do so are similar to those given in Chapter 16.

This chapter focuses on orthonormal Daubechies wavelets. There are several results for redundant sparsifying transforms. Closely mirroring the results of Chapter 12, but also working in the infinite-dimensional setting of Chapter 14, nonuniform recovery guarantees for tight frames in terms of the local numbers of measurements m_k and local sparsities s_k were shown in [394]. Uniform guarantees relating the total sparsity s to the total number of measurements m were shown in the finite-dimensional, tight-frame setting in [300]. In particular, the inverse linear law was shown to be sufficient for recovery from discrete, one-dimensional Fourier samples with the discrete Haar wavelet frame. This extends Theorem 13.19 to the nonorthogonal setting. Extensions to the nontight and infinite-dimensional case (along the lines of Chapter 14) have been shown in [31], along with applications to electrical impedance tomography. For the special case of shearlets (see §9.11), a Fourier sampling strategy and uniform recovery guarantee (based on sparsity, not sparsity in levels) has been shown in [310].

16 Recovery Guarantees for Wavelet-Based Compressive Imaging

Having introduced the various sampling schemes in the previous chapter and summarized the corresponding measurement conditions, we now present the formal recovery guarantees and their proofs. We first specify the decoders and precise recovery guarantees in §16.1. Next, in §16.2, we interpret these guarantees in terms of wavelet approximation theory – considered previously in Chapter 10 – by providing error bounds for piecewise smooth function approximation via compressed sensing. We then state our main results in §16.3, before presenting their proofs in §16.4. The proofs of the recovery guarantees are based on the main results from Chapter 14, Theorems 14.5 and 14.7, specialized to the case of Fourier or Walsh sampling with wavelets. Consequently, they involve two main technical steps: establishing the balancing property and estimating the local coherences. These tasks form the core of this chapter.

16.1 Decoders and Recovery Guarantees

Our main results in this chapter assert accurate and stable recovery for the weighted QCBP and SR-LASSO decoders. In order to save unnecessary repetitions, we now specify the types of guarantees we prove.

16.1.1 Formulation as a Compressed Sensing Problem

We follow the setup of Chapter 14 and consider the Hilbert space $L^2([0,1])$ or $L^2([0,1]^2)$. Write $\Phi = \{\phi_i\}_{i\in\mathbb{N}}$ for the sparsity basis and $\Upsilon = \{\upsilon_i\}_{i\in\mathbb{N}}$ for either the Fourier or Walsh sampling basis. We let

$$U = \left(\langle \phi_j, \upsilon_i \rangle\right)_{i,j\in\mathbb{N}} \tag{16.1}$$

denote the infinite change-of-basis matrix between Φ and Υ. As described in §15.3.1, Φ is the periodized Daubechies wavelet basis of order $p \geq 1$ with smoothness $q \geq 0$ and coarsest scale j_0 as in (9.49). Given some fixed $r \geq 2$, we write $\mathbf{M} = (M_1, \ldots, M_r)$ for the corresponding sparsity levels, where M_k is given by (9.47) (one dimension) or (9.48) (two dimensions), and $\mathbf{s} = (s_1, \ldots, s_r)$ for the local sparsities.

We consider the DS, DIS and DAS sampling schemes introduced in Chapter 15. As we show later, each of these is equivalent to a certain $(\mathbf{m}, \mathbf{N})$-multilevel random sampling scheme (in the sense of Definition 11.13) applied to the matrix (16.1). Write Ω for this scheme and D for the corresponding diagonal scaling matrix defined in (14.11). Then the measurements take the form

$$y = P_\Omega DUd + e \in \mathbb{C}^m, \tag{16.2}$$

where $e \in \mathbb{C}^m$ is noise and $d \in \ell^2(\mathbb{N})$ is the infinite vector of wavelet coefficients of the unknown continuous image $f \in L^2([0,1])$ or $f \in L^2([0,1]^2)$. We also write $A = P_\Omega DUP_M \in \mathbb{C}^{m \times M}$ as before, where $M = M_r$. Define weights $\{w_i\}_{i=1}^{\infty}$ as in (14.13)–(14.14) for $i = 1, \ldots, M$ and (for concreteness) $w_i = 1$ for $i > M$. For convenience, we also write s for the total sparsity and m for the total number of measurements.

16.1.2 Recovery Guarantees

With this in hand, the (uniform) recovery guarantees we prove in this chapter take the following form:

(A) Let $d \in \ell^2(\mathbb{N})$, $y = P_\Omega DUd + e \in \mathbb{C}^m$ and suppose that $\|e\|_{\ell^2} \leq \eta/2$ and $\|P_M^\perp d\|_{\ell^1} \leq c_p \eta$ for a certain constant $c_p > 0$. Then every minimizer $\hat{d}$ of the weighted QCBP decoder

$$\min_{z \in \mathbb{C}^M} \|z\|_{\ell^1_w} \text{ subject to } \|Az - y\|_{\ell^2} \leq \eta \tag{16.3}$$

satisfies

$$\|\hat{d} - d\|_{\ell^2} \lesssim \frac{\sigma_{\mathbf{s},\mathbf{M}}(P_M d)_{\ell^1_w}}{r^{1/4}\sqrt{s}} + r^{1/4}\eta + \|P_M^\perp d\|_{\ell^2}. \tag{16.4}$$

(B) Let $d \in \ell^2(\mathbb{N})$, $y = P_\Omega DUd + e \in \mathbb{C}^m$ and suppose that $c/\sqrt{rs} \leq \lambda \leq c_p/\sqrt{rs}$ for a certain constant $c_p > 0$ and any $0 < c \leq c_p$. Then every minimizer $\hat{d}$ of the weighted SR-LASSO decoder

$$\min_{z \in \mathbb{C}^M} \lambda \|z\|_{\ell^1_w} + \|Az - y\|_{\ell^2}, \tag{16.5}$$

satisfies

$$\|\hat{d} - d\|_{\ell^2} \lesssim \frac{\sigma_{\mathbf{s},\mathbf{M}}(P_M d)_{\ell^1_w}}{r^{1/4}\sqrt{s}} + \frac{r^{1/4}}{c}\left(\|e\|_{\ell^2} + \|P_M^\perp d\|_{\ell^1}\right) + \|P_M^\perp d\|_{\ell^2}. \tag{16.6}$$

In our subsequent results, we give conditions on $\mathbf{m}$ and $\mathbf{s}$ for (A) and (B) to hold. Note that, as in Chapter 14, we consider the minimizer $\hat{d}$ as either an element of $\mathbb{C}^M$ or $\ell^2(\mathbb{N})$ (i.e. extended by zero). Also as before (see Remark 15.1), the constants implied by the symbols $\lesssim$, $\gtrsim$ and $\asymp$ may depend on p in this chapter.

16.2 What does this Mean? Near-Optimal Wavelet Approximation

Upon viewing (16.4) and (16.6), the reader may justifiably wonder exactly what they mean in terms of accuracy of the recovered function. To gain some insight, in this section we adopt the approach of Chapter 10 and consider how these error bounds behave for classes of piecewise smooth functions.

Proposition 16.1 *Suppose that* $f \in PC^{\alpha}([0,1])$, *where* $\alpha = k + \beta > 1/2$ *with* $k \in \mathbb{N}_0$ *and* $0 < \beta \leq 1$. *Consider the periodized Daubechies wavelet basis (Definition 9.23) of order* $p > k$ *with* j_0 *as in (9.49). Then there exist* $c_1, c_2 > 0$ *depending on* p *and* α *only such that the following holds. For every* $s \geq 2$ *satisfying* $s/\sqrt{\log(s)} \geq c_2(\mathcal{N}(f))^2$, *there is a choice of* $r \geq 1$ *and local sparsities* $\mathbf{s} = (s_1, \ldots, s_r)$ *with* $s_1 + \cdots + s_r \leq s$ *such that, with weights* w_i *as in (14.13)–(14.14),*

$$\frac{\sigma_{\mathbf{s},\mathbf{M}}(P_M d)_{\ell^1_w}}{r^{1/4}\sqrt{s}} + r^{1/4} \|P_M^{\perp} d\|_{\ell^1} + \|P_M^{\perp} d\|_{\ell^2} \leq c_1 \|f\|_{PC^{\alpha}} / s^{\alpha}.$$

Proposition 16.2 *Let* $f \in BV([0,1])$ *and consider the periodized Daubechies wavelet basis of order* $p \geq 1$ *with* j_0 *as in (9.49). Then there exists a* $c > 0$ *depending on* p *only such that the following holds. For every* $s \geq 1$ *there is a choice of* $r \geq 1$ *and local sparsities* $\mathbf{s} = (s_1, \ldots, s_r)$ *with* $s_1 + \cdots + s_r \leq s$ *such that, with weights* w_i *as in (14.13)–(14.14),*

$$\frac{\sigma_{\mathbf{s},\mathbf{M}}(P_M d)_{\ell^1_w}}{r^{1/4}\sqrt{s}} + r^{1/4} \|P_M^{\perp} d\|_{\ell^1} + \|P_M^{\perp} d\|_{\ell^2} \leq c V(f)/s.$$

Upon comparison with Theorems 10.5 and 10.7, respectively, we conclude the following. For the same function classes, there always exists a choice of sparsity levels $\mathbf{s}$ so that the compressed sensing errors (16.4) and (16.6) obey the same error bound in terms of the total sparsity s as the best s-term approximation. Using this, and measurement conditions stated later in Theorems 16.3 and 16.7, we deduce:

> Infinite-dimensional compressed sensing with Fourier or Walsh measurements is optimal (up to log factors) for approximating functions in the $BV([0,1])$ and $PC^{\alpha}([0,1])$ spaces. Specifically, there exists a sampling scheme (the DS scheme with suitable $\mathbf{m}$) for which m Fourier or Walsh samples lead to errors behaving like $m^{-\alpha}$ and m^{-1}, respectively as $m \to \infty$, up to log terms.

Note that working in the infinite-dimensional compressed sensing framework is crucial here, since it avoids the discretization errors that are incurred in the finite-dimensional setup through the use of discrete transforms (e.g. the wavelet crime – see §9.10.3).

Proof of Proposition 16.1 We use similar ideas to those employed in the proof of Theorem 10.5. Notice that the condition on s implies that

$$s \geq c_3(\mathcal{N}(f))^2 \geq c_3 \mathcal{N}(f) \geq c_3, \qquad s/\log(s) \geq c_4 \mathcal{N}(f), \tag{16.7}$$

where c_3, c_4 depend on p and α only. Let

$$r = \left\lceil \max\left\{(2\alpha+1), \frac{\alpha+3/2}{\alpha-1/2}\right\} \log_2(s) \right\rceil - j_0 \qquad \bar{r} = \lfloor \log_2(s/2) \rfloor - j_0,$$

and note that $r \geq (2\alpha+1)\log_2(s) - j_0 - 1 \geq 2\alpha \log_2(s) - j_0 \geq \bar{r} \geq 1$, since $\alpha > 1/2$ and $s \geq c_3$. Let $c \geq 1$ be chosen large enough so that the number of wavelets $\psi_{j,n}$ at a given scale crossing a discontinuity of f^{ext} is at most $c\mathcal{N}(f)$, and define

$$\tilde{r} = \bar{r} + \left\lfloor \frac{3}{2(\alpha - 1/2)} \log_2 \left(\frac{(2^{2(\alpha-1/2)/3} - 1)s}{8c\mathcal{N}(f)} \right) \right\rfloor .$$

Observe that $\bar{r} \le \tilde{r}$ and

$$\tilde{r} \le \log_2(s) + \frac{3}{2(\alpha - 1/2)} \log_2(s) + c_\alpha - j_0 - 1 \le \frac{\alpha + 3/2}{\alpha - 1/2} \log_2(s) - j_0 - 1 \le r.$$

Here c_α is a fixed constant depending on α. In the second step we used (16.7) to assert that $c_\alpha \le \frac{1/2}{\alpha - 1/2} \log_2(s)$ whenever $s \ge c_3$. Now let

$$s_k = \begin{cases} 2^{k+j_0-1} & k = 1, \ldots, \bar{r} \\ \left\lceil \frac{2^{2(\alpha-1/2)/3} - 1}{8} s 2^{-2(\alpha-1/2)(k-\bar{r})/3} \right\rceil & k = \bar{r}+1, \ldots, \tilde{r} \\ \lceil c\mathcal{N}(f) \rceil & k = \tilde{r}+1, \ldots, r \end{cases} .$$

Notice that s_k is equal to the size of the wavelet scale when $1 \le k \le \bar{r}$ and s_k is at least $c\mathcal{N}(f)$ otherwise (this is trivial for the case $\tilde{r} < k \le r$ and holds for $\bar{r} < k \le \tilde{r}$ because of the definition of $\tilde{r}$). In particular, s_k allows us to capture all the wavelet coefficients corresponding to wavelets crossing a discontinuity of f. We now show that this choice of s_k is valid, i.e. $s_k \le 2^{k+j_0-1}$ for all k and $s_1 + \cdots + s_r \le s$. Consider the first condition. Clearly this holds for $1 \le k \le \bar{r}$. If $\tilde{r} < k \le r$ then we have

$$2^{k+j_0-1} \ge 2^{\bar{r}+j_0} \ge s/4 \ge \lceil c\mathcal{N}(f) \rceil = s_k,$$

since $s \ge c_3 \mathcal{N}(f)$. Finally, if $\bar{r} < k \le \tilde{r}$ we have

$$s_k \le \left\lceil \frac{2^{2(\alpha-1/2)/3} - 1}{8} s 2^{-2(\alpha-1/2)/3} \right\rceil < \left\lceil \frac{s}{8} \right\rceil \le \frac{s}{4} \le 2^{\bar{r}+j_0} \le 2^{k+j_0-1},$$

since $s \ge c_3$. Hence the first condition holds. Now consider the second condition:

$$\begin{aligned} \sum_{k=1}^{r} s_k &\le 2^{\bar{r}+j_0} + \sum_{k=\bar{r}+1}^{\tilde{r}} \left(\frac{2^{2(\alpha-1/2)/3} - 1}{4} s 2^{-2(\alpha-1/2)(k-\bar{r})/3} + 1 \right) + r\lceil c\mathcal{N}(f) \rceil \\ &\le \frac{s}{2} + \frac{2^{2(\alpha-1/2)/3} - 1}{4} s \frac{1}{2^{2(\alpha-1/2)/3} - 1} + r(c\mathcal{N}(f) + 2) \\ &\le \frac{s}{2} + \frac{s}{4} + 3rc\mathcal{N}(f). \end{aligned}$$

Here we have used the fact that $c, \mathcal{N}(f) \ge 1$. Since $s/\log(s) \ge c_4 \mathcal{N}(f)$, we deduce that $s_1 + \cdots + s_r \le s$. We therefore conclude that this choice of local sparsities is valid.

With this in hand, we now use Lemma 10.10 and the choice of weights to get

$$
\begin{aligned}
\frac{\sigma_{\mathbf{s},\mathbf{M}}(P_M d)_{\ell^1_w}}{r^{1/4}\sqrt{s}} &\lesssim \|f\|_{PC^\alpha} \sum_{k=\bar{r}+1}^{r} \frac{1}{r^{1/4}\sqrt{s_k}} 2^{-(\alpha-1/2)k} \\
&\lesssim \|f\|_{PC^\alpha} \left(\frac{2^{-(\alpha-1/2)\bar{r}}}{\sqrt{s}} \sum_{k=\bar{r}+1}^{\bar{r}} 2^{-2(\alpha-1/2)(k-\bar{r})/3} + \frac{1}{\sqrt{\mathcal{N}(f)}} 2^{-(\alpha-1/2)\bar{r}} \right) \\
&\lesssim \|f\|_{PC^\alpha} \left(s^{-\alpha} + \frac{1}{\sqrt{\mathcal{N}(f)}} s^{-(\alpha-1/2)} \left(\frac{s}{c\mathcal{N}(f)} \right)^{-3/2} \right) \\
&\lesssim \|f\|_{PC^\alpha} s^{-\alpha} \left(1 + \mathcal{N}(f)/s\right) \lesssim \|f\|_{PC^\alpha} s^{-\alpha},
\end{aligned}
$$

since $s \geq c_3 \mathcal{N}(f)$. Here the constant implied by symbol $\lesssim$ depends on α as well as p. Also by Lemma 10.10,

$$
\begin{aligned}
r^{1/4}\|P_M^{\perp} d\|_{\ell^1} + \|P_M^{\perp} d\|_{\ell^2} &\leq (r^{1/4}+1)\|P_M^{\perp} d\|_{\ell^1} \\
&\lesssim (\log(s))^{1/4} \|f\|_{PC^\alpha} \sum_{k>r} \left(2^{-(\alpha-1/2)k} + \mathcal{N}(f) 2^{-k/2} \right) \\
&\lesssim (\log(s))^{1/4} \|f\|_{PC^\alpha} \mathcal{N}(f) s^{-\alpha-1/2} \\
&\lesssim \|f\|_{PC^\alpha} s^{-\alpha},
\end{aligned}
$$

where in the last step we use the fact that $s/\sqrt{\log(s)} \geq c_2(\mathcal{N}(f))^2$. Combining this with the previous estimate completes the proof. □

Proof of Proposition 16.2 We may assume that $s \geq c_1$ for some constant c_1 depending on p. Let

$$
\bar{r} = \lfloor \log_2(s/2) \rfloor - j_0, \quad r = \lfloor 2\log_2(s(\log_2(s))^{1/4}) \rfloor - j_0,
$$

and note that $1 \leq \bar{r} \leq r$ since $s \geq c_1$. We now set

$$
s_k = \begin{cases} 2^{k+j_0-1} & k = 1, \ldots, \bar{r} \\ \lceil 2^{(\bar{r}-k)/3}(2^{1/3}-1)s/8 \rceil & k = \bar{r}+1, \ldots, r \end{cases},
$$

and observe that

$$
\sum_{k=1}^{r} s_k \leq 2^{\bar{r}+j_0} + \sum_{k=\bar{r}+1}^{r} 2^{(\bar{r}-k)/3}(2^{1/3}-1)s/8 + r \leq s/2 + s/8 + r \leq s,
$$

since $r \leq 3s/8$ for $s \geq c_1$. Note also that $s_k \leq 2^{k+j_0-1}$ for all k. Hence this choice of local sparsities is valid. With this in hand, we now apply Lemma 10.11 to get

$$
\begin{aligned}
\frac{\sigma_{\mathbf{s},\mathbf{M}}(P_M d)_{\ell^1_w}}{r^{1/4}\sqrt{s}} &\lesssim V(f) \sum_{k=\bar{r}+1}^{r} \frac{1}{\sqrt{s_k}} 2^{-k/2} \lesssim \frac{V(f) 2^{-\bar{r}/6}}{\sqrt{s}} \sum_{k=\bar{r}+1}^{r} 2^{-k/3} \\
&\lesssim \frac{V(f) 2^{-\bar{r}/2}}{\sqrt{s}} \lesssim \frac{V(f)}{s},
\end{aligned}
$$

and

$$\begin{aligned} r^{1/4}\|P_M^{\perp} d\|_{\ell^1} + \|P_M^{\perp} d\|_{\ell^2} &\leq (r^{1/4}+1)\|P_M^{\perp} d\|_{\ell^1} \\ &\lesssim (\log(s))^{1/4} V(f) \sum_{k>r} 2^{-k/2} \\ &\lesssim (\log(s))^{1/4} V(f) (s(\log(s))^{1/4})^{-1} \lesssim V(f)/s. \end{aligned}$$

This gives the result. □

Note that, while these results give the same error rates as those shown in Theorems 10.5 and 10.7 for the best s-term approximation, the choice of the parameters s_k and r is somewhat different. For instance in the BV setting, Theorem 10.7 requires a maximum wavelet scale $j \approx 2\log_2(s)$, whereas the proof of Proposition 16.2 uses the slightly larger maximal scale $j \approx 2\log_2(s(\log(s))^{1/4})$.

16.3 Main Recovery Guarantees

We now move on to the formal recovery guarantees for Fourier and Walsh sampling.

16.3.1 Fourier Sampling

We commence with the one-dimensional Fourier DS scheme (Definition 15.6):

Theorem 16.3 (Fourier sampling, DS scheme) *Let $0 < \varepsilon < 1$, $r \geq 2$ and consider the Fourier DS scheme of order $\mathbf{m} = (m_1, \ldots, m_r)$. Suppose that*

$$m_k \gtrsim \left(s_k + \sum_{l=1}^{k-1} s_l 2^{-(2q+1)(k-l)} + \sum_{l=k+1}^{r} s_l 2^{-(2p+1)(l-k)} \right) \cdot L, \qquad k = 1, \ldots, r,$$

where $L = r^3 \cdot \log(2m) \cdot \log^2(rs) + r \cdot \log(\varepsilon^{-1})$. Then statements (A) and (B) hold with probability at least $1 - \varepsilon$.

Next, we consider the two-dimensional case:

Theorem 16.4 (Fourier sampling, DIS scheme) *Let $0 < \varepsilon < 1$, $r \geq 2$ and consider the Fourier DIS scheme of order $\mathbf{m} = (m_1, \ldots, m_r)$. Suppose that*

$$m_k \gtrsim \left(s_k + \sum_{l=1}^{k-1} s_l 2^{-2q(k-l)} + \sum_{l=k+1}^{r} s_l 2^{-2(p+1)(l-k)} \right) \cdot L,$$

where $L = r^3 \cdot \log(2m) \cdot \log^2(rs) + r \cdot \log(\varepsilon^{-1})$. Then statements (A) and (B) hold with probability at least $1 - \varepsilon$.

Theorem 16.5 (Fourier sampling, DAS scheme) *Let $0 < \varepsilon < 1$, $r \geq 2$ and consider the Fourier DAS scheme of order $\mathbf{m} = (m_{k_1,k_2})_{k_1,k_2=1}^{r}$. Suppose that*

$$m_{k_1,k_2} \gtrsim \mathcal{M}(\mathbf{s}, k_1, k_2) \cdot L, \qquad k_1, k_2 = 1, \ldots, r, \tag{16.8}$$

where $L = r^3 \cdot \log(2m) \cdot \log^2(rs) + r \cdot \log(\varepsilon^{-1})$ *and* $\mathcal{M}$ *is as in §15.3.3. Then statements (A) and (B) hold with probability at least* $1 - \varepsilon$.

16.3.2 Walsh Sampling with Haar Wavelets

We now consider Walsh sampling. First, we look at the special case of Haar wavelets. Since the corresponding change-of-basis matrix U is block diagonal in this case, we have the following simpler result:

Theorem 16.6 (Walsh sampling with Haar, DS and DIS schemes) *Let* $0 < \varepsilon < 1$, $r \geq 2$ *and consider the Walsh DS (one dimension) or DIS (two dimensions) scheme of order* $\mathbf{m} = (m_1, \ldots, m_r)$. *Suppose that*

$$m_k \gtrsim s_k \cdot L,$$

where $L = r^3 \cdot \log(2m) \cdot \log^2(rs) + r \cdot \log(\varepsilon^{-1})$. *Then statements (A) and (B) hold with probability at least* $1 - \varepsilon$.

16.3.3 Walsh Sampling with Higher-Order Wavelets

Notice that, in all the above cases, the samples are drawn from the lowest N Fourier or Walsh frequencies, where $N = 2^{j_0+r-1}$ in one dimension and $N = 2^{2(j_0+r-1)}$ in two dimensions. This follows from the definitions of the sampling schemes in §15.2.2 (note that we have redefined N in the two-dimensional case here to be consistent with its later use). In particular, $M = M_r = N$ or, in the language of Chapter 14, the sparsity bandwidth is equal to the sampling bandwidth. As we prove later, the balancing property (Definition 14.2) holds with $N = M$ in the Fourier case for any wavelet and in the Walsh case for the Haar wavelet. Unfortunately, this is no longer true in the Walsh case when considering higher-order wavelets. Hence we need to slightly modify the setup.

We do this by concatenating a number of the sets in the dyadic partition into a single larger set. Consider the one-dimensional case. Let $r \geq 1$ and $M = M_r = 2^{j_0+r-1}$ be the sparsity bandwidth. Suppose that $\mathcal{B} = \{B_k\}_{k \in \mathbb{N}}$ is the dyadic partition of $\mathbb{N}_0$ (Definition 15.4). We now let $N = 2^{j_0+r+t-1}$ be the sampling bandwidth, where $t \geq 0$ will be chosen later, and define a new partition of $\{0, \ldots, N-1\}$ as follows:

$$\widetilde{B}_k = \begin{cases} B_k & k = 1, \ldots, r-1 \\ B_r \cup \cdots \cup B_{r+t} & k = r \end{cases}. \tag{16.9}$$

In other words, the first $r - 1$ partition elements are unchanged, with only the final one being modified to increase the sampling bandwidth to the desired value of N. Now suppose that the Walsh DS sampling scheme is based on this modified partition. Then we have the following recovery guarantee:

Theorem 16.7 (Walsh sampling, DS scheme) *Let* $0 < \varepsilon < 1$, $r \geq 2$ *and consider the Walsh DS scheme of order* $\mathbf{m} = (m_1, \ldots, m_r)$ *with the partition modified as in (16.9).*

Suppose that the number of vanishing moments $p \geq 3$, $t = c_p$ *for a certain constant* $c_p > 0$ *and*

$$m_k \gtrsim \left(s_k + \sum_{l=1}^{k-1} s_l 2^{-(k-l)} + \sum_{l=k+1}^{r} s_l 2^{-(l-k)} \right) \cdot L, \quad k = 1, \ldots, r,$$

where $L = r^3 \cdot \log(2m) \cdot \log^2(rs) + r \cdot \log(\varepsilon^{-1})$. *Then statements (A) and (B) hold with probability at least* $1 - \varepsilon$. *If* $p = 2$, *then the same conclusion holds, provided the factor* $2^{-(k-l)}$ *in the first sum is replaced by* $2^{-(2\alpha-1)(k-l)}$, *where* $\alpha \approx 0.5500$ *is the Hölder exponent of the DB2 wavelet (see Table 9.3).*

We next consider the two-dimensional case. Let $r \geq 2$, $M = M_r = 2^{2(j_0+r-1)}$ denote the sparsity bandwidth and write $N = 2^{2(j_0+r+t-1)}$ for the sampling bandwidth, where $t \geq 0$. Suppose that $\mathcal{B}^{(2)} = \{B^{(2)}_{k_1,k_2}\}_{k_1,k_2 \in \mathbb{N}}$ is the dyadic anisotropic partition of $\mathbb{N}_0^2$ (Definition 15.5). Then we define a new partition

$$\{\widetilde{B}^{(2)}_{k_1,k_2}\}^{r}_{k_1,k_2=1}, \tag{16.10}$$

as follows. First,

$$\widetilde{B}^{(2)}_{k_1,k_2} = B^{(2)}_{k_1,k_2}, \qquad k_1, k_2 = 1, \ldots, r-1.$$

Then

$$\widetilde{B}^{(2)}_{k_1,r} = B^{(2)}_{k_1,r} \cup \cdots \cup B^{(2)}_{k_1,r+t}, \qquad k_1 = 1, \ldots, r-1,$$
$$\widetilde{B}^{(2)}_{r,k_2} = B^{(2)}_{r,k_2} \cup \cdots \cup B^{(2)}_{r+t,k_2}, \qquad k_2 = 1, \ldots, r-1,$$

and finally,

$$\widetilde{B}^{(2)}_{r,r} = \bigcup_{l_1,l_2=0}^{t} B^{(2)}_{r+l_1,r+l_2}.$$

Similar to the one-dimensional case, in this new partition only those elements that lie on the 'boundary' are modified. Notice that (16.10) forms a partition of the set

$$\{0, \ldots, 2^{j_0+r+t-1} - 1\}^2,$$

corresponding to the lowest N Walsh frequencies. We now have the following result:

Theorem 16.8 (Walsh sampling, DAS scheme) *Let* $0 < \varepsilon < 1$, $r \geq 2$ *and consider the Walsh DAS scheme of order* $\mathbf{m} = (m_{k_1,k_2})^{r}_{k_1,k_2=1}$ *with partition modified as in (16.10). Suppose that the number of vanishing moments* $p \geq 3$, $t = c_p$ *for a certain constant* $c_p > 0$, *and*

$$m_{k_1,k_2} \gtrsim \left(\sum_{l=1}^{r} s_l 2^{-|k_1-l|-|k_2-l|} \right) \cdot L, \quad k_1, k_2 = 1, \ldots, r, \tag{16.11}$$

where $L = r^3 \cdot \log(2m) \cdot \log^2(rs) + r \cdot \log(\varepsilon^{-1})$. *Then statements (A) and (B) hold with probability at least* $1 - \varepsilon$.

We have, for succinctness, excluded the case $p = 2$ from this theorem. A measurement condition could be readily derived in this case by changing the factor $2^{-|k_1-l|-|k_2-l|}$ in a similar way to the modification made in one dimension in Theorem 16.7.

16.4 Proofs of the Recovery Guarantees

We now prove Theorems 16.3–16.8. The first step is to recast each problem as a special case of the problem considered in Chapter 14. This is done by specifying the sampling and sparsity levels (§16.4.1–§16.4.3), which then induces a block structure on the change-of-basis matrix U. Once we have this, the next steps are to establish the balancing property (§16.4.4 and §16.4.5) and to estimate the various local coherences (§16.4.6 and §16.4.7). Having done this, the final arguments are then presented in §16.4.8.

16.4.1 Sparsity Basis and Levels

While the sparsity basis and levels were already defined in §16.1.1 – in particular, the sparsity levels M_k are given by (9.47) in one dimension and (9.48) in two dimensions – it is now useful to introduce some additional notation. Let Φ denote the sparsity basis. Notice that the sparsity levels partition this basis into subsets

$$\Phi = \Phi_1 \cup \Phi_2 \cup \cdots .$$

In one dimension, these sets are given by

$$\begin{aligned} \Phi_1 &= \{\varphi^{\mathrm{per}}_{j_0,n} : n = 0, \ldots, 2^{j_0} - 1\}, \\ \Phi_k &= \{\psi^{\mathrm{per}}_{j_0+k-2,n} : n = 0, \ldots, 2^{j_0+k-2} - 1\}, \quad k \geq 2. \end{aligned} \tag{16.12}$$

In particular, Φ_1 is an orthonormal basis for the (periodized) multiresolution space $V^{\mathrm{per}}_{j_0}$ and Φ_k is an orthonormal basis for the detail space $W^{\mathrm{per}}_{j_0+k-2}$ (recall §9.7.1). Note that

$$|\Phi_1| = 2^{j_0}, \qquad |\Phi_k| = 2^{j_0+k-2}, \quad k \geq 2.$$

In two dimensions, these sets are given by

$$\begin{aligned} \Phi_1 &= \{\psi^{\mathrm{per},(0,0)}_{j_0,n} : n = (n_1, n_2),\ n_1, n_2 = 0, \ldots, 2^{j_0} - 1\}, \\ \Phi_k &= \{\psi^{\mathrm{per},(e)}_{j_0+k-2,n} : n = (n_1, n_2),\ n_1, n_2 = 0, \ldots, 2^{j_0+k-2} - 1,\ e \in \{0,1\}^2 \backslash \{0\}\}, \end{aligned} \tag{16.13}$$

and they constitute orthonormal bases for the two-dimensional multiresolution $V^{(2),\mathrm{per}}_{j_0}$ and detail $W^{(2),\mathrm{per}}_{j_0+k-2}$ spaces, respectively (recall §9.8.2). We also have

$$|\Phi_1| = 2^{2j_0}, \qquad |\Phi_k| = 3 \times 2^{2(j_0+k-2)}, \quad k \geq 2.$$

16.4.2 Sampling Levels and Block Structure of U: DS and DIS Schemes

We now describe the sampling levels. The main challenge is one of notation: the Fourier and Walsh bases are indexed over $\mathbb{Z}^d$ and $\mathbb{N}_0^d$, respectively, whereas in Chapter 14 we assume an indexing over $\mathbb{N}$. Describing the sampling levels is equivalent to partitioning each basis into finite subsets of basis elements. Note that we do not need to fully specify an ordering of the Fourier or Walsh bases over $\mathbb{N}$, just this partition. This is because the multilevel sampling scheme samples uniformly within dyadic regions, and therefore the *intra-level* ordering of the sampling basis is of no consequence. In particular, in the Walsh case this means that it also does not matter whether we consider the Paley or the sequency ordering (recall from §2.4.3 that these two orderings have the same dyadic structure). Therefore, without loss of generality, we consider the Paley ordering henceforth.

Consider the one-dimensional case. As in §16.1.1, let Υ denote the sampling basis and $\mathcal{B} = \{B_k\}$ be the dyadic partition of either $\mathbb{Z}$ in the Fourier case or $\mathbb{N}_0$ in the Walsh case (Definition 15.4). We now partition Υ as follows:

$$\Upsilon = \Upsilon_1 \cup \Upsilon_2 \cup \cdots, \qquad \Upsilon_k = \{\upsilon_i : i \in B_k\}.$$

The first sampling level now corresponds to Υ_1, the second to Υ_2 and so forth. Note that

$$|\Upsilon_1| = 2^{j_0}, \qquad |\Upsilon_k| = 2^{j_0+k-2}, \quad k = 2, 3, \ldots,$$

which gives the sampling levels

$$N_k = 2^{j_0+k-1}, \quad k = 1, 2, \ldots. \tag{16.14}$$

From this, it follows immediately that the DS scheme is equivalent to the $(\mathbf{m}, \mathbf{N})$-multilevel random sampling scheme applied to the matrix (16.1) with this choice of levels. This and the sparsity levels (9.47) endow U with the block structure

$$U = \begin{pmatrix} U^{(1,1)} & U^{(1,2)} & \cdots \\ U^{(2,1)} & U^{(2,2)} & \cdots \\ \vdots & \vdots & \ddots \end{pmatrix}, \tag{16.15}$$

where $U^{(k,l)}$ is the change-of-basis matrix between Υ_k and Φ_l, with Φ_l as in (16.12).

Now consider the DIS sampling scheme in two dimensions. Let Υ denote the sampling basis and $\overline{\mathcal{B}}^{(2)} = \{\overline{B}_k^{(2)}\}$ denote the dyadic isotropic partition of $\mathbb{Z}^2$ or $\mathbb{N}_0^2$ (Definition 15.5). Then we partition Υ in an identical way, by writing

$$\Upsilon = \Upsilon_1 \cup \Upsilon_2 \cup \cdots, \qquad \Upsilon_k = \{\upsilon_i : i \in \overline{B}_k^{(2)}\}.$$

Since

$$|\Upsilon_1| = 2^{2j_0}, \qquad |\Upsilon_k| = 3 \times 2^{2(j_0+k-2)}, \quad k = 2, 3, \ldots,$$

the DIS scheme corresponds to the $(\mathbf{m}, \mathbf{N})$-multilevel random sampling scheme applied to (16.1) with the sampling levels

$$N_k = 2^{2(j_0+k-1)}, \quad k = 1, 2, \ldots. \tag{16.16}$$

In combination with the sparsity levels (9.48), this yields a block structure as in (16.15), where $U^{(k,l)}$ is the change-of-basis matrix between Υ_k and Φ_l, and Φ_l is as in (16.13).

16.4.3 Sampling Levels and Block Structure of U: DAS Scheme

The DAS scheme requires some additional care. Let $\mathcal{B}^{(2)} = \{B^{(2)}_{k_1,k_2}\}$ be the dyadic anisotropic partition of $\mathbb{Z}^2$ or $\mathbb{N}_0^2$ (Definition 15.5). Then we first partition the sampling basis Υ as

$$\bigcup_{k_1,k_2\in\mathbb{N}} \Upsilon_{k_1,k_2}, \qquad \Upsilon_{k_1,k_2} = \{\upsilon_i : i \in B^{(2)}_{k_1,k_2}\}.$$

We assume these sets are ordered as follows:

$$\Upsilon_{1,1} \cup (\Upsilon_{2,1} \cup \Upsilon_{2,2} \cup \Upsilon_{1,2}) \cup \cdots \cup (\Upsilon_{k,1} \cup \cdots \cup \Upsilon_{k,k} \cup \cdots \cup \Upsilon_{1,k}) \cup \cdots .$$

In other words, we order the sets according to increasing $k = \max\{k_1, k_2\}$ (the ordering within each fixed value of k is arbitrary). When combined with the sparsity levels (9.48), this endows U with the following block structure:

$$U = \begin{pmatrix} U^{(1,1,1)} & U^{(1,1,2)} & U^{(1,1,3)} & \cdots \\ U^{(2,1,1)} & U^{(2,1,2)} & U^{(2,1,3)} & \cdots \\ U^{(2,2,1)} & U^{(2,2,2)} & U^{(2,2,3)} & \cdots \\ U^{(1,2,1)} & U^{(1,2,2)} & U^{(1,2,3)} & \cdots \\ U^{(3,1,1)} & U^{(3,1,2)} & U^{(3,1,3)} & \cdots \\ \vdots & \vdots & \vdots & \ddots \end{pmatrix}. \tag{16.17}$$

Observe that

$$U^{(k_1,k_2,l)} \in \mathbb{C}^{|B^{(2)}_{k_1,k_2}|\times(M_l-M_{l-1})},$$

and

$$|B^{(2)}_{k_1,k_2}| = 2^{2j_0+k_1+k_2+\delta_{k_1-1}+\delta_{k_2-1}-4},$$

with δ_k denoting the Kronecker delta. In particular, $U^{(k_1,k_2,l)}$ is the change-of-basis matrix between Υ_{k_1,k_2} and Φ_l. Unlike in the previous cases, we do not worry about explicitly writing down the sampling levels N_k in this case.

Upon inspecting (16.17), it is clear that the DAS scheme is equivalent to an $(\mathbf{m},\mathbf{N})$-multilevel random sampling scheme with r^2 sampling levels, which is more than the number of sparsity levels r. The DAS scheme differs from the DS and DIS schemes in this respect. In particular, this means that the main results of Chapter 14 do not apply. Fortunately, they are easily generalized to the case where the number of sampling levels exceeds the number of sparsity levels. This task is addressed in Theorem 16.23, which in turn leads to the main results for the DAS scheme.

16.4.4 The Balancing Property for Fourier Sampling

With the levels structure in hand, we now progress to the next stage of the proof: establishing the balancing property. We commence with Fourier sampling.

Lemma 16.9 *Let φ be the scaling function of the Daubechies wavelet of order p. Then*

$$\inf_{|\omega|\leq\pi} |\mathcal{F}\varphi(\omega)|^2 > 0.$$

Proof Recall that φ is given by Theorem 9.14. Part (b) of this theorem and (9.25) imply that $\mathcal{F}\varphi(0) = 1$, and Lemma 9.15 implies that $\mathcal{F}\varphi$ is continuous at $\omega = 0$. Using (9.25) once more, we see that

$$\mathcal{F}\varphi(\omega) = \mathcal{F}\varphi(\omega/2^N) \prod_{j=1}^{N} m_0(\omega/2^j),$$

for any N. The result now follows from the continuity of $\mathcal{F}\varphi$, the fact that $\mathcal{F}\varphi(0) \neq 0$ and property (c) of Theorem 9.14. □

Theorem 16.10 (Balancing property for Fourier sampling, $d = 1$) *Let $r \geq 2$ and U be the infinite change-of-basis matrix for the periodized Daubechies wavelet and Fourier bases of $L^2([0,1])$, ordered as in (16.15). If $N = M = 2^{j_0+r-1}$ then U has the balancing property with constant*

$$\theta = \inf_{|\omega|\leq\pi} |\mathcal{F}\varphi(\omega)|^2 > 0.$$

Moreover, for each $0 < \theta < 1$ there exists $c_{\theta,p} \in \mathbb{N}_0$ such that the balancing property with constant θ holds whenever $N \geq c_{\theta,p} M$.

Proof Since $P_M - P_M U^* P_N U P_M$ is nonnegative definite, we have

$$\begin{aligned}
\|P_M U^* P_N U P_M - P_M\|_{\ell^2}^2 &= \sup_{\substack{x \in P_M(\ell^2(\mathbb{N})) \\ \|x\|_{\ell^2}=1}} \langle (P_M - P_M U^* P_N U P_M)x, x\rangle \\
&= \sup_{\substack{x \in P_M(\ell^2(\mathbb{N})) \\ \|x\|_{\ell^2}=1}} \left(\|P_M x\|_{\ell^2}^2 - \|P_N U P_M x\|_{\ell^2}^2 \right) \\
&= 1 - \inf_{\substack{x \in P_M(\ell^2(\mathbb{N})) \\ \|x\|_{\ell^2}=1}} \|P_N U P_M x\|_{\ell^2}^2.
\end{aligned}$$

Hence the balancing property holds with constant θ if and only if

$$\sigma_{\min}(P_N U P_M) = \inf_{\substack{x \in P_M(\ell^2(\mathbb{N})) \\ \|x\|_{\ell^2}=1}} \|P_N U P_M x\|_{\ell^2} \geq \sqrt{\theta}. \tag{16.18}$$

Here $\sigma_{\min}(P_N U P_M) = \sigma_M(P_N U P_M)$ is the minimum singular value of $P_N U P_M$. Let $x \in P_M(\ell^2(\mathbb{N}))$ with $\|x\|_{\ell^2} = 1$ and write $g = \mathcal{T}_\Phi x$, where $\mathcal{T}_\Phi$ is the synthesis operator (14.4) of the wavelet basis Φ. Note that $\|g\|_{L^2} = \|x\|_{\ell^2} = 1$,

$$g \in V_{j_0}^{\mathrm{per}} \oplus W_{j_0}^{\mathrm{per}} \oplus \cdots \oplus W_{j_0+r-2}^{\mathrm{per}} = V_{j_0+r-1}^{\mathrm{per}}$$

(the equality follows from standard properties of the multiresolution and detail spaces – see §9.7.1) and

$$\|P_N U P_M x\|_2^2 = \sum_{\omega=-N/2+1}^{N/2} |\langle g, \upsilon_\omega \rangle_{L^2}|^2,$$

where $\{\upsilon_\omega\}$ is the Fourier basis. Conversely, every $g \in V^{\text{per}}_{j_0+r-1}$ with $\|g\|_{L^2} = 1$ is equivalent to a vector of coefficients $x \in P_M(\ell^2(\mathbb{N}))$ with $\|x\|_{\ell^2} = 1$. Hence

$$\inf_{\substack{x\in\mathbb{C}^M \\ \|x\|_{\ell^2}=1}} \|P_N U P_M x\|^2_{\ell^2} = \inf_{\substack{g\in V^{\text{per}}_{j_0+r-1} \\ \|g\|_{L^2}=1}} \left\{ \sum_{\omega=-N/2+1}^{N/2} |\langle g, \upsilon_\omega \rangle_{L^2}|^2 \right\}. \tag{16.19}$$

Fix a $g \in V^{\text{per}}_{j_0+r-1}$ with $\|g\|_{L^2} = 1$ and write

$$g = \sum_{n=0}^{M-1} z_n \varphi^{\text{per}}_{j_0+r-1,n},$$

where $\|z\|_{\ell^2} = \|g\|_{L^2} = 1$ and $z = (z_n)_{n=0}^{M-1}$. We now make the following observation. Consider $\psi^{\text{per},(e)}_{j,n}$, where $e = 0, 1$, as function on the real line that is zero outside $[0,1]$ (recall that $\psi^{(e)}$ is shorthand notation for the scaling function φ when $e = 0$ and the wavelet ψ when $e = 1$). Then, by the definition (9.37) of the periodization operation,

$$\mathcal{F}\psi^{\text{per},(e)}_{j,n}(2\pi\omega) = \int_0^1 \psi^{\text{per},(e)}_{j,n}(x)\mathrm{e}^{-2\pi\mathrm{i}\omega x}\,\mathrm{d}x = \sum_{k\in\mathbb{Z}} \mathrm{e}^{2\pi\mathrm{i}k\omega} \int_k^{k+1} \psi^{(e)}_{j,n}(x)\mathrm{e}^{-2\pi\mathrm{i}\omega x}\,\mathrm{d}x.$$

If $\omega \in \mathbb{Z}$ this gives $\mathcal{F}\psi^{\text{per},(e)}_{j,n}(2\pi\omega) = \mathcal{F}\psi^{(e)}_{j,n}(2\pi\omega)$. Hence, using Table E.1 we get

$$\mathcal{F}\psi^{\text{per},(e)}_{j,n}(2\pi\omega) = 2^{-j/2}\mathrm{e}^{-2\pi\mathrm{i}n\omega/2^j}\mathcal{F}\psi^{(e)}(2\pi\omega/2^j), \quad \omega \in \mathbb{Z}. \tag{16.20}$$

Returning to g and applying (16.20), we now get

$$\langle g, \upsilon_\omega \rangle = M^{-1/2}\mathcal{F}\varphi(2\pi\omega/M)G(\omega/M),$$

where $G(x) = \sum_{n=0}^{M-1} z_n \mathrm{e}^{-2\pi\mathrm{i}nx}$ is a 1-periodic function. Therefore

$$\sum_{\omega=-N/2+1}^{N/2} |\langle g, \upsilon_\omega \rangle_{L^2}|^2 = M^{-1} \sum_{\omega=-N/2+1}^{N/2} |\mathcal{F}\varphi(2\pi\omega/M)|^2\,|G(\omega/M)|^2. \tag{16.21}$$

Suppose first that $N = M$. Then, since G is 1-periodic, we deduce that

$$\sum_{\omega=-M/2+1}^{M/2} |\langle g, \upsilon_\omega \rangle_{L^2}|^2 \geq \inf_{|\omega|\leq\pi} |\mathcal{F}\varphi(\omega)|^2\, M^{-1} \sum_{i=0}^{M-1} |G(i/M)|^2.$$

Let $\mathcal{F}(z)$ denote the DFT of the vector $z \in \mathbb{C}^M$ (Definition E.1). Then $G(i/M) = (\mathcal{F}(z))_{i+1}$, and therefore

$$M^{-1}\sum_{i=0}^{M-1} |G(i/M)|^2 = M^{-1}\|\mathcal{F}(z)\|^2_{\ell^2} = \|z\|^2_{\ell^2} = \|g\|^2_{L^2} = 1.$$

This gives

$$\sum_{\omega=-M/2+1}^{M/2} |\langle g, \upsilon_\omega \rangle_{L^2}|^2 \geq \inf_{|\omega|\leq\pi} |\mathcal{F}\varphi(\omega)|^2 = \theta.$$

Since g was arbitrary, we deduce from (16.18) and (16.19) that the balancing property holds for $N = M$ with this value of θ.

For the second result, notice that the left-hand side of (16.18) is a nondecreasing function of N. Hence, we may assume without loss of generality that $N = 2PM$ for some $P \in \mathbb{N}$. Then (16.21) can be expressed as

$$\begin{aligned}\sum_{\omega=-N/2+1}^{N/2} |\langle g, \upsilon_\omega \rangle_{L^2}|^2 &= M^{-1} \sum_{p=-P}^{P-1} \sum_{n=1}^{M} \left| \mathcal{F}\varphi\left(2\pi \frac{pM+n}{M}\right)\right|^2 \left| G\left(\frac{pM+n}{M}\right)\right|^2 \\ &= M^{-1} \sum_{n=1}^{M} |G(n/M)|^2 \sum_{p=-P}^{P-1} |\mathcal{F}\varphi(2p\pi + 2\pi n/M)|^2 \\ &\geq \inf_{\omega \in [0,2\pi]} \sum_{p=-P}^{P-1} |\mathcal{F}\varphi(2p\pi + \omega)|^2 M^{-1} \sum_{i=0}^{M-1} |G(i/M)|^2 \\ &= \inf_{\omega \in [0,2\pi]} \sum_{p=-P}^{P-1} |\mathcal{F}\varphi(2p\pi + \omega)|^2.\end{aligned}$$

Hence it suffices to show that for each $0 < \theta < 1$ there exists a $P \in \mathbb{N}$ such that

$$\inf_{\omega \in [0,2\pi]} \sum_{p=-P}^{P-1} |\mathcal{F}\varphi(2p\pi + \omega)|^2 \geq \theta.$$

Recall from Lemma 9.8 that $\sum_{p\in\mathbb{Z}} |\mathcal{F}\varphi(2p\pi+\omega)|^2 = 1$ a.e. $\omega \in \mathbb{R}$ since $\{\varphi(\cdot-k) : k \in \mathbb{Z}\}$ is an orthonormal system. In particular, for every $\omega \in [0, 2\pi]$ there exists a $P_\omega \in \mathbb{N}$ such that

$$\sum_{p=-P_\omega}^{P_\omega-1} |\mathcal{F}\varphi(2p\pi + \omega)|^2 \geq 2\theta.$$

Since $\mathcal{F}\varphi$ is continuous, the function on the left-hand side is also continuous. Hence there is a neighbourhood $U_\omega \subset \mathbb{R}$ containing ω for which

$$\sum_{p=-P_\omega}^{P_\omega-1} |\mathcal{F}\varphi(2p\pi + \omega')|^2 \geq \theta, \quad \forall \omega' \in U_\omega.$$

Note that $[0, 2\pi]$ is compact and $\bigcup_{\omega\in[0,2\pi]} U_\omega$ is a cover for it. Hence $[0, 2\pi]$ has a finite subcover $\bigcup_{j=1}^{J} U_{\omega_j}$, for some finite set of values $\omega_1, \ldots, \omega_J \in [0, 2\pi]$. We now let $P = \max\{P_{\omega_1}, \ldots, P_{\omega_J}\}$ to deduce that

$$\sum_{p=-P}^{P-1} |\mathcal{F}\varphi(2p\pi + \omega)|^2 \geq \theta, \quad \forall \omega \in [0, 2\pi],$$

as required. This completes the proof. □

The following result extends Theorem 16.10 to the two-dimensional case:

Theorem 16.11 (Balancing property for Fourier sampling, $d = 2$) *Let $r \geq 2$ and U be the infinite change-of-basis matrix for the periodized Daubechies wavelet and Fourier* *bases of* $L^2([0,1]^2)$*, ordered as in (16.15) or (16.17). If* $N = M = 2^{2(j_0+r-1)}$ *then the balancing property holds with*

$$\theta \geq \inf_{|\omega| \leq \pi} |\mathcal{F}\varphi(\omega)|^4.$$

For simplicity, we do not consider the second part of Theorem 16.10, although it can also be generalized to two dimensions.

Proof Given orthonormal bases $\{\upsilon_i\}_{i\in\mathbb{N}}$ and $\{\phi_j\}_{j\in\mathbb{N}}$, notice that the balancing property depends only on $\mathrm{span}\{\phi_1, \ldots, \phi_M\}$ and not the sparsity basis vectors themselves. Hence, for the Fourier-wavelets problem, the balancing property depends only on the subspace $V^{\mathrm{per},(2)}_{j_0+r-1}$, as this is precisely the span of the first M wavelets in the given ordering. Therefore we may replace $P_M U P_M$ by a new matrix $U' \in \mathbb{C}^{M\times M}$ corresponding to the tensor-product orthonormal basis of scaling functions for $V^{\mathrm{per},(2)}_{j_0+r-1}$.

Note that the balancing property is also independent of the ordering of the first M sampling basis functions $\{\upsilon_1, \ldots, \upsilon_M\}$. Moreover, the first $M = 2^{2(j_0+r-1)}$ rows in either ordering (16.15) or (16.17) are the same, up to possible permutations. Hence we may order the first M Fourier basis functions lexicographically so that the matrix U' has a Kronecker product structure. This gives $U' = U'' \otimes U''$, where U'' is precisely the change-of-basis matrix for the first $\sqrt{M}$ one-dimensional scaling functions and first $\sqrt{M}$ one-dimensional Fourier basis functions.

Recall from (16.18) that the balancing property holds with constant θ if and only if

$$\sigma_M(U) = \sigma_M(U') \geq \sqrt{\theta}.$$

By properties of Kronecker products (see §A.9), we have $\sigma_M(U') = (\sigma_{\sqrt{M}}(U''))^2$. But $\sigma_{\sqrt{M}}(U'')$ pertains to the balancing property for the one-dimensional Fourier-wavelets problem. In particular, Theorem 16.10 gives that $\sigma_{\sqrt{M}}(U'') \geq \inf_{|\omega|\leq\pi} |\mathcal{F}\varphi(\omega)|$. The result now follows. □

16.4.5 The Balancing Property for Walsh Sampling

We now consider Walsh sampling. We commence with the Haar wavelet case:

Theorem 16.12 (Balancing property for Walsh sampling with Haar) *Let* $r \geq 2$*,* U *be the infinite change-of-basis matrix for the Haar wavelet and Walsh bases of either* $L^2([0,1])$ *or* $L^2([0,1]^2)$*, ordered as in (16.15). Let* $M = 2^{r-1}$ *(one dimension) or* $M = 2^{2(r-1)}$ *(two dimensions). Then* $P_M U P_M$ *is unitary and therefore the balancing property holds with* $\theta = 1$ *when* $N = M$*.*

Proof Consider the one-dimensional case first. Recall from §16.4.1 that

$$\mathrm{span}\,(\Phi_1) = V^{\mathrm{per}}_0, \quad \mathrm{span}(\Phi_{j+2}) = W^{\mathrm{per}}_j, \quad j = 0, 1, \ldots,$$

where V^{per}_0 and W^{per}_j denote multiresolution and detail spaces for the Haar wavelet (we continue to use the superscript 'per' here to highlight that these are the Haar multiresolution and detail spaces of $L^2([0,1])$ and not $L^2(\mathbb{R})$ – the Haar wavelet is, of course, unchanged by periodization). Lemma F.6 gives

$$\text{span}(\Upsilon_1) = \text{span}\{\upsilon_0\} = \text{span}\{\varphi\} = V_0^{\text{per}},$$

and, for $j = 0, 1, \ldots,$

$$\text{span}\left(\Upsilon_{j+2}\right) = \text{span}\{\upsilon_{2^j+m} : m = 0, \ldots, 2^j - 1\} = W_j^{\text{per}} = \text{span}(\Phi_{j+2}). \tag{16.22}$$

Recalling that $V_0^{\text{per}} \oplus W_0^{\text{per}} \oplus \cdots W_{r-2}^{\text{per}} = V_{r-1}^{\text{per}}$, we also get

$$\text{span}(\Phi_1 \cup \cdots \cup \Phi_r) = \text{span}(\Upsilon_1 \cup \cdots \cup \Upsilon_r) = V_{r-1}^{\text{per}}. \tag{16.23}$$

Therefore the first $M = 2^{r-1}$ Walsh functions and Haar wavelets span the same space. Since they are both orthonormal bases for this space, it follows (recall Remark 14.4) that their change-of-basis matrix $P_M U P_M$ is unitary.

Now consider the two-dimensional case. Note that

$$\text{span}(\Phi_1) = V_0^{\text{per},(2)}, \qquad \text{span}(\Phi_{j+2}) = W_j^{\text{per},(2)}, \quad j = 0, 1, \ldots,$$

where $V_0^{\text{per},(2)}$ and $W_j^{\text{per},(2)}$ are the two-dimensional Haar multiresolution and detail spaces. We next examine the Υ_k. Observe that $\text{span}(\Upsilon_1) = V_0^{\text{per},(2)}$. We now claim that

$$\text{span}(\Upsilon_{j+2}) = W_j^{\text{per},(2)}, \quad j = 0, 1, \ldots.$$

To see why this holds, note that we can write Υ_{j+2} as

$$\Upsilon_{j+2} = \bigcup_{(e_1,e_2)\in\{0,1\}^2\setminus\{0\}} \left\{\upsilon_{2^j e_1+m_1} \otimes \upsilon_{2^j e_2+m_2} : m_1, m_2 = 0, \ldots, 2^j - 1\right\},$$

where υ_n is the one-dimensional Walsh function (recall from §2.4.2 that the two-dimensional Walsh functions are tensor products of the one-dimensional Walsh functions). Hence, by (16.22) and (16.23), we get

$$\text{span}\left(\Upsilon_{j+2}\right) = (V_j^{\text{per}} \otimes W_j^{\text{per}}) \oplus (W_j^{\text{per}} \otimes V_j^{\text{per}}) \oplus (W_j^{\text{per}} \otimes W_j^{\text{per}}) = W_j^{\text{per},(2)},$$

as required. Here we also recall from §9.8 that $W_j^{\text{per},(2)}$ is a direct sum of these three spaces. It now follows that $\text{span}(\Upsilon_k) = \text{span}(\Phi_k)$ for $k = 1, 2, \ldots$. In particular, the first $M = 2^{2(r-1)}$ Walsh functions and Haar wavelets span the same space, specifically,

$$\text{span}(\Phi_1 \cup \cdots \cup \Phi_r) = \text{span}(\Upsilon_1 \cup \cdots \cup \Upsilon_r) = V_{r-1}^{\text{per},(2)}.$$

Hence we once more deduce the result. □

We next consider the general case:

Theorem 16.13 (Balancing property for Walsh sampling) *Let $r \geq 2$, U be the infinite change-of-basis matrix for the periodized Daubechies wavelet and Walsh bases of either $L^2([0,1])$ or $L^2([0,1]^2)$, ordered as in (16.15) or (16.17), respectively. Let $M = 2^{j_0+r-1}$ (one dimension) or $M = 2^{2(j_0+r-1)}$ (two dimensions). Then for each $0 < \theta < 1$ there exists $c_{\theta,p} \in \mathbb{N}$ such that the balancing property with constant θ holds for all $N \geq c_{\theta,p} M$.*

To prove this theorem, we first require the following two lemmas. For these, we recall the definition (2.24) of the Walsh transform $\mathcal{H}\colon L^2([0,1)) \to \ell^2(\mathbb{N}_0)$. We also recall that the Paley ordering is being used throughout this section.

Lemma 16.14 *Consider the one-dimensional periodized Daubechies wavelets $\psi^{\mathrm{per},(e)}_{j,n}$ of order $p \geq 1$. Then*

$$\langle \psi^{\mathrm{per},(e)}_{j,n}, \upsilon_i \rangle_{L^2} = 2^{-j/2} \sum_{l=-p+1}^{p-1} \upsilon_i\left(\frac{n+l}{2^j}\right) \mathcal{H}\left(\psi^{(e)}(\cdot + l)|_{[0,1)}\right)\left(\lfloor i/2^j \rfloor\right),$$

for $e \in \{0,1\}$, $n = 0,\ldots,2^j-1$, $j = j_0, j_0+1,\ldots$ and $i \in \mathbb{N}_0$, where, on the right-hand side, υ_i is the 1-periodic extension of the Walsh function to $\mathbb{R}$.

Proof We first note the following. Let $x \in [0,1)$ and $n \in \{0,\ldots,2^j-1\}$ and write them in terms of their dyadic expansions (recall §2.4.1) as $x = \sum_{k=1}^{\infty} x_k 2^{-k}$ and $n = \sum_{k=1}^{j} n_k 2^{k-1}$, where $x_k, n_k \in \{0,1\}$. Let $\oplus$ denote the binary addition operation defined in §F.2. Then

$$\frac{x}{2^j} + \frac{n}{2^j} = \sum_{l=j+1}^{\infty} x_{l-j} 2^{-l} + \sum_{l=1}^{j} n_{j+1-l} 2^{-l} = \frac{x}{2^j} \oplus \frac{n}{2^j}, \tag{16.24}$$

since the two terms have no common binary digits. Now suppose that $p-1 \leq n \leq 2^j - p$. Then $\mathrm{supp}(\psi^{(e)}_{j,n}) = [(-p+1+n)/2^j, (p+n)/2^j] \subseteq [0,1]$ by (9.39) and $\psi^{\mathrm{per},(e)}_{j,n} = \psi^{(e)}_{j,n}$ by (9.40). Hence

$$\begin{aligned}
\langle \psi^{\mathrm{per},(e)}_{j,n}, \upsilon_i \rangle_{L^2} &= \int_{(-p+1+n)/2^j}^{(p+n)/2^j} 2^{j/2} \psi^{(e)}(2^j x - n) \upsilon_i(x) \,\mathrm{d}x \\
&= 2^{-j/2} \int_{-p+1}^{p} \psi^{(e)}(x) \upsilon_i(2^{-j}(x+n)) \,\mathrm{d}x.
\end{aligned}$$

We now split the interval $[-p+1, p]$ into subintervals of length one and use (16.24) and Lemma F.3 to get

$$\begin{aligned}
\langle \psi^{\mathrm{per},(e)}_{j,n}, \upsilon_i \rangle_{L^2} &= 2^{-j/2} \sum_{l=-p+1}^{p-1} \int_0^1 \psi^{(e)}(x+l) \upsilon_i\left(\frac{x+n+l}{2^j}\right) \mathrm{d}x \\
&= 2^{-j/2} \sum_{l=-p+1}^{p-1} \int_0^1 \psi^{(e)}(x+l) \upsilon_i\left(\frac{x}{2^j} \oplus \frac{n+l}{2^j}\right) \mathrm{d}x \\
&= 2^{-j/2} \sum_{l=-p+1}^{p-1} \upsilon_i\left(\frac{n+l}{2^j}\right) \int_0^1 \psi^{(e)}(x+l) \upsilon_i\left(\frac{x}{2^j}\right) \mathrm{d}x \\
&= 2^{-j/2} \sum_{l=-p+1}^{p-1} \upsilon_i\left(\frac{n+l}{2^j}\right) \mathcal{H}\left(\psi^{(e)}(\cdot + l)|_{[0,1)}\right)\left(\lfloor i/2^j \rfloor\right).
\end{aligned}$$

This gives the result for the case $p-1 \leq n \leq 2^j - p$. Now suppose that $0 \leq n \leq p-2$.

Then (9.41) gives

$$\langle \psi^{\text{per},(e)}_{j,n}, \upsilon_i \rangle_{L^2} = I_1 + I_2 := 2^{j/2} \int_0^{(p+n)/2^j} \psi^{(e)}(2^j x - n) \upsilon_i(x) \,\mathrm{d}x$$
$$+ 2^{j/2} \int_{(-p+1+n+2^j)/2^j}^{1} \psi^{(e)}(2^j x - 2^j - n) \upsilon_i(x) \,\mathrm{d}x.$$

Consider the first integral. We again split into intervals of length one and write

$$I_1 = 2^{-j/2} \sum_{l=-n}^{p-1} \int_0^1 \psi^{(e)}(x+l) \upsilon_i \left(\frac{x+n+l}{2^j} \right) \mathrm{d}x.$$

Note that $0 \leq n + l < 2p - 2 < 2^{j_0} \leq 2^j$ since j_0 is given by (9.49). Therefore, by the same arguments,

$$I_1 = 2^{-j/2} \sum_{l=-n}^{p-1} \upsilon_i \left(\frac{n+l}{2^j} \right) \mathcal{H} \left(\psi^{(e)}(\cdot + l)|_{[0,1)} \right) \left(\lfloor i/2^j \rfloor \right).$$

Similarly, for the second integral we obtain

$$I_2 = 2^{-j/2} \sum_{l=-p+1}^{-n-1} \upsilon_i \left(\frac{2^j + n + l}{2^j} \right) \mathcal{H} \left(\psi^{(e)}(\cdot + l)|_{[0,1)} \right) \left(\lfloor i/2^j \rfloor \right).$$

We now replace $\frac{2^j+n+l}{2^j}$ by $\frac{n+l}{2^j}$, since υ_i is 1-periodic, and combine with the expression for I_1 to obtain the result in this case as well. The case $2^j - p < n < 2^j$ is similar. □

For the second lemma, we also recall the definition of the Hölder space $C^\alpha([0,1])$, Definition 10.3:

Lemma 16.15 *Suppose that $f \in C^\alpha([0,1])$ for some $0 < \alpha \leq 1$. Then the Walsh transform of f satisfies*

$$|\mathcal{H} f(i)| \leq \|f\|_{C^\alpha} (i+1)^{-\alpha}.$$

Proof Clearly the result holds for $i = 0$, since $\upsilon_0 \equiv 1$. Suppose now that $2^j \leq i < 2^{j+1}$ for some $j \in \mathbb{N}_0$. Observe that the $(j+1)$th digit in the binary expansion $(i_k)_{k=1}^\infty$ of i satisfies $i_{j+1} = 1$. Hence $\upsilon_i(2^{-j-1}) = (-1)^{i_{j+1}} = -1$ by (2.23). Now consider the function $f(x \oplus 2^{-j-1})$. By Lemma F.4 we have

$$\int_0^1 f(x \oplus 2^{-j-1}) \upsilon_i(x) \,\mathrm{d}x = \upsilon_i(2^{-j-1}) \mathcal{H} f(i) = -\mathcal{H} f(i).$$

Therefore

$$2\mathcal{H} f(i) = \int_0^1 \left(f(x) - f(x \oplus 2^{-j-1}) \right) \upsilon_i(x) \,\mathrm{d}x.$$

Observe that $|x - x \oplus 2^{-j-1}| = 2^{-j-1}$, since x and $x \oplus 2^{-j-1}$ differ by exactly one in their $(j+1)$th binary digits. Hence, since $f \in C^\alpha([0,1])$ we deduce that

$$|\mathcal{H} f(i)| \leq \frac{1}{2} 2^{-(j+1)\alpha} \|f\|_{C^\alpha} \leq (i+1)^{-\alpha} \|f\|_{C^\alpha}.$$

This gives the result. □

Proof of Theorem 16.13 The proof is generally similar to that of Theorem 16.10. Consider the one-dimensional case first and recall that the left-hand side of (16.18) is nondecreasing in N. Hence without loss of generality we may take $N = 2^{j_0+r+t-1}$ for some $t \in \mathbb{N}_0$. Observe that

$$\|P_M U^* P_N U P_M - P_M\|_{\ell^2} = \|P_M U^* P_N^\perp U P_M\|_{\ell^2} = \|P_N^\perp U P_M\|_{\ell^2}^2,$$

since U is unitary, and

$$\sup_{\substack{x \in \mathbb{C}^M \\ \|x\|_{\ell^2}=1}} \|P_N^\perp U P_M x\|_{\ell^2}^2 = \sup_{\substack{g \in V_{j_0+r-1}^{\mathrm{per}} \\ \|g\|_{L^2}=1}} \left\{ \sum_{i \geq N} |\langle g, \upsilon_i \rangle_{L^2}|^2 \right\}. \tag{16.25}$$

Let $j = j_0 + r - 1$ so that $M = 2^j$ and $N = 2^{j+t}$. As before, fix a $g \in V_j^{\mathrm{per}}$ with $\|g\|_{L^2} = 1$ and write $g = \sum_{n=0}^{M-1} z_n \varphi_{j,n}^{\mathrm{per}}$, where $\|z\|_{\ell^2} = \|g\|_{L^2} = 1$ and $z = (z_n)_{n=0}^{M-1}$. Then Lemma 16.14 gives

$$\langle g, \upsilon_i \rangle_{L^2} = 2^{-j/2} \sum_{l=-p+1}^{p-1} a_{i,j,l} \sum_{n=0}^{M-1} z_n \upsilon_i \left(\frac{n+l}{2^j} \right),$$

where

$$a_{i,j,l} = \mathcal{H}\left(\psi^{(0)}(\cdot + l)|_{[0,1)}\right)\left(\lfloor i/2^j \rfloor\right).$$

Hence

$$\sqrt{\sum_{i \geq N} |\langle g, \upsilon_i \rangle_{L^2}|^2} \leq \sum_{l=-p+1}^{p-1} \sqrt{\sum_{i \geq N} |a_{i,j,l}|^2 2^{-j} \left| \sum_{n=0}^{M-1} z_n \upsilon_i \left(\frac{n+l}{2^j} \right) \right|^2}. \tag{16.26}$$

Consider the terms $a_{i,j,l}$. Recall from §9.6 that the Daubechies wavelet and scaling function are, for $p \geq 2$, α-Hölder continuous with values of α given in Table 9.3. Hence

$$|a_{i,j,l}| \lesssim (i/2^j)^{-\min\{\alpha,1\}},$$

by Lemma 16.15. Returning to (16.26), suppose now that we write $i \geq N$ in the form $i = 2^j k + m$, where $k \geq 2^t$ and $0 \leq m < 2^j$. Then

$$\sqrt{\sum_{i \geq N} |\langle g, \upsilon_i \rangle_{L^2}|^2} \lesssim \sum_{l=-p+1}^{p-1} \sqrt{\sum_{k \geq 2^t} k^{-2\min\{\alpha,1\}} 2^{-j} \sum_{m=0}^{2^j-1} \left| \sum_{n=0}^{M-1} z_n \upsilon_{2^j k+m} \left(\frac{n+l}{2^j} \right) \right|^2}.$$

We now claim that

$$\upsilon_{2^j k+m}\left(\frac{n+l}{2^j} \right) = \upsilon_m \left(\frac{n+l}{2^j} \right). \tag{16.27}$$

Notice first that $2^j k + m = 2^j k \oplus m$ since $2^j k$ has zeroes in its first j binary decimals and m is nonzero in its first j binary decimals only. Now suppose that $p-1 \leq n \leq 2^j - p$ so that $\frac{n+l}{2^j} \in [0,1)$. Then, by Lemma F.3,

$$\upsilon_{2^j k+m}\left(\frac{n+l}{2^j} \right) = \upsilon_{2^j k}\left(\frac{n+l}{2^j} \right) \upsilon_m \left(\frac{n+l}{2^j} \right).$$

Since the binary expansion of $\frac{n+l}{2^j}$ is nonzero in its first j terms only, whereas the binary expansion of $2^j k$ is zero in its first $j+1$ entries, we have $\upsilon_{2^j k}\left(\frac{n+l}{2^j}\right) = 1$. This gives the result for this case. Next suppose that $0 \leq n < p-1$. Then, using the definition (9.49) of j_0 and the fact that $j > j_0$, we have $\frac{n+l+p-1}{2^j} \in [0,1)$ and therefore by periodicity and similar arguments to the previous case,

$$\begin{aligned}\upsilon_{2^j k+m}\left(\frac{n+l}{2^j}\right) &= \upsilon_{2^j k+m}\left(\frac{n+l+p-1}{2^j}\right) \\ &= \upsilon_{2^j k}\left(\frac{n+l+p-1}{2^j}\right)\upsilon_m\left(\frac{n+l+p-1}{2^j}\right) = \upsilon_m\left(\frac{n+l}{2^j}\right).\end{aligned}$$

The case $2^j - p < n < 2^j$ is similar. Hence the claim (16.27) is proved.

Using this claim, we deduce that

$$\sqrt{\sum_{i \geq N} |\langle g, \upsilon_i \rangle_{L^2}|^2} \lesssim (2^t)^{1/2-\min\{\alpha,1\}} \max_{-p<l<p} \sqrt{2^{-j} \sum_{m=0}^{2^j-1} \left| \sum_{n=0}^{2^j-1} z_n \upsilon_m\left(\frac{n+l}{2^j}\right)\right|^2}.$$

Here, we used the fact that $\alpha > 1/2$ for every Daubechies wavelet (see Table 9.3). For $l = 0$, the term under the square-root is equal to $2^{-j}\|\mathcal{H}(z)\|_{\ell^2}^2$, where $\mathcal{H}$ is the discrete Walsh–Hadamard transform (2.28) of z, and for $l \neq 0$ it is equal to $2^{-j}\|\mathcal{H}(z')\|_{\ell^2}^2$ where z' is a permutation of the entries of z. Since $\|\mathcal{H}(x)\|_{\ell^2} = 2^{j/2}\|x\|_{\ell^2}$, $\forall x$, and $\|z\|_{\ell^2} = \|g\|_{L^2} = 1$ we deduce that

$$\sqrt{\sum_{i \geq N} |\langle g, \upsilon_i \rangle_{L^2}|^2} \lesssim (2^t)^{1/2-\min\{\alpha,1\}}.$$

Substituting this into (16.25), we see that the balancing property holds whenever

$$(2^t)^{1/2-\min\{\alpha,1\}} \lesssim \sqrt{1-\theta},$$

or equivalently $2^t \geq c_{\theta,p}$. This completes the proof for the one-dimensional case. In the two-dimensional case we argue as in the proof of Theorem 16.11. □

We remark in passing that this proof relied crucially on the sharp values for the Hölder exponent of the Daubechies wavelet that were given in Table 9.3. Specifically, the fact that $\alpha > 1/2$ for $p = 2$. In particular, one cannot use the wavelet smoothness parameter q to infer a bound for the Hölder exponent here, as in (9.24), since this would fail to give $\alpha > 1/2$ when $p = 2$.

16.4.6 Local Coherence Estimates for Fourier Sampling

We now consider the various local coherence estimates. The first result formalizes the arguments presented in §11.1.3 on the frequency concentration of Daubechies wavelets:

Theorem 16.16 (Fourier DS local coherences) *Let U be the infinite change-of-basis matrix for the periodized Daubechies wavelet and Fourier bases of $L^2([0,1])$, with blocks $U^{(k,l)}$ as in (16.15). Then the local coherences satisfy*

$$\mu\left(U^{(k,l)}\right) \lesssim \begin{cases} 2^{-(2q+1)(k-l)} & k \geq l \\ 2^{-(2p+1)(l-k)} & k < l \end{cases}, \qquad k,l = 1,2,\ldots.$$

We first require the following lemma:

Lemma 16.17 *Let U be the infinite change-of-basis matrix for the periodized Daubechies wavelet and Fourier bases of $L^2([0,1])$, with blocks $U^{(k,l)}$ as in (16.15). Then, for $k = 1,2,\ldots$,*

$$\mu\left(U^{(k,l)}\right) = 2^{k-l+\delta_{k-1}} \max_{\omega \in B_k} \left|\mathcal{F}\psi(2\pi\omega/2^{j_0+l-2})\right|^2, \quad l > 1,$$

and

$$\mu\left(U^{(k,1)}\right) = 2^{k-1+\delta_{k-1}} \max_{\omega \in B_k} \left|\mathcal{F}\varphi(2\pi\omega/2^{j_0})\right|^2,$$

where $\{B_k\}$ is the dyadic partition of $\mathbb{Z}$ of index j_0 (Definition 15.4).

Proof By definition,

$$\mu\left(U^{(k,l)}\right) = |B_k| \max_{\omega \in B_k} \max_{0 \leq n < 2^{j_0+l-2}} \left|\mathcal{F}\psi^{\text{per}}_{j_0+l-2,n}(2\pi\omega)\right|^2, \quad l > 1,$$

and

$$\mu\left(U^{(k,1)}\right) = |B_k| \max_{\omega \in B_k} \max_{0 \leq n < 2^{j_0}} \left|\mathcal{F}\varphi^{\text{per}}_{j_0,n}(2\pi\omega)\right|^2.$$

Note that $|B_k| = 2^{j_0+k+\delta_{k-1}-2}$. The result now follows from (16.20). □

Proof of Theorem 16.16 By the previous lemma, it suffices to estimate the Fourier transform of the wavelet and scaling function in different regions of frequency space. First, suppose that $k \geq l \geq 1$. Then $|\omega| \geq 2^{j_0+k-3}$ for $\omega \in B_k$, and the smoothness condition (9.34) gives

$$|\mathcal{F}\psi(2\pi\omega/2^{j_0+l-2})| \lesssim 2^{-(q+1)(k-l)}, \qquad |\mathcal{F}\varphi(2\pi\omega/2^{j_0+l-2})| \lesssim 2^{-(q+1)(k-l)}$$

(note that (9.34) also holds for the mother wavelet, since it is a finite linear combination of scaling functions). The first result now follows from Lemma 16.17.

For the second result, we need to bound $|\mathcal{F}\psi(2\pi\omega)|$ for $|\omega| \ll 1$. Since the wavelet has p vanishing moments, Proposition 9.12 implies that $\mathcal{F}\psi$ and its first $p-1$ derivatives vanish at $\omega = 0$. Hence

$$|\mathcal{F}\psi(2\pi\omega)| \lesssim |\omega|^p, \quad \forall |\omega| \leq 1. \tag{16.28}$$

Now $l > k \geq 1$. Then $|\omega|/2^{j_0+l-2} \leq 2^{j_0+k-2}/2^{j_0+l-2} \leq 1$ for all $\omega \in B_k$. Therefore, by (16.28) and the previous lemma,

$$\mu\left(U^{(k,l)}\right) \leq 2^{1+k-l} \max_{|\omega| \leq 2^{j_0+k-2}} |\mathcal{F}\psi(2\pi\omega/2^{j_0+l-2})|^2 \lesssim 2^{k-l}2^{2p(k-l)}.$$

The result now follows immediately. □

We next consider the two-dimensional case. First, we consider the DIS setting:

Theorem 16.18 (Fourier DIS local coherences) *Let U be the infinite change-of-basis matrix for the periodized Daubechies wavelet and Fourier bases of $L^2([0,1]^2)$, with blocks $U^{(k,l)}$ as in (16.15). Then the local coherences satisfy*

$$\mu\left(U^{(k,l)}\right) \lesssim \begin{cases} 2^{-2q(k-l)} & k \geq l \\ 2^{-2(p+1)(l-k)} & k < l \end{cases}, \qquad k,l = 1,2,\ldots.$$

This theorem will in fact be derived as a consequence of the following result, which addresses the DAS case:

Theorem 16.19 (Fourier DAS local coherences) *Let U be the infinite change-of-basis matrix for the periodized Daubechies wavelet and Fourier bases of $L^2([0,1]^2)$, with blocks $U^{(k_1,k_2,l)}$ as in (16.17). Then the local coherences satisfy*

$$\mu\left(U^{(k_1,k_2,l)}\right) \lesssim \begin{cases} 2^{-(2q+1)((k_1-l)+(k_2-l))} & k_1,k_2 \geq l \\ 2^{-(2q+1)(k_1-l)-(l-k_2)} & k_1 \geq l, k_2 < l \\ 2^{-(l-k_1)-(2q+1)(k_2-l)} & k_1 < l, k_2 \geq l \\ 2^{-(2p+1)(l-k_1)-(l-k_2)} & k_2 \leq k_1 < l \\ 2^{-(l-k_1)-(2p+1)(l-k_2)} & k_1 \leq k_2 < l \end{cases},$$

for $k_1, k_2, l = 1, 2, \ldots$. In particular,

$$\mu\left(U^{(k_1,k_2,l)}\right) \lesssim 2^{-|k_1-l|-|k_2-l|}.$$

Proof For $k, l \in \mathbb{N}$ and $e \in \{0,1\}$, define

$$F^{(e)}_{k,l} = |B_k| \max_{\omega \in B_k} \max_{0 \leq n < 2^{l+j_0-2}} \left| \mathcal{F}\psi^{\text{per},(e)}_{j_0+l-2,n}(2\pi\omega) \right|^2.$$

Then, from the proof of Theorem 16.16, we note that

$$F^{(e)}_{k,l} \lesssim 2^{-(2q+1)(k-l)}, \quad k \geq l,\ e \in \{0,1\},$$

and

$$F^{(1)}_{k,l} \lesssim 2^{-(2p+1)(l-k)}, \quad k < l.$$

Also, since $F^{(0)}_{k,l} \lesssim 2^{k-l} \max_{\omega \in B_k} |\mathcal{F}\varphi(2\pi\omega/2^{l+j_0-2})|^2 \lesssim 2^{k-l}$, we have

$$F^{(0)}_{k,l} \lesssim 2^{-(l-k)}, \quad k < l.$$

Hence

$$F^{(e)}_{k,l} \lesssim \begin{cases} 2^{-(2q+1)(k-l)} & k \geq l, \\ 2^{-(2pe+1)(l-k)} & k < l \end{cases} \qquad e \in \{0,1\}. \tag{16.29}$$

Now let $k_1, k_2 \in \mathbb{N}$. Then, by (16.29), and the definition of $U^{(k_1,k_2,l)}$,

$$\mu\left(U^{(k_1,k_2,1)}\right) = F^{(0)}_{k_1,2} F^{(0)}_{k_2,2} \lesssim 2^{-(2q+1)(|k_1-1|+|k_2-1|)},$$

and for $k_1, k_2 \geq l > 1$,

$$\mu\left(U^{(k_1,k_2,l)}\right) = \max_{\substack{e \in \{0,1\}^2 \\ e \neq 0}} \left\{ F^{(e_1)}_{k_1,1} F^{(e_2)}_{k_2,1} \right\} \lesssim 2^{-(2q+1)(|k_1-l|+|k_2-l|)}.$$

This gives the first result. Now suppose that $k_1 \geq l$ and $k_2 < l$. Then

$$\mu\left(U^{(k_1,k_2,l)}\right) = \max_{\substack{e \in \{0,1\}^2 \\ e \neq 0}} \left\{ F^{(e_1)}_{k_1,l} F^{(e_2)}_{k_2,l} \right\} \lesssim 2^{-(2q+1)(k_1-l)} 2^{-(l-k_2)},$$

which gives the second result. The third result follows merely by interchanging k_1 and k_2. Now suppose that $k_2 \leq k_1 < l$. Then

$$\mu\left(U^{(k_1,k_2,l)}\right) = \max_{\substack{e \in \{0,1\}^2 \\ e \neq 0}} \left\{ F^{(e_1)}_{k_1,l} F^{(e_2)}_{k_2,l} \right\} \lesssim \max_{\substack{e \in \{0,1\}^2 \\ e \neq 0}} \left\{ 2^{-(2pe_1+1)(l-k_1)-(2pe_2+1)(l-k_2)} \right\}.$$

Since $l - k_1 \leq l - k_2$, this maximum is attained at $e_1 = 1$ and $e_2 = 0$, giving

$$\mu\left(U^{(k_1,k_2,l)}\right) \lesssim 2^{-(2p+1)(l-k_1)-(l-k_2)},$$

as required. For the final result we once again interchange k_1 and k_2. □

Proof of Theorem 16.18 By definition

$$\mu\left(U^{(k,l)}\right) = |\bar{B}^{(2)}_k| \max \left\{ \frac{\mu\left(U^{(k_1,k_2,l)}\right)}{|B^{(2)}_{k_1,k_2}|} : 1 \leq k_1, k_2 \leq k,\ \max\{k_1, k_2\} = k \right\}.$$

Without loss of generality, suppose that $1 \leq k_1 \leq k_2 = k$. Then

$$|\bar{B}^{(2)}_k| \frac{\mu\left(U^{(k_1,k_2,l)}\right)}{|B^{(2)}_{k_1,k_2}|} \lesssim 2^{2k} \frac{\mu\left(U^{((k_1,k),l)}\right)}{2^{k_1+k}} = \frac{\mu\left(U^{((k_1,k),l)}\right)}{2^{k_1-k}}.$$

Applying Theorem 16.19, we get

$$|\bar{B}^{(2)}_k| \frac{\mu\left(U^{((k_1,k),l)}\right)}{|B^{(2)}_{(k_1,k)}|} \lesssim \begin{cases} 2^{-(2q+2)k_1-2qk+2(2q+1)l} & k \geq k_1 \geq l \\ 2^{-2q(k-l)} & k \geq l \geq k_1 \\ 2^{-2(p+1)(l-k)} & l \geq k \geq k_1 \end{cases}.$$

From this we deduce that

$$|\bar{B}^{(2)}_k| \max \left\{ \frac{\mu\left(U^{((k_1,k),l)}\right)}{|B^{(2)}_{(k_1,k)}|} : k_1 = 1, \ldots, k \right\} \lesssim \begin{cases} 2^{-2q(k-l)} & k \geq l \\ 2^{-2(p+1)(l-k)} & k < l \end{cases},$$

as required. □

16.4.7 Local Coherence Estimates for Walsh Sampling

We now consider Walsh sampling:

Theorem 16.20 (Walsh DS local coherences) *Let U be the infinite change-of-basis matrix for the periodized Daubechies wavelet and Walsh bases of $L^2([0,1])$, with blocks $U^{(k,l)}$ as in (16.15). If the order $p \geq 3$, then*

$$\mu\left(U^{(k,l)}\right) \lesssim \begin{cases} 2^{-(k-l)} & k \geq l \\ 2^{-(l-k)} & k < l \end{cases}, \qquad k,l = 1,2,\ldots. \tag{16.30}$$

Conversely, if $p = 2$, then

$$\mu\left(U^{(k,l)}\right) \lesssim \begin{cases} 2^{-(2\alpha-1)(k-l)} & k \geq l \\ 2^{-(l-k)} & k < l \end{cases}, \qquad k,l = 1,2,\ldots, \tag{16.31}$$

where $\alpha \approx 0.5500$ is the Hölder continuity of the wavelet (see Table 9.3).

Proof First, notice that Lemma 16.14 gives

$$|\langle \psi^{\mathrm{per},(e)}_{j,n}, \upsilon_i \rangle_{L^2}| \leq 2^{1-j/2} p \max_{-p<l<p} \left\{ \left| \mathcal{H}\left(\psi^{(e)}_{0,l}|_{[0,1)}\right)\left(\lfloor i/2^j \rfloor\right) \right| \right\}. \tag{16.32}$$

Let $i \in B_k$, where B_k is the kth element in the dyadic partition of $\mathbb{N}_0$. Then $i \gtrsim 2^k$ and Lemma 16.15 gives that

$$|\langle \psi^{\mathrm{per},(e)}_{j,n}, \upsilon_i \rangle_{L^2}| \lesssim 2^{-j/2}\left(1 + 2^{k-j}\right)^{-\min\{\alpha,1\}}.$$

Therefore, since $|B_k| \lesssim 2^k$ and $U^{(k,l)}$ corresponds to wavelets at scale $j_0 + l - 2$ and Walsh frequencies in B_k, we get

$$\mu\left(U^{(k,l)}\right) \lesssim 2^{k-l}\left(1 + 2^{k-l}\right)^{-2\min\{\alpha,1\}}.$$

If $k < l$ we deduce that $\mu(U^{(k,l)}) \lesssim 2^{-(l-k)}$. Conversely, when $k \geq l$ we obtain $\mu(U^{(k,l)}) \lesssim 2^{-(2\min\{\alpha,1\}-1)(k-l)}$. We now appeal to Table 9.3. □

As in the proof of Theorem 16.13, we note that this argument relied crucially on the sharp values for the Hölder exponent α given in Table 9.3, in particular, the fact that $\alpha > 1$ for $p \geq 3$.

Next, we consider the two-dimensional case:

Theorem 16.21 (Walsh DAS local coherences) *Let U be the infinite change-of-basis matrix for the periodized Daubechies wavelet and Walsh bases of $L^2([0,1]^2)$, with blocks $U^{(k_1,k_2,l)}$ as in (16.17). If $p \geq 3$, then the local coherences satisfy*

$$\mu\left(U^{(k_1,k_2,l)}\right) \lesssim 2^{-|k_1-l|-|k_2-l|}, \qquad k_1,k_2,l = 1,2,\ldots.$$

Proof The argument is similar to (in fact, simpler than) that of Theorem 16.19, and proceeds by using Theorem 16.20 instead of Theorem 16.16. We omit the details. □

We have excluded the case $p = 2$ here, but it could be considered as well, with suitable modifications along the same line as Theorem 16.20. Finally, we also consider the case of Haar wavelets (i.e. $p = 1$):

Theorem 16.22 (Walsh–Haar DS and DIS local coherences) *Let U be the infinite change-of-basis matrix for the Haar wavelet and Walsh bases of $L^2([0,1])$ or $L^2([0,1]^2)$, with blocks $U^{(k,l)}$ as in (16.15). Then U is block diagonal, $U^{(k,l)} = 0$ for $k \neq l$, and its diagonal blocks are incoherent with*

$$\mu(U^{(k,k)}) = \begin{cases} 1 & d = 1 \\ 3 - 2\delta_{k-1} & d = 2 \end{cases}, \qquad k = 1, 2, \ldots .$$

Proof Consider the one-dimensional case first. The matrix $U^{(k,l)}$ is the change-of-basis matrix between the bases Υ_k and Φ_l. As shown in the proof of Theorem 16.12, $\mathrm{span}(\Upsilon_1) = \mathrm{span}(\Phi_1) = V_0^{\mathrm{per}}$ and $\mathrm{span}(\Upsilon_{j+2}) = \mathrm{span}(\Phi_{j+2}) = W_j^{\mathrm{per}}$ for $j = 0, 1, \ldots$. These spaces are orthogonal, and therefore $\mu(U^{(k,l)}) = 0$ for $k \neq l$.

Since $\langle \varphi, \upsilon_0 \rangle_{L^2} = \|\varphi\|_{L^2}^2 = 1$, we immediately get that $\mu(U^{(1,1)}) = 1$. The fact that $\mu(U^{(k,k)}) = 1$ for $k \geq 2$ also follows from Lemma F.6, since this shows that the coefficients of the Walsh function $\upsilon_{2^{k-2}+n}$ in the Haar basis are precisely $2^{-(k-2)/2}$ in magnitude, and $U^{(k,k)}$ is itself of size $2^{k-2} \times 2^{k-2}$ for $k \geq 2$.

Now consider the two-dimensional case. To deduce block diagonality, we recall the proof of Theorem 16.12 once more and then argue in the same way as above. Now consider the coherences $\mu(U^{(k,k)})$. It is once more immediate that $\mu(U^{(1,1)}) = 1$. Suppose that $k \geq 2$. Observe that the one-dimensional basis functions satisfy $|\langle \upsilon_m, \varphi_{j,n} \rangle| \leq \|\upsilon_m\|_{L^\infty} \|\varphi_{j,n}\|_{L^1} = 2^{-j/2}$ and likewise for $\psi_{j,n}$. Since $U^{(k,k)}$ is of size $3 \times 2^{2(k-2)}$ we immediately deduce that $\mu(U^{(k,k)}) \leq 3$ for $k \geq 2$. Equality follows by observing that there must be at least some entries of $U^{(k,k)}$ of magnitude exactly $2^{-(k-2)}$, due once more to Lemma F.6. □

16.4.8 Proofs of Theorems 16.3–16.8

We are now finally ready to prove the main theorems. We divide these proofs into several cases:

Proof of Theorems 16.3, 16.4 and 16.6 We will use Theorem 14.5 for (A) and Theorem 14.7 for (B). For both, we first need to show that conditions (i) and (ii) of Theorem 14.5 hold (condition (iii) holds by construction).

In the Fourier case (Theorems 16.3 and 16.4), condition (i) follows from either Theorem 16.10 (one dimension) or Theorem 16.11 (two dimensions), and holds with $\theta \geq c_p$, where $c_p > 0$. In the Walsh–Haar case (Theorem 16.6), (i) holds with $N = M$ and $\theta = 1$ (Theorem 16.12). In all cases, condition (ii) follows immediately from this, the assumptions on the m_k and the coherence bounds of Theorems 16.16, 16.18 or 16.22.

Next, we need to estimate the term $\|P_\Omega D U P_M^\perp d\|_{\ell^2}$. In the Walsh–Haar case this is zero, since U is block diagonal (Theorem 16.22) and $\Omega \subseteq \{1, \ldots, M\}$. Thus we need only consider the Fourier case. Lemma 14.6 gives

$$\|P_\Omega D U P_M^\perp d\|_{\ell^2}^2 \leq \left(\sum_{k=1}^{r} \mu\left(P_{N_k}^{N_{k-1}} U P_M^\perp\right) \right) \|P_M^\perp d\|_{\ell^1}^2 . \tag{16.33}$$

Since $M = M_r$, we may use Theorem 16.16 (one dimension) or Theorem 16.18 (two dimensions) to obtain

$$\mu\left(P_{N_k}^{N_{k-1}} U P_M^{\perp}\right) = \sup_{l>r} \mu\left(U^{(k,l)}\right) \lesssim 2^{-(r-k)}, \quad k = 1, \ldots, r.$$

Hence $\sum_{k=1}^{r} \mu\left(P_{N_k}^{N_{k-1}} U P_M^{\perp}\right) \leq c_p$ for some (possibly different) $c_p > 0$, and therefore

$$\|P_\Omega D U P_M^{\perp} d\|_{\ell^2} \leq c_p \|P_M^{\perp} d\|_{\ell^1}. \tag{16.34}$$

In particular, we have shown that $\|P_\Omega D U P_M^{\perp} d\|_{\ell^2} \leq \eta/2$ whenever $\|P_M^{\perp} d\|_{\ell^1} \leq c_p \eta$. Hence, upon recalling that $\theta \geq c_p$, conclusion (A) follows immediately from Theorem 14.5. For (B), we use Theorem 14.7 instead, and (16.34) once more. □

We next consider the proof of Theorem 16.7. For this, we first require a couple of changes, due to the modified partition defined in (16.9). To this end, let us write the matrix $P_N U$ in block form as

$$P_N U = \begin{pmatrix} U^{(1,1)} & U^{(1,2)} & \cdots \\ \vdots & \vdots & \ddots \\ U^{(r-1,1)} & U^{(r-1,2)} & \cdots \\ \widetilde{U}^{(r,1)} & \widetilde{U}^{(r,2)} & \cdots \end{pmatrix}, \tag{16.35}$$

where the matrix

$$\widetilde{U}^{(r,l)} \in \mathbb{C}^{(N_{r+t} - N_{r-1}) \times (M_l - M_{l-1})}$$

is the change-of-basis matrix between the functions $\widetilde{\Upsilon}_r = \{v_i : i \in \widetilde{B}_r\}$ and Φ_l. In particular, we observe that $\widetilde{U}^{(r,l)}$ can be expressed as

$$\widetilde{U}^{(r,l)} = \begin{pmatrix} U^{(r,l)} \\ \vdots \\ U^{(r+t,l)} \end{pmatrix}. \tag{16.36}$$

Proof of Theorem 16.7 As in the previous proof we show that conditions (i) and (ii) of Theorem 14.5 hold, and then estimate $\|P_\Omega D U P_M^{\perp} d\|_{\ell^2}$.

Theorem 16.13 and the fact that $t = c_p$ for some suitable c_p imply that condition (i) holds with $\theta \geq 1/2$ (the factor $1/2$ is arbitrary). Now consider (ii). The conditions on the m_k for $k = 1, \ldots, r-1$ follow immediately from Theorem 16.20. For m_r, we need a small adjustment. Since the final level in the decomposition (16.35) is based on the concatenated matrices $\widetilde{U}^{(r,l)}$, for condition (ii) to hold when $k = r$ we require

$$m_r \gtrsim \left(\sum_{l=1}^{r} s_l \mu\left(\widetilde{U}^{(r,l)}\right)\right) \cdot L. \tag{16.37}$$

Using (16.36) and Theorem 16.20, we estimate the corresponding local coherences as follows. If $1 \leq l \leq r$, then

$$\begin{aligned}\mu\left(\widetilde{U}^{(r,l)}\right) &= (N_{r+t} - N_{r-1}) \max\left\{\frac{\mu\left(U^{(r,l)}\right)}{(N_r - N_{r-1})}, \ldots, \frac{\mu\left(U^{(r+t,l)}\right)}{(N_{r+t} - N_{r+t-1})}\right\} \\ &\lesssim 2^{r+t} \frac{2^{-(2\min\{\alpha,1\}-1)(r-l)}}{2^r} \\ &\lesssim 2^{-(2\min\{\alpha,1\}-1)(r-l)}.\end{aligned}$$

Here, in the final step we use the fact that $t = c_p$. Repeating this procedure for $l > r$ (this will be needed later in the proof), we conclude that

$$\mu\left(\widetilde{U}^{(r,l)}\right) \lesssim \begin{cases} 2^{-(2\min\{\alpha,1\}-1)(r-l)} & l \leq r \\ 2^{-(l-r)} & l > r \end{cases}, \qquad l = 1, 2, \ldots. \tag{16.38}$$

In particular, (16.37) is implied by

$$m_r \gtrsim \left(\sum_{l=1}^{r} s_l 2^{-(2\min\{\alpha,1\}-1)(r-l)}\right) \cdot L,$$

which is an assumption in Theorem 16.7.

It remains to bound $\|P_\Omega D U P_M^\perp d\|_{\ell^2}$. To do this, we argue as in the previous proof, replacing the matrix $P_{N_r}^{N_{r-1}} U P_M^\perp$ in the final term in (16.33) by $P_{N_{r+t}}^{N_{r-1}} U P_M^\perp$, and using the coherence estimate (16.38) for the modified matrices. □

We now move on to the proofs of Theorems 16.5 and 16.8. Recall that in these cases there are r^2 sampling levels and only r sparsity levels. Hence we first need generalizations of Theorems 14.5 and 14.7. We summarize these as follows:

Theorem 16.23 *The conclusions of Theorems 14.5 and 14.7 remain valid when the* $(\mathbf{m}, \mathbf{N})$*-multilevel random sampling scheme consists of* $r' \neq r$ *levels, where* $\mathbf{N} = (N_1, \ldots, N_{r'})$ *are the sampling levels,* $N_{r'} = N$ *and the local numbers of measurements* $\mathbf{m} = (m_1, \ldots, m_{r'})$ *satisfy*

$$m_k \gtrsim \theta^{-2} \cdot \left(\sum_{l=1}^{r} s_l \mu\left(U^{(k,l)}\right)\right) \cdot L, \quad k = 1, \ldots, r', \tag{16.39}$$

instead of (14.17), where $L = r^2 \cdot \log(2m) \cdot \log^2(rs/\theta) \cdot \log(M) + r \cdot \log(\varepsilon^{-1})$.

Proof As in the proofs of Theorems 14.5 and 14.7, it suffices to show that A has the QCBP and SR-LASSO uniform recovery properties of order $(\mathbf{s}, \mathbf{M})$ with suitable constants. Since the balancing property holds, the matrix $\mathbb{E}(A^*A) = P_M U^* P_N U P_M = G^*G$ is positive definite and G satisfies the same bounds as those given in the proof of Theorem 14.5, i.e. $\|G^{-1}\|_{\ell^2} \leq 1/\sqrt{\theta}$ and $\|G\|_{\ell^2} \leq 1$. We also note that A is precisely the matrix that arises from sampling according to the nondegenerate collection $C = \{\mathcal{A}_i\}_{i=1}^m$ that corresponds to the $(\mathbf{m}, \mathbf{N})$-multilevel random sampling scheme applied to $P_N U P_M$. Arguing as in (11.16), we see that the local coherence $\mu_l(\mathcal{A}_i)$ satisfies

$$\mu_l(\mathcal{A}_i) \leq \frac{m}{m_k} \mu(U^{(k,l)}),$$

when i belongs to the kth block of measurements. The result now follows from Theorem 13.14, Remark 13.13 and (16.39). □

Proof of Theorem 16.5 We argue as in the proof of Theorems 16.3 and 16.4, using Theorem 16.23 with $r' = r^2$ instead of Theorems 14.5 and 14.7. Condition (i) is unchanged. The modified version of condition (ii), i.e. (16.39), also follows, since

$$\sum_{l=1}^{r} s_l \mu(U^{(k_1,k_2,l)}) \lesssim \mathcal{M}(\mathbf{s}, k_1, k_2),$$

due to Theorem 16.19 and the definition of $\mathcal{M}(\mathbf{s}, k_1, k_2)$. It remains to estimate the term $\|P_\Omega DUP_M^\perp d\|_{\ell^2}$. Lemma 14.6 gives

$$\|P_\Omega DUP_M^\perp d\|_{\ell^2}^2 \leq \left(\sum_{k_1,k_2=1}^{r} \sup_{l>r} \mu\left(U^{(k_1,k_2,l)}\right) \right) \|P_M^\perp d\|_{\ell^1}^2.$$

From Theorem 16.19 we see that

$$\sum_{k_1,k_2=1}^{r} \sup_{l>r} \mu\left(U^{k_1,k_2,l}\right) \lesssim \sum_{k_1,k_2=1}^{r} 2^{-(r-k_1)-(r-k_2)} \lesssim 1.$$

Hence $\|P_\Omega DUP_M^\perp d\|_{\ell^2} \lesssim \|P_M^\perp d\|_{\ell^1}$, as required. □

For the Walsh case, we once again require several modifications. Consider the modified partition (16.10) and let $N = 2^{2(j_0+r+t-1)}$. Then we can write $P_N U$ in block form

$$P_N U = \begin{pmatrix} U^{(1,1,1)} & U^{(1,1,2)} & U^{(1,1,3)} & \cdots \\ U^{(2,1,1)} & U^{(2,1,2)} & U^{(2,1,3)} & \cdots \\ U^{(2,2,1)} & U^{(2,2,2)} & U^{(2,2,3)} & \cdots \\ U^{(1,2,1)} & U^{(1,2,2)} & U^{(1,2,3)} & \cdots \\ \vdots & \vdots & \vdots & \ddots \\ \widetilde{U}^{(r,1,1)} & \widetilde{U}^{(r,1,2)} & \widetilde{U}^{(r,1,3)} & \cdots \\ \vdots & \vdots & \vdots & \ddots \\ \widetilde{U}^{(r,r,1)} & \widetilde{U}^{(r,r,2)} & \widetilde{U}^{(r,r,3)} & \cdots \\ \vdots & \vdots & \vdots & \ddots \\ \widetilde{U}^{(1,r,1)} & \widetilde{U}^{(1,r,2)} & \widetilde{U}^{(1,r,3)} & \cdots \end{pmatrix}, \tag{16.40}$$

where $\widetilde{U}^{(k_1,k_2,l)}$ is the change-of-basis matrix between $\widetilde{\Upsilon}_{k_1,k_2} = \{v_i : i \in \widetilde{B}^{(2)}_{k_1,k_2}\}$ and Φ_l.

Proof of Theorem 16.8 We modify the steps of the previous proofs as needed. Condition (i) holds with $\theta \geq 1/2$. This is due to Theorem 16.13 and the fact that $t = c_p$ for suitable c_p. For condition (ii), we first note that the modified matrix $\widetilde{U}^{(r,k,l)}$, $k = 1, \ldots, r-1$, is a vertical concatenation of the matrices $U^{(r,k,l)}, \ldots, U^{(r+t,k,l)}$, and similarly for $\widetilde{U}^{(k,r,l)}$, $k = 1, \ldots, r-1$. On the other hand, the matrix $\widetilde{U}^{(r,r,l)}$ is a vertical concatenation of the matrices $\{U^{(r+l_1,r+l_2,t)} : l_1, l_2 = 0, \ldots, t\}$. Hence, we can perform a similar calculation to that carried out in the proof of Theorem 16.7 to estimate the coherences of these modified matrices. Condition (ii) then follows from Theorem 16.21. Finally, we estimate $\|P_\Omega D U P_M^\perp d\|_{\ell^2}$. The modified matrices aside, the argument is identical to that of the Fourier case considered previously. We omit the details. □

Remark 16.24 In §15.4.1 we considered a variant of the DS, DIS and DAS schemes where the sampling within each partition element was nonuniform. This can be analysed in a straightforward manner. Let $\mathbf{N} = (N_1, \ldots, N_{r'})$ be sampling levels, where $N_{r'} = N$, $\mathbf{m} = (m_1, \ldots, m_{r'})$ be local numbers of measurements, and for each k, let $p^{(k)} = (p_i^{(k)})_{i=N_{k-1}+1}^{N_k}$ be a discrete probability distribution on the indices $\{N_{k-1}+1, \ldots, N_k\}$. Notice that we also permit $r' \geq r$ sampling levels here, in order to encompass the DIS case as well. Analogous to Definition 11.13, we call Ω an $(\mathbf{m}, \mathbf{N})$-*variable density* multilevel random sampling scheme if $\Omega = \Omega_1 \cup \cdots \cup \Omega_{r'}$, where, for each k, Ω_k consists of m_k indices chosen independently from $\{N_{k-1}+1, \ldots, N_k\}$ according to $p^{(k)}$ if $m_k < N_k - N_{k-1}$, and $\Omega_k = \{N_{k-1}+1, \ldots, N_k\}$ otherwise.

The matrix A that arises from such a scheme corresponds to a particular nondegenerate collection $C = \{\mathcal{A}_i\}_{i=1}^m$. As in §11.4.5, this is defined as follows. For $m_1 + \cdots + m_{k-1} < i \leq m_1 + \cdots + m_k$ we set $\mathcal{A}_i = \sqrt{m} U^* e_i$ if $m_k = N_k - N_{k-1}$, otherwise we set $\mathcal{A}_i = \mathcal{A}^{(k)}$, where $\mathcal{A}^{(k)}$ is the family of scaled rows of $P_N U P_M$ drawn according to the nonuniform probability distribution $p^{(k)}$. To be precise, $a \sim \mathcal{A}^{(k)}$ if

$$\mathbb{P}\left(a = \sqrt{\frac{m}{m_k p_i^{(k)}}} P_M U^* P_N e_i^* \right) = p_i^{(k)}, \quad i = N_{k-1}+1, \ldots, N_k.$$

A measurement condition for such a matrix is easily derived by arguing as in the proof of Theorem 16.23. Calculating the coherences $\mu_l(\mathcal{A}_i)$ for this new collection gives

$$\mu_l(\mathcal{A}_i) \leq \frac{m}{m_k} \max_{N_{k-1} < i \leq N_k} \max_{M_{l-1} < j \leq M_l} \frac{|u_{ij}|^2}{p_i^{(k)}} \leq \frac{m}{m_k} \frac{1}{P^{(k)}} \mu(U^{(k,l)}),$$

where $P^{(k)} = (N_k - N_{k-1}) \min_{N_{k-1} < i \leq N_k} \{p_i^{(k)}\}$. Hence the measurement condition takes the form

$$m_k \gtrsim \theta^{-2} \cdot \frac{1}{P^{(k)}} \left(\sum_{l=1}^{r} s_l \mu(U^{(k,l)}) \right) \cdot L, \quad k = 1, \ldots, r'.$$

Up to the factor $P^{(k)}$, this is identical to (16.39). In particular, we have established the claim made previously in §15.4.1. Namely, a sufficient measurement condition for variable-density sampling within the sampling levels arises by simply taking the corresponding measurement condition for uniform sampling within the levels and dividing the right-hand side by the factor $P^{(k)}$.

Notes

Propositions 16.1 and 16.2 provide justification for the sparsity in levels model in the setting of wavelet approximation. They allow one to concretely relate compressed sensing to nonlinear wavelet approximation theory. Consider, for instance, $f \in PC^\alpha([0,1])$.

Then, applying Theorem 16.3, it is not difficult to show that compressed sensing from (noiseless) Fourier measurements produces an approximation $\hat{f}$ to f for which

$$\|\hat{f} - f\|_{L^2} \lesssim \|f\|_{PC^\alpha} \frac{(\log(m))^{6\alpha}}{m^\alpha}.$$

Hence, Fourier sampling is near-optimal for the approximation of PC^α functions.

The large log factor is a potential cause for concern. Fortunately, through a more refined selection of the local sparsities $\mathbf{s}$ and measurements $\mathbf{m}$ it can be shown [7] that one can obtain, via compressed sensing, an approximation from m Fourier samples that achieves the rate

$$\|\hat{f} - f\|_{L^2} \lesssim \|f\|_{PC^\alpha} \frac{(\log(m))^{13/4+\delta}}{m^\alpha}, \tag{16.41}$$

for any fixed $0 < \delta < 1$. In particular, this provides a justification for the benefit of Fourier sampling over random Gaussian sampling – the reader will recall the experiments in Chapter 1 that empirically demonstrated this phenomenon. Indeed, random Gaussian sampling yields the error bound

$$\|\hat{f} - f\|_{L^2} \lesssim \|f\|_{PC^\alpha} \frac{(\log(m))^{\alpha}}{m^\alpha}$$

(see [7]), which is worse than (16.41) for sufficiently large α. As noted in [7], the factor 13/4 is likely not sharp. In [7] it was also shown that there is a sampling strategy – albeit not a Fourier sampling strategy – which achieves an $\mathcal{O}\left(m^{-\alpha}\right)$ error without log terms. It is based on sparsity in levels and a two-level sampling scheme that acquires the coarse-scale wavelet coefficients directly and then uses random Gaussian sampling for the fine scales. In other words, there is an *encoder–decoder pair* based on compressed sensing that achieves an $m^{-\alpha}$ rate over $PC^\alpha([0,1])$ without any log factors.

Theorems 16.3–16.8 are new, although a variant of Theorem 16.7 based on boundary-corrected Daubechies wavelets was shown earlier in [3]. The coherence estimates for Walsh sampling were shown in [34]. One could also consider boundary-corrected wavelets in the Fourier setting as well, with some additional technical hurdles (much as in the Walsh case with periodic wavelets) to ensure the balancing property.

Theorem 16.22 on the block diagonality of the Walsh–Haar matrix follows from Lemma F.6, which is a classical result relating the Walsh and Haar bases. See, for example, [232, §1.3]. See also [361, 362].

Theorem 16.10 is based on a result proved in [19], which considered a slightly different setup. Similarly, a version of Theorem 16.13 for boundary-corrected wavelets was shown in [257]. We have used much the same arguments for the periodized wavelets. For more on the theoretical analysis of reconstructions from binary measurements, see for example, [107, 458].

17 Total Variation Minimization

The previous two chapters focused on wavelets. In this chapter, we consider the discrete gradient transform and the corresponding TV minimization problem. We commence in §17.1 with the formal definition of the discrete gradient operator and TV semi-norm. Next, in §17.2 we demonstrate two curious phenomena. First, it is possible to recover a gradient-sparse image from a small number of its Fourier samples taken randomly and uniformly, unlike in the case of wavelet sparsity. However, and second, the recovery is significantly enhanced by sampling with a variable-density scheme. The main recovery guarantees for TV minimization, which are stated in §17.3, explain this phenomenon. They assert near-optimal accuracy and stability in the recovery of the image gradient from uniform random Fourier samples, yet suboptimal accuracy and stability in the recovery of the image itself. On the other hand, augmenting these samples with suitable variable-density Fourier samples ensures near optimality of both the recovered gradient *and* the recovered image. Proofs are given in §17.4. Since these results are specific to Fourier sampling, in §17.5 we provide recovery guarantees for more general sampling operators, which includes Walsh sampling. Finally, we conclude in §17.6 by discussing some limitations of the analysis. In particular, as seen in previous chapters, we show that the best sampling strategy is in practice image dependent, a phenomenon that is not apparent from the recovery guarantees given in §17.3 and §17.5.

17.1 Definitions

We consider discrete images in one or two dimensions at resolution $N = 2^r$, where $r \geq 1$ is an integer. We write $x = (x_i)_{i=1}^N$ for a one-dimensional discrete image. As in §2.1, we write $X = (X_{i_1,i_2})_{i_1,i_2=1}^N \in \mathbb{C}^{N \times N}$ for a two-dimensional discrete image and $\mathrm{vec}(X) = x = (x_i)_{i=1}^{N^2}$ for its vectorization.

Definition 17.1 (Discrete gradient and TV semi-norm, $d = 1$) The *one-dimensional discrete gradient operator* $\nabla : \mathbb{C}^N \to \mathbb{C}^N$ is defined by

$$(\nabla x)_i = x_{i+1} - x_i, \quad i = 1, \ldots, N,$$

for $x = (x_i)_{i=1}^N$, where $x_{N+1} = x_1$. The one-dimensional *Total Variation (TV)* semi-norm $\|\cdot\|_{TV}$ is defined by

$$\|x\|_{TV} = \|\nabla x\|_{\ell^1}.$$

This definition imposes periodic boundary conditions, the value x_{N+1} being identified with x_1. Other definitions are possible. However, this version is particularly useful for both theory and computations, since it endows the gradient operator ∇ with a circulant structure. Specifically, ∇ can be represented as the $N \times N$ circulant matrix

$$\nabla = \begin{pmatrix} -1 & 1 & & & \\ & -1 & 1 & & \\ & & \ddots & \ddots & \\ 1 & & & & -1 \end{pmatrix}. \tag{17.1}$$

Definition 17.2 The *two-dimensional vertical and horizontal gradient operators* $\nabla_1 \colon \mathbb{C}^{N\times N} \to \mathbb{C}^{N\times N}$ and $\nabla_2 \colon \mathbb{C}^{N\times N} \to \mathbb{C}^{N\times N}$ are defined by

$$(\nabla_1 X)_{i_1,i_2} = X_{i_1+1,i_2} - X_{i_1,i_2}, \quad (\nabla_2 X)_{i_1,i_2} = X_{i_1,i_2+1} - X_{i_1,i_2}, \qquad i_1, i_2 = 1,\dots,N,$$

respectively for $X = (X_{i_1,i_2})_{i_1,i_2=1}^N$, where $X_{i_1,N+1} = X_{i_1,1}$ and $X_{N+1,i_2} = X_{1,i_2}$ for $i_1, i_2 = 1,\dots,N$.

In two dimensions there is more than one way to define the corresponding total variation semi-norm:

Definition 17.3 (Discrete gradient and TV semi-norm, $d = 2$) The two-dimensional *isotropic discrete gradient operator* $\nabla \colon \mathbb{C}^{N\times N} \to \mathbb{C}^{N\times N}$ is defined by

$$\nabla X = \nabla_1 X + \mathrm{i}\nabla_2 X,$$

where i is the imaginary unit. The two-dimensional *anisotropic discrete gradient operator* $\nabla \colon \mathbb{C}^{N\times N} \to \mathbb{C}^{N\times 2N}$ is defined by

$$\nabla X = (\nabla_1 X | \nabla_2 X).$$

In either case, the two-dimensional TV semi-norm is defined by

$$\|X\|_{TV} = \|\nabla X\|_{\ell^{1,1}},$$

where $\|\cdot\|_{\ell^{1,1}}$ denotes the matrix $\ell^{1,1}$-norm (see (A.14)).

For convenience, if $x = \mathrm{vec}(X)$ is the vectorization of X we will also use the notation ∇x and $\|x\|_{TV}$ from now on to denote ∇X and $\|X\|_{TV}$, respectively.

Writing out the $\ell^{1,1}$-norm in each of the above cases gives

$$\|X\|_{TV} = \|X\|_{TV_i} = \sum_{i_1,i_2=1}^{N} \sqrt{|X_{i_1+1,i_2} - X_{i_1,i_2}|^2 + |X_{i_1,i_2+1} - X_{i_1,i_2}|^2},$$

for the isotropic TV semi-norm, which is denoted by $\|\cdot\|_{TV_i}$ for emphasis, and

$$\|X\|_{TV} = \|X\|_{TV_a} = \sum_{i_1,i_2=1}^{N} \left(|X_{i_1+1,i_2} - X_{i_1,i_2}| + |X_{i_1,i_2+1} - X_{i_1,i_2}|\right),$$

for the anisotropic TV semi-norm, which is denoted by $\|\cdot\|_{TV_a}$. Both versions of the TV semi-norm are used in practical compressive imaging. We shall not dwell on the differences between the two. However, we do note in passing that

$$\|X\|_{TV_i} \leq \|X\|_{TV_a} \leq \sqrt{2}\|X\|_{TV_i}. \tag{17.2}$$

For the sake of consistency, we henceforth consider the isotropic TV semi-norm, unless otherwise stated, and simply write $\|\cdot\|_{TV}$. The theoretical results presented later can, however, be adapted to the anisotropic case.

Consider a discrete image $x \in \mathbb{C}^{N^d}$, where $d = 1, 2$. Let $A \in \mathbb{C}^{m \times N^d}$ be a measurement matrix and

$$y = Ax + e \in \mathbb{C}^m$$

be noisy measurements of x. For the remainder of this chapter, we focus on the quadratically constrained TV minimization problem

$$\min_{z \in \mathbb{C}^{N^d}} \|z\|_{TV} \text{ subject to } \|Az - y\|_{\ell^2} \leq \eta, \tag{17.3}$$

where $\eta \geq 0$ is such that $\|e\|_{\ell^2} \leq \eta$. Note that one could also consider the LASSO or SR-LASSO instead (see Chapter 6), but for simplicity we will not do this.

17.2 Two Curious Experiments

As seen in previous chapters, effective Fourier sampling strategies for wavelet sparsity are of variable-density type and feature denser sampling at low frequencies than at high frequencies. Recall from §11.1.1 that wavelet sparsifying transforms yield poor recovery from samples taken uniformly at random. In Fig. 17.1 we show the reconstruction of an image from uniform random Fourier samples using either wavelets or TV minimization. As expected, wavelets give a very poor reconstruction. However, TV minimization gives a much more palatable recovery, especially at the higher sampling percentage. Although there are still artefacts, the visual quality of the image is substantially better.

The first theoretical results in the next section explain this observation. In particular, they show that recovery is possible with TV minimization from uniform random Fourier samples. However, they also show that the accuracy and stability estimates for the recovery of the image are not optimal.

This raises the following question: what is a more effective sampling strategy for TV minimization? In Fig. 17.2 we consider variable-density Fourier sampling, according to the inverse square law. As is evident, the reconstruction is significantly better than that obtained from uniform random samples in Fig. 17.1. Our second set of theoretical results strives to explain this phenomenon. Specifically, they show that variable-density sampling leads to better accuracy and stability estimates than uniform random sampling.

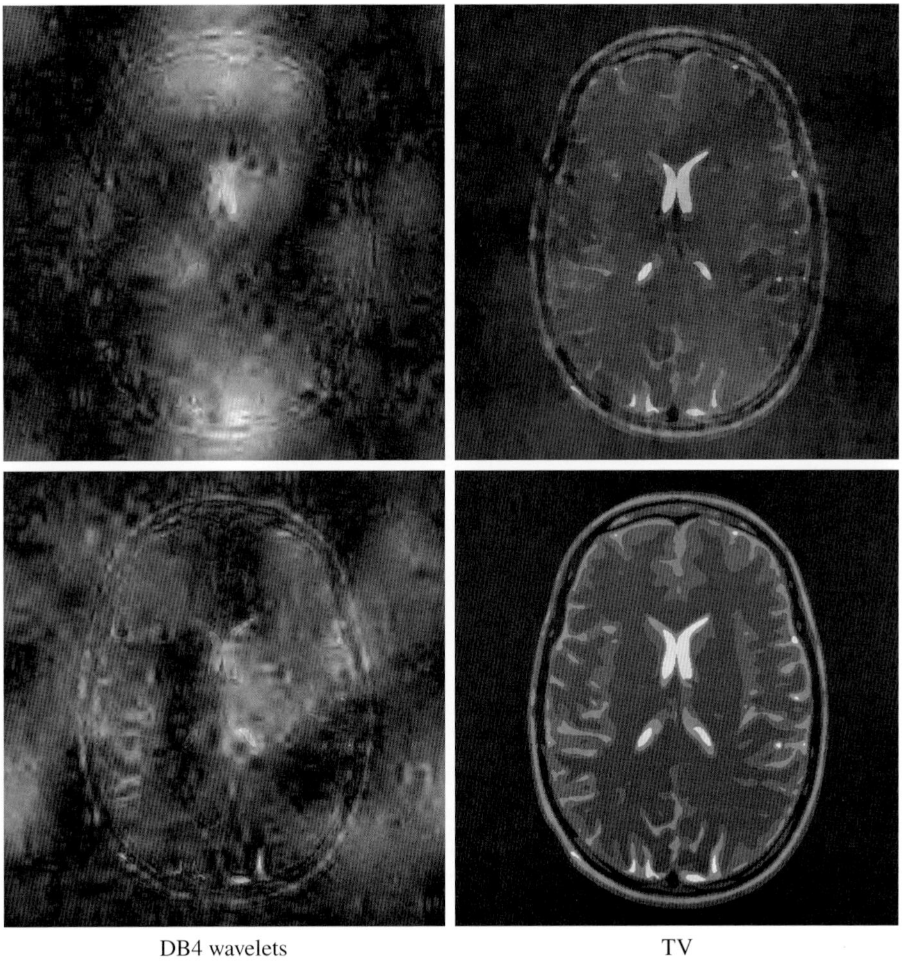

Figure 17.1 Recovery of the discrete 512×512 GLPU phantom from 10% (top row) or 15% (bottom row) uniform random Fourier samples with different sparsifying transforms.

17.3 Recovery Guarantees for Fourier Sampling

We now present recovery guarantees for Fourier sampling. We write $F \in \mathbb{C}^{N \times N}$ or $F \in \mathbb{C}^{N^2 \times N^2}$ for the one- or two-dimensional Fourier matrix (Definition 2.1).

17.3.1 Uniform Random Sampling

We first consider uniform random sampling (Definition 4.1):

Theorem 17.4 (Uniform random Fourier sampling, $d = 1$) *Let $0 < \varepsilon < 1$, $N \geq s, m \geq 2$ and $\Omega = \Omega_1 \cup \Omega_2$, where $\Omega_1 \subseteq \{-N/2+1, \ldots, N/2\}$ is a uniform random sampling*

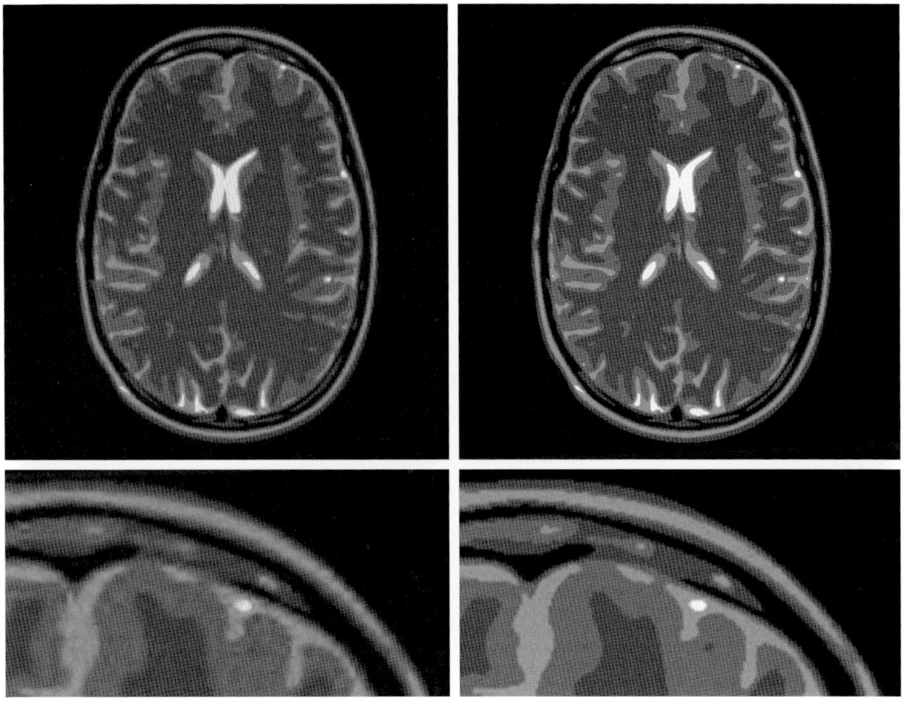

Figure 17.2 Recovery of the discrete 512×512 GLPU phantom from 10% variable density Fourier samples taken according to the inverse square law (4.2) with different sparsifying transforms. Top row: Full image. Bottom row: Crops.

scheme of order m and $\Omega_2 = \{0\}$. Let $A = m^{-1/2} P_\Omega F$ and suppose that

$$m \gtrsim s \cdot \left(\log^3(s) \cdot \log(N) + \log(\varepsilon^{-1})\right).$$

Then the following holds with probability at least $1 - \varepsilon$. For all $x \in \mathbb{C}^N$ and $y = Ax + e \in \mathbb{C}^m$, every minimizer $\hat{x} \in \mathbb{C}^N$ of (17.3) with parameter $\eta \geq \|e\|_{\ell^2}$ satisfies

$$\|\nabla x - \nabla \hat{x}\|_{\ell^2} \lesssim \frac{\sigma_s(\nabla x)_{\ell^1}}{\sqrt{s}} + \eta, \quad \|x - \hat{x}\|_{TV} \lesssim \sigma_s(\nabla x)_{\ell^1} + \sqrt{s}\eta, \tag{17.4}$$

and

$$\frac{\|x - \hat{x}\|_{\ell^2}}{\sqrt{N}} \lesssim \sigma_s(\nabla x)_{\ell^1} + \sqrt{s}\eta. \tag{17.5}$$

Theorem 17.5 (Uniform random Fourier sampling, $d = 2$) *Let $0 < \varepsilon < 1$, $N^2 \geq s, m \geq 2$ and $\Omega = \Omega_1 \cup \Omega_2$, where $\Omega_1 \subseteq \{-N/2 + 1, \ldots, N/2\}^2$ is a uniform random sampling scheme of order m and $\Omega_2 = \{(0, 0)\}$. Let $A = m^{-1/2} P_\Omega F$ and suppose that*

$$m \gtrsim s \cdot \left(\log^3(s) \cdot \log(N) + \log(\varepsilon^{-1})\right).$$

Then the following holds with probability at least $1-\varepsilon$. *For all* $x \in \mathbb{C}^{N^2}$ *and* $y = Ax+e \in \mathbb{C}^m$, *every minimizer* $\hat{x} \in \mathbb{C}^{N^2}$ *of (17.3) with parameter* $\eta \geq \|e\|_{\ell^2}$ *satisfies*

$$\|\nabla x - \nabla \hat{x}\|_{\ell^2} \lesssim \frac{\sigma_s(\nabla x)_{\ell^1}}{\sqrt{s}} + \eta, \quad \|x - \hat{x}\|_{TV} \lesssim \sigma_s(\nabla x)_{\ell^1} + \sqrt{s}\eta, \tag{17.6}$$

and

$$\|x - \hat{x}\|_{\ell^2} \lesssim \sigma_s(\nabla x)_{\ell^1} + \sqrt{s}\eta. \tag{17.7}$$

Here, we remind the reader that P_Ω is simply a shorthand for $P_{\varrho^{-1}(\Omega)}$, where $\varrho\colon \{1,\dots, N^d\} \to \{-N/2+1,\dots,N/2\}^d$ is the bijection (2.14). See Remark 12.13.

Observe that the condition on m is precisely the same as that which ensures that the randomly subsampled Fourier matrix $m^{-1/2}P_{\Omega_1}F$ has the RIP of order s (see §5.6.4). As we see later, this is a crucial element of the proof.

17.3.2 Variable-Density Sampling

We now consider variable-density sampling (Definition 4.4). Specifically, in the following results we augment the measurements with samples taken according to the inverse linear law (4.1) in one dimension or the inverse square law (4.2) in two dimensions.

Theorem 17.6 (Variable-density Fourier sampling, $d = 1$) *Let* $0 < \varepsilon < 1$, $N \geq s, m \geq 2$ *and* $\Omega = \Omega_1 \cup \Omega_2 \subseteq \{-N/2+1,\dots,N/2\}$, *where* Ω_1 *is a uniform random sampling scheme of order* m *and* Ω_2 *is a variable-density sampling scheme of order* m *corresponding to the inverse linear law (4.1). Let* $A = m^{-1/2}P_\Omega F$ *and suppose that*

$$m \gtrsim s \cdot \log(N) \cdot \left(\log^2(s) \cdot \log(s\log(N)) \cdot \log(N) + \log(2\varepsilon^{-1})\right). \tag{17.8}$$

Then the following holds with probability at least $1-\varepsilon$. *For all* $x \in \mathbb{C}^N$ *and* $y = Ax+e \in \mathbb{C}^m$, *every minimizer* $\hat{x} \in \mathbb{C}^N$ *of (17.3) with parameter* $\eta \geq \|e\|_{\ell^2}$ *satisfies*

$$\|\nabla x - \nabla \hat{x}\|_{\ell^2} \lesssim \frac{\sigma_s(\nabla x)_{\ell^1}}{\sqrt{s}} + \eta, \quad \|x - \hat{x}\|_{TV} \lesssim \sigma_s(\nabla x)_{\ell^1} + \sqrt{s}\eta, \tag{17.9}$$

and

$$\frac{\|x - \hat{x}\|_{\ell^2}}{\sqrt{N}} \lesssim \frac{\sigma_s(\nabla x)_{\ell^1}}{s} + \left(\sqrt{\frac{\log(N)}{N}} + \frac{1}{\sqrt{s}}\right)\eta. \tag{17.10}$$

Theorem 17.7 (Variable-density Fourier sampling, $d = 2$) *Let* $0 < \varepsilon < 1$, $N^2 \geq s, m \geq 2$ *and* $\Omega = \Omega_1 \cup \Omega_2 \subseteq \{-N/2+1,\dots,N/2\}^2$, *where* Ω_1 *is a uniform random sampling scheme of order* m *and* Ω_2 *is a variable-density sampling scheme of order* m *corresponding to the inverse square law (4.2). Let* $A = m^{-1/2}P_\Omega F$ *and suppose that*

$$m \gtrsim s \cdot \log^3(N) \cdot \left(\log^3(s\log(N)) \cdot \log(N) + \log(2\varepsilon^{-1})\right). \tag{17.11}$$

Then the following holds with probability at least $1-\varepsilon$. *For all* $x \in \mathbb{C}^{N^2}$ *and* $y = Ax+e \in \mathbb{C}^m$, *every minimizer* $\hat{x} \in \mathbb{C}^{N^2}$ *of (17.3) with parameter* $\eta \geq \|e\|_{\ell^2}$ *satisfies*

$$\|\nabla x - \nabla \hat{x}\|_{\ell^2} \lesssim \frac{\sigma_s(\nabla x)_{\ell^1}}{\sqrt{s}} + \eta, \quad \|x - \hat{x}\|_{TV} \lesssim \sigma_s(\nabla x)_{\ell^1} + \sqrt{s}\eta, \tag{17.12}$$

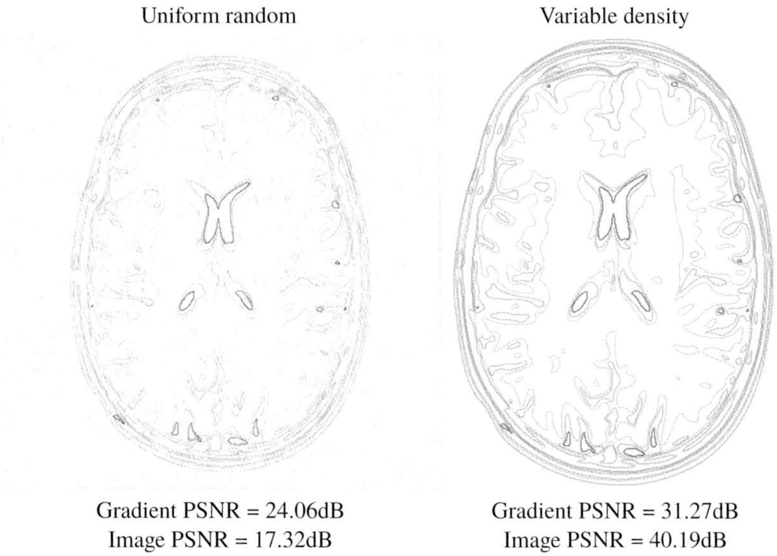

Figure 17.3 Recovery of $|\nabla x|$, where ∇ is the isotropic discrete gradient operator and x is the discrete 512×512 GLPU phantom, from 10% samples. Left: Uniform random sampling. Right: Variable-density sampling according to the inverse square law (4.2). The greyscale has been reversed for visualization purposes.

and

$$\|x - \hat{x}\|_{\ell^2} \lesssim \frac{\sigma_s(\nabla x)_{\ell^1}}{\sqrt{s}} + \eta\sqrt{\log(N)}. \qquad (17.13)$$

17.3.3 Discussion

These four theorems demonstrate the following. On the one hand, uniform random sampling provides stable and accurate recovery of the image gradient ∇x, with the latter measured in terms of the best s-term approximation error $\sigma_s(\nabla x)_{\ell^1}$. On the other hand, without the additional variable-density samples, the recovery of the image itself is worse by a factor of roughly $\sqrt{s}$.

This phenomenon can be seen in practice. In Fig. 17.3 we show the recovery of $|\nabla x|$ from the experiments conducted previously in Figs 17.1 and 17.2. As expected, the recovery of the gradient is much more consistent across the two sampling strategies than the recovery of image x. In Fig. 17.4 we present a more comprehensive demonstration of this effect. Here we perturb either the image x (to study accuracy) or the measurements y (to study stability) and compute the error in the reconstructed image and its gradient. We use the SL phantom, since its gradient is exactly sparse, and compare the recovery from uniform random and variable-density samples. As predicted, the image recovery is better for variable-density samples than uniform random samples, whereas the gradient recoveries are very similar.

Intuitively, this phenomenon can be explained as follows. Since it has periodic boundary conditions, the gradient operator ∇ is diagonalized by the Fourier matrix F, i.e.

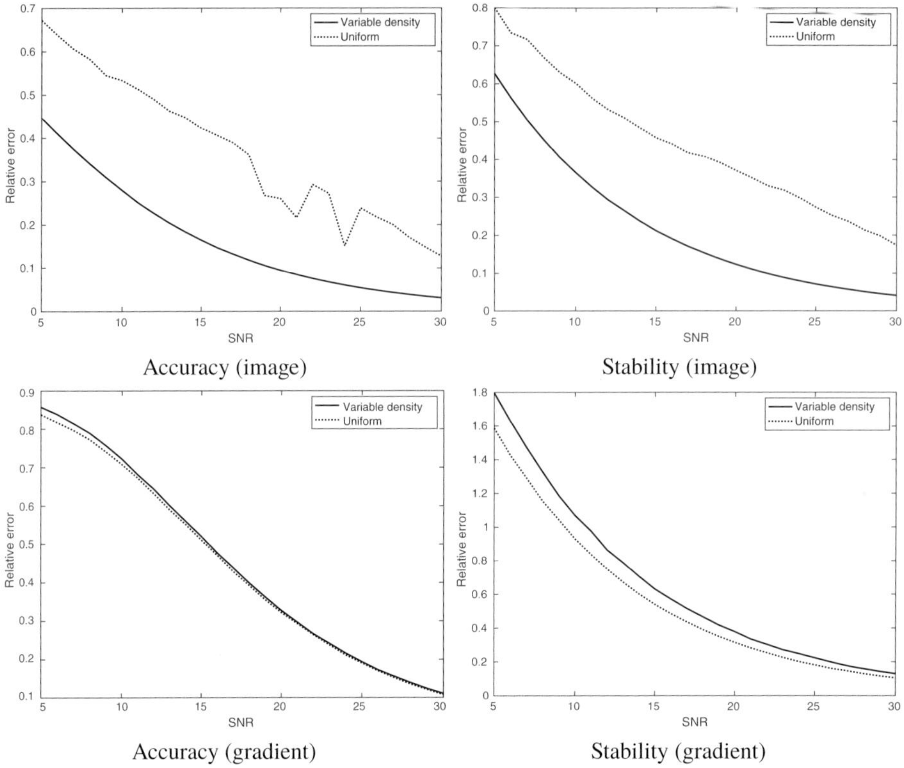

Figure 17.4 Recovery of the discrete 256×256 SL phantom from 25% Fourier measurements using either uniform random sampling or variable-density sampling according to (4.2). The horizontal axis shows the signal-to-noise ratio (SNR) of the perturbation and the vertical axis shows the relative error in the recovered image (top row) or recovered image gradient (bottom row). For the accuracy experiment (left), the image x is randomly perturbed to $x + h$. The SNR and relative error are defined as $20 \log_{10}(\|x\|_{\ell^2} / \|h\|_{\ell^2})$ and $\|\hat{x} - (x + h)\|_{\ell^2} / \|x + h\|_{\ell^2}$ (top row) or $\|\nabla(\hat{x} - (x + h))\|_{\ell^2} / \|\nabla(x + h)\|_{\ell^2}$ (bottom row), respectively, where $\hat{x}$ is the reconstruction of $x + h$. For the stability experiment, the measurements y are randomly perturbed to $y + h$. The SNR and relative error are defined as $20 \log_{10}(\|y\|_{\ell^2} / \|h\|_{\ell^2})$ and $\|\hat{x} - x\|_{\ell^2} / \|x\|_{\ell^2}$ (top row) or $\|\nabla(\hat{x} - x)\|_{\ell^2} / \|\nabla x\|_{\ell^2}$ (bottom row), respectively, where $\hat{x}$ is the reconstruction obtained from measurements $y + h$.

$F\nabla = DF$ for some diagonal matrix D. Hence the recovery of the image gradient ∇x reduces to the problem of recovering a sparse vector from samples of its Fourier transform. The Fourier matrix F is perfectly incoherent, therefore we expect accurate and stable recovery of ∇x from uniform random samples.

Now consider the image recovery. Since the constant vector lies in the null space of the gradient operator, it is generally impossible to recover x from ∇x alone. This is why the zero frequency is added in Theorems 17.4 and 17.5. However, the accuracy and stability of the image recovery is worse, since the gradient operator ∇ is ill-conditioned for large N. In particular, smooth functions (i.e. image textures) lie approximately in its null space. Yet, the Fourier transform of a smooth function decays rapidly with increasing frequency.

Hence, adding variable-density samples overcomes this issue by sampling more densely near the origin, thus stabilizing the recovery of the smooth image components.

Remark 17.8 A major difference between the two sets of results is that the one-dimensional image recovery bounds (17.5) and (17.10) involve a $1/\sqrt{N}$ factor, whereas the two-dimensional bounds (17.7) and (17.13) do not. The reason for this factor can be explained by viewing x as the discretization of a continuous image $f\colon [0,1]^d \to \mathbb{R}$. Indeed, suppose that $x \in \mathbb{C}^{N^d}$ is the discretization of f at resolution N, see (2.5). Then

$$\|f\|_{L^p}^p \approx N^{-d}\|x\|_{\ell^p}^p,$$

for large N, and, in particular, $\|f\|_{L^2} \approx N^{-d/2}\|x\|_{\ell^2}$. Moreover, assuming sufficient smoothness of f and taking finite differences, the total variation $V(f)$ of f satisfies

$$V(f) = \int_{[0,1]^d} \sqrt{\sum_{j=1}^{d} \left|\frac{\partial f}{\partial t_j}\right|^2}\, \mathrm{d}t \approx N^{1-d}\|x\|_{TV}.$$

Hence, for $d = 1$ one has

$$\|x\|_{\ell^2}/\sqrt{N} \approx \|f\|_{L^2}, \qquad V(f) \approx \|x\|_{TV},$$

which explains the $1/\sqrt{N}$ factor in (17.5) and (17.10), whereas when $d = 2$ one has

$$\|x\|_{\ell^2}/N \approx \|f\|_{L^2}, \qquad V(f) \approx \|x\|_{TV}/N,$$

which explains the absence of this factor in (17.7) and (17.13).

17.4 Proofs

We now prove Theorems 17.4–17.7. This is divided into three parts. In the first part, we establish accurate and stable recovery of the gradient ∇x. This is derived from the set Ω_1, and exploits the fact that the discrete gradient operator is diagonalized by the Fourier matrix. Next we address the recovery of the image itself. In the case of uniform random sampling, we first establish the following discrete version of *Poincaré's inequality*:

$$\begin{aligned} \|z\|_{\ell^2} &\leq \|Az\|_{\ell^2} + \sqrt{N}\|z\|_{TV}, \quad \forall z \in \mathbb{C}^N, \\ \|z\|_{\ell^2} &\leq \|Az\|_{\ell^2} + \sqrt{2}\|z\|_{TV}, \quad \forall z \in \mathbb{C}^{N^2}. \end{aligned} \tag{17.14}$$

The estimates for $\|\hat{x} - x\|_{\ell^2}$ then follow immediately by setting $z = \hat{x} - x$ and using the existing gradient error bounds.

The case of variable-density sampling requires substantially more effort. It involves using the variable-density samples Ω_2 to prove a strengthened version of (17.14):

$$\begin{aligned} \|z\|_{\ell^2} &\lesssim \sqrt{\log(N)}\|Az\|_{\ell^2} + \sqrt{N}\|z\|_{TV}/s, \quad \forall z \in \mathbb{C}^N, \\ \|z\|_{\ell^2} &\lesssim \sqrt{\log(N)}\|Az\|_{\ell^2} + \|z\|_{TV}/\sqrt{s}, \quad \forall z \in \mathbb{C}^{N^2}. \end{aligned} \tag{17.15}$$

Perhaps surprisingly, the proof of this inequality uses Haar wavelets. Specifically, it relies on the fact that the Haar basis Φ is incoherent with variable-density Fourier sampling, and therefore a suitably rescaled version of $A\Phi$ satisfies the RIP. To obtain (17.15), one then uses the fact that discrete Haar wavelet coefficients can be bounded in terms of the TV semi-norm, similar to what was done in the continuous setting in §10.4. With (17.15) in hand, the bounds for $\|x - x\|_{\ell^2}$ follow once more from the existing gradient error bounds.

17.4.1 Part I: Gradient Recovery

The one-dimensional discrete gradient operator (17.1) is a circulant matrix, hence it is diagonalized by the Fourier matrix:

$$F\nabla = \operatorname{diag}(d)F, \tag{17.16}$$

where $d = (d_i)_{i=1}^N \in \mathbb{C}^N$ has entries $d_i = \exp(2\pi \mathrm{i}\varrho(i)/N) - 1$. We informally refer to (17.16) as the *commuting property* of the discrete gradient operator with the Fourier matrix.

A similar situation arises in two dimensions. Let $\nabla_1 \in \mathbb{R}^{N^2 \times N^2}$ and $\nabla_2 \in \mathbb{R}^{N^2 \times N^2}$ denote the matrices of the horizontal and vertical gradient operators, respectively. Then

$$\nabla_1 = I \otimes \nabla, \quad \nabla_2 = \nabla \otimes I,$$

where ∇ is the one-dimensional discrete gradient matrix and $\otimes$ is the Kronecker product. Recall that the two-dimensional Fourier matrix $F = F^{(2)} \in \mathbb{C}^{N^2 \times N^2}$ is defined as

$$F^{(2)} = F \otimes F,$$

where $F \in \mathbb{C}^{N \times N}$ is the one-dimensional Fourier matrix. Hence, using standard properties of Kronecker products (see §A.9), we get

$$F^{(2)}\nabla_1 = (I \otimes \operatorname{diag}(d))\, F^{(2)}, \qquad F^{(2)}\nabla_2 = (\operatorname{diag}(d) \otimes I)\, F^{(2)}. \tag{17.17}$$

Since the isotropic two-dimensional discrete gradient operator is given by $\nabla = \nabla^{(2)} = \nabla_1 + \mathrm{i}\nabla_2$, this implies the commuting property

$$F^{(2)}\nabla^{(2)} = DF^{(2)}, \tag{17.18}$$

where D is the diagonal matrix $D = I \otimes \operatorname{diag}(d) + \mathrm{i}\operatorname{diag}(d) \otimes I$.

Proof of Theorems 17.4–17.7 (gradient error) We now show the gradient recovery estimates (17.4), (17.6), (17.9) and (17.12). In all cases, notice first that

$$A = \begin{pmatrix} A_1 \\ A_2 \end{pmatrix}, \qquad A_i = \frac{1}{\sqrt{m}} P_{\Omega_i} F, \quad i = 1, 2. \tag{17.19}$$

The matrix A_1 is a randomly subsampled unitary matrix in the sense of Definition 5.6. The normalized Fourier matrix is perfectly incoherent. Hence Theorem 5.27 gives that (with probability at least $1 - \varepsilon$) A_1 has the RIP of order s with constant $\delta_s \leq 1/4$ whenever

$$m \gtrsim s \cdot \left(\log^3(s) \cdot \log(N) + \log(\varepsilon^{-1})\right)$$

(the factor $1/4$ is arbitrary; any constant less than $\sqrt{2} - 1$ will suffice). This condition holds due to the assumption on m. Lemma 5.20 now implies that A_1 has the rNSP with constants $\rho \leq \sqrt{2}/3$ and $\gamma \leq \sqrt{20}/3$. Hence, we may apply Lemma 5.15 to $\nabla\hat{x}$ and ∇x and use the fact that

$$\|\nabla\hat{x}\|_{\ell^1} = \|\hat{x}\|_{TV} \leq \|x\|_{TV} = \|\nabla x\|_{\ell^1},$$

since $\hat{x}$ is a minimizer and x is feasible for (17.3), to get

$$\|\hat{x} - x\|_{TV} = \|\nabla\hat{x} - \nabla x\|_{\ell^1} \lesssim \sigma_s(\nabla x)_{\ell^1} + \sqrt{s}\|A_1\nabla(\hat{x} - x)\|_{\ell^2}.$$

Consider the second term. When $d = 1$ the commuting property (17.16) gives

$$A_1\nabla = \frac{1}{\sqrt{m}}P_{\Omega_1}F\nabla = \frac{1}{\sqrt{m}}P_{\Omega_1}\mathrm{diag}(d)F.$$

Using this and the bound $\|d\|_{\ell^\infty} \leq 2$ we obtain

$$\begin{aligned}\|A_1\nabla(\hat{x} - x)\|_{\ell^2} = \frac{1}{\sqrt{m}}\|P_{\Omega_1}\mathrm{diag}(d)F(\hat{x} - x)\|_{\ell^2} &\leq \frac{2}{\sqrt{m}}\|P_{\Omega_1}F(\hat{x} - x)\|_{\ell^2} \\ &= 2\|A_1(\hat{x} - x)\|_{\ell^2} \\ &\leq 2\|A(\hat{x} - x)\|_{\ell^2} \leq 4\eta,\end{aligned} \tag{17.20}$$

where in the last step we use the fact that x and $\hat{x}$ are both feasible. Similarly, when $d = 2$ we use (17.18) to get

$$\|A_1\nabla(\hat{x} - x)\|_{\ell^2} \leq 4\|A_1(\hat{x} - x)\|_{\ell^2} \leq 8\eta. \tag{17.21}$$

Therefore, in both cases, we deduce that

$$\|\hat{x} - x\|_{TV} \lesssim \sigma_s(\nabla x)_{\ell^1} + \sqrt{s}\eta,$$

which gives the first set of bounds. Next, applying Lemma 5.16 we get

$$\|\nabla\hat{x} - \nabla x\|_{\ell^2} \lesssim \sigma_s(\nabla x)_{\ell^1}/\sqrt{s} + \|A_1\nabla(\hat{x} - x)\|_{\ell^2}.$$

To complete the proof, we use (17.20) or (17.21) once more. □

17.4.2 Part II: Image Recovery for Uniform Random Sampling

Having shown recovery guarantees for the gradient, we now show the recovery bounds for the image x itself. In this section, we consider uniform random sampling (i.e. $\Omega_2 = \{0\}$).

Lemma 17.9 (Poincaré's inequality, $d = 1$) *Let $x \in \mathbb{C}^N$ satisfy $\sum_{i=1}^N x_i = 0$. Then*

$$\|x\|_{\ell^2} \leq \sqrt{N}\|x\|_{TV}. \tag{17.22}$$

Proof Suppose that $1 \leq j < i \leq N$. Then

$$x_i - x_j = \sum_{l=j+1}^{i}(x_l - x_{l-1}).$$

Conversely, if $1 \leq i < j \leq N$ then

$$x_i - x_j = -\sum_{l=i+1}^{j}(x_l - x_{l-1}).$$

Hence, summing over i and using the fact that $\sum_{i=1}^{N} x_i = 0$ gives

$$N x_j = \sum_{i=1}^{j-1} \sum_{l=i+1}^{j} (x_l - x_{l-1}) - \sum_{i=j+1}^{N} \sum_{l=j+1}^{i} (x_l - x_{l-1}).$$

We deduce that $N|x_j| \leq N\|x\|_{TV}$, $\forall j = 1, \ldots, N$. Hence $\|x\|_{\ell^2}^2 = \sum_{j=1}^{N} |x_j|^2 \leq N\|x\|_{TV}^2$, as required. □

Lemma 17.10 (Poincaré's inequality, $d = 2$) *Let $X = (X_{i_1,i_2}) \in \mathbb{C}^{N\times N}$ satisfy $\sum_{i_1,i_2=1}^{N} X_{i_1,i_2} = 0$. Then*

$$\|X\|_{\ell^{2,2}} \leq \|X\|_{TV_a} \leq \sqrt{2}\|X\|_{TV_i}, \tag{17.23}$$

where $\|\cdot\|_{TV_a}$ and $\|\cdot\|_{TV_i}$ are the anisotropic and isotropic TV semi-norms, respectively.

Proof Write $X_{i_1,i_2} - X_{j_1,j_2} = X_{i_1,i_2} - X_{i_1,j_2} + X_{i_1,j_2} - X_{j_1,j_2}$. For $1 \leq i_1 < j_1 \leq N$ and $1 \leq i_2 < j_2 \leq N$ we have

$$X_{i_1,i_2} - X_{j_1,j_2} = -\sum_{l=i_2+1}^{j_2} (X_{i_1,l} - X_{i_1,l-1}) - \sum_{m=i_1+1}^{j_1} \left(X_{m,j_2} - X_{m-1,j_2}\right).$$

Similarly,

$$X_{i_1,i_2} - X_{j_1,j_2} = -\sum_{l=i_2+1}^{j_2} (X_{i_1,l} - X_{i_1,l-1}) + \sum_{m=j_1+1}^{i_1} \left(X_{m,j_2} - X_{m-1,j_2}\right),$$

for $1 \leq j_1 < i_1 \leq N$ and $1 \leq i_2 < j_2 \leq N$,

$$X_{i_1,i_2} - X_{j_1,j_2} = \sum_{l=j_2+1}^{i_2} (X_{i_1,l} - X_{i_1,l-1}) - \sum_{m=i_1+1}^{j_1} \left(X_{m,j_2} - X_{m-1,j_2}\right),$$

for $1 \leq i_1 < j_1 \leq N$ and $1 \leq j_2 < i_2 \leq N$, and

$$X_{i_1,i_2} - X_{j_1,j_2} = \sum_{l=j_2+1}^{i_2} (X_{i_1,l} - X_{i_1,l-1}) + \sum_{m=j_1+1}^{i_1} \left(X_{m,j_2} - X_{m-1,j_2}\right),$$

for $1 \leq j_1 < i_1 \leq N$ and $1 \leq j_2 < i_2 \leq N$. Summing over j_1 and j_2 and taking absolute values, we get

$$N^2|X_{i_1,i_2}| \leq \sum_{j_1,j_2=1}^{N} \sum_{l=1}^{N} |X_{i_1,l} - X_{i_1,l-1}| + \sum_{j_1,j_2=1}^{N} \sum_{m=1}^{N} |X_{m,j_2} - X_{m-1,j_2}|,$$

and therefore

$$|X_{i_1,i_2}| \leq \sum_{l=1}^{N} |X_{i_1,l} - X_{i_1,l-1}| + \frac{1}{N} \sum_{m,j_2=1}^{N} |X_{m,j_2} - X_{m-1,j_2}|.$$

Symmetry gives

$$|X_{i_1,i_2}| \leq \sum_{l=1}^{N} |X_{l,i_2} - X_{l-1,i_2}| + \frac{1}{N} \sum_{m,j_2=1}^{N} |X_{m,j_2} - X_{m,j_2-1}|,$$

and hence

$$\|X\|_{\ell^{2,2}}^2 = \sum_{i_1,i_2=1}^{N} |X_{i_1,i_2}|^2 \leq \left(\sum_{i_1,l=1}^{N} |X_{i_1,l} - X_{i_1,l-1}| + \sum_{m,j_2=1}^{N} |X_{m,j_2} - X_{m-1,j_2}| \right)$$
$$\times \left(\sum_{l,i_2=1}^{N} |X_{l,i_2} - X_{l-1,i_2}| + \sum_{m,j_2=1}^{N} |X_{m,j_2} - X_{m,j_2-1}| \right),$$

which is precisely $\|X\|_{TV_a}^2$. To complete the proof, we use (17.2). □

Note that the lemmas could both be obtained as simple corollaries of Poincaré's inequality for functions in $BV([0,1]^d)$. We have opted to give direct proofs instead.

Lemma 17.11 (Poincaré's inequality for A) *If A is the measurement matrix of Theorem 17.4 then*

$$\|z\|_{\ell^2} \leq \|Az\|_{\ell^2} + \sqrt{N}\|z\|_{TV}, \quad \forall z \in \mathbb{C}^N,$$

and if A is the measurement matrix of Theorem 17.5 then

$$\|z\|_{\ell^2} \leq \|Az\|_{\ell^2} + \sqrt{2}\|z\|_{TV}, \quad \forall z \in \mathbb{C}^{N^2}.$$

Proof Let $z \in \mathbb{C}^N$ and define $\bar{z} = (\bar{z}_i)_{i=1}^N$ by $\bar{z}_i = z_i - \frac{1}{N}\sum_{j=1}^N z_j$. Then $\sum_{i=1}^N \bar{z}_i = 0$ and the Poincaré inequality (17.22) gives

$$\|\bar{z}\|_{\ell^2} \leq \sqrt{N}\|\bar{z}\|_{TV} = \sqrt{N}\|z\|_{TV}.$$

Observe that $\sum_{j=1}^N z_j = (Fz)_1$. Hence

$$\|z\|_{\ell^2} \leq \frac{1}{\sqrt{N}}|(Fz)_1| + \sqrt{N}\|z\|_{TV} \leq \sqrt{\frac{m}{N}}\|A_2 z\|_{\ell^2} + \sqrt{N}\|z\|_{TV} \leq \|Az\|_{\ell^2} + \sqrt{N}\|z\|_{TV},$$

since $m \leq N$ by assumption. This gives the first result. For the second result we argue in a near-identical manner, replacing (17.22) by (17.23). □

Proof of Theorems 17.4 and 17.5 (image error) We now prove (17.5) and (17.7). Lemma 17.11 gives

$$\|\hat{x} - x\|_{\ell^2} \leq C\left(\|A(\hat{x} - x)\|_{\ell^2} + \|\nabla\hat{x} - \nabla x\|_{\ell^1}\right),$$

where $C = \sqrt{N}$ or $C = \sqrt{2}$ in the one- or two-dimensional cases, respectively. We now apply the previously derived bounds for $\|\nabla\hat{x} - \nabla x\|_{\ell^1} = \|\hat{x} - x\|_{TV}$ given in (17.4) and (17.6) and use the fact that $\|A(\hat{x} - x)\|_{\ell^2} \leq 2\eta$ to obtain

$$\|\hat{x} - x\|_{\ell^2}/C \lesssim \sqrt{s}\eta + \sigma_s(\nabla x)_{\ell^1}.$$

This gives the result. □

17.4.3 Part III: Image Recovery for Variable-Density Sampling

For variable-density sampling, the improved image recovery error bounds stem from the following strengthened version of Lemma 17.11:

Lemma 17.12 (Strengthened Poincaré's inequality for A) *Under the conditions of Theorem 17.6, the following holds with probability at least* $1 - \varepsilon/2$*:*

$$\|x\|_{\ell^2} \lesssim \sqrt{\log(N)}\|Ax\|_{\ell^2} + \sqrt{N}\|x\|_{TV}/s, \quad \forall x \in \mathbb{C}^N. \tag{17.24}$$

Under the conditions of Theorem 17.7, the following holds with probability at least $1 - \varepsilon/2$*:*

$$\|x\|_{\ell^2} \lesssim \sqrt{\log(N)}\|Ax\|_{\ell^2} + \|x\|_{TV}/\sqrt{s}, \quad \forall x \in \mathbb{C}^{N^2}. \tag{17.25}$$

This lemma is proved next. First, however, we show how it implies the main results:

Proof of Theorems 17.6 and 17.7 (image error) We now prove (17.10) and (17.13). The conditions on m and the arguments given in §17.4.1 demonstrate that the gradient error bound (17.9) (one dimension) or (17.12) (two dimensions) holds with probability exceeding $1 - \varepsilon/2$. Furthermore, Lemma 17.12 shows that the strengthened Poincaré inequality (17.24) or (17.25) holds with probability at least $1 - \varepsilon/2$. Hence (17.9) and (17.24) (respectively (17.12) and (17.25)) hold simultaneously with probability at least $1 - \varepsilon$. To obtain the image recovery error estimate we now apply (17.24) or (17.25) to $\hat{x} - x$, and then use (17.9) or (17.12) and the feasibility of $\hat{x}$ and x. □

17.4.4 Discrete Haar Coefficients and the TV Semi-norm

To prove Lemma 17.12, we first need to derive a relation between discrete Haar wavelet coefficients and the TV semi-norm. Write $\Phi \in \mathbb{R}^{N \times N}$ or $\Phi \in \mathbb{R}^{N^2 \times N^2}$ for the discrete Haar wavelet sparsifying transform in one or two dimensions, respectively (see §9.10.5).

Lemma 17.13 *Let* $x \in \mathbb{C}^N$ *satisfy* $\sum_{i=1}^N x_i = 0$ *and* $d = \Phi^* x$ *be its discrete Haar wavelet coefficients. If* $\pi \colon \{1, \ldots, N\} \to \{1, \ldots, N\}$ *is a bijection that gives a nonincreasing rearrangement of the entries of* d *in absolute value, then*

$$|d_{\pi(i)}| \lesssim \sqrt{N}\|x\|_{TV}/i^{3/2}, \quad i = 1, \ldots, N.$$

Proof Let $BV([0, 1])$ be the space of bounded variation functions on $[0, 1]$ (Definition 10.6) and define $f \in BV([0, 1])$ by

$$f(t) = \sqrt{N}x_{i+1} \quad i/N \leq t < (i + 1)/N, \quad i = 0, \ldots, N - 1.$$

Observe that

$$\|f\|_{L^2} = \|x\|_{\ell^2}, \qquad V(f) = \sqrt{N}\sum_{i=1}^N |x_i - x_{i-1}| = \sqrt{N}\|x\|_{TV},$$

where $V(f)$ is the total variation of f (see Definition 10.6 once more). Note also that the first N Haar wavelet coefficients of f are precisely the coefficients d of x (this follows from Remark 9.30 and the fact that f is piecewise constant). Hence Proposition 10.1 and Theorem 10.7 give

$$|d_{\pi(i)}| \lesssim V(f)/i^{3/2} = \sqrt{N}\|x\|_{TV}/i^{3/2},$$

as required. □

A similar result, which we shall not prove, also holds in two dimensions:

Lemma 17.14 *Let $x \in \mathbb{C}^{N^2}$ be a vectorized two-dimensional image satisfying $\sum_{i=1}^{N^2} x_i = 0$ and $d = \Phi^* x$ be its discrete Haar wavelet coefficients. If $\pi : \{1, \ldots, N^2\} \to \{1, \ldots, N^2\}$ is a bijection that gives a nonincreasing rearrangement of the entries of d in absolute value, then*

$$|d_{\pi(i)}| \lesssim \|x\|_{TV}/i, \quad i = 1, \ldots, N^2.$$

17.4.5 Poincaré Inequality for Haar-Incoherent Measurements

We now use these estimates to prove the following versions of Poincaré's inequality for a measurement matrix B that is incoherent with the discrete Haar basis, in the sense that the product $B\Phi$ satisfies the RIP:

Lemma 17.15 (Poincaré's inequality for Haar-incoherent measurements, $d = 1$) *Let $B \in \mathbb{C}^{m\times N}$ and suppose that $B\Phi$ has the RIP of order $5k$ with constant $\delta \le 1/2$. Then*

$$\|x\|_{\ell^2} \lesssim \|x\|_{TV}\sqrt{N}/k + \|Bx\|_{\ell^2}, \quad \forall x \in \mathbb{C}^N.$$

Lemma 17.16 (Poincaré's inequality for Haar-incoherent measurements, $d = 2$) *Let $B \in \mathbb{C}^{m\times N^2}$ and suppose that $B\Phi$ has the RIP of order $5k$ with constant $\delta \le 1/2$. Then*

$$\|x\|_{\ell^2} \lesssim \|x\|_{TV} \log(N^2/k)/\sqrt{k} + \|Bx\|_{\ell^2}, \quad \forall x \in \mathbb{C}^{N^2}.$$

Note that neither the condition $\delta \le 1/2$ nor the factor 5 in the RIP order are sharp. This is of little consequence for what follows.

The proofs of these lemmas are based on the following result:

Lemma 17.17 *Let $\gamma \in \mathbb{N}$ and suppose that $A \in \mathbb{C}^{m\times N}$ has the RIP of order $5k\gamma^2$ with constant $\delta \le 1/2$. Let $d \in \mathbb{C}^N$ and suppose that there is a set $\Delta \subseteq \{1, \ldots, N\}$ with $|\Delta| \le k$ such that*

$$\|P_\Delta^\perp d\|_{\ell^1} \le \gamma\|P_\Delta d\|_{\ell^1} + \sigma,$$

for some $\sigma \ge 0$. Then

$$\|d\|_{\ell^2} \lesssim \frac{\sigma}{\gamma\sqrt{k}} + \|Ad\|_{\ell^2}.$$

Proof Define $s = k\gamma^2$. Let Δ_1 be the index set corresponding to the largest $4s$ entries of $P_\Delta^\perp d$, Δ_2 be the index set corresponding to the next largest $4s$ entries of $P_\Delta^\perp d$, and so forth. Then

$$\sum_{j\ge 2} \|P_{\Delta_j} d\|_{\ell^2} \le \frac{1}{2\sqrt{s}} \sum_{j\ge 1} \|P_{\Delta_{j-1}} d\|_{\ell^1} = \frac{\|P_\Delta^\perp d\|_{\ell^1}}{2\gamma\sqrt{k}} \le \frac{1}{2\sqrt{k}}\|P_\Delta d\|_{\ell^1} + \frac{\sigma}{2\gamma\sqrt{k}}.$$

Hence

$$\sum_{j\geq 2} \|P_{\Delta_j} d\|_{\ell^2} \leq \frac{1}{2}\|P_\Delta d\|_{\ell^2} + \frac{\sigma}{2\gamma\sqrt{k}}. \tag{17.26}$$

Now consider $\|Ad\|_{\ell^2}$. Since A has the RIP of order $5k\gamma^2 \geq (4\gamma^2+1)k = |\Delta \cup \Delta_1|$, we have

$$\begin{aligned}
\|Ad\|_{\ell^2} &\geq \|AP_{\Delta\cup\Delta_1} d\|_{\ell^2} - \sum_{j\geq 2} \|AP_{\Delta_j} d\|_{\ell^2} \\
&\geq \sqrt{1-\delta}\|P_{\Delta\cup\Delta_1} d\|_{\ell^2} - \sqrt{1+\delta}\left(\frac{1}{2}\|P_\Delta d\|_{\ell^2} + \frac{\sigma}{2\gamma\sqrt{k}}\right) \\
&\geq \left(\sqrt{1-\delta} - \frac{1}{2}\sqrt{1+\delta}\right)\|P_{\Delta\cup\Delta_1} d\|_{\ell^2} - \frac{\sqrt{1+\delta}\sigma}{2\gamma\sqrt{k}}.
\end{aligned}$$

Since $\delta \leq 1/2$, we deduce that

$$\|P_{\Delta\cup\Delta_1} d\|_{\ell^2} \lesssim \frac{\sigma}{\gamma\sqrt{k}} + \|Ad\|_{\ell^2}.$$

Furthermore, (17.26) gives

$$\|P^\perp_{\Delta\cup\Delta_1} d\|_{\ell^2} \leq \sum_{j\geq 2} \|P_{\Delta_j} d\|_{\ell^2} \leq \frac{1}{2}\|P_{\Delta\cup\Delta_1} d\|_{\ell^2} + \frac{\sigma}{2\gamma\sqrt{k}}.$$

The result now follows by writing $\|d\|_{\ell^2} \leq \|P_{\Delta\cup\Delta_1} d\|_{\ell^2} + \|P^\perp_{\Delta\cup\Delta_1} d\|_{\ell^2}$. □

Proof of Lemmas 17.15 and 17.16 We may assume that x has mean zero. Let $A = B\Phi$, $d = \Phi^* x$ and Δ be the index set of the largest k entries of d in absolute value. An application of Lemma 17.17 with the trivial choices $\gamma = 1$ and $\sigma = \|P^\perp_\Delta d\|_{\ell^1}$ gives

$$\|x\|_{\ell^2} = \|d\|_{\ell^2} \lesssim \|P^\perp_\Delta d\|_{\ell^1}/\sqrt{k} + \|B\Phi d\|_{\ell^2} = \|P^\perp_\Delta d\|_{\ell^1}/\sqrt{k} + \|Bx\|_{\ell^2}.$$

In the one-dimensional case, we use Lemma 17.13 to obtain

$$\|P^\perp_\Delta d\|_{\ell^1} = \sum_{i=k+1}^{N} |d_{\pi(i)}| \lesssim \sqrt{N}\|x\|_{TV}/\sqrt{k}.$$

This completes the proof of Lemma 17.15. For the proof of Lemma 17.16 we simply use Lemma 17.14 instead. □

As the reader will have noticed, Lemma 17.17 is substantially more general than what is needed in the above proof. Its generality will be useful in §17.5.

17.4.6 Final Arguments

We are now finally ready to give the proof of Lemma 17.12:

Proof of Lemma 17.12 Consider the one-dimensional case first. We proceed much like in Remark 12.15. Let $U = N^{-1/2}F\Phi$ be the unitary discrete Fourier–Haar matrix, and define the isotropic family $\mathcal{A}$ defined by $a \sim \mathcal{A}$ if $\mathbb{P}(a = U^* e_{\varrho^{-1}(\omega)}/\sqrt{\pi_\omega}) = \pi_\omega$ for

$-N/2 < \omega \leq N/2$, where $\pi = \{\pi_\omega\}$ is the inverse linear law (4.1). Let $A' \in \mathbb{C}^{m\times N}$ be the measurement matrix corresponding to this family, and recall from (12.43) that $A' = DA_2\Phi$, where A_2 is the matrix defined in (17.19). Since π is the inverse linear law, (12.78) with $\alpha = 1$ gives that $\|D\|_{\ell^2} \lesssim \sqrt{\log(N)}$.

Lemma 13.20 and (17.8) imply that, with probability at least $1 - \varepsilon/2$, A' has the RIP of order $5s$ with constant $\delta \leq 1/2$. We now apply Lemma 17.15 with $B = A'\Phi^*$ to get

$$\|x\|_{\ell^2} \lesssim \sqrt{N}\|x\|_{TV}/s + \|A'\Phi^* x\|_{\ell^2}.$$

Consider the second term. Since $A' = DA_2\Phi$, we have

$$\|A'\Phi^* x\|_{\ell^2} \leq \|D\|_{\ell^2}\|A_2 x\|_{\ell^2} \lesssim \sqrt{\log(N)}\|Ax\|_{\ell^2}.$$

This completes the proof for the one-dimensional case.

The two-dimensional case is similar. Let $U = N^{-1}F\Phi \in \mathbb{C}^{N^2\times N^2}$ be the unitary discrete Fourier–Haar matrix in two dimensions and $\mathcal{A}$ be the analogous isotropic family. Lemma 13.20 and (17.11) imply that the measurement matrix $A' \in \mathbb{C}^{m\times N^2}$ corresponding to this family has the RIP of order $5k$ with constant $\delta \leq 1/2$, where $k = \lceil s\log^2(N)\rceil$. Lemma 17.16 with $B = A'\Phi^*$ now gives

$$\|x\|_{\ell^2} \lesssim \|x\|_{TV}/\sqrt{s} + \|A'\Phi^* x\|_{\ell^2}.$$

By the same arguments as before, we have $\|A'\Phi^* x\|_{\ell^2} \lesssim \sqrt{\log(N)}\|Ax\|_{\ell^2}$. Hence the result now follows. □

17.5 Recovery Guarantees for Haar-Incoherent Measurements

Thus far, we have focused on Fourier sampling, with our proofs relying critically on the commuting property of the discrete gradient operator with the Fourier matrix. This property is absent for other sampling operators, and notably, for Walsh sampling. In this section, we prove a recovery guarantee for TV minimization in a more general setting. For reasons discussed in the Notes section, we consider the two-dimensional case only.

Theorem 17.18 *Let $N \geq s \geq 2$, $\Phi \in \mathbb{R}^{N^2\times N^2}$ be the matrix of the two-dimensional discrete Haar wavelet sparsifying transform and $A \in \mathbb{C}^{m\times N^2}$. Suppose that $A\Phi$ has the RIP of order $t \gtrsim s\cdot\log(N)\cdot\log^2(2N^2/s)$ with constant $\delta \leq 1/2$. Then for all $x \in \mathbb{C}^{N^2}$ and $y = Ax + e$, every minimizer $\hat{x} \in \mathbb{C}^{N^2}$ of (17.3) with parameter $\eta \geq \|e\|_{\ell^2}$ satisfies*

$$\|\hat{x} - x\|_{\ell^2} \lesssim \frac{\sigma_s(\nabla x)_{\ell^1}}{\sqrt{s\log(N)}} + \eta.$$

Proof Let $z = \hat{x} - x$ and $d = \Phi^* z$ be its discrete Haar coefficients. We may assume that z has mean zero. Let $\pi\colon \{1,\ldots,N^2\} \to \{1,\ldots,N^2\}$ be a nonincreasing rearrangement of the entries of d in absolute value. We first claim that

$$\sum_{j=k+1}^{N^2} |d_{\pi(j)}| \lesssim \log(N^2/k)\left(\sum_{j=1}^{k} |d_{\pi(j)}| + \sigma_s(\nabla x)_{\ell^1}\right), \tag{17.27}$$

where $k = \lceil 6s \log_2(N) \rceil$. To show this, we first apply Lemma 17.14 to obtain

$$\sum_{j=k+1}^{N^2} |d_{\pi(j)}| \lesssim \log(N^2/k) \|\nabla z\|_{\ell^1}. \tag{17.28}$$

Now consider $\|\nabla z\|_{\ell^1}$. Let Δ be the index set of the largest s entries of ∇x in absolute value. It is straightforward to see that

$$\|P_\Delta^\perp \nabla z\|_{\ell^1} \leq 2\sigma_s(\nabla x)_{\ell^1} + \|P_\Delta \nabla z\|_{\ell^1}. \tag{17.29}$$

See, for instance, (13.11). Let $\phi_1, \ldots, \phi_{N^2} \in \mathbb{C}^{N^2}$ denote the two-dimensional discrete Haar basis, and

$$\Lambda = \{j : (\nabla \phi_j)_i \neq 0 \text{ for some } i \in \Delta\}$$

be the index set of those Haar wavelets that are nonconstant on Δ. Note that for each scale, there are at most six wavelets for which $(\nabla \phi_j)_i \neq 0$ for each fixed i. Hence, there are at most $6 \log_2(N)$ in total. It follows that $|\Lambda| \leq 6s \log_2(N) \leq k$. Write $z = \sum_{j \in \Lambda} d_j \phi_j + \sum_{j \notin \Lambda} d_j \phi_j$. Then $P_\Delta \nabla z = \sum_{j \in \Lambda} d_j P_\Delta \nabla \phi_j$ by construction, and therefore

$$\|P_\Delta \nabla z\|_{\ell^1} \leq \sum_{j \in \Lambda} |d_j| \|\nabla \phi_j\|_{\ell^1} \leq 8 \sum_{j \in \Lambda} |d_j|.$$

Here, in the second step we use the fact that $\|\nabla \phi_j\|_{\ell^1} \leq 8$, which follows easily from the definition of the ϕ_j. Combining this with (17.29), we have

$$\|\nabla z\|_{\ell^1} \leq 2\sigma_s(\nabla x)_{\ell^1} + 16 \sum_{j \in \Lambda} |d_j| \leq 2\sigma_s(\nabla x)_{\ell^1} + 16 \sum_{j=1}^{k} |d_{\pi(j)}|,$$

where in the second step we use the definition of π and the fact that $|\Lambda| \leq k$. Substituting this into (17.28) now yields (17.27).

To complete the proof we apply Lemma 17.17 with the matrix $A\Phi$ and with $\gamma = \lceil \log(N^2/k) \rceil$, $\sigma = \gamma \sigma_s(\nabla x)_{\ell^1}$ and $\Delta = \{\pi(1), \ldots, \pi(k)\}$. The matrix $A\Phi$ satisfies the RIP of order $5k\gamma^2 \lesssim s \log(N) \log^2(2N^2/s)$. Hence

$$\|\hat{x} - x\|_{\ell^2} = \|d\|_{\ell^2} \lesssim \frac{\sigma}{\gamma \sqrt{k}} + \|A\Phi d\|_{\ell^2} \lesssim \frac{\sigma_s(\nabla x)_{\ell^1}}{\sqrt{s \log(N)}} + \|A(\hat{x} - x)\|_{\ell^2}.$$

The result now follows after noting that $\|A(\hat{x} - x)\|_{\ell^2} \leq 2\eta$. □

This result asserts that every measurement matrix that is incoherent with the Haar wavelet basis – in the sense that $A\Phi$ has the RIP of sufficient order – yields accurate and stable recovery via TV minimization. A Gaussian random matrix certainly has this property with high probability, provided

$$m \gtrsim s \cdot \log(N) \cdot \log^3(2N^2/s).$$

This follows from the universality of Gaussian matrices (Remark 5.26) and the concentration bounds Lemmas 5.24 and 5.25. Of more relevance to imaging, however, is the case of Walsh measurements:

Theorem 17.19 (Variable-density Walsh sampling, $d = 2$) *Let $0 < \varepsilon < 1$, $N^2 \geq s \geq 2$ and $\Omega \subseteq \{0, \ldots, N-1\}^2$ be a variable-density sampling scheme of order m corresponding to the inverse square law (4.6). Let $A = m^{-1/2} P_\Omega H$, where $H \in \mathbb{R}^{N^2 \times N^2}$ is the two-dimensional sequency-ordered Hadamard matrix (see §2.4.4), and suppose that*

$$m \gtrsim s \cdot \log^2(2N^2/s) \cdot \log^2(N) \cdot \left(\log^3(s \log(N)) \cdot \log(N) + \log(\varepsilon^{-1})\right).$$

Then the following holds with probability at least $1 - \varepsilon$. For all $x \in \mathbb{C}^{N^2}$ and $y = Ax + e$, every minimizer $\hat{x} \in \mathbb{C}^{N^2}$ of (17.3) with parameter $\eta \geq \|e\|_{\ell^2}$ satisfies

$$\|x - \hat{x}\|_{\ell^2} \lesssim \frac{\sigma_s(\nabla x)_{\ell^1}}{\sqrt{s \log(N)}} + \eta \sqrt{\log(N)}.$$

As before, P_Ω in this theorem is simply shorthand for $P_{\varrho^{-1}(\Omega)}$, where $\varrho \colon \{1, \ldots, N^d\} \to \{0, \ldots, N-1\}^d$ is the composition of the lexicographical ordering (2.2) and the integer shift $\{1, \ldots, N\}^d \to \{0, \ldots, N-1\}^d$.

Similar to Fourier sampling, this result asserts accurate and stable recovery of the image x from roughly s Walsh measurements, up to log factors, taken according to the appropriate variable-density strategy. Unlike the Fourier case, however, there is no recovery guarantee for the image gradient. Moreover, the log factor is larger by roughly $\log(N)$ than in the Fourier case. Both differences stem from the lack of the commuting property in this case, which means the proof strategy is quite different.

To prove Theorem 17.19, we first require the following lemma. This result is the equivalent of Lemma 13.20 (with $\alpha = 1$) for Walsh sampling. For completeness, the following lemma also considers the one-dimensional case:

Lemma 17.20 *Let $d = 1, 2$, $0 < \delta, \varepsilon < 1$, $N^d \geq s \geq 2$ and $U = N^{-d/2} H \Phi \in \mathbb{R}^{N^d \times N^d}$, where $H \in \mathbb{R}^{N^d \times N^d}$ is the sequency-ordered Hadamard matrix and $\Phi \in \mathbb{R}^{N^d \times N^d}$ is the discrete Haar wavelet sparsifying transform. Let $\mathcal{A}$ be the isotropic family defined by $a \sim \mathcal{A}$ if*

$$\mathbb{P}\left(a = U^* e_{\varrho^{-1}(n)} / \sqrt{\pi_n}\right) = \pi_n, \quad n \in \{0, \ldots, N-1\}^d,$$

where π corresponds to inverse linear law (4.5) ($d = 1$) or inverse square law (4.6) ($d = 2$). Suppose that $A' \in \mathbb{R}^{m \times N^d}$ is the measurement matrix corresponding to this family, and let

$$m \gtrsim \delta^{-2} \cdot s \cdot \log(N) \cdot \left(\log(s \log(N)) \cdot \log^2(s) \cdot \log(N) + \log(\varepsilon^{-1})\right).$$

Then, with probability at least $1 - \varepsilon$, the matrix A' has the RIP of order s with constant $\delta_s \leq \delta$.

Proof The result follows from Corollary 13.15 after showing that $\mu(\mathcal{A}) \lesssim \log(N)$. Consider the one-dimensional case. Recall that the first $N = 2^r$ one-dimensional Haar and Walsh basis functions are constant on intervals of length 2^{-r}. Suppose that $n = 2^j + m$ for some $0 \leq m < 2^j$. Then Lemma F.6 and (2.26) give that $|\langle \upsilon_{2^j+m}, \psi_{j,n} \rangle| = 2^{-j/2}$ and

$|\langle \upsilon_{2^j+m}, \psi_{l,n} \rangle| = 0$ for $l \neq j$, where υ_{2^j+m} is the sequency-ordered Walsh function. It now follows immediately that

$$\|U^* e_{\varrho^{-1}(n)}\|^2_{\ell^\infty} \leq 2^{-j} \lesssim 1/\max\{1, n\}.$$

To complete the proof, we recall that

$$\mu(\mathcal{A}) = \max_{n=0,\ldots,N-1} \left\{ \|U^* e_{\varrho^{-1}(n)}\|^2_{\ell^\infty} / \pi_n \right\},$$

and then use the definition of π_n and the fact that $C_N \asymp 1/\log(N)$ as $N \to \infty$. The two-dimensional case is similar. □

Proof of Theorem 17.19 Let A' be as in Lemma 17.20. This lemma and the condition on m imply that A' has the RIP of order $t \gtrsim s \log(N^2) \log^2(2N^2/s)$. To complete the proof, much like in Remark 12.15 we cannot simply invoke Theorem 17.18, since the measurement matrix $A = m^{-1/2} P_\Omega H$ is not scaled in such a way for $A\Phi$ to have the RIP. Instead, we follow the same steps as its proof, making adjustments where needed. Let $z = \hat{x} - x$, $d = \Phi^* z$ be its Haar coefficients and $k = \lceil 6s \log_2(N) \rceil$. Then (17.27) holds (this property does not depend on the measurement matrix). We now apply Lemma 17.17 using the matrix A' and the values $\gamma = \log(N^2/k)$ and $\sigma = \gamma \sigma_s(\nabla x)_{\ell^1}$. This gives

$$\|\hat{x} - x\|_{\ell^2} = \|d\|_{\ell^2} \lesssim \sigma_s(\nabla x)_{\ell^1} / \sqrt{s \log(N)} + \|A'd\|_{\ell^2}.$$

Observe that $\|A'd\| = \|A'\Phi^*(\hat{x} - x)\| \lesssim \sqrt{\log(N)} \|A(\hat{x} - x)\|_{\ell^2}$, where the last inequality follows by essentially the same arguments as those that gave (12.78) in the Fourier case. Hence, the feasibility of x and $\hat{x}$ yields

$$\|\hat{x} - x\|_{\ell^2} \lesssim \sigma_s(\nabla x)_{\ell^1} / \sqrt{s \log(N)} + \sqrt{\log(N)} \eta,$$

as required. □

17.6 Structure-Dependent Sampling

To conclude this chapter, we return to the theme of local structure in the context of Fourier sampling (Walsh sampling could also be considered). As has now been shown, the inverse linear law (in one dimension) or the inverse square law (in two dimensions) yields better recovery than uniform random sampling for TV minimization. But are these the best sampling patterns in practice? The answer – which should come of little surprise given the discussion in §15.1.2 on wavelets – is no. Table 17.1 illustrates this phenomenon. It performs the same experiment as in Table 15.1 (which considered a DB4 wavelet sparsifying transform), and for each image and sampling percentage reports the value of α in the power-law sampling scheme (15.3) that gives the highest PSNR. Note that the value $\alpha = 1$ corresponds to the theoretical result, Theorem 17.7.

There are two main observations. First, the optimal α depends on the image, resolution and sampling percentage, and generally does not correspond to $\alpha = 1$. As expected, the more complex the image, the larger this optimal value. This is precisely Principle #3 of Chapter 4 in practice. Second, upon comparing with Table 15.1, we see that the optimal

Table 17.1 The value of α that gives the highest PSNR reconstruction for a given test image (see Fig. 2.2), resolution and sampling percentage. The value of α is chosen from the set $\{0.50, 0.75, 1.00, 1.25, 1.50, 1.75, 2.00, 2.25, 2.50, 2.75, 3.00\}$. The corresponding PSNR values are given below each line of α values.

Image/Percentage	5%	10%	15%	20%	25%	30%	35%	40%
Dog (256 × 256)	2.75	2.25	2.50	2.75	2.25	2.75	3.00	2.25
	26.03	28.27	29.84	31.17	32.30	33.35	34.45	35.49
Dog (512 × 512)	2.50	2.25	2.75	3.00	2.75	2.75	2.75	3.00
	27.14	29.42	31.11	32.51	33.76	34.99	36.15	37.30
Brain (256 × 256)	2.50	2.00	1.75	1.50	1.50	1.50	1.25	1.25
	21.23	24.69	27.06	28.97	30.83	32.33	34.03	35.77
Brain (512 × 512)	2.00	1.75	1.50	1.50	1.25	1.25	1.00	1.00
	27.11	31.32	34.27	36.71	38.88	40.93	42.88	44.98
Peppers (256 × 256)	2.00	2.00	1.50	1.75	1.50	1.25	1.25	1.25
	29.33	32.74	35.33	37.15	38.83	40.33	41.63	42.99
Peppers (512 × 512)	1.25	1.75	1.50	1.50	1.25	1.00	1.00	0.75
	30.72	33.62	34.99	35.90	36.62	37.37	37.85	38.59
Kopp (256 × 256)	1.50	1.25	1.25	1.00	1.00	1.00	1.00	0.75
	36.46	39.76	42.02	43.98	45.69	47.22	48.71	50.04
Kopp (512 × 512)	1.25	1.25	1.25	1.25	1.25	1.25	1.25	1.25
	39.92	43.26	45.52	47.32	48.72	49.93	51.02	52.10

value of α also depends on whether a wavelet or discrete gradient sparsifying transform is employed. This confirms another component of Principle #3.

We remark in passing that it is possible to derive measurement conditions for TV minimization with other values of α, in a similar manner to what was done in §13.4.4 for the Fourier–Haar wavelet problem. But these would depend algebraically on N in much the same way; an observation that comes as no surprise since the RIP of the Fourier–Haar matrix was a key part of the above proofs. Hence, we find ourselves in a similar position to that described in §11.2.1 for wavelets: the theoretically optimal sampling map for sparse recovery is generally not the best choice in practice. Could one therefore derive a local theory of sampling for gradient sparsifying transforms, as we did in the previous chapters for wavelets? Unfortunately, this remains an open problem (see the Notes section).

Notes

TV minimization is a concept predating compressed sensing. It was introduced to imaging in the seminal work of Rudin, Osher & Fatemi [424] and has been widely used for image restoration tasks such as denoising, deblurring and inpainting. See [130] for an overview. As a result, it is unsurprising that TV minimization was considered in some of the first works on compressed sensing and its applications [121, 336, 337].

Our focus in this chapter is TV minimization for compressed sensing. We have left out a large literature on theoretical results for TV minimization for denoising and other inverse problems. See, for example, [129, 272] and references therein.

The first result for compressed sensing via TV minimization was shown in [121], which proved exact recovery of an exactly gradient sparse image from $m \gtrsim s \cdot \log(N)$ Fourier measurements taken uniformly at random. Accurate and stable recovery was shown by Needell & Ward in the two-dimensional case [373], and later the d-dimensional case for $d \geq 2$ [372]. In particular, these works were the first to exploit (in the compressed sensing context) the connection between the TV semi-norm and Haar wavelet coefficients, which is a key step in obtaining the strengthened Poincaré inequality (17.15). Recovery guarantees for Fourier sampling were shown by Krahmer & Ward [302] and Poon [393]. The former addresses uniform recovery, while the latter considers nonuniform recovery. The work [393] was the first to explore the effect of structured sampling on the recovery – specifically, the differences between uniform random and variable-density sampling.

The main results in this chapter are a combination of [302] and [393]. As in [393], they consider both uniform random and variable-density sampling. However, the results in [393] are nonuniform (and obtained using the weak RIP of [118]), whereas Theorems 17.4–17.7 are uniform, much like those in [302]. The recovery guarantees in [393] assert recovery from $m \gtrsim s \cdot \log(N)$ measurements, but the corresponding error bounds contain log factors. Uniform recovery techniques allow one to remove the log factors from the error bounds, at the expense of increased log factors in the measurement conditions. The recovery guarantees shown in this chapter are comparable in this respect to those of [302]. In [302] the measurement condition is $m \gtrsim s \cdot \log^5(N) \cdot \log^3(s)$, under the additional assumption that $s \gtrsim \log(N)$. The proof technique pursued herein differs from that of [302] in that it exploits the commuting property of the discrete gradient operator with the Fourier matrix. This is similar in this regard to the approach of [393]. Doing so culminates in a somewhat smaller log factor in Theorem 17.7 over that of [302], taking the form $\log^4(N) \cdot \log^3(s)$ under the same condition on s. The results of [302] also require the noise to be bounded in a certain weighted norm (see Remark 12.15), a condition which this analysis avoids. The noise term aside, the main result in §17.5 (which does not require the commuting property) is based on [373, Thm. 6]. The application to Walsh sampling (Theorem 17.19) appears to be new.

Note that the results shown in this chapter have also recently been improved (by one log factor) and generalized to the case of d-dimensional images, $d \geq 3$, in [12]. As an interesting postscript to §17.6, it was shown in [12] that the best Fourier sampling strategy – i.e. the one that gives a near-optimal measurement condition for gradient sparse images – is no longer isotropic when $d \geq 3$. In particular, power-law sampling ceases to be theoretically optimal in higher dimensions.

For $d \geq 2$, Needell & Ward showed how to construct a measurement matrix by concatenating several matrices that have the RIP so as to ensure accurate and stable recovery [372, 373]. In essence, this ensures the measurement matrix commutes with the discrete gradient operator. This has the advantage of decreasing the number of log factors in the measurement condition.

Our focus in this chapter has been on Fourier or Walsh sampling. For recovery guarantees for TV minimization with Gaussian (or more generally, subgaussian) measurements, we refer to [105, 298]. An interesting feature of Gaussian measurements is that, in one dimension, necessary and sufficient conditions for exact recovery of arbitrary gradient sparse vectors are $m \gtrsim \sqrt{sN}$ and $m \gtrsim \sqrt{sN} \cdot \log(N)$, respectively. Conversely, as noted, only $m \gtrsim s \cdot \log(N)$ Fourier measurements are sufficient for exact recovery – a much more appealing result in the regime $s \ll N$.

In Theorem 17.18 we considered the two-dimensional case only. It is straightforward to see that following the same proof steps in one dimension (in particular, using Lemma 17.13 as opposed to Lemma 17.14) would require $A\Phi$ to satisfy an RIP of order $t \gtrsim N$. This is, of course, meaningless. Such a poor result is perhaps unsurprising, given that even Gaussian measurements (which, as noted, are Haar incoherent) require $m \gtrsim \sqrt{sN}$ measurements for exact recovery in one dimension. Note that the results in [105, 298] for Gaussian measurements use specific tools such as the *Gaussian mean width* that are not applicable to Fourier or Walsh measurements.

In this chapter, the discrete gradient operator is defined with periodic boundary conditions. This is useful both for the numerical implementation of (17.3) (see, for instance, [229]) and, as seen herein, for the theory. However, it is not essential. The theoretical results in [298, 372, 373] consider nonperiodic versions of the gradient operator.

Lemma 17.14 can be found in [373, Prop. 8]. Its proof is structurally similar to that of Lemma 17.13 in that a discrete image is isometrically embedded as a function $f : [0, 1]^2 \to \mathbb{C}$ of bounded variation, and then one uses known results on the Haar wavelet coefficients of BV functions (see [154, Thm. 8.1] or [150, Thm. 1.1]) combined with the bound $V(f) \leq \|X\|_{TV_i}$ (see [373, Lem. 14]).

Structure dependence in compressive imaging with TV minimization was first considered in [393]. As shown therein, if the edges of a one-dimensional image are sufficiently *well separated* then recovery can be achieved using low-frequency Fourier samples only. This is related to the *superresolution* problem [116], mentioned briefly in the Notes section of Chapter 14. More recently, a result of similar nature has been shown for random Gaussian sampling: for one-dimensional images with well-separated edges the measurement condition improves from $m \gtrsim \sqrt{sN} \cdot \log(N)$ to $m \gtrsim s \cdot \log^2(N)$ [227]. However, as remarked in §17.6, a more precise understanding of how local gradient structure, especially in two dimensions, influences the best choice of (Fourier or Walsh) sampling strategy is currently lacking.

Part V

From Compressed Sensing to Deep Learning

Summary of Part V

The focus of Parts II–IV of this book has been on reconstruction procedures that are *model-based*, since they impose a specific model (e.g. sparsity in wavelets) on the images to be recovered, and *untrained*, since no database of images is used to design the reconstruction scheme. Yet in many imaging applications, training data is available. It is therefore natural to ask how one might use this data to devise better, *data-driven* reconstruction schemes. As discussed in §4.7, the classical approach to doing this is dictionary learning. In this final part of the book, we examine the latest, and arguably most active, area of research in this direction: namely, *neural networks* and *deep learning* for compressive imaging. We aim to highlight the potential of such approaches, as well as some of their pitfalls.

We commence in Chapter 18 with a general introduction to neural networks and deep learning. In recent years, deep learning has emerged as a powerful framework for a wide range of historically challenging computational problems, including image classification, speech recognition and natural language translation. It is now used to perform such tasks on an everyday basis. As deep learning developed outside of the realm of image reconstruction, this chapter detours into the world of machine learning, in particular, the classification problem. Besides introducing the main concepts, we also discuss tasks such as architecture design and training. Our purpose is not to be exhaustive, but rather to convey to the reader a flavour of this large topic.

Towards the end of this chapter, we highlight an intriguing phenomenon in deep learning. While trained neural networks are often highly successful on machine learning tasks such as image classification, they also exhibit *instabilities*. That is, a small change to the input image (imperceivable to the human eye) can cause the network to classify it incorrectly. Such perturbations are often *universal* and *transferrable*. We show how to construct these perturbations via the *DeepFool* algorithm.

Chapters 19–21 return to compressive imaging. In Chapter 19 we describe current approaches for applying deep learning to image reconstruction. Next, in Chapter 20 our focus turns to the two main criteria that dominate this book: accuracy and stability. The instabilities highlighted in Chapter 18 for classification problems suggest neither may be guaranteed, and indeed, we demonstrate that current deep learning approaches for image reconstruction have a tendency to be unstable (Key Point #10 of Chapter 1). A focal point of Chapter 20 is examining, both theoretically and numerically, the subtle tradeoff between accuracy and stability. We end this chapter by showing that instability in deep learning, when it occurs, cannot easily be remedied by changing the training setup.

This raises a key question: given that existing deep learning procedures may be unstable and unable to be easily stabilized, can accurate and stable neural networks for compressive imaging actually be computed? Since even simple-looking optimization problems such as QCBP are formally uncomputable (Key Point #6), this matter is unsurprisingly quite delicate. Fortunately, in Chapter 21, we answer this in the affirmative by showing the existence of computable neural networks that match the performance of compressed sensing (Key Point #11). With this fresh in our mind, we end this book with an epilogue containing some thoughts on the future of compressive imaging.

18 Neural Networks and Deep Learning

We begin this chapter in §18.1 by introducing some of the basic elements of supervised machine learning. We define neural networks in §18.2 before discussing their classical approximation properties in §18.3. In §18.4 and §18.5 we consider important practical matters such as architecture design and training. Then in §18.6 we briefly describe the overwhelming success that deep learning has had in image classification tasks. Finally, in §18.7 we consider instabilities in classification and their potential consequences, before providing some mathematical insights in §18.8 as to why they occur.

18.1 Supervised Machine Learning

In *supervised* machine learning, the objective is to compute (*learn*) a mapping f from an input space $\mathbb{U}$ (typically a subset of $\mathbb{R}^n$) to an output space $\mathbb{V}$ (typically a subset of $\mathbb{R}^p$) using a set of data

$$\Theta = \{(u_i, v_i)\}_{i=1}^K, \qquad u_i \in \mathbb{U},\ v_i \in \mathbb{V}, \tag{18.1}$$

known as the *training set*. The u_is are the *examples* and the v_is are the *labels*. For instance, each u_i could be an image and v_i could take value either $+1$ or -1 depending on whether the image showed a cat or a dog. This is a so-called *binary classification* problem. The goal is to compute, using only the training data Θ, a mapping $f : u \mapsto v$ that takes an image as its input and produces a label $+1$ or -1 as its output. More generally, in *multiclass classification* one seeks a mapping f that labels an input u according to any one of a number of classes, e.g. cats, dogs, elephants and so forth.

Image reconstruction can be cast as a supervised learning problem. In the discrete setting, we let $\mathbb{U} \subseteq \mathbb{C}^m$ and $\mathbb{V} \subseteq \mathbb{C}^N$ and consider a training set

$$\Theta = \{(y_i, x_i)\}_{i=1}^K, \qquad y_i = Ax_i,$$

where $\{x_i\}$ is a database of images and, for each i, $y_i = Ax_i$ is the corresponding vector of measurements. For example, in medical imaging this may be a database of MRI scans of the brain. The objective is to find a mapping which takes measurements y and produces (an approximation to) the underlying image x. We consider this further in Chapter 19.

Returning to the general setting, the first question to ask is: what sort of mapping f is desirable? Clearly, one would like small *training error*, i.e. $f(u_i) \approx v_i$ for $i = 1, \dots, K$. But it is usually not sufficient for a mapping to simply reproduce the training set well. A mapping should also have good *generalization*: it should perform well on a large class of new *instances* $(u, v) \in \mathbb{U} \times \mathbb{V}$ that are close to, but not part of the training set.

In practice, generalization is typically measured using a second set of data, known as the *test set*. This is a set $\overline{\Theta} = \{(\overline{u}_i, \overline{v}_i)\}_{i=1}^{\overline{K}}$ that is not used in the learning process but is used to examine the performance of the learned mapping. Good generalization is commonly equated with a small *test error*, i.e. $f(\overline{u}_i) \approx \overline{v}_i$ for $i = 1, \ldots, \overline{K}$. Often, one may also have a third set $\widetilde{\Theta} = \{(\widetilde{u}_i, \widetilde{v}_i)\}_{i=1}^{\widetilde{K}}$, known as the *validation set*. This is used in the learning process in order to tune the parameters of the learning algorithm. In practice, it is common to reserve a proportion of the original training set as the validation set.

Returning to the original task, in order to perform supervised learning one first needs to decide what type of mappings to consider, and then how to compute a suitable mapping from the training data – a process known as *training the model*. In deep learning, such mappings are chosen as *neural networks*. We introduce neural networks in the next several sections. Then in §18.5 we explain how to train a neural network from data.

18.2 Neural Networks

Neural networks (sometimes referred to as *artificial* neural networks) can be viewed as extensions of so-called *perceptrons*.

18.2.1 Perceptrons

A perceptron is a type of binary classification function. It takes the form

$$\mathrm{P}\colon \mathbb{R}^n \to \mathbb{R},\ u \mapsto \sigma(w^\top u + b), \tag{18.2}$$

where $w \in \mathbb{R}^n$ is a *weight* vector, $b \in \mathbb{R}$ is a *bias* and $\sigma\colon \mathbb{R} \to \mathbb{R}$ is an *activation* function. Classically, σ is taken as the sign function, so that $\sigma(x) = 1$ if $x > 0$ and $\sigma(x) = -1$ otherwise. Since the equation $w^\top u + b = 0$ defines a hyperplane in $\mathbb{R}^n$, the function P is an example of a *linear classifier* function: points are classified depending on which side of the hyperplane they lie. Learning a perceptron corresponds to using a training set Θ to determine values of the *parameters* $w \in \mathbb{R}^n$ and $b \in \mathbb{R}$.

In practice, it is often desirable to replace the sign function with a nonbinary activation function that accounts for the intensity of $w^\top x + b$. Two common choices are the *sigmoid* $\sigma(x) = (1 + \mathrm{e}^{-x})^{-1}$ and *hyperbolic tangent* $\sigma(x) = \tanh(x)$. The former takes values between 0 and +1, while the latter takes values between −1 and +1. A third common activation function is the *Rectified Linear Unit (ReLU)*, defined as $\sigma(x) = \max\{0, x\}$. Note that, unlike the others, this activation is unbounded. Several of these activation functions are shown in Fig. 18.1.

The perceptron (18.2) has output dimension one. More generally, we may consider a perceptron with output dimension p. This is defined as

$$\mathrm{P}\colon \mathbb{R}^n \to \mathbb{R}^p,\ u \mapsto \sigma(Wu + b),$$

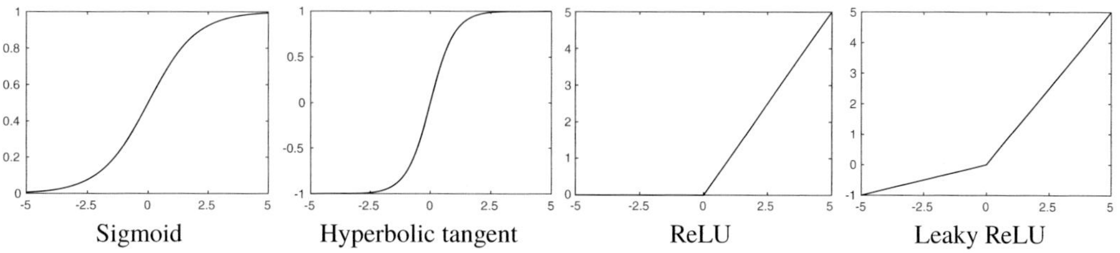

Figure 18.1 Common choices for activation function σ. The leaky ReLU is defined as $\sigma(x) = \max\{0.2x, x\}$. It is a modification of the ReLU activation function where the flat region is replaced by a linear function of small slope.

where $W \in \mathbb{R}^{p\times n}$ is the weight matrix, $b \in \mathbb{R}^p$ is the bias vector and σ is interpreted componentwise, i.e. $(\sigma(z))_i = \sigma(z_i)$ for $z = (z_i)_{i=1}^p \in \mathbb{R}^p$.

18.2.2 Feedforward Neural Networks

We are now ready to define neural networks. In the following definition, we introduce the class of so-called *feedforward* neural networks. These are simply mappings that are formed by composing a finite number of perceptrons:

Definition 18.1 (Feedforward neural network) A *feedforward (multilayer perceptron) neural network* is a mapping $\mathrm{N}\colon \mathbb{R}^n \to \mathbb{R}^p$ defined as

$$\begin{aligned} a^{(0)} &= u \in \mathbb{R}^n, \\ a^{(l)} &= \sigma(W^{(l)}a^{(l-1)} + b^{(l)}) \in \mathbb{R}^{n_l}, \quad l = 1, 2, \ldots, L, \\ \mathrm{N}(u) &= a^{(L)}, \end{aligned} \tag{18.3}$$

where σ is an *activation function* that acts componentwise, $W^{(l)} \in \mathbb{R}^{n_l\times n_{l-1}}$ are the *weights*, $b^{(l)} \in \mathbb{R}^{n_l}$ are the *biases* and $n_0 = n$ and $n_L = p$.

Let $A^{(l)}$ denote the affine map $A^{(l)}\colon x \mapsto W^{(l)}x + b^{(l)}$. Then we can write $\mathrm{N}(u)$ as the composition

$$\mathrm{N}(u) = \sigma \circ A^{(L)} \circ \sigma \circ A^{(L-1)} \circ \cdots \circ \sigma \circ A^{(1)}(u). \tag{18.4}$$

The action of N on an input u can therefore be viewed as *feeding* (or *propagating*) it forwards through the network via an alternating sequence of affine maps and nonlinear activations.

It is common to visualize a neural network as a graph, where the nodes of the graph (also called the *units*) are the *neurons* and the entries of the $W^{(l)}$ are the weights assigned to the edges of the graph. An example is shown in Fig. 18.2. We interpret a neural network as flowing information from left to right across this graph. In particular, at a given *layer*, each neuron does the following: it takes a weighted linear combination of the outputs of the neurons from the previous layer, applies a bias, applies the nonlinear activation function and then finally feeds this information forward to the next layer. The calculation

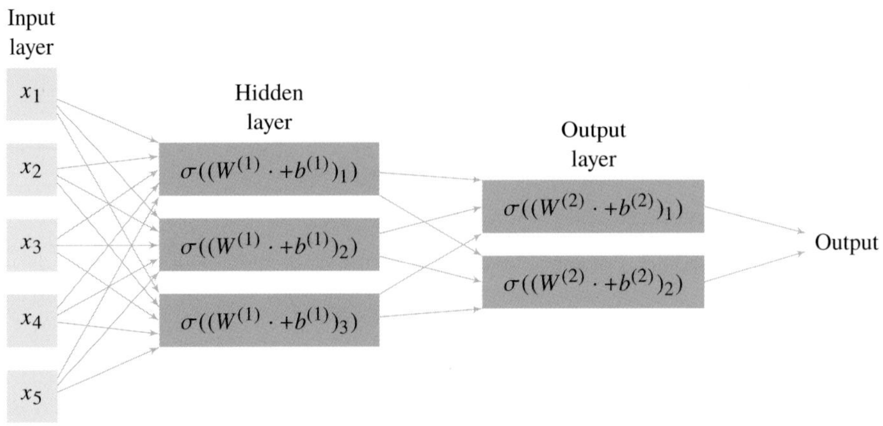

Figure 18.2 A diagram of a neural network with a single hidden layer and widths $n_0 = 5$, $n_1 = 3$ and $n_2 = 2$.

then proceeds in the same manner in the next layer and so forth across the network until one reaches the output layer.

Note that there are numerous variations on the theme of Definition 18.1. A typical one involves forgoing the nonlinear activation in the final layer, so that

$$\mathrm{N}(u) = W^{(L)} a^{(L-1)} + b^{(L)}. \tag{18.5}$$

This is particularly important if the activation function used is uniformly bounded (e.g. the sigmoid), since one often does want the output of the network to lie in the same range. We will encounter several other variations later in this chapter.

18.2.3 Neural Network Architectures

We now introduce several further pieces of standard terminology. The weights $W^{(l)}$ and biases $b^{(l)}$ parametrize a neural network N, and are accordingly referred to as its *parameters*. Taking their dimensions into account, we see that the number of parameters is therefore

$$d = (n_1 \times n_0 + n_2 \times n_1 + \cdots + n_L \times n_{L-1}) + (n_1 + n_2 + \cdots + n_L). \tag{18.6}$$

The quantity L is termed the *depth* of the network and each value of $l = 0, \ldots, L$ corresponds to a layer. The first layer $l = 0$ is the *input* layer and the last layer $l = L$ is the *output* layer. Layers $l = 1, \ldots, L-1$ are *hidden* layers. The values $n_1, \ldots, n_{L-1}$ are referred to as the *widths* of the hidden layers. Informally, we say a neural network is a *deep* neural network if it has more than a handful of layers. If not, then it is a *shallow* neural network.

The *architecture* of a neural network consists of the following:

(i) the depth L;
(ii) the parameters $n_1, \ldots, n_{L-1}$, the widths of the hidden layers;

(iii) the activation function σ.

We are free to choose these quantities ourselves – a process known as *designing* the neural network architecture. We discuss this further in §18.4.

Let $\mathbf{n} = (n_0, \dots, n_L) \in \mathbb{N}^{L+1}$ be the vector of widths, where we also include the input and output dimensions n_0 and n_L for convenience. We write either $\mathcal{N}$, $\mathcal{N}_\mathbf{n}$ or $\mathcal{N}_{\mathbf{n},\sigma}$ when we wish to make the dependence on $\mathbf{n}$ and σ explicit, for the family of neural networks with a given architecture. Note that the family $\mathcal{N}_\mathbf{n}$ is parametrized by the weight matrices $W^{(l)}$ and bias vectors $b^{(l)}$:

$$\mathcal{N}_\mathbf{n} = \Big\{\text{Neural networks N with weights and biases } \{W^{(l)}, b^{(l)}\}_{l=1}^{L}, \\ \text{where } W^{(l)} \in \mathbb{R}^{n_l \times n_{l-1}} \text{ and } b^{(l)} \in \mathbb{R}^{n_l}, \text{ and activation } \sigma\Big\}.$$

This is known as a family of *fully connected* neural networks, since the weight matrices are allowed to take arbitrary values. In particular, they can be dense matrices, in which case each neuron in the graph is connected to each neuron in the layer adjacent to it.

As noted, there are various ways to modify or extend Definition 18.1. One way is to include different activation functions at each layer, i.e. we replace (18.4) with

$$\mathrm{N}(u) = \sigma^{(L)} \circ A^{(L)} \circ \sigma^{(L-1)} \circ A^{(L-1)} \circ \dots \circ \sigma^{(1)} \circ A^{(1)}(u).$$

In this case, we write $\mathcal{N}_{\mathbf{n},\sigma}$ for the resulting family, where $\sigma = (\sigma^{(1)}, \dots, \sigma^{(L)})$. A particular instance of this setup is when $\sigma^{(1)} = \dots = \sigma^{(L-1)} = \sigma$ and $\sigma^{(L)} = \widetilde{\sigma}$. In other words, the same activation function is used in all layers besides the final one. This includes the case of the identity map $\widetilde{\sigma}(x) = x$ where, as in (18.5), the final layer is not subject to a nonlinear activation.

18.3 The Universal Approximation Theorem

When solving a supervised machine learning problem, it is common to assume that there is an unknown labelling function (the *ground truth*) that is being approximated. One may therefore ask: why use a neural network to approximate this function? To answer this question, one can look to the *approximation theory* of neural networks. The classical result in this area, referred to as the *universal approximation theorem*, gives credence to the use of neural networks as an approximation tool. It demonstrates that shallow neural networks with one hidden layer can approximate *any* continuous function:

Theorem 18.2 (Universal approximation theorem) *Let $\sigma \in C(\mathbb{R})$ and define the class of real-valued neural networks with one hidden layer*

$$\mathcal{M}(\sigma) = \left\{ x \in \mathbb{R}^n \mapsto \sum_{i=1}^{r} c_i \sigma\left(w_i^\top x + b_i\right) \in \mathbb{R} : w_i \in \mathbb{R}^n,\ b_i, c_i \in \mathbb{R}, r \in \mathbb{N} \right\}. \quad (18.7)$$

Then $\mathcal{M}(\sigma)$ is dense in $C(\mathbb{R}^n)$ in the topology of uniform convergence on compact sets if and only if σ is not a polynomial.

This result means the following. Given any $f \in C(\mathbb{R}^n)$, $\epsilon > 0$ and compact set $K \subset \mathbb{R}^n$, there exists a $g \in \mathcal{M}(\sigma)$ such that $\max_{x\in K} |f(x) - g(x)| < \epsilon$. Notice that (18.7) is a class of neural networks with one hidden layer, where the output bias $b^{(2)}$ is set to zero and where the output layer is not subject to a nonlinear activation. Clearly, the theorem would fail to hold if σ were applied on the final layer, since the theorem includes, for instance, the sigmoid activation function, which produces an output bounded between zero and one. We also note that this result extends readily to discontinuous functions on compact sets. Indeed, $C(K)$ is dense in $L^p(K)$ for every compact set K and $1 \leq p < \infty$, hence so is $\mathcal{M}(\sigma)$.

Since it will be of use later, we now list a second classical result in neural network approximation theory. This pertains to their ability to interpolate data:

Theorem 18.3 (Universal interpolation theorem) *Let $\sigma \in C(\mathbb{R})$ and assume that σ is not a polynomial. Then for every k distinct points $\{x_j\}_{j=1}^k \subset \mathbb{R}^n$ and associated data $\{y_j\}_{j=1}^k \subset \mathbb{R}$ there exist $\{w_j\}_{j=1}^k \subset \mathbb{R}^n$, $\{b_j\}_{j=1}^k \subset \mathbb{R}$ and $\{c_j\}_{j=1}^k \subset \mathbb{R}$ such that*

$$\sum_{j=1}^{k} c_j \sigma(w_j^\top x_i + b_j) = y_i, \qquad i = 1, \ldots, k.$$

Theorems 18.2 and 18.3 provide important insight into the approximation capabilities of neural networks. It is important to note, however, that they do not generally prescribe practical strategies for constructing good neural networks from training data. They are, in other words, *existence theorems*.

Overall, these results imply that the class of neural networks with one hidden layer is already extremely rich. There are, however, many reasons for considering deeper networks. In particular, they can often approximate complicated functions more efficiently (in terms of the number of parameters) than shallow networks. We omit any discussion on the approximation theory of deeper networks – see the Notes section for references.

18.4 Architecture Design and Extensions

We now turn our attention towards the practical construction of neural networks. Given a supervised learning problem to solve (e.g. a classification problem) it is up to the user to choose the network architecture. Good architecture design has been instrumental in the breakthrough success that deep learning has achieved in recent years. While there are few fully rigorous means of doing this, various different strategies are used in applications. The intricacies of practical architecture design are largely outside the scope of this book. However, in this section we briefly discuss some of the key components that go into this, especially in the context of imaging tasks. In §19.2 we discuss architecture design for image reconstruction in a little more detail.

18.4.1 Convolutional Layers

The first practical concern in architecture design is that the number of parameters (18.6) in a fully connected neural network architecture can grow extremely large for even moderate sizes of $\mathbf{n}$ and L. For problems involving images, where the input dimension n is often large, it may simply be infeasible to have so many parameters. To overcome this issue, one typically restricts the weight matrices to belong to a subclass that is defined by a smaller number of parameters.

One way to do this is to consider sparse weight matrices, leading to so-called *sparsely connected* layers. However, for imaging problems in particular, it is more common to restrict the weight matrices to be convolutions. If a weight matrix $W^{(l)}$ is a convolution, we refer to the corresponding layer as a *convolutional layer*. A convolutional layer has far fewer parameters to train than in the general case. Matrix–vector multiplications with $W^{(l)}$ can also be performed efficiently. This contrasts with a *fully connected* layer, in which $W^{(l)}$ is an arbitrary dense matrix. A neural network with predominantly convolutional layers is termed a *Convolutional Neural Network (CNN)*. Such networks have been key to the success of deep learning in imaging tasks.

In one dimension, a typical example of a convolution is the following:

$$\begin{pmatrix} 1 & -1 & & & \\ & 1 & -1 & & \\ & & \ddots & \ddots & \\ & & & 1 & -1 \end{pmatrix} \in \mathbb{R}^{n \times (n+1)}. \tag{18.8}$$

This corresponds to convolution with the filter $(1, -1)$ of *length* two. Of course, we recognize this as a (nonperiodic) discrete gradient operator (recall Chapter 17). Hence, this mapping extracts the edges of an image – important features which may be useful in, for instance, classification. This example helps motivate the use of convolutional neural networks in imaging tasks. In general, convolutional layers provide translation invariance and locality, properties which are considered useful in such problems.

Note that we can also change the length of the convolution filter, as well as its *stride*. In (18.8) the convolution has stride one. In the following example:

$$\begin{pmatrix} 1 & 2 & 2 & 1 & & & & & \\ & & 1 & 2 & 2 & 1 & & & \\ & & & & 1 & 2 & 2 & 1 & \\ & & & & \ddots & \ddots & \ddots & \ddots & \\ & & & & & 1 & 2 & 2 & 1 \end{pmatrix} \in \mathbb{R}^{n \times (2n+2)},$$

the filter $(1, 2, 2, 1)$ has length four and stride two. This convolution takes input of length $2n + 2$. If an input happens to have length less than $2n + 2$, one typically zero pads it to obtain the correct length before applying the convolution.

In practice, image data is either two-dimensional (for greyscale images) or three-dimensional (for colour images). In these cases, the filter takes the form of a matrix or tensor, respectively, and the convolutional layer applies this filter across the corresponding patches of the input data.

18.4.2 Pooling, Upsampling and Downsampling

Another common type of layer, which often follows a convolutional layer, is a *pooling* layer. In one dimension, such a layer takes the form

$$\begin{pmatrix} x_1 \\ x_2 \\ \vdots \\ x_n \end{pmatrix} \mapsto \begin{pmatrix} \max\{x_1, x_2\} \\ \max\{x_3, x_4\} \\ \vdots \\ \max\{x_{n-1}, x_n\} \end{pmatrix} \quad \text{or} \quad \begin{pmatrix} x_1 \\ x_2 \\ \vdots \\ x_n \end{pmatrix} \mapsto \begin{pmatrix} \frac{1}{2}(x_1 + x_2) \\ \frac{1}{2}(x_3 + x_4) \\ \vdots \\ \frac{1}{2}(x_{n-1} + x_n) \end{pmatrix}.$$

The former is known as a *max-pooling* layer and the latter as an *average-pooling* layer. For two or three-dimensional input, the pooling operation is done over blocks of neighbouring pixels. By doing this, pooling helps reduce the sensitivity of the network to small changes in the position of a feature in the image. This is referred to as *local translation invariance.*

In many applications – for example, classification – the input dimension n is significantly larger than the output dimension p. Convolution (with stride greater than one) and pooling can both be used to achieve *downsampling* so as to effect such a reduction in dimension. *Upsampling* can also be achieved using so-called *transposed* convolutions and *unpooling* operations.

18.4.3 Skip Connections

Another common practice in architecture design is to allow so-called *skip connections.* Here the input to the network is also allowed to propagate directly to the later layers without going through the earlier layers. An example of such an architecture is the two-layer network

$$\mathrm{N}(x) = \sigma \circ A^{(2)} \left(x + \sigma \circ A^{(1)}(x) \right), \tag{18.9}$$

where $A^{(1)}$ and $A^{(2)}$ are affine maps. In other words, the input to the second layer is a linear combination of x and the result of the first layer $\sigma \circ A^{(1)}(x)$. Skip connections such as (18.9) are often concatenated to build deeper networks, leading to a so-called *ResNet* (Residual Network). Such skip connections are 'local'. One may also build 'global' skip connections, where the input of a deep network is combined into its last few layers. See §19.2.3 for an example of this in image reconstruction.

Skip connections are commonly employed in imaging tasks. A motivation for their use is that it can be easier to train a network if it does not have to preserve the input image x through the layers. Specifically, they assist in the training process by helping to mitigate the so-called *vanishing gradient* problem (see later).

Remark 18.4 Pooling layers and skip connections are, in general, not permitted in the original definition of a neural network, Definition 18.1. However, if the activation function is a ReLU function, both these layers can be realized within this definition. Indeed, if $\sigma(x) = \max\{0, x\}$ is a ReLU, then

$$x = \sigma(x) - \sigma(-x).$$

Moreover,

$$\max\{x_1, x_2\} = \frac{1}{2}(x_1 + x_2 + |x_1 - x_2|),$$

can also be written as a combination of ReLUs, since $|x| = \sigma(x) + \sigma(-x)$.

18.5 Training a Neural Network

Suppose we have fixed an architecture, i.e. a family of neural networks $\mathcal{N}$. *Training* is the process of computing a suitable neural network $\mathrm{N} \in \mathcal{N}$ from a given training set $\Theta = \{(u_i, v_i)\}_{i=1}^{K} \subset \mathbb{R}^n \times \mathbb{R}^p$. This is typically done by solving an optimization problem

$$\min_{\mathrm{N}\in\mathcal{N}} \mathrm{Cost}\left((\mathrm{N}(u_i))_{i=1}^{K}, (v_i)_{i=1}^{K}\right), \tag{18.10}$$

where $\mathrm{Cost}\colon \mathbb{R}^{pK} \times \mathbb{R}^{pK} \to [0,\infty)$ is a *cost* function (or *loss* function).

Typically, the cost function can be decomposed as a sum of separable cost functions over the training data, so that it takes the form

$$\frac{1}{K}\sum_{i=1}^{K} \mathrm{Cost}_i(\mathrm{N}(u_i), v_i), \tag{18.11}$$

where $\mathrm{Cost}_i\colon \mathbb{R}^p \times \mathbb{R}^p \to [0,\infty)$. A standard example is the ℓ^2-loss (also called the *mean-squared* loss, *least-squares* loss or *empirical risk*), in which case the problem (18.10) becomes

$$\min_{\mathrm{N}\in\mathcal{N}} \frac{1}{K}\sum_{i=1}^{K} \frac{1}{2}\|\mathrm{N}(u_i) - v_i\|_{\ell^2}^2.$$

Note that the factors $1/K$ and $1/2$ are often included for convenience (see later).

Since $\mathcal{N}$ is parametrized by the weights and biases, the optimization problem (18.10) can be reformulated as a standard optimization problem over $\mathbb{R}^d$, where d is the number of parameters, i.e. (18.6) in the case of a fully connected network. In other words, (18.10) can be recast in the form

$$\min_{w\in\mathbb{R}^d} f(w), \tag{18.12}$$

where the vector w contains the weights and biases. While benign looking, this problem is nonlinear and nonconvex. There is usually little prospect of computing global minimizers of it. It is also a large-scale problem, since most powerful deep networks involve many parameters. As discussed in §18.6, modern neural networks for image classification involve tens of millions of parameters. As a result, successfully training a neural network is a major computational challenge, one that usually requires substantial computing power and hundreds of hours of computation time.

18.5.1 Gradient Descent and Stochastic Gradients

Due to its extremely large size, (approximate) solutions of (18.12) are usually computed with first-order optimization methods (recall Chapter 7). These are based on variations of gradient descent. Recall that gradient descent produces a sequence

$$w_{i+1} = w_i - \tau_i \nabla f(w_i), \quad i = 0, 1, \ldots, \tag{18.13}$$

from an initial point $w_0 \in \mathbb{R}^d$, where $\tau_i > 0$ is the stepsize. In the context of machine learning, τ_i is called the *learning rate* and, to distinguish it from the network parameters (the weights and biases), it is often referred to as a *hyperparameter*. It is also common practice to vary τ_i with each iteration; see Remark 18.5 below.

As discussed above, the cost function $f(w)$ can typically be expressed as

$$f(w) = \frac{1}{K} \sum_{j=1}^{K} f_j(w), \tag{18.14}$$

where $f_j \colon \mathbb{R}^d \to [0, \infty)$ corresponds to the jth element in the training set. Therefore, calculating the gradient

$$\nabla f = \frac{1}{K} \sum_{j=1}^{K} \nabla f_j$$

requires one pass through all of the training data. When the amount of training data is large, as it often is in practice, this ceases to be computationally feasible. An alternative is to use so-called *stochastic gradients*. Here, at step i, we replace (18.13) by the following:

(i) Pick an integer j uniformly at random from $\{1, \ldots, K\}$.
(ii) Update $w_{i+1} = w_i - \tau_i \nabla f_j(w_i)$.

In other words, stochastic gradients use one training element (indexed by j) as a substitute for the whole dataset at each iteration. Perhaps remarkably, this crude approximation can often produce good results in practice.

There are several variations of stochastic gradients. One is to sample without replacement, thus ensuring that no training point is repeated. In this form of stochastic gradient, K steps of the iteration correspond to one full pass through the training data. This is known as an *epoch*. Another variation is so-called *mini-batch* stochastic gradient. Here the full cost function (18.14) is replaced by a small sample average. Specifically, given a batch size parameter $r \ll K$, the update step is:

(i) Pick $j_1, \ldots, j_r$ uniformly at random from $\{1, \ldots, K\}$.
(ii) Update $w_{i+1} = w_i - \tau_i \frac{1}{r} \sum_{k=1}^{r} \nabla f_{j_k}(w_i)$.

It is also possible to perform mini-batch stochastic gradient without replacement, in which case one epoch equates to K/r steps of the iteration. Like the learning rate, the mini-batch size r is another hyperparameter to be chosen. Computational considerations such as memory often inform this choice.

On the face of it, it may seem surprising that (mini-batch) stochastic gradient can work effectively. After all, the gradient is approximated from a very small sample size. But in practice, it often does. One explanation for this is that standard training sets typically contain many redundancies, e.g. similar images in the case of image classification. Hence, it is not necessary to pass through the whole dataset to obtain a good estimate for the gradient. A random sample may do almost as good a job, while using significantly less computing time.

Remark 18.5 In practice, choosing the learning rate τ_i is crucial to successful training. This is known as setting the learning rate *schedule*. It is common to use a decreasing learning rate to take into account the fact that stochastic gradient only produces an approximation of the true gradient. Various different schedules are used in practice, such as linearly or exponentially decreasing schedules.

Remark 18.6 Gradient descent or stochastic gradients are vanilla methods for solving the optimization problem (18.12). Performance can often be improved by using accelerated gradient methods, a topic discussed previously in Chapter 7. One such enhancement is *gradient descent with momentum*, in which case the update rule takes the form

$$z_{i+1} = \alpha z_i - \tau \nabla f(w_i), \quad w_{i+1} = w_i + z_{i+1}.$$

Here $\alpha > 0$ is the momentum parameter and $\tau > 0$ is the learning rate. As with all acceleration schemes, momentum helps to mitigate the zigzag behaviour of standard gradient descent by incorporating memory into the update. There are also various alternatives, for example *AdaGrad*, *RMSProp* and *Adam*. In practice, carefully choosing an optimization method and its hyperparameters is usually a vital step towards successful training.

18.5.2 Backpropagation

In order to apply gradient descent or stochastic gradients, we need to compute the gradient of each cost function f_i with respect to w, the vector containing the weights and biases. These gradients can be evaluated via the celebrated *backpropagation formulae*.

For simplicity, in this section we assume that these cost functions are defined by the ℓ^2-loss. Hence, letting (u, v) be a generic element of the training set, we consider the function

$$f(w) = \frac{1}{2}\|\mathrm{N}(u; w) - v\|_{\ell^2}^2,$$

where N is the neural network with weights and biases defined by the vector w. We now introduce some additional notation. First, let

$$z^{(l)} = W^{(l)} a^{(l-1)} + b^{(l)} \in \mathbb{R}^{n_l}, \quad l = 1, \ldots, L,$$

so that $a^{(l)}$, the output of the lth layer, is given by

$$a^{(l)} = \sigma(z^{(l)}), \quad l = 1 \ldots, L.$$

Next, we define $\delta^{(l)} \in \mathbb{R}^{n_l}$ by

$$\delta^{(l)} = \nabla_{z^{(l)}} f, \quad l = 1, \ldots, L,$$

where the right-hand side is the gradient of the cost function f with respect to the variable $z^{(l)}$. We also write $\nabla_{W^{(l)}} f$ and $\nabla_{b^{(l)}} f$ for the gradients of f with respect to the weights and biases, respectively. Finally, we let $x \odot y \in \mathbb{R}^n$ denote the entrywise (Hadamard) product of two vectors $x, y \in \mathbb{R}^n$.

Lemma 18.7 (Backpropagation formulae) *We have*

$$\begin{aligned}
\delta^{(L)} &= \sigma'(z^{(L)}) \odot (a^{(L)} - y), \\
\delta^{(l)} &= \sigma'(z^{(l)}) \odot (W^{(l+1)})^{\top} \delta^{(l+1)}, \quad l = 1, \ldots, L-1, \\
\nabla_{b^{(l)}} f &= \delta^{(l)}, \quad l = 1, \ldots, L, \\
\nabla_{W^{(l)}} f &= \delta^{(l)} (a^{(l-1)})^{\top}, \quad l = 1, \ldots, L.
\end{aligned}$$

This lemma is nothing more than the chain rule applied to f. But significantly, it allows the gradients of f to be computed by propagating through the network's layers in reverse order, starting from the final layer and ending with the input layer. The resulting procedure is known as *backpropagation*.

18.5.3 An Algorithm for Training

With this in hand, we now have a basic algorithm for training a neural network. This is shown in Algorithm 18.1. Notice that each step of the outer while loop requires one forward propagation through the network (the first for loop) to compute the $a^{(l)}$ and $z^{(l)}$, followed by one backpropagation (the second for loop) to compute the $\delta^{(l)}$ in order to evaluate the gradients needed for the stochastic gradient update (the third for loop).

Two key implementation details are missing from Algorithm 18.1. The first is the choice of initial weights and biases. Since the optimization problem is nonconvex and computationally intensive, the choice of initial point can have a significant effect on the output it converges to, or indeed, whether it converges in the first place. It is common practice to initialize the parameters randomly, with values drawn from a normal or uniform distribution with zero mean and a given variance. Choosing the right variance is important, and several heuristics exist for doing this. Second, no stopping criteria are given for the algorithm. Typical choices involve either running for a fixed number of epochs or halting when a sufficiently small training or validation error is achieved (see next). Naturally, good stopping criteria can have a significant positive effect on the produced output.

Architecture design also plays an important role in training. There is usually a tradeoff between *expressivity* – that is, the existence of networks that can approximate complicated functions – and *trainability*, i.e. the ability to compute such networks with an optimization algorithm from training data. Choosing an architecture that is simultaneously expressible and trainable is often crucial to successful deep learning.

Common issues that can affect training are the *vanishing* and *exploding* gradients problems. This is where the gradients of the cost function either become very small during training, meaning one ceases to explore the optimization landscape effectively, or they blow up, meaning that the gradient update moves the iterates a long way, often not in a desirable direction. The ResNet architecture can help avoid the vanishing gradients problem. The exploding gradients problem is often treated by *gradient clipping*, wherein the computed gradient values are restricted (clipped) to some fixed maximum value.

Algorithm 18.1: Training a neural network via stochastic gradients

input: training set $\{(u_i, v_i)\}_{i=1}^K$, activation function σ, learning rate τ, initial weights and biases $\{W^{(l)}, b^{(l)}\}_{l=1}^L$
output: weights and biases $\{W^{(l)}, b^{(l)}\}_{l=1}^L$

while *not converged* **do**
  Choose j uniformly and randomly from $\{1, \ldots, K\}$
  Set $u = u_j$, $a^{(0)} = u$ and $v = v_j$
  for $l = 1$ *to* $l = L$ **do**
    $z^{(l)} = W^{(l)} a^{(l-1)} + b^{(l)}$
    $a^{(l)} = \sigma(z^{(l)})$
  end
  $\delta^{(L)} = \sigma'(z^{(L)}) \odot (a^{(L)} - v)$
  for $l = L - 1$ *downto* $l = 1$ **do**
    $\delta^{(l)} = \sigma'(z^{(l)}) \odot (W^{(l+1)})^\top \delta^{(l+1)}$
  end
  for $l = L$ *downto* $l = 1$ **do**
    $W^{(l)} = W^{(l)} - \tau \delta^{(l)} (a^{(l-1)})^\top$
    $b^{(l)} = b^{(l)} - \tau \delta^{(l)}$
  end
end

18.5.4 Underfitting, Overfitting and Regularization

The objective of training is to obtain a network that has good generalization performance. Whether or not this is possible naturally depends on the network architecture, the training data Θ, the choice of cost function and the optimization algorithm.

There are two common phenomena that can cause poor generalization. The first is so-called *underfitting*. This occurs when the trained network has a large training error, i.e. it performs poorly over the training set itself. Underfitting is often a consequence of choosing an architecture with too few parameters – in other words, one that is insufficiently expressible. Conversely, a network *overfits* if it achieves a small or even zero training error, but generalizes poorly. This may occur when the architecture has too many parameters and when the cost function promotes only fidelity to the training data.

There are several ways to mitigate overfitting. One way is to add an additional term to the cost function that is independent of the training set Θ and depends only on the network N. This is known as *regularization*. Specifically, one replaces the cost function in (18.10) with

$$\mathrm{Cost}\left((\mathrm{N}(u_i))_{i=1}^K, (v_i)_{i=1}^K\right) + \lambda J(\mathrm{N}), \tag{18.15}$$

where $J : \mathcal{N} \to [0, \infty)$ is a *regularization function* and $\lambda \geq 0$ is a *regularization parameter*. The first term in (18.15) is often called the *fidelity* term (it promotes approximate fitting of the data) and the second term the *regularization* term. Like the learning rate τ, the scalar $\lambda \geq 0$ is another hyperparameter of the training procedure that requires

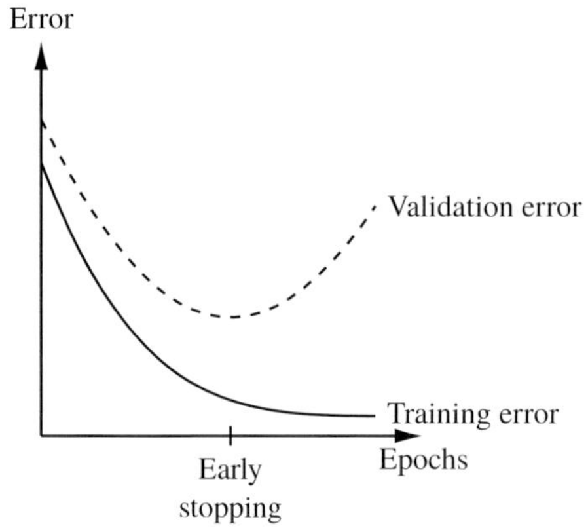

Figure 18.3 A typical scenario in early stopping. The training and validation errors are shown versus the number of epochs. The training error decreases with each epoch, whereas the validation error reaches a minimum and then begins to increase. In early stopping, the optimization algorithm is stopped when the validation error starts to increase.

tuning. A typical regularization function is the quadratic function

$$J(\mathrm{N}) = \sum_{l=1}^{L} \|W^{(l)}\|_F^2,$$

where $\|\cdot\|_F$ is the Frobenius norm and $W^{(l)}$ are the weight matrices associated with N. This type of regularization aims to mitigate against large weights, which may cause the network to overfit the training data.

Another strategy to avoid overfitting is *early stopping* of the optimization algorithm. This can be done as follows. The set $\Theta = \{(u_i, v_i)\}_{i=1}^K$ is first divided into two subsets: a training set that will be used to train the network and a validation set, which is not used to train the network, but instead used to examine its generalization performance. Overfitting occurs when the network performs well on the training set but has a large *validation error*, i.e. it performs poorly on the validation set. Hence this leads to a simple strategy. After each step of the optimization algorithm, compute the validation error and halt the algorithm once this error ceases to decrease. This strategy is visualized in Fig. 18.3. It is referred to as early stopping since the algorithm often halts when the derivatives of the objective function are still quite large – in other words, the output is not an approximate stationary point of the objective function.

Another strategy to avoid overfitting is *data augmentation*. Overfitting can be attributed to having too little training data for the network architecture, with training yielding a network that interpolates the data but performs poorly in between data points. In data augmentation one uses invariances in the problem to increase the amount of data. A typical example is image classification, where one expects an image's label to be unchanged if it is rotated, reflected or translated. Performing such operations (whatever is allowable within the particular problem) can significantly increase the size of the dataset and thus help mitigate overfitting.

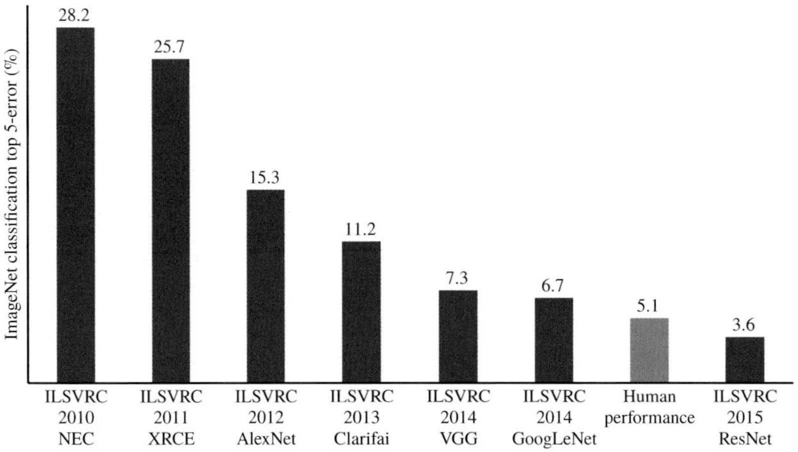

Figure 18.4 Winners of the ImageNet Large Scale Visual Recognition Challenge (ILSVRC). All of the winners since 2012 are based on deep learning.

18.6 The Success of Deep Learning

We have now described the basics of neural networks and deep learning. As the reader will hopefully have gathered, this is not straightforward. Solving a supervised machine learning problem with deep learning involves careful choices of the network architecture, optimization algorithm and hyperparameters, and then, once these decisions have been made, significant computational resources to train the large number of parameters.

Fortunately, many of these tasks are nowadays made much easier by the availability of specialist hardware such as Graphical Processing Units (GPUs) and software (e.g. TensorFlow, PyTorch, MXNet). Moreover, it has proved an extremely worthwhile endeavour. Deep learning has achieved notable and high-profile successes, yielding state-of-the-art performance on a range of challenging machine learning problems.

While not attempting a full review of these successes, it is worth pointing out one exemplar: namely, image classification. The beginning of the popular deep learning revolution is often dated to 2012, when a deep learning-based classifier named *AlexNet* not only won the *ImageNet Large Scale Visual Recognition Challenge (ILSVRC)*, but achieved an error reduction of nearly 10 percentage points over the previous year's winner.[1] AlexNet was a convolutional neural network with five convolutional layers and approximately 60 million parameters, trained using a GPU on a training set of roughly 1.2 million images (which was augmented).

This was a remarkable improvement on previous image classification algorithms. Since then, all winners of the ILSVRC contest have employed deep learning based on convolutional neural networks. Figure 18.4 lists these winners and their error rates. In less than a decade, the error rate was reduced from close to 30% to less than 4%. In 2015, deep learning achieved another milestone when this error rate was reduced below 5%, which is the error rate incurred by humans. This was achieved with a ResNet architecture.

[1] ImageNet is an image database of over 14 million labelled images for development and testing of visual object recognition algorithms. The ILSVRC competition has run annually since 2010. Prior to 2012, the winners were not based on deep learning.

As a result of this performance, the term 'superhuman' has been used to describe deep learning's ability to carry out image classification. Suffice to say, it is now the method of choice for most image classification tasks.

18.7 Instabilities in Deep Learning

It is hard to overstate the level of success that deep learning has achieved in recent years on this and many other machine learning problems. One may therefore be tempted to think that little can possibly go wrong. Unfortunately, we end this chapter on a more sober note. While trained neural networks for classification can perform extremely well, they also have a tendency to be highly unstable.

18.7.1 The Devil in the Details: Small Perturbations Change Labels

Around 2014, it was observed that neural networks had some unusual and quite alarming properties. In particular, while they are extremely good at classifying large classes of images, they are also greatly affected by certain perturbations to their input.

To be more precise, given a trained classifier C and an input image x_0, it was shown that it is possible to find a visually imperceptible perturbation r for which the network misclassified the image $x_0 + r$, i.e.

$$\mathrm{C}(x_0) \neq \mathrm{C}(x_0 + r).$$

Figure 18.5 demonstrates this phenomenon. Each image has been perturbed in a small (and barely visible) way, yet this causes the classifier to produce a clearly incorrect label. Note that this perturbation is not random. It was purposefully constructed in each case to produce such an effect. For this reason, it is commonly referred to as an *adversarial perturbation* and, imagining a malicious actor, the procedure for creating it is termed an *adversarial attack*.

18.7.2 Constructing Adversarial Perturbations via DeepFool

These instabilities are troubling – we will touch on some of their potential real-world consequences later. But first, it is worth explaining how such adversarial perturbations can be constructed. While there are a number of different ways to do this, in this section we describe a method known as *DeepFool*.

We first consider the case of binary (two-class) classification. Suppose that the classifier $\mathrm{C}: \mathbb{R}^n \to \{+1, -1\}$ takes the form $\mathrm{C}(x) = \mathrm{sign}(f(x))$, where $f: \mathbb{R}^n \to \mathbb{R}$ is continuous and differentiable and sign is the usual sign function. Let x_0 be the image we wish to perturb. To find a perturbation r, the idea is to solve the optimization problem

$$\min_{r \in \mathbb{R}^n} \|r\|_{\ell^2} \text{ subject to } \mathrm{sign}(f(x_0 + r)) \neq \mathrm{sign}(f(x_0)). \tag{18.16}$$

Solving this problem produces a perturbation $\hat{r}$ of minimal ℓ^2-norm that changes the label of the image x_0.

wool | Indian elephant | Indian elephant | African grey

African grey | grey fox | macaw | three-toed sloth

Figure 18.5 Instabilities in deep learning for image classification. Perturbed images and the labels produced by the classifier are shown. Although the perturbation is invisible to the human eye in each case, it causes the classifier to produce an incorrect label. Image reproduced courtesy of Seyed-Mohsen Moosavi-Dezfooli, Alhussein Fawzi, Omar Fawzi and Pascal Frossard.

This is a nonlinear and generally nonconvex optimization problem. Hence we need a method for computing (approximate) solutions to it. For simplicity, suppose first that $f(x) = w^\top x + b$ is an affine function, so that $\mathrm{C}(x)$ is a linear classifier. Then the *decision boundary* – that is, the boundary between regions of the input space $\mathbb{R}^n$ that are assigned label $+1$ and those assigned label -1 – is precisely the hyperplane

$$H = \{x \in \mathbb{R}^n : w^\top x + b = 0\}.$$

Hence, the minimum ℓ^2-norm perturbation $\hat{r}$ required to change the label of x_0 should move x_0 to its closest point on H. This can be obtained via the orthogonal projection onto H, yielding the following explicit formula:

$$\hat{r} = -\frac{(w^\top x_0 + b)}{\|w\|_{\ell^2}^2} w = -\frac{f(x_0)}{\|w\|_{\ell^2}^2} w. \tag{18.17}$$

Figure 18.6 illustrates this procedure.

Now suppose that $f: \mathbb{R}^n \to \mathbb{R}$ is an arbitrary differentiable function. It is no longer possible to minimize (18.16) exactly, so we instead adopt an iterative procedure. Suppose that we linearize f around x_0,

$$f(x_0 + r) \approx f(x_0) + \nabla f(x_0)^\top r.$$

Then we replace (18.16) by the linearized problem

$$\min_{r \in \mathbb{R}^n} \|r\|_{\ell^2} \text{ subject to } f(x_0) + \nabla f(x_0)^\top r = 0.$$

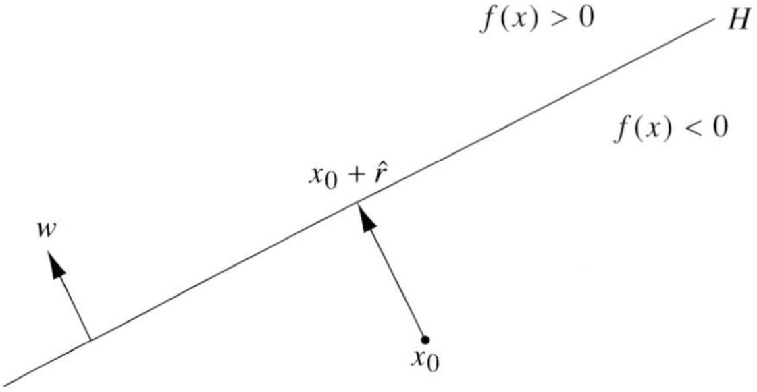

Figure 18.6 The minimum-norm perturbation $\hat{r}$ required to move x_0 to the decision boundary of a linear classifier $f(x) = w^\top x + b$.

Algorithm 18.2: DeepFool for binary classifiers

input: image x_0, classifier function f
output: perturbation $\hat{r}$

Set $i = 0, \hat{r} = 0$
while $\text{sign}(f(x_i)) = \text{sign}(f(x_0))$ **do**
  $r_i = -\frac{f(x_i)}{\|\nabla f(x_i)\|_{\ell 2}^2} \nabla f(x_i)$
  $x_{i+1} = x_i + r_i$
  $\hat{r} = \hat{r} + r_i$
  $i = i + 1$
end

In view of (18.17), the solution r_0 of this problem is precisely

$$r_0 = -\frac{f(x_0)}{\|\nabla f(x_0)\|_{\ell 2}^2} \nabla f(x_0).$$

Naturally, since an approximation was performed, the perturbed image $x_1 = x + r_0$ may not have succeeded in changing the label of x. The idea now is to linearize f around x_1 and then repeat the procedure, giving a perturbation r_1 and a new image $x_2 = x_1 + r_1 = x_0 + r_0 + r_1$. One now continues in this way to produce a sequence of perturbed images x_i. The result is the iteration described in Algorithm 18.2. Notice that this iteration either halts at some finite i if x_i has a label different to that of x_0, or in the limit $i \to \infty$ it produces an image that lies on the decision boundary of the classifier. In the latter case, one typically multiplies the final perturbation $\hat{r}$ by a constant $1 + \delta$, where $\delta \ll 1$, to produce a perturbation lying on the other side of the decision boundary.

Since (18.16) is generally nonconvex, we do not claim that Algorithm 18.2 produces a local minimum. However, that is not the main concern. Provided it does not run for too many iterations, Algorithm 18.2 is expected to produce a perturbation $\hat{r}$ that is small in magnitude and changes the label of x_0.

Algorithm 18.2 pertains to binary classification. Now consider a multiclass classification problem with $p \geq 2$ distinct classes. We assume a *one-versus-all* framework, where $C: \mathbb{R}^n \to \{1, \ldots, p\}$ takes the form $C(x) = \sigma(f(x))$, with $f: \mathbb{R}^n \to \mathbb{R}^p$ continuous and

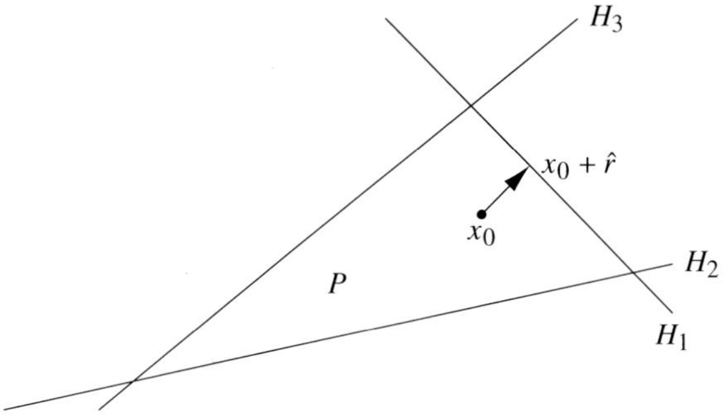

Figure 18.7 The minimum-norm perturbation $\hat{r}$ required to change the label of x_0 with label $k_0 = 4$ for a linear classifier $f(x) = Wx + b$ with $p = 4$ classes. The polytope P is the triangular region.

differentiable and $\sigma \colon \mathbb{R}^p \to \{1, \dots, p\}$ defined by

$$\sigma(z) = \min\{k : z_k \geq z_i,\ \forall i = 1, \dots, p\}, \qquad z = (z_k)_{k=1}^{p}. \tag{18.18}$$

Let x_0 be an image with label $k_0 \in \{1, \dots, p\}$, i.e. $\mathrm{C}(x_0) = k_0$. Then to construct a perturbation r we seek to solve the problem

$$\min_{r \in \mathbb{R}^n} \|r\|_{\ell^2} \text{ such that } f_k(x_0 + r) \geq f_{k_0}(x_0 + r) \text{ for some } k \neq k_0, \tag{18.19}$$

where f_k denotes the kth component of f.

As before, we first consider the case where f is an affine function, i.e. $f(x) = Wx + b$ for some $W \in \mathbb{R}^{p \times n}$ and $b \in \mathbb{R}^p$. Define the hyperplanes

$$H_k = \{x : f_k(x) = f_{k_0}(x)\}, \qquad k \neq k_0,$$

and notice that x_0 belongs to the polyhedron

$$P = \bigcap_{\substack{k=1 \\ k \neq k_0}}^{p} \{x : f_{k_0}(x) \geq f_k(x)\},$$

whose faces are the hyperplanes H_k. Hence, the minimum-norm perturbation $\hat{r}$ should project x_0 onto the closest such hyperplane. This is illustrated in Fig. 18.7. In view of (18.17), the perturbation $\hat{r}$ is given by

$$\hat{r} = -\frac{(f_{\hat{k}}(x_0) - f_{k_0}(x_0))}{\|\nabla f_{\hat{k}}(x_0) - \nabla f_{k_0}(x_0)\|_{\ell^2}^2} \left(\nabla f_{\hat{k}}(x_0) - \nabla f_{k_0}(x_0)\right),$$

where

$$\hat{k} = \operatorname*{argmin}_{k \neq k_0} \frac{|f_k(x_0) - f_{k_0}(x_0)|}{\|\nabla f_k(x_0) - \nabla f_{k_0}(x_0)\|_{\ell^2}}.$$

This solves (18.19) in the case of a linear classifier. For a nonlinear classifier, we proceed as in the binary case, using an iterative procedure based on local linearization around each iterate. Doing so leads to Algorithm 18.3.

To summarize, in Algorithms 18.2 and 18.3 we have obtained procedures for constructing adversarial perturbations of binary and multiclass classifier functions of the form $\mathrm{C}(x) = \sigma(f(x))$. Note that both procedures require us to compute gradients of the

Algorithm 18.3: DeepFool for multiclass classifiers

input: image x_0, label k_0, classifier function f
output: perturbation $\hat{r}$

Set $i = 0$, $\hat{r} = 0$
while $k_i = k_0$ **do**
  for $k \neq k_0$ **do**
    $w'_k = \nabla f_k(x_i) - \nabla f_{k_0}(x_i)$
    $f'_k = f_k(x_i) - f_{k_0}(x_i)$
  end
  $k_i = \underset{k \neq k_0}{\operatorname{argmin}} \frac{|f'_k|}{\|w'_k\|_{\ell 2}}$
  $r_i = -\frac{f'_{k_i}}{\|w'_{k_i}\|^2_{\ell 2}} w'_{k_i}$
  $x_{i+1} = x_i + r_i$
  $\hat{r} = \hat{r} + r_i$
  $i = i + 1$
end

function f. However, in the case of a trained neural network, this can be done efficiently using backpropagation, as long as the weights and biases of the network are known. As we discuss in the Notes section, this means that DeepFool is a type of *whitebox* attack.

18.7.3 Universality and Transferability

Algorithms 18.2 and 18.3 are designed to construct a perturbation of a specific image x_0. If the resulting perturbation is applied to a different image x_1, it will likely not cause a misclassification. Perhaps surprisingly, it is also possible to construct *universal* adversarial perturbations. Such a perturbation is designed to simultaneously misclassify a large number of images from a given dataset.

Figure 18.8 shows examples of universal adversarial perturbations for six different trained neural network classifiers. When applied to the ImageNet validation dataset, these perturbations achieve a *fooling rate* of over 75% for each network (i.e. 75% of the images in the dataset were misclassified when subjected to this perturbation), and for several of the networks this rate is over 90%. These rates are given in Table 18.1. We omit the description of the algorithm used to construct these perturbations. We note in passing, though, that it is based on repeatedly applying the algorithms described above (which construct single-image perturbations) while iterating over the dataset of images. See the Notes section for further information.

Interestingly, these perturbations are not only universal, they are also *transferrable*. That is, the perturbation constructed to fool one network can also be used to fool another network. Table 18.1 shows this effect for the networks considered in Fig. 18.8. In each case, the perturbation from one network is able to fool a significant proportion of images for any one of the other networks.

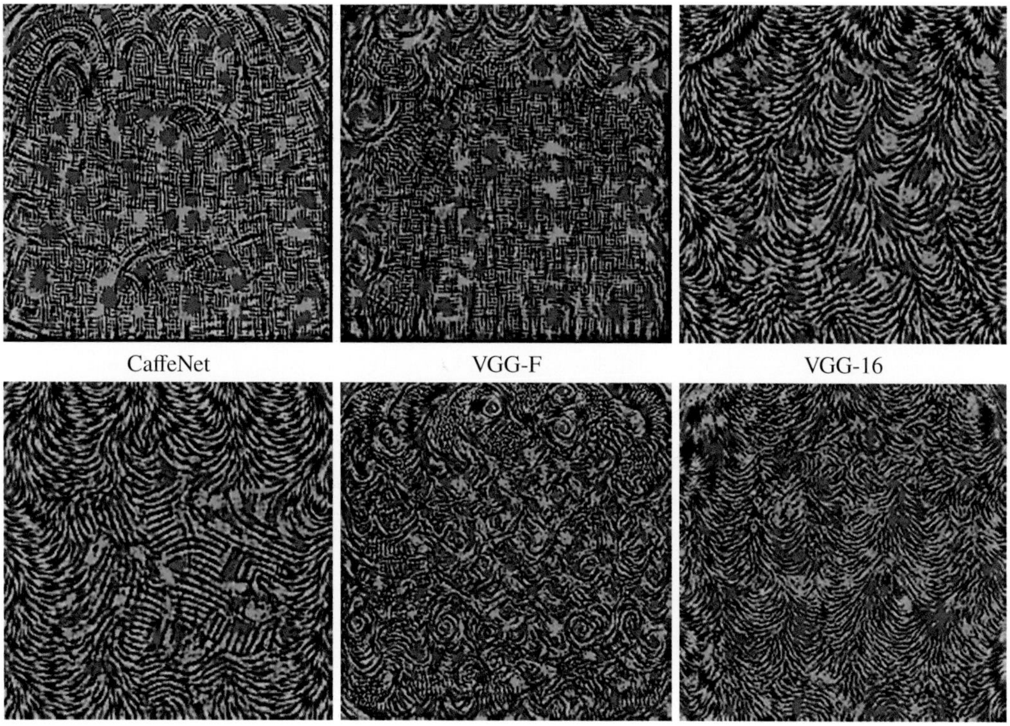

Figure 18.8 Universal perturbations that were computed for different trained networks (listed below each image) using the ImageNet validation dataset, which consists of 50,000 images. In each case, the perturbation fools over 75% of the images in the dataset. Precise fooling rates are shown in Table 18.1. Image reproduced courtesy of Seyed-Mohsen Moosavi-Dezfooli, Alhussein Fawzi, Omar Fawzi and Pascal Frossard.

18.7.4 Consequences and Defences

We have now seen how to construct adversarial perturbations. But what does this mean for real-world deep learning systems? Clearly, there are some applications where adversarial perturbations may have few consequences (being mistagged in a Facebook photo is unlikely to cause many of us sleepless nights). Yet, there are many real-world problems where the consequences are potentially far reaching. Although a detailed discussion on this topic is outside the scope of this book, we note in passing that adversarial attacks have been constructed in a range of practical settings – see the Notes section for further information. For example, self-driving cars rely crucially on accurately recognizing road features such as cars, traffic signs and pedestrians. Real-world adversarial perturbations have been constructed to fool these systems by placing adversarial patches on stop signs. Similarly, facial recognition algorithms for surveillance have been fooled into misclassification by specially designed adversarial eyeglasses, and in medical diagnosis, adding a perturbation or even simply rotating an image of a melanoma has been shown

Table 18.1 Fooling rates for different networks when subject to the universal adversarial perturbations shown in Fig. 18.8. The rows indicate the architecture for which the universal adversarial perturbation was computed and the columns indicate the architecture to which the perturbation was applied. Table reproduced courtesy of Seyed-Mohsen Moosavi-Dezfooli, Alhussein Fawzi, Omar Fawzi and Pascal Frossard.

	VGG-F	CaffeNet	GoogLeNet	VGG-16	VGG-19	ResNet-152
VGG-F	**93.7%**	71.8%	48.4%	42.1%	42.1%	47.4%
CaffeNet	74.0%	**93.3%**	47.7%	39.9%	39.9%	48.0%
GoogLeNet	46.2%	43.8%	**78.9%**	39.2%	39.8%	45.5%
VGG-16	63.4%	55.8%	56.5%	**78.3%**	73.1%	63.4%
VGG-19	64.0%	57.2%	53.6%	73.5%	**77.8%**	58.0%
ResNet-152	46.3%	46.3%	50.5%	47.0%	45.5%	**84.0%**

to cause it to be misclassified. The latter was part of a demonstration on how adversarial attacks may be used to commit medical insurance fraud.

The discovery of adversarial perturbations has also led to a recent flurry of activity on *defences* against such attacks. Broadly speaking, a defence is any procedure that seeks to improve the robustness of a classifier to adversarial perturbations. However, no strategy has proved uniformly successful thus far. Universality and transferability highlight the pervasive nature of instabilities in deep learning and the difficulty in creating effective defences. For instance, they potentially make adversarial attacks more easily realizable, since an adversary may not need to have access to the network's parameters in order to fool it. In other words, adversarial attacks cannot necessarily be defended against simply by hiding the network's parameters from the user.

18.8 Why do Instabilities Occur?

Having described the instability of deep learning and its consequences, we close this chapter with some theoretical insights into why this occurs. In particular, we now show that this can be attributed to the so-called *false structure* phenomenon.

Consider a binary labelling function

$$\mathrm{C}_0 \colon \mathbb{U} \subset \mathbb{R}^n \to \mathbb{V} = \{+1, -1\}. \tag{18.20}$$

This function serves as the ground truth that we seek to approximate with a learned classifier C. Since C_0 is either constant or discontinuous, it will itself be unstable at certain points, unless it happens to be constant. In order to make meaningful statements, we therefore restrict the set of inputs so that it does not come too close to the decision boundary. Given $\delta > 0$, we let

$$\mathbb{U}_\delta := \{x \in \mathbb{U} : \mathrm{C}_0(x+y) = \mathrm{C}_0(x), \forall y : x+y \in \mathbb{U}, \|y\|_{\ell^\infty} < \delta\}. \tag{18.21}$$

We assume that $\mathbb{U}_\delta \neq \emptyset$ for all sufficiently small $\delta > 0$. In this case $\mathrm{C}_0|_{\mathbb{U}_\delta}$ is stable to small perturbations. However, as we now see, a learned classifier C may easily become unstable, even when restricted to $\mathbb{U}_\delta$.

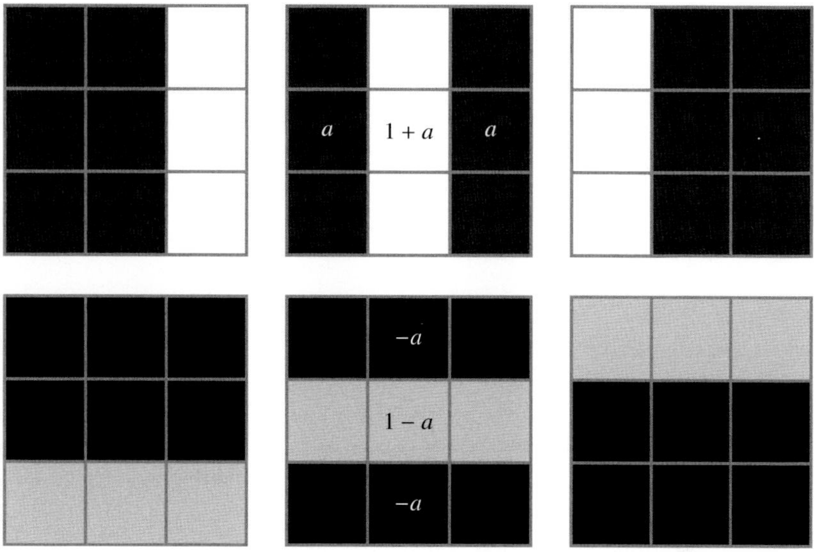

Figure 18.9 3 × 3 images with either horizontal or vertical stripes. Vertical stripes (top row) are assigned the value a (dark) or $1 + a$ (light), and horizontal stripes (bottom row) are assigned the values $-a$ and $1 - a$. These images are coloured as follows: $-1/4$ represents black, $1 + 1/4$ represents white, and numbers in between $-1/4$ and $1 + 1/4$ represent shades of grey.

18.8.1 Instabilities in Shallow Neural Networks

As an example, consider the set of 3×3 images with a light stripe that is either horizontal or vertical. Let $\mathbb{U}$ denote the collection of all such images where, in the vertical case, the light stripe takes the value $1 + a$ and the dark stripes take the value a for some $0 \leq a \leq 1/4$, and, in the horizontal case, the light stripe takes the value $1 - a$ and the dark stripes take the value $-a$. This is illustrated in Fig. 18.9. Next, define the binary labelling function

$$\mathrm{C}_0(x) = \begin{cases} +1 & \text{if } x \text{ has a horizontal light stripe,} \\ -1 & \text{if } x \text{ has a vertical light stripe.} \end{cases}$$

Note that C_0, in fact, is completely stable on $\mathbb{U}$: no restriction to the subdomain $\mathbb{U}_\delta$ is required in this case.

Now consider the one-layer neural network defined by

$$\mathrm{C}(x) = \begin{cases} +1 & \text{if the sum of the pixel values is } \leq 3, \\ -1 & \text{if the sum of the pixel values is } > 3. \end{cases}$$

While simple, this network has a remarkable success rate. Indeed, it succeeds on uncountably many inputs, and fails on just one case ($a = 0$). However, it is also completely unstable. Indeed, a small, constant perturbation to the pixel values of the input image can cause C to give the wrong answer, even though C_0 is completely stable to such a perturbation. Being small, such a perturbation is also invisible to the human eye.

This example illustrates that a classifier may be successful, but do so for completely the wrong reasons. Indeed, C succeeds in this example since it captures the offset of the image. This is a simple, but ultimately false, structure. Conversely, it fails to capture the more complicated, true structure, namely, the stripe. The inevitable result is that it is unstable to small perturbations.

18.8.2 Instabilities in Deeper Networks

The classifier C in the previous example is extremely simple. One can imagine that a deeper network would capture the more complicated structure of this problem, hence leading to better stability. This begs the following question: do instabilities occur in trained neural networks for classification when the networks are deep? As we now show, the answer to this question is yes.

In order to avoid contrived examples, we need to ensure that the data that comprises the training and test sets is well separated. Once more, we also restrict the input domain away from the decision boundary of the ground truth labelling function. Specifically, given C_0 and $\mathbb{U}_\delta$ is as in (18.21), we define the family of well-separated and stable sets with separation at least $\delta > 0$ as

$$\mathcal{S}(C_0, \delta) = \left\{ \{x_i\}_{i=1}^r \subseteq \mathbb{U}_\delta : r \in \mathbb{N},\ \|x_j\|_{\ell^\infty} \leq 1, \min_{i \neq j} \|x_i - x_j\|_{\ell^\infty} \geq \delta \right\}.$$

Let K be the size of training set and define the set of cost functions

$$\mathcal{CF}_K = \left\{ \mathrm{Cost}\colon \mathbb{R}^{nK} \times \mathbb{R}^{nK} \to [0, \infty) : \mathrm{Cost}(u, v) = 0 \Leftrightarrow u = v \right\}.$$

In the following result, we consider families of fully connected, feedforward neural networks $\mathcal{N}_\mathbf{n}$ of the form

$$N(u) = A^{(L)} \circ \sigma \circ A^{(L-1)} \circ \cdots \circ \sigma \circ A^{(1)}(u),$$

where $\sigma(x) = \max\{0, x\}$ is the ReLU activation function and the $A^{(l)}$ are affine maps. Note that the ReLU activation is not applied in the final layer.

Theorem 18.8 *There is an uncountable family $\mathcal{F}$ of classification functions $C\colon \mathbb{R}^{n_0} \to \{+1, -1\} \subset \mathbb{R}$ with the following property. For every $C \in \mathcal{F}$ and network architecture $\mathbf{n} = (n_0, \ldots, n_L)$ with $n_0, L \geq 2$ and $n_L = 1$, $\epsilon > 0$ and integers K, S with $K \geq 3(n_1 + 1) \cdots (n_{L-1} + 1)$, there exist uncountably many nonintersecting training sets $\mathbb{T} = \{x_1, \ldots, x_K\} \subseteq \mathcal{S}(C_0, \delta(K + S))$ of size K (where $\delta(n) := ((4n + 3)(2n + 2))^{-1}$) and uncountably many nonintersecting test sets $\overline{\mathbb{T}} = \{y_1, \ldots, y_S\} \subseteq \mathcal{S}(C_0, \delta(K + S))$ of size S such that the following holds. For every* Cost $\in \mathcal{CF}_K$ *there is a neural network $\widehat{N} \in \mathcal{N}_\mathbf{n}$ with*

$$\widehat{N} \in \underset{N \in \mathcal{N}_\mathbf{n}}{\mathrm{argmin}}\, \mathrm{Cost}(u, v), \qquad u = (N(x_i))_{i=1}^K,\ v = (C(x_i))_{i=1}^K, \tag{18.22}$$

such that

$$\widehat{N}(x) = C(x) \quad \forall x \in \mathbb{T} \cup \overline{\mathbb{T}}. \tag{18.23}$$

However, there are uncountably many $v \in \mathbb{R}^{n_0}$ *such that*

$$|\widehat{\mathrm{N}}(v) - \mathrm{C}(v)| \geq 1/2, \qquad \|v - x\|_{\ell^\infty} \leq \epsilon \text{ for some } x \in \mathbb{T}. \tag{18.24}$$

On the other hand, there exists a neural network $\breve{\mathrm{N}} \notin \mathcal{N}_{\mathbf{n}}$ *such that* $\breve{\mathrm{N}}(x) = \mathrm{C}(x)$ *for all* $x \in B_{\delta(K+S)}(\mathbb{T} \cup \overline{\mathbb{T}})$*, where*

$$B_{\delta(K+S)}(\mathbb{T} \cup \overline{\mathbb{T}}) = \left\{ z \in \mathbb{R}^{n_0} : \exists x \in \mathbb{T} \cup \overline{\mathbb{T}}, \|x - z\|_{\ell^\infty} \leq \delta(K+s) \right\}.$$

This theorem generalizes the example discussed in §18.8.1 to arbitrarily deep networks – indeed, its proof is based on similar reasoning to this example. It implies the following. First, there are uncountably many classification functions that will cause trained neural networks (i.e. minimizers of (18.22)) to be unstable. Moreover, this happens for uncountably many distinct training sets. Hence, instability is not a rare event, but a potentially common occurrence. Second, the trained network may succeed on (arbitrarily large) training sets and test sets, see (18.23). Yet, as shown in (18.24) there are uncountably many cases where the network will fail, and these examples can be made arbitrarily close to the training set. Third, even though the trained network is unstable, there exists another network (with a different architecture) that succeeds on the same set of inputs, yet is also completely stable.

This last point implies that there is nothing wrong with the class of neural networks per se. It is just that there is no clear way to compute this network via training. Indeed, even if we changed the architecture accordingly, there is nothing to stop the same phenomenon from occurring within this new class.

Notes

Deep learning has garnered unprecedented levels of interest since AlexNet, developed by Krizhevsky, Sutskever & Hinton [303], achieved breakthrough success at the ILSVRC contest in 2012. It is the epitome of a 'hot topic', and, to the best of our knowledge, only the second topic mentioned in this book to have been featured on the cover of the *New York Times* [350] (the other being Karmarkar's algorithm for linear programming). For more information on ImageNet and ILSVRC, see [425].

Neural networks have a long history, dating back to the 1950s. Many of the components that go into deep learning, such as training via backpropagation, are classical. However, the contemporary rise of deep learning began after 2000, as computational resources such as GPUs became available to train deep convolutional networks, as well as large amounts of publicly available training data. For more historical information and context, see [317, 428].

There are numerous overviews of deep learning. We have found the survey article by Higham & Higham [265] to be amongst the most accessible. As noted, this chapter is not intended as a comprehensive guide to implementing deep learning in practice. As such, we have barely touched upon many important topics that are vital to successful implementations, such as architecture design, choice of optimization algorithm, hyperparameter selection and initialization. We refer to [233] for an in-depth introduction to these topics.

For an introduction to the classical approximation theory of shallow neural networks, including estimates on the rate (or *degree*) of approximation, see [390]. Theorems 18.2 and 18.3 are Theorems 3.1 and 5.1, respectively therein. Density of neural networks (Theorem 18.2) was first considered in the works of Cybenko [161] and Hornik [268]. See [390] for an overview of this literature. Spurred by deep learning, there is now a growing literature on the approximation theory of deeper networks [11,46,68,242,246, 325,387,431,474,516,517]. It is important to note that this work does not typically explain the practical performance of deep learning, as results therein are generally of existence type only. A comprehensive mathematical understanding of the success of deep learning is currently lacking. See [345,482] and references therein for some work in this direction. The presence of adversarial perturbations suggests this is a very subtle matter.

Convolutional neural networks are a classical concept, dating back to the 1980s [428]. ResNets were used in the winning entry for the 2015 ILSVRC competition [261]. Their use, however, is not limited to classification. Convolutional layers are found in most architectures for image restoration and image reconstruction.

For more information regarding optimization for deep learning, see [233, Chpt. 8], [84] and references therein. These also include descriptions of the AdaGrad, RMSProp and Adam methods which were mentioned in Remark 18.6. A proof of Lemma 18.7 can be found in [265]. Regularization is a classical approach, dating back at least to [304]. See also [413]. It is sometimes known as *weight decay*. For more on overfitting and how to avoid it, see [233, Chpt. 7,8]. Besides those already mentioned, other approaches to improve training include *bagging*, *dropout* and *batch normalization*.

The susceptibility of neural networks to perturbations was first shown in [454]. Since then, the study of adversarial attacks has become a subject in its own right. This subject deals with the construction of attacks, the understanding of why they occur, their potential consequences in applications, and perhaps most importantly, methods for defending against them [44,275,277,341,429,463,503,511]. Amongst the most well-known defences is so-called *adversarial training* [41,44,235,275,307,341,441,463,488]. We discuss this further in the context of image reconstruction in §20.5. The current situation in this field has been likened to an 'arms race' [499], with new defence strategies leading to new attacks and vice versa. So far, no defence strategy has achieved complete success. Attacks on self-driving cars based on manipulating stop signs were shown in [201], and attacks based on eyeglasses and clothing patches for fooling surveillance systems in [435] and [459], respectively. See [210] for a discussion on adversarial attacks in medical diagnosis and their potential application to medical insurance fraud. Another line of work has demonstrated a 'dual' phenomenon to adversarial perturbations [203], where images that are unrecognizable to the human eye are classified with high confidence by neural networks [380]. For extensive reviews on adversarial attacks, including further discussion on why deep learning is susceptible to these perturbations, see [30,128,203,499].

One of the earliest methods for generating perturbations was the *Fast Gradient Sign Method (FGSM)* [235]. DeepFool was introduced by Moosavi-Dezfooli, Fawzi & Frossard [360]. §18.7.2 is based on this paper.

DeepFool is a type of whitebox attack, in that it requires the network's parameters in order to compute its gradients and thus compute the adversarial perturbation. Blackbox attacks are also possible. DeepFool is also a *nontargeted* attack: it simply aims to cause misclassification without caring about the resulting label. *Targeted* attacks, in which one seeks to cause a specific misclassification, can also be achieved. See [499].

Universal adversarial perturbations were first shown by Moosavi-Dezfooli, Fawzi, Fawzi & Frossard [359]. Figures 18.5 and 18.8 are from this paper, as is Table 18.1. For more information about these experiments, including the networks listed in Fig. 18.5 and Table 18.1 and the algorithm used to construct the perturbations, see [359].

The stripes example of §18.8 is due to [203]. Theorem 18.8 and its proof can be found in [52]. For further discussion on false structures, see [457] and references therein.

19 Deep Learning for Compressive Imaging

The purpose of this chapter is to give a short introduction to the application of deep learning to compressive imaging. We begin in §19.1 with a brief motivation. Then in §19.2 we describe some of the different ways to apply neural networks and deep learning to the image reconstruction problem. In §19.3 we introduce the experimental setup that is used in the next chapter to examine the performance of deep learning, including the particular networks that are considered. Finally, motivated by the instability issue discussed in §18.7 for classification problems, in §19.4 we introduce a computational framework for investigating instabilities of neural networks for image reconstruction.

A word of caution: at the time of writing, deep learning for compressive imaging is a rapidly evolving topic. For this reason, we have chosen to briefly survey some of its general principles, rather than attempt a broader survey of the many different methods that have recently been proposed. The Notes section contains references for further reading. For the purposes of experimental comparison, we have selected networks that are currently amongst the most well known.

19.1 Why Go Beyond Compressed Sensing

The answer, simply put, is because we are greedy: we want higher-accuracy reconstructions from fewer measurements. More precisely, there are at least five limitations of compressed sensing that deep learning seeks to address:

(i) Compressed sensing is model-based. A fixed model such as sparsity (or sparsity in levels) in wavelets may not be optimal for a particular modality such as MRI.
(ii) Given a model, compressed sensing requires one to *handcraft* a reconstruction procedure (e.g. ℓ^1-minimization) that exploits this structure. It may be challenging to craft an effective reconstruction procedure for a more sophisticated image model.
(iii) Optimization-based recovery procedures are slow.
(iv) Tuning the parameters of an iterative optimization solver is delicate, and can have a significant effect on reconstruction quality.
(v) Compressed sensing approaches typically require accurate sensor calibration.

Of course, (i) does not require deep learning per se. Dictionary learning (see §4.7) could be used to overcome this limitation. But dictionary learning generally leads to slower computations and additional sensitivity to the optimization parameters. In theory at least, neural networks, once trained, could be faster than optimization-based approaches. Reconstruction involves only a single forwards propagation through the network, with the expensive computations being performed offline during the training phase. Deep learning is also a more flexible methodology: in a sense, it implicitly learns a nonlinear sparsifying transform directly from data. The success of deep learning on image classification tasks indicates that neural networks can effectively encode important image features, an ability that one naturally looks to exploit in the related task of image reconstruction.

19.2 Deep Learning for Inverse Problems

We now describe some of the current deep learning methodologies for solving discrete, linear inverse problems. Throughout, we consider the problem of recovering an unknown vector $x \in \mathbb{C}^N$ from measurements $y = Ax + e \in \mathbb{C}^m$, where $A \in \mathbb{C}^{m \times N}$. Note that while our main focus is on imaging, most of the theoretical results we develop in the next chapter also apply to this abstract setting.

To apply deep learning to this problem, we assume there is a training set

$$\Theta = \{(y_i, x_i)\}_{i=1}^K \subset \mathbb{C}^m \times \mathbb{C}^N, \qquad y_i = Ax_i + e_i,$$

consisting of images x_i and their (noisy) measurements y_i. The goal is to use this data to construct a reconstruction map $\mathrm{R}\colon \mathbb{C}^m \to \mathbb{C}^N$ that performs well on the images of interest in the given modality.

Remark 19.1 In problems such as MRI it is common to encounter a complex input $y \in \mathbb{C}^m$ and output $x \in \mathbb{C}^N$. There are two standard ways to deal with this when using neural networks. First, one can associate $y \in \mathbb{C}^m$ with a vector $y' \in \mathbb{R}^{2m}$ consisting of the real and imaginary parts of y, then design a real-valued network $\mathrm{N}\colon \mathbb{R}^{2m} \to \mathbb{R}^{2N}$ whose output $x' = \mathrm{N}(y')$ is likewise associated with a complex image $x \in \mathbb{C}^N$. Second, one simply allows *complex-valued* neural networks, i.e. networks for which the weights and biases are complex and for which the activation functions are mappings $\sigma\colon \mathbb{C} \to \mathbb{C}$. This is a little more challenging when it comes to training as it requires complex versions of standard operations such as backpropagation. However, it is more convenient when it comes to theory. Except when stated otherwise, we consider this latter approach from now on. We denote a complex-valued neural network as $\mathrm{N}\colon \mathbb{C}^m \to \mathbb{C}^N$.

19.2.1 Denoiser Networks

Image denoising is the task of recovering an image x from a noisy version of itself $x' = x + e$. To apply deep learning to this problem, one considers a training set

$$\Theta = \{(x_i + e_i, x_i)\}_{i=1}^K \subset \mathbb{C}^N \times \mathbb{C}^N.$$

Typically, the noise e_i is drawn from some specific distribution, and hence the objective is to train a neural network $\mathrm{N}\colon \mathbb{C}^N \to \mathbb{C}^N$ that can denoise new images when the noise is drawn from the same distribution. It transpires that neural networks are particularly well suited to this task. They now provide state-of-the-art denoiser performance – see the

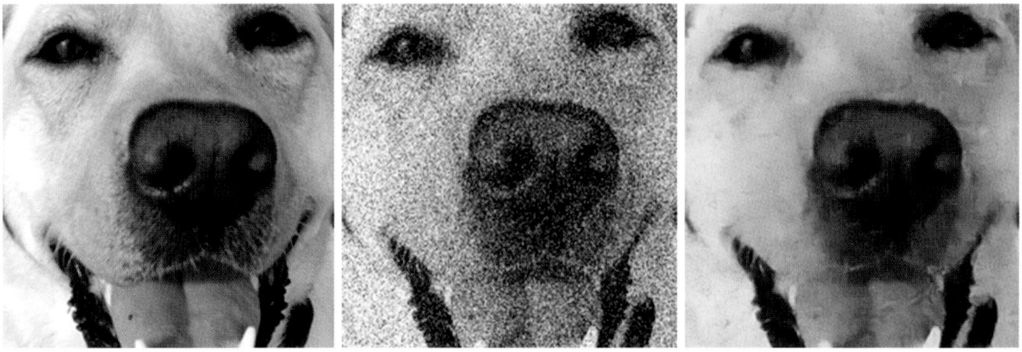

(a) Original (b) Noisy (c) Denoised

Figure 19.1 Denoising the 512×512 dog image via deep learning. (a) The (cropped) original image x. (b) Noisy image $x + e$. (c) The denoised image $\mathrm{N}(x + e)$, where N is a trained convolutional neural network.

Notes section for further information. Figure 19.1 shows an example of image denoising using a trained neural network.

Now consider the inverse problem of recovering x from measurements $y = Ax+e$. In a *denoiser network* one first preprocesses the measurements y by applying a classical (and typically computationally cheap) reconstruction $\mathrm{R}_0 : \mathbb{C}^m \to \mathbb{C}^N$. For instance, in Fourier imaging this may be a zero-padded inverse FFT; in Radon imaging it may be a zero-padded filtered back-projection. In either case, $\mathrm{R}_0(y) = By$ simply applies a linear map to y. As discussed in Chapters 3 and 4, these maps typically give poor reconstructions that exhibit significant artefacts. Hence, $\mathrm{R}_0(y)$ can be considered a noisy version of x, with structured noise depending on the modality and the choice of R_0. A neural network $\mathrm{N} : \mathbb{C}^N \to \mathbb{C}^N$ is then trained to clean up these artefacts, giving the overall reconstruction map as the composition $\mathrm{R} = \mathrm{N} \circ \mathrm{R}_0 : \mathbb{C}^m \to \mathbb{C}^N$. This approach is sometimes referred to as *image-domain* learning.

Figure 19.2 shows an example of the denoiser approach based on the so-called Ell 50 and Med 50 networks (see §19.3). The middle column shows the reconstruction $\mathrm{R}_0(y)$ obtained via filtered back-projection. Its characteristic artefacts are clearly visible. The third column shows the result of the neural network that has been trained to remove these artefacts. The improvement in quality is significant.

An advantage of denoiser networks is that they naturally incorporate the knowledge of the physics of the problem into the reconstruction procedure through the preprocessor R_0. A disadvantage is that the network N does not see the data y, but rather the noisy image $\mathrm{R}_0(y)$. Hence, any features lost in the process $y \mapsto \mathrm{R}_0(y)$, e.g. due to inaccurate modelling of the underlying physics, cannot be restored in the final reconstruction.

19.2.2 Learn the Physics

Denoiser networks are hybrid model-based and data-driven approaches: the model-based reconstruction R_0 is postprocessed by the data-driven neural network N. By contrast,

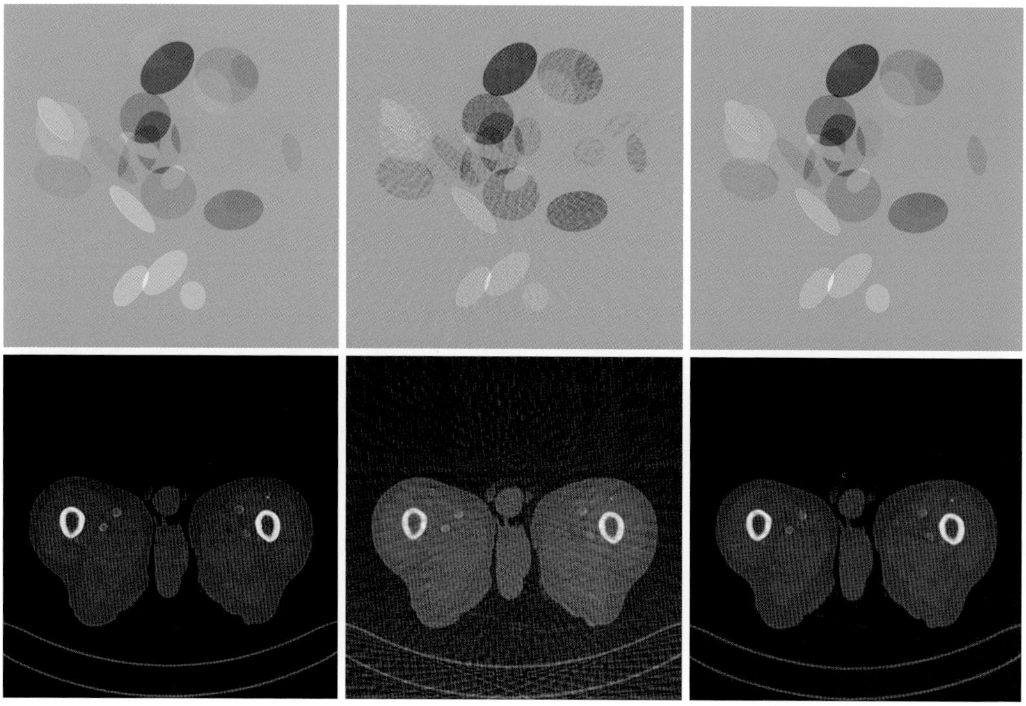

(a) Original (b) Filtered back projection (c) Deep learning

Figure 19.2 Recovery from discrete Radon measurements taken at 50 equally spaced angles. (a) Original image x. (b) Zero-padded filtered back-projection reconstruction $\mathrm{R}_0(y) = By$. (c) Deep learning reconstruction $\mathrm{R}(y) = \mathrm{N} \circ \mathrm{R}_0(y)$, where N is either the Ell 50 (top) or Med 50 (bottom) neural network.

the *learn-the-physics* (or *fully trained*) approach is fully data driven. Here, one trains a neural network $\mathrm{N}: \mathbb{C}^m \to \mathbb{C}^N$ that maps directly from the measurement space $\mathbb{C}^m$ to the image space $\mathbb{C}^N$ without using the forwards operator A or the preprocessor R_0.

The advantages of this approach are that it is conceptually simple and does not rely on inexact physical modelling of the imaging problem. Indeed, fully trained approaches do not suffer from the potential loss of information that denoiser networks do when performing the preprocessing step $y \mapsto \mathrm{R}_0(y)$. The AUTOMAP network introduced in §19.3 is an example of this type of approach. Figure 19.3 gives an example of image reconstruction via this network.

This approach has two main disadvantages. First, since the physics is unlikely to be represented by convolution operators only, it is generally necessary to have several fully connected layers. This makes training more computationally intensive since the number of network parameters can become very large. This also means that a large amount of training data is needed. As a result, fully trained approaches are theoretically limited to low-resolution imaging problems. A second disadvantage is that such approaches

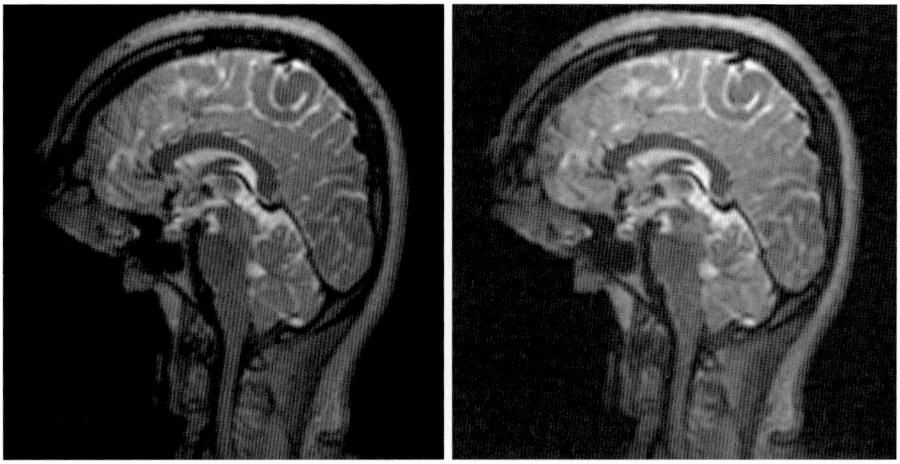

Original Reconstruction

Figure 19.3 MRI reconstruction using the AUTOMAP network (see §19.3). Left: Original image. Right: Reconstruction from 60% Fourier measurements.

are inflexible. Any change to the forwards model – for instance, changing the sampling pattern in MRI or the number of angles in X-ray CT – requires the model to be retrained.

19.2.3 Examples of Architecture Design

In order to implement either of the previous two approaches, one first needs to fix a network architecture. As noted in Chapter 18, this is an intricate matter. We now describe typical architectures for each approach.

The *U-net*, which is shown in Fig. 19.4, is a popular denoiser network architecture. It is *fully convolutional* in the sense that it only involves convolution operations, pooling and upsampling. The network consists of two *paths*. First, a *contracting path* reduces the size of the input through a sequence of convolution and pooling layers. This is reminiscent of convolutional neural networks for classification problems, where the desired output dimension (equal to the number of labels) is much smaller than the input dimension (equal to the image size). Second, an *expansive path* performs a series of convolutions and upsampling operations to give an output dimension of the same size as the input. Skip connections (see §18.4.3) are included in order to transfer coarse image information from the early layers to the later layers.

The U-net has been used very successfully in image segmentation. A modification for X-ray CT reconstruction, termed *FBPConvNet*, is used in the Ell 50 and Med 50 networks. One modification made by FBPConvNet is to add an additional skip connection between the input and output layer, so that the network has a ResNet form (see §18.4.3). In other words, the network learns the difference between the noisy input and the denoised output. As noted in §18.4.3, this is done primarily to make training easier.

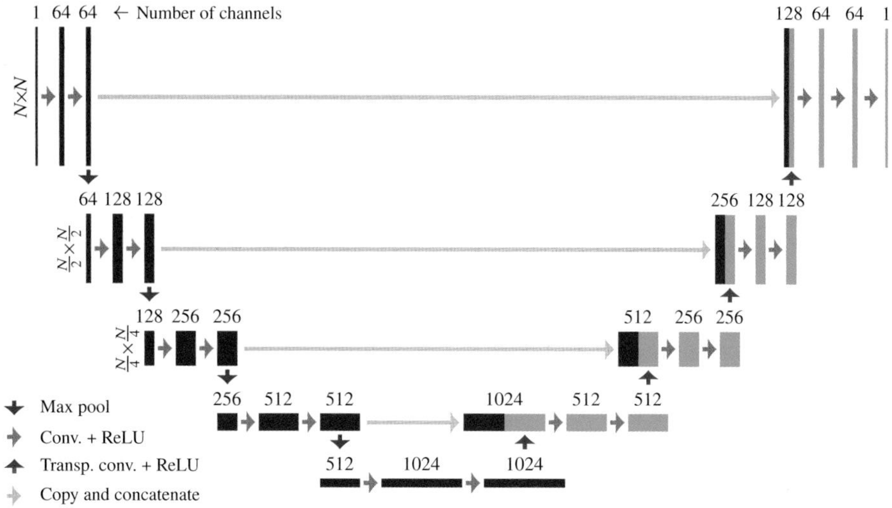

Figure 19.4 A schematic of the U-net architecture. The input image is viewed as an $N \times N \times 1$ tensor with one channel. The left side of the 'U' applies a sequence of alternating convolutional layers and max-pooling operations to produce a $N/16 \times N/16 \times 1024$ tensor. The right side of the 'U' then alternates convolutions and transpose convolutions (which perform upsampling) to give an output of the same size of as the input. The grey arrows indicate the skip connections.

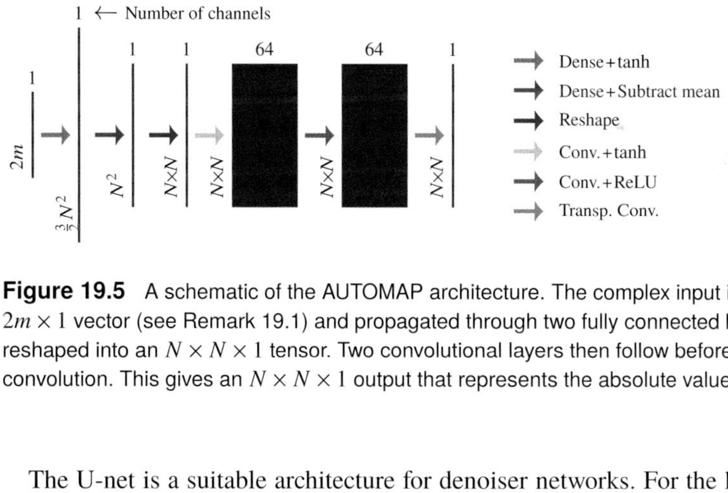

Figure 19.5 A schematic of the AUTOMAP architecture. The complex input is reshaped into a $2m \times 1$ vector (see Remark 19.1) and propagated through two fully connected layers before being reshaped into an $N \times N \times 1$ tensor. Two convolutional layers then follow before a final transpose convolution. This gives an $N \times N \times 1$ output that represents the absolute value image $|x|$.

The U-net is a suitable architecture for denoiser networks. For the learn-the-physics approach, as mentioned, the architecture should have several fully connected layers. Figure 19.5 shows a typical architecture. The first two layers are fully connected matrices of size $25{,}000 \times 2m$ and $N^2 \times 25{,}000$, respectively, where N is the image size and m is the number of measurements. The first fully connected layer is followed by a hyperbolic tangent activation function, and the second fully connected layer is followed by a layer which subtracts the mean from the output of the layer and then reshapes the output into an $N \times N$ image. After that, there is a series of two convolutional layers before a final transpose convolutional layer which produces the output.

19.2.4 Unravelling

The previous approaches to architecture design are somewhat ad hoc: they use various heuristics to obtain architectures that work well in practice. For image reconstruction, a rather more principled way to approach this task is to start with an iterative optimization algorithm for solving, for instance, QCBP or LASSO, and then *unravel* it.

Recall from Chapter 7 that many optimization algorithms involve alternating applications of fixed affine maps (related to the matrix A) and nonlinear functions (typically proximal maps). For example, consider the U-LASSO problem

$$\min_{x \in \mathbb{R}^N} g(x) + \frac{1}{2}\|Ax - y\|_{\ell^2}^2, \tag{19.1}$$

where g is a generic convex regularization function. The forward–backward splitting method for this problem (see §7.4.1) is given by

$$x_{n+1} = \mathrm{prox}_{\tau g}(x_n - \tau A^\top(Ax_n - y)), \quad n = 0, 1, \ldots, \tag{19.2}$$

where $\mathrm{prox}_{\tau g}$ is the proximal map of τg. Note that $\mathrm{prox}_{\tau g}$ often acts componentwise. For example, when g is the ℓ^1-norm it is precisely the soft thresholding operator $\mathcal{S}_\tau$ (Definition 7.4). Hence, the operation $x_n \mapsto x_{n+1}$ can be interpreted as the action of one layer of a neural network with nonlinear activation $\mathcal{S}_\tau$, and k steps of forward–backward splitting can be viewed as the action of a neural network with k layers.

In general, unravelling yields a neural network architecture from which the components, i.e. the affine maps, can then be learned. The optimization parameters (e.g. the stepsize τ, LASSO parameter) may also be learned, as well as the activation functions themselves. For instance, one may parametrize the activation functions as piecewise linear functions and then learn the parameters of this parametrization.

The MRI-VN network used later is an example of the unravelling principle. Unravelling will also be the focal point of Chapter 21.

Unravelling is a hybrid model-based and data-driven approach: a model-based optimization scheme is unravelled, and then used as the architecture in training. Its advantage is that it gives a principled way to design architectures, and theoretically at least, one is guaranteed a choice of weights and biases for which the resulting network possesses the same accuracy and stability as compressed sensing. A disadvantage is that the architecture is closely linked to the optimization algorithm that was unravelled. Moreover, effective optimization algorithms often employ stopping criteria that are dependent on the input (e.g. the primal–dual gap). By contrast, unravelling usually assumes an *a priori* fixed number of iterations.

19.2.5 Learning the Proximal Map

Consider the U-LASSO problem (19.1) and the forward–backward splitting method (19.2). By definition (see (D.12)), the proximal map is given by

$$\mathrm{prox}_{\tau g}(u) = \underset{z \in \mathbb{R}^N}{\mathrm{argmin}} \left\{ \tau g(z) + \frac{1}{2}\|u - z\|_{\ell^2}^2 \right\}, \quad u \in \mathbb{R}^N.$$

Hence $u \mapsto \mathrm{prox}_{\tau g}(u)$ can be interpreted as a regularization-based denoising procedure. When given a noisy image $x' = x + e$ as its input, $\mathrm{prox}_{\tau g}$ denoises it by solving a LASSO-type regularization problem involving the function g. With this in mind, (19.2) can be interpreted as follows. First, the *data fidelity* update

$$x_n \mapsto x_{n+1/2} = x_n - \tau A^\top (A x_n - y) \tag{19.3}$$

is performed. Observe that $(A x_{n+1/2} - y) = (I - \tau A A^\top)(A x_n - y)$. Hence if the stepsize τ satisfies $\tau \|A\|_{\ell^2}^2 < 1$, this update promotes fidelity of $A x_{n+1/2}$ to the measurements y. Next, the image $x_{n+1/2}$ is denoised via the proximal map, giving $x_{n+1} = \mathrm{prox}_{\tau g}(x_{n+1/2})$.

Regularization-based denoising – for instance, TV regularization, which corresponds to the choice $g(\cdot) = \|\cdot\|_{TV}$ – is a well-known denoising procedure. But it is no longer considered state-of-the-art. On the other hand, neural networks are excellent denoisers. This leads to another means to apply deep learning to image reconstruction: namely, fix a finite number of steps of a given optimization algorithm, replace the proximal maps by neural networks, and then train their parameters. The Deep MRI network discussed next is an example of this procedure. Note that this leads to a type of *recurrent* neural network architecture if the same neural network is used for each proximal map. Variations include using different networks for each proximal map, learning the coefficients in the update (19.3), incorporating additional memory into the optimization solver, and so forth.

19.3 Experimental Setup

In the next chapter, we present a series of experiments comparing trained neural networks and compressed sensing. We now briefly describe the experimental setup. The Notes section contains further information and references.

The networks we consider, some of which have already been mentioned in the previous section, are listed in Table 19.1. Note that each network is designed for a particular modality and trained using a specific sampling strategy. Hence, each network is associated with a particular measurement matrix $A \in \mathbb{C}^{m \times N}$. Throughout, if A is not specified it is assumed to be as prescribed by this table.

For compressed sensing, we consider several different approaches. Generally, we use the procedure described in §4.8 based on iterative reweighting and a combination of shearlets and TGV. This is used except when explicitly stated otherwise, or whenever the parallel MRI problem is considered (i.e. for comparison with the MRI-VN network). In this latter case, we use the CS SENSE reconstruction (3.20) with wavelets.

Henceforth, we write $\mathrm{R}_{\mathrm{dl}} : \mathbb{C}^m \to \mathbb{C}^N$ for a reconstruction map based on any of these deep learning procedures and $\mathrm{R}_{\mathrm{cs}} : \mathbb{C}^m \to \mathbb{C}^N$ for a reconstruction map based on any of the compressed sensing procedures.

Table 19.1 A description of the trained neural networks considered in this and the next chapter. Further information can be found in the Notes section.

Name	Modality	Description
AUTOMAP	Single-coil MRI	Developed for low-resolution single-coil MRI with 60% subsampling. The training set consists of brain images with white noise added to the Fourier samples.
DAGAN	Single-coil MRI	Developed for medium-resolution single-coil MRI with 20% subsampling. Trained on a set of brain images.
Deep MRI	Single-coil MRI	Developed for medium-resolution single-coil MRI with 33% subsampling. Trained on a set of detailed cardiac MR images.
Ell 50	CT	Developed for CT or any Radon transform-based imaging problem. Uses the FBPConvNet architecture. Trained on images containing ellipses only (hence the name Ell 50). The number 50 refers to the number of angles used in the sampling.
Med 50	CT	Exactly the same architecture and sampling scheme as Ell 50. However, it is trained using medical images (hence the name Med 50) from the Mayo Clinic database.
MRI-VN	Parallel MRI	Developed for medium to high-resolution parallel MRI with 15 coils and 15% subsampling. Trained on a set of knee images.

19.4 Testing for Instabilities in Neural Networks for Compressive Imaging

To examine the performance of these networks, we need a way of constructing adversarial perturbations for image reconstruction problems, similar to what was done via DeepFool for classification problems. We now describe this procedure.

Let $\mathrm{R}\colon \mathbb{R}^m \to \mathbb{R}^N$ be a reconstruction map, $x \in \mathbb{R}^N$ be an image we seek to perturb and $y = Ax \in \mathbb{R}^m$ be its measurements. For convenience, we consider problems over the reals in this section (recall Remark 19.1). Inspired by the approach of §18.7, a first idea is to solve

$$\min_{r \in \mathbb{R}^N} \|r\|_{\ell^2} \text{ subject to } \|\mathrm{R}(y + Ar) - \mathrm{R}(y)\|_{\ell^2} \geq \delta,$$

where $\delta > 0$ controls the magnitude of the effect of the perturbation on the output. However, this approach is problematic since it may be infeasible for certain values of δ and it is difficult to know *a priori* how to set δ. A better approach is to use the unconstrained LASSO-type formulation

$$\max_{r \in \mathbb{R}^N} \frac{1}{2}\|\mathrm{R}(y + Ar) - \mathrm{R}(y)\|^2_{\ell^2} - \frac{\lambda}{2}\|r\|^2_{\ell^2},$$

where $\lambda > 0$ is a parameter. We consider this formulation from now on. Note that solving this problem will create one type of perturbation. More generally, one could consider the problem

$$\max_{r \in \mathbb{R}^N} \frac{1}{2}\|\mathrm{R}(y + Ar) - p\|_{\ell^2}^2 - \frac{\lambda}{2}\|r\|_{\ell^2}^2, \tag{19.4}$$

where $p \in \mathbb{R}^N$ is not necessarily equal to $\mathrm{R}(y)$. Different choices of p will then lead to different types of perturbations. A standard choice is to set $p = x$.

The problem (19.4) can be solved via gradient ascent. Let

$$f_{y,p,\lambda}(r) = \frac{1}{2}\|\mathrm{R}(y + Ar) - p\|_{\ell^2}^2 - \frac{\lambda}{2}\|r\|_{\ell^2}^2$$

be the objective function. Then the gradient of $f_{y,p,\lambda}$ is given by

$$\nabla f_{y,p,\lambda}(r) = A^\top \nabla g_p(y + Ar) - \lambda r, \qquad g_p(z) = \|\mathrm{R}(z) - p\|_{\ell^2}^2. \tag{19.5}$$

Note that if R is a neural network, then the gradient ∇g_p can easily be computed via backpropagation. A single gradient ascent update step therefore takes the form

$$r_{i+1} = r_i + \tau \left(A^\top \nabla g_p(y + Ar_i) - \lambda r_i \right),$$

where τ is the learning rate. In practice, however, it is typically more efficient to use an accelerated version of gradient ascent, for instance, gradient ascent with momentum (see Remark 18.6). In this case, the update step is

$$v_{i+1} = \alpha v_i + \tau \left(A^\top \nabla g_p(y + Ar_i) - \lambda r_i \right) \quad r_{i+1} = r_i + v_{i+1}, \tag{19.6}$$

where $\alpha > 0$ is the momentum parameter.

Algorithm 19.1 summarizes this procedure. Note that the additional parameter $\beta > 0$ in this algorithm is simply a scaling factor that is used to account for the dynamic range of the input images.

Remark 19.2 In contrast to most algorithms in this book, we are not concerned with whether or not the iteration (19.6) converges to a local maximum of (19.4). Rather, our goal is a qualitative one. We simply use (19.6) to construct perturbations that are not too large and for which the recovered image is significantly impacted in a visual sense (i.e. in the eyeball metric). Generally speaking, smaller perturbations that give milder artefacts are obtained by stopping after fewer iterations, while larger perturbations that give worse artefacts are obtained by running more iterations. In the experiments shown in the next chapter, the number of iterations is manually tuned.

Remark 19.3 Much as when training a neural network, an appropriate choice of the optimization parameters $\alpha, \tau > 0$ in Algorithm 19.1 is quite important. For Radon sampling, in particular, this can be quite challenging. This issue can be mitigated by replacing the matrix–vector multiplication with $A^\top$, which corresponds to the (discretized and zero-padded) back-projection operator, by multiplication with the filtered back-projection operator $B \in \mathbb{R}^{N \times m}$. See §2.3 for background on these operators. In effect, the filtering operation regularizes the gradient step, making it less sensitive to parameter choices. The Radon sampling experiments performed in the next chapter use this modification.

Algorithm 19.1: Constructing adversarial perturbations for inverse problems

input: image $x \in \mathbb{R}^N$, measurement matrix $A \in \mathbb{R}^{m \times N}$, reconstruction map R,
maximum number of iterations M, parameters $\lambda, \alpha, \tau, \beta > 0$ and $p \in \mathbb{R}^N$
output: Perturbation $\hat{r} = r_M$

Let g_p be as in (19.5) and set $y = Ax$, $v_0 = 0$ and $i = 0$.
Draw r_0 from the uniform distribution on $[0, \beta]^N$.
for $i = 0, \ldots, M$ **do**
$v_{i+1} = \alpha v_i + \tau \left(A^\top \nabla g_p(y + Ar_i) - \lambda r_i \right)$
$r_{i+1} = r_i + v_{i+1}$
end

Notes

As noted at the beginning of this chapter, many different deep learning approaches have recently been proposed for compressive imaging. Rather than attempting to survey the current landscape, we have instead chosen to briefly highlight some of the main flavours of deep learning for compressive imaging. For overviews of the many different methods, see [25,42,333,353,384,411,520]. For MRI-specific approaches, see [294,324,334,426]. While medical imaging has been a driving force, deep learning has also been applied to various other imaging modalities, such as optical imaging, microscropy and seismic imaging [384].

To date, deep learning has arguably progressed further in image restoration tasks such as denoising, deblurring and inpainting than it has in image reconstruction. See [353, 411] and references therein. It now offers state-of-the-art denoiser performance, for example, equalling or surpassing well-known denoising techniques such as BM3D (Block-Matching and 3D Filtering) [162] which uses sparsity and self-similarity of image patches. Indeed, the experiment in Fig. 19.1 was performed using Matlab's `denoiseImage` command with the option `'DnCNN'`. This uses a pre-trained convolutional neural network for image denoising that was developed in [522]. Since this network only takes greyscale inputs, each of the RGB channels in Fig. 19.1 was denoised separately and then combined.

It is worth noting that using neural networks for imaging tasks is not a new idea. As observed in [353, 411], they were used as early as 1988 for image restoration [525] and in 1991 for image reconstruction in SPECT [211]. But these approaches were largely forgotten until recent years.

For further discussion on complex-valued neural networks (Remark 19.1), see [426, 462] and references therein.

The Ell 50 and Med 50 networks were introduced in [278]. Many other denoiser networks have also been proposed in the literature. We refer to [42, Sec. 5.1.5] and [411, Sec. VI.A] for overviews. A related approach is to seek to use a neural network as a *preprocessor*: that is, use a network to fill in the missing k-space data (in the case of MRI) or projection data (in the case of X-ray CT), followed by a classical inversion [294,411]. This is sometimes referred to as *sensor-domain learning*.

While there had been several prior attempts, the learn-the-physics methodology first gained wider attention through the AUTOMAP network [527]. See [42, Sec. 5.1.3] for an overview of work in this direction. As noted therein, this approach cannot currently solve large-scale problems, due to its need for fully connected layers to model the physics. In [527], for instance, the network was trained to recover 128×128 MRI images – a low resolution by modern standards.

Fully convolutional neural networks for image segmentation were introduced in [331], and developed further in [420] for biomedical images. The U-Net is from this latter paper. This network was adapted for X-ray CT reconstruction in [278], leading to FBPConvNet. It has also been adapted for various image restoration tasks [333]. Figure 19.4 is based on [278].

See the Notes section of Chapter 21 for more information on unravelling. Compressive imaging strategies based on learned proximal mappings have been developed in various venues. See [26,134,175,349,427] and references therein. The connection between proximal maps and denoising has also been exploited in other ways. In the *Plug-and-Play Prior (P^3)* method [481], one replaces the proximal map by an off-the-shelf denoising algorithm. This could be a trained neural network, in which case the overall reconstruction mapping is also a neural network, or the BM3D denoiser [162], in which case it is not. A related approach is *Regularization by Denoising (RED)* [417]. Note that P^3 and RED are not deep learning approaches per se, since any off-the-shelf denoiser may be used. See [27] for an overview.

As discussed in [384], deep learning approaches can be broadly categorized into methods that require full knowledge of A, methods that require knowledge of A only in the reconstruction phase and not in the training phase, and methods that require no knowledge of A. Denoiser networks belong to the first category, plug-and-play methods to the second, and fully trained approaches to the third. Methods in the second category are arguably more flexible, since they do not require retraining if the reconstruction problem changes. Another method in this category is so-called *compressed sensing using generative models* [82]. A fourth category consists of problems where A is partially known, for example, problems with unknown calibration parameters. In this case, these parameters can also be learned in the training process. See [384] and references therein.

See [36] for further information about the networks listed in Table 19.1 and the compressed sensing procedures used for comparison purposes. AUTOMAP was introduced in [527], DAGAN in [512], Deep MRI in [427], Ell 50 and Med 50 in [278] and MRI-VN in [253]. The technique described in §19.4 is also from [36].

20 Accuracy and Stability of Deep Learning for Compressive Imaging

We now examine deep learning for image reconstruction from the perspective of accuracy and stability. We do this in both a theoretical and experimental manner, using the networks listed in §19.3 for the latter. As throughout this book, our perspective is deterministic, as opposed to statistical.

We commence in §20.1 with an exploration of accuracy through so-called *optimal maps*. Next, in §20.2 we consider instabilities in deep learning. Experimentally, we establish the existence of instabilities for all the networks considered. These instabilities cause a myriad of different effects, ranging from clearly nonphysical artefacts to artefacts that are hard to dismiss as such. Next, we give a key theoretical insight. Deep learning approaches can become unstable because they may lack *kernel awareness*. There is typically nothing to prohibit a network from being trained to recover two images whose difference lies close to the null space of the measurement matrix. This leads to specific, worst-case perturbations which cause bad artefacts. However, we show that generic noise added to the measurements can also cause bad artefacts with nonzero probability.

The conclusion of these two sections is that there is a delicate tradeoff between accuracy and stability. In §20.3 we explore this tradeoff experimentally. Next, in §20.4 we examine it theoretically in connection with compressed sensing. We develop scenarios where the instability of deep learning is caused first by its over-performance, and second, by the addition of further training data. Finally, in §20.5 we consider potential remedies for instabilities. These include methods that are known to achieve (partial) success in protecting against adversarial attacks in classification problems, such as adversarial training and *Generative Adversarial Networks (GANs)*. However, as we explain, these may be of limited efficacy when applied to image reconstruction.

20.1 Optimal Maps

As noted, in compressed sensing one imposes an *explicit* structure (e.g. sparsity or sparsity in levels), and then designs a recovery procedure which, under conditions such as the rNSP, accurately recovers images that (approximately) possess this structure. By contrast, the idea of learning is to try to learn a structure *implicitly* from training data. This raises the question: what do we seek to learn? We now discuss this matter through the idea of optimal maps.

Note that since our goal is to study accuracy, we assume noise-free measurements in this section.

20.1.1 The Inverse Problem Triple

For reasons of generality, we consider $\mathbb{C}^N$ equipped with an arbitrary metric d throughout this section. We describe an inverse problem in terms of a triple $\{A, \mathbb{M}_1, \mathbb{M}_2\}$, where

(i) $A \in \mathbb{C}^{m\times N}$ is the sampling operator;
(ii) $\mathbb{M}_1 \subseteq \mathbb{C}^N$ is the *domain*, it is a metric space with the metric d;
(iii) $\mathbb{M}_2 = A(\mathbb{M}_1) \subseteq \mathbb{C}^m$ is the *range*.

The idea is that $\mathbb{M}_1$ represents the images of interest. Thus, in compressed sensing we impose $\mathbb{M}_1$, whereas in deep learning we access it via the training data $\{(Ax_i, x_i)\}_{i=1}^K \subseteq \mathbb{M}_2 \times \mathbb{M}_1$. Given such a triple, the objective is to construct a *reconstruction map* R taking inputs $y = Ax \in \mathbb{M}_2$ and producing outputs in $\mathbb{C}^N$. In order to cover scenarios such as compressed sensing, where the reconstruction is obtained by solving a convex optimization problem, it is necessary to consider multivalued maps. As in Remark 5.11, we denote a multivalued map using double arrows, i.e.

$$\mathrm{R}\colon \mathbb{M}_2 \rightrightarrows \mathbb{C}^N.$$

In compressed sensing, R is, for example, the QCBP decoder (i.e. the set of minimizers of the QCBP minimization problem). In deep learning, R is a trained neural network. Either way, we assume that the set $\mathrm{R}(y)$ is bounded for all $y \in \mathbb{M}_2$.

Since R may be multivalued, we need a way to measure the distance between two sets $X, Y \subset \mathbb{C}^N$. We do this via the Hausdorff distance. This is defined as

$$\mathrm{dist}(X, Y) = \max\left\{\sup_{x\in X}\inf_{y\in Y} d(x, y), \sup_{y\in Y}\inf_{x\in X} d(x, y)\right\},$$

where d is the metric on $\mathbb{C}^N$. With slight abuse of notation we denote the singleton $\{x\} \subset \mathbb{C}^N$ simply as x.

20.1.2 Optimal and Approximately Optimal Maps

Let $\{A, \mathbb{M}_1, \mathbb{M}_2\}$ be an inverse problem triple. We are interested in how well reconstruction can be performed for this problem. This motivates the following definition:

Definition 20.1 (Optimal map) Let d be a metric on $\mathbb{C}^N$, $\mathbb{M}_1 \subset \mathbb{C}^N$, $A \in \mathbb{C}^{m\times N}$ and $\mathbb{M}_2 = A(\mathbb{M}_1)$. The *optimality constant* of $\{A, \mathbb{M}_1\}$ is

$$c_{\mathrm{opt}}(A, \mathbb{M}_1) = \inf_{\mathrm{R}:\mathbb{M}_2\rightrightarrows\mathbb{C}^N} \sup_{x\in\mathbb{M}_1} \mathrm{dist}(\mathrm{R}(Ax), x). \tag{20.1}$$

A map $\mathrm{R}\colon \mathbb{M}_2 \rightrightarrows \mathbb{C}^N$ is an *optimal map* for $\{A, \mathbb{M}_1\}$ if it attains the infimum in (20.1).

The optimal map is the best possible reconstruction map for the given triple. However, such a map may not exist in practice, since the infimum in (20.1) may fail to be attained. Hence we also define:

Definition 20.2 (Approximately optimal maps) Let d be a metric on $\mathbb{C}^N$, $\mathbb{M}_1 \subset \mathbb{C}^N$, $A \in \mathbb{C}^{m\times N}$ and $\mathbb{M}_2 = A(\mathbb{M}_1)$. A family of *approximately optimal maps* for $\{A, \mathbb{M}_1\}$ is a collection of maps $\mathrm{R}_\varepsilon : \mathbb{M}_2 \rightrightarrows \mathbb{C}^N$, $0 < \varepsilon \leq 1$, such that

$$\sup_{x\in\mathbb{M}_1} \mathrm{dist}(\mathrm{R}_\varepsilon(Ax), x) \leq c_{\mathrm{opt}}(A, \mathbb{M}_1) + \varepsilon, \quad \forall \varepsilon. \tag{20.2}$$

20.1.3 An Intriguing Paradox

Consider a triple $\{A, \mathbb{M}_1, \mathbb{M}_2\}$, where $\mathbb{M}_2 = A(\mathbb{M}_1)$, and a training set $\Theta \subseteq \mathbb{M}_2 \times \mathbb{M}_1$. We now pose the following question: are reconstruction maps obtained through learning optimal, or approximately optimal? Unfortunately, as the following theorem shows, the answer to this question can be negative:

Theorem 20.3 (Absence of optimal maps) *Let d be a metric on $\mathbb{C}^N$ that is induced by a norm, $A \in \mathbb{C}^{m\times N}\backslash\{0\}$, where $m < N$, $K \in \{2, \ldots, \infty\}$, $\delta \leq 1/5$ and $B \subset \mathbb{C}^N$ be the closed unit ball with respect to d. Then the following holds:*

(a) *There are uncountably many domains $\mathbb{M}_1 \subset B$ such that, for each $\mathbb{M}_1$ there are uncountably many sets $\Theta \subseteq \{(Ax, x) : x \in \mathbb{M}_1\}$, $|\Theta| = K$, with the following properties. Every map $\mathrm{R}: \mathbb{M}_2 \to \mathbb{C}^N$ (potentially multivalued $\mathrm{R}: \mathbb{M}_2 \rightrightarrows \mathbb{C}^N$) that satisfies*

$$\mathrm{dist}(\mathrm{R}(Ax), x) \leq \delta, \qquad \forall (Ax, x) \in \Theta \tag{20.3}$$

is not an optimal map. Moreover, the collection of such mappings does not contain a family of approximately optimal maps. If K is finite, one can choose $\mathbb{M}_1$ with $|\mathbb{M}_1| = K + 1$, in which case there is at least one Θ with the above property.

(b) *There are uncountably many domains $\mathbb{M}_1 \subset B$ with $|\mathbb{M}_1| = K$ such that there does not exist a map $\mathrm{R}: \mathbb{M}_2 \to \mathbb{C}^N$ (nor a multivalued map $\mathrm{R}: \mathbb{M}_2 \rightrightarrows \mathbb{C}^N$) satisfying*

$$\mathrm{dist}(\mathrm{R}(Ax), x) \leq \delta, \qquad \forall (Ax, x) \in \mathbb{M}_2 \times \mathbb{M}_1.$$

Recall that the objective of training is to compute a map that achieves small training error. In other words, if Θ is a training set, the learned map R should satisfy (20.3) for some suitable value of δ.[1] Part (a) of this theorem shows that successful training, i.e. (20.3), may not yield an optimal map. Thus, learning may be of limited effectiveness in producing maps that perform well over the domain $\mathbb{M}_1$. More dramatically, (b) shows that it may not be possible to achieve a small error over the whole domain in the first place. In particular, there are domains $\mathbb{M}_1$, even domains of finite size, that cannot be implicitly learned.

An example of this phenomenon is shown in Fig. 20.1. The network used performs well on the left image, which lies in the training set, but struggles to recover the right image, which is close to the training set, but not in it. This suggests that it may not be an optimal map. Conversely, compressed sensing performs consistently on both images.

[1] One may typically define the training error as $\left(\frac{1}{|\Theta|}\sum_{(Ax,x)\in\Theta}(\mathrm{dist}(\mathrm{R}(Ax), x))^2\right)^{1/2}$. For example, if d is induced by the ℓ^2-norm then this is just the usual ℓ^2-loss over the training data. Hence, if the training error is at most ε then (20.3) holds with $\delta \leq \sqrt{K}\varepsilon$.

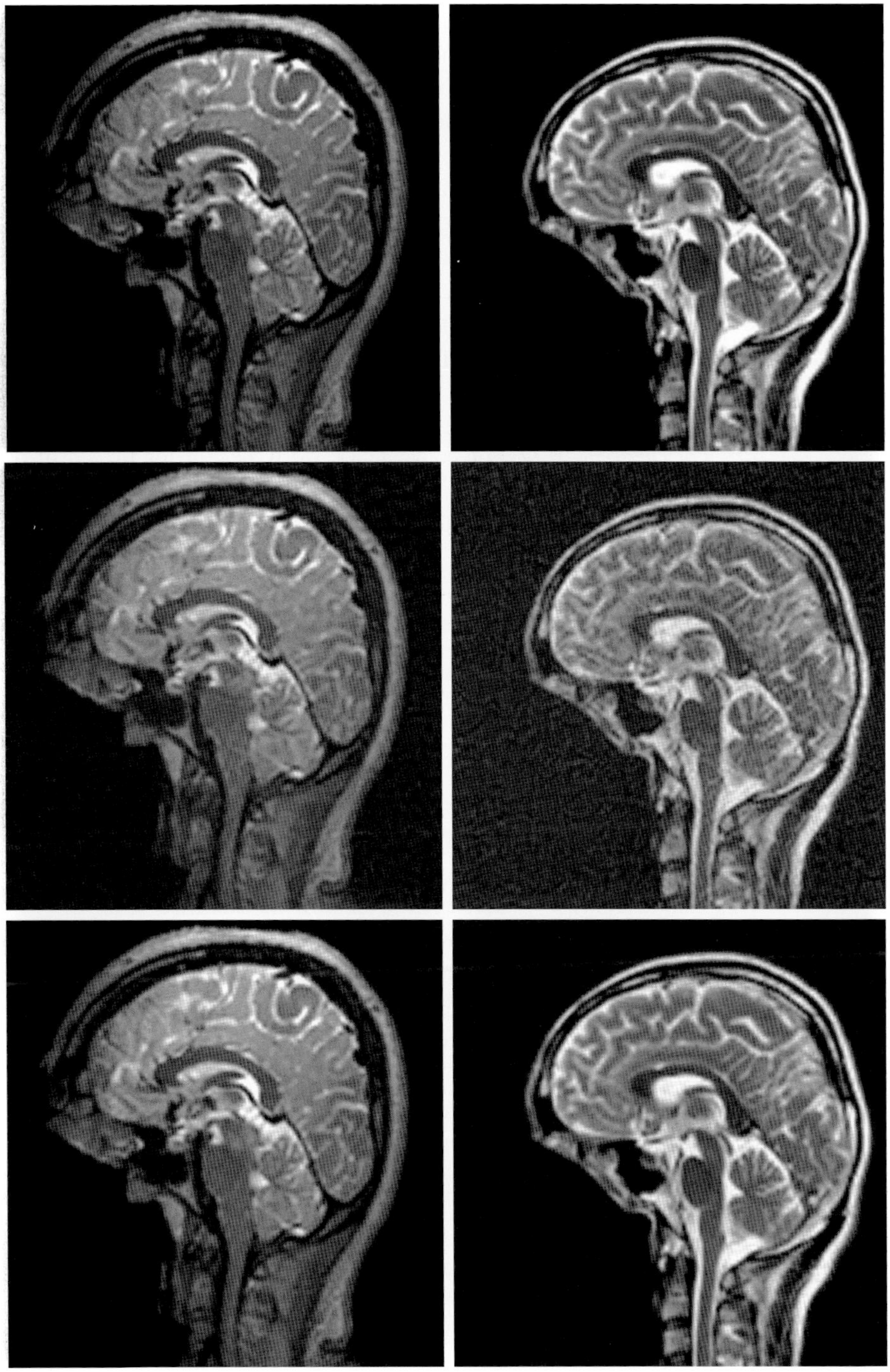

Figure 20.1 Comparison of AUTOMAP R_{dl} and compressed sensing R_{cs} for recovering two images from 60% Fourier measurements (see §19.3). Top row: Original images. Middle row: AUTOMAP reconstructions. Bottom row: Compressed sensing reconstructions. The left image is a typical image from the training set that was used to train the AUTOMAP network. The right image is based on the 'brain' image (see Fig. 2.2) but it has been altered to make it appear more similar to the images in the training set. It is not part of the training set.

It is worth observing that Theorem 20.3 is not a statement about overfitting. Recall that overfitting occurs when a network performs well on the training set, but poorly on a test set. It can arise either through the choice of architecture – i.e. the architecture does not have enough capacity to simultaneously fit the training set and test set – or by the type of training performed, since certain cost functions may promote overfitting more than others. Overfitting is therefore specific to the particular setup (choice of architecture and cost function). Conversely, Theorem 20.3 applies to *all* mappings. Theorem 18.3 states that there always exists a network (of a suitable architecture) that attains (20.3) whenever K is finite. However, by Theorem 20.3, such a map still cannot be optimal.

Note that the condition $\delta \leq 1/5$ in Theorem 20.3 is related to the assumption that $\mathbb{M}_1$ be a subset of the unit ball B. The theorem holds for arbitrary $\delta > 0$, provided this ball is suitably enlarged.

Proof of Theorem 20.3 For convenience we write $\|\cdot\|$ for the norm by which d is induced. We commence with the proof of (b). First, let $\{x_1, \ldots, x_K\}$ be K distinct elements in $(\mathrm{Ker}(A))^\perp$ such that $\|x_1\| = 1/2$ and $0 < \|x_j\| \leq 1$ otherwise. Note that such elements exist since $\mathrm{rank}(A) \geq 1$. As $m < N$ there is a $z_1 \in \mathrm{Ker}(A)$ with $\|z_1\| = 1/2$. Let $\mathbb{M}_1 = \{x_1 + z_1, x_1, \ldots, x_K\}$ and observe that $\mathbb{M}_1 \subset B$. We now argue by contradiction. Suppose that there is a map $\mathrm{R} \colon \mathbb{M}_2 \rightrightarrows \mathbb{C}^N$ with

$$\mathrm{dist}(\mathrm{R}(Ax), x) \leq \delta, \qquad \forall x \in \mathbb{M}_1. \tag{20.4}$$

In particular, $\mathrm{dist}(\mathrm{R}(Ax_1), x_1) \leq \delta$. But since $z_1 \in \mathrm{Ker}(A)$, we also have $\mathrm{R}(A(x_1+z_1)) = \mathrm{R}(Ax_1)$ and therefore

$$\mathrm{dist}(\mathrm{R}(A(x_1 + z_1)), x_1 + z_1) \geq \|z_1\| - \mathrm{dist}(\mathrm{R}(Ax_1), x_1) \geq \|z_1\| - \delta \geq 1/2 - 1/5 > \delta.$$

This contradicts (20.4). Given K, this shows the existence of an $\mathbb{M}_1$ with the desired properties. In order to get uncountably many different $\mathbb{M}_1$s, we can simply multiply this choice of $\mathbb{M}_1$ by complex numbers of modulus one.

To prove (a) we use the setup from the proof of (b). Let $\mathbb{M}_1$ be as defined previously and set $\Theta = \{(Ax_i, x_i)\}_{i=1}^K$. Define the map $\mathrm{R}_0 \colon \mathbb{M}_2 \to \mathbb{C}^N$ by

$$\mathrm{R}_0(y) = \begin{cases} x_1 + \frac{1}{2} z_1 & \text{if } y = Ax_1 \\ x_1 + \frac{1}{2} z_1 & \text{if } y = A(x_1 + z_1) \\ x_j & \text{if } y = Ax_j,\ j \in \{2, \ldots, K\} \end{cases}. \tag{20.5}$$

This map is well defined since A is injective when restricted to $(\mathrm{Ker}(A))^\perp$ (as $Az_1 = 0$ the second line is not strictly needed – we write it for clarity). Then, by (20.5),

$$\begin{aligned} c_{\mathrm{opt}}(A, \mathbb{M}_1) &\leq \sup_{x \in \mathbb{M}_1} \mathrm{dist}(\mathrm{R}_0(Ax), x) \\ &= \max \left\{ \sup_{j \geq 1} \|\mathrm{R}_0(Ax_j) - x_j\|, \|\mathrm{R}_0(A(x_1 + z_1)) - (x_1 + z_1)\| \right\} \\ &= 1/4. \end{aligned} \tag{20.6}$$

However, for every map $\mathrm{R}\colon \mathbb{M}_2 \rightrightarrows \mathbb{C}^N$ that satisfies (20.3) we have

$$\begin{aligned}\sup_{x\in\mathbb{M}_1} \mathrm{dist}(\mathrm{R}(Ax), x) \geq \mathrm{dist}(\mathrm{R}(A(x_1+z_1)), x_1+z_1) &= \mathrm{dist}(\mathrm{R}(Ax_1), x_1+z_1)\\ &\geq \|z_1\| - \delta\\ &\geq 1/2 - 1/5 > 1/4.\end{aligned}$$

Thus, it follows from (20.6) that R is not an optimal map. Furthermore, it is clear that no family of maps that satisfy (20.3) can be approximately optimal. □

20.1.4 The Desired Mapping May Not be Learned

Theorem 20.3 is a seemingly paradoxical result. To understand this better, it is informative to compare it to the classification problem. In binary classification one often assumes a class of images $\mathbb{M}$ and a ground truth labelling function $\mathrm{C}_0\colon \mathbb{M} \to \{+1,-1\}$. The function C_0 is well defined over $\mathbb{M}$ and the goal is to approximate it; by definition, C_0 is the optimal map for the problem. Through learning, we construct an approximation to C_0 from the training set

$$\Theta = \{(x_i, \mathrm{C}_0(x_i))\}_{i=1}^K,$$

which is simply a finite subset of the graph $\{(x, \mathrm{C}_0(x)) : x \in \mathbb{M}\}$ of C_0.

Now consider the inverse problem, where the training set takes the form

$$\Theta = \{(y_i, x_i)\}_{i=1}^K, \qquad y_i = Ax_i. \tag{20.7}$$

In contrast to the classification problem, there is no reason why Θ should arise from sampling the graph $\{(y, \mathrm{R}(y)) : y \in \mathbb{M}_2\}$ of an optimal (or approximately optimal) map R for the inverse problem. Theorem 20.3 asserts that this may not occur in general. In other words, any map R for which $\mathrm{dist}(\mathrm{R}(y_i), x_i) \leq \delta$, $i = 1, \ldots, K$, may not be an optimal map. Therefore, learning, which is usually done by seeking a small training error, may not succeed in the objective of producing optimal maps.

Note that the root cause of this scenario is the noninvertibility of A. If $A \in \mathbb{C}^{N\times N}$ is invertible, then $\mathrm{R}(y) = A^{-1}y$ is an optimal map and the training set (20.7) is indeed a subset of its graph. Of course, this situation is often irrelevant for the applications considered in this book.

20.2 Examining Instabilities in Deep Learning for Compressive Imaging

Having discussed accuracy in the previous section, we now consider stability. In §18.7 we raised the issue of instabilities of deep learning for image classification. This begs the question: can instabilities also arise in deep learning for compressive imaging? Unfortunately, the answer to this question is yes. Moreover, given the continuous nature of the output (versus the discrete output of typical classifiers), such instabilities can cause a range of different artefacts in the recovered images.

Figures 20.2–20.4 demonstrate unstable behaviour for three of the networks listed in §19.3. In each case, a perturbation r of the image x is constructed by Algorithm 19.1,

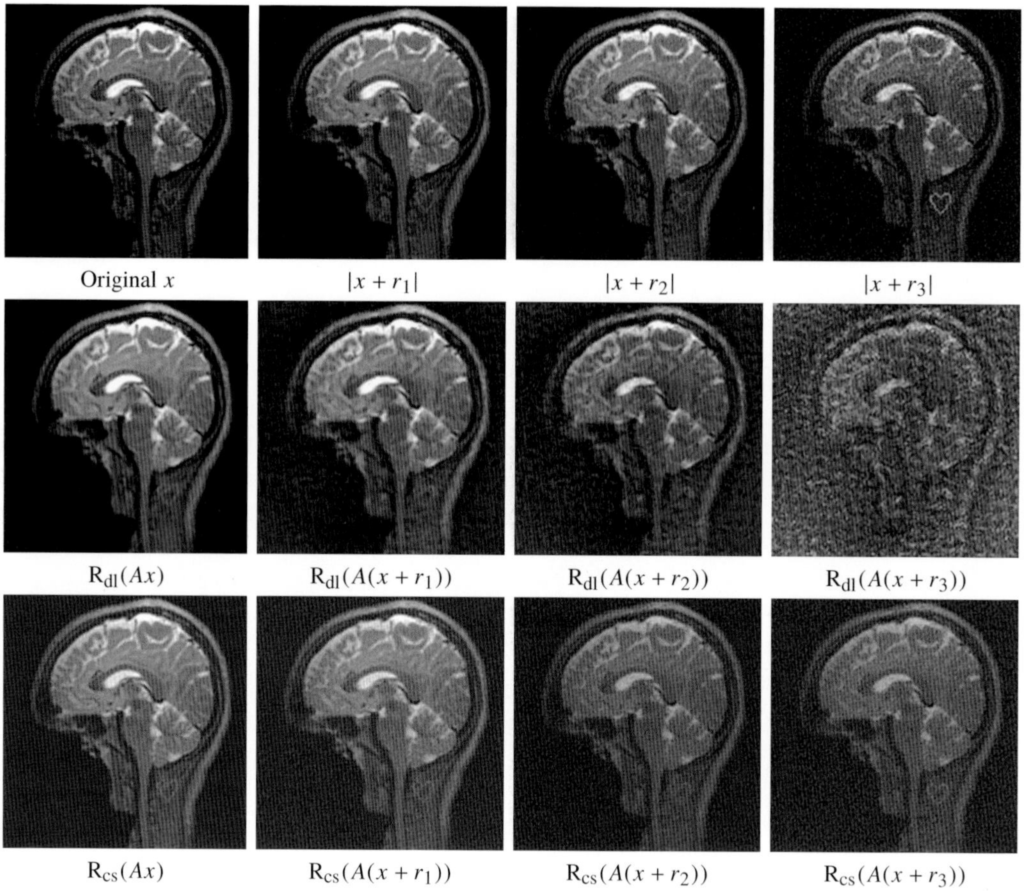

Figure 20.2 The effect of perturbations on the AUTOMAP network R_{dl}. Perturbations $\tilde{r}_1, \tilde{r}_2, \tilde{r}_3$ of increasing norm $\|\tilde{r}_1\|_{\ell^2} < \|\tilde{r}_2\|_{\ell^2} < \|\tilde{r}_3\|_{\ell^2}$ are added to the measurements $y = Ax$. To visualize these perturbations we show the perturbed absolute value image $|x + r_j|$, where $r_j = A^\dagger \tilde{r}_j$. Top row: Original image x and perturbed images $|x + r_j|$. Middle row: Recovery using R_{dl}. Bottom row: Recovery using compressed sensing R_{cs}. A detail in the form of a heart (with varying intensity) is added to the images to help visualize the loss in quality.

leading to a perturbation $\tilde{r} = Ar$ of the measurements. The perturbed image $x + r$ is barely distinguishable from x, yet the perturbation $\tilde{r}$ has a clear visual effect on the recovered image. As highlighted in Fig. 20.3, the different perturbations can cause artefacts that are clearly unphysical, e.g. in the case $r = r_2$, but more worryingly for practical purposes, also seemingly physical, e.g. the case $r = r_1$ (see the regions indicated by the arrows). Note that all the networks recover the original image x well. But their performance is greatly affected by these small perturbations. By contrast, the compressed sensing reconstruction appears stable, at least to the same perturbations that cause instabilities in the various networks. Later, in Chapter 21, we will show the stability of a compressed sensing-based reconstruction to similar worst-case perturbations.

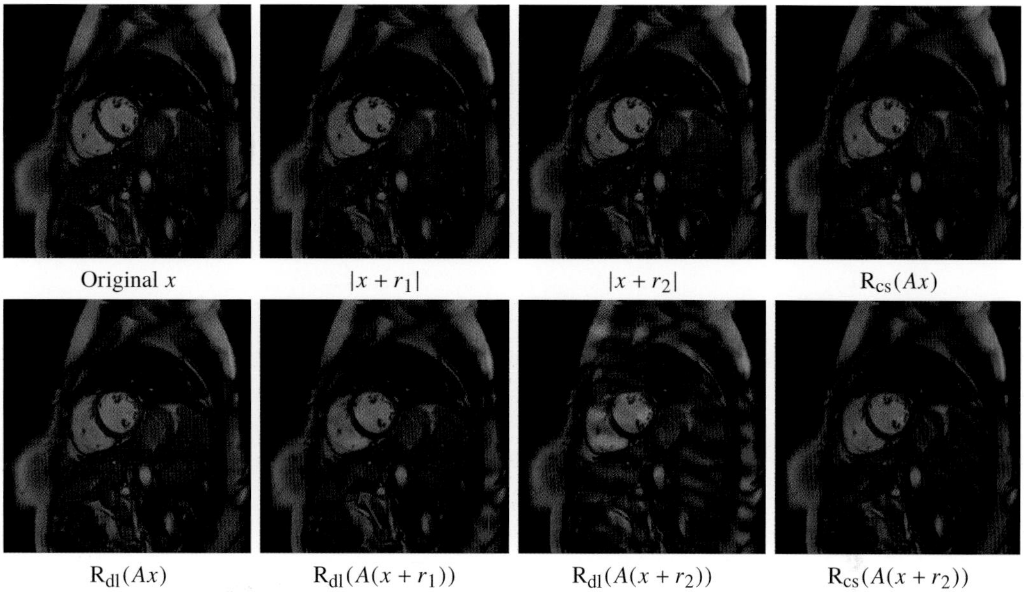

Figure 20.3 The effect of perturbations on the Deep MRI network R_{dl}. Perturbations $\|r_1\|_{\ell^2} < \|r_2\|_{\ell^2}$ of the original image x are constructed, giving perturbations $\tilde{r}_i = Ar_i$ of the measurements. Top row: Original and perturbed images. Bottom row: Recovery using R_{dl}. The right column shows the compressed sensing reconstruction R_{cs}.

20.2.1 The Universal Instability Theorem

Having observed them empirically, we now explore instabilities from a theoretical perspective. Seeking generality, let d_1 and d_2 be metrics on $\mathbb{C}^N$ and $\mathbb{C}^m$, respectively and $R: \mathbb{C}^m \to \mathbb{C}^N$ be a reconstruction map. To avoid unnecessary complications, we consider only single-valued maps in this section.

A standard way of studying stability of a mapping R is via its Lipschitz constant. Given $\varepsilon > 0$, we define the *ε-Lipschitz constant* of R at $y \in \mathbb{C}^m$ as

$$L_\varepsilon(R, y) = \sup_{\substack{z \in \mathbb{C}^m \\ 0 < d_2(z,y) \leq \varepsilon}} \frac{d_1(R(z), R(y))}{d_2(z, y)}.$$

Observe that a large ε-Lipschitz constant at $y \in \mathbb{C}^m$ implies that there is a perturbed input $\tilde{y}$ within the ε-ball centred at y that causes a large change in the output $R(\tilde{y})$ relative to $R(y)$.

Theorem 20.4 (Universal instability theorem) *Let $A \in \mathbb{C}^{m \times N}$, d_1 and d_2 be metrics on $\mathbb{C}^N$ and $\mathbb{C}^m$, respectively and $R: \mathbb{C}^m \to \mathbb{C}^N$ be continuous. Suppose that there exist $x, x' \in \mathbb{C}^N$ and $\eta > 0$ such that*

$$d_1(R(Ax), x) < \eta, \quad d_1(R(Ax'), x') < \eta, \tag{20.8}$$

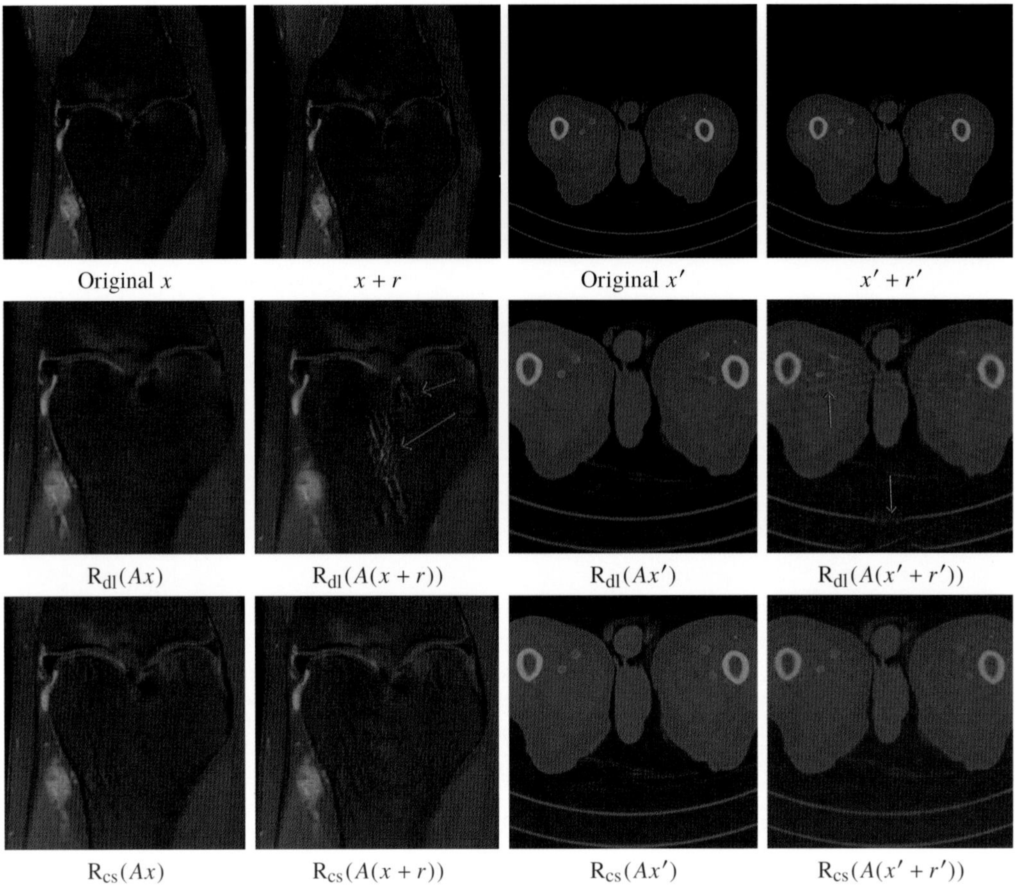

Figure 20.4 The effect of perturbations on the MRI-VN (left) and Med 50 (right) networks. Perturbations r and r' of the original images x and x' are constructed, giving perturbations $\tilde{r} = Ar$ and $\tilde{r}' = \tilde{A}r'$ of the measurements. Here A is a subsampled discrete Fourier transform and $\tilde{A}$ is the subsampled discrete Radon transform – see Table 19.1. Top row: Original and perturbed images. Middle row: Reconstructions obtained by the networks. Bottom row: Compressed sensing reconstructions R_{cs}.

and

$$d_2(Ax, Ax') \leq \eta. \tag{20.9}$$

Then the following hold:

(a) *There is a closed nonempty ball $B_y \subset \mathbb{C}^m$ centred at $y = Ax$ such that the local ε-Lipschitz constant at any $\tilde{y} \in B_y$ is bounded from below. In particular,*

$$L_\varepsilon(\mathrm{R}, \tilde{y}) \geq \frac{1}{\eta}\left(d_1(x, x') - 2\eta\right), \quad \varepsilon \geq \eta. \tag{20.10}$$

(b) *Suppose that the metrics are translation invariant.*[2] *Then there is a* $z \in \mathbb{C}^N$ *with* $d_1(0, z) \geq d_1(x, x')$, *an* $e \in \mathbb{C}^m$ *with* $d_2(0, e) \leq \eta$ *and closed nonempty balls* B_x, B_e *and* B_z *centred at* x, e *and* z, *respectively, such that*

$$d_1(\mathrm{R}(A\tilde{x} + \tilde{e}), \tilde{x} + \tilde{z}) \leq \eta, \quad \forall \tilde{x} \in B_x, \tilde{e} \in B_e, \tilde{z} \in B_z.$$

(c) *Suppose that the metrics are translation invariant. Then there is a* $z \in \mathbb{C}^N$ *with* $d_1(0, z) \geq d_1(x, x')$, *an* $e \in \mathbb{C}^m$ *with* $d_2(0, e) \leq \eta$ *and closed nonempty balls* B_x, B_e *and* B_z *centred at* x, e *and* z, *respectively, such that*

$$d_1(\mathrm{R}(A(\tilde{x} + \tilde{z}) + \tilde{e}), \tilde{x}) \leq \eta, \quad \forall \tilde{x} \in B_x, \tilde{e} \in B_e, \tilde{z} \in B_z.$$

This theorem states the following. Consider a reconstruction map R that performs sufficiently well, i.e. (20.8), on two elements $x, x' \in \mathbb{C}^N$ which are not close themselves, but whose difference lies close to the null space of A, i.e. (20.9). In other words, the map R *over-performs*: it has no right to recover both x and x' well, since the inputs Ax and Ax' that it sees are similar. Then (a) states that such a map is necessarily unstable, with its Lipschitz constant in a ball around $y = Ax$ scaling like $1/\eta$. In particular, the more it over-performs, the worse the instability becomes.

In addition, (b) states that such a map produces *false positives* and (c) states that it produces *false negatives*. In (b), for instance, perturbing the input Ax by a small amount to $Ax + e$ causes the map to switch from recovering x to recovering $x + z$. This is a false positive. If x represents a healthy brain and z a tumour, so that $x + z$ is an unhealthy brain, a small perturbation in the input causes the mapping to reconstruct the cancerous brain $x + z$ rather than the true healthy brain x.

Proof of Theorem 20.4 Consider part (a). Using (20.9), the fact that $\varepsilon \geq \eta$ and applying the triangle inequality twice gives

$$\begin{aligned} L_\varepsilon(\mathrm{R}, y) = \sup_{0 < d_2(z,y) \leq \varepsilon} \frac{d_1(\mathrm{R}(z), \mathrm{R}(y))}{d_2(z, y)} &\geq \frac{d_1(\mathrm{R}(Ax'), \mathrm{R}(Ax))}{d_2(Ax', Ax)} \\ &\geq \frac{d_1(x', x) - d_1(\mathrm{R}(Ax), x) - d_1(\mathrm{R}(Ax'), x')}{d_2(Ax', Ax)}. \end{aligned}$$

Thus, using (20.8) and (20.9) we obtain

$$L_\varepsilon(\mathrm{R}, y) > \frac{d_1(x', x) - 2\eta}{\eta}.$$

The continuity of R now implies that

$$L_\varepsilon(\mathrm{R}, \tilde{y}) \geq \frac{1}{\eta} \left(d_1(x, x') - 2\eta \right),$$

for all $\tilde{y} \in B_y$, where B_y is some ball around $y = Ax$.

For part (b), let $z = x' - x$ and $e = A(x' - x)$ and observe that $d_1(0, z) = d_1(x, x')$ and $d_2(0, e) \leq \eta$. This follows from the fact that the metrics are translation invariant and (20.9). Moreover by (20.8),

$$d_1(\mathrm{R}(Ax + e), x + z) = d_1(\mathrm{R}(Ax'), x') < \eta.$$

[2] A metric d on a vector space $\mathbb{V}$ is *translation invariant* if $d(x + z, y + z) = d(x, y)$ for all $x, y, z \in \mathbb{V}$.

The result follows once more from the continuity of R. Part (c) is identical. □

Theorem 20.4 is deliberately formulated with weak conditions so as to demonstrate the ease with which a mapping can become unstable. However, while bad perturbations always arise in a certain ball, it says nothing about the size of these balls. For this one needs slightly stronger assumptions:

Theorem 20.5 *Let $m \leq N$, $A \in \mathbb{C}^{m\times N}$ be full rank, $\mathrm{R}\colon \mathbb{C}^m \to \mathbb{C}^N$ be continuous and consider $\mathbb{C}^m$ and $\mathbb{C}^N$ equipped with their respective ℓ^2-norms. Suppose that there exists $x \in (\mathrm{Ker}(A))^{\perp}$, $x' \in \mathbb{C}^N$ and $r_1 > 0$ such that*

$$\|x' - \mathrm{R}(Ax')\|_{\ell^2} \leq \eta, \quad \|z - \mathrm{R}(Az)\|_{\ell^2} \leq \eta, \quad \|A(x'-z)\|_{\ell^2} \leq \eta, \quad \forall z \in B_x,$$

where B_x is the open ball of radius r_1 centred at x. Then there is a closed ball $B_y \subset \mathbb{C}^m$ of radius $r_2 \geq \sigma_{\min}(A) r_1$ centred at $y = Ax$ such that, for every $\tilde{y} \in B_y$, the local ε-Lipschitz constant satisfies

$$L_\varepsilon(\mathrm{R}, \tilde{y}) \geq \frac{1}{\eta}\left(\mathrm{dist}(x', B_x) - 2\eta\right),$$

where $\mathrm{dist}(x', B_x) = \inf\{\|x' - z\|_{\ell^2} : z \in B_x\}$.

Proof Define the ball B_y by $\tilde{y} \in B_y$ if $\|y - \tilde{y}\|_{\ell^2} \leq \sigma_{\min}(A) r_1$. Fix $\tilde{y} \in B_y$ and write $\tilde{x} = A^{\dagger}\tilde{y} \in (\mathrm{Ker}(A))^{\perp}$. Since $x \in (\mathrm{Ker}(A))^{\perp}$ and A is full rank, we have $x = A^{\dagger} y$. In particular, $\|\tilde{x} - x\|_{\ell^2} \leq 1/\sigma_{\min}(A)\|\tilde{y} - y\|_{\ell^2} \leq r_1$. Hence $\tilde{x} \in B_x$. Set $e = A(x' - \tilde{x})$ and observe that $\|e\|_{\ell^2} \leq \eta \leq \varepsilon$. Then, since $A\tilde{x} = \tilde{y}$, we have

$$\begin{aligned} L_\varepsilon(\mathrm{R}, \tilde{y}) &\geq \frac{\|\mathrm{R}(A\tilde{x} + e) - \mathrm{R}(A\tilde{x})\|_{\ell^2}}{\|e\|_{\ell^2}} \geq \frac{\|\mathrm{R}(Ax') - \mathrm{R}(A\tilde{x})\|_{\ell^2}}{\eta} \\ &\geq \frac{\|x' - \tilde{x}\|_{\ell^2} - \|x' - \mathrm{R}(Ax')\|_{\ell^2} - \|\tilde{x} - \mathrm{R}(A\tilde{x})\|_{\ell^2}}{\eta} \\ &\geq \frac{\mathrm{dist}(x', B_x) - 2\eta}{\eta}, \end{aligned}$$

as required. □

Note that the assumption that A be full rank is not unreasonable. In Fourier imaging, for instance, this holds whenever the sampling scheme consists of m distinct frequencies. Moreover, if $A = N^{-1/2} P_\Omega F$, then $\sigma_{\min}(A) = 1$.

20.2.2 Consequences of the Universal Instability Theorem

We now discuss several consequences of Theorems 20.4 and 20.5. The first, which follows without further explanation, is as follows:

> Stable mappings must be *kernel aware*: they must avoid recovering two distinct elements whose difference lies close to the null space of A.

Of course, kernel awareness lies at the heart of compressed sensing via properties such as the rNSP. On the other hand:

Instabilities and false positives and negatives can easily arise in learning.

Theorem 18.3 implies that it is easy to set up a neural network architecture that has the capacity to interpolate any two distinct images. Moreover, in imaging problems the measurement matrix A often has a large null space. For example, if the image size is 256×256 and the sampling percentage is 25% then the null space has dimension at least $0.75 \times 256^2 = 49{,}152$. Hence, for any moderately sized network architecture there may be many ways in which (20.8) and (20.9) can arise. If x and x' happen to also be members of the training set, then (20.8) occurs whenever the training error is small. Hence, the universal instability theorem implies that if the training set contains at least two elements whose difference lies close to the null space, then successful training (i.e. small training error) must lead to instabilities.

Figure 20.5 demonstrates this phenomenon. It shows the recovery of images x and x', where x' is identical to x except for a small structural change that represents a tumour. The tumour $z = x' - x$ is localized in space and its Fourier transform is approximately zero at low frequencies. The measurement matrix A is a subsampled discrete Fourier transform, and takes mainly low-frequency measurements, as is typical in practice. Hence, z lies close to $\mathrm{Ker}(A)$. A neural network R_{dl} was trained to recover both x' and x well from their respective measurements. But, as Theorem 20.4 implies, and this figure confirms, the result is false positives (a small perturbation of $y = Ax$ results in the presence of a tumour in the reconstruction) and false negatives (a small perturbation of $y' = Ax'$ leads to the absence of the tumour in the reconstruction).

The next consequence concerns the abundance of instabilities:

Instabilities are stable.

Theorem 20.4 states that, even in the most general setting, there is always a ball of bad perturbations. With stronger assumptions such as in Theorem 20.5, the size of this ball can also be quantified. This effect is illustrated in Fig. 20.6, which is based on the example shown previously in Fig. 20.3. The network reconstructs the image x from the measurements $A(x + r_1 + v)$, where v is a random perturbation and r_1 is the original perturbation constructed in Fig. 20.3. The result of the additional perturbation v is a similar artefact to that seen in Fig. 20.3 for the original perturbation r_1.

20.2.3 The Prevalence of Bad Perturbations

While this discussion confirms that bad perturbations do not constitute a set of measure zero, it is natural to ask how likely these perturbations are to arise in practical imaging scenarios. Indeed, one might hope that such bad perturbations might not occur, since in practice the measurements may only be subject to Gaussian (or some other random) noise. Unfortunately, our next conclusion is the following:

Random noise can cause bad perturbations to occur with nonzero probability.

Suppose the measurements Ax are perturbed to $Ax + e$, where e is a realization of a mean-zero random variable. Then, under the assumptions of Theorem 20.4 and subject

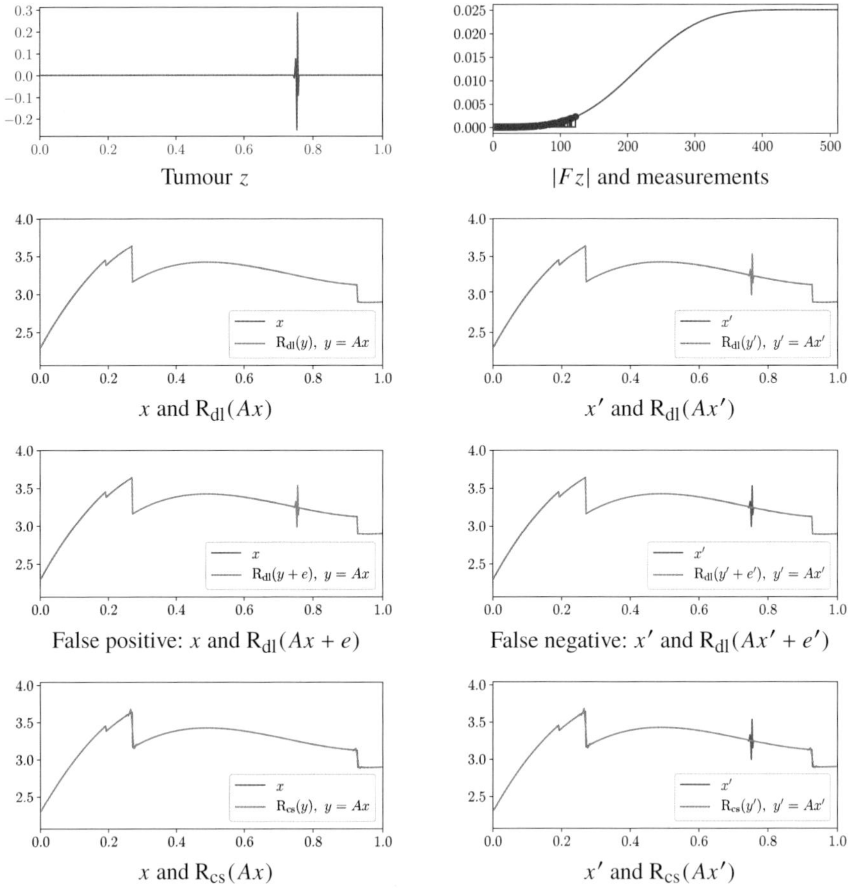

Figure 20.5 A neural network $R_{dl} : \mathbb{C}^m \to \mathbb{C}^N$ is trained to approximately recover two one-dimensional images x and $x' = x + z$ from measurements $y = Ax$ and $y = Ax'$, respectively. Here $\|z\|_{\ell^2} = 0.4$, $\eta = \|Az\|_{\ell^2} = 5.566 \times 10^{-3}$ and $A = P_\Omega F$ is a subsampled Fourier matrix. Top row: The tumour z and the magnitude of its Fourier transform Fz. The red dots indicate the measurements corresponding to Ω. Second row: Images x and x' and their reconstructions via R_{dl}. Third row: Perturbations e and e' are added to the measurements, leading to a false positive in the recovery of x via R_{dl} and a false negative in the recovery of x'. Fourth row: Recovery via compressed sensing R_{cs} based on QCBP with wavelets. The compressed sensing reconstruction does not recover z as it lies close to $\mathrm{Ker}(A)$.

to mild conditions on this random variable, one has

$$\mathbb{P}\left(d_1(\mathrm{R}(Ax + e), x + z) \leq \eta\right) \geq c_1 > 0,$$

and

$$\mathbb{P}\left(d_1(\mathrm{R}(A(x + z) + e), x) \leq \eta\right) \geq c_2 > 0,$$

for constants $c_1, c_2 > 0$ depending on the distribution of e and the size of the balls guaranteed by Theorem 20.4. Hence significant image artefacts arise with nonzero

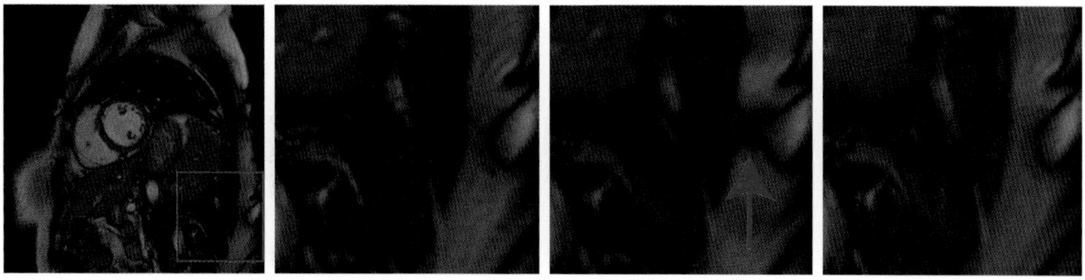

$|x + r_1 + v|$ $|x + r_1 + v|$ (cropped) $\mathrm{R}_{\mathrm{dl}}(A(x + r_1 + v))$ $\mathrm{R}_{\mathrm{cs}}(A(x + r_1 + v))$

Figure 20.6 The effect of random perturbations of bad perturbations on the Deep MRI network R_{dl}. The perturbation v is first defined as $v = A^{\dagger} e$, where $e \in \mathbb{C}^m$ is a complex Gaussian random vector. Then v is rescaled so that $\|v\|_{\ell^2} = \frac{1}{4}\|r_1\|_{\ell^2}$, where r_1 is the perturbation from Fig. 20.3.

probability. An example of this phenomenon is shown in Fig. 20.7. The network considered is unstable with respect to Gaussian noise, which causes the false dark area indicated by the red arrows.

On the other hand, the measurements in many imaging scenarios are also corrupted by additional effects beyond generic, random noise. In MRI, for instance, patient motion or small anatomical changes can cause specific perturbations in the measurements. In this case, one may model the corrupted measurements as

$$Ax + e, \qquad e = e_c + e_g,$$

where e_c is a random variable that accounts for the nongeneric part of the perturbation and e_g is a mean-zero random variable accounting for its generic part. Finding a good model for e_c may be challenging. In part, this is why much of this book focuses on noise bounds that are *adversarial*, i.e. they depend on $\|e\|_{\ell^2}$ and hold for every $e \in \mathbb{C}^m$ without making any assumption that e is drawn from a certain distribution. On the other hand, since the instabilities established in Theorem 20.4 are stable, if a realization $\tilde{e}_c$ of e_c results in a bad perturbation, then one has

$$\mathbb{P}\left(d_1(\mathrm{R}(Ax + e_c + e_g), x + z) \leq \eta | e_c = \tilde{e}_c\right) \geq 1 - \delta > 0,$$

and

$$\mathbb{P}\left(d_1(\mathrm{R}(A(x + z) + e_c + e_g), x) \leq \eta | e_c = \tilde{e}_c\right) \geq 1 - \delta > 0,$$

where $\delta > 0$ is a constant (depending on the distribution of e_g and the size of the balls) which is typically small. Hence this represents a high-probability event. We conclude:

> Generic noise added to a bad perturbation will generally not counteract the artefacts that perturbation causes.

An example of this phenomenon was shown previously in Fig. 20.6. Another reason this effect is of interest is that adding generic noise has been used as a way to defend against adversarial perturbations in classification problems. Yet, this argument suggests it may be of limited use in counteracting instabilities in image reconstruction.

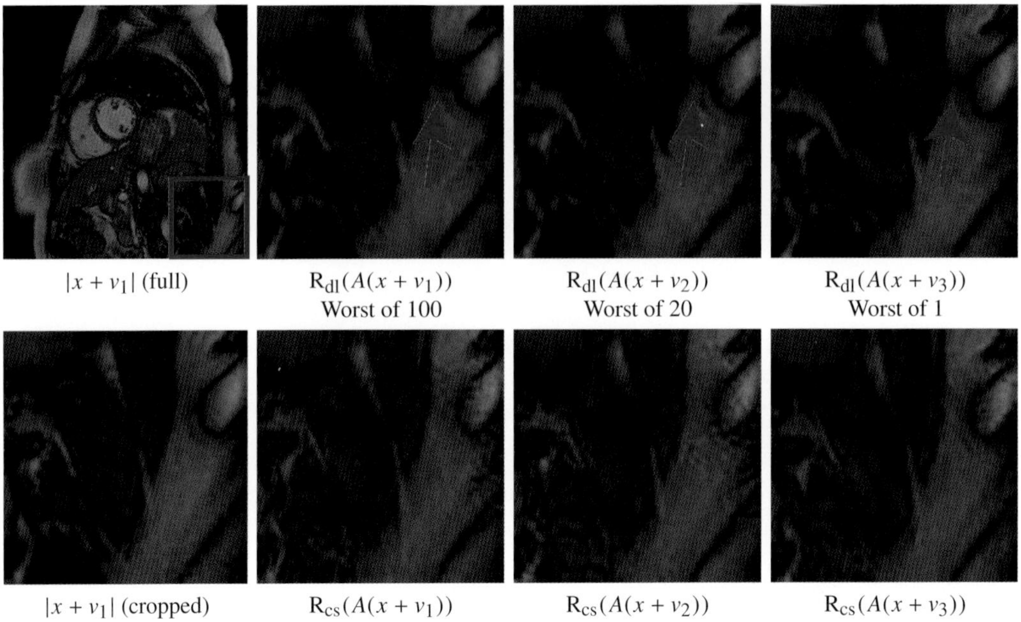
$|x + v_1|$ (full)
$R_{dl}(A(x + v_1))$
Worst of 100
$R_{dl}(A(x + v_2))$
Worst of 20
$R_{dl}(A(x + v_3))$
Worst of 1
$|x + v_1|$ (cropped)
$R_{cs}(A(x + v_1))$
$R_{cs}(A(x + v_2))$
$R_{cs}(A(x + v_3))$

Figure 20.7 The effect of random perturbations on the Deep MRI network R_{dl}. In the second column, 100 random Gaussian vectors $w_j \in \mathbb{C}^N$ were drawn and the one that gave the worst reconstruction via R_{dl} (upon visual inspection) was chosen and labelled v_1. The third and fourth columns repeat the same experiment with 20 and one new random vectors, respectively, giving perturbations v_2 and v_3. All images are crops of the same region. The full image $x + v_1$ is shown in the first column for illustration.

20.3 The Stability versus Performance Tradeoff

We have now seen that trained neural networks may not yield optimal maps, and moreover, they may become unstable when they attempt to over-perform. This points towards a delicate tradeoff between accuracy and stability. If one designs a network architecture and trains it, then the better it performs on a large class of images, the more prone it is to exhibiting instabilities.

An illustration of this tradeoff is shown in Fig. 20.8. The Deep MRI network clearly outperforms compressed sensing across a range of different subsampling percentages. Yet, as shown in Figs 20.3, 20.6 and 20.7, the former is highly susceptible to instabilities, while the latter is not.

In Fig. 20.9 we explore this tradeoff for other networks. To do this, we add a small, but clearly visible detail to each image and study whether or not the network can recover it. Given an image x we add a perturbation r, where r is a detail that is visible in the perturbed image $x + r$, and check whether or not r is still visible in the reconstructed image $R(A(x + r))$. The details used are the four card suits ♠, ♥, ♦, ♣ and the text CAN U SEE IT, none of which were present in the datasets used to train the various networks. If a network is able to recover these basic details well it is likely to recover other details of the same size. However, if the network fails on these details, it is liable

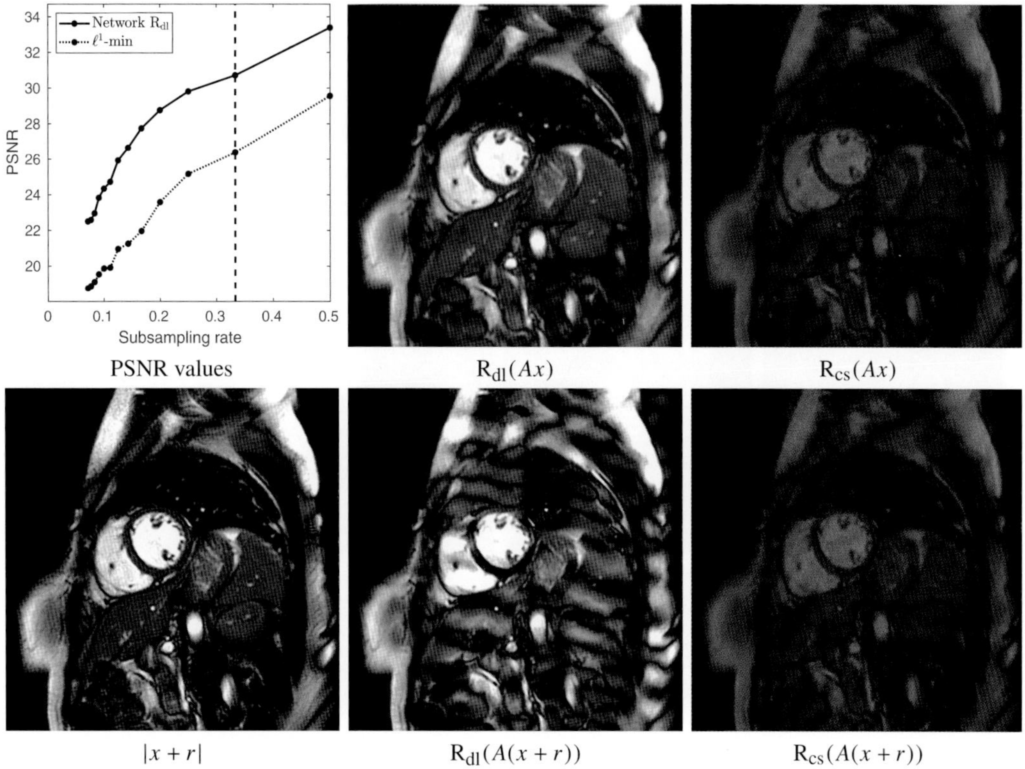

Figure 20.8 Comparison between the Deep MRI network R_{dl} and compressed sensing R_{cs} based on QCBP with wavelets. In all experiments $A \in \mathbb{C}^{m \times N}$ is a subsampled Fourier matrix. Top left: PSNR values against subsampling rate. The dashed line indicates the subsampling rate at which the network was trained. Top middle and right: Reconstructions of x based on 33% subsampling. In the bottom row these reconstructions are compared on a perturbed image $x + r$, where r is constructed to cause artefacts in R_{dl}.

to fail on other details as well. Hence, recovery of these details examines the accuracy of the network at recovering small features.

Figure 20.9 shows improving performance with respect to these details from the top row to the bottom row. The Ell 50 network (top row) washes out these details almost entirely, whereas the Deep MRI network (bottom row) recovers them very well. However, exactly as one expects, this improvement from top to bottom is precisely the opposite of the stability trend. The Ell 50 network is very stable (not shown), while the other networks are increasingly unstable (see Figs 20.3 and 20.4).

Having done this, we conclude this section by examining a related phenomenon, which is the performance of the networks as the sampling rate is increased. This is shown in Fig. 20.10. While each has been trained at a specific sampling rate, indicated by the dashed line, it is not unreasonable to hope that the network will produce better reconstructions when more measurements are supplied it. Unfortunately, for three of the networks, increasing the sampling rate actually worsens their performance. Theoretically,

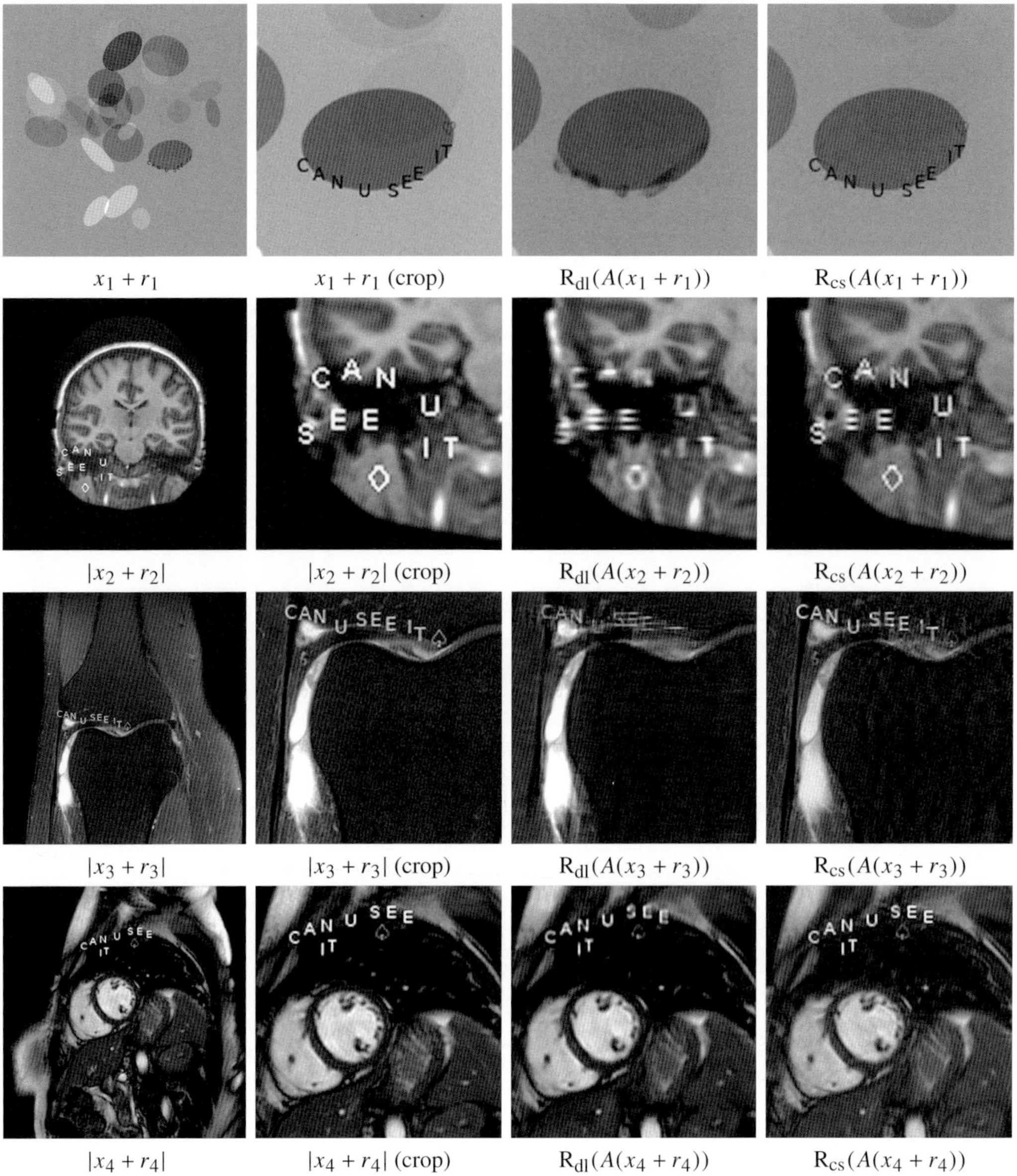

Figure 20.9 The effect of structural perturbations on the Ell 50, DAGAN, MRI-VN and Deep MRI networks (top to bottom). First two columns: Perturbed images $x_i + r_i$. Third column: Neural network reconstructions R_{dl}. Fourth column: Compressed sensing reconstructions R_{cs}. In each case, the measurement matrix A_i corresponds to the modality listed in Table 19.1.

this suggests that understanding the performance of a trained neural network is a quite subtle question. A practical consequence of this effect is that a network may need to be trained separately for each desired sampling pattern in order to ensure the best performance.

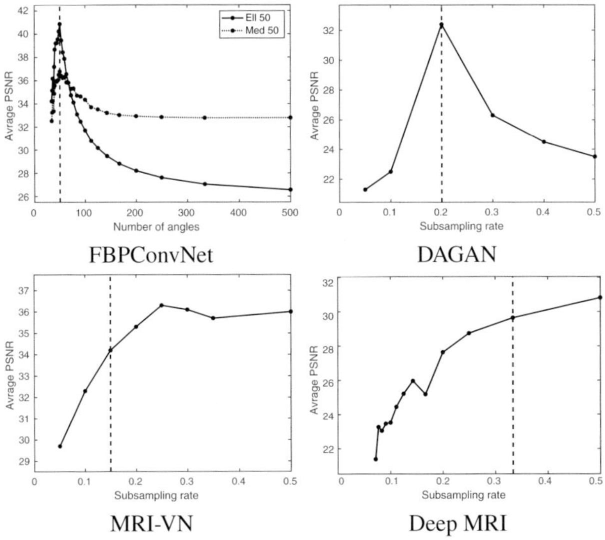

Figure 20.10 PSNR versus subsampling rate for different networks. In each case, the dashed line indicates the subsampling rate at which the network was trained.

20.4 The Tradeoff for Compressed Sensing and Deep Learning

Having explored it empirically, we now investigate the accuracy–stability tradeoff from a theoretical perspective. We do this by comparing deep learning and compressed sensing on two standard imaging scenarios, namely, Fourier and Walsh sampling. In order to make such a comparison, we consider scenarios in which there are theoretical guarantees on performance, and then examine the stability of methods that strive to achieve further gains in accuracy.

Throughout this section, we consider discrete, one-dimensional images $x \in \mathbb{C}^N$, where $N = 2^{r-1}$ for some $r \geq 3$. We let $F \in \mathbb{C}^{N\times N}$ denote the one-dimensional Fourier matrix (Definition 2.1) and $H \in \mathbb{R}^{N\times N}$ denote the one-dimensional sequency-ordered Hadamard matrix (Definition 2.8). Following §11.6, we define sampling levels $\mathbf{N} = (N_1, \ldots, N_r)$ with $N_k = 2^{k-1}$ (although §11.6 only considered the Fourier case, these levels also apply in the Walsh case – see Chapter 16). Given an $(\mathbf{m}, \mathbf{N})$-multilevel random sampling scheme Ω (Definition 11.13), we define the corresponding multilevel subsampled unitary matrix (Definition 11.14) as

$$A = P_\Omega D U, \tag{20.11}$$

where $U = N^{-1/2}F$ (Fourier) or $U = N^{-1/2}H$ (Walsh) and D is the diagonal scaling matrix with entries

$$D_{ii} = \begin{cases} \sqrt{\frac{N_k - N_{k-1}}{m_k}} & m_k \neq 0 \\ 1 & m_k = 0 \end{cases}, \quad i = N_{k-1}+1, \ldots, N_k,\ k = 1, \ldots, r.$$

We consider (multivalued) mappings from $\mathrm{R}\colon \mathbb{C}^m \rightrightarrows \mathbb{C}^N$ and we equip both $\mathbb{C}^m$ and $\mathbb{C}^N$ with the ℓ^2-norm. For convenience, we now also define the ε-Lipschitz constant of a mapping $\mathrm{R}\colon \mathbb{C}^m \rightrightarrows \mathbb{C}^N$ over a set $\mathbb{M}_2 \subseteq \mathbb{C}^m$. This is simply the supremum of the ε-Lipschitz constants $L_\varepsilon(\mathrm{R}, y)$ for $y \in \mathbb{M}_2$:

$$L_{\varepsilon}(\mathrm{R}, \mathbb{M}_2) = \sup_{y \in \mathbb{M}_2} L_{\varepsilon}(\mathrm{R}, y) = \sup_{y \in \mathbb{M}_2} \sup_{\substack{e \in \mathbb{C}^m \\ 0 < \|e\|_{\ell^2} \leq \varepsilon}} \frac{\mathrm{dist}(\mathrm{R}(y+e), \mathrm{R}(y))}{\|e\|_{\ell^2}}.$$

Here, dist is the corresponding Hausdorff distance.

Finally, we let $\Phi \in \mathbb{R}^{N \times N}$ be the one-dimensional discrete Haar wavelet transform. We write $\mathbf{M} = (M_1, \ldots, M_r)$ for the corresponding sparsity levels, where $M_k = 2^{k-1}$ (see §11.6), $\mathbf{s} = (s_1, \ldots, s_r)$ for the local sparsities and $s = s_1 + \cdots + s_r$ for the total sparsity. We define the compressed sensing reconstruction map $\mathrm{R}_{\mathrm{cs}} : \mathbb{C}^m \rightrightarrows \mathbb{C}^N$ in terms of the weighted SR-LASSO decoder as

$$\mathrm{R}_{\mathrm{cs}}(y) = \operatorname*{argmin}_{z \in \mathbb{C}^N} \left\{ \lambda \|\Phi^* z\|_{\ell^1_w} + \|Az - y\|_{\ell^2} \right\}, \tag{20.12}$$

where, as per usual, the weights $w = (w_i)_{i=1}^N$ are given by (13.2)–(13.3). Note that one could also consider the weighted QCBP decoder in this section, albeit with some additional technicalities.

20.4.1 Over-performance Implies Instability

We now present our first result, which is based on Walsh sampling. It illustrates the following principle:

Compressed sensing is sometimes optimal, but may be outperformed at the cost of instability.

Theorem 20.6 *Let $0 < \nu < 1$ and consider Walsh measurements. There are at least $2^{(r-1)(r-2)/2}$ choices of local sparsities $\mathbf{s}$ such that, for each such $\mathbf{s}$ and each $0 < \gamma < 1/2$, there are uncountably many domains $\mathbb{M}_1, \widetilde{\mathbb{M}}_1 \subset \mathbb{C}^N$, $|\mathbb{M}_1| = |\widetilde{\mathbb{M}}_1| = \infty$, for which the following holds. If Ω is an $(\mathbf{m}, \mathbf{N})$-multilevel random sampling scheme with*

$$m_k = \left\lceil C \cdot s_k \cdot \left(\log^3(N) \cdot \log(2m) \cdot \log^2(\log(N)s) + \log(N) \cdot \log(\nu^{-1}) \right) \right\rceil, \tag{20.13}$$

for $k = 1, \ldots, r$, where $C > 0$ is a numerical constant and $m = m_1 + \cdots + m_r$, A is as in (20.11), $\mathbb{M}_2 = A(\mathbb{M}_1)$ and $\widetilde{\mathbb{M}}_2 = A(\widetilde{\mathbb{M}}_1)$, then:

(a) With probability at least $1 - \nu$, the map R_{cs} defined by (20.12) is an optimal map for $\{A, \mathbb{M}_1\}$ (Definition 20.1) whenever $\lambda \leq \frac{1}{2\sqrt{2}\sqrt{rs}}$, and the optimality constant satisfies $c_{\mathrm{opt}}(A, \mathbb{M}_1) = 0$. Moreover,

$$L_{\varepsilon}(\mathrm{R}_{\mathrm{cs}}, \mathbb{M}_2) \lesssim \frac{r^{1/4}}{\sqrt{rs}\lambda}, \qquad \forall \varepsilon > 0,$$

and in particular, $L_{\varepsilon}(\mathrm{R}_{\mathrm{cs}}, \mathbb{M}_2) \lesssim r^{1/4}$ if $\frac{1}{\sqrt{rs}} \lesssim \lambda \leq \frac{1}{2\sqrt{2}\sqrt{rs}}$.

(b) For each $0 < \delta \leq \gamma$, every map $\mathrm{R} : \mathbb{C}^m \rightrightarrows \mathbb{C}^N$ that satisfies

$$\mathrm{dist}(\mathrm{R}(Ax), x) \leq \delta, \qquad \forall x \in \widetilde{\mathbb{M}}_1 \tag{20.14}$$

also satisfies

$$\sup_{x \in \widetilde{\mathbb{M}}_1} \mathrm{dist}(\mathrm{R}(Ax), x) \leq \gamma \sup_{x \in \widetilde{\mathbb{M}}_1} \mathrm{dist}(\mathrm{R}_{\mathrm{cs}}(Ax), x). \tag{20.15}$$

However, if $\frac{1}{\sqrt{rs}} \lesssim \lambda \leq \frac{1}{2\sqrt{2}\sqrt{rs}}$ *then*

$$L_{\varepsilon}(\mathrm{R}_{\mathrm{cs}}, \widetilde{\mathbb{M}}_2) \lesssim r^{1/4}, \quad \forall \varepsilon > 0, \tag{20.16}$$

with probability at least $1 - \nu$, *whereas*

$$L_{\varepsilon}(\mathrm{R}, \widetilde{\mathbb{M}}_2) \geq \frac{1}{\gamma}, \quad \varepsilon \geq \gamma. \tag{20.17}$$

This theorem demonstrates that compressed sensing may be optimal on one domain $\mathbb{M}_1$, but on another domain $\widetilde{\mathbb{M}}_1$ a learning-based procedure will be provably better. As shown in (20.15), such an improvement can be arbitrarily good. However, this comes at the price of instability. As demonstrated by (20.15) and (20.17), the better the performance, the more unstable the map R. Conversely, the Lipschitz constant of the compressed sensing map grows at worst like $r^{1/4} \lesssim (\log(N))^{1/4}$, so it is, for all intents and purposes, bounded.

Figure 20.8 gives an illustration of how this phenomenon may occur in practice. The network consistently outperforms compressed sensing, but in doing so it forfeits stability.

Proof of Theorem 20.6 Fix $1 \leq k \leq r$ and let $\mathbf{s}$ be such that $s_k = 0$ and $s = s_1 + \cdots + s_r \geq 2$. In particular, $s_j \geq 1$ for at least one $j \neq k$. We derive a lower bound on the number of such patterns at the end of the proof.

We begin with (a). Let $\mathbb{M}_1$ be a countably infinite subset of $\Phi(\Sigma_{\mathbf{s},\mathbf{M}})$, where $\Sigma_{\mathbf{s},\mathbf{M}}$ is the set of $(\mathbf{s}, \mathbf{M})$-sparse vectors (Definition 11.2), and Ω be an $(\mathbf{m}, \mathbf{N})$-multilevel random sampling scheme satisfying (20.13). Recall from Theorem 16.22 that the matrix $U = N^{-1/2} H\Phi$ is block diagonal and each block is perfectly incoherent. Hence Corollary 13.17, (20.13) and the fact that $s \geq 2$ imply that the matrix $A\Phi$ has the SR-LASSO uniform recovery property (see Definition 13.2) of order $(\mathbf{s}, \mathbf{M})$ with constant $\tau = 2\sqrt{2}$. Due to the condition on λ, we get

$$\mathrm{dist}(\mathrm{R}_{\mathrm{cs}}(Ax + e), x) \lesssim r^{1/4} \left(\frac{\sigma_{\mathbf{s},\mathbf{M}}(\Phi^* x)_{\ell^1_w}}{\sqrt{rs}} + \frac{1}{\sqrt{rs}\lambda} \|e\|_{\ell^2} \right), \tag{20.18}$$

for all $x \in \mathbb{C}^N$ and $e \in \mathbb{C}^m$, with probability at least $1 - \nu$. In particular,

$$\mathrm{dist}(\mathrm{R}_{\mathrm{cs}}(Ax), x) = 0 \quad \forall x \in \Phi(\Sigma_{\mathbf{s},\mathbf{M}}), \tag{20.19}$$

which implies that $\mathrm{dist}(\mathrm{R}_{\mathrm{cs}}(Ax), x) = 0$, $\forall x \in \mathbb{M}_1$. Therefore R_{cs} is an optimal map. Now let $x \in \Phi(\Sigma_{\mathbf{s},\mathbf{M}})$ and $e \in \mathbb{C}^m$ with $0 < \|e\|_{\ell^2} \leq \varepsilon$. Then, by (20.18) and (20.19),

$$\mathrm{dist}(\mathrm{R}_{\mathrm{cs}}(Ax + e), \mathrm{R}_{\mathrm{cs}}(Ax)) = \mathrm{dist}(\mathrm{R}_{\mathrm{cs}}(Ax + e), x) \lesssim \frac{r^{1/4}}{\sqrt{rs}\lambda} \|e\|_{\ell^2}.$$

It follows that

$$L_{\varepsilon}(\mathrm{R}_{\mathrm{cs}}, \mathbb{M}_2) \leq L_{\varepsilon}(\mathrm{R}_{\mathrm{cs}}, A\Phi(\Sigma_{\mathbf{s},\mathbf{M}})) \lesssim \frac{r^{1/4}}{\sqrt{rs}\lambda}, \tag{20.20}$$

which completes the proof of (a).

We now consider (b). Let $u \in \mathbb{C}^N$ satisfy $\|u\|_{\ell^2} = 1$ and $u_i = 0$ for $i \notin \{N_{k-1} + 1, \ldots, N_k\}$. Set $z_1 = \Phi u$ and let $z_2 \in \mathbb{M}_1 \backslash \{0\}$. Let $z = z_1 + \frac{\kappa}{\|z_2\|_{\ell^2}} z_2$, where $\kappa > 0$ is a parameter to be chosen later, and define

$$\widetilde{\mathbb{M}}_1 = \mathbb{M}_1 \cup \{0, z\}.$$

Since $m_k = 0$ and U is block diagonal, it follows that $z_1 \in \mathrm{Ker}(A)$. Hence, by (20.19), the fact that $\|z_1\|_{\ell^2} = 1$ (since Φ is unitary) and the assumption (20.14) on R, we have

$$\begin{aligned}
\gamma \sup_{x \in \widetilde{\mathbb{M}}_1} \mathrm{dist}(\mathrm{R}_{\mathrm{cs}}(Ax), x) \geq \gamma \mathrm{dist}(\mathrm{R}_{\mathrm{cs}}(Az), z) &= \gamma \mathrm{dist}\left(\mathrm{R}_{\mathrm{cs}}\left(A \frac{\kappa}{\|z_2\|_{\ell^2}} z_2\right), z\right) \\
&= \gamma \left\| \frac{\kappa}{\|z_2\|_{\ell^2}} z_2 - z \right\|_{\ell^2} \\
&= \gamma \|z_1\|_{\ell^2} \\
&\geq \delta \geq \sup_{x \in \widetilde{\mathbb{M}}_1} \mathrm{dist}(\mathrm{R}(Ax), x),
\end{aligned}$$

which establishes (20.15). Now consider (20.17). The conditions on $\mathbf{m}$ imply that the matrix $A\Phi$ has the RIPL of order $(\mathbf{s}, \mathbf{M})$. Hence

$$\|Az\|_{\ell^2} = \frac{\kappa}{\|z_2\|_{\ell^2}} \|Az_2\|_{\ell^2} \leq 2\kappa \frac{\|\Phi z_2\|_{\ell^2}}{\|z_2\|_{\ell^2}} = 2\kappa.$$

Therefore, if $2\kappa \leq \varepsilon$, then

$$L_\varepsilon(\mathrm{R}, \widetilde{\mathbb{M}}_2) \geq L_\varepsilon(\mathrm{R}, 0) \geq \frac{\mathrm{dist}(\mathrm{R}(Az), \mathrm{R}(0))}{\|Az\|_{\ell^2}} \geq \frac{\|z\|_{\ell^2} - 2\delta}{2\kappa} \geq \frac{1 - 2\gamma}{2\kappa}.$$

Setting $\kappa = (1 - 2\gamma)/(2/\gamma) \leq \varepsilon/2$ now gives $L_\varepsilon(\mathrm{R}, \widetilde{\mathbb{M}}_2) \geq 1/\gamma$. Therefore (20.17) holds.

On the other hand, for the mapping R_{cs} we have

$$L_\varepsilon(\mathrm{R}_{\mathrm{cs}}, \widetilde{\mathbb{M}}_2) = \max\left\{L_\varepsilon(\mathrm{R}_{\mathrm{cs}}, \mathbb{M}_2), L_\varepsilon(\mathrm{R}_{\mathrm{cs}}, 0), L_\varepsilon(\mathrm{R}_{\mathrm{cs}}, Az)\right\}.$$

Observe that

$$\max\left\{L_\varepsilon(\mathrm{R}_{\mathrm{cs}}, \mathbb{M}_2), L_\varepsilon(\mathrm{R}_{\mathrm{cs}}, 0)\right\} \leq L_\varepsilon(\mathrm{R}_{\mathrm{cs}}, A\Phi(\Sigma_{\mathbf{s},\mathbf{M}})).$$

Also, since $Az = \frac{\kappa}{\|z_2\|_{\ell^2}} Az_2$, we have

$$L_\varepsilon(\mathrm{R}_{\mathrm{cs}}, Az) = L_\varepsilon\left(\mathrm{R}_{\mathrm{cs}}, \frac{\kappa}{\|z_2\|_{\ell^2}} Az_2\right) \leq L_\varepsilon(\mathrm{R}_{\mathrm{cs}}, A\Phi(\Sigma_{\mathbf{s},\mathbf{M}})).$$

Hence, combining the above arguments with (20.20), we deduce that

$$L_\varepsilon(\mathrm{R}_{\mathrm{cs}}, \widetilde{\mathbb{M}}_2) \leq L_\varepsilon(\mathrm{R}_{\mathrm{cs}}, A\Phi(\Sigma_{\mathbf{s},\mathbf{M}})) \lesssim \frac{r^{1/4}}{\sqrt{rs\lambda}},$$

which gives (20.16).

The statement about uncountably many domains $\mathbb{M}_1$ and $\widetilde{\mathbb{M}}_1$ follows by multiplying the above choices by complex numbers of modulus one. To complete the proof, it remains to show that there are at least $2^{(r-1)(r-2)/2}$ choices of $\mathbf{s}$ for which $s_k = 0$ for some $1 \leq k \leq r$ and $s = s_1 + \cdots + s_r \geq 2$. Consider the case where $s_1 = 0$ and $s_k \geq 1$

for $k > 1$. Notice that $s = s_1 + \cdots + s_r \geq r - 1 \geq 2$ by assumption on r. Since the sparsity levels are of size $1, 1, 2, \ldots, 2^{r-2}$ there are exactly

$$\prod_{k=0}^{r-2} 2^k = 2^{\sum_{k=1}^{r-2} k} = 2^{(r-1)(r-2)/2}$$

such choices for $\mathbf{s}$. This gives the result. □

20.4.2 Extra Training Data May Cause Instabilities

Our second result, which is based on Fourier sampling, illustrates the following:

> Compressed sensing and deep learning may both be optimal, but adding two more elements to the training set may destabilize deep learning.

For this result, we need to consider classes of neural networks that are sufficiently rich. Specifically:

Definition 20.7 Let $K \in \mathbb{N}$. A class $\mathcal{N}$ of neural networks $\mathrm{N}\colon \mathbb{C}^m \to \mathbb{C}^N$ is *K-interpolatory* if for every $\{x_j\}_{j=1}^K \subset \mathbb{C}^N$ and $\{y_j\}_{j=1}^K \subset \mathbb{C}^m$ there exists a neural network $\mathrm{N} \in \mathcal{N}$ such that $\mathrm{N}(y_j) = x_j$, $\forall j = 1, \ldots, K$.

We shall not discuss conditions on general neural network architectures that ensure this property. We do recall in passing, however, that Theorem 18.3 gives explicit conditions in the case of one-layer networks.

Theorem 20.8 *Let $0 < \nu < 1$, $K, M \in \mathbb{N}$ with $M \geq K$ and consider Fourier measurements. For every choice of local sparsities $\mathbf{s}$ with $s = s_1 + \cdots + s_r \geq 2$ there are uncountably many sets $\{x_i\}_{i=1}^K$ of size K and domains $\mathbb{M}_1 \supset \{x_i\}_{i=1}^K$ of size M for which the following holds. If Ω is an $(\mathbf{m}, \mathbf{N})$-multilevel random sampling scheme with*

$$m_k = \left\lceil C \cdot \left(s_k + \sum_{l=1}^{k-1} s_l 2^{-(k-l)} + \sum_{l=k+1}^{r} s_l 2^{-3(l-k)} \right) \cdot L \right\rceil, \quad k = 1, \ldots, r, \tag{20.21}$$

where $C > 0$ is a numerical constant, $L = \log^3(N) \cdot \log(2m) \cdot \log^2(\log(N)s) + \log(N) \cdot \log(\nu^{-1})$ and $m = m_1 + \cdots + m_r < N$, A is as in (20.11) and $\mathbb{M}_2 = A(\mathbb{M}_1)$, then:

(a) With probability at least $1 - \nu$, the map R_{cs} defined by (20.12) is an optimal map for $\{A, \mathbb{M}_1\}$ whenever $\lambda \leq \frac{1}{2\sqrt{2}\sqrt{rs}}$, and the optimality constant satisfies $c_{\mathrm{opt}}(A, \mathbb{M}_1) = 0$. Moreover,

$$L_\varepsilon(\mathrm{R}_{\mathrm{cs}}, \mathbb{M}_2) \lesssim \frac{r^{1/4}}{\sqrt{rs\lambda}}, \quad \forall \varepsilon > 0,$$

and in particular, $L_\varepsilon(\mathrm{R}_{\mathrm{cs}}, \mathbb{M}_2) \lesssim r^{1/4}$ if $\frac{1}{\sqrt{rs}} \lesssim \lambda \leq \frac{1}{2\sqrt{2}\sqrt{rs}}$.

(b) Let $\mathcal{N}$ be a class of neural networks that is $\max\{M, K+1\}$*-interpolatory. Then there exists an*

$$\widehat{\mathrm{N}} \in \underset{\mathrm{N} \in \mathcal{N}}{\mathrm{argmin}} \frac{1}{K} \sum_{i=1}^{K} \frac{1}{2} \| x_i - \mathrm{N}(Ax_i) \|_{\ell^2}^2, \tag{20.22}$$

that is an optimal map for $\{A, \mathbb{M}_1\}$. *However, for every* $0 < \gamma < 1$ *there are uncountably many sets* $\{x_{K+1}, x_{K+2}\}$, *where* $\|x_{K+1} - x_j\|_{\ell^2}, \|x_{K+2} - x_i\|_{\ell^2} \leq \gamma$ *for some* $1 \leq i, j \leq K$, *such that every*

$$\breve{\mathrm{N}} \in \underset{\mathrm{N} \in \mathcal{N}}{\operatorname{argmin}} \frac{1}{K+2} \sum_{i=1}^{K+2} \frac{1}{2} \|x_i - \mathrm{N}(Ax_i)\|_{\ell^2}^2 \tag{20.23}$$

satisfies

$$L_\varepsilon(\breve{\mathrm{N}}, \mathbb{M}_2) \geq \frac{1}{\gamma}, \qquad \varepsilon \geq \gamma.$$

Theorem 20.8 illustrates how fragile the training process can be. A neural network $\widehat{\mathrm{N}}$ obtained via (20.22) as a minimizer of the standard ℓ^2-loss function may result in an optimal map. But adding two additional elements to the training set causes instabilities: every minimizer of the ℓ^2-loss function (20.23) over the augmented training set has a large Lipschitz constant. Perhaps bizarrely, these new elements can be arbitrarily close to the original training set – they may simply be noisy versions of images in the original training set – yet the instability worsens the closer they become.

Proof of Theorem 20.8 Consider (a). Pick $\mathbb{M}_1$ as a subset of $\Phi(\Sigma_{\mathbf{s},\mathbf{M}})$ of size M and let Ω be an $(\mathbf{m}, \mathbf{N})$-multilevel random sampling scheme satisfying (20.21). The remainder of the proof is nearly identical to that of part (a) of Theorem 20.6. The only difference is the use of Theorem 13.18 to assert that $A\Phi$ has the SR-LASSO uniform recovery property, since we consider Fourier sampling in this theorem.

Consider (b). Since $\mathcal{N}$ is M-interpolatory and $|\mathbb{M}_1| = M$ the first result follows immediately. For the second result, write $x_{K+i} = x_i + z_i$ for $i = 1, 2$. Since $m \leq N - 1$ we may choose $z_2 \in \mathrm{Ker}(A)$ with $\|z_2\|_{\ell^2} = \gamma/4$. We now claim that there is a $z_1 \in \mathbb{C}^N$ that satisfies $\|z_1\|_{\ell^2} = \gamma$ and $0 < \|Az_1\|_{\ell^2} \leq \gamma^2/2$. Indeed, let $u \in \mathrm{Ker}(A)$ and $v \in (\mathrm{Ker}(A))^\perp$ be unit vectors and set

$$z_1 = (\gamma^2 - \beta^2)^{1/2} u + \beta v, \qquad \beta = \gamma^2/(2\|A\|_{\ell^2}).$$

Notice that $\|A\|_{\ell^2} \geq 1$, since $A = P_\Omega D U$, where U is unitary and D is diagonal with diagonal entries at least one. Therefore $\beta \leq \gamma^2/2 < \gamma$, which implies that z_1 is well defined. Also $\|z\|_{\ell^2}^2 = (\gamma^2 - \beta^2)\|u\|_{\ell^2}^2 + \beta^2\|v\|_{\ell^2}^2 = \gamma^2$, since $u \perp v$ and $\|u\|_{\ell^2} = \|v\|_{\ell^2} = 1$, and $\|Az_1\|_{\ell^2} = \beta\|Av\|_{\ell^2} \leq \beta\|A\|_{\ell^2} = \gamma^2/2$. This establishes the claim. To get uncountably many such x_{K+1} and x_{K+2}, we can simply multiply z_1 and z_2 by complex numbers of modulus one.

Since $\mathcal{N}$ is $(K+1)$-interpolatory, there exists an $\mathrm{N} \in \mathcal{N}$ with $\mathrm{N}(Ax_i) = x_i$ for $i = 1, \ldots, K+1$. Notice that $Ax_{K+2} = Ax_2$. Hence

$$\|x_i - \breve{\mathrm{N}}(Ax_i)\|_{\ell^2} \leq \|x_{K+2} - \mathrm{N}(Ax_{K+2})\|_{\ell^2} = \|x_{K+2} - x_2\|_{\ell^2}, \quad i = 1, \ldots, K+2.$$

As $0 < \|Az_1\|_{\ell^2} \leq \gamma^2/2 \leq \varepsilon$, this gives

$$L_\varepsilon(\breve{\mathrm{N}}, \mathbb{M}_2) \geq \frac{\|\breve{\mathrm{N}}(Ax_1 + Az_1) - \breve{\mathrm{N}}(Ax_1)\|_{\ell^2}}{\|Az_1\|_{\ell^2}} \geq \frac{\|\breve{\mathrm{N}}(Ax_{K+1}) - \breve{\mathrm{N}}(Ax_1)\|_{\ell^2}}{\gamma^2/2},$$

and therefore

$$\begin{aligned} L_{\varepsilon}(\breve{\mathrm{N}}, \mathbb{M}_2) &\geq \frac{\|x_{K+1} - x_1\|_{\ell^2} - \|\breve{\mathrm{N}}(Ax_{K+1}) - x_{K+1}\|_{\ell^2} - \|\breve{\mathrm{N}}(Ax_1) - x_1\|_{\ell^2}}{\gamma^2/2} \\ &\geq \frac{\|x_{K+1} - x_1\|_{\ell^2} - 2\|x_{K+2} - x_2\|_{\ell^2}}{\gamma^2/2} \\ &= \frac{\|z_1\|_{\ell^2} - 2\|z_2\|_{\ell^2}}{\gamma^2/2} = \frac{\gamma/2}{\gamma^2/2} = \frac{1}{\gamma}, \end{aligned}$$

as required. □

20.5 Can Instabilities be Remedied?

Having seen how trained neural networks can be unstable, in this final section we consider whether there is a straightforward way to remedy this situation. Of course, if stability alone were our only goal, the answer would be simple: the zero network is a highly stable, but entirely useless network. The challenge, as discussed previously in §20.4, is combining stability with performance.

In this section, we study three possible approaches for remedying instabilities, including several that are known to achieve at least partial success in mitigating adversarial attacks in image classification. Unfortunately, our main conclusion is negative:

> Instabilities cannot easily be remedied by modifying the training setup.

In particular, we show that mechanisms that drive instabilities, such as an absence of kernel awareness (Theorem 20.4), are not easily avoided in learning.

20.5.1 Regularization and Adversarial Training

We first consider three popular techniques:

1. Regularization
2. Adversarial training
3. Adversarial training using Generative Adversarial Networks (GANs).

These three approaches can be studied in a unified manner, in which one considers training a neural network by solving the following optimization problem:

$$\min_{\mathrm{N} \in \mathcal{N}} \max_{J \in \mathcal{K}} \frac{1}{|\Theta|} \sum_{(y,x) \in \Theta} \frac{1}{2} \|x - \mathrm{N}(y)\|_{\ell^2}^2 + \lambda J(\mathrm{N}, \Theta) \tag{20.24}$$

(for simplicity, we consider the ℓ^2-cost function only in this section). Here $\Theta = \{(y_i, x_i)\}_{i=1}^K$ is the training set, $0 \leq \lambda < \infty$ is the regularization parameter, $J \colon \mathcal{N} \times \mathcal{E} \to [0, \infty)$, where $\mathcal{E}$ is some family of training data, and $\mathcal{K}$ is a suitable class of functions such that the maximum is attained. Each of the techniques listed above can be seen as an example of this general approach:

1. Regularization was previously discussed in §18.5.4. It is an example of (20.24) with $\mathcal{K} = \{J\}$ being a singleton, where $J : \mathcal{N} \to [0, \infty)$ is independent of Θ.
2. In adversarial training, we consider a class $\mathcal{L}$ of functions of the form $\mathrm{L}: \mathcal{N} \times \mathbb{C}^m \to \mathbb{C}^m$. We define

$$J_{\mathrm{L}}(\mathrm{N}, \Theta) = \frac{1}{|\Theta|} \sum_{(y,x)\in\Theta} \frac{1}{2} \|\mathrm{N}(y + \mathrm{L}(\mathrm{N}, y)) - x\|_{\ell^2}^2,$$

and

$$\mathcal{K} = \{J_{\mathrm{L}} : \mathrm{L} \in \mathcal{L}\}. \tag{20.25}$$

The idea is that $\mathrm{L}(\mathrm{N}, y)$ provides a potential bad perturbation for the network N at the input y. Hence (20.24) becomes a game between two adversaries: one player aims to find a network $\mathrm{N} \in \mathcal{N}$ which reconstructs the training set as well as possible, and the other player aims to find a function $\mathrm{L} \in \mathcal{L}$ which affects these reconstructions in as bad a way as possible. The hope is that the network that results from playing this game should be more stable.
3. This is a special case of adversarial training in which neural networks are used both for the reconstruction map and for constructing the bad perturbations. Specifically, we let $\varepsilon > 0$ and consider a second class of neural networks $\mathcal{N}'$. Then we define

$$\mathcal{L} = \{\mathrm{N}' \in \mathcal{N}' : \|\mathrm{N}'\|_{\ell^p} \leq \varepsilon\}, \qquad \|\mathrm{N}'\|_{\ell^p} = \sup_{\substack{y\in\mathbb{C}^m \\ \|y\|_{\ell^p}\leq 1}} \|\mathrm{N}'(y)\|_{\ell^p},$$

for some $1 \leq p \leq \infty$. Note that different choices of p will provide different types of robustness. The restriction $\|\mathrm{N}'\|_{\ell^p} \leq \varepsilon$ aims to tailor the network to the noise level expected in the particular problem.

Remark 20.9 The rationale for the adversarial training is as follows. Ideally, we would like to solve the following problem:

$$\min_{\mathrm{N}\in\mathcal{N}} \frac{1}{|\Theta|} \sum_{(y,x)\in\Theta} \max_{\|z\|_{\ell^p}\leq\varepsilon} \left\{ \frac{1}{2}\|x - \mathrm{N}(y)\|_{\ell^2}^2 + \frac{\lambda}{2}\|x - \mathrm{N}(y + z)\|_{\ell^2}^2 \right\}.$$

In other words, for each training point $(y, x) \in \Theta$ we find the worst-case perturbation z in the ε-ball around y, in the sense that it maximizes the reconstruction error $\|x - \mathrm{N}(y + z)\|_{\ell^2}$. However, this problem is typically not computationally feasible, since it involves solving a separate maximization problem for each element of the training set. Hence, the idea is to parametrize these perturbations as $z \approx \mathrm{L}(\mathrm{N}, y)$, where $\mathrm{L}: \mathcal{N} \times \mathbb{C}^m \to \mathbb{C}^m$ is a mapping belonging to some class of mappings $\mathcal{L}$ (e.g. a class of neural networks in the case of GANs). The the minimization problem then becomes

$$\min_{\mathrm{N}\in\mathcal{N}} \max_{\mathrm{L}\in\mathcal{L}} \frac{1}{|\Theta|} \sum_{(y,x)\in\Theta} \left\{ \frac{1}{2}\|x - \mathrm{N}(y)\|_{\ell^2}^2 + \frac{\lambda}{2}\|x - \mathrm{N}(y + \mathrm{L}(\mathrm{N}, y))\|_{\ell^2}^2 \right\},$$

which is exactly (20.24) with $\mathcal{K}$ as in (20.25).

Regardless of which procedure one uses, a key question is how to set the regularization parameter λ in (20.24). If λ is too small, the network is liable to be unstable, but if λ

is too large, the network is liable to be stable but lack performance. To investigate this question, we now define the following:

Definition 20.10 Let $\{A, \mathbb{M}_1\}$, a class of neural networks $\mathcal{N}$, a class of functions $\mathcal{K}$ of the above form and a training set Θ be given. A number $0 \le \lambda < \infty$ is *optimal* for $\{\{A, \mathbb{M}_1\}, \mathcal{N}, \mathcal{K}, \Theta\}$ if there is a minimizer of (20.24) that is an optimal map for $\{A, \mathbb{M}_1\}$.

Theorem 20.11 below reveals the following issue:

Setting the regularization parameter λ in (20.24) is a highly delicate, and ironically, highly unstable problem depending on the sampling scheme.

In this result, we consider classes of real-valued ReLU neural networks $\mathcal{N} = \mathcal{N}_{\mathbf{n}}$. If the input $y \in \mathbb{C}^m$ is complex valued, then, as in Remark 19.1, we assume the network receives an input $y' \in \mathbb{R}^{2m}$ corresponding to the real and imaginary parts of y and produces an output in $\mathbb{R}^{2N}$ corresponding to a complex vector in $\mathbb{C}^N$. Further, we also assume the network can take an input of size less than m (or $2m$ in the complex case). This is done by suitably zero padding the input.

Theorem 20.11 *Let $U \in \mathbb{C}^{N \times N}$ be an invertible matrix with $N \ge 4$. Then there are $2^N - 2N - 2$ sampling patterns $\widetilde{\Omega}$ and for each of them a sampling pattern Ω, $|\Omega| \ne N$, such that if $A = P_\Omega U$ and $\widetilde{A} = P_{\widetilde{\Omega}} U$ then the following holds. Let $M \in \{2, \ldots, \infty\}$, $m = \max\{|\Omega|, |\widetilde{\Omega}|\}$, $\mathcal{N}_{\mathbf{n}}$ be any class of ReLU neural networks with at least one hidden layer, where $\mathbf{n} = (m, n_1, \ldots, n_{L-1}, N)$, $n_l \ge 2m$, in the real case and $\mathbf{n} = (2m, n_1, \ldots, n_{L-1}, 2N)$, $n_l \ge 4m$, in the complex case, and consider* (20.24)*. Then there exists a $0 \le \lambda_{\mathrm{opt}} < \infty$ and uncountably many domains $\mathbb{M}_1$ of size M such that for each $\mathbb{M}_1$ there are uncountably many training sets*

$$\Theta = \{(Ax_i, x_i)\}_{i=1}^K \subset A(\mathbb{M}_1) \times \mathbb{M}_1, \qquad \widetilde{\Theta} = \{(\widetilde{A}\tilde{x}_i, \tilde{x}_i)\}_{i=1}^{\widetilde{K}} \subset \widetilde{A}(\mathbb{M}_1) \times \mathbb{M}_1,$$

with $K, \widetilde{K} < \infty$ and possibly with $\{x_i\}_{i=1}^K = \{\tilde{x}_i\}_{i=1}^{\widetilde{K}}$, for which λ_{opt} is optimal for $\{\{A, \mathbb{M}_1\}, \mathcal{N}, \mathcal{K}, \Theta\}$ and $\{\{\widetilde{A}, \mathbb{M}_1\}, \mathcal{N}, \mathcal{K}, \widetilde{\Theta}\}$. However, there exists an uncountable set $\mathbb{S} \subseteq \mathbb{C}^N$ such that:

(a) If $(\widetilde{A}x, x)$, $x \in \mathbb{S}$, is either added to the training set $\widetilde{\Theta}$, or replaces a specific element in $\widetilde{\Theta}$, then either there is no element of

$$\underset{\mathrm{N} \in \mathcal{N}}{\operatorname{argmin}} \max_{J \in \mathcal{K}} \frac{1}{|\widetilde{\Theta}|} \sum_{(\tilde{y}, \tilde{x}) \in \widetilde{\Theta}} \frac{1}{2} \|\tilde{x} - \mathrm{N}(\tilde{y})\|_{\ell^2}^2 + \lambda J(\mathrm{N}, \widetilde{\Theta}), \tag{20.26}$$

that is an optimal map for $\{\widetilde{A}, \mathbb{M}_1\}$ for any $0 \le \lambda < \infty$, or there is another $\tilde{\lambda}_{\mathrm{opt}} \ne \lambda_{\mathrm{opt}}$ that is optimal for $\{(\widetilde{A}, \mathbb{M}_1), \mathcal{N}, \widetilde{\Theta}\}$ whereas λ_{opt} is not.

(b) Given any subset $\mathbb{V} \subset \mathbb{S}$, if $\{(Ax, x) : x \in \mathbb{V}\}$ is either added to Θ or replaces elements in Θ, then λ_{opt} is still optimal for $\{\{A, \mathbb{M}_1\}, \mathcal{N}, \mathcal{K}, \Theta\}$.

This theorem, whose proof we defer until §20.5.4, states that there are many sampling patterns Ω and $\widetilde{\Omega}$, training sets Θ and $\widetilde{\Theta}$ and a large set $\mathbb{S}$ for which the following holds. When considering the sampling pattern $\widetilde{\Omega}$, setting the parameter λ is unstable with respect to changes in $\widetilde{\Theta}$ using elements from $\mathbb{S}$. On the other hand, setting the parameter λ is stable with respect to changes in Θ using the same elements from $\mathbb{S}$ when considering the sampling pattern Ω. Hence, changes to the training sets from the same set $\mathbb{S}$ can give vastly different results. The conclusion is therefore that, unless one has prior information about the training data, or a potential way of learning this information, setting the parameter λ is a delicate affair. Ironically, one ends up with a potentially unstable problem in order to fix the instability issue in the original problem.

20.5.2 Enforcing Consistency

Enforcing *consistency* is another approach to try to improve the robustness of a reconstruction map. If $\mathrm{R}\colon \mathbb{C}^m \to \mathbb{C}^N$ is a reconstruction map (it need not be a neural network) then consistency is the condition that $\mathrm{R}(y)$ agrees with the measurements y, i.e.

$$A\hat{x} = y, \text{ where } \hat{x} = \mathrm{R}(y),\ y = Ax,\ x \in \mathbb{M}_1.$$

This is a quite natural condition to enforce. However, as can be seen via Theorem 20.4, it does nothing to prevent instabilities. Indeed, the conditions

$$d_1(\mathrm{R}(Ax), x) < \eta, \quad d_1(\mathrm{R}(Ax'), x') < \eta, \quad d_2(Ax, Ax') \le \eta \tag{20.27}$$

pertain to the quality of R as an approximation, and are unrelated to its consistency. In fact, if $\mathrm{R}(Ax) = x$ and $\mathrm{R}(Ax') = x'$, i.e. R recovers x and x' perfectly, then clearly R is also consistent for x and x'.

In practice, enforcing exact consistency may be challenging. A rather general approach to approximate consistency is to consider a set $\mathbb{S} \subset \mathbb{C}^N$ which either contains the images of interest, or approximates these images well. Then, one defines the reconstruction map

$$\mathrm{R}\colon \mathbb{C}^m \to \mathbb{C}^N,\ y \mapsto \mathrm{R}(y) \in \underset{z\in\mathbb{S}}{\operatorname{argmin}} \frac{1}{2}\|Az - y\|_{\ell^2}^2. \tag{20.28}$$

However, if x and x' satisfy $d_2(Ax, Ax') \le \eta$ and additionally, $x, x' \in \mathbb{S}$, then (20.27) still holds, and thus instabilities still occur.

20.5.3 Training with Multiple Sampling Patterns

We have seen in Fig. 20.10 that trained neural networks may be brittle to changes in the sampling pattern. A third approach to try to improve the robustness of deep learning is to train with many different sampling patterns at once. Specifically, suppose the measurements are obtained as in Theorem 20.11 via an invertible matrix U. We now consider the reconstruction map N as a mapping $\mathbb{C}^N \to \mathbb{C}^N$ and the measurement vector y as an element of $\mathbb{C}^N$, where the components in y that correspond to the indices that are not sampled are set to zero. The map N is constructed by training on the data $\{(y_{ij}, x_j) : j = 1, \ldots, K, i = 1, \ldots, L\}$, where $y_{ij} = P_{\Omega_i} U x_j$ and Ω_i is the ith sampling pattern. For instance, one may define

$$\widehat{\mathrm{N}} \in \underset{\mathrm{N}\in\mathcal{N}}{\operatorname{argmin}} \frac{1}{KL} \sum_{j=1,i=1}^{K,L} \frac{1}{2}\|x_i - \mathrm{N}(P_{\Omega_j} U x_i)\|_{\ell^2}^2. \tag{20.29}$$

Once the network is trained, it is used to reconstruct an image x from measurements $y = P_\Omega U x$ acquired from a given sampling pattern Ω of size $|\Omega| = m$ (which may or may not be equal to Ω_i for some i). In particular, even though it is trained using $\Omega_1, \ldots, \Omega_L$, when used as a reconstruction map it only has access to the measurements from a single sampling pattern of size m, and not all L sampling patterns used in the training.

This type of training also does not avoid instabilities. In fact, it may make them more likely. Training on more data, as in (20.29), can potentially improve the performance of the reconstruction map $\widehat{\mathrm{N}}$, making it easier to achieve the conditions

$$d_1(\mathrm{N}(P_\Omega U x), x) < \eta, \quad d_1(\mathrm{N}(P_\Omega U x'), x') < \eta, \quad d_1(x, x') \gg \eta.$$

Yet, the amount and variety of the training data is completely unrelated to the null space of $P_\Omega U$. Hence, it does nothing to mitigate against the condition

$$d_2(P_\Omega U x, P_\Omega U x') \leq \eta.$$

As it happens, the network used in Figs 20.3, 20.6 and 20.8 was trained with multiple sampling patterns. However, it still exhibits instabilities.

20.5.4 Proof of Theorem 20.11

We conclude this section with the proof of the main result stated earlier:

Proof of Theorem 20.11 We first define Ω, $\widetilde{\Omega}$, $\mathbb{M}_1$, Θ and $\widetilde{\Theta}$. Let $\widetilde{\Omega} \subset \{1, \ldots, N\}$ with $2 \leq |\widetilde{\Omega}| \leq N - 2$ and note that there are $2^N - 2N - 2$ different choices of $\widetilde{\Omega}$. Also, let $\Omega = \widetilde{\Omega} \cup \{j\}$ where $j \notin \widetilde{\Omega}$, and notice that $|\Omega| < N$ since $|\widetilde{\Omega}| \leq N - 2$. Choose $\mathbb{M}_1 \subset (\mathrm{Ker}(\widetilde{A}))^\perp$ of size M, and if M is infinite, choose $\mathbb{M}_1$ to be countable. Multiplying $\mathbb{M}_1$ by any real number we clearly get uncountably many different choices of $\mathbb{M}_1$. For ease of notation let $\mathbb{M}_2 = A(\mathbb{M}_1)$ and $\widetilde{\mathbb{M}}_2 = \tilde{A}(\mathbb{M}_1)$.

Choose $i \in \widetilde{\Omega}$. Let $\widetilde{\Theta} \subset \widetilde{\mathbb{M}}_2 \times \mathbb{M}_1$ be any finite, nonzero collection such that there is exactly one pair $(\hat{y} = \widetilde{A}\hat{x}, \hat{x}) \in \widetilde{\Theta}$ such that

$$\widetilde{\Theta} \backslash \{(\hat{y}, \hat{x})\} \subset \{(\tilde{y}, \tilde{x}) : \tilde{y} = \widetilde{A}\tilde{x},\ P_{\{i\}}\tilde{y} = 0\}, \quad P_{\{i\}}\hat{y} \neq 0, \quad P_{\widetilde{\Omega}\backslash\{i\}}\hat{y} = 0. \tag{20.30}$$

Note that such a choice is possible since $|\widetilde{\Omega}| \geq 2$. Choose any finite, nonempty $\Theta \subset \mathbb{M}_2 \times \mathbb{M}_1$. As both Θ and $\widetilde{\Theta}$ can be multiplied by any real number then, without changing any of the properties outlined above, we clearly have that there are uncountably many different choices of Θ and $\widetilde{\Theta}$. Note that

$$\widetilde{A}^\dagger y = x \text{ if } y = \widetilde{A}x, \quad x \in \mathbb{M}_1, \tag{20.31}$$

where $\widetilde{A}^\dagger$ denotes the pseudoinverse. This fact will be crucial later in the proof.

For convenience, we denote all neural networks in what follows as taking complex input and producing complex output, with this being understood in the sense discussed directly before the statement of Theorem 20.11. Consider the L-layer ReLU neural network $\widetilde{\mathrm{N}} \colon \mathbb{C}^{|\widetilde{\Omega}|} \to \mathbb{C}^N$ defined by

$$\widetilde{\mathrm{N}}(y) = \widetilde{A}^\dagger W_2 \sigma(\ldots \sigma(W_1 W_2 \sigma(W_1 W_2 \sigma(W_1 y)))),$$

where

$$W_1 = (1,-1)^\top \otimes I_{|\widetilde{\Omega}|}, \quad W_2 = (1,-1) \otimes I_{|\widetilde{\Omega}|}, \tag{20.32}$$

where I_d denotes the $d \times d$ identity matrix of size and $\otimes$ denotes the Kronecker product. Observe that

$$W_2\sigma(W_1\tilde{y}) = W_2 \begin{pmatrix} \sigma(\tilde{y}) \\ \sigma(-\tilde{y}) \end{pmatrix} = \sigma(\tilde{y}) - \sigma(-\tilde{y}) = \tilde{y},$$

where the last equality is due to the fact that σ is the ReLU activation function. Hence, for every $(\tilde{y} = \widetilde{A}\tilde{x}, \tilde{x}) \in \widetilde{\mathbb{M}}_2 \times \mathbb{M}_1$, we have

$$\widetilde{\mathrm{N}}(\tilde{y}) = \widetilde{A}^\dagger W_2\sigma(\cdots \sigma(W_1W_2\sigma(W_1W_2\sigma(W_1\tilde{y})))) = \widetilde{A}^\dagger \tilde{y} = \tilde{x}. \tag{20.33}$$

Also, recalling that $\mathbf{n} = (m, n_1, \ldots, n_{L-1}, N)$, $m = \max\{|\Omega|, |\widetilde{\Omega}|\}$ and the assumption that $n_j \geq 2m$, it is clear that by suitably padding W_j with zeros we can without loss of generality assume that $\widetilde{\mathrm{N}} \in \mathcal{N}_{\mathbf{n}}$. Hence, by setting λ_{opt} to zero, and using (20.33) we have that

$$\max_{J\in\mathcal{K}} \frac{1}{|\widetilde{\Theta}|} \sum_{(\tilde{y},\tilde{x})\in\widetilde{\Theta}} \frac{1}{2}\|\tilde{x} - \widetilde{\mathrm{N}}(\tilde{y})\|_{\ell^2}^2 + \lambda_{\mathrm{opt}} J(\widetilde{\mathrm{N}}, \widetilde{\Theta}) = 0. \tag{20.34}$$

We use choice of λ_{opt} throughout the argument. We first claim that λ_{opt} is optimal for $\{\{\widetilde{A}, \mathbb{M}_1\}, \mathcal{N}, \mathcal{K}, \widetilde{\Theta}\}$. Since (20.34) implies that $\widetilde{\mathrm{N}}$ is a minimizer of (20.26) for $\lambda = \lambda_{\mathrm{opt}}$ we only need to show that $\widetilde{\mathrm{N}}$ is an optimal map for $\{\widetilde{A}, \mathbb{M}_1\}$. To see this, we use (20.33) to obtain

$$c_{\mathrm{opt}}(\widetilde{A}, \mathbb{M}_1) = \inf_{\mathrm{R}:\widetilde{\mathbb{M}}_2 \rightrightarrows \mathbb{C}^N} \sup_{x\in\mathbb{M}_1} \mathrm{dist}(\mathrm{R}(\widetilde{A}x), x) \leq \sup_{x\in\mathbb{M}_1} \mathrm{dist}(\widetilde{\mathrm{N}}(\widetilde{A}x), x) = 0. \tag{20.35}$$

Hence the claim that λ_{opt} is optimal for $\{\{\widetilde{A}, \mathbb{M}_1\}, \mathcal{N}, \mathcal{K}, \widetilde{\Theta}\}$ holds. That λ_{opt} is also optimal for $\{\{A, \mathbb{M}_1\}, \mathcal{N}, \Theta\}$, will be shown when we consider part (b).

We now define $\mathbb{S}$. Note that $\mathrm{Ker}(\widetilde{A}) \cap (\mathrm{Ker}(A))^\perp$ is nonzero by our choice of Ω. We choose a nonzero $x \in \mathrm{Ker}(\widetilde{A}) \cap (\mathrm{Ker}(A))^\perp$ and let $z = \hat{x} + x$ where $\hat{x}$ is from (20.30). We then define $\mathbb{S}$ as any uncountable collection of nonzero multiples of z.

We are now ready to show (a). Note that it is enough to show that λ_{opt} is no longer optimal if we add or replace a specific element of $\widetilde{\Theta}$ with an element from $\mathbb{S}$. First, suppose that we replace $(\hat{y}, \hat{x}) \in \widetilde{\Theta}$ by $(\hat{y}, \hat{x} + x)$. Define the neural network $\mathrm{N} \in \mathcal{N}$ by

$$\mathrm{N}(x) = CW_2\sigma(\cdots \sigma(W_1W_2\sigma(W_1W_2\sigma(W_1x)))), \tag{20.36}$$

where W_1 and W_2 are as in (20.32) and

$$C = \widetilde{A}^\dagger P_{\widetilde{\Omega}\setminus\{i\}} + \left(\frac{1}{e_i^\top \hat{y}}(\hat{x} + x) \otimes e_i^\top\right).$$

Observe that $\mathrm{N}(\tilde{y}) = \widetilde{\mathrm{N}}(\tilde{y}) = \tilde{x}$ for $(\tilde{y}, \tilde{x}) \in \widetilde{\Theta}$ with $P_{\{i\}}\tilde{y} = 0$. Also, (20.30) gives

$$\mathrm{N}(\hat{y}) = \left(\widetilde{A}^\dagger P_{\widetilde{\Omega}\setminus\{i\}} + \left(\frac{1}{\hat{y}^i}(\hat{x} + x) \otimes e_i^\top\right)\right) \hat{y} = \hat{x} + x,$$

for $(\hat{y}, \hat{x} + x) \in \widetilde{\Theta}$. Hence, the objective function in (20.26) is zero at N whenever $\lambda = \lambda_{\text{opt}}$. Thus, every

$$\widehat{\mathrm{N}} \in \operatorname*{argmin}_{\mathrm{N} \in \mathcal{N}} \max_{J \in \mathcal{K}} \frac{1}{|\widetilde{\Theta}|} \sum_{(\tilde{y}, \tilde{x}) \in \widetilde{\Theta}} \frac{1}{2} \| \tilde{x} - \mathrm{N}(\tilde{y}) \|_{\ell^2}^2 + \lambda_{\text{opt}} J(\mathrm{N}, \widetilde{\Theta}) \tag{20.37}$$

must satisfy $\widehat{\mathrm{N}}(\hat{y}) = \hat{x} + x$, which means that

$$\sup_{x \in \mathbb{M}_1} \operatorname{dist}(\widehat{\mathrm{N}}(\widetilde{A}x), x) \neq 0.$$

It follows from (20.35) that $\widehat{\mathrm{N}}$ is not an optimal map. Hence λ_{opt} is no longer optimal for $\{\{\widetilde{A}, \mathbb{M}_1\}, \mathcal{N}, \mathcal{K}, \widetilde{\Theta}\}$.

Now consider the case where $(\hat{y}, \hat{x} + x)$ is added to $\widetilde{\Theta}$. Let $\widetilde{\mathrm{N}}$ be the neural network defined by (20.36) with

$$C = \widetilde{A}^{\dagger} P_{\widetilde{\Omega} \setminus \{i\}} + \left(\frac{1}{e_i^{\top} \hat{y}} \left(\hat{x} + \frac{1}{2} x \right) \otimes e_i^{\top} \right).$$

Observe that $\widetilde{\mathrm{N}}(\tilde{y}) = \tilde{x}$ for $(\tilde{y}, \tilde{x}) \in \widetilde{\Theta}$ with $P_{\{i\}} \tilde{y} = 0$. Also, (20.30) gives that

$$\widetilde{\mathrm{N}}(\hat{y}) = \left(\widetilde{A}^{\dagger} P_{\widetilde{\Omega} \setminus \{i\}} + \left(\frac{1}{\hat{y}^i} \left(\hat{x} + \frac{1}{2} x \right) \otimes e_i^{\top} \right) \right) \hat{y} = \hat{x} + \frac{1}{2} x,$$

for $(\hat{y}, \hat{x} + x), (\hat{y}, \hat{x}) \in \widetilde{\Theta}$. Hence

$$\frac{1}{|\widetilde{\Theta}|} \sum_{(\tilde{y}, \tilde{x}) \in \widetilde{\Theta}} \frac{1}{2} \| \tilde{x} - \widetilde{\mathrm{N}}(\tilde{y}) \|_{\ell^2}^2 + \lambda_{\text{opt}} J(\widetilde{\mathrm{N}}) = \frac{1}{2|\widetilde{\Theta}|} \left\| \frac{1}{2} x \right\|_{\ell^2}^2,$$

and therefore every minimizer N of (20.37) satisfies

$$\max_{J \in \mathcal{K}} \frac{1}{|\widetilde{\Theta}|} \sum_{(\tilde{y}, \tilde{x}) \in \widetilde{\Theta}} \frac{1}{2} \| \tilde{x} - \mathrm{N}(\tilde{y}) \|_{\ell^2}^2 + \lambda_{\text{opt}} J(\mathrm{N}, \widetilde{\Theta}) \leq \frac{1}{8|\widetilde{\Theta}|} \|x\|_{\ell^2}^2. \tag{20.38}$$

However, by (20.35), every optimal map R for $(\widetilde{A}, \mathbb{M}_1)$ satisfies

$$\sup_{x \in \mathbb{M}_1} \operatorname{dist}(\mathrm{R}(\widetilde{A}x), x) = 0.$$

Thus,

$$\frac{1}{|\widetilde{\Theta}|} \sum_{(\tilde{y}, \tilde{x}) \in \widetilde{\Theta}} \frac{1}{2} \| \tilde{x} - \mathrm{R}(\tilde{y}) \|_{\ell^2}^2 = \frac{1}{2|\widetilde{\Theta}|} \|x\|_{\ell^2}^2,$$

and therefore, by (20.38), no minimizer N of (20.37) can be an optimal map for $\{\widetilde{A}, \mathbb{M}_1\}$. Hence λ_{opt} is not optimal for $\{(\widetilde{A}, \mathbb{M}_1, \mathcal{N}, \mathcal{K}, \widetilde{\Theta})\}$.

Now consider part (b). Let $\mathbb{D} \subset \mathbb{M}_1 \cup \mathbb{S}$ be any finite nonempty set, and let

$$\Theta = \{(Ax, x) : x \in \mathbb{D}\}.$$

We shall prove that λ_{opt} is optimal for $\{\{A, (\operatorname{Ker}(A))^{\perp}\}, \mathcal{N}, \mathcal{K}, \Theta\}$ for any such Θ. Note that this is a stronger statement than in the theorem, as

$$\mathbb{M}_1 \cup \mathbb{S} \subset (\operatorname{Ker}(A))^{\perp}.$$

From (20.35) it is clear that $y \mapsto A^\dagger y$ is an optimal map for $\{A, (\mathrm{Ker}(A))^\perp\}$. Using the network $\widetilde{\mathrm{N}}$ from (20.33), where $\tilde{A}^\dagger$ is replaced by $A^\dagger$ in the last layer, it is clear that $\widetilde{\mathrm{N}}$ is an optimal map, and a minimizer of (20.37) for λ_{opt} when we replace $\widetilde{\Theta}$ by Θ. Thus λ_{opt} is optimal for $\{\{A, (\mathrm{Ker}(A))^\perp\}, \mathcal{N}, \mathcal{K}, \Theta\}$. □

Notes

The instability phenomenon in deep learning for compressive imaging was shown experimentally in [36]; see also [271] for some related work in the limited-angle CT problem. Figures 20.2, 20.3, 20.4, 20.6 and 20.9 are from [36]. Figure 20.1 is from [236]. The image used is from the MGH–USC HCP public dataset [202]. Figures 20.5, 20.7 and 20.8 are also from [236]. We refer to these papers for full details of the experiments.

The main theoretical results in this chapter, Theorems 20.4, 20.5, 20.6, 20.8 and 20.11, are based on [236]. Note that Theorems 20.6 and 20.8 are slightly different to those proved in [236], which used the QCBP decoder. Here we have used the SR-LASSO decoder as it somewhat simplifies the arguments.

As observed in the Notes section of Chapter 18, there have been extensive efforts on improving the robustness of deep learning in classification. Adversarial training using a regularization formulation, much as in §20.5.1, has played a considerable role [235,275,307,402,488,508]. GANs [234] have proved particularly popular [39,488,508]. Injecting noise into the input image was used in [155] to improve the robustness of classifier networks. Far less progress has to date been made in image reconstruction, although results have recently begun to emerge [402]. For approaches focusing on consistency, see [25,70,134,249,456]. As noted, training with multiple sampling patterns has been used, for example, in the Deep MRI network [427].

21 Stable and Accurate Neural Networks for Compressive Imaging

In the previous chapter, we saw that deep learning approaches face difficulties in simultaneously ensuring stability and accuracy. Methods that perform too well are liable to be unstable, while methods that are stable tend to lack performance. This raises the following question: where does the *accuracy–stability barrier* lie for compressive imaging? And more pointedly: do accurate and stable neural networks for compressive imaging even exist, and if so, can they be computed by an algorithm? The purpose of this chapter is to answer this question in the affirmative. The main results we prove establish the existence of algorithms for computing neural networks whose accuracy and stability are as good, up to constants, as compressed sensing.

Our basis for this will be unravelling, a topic already discussed in §19.2.4. Note that unravelling an optimization method does not mean that asymptotically, as the number of iterations (i.e. layers) grows, the output of the resulting network will converge to a minimizer of the underlying optimization problem. Indeed, Theorem 8.18 and the numerical example in §7.1 demonstrated how delicate computing minimizers can be: in general, no algorithm can compute minimizers of the standard compressed sensing optimization problems to arbitrary accuracy. Nevertheless, while unravelling does not yield convergence to a minimizer, we now show that the standard compressed sensing assumptions (e.g. the rNSP and its variants) are sufficient to ensure that the neural networks resulting from it possess the standard accuracy and stability bounds of compressed sensing.

We begin in §21.1 with a formal definition of computability for neural networks. This mirrors the previous developments in §8.6. Next, in §21.2 we take a closer look at unravelling ISTA, and then in §21.3 we consider unravelling the primal–dual iteration. Our main results are presented in §21.4, which deals with the abstract compressed sensing setting, and §21.5, which focuses on compressive imaging.

21.1 Algorithms for Computing Neural Networks

It is trivial to assert the existence of stable and accurate neural networks for compressive imaging. Take a reconstruction map R defined by another approach, e.g. $R = R_{cs}$ for some suitable compressed sensing procedure, and then use the universal approximation theorem (Theorem 18.2) to approximate it to arbitrary accuracy with a neural network. Yet this is highly dissatisfying. It does not assert the existence of an algorithm which can actually compute such a network. Indeed, even just evaluating R usually involves computing a minimizer of an optimization problem, which, as we know from Chapter 8, cannot generally be done to arbitrary accuracy.

To formalize the mathematical question of computability of neural networks, we first recall the notion of inverse problem triples introduced in §20.1. For reasons that will become clear later, we now consider a slight generalization of this approach. We define a triple $\{A, \mathbb{M}_1, \mathbb{M}_2\}$, where

(i) $A \in \mathbb{C}^{m \times N}$ is the sampling operator,
(ii) $\mathbb{M}_1 \subseteq \mathbb{C}^N \times \mathbb{C}^m$ is the *domain*,
(iii) $\mathbb{M}_2 = \{Ax + e : (x, e) \in \mathbb{M}_1\} \subseteq \mathbb{C}^m$ is the *range*.

Note that we may also allow $\mathbb{M}_1$ to depend on A (of course, $\mathbb{M}_2$ depends on A).

Next, we define what we mean by training sets:

Definition 21.1 A *training set* is a set

$$\iota = \iota_A = \{(A, Ax_k, x_k) : k \in \mathbb{N}\}, \tag{21.1}$$

where $A \in \mathbb{C}^{m \times N}$ is a matrix and $x_k \in \mathbb{C}^N$ for $k \in \mathbb{N}$. A *family of training sets* is a collection of the form

$$\mathcal{I} = \{\iota_A : A \in \mathcal{A}\}, \tag{21.2}$$

for some $\mathcal{A} \subset \mathbb{C}^{m \times N}$.

For each $A \in \mathcal{A}$, the training set ι_A is the set of information from which the corresponding neural network is to be constructed. We do not specify how this training data is provided. However, we do assume that it is at most countable. Note that we choose to index ι over the natural numbers $\mathbb{N}$ simply for convenience. If there are only $K < \infty$ training images, we merely set $x_k = 0$ for all $k > K$. In particular, if there are no training images, then $\iota_A = \{(A, 0, 0)\}$, so that the training set consists solely of the matrix A. We also note that the setup described by Definition 21.1 includes fully trained approaches (see §19.2.2). In that case, the information about the matrix A, i.e. the first component of ι_A, is simply not used in the construction of the network.

With this in hand, we now formulate the following question:

> Given $\zeta > 0$ and a family of training sets $\mathcal{I}$, does there exist an algorithm which can, for each $\iota = \iota_A \in \mathcal{I}$, compute a neural network $\mathrm{N}_\iota : \mathbb{C}^m \to \mathbb{C}^N$ that satisfies $\|\mathrm{N}_\iota(Ax + e) - x\|_{\ell^2} \leq \zeta$ for every $(x, e) \in \mathbb{M}_1$?

Note that this question could be posed with any metric on $\mathbb{C}^N$. We use the ℓ^2-norm for simplicity and for its practical relevance.

While this question is of the right flavour, there is one key ingredient missing. For much the same reasons as those described in §7.1.2 – namely, that real numbers can only be represented approximately on a computer – the training data is generally subject to inaccuracies. Thus, in order to discuss computability, we need to consider a formulation where we can only access approximations of the training data to finite, but arbitrary precision. To do this, we now follow a similar setup to that described in §8.4 (the reader may wish to refer to this section for additional details).

We consider input approximations that are given as infinite sequences. Specifically, if $\iota = \iota_A = \{(A, Ax_k, x_k) : k \in \mathbb{N}\} \in \mathcal{I}$ is an input, we consider mappings of the form $\tilde{\iota} = \tilde{\iota}_A : \mathbb{N} \times \mathbb{N} \to \mathbb{C}^{m \times N} \times \mathbb{C}^m \times \mathbb{C}^N$ that satisfy

$$\|\tilde{\iota}(k, n) - (A, Ax_k, x_k)\| \leq 10^{-n}, \quad \forall k, n \in \mathbb{N},$$

where $\|(A, y, x)\| = \max\{\|A\|_{\ell^2}, \|y\|_{\ell^2}, \|x\|_{\ell^2}\}$. As in §8.4, we often refer to $\tilde{\iota}$ as an *oracle* for the training set ι. Note that we will often drop the subscript A and simply write $\iota \in \mathcal{I}$ and $\tilde{\iota} \in \widetilde{\mathcal{I}}$ whenever the meaning is clear.

Next, given a family of training sets as in (21.2), we define the set of all oracles as

$$\overline{\mathcal{I}} = \bigcup_{A \in \mathcal{A}} \{\tilde{\iota}_A : \|\tilde{\iota}_A(k, n) - (A, Ax_k, x_k)\| \leq 10^{-n}, \ \forall k, n \in \mathbb{N}\}. \tag{21.3}$$

As before, it may occasionally be undesirable to consider all possible oracles (see Remark 8.11). Hence, we define an *oracle class* as a set $\widetilde{\mathcal{I}} \subseteq \overline{\mathcal{I}}$ with the property that for each $\iota \in \mathcal{I}$ there is at least one $\tilde{\iota} \in \widetilde{\mathcal{I}}$ that is an oracle for ι. Usually, one will consider $\widetilde{\mathcal{I}} = \overline{\mathcal{I}}$, in particular, we require that the algorithm works for all possible oracles.

With this in hand, we are are now ready to define what we mean by an arithmetic algorithm for neural networks. The following is analogous to Definition 8.13:

Definition 21.2 (Arithmetic algorithm for neural networks) Let $\mathcal{I}$ be a class of inputs of the form (21.2) and $\widetilde{\mathcal{I}}$ be an oracle class for $\mathcal{I}$. An *arithmetic algorithm* (with radicals) for a class of neural networks $\mathcal{N}$ is a mapping $\mathrm{A} : \widetilde{\mathcal{I}} \times \mathbb{N} \to \mathcal{N}$ such that $\mathrm{A}(\cdot, k)$ is a general algorithm for each $k \in \mathbb{N}$, and there is a BSS (Blum–Shub–Smale) machine such that for each $k \in \mathbb{N}$ and $\tilde{\iota} \in \widetilde{\mathcal{I}}$, the mapping $k \mapsto \mathrm{A}(\tilde{\iota}, k)$ is executable on this machine with a node (subroutine) for the operation $a \mapsto \sqrt{a}$, $a > 0$, and a node for any oracle $\tilde{\iota}$.

In what follows, we will typically write $\mathrm{A}(\iota, k)$ for an input $\iota \in \mathcal{I}$ rather than $\mathrm{A}(\tilde{\iota}, k)$, where $\tilde{\iota}$ is an oracle for ι. This is much the same as was done in §8.4 (see Remark 8.16).

Remark 21.3 The requirement that $\mathrm{A} : \widetilde{\mathcal{I}} \times \mathbb{N} \to \mathcal{N}$ may seem strange given that A must be implementable on a BSS machine and hence must output a vector. To make sense of this we can simply identify each $\mathrm{N} \in \mathcal{N}$ with the vector containing its weights and biases.

21.2 Unravelled ISTA

We now turn our attention to constructing such algorithms. As mentioned, our method for doing so is based on unravelling. Hence, we begin in this section by taking another look at arguably the simplest unravelling procedure, which is based on the ISTA algorithm for solving the U-LASSO problem

$$\min_{z \in \mathbb{C}^N} \lambda \|x\|_{\ell^1} + \|Ax - y\|_{\ell^2}^2. \tag{21.4}$$

This algorithm was defined in Algorithm 7.1 for real variables, with its extension to complex variables being described in Remark 7.6.

Suppose we apply $L \geq 1$ steps of (the complex version of) ISTA to (21.4) with a fixed initial point x_0. Then the mapping from the input y to the output can be expressed as a map $\mathrm{N}\colon \mathbb{C}^m \to \mathbb{C}^N$, defined by

$$\begin{aligned} a^{(0)} &= y, \\ a^{(1)} &= \mathcal{S}_{\lambda\tau}\left((I - 2\tau A^*A)x_0 + 2\tau A^* a^{(0)}\right), \\ a^{(l)} &= \mathcal{S}_{\lambda\tau}\left((I - 2\tau A^*A)a^{(l-1)} + 2\tau A^* y\right), \quad l = 2, \dots, L, \\ \mathrm{N}(y) &= a^{(L)}, \end{aligned}$$

where $\mathcal{S}_{\lambda\tau}$ is the complex soft thresholding operator (see Definition 7.4 and Remark 7.6). We now readily identify this as a complex-valued neural network (see Remark 19.1). This network has L layers, its weights are given by

$$W_1 = 2\tau A^* \in \mathbb{C}^{N\times m}, \qquad W_2 = \cdots = W_L = I - 2\tau A^*A \in \mathbb{C}^{N\times N},$$

its biases by

$$b_1 = (I - 2\tau A^*A)x_0 \in \mathbb{C}^N, \qquad b_2 = \cdots = b_L = 2\tau A^* y \in \mathbb{C}^N,$$

and the activation function by $\mathcal{S}_{\lambda\tau}$. Recall that $\mathcal{S}_{\lambda\tau}$ acts componentwise on a vector.

Unravelling ISTA leads to a simple neural network architecture. However, the reader may have noticed that this network is not quite in the standard feedforward form (Definition 18.1), since the biases $b_l = b_l(y)$ for $l = 2, \dots, L$ are linear maps of the input y. Allowing the biases to be linear, or more generally, affine maps of the input is typical in unravelled optimization schemes. This is by no means a substantial modification. It can also be viewed as a skip connection – a standard approach in neural network architecture design, see §18.4.3 – between the input and the corresponding layer. We shall continue to employ this modification throughout the rest of this chapter.

Remark 21.4 There are several ways of incorporating skip connections in neural networks. As discussed in Remark 18.4, ReLU networks immediately allow for skip connections. Alternatively, one can simply alter Definition 18.1 to allow for pointwise activation functions that are potentially different in each component. We do this later in §21.3.2. Either way, any network with biases that depend affinely on the input can be rewritten as another network (with a slightly different architecture) with constant weights and biases.

Remark 21.5 While the soft thresholding operator $\mathcal{S}_\tau$ is not a 'classical' nonlinear activation function such as a ReLU or sigmoid, it is not unreasonable. As noted, it acts componentwise on a vector, like a standard activation function. In the real case, it can also be expressed as a combination of two ReLU functions:

$$\mathcal{S}_1(x) = \sigma(x-1) - \sigma(-x-1) = \begin{pmatrix} 1 \\ -1 \end{pmatrix}^\top \sigma\left(\begin{pmatrix} 1 \\ -1 \end{pmatrix} x - \begin{pmatrix} 1 \\ 1 \end{pmatrix}\right), \qquad \sigma(x) = \max\{0, x\}.$$

This does not hold in the complex case, since the ReLU is not defined for complex numbers. However, there are various different generalizations of the ReLU function to complex networks. One of these is the *modReLU function*, which is defined by

$$\sigma(z) = \begin{cases} (|z| + b)\frac{z}{|z|} & |z| + b \geq 0 \\ 0 & \text{otherwise} \end{cases},$$

where $b \in \mathbb{R}$ is a (learnable) parameter. However, when $b = -\tau$ this is precisely the soft thresholding operator $\mathcal{S}_\tau$. Notice that $\mathcal{S}_\tau$, and therefore the modReLU function, can also be expressed in terms of the real ReLU function as follows:

$$\mathcal{S}_\tau(z) = \sigma(|z| - \tau)\frac{z}{|z|}, \qquad \sigma(x) = \max\{0, x\}.$$

21.3 Unravelling the Primal–Dual Iteration

The previous example illustrates the basic principle of unravelling: namely, take a fixed number of iterations of an iterative algorithm for solving either QCBP, U-LASSO or some other optimization problem, and then reinterpret each step as a layer of a neural network. We could potentially continue to work with the U-LASSO problem and ISTA in what follows. However, for the reasons discussed in Chapters 6 and 14, we now consider the (weighted) square-root LASSO problem

$$\min_{z \in \mathbb{C}^N} \lambda \|z\|_{\ell^1_w} + \|Az - y\|_{\ell^2}, \tag{21.5}$$

instead. Since neither term in the objective function is differentiable, we can no longer use a standard forward–backward splitting method such as ISTA to solve this problem. As in §7.5, we shall now employ the primal–dual iteration.

21.3.1 The Primal–Dual Iteration for Complex, Weighted SR-LASSO

First, we need to derive the primal–dual iteration for (21.5). In the real and unweighted case, this is given by Algorithm 7.5. The extension of this algorithm to complex variables proceeds, as above, by replacing $A^\top$ by A^* and $\mathcal{S}_\lambda$ by the complex soft thresholding operator. To extend it to the weighted case, we notice that the scalar soft thresholding operator satisfies $\mathcal{S}_{\tau w}(z) = w\mathcal{S}_\tau(z/w)$ for real and positive w. Hence, if $W = \mathrm{diag}(w_1, \ldots, w_N)$ is the diagonal matrix of weights, then

$$\mathrm{prox}_{\lambda \|\cdot\|_{\ell^1_w}}(z) = W\mathcal{S}_\lambda(W^{-1}z), \qquad z \in \mathbb{R}^N.$$

With this, we now have all the ingredients needed to extend the primal–dual iteration to (21.5). This is shown in Algorithm 21.1.

21.3.2 A Class of Neural Networks for Unravelled Schemes

As was discussed above, unravelling typically yields neural networks that are not quite of the standard feedforward type (Definition 18.1). With this in mind, we now define a general class of neural networks with which to describe unravelled schemes based on

Algorithm 21.1: The primal–dual iteration for the complex, weighted SR-LASSO problem (21.5)

input: measurements y, measurement matrix A, diagonal weight matrix W, parameter $\lambda > 0$, stepsizes $\tau, \sigma > 0$, initial points (x_0, ξ_0)

output: $\tilde{x}$, an approximate minimizer of (21.5)

for $n = 0, 1, \ldots$ **do**

$x_{n+1} = W \mathcal{S}_{\tau\lambda}(W^{-1}(x_n - \tau A^* \xi_n))$

$\zeta = \xi_n + \sigma A(2x_{n+1} - x_n) - \sigma y$

$\xi_{n+1} = \min\left\{1, \frac{1}{\|\zeta\|_{\ell^2}}\right\} \zeta$

end

methods such as the primal–dual iteration and ISTA. Specifically, we consider complex-valued feedforward neural networks $\mathrm{N}\colon \mathbb{C}^m \to \mathbb{C}^N$ of the form

$$\mathrm{N}(y) = A^{(L)} \circ \sigma^{(L-1)} \circ A^{(L-1)} \circ \ldots \circ \sigma^{(1)} \circ A^{(1)}(y),$$

where $L \geq 2$ and, for each $l = 1, \ldots, L$, $A^{(l)}\colon \mathbb{C}^{n_{l-1}} \to \mathbb{C}^{n_l}$ is an affine map of the form

$$A^{(l)}(x) = W^{(l)} x + b^{(l)}(y), \qquad W^{(l)} \in \mathbb{C}^{n_l \times n_{l-1}}, \tag{21.6}$$

whose biases $b^{(l)}(y)$ are themselves an affine map of the input y, i.e.

$$b^{(l)}(y) = R^{(l)} y + c^{(l)}, \qquad R^{(l)} \in \mathbb{C}^{n_l \times m},\ c^{(l)} \in \mathbb{C}^{n_l}. \tag{21.7}$$

Here $n_0 = m$ and $n_L = N$.[1] The activation functions $\sigma^{(l)}\colon \mathbb{C}^{n_l} \to \mathbb{C}^{n_l}$ are permitted to take one of the two following forms:

(i) There is an index set $I^{(l)} \subseteq \{1, \ldots, n_l\}$ such that $\sigma^{(l)}$ acts componentwise on those components of the input vector with indices in $I^{(l)}$ while leaving the rest unchanged.

(ii) There is a nonlinear function $\rho^{(l)}\colon \mathbb{C} \to \mathbb{C}$ such that, if the input vector x to the layer takes the form

$$x = \begin{pmatrix} x_1 \\ u \\ v \end{pmatrix},$$

where x_1 is a scalar and u and v are (possibly) vectors, then

$$\sigma^{(l)}\colon x \mapsto \begin{pmatrix} 0 \\ \rho^{(l)}(x_1) u \\ v \end{pmatrix}.$$

We denote the class of networks of this form as $\mathcal{N}^* = \mathcal{N}^*_{\mathbf{n},L,q}$, where

$$\mathbf{n} = (n_0 = m, n_1, \ldots, n_{L-1}, n_L = N),$$

[1] The affine dependence (21.7) means that computing the biases of the network is equivalent to computing the matrices $R^{(l)}$ and vectors $c^{(l)}$.

L denotes the number of layers and q is the number of different nonlinear activation functions employed.

Remark 21.6 While convenient, having both (i) and (ii) is not strictly necessary. The second type (ii) can be re-expressed using a combination of the componentwise logarithm and exponential functions. Indeed,

$$\begin{pmatrix} x_1 \\ u \\ v \end{pmatrix} \overset{(a)}{\longmapsto} \begin{pmatrix} \log(\rho^{(l)}(x_1)) \\ \log(u) \\ v \end{pmatrix} \overset{(b)}{\longmapsto} \begin{pmatrix} 0 \\ \log((\rho^{(l)}(x_1)) + \log(u) \\ v \end{pmatrix} \overset{(c)}{\longmapsto} \begin{pmatrix} 0 \\ \rho^{(l)}(x_1)u \\ v \end{pmatrix}.$$

Step (a) involves operations of type (i) using $\rho^{(l)}$ and the componentwise logarithm function, step (b) is an affine (in fact, linear) map and step (c) is a map of type (i) involving the componentwise exponential function. Therefore, (ii) can be expressed as a several layer network with activation functions of type (i). An alternative (which avoids exponentials and, potentially undefined, logarithms) is to use componentwise squaring:

$$\begin{pmatrix} x_1 \\ u \\ v \end{pmatrix} \mapsto \begin{pmatrix} \rho^{(l)}(x_1) \\ u \\ v \end{pmatrix} \mapsto \begin{pmatrix} \rho^{(l)}(x_1)\mathbb{I} \\ u \\ \rho^{(l)}(x_1)\mathbb{I} + u \\ v \end{pmatrix} \mapsto \begin{pmatrix} (\rho^{(l)}(x_1))^2\mathbb{I} \\ u^2 \\ (\rho^{(l)}(x_1)\mathbb{I} + u)^2 \\ v \end{pmatrix}$$

$$\mapsto \begin{pmatrix} 0 \\ \frac{1}{2}\left((\rho^{(l)}(x_1)\mathbb{I} + u)^2 - (\rho^{(l)}(x_1))^2\mathbb{I} - u^2\right) \\ v \end{pmatrix} = \begin{pmatrix} 0 \\ \rho^{(l)}(x_1)u \\ v \end{pmatrix}.$$

Here, $\mathbb{I}$ denotes the vector of ones and x^2 is the componentwise square of a vector x.

21.3.3 Expressing the Primal–Dual Iteration as a Neural Network

We now show that L steps of the primal–dual iteration can be expressed as a neural network of the above form. We commence by examining a single step of this method. To this end, we first note the following:

Lemma 21.7 *The map $\mathbb{C}^N \to \mathbb{C}^N$ given by*

$$x \mapsto \min\left\{1, \frac{1}{\|x\|_{\ell^2}}\right\} x$$

can be expressed as a neural network $\mathrm{N} \in \mathcal{N}^*_{\mathbf{n},3,2}$, where $\mathbf{n} = (N, 2N, N+1, N)$ and the biases are all zero (in particular, independent of the input x).

Proof Let $x = (x_i)_{i=1}^N$ and define the scalar function $\rho(t) = \min\{1, 1/\sqrt{|t|}\}$, $t \in \mathbb{C}$. Then we can write

$$x \overset{(a)}{\longmapsto} \begin{pmatrix} x \\ x \end{pmatrix} \overset{(b)}{\longmapsto} \begin{pmatrix} |x_1|^2 \\ \vdots \\ |x_N|^2 \\ x \end{pmatrix} \overset{(c)}{\longmapsto} \begin{pmatrix} z \\ x \end{pmatrix} \overset{(d)}{\longmapsto} \begin{pmatrix} 0 \\ \rho(z)\,x \end{pmatrix} \overset{(e)}{\longmapsto} \rho(z)\,x,$$

where $z = \sum_{i=1}^{N} |x_i|^2$. Notice that (a), (c) and (e) are simply linear maps. The map (b) applies elementwise squaring, which is an allowed nonlinear activation of type (i). The map (d) is also of the allowed form. It involves multiplying the last n entries of the input vector by the result of the scalar function ρ acting on the first entry z, which means it is of type (ii). This gives the result. □

As shown in Theorem 7.8, error estimates for the primal–dual iteration are available for the ergodic sequence $X_n = \frac{1}{n}\sum_{i=1}^{n} x_i$, where x_i is the ith iterate of the iteration. Hence, to formulate the primal–dual iteration (Algorithm 21.1) as a neural network with guarantees, we now consider the iterative update step

$$\begin{pmatrix} X_n \\ x_n \\ \xi_n \end{pmatrix} \in \mathbb{C}^{2N+m} \mapsto \begin{pmatrix} X_{n+1} \\ x_{n+1} \\ \xi_{n+1} \end{pmatrix} \in \mathbb{C}^{2N+m}. \tag{21.8}$$

Lemma 21.8 *The update (21.8) can be performed by a neural network* $\mathrm{N} \in \mathcal{N}^*_{\mathbf{n},4,3}$, *where* $\mathbf{n} = (2N+m, 2N+m, 2(N+m), 2N+m+1, 2N+m)$ *and the biases depend (affinely) on* y *only. Moreover, the nonlinear activations are independent of* n.

Proof In view of Algorithm 21.1, we can write (21.8) as

$$\begin{pmatrix} X_n \\ x_n \\ \xi_n \end{pmatrix} \overset{(a)}{\longmapsto} \begin{pmatrix} X_n \\ W^{-1}(x_n - \tau A^* \xi_n) \\ \xi_n - \sigma A x_n \end{pmatrix}$$

$$\overset{(b)}{\longmapsto} \begin{pmatrix} X_n \\ \mathcal{S}_{\tau\lambda}(W^{-1}(x_n - \tau A^* \xi_n)) \\ \xi_n - \sigma A x_n \end{pmatrix} \overset{(c)}{\longmapsto} \begin{pmatrix} X_{n+1} \\ x_{n+1} \\ \zeta \end{pmatrix} \overset{(d)}{\longmapsto} \begin{pmatrix} X_{n+1} \\ x_{n+1} \\ \xi_{n+1} \end{pmatrix}.$$

Notice that (a) applies a linear map and (b) applies $\mathcal{S}_{\tau\lambda}$ to the middle component of its input. Since $\mathcal{S}_{\tau\lambda}$ is an elementwise operation, this is a nonlinear activation of the allowed type. The map (c) is an affine map with bias depending on y only. Hence

$$\begin{pmatrix} X_n \\ x_n \\ \xi_n \end{pmatrix} \mapsto \begin{pmatrix} X_{n+1} \\ x_{n+1} \\ \zeta \end{pmatrix}$$

is the action of a neural network $\mathrm{N}' \in \mathcal{N}^*_{(2N+m,2N+m,2N+m),2,1}$. The operation (d) computes $\xi_{n+1} = \min\{1, 1/\|\zeta\|_{\ell^2}\}\zeta$. As shown in Lemma 21.7, this operation can be performed with a neural network of size $(m, 2m, m+1, m)$ with $L = 3$ layers and $q = 2$ activation functions. Embedding this into the larger network, we see that the operation (d) can be expressed as the action of a neural network

$$\mathrm{N}'' \in \mathcal{N}^*_{(2N+m,2(N+m),2N+m+1,2N+m),3,2},$$

whose biases are independent of y. Hence the update (21.8) is the action of N' followed by N''. Notice that the composition of two affine maps of the form (21.6)–(21.7) can be expressed as a single affine map of the same form. Hence, concatenating the two networks N' and N'', we deduce that (21.8) can be expressed as a single neural network $\mathrm{N} \in \mathcal{N}^*_{\mathbf{n},4,3}$ with biases depending on y only. This completes the proof. □

We are now ready to show that the unravelled primal–dual iteration can be expressed as a neural network:

Theorem 21.9 (Unravelled primal–dual iteration) *Let* $X_n = \frac{1}{n}\sum_{i=1}^{n} x_i$ *be the ergodic sequence produced at the nth step of the primal–dual iteration (Algorithm 21.1) with input* $y \in \mathbb{C}^m$ *and initial point* $(x_0, \xi_0) \in \mathbb{C}^N \times \mathbb{C}^m$*. Then*

$$X_n = \mathrm{N}(y),$$

where $\mathrm{N} \in \mathcal{N}^*_{\mathbf{n},3n+1,3}$ *and*

$$\mathbf{n} = (m, \underbrace{2N + m, 2(N + m), 2N + m + 1}_{n \text{ times}}, N). \tag{21.9}$$

Note that (21.9) means that the middle term, which consists of three numbers, is repeated n times to give a vector $\mathbf{n}$ of length $3n + 2$.

Proof Lemma 21.8 gives that the update step (21.8) can be performed by a neural network $\mathrm{N}_n \in \mathcal{N}^*_{\mathbf{n},4,3}$, where $\mathbf{n} = (2N + m, 2N + m, 2(N + m), 2N + m + 1, 2N + m)$ and the biases depend on y only. Hence, letting $X_0 = 0$, the map $y \mapsto X_n$ can be written as

$$y \mapsto \begin{pmatrix} X_0 \\ x_0 \\ \xi_0 \end{pmatrix} \mapsto \begin{pmatrix} X_n \\ x_n \\ \xi_n \end{pmatrix} \mapsto X_n.$$

The first and third arrows are actions of affine maps and the middle arrow is the action of the composition $\mathrm{N}_{n-1} \circ \cdots \circ \mathrm{N}_0$. Using the compositional properties of the affine maps, as in the proof of Lemma 21.8, and the fact that the activation functions in N_k are independent of k now gives the result. □

21.4 Stable and Accurate Neural Networks for Compressed Sensing

We are now ready to establish the main results of this chapter. We first consider the abstract compressed sensing case, before focusing on compressive imaging in §21.5.

21.4.1 Stable and Accurate Recovery Under the Weighted rNSPL

We commence with the following lemma, which is based on the weighted rNSPL (Definition 13.5). This can be viewed as a generalization of Theorem 8.7 to the weighted and levels case. At this stage, we also recall Definition 21.1:

Lemma 21.10 *Let* $\alpha > 0$ *and consider any family of training sets* $\mathcal{T} = \{\iota_A : A \in \mathcal{A}\}$*, where* $\mathcal{A}$ *is a collection of matrices* $A \in \mathbb{C}^{m\times N}$*,* $\|A\|_{\ell^2} \leq \alpha$*, that have the weighted rNSPL of order* $(\mathbf{s}, \mathbf{M})$ *with weights* w *of the form (13.2)–(13.3) and constants* $0 < \rho < 1$

and $\gamma > 0$*. Let* $\widetilde{\mathcal{I}}$ *be any oracle class for* $\mathcal{I}$, $0 < \lambda \leq C_1/(C_2\sqrt{rs})$, *where*

$$C_1 = \left(\frac{\rho+1}{2} + (\rho+3)\frac{r^{1/4}}{4}\right)\left(\frac{3+\rho}{1-\rho}\right),$$
$$C_2 = \left(\frac{3+\rho}{1-\rho} + \frac{7+\rho}{1-\rho}\frac{r^{1/4}}{2}\right)\left(\frac{\rho+1}{2\rho}\right)\gamma, \tag{21.10}$$

$x_0 \in \mathbb{C}^N$ *be arbitrary and* $\tau, \sigma > 0$ *satisfy* $\tau\sigma(\alpha+1)^2 \leq 1$*. Then, for each* $n \geq 1$*, there is an arithmetic algorithm* $\mathrm{A}\colon \widetilde{\mathcal{I}} \times \mathbb{N} \to \mathcal{N}^*$*, where* $\mathcal{N}^* = \mathcal{N}^*_{\mathbf{n}_n, 3n+1, 3}$ *and*

$$\mathbf{n}_n = (m, \underbrace{2N+m, 2(N+m), 2N+m+1}_{n \text{ times}}, N),$$

that satisfies

$$\|x - \mathrm{A}(\iota, k)(y)\|_{\ell^2} \leq 2C_1 \frac{\sigma_{\mathbf{s},\mathbf{M}}(x)_{\ell^1_w}}{\sqrt{rs}} + \frac{C_1}{\sqrt{rs}\lambda}\left(\frac{\tau^{-1}\|x - x_0\|^2_{\ell^2} + \sigma^{-1}}{n}\right)$$
$$+ \left(C_2 + \frac{C_1}{\lambda\sqrt{rs}}\right)\|e\|_{\ell^2},$$

where $\sigma_{\mathbf{s},\mathbf{M}}(x)_{\ell^1_w}$ *is as in (12.4). This holds for every* $\iota = \iota_A \in \mathcal{I}$, $x \in \mathbb{C}^N$ *and* $y = Ax + e \in \mathbb{C}^m$*, and for all* k *satisfying*

$$10^{-k} \leq \frac{1-\rho}{\gamma(2\sqrt{rs} + \rho + 1)}. \tag{21.11}$$

Note that the only aspect of $\mathcal{I}$ that is fixed in the above result is the set of matrices $\mathcal{A}$. For each $A \in \mathcal{A}$, the corresponding training images $\{x_k\}_{k\in\mathbb{N}}$ can be arbitrary.

Proof We first define the algorithm $\mathrm{A}\colon \widetilde{\mathcal{I}} \times \mathbb{N} \to \mathcal{N}^*$. Let $\iota = \iota_A$ be as in (21.1) for $A \in \mathcal{A}$ and $\tilde{\iota}_A \in \widetilde{\mathcal{I}}$ be an oracle for ι_A. Let A' denote the first component of $\tilde{\iota}_A(l,k)$ for any l and, given $y \in \mathbb{C}^m$, let X_n be the vector defined in Theorem 21.9 that arises from applying n steps of the primal–dual iteration with the matrix A'. We now set $\mathrm{A}(\iota,k)(y) = X_n$. It is clear from Theorem 21.9 and its proof that this is an arithmetic algorithm in the sense of Definition 21.2.

Consider the matrix A'. A straightforward extension of Lemma 8.5 gives that if

$$\|A - A'\|_{\ell^2} \leq \delta < \frac{1-\rho}{\gamma(\sqrt{rs}+1)}, \tag{21.12}$$

then A' also has the weighted rNSPL with constants

$$\rho' = \frac{\rho + \gamma\delta\sqrt{rs}}{1-\gamma\delta} < 1, \qquad \gamma' = \frac{\gamma}{1-\gamma\delta}. \tag{21.13}$$

By construction, we have $\|A - A'\|_{\ell^2} \leq 10^{-k}$. Hence (21.11) implies that (21.12) holds with $\delta = 10^{-k}$. Using (21.13) and (21.11) once more, we deduce that A' has the weighted rNSPL with constants

$$\rho' \leq \frac{\rho+1}{2}, \qquad \gamma' \leq \frac{\rho+1}{2\rho}\gamma.$$

The rest of the proof uses similar arguments to those developed in §8.2. First, consider (21.5) with A' in place of A, and write this as $\min_{z \in \mathbb{C}^N} f(A'z) + g(z)$, where $f(z) = \|z - y\|_{\ell^2}$ and $g(z) = \lambda \|z\|_{\ell^1_w}$. The Lagrangian of this problem is

$$\mathcal{L}(x, \xi) = \mathrm{Re}\,\langle \xi, A'x \rangle - f^*(\xi) + g(x),$$

where $f^*(\xi)$ is the (complex) convex conjugate of f, defined by

$$f^*(\xi) = \max_{z \in \mathbb{C}^m} \mathrm{Re}\,\langle \xi, z \rangle - \|z - y\|_{\ell^2},$$

and the associated saddle point problem is

$$\min_{x \in \mathbb{C}^N} \max_{\xi \in \mathbb{C}^m} \mathcal{L}(x, \xi). \tag{21.14}$$

Using Table D.1 and (D.10), we see that

$$f^*(\xi) = \mathrm{Re}\,\langle \xi, y \rangle + \max_{z \in \mathbb{C}^m} \mathrm{Re}\,\langle \xi, z \rangle - \|z\|_{\ell^2} = \mathrm{Re}\,\langle \xi, y \rangle + \delta_B(\xi),$$

where $B = \{z : \|z\|_{\ell^2} \leq 1\} \subset \mathbb{C}^m$ and δ_B is as in (D.3).[2] Hence the Lagrangian can be expressed as

$$\mathcal{L}(x, \xi) = \mathrm{Re}\,\langle \xi, A'x - y \rangle - \delta_B(\xi) + \lambda \|x\|_{\ell^1_w}.$$

Observe that $\|A'\|_{\ell^2} \leq \|A\|_{\ell^2} + 10^{-k} \leq \alpha + 1$. Hence, by the assumption on τ and σ, we have $\tau\sigma \|A'\|_{\ell^2}^2 \leq 1$. We now argue exactly as in the proof of Lemma 8.6 to get

$$\lambda \|X_n\|_{\ell^1_w} + \|A'X_n - y\|_{\ell^2} - \left(\lambda \|x\|_{\ell^1_w} + \|A'x - y\|_{\ell^2} \right) \leq \frac{\tau^{-1} \|x - x_0\|_{\ell^2}^2 + \sigma^{-1}}{n}.$$

We next apply Lemma 13.7 with $z = X_n$, recalling that $\xi = rs$ and $\zeta = s$ for this choice of weights. This gives

$$\begin{aligned}
\|X_n - x\|_{\ell^2} &\leq C_1 \left(\frac{2\sigma_{\mathbf{s},\mathbf{M}}(x)_{\ell^1_w} + \|X_n\|_{\ell^1_w} - \|x\|_{\ell^1_w}}{\sqrt{rs}} \right) + C_2 \|A'(X_n - x)\|_{\ell^2} \\
&\leq 2C_1 \frac{\sigma_{\mathbf{s},\mathbf{M}}(x)_{\ell^1_w}}{\sqrt{rs}} + \frac{C_1}{\sqrt{rs}\lambda} \left(\lambda \|X_n\|_{\ell^1_w} + \|A'X_n - y\|_{\ell^2} - \lambda \|x\|_{\ell^1_w} \right) \\
&\quad + C_2 \|e\|_{\ell^2}.
\end{aligned}$$

The result now follows from the previous estimate. □

21.4.2 Conventional Compressed Sensing

With this in hand, we now show the existence of computable neural networks that match the performance of standard compressed sensing.

Following §21.1, we first need to define the domain $\mathbb{M}_1$ and range $\mathbb{M}_2$. Let $\zeta > 0$ and $A \in \mathbb{C}^{m \times N}$. Then we set

$$\mathbb{M}_1 = \left\{ (x, e) \in \mathbb{C}^N \times \mathbb{C}^m : \|x\|_{\ell^2} \leq 1,\ CS_s(x, e) \leq \zeta \right\}, \tag{21.15}$$

[2] The reader will notice that §8.2 considered only real variables, whereas we now work with complex variables. It is a straightforward exercise, following ideas from §7.2.3, to show that everything extends as described to the complex case.

and

$$\mathbb{M}_{\zeta,s} = \mathbb{M}_2 = \{Ax + e : (x, e) \in \mathbb{M}_1\}, \tag{21.16}$$

where

$$CS_s(x, e) = \frac{\sigma_s(x)_{\ell^1}}{\sqrt{s}} + \|e\|_{\ell^2}$$

is as in (8.2). In other words, $\mathbb{M}_{\zeta,s}$ is the set of measurements $y = Ax + e$ from which the underlying vector x can be stably and accurately (in the sense of standard sparsity) recovered via compressed sensing whenever A has the rNSP. We now have the following:

Theorem 21.11 *Let $\alpha > 0$ and consider any family of training sets $\mathcal{I} = \{\iota_A : A \in \mathcal{A}\}$, where $\mathcal{A}$ is a set of matrices $A \in \mathbb{C}^{m\times N}$, $\|A\|_{\ell^2} \leq \alpha$, that have the rNSP of order s with constants $0 < \rho < 1$ and $\gamma > 0$. Let $\widetilde{\mathcal{I}}$ be any oracle class for $\mathcal{I}$. Then there is an arithmetic algorithm $\mathrm{A}\colon \widetilde{\mathcal{I}} \times \mathbb{N} \to \mathcal{N}^*$, where $\mathcal{N}^* = \mathcal{N}^*_{\mathbf{n}_n,3n+1,3}$, $n = \lceil(\alpha + 1)/\zeta\rceil$ and*

$$\mathbf{n} = (m, \underbrace{2N + m, 2(N + m), 2N + m + 1}_{n \text{ times}}, N),$$

that satisfies

$$\|x - \mathrm{A}(\iota, k)(y)\|_{\ell^2} \leq 4\max\{C_1, C_2\}\zeta, \qquad \forall y = Ax + e \in \mathbb{M}_{\zeta,s}, \tag{21.17}$$

where C_1 and C_2 are as in (21.10) with $r = 1$. This holds whenever k is such that

$$10^{-k} \leq \frac{1-\rho}{\gamma(2\sqrt{s} + \rho + 1)}.$$

Proof We apply Lemma 21.10 with $r = 1$, $\lambda = C_1/(C_2\sqrt{s})$, where C_1, C_2 are as in (21.10), $x_0 = 0$ and $\tau = \sigma = (\alpha + 1)^{-1}$. This gives an arithmetic algorithm A with

$$\|x - \mathrm{A}(\iota, k)(y)\|_{\ell^2} \leq 2C_1\frac{\sigma_s(x)_{\ell^1}}{\sqrt{s}} + C_2\left(\frac{(\alpha + 1)(\|x\|^2_{\ell^2} + 1)}{n}\right) + 2C_2\|e\|_{\ell^2},$$

for all $y = Ax + e \in \mathbb{M}_{\zeta,s}$. Hence

$$\|x - \mathrm{A}(\iota, k)(y)\|_{\ell^2} \leq 2\max\{C_1, C_2\}\left(CS_s(x, e) + \frac{\alpha + 1}{n}\right) \leq 4\max\{C_1, C_2\}\zeta,$$

where in the second step we use (21.16) and the fact that $n \geq (\alpha + 1)/\zeta$. □

It is informative to compare this result with the corresponding error bound for the exact SR-LASSO decoder in the sparse case. Let $\mathrm{R}_\iota\colon \mathbb{C}^m \rightrightarrows \mathbb{C}^N$ be defined by

$$\mathrm{R}_\iota(y) = \underset{z\in\mathbb{C}^N}{\operatorname{argmin}} \left\{\lambda\|z\|_{\ell^1} + \|Az - y\|_{\ell^2}\right\}.$$

Then Theorem 6.5 and the choice $\lambda = C_1/(C_2\sqrt{s})$ give that, under the same conditions on A, the map R_ι satisfies

$$\mathrm{dist}(x, \mathrm{R}_\iota(y)) \leq 2\max\{C_1, C_2\}\zeta, \qquad \forall y = Ax + e \in \mathbb{M}_{\zeta,s},$$

where dist is the Hausdorff distance between bounded subsets of $\mathbb{C}^N$ induced by the ℓ^2-norm. Up to constants, this is identical to the error bound for $\mathrm{N}_\iota = \mathrm{A}(\iota, k)$ given in

(21.17). Hence, the network N_ι computed by the algorithm is as stable and accurate as compressed sensing based on the exact reconstruction map R_ι.

Note that the depth of the network in Theorem 21.11 depends on the bound α for $\|A\|_{\ell^2}$. See Remark 8.8 for more discussion on this term.

21.5 Stable and Accurate Neural Networks for Compressive Imaging

We now move on to compressive imaging. For simplicity, we consider only wavelet sparsity (in levels) as our measure of accuracy, although discrete gradient sparsity could also be considered along the lines of Chapter 17. As throughout this book, we first treat the one-dimensional discrete Fourier–Haar problem, before addressing the case of higher-order wavelets in one and two dimensions with both Fourier and Walsh sampling.

21.5.1 The One-Dimensional Discrete Fourier–Haar Wavelet Setting

Consider the setup of §11.6. Let $N = 2^{r-1}$, $r \geq 2$ and $\mathbf{N}$ and $\mathbf{M}$ be the sampling and sparsity levels defined therein. Fix local numbers of measurements $\mathbf{m} = (m_1, \ldots, m_r)$. We consider the class $\mathcal{A}$ of matrices $A \in \mathbb{C}^{m \times N}$ of the form

$$A = \frac{1}{\sqrt{N}} P_\Omega D F, \qquad (21.18)$$

where $F \in \mathbb{C}^{N \times N}$ is the DFT matrix, D is as in Definition 11.14 and Ω is an $(\mathbf{m}, \mathbf{N})$-multilevel random sampling scheme.

Write $\Phi \in \mathbb{R}^{N \times N}$ for the one-dimensional discrete Haar wavelet transform. Given $\zeta > 0$, we define

$$\mathbb{M}_1 = \{(x, e) \in \mathbb{C}^N \times \mathbb{C}^m : \|x\|_{\ell^2} \leq 1,\ CS_{\mathbf{s},\mathbf{M}}(x, e) \leq \zeta\}, \qquad (21.19)$$

and

$$\mathbb{M}_{\zeta,\mathbf{s},\mathbf{M}} = \mathbb{M}_2 = \{Ax + e : (x, e) \in \mathbb{M}_1\}, \qquad (21.20)$$

where

$$CS_{\mathbf{s},\mathbf{M}}(x, e) = \frac{\sigma_{\mathbf{s},\mathbf{M}}(\Phi^* x)_{\ell^1_w}}{r^{1/4}\sqrt{s}} + r^{1/4}\|e\|_{\ell^2},$$

and the weights w are as in (13.2)–(13.3). In other words, we consider the class of measurement vectors y which are noisy Fourier samples of discrete, one-dimensional images that are compressible in Haar wavelets.

Theorem 21.12 *Let $\zeta > 0$ and consider any family of training sets $\mathcal{I} = \{\iota_A : A \in \mathcal{A}\}$, where $\mathcal{A}$ is as defined above and where the m_k satisfy*

$$m_k \gtrsim \left(s_k + \sum_{l=1}^{k-1} s_l 2^{-(k-l)} + \sum_{l=k+1}^{r} s_l 2^{-3(l-k)} \right) \cdot L, \quad k = 1, \ldots, r, \qquad (21.21)$$

for $L = \log^3(N) \cdot \log(2m) \cdot \log^2(\log(N)s) + \log(N) \cdot \log(\varepsilon^{-1})$. *Consider the class* $\mathcal{N}^* = \mathcal{N}^*_{\mathbf{n},3n+1,3}$, *where* $n = \lceil C_{\mathbf{s},\mathbf{M}}/\zeta \rceil$,

$$C_{\mathbf{s},\mathbf{M}} = \sqrt{\sqrt{r} \max_{l=1,\dots,r} \left\lceil \frac{M_l - M_{l-1}}{s_l} \right\rceil}$$

and

$$\mathbf{n} = (m, \underbrace{2N+m, 2(N+m), 2N+m+1}_{n \text{ times}}, M).$$

Then there is an arithmetic algorithm $\mathrm{A}\colon \widetilde{\mathcal{I}} \times \mathbb{N} \to \mathcal{N}^*$ *such that*

$$\|x - \mathrm{A}(\iota, k)(y)\|_{\ell^2} \lesssim \zeta, \qquad \forall y = Ax + e \in \mathbb{M}_{\zeta,\mathbf{s},\mathbf{M}}, \tag{21.22}$$

with probability at least $1 - \varepsilon$, *whenever* k *satisfies*

$$10^{-k} \leq \frac{1}{\sqrt{2}(4\sqrt{rs} + 3)}.$$

Remark 21.13 The 'with probability at least $1 - \varepsilon$' statement in this theorem is understood as follows. Each draw of an $(\mathbf{m}, \mathbf{N})$-multilevel random sampling scheme Ω yields a matrix $A \in \mathcal{A}$ as in (21.18), which in turn defines a training set $\iota = \iota_A \in \mathcal{I}$. Hence the result states that (21.22) holds with probability $1 - \varepsilon$ for training sets drawn randomly according to this model.

As in the previous case, to put this result in context we consider the weighted SR-LASSO decoder

$$\mathrm{R}_\iota\colon \mathbb{C}^m \rightrightarrows \mathbb{C}^N, \quad \mathrm{R}_\iota(y) = \operatorname*{argmin}_{z \in \mathbb{C}^N} \left\{ \lambda \|\Phi^* z\|_{\ell^1_w} + \|Az - y\|_{\ell^2} \right\}, \quad \lambda = \frac{1}{2\sqrt{2}\sqrt{rs}}.$$

Theorem 13.18 and the condition (21.21) on the m_k imply that

$$\operatorname{dist}(x, \mathrm{R}_\iota(y)) \lesssim \zeta, \qquad \forall y = Ax + e \in \mathbb{M}_{\zeta,\mathbf{s},\mathbf{M}},$$

where dist is once again the Hausdorff metric induced by the ℓ^2-norm. Hence the conclusion is the same. For the given class of inputs, one can compute a neural network $\mathrm{N}_\iota = \mathrm{A}(\iota, k)$ that achieves the same recovery error ζ (up to constants) as the compressed sensing reconstruction map R_ι. Moreover, the depth and width are controlled by the input class. Indeed, the maximum width of a hidden layer is no more than $4N$ and, since $M_l - M_{l-1} \leq M = N$ in this case, the depth is bounded by $r^{1/4}\sqrt{N}/\zeta$.

Proof of Theorem 21.12 We follow arguments given in Chapter 13 for the weighted SR-LASSO decoder. As in Theorem 13.18, the conditions on $\mathbf{m}$ assert that the matrix $A\Phi$ has the RIPL (note that $G = I$ in this case) of order $(\mathbf{t}, \mathbf{M})$ with constant $\delta = 1/2$, where $\mathbf{t}$ is as in (13.15) with weights (13.2)–(13.3). Hence Lemma 13.8 implies that $A\Phi$ has the weighted rNSPL with constants $\rho = 1/2$ and $\gamma = 1/\sqrt{1-\delta} = \sqrt{2}$.

We now wish to apply Lemma 21.10 to the class of matrices $\{A\Phi : A \in \mathcal{A}\}$. To do this, we first need to bound $\|A\Phi\|_{\ell^2}$ for $A \in \mathcal{A}$. We do this by extending the argument used in Remark 8.8. Let $x \in \mathbb{C}^N$ be arbitrary and consider $\|A\Phi x\|_{\ell^2}$. For $l = 1, \dots, r$, let $\Delta_{l,1}, \Delta_{l,2}, \ldots$ be a partition of $\{M_{l-1} + 1, \ldots, M_l\}$ into index sets of size at most s_l. Let $\Delta_i = \Delta_{1,i} \cup \cdots \cup \Delta_{r,i}$, and notice that $\Delta_1, \Delta_2, \ldots$ gives a partition of $\{1, \ldots, N\}$. The number of such sets needed for this partition is

$$\max_{l=1,\ldots,r} \left\lceil \frac{M_l - M_{l-1}}{s_l} \right\rceil. \tag{21.23}$$

Now, since $A\Phi$ has the RIPL of order $(\mathbf{t}, \mathbf{M})$ and $t_l \geq s_l$ for all l, it has the RIPL of order $(\mathbf{s}, \mathbf{M})$. Therefore

$$\|A\Phi x\|_{\ell^2} \leq \sum_i \|A\Phi P_{\Delta_i} x\|_{\ell^2} \leq \sqrt{2} \sum_i \|P_{\Delta_i} x\|_{\ell^2} \leq \sqrt{2 \max_{l=1,\ldots,r} \left\lceil \frac{M_l - M_{l-1}}{s_l} \right\rceil} \|x\|_{\ell^2}.$$

Therefore, since $x \in \mathbb{C}^N$ was arbitrary, we obtain

$$\|A\Phi\|_{\ell^2} \leq \alpha, \qquad \alpha = \sqrt{2 \max_{l=1,\ldots,r} \left\lceil \frac{M_l - M_{l-1}}{s_l} \right\rceil}. \tag{21.24}$$

We now apply Lemma 21.10 with this choice of α and with $\lambda = C_1/(C_2\sqrt{rs})$, $x_0 = 0$ and $\tau = \sigma = (\alpha + 1)^{-1}$. This gives an arithmetic algorithm A for which

$$\|d - \mathrm{A}(\iota, k)(y)\|_{\ell^2} \leq 2C_1 \frac{\sigma_{\mathbf{s},\mathbf{M}}(d)_{\ell^1}}{\sqrt{rs}} + C_2 \left(\frac{(\alpha + 1)(\|d\|_{\ell^2}^2 + 1)}{n} \right) + 2C_2 \|e\|_{\ell^2},$$

for all $y = Ax + e \in \mathbb{M}_{\zeta,s}$, where $d = \Phi^* x$ and C_1, C_2 are as in (21.10). Observe that $C_1, C_2 \lesssim r^{1/4}$ in this case. Since Φ is unitary and $\|x\|_{\ell^2} \leq 1$, this gives

$$\|x - \Phi\mathrm{A}(\iota, k)(y)\|_{\ell^2} \lesssim \zeta + \frac{r^{1/4}(\alpha + 1)}{n} \lesssim \zeta, \tag{21.25}$$

where in the second step we use (21.24) and the definition of n. Notice that $\Phi\mathrm{A}(\iota, k) \in \mathcal{N}^*_{\mathbf{n},3n+1,3}$ since Φ is a linear map. Also, it is clear that the map $(\iota, k) \mapsto \Phi\mathrm{A}(\iota, k)$ is an arithmetic algorithm. Hence the result follows after relabelling A. □

21.5.2 The General Setting

We now proceed to the general case of Fourier or Walsh sampling in one or two dimensions. For this, we follow the setup of Chapters 14–16. In particular, we consider continuous images $f \in L^2([0,1])$ or $f \in L^2([0,1]^2)$. Since this setup is infinite dimensional, a little care is needed to reformulate the problem in a way suitable for the tools of §21.1. We do this by using a wavelet basis to discretize these spaces. Specifically, let $\Phi \subset L^2([0,1])$ or $\Phi \subset L^2([0,1]^2)$ be the periodized Daubechies wavelet basis of order p (Definition 9.23) and $d = \mathcal{T}_\Phi^* f$ be the wavelet coefficients of f, where $\mathcal{T}_\Phi^*$ is the analysis operator of Φ (see §14.2). We assume that f is sampled using either the Fourier or Walsh basis. Hence, as in (16.2), the measurement can be expressed as

$$y = P_\Omega D U d + e,$$

where U is the infinite change-of-basis matrix between the sampling and sparsity bases, Ω is a multilevel random sampling scheme, D is as in (14.11) and $e \in \mathbb{C}^m$ is noise. Let $M = M_r$ be the sparsity bandwidth, and write

$$y = AP_M d + P_\Omega DUP_M^\perp d + e, \qquad A = P_\Omega DUP_M.$$

With this in hand, we now let $\mathcal{A}$ be the family of $m \times M$ matrices of this form, i.e. $A \in \mathcal{A}$ if $A = P_\Omega DUP_M$ for some multilevel random sampling scheme Ω.

Remark 21.14 Expressing y in terms of the wavelet coefficients d is equivalent to expressing y in terms of f directly (since Φ is an orthonormal basis). In Fourier sampling, for instance, the measurements $y = P_\Omega DUd + e$ are completely equivalent to

$$\{b_\omega \mathcal{F} f(2\pi\omega) + e_\omega : \omega \in \Omega\},$$

where b_ω is the (suitably indexed) diagonal entry of D. The latter is perhaps more natural, since it does not rely on an orthonormal basis. However, it is convenient to write y in terms of the wavelet coefficients in what follows. One can then simply view the matrix A as a discretization of the true Fourier sampling operator $\mathcal{F}$ obtained by replacing the function f by its truncated wavelet expansion of order M.

Next, let $\mathbf{M}$ be the sparsity levels for the wavelet sparsity basis, as defined in §16.1.1, and $\mathbf{s}$ be the local sparsities. Given $\zeta > 0$, we consider the class $\mathbb{M}_2 = \mathbb{M}_{\zeta,\mathbf{s},\mathbf{M}} \subseteq \mathbb{C}^m$ of measurement vectors $y \in \mathbb{C}^m$ of the form

$$y = P_\Omega DUd + e, \qquad d = \mathcal{T}_\Phi^* f, \tag{21.26}$$

for some $f \in L^2([0,1])$ or $f \in L^2([0,1]^2)$ and noise $e \in \mathbb{C}^m$ satisfying

$$\|f\|_{L^2} \le 1, \quad \mathcal{CS}_{\mathbf{s},\mathbf{M}}(d,e) \le \zeta, \tag{21.27}$$

where

$$\mathcal{CS}_{\mathbf{s},\mathbf{M}}(d,e) = \frac{\sigma_{\mathbf{s},\mathbf{M}}(P_M d)_{\ell^1_w}}{r^{1/4}\sqrt{s}} + r^{1/4}\left(\|e\|_{\ell^2} + \|P_M^\perp d\|_{\ell^1}\right) + \|P_M^\perp d\|_{\ell^2},$$

and the weights w are as in (14.13)–(14.14). In other words, we consider the class of measurement vectors which are noisy Fourier or Walsh samples of continuous images that are compressible in the Daubechies wavelet basis of order p.

We have now defined the relevant family $\mathcal{A}$ and class $\mathbb{M}_2$ for the problem. Before stating the main result, we require one additional modification. In the finite-dimensional case, the output of a reconstruction map is a discrete image, i.e. a vector in $\mathbb{C}^N$. Working in the infinite-dimensional case, we now consider function space-valued maps, i.e. $\mathrm{R}: \mathbb{C}^m \to L^2([0,1])$ or $\mathrm{R}: \mathbb{C}^m \to L^2([0,1]^2)$. In the case of the neural network, the only change we need to make is to allow the weight matrix in the final layer to be a function of the spatial variable.[3]

Theorem 21.15 *Let $\zeta > 0$ and $d = 1, 2$. Let $\mathcal{T} = \{\iota_A : A \in \mathcal{A}\}$ be any family of training sets, where $\mathcal{A}$ is as defined above and where $\mathbf{m}$ satisfies the conditions of either Theorem 16.3 (Fourier sampling, DS scheme), Theorem 16.4 (Fourier sampling,*

[3] This is done solely for the sake of having clear theoretical statements. In practice, the reconstruction map would most likely be evaluated on a finite grid. In this case, one could simply consider a neural network $\mathrm{N}: \mathbb{C}^m \to \mathbb{C}^N$, where N is the grid size.

DIS scheme), Theorem 16.5 (Fourier sampling, DAS scheme), Theorem 16.7 (Walsh sampling, DS scheme), Theorem 16.6 (Walsh sampling with Haar, DS and DIS schemes) or Theorem 16.8 (Walsh sampling, DAS scheme). Consider the class $\mathcal{N}^* = \mathcal{N}^*_{\mathbf{n},3n+1,3}$, *where* $n = \lceil C_{\mathbf{s},\mathbf{M}}/\zeta \rceil$,

$$C_{\mathbf{s},\mathbf{M}} = \sqrt{\sqrt{r} \max_{l=1,\dots,r} \left\lceil \frac{M_l - M_{l-1}}{s_l} \right\rceil}$$

and

$$\mathbf{n} = (m, \underbrace{2N+m, 2(N+m), 2N+m+1}_{n \text{ times}}, M).$$

Then there is an arithmetic algorithm $\mathrm{A}\colon \widetilde{\mathcal{I}} \times \mathbb{N} \to \mathcal{N}^*$ *and a vector-valued function* $W\colon [0,1]^d \to \mathbb{R}^M$ *such that, with probability at least* $1-\varepsilon$,

$$\|f - W(\cdot)^\top \mathrm{A}(\iota, k)(y)\|_{L^2} \lesssim \zeta, \qquad \forall y \in \mathbb{M}_{\zeta,\mathbf{s},\mathbf{M}}, \tag{21.28}$$

where f *and* e *are as in (21.26)–(21.27). This holds provided* k *satisfies*

$$10^{-k} \leq \frac{1}{c_p(4\sqrt{rs}+3)},$$

where $c_p > 0$ *depends on the wavelet order* p *only.*

As in Theorem 21.12, the 'with probability at least $1-\varepsilon$' statement in this theorem is understood in the sense described in Remark 21.13. Note also that the constant implied by the symbol $\lesssim$ in (21.28) depends on the wavelet order p, as was previously the case in Chapters 15 and 16.

Like with earlier results, we can compare Theorem 21.15 against the weighted SR-LASSO decoder. Specifically, let $\mathrm{R}_\iota\colon \mathbb{C}^m \rightrightarrows L^2([0,1]^d)$ be defined as

$$\mathrm{R}_\iota(y) = \left\{ \mathcal{T}_\Phi \hat{d} : \hat{d} \in \operatorname*{argmin}_{z \in \mathbb{C}^M} \left\{ \lambda \|z\|_{\ell^1_w} + \|Az - y\|_{\ell^2} \right\} \right\}, \qquad y \in \mathbb{M}_{\zeta,\mathbf{s},\mathbf{M}}.$$

Due to Parseval's identity, the results shown in Chapter 16 assert that

$$\operatorname{dist}(f, \mathrm{R}_\iota(y)) \lesssim \zeta, \quad \forall y = P_\Omega U d + e \in \mathbb{M}_{\zeta,\mathbf{s},\mathbf{M}},\ f = \mathcal{T}_\Phi d,$$

where dist is the Hausdorff distance between compact subsets of $L^2([0,1])$ or $L^2([0,1]^2)$. Therefore, this result yields the main conclusion of this chapter. It is possible to compute a neural network (of controllable width and depth) for reconstructing one- or two-dimensional images from Fourier or Walsh samples that achieves the same recovery error bound as compressed sensing with wavelets.

Proof of Theorem 21.15 The proof, which is similar to that of Theorem 21.12, involves modifying arguments given previously in Chapters 14 and 16 for the weighted SR-LASSO decoder. First, as in §16.4.8, we notice that the conditions on $\mathbf{m}$ given in Theorems 16.3, 16.4, 16.6 and 16.7 imply that conditions (i) and (ii) of Theorem 14.5 hold with $\theta \gtrsim 1$, and in the case of Theorems 16.5 and 16.8 they imply that (i) holds, with

(ii) being replaced by (16.39) for the same value $\theta \gtrsim 1$. Condition (iii) of Theorem 14.5 also holds in all cases due to the choice of weights.

We now argue as in the proof of Theorem 14.5. Using the proof of Theorem 13.14, we observe that the matrix $A = P_\Omega D U P_M$ has the G-RIPL of order $(\mathbf{t}, \mathbf{M})$ with constant $\delta = 1/2$, where $\mathbf{t}$ is as in (13.15). Here $G \in \mathbb{C}^{M\times M}$ is the unique positive-definite square root of the matrix $P_M U^* P_N U P_M$. It follows immediately from Lemma 13.8 that A has the weighted rNSPL of order $(\mathbf{s}, \mathbf{M})$ with constants $\rho = 1/2$ and $\gamma = \sqrt{2}\|G^{-1}\|_{\ell^2}$. Since the balancing property (Definition 14.2) holds with constant $\theta \geq c_p$, we have $\|G^{-1}\|_{\ell^2} = \sqrt{\|(P_M U^* P_N U P_M)^{-1}\|_{\ell^2}} \leq 1/\sqrt{\theta} \lesssim 1$. Therefore $\gamma \lesssim 1$.

We next estimate $\|A\|_{\ell^2}$. Similar to the proof of Theorem 21.12, for $l = 1, \ldots, r$ let $\Delta_{l,1}, \Delta_{l,2}, \ldots$ be a partition of $\{M_{l-1}+1, \ldots, M_l\}$ into index sets of size at most s_l. Let $\Delta_i = \Delta_{1,i} \cup \cdots \cup \Delta_{r,i}$, and notice that $\Delta_1, \Delta_2, \ldots$ gives a partition of $\{1, \ldots, M\}$. The number of such sets needed is given by (21.23) once more. Since A has the G-RIPL of order $(\mathbf{t}, \mathbf{M})$ and $t_l \geq s_l$ for all l, it has the G-RIPL of order $(\mathbf{s}, \mathbf{M})$. Therefore

$$\|Ax\|_{\ell^2} \leq \sum_i \|AP_{\Delta_i} x\|_{\ell^2} \leq \sqrt{2} \sum_i \|GP_{\Delta_i} x\|_{\ell^2}.$$

Since $\|G\|_{\ell^2}^2 = \|P_M U^* P_N U P_M\|_{\ell^2} \leq 1$ and x was arbitrary, we deduce that

$$\|A\|_{\ell^2} \leq \alpha, \qquad \alpha = \sqrt{2 \max_{l=1,\ldots,r} \left\lceil \frac{M_l - M_{l-1}}{s_l} \right\rceil}.$$

We now apply Lemma 21.10 with $\lambda = C_1/(C_2\sqrt{rs})$, $x_0 = 0$ and $\tau = \sigma = (\alpha+1)^{-1}$. Noticing that $C_1, C_2 \lesssim r^{1/4}$, this gives an arithmetic algorithm A for which

$$\|d' - \mathrm{A}(\iota, k)(Ad' + e')\|_{\ell^2} \lesssim \frac{\sigma_{\mathbf{s},\mathbf{M}}(d')_{\ell^1_w}}{r^{1/4}\sqrt{s}} + r^{1/4}\left(\frac{(\alpha+1)(\|d'\|_{\ell^2}^2 + 1)}{n}\right) + r^{1/4}\|e'\|_{\ell^2},$$

for all $d' \in \mathbb{C}^M$ and $e' \in \mathbb{C}^m$, where $\iota = \iota_A \in \mathcal{I}$. Now consider $y = P_\Omega D U d + e \in \mathbb{M}_{\zeta,\mathbf{s},\mathbf{M}}$, where d and e satisfy (21.27) with $f = \mathcal{T}_\Phi d$. Write $d' = P_M d$ and $e' = e + P_\Omega D U P_M^\perp d$ so that

$$y = P_\Omega D U d + e = Ad' + e'.$$

Recall from the arguments given in §16.4.8 that $\|P_\Omega D U P_M^\perp d\|_{\ell^2} \lesssim \|P_M^\perp d\|_{\ell^1}$. Since we also have $\|d'\|_{\ell^2} \leq \|d\|_{\ell^2} = \|f\|_{L^2} \leq 1$, this gives

$$\|P_M d - \mathrm{A}(\iota, k)(y)\|_{\ell^2} \lesssim \frac{\sigma_{\mathbf{s},\mathbf{M}}(P_M d)_{\ell^1_w}}{r^{1/4}\sqrt{s}} + r^{1/4}\left(\|e\|_{\ell^2} + \|P_M^\perp d\|_{\ell^1}\right) + \frac{r^{1/4}(\alpha+1)}{n}.$$

Using the definition of n and α, we deduce that

$$\|P_M d - \mathrm{A}(\iota, k)(y)\|_{\ell^2} \lesssim \zeta.$$

To complete the proof, we let W be the vector-valued function $W(t) = \{\phi_j(t)\}_{j=1}^M$, $t \in [0,1]^d$, where $\phi_1, \ldots, \phi_M$ are the first M wavelet functions. This, Parseval's identity and the fact that $\|P_M^\perp d\|_{\ell^2} \leq \zeta$ now give the result. ☐

21.5.3 Demonstrating Stability and Accuracy in Practice

Having shown that it is possible to compute neural networks that possess the same stability and accuracy guarantees as compressed sensing, we now conclude by demonstrating this result in practice. Since the mappings constructed are neural networks, we can apply Algorithm 19.1 to them to test their robustness to worst-case perturbations (with the caveat that finding no bad perturbations with this algorithm is only a strong indication of stability, and not a rigorous demonstration of it). Note that this is not possible when a compressed sensing reconstruction is computed using a blackbox optimization solver, since Algorithm 19.1 requires the gradients of the reconstruction map.

In Fig. 21.1 we compare the stable neural network of Theorem 21.15 against the AUTOMAP network that was considered in previous chapters. As was already seen in Chapter 20, the latter is unstable and greatly affected by perturbations computed via Algorithm 19.1. On the other hand, the former shows good robustness to the worst-case perturbations computed via this algorithm. This highlights the theoretical stability that was established in Theorem 21.15. Moreover, the stable neural network also reconstructs unperturbed images to the same quality as the AUTOMAP network, thus demonstrating the claimed accuracy of this approach.

Notes

The unravelling approach for neural network architecture design was first considered by Gregor & LeCun in [239] for the sparse coding problem. They used ISTA, as described in §21.2. This was extended to the compressed sensing setting and generalized in [521], which introduced so-called *ISTA-Net*. Deep neural networks based on unravelling the ADMM optimization algorithm, known as *ADMM-Net* and *ADMM-CSNet*, were developed in [514, 515]. The MRI-VN network [253] considered in Chapter 19 is another unravelled network, based on gradient descent applied to a U-LASSO-type problem with regularization term based on the so-called Field of Experts model [421]. ADMM-Net, ADMM-CSNet and MRI-VN train not only weights and biases, but also the activation functions. For instance, in the former the activation function is a learned piecewise linear function. Unravelling the primal–dual iteration was considered in [26, 489]. Other unravelling approaches have also been developed based on Neumann series [228], block coordinate descent [149], approximate message passing [355] and various others.

For more information on unravelling, see [42, 324, 353, 358, 411]. For more on extensions of the ReLU function to complex numbers, see [462]. The modReLU function was introduced in [40]. Figure 21.1 is from [36].

The approach pursued in this chapter is based on [35]. This work also establishes theoretical results on uncomputability of neural networks for inverse problems, of a similar flavour to Theorem 8.18. Note that we have chosen to unravel the weighted SR-LASSO decoder. One can also unravel other decoders – such as (weighted) QCBP and U-LASSO – and then use the same compressed sensing tools to show similar results. We remark also that [35] does not assume functions such as the square-root can be computed exactly (as we do). It also establishes stability of the constructed networks to the errors induced by these inexact computations.

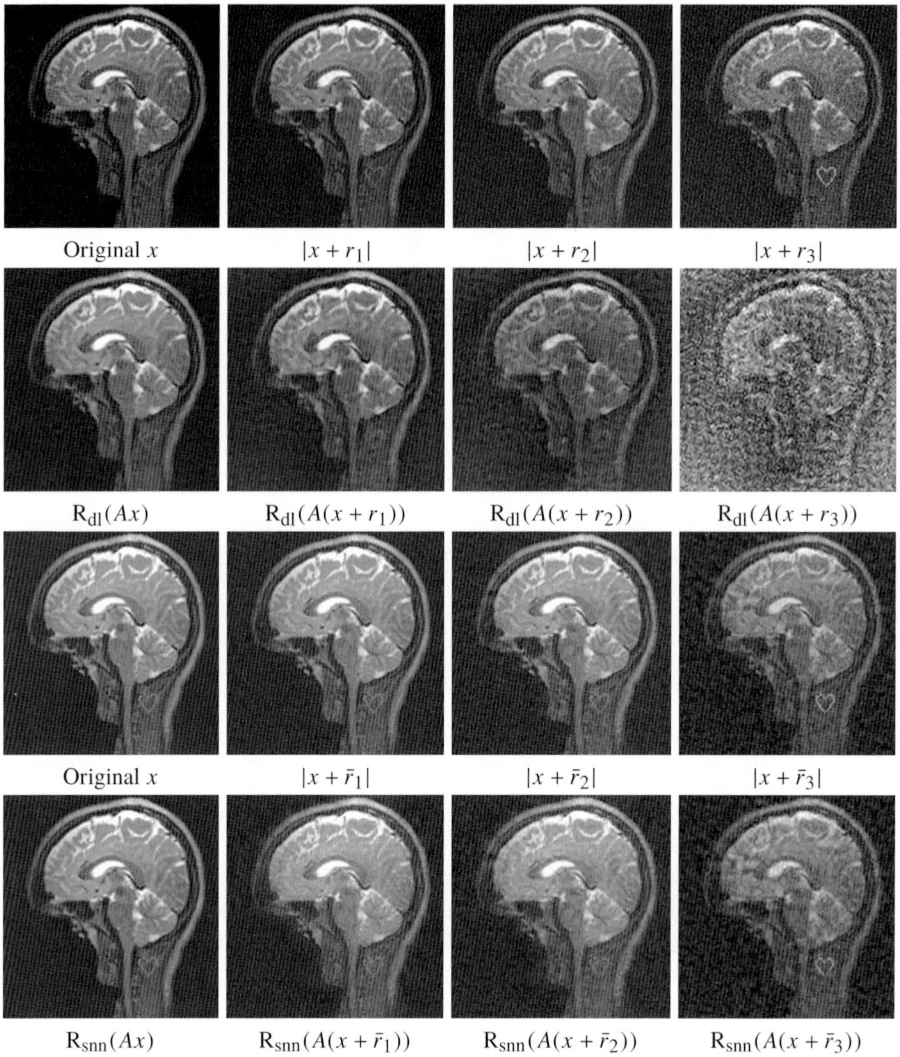

Figure 21.1 The effect of perturbations on the AUTOMAP network $\mathrm{R_{dl}}$ and the stable neural network $\mathrm{R_{snn}}$ of Theorem 21.15, which is based on 1000 layers. The experiment is performed as in Fig. 20.2, except that $\bar{r}_1, \bar{r}_2, \bar{r}_3$ are now constructed as adversarial perturbations for $\mathrm{R_{snn}}$ using Algorithm 19.1. First row: Original image x with perturbed images $|x + r_j|$. Second row: Recovery using $\mathrm{R_{dl}}$. Third row: Original image x with perturbed images $|x + \bar{r}_j|$. Fourth row: Recovery using $\mathrm{R_{snn}}$.

It is notable that the neural networks derived in this chapter are quite deep. Specifically, the number of layers scales like $1/\zeta$, where ζ is the target accuracy. The main results in [35] show that neural networks with similar guarantees, but depth scaling like $\log(\zeta^{-1})$ instead of $1/\zeta$, can also be computed. This is done by replacing the standard optimization scheme – which converges with rate $O(1/n)$ – by one involving an efficient restart procedure, so as to obtain a linear order of convergence. As shown in [35], this leads to practical, and relatively shallow networks for compressive imaging. For brevity, we have chosen to present the more simple case only in this chapter.

Epilogue

The rise of compressed sensing in the mid-2000s revolutionized image reconstruction, as researchers developed the theory and techniques for exploiting low-dimensional image structures using suitably designed sampling strategies. Compressed sensing ushered in a new era and a new field, known as compressive imaging.

As Part I of this book described, there is now an increasingly complete picture of how to best apply compressed sensing to imaging. The key considerations of Chapter 3 are now well understood in many different applications. We also understand how to boost performance, as discussed in Chapter 4. Equally importantly, we understand theoretically the extent to which compressed sensing for imaging meets the holy grail of image reconstruction: namely, Objectives #1–4 of Chapter 1. We have a comprehensive mathematical framework that guarantees accuracy (up to the prescribed image model) and stability, and shows how measurements should be acquired to achieve these bounds. We also know that it is possible to compute such reconstructions down to the accuracy needed and, because of efficient first-order optimization algorithms for large-scale problems, how to do so in reasonable computing time (Chapters 7 and 8).

In other words, compressive imaging has come far. Yet we are now in the midst of a second revolution, driven by the great potential of machine learning [486]. Progress over the last couple of years has been rapid. The FDA, for example, has already granted approval for the use of deep learning techniques to several commercial CT vendors [411]. In MRI, efforts such as the fastMRI challenge [295, 365] are providing valuable mechanisms to rapidly advance machine learning research within the field. This trend seems set to continue apace over the coming years. After all, most, if not all, applications where accurate image reconstruction from limited measurements is necessary can potentially benefit from data-driven approaches.

There are, however, some significant challenges. Arguably, deep learning does not currently meet the usual standards for robustness and reliability that have been the traditional pillars in the field. This raises significant concerns, especially for applications within critical sectors such as healthcare.

We now discuss several of these challenges.

Accuracy and stability. Chapter 20 demonstrates that stability is a pernicious issue for deep learning approaches. Guaranteed accuracy is also elusive: as shown in §20.3, certain approaches can struggle to recover details outside their training sets. This, of course, is an instance of one of the most profound questions in deep learning research: namely, understanding how well trained networks generalize away from the training set. Very much related to this is the unpredictability of the artefacts generated by trained neural networks, as shown in §20.2, making failure cases potentially impossible to recognize.

Sampling. The great achievement of compressed sensing was to connect the matter of sampling with low-dimensional image models. Yet nothing is known about how to optimize sampling for deep learning approaches. Should the sampling strategy also be learned? Perhaps. But it is not clear how this might lead to any guarantees on performance. Since the sampling strategy is difficult to alter in some applications or may even be fixed, a related problem is to understand the extent to which training data can be used to enhance reconstructions from relatively poor measurements. Recall the point made in §4.6 to this effect.

Efficiency. It has been argued that neural networks improve the speed of image reconstruction, as once they are trained, reconstruction requires a single forward pass through the network. This, of course, means the network cannot be too deep. But without guarantees on accuracy and stability, it is hard to see how such an improvement can be quantified. Chapter 20 constructs neural networks that can perform as well as compressed sensing. Yet these offer no benefit in terms of accuracy, stability or computational efficiency. Improving these results would be an interesting place to start.

Datasets. The use of data-driven strategies also raises another issue: namely, the size and quality of datasets. The success of deep learning in image classification is owed in great part to the vast quantity of training data available. By contrast, image reconstruction datasets are orders of magnitude smaller [327,353,411,436]. Real data is often difficult to obtain, and while synthetic data is often much easier to generate, using it carries the risk of the inverse crime (§4.4). The unpredictable performance of deep learning when the measurement model is changed – even, as shown in Fig. 20.10, when that change involves simply increasing the number of measurements – makes this a particular concern.

What to do? First, it is worth asking the question whether we care in practice. This, of course, depends on the application – medical imaging places a high price on reliable images, other applications potentially less so – the type and prevalence of instabilities, and our ability to detect them. In some applications, a trained network that produces correct-looking images most of the time and does so efficiently might be good enough. On the other hand, rather than curing instabilities completely, it is worth investigating whether they can be effectively detected – for example, by quantifying the uncertainty in a neural network reconstruction. Efforts in this direction are already in progress. However, we feel that this should not be a get-out-of-jail-free card that allows one to avoid dealing with the instability issue in the first place.

It will come as little surprise to the reader that we feel that these challenges will only be solved through the development of solid mathematical foundations. In Chapter 20 we probed the *accuracy–stability barrier* for deep learning in image reconstruction. Next, in Chapter 21, we combined the mathematical tools from Parts II–IV of this book to, in effect, show a lower bound on performance. How far this bound can be pushed, especially when training data enters the picture, is a tantalizing question for the future. Hopefully, these tools give a solid place from which to start. The connection between compressed sensing and neural networks via unravelling, as used in Chapter 21, seems a fruitful one to exploit further. A singular challenge herein is to better describe the class of objects to be recovered. Compressed sensing imposes models such as sparsity or sparsity in levels. However, both of these models are too crude a description for the mysterious set of 'natural images', a class mathematicians have struggled to describe for decades. In tandem with this effort, we also need to examine the question of upper bounds: that is, how well can a stable method perform for a given class? Tools such as the balancing property and stable sampling rate (Chapter 14) may prove useful in addressing these questions.

Computability should remain a key component of going forwards. Chapter 8 shows that we have been lucky so far in this regard. The convex optimization problems we wish to solve in compressed sensing turn out to be computable down to the accuracy we need. While preparing this book, we often found ourselves speculating whether the compressed sensing revolution would have happened at all had the impossibility theorem (Theorem 8.18) been known at the time. The answer is probably yes, but the speed of uptake from practitioners may well have been slower. This serves as an important reminder about the trust we place in computations. With the rise of nonconvex optimization problems as training procedures, the computability question becomes all the more important.

This brings us to a somewhat philosophical moment. Given the current optimism associated with deep learning – not just in imaging, but across a broad spectrum of computational tasks[1] – it is tempting to draw a parallel with a particularly important era in the history of mathematics, the transition from the nineteenth to the twentieth century. Hilbert, who provided the famous list of 23 important mathematical problems for the twentieth century, was convinced that mathematics could solve any logical problem through an algorithm. Yet this optimism turned out to be misplaced. Gödel, Turing and others turned Hilbert's view upside down by demonstrating fundamental barriers on what mathematics can prove and what algorithms can compute.[2] However, this did not stop mathematics and computer science from thriving as academic fields. Rather, it led to a rich theory describing the boundaries of what is possible to achieve.

Will the present moment parallel this story? Will there be a rich theory on the boundaries of what deep learning can achieve, and will there be researchers playing the roles of Gödel and Turing in leading the way? Having already quoted Hilbert's list of

[1] An example of such optimism being Geoffrey Hinton's well-known declaration that 'they should stop training radiologists now'.

[2] A particular example of Hilbert's confidence was the formulation of his 10th problem: 'Given a diophantine equation with any number of unknown quantities and with rational integral numerical coefficients: To find an algorithm according to which it can be determined by a finite number of operations whether the equation is solvable in rational integers'. The original formulation for 'algorithm' was the German word 'verfahren', which can best be translated as 'method' or 'procedure'. Modern statements of the problem typically use the word 'algorithm'. The formulation of the problem suggested a strong optimism that this could be done; it did not even suggest that it might be impossible. Yet no such algorithm exists. The celebrated work of Davis, Matiyasevich, Putnam and Robinson showed that this is a non-computable problem [352].

problems for the twentieth century, it is also timely to remember Smale's problems for the twenty-first century, particularly his 18th problem.[3]

We very much hope so. However, it is also worth mentioning the methodology that predominates within much of deep learning and artificial intelligence research. After NeurIPS 2017, a rather vibrant exchange took place between Ali Rahimi (winner of the test of time award at the conference) and deep learning pioneer Yann LeCun over the former's likening of modern machine learning, due to its trial-and-error focus, to 'alchemy'. Regardless of one's opinion on this issue, it is clear that a trial-and-error-based approach will not be able to assess the limitations of deep learning, much like the alchemists would never discover their own limitations. Hence, a new research methodology for understanding these limitations is needed. This may be as important to the twenty-first century as the foundational contributions of Gödel and Turing were to the twentieth.

It is with this thought that we end this book. Regrettably we have to leave this exploration of the world of compressive imaging in the midst of an exciting and unpredictable time. But a line has to be drawn somewhere, and now seems an appropriate point to do so – something that no doubt makes our publisher happy. Nevertheless, we hope to have conveyed to the reader the vibrancy of the field: one which spans a wide range of its disciplines, but at its core relies on foundational mathematical principles; one which has gone through one revolution, and now seems to be undergoing another; or, in other words, one that continues to be an arena for exciting research. We look forward to watching, reading and contributing to its next evolution.

[3] This is titled 'Limits of Intelligence' and asks 'What are the limits of intelligence, both artificial and human?' [445].

Appendices

Summary of the Appendices

In these appendices we present some background material that is used throughout this book. We have divided this material into five topics: linear algebra (Appendix A), functional analysis (Appendix B), probability (Appendix C), convex analysis and convex optimization (Appendix D) and Fourier transforms and series (Appendix E). We also have one further appendix. Appendix F gives additional information on Walsh functions and the Walsh transforms, which were previously introduced in Chapter 2. It also contains proofs of several of the results listed therein. This appendix is more specialized than the others.

Our coverage of these topics is purposefully not comprehensive: we have generally only included material that is needed in this book. We also largely omit proofs. Where relevant, we give references for further reading.

Appendix A: Linear Algebra

A.1 Norms

Let $\mathbb{V}$ be a vector space over the field $\mathbb{F} = \mathbb{R}$ or $\mathbb{F} = \mathbb{C}$. A *norm* on $\mathbb{V}$ is a function $\|\cdot\|: \mathbb{V} \to \mathbb{R}$ that satisfies, for all $x, y \in \mathbb{V}$ and $\alpha \in \mathbb{F}$,

(i) $\|x\| \geq 0$ and $\|x\| = 0$ if and only if $x = 0$,
(ii) $\|\alpha x\| = |\alpha|\|x\|$,
(iii) $\|x + y\| \leq \|x\| + \|y\|$.

Property (iii) is referred to as the *triangle inequality.*

We now consider the vector space $\mathbb{V} = \mathbb{C}^n$ of complex-valued (column) vectors of length n.

Definition A.1 (ℓ^p-norm) Let $1 \leq p \leq \infty$. The *ℓ^p-norm* on $\mathbb{C}^n$ is

$$\|x\|_{\ell^p} := \begin{cases} \left(\sum_{i=1}^n |x_i|^p\right)^{1/p} & 1 \leq p < \infty \\ \max_{i=1,\ldots,n} |x_i| & p = \infty \end{cases}, \quad x = (x_i)_{i=1}^n \in \mathbb{C}^n. \tag{A.1}$$

When $p = 2$, the ℓ^2-norm is also referred to as the *Euclidean* norm. Note that (A.1) makes sense for $0 < p < 1$, but it no longer defines a norm since the triangle inequality fails to hold. It does, however, define a *quasi-norm*, since the bound $\|x + y\|_{\ell^p} \leq 2^{1/p-1}(\|x\|_{\ell^p} + \|y\|_{\ell^p})$ holds for all $x, y \in \mathbb{C}^n$ when $0 < p < 1$.

Any two norms $\|\cdot\|$ and $|||\cdot|||$ on $\mathbb{C}^n$ are *equivalent*. That is, there are constants $c_1, c_2 > 0$ such that $c_1\|x\| \leq |||x||| \leq c_2\|x\|$, $\forall x \in \mathbb{C}^n$. In the case of the ℓ^p-norms, we have

$$\|x\|_{\ell^p} \leq \|x\|_{\ell^q} \leq n^{1/q-1/p}\|x\|_{\ell^p}, \quad \forall x \in \mathbb{C}^n,\ 1 \leq q \leq p.$$

The *Euclidean inner product* on $\mathbb{C}^n$ is

$$\langle x, y \rangle = \sum_{i=1}^n x_i \overline{y_i}, \quad x, y \in \mathbb{C}^n. \tag{A.2}$$

Note that the ℓ^2-norm of vector $x \in \mathbb{C}^n$ is precisely its *Euclidean length*: $\|x\|_{\ell^2} = \sqrt{\langle x, x \rangle}$. The *Cauchy–Schwarz inequality* states that

$$|\langle x, y \rangle| \leq \|x\|_{\ell^2}\|y\|_{\ell^2}, \quad x, y \in \mathbb{C}^n.$$

This is a special case of *Hölder's inequality*, which states that

$$|\langle x, y \rangle| \leq \|x\|_{\ell^p}\|y\|_{\ell^q}, \quad x, y \in \mathbb{C}^n, \tag{A.3}$$

for all $1 \leq p \leq \infty$, where $1 \leq q \leq \infty$ is given by

$$\frac{1}{p} + \frac{1}{q} = 1, \tag{A.4}$$

with the convention that $q = \infty$ when $p = 1$ and vice versa.

Let $\|\cdot\|$ be a norm on $\mathbb{C}^n$. Its *dual* norm $\|\cdot\|'$ is defined by

$$\|x\|' = \sup\left\{\frac{|\langle x, y\rangle|}{\|y\|} : y \in \mathbb{C}^n, y \neq 0\right\} = \sup\left\{\frac{\mathrm{Re}\,(\langle x, y\rangle)}{\|y\|} : y \in \mathbb{C}^n, y \neq 0\right\}, \tag{A.5}$$

where $\langle \cdot, \cdot \rangle$ is as in (A.2). This is a norm. The dual of $\|\cdot\|'$ is the original norm $\|\cdot\|$. For the ℓ^p-norm, one has $\|\cdot\|'_{\ell^p} = \|\cdot\|_{\ell^q}$ where q is given by (A.4). In particular, the ℓ^2-norm is *self-dual*: $\|\cdot\|'_{\ell^2} = \|\cdot\|_{\ell^2}$.

Given a norm $\|\cdot\|$, a vector $y \in \mathbb{C}^n$ and a positive scalar $r > 0$, the sets

$$\{x \in \mathbb{C}^n : \|x - y\| < r\}, \qquad \{x \in \mathbb{C}^n : \|x - y\| \leq r\}$$

are called the open and closed *balls of radius r centred at y*. When $r =$ and $y = 0$ they are the (open and closed) *unit balls* of $\|\cdot\|$. If $\|\cdot\| = \|\cdot\|_{\ell^p}$, they are termed *$\ell^p$-balls.*

Note that the supremum in (A.5) can always be replaced by a supremum over the unit ball or its boundary, e.g.

$$\|x\|' = \sup\left\{|\langle x, y\rangle| : y \in \mathbb{C}^n, \|y\| \leq 1\right\} = \sup\left\{|\langle x, y\rangle| : y \in \mathbb{C}^n, \|y\| = 1\right\}. \tag{A.6}$$

The same applies to all similar quantities considered below.

A.2 Orthogonality and Orthonormal Bases

Two vectors $x, y \in \mathbb{C}^n$ are *orthogonal* if $\langle x, y\rangle = 0$. This is commonly written as $x \perp y$. Two subspaces $U, V \subseteq \mathbb{C}^n$ are *orthogonal* if $x \perp y$ for all $x \in U$ and $y \in V$.

A set S of nonzero vectors is *orthogonal* if $x \perp y$ whenever $x, y \in S$ and $x \neq y$. Orthogonal vectors are linearly independent. Hence any n orthogonal vectors in $\mathbb{C}^n$ form a basis, a so-called *orthogonal* basis. In other words, $\{\phi_i\}_{i=1}^n$ is an orthogonal basis if and only if

$$\langle \phi_i, \phi_j\rangle = 0, \quad i \neq j,\ i, j = 1, \ldots, n.$$

If, in addition, the vectors have unit length, i.e.

$$\langle \phi_i, \phi_i\rangle = 1, \quad i = 1, \ldots, n,$$

then $\{\phi_i\}_{i=1}^n$ is an *orthonormal* basis. Note that the coordinate vectors $\{e_i\}_{i=1}^n$, where $e_i = (\delta_{ij})_{j=1}^n$, form an orthonormal basis of $\mathbb{C}^n$, the so-called *canonical* (or *standard*) basis. Here δ_{ij} is the Kronecker delta.

If $\{\phi_i\}_{i=1}^n$ is an orthonormal basis, then every $x \in \mathbb{C}^n$ can be written as

$$x = \sum_{i=1}^n d_i \phi_i, \qquad d_i = \langle x, \phi_i\rangle.$$

We refer to d_i as the *coefficients* of x in this basis. Equivalently, $x = \Phi d$, where $\Phi = (\phi_1 | \cdots | \phi_n) \in \mathbb{C}^{n \times n}$ is the matrix whose ith column is ϕ_i and $d = (d_i)_{i=1}^n$ is the *vector of coefficients* of x.

A.3 Matrices

In this section we consider the space $\mathbb{C}^{m \times n}$ of complex $m \times n$ matrices.

Let $A = (a_{ij})_{i,j=1}^{m,n} \in \mathbb{C}^{m \times n}$. The *range* of A is $\mathrm{Ran}(A) = \{Ax : x \in \mathbb{C}^n\}$ and the *null space* of A is $\mathrm{Ker}(A) = \{x \in \mathbb{C}^n : Ax = 0\}$. The rank of A, denoted $\mathrm{rank}(A)$, is the dimension of $\mathrm{Ran}(A)$, and the *nullity* of A, denoted $\mathrm{null}(A)$, is the dimension of $\mathrm{Ker}(A)$. The *rank–nullity formula* states that $\mathrm{rank}(A) + \mathrm{null}(A) = n$.

The rank of A is equal to its number of linearly independent columns (sometimes called the *column rank*). It is also equal to the number of linearly independent rows of A (the so-called *row rank*). In particular, $\mathrm{rank}(A) \leq \min\{m, n\}$. A matrix is *full rank* if $\mathrm{rank}(A) = \min\{m, n\}$.

Let $A = (a_{ij})_{i,j=1}^{m,n} \in \mathbb{C}^{m \times n}$ be an $m \times n$ matrix. Its *transpose* is the $n \times m$ matrix

$$A^\top = (a_{ji})_{i,j=1}^{n,m},$$

and its *adjoint* (also known as *Hermitian conjugate*) is the $n \times m$ matrix

$$A^* = (\overline{a_{ji}})_{i,j=1}^{n,m}.$$

A matrix is *symmetric* if $A = A^\top$ and *self-adjoint* (also known as *Hermitian*) if $A = A^*$. A self-adjoint matrix $A \in \mathbb{C}^{n \times n}$ has real eigenvalues $\lambda_1, \ldots, \lambda_n$ and an orthonormal basis $\{q_i\}_{i=1}^n$ of eigenvectors. Equivalently, it has an *eigenvalue decomposition*

$$A = Q \Lambda Q^*, \tag{A.7}$$

where $Q = (q_1 | \ldots | q_n) \in \mathbb{C}^{n \times n}$ is the matrix whose columns are the orthonormal eigenvectors of A and $\Lambda = \mathrm{diag}(\lambda_1, \ldots, \lambda_n)$ is the diagonal matrix of eigenvalues.

The matrix Q is an example of a unitary matrix. A matrix $U \in \mathbb{C}^{n \times n}$ is *unitary* if its inverse is equal to its adjoint. That is,

$$U^* U = U U^* = I, \tag{A.8}$$

where I is the identity matrix. If $U \in \mathbb{R}^{n \times n}$ is a real $n \times n$ matrix then (A.8) is equivalent to $U^\top U = U U^\top = I$, in which case U is often referred to as *orthogonal*. Note that unitary matrices preserve lengths and inner products, i.e.

$$\langle Ux, Uy \rangle = \langle x, y \rangle, \qquad \|Ux\|_{\ell^2} = \|x\|_{\ell^2}, \qquad \forall x, y \in \mathbb{C}^N. \tag{A.9}$$

Orthonormal bases and unitary matrices are equivalent. If $\{\phi_i\}_{i=1}^n$ is an orthonormal basis of $\mathbb{C}^n$ then the matrix

$$\Phi = (\phi_1 | \cdots | \phi_n) \in \mathbb{C}^{n \times n}$$

is unitary. Conversely, if Φ is unitary then its columns form an orthonormal basis.

A matrix $A \in \mathbb{C}^{n \times n}$ is *positive definite* if it is self-adjoint and if

$$x^* A x > 0, \quad \forall x \in \mathbb{C}^n \backslash \{0\}.$$

It is *nonnegative definite* (sometimes known as *positive semi-definite*) if $>$ is replaced by $\geq$ in the above expression. A matrix is positive (nonnegative) definite if and only if all its eigenvalues are positive (nonnegative).

A positive (nonnegative)-definite matrix A has a unique positive (nonnegative)-definite square root. That is, a positive (nonnegative)-definite matrix B that satisfies $B^2 = A$. This matrix can be written explicitly in terms of the eigenvalue decomposition (A.7) as $B = Q\sqrt{\Lambda}Q^*$, where $\sqrt{\Lambda} = \mathrm{diag}(\sqrt{\lambda_1}, \ldots, \sqrt{\lambda_n})$.

An $n \times n$ matrix P is an *orthogonal projection* if $P^* = P$ and $P^2 = P$. The range and kernel of P are orthogonal subspaces and they form a direct sum:

$$\mathrm{Ran}(P) \oplus \mathrm{Ker}(P) = \mathbb{C}^n.$$

This means that every vector $x \in \mathbb{C}^n$ has the unique decomposition $x = u + v = Px + (I - P)x$ with $u = Px \in \mathrm{Ran}(P)$ and $v = (I - P)x \in \mathrm{Ker}(P)$. The matrix $P^\perp = I - P$ is also an orthogonal projection, the so-called *complementary projection*. It satisfies $\mathrm{Ran}(P^\perp) = \mathrm{Ker}(P)$ and $\mathrm{Ker}(P^\perp) = \mathrm{Ran}(P)$. Since Px and $P^\perp x$ are orthogonal vectors, one also has

$$\|Px\|_{\ell^2}^2 + \|P^\perp x\|_{\ell^2}^2 = \|x\|_{\ell^2}^2, \quad \forall x \in \mathbb{C}^n.$$

In particular, $\|Px\|_{\ell^2} \leq \|x\|_{\ell^2}$ and $\|P^\perp x\|_{\ell^2} \leq \|x\|_{\ell^2}$ for all x.

If $\mathrm{rank}(P) = k$ and $\{q_i\}_{i=1}^k$ is an orthonormal basis for $\mathrm{Ran}(P)$ then P can be expressed as a sum of rank-one matrices as $P = \sum_{i=1}^k q_i q_i^*$. If this basis is extended to an orthonormal basis $\{q_i\}_{i=1}^n$ of $\mathbb{C}^n$ then $P^\perp = \sum_{i=k+1}^n q_i q_i^*$.

A.4 Matrix Norms

Let $\|\cdot\|_{(a)}$ and $\|\cdot\|_{(b)}$ be norms on $\mathbb{C}^n$ and $\mathbb{C}^m$, respectively. The *induced matrix norm* on $\mathbb{C}^{m\times n}$ is defined as

$$\|A\|_{(a,b)} = \sup\left\{\frac{\|Ax\|_{(b)}}{\|x\|_{(a)}} : x \in \mathbb{C}^n, x \neq 0\right\}, \tag{A.10}$$

or equivalently (recall (A.6)), as

$$\|A\|_{(a,b)} = \sup\left\{\|Ax\|_{(b)} : x \in \mathbb{C}^n, \|x\|_{(a)} \leq 1\right\} = \sup\left\{\|Ax\|_{(b)} : x \in \mathbb{C}^n, \|x\|_{(a)} = 1\right\}.$$

An immediate consequence of this definition is that

$$\|Ax\|_{(b)} \leq \|A\|_{(a,b)}\|x\|_{(a)}, \quad \forall x \in \mathbb{C}^n.$$

If $\|\cdot\|_{(c)}$ is a norm on $\mathbb{C}^p$ then one also has

$$\|BA\|_{(a,c)} \leq \|A\|_{(a,b)}\|B\|_{(b,c)}, \quad \forall A \in \mathbb{C}^{m\times n},\ B \in \mathbb{C}^{p\times m}. \tag{A.11}$$

If $\|\cdot\|_{(a)} = \|\cdot\|_{\ell^p}$ and $\|\cdot\|_{(b)} = \|\cdot\|_{\ell^q}$ for some $1 \leq p, q \leq \infty$ then (A.10) is the *matrix* (ℓ^p, ℓ^q)*-norm*. If $p = q$ it is the *matrix* ℓ^p*-norm*. We denote the latter as $\|A\|_{\ell^p}$, i.e.

$$\|A\|_{\ell^p} = \sup\left\{\frac{\|Ax\|_{\ell^p}}{\|x\|_{\ell^p}} : x \in \mathbb{C}^n, x \neq 0\right\}. \tag{A.12}$$

Not all matrix norms are induced by vector norms as in (A.12). The most common example of a noninduced matrix norm is the *Frobenius norm*, which is defined as

$$\|A\|_F = \sqrt{\sum_{i=1}^{n}\sum_{j=1}^{m}|a_{ij}|^2}, \qquad A = (a_{ij})_{i,j=1}^{m,n}. \tag{A.13}$$

This is precisely the ℓ^2-norm of the vectorization of A. It can also be written as

$$\|A\|_F = \sqrt{\mathrm{Tr}(A^*A)} = \sqrt{\mathrm{Tr}(AA^*)},$$

where Tr denotes the trace of a matrix. The multiplicative property (A.11) also holds for the Frobenius norm, i.e. $\|BA\|_F \leq \|A\|_F\|B\|_F$.

The Frobenius norm is a type of *matrix $\ell^{p,q}$-norm*. This family of norms is defined as

$$\|A\|_{\ell^{p,q}} = \left(\sum_{i=1}^{n}\left(\sum_{j=1}^{m}|a_{ij}|^p\right)^{q/p}\right)^{1/q}, \tag{A.14}$$

where $1 \leq p, q \leq \infty$ (with suitable modifications when $p = \infty$ or $q = \infty$). The Frobenius norm corresponds to $p = q = 2$.

Both the matrix ℓ^2-norm and the Frobenius norm are *unitarily invariant*. That is,

$$\|UAV\|_{\ell^2} = \|A\|_{\ell^2}, \qquad \|UAV\|_F = \|A\|_F,$$

for all unitary matrices $U \in \mathbb{C}^{m\times m}$ and $V \in \mathbb{C}^{n\times n}$. This follows immediately from (A.8), (A.9) and the definitions of the two norms.

A.5 Further Properties of the Matrix ℓ^2-Norm

The matrix ℓ^2-norm also has the equivalent definition

$$\|A\|_{\ell^2} = \sqrt{\lambda_{\max}(A^*A)} = \sigma_{\max}(A),$$

where $\lambda_{\max}(A^*A)$ is the largest eigenvalue of A^*A and $\sigma_{\max}(A)$ is the largest singular value of A (defined next). In particular, if A is self-adjoint then $\|A\|_{\ell^2}$ is equal to the largest eigenvalue of A in absolute value.

For an arbitrary matrix A, one also has

$$\|A\|_{\ell^2} = \sqrt{\|A^*A\|_{\ell^2}} = \sqrt{\|AA^*\|_{\ell^2}}. \tag{A.15}$$

Moreover, since the vector ℓ^2-norm is self-dual, one has

$$\|A\|_{\ell^2} = \sup_{\substack{x\neq 0\\ y\neq 0}}\left\{\frac{|\langle Ax, y\rangle|}{\|x\|_{\ell^2}\|y\|_{\ell^2}}\right\} = \sup_{\substack{x\neq 0\\ y\neq 0}}\left\{\frac{\mathrm{Re}\,(\langle Ax, y\rangle)}{\|x\|_{\ell^2}\|y\|_{\ell^2}}\right\}.$$

If A is self-adjoint then this supremum is achieved when $y = x$. This gives

$$\|A\|_{\ell^2} = \sup_{x\neq 0}\left\{\frac{|\langle Ax, x\rangle|}{\|x\|_{\ell^2}^2}\right\}. \tag{A.16}$$

If A is also nonnegative definite, then $\langle Ax, x\rangle$ is nonnegative, and therefore

$$\|A\|_{\ell^2} = \sup_{x\neq 0}\left\{\frac{\langle Ax, x\rangle}{\|x\|^2_{\ell^2}}\right\}.$$

A.6 The Singular Value Decomposition

The *(full) Singular Value Decomposition (SVD)* of a matrix $A \in \mathbb{C}^{m\times n}$ is

$$A = U\Sigma V^*,$$

where $U \in \mathbb{C}^{m\times m}$ and $V \in \mathbb{C}^{n\times n}$ are unitary and $\Sigma \in \mathbb{R}^{m\times n}$ is diagonal and its diagonal entries

$$\sigma_1 \geq \sigma_2 \geq \cdots \sigma_p \geq 0, \qquad p = \min\{m, n\}$$

are nonnegative and ordered. The columns $u_i \in \mathbb{C}^m$ and $v_j \in \mathbb{C}^n$ of U and V are the *left-singular vectors* and *right-singular vectors*, respectively, and the σ_i are the *singular values*. We commonly denote σ_1 as $\sigma_{\max}$ and σ_p as $\sigma_{\min}$, and refer to them as the *maximum* and *minimum* singular values, respectively.

Here we list several properties of the SVD:

(i) Every matrix A has a singular value decomposition. Its singular values are unique.
(ii) The rank of A is equal to its number of nonzero singular values.
(iii) The nonzero singular values of A are equal to the square roots of the nonzero eigenvalues of AA^* and A^*A.
(iv) If A is self-adjoint then its singular values are the absolute values of its eigenvalues.

The matrix ℓ^2-norm and the Frobenius norm can both be expressed in terms of the singular values. Specifically,

$$\|A\|_{\ell^2} = \sigma_1, \qquad \|A\|_F = \sqrt{\sigma_1^2 + \cdots + \sigma_p^2}.$$

Norms such as these that are functions of the singular values only are referred to as *Schatten norms*.

A.7 Least Squares and the Pseudoinverse

Let $A \in \mathbb{C}^{m\times n}$ with $m \geq n$. In this case, A is described as a *tall* matrix. Suppose that $y \in \mathbb{C}^m$. Then the *least-squares problem* is

$$\min_{z\in\mathbb{C}^n} \|Az - y\|_{\ell^2}. \tag{A.17}$$

A vector $x \in \mathbb{C}^n$ is a solution of this problem if and only if it is a solution of the *normal equations*

$$A^*Az = A^*y.$$

The matrix A^*A is invertible if and only if A is full rank. Hence (A.17) has a unique solution x if and only if A is full rank, i.e. $\mathrm{rank}(A) = \min\{m, n\} = n$. This solution is then given by

$$x = (A^*A)^{-1}A^*y. \tag{A.18}$$

The following lemma is particularly useful:

Lemma A.2 *Suppose that $A \in \mathbb{C}^{m\times n}$ with $m \geq n$ and $\|I - A^*A\|_{\ell^2} \leq \eta < 1$. Then A is full rank and its maximum and minimum singular values satisfy*

$$\sqrt{1-\eta} \leq \sigma_{\min} \leq \sigma_{\max} \leq \sqrt{1+\eta}.$$

Proof Let $U\Sigma V^*$ be the SVD of A. The unitary invariance of the ℓ^2-norm gives

$$\|I - A^*A\|_{\ell^2} = \|VV^* - V\Sigma^\top\Sigma V^*\|_{\ell^2} = \|I - \Sigma^\top\Sigma\|_{\ell^2}.$$

The matrix $I - \Sigma^\top\Sigma$ is diagonal with diagonal entries $1 - \sigma_i^2$, $i = 1, \ldots, n$. Since it is diagonal, its ℓ^2-norm is equal to its maximum diagonal entry in absolute value, i.e.

$$\|I - \Sigma^\top\Sigma\|_{\ell^2} = \max_{i=1,\ldots,n} |1 - \sigma_i^2|.$$

Hence $|1 - \sigma_i^2| \leq \eta$ for all i, or equivalently

$$\sqrt{1-\eta} \leq \sigma_i \leq \sqrt{1+\eta}, \quad i = 1, \ldots, n.$$

In particular, $\sigma_n > 0$ which implies that A is full rank. This gives the result. □

The matrix in (A.18) is known as the *pseudoinverse* of A and denoted

$$A^\dagger = (A^*A)^{-1}A^* \in \mathbb{C}^{n\times m}. \tag{A.19}$$

Every matrix (of any size and rank) has a unique pseudoinverse. In the general case, $A^\dagger \in \mathbb{C}^{n\times m}$ is defined as the unique matrix satisfying the following four conditions:

(i) $AA^\dagger A = A$,
(ii) $A^\dagger AA^\dagger = A^\dagger$,
(iii) $(AA^\dagger)^* = AA^\dagger$,
(iv) $(A^\dagger A)^* = A^\dagger A$.

When A is tall and full rank, it is straightforward to show that (A.19) satisfies (i)–(iv). If A is square and invertible then its pseudoinverse is equal to its inverse, i.e. $A^\dagger = A^{-1}$.

In general, the pseudoinverse of $A \in \mathbb{C}^{m\times n}$ can be expressed in terms of its SVD $U\Sigma V^*$. Specifically,

$$A^\dagger = V\Sigma^\dagger U^*,$$

where $\Sigma^\dagger \in \mathbb{R}^{n\times m}$, the pseudoinverse of Σ, is the diagonal matrix with ith entry $1/\sigma_i$ if $\sigma_i > 0$ and zero otherwise. In particular, the ℓ^2-norm of the pseudoinverse satisfies $\|A^\dagger\|_{\ell^2} = 1/\sigma_r$, where $r = \mathrm{rank}(A)$.

When A is tall, the vector $x = A^\dagger y$ is always a solution of (A.17), regardless of whether or not A is full rank. If A is not full rank then it is the (unique) solution with smallest ℓ^2-norm amongst all possible solutions of (A.17).

Now suppose that $A \in \mathbb{C}^{m\times n}$ with $m < n$. Such an A is described as a *fat* matrix. It is full rank if and only if the matrix AA^* is invertible. In that case, its pseudoinverse is given by $A^\dagger = A^*(AA^*)^{-1}$.

Much like in the case of a tall matrix, the pseudoinverse $A^\dagger$ of a fat matrix yields solutions to a certain optimization problem. Specifically, if $y \in \mathrm{Ran}(A)$ then the vector $x = A^\dagger y$ is the unique solution of the ℓ^2-minimization problem

$$\min_{z\in\mathbb{C}^n} \|z\|_{\ell^2} \text{ subject to } Az = y.$$

A.8 Circulant Matrices and Convolution

A circulant matrix $C \in \mathbb{C}^{n\times n}$ is a matrix generated by cyclic shifts of a single vector $c = (c_i)_{i=0}^{n-1}$:

$$C = \begin{pmatrix} c_0 & c_{n-1} & \cdots & c_2 & c_1 \\ c_1 & c_0 & \cdots & c_3 & c_2 \\ \vdots & \vdots & \ddots & \vdots & \vdots \\ c_{n-2} & c_{n-3} & \cdots & c_0 & c_{n-1} \\ c_{n-1} & c_{n-2} & \cdots & c_1 & c_0 \end{pmatrix}.$$

The action $x \mapsto Cx$ is the *circular convolution* of the vectors $x = (x_i)_{i=0}^{n-1}$ and c:

$$Cx = c \star x, \qquad (c\star x)_i = \sum_{j=0}^{n-1} x_j c_{i-j} \tag{A.20}$$

(here $i - j$ is taken modulo n). Every circulant matrix is diagonalized by the $n\times n$ Fourier matrix F (Definition 2.1). Specifically,

$$C = F^{-1}\mathrm{diag}(d)F,$$

where $d = Fc$. This is equivalent to the statement that convolution is multiplication in the Fourier domain: namely,

$$F(c\star x) = (Fc) \odot (Fx), \qquad \forall x, c \in \mathbb{C}^n,$$

where $\odot$ is the entrywise (Hadamard) product of two vectors.

A.9 Kronecker products of matrices

The Kronecker product of an $m\times n$ matrix A and a $p\times q$ matrix B is the $mp\times nq$ matrix

$$A\otimes B = \begin{pmatrix} a_{11}B & \cdots & a_{1n}B \\ \vdots & \ddots & \vdots \\ a_{m1}B & \cdots & a_{mn}B \end{pmatrix} \in \mathbb{C}^{mp\times nq}.$$

The Kronecker product is linear in both its entries:

$$A \otimes (B + C) = A \otimes B + A \otimes C,$$
$$(A + B) \otimes C = A \otimes C + B \otimes C,$$
$$A \otimes (cB) = c(A \otimes B),$$
$$(cA) \otimes B = c(A \otimes B).$$

It is also associative:

$$A \otimes (B \otimes C) = (A \otimes B) \otimes C.$$

Further, if A, B, C and D are matrices such that AC and BD are well defined, then

$$(A \otimes B)(C \otimes D) = (AC) \otimes (BD).$$

In particular, $A \otimes B$ is invertible if and only if A and B are invertible, and

$$(A \otimes B)^{-1} = A^{-1} \otimes B^{-1},$$

in this case.

For general A and B, the pseudoinverse of $A \otimes B$ is given by $(A \otimes B)^{\dagger} = A^{\dagger} \otimes B^{\dagger}$, and the adjoint and transpose of $A \otimes B$ are given by

$$(A \otimes B)^{*} = A^{*} \otimes B^{*}, \qquad (A \otimes B)^{\top} = A^{\top} \otimes B^{\top}.$$

The singular values of $A \otimes B$ are the products of the singular values of A and the singular values of B (if A and B are square, the same property also holds for the eigenvalues). In particular, $\mathrm{rank}(A \otimes B) = \mathrm{rank}(A)\mathrm{rank}(B)$ and $\|A \otimes B\|_{\ell^2} = \|A\|_{\ell^2}\|B\|_{\ell^2}$.

Let $A^{(k)} = (a^{(k)}_{ij})^{n}_{i,j=1}$ be $n \times n$ matrices for $k = 1, \ldots, d$. Then the d-fold Kronecker product $A^{(1)} \otimes \cdots \otimes A^{(d)} \in \mathbb{C}^{n^d \times n^d}$ has entries

$$\left(A^{(1)} \otimes \cdots \otimes A^{(d)}\right)_{ij} = \prod_{k=1}^{d} a^{(k)}_{\varsigma(i)_k, \varsigma(j)_k}, \tag{A.21}$$

where $\varsigma : \{1, \ldots, n^d\} \to \{1, \ldots, n\}^d$ is the lexicographical ordering (2.2) and, for $i \in \{1, \ldots, N^d\}$, $\varsigma(i)_k$ is the kth entry of $\varsigma(i)$.

Appendix B: Functional Analysis

B.1 Metric Spaces

A *metric space* $(\mathbb{M}, d)$ is a pair consisting of a set $\mathbb{M}$ and *metric* $d \colon \mathbb{M} \times \mathbb{M} \to \mathbb{R}$ that satisfies, for all $x, y, z \in \mathbb{M}$,

(i) $d(x, y) = 0$ if and only if $x = y$,
(ii) $d(x, y) = d(y, x)$,
(iii) $d(x, z) \leq d(x, y) + d(y, z)$.

Property (iii) is known as the *triangle inequality* for metrics. Note that (i)–(iii) imply that $d(x, y) \geq 0$, $\forall x, y \in \mathbb{M}$.

A sequence $\{x_i\}_{i=1}^{\infty} \subseteq \mathbb{M}$ is *convergent* in $(\mathbb{M}, d)$ if there exists an $x \in \mathbb{M}$ such that $d(x_i, x) \to 0$ as $i \to \infty$. We write $x = \lim_{i\to\infty} x_i$ and call x the *limit* of the sequence. A sequence $\{x_i\}_{i=1}^{\infty}$ is a *Cauchy sequence* if for each $\epsilon > 0$ there exists an n such that $d(x_i, x_j) \leq \epsilon$ whenever $i, j \geq n$. A metric space is *complete* if every Cauchy sequence in $\mathbb{M}$ has a limit in $\mathbb{M}$.

The *open ball* of radius $r > 0$ around a point $x \in \mathbb{M}$ is the set

$$B(x, r) = \{y \in \mathbb{M} : d(x, y) < r\}.$$

A set $X \subseteq \mathbb{M}$ is *open* if for every $x \in X$ there exists an $r > 0$ such that $B(x, r) \subseteq X$. A set X is a *neighbourhood* of a point $x \in \mathbb{M}$ if $B(x, r) \subseteq X$ for some $r > 0$.

A set $Y \subseteq \mathbb{M}$ is *closed* if its complement $Y^c = \mathbb{M} \backslash Y$ is open. Equivalently, Y is closed if the limit of every convergent sequence of terms in Y also belongs to Y. The *closed ball* of radius $r > 0$ around a point $x \in \mathbb{M}$ is

$$B(x, r) = \{y \in \mathbb{M} : d(x, y) \leq r\}.$$

It is a closed set.

The *closure* of a set $U \subseteq \mathbb{M}$ is the set $\overline{U} \supseteq U$ consisting of all limit points of convergent sequences in U:

$$\overline{U} = \{u \in \mathbb{M} : u = \lim_{i\to\infty} u_i,\ \{u_i\} \subseteq U\}.$$

Hence a subset U is closed if and only if it is equal to its own closure, i.e. $\overline{U} = U$. A subset $U \subseteq \mathbb{M}$ is *dense* in the metric space $(\mathbb{M}, d)$ if $\overline{U} = \mathbb{M}$. A metric space is *separable* if it has a countable, dense subset.

B.2 Banach and Hilbert Spaces

A *normed vector space* is a vector space $\mathbb{V}$ with a norm $\|\cdot\|$. It is a metric space with metric $d(x, y) = \|x - y\|$. A normed vector space is a *Banach space* if it is complete as a metric space. Every finite-dimensional normed vector space is a Banach space.

Let $\mathbb{V}$ be a vector space over $\mathbb{F} = \mathbb{R}$ or $\mathbb{F} = \mathbb{C}$. Then $\mathbb{V}$ is an *inner product space* if $\mathbb{V}$ has an *inner product*: that is, a map $\langle\cdot,\cdot\rangle\colon \mathbb{V}\times\mathbb{V} \to \mathbb{F}$ that satisfies

(i) $\langle x, y\rangle = \overline{\langle y, x\rangle}$,
(ii) $\langle ax, y\rangle = a\langle x, y\rangle$ and $\langle x + y, z\rangle = \langle x, z\rangle + \langle y, z\rangle$,
(iii) $\langle x, x\rangle \geq 0$ and $\langle x, x\rangle = 0$ if and only if $x = 0$,

for all $x, y, z \in V$ and $a \in \mathbb{F}$. An inner product space is a normed space, with norm $\|x\| = \sqrt{\langle x, x\rangle}$. A *Hilbert space* $\mathbb{H}$ is an inner product space which is a Banach space with respect to this norm. The vector space $\mathbb{C}^n$ with the Euclidean inner product (A.2) is a Hilbert space.

In every Hilbert space $(\mathbb{H}, \langle\cdot,\cdot\rangle)$, the *Cauchy–Schwarz inequality* holds:

$$|\langle x, y\rangle| \leq \|x\|\|y\|, \quad \forall x, y \in \mathbb{H}.$$

Note that we often write $\langle\cdot,\cdot\rangle_{\mathbb{H}}$ instead of $\langle\cdot,\cdot\rangle$, so as to make it clear that $\langle\cdot,\cdot\rangle$ is an inner product on the space $\mathbb{H}$.

B.3 The ℓ^p and L^p Spaces

Definition B.1 (ℓ^p-space) Let $1 \leq p \leq \infty$. The space $\ell^p(\mathbb{N})$ consists of all complex infinite sequences $x = (x_i)_{i=1}^{\infty}$, $x_i \in \mathbb{C}$, for which $\|x\|_{\ell^p} < \infty$, where

$$\|x\|_{\ell^p} = \begin{cases} \left(\sum_{i=1}^{\infty} |x_i|^p\right)^{1/p} & 1 \leq p < \infty \\ \sup_{i=1,\ldots,\infty} |x_i| & p = \infty \end{cases}$$

The $\ell^p(\mathbb{N})$ spaces are Banach spaces. The space $\ell^2(\mathbb{N})$ is a Hilbert space with the inner product

$$\langle x, y\rangle = \sum_{i,j=1}^{\infty} x_i \overline{y_i}.$$

Hölder's inequality extends to these spaces. Specifically, if $x \in \ell^p(\mathbb{N})$ and $y \in \ell^q(\mathbb{N})$, where $\frac{1}{p} + \frac{1}{q} = 1$, then $z = (x_i\overline{y_i})_{i=1}^{\infty} \in \ell^1(\mathbb{N})$ and

$$|\langle x, y\rangle| \leq \|z\|_{\ell^1} \leq \|x\|_{\ell^p}\|y\|_{\ell^q}.$$

Definition B.2 (L^p-space) Let $1 \leq p < \infty$ and D be a measurable subset of $\mathbb{R}^d$. The space $L^p(D)$ consists of all Lebesgue measurable functions $f\colon D \to \mathbb{C}$ for which

$$\int_D |f(t)|^p \, dt < \infty. \tag{B.1}$$

The norm on $L^p(D)$ is

$$\|f\|_{L^p} = \left(\int_D |f(t)|^p \, \mathrm{d}t \right)^{1/p}.$$

For $p = \infty$, the space $L^\infty(D)$ consists of all measurable functions that are essentially bounded, i.e.

$$\|f\|_{L^\infty} := \inf\{M \geq 0 : |f(t)| \leq M \text{ almost everywhere}\} < \infty.$$

On occasion we write $\|\cdot\|_{L^p(D)}$ to make the dependence on D explicit.

This definition is not technically correct. To be precise, $L^p(D)$ consists of equivalence classes of functions satisfying (B.1) that differ on sets of Lebesgue measure zero. For the purposes of this book, this technicality can be ignored.

The spaces $L^p(D)$ are Banach spaces for $1 \leq p \leq \infty$. The space $L^2(D)$ is a Hilbert space with inner product

$$\langle f, g \rangle_{L^2} = \int_D f(t)\overline{g(t)} \, \mathrm{d}t.$$

As above, we write $\langle \cdot, \cdot \rangle_{L^2(D)}$ when needed. One also has the following version of Hölder's inequality for the L^p-spaces. If $f \in L^p(\mathbb{R})$ and $g \in L^q(\mathbb{R})$, where $\frac{1}{p} + \frac{1}{q} = 1$, then $f\overline{g} \in L^1(\mathbb{R})$ and

$$\left| \int_D f(t)\overline{g(t)} \, \mathrm{d}t \right| \leq \int_D |f(t)||g(t)| \, \mathrm{d}t \leq \|f\|_{L^p} \|g\|_{L^q}.$$

When $p = q = 2$ this gives the Cauchy–Schwarz inequality for the space $L^2(D)$.

B.4 Operators between Normed Spaces

A linear operator $\mathcal{T} : \mathbb{V}_1 \to \mathbb{V}_2$ between normed spaces $(\mathbb{V}_1, \|\cdot\|_{\mathbb{V}_1})$ and $(\mathbb{V}_2, \|\cdot\|_{\mathbb{V}_2})$ is *bounded* if

$$\|\mathcal{T}x\|_{\mathbb{V}_2} \leq M\|x\|_{\mathbb{V}_1}, \quad \forall x \in \mathbb{V}_1,$$

for some $M > 0$. The *operator norm* of $\mathcal{T}$, denoted $\|\mathcal{T}\|_{\mathbb{V}_1 \to \mathbb{V}_2}$, is the smallest such constant M, i.e.

$$\|\mathcal{T}\|_{\mathbb{V}_1 \to \mathbb{V}_2} = \sup \left\{ \frac{\|\mathcal{T}x\|_{\mathbb{V}_2}}{\|x\|_{\mathbb{V}_1}} : x \in \mathbb{V}_1, \ x \neq 0 \right\}.$$

If $\mathbb{V}_1 = \mathbb{V}_2 = \mathbb{V}$, we simply write $\|\mathcal{T}\|_{\mathbb{V}}$.

Let $\mathcal{A} : \mathbb{H}_1 \to \mathbb{H}_2$ be a bounded operator between Hilbert spaces $(\mathbb{H}_1, \langle \cdot, \cdot \rangle_{\mathbb{H}_1})$ and $(\mathbb{H}_2, \langle \cdot, \cdot \rangle_{\mathbb{H}_2})$. Its *adjoint* is the unique bounded operator $\mathcal{A}^* : \mathbb{H}_2 \to \mathbb{H}_1$ with $\langle \mathcal{A}x_1, x_2 \rangle_{\mathbb{H}_2} = \langle x_1, \mathcal{A}^* x_2 \rangle_{\mathbb{H}_1}$ for all $x_1 \in \mathbb{H}_1$, $x_2 \in \mathbb{H}_2$. A bounded operator $\mathcal{A} : \mathbb{H} \to \mathbb{H}$ on a Hilbert space $(\mathbb{H}, \langle \cdot, \cdot \rangle_{\mathbb{H}})$ is *self-adjoint* if $\mathcal{A} = \mathcal{A}^*$. For a self-adjoint operator, one has

$$\|\mathcal{A}\|_{\mathbb{H}} = \sup_{\substack{x \in \mathbb{H} \\ x \neq 0}} \left\{ \frac{|\langle \mathcal{A}x, x \rangle|}{\|x\|} \right\}.$$

A bounded operator $\mathcal{U}\colon \mathbb{H} \to \mathbb{H}$ is *unitary* if $\mathcal{U}^*\mathcal{U} = \mathcal{U}\mathcal{U}^* = \mathcal{I}$, where $\mathcal{I}\colon \mathbb{H} \to \mathbb{H}$ is the identity operator.

B.5 Orthogonality in Hilbert Spaces

Two elements f and g of a Hilbert space $(\mathbb{H}, \langle\cdot,\cdot\rangle_{\mathbb{H}})$ are *orthogonal* if $\langle f, g\rangle_{\mathbb{H}} = 0$. We write $f \perp g$. Two subspaces $F, G \subseteq \mathbb{H}$ are *orthogonal* if $f \perp g$ for all $f \in F$ and $g \in G$. If F and G are orthogonal, closed subspaces of $\mathbb{H}$, their *direct sum* is

$$F \oplus G = \{f + g : f \in F, g \in G\}.$$

The symbol $\oplus$ means that every $h \in F \oplus G$ has a unique decomposition as $h = f + g$ with $f \in F$ and $g \in G$.

If F is a subspace of $\mathbb{H}$, its *orthogonal complement* is

$$F^{\perp} = \{g \in H : f \perp g, \forall f \in F\}.$$

This set is always a closed subspace of $\mathbb{H}$. If F is also closed, then one has the direct sum $\mathbb{H} = F \oplus F^{\perp}$. If F is not closed, then $\mathbb{H} = \overline{F} \oplus F^{\perp}$, where $\overline{F}$ is the closure of F in H.

An *orthogonal projection* on a Hilbert space $(\mathbb{H}, \langle\cdot,\cdot\rangle)$ is a linear mapping $\mathcal{P}\colon \mathbb{H} \to \mathbb{H}$ satisfying $\mathcal{P}^* = \mathcal{P}$ and $\mathcal{P}^2 = \mathcal{P}$. The operator norm of a nonzero orthogonal projection satisfies $\|\mathcal{P}\|_{\mathbb{H}} = 1$. The range $\operatorname{Ran}(\mathcal{P}) = \{\mathcal{P}x : x \in \mathbb{H}\}$ of an orthogonal projection is closed, as is its null space $\operatorname{Ker}(\mathcal{P}) = \{x \in \mathbb{H} : \mathcal{P}x = 0\}$. They yield the orthogonal decomposition

$$\operatorname{Ran}(\mathcal{P}) \oplus \operatorname{Ker}(\mathcal{P}) = \mathbb{H}.$$

Conversely, for every closed subspace G of $\mathbb{H}$ there exists an orthogonal projection $\mathcal{P}$ with $\operatorname{Ran}(\mathcal{P}) = G$ and $\operatorname{Ker}(\mathcal{P}) = G^{\perp}$.

If $\mathcal{P}$ is an orthogonal projection then $\mathcal{P}^{\perp} = \mathcal{I} - \mathcal{P}$ is also an orthogonal projection, the *complementary projection*. It satisfies $\operatorname{Ran}(\mathcal{P}^{\perp}) = \operatorname{Ker}(\mathcal{P})$ and $\operatorname{Ker}(\mathcal{P}^{\perp}) = \operatorname{Ran}(\mathcal{P})$. Every $f \in \mathbb{H}$ can be expressed as $f = \mathcal{P}f + \mathcal{P}^{\perp}f$ and one has $\|\mathcal{P}f\|_{\mathbb{H}}^2 + \|\mathcal{P}^{\perp}f\|_{\mathbb{H}}^2 = \|f\|_{\mathbb{H}}^2$.

B.6 Orthonormal Bases of Hilbert Spaces

An *orthonormal system* in a Hilbert space is a collection $\{\phi_i\}_{i\in I} \subset \mathbb{H}$ for which $\langle \phi_i, \phi_j\rangle = \delta_{ij}$. An orthonormal system is an *orthonormal basis* if its linear span

$$\operatorname{span}(\{\phi_i\}_{i\in I}) = \left\{ \sum_{i\in J} x_i\phi_i : x_i \in \mathbb{C},\ J \subset I,\ |J| < \infty \right\}$$

is dense in $\mathbb{H}$. A Hilbert space is separable if and only if it has a countable orthonormal basis. The space $\ell^2(\mathbb{N})$ is separable. It has an orthonormal basis consisting of the sequences $\{e_i\}_{i\in\mathbb{N}}$, where

$$e_i = (\delta_{ij})_{j\in\mathbb{N}}, \quad i \in \mathbb{N}.$$

The basis $\{e_i\}_{i\in\mathbb{N}}$ is called the *canonical* (or *standard*) basis of $\ell^2(\mathbb{N})$. The space $L^2(D)$ is also separable.

Theorem B.3 *Let $\{\phi_i\}_{i\in\mathbb{N}}$ be an orthonormal system in a Hilbert space $\mathbb{H}$. Then the following are equivalent:*

(a) $\{\phi_i\}_{i\in\mathbb{N}}$ is an orthonormal basis;
(b) $f = \sum_{i\in\mathbb{N}}\langle f, \phi_i\rangle\phi_i$, $\forall f \in \mathbb{H}$;
(c) $\langle f, g\rangle = \sum_{i\in\mathbb{N}}\langle f, \phi_i\rangle\overline{\langle g, \phi_i\rangle}$, $\forall f, g \in \mathbb{H}$;
(d) $\sum_{i\in\mathbb{N}} |\langle f, \phi_i\rangle|^2 = \|f\|^2$, $\forall f \in \mathbb{H}$;
(e) If $\langle f, \phi_i\rangle = 0$, $\forall i \in \mathbb{N}$, then $f = 0$.

Property (b) states that every $f \in \mathbb{H}$ has a convergent expansion whose terms are given by the *coefficients* $\langle f, \phi_i\rangle$ of f in $\{\phi_i\}_{i\in\mathbb{N}}$. Property (d) is referred to as *Parseval's identity*. In particular, it implies that the sequence of coefficients $(\langle f, \phi_i\rangle)_{i\in\mathbb{N}}$ of any $f \in \mathbb{H}$ is an element of $\ell^2(\mathbb{N})$.

A consequence of Theorem B.3 is that the *analysis operator*

$$\mathcal{S}\colon \mathbb{H} \to \ell^2(\mathbb{N}), f \mapsto \{\langle f, \phi_i\rangle\}_{i\in\mathbb{N}}$$

of an orthonormal basis $\{\phi_i\}_{i\in\mathbb{N}}$ is an *isometric isomorphism*. That is to say, $\mathcal{S}$ is a bijective, norm-preserving map between $\mathbb{H}$ and $\ell^2(\mathbb{N})$. In particular, every separable, infinite-dimensional Hilbert space is isometrically isomorphic to $\ell^2(\mathbb{N})$. The inverse $\mathcal{T}$ of $\mathcal{S}$ is equal to its adjoint, $\mathcal{T} = \mathcal{S}^{-1} = \mathcal{S}^*$, and is given explicitly by

$$\mathcal{T} : \ell^2(\mathbb{N}) \to \mathbb{H}, x = (x_i)_{i\in\mathbb{N}} \mapsto \sum_{i\in\mathbb{N}} x_i\phi_i.$$

This is known as the *synthesis operator* of $\{\phi_i\}_{i\in\mathbb{N}}$.

Appendix C: Probability

C.1 Definition and Basic Properties

Definition C.1 (Probability space) A *probability space* $(\Omega, \Sigma, \mathbb{P})$ consists of three components:

1. A nonempty set Ω, known as the *sample space*.
2. A set of subsets Σ of Ω that forms a σ*-algebra*. That is,
   (i) $\Omega \in \Sigma$,
   (ii) if $E \in \Sigma$ then $E^c = \Omega \backslash E \in \Sigma$ (Σ is closed under complements),
   (iii) if $E_i \in \Sigma$, $i = 1, 2, \ldots$, then $E_1 \cup E_2 \cup \cdots \in \Sigma$ (Σ is closed under countable unions).
3. A mapping $\mathbb{P} \colon \Sigma \to [0, 1]$, referred to as a *probability measure*, that satisfies
   (i) $\mathbb{P}(\Omega) = 1$,
   (ii) if $E_i \in \Sigma$, $i = 1, 2, \ldots$ are *pairwise disjoint*, i.e. $E_i \cap E_j = \emptyset$ for $i \neq j$, then

$$\mathbb{P}\left(\bigcup_{i=1}^{\infty} E_i\right) = \sum_{i=1}^{\infty} \mathbb{P}(E_i).$$

The elements of Σ are called *events*. The *probability* of an event $E \in \Sigma$ is $\mathbb{P}(E)$, and is also denoted as

$$\mathbb{P}(E) = \int_E \mathrm{d}\mathbb{P}(\omega).$$

We say that an event E occurs *almost surely* if $\mathbb{P}(E) = 1$.

Several standard properties follow immediately from conditions 1–3:

(a) The empty set $\emptyset = \Omega^c$ is an element of Σ.
(b) Σ is closed under countable intersections.
(c) If $E \in \Sigma$ then $\mathbb{P}(E^c) = 1 - \mathbb{P}(E)$. In particular, $\mathbb{P}(\emptyset) = 0$.
(d) If $E_1, E_2 \in \Sigma$ then $\mathbb{P}(E_1) \leq \mathbb{P}(E_2)$ whenever $E_1 \subseteq E_2$, and in general,

$$\mathbb{P}(E_1 \cup E_2) = \mathbb{P}(E_1) + \mathbb{P}(E_2) - \mathbb{P}(E_1 \cap E_2).$$

It follows from (d) that $\mathbb{P}(E_1 \cup E_2) \leq \mathbb{P}(E_1) + \mathbb{P}(E_2)$ for all $E_1, E_2 \in \Sigma$. Applying this inequality repeatedly gives

$$E_1, \ldots, E_n \in \Sigma \quad \Rightarrow \quad \mathbb{P}(E_1 \cup \cdots \cup E_n) \leq \mathbb{P}(E_1) + \cdots + \mathbb{P}(E_n). \tag{C.1}$$

This is known as the *union bound*.

The *conditional probability* of an event E given an event F with $\mathbb{P}(F) \neq 0$ is

$$\mathbb{P}(E|F) = \frac{\mathbb{P}(E \cap F)}{\mathbb{P}(F)}.$$

Two events E and F are *independent* if $\mathbb{P}(E \cap F) = \mathbb{P}(E)\mathbb{P}(F)$. If $\mathbb{P}(F) \neq 0$, this is equivalent to $\mathbb{P}(E|F) = \mathbb{P}(E)$. For (not necessarily independent) events E and F with $\mathbb{P}(F) \neq 0$, *Bayes' rule* states that

$$\mathbb{P}(E|F) = \frac{\mathbb{P}(F|E)\mathbb{P}(E)}{\mathbb{P}(F)}.$$

In general, events $\{E_i : i \in I\}$ are independent if $\mathbb{P}\left(\cap_{j \in J} E_j\right) = \prod_{j \in J} \mathbb{P}(E_j)$ for every subset $J \subseteq I$.

Events $\{E_i : i \in I\}$ form a *partition* of Ω if they are pairwise disjoint and their union $\cup_{i \in I} E_i$ is equal to Ω. The *law of total probability* states that

$$\mathbb{P}(F) = \sum_{i \in I} \mathbb{P}(F|E_i)\mathbb{P}(E_i), \tag{C.2}$$

for every event F, whenever $\{E_i : i \in I\}$ is a partition.

C.2 Random Variables

Definition C.2 (Random variable) A (real-valued) *random variable* on a probability space $(\Omega, \Sigma, \mathbb{P})$ is a function $X \colon \Omega \to \mathbb{R}$ that is *measurable* on (Ω, Σ). That is, the preimage $X^{-1}(B) = \{\omega : X(\omega) \in B\} \in \Sigma$ for every Borel-measurable subset $B \subseteq \mathbb{R}$.

All functions encountered in this book are measurable. We are often concerned with the probability of the event $\{\omega : X(\omega) \in B\}$. We use the following shorthand notation:

$$\mathbb{P}(X \in B) = \mathbb{P}\left(\{\omega : X(\omega) \in B\}\right).$$

The *(cumulative) distribution function* $F_X \colon \mathbb{R} \to [0, 1]$ of a random variable X is

$$F_X(x) = \mathbb{P}(X \leq x), \quad x \in \mathbb{R},$$

where, similarly, $\mathbb{P}(X \leq x) = \mathbb{P}(\{\omega : X(\omega) \leq x\})$. A random variable is *absolutely continuous* if F_X can be expressed as

$$F_X(x) = \int_{-\infty}^{x} f_X(t)\, \mathrm{d}t,$$

for some nonnegative and integrable function f_X known as the *Probability Density Function (PDF)* of X. When it exists, this function has the property

$$\mathbb{P}(X \in B) = \int_B f_X(t)\, \mathrm{d}t,$$

for all Borel-measurable sets B.

If X is a random variable and $g \colon \mathbb{R} \to \mathbb{R}$ is a Borel-measurable function then $Y = g(X)$ is a random variable. Its distribution function is $F_Y(y) = \mathbb{P}(g(X) \leq y)$.

A random variable X follows the *normal (or Gaussian) distribution* $\mathcal{N}(\mu, \sigma^2)$ with *mean* $\mu \in \mathbb{R}$ and *variance* $\sigma^2 > 0$ if it has probability density function

$$f(t) = \frac{1}{\sqrt{2\pi\sigma^2}} \exp\left(-\frac{(t-\mu)^2}{2\sigma^2}\right).$$

The *standard* normal distribution is $\mathcal{N}(0, 1)$.

In general, if X has a distribution denoted by $\mathcal{D}$, then we write $X \sim \mathcal{D}$. In particular, $X \sim \mathcal{N}(\mu, \sigma^2)$ if X follows the normal distribution with mean μ and variance σ^2.

C.3 Joint Distributions and Independence

Let $X_1, \ldots, X_n$ be random variables on a common probability space $(\Omega, \Sigma, \mathbb{P})$. Their *joint distribution* is the function

$$F_{X_1,\ldots,X_n}(x_1, \ldots, x_n) = \mathbb{P}(X_1 \leq x_1, \ldots, X_n \leq x_n), \quad x_1, \ldots, x_n \in \mathbb{R}. \tag{C.3}$$

The random variables $X_1, \ldots, X_n$ have *joint probability density function* if $f_{X_1,\ldots,X_n}$ if

$$\mathbb{P}((X_1, \ldots, X_n) \in B) = \int_B f_{X_1,\ldots,X_n}(t_1, \ldots, t_n)\, \mathrm{d}t_1 \cdots \mathrm{d}t_n,$$

for every Borel-measurable set $B \subseteq \mathbb{R}^n$. The random variables $X_1, \ldots, X_n$ are *independent* if their joint distribution is the product of their individual distributions:

$$F_{X_1,\ldots,X_n}(x_1, \ldots, x_n) = \prod_{i=1}^{n} F_{X_i}(x_i).$$

The same also applies to the joint PDF, if it exists. If $X_1, \ldots, X_n$ are independent and have the same distribution function they are said to be *independent and identically distributed (i.i.d.)*.

A *random vector* is a vector of n random variables on a common probability space $(\Omega, \Sigma, \mathbb{P})$. A random matrix is defined in the same way. A complex random vector $Z = X + \mathrm{i}Y$ is equivalent to the real random vector $(X, Y) \in \mathbb{R}^{2n}$ and likewise for a complex random matrix. A collection $X^{(1)}, \ldots, X^{(m)}$ of random vectors or matrices is *independent* if

$$F_{X^{(1)},\ldots,X^{(m)}}(x^{(1)}, \ldots, x^{(m)}) = \prod_{i=1}^{m} F_{X^{(i)}}(x^{(i)}),$$

where $F_{X^{(i)}}(x^{(i)})$ is the distribution function of $X^{(i)}$. This, as in (C.3), is the joint distribution of its components.

C.4 Expectation and Variance

The *expectation* (or *mean*) of a random variable is

$$\mathbb{E}(X) = \int_\Omega X(\omega)\, \mathrm{d}\mathbb{P}(\omega).$$

If X and Y are random variables then

$$\mathbb{E}(aX + bY) = a\mathbb{E}(X) + b\mathbb{E}(Y), \qquad a, b \in \mathbb{R}.$$

Moreover, if X and Y are independent, then the random variable XY satisfies

$$\mathbb{E}(XY) = \mathbb{E}(X)\mathbb{E}(Y).$$

If X has PDF f_X and $g : \mathbb{R} \to \mathbb{R}$ is measurable then the random variable $Y = g(X)$ has expectation

$$\mathbb{E}(g(X)) = \int_\Omega f_X(x) g(x)\, \mathrm{d}x.$$

In particular, setting $g(x) = x^p$ for $p \in \mathbb{N}$ gives the *moments* $\mathbb{E}(X^p)$ of X, and setting $g(x) = |x|^p$ for $p > 0$ gives the *absolute moments* $\mathbb{E}(|X|^p)$ of X. Hölder's inequality for expectations states that

$$|\mathbb{E}(XY)| \le \mathbb{E}(|XY|) \le \left(\mathbb{E}(|X|^p)\right)^{1/p} \left(\mathbb{E}(|X|^q)\right)^{1/q}, \tag{C.4}$$

where $\frac{1}{p} + \frac{1}{q} = 1$. When $p = q = 2$ this is the Cauchy–Schwarz inequality for expectations.

If $X = (X_{ij})_{i,j=1}^{m,n}$ is a random matrix or vector, then its expectation is the matrix or vector $\mathbb{E}(X) = (\mathbb{E}(X_{ij}))_{i,j=1}^{m,n}$.

The *variance* of a random variable X is

$$\mathrm{Var}(X) = \mathbb{E}\left((X - \mathbb{E}(X))^2\right) = \mathbb{E}(X^2) - (\mathbb{E}(X))^2,$$

and its *standard deviation* is $\sqrt{\mathrm{Var}(X)}$. Observe that $\mathrm{Var}(aX) = a^2\mathrm{Var}(X)$, and if X and Y are independent, $\mathrm{Var}(X + Y) = \mathrm{Var}(X) + \mathrm{Var}(Y)$. If $X \sim \mathcal{N}(\mu, \sigma^2)$ is normally distributed, then $\mathbb{E}(X) = \mu$ and $\mathrm{Var}(X) = \sigma^2$.

Appendix D: Convex Analysis and Convex Optimization

In this appendix we present elements of convex analysis and convex optimization. For further information, see [53,55,56,90,191,414]. Throughout this appendix, $\mathbb{V}$ is a finite-dimensional vector space over the field $\mathbb{R}$ with an inner product $\langle \cdot, \cdot \rangle$ and corresponding norm $\|\cdot\|$ defined by $\|x\| = \sqrt{\langle x, x \rangle}$. Typically, $\mathbb{V} = \mathbb{R}^n$ with the Euclidean inner product.

D.1 Convex Sets and Convex Functions

A set $C \subseteq \mathbb{V}$ is *convex* if

$$x, y \in C,\ t \in [0,1] \quad \Rightarrow \quad tx + (1-t)y \in C.$$

An example of a convex set is $\{x \in \mathbb{R}^N : \|Ax - y\|_{\ell^2} \leq \eta\}$, where $A \in \mathbb{R}^{m \times N}$ and $y \in \mathbb{R}^m$. Notice that this is the feasible set for the QCBP problem (5.18).

In general, we work with extended-valued functions $f \colon \mathbb{V} \to [-\infty, \infty] := \mathbb{R} \cup \{\pm\infty\}$. The *epigraph* of f is the set

$$\mathrm{epi}(f) = \{(x,t) : f(x) \leq t,\ x \in \mathbb{V},\ t \in \mathbb{R}\},$$

and the *domain* of f is $\mathrm{dom}(f) = \{x \in \mathbb{V} : f(x) \neq +\infty\}$. An extended-valued function is called *proper* if it is nowhere equal to $-\infty$ and there exists an $x \in \mathbb{V}$ for which $f(x) < \infty$, i.e. $\mathrm{dom}(f)$ is nonempty.

An extended-valued function f is *convex* if its epigraph is a convex set. If f is proper, then it is convex if and only if $\mathrm{dom}(f)$ is convex and

$$f(tx + (1-t)y) \leq tf(x) + (1-t)f(y), \qquad \forall x, y \in \mathrm{dom}(f),\ 0 \leq t \leq 1. \tag{D.1}$$

If strict inequality holds for all $y \neq x$ and $0 < t < 1$, then f is *strictly convex*. Moreover, f is *strongly convex* if (D.1) is replaced by

$$\begin{aligned} f(tx + (1-t)y) \leq\, & tf(x) + (1-t)f(y) - \frac{\sigma}{2} t(1-t)\|x - y\|^2, \\ & \forall x, y \in \mathrm{dom}(f),\ 0 \leq t \leq 1, \end{aligned} \tag{D.2}$$

for some $\sigma > 0$. We call σ the strong convexity *parameter* of f. Notice that f is strongly convex if and only if the function $f(\cdot) - \frac{\sigma}{2}\|\cdot\|^2$ is convex.

We now list several elementary facts about convex functions:

(a) The function $f(x) = |||x|||$ is convex for any norm $|||\cdot|||$ on $\mathbb{V}$.

(b) If $f, g\colon \mathbb{V} \to \mathbb{R}$ are convex and $a, b \geq 0$, then $af + bg$ is also convex.
(c) If $f\colon \mathbb{R}^m \to \mathbb{R}$ is convex then so is the function $x \mapsto f(Ax + b)$, where $A \in \mathbb{R}^{m\times n}$ and $b \in \mathbb{R}^m$.
(d) If $f\colon \mathbb{V} \to \mathbb{R}$ is convex and $g\colon \mathbb{R} \to \mathbb{R}$ is convex and nondecreasing over the range of f, then the composition $x \mapsto g(f(x))$ is convex.

Properties (a)–(c) imply in particular that the function

$$f\colon \mathbb{R}^N \to \mathbb{R},\ x \mapsto \lambda\|x\|_{\ell^1} + \|Ax - y\|_{\ell^2}$$

is convex. The reader will recall that the minimization of this function is precisely the SR-LASSO problem (6.4). Moreover, the function $x \mapsto \|Ax - y\|^2_{\ell^2}$ is also convex, since $x \mapsto \|Ax - y\|_{\ell^2}$ is convex and the function $t \mapsto t^2$ is convex and nondecreasing on $[0, \infty)$. It now follows from (d) that the function

$$f\colon \mathbb{R}^N \to \mathbb{R},\ x \mapsto \lambda\|x\|_{\ell^1} + \|Ax - y\|^2_{\ell^2},$$

minimized in the U-LASSO problem (6.2) is convex as well.

It is useful to have a weaker notion of continuity for extended-valued functions. A function $f\colon \mathbb{V} \to [-\infty, \infty]$ is *lower semicontinuous* at $x \in \mathbb{V}$ if $f(x) \leq \liminf_{n\to\infty} f(x_n)$ for all sequences $\{x_n\} \subset \mathbb{V}$ for which $x_n \to x$ as $n \to \infty$. It is *lower semicontinuous* if it is lower semicontinuous at each point in $\mathbb{V}$. Note that a function is lower semicontinuous if and only if it is *closed*: that is, its epigraph $\mathrm{epi}(f)$ is a closed set.

Let $C \subseteq \mathbb{V}$. The *indicator function* $\delta_C\colon \mathbb{V} \to (-\infty, \infty]$ is defined by

$$\delta_C(x) = \begin{cases} 0 & x \in C \\ +\infty & \text{otherwise} \end{cases}. \tag{D.3}$$

Observe that $\mathrm{dom}(\delta_C) = C$. Furthermore, δ_C is lower semicontinuous if and only if C is closed and convex if and only if C is a convex set.

D.2 Subdifferentials

Let $f\colon \mathbb{V} \to (-\infty, \infty]$ be convex. A point $z \in \mathbb{C}$ is a *subgradient* of f at a point $x \in \mathbb{V}$ if

$$f(y) \geq f(x) + \langle z, y - x\rangle, \quad \forall y \in \mathbb{V}.$$

The *subdifferential* of f at $x \in \mathbb{V}$ is the set of subgradients at x:

$$\partial f(x) = \{z \in \mathbb{V} : f(y) \geq f(x) + \langle z, y - x\rangle,\ \forall y \in \mathbb{V}\}.$$

The subdifferential may be considered an extension of the gradient to nondifferentiable functions. If $f\colon \mathbb{R}^n \to \mathbb{R}$ is differentiable at x, then $\partial f(x) = \{\nabla f(x)\}$. We note also that if $f\colon \mathbb{V} \to \mathbb{R}$ then its subdifferential sets are always nonempty.

Consider the function $f\colon \mathbb{R} \to \mathbb{R}$, $x \mapsto |x|$. This function is differentiable everywhere except for $x = 0$, at which point its subdifferential is the interval $[-1, 1]$. Hence

$$\partial f(x) = \begin{cases} -1 & x < 0 \\ [-1, 1] & x = 0 \\ +1 & x > 0 \end{cases}.$$

Notice that $[-1, 1]$ is the unit ball in $\mathbb{R}$ with respect to $|\cdot|$. More generally, if $f : \mathbb{V} \to \mathbb{R}, x \mapsto |||x|||$, where $|||\cdot|||$ is a norm on $\mathbb{V}$, then

$$\partial f(0) = \{z : |||z|||' \le 1\} \subset \mathbb{V}$$

is the unit ball with respect to the dual norm $|||\cdot|||'$.

D.3 Convex Optimization

Let $f : \mathbb{V} \to (-\infty, \infty]$ be a proper, convex function. A *convex optimization problem* is a problem of the form

$$\min_{x \in \mathbb{V}} f(x). \tag{D.4}$$

Let $C \subseteq \mathbb{V}$ be a convex set. Then the problem

$$\min_{x \in C} f(x)$$

can easily be recast in the form (D.4) by replacing $f(x)$ by $f(x) + \delta_C(x)$, where δ_C is the indicator function of C, given by (D.3). Notice that the sets

$$\{z \in \mathbb{R}^N : Az = y\}, \qquad \{z \in \mathbb{R}^N : \|Az - y\| \le \eta\}$$

are convex. Hence BP (5.15) and QCBP (5.18) are both convex optimization problems. For instance, we may write the former as

$$\min_{x \in \mathbb{R}^N} \|x\|_{\ell^1} + \delta_{\{z : Az = y\}}(x).$$

Consider the general formulation (D.4). A *local minimizer* of f is a point $\hat{x} \in \mathbb{V}$ for which $f(x) \ge f(\hat{x})$ in some neighbourhood of $\hat{x}$. A *global minimizer* of f is a point $\hat{x} \in \mathbb{V}$ for which $f(x) \ge f(\hat{x})$ for all $x \in \mathbb{V}$. We denote the set of global minimizers using argmin, i.e.

$$\operatorname*{argmin}_{x \in \mathbb{V}} f(x) = \{\hat{x} \in \mathbb{V} : f(x) \ge f(\hat{x}), \forall x \in \mathbb{V}\}.$$

The problem (D.4) has the following four fundamental properties:

(a) Every local minimizer is a global minimizer.
(b) The set of minimizers is convex.
(c) If f is strictly convex then it has at most one minimizer.
(d) If f is lower semicontinuous and strongly convex with parameter $\sigma > 0$ then it has a unique minimizer $\hat{x} \in \mathbb{V}$. This satisfies $f(x) \ge f(\hat{x}) + \frac{\sigma}{2}\|x - \hat{x}\|^2$ for all $x \in \mathbb{V}$.

Property (a) states that local equals global for convex optimization, a feature that makes convex problems highly appealing and algorithmically tractable.

Fermat's optimality condition gives a characterization of minimizers of a convex optimization problem in terms of the subdifferential. It states that

$$\hat{x} \in \mathbb{V} \text{ is a minimizer of } f(x) \text{ over } \mathbb{V} \text{ if and only if } 0 \in \partial f(\hat{x}). \tag{D.5}$$

This generalizes the classical condition that the minimizers of a continuously differentiable, convex function $f\colon \mathbb{R}^n \to \mathbb{R}$ are precisely its *stationary points*, i.e. those for which $\nabla f(\hat{x}) = 0$.

Let $C \subseteq \mathbb{V}$ be a closed, nonempty and convex set and $y \in \mathbb{V}$. The function $x \mapsto \|x - y\|^2$ is strictly convex and the problem $\min_{x \in C} \|x - y\|^2$ has a unique minimizer. Therefore the mapping

$$\operatorname{proj}_C\colon \mathbb{V} \to C, \quad y \mapsto \operatorname*{argmin}_{x \in C} \|x - y\|^2 \tag{D.6}$$

is well defined. It is called the *projection onto C*.

If $C = \{x : \|x\|_{\ell^2} \leq 1\} \subset \mathbb{R}^n$ is the unit ℓ^2-ball then

$$\operatorname{proj}_C(x) = \min\left\{1, \frac{1}{\|x\|_{\ell^2}}\right\} x, \tag{D.7}$$

and if $C = \{x : \|x\|_{\ell^\infty} \leq 1\} \subset \mathbb{R}^n$ is the unit ℓ^∞-ball then

$$(\operatorname{proj}_C(x))_i = \begin{cases} x_i & |x_i| \leq 1 \\ \operatorname{sign}(x_i) & \text{otherwise} \end{cases}, \qquad i = 1, \ldots, n. \tag{D.8}$$

Both results follow straightforwardly from the definition (D.6).

D.4 The Convex Conjugate

Let $f\colon \mathbb{V} \to (-\infty, \infty]$ be proper. Its *convex conjugate* (also known as the *Fenchel conjugate* or *Legendre–Fenchel conjugate*) is the function

$$f^*(\xi) = \max_{x \in \mathbb{V}} \langle \xi, x \rangle - f(x), \quad \xi \in \mathbb{V}.$$

This function f^* is always convex and lower semicontinuous, regardless of whether or not f is. *Fenchel's inequality* states that

$$f(x) + f^*(\xi) \geq \langle \xi, x \rangle, \quad \forall x, \xi \in \mathbb{V}. \tag{D.9}$$

The *biconjugate* (also known as the *convex relaxation*) of f, denoted f^{**}, is the conjugate of f^*, i.e. $(f^*)^*$. In general, one has

$$f(x) \geq f^{**}(x), \quad \forall x \in \mathbb{V}.$$

In fact, f^{**} is the largest convex and lower semicontinuous function for which this holds. Hence, if f is convex and lower semicontinuous, then $f^{**} = f$.

Let $f(x) = |||x|||$, where $|||\cdot|||$ is a norm on $\mathbb{R}^n$. Then

$$f^*(\xi) = \delta_{B'}(\xi), \tag{D.10}$$

where $B' = \{\xi : |||\xi|||' \leq 1\}$ is the closed unit ball with respect to the dual norm $|||\cdot|||'$ of $|||\cdot|||$ and $\delta_{B'}$ is the indicator function of B', as in (D.3). To see this, write

$$f^*(\xi) = \max_{x \in \mathbb{V}} \langle \xi, x \rangle - |||x|||.$$

$f(x)$	$f^*(\xi)$
$\alpha g(x)$	$\alpha g^*(\xi/\alpha)$
$\alpha g(x/\alpha)$	$\alpha g^*(\xi)$
$g(x-z)$	$g^*(\xi)+\langle z,\xi\rangle$

Table D.1 Calculus rules for the convex conjugate. Here $\alpha > 0$ and $z \in \mathbb{V}$.

Suppose first that $|||\xi|||' > 1$. Then there exists an x such that $\langle x, \xi\rangle > |||x|||$. Hence

$$\langle \xi, tx\rangle - |||tx||| = t\left(\langle x, \xi\rangle - |||x|||\right).$$

Allowing $t \to +\infty$ gives that $f^*(\xi) = +\infty$ in this case. Conversely, if $|||\xi|||' \leq 1$ then $\langle \xi, x\rangle - |||x||| \leq |||\xi|||'|||x||| - |||x||| \leq 0$ for all x, with equality holding when $x = 0$. This gives $f^*(\xi) = 0$, as required.

When considering more complicated functions, it is useful to have various calculus rules for convex conjugates. Several such rules, all of which follow straightforwardly from the definition, are summarized in Table D.1.

The convex conjugate and subdifferential are related by the *Legendre–Fenchel identity*. Suppose that $f\colon \mathbb{V} \to (-\infty, \infty]$ is proper, convex and lower semicontinuous. Then this identity states that

$$x \in \partial f^*(\xi) \quad \Leftrightarrow \quad \xi \in \partial f(x) \quad \Leftrightarrow \quad f(x) + f^*(\xi) = \langle \xi, x\rangle. \tag{D.11}$$

Here, the first equivalence describes a sense in which ∂f and ∂f^* are inverses of each other. The second equivalence actually holds without the requirement that f be lower semicontinuous. It gives the conditions under which Fenchel's inequality (D.9) holds with equality.

To conclude this section, it is instructive to consider the convex relaxation (biconjugate) of the ℓ^0-norm (5.2). Recall that this is used in §5.4 to motivate ℓ^1-minimization problems for compressed sensing. First, let $f(x) = \|x\|_{\ell^0}$. Then

$$f^*(\xi) = \max_x \langle \xi, x\rangle - \|x\|_{\ell^0} = \delta_{\{0\}}(\xi)$$

is the indicator function of the set $\{0\}$. From this, using the definition of the convex conjugate once more, it follows that $f^{**}(x) = 0$. This is *not* the ℓ^1-norm. To view the ℓ^1-norm as a convex relaxation of the ℓ^0-norm, we need to consider its restriction to a suitable unit ball. Let

$$f(x) = \begin{cases} \|x\|_{\ell^0} & \|x\|_{\ell^\infty} \leq 1 \\ +\infty & \text{otherwise} \end{cases}.$$

Then

$$f^*(\xi) = \max_{\|x\|_{\ell^\infty}\leq 1} \langle \xi, x\rangle - \|x\|_{\ell^0} = \sum_i \max_{|x_i|\leq 1}\left(\xi_i x_i - \mathbb{I}_{\mathbb{R}\setminus\{0\}}(x_i)\right) = \sum_i \max\{|\xi_i| - 1, 0\},$$

and therefore

$$f^{**}(x) = \max_\xi \langle x, \xi\rangle - f^*(\xi) = \sum_i \max_{\xi_i}\left(x_i\xi_i - \max\{|\xi_i| - 1, 0\}\right).$$

The function $\xi \mapsto x\xi - \max\{|\xi| - 1, 0\}$ is piecewise linear with slope $x+1$ when $\xi < -1$, slope x when $-1 \leq \xi \leq 1$ and slope $x-1$ when $\xi > 1$. If $|x| \leq 1$ it has a finite maximum equal to $|x|$, and if $|x| > 1$ its maximum is $+\infty$. Therefore

$$f^{**}(x) = \begin{cases} \|x\|_{\ell^1} & \|x\|_{\ell^\infty} \leq 1 \\ +\infty & \text{otherwise} \end{cases}.$$

Thus, the biconjugate (convex relaxation) of f, the ℓ^0-norm restricted to the unit ℓ^∞-ball, is equal to the ℓ^1-norm restricted to the same ball.

D.5 The Proximal Map

The proximal map of a convex function is a natural extension of the projection proj_C onto a convex set. Let $f\colon \mathbb{V} \to (-\infty, \infty]$ be proper, convex and lower semicontinuous. Then the function

$$y \mapsto f(y) + \frac{1}{2}\|y - x\|^2$$

is proper, lower semicontinuous and strongly convex, and therefore has a unique minimizer over $\mathbb{V}$. The *proximal mapping* of f is defined as

$$\text{prox}_f(x) = \underset{y \in \mathbb{V}}{\text{argmin}} \left\{ f(y) + \frac{1}{2}\|y - x\|^2 \right\}, \qquad x \in \mathbb{V}. \tag{D.12}$$

Notice that if $f = \delta_C$ is the indicator function of a closed and convex set C, then

$$\text{prox}_f(x) = \underset{y \in C}{\text{argmin}} \frac{1}{2}\|y - x\|^2 = \text{proj}_C(x) \tag{D.13}$$

simply reduces to the projection onto C.

Consider the absolute value function $f\colon \mathbb{R} \to \mathbb{R}$, $x \mapsto \tau|x|$, where $\tau > 0$ is a parameter. It is a simple exercise to show that

$$\text{prox}_f(x) = \mathcal{S}_\tau(x) = \begin{cases} \text{sign}(x)(|x| - \tau) & |x| \geq \tau \\ 0 & |x| < \tau \end{cases}, \tag{D.14}$$

where $\mathcal{S}_\tau$ is the scalar soft thresholding operator (see Definition 7.4).

For calculating the proximal mapping of more complicated functions, it is useful to have some calculus rules. Several such rules are listed in Table D.2. The third rule allows one to derive the proximal map of the ℓ^1-norm. Specifically, by this formula and (D.14), we find that $\text{prox}_{\tau\|\cdot\|_{\ell^1}}(x) = (\mathcal{S}_\tau(x_i))_{i=1}^n$ for $x = (x_i)_{i=1}^n \in \mathbb{R}^n$. Hence

$$\text{prox}_{\tau\|\cdot\|_{\ell^1}} = \mathcal{S}_\tau \tag{D.15}$$

is the *vector* soft thresholding operator (see Definition 7.4).

The proximal mapping can also be characterized in terms of subdifferentials by applying Fermat's condition to the minimization problem (D.12). Specifically,

$$u = \text{prox}_f(x) \quad \Leftrightarrow \quad x \in u + \partial f(u). \tag{D.16}$$

$f(x)$	$\text{prox}_f(x)$
$g(\lambda x + a)$	$\lambda^{-1}(\text{prox}_{\lambda^2 g}(\lambda x + a) - a)$
$\lambda g(x/\lambda)$	$\lambda \text{prox}_{g/\lambda}(x/\lambda)$
$\sum_{i=1}^n g_i(x_i)$	$(\text{prox}_{g_i}(x_i))_{i=1}^n$

Table D.2 Calculus rules for the proximal map. Here $g : \mathbb{V} \to (-\infty, \infty]$ and $\lambda \neq 0$. In the third row, $\mathbb{V} = \mathbb{R}^n$, $g_i : \mathbb{R} \to \mathbb{R}$ for each i and $x = (x_i)_{i=1}^n$.

This result means one may write

$$\text{prox}_f = (I + \partial f)^{-1} \tag{D.17}$$

as the *resolvent* of the operator ∂f (note that, unlike ∂f, the resolvent is single-valued – it can be interpreted as a mapping from $\mathbb{V}$ to $\mathbb{V}$).

Consider the convex optimization problem (D.4). By Fermat's optimality condition (D.5), a point $\hat{x}$ is a minimizer if and only if $0 \in \partial f(\hat{x})$. Multiplying by $\tau > 0$ and adding $\hat{x}$ to both sides, this is equivalent to $\hat{x} \in \hat{x} + \tau \partial f(\hat{x})$. Hence, by (D.16), a point $\hat{x}$ is a minimizer of (D.4) if and only if it satisfies the *fixed-point* equation $\hat{x} = \text{prox}_{\tau f}(\hat{x})$:

$$\hat{x} \in \underset{x \in \mathbb{V}}{\text{argmin}} f(x) \quad \Leftrightarrow \quad \hat{x} = \text{prox}_{\tau f}(\hat{x}).$$

As elaborated upon in §7.4 and 7.5, this suggests a close connection between fixed-point iterations and proximal map-based algorithms for solving convex optimization problems.

Suppose now that $u = \text{prox}_f(x)$. Then $x - u \in \partial f(u)$ by (D.16) and therefore (D.11) gives $u \in \partial f^*(x - u)$, or equivalently $x \in (x - u) + \partial f^*(x - u)$. Hence, by (D.16) once more, $x - u = \text{prox}_{f^*}(x)$. We deduce *Moreau's identity*:

$$\text{prox}_f(x) + \text{prox}_{f^*}(x) = x, \quad \forall x \in \mathbb{V}.$$

In particular, this implies that prox_{f^*} can easily be calculated once prox_f has been calculated, or vice versa. Using Tables D.1 and D.2, one also has the following more general version of Moreau's identity:

$$\text{prox}_{\tau f}(x) + \tau \text{prox}_{\tau^{-1} f^*}(x/\tau) = x, \quad \forall x \in \mathbb{V},\ \tau > 0. \tag{D.18}$$

As an example, we now show how this identity can be used to give another proof of (D.15). Let $f(x) = \|x\|_{\ell^1}$. Then, as shown in (D.10), $f^*(\xi) = \delta_{B'}(\xi)$, where $B' = \{\xi : \|\xi\|_{\ell^\infty} \leq 1\}$ is the closed unit ℓ^∞-ball. Hence

$$\text{prox}_{\tau \|\cdot\|_{\ell^1}}(x) = x - \tau \text{prox}_{\tau^{-1} \delta_{B'}}(x/\tau).$$

We now apply (D.13) to get

$$\text{prox}_{\tau \|\cdot\|_{\ell^1}}(x) = x - \tau \text{proj}_{B'}(x/\tau).$$

Since B' is the unit ℓ^∞-ball, (D.8) gives

$$(\text{prox}_{\tau \|\cdot\|_{\ell^1}}(x))_i = x_i - \tau \begin{cases} x_i/\tau & |x_i| \leq \tau \\ \text{sign}(x_i) & \text{otherwise} \end{cases}, \qquad i = 1, \ldots, n.$$

Therefore, writing $x_i = \text{sign}(x_i)|x_i|$, we obtain

$$(\text{prox}_{\tau \|\cdot\|_{\ell^1}}(x))_i = \begin{cases} 0 & |x_i| \leq \tau \\ \text{sign}(x_i)(|x_i| - \tau) & \text{otherwise} \end{cases} = S_\tau(x_i), \qquad i = 1, \ldots, n,$$

as required.

Appendix E: Fourier Transforms and Series

E.1 The Fourier Transform

Let $d \geq 1$ and $x = (x_1, \ldots, x_d) \in \mathbb{R}^d$, $\omega = (\omega_1, \ldots, \omega_d) \in \mathbb{R}^d$ denote the spatial and frequency variables, respectively. The *Fourier transform* and *inverse Fourier transform* are the linear operators defined by

$$\mathcal{F}f(\omega) = \int_{\mathbb{R}^d} f(x)\mathrm{e}^{-\mathrm{i}\omega\cdot x}\,\mathrm{d}x, \qquad f \in L^1(\mathbb{R}^d),$$

and

$$\mathcal{F}^{-1}g(x) = \frac{1}{(2\pi)^d}\int_{\mathbb{R}^d} g(\omega)\mathrm{e}^{\mathrm{i}\omega\cdot x}\,\mathrm{d}\omega, \qquad g \in L^1(\mathbb{R}^d),$$

respectively. Here $\omega \cdot x = \omega_1 x_1 + \cdots + \omega_d x_d$. They are inverses of each other in the sense that

$$\mathcal{F}^{-1}(\mathcal{F}f) = \mathcal{F}(\mathcal{F}^{-1}f) = f, \qquad f, \mathcal{F}f, \mathcal{F}^{-1}f \in L^1(\mathbb{R}^d).$$

The Fourier transform preserves the L^2-inner product up to a constant. Specifically, *Plancherel's theorem* states that

$$\int_{\mathbb{R}^d} f(x)\overline{g(x)}\,\mathrm{d}x = (2\pi)^{-d}\int_{\mathbb{R}^d} \mathcal{F}f(\omega)\overline{\mathcal{F}g(\omega)}\,\mathrm{d}\omega, \tag{E.1}$$

for all $f, g \in L^1(\mathbb{R}^d) \cap L^2(\mathbb{R}^d)$. In particular,

$$\|f\|_{L^2} = (2\pi)^{-d/2}\|\mathcal{F}f\|_{L^2},$$

and therefore $\mathcal{F}f \in L^2(\mathbb{R}^d)$. An important consequence of this theorem is that the Fourier transform can be uniquely extended to a bounded linear operator $\mathcal{F} : L^2(\mathbb{R}^d) \to L^2(\mathbb{R}^d)$. This operator is unitary up to a constant: its inverse $\mathcal{F}^{-1}$ is equal to $(2\pi)^{-d}$ times its adjoint $\mathcal{F}^*$.

Several key properties of the one-dimensional Fourier transform are summarized in Table E.1. They are proved easily from its definition. All have straightforward analogues in $d \geq 1$ dimensions.

Table E.1 Properties of the one-dimensional Fourier transform. Here $a, b \in \mathbb{R}$, $b \neq 0$ are scalars and f, g are functions. The function $f^{(k)}$ is the kth derivative of f.

Function	$f(x)$	$\mathcal{F}g(x)$	$f(x-a)$	$\mathrm{e}^{\mathrm{i}ax}f(x)$
Fourier transform	$\mathcal{F}f(\omega)$	$2\pi g(-\omega)$	$\mathrm{e}^{-\mathrm{i}a\omega}\mathcal{F}f(\omega)$	$\mathcal{F}f(\omega-a)$
Function	$f(x/b)$	$f^{(k)}(x)$	$(-\mathrm{i}x)^k f(x)$	$\overline{f(t)}$
Fourier transform	$\lvert b\rvert\mathcal{F}f(b\omega)$	$(\mathrm{i}\omega)^k\mathcal{F}f(\omega)$	$(\mathcal{F}f)^{(k)}(\omega)$	$\overline{\mathcal{F}f(-\omega)}$

E.2 The Fourier Basis

A function $f\colon \mathbb{R} \to \mathbb{C}$ is *periodic* with *period* $T > 0$ if

$$f(x) = f(x+nT), \quad \forall x \in \mathbb{R}, n \in \mathbb{Z}.$$

A periodic function can be identified with a function on the one-dimensional torus $\mathbb{T} = \mathbb{R}/(T\mathbb{Z})$. Let $L^2(\mathbb{T})$ be the Hilbert space of square-integrable functions $f\colon \mathbb{T} \to \mathbb{C}$, equipped with the inner product

$$\langle f, g\rangle_{L^2} = \frac{1}{T}\int_{\mathbb{T}} f(x)\overline{g(x)}\,\mathrm{d}x.$$

The *Fourier basis* of $L^2(\mathbb{T})$ is the orthonormal basis

$$\{\upsilon_\omega\}_{\omega\in\mathbb{Z}}, \quad \upsilon_\omega(x) = \mathrm{e}^{2\pi\mathrm{i}\omega x/T}, \ x \in \mathbb{T}. \tag{E.2}$$

Similarly, if $\mathbb{T}^d = \mathbb{R}^d/(T\mathbb{Z})^d$ denotes the d-dimensional torus, the orthonormal Fourier basis of $L^2(\mathbb{T}^d)$ (equipped with the analogous inner product) is

$$\{\upsilon_\omega\}_{\omega\in\mathbb{Z}^d}, \quad \upsilon_\omega(x) = \mathrm{e}^{2\pi\mathrm{i}\omega\cdot x/T}, \ x = (x_1,\ldots,x_d) \in \mathbb{T}^d. \tag{E.3}$$

Let $f \in L^2(\mathbb{T}^d)$. Then f has the L^2-convergent *Fourier series* expansion

$$f = \sum_{\omega\in\mathbb{Z}^d} \langle f, \upsilon_\omega\rangle_{L^2}\upsilon_\omega. \tag{E.4}$$

The values $\langle f, \upsilon_\omega\rangle_{L^2}$ are the *Fourier coefficients* of f.

Fourier coefficients are directly related to samples of the Fourier transform at equispaced points. Indeed, every function $f \in L^2(\mathbb{T}^d)$ can be identified with a function $\tilde{f} \in L^2(\mathbb{R}^d)$ that is zero outside the unit cube $[0, 1]^d$. Then

$$\langle f, \upsilon_\omega\rangle_{L^2} = T^{-1}\mathcal{F}\tilde{f}(2\pi\omega). \tag{E.5}$$

For convenience, we usually do not worry about the distinction between f and $\tilde{f}$, and simply write $\mathcal{F}f$ instead of $\mathcal{F}\tilde{f}$ in (E.5).

A function f is a *trigonometric polynomial* if it has only finitely many nonzero Fourier coefficients. In one dimension, for example, a trigonometric polynomial takes the form

$$f(x) = \sum_{\omega=-N_1}^{N_2} d_\omega \mathrm{e}^{2\pi\mathrm{i}\omega x},$$

for $N_1, N_2 \in \mathbb{N}_0$, where $\{d_\omega\}_{\omega=-N_1}^{N_2}$ are its *coefficients*.

E.3 The Discrete Fourier Transform

Definition E.1 (Discrete Fourier transform) The one-dimensional *Discrete Fourier Transform (DFT)* of a vector $x \in \mathbb{C}^N$ is defined as

$$(\mathcal{F}(x))_i = \sum_{j=1}^{N} x_j \exp(-2\pi \mathrm{i}(i-1)(j-1)/N), \quad i = 1, \ldots, N.$$

Its inverse, the *Inverse Discrete Fourier Transform (IDFT)*, is

$$\left(\mathcal{F}^{-1}(y)\right)_i = \frac{1}{N} \sum_{j=1}^{N} y_j \exp(2\pi \mathrm{i}(i-1)(j-1)/N), \quad i = 1, \ldots, N.$$

The map $\mathcal{F} : \mathbb{C}^N \to \mathbb{C}^N$ satisfies

$$\mathcal{F}^{-1} = N^{-1}\mathcal{F}^*,$$

where $\mathcal{F}^*$ is the adjoint of $\mathcal{F}$. In particular, $\mathcal{F}$ is a unitary map of $\mathbb{C}^N$ up to a constant, with $\|\mathcal{F}(x)\|_{\ell^2} = \sqrt{N}\|x\|_{\ell^2}$.

DFTs are instrumental in many computations in the modern world. This stems from the fact that the operations $x \mapsto \mathcal{F}(x)$ and $y \mapsto \mathcal{F}^{-1}(y)$ can be computed efficiently. This is done via the famous *Fast Fourier Transform (FFT)* algorithm, and requires only $O(N\log(N))$ arithmetic operations. This translates into significantly less computational time than matrix–vector multiplication in the general case, which involves $O(N^2)$ arithmetic operations.

Appendix F: Properties of Walsh Functions and the Walsh Transform

In this final appendix, we describe several properties of Walsh functions that were mentioned in Chapter 2. Since many of these results are less standard, unlike in other appendices we now give proofs of most results. For in-depth overviews of Walsh functions, see [54, 224, 232].

F.1 Sign Changes

We first describe the sign pattern of the Paley-ordered Walsh functions introduced in Definition 2.6. Define the dyadic intervals

$$I_k^j = [k/2^j, (k+1)/2^j), \quad k = 0, \ldots, 2^j - 1, \; j = 0, 1, 2, \ldots. \tag{F.1}$$

Note that the intervals $\{I_k^j\}_{k=0}^{2^j-1}$ form a partition of $[0, 1)$ for each fixed j.

Lemma F.1 *Let $n \in \mathbb{N}$ and $j \in \mathbb{N}_0$ be such that $2^j \leq n < 2^{j+1}$. The Paley-ordered Walsh function υ_n^P is constant on each interval I_k^{j+1} and takes value $+1$ on I_0^{j+1}. Moreover, for every two consecutive intervals I_{2k}^{j+1} and I_{2k+1}^{j+1} it takes value $+1$ on precisely one of them, and -1 on the other.*

Proof The integer n has a binary expansion of the form (2.22), where $n_{j+1} = 1$, $n_i \in \{0, 1\}$ for $i = 1, \ldots, j$ and $n_i = 0$ otherwise. Notice that the first $j + 1$ binary digits $x_1, \ldots, x_{j+1}$ of every $x \in I_k^{j+1}$ are fixed. The first result now follows immediately from the definition (2.23). For the second, observe that $x_{j+1} = 0$ if $x \in I_{2k}^{j+1}$ and $x_{j+1} = 1$ if $x \in I_{2k+1}^{j+1}$. Since $n_{j+1} = 1$ we obtain the result. □

This result is demonstrated in Fig. 2.4, which plots the first 16 Walsh functions.

F.2 Binary Addition, Translation and Scaling

We now present several further properties of Walsh functions. We first define an addition operation $\oplus$ on $\{0, 1\}^{\mathbb{N}}$. Given $\dot{x} = (x_i)_{i \in \mathbb{N}}$ and $\dot{y} = (y_i)_{i \in \mathbb{N}}$ in $\{0, 1\}^{\mathbb{N}}$, let

$$\dot{x} \oplus \dot{y} = (|x_i - y_i|)_{i \in \mathbb{N}} \in \{0, 1\}^{\mathbb{N}}.$$

The quantity $|x_i - y_i|$ is precisely the XOR (eXclusive OR) of the binary numbers x_i and y_i, equal to zero if $x_i = y_i$ and one if $x_i \neq y_i$. The operation $\oplus$ makes $\{0, 1\}^{\mathbb{N}}$ into a commutative group.

Recall the subset $G \subset \{0, 1\}^{\mathbb{N}}$ and the bijection $g\colon [0, 1) \to G$ introduced in §2.4.1. We use $\oplus$ to define an addition operation on $[0, 1)$ in the obvious way: namely,

$$x \oplus y = g^{-1}(g(x) \oplus g(y)).$$

Note that this operation is not necessarily defined for all x and y, since G is not a subgroup of $(\{0, 1\}^{\mathbb{N}}, \oplus)$. For example, adding $(1, 0, 1, 0, 1, \ldots)$ and $(0, 1, 0, 1, 0, \ldots)$ gives the sequence $(1, 1, 1, 1, 1, \ldots) \notin G$. Fortunately, one has the following:

Lemma F.2 *For fixed $y \in [0, 1)$, the sum $x \oplus y$ is defined for all but at most countably many points $x \in [0, 1)$. If y is a dyadic rational, then $x \oplus y$ is defined for all $x \in [0, 1)$.*

See the Notes section for details. We can also define $n \oplus m$ for $n, m \in \mathbb{N}$ in the obvious way, using the binary expansions of n and m. Here the operation is defined for all $n, m \in \mathbb{N}$, since the set H introduced in §2.4.1 forms a subgroup of $(\{0, 1\}^{\mathbb{N}}, \oplus)$.

With this in hand, we can now establish several further properties of the Walsh functions. Note that these are analogous to standard properties of the Fourier basis.

Lemma F.3 *Let $n, m, k \in \mathbb{N}_0$ and $x, y \in [0, 1)$. Then*

$$\begin{aligned} \upsilon_n(x \oplus y) &= \upsilon_n(x)\upsilon_n(y) \text{ whenever } x \oplus y \text{ is defined,} \\ \upsilon_n(x)\upsilon_m(x) &= \upsilon_{n \oplus m}(x), \\ \upsilon_n(2^{-k}x) &= \upsilon_{\lfloor n/2^k \rfloor}(x). \end{aligned}$$

Proof Suppose that $x \oplus y$ is defined. Then

$$\upsilon_n(x \oplus y) = (-1)^{\sum_{i=1}^{\infty} n_i |x_i - y_i|} = (-1)^{\sum_{i=1}^{\infty} n_i (x_i + y_i)} = \upsilon_n(x)\upsilon_n(y),$$

which gives the first result. The second result follows similarly. For the third, we have

$$\upsilon_n(2^{-k}x) = (-1)^{\sum_{i=1}^{k} 0 \cdot n_i + \sum_{i=k+1}^{\infty} n_i x_{i-k}} = (-1)^{\sum_{i=1}^{\infty} n_{k+i} x_i} = \upsilon_{\lfloor n/2^k \rfloor}(x),$$

as required. □

The following lemma demonstrates that the Walsh transform (2.24) has a translational property similar to that of the Fourier transform (see Table E.1):

Lemma F.4 *Let $z \in [0, 1)$, $f \in L^2([0, 1))$ and define $f_z(x) = f(x \oplus z)$. Then $f_z \in L^2([0, 1))$ and*

$$\mathcal{H} f_z(i) = \upsilon_i(z)\mathcal{H} f(i), \quad i = 0, 1, 2, \ldots .$$

Proof It can be shown that the Lebesgue integral is translation invariant with respect to $\oplus$, i.e.

$$\int_0^1 f(t \oplus x)\, \mathrm{d}t = \int_0^1 f(t)\, \mathrm{d}t, \tag{F.2}$$

for every Lebesgue integrable function f (see the Notes section). Note that $f(t \oplus x)$ is defined almost everywhere, due to Lemma F.2. Now consider $\mathcal{H} f_z(i)$. Since $(t \oplus z) \oplus z = t$, this property and Lemma F.3 give

$$\mathcal{H} f_z(i) = \int_0^1 f(t \oplus z) \upsilon_i(t) \, \mathrm{d}t = \int_0^1 f(t) \upsilon_i(t \oplus z) \, \mathrm{d}t = \upsilon_i(z) \int_0^1 f(t) \upsilon_i(t) \, \mathrm{d}t,$$

as required. □

F.3 Orthonormality and Relation to Haar Wavelets

We now show that the Walsh functions $\{\upsilon_n\}_{n \in \mathbb{N}_0}$ form an orthonormal basis of $L^2([0,1))$. We first show that they are orthonormal.

Lemma F.5 (Orthonormality of Walsh functions) *For $n, m \in \mathbb{N}_0$, the Walsh functions satisfy*

$$\int_0^1 \upsilon_n(x) \upsilon_m(x) \, \mathrm{d}x = \delta_{nm}.$$

Proof The integrand is equal to $\upsilon_{n \oplus m}(x)$ (Lemma F.3). Suppose first that $m \neq n$ and write $l = n \oplus m \geq 1$. Let $j \in \mathbb{N}_0$ be such that $2^j \leq l < 2^{j+1}$. Then

$$\int_0^1 \upsilon_l(x) \, \mathrm{d}x = \sum_{k=0}^{2^j - 1} \int_{I_k^j} \upsilon_l(x) \, \mathrm{d}x,$$

where the I_k^j are as in (F.1). Observe that $I_k^j = I_{2k}^{j+1} \cup I_{2k+1}^{j+1}$. Also, from Lemma F.1 we have that υ_l is equal to $+1$ on one of these intervals and -1 on the other. Hence

$$\int_{I_k^j} \upsilon_l(x) \, \mathrm{d}x = 0,$$

and therefore $\int_0^1 \upsilon_l(x) \, \mathrm{d}x = 0$, as required. On the other hand, when $m = n$ we simply have $\upsilon_{n \oplus n}(x) = \upsilon_0(x) \equiv 1$. This completes the proof. □

We now show the Walsh functions form a basis. To do this, we first derive the following relationship between the Walsh functions and Haar wavelets (Example 9.2):

Lemma F.6 (Walsh functions and Haar wavelets) *Let $\{\upsilon_n\}_{n \in \mathbb{N}_0}$ denote the Paley-ordered Walsh functions and $\{\varphi\} \cup \{\psi_{j,n} : n = 0, \ldots, 2^j - 1, \ j = 0, 1, 2 \ldots\}$ denote the orthonormal Haar wavelet basis of $L^2([0,1))$. Then $\upsilon_0 = \varphi$ and, for $j = 0, 1, 2, \ldots$,*

$$\mathrm{span}\{\upsilon_{2^j + n} : n = 0, \ldots, 2^j - 1\} = \mathrm{span}\{\psi_{j,n} : n = 0, \ldots, 2^j - 1\} = W_j^{\mathrm{per}}, \tag{F.3}$$

where $W_j^{\mathrm{per}} \subset L^2([0,1))$ is the jth wavelet space corresponding to the Haar wavelet on $[0,1)$. Moreover, one has

$$\upsilon_{2^j + m} = 2^{-j/2} \sum_{n=0}^{2^j - 1} \upsilon_n(m/2^j) \psi_{j,n}, \quad m = 0, \ldots, 2^j - 1, \ j = 0, 1, 2, \ldots, \tag{F.4}$$

and

$$\psi_{j,m} = 2^{-j/2} \sum_{n=0}^{2^j-1} \upsilon_n(m/2^j)\upsilon_{2^j+n}, \quad m = 0, \ldots, 2^j - 1, \; j = 0, 1, 2, \ldots. \tag{F.5}$$

Proof Both υ_0 and φ are constant functions with unit L^2-norm on $[0, 1)$. Hence $\upsilon_0 = \varphi$, which gives the first part of the result. Clearly (F.3) follows immediately from (F.4) and (F.5). Hence we now show these relations.

Consider υ_{2^j+m}, where $j \geq 0$ and $m = 0, \ldots, 2^j - 1$. Lemma F.1 implies that this function is uniquely defined by the values it takes on the intervals I_k^{j+1}, $k = 0, \ldots, 2^j - 1$. We also notice that $\psi_{j,n}$ can be written as

$$\psi_{j,n}(x) = \begin{cases} 2^{j/2} & x \in I_{2n}^{j+1} \\ -2^{j/2} & x \in I_{2n+1}^{j+1} \\ 0 & \text{otherwise} \end{cases}.$$

Let $x \in I_{2k+e}^{j+1}$, where $e \in \{0, 1\}$ and $k = 0, \ldots, 2^j - 1$. Then

$$2^{-j/2} \sum_{n=0}^{2^j-1} \upsilon_n(m/2^j)\psi_{j,n}(x) = (-1)^e \upsilon_k(m/2^j).$$

To derive (F.4), it suffices to show that this is equal to $\upsilon_{2^j+m}(x)$. Write k and m in their binary expansions (2.22) as $k = \sum_{i=1}^{j} k_i 2^{i-1}$ and $m = \sum_{i=1}^{j} m_i 2^{i-1}$. Observe that

$$\frac{m}{2^j} = \sum_{i=1}^{j} m_i 2^{i-j-1} = \sum_{i=1}^{j} m_{j+1-i} 2^{-i}.$$

Hence

$$(-1)^e \upsilon_k(m/2^j) = (-1)^{e+\sum_{i=1}^{j} k_i m_{j+1-i}} = (-1)^{e+\sum_{i=1}^{j} k_{j+1-i} m_i}. \tag{F.6}$$

On the other hand, if $x \in I_{2k+e}^{j+1}$ then $\upsilon_{2^j+m}(x) = \upsilon_{2^j+m}((2k + e)/2^{j+1})$. Since

$$\frac{2k + e}{2^{j+1}} = \sum_{i=1}^{j} k_i 2^{i-j-1} + \frac{e}{2^{j+1}} = \sum_{i=1}^{j} k_{j+1-i} 2^{-i} + \frac{e}{2^{j+1}},$$

and $2^j + m = \sum_{i=1}^{j} m_i 2^{i-1} + 2^j$, we have

$$\upsilon_{2^j+m}(x) = \upsilon_{2^j+m}((2k + e)/2^{j+1}) = (-1)^{e+\sum_{i=1}^{j} k_{j+1-i} m_i}.$$

This is equal to the right-hand side of (F.6), and therefore $(-1)^e \upsilon_k(m/2^j) = \upsilon_{2^j+m}(x)$, as required.

Now consider (F.5). Let H denote the $2^j \times 2^j$ Paley-ordered Hadamard matrix (Definition 2.8). Then (F.4) is equivalent to

$$\upsilon_{2^j+n} = 2^{-j/2} \sum_{l=0}^{2^j-1} H_{l+1,n+1} \psi_{j,l}.$$

Hence

$$\sum_{n=0}^{2^j-1} \upsilon_n(m/2^j)\upsilon_{2^j+n} = 2^{-j/2} \sum_{n=0}^{2^j-1} \sum_{l=0}^{2^j-1} H_{l+1,n+1} H_{n+1,m+1} \psi_{j,l} = 2^{-j/2} \sum_{l=0}^{2^j-1} (H^2)_{l+1,m+1} \psi_{j,l}.$$

However, H is symmetric and satisfies $H^2 = H^\top H = 2^j I$ (Proposition F.10). Using this we immediately deduce (F.5). □

We now state the main result:

Theorem F.7 *The Walsh functions $\{\upsilon_n\}_{n\in\mathbb{N}_0}$ form an orthonormal basis of $L^2([0,1))$.*

Proof The Walsh functions are orthonormal (Lemma F.5), and Lemma F.6 implies that the first 2^j Walsh functions span the same space as the first 2^j Haar wavelet functions. Since Haar wavelets form a basis of $L^2([0,1))$, we immediately deduce the result. □

F.4 The Paley and Sequency Orderings

The next result describes the relationship between the Paley-ordered Walsh functions and sequency-ordered Walsh functions introduced in Definition 2.7:

Lemma F.8 *Let υ_n^P and υ_n^S denote the Paley- and sequency-ordered Walsh functions, respectively. Then*

$$\upsilon_n^S = \upsilon_{h(n)}^P, \quad n \in \mathbb{N}_0,$$

where $h(n) = n \oplus \lfloor n/2 \rfloor \in \mathbb{N}_0$.

Proof Let n have the binary expansion $(n_i)_{i=1}^\infty$. Then $\lfloor n/2 \rfloor$ has the binary expansion $(n_{i+1})_{i=1}^\infty$. Hence $h(n)$ has the binary expansion $(|n_i - n_{i+1}|)_{i=1}^\infty$. The result now follows immediately from the definitions of υ_n^S and υ_n^P. □

The quantity $h(n)$ is known as the *Gray code* of $n \in \mathbb{N}_0$. The Gray code is an alternative way to represent $\mathbb{N}_0$ using binary expansions. In this code, every two consecutive integers have binary expansions which differ by precisely one binary digit. For example, the numbers 4, 5 and 6 have the binary expansions 100, 101 and 110, respectively. However, in the Gray code, they are represented as 110, 111 and 101.

Lemma F.9 *The mapping $h: \mathbb{N}_0 \to \mathbb{N}_0$ is a bijection. Moreover, for every $j = 0, 1, 2, \ldots$,*

$$h(\{2^j, \ldots, 2^{j+1}-1\}) = \{2^j, \ldots, 2^{j+1}-1\}. \tag{F.7}$$

Proof We prove that h is injective and that (F.7) holds, which in turn implies surjectivity and therefore bijectivity. Suppose first that $h(n) = h(m)$ for $n, m \in \mathbb{N}_0$ and write $(n_i)_{i=1}^\infty$ and $(m_i)_{i=1}^\infty$ for their binary expansions. Then $|n_i - n_{i+1}| = |m_i - m_{i+1}|$ for all $i = 1, 2, \ldots$. Let j be such that $n_i = m_i = 0$ for $i > j$. Hence $|n_j| = |m_j|$, which implies that $n_j = m_j$, $|n_{j-1} - n_j| = |m_{j-1} - m_j|$, which implies that $n_{j-1} = m_{j-1}$ and so forth. We deduce that $n_i = m_i$ for $i = 1, \ldots, j$, and therefore $n = m$. Hence h is injective.

We now show (F.7). Let $2^j \leq n < 2^{j+1}$. Then n has binary expansion $(n_i)_{i=1}^{\infty}$, where $n_{j+1} = 1$, $n_i \in \{0, 1\}$ for $i = 1, \ldots, j$ and $n_i = 0$ otherwise. Hence $h(n)$ has binary expansion $\left(|n_1 - n_2|, \ldots, |n_j - 1|, 1, 0, 0, \ldots\right)$ and therefore $2^j \leq h(n) < 2^{j+1}$. The result now follows from the injectivity of h. □

Note that the relation (2.26) follows immediately from these two lemmas.

F.5 Properties of the Hadamard Matrix

We now present some properties of the (Paley- or sequency-ordered) Hadamard matrix (Definition 2.8).

Proposition F.10 *Let $N = 2^r$ and H be the Paley- or sequency-ordered Hadamard matrix of size $N \times N$. Then H is real and symmetric and satisfies*

$$N^{-1} H^\top H = I.$$

Proof Since the sequency-ordered Hadamard matrix is a row permutation (according to the Gray code) of the Paley-ordered Hadamard matrix, we need only consider one. Let H be the Paley-ordered Hadamard matrix. The Walsh functions are real-valued, hence so is H. Now let $0 \leq n, m < 2^r$ and write $n = \sum_{i=1}^{r} n_i 2^{i-1}$ and $m = \sum_{i=1}^{r} m_i 2^{i-1}$. Since $n/2^r$ has the binary expansion $n/2^r = \sum_{i=1}^{r} n_i 2^{i-r-1} = \sum_{j=1}^{r} n_{r+1-j} 2^{-j}$ we have

$$\upsilon_m(n/2^r) = (-1)^{\sum_{i=1}^{r} m_i n_{r+1-i}}.$$

Similarly, $m/2^r = \sum_{j=1}^{r} m_{r+1-j} 2^{-j}$, and therefore

$$\upsilon_n(m/2^r) = (-1)^{\sum_{i=1}^{r} n_i m_{r+1-i}}.$$

Since $\sum_{i=1}^{r} m_i n_{r+1-i} = \sum_{i=1}^{r} n_i m_{r+1-i}$ we deduce that $\upsilon_m(n/2^r) = \upsilon_n(m/2^r)$. Therefore H is symmetric. Now let $0 \leq m, n < 2^r$. By Lemmas F.1 and F.5,

$$\begin{aligned}\left(H^\top H\right)_{m+1,n+1} &= \sum_{k=0}^{2^r-1} \upsilon_m(k/2^r)\upsilon_n(k/2^r) = 2^r \sum_{k=0}^{2^r-1} \int_{I_k^r} \upsilon_m(x)\upsilon_n(x)\,\mathrm{d}x \\ &= 2^r \int_0^1 \upsilon_m(x)\upsilon_n(x)\,\mathrm{d}x = 2^r \delta_{nm}.\end{aligned}$$

This gives the result. □

The second result considers the relation between the Paley-ordered Hadamard matrix and the ordinary Hadamard matrix (Definition 2.9):

Proposition F.11 *Let $N = 2^r$. Then the ordinary and Paley-ordered Hadamard matrices have the same rows. Specifically, for $m = 0, \ldots, r-1$ the $(m+1)$th row of the ordinary Hadamard matrix is the $(b(m)+1)$th row of the Paley-ordered Hadamard matrix, where b is the bit-reversal permutation*

$$b \colon \{0, \ldots, 2^r - 1\} \to \{0, \ldots, 2^r - 1\},\ n = \sum_{i=1}^{r} n_i 2^{i-1} \mapsto b(n) = \sum_{i=1}^{r} n_{r+1-i} 2^{i-1}.$$

Proof Let H be the ordinary Hadamard matrix. It is straightforward to see that its entries are

$$H_{m+1,n+1} = (-1)^{\sum_{i=1}^{r} n_i m_i}, \qquad m, n = 0, \ldots, 2^r - 1, \tag{F.8}$$

where $n = \sum_{i=1}^{r} n_i 2^{i-1}$ and $m = \sum_{i=1}^{r} m_i 2^{i-1}$ are the binary expansions of n and m, respectively. By this and the definition of the Paley-ordered Walsh function, we have

$$H_{m+1,n+1} = \upsilon_n \left(\sum_{i=1}^{r} m_i 2^{-i} \right) = \upsilon_n \left(\frac{\sum_{i=1}^{r} m_{r+1-i} 2^{i-1}}{2^r} \right) = \upsilon_n \left(\frac{b(m)}{2^r} \right).$$

The right-hand side is the $(b(m) + 1, n + 1)$th entry of the Paley-ordered Hadamard matrix. This gives the result. □

F.6 The Fast Walsh–Hadamard Transform

Finally, we discuss the DHT (see §2.4.4) and its associated fast transform. First, we observe that matrix–vector multiplications with the ordinary Hadamard matrix can be computed efficiently in $\mathcal{O}(N \log(N))$ arithmetic operations. This is realized by a divide-and-conquer approach. Let $x \in \mathbb{C}^N$ and write

$$x = \begin{pmatrix} x^{(1)} \\ x^{(2)} \end{pmatrix}, \qquad x^{(1)}, x^{(2)} \in \mathbb{C}^{N/2}.$$

Then the operation

$$x \mapsto H_r x = \begin{pmatrix} H_{r-1} x^{(1)} + H_{r-1} x^{(2)} \\ H_{r-1} x^{(1)} - H_{r-1} x^{(2)} \end{pmatrix}$$

can be evaluated by two matrix–vector multiplications with the Hadamard matrix H_{r-1} of size $N/2$, followed by a vector addition and subtraction. Applying this formula recursively leads to an $\mathcal{O}(N \log(N))$ algorithm for computing $H_r x$. Note that this divide-and-conquer procedure is similar to, and in fact rather simpler than, the one that underlies the FFT.

Due to Proposition F.11, we see that matrix–vector multiplications with either the Paley- or sequency-ordered Hadamard matrix can also be performed in $\mathcal{O}(N \log(N))$ time, since these matrices are just row permutations of the ordinary Hadamard matrix. As mentioned in §2.4.4, we refer to this process as the Fast Walsh–Hadamard Transform (FHT).

Notes

Lemma F.2 is based on [232, 1.2.1]. The observation (F.2) that the Lebesgue integral is translation invariant with respect to $\oplus$ can be found in [232, pp. 35–36].

Notation

Sets and spaces

$\mathbb{Z}, \mathbb{N}_0, \mathbb{N}$	Integers, nonnegative integers or positive integers
$\mathbb{R}, \mathbb{C}$	Real or complex numbers
$\mathbb{R}^n, \mathbb{C}^n$	Vector space of real or complex vectors of length n
$\mathbb{R}^{m\times n}, \mathbb{C}^{m\times n}$	Vector space of real or complex $m \times n$ matrices
$\{e_i\}_{i=1}^n$	Canonical basis of $\mathbb{R}^n$ or $\mathbb{C}^n$
$\langle \cdot, \cdot \rangle$	Typically, the Euclidean inner product on $\mathbb{R}^n$ or $\mathbb{C}^n$

Numbers, vectors and matrices

$\mathrm{Re}\,(z), \mathrm{Im}\,(z)$	Real and imaginary parts of a complex number z
$\overline{z}$	Complex conjugate of a complex number z
$\mathrm{sign}(z)$	Sign of number $z \in \mathbb{C}$ or vector $z \in \mathbb{C}^n$
$A^\top, A^*$	Transpose and adjoint of a matrix A
$\mathrm{Ran}(A), \mathrm{Ker}(A)$	Range and null space of a matrix A
$A^{-1}, A^\dagger$	Inverse and pseudoinverse of a matrix A
$A \otimes B$	Kronecker product of matrices A and B

Norms

$\|\cdot\|$	Generic norm
$\|x\|_{\ell^p}$	ℓ^p-norm of a vector x
$\|A\|_{\ell^p}$	Induced ℓ^p-norm of a matrix A
$\|A\|_{\ell^{p,q}}$	$\ell^{p,q}$-norm of a matrix A
$\|\cdot\|_{TV}$	TV semi-norm

Function spaces

$(\mathbb{M}, d)$	Metric space with metric d
$(\mathbb{H}, \langle \cdot, \cdot \rangle_{\mathbb{H}})$	Hilbert space with inner product $\langle \cdot, \cdot \rangle_{\mathbb{H}}$
$\ell^p(\mathbb{N}), \|\cdot\|_{\ell^p}$	Space of ℓ^p-summable sequences and its norm
$L^p(D), \|\cdot\|_{L^p}$	L^p-space over a domain D and its norm
$\langle \cdot, \cdot \rangle_{L^2}$	L^2-inner product on $L^2(D)$

$C^\alpha([a,b])$, $\|\cdot\|_{C^\alpha}$	Space of α-Hölder continuous functions on $[a,b]$ and its norm
$V(f)$, $V(f;[a,b])$	Total variation of a function f on $[ab]$
$BV([a,b])$	Space of functions of bounded variation on $[a,b]$

Transforms

$\mathcal{F}$	Continuous or discrete Fourier transform
$\mathcal{H}$	Continuous Walsh transform or discrete Walsh–Hadamard transform
Ω	Finite set of frequencies sampled
F	Fourier matrix
H	Hadamard matrix
Φ	Sparsifying transform
$\{\phi_j\}_{j=1}^M$	Sparsity basis, the columns of Φ
∇	Discrete gradient operator

Discrete reconstruction problem

X	Discrete image to be recovered
x	Vector to be recovered
N	Resolution of the discrete image to be recovered
m	Number of measurements
A	Measurement matrix
e	Measurement noise
y	Measurements, i.e. $y = Ax + e$
R	Reconstruction map, $\mathbb{C}^m \rightrightarrows \mathbb{C}^N$
$\hat{x}$	Reconstruction of x

Sets and projections

Δ^c	Complement of a set Δ
P_Δ	Orthogonal projection with range $\mathrm{span}\{e_i : i \in \Delta\}$
$P_\Delta^\perp$	Equal to P_{Δ^c}
P_M	Equal to $P_{\{1,\ldots,M\}}$
$P_{M_2}^{M_1}$	Equal to $P_{\{M_1+1,\ldots,M_2\}}$

Compressed sensing

$\mathrm{supp}(x)$	The support of a vector x
s	Sparsity
r	Number of (sparsity or sampling) levels
$\mathbf{M} = (M_1, \ldots, M_r)$	Sparsity levels

$\mathbf{s} = (s_1, \ldots, s_r)$	Local sparsities
Σ_s, $\Sigma_{\mathbf{s},\mathbf{M}}$	Set of s-sparse or $(\mathbf{s}, \mathbf{M})$-sparse vectors
D_s, $D_{\mathbf{s},\mathbf{M}}$	The set of all possible support sets of an exactly s-sparse or $(\mathbf{s}, \mathbf{M})$-sparse vector
$\sigma_s(x)_{\ell^p}$, $\sigma_{\mathbf{s},\mathbf{M}}(x)_{\ell^p}$	The ℓ^p-norm best s-term or $(\mathbf{s}, \mathbf{M})$-term approximation error of a vector x
$\mu(U)$	Coherence of a matrix U
$\mathcal{A}$	Family of random vectors in $\mathbb{C}^N$
$C = \{\mathcal{A}_i\}_{i=1}^m$	Collection of families of random vectors $\mathcal{A}_i$
$\mu(\mathcal{A})$, $\mu(C)$	Coherence of a family $\mathcal{A}$ or collection C
$\mu_l(\mathcal{A})$	lth local coherence of a family $\mathcal{A}$
$\mathbf{N} = (N_1, \ldots, N_r)$	Sampling levels
$\mathbf{m} = (m_1, \ldots, m_r)$	Local numbers of measurements
$U^{(k,l)}$	Block of a matrix U corresponding to the kth sampling and lth sparsity level

Wavelets

ψ, φ	Mother wavelet and scaling function
V_j, W_j	Wavelet multiresolution and detail spaces
j, n	Scale and translation indices
$\psi_{j,n}$, $\varphi_{j,n}$	Dilated and translated wavelet and scaling function
$\psi_{j,n}^{(e)}$	Alternative notation for $\varphi_{j,n}$ $(e = 0)$ and $\psi_{j,n}$ $(e = 1)$
$\psi_{j,n}^{\mathrm{per},(e)}$	Periodized wavelet and scaling function
p, q	Daubechies wavelet order and smoothness parameter
$\mathcal{W}$, $\mathcal{W}^{-1}$	Discrete Wavelet Transform (DWT) and its inverse
W	Matrix representing the DWT

Neural networks

$\Theta = \{(u_i, v_i)\}_{i=1}^K$	Training set
N	Neural network
$W^{(l)}$, $b^{(l)}$	Weights and biases
σ	Activation function
L	Number of layers
$\mathbf{n} = (n_0, \ldots, n_L)$	Widths of the network layers
$\mathcal{N}$, $\mathcal{N}_{\mathbf{n}}$, $\mathcal{N}_{\mathbf{n},\sigma}$	Family of neural networks
Cost	Cost function to minimize

Miscellaneous

$\mathbb{P}$	Probability
$\mathbb{E}$	Expectation

δ_{ij}	Kronecker delta
δ_i	Kronecker delta δ_{i0}
$\lesssim, \gtrsim$	Inequality up to a constant: $a \lesssim b$ if $a \leq cb$ for some constant $c \geq 0$ independent of all parameters, and likewise for $a \gtrsim b$
$\asymp$	Equivalence up to constants: $a \asymp b$ if $a \lesssim b$ and $a \lesssim b$
$f \otimes g$	Tensor product of functions f and g
argmin	Set of (global) minimizers of an optimization problem

Abbreviations

BP	Basis Pursuit
C-LASSO	Constrained LASSO
CNN	Convolutional Neural Network
CT	Computed Tomography
DAS	Dyadic Anisotropic Sampling
DBp	Daubechies wavelet of order p
DFT	Discrete Fourier Transform
DHT	Discrete Walsh–Hadamard Transform
DIS	Dyadic Isotropic Sampling
DWT	Discrete Wavelet Transform
FFT	Fast Fourier Transform
FHT	Fast Walsh–Hadamard Transform
FISTA	Fast ISTA
FWT	Fast Wavelet Transform
G-RIC (G-RICL)	G-adjusted Restricted Isometry Constant (in Levels)
G-RIP (G-RIPL)	G-adjusted Restricted Isometry Property (in Levels)
ISTA	Iterative Shrinkage-Thresholding Algorithm
LASSO	Least Absolute Shrinkage and Selection Operator
MRA	MultiResolution Analysis
MRI	Magnetic Resonance Imaging
NESTA	NESTerov's Algorithm for QCBP
NSP	Null Space Property
PSNR	Peak Signal-to-Noise Ratio
QCBP	Quadratically-Constrained Basis Pursuit
ReLU	Rectified Linear Unit
RIC (RICL)	Restricted Isometry Constant (in Levels)
RIP (RIPL)	Restricted Isometry Property (in Levels)
rNSP (rNSPL)	robust Null Space Property (in Levels)
SR-LASSO	Square-Root LASSO
SVD	Singular Value Decomposition
TV	Total Variation
U-LASSO	Unconstrained LASSO

References

[1] The USC-SIPI Image Database. `http://sipi.usc.edu/database/`.

[2] B. Adcock. Infinite-dimensional compressed sensing and function interpolation. *Found. Comput. Math.*, 18(3):661–701, 2018.

[3] B. Adcock, V. Antun, and A. C. Hansen. Uniform recovery in infinite-dimensional compressed sensing and applications to structured binary sampling. *arXiv:1905.00126*, 2019.

[4] B. Adcock, A. Bao, and S. Brugiapaglia. Correcting for unknown errors in sparse high-dimensional function approximation. *Numer. Math.*, 142(3):667–711, 2019.

[5] B. Adcock, A. Bao, J. D. Jakeman, and A. Narayan. Compressed sensing with sparse corruptions: Fault-tolerant sparse collocation approximations. *SIAM/ASA J. Uncertain. Quantif.*, 6(4):1424–1453, 2018.

[6] B. Adcock, C. Boyer, and S. Brugiapaglia. On oracle-type local recovery guarantees in compressed sensing. *Inf. Inference (in press)*, 2020.

[7] B. Adcock, S. Brugiapaglia, and M. King-Roskamp. Do log factors matter? On optimal wavelet approximation and the foundations of compressed sensing. *Found. Comput. Math. (in press)*, 2021.

[8] B. Adcock, S. Brugiapaglia, and M. King-Roskamp. Iterative and greedy algorithms for the sparsity in levels model in compressed sensing. In D. V. D. Ville, M. Papadakis, and Y. M. Lu, editors, *Wavelets and Sparsity XVIII*, volume 11138, pages 76–89. International Society for Optics and Photonics, SPIE, 2019.

[9] B. Adcock, S. Brugiapaglia, and M. King-Roskamp. The benefits of acting locally: reconstruction algorithms for sparse in levels signals with stable and robust recovery guarantees. *arXiv:2006.1338*, 2020.

[10] B. Adcock, S. Brugiapaglia, and C. G. Webster. Compressed sensing approaches for polynomial approximation of high-dimensional functions. In H. Boche, G. Caire, R. Calderbank, M. März, G. Kutyniok, and R. Mathar, editors, *Compressed Sensing and its Applications: Second International MATHEON Conference 2015*, Applied and Numerical Harmonic Analysis, pages 93–124. Birkhäuser, Cham, 2017.

[11] B. Adcock and N. Dexter. The gap between theory and practice in function approximation with deep neural networks. *SIAM J. Math. Data Sci. (in press)*, 2021.

[12] B. Adcock, N. Dexter, and Q. Xu. Improved recovery guarantees and sampling strategies for tv minimization in compressive imaging. *arXiv:2009.08555*, 2020.

[13] B. Adcock, M. Gataric, and A. C. Hansen. On stable reconstructions from nonuniform Fourier measurements. *SIAM J. Imaging Sci.*, 7(3):1690–1723, 2014.

[14] B. Adcock, M. Gataric, and A. C. Hansen. Weighted frames of exponentials and stable recovery of multidimensional functions from nonuniform fourier samples. *Appl. Comput. Harmon. Anal.*, 42(3):508–535, 2017.

[15] B. Adcock and A. C. Hansen. A generalized sampling theorem for stable reconstructions in arbitrary bases. *J. Fourier Anal. Appl.*, 18(4):685–716, 2012.

[16] B. Adcock and A. C. Hansen. Stable reconstructions in Hilbert spaces and the resolution of the Gibbs phenomenon. *Appl. Comput. Harmon. Anal.*, 32(3):357–388, 2012.

[17] B. Adcock and A. C. Hansen. Generalized sampling and infinite-dimensional compressed sensing. *Found. Comput. Math.*, 16(5):1263–1323, 2016.

[18] B. Adcock, A. C. Hansen, and C. Poon. Beyond consistent reconstructions: optimality and sharp bounds for generalized sampling, and application to the uniform resampling problem. *SIAM J. Math. Anal.*, 45(5):3114–3131, 2013.

[19] B. Adcock, A. C. Hansen, and C. Poon. On optimal wavelet reconstructions from Fourier samples: linearity and universality of the stable sampling rate. *Appl. Comput. Harmon. Anal.*, 36(3):387–415, 2014.

[20] B. Adcock, A. C. Hansen, C. Poon, and B. Roman. Breaking the coherence barrier: a new theory for compressed sensing. *Forum Math. Sigma*, 5, 2017.

[21] B. Adcock, A. C. Hansen, and B. Roman. The quest for optimal sampling: computationally efficient, structure-exploiting measurements for compressed sensing. In H. Boche, R. Calderbank, G. Kutyniok, and J. Vybíral, editors, *Compressed Sensing and its Applications: MATHEON Workshop 2013*, Applied and Numerical Harmonic Analysis, pages 143–167. Birkhäuser, Cham, 2015.

[22] B. Adcock, A. C. Hansen, and B. Roman. A note on compressed sensing of structured sparse wavelet coefficients from subsampled Fourier measurements. *IEEE Signal Process. Lett.*, 23(5):732–736, 2016.

[23] B. Adcock, A. C. Hansen, and A. Shadrin. A stability barrier for reconstructions from Fourier samples. *SIAM J. Numer. Anal.*, 52(1):125–139, 2014.

[24] B. Adcock and Y. Sui. Compressive Hermite interpolation: sparse, high-dimensional approximation from gradient-augmented measurements. *Constr. Approx.*, 50(1):167–207, 2019.

[25] J. Adler and O. Öktem. Solving ill-posed inverse problems using iterative deep neural networks. *Inverse Problems*, 33(12):124007, 2017.

[26] J. Adler and O. Öktem. Learned primal-dual reconstruction. *IEEE Trans. Med. Imag.*, 37(6):1322–1332, 2018.

[27] R. Ahmad, C. A. Bouman, G. T. Buzzard, S. Chan, S. Liu, E. T. Reehorst, and P. Schniter. Plug-and-play methods for magnetic resonance imaging: using denoisers for image recovery. *IEEE Signal Process. Mag.*, 37(1):105–116, 2020.

[28] R. Ahmad and P. Schniter. Iteratively reweighted ℓ_1 approaches to sparse composite regularization. *IEEE Trans. Comput. Imag.*, 1(4):220–235, 2015.

[29] M. E. Ahsen and M. Vidyasagar. Error bounds for compressed sensing algorithms with group sparsity: a unified approach. *Appl. Comput. Harmon. Anal.*, 43(2):212–232, 2017.

[30] N. Akhtar and A. Mian. Threat of adversarial attacks on deep learning in computer vision: a survey. *IEEE Access*, 6:14410–14430, 2018.

[31] G. S. Alberti and M. Santacesaria. Infinite dimensional compressed sensing from anisotropic measurements and applications to inverse problems in PDE. *Appl. Comput. Harmon. Anal.*, 50:105–146, 2021.

[32] L. Ambrosio, N. Fusco, and D. Pallara. *Functions of Bounded Variation and Free Discontinuity Problems*. Oxford Mathematical Monographs. Clarendon Press, Oxford, 2000.

[33] J. Andersson and J.-O. Strömberg. On the theorem of uniform recovery of random sampling matrices. *IEEE Trans. Inf. Theory*, 60(3):1700–1710, 2014.

[34] V. Antun. Coherence estimates between Hadamard matrices and Daubechies wavelets. Master's thesis, University of Oslo, 2016.

[35] V. Antun, M. J. Colbrook, and A. C. Hansen. Can stable and accurate neural networks be computed? – On barriers of deep learning and Smale's 18th problem. *arXiv:2101.08286*, 2021.

[36] V. Antun, F. Renna, C. Poon, B. Adcock, and A. C. Hansen. On instabilities of deep learning in image reconstruction and the potential costs of AI. *Proc. Natl. Acad. Sci. USA*, 117(48):30088–30095, 2020.

[37] V. Antun and Ø. Ryan. On the unification of schemes and software for wavelets on the interval. *Acta Appl. Math. (in press)*, 2021.

[38] G. R. Arce, D. J. Brady, L. Carin, H. Arguello, and D. Kittle. Compressive coded aperture spectral imaging: an introduction. *IEEE Signal Process. Mag.*, 31(1):105–115, 2014.

[39] M. Arjovsky, S. Chintala, and L. Bottou. Wasserstein generative adversarial networks. In D. Precup and Y. W. Teh, editors, *Proceedings of the 34th International Conference on Machine Learning*, volume 70 of *Proceedings of Machine Learning Research*, pages 214–223. PMLR, 2017.

[40] M. Arjovsky, A. Shah, and Y. Bengio. Unitary evolution recurrent neural networks. In M. F. Balcan and K. Q. Weinberger, editors, *Proceedings of The 33rd International Conference on Machine Learning*, volume 48, pages 1120–1128. Proceedings of Machine Learning Research, 2016.

[41] A. Arnab, O. Miksik, and P. H. Torr. On the robustness of semantic segmentation models to adversarial attacks. In *2018 IEEE/CVF Conference on Computer Vision and Pattern Recognition*, pages 888–897, 2018.

[42] S. Arridge, P. Maass, O. Öktem, and C.-B. Schönlieb. Solving inverse problems using data-driven models. *Acta Numer.*, 28:1–174, 2019.

[43] M. S. Asif, A. Ayremlou, A. C. Sankaranarayanan, A. Veeraraghavan, and R. G. Baraniuk. Flatcam: thin, bare-sensor cameras using coded aperture and computation. *IEEE Trans. Comput. Imag. (in press)*, 2021.

[44] A. Athalye, N. Carlini, and D. Wagner. Obfuscated gradients give a false sense of security: circumventing defenses to adversarial examples. In J. Dy and A. Krause, editors, *Proceedings of the 35th International Conference on Machine Learning*, volume 80 of *Proceedings of Machine Learning Research*, pages 274–283. PMLR, 2018.

[45] P. Babu and P. Stoica. Connection between SPICE and Square-Root LASSO for sparse parameter estimation. *Signal Process.*, 95:10–14, 2014.

[46] F. Bach. Breaking the curse of dimensionality with convex neural networks. *J. Mach. Learn. Res.*, 18(19):1–53, 2017.

[47] L. Baldassarre, Y.-H. Li, J. Scarlett, B. Gözcü, I. Bogunovic, and V. Cevher. Learning-based compressive subsampling. *IEEE J. Sel. Topics Signal Process.*, 10(4):809–822, 2016.

[48] R. G. Baraniuk, V. Cevher, M. F. Duarte, and C. Hedge. Model-based compressive sensing. *IEEE Trans. Inf. Theory*, 56(4):1982–2001, 2010.

[49] R. G. Baraniuk, T. Goldstein, A. C. Sankaranarayanan, C. Studer, A. Veeraraghavan, and M. B. Wakin. Compressive video sensing: algorithms, architectures, and applications. *IEEE Signal Process. Mag.*, 34(1):52–66, 2017.

[50] H. H. Barrett and K. J. Myers. *Foundations of Image Science*. Wiley–Interscience, Hoboken, NJ, 2004.

[51] A. Bastounis and A. C. Hansen. On the absence of uniform recovery in many real-world applications of compressed sensing and the restricted isometry property and nullspace property in levels. *SIAM J. Imaging Sci.*, 10(1):335–371, 2017.

[52] A. Bastounis, A. C. Hansen, and V. Vlačić. The extended Smale's 9th problem – on computational barriers and paradoxes in estimation, regularisation, computer-assisted proofs, and learning. *Preprint*, 2021.

[53] H. H. Bauschke and P. L. Combettes. *Convex Analysis and Monotone Operator Theory in Hilbert Spaces*. CMS Books in Mathematics. Springer, New York, NY, 2011.

[54] K. G. Beauchamp. *Walsh Functions and their Applications*. Academic Press, London, 1975.

[55] A. Beck. *Introduction to Nonlinear Optimization: Theory, Algorithms, and Applications with MATLAB*. MOS-SIAM Series on Optimization. Society for Industrial and Applied Mathematics, Philadelphia, PA, 2014.

[56] A. Beck. *First-Order Methods in Optimization*. MOS-SIAM Series on Optimization. Society for Industrial and Applied Mathematics, Philadelphia, PA, 2017.

[57] A. Beck and M. Teboulle. A fast iterative shrinkage-thresholding algorithm for linear inverse problems. *SIAM J. Imaging Sci.*, 2(1):183–202, 2009.

[58] A. Beck and M. Teboulle. Gradient-based algorithms with applications to signal-recovery problems. In D. P. Palomar and Y. C. Eldar, editors, *Convex Optimization in Signal Processing and Communications*, pages 42–88. Cambridge University Press, Cambridge, 2009.

[59] A. Beck and M. Teboulle. Smoothing and first order methods: a unified framework. *SIAM J. Optim.*, 22(2):557–580, 2012.

[60] S. Becker, J. Bobin, and E. J. Candès. NESTA: A fast and accurate first-order method for sparse recovery. *SIAM J. Imaging Sci.*, 4(1):1–39, 2011.

[61] S. R. Becker. *Practical Compressed Sensing: Modern Data Acquisition and Signal Processing*. PhD thesis, Stanford University, 2011.

[62] A. Belloni, V. Chernozhukov, and L. Wang. Square-root lasso: pivotal recovery of sparse signals via conic programming. *Biometrika*, 98(4):791–806, 2011.

[63] A. Belloni, V. Chernozhukov, and L. Wang. Pivotal estimation via square-root Lasso in nonparametric regression. *Ann. Statist.*, 42(2):757–788, 2014.

[64] A. Ben-Tal and A. Nemirovski. Interior Point Polynomial Time Methods in Convex Programming. Available online at `www2.isye.gatech.edu/~nemirovs/`, 1996.

[65] A. Ben-Tal and A. Nemirovski. Lectures on Modern Convex Optimization: Analysis, Algorithms, and Engineering Applications. Available online at `www2.isye.gatech.edu/~nemirovs/`, 2000.

[66] A. Ben-Tal and A. Nemirovski. *Lectures on Modern Convex Optimization: Analysis, Algorithms, and Engineering Applications*. MOS-SIAM Series on Optimization. Society for Industrial and Applied Mathematics, Philadelphia, PA, 2001.

[67] A. Berk, Y. Plan, and O. Yilmaz. Sensitivity of ℓ_1 minimization to parameter choice. *Inf. Inference (in press)*, 2020.

[68] J. Berner, P. Grohs, and A. Jentzen. Analysis of the generalization error: empirical risk minimization over deep artificial neural networks overcomes the curse of dimensionality in the numerical approximation of Black–Scholes partial differential equations. *SIAM J. Math. Data Sci.*, 2(3):631–657, 2020.

[69] P. J. Bickel, Y. Ritov, and A. B. Tsybakov. Simultaneous analysis of Lasso and Dantzig selector. *Ann. Statist.*, 37(4):1705–1732, 2009.

[70] S. A. Bigdeli, M. Zwicker, P. Favaro, and M. Jin. Deep mean-shift priors for image restoration. In *Advances in Neural Information Processing Systems*, pages 763–772, 2017.

[71] J. Bigot, C. Boyer, and P. Weiss. An analysis of block sampling strategies in compressed sensing. *IEEE Trans. Inf. Theory*, 62(4):2125–2139, 2016.

[72] E. G. Birgin, J. M. Martínez, and M. Raydan. Nonmonotone spectral projected gradient methods on convex sets. *SIAM J. Optim.*, 10(4):1196–1211, 2000.

[73] D. Birkes and Y. Dodge. *Alternative Methods of Regression*. Wiley-Interscience, New York, 1993.

[74] M. Blaimer, F. Breuer, M. Mueller, R. Heidemann, M. Griswold, and P. Jakob. SMASH, SENSE, PILS, GRAPPA: how to choose the optimal method. *Top. Magn. Reson. Imaging*, 15(4):223–236, 2004.

[75] K. T. Block, M. Uecker, and J. Frahm. Suppression of MRI truncation artifacts using total variation constrained data extrapolation. *Int. J. Biomed. Imaging*, 2008:184123, 2008.

[76] L. Blum, F. Cucker, M. Shub, and S. Smale. *Complexity and Real Computation*. Springer, New York, NY, 1998.

[77] L. Blum, M. Shub, and S. Smale. On a theory of computation and complexity over the real numbers: NP-completeness, recursive functions and universal machines. *Bull. Amer. Math. Soc.*, 21(1):1–46, 1989.

[78] T. Blumensath and M. E. Davies. Iterative thresholding for sparse approximations. *J. Fourier Anal. Appl.*, 14(5):629–654, 2008.

[79] T. Blumensath and M. E. Davies. Iterative hard thresholding for compressed sensing. *Appl. Comput. Harmon. Anal.*, 27(3):265–274, 2009.

[80] B. G. Bodmann, A. Flinth, and G. Kutyniok. Compressed sensing for analog signals. *arXiv:1803.04218*, 2018.

[81] V. Boominathan, J. K. Adams, M. S. Asif, B. W. Avants, J. T. Robinson, R. G. Baraniuk, A. C. Sankaranarayanan, and A. Veeraraghavan. Lensless imaging: a computational renaissance. *IEEE Signal Process. Mag.*, 33(5):23–35, 2016.

[82] A. Bora, A. Jalal, E. Price, and A. G. Dimakis. Compressed sensing using generative models. In *International Conference on Machine Learning*, pages 537–546, 2017.

[83] A. Böttcher. Infinite matrices and projection methods. In *Lectures on Operator Theory and its Applications*, volume 3 of *Fields Institute Monographs*, pages 1–72. American Mathematical Society, Providence, RI, 1996.

[84] L. Bottou, F. E. Curtis, and J. Nocedal. Optimization methods for large-scale machine learning. *SIAM Rev.*, 60(2):223–311, 2018.

[85] S. Boucheron, G. Lugosi, and P. Massart. *Concentration Inequalities: A Nonasymptotic Theory of Independence*. Oxford University Press, Oxford, 2013.

[86] J. Bourgain. An improved estimate in the restricted isometry problem. In B. Klartag and E. Milman, editors, *Geometric Aspects of Functional Analysis*, volume 2116 of *Lecture Notes in Mathematics*, pages 65–70. Springer, Cham, 2014.

[87] A. Bourrier, M. E. Davies, T. Peleg, P. Pérez, and R. Gribonval. Fundamental performance limits for ideal decoders in high-dimensional linear inverse problems. *IEEE Trans. Inf. Theory*, 60(12):7928–7946, 2014.

[88] S. Boyd and N. Parikh. Proximal algorithms. *Foundations and Trends in Optimization*, 1(3):123–231, 2013.

[89] S. Boyd, N. Parikh, E. Chu, B. Peleato, and J. Eckstein. Distributed optimization and statistical learning via the alternating direction method of multipliers. *Foundations and Trends in Machine Learning*, 3(1):1–122, 2011.

[90] S. Boyd and L. Vandenberghe. *Convex Optimization*. Cambridge University Press, Cambridge, 2004.

[91] C. Boyer, J. Bigot, and P. Weiss. Compressed sensing with structured sparsity and structured acquisition. *Appl. Comput. Harmon. Anal.*, 46(2):312–350, 2019.

[92] C. Boyer, N. Chauffert, P. Ciuciu, J. Kahn, and P. Weiss. On the generation of sampling schemes for magnetic resonance imaging. *SIAM J. Imaging Sci.*, 9(4):2039–2072, 2016.

[93] C. Boyer, P. Weiss, and J. Bigot. An algorithm for variable density sampling with block-constrained acquisition. *SIAM J. Imaging Sci.*, 7(2):1080–1107, 2014.

[94] D. J. Brady. *Optical Imaging and Spectroscopy*. Wiley, Hoboken, NJ, 2009.

[95] D. J. Brady, K. Choi, D. L. Marks, R. Horisaki, and S. Lim. Compressive holography. *Opt. Express*, 17(15):13040–13049, 2009.

[96] K. Bredies, K. Kunisch, and T. Pock. Total generalized variation. *SIAM J. Imaging Sci.*, 3(3):492–526, 2010.

[97] S. Brugiapaglia and B. Adcock. Robustness to unknown error in sparse regularization. *IEEE Trans. Inf. Theory*, 64(10):6638–6661, 2018.

[98] T. A. Bubba, G. Kutyniok, M. Lassas, M. März, W. Samek, S. Siltanen, and V. Srinivasan. Learning the invisible: a hybrid deep learning-shearlet framework for limited angle computed tomography. *Inverse Problems*, 35(6):064002, 2019.

[99] S. Bubeck. Convex optimization: algorithms and complexity. *Foundations and Trends in Machine Learning*, 8(3–4):231–358, 2015.

[100] F. Bunea, J. Lederer, and Y. She. The group square-root Lasso: theoretical properties and fast algorithms. *IEEE Trans. Inf. Theory*, 60(2):1313–1325, 2014.

[101] M. Burger, M. Möller, M. Benning, and S. Osher. An adaptive inverse scale space method for compressed sensing. *Math. Comp.*, 82(281):269–299, 2013.

[102] M. Burger, A. Sawatzky, and G. Steidl. First order algorithms in variational image processing. In R. Glowinski, S. J. Osher, and W. Yin, editors, *Splitting Methods in Communication, Imaging, Science, and Engineering*, pages 345–407. Springer, Berlin, 2016.

[103] P. Bürgisser and F. Cucker. *Condition: The Geometry of Numerical Algorithms*. Grundlehren der mathematischen Wissenschaften. Springer, Berlin, 2013.

[104] J. Cahill and D. G. Mixon. Robust width: a characterization of uniformly stable and robust compressed sensing. *arXiv:1408.4409*, 2018.

[105] J.-F. Cai and W. Xu. Guarantees of total variation minimization for signal recovery. *Inf. Inference*, 4(4):328–353, 2015.

[106] T. Cai and A. Zhang. Sparse representation of a polytope and recovery of sparse signals and low-rank matrices. *IEEE Trans. Inf. Theory*, 60(1):122–132, 2014.

[107] R. Calderbank, A. Hansen, B. Roman, and L. Thesing. On reconstructing functions from binary measurements. In H. Boche, G. Caire, R. Calderbank, G. Kutyniok, R. Mathar, and P. Petersen, editors, *Compressed Sensing and Its Applications: Third International MATHEON Conference 2017*, Applied and Numerical Harmonic Analysis, pages 97–128. Birkhäuser, Cham, 2019.

[108] E. J. Candès. Compressive sampling. In M. Sanz-Solé, J. Soria, J. L. Varona, and J. Verdera, editors, *Proceedings of the International Congress of Mathematicians, Madrid 2006*, pages 1433–1452. American Mathematical Society, Providence, RI, 2006.

[109] E. J. Candès. The restricted isometry property and its implications for compressed sensing. *C. R. Math. Acad. Sci. Paris*, 346(9–10):589–592, 2008.

[110] E. J. Candès and D. L. Donoho. Ridgelets: a key to high dimensional intermittency? *Philos. Trans. Roy. Soc. A*, 357(1760):2495–2509, 1999.

[111] E. J. Candès and D. L. Donoho. Curvelets—a surprisingly effective nonadaptive representation for objects with edges. In C. Rabut, A. Cohen, and L. L. Schumaker, editors, *Curves and Surfaces*, pages 105–120. Vanderbilt University Press, Nashville, TN, 2000.

[112] E. J. Candès and D. L. Donoho. Recovering edges in ill-posed inverse problems: optimality of curvelet frames. *Ann. Statist.*, 30(3):784–842, 2002.

[113] E. J. Candès and D. L. Donoho. New tight frames of curvelets and optimal representations of objects with piecewise C^2 singularities. *Comm. Pure Appl. Math.*, 57(2):219–266, 2004.

[114] E. J. Candès, Y. C. Eldar, D. Needell, and P. Randall. Compressed sensing with coherent and redundant dictionaries. *Appl. Comput. Harmon. Anal.*, 31(1):59–73, 2010.

[115] E. J. Candès, Y. C. Eldar, T. Strohmer, and V. Voroninski. Phase retrieval via matrix completion. *SIAM J. Imaging Sci.*, 6(1):199–225, 2013.

[116] E. J. Candès and C. Fernandez-Granda. Towards a mathematical theory of super-resolution. *Comm. Pure Appl. Math.*, 67(6):906–956, 2014.

[117] E. J. Candès, X. Li, and M. Soltanolkotabi. Phase retrieval via Wirtinger flow: theory and algorithms. *IEEE Trans. Inf. Theory*, 61(4):1985–2007, 2015.

[118] E. J. Candès and Y. Plan. A probabilistic and RIPless theory of compressed sensing. *IEEE Trans. Inf. Theory*, 57(11):7235–7254, 2011.

[119] E. J. Candès and J. Romberg. l1-magic. `https://statweb.stanford.edu/~candes/software/l1magic/`.

[120] E. J. Candès and J. Romberg. Sparsity and incoherence in compressive sampling. *Inverse Problems*, 23(3):969–985, 2007.

[121] E. J. Candès, J. Romberg, and T. Tao. Robust uncertainty principles: exact signal reconstruction from highly incomplete frequency information. *IEEE Trans. Inf. Theory*, 52(2):489–509, 2006.

[122] E. J. Candès, T. Strohmer, and V. Voroninski. Phaselift: exact and stable signal recovery from magnitude measurements via convex programming. *Comm. Pure Appl. Math.*, 66(8):1241–1274, 2013.

[123] E. J. Candès and T. Tao. Near optimal signal recovery from random projections: universal encoding strategies? *IEEE Trans. Inf. Theory*, 52(12):5406–5425, 2006.

[124] E. J. Candès and T. Tao. The Dantzig selector: statistical estimation when p is much larger than n. *Ann. Statist.*, 35(6):2313–2351, 2007.

[125] E. J. Candès and M. B. Wakin. An introduction to compressive sampling. *IEEE Signal Process. Mag.*, 25(2):21–30, 2008.

[126] E. J. Candès, M. B. Wakin, and S. P. Boyd. Enhancing sparsity by reweighted ℓ_1 minimization. *J. Fourier Anal. Appl.*, 14(5):877–905, 2008.

[127] P. G. Casazza and O. Christensen. Approximation of the inverse frame operator and applications to Gabor frames. *J. Approx. Theory*, 103(2):338–356, 2000.

[128] A. Chakraborty, M. Alam, V. Dey, A. Chattopadhyay, and D. Mukhopadhyay. Adversarial attacks and defences: a survey. *arXiv:1810.00069*, 2018.

[129] A. Chambolle, V. Duval, G. Peyré, and C. Poon. Geometric properties of solutions to the total variation denoising problem. *Inverse Problems*, 33(1):015002, 2016.

[130] A. Chambolle, M. Novaga, D. Cremers, and T. Pock. An introduction to total variation for image analysis. In M. Fornasier, editor, *Theoretical Foundations and Numerical Methods for Sparse Recovery*, volume 9 of *Radon Series in Computational and Applied Mathematics*, pages 263–340. de Gruyter, Berlin, 2010.

[131] A. Chambolle and T. Pock. A first-order primal-dual algorithm for convex problems with applications to imaging. *J. Math. Imaging Vision*, 40(1):120–145, 2011.

[132] A. Chambolle and T. Pock. An introduction to continuous optimization for imaging. *Acta Numer.*, 25:161–319, 2016.

[133] A. Chambolle and T. Pock. On the ergodic convergence rates of a first-order primal-dual algorithm. *Math. Program.*, 159(1–2):253–287, 2016.

[134] J. H. R. Chang, C. Li, B. Póczos, B. V. K. Vijaya Kumar, and A. C. Sankaranarayanan. One network to solve them all – solving linear inverse problems using deep projection models. In *2017 IEEE International Conference on Computer Vision (ICCV)*, pages 5888–5897, 2017.

[135] R. Chartrand. Fast algorithms for nonconvex compressive sensing: MRI reconstruction from very few data. In *2009 IEEE International Symposium on Biomedical Imaging: From Nano to Macro*, pages 262–265, 2009.

[136] N. Chauffert, P. Ciuciu, J. Kahn, and P. Weiss. Variable density sampling with continuous trajectories. *SIAM J. Imaging Sci.*, 7(4):1962–1992, 2014.

[137] C. E. Chávez, F. Alonzo-Atienza, and D. Álvarez. Avoiding the inverse crime in the Inverse Problem of electrocardiography: estimating the shape and location of cardiac ischemia. In *Computing in Cardiology 2013*, volume 687–690, 2013.

[138] G.-H. Chen, J. Tang, and S. Leng. Prior image constrained compressed sensing (PICCS): a method to accurately reconstruct dynamic CT images from highly undersampled projection data sets. *Med. Phys.*, 35(2):660–663, 2008.

[139] J. Chen and X. Huo. Theoretical results on sparse representations of multiple-measurement vectors. *IEEE Trans. Signal Process.*, 54(12):4634–4643, 2006.

[140] S. S. Chen, D. L. Donoho, and M. A. Saunders. Atomic decomposition by basis pursuit. *SIAM J. Sci. Comput.*, 20(1):33–61, 1998.

[141] M. Cheraghchi, V. Guruswami, and A. Velingker. Restricted isometry of Fourier matrices and list decodability of random linear codes. *SIAM J. Comput.*, 42(5):1888–1914, 2013.

[142] Y. Chi, L. L. Scharf, A. Pezeshki, and R. Calderbank. Sensitivity to basis mismatch in compressed sensing. *IEEE Trans. Signal Process.*, 59(5):2182–2195, 2011.

[143] A. Chkifa, N. Dexter, H. Tran, and C. G. Webster. Polynomial approximation via compressed sensing of high-dimensional functions on lower sets. *Math. Comp.*, 87(311):1415–1450, 2018.

[144] H. Choi and R. G. Baraniuk. Wavelet statistical models and Besov spaces. In M. A. Unser, A. Aldroubi, and A. F. Laine, editors, *Wavelet Applications in Signal and Image Processing VII*, volume 3813, pages 489–501. International Society for Optics and Photonics, SPIE, 1999.

[145] O. Christensen and T. Strohmer. The finite section method and problems in frame theory. *J. Approx. Theory*, 133(2):221–237, 2005.

[146] I.-Y. Chun and B. Adcock. Compressed sensing and parallel acquisition. *IEEE Trans. Inf. Theory*, 63(8):4860–4882, 2017.

[147] I.-Y. Chun, B. Adcock, and T. Talavage. Efficient compressed sensing SENSE pMRI reconstruction with joint sparsity promotion. *IEEE Trans. Med. Imag.*, 31(1):354–368, 2016.

[148] I.-Y. Chun and J. A. Fessler. Convolutional dictionary learning: acceleration and convergence. *IEEE Trans. Image Process.*, 27(4):1697–1712, 2018.

[149] I.-Y. Chun and J. A. Fessler. Deep BCD-net using identical encoding-decoding CNN structures for iterative image recovery. In *2018 IEEE 13th Image, Video, and Multidimensional Signal Processing Workshop (IVMSP)*, pages 1–5, 2018.

[150] A. Cohen, W. Dahmen, I. Daubechies, and R. DeVore. Harmonic analysis of the space BV. *Rev. Mat. Iberoam.*, 19(1):235–263, 2003.

[151] A. Cohen, W. Dahmen, and R. A. DeVore. Compressed sensing and best k-term approximation. *J. Amer. Math. Soc.*, 22(1):211–231, 2009.

[152] A. Cohen, I. Daubechies, and J.-C. Feauveau. Biorthogonal bases of compactly supported wavelets. *Comm. Pure Appl. Math.*, 45(5):485–560, 1992.

[153] A. Cohen, I. Daubechies, and P. Vial. Wavelet bases on the interval and fast algorithms. *Appl. Comput. Harmon. Anal.*, 1(1):54–81, 1993.

[154] A. Cohen, R. DeVore, P. Petrushev, and H. Xu. Nonlinear approximation and the space $BV(\mathbb{R}^2)$. *Amer. J. Math.*, 121(3):587–628, 1999.

[155] J. Cohen, E. Rosenfeld, and J. Z. Kolter. Certified adversarial robustness via randomized smoothing. In *International Conference on Machine Learning*, pages 1310–1320, 2019.

[156] R. R. Coifman, F. Geshwind, and Y. Meyer. Noiselets. *Appl. Comput. Harmon. Anal.*, 10(1):27–44, 2001.

[157] D. Colton and R. Kress. *Integral Equation Methods in Scattering Theory*. Classics in Applied Mathematics. Society for Industrial and Applied Mathematics, Philadelphia, PA, 2013.

[158] P. L. Combettes and J.-C. Pesquet. Proximal splitting methods in signal processing. In H. H. Bauschke, R. S. Burachik, P. L. Combettes, V. Elser, D. R. Luke, and H. Wolkowicz, editors, *Fixed-Point Algorithms for Inverse Problems in Science and Engineering*, volume 49 of *Springer Optimization and Its Applications*, pages 185–212. Springer, New York, NY, 2011.

[159] L. Condat. A primal-dual splitting method for convex optimization involving lipschitzian, proximable and linear composite terms. *J. Optim. Theory App.*, 158(2):460–479, 2013.

[160] M. S. Crouse, R. D. Nowak, and R. G. Baraniuk. Wavelet-based statistical signal processing using hidden Markov models. *IEEE Trans. Signal Process.*, 46(4):886–902, 1998.

[161] G. Cybenko. Approximation by superposition of a sigmoidal function. *Math. Control, Signals, and Systems*, 2(4):303–314, 1989.

[162] K. Dabov, A. Foi, V. Katkovnik, and K. Egiazarian. Image denoising by sparse 3-D transform-domain collaborative filtering. *IEEE Trans. Image Process.*, 16(8):2080–2095, 2007.

[163] I. Dassios, K. Fountoulakis, and J. Gondzio. A preconditioner for a primal-dual Newton conjugate gradient method for compressed sensing problems. *SIAM J. Sci. Comput.*, 37(6):A2783–A2812, 2015.

[164] I. Daubechies. *Ten Lectures on Wavelets*. CBMS-NSF Regional Conference Series in Applied Mathematics. Society for Industrial and Applied Mathematics, Philadelphia, PA, 1992.

[165] I. Daubechies, M. Defrise, and C. De Mol. An iterative thresholding algorithm for linear inverse problems with a sparsity constraint. *Comm. Pure Appl. Math.*, 57(11):1413–1457, 2004.

[166] I. Daubechies, R. DeVore, M. Fornasier, and C. S. Güntürk. Iteratively re-weighted least squares minimization for sparse recovery. *Comm. Pure Appl. Math.*, 63(1):1–38, 2010.

[167] M. A. Davenport, M. F. Duarte, Y. C. Eldar, and G. Kutyniok. Introduction to compressed sensing. In Y. C. Eldar and G. Kutyniok, editors, *Compressed Sensing: Theory and Applications*, pages 1–64. Cambridge University Press, Cambridge, 2012.

[168] M. A. Davenport and J. Romberg. An overview of low-rank matrix recovery from incomplete observations. *IEEE J. Sel. Topics Signal Process.*, 10(4):602–622, 2016.

[169] M. A. Davenport and M. B. Wakin. Compressive sensing of analog signals using discrete prolate spheroidal sequences. *Appl. Comput. Harmon. Anal.*, 33(3):438–472, 2012.

[170] M. E. Davies and Y. C. Eldar. Rank awareness in joint sparse recovery. *IEEE Trans. Inf. Theory*, 58(2):1135–1146, 2012.

[171] A. H. Delaney and Y. Bresler. Globally convergent edge-preserving regularized reconstruction: an application to limited-angle tomography. *IEEE Trans. Image Process.*, 7(2):202–221, 1998.

[172] A. Denițiu, S. Petra, C. Schnörr, and C. Schnörr. Phase transitions and cosparse tomographic recovery of compound solid bodies from few projections. *Fundam. Inform.*, 135(1–2):73–102, 2014.

[173] R. DeVore, G. Petrova, and P. Wojtaszczyk. Instance-optimality in probability with an ℓ_1-minimization decoder. *Appl. Comput. Harmon. Anal.*, 27(3):275–288, 2009.

[174] R. A. DeVore. Nonlinear approximation. *Acta Numer.*, 7:51–150, 1998.

[175] S. Diamond, V. Sitzmann, F. Heide, and G. Wetzstein. Unrolled optimization with deep priors. *arXiv:1705.08041*, 2017.

[176] M. N. Do and M. Vetterli. The contourlet transform: an efficient directional multiresolution image representation. *IEEE Trans. Image Process.*, 14(12):2091–2106, 2005.

[177] T. T. Do, L. Gan, N. H. Nguyen, and T. D. Tran. Fast and efficient compressive sensing using structurally random matrices. *IEEE Trans. Signal Process.*, 60(1):139–154, 2011.

[178] M. Doneva. Mathematical models for magnetic resonance imaging reconstruction: an overview of the approaches, problems, and future research areas. *IEEE Signal Process. Mag.*, 37(1):24–32, 2020.

[179] D. L. Donoho. Compressed sensing. *IEEE Trans. Inf. Theory*, 52(4):1289–1306, 2006.

[180] D. L. Donoho and M. Elad. Optimally sparse representation in general (non-orthogonal) dictionaries via ℓ^1 minimization. *Proc. Natl. Acad. Sci. USA*, 100(5):2197–2002, 2003.

[181] D. L. Donoho and X. Huo. Uncertainty principles and ideal atomic decomposition. *IEEE Trans. Inf. Theory*, 47(7):2845–2862, 2001.

[182] D. L. Donoho, A. Maleki, and A. Montanari. Message-passing algorithms for compressed sensing. *Proc. Natl. Acad. Sci. USA*, 106(45):18914–18919, 2009.

[183] D. L. Donoho and J. Tanner. Observed universality of phase transitions in high-dimensional geometry, with implications for modern data analysis and signal processing. *Philos. Trans. Roy. Soc. A*, 367(1906):4273–4293, 2009.

[184] D. Dorsch and H. Rauhut. Refined analysis of sparse MIMO radar. *J. Fourier Anal. Appl.*, 23(3):485–529, 2017.

[185] J. Douglas and H. Rachford. On the numerical solution of heat conduction problems in two or three space variables. *Trans. Amer. Math. Soc.*, 82(2):421–439, 1956.

[186] M. F. Duarte, M. A. Davenport, D. Takhar, J. Laska, K. Kelly, and R. G. Baraniuk. Single-pixel imaging via compressive sampling. *IEEE Signal Process. Mag.*, 25(2):83–91, 2008.

[187] M. F. Duarte and Y. C. Eldar. Structured compressed sensing: from theory to applications. *IEEE Trans. Signal Process.*, 59(9):4053–4085, 2011.

[188] B. Dumitrescu and P. Irofti. *Dictionary Learning: Algorithms and Applications*. Springer, Cham, 2018.

[189] V. Duval and G. Peyré. Exact support recovery for sparse spikes deconvolution. *Found. Comput. Math.*, 15(5):1315–1355, 2015.

[190] B. Efron, T. Hastie, I. Johnstone, and R. Tibshirani. Least angle regression. *Ann. Statist.*, 32(2):407–499, 2004.

[191] I. Ekeland and R. Témam. *Convex Analysis and Variational Problems*. Classics in Applied Mathematics. Society for Industrial and Applied Mathematics, Philadelphia, PA, 1999.

[192] M. Elad. *Sparse and Redundant Representations: From Theory to Applications in Signal and Image Processing*. Springer, New York, NY, 2010.

[193] M. Elad and A. M. Bruckstein. A generalized uncertainty principle and sparse representation in pairs of bases. *IEEE Trans. Inf. Theory*, 48(9):2558–2567, 2002.

[194] M. Elad, P. Milanfar, and R. Rubinstein. Analysis versus synthesis in signal priors. *Inverse Problems*, 23(3):947, 2007.

[195] Y. C. Eldar and G. Kutyniok, editors. *Compressed Sensing: Theory and Applications*. Cambridge University Press, Cambridge, 2012.

[196] Y. C. Eldar and M. Mishali. Robust recovery of signals from a structured union of subspaces. *IEEE Trans. Inf. Theory*, 55(11):5302–5316, 2009.

[197] Y. C. Eldar and H. Rauhut. Average case analysis of multichannel sparse recovery using convex relaxation. *IEEE Trans. Inf. Theory*, 56(1):505–519, 2010.

[198] C. L. Epstein. *Introduction to the Mathematics of Medical Imaging*. Other Titles in Applied Mathematics. Society for Industrial and Applied Mathematics, 2nd edition, 2007.

[199] E. Esser. Applications of Lagrangian-based alternating direction methods and connections to split Bregman. *Preprint*, 2009.

[200] E. Esser, X. Zhang, and T. F. Chan. A general framework for a class of first order primal-dual algorithms for convex optimization in imaging science. *SIAM J. Imaging Sci.*, 3(4):1015–1046, 2010.

[201] I. Evtimov, K. Eykholt, E. Fernandes, T. Kohno, B. Li, A. Prakash, A. Rahmati, and D. Song. Robust physical-world attacks on machine learning models. In *2018 IEEE/CVF Conference on Computer Vision and Pattern Recognition*, pages 1625–1634, 2018.

[202] Q. Fan, T. Witzel, A. Nummenmaa, K. R. A. Van Dijk, J. D. Van Horn, M. K. Drews, L. H. Somerville, M. A. Sheridan, R. M. Santillana, J. Snyder, T. Hedden, E. E. Shaw, M. O. Hollinshead, V. Renvall, R. Zanzonico, B. Keil, S. Cauley, J. R. Polimeni, D. Tisdall, R. L. Buckner, V. J. Wedeen, L. L. Wald, A. W. Toga, and B. R. Rosen. MGH–USC human connectome project datasets with ultra-high *b*-value diffusion MRI. *Neuroimage*, 124(Pt B):1108–1114, 2016.

[203] A. Fawzi, S. Moosavi-Dezfooli, and P. Frossard. The robustness of deep networks: a geometrical perspective. *IEEE Signal Process. Mag.*, 34(6):50–62, 2017.

[204] T. G. Feeman. *The Mathematics of Medical Imaging: A Beginner's Guide*. Springer Undergraduate Texts in Mathematics and Technology. Springer, Cham, 2015.

[205] J. A. Fessler. Model-based image reconstruction for MRI. *IEEE Signal Process. Mag.*, 27(4):81–89, 2010.

[206] J. A. Fessler. Optimization methods for magnetic resonance image reconstruction: key models and optimization algorithms. *IEEE Signal Process. Mag.*, 37(1):33–40, 2020.

[207] J. A. Fessler and B. P. Sutton. Nonuniform fast Fourier transforms using min-max interpolation. *IEEE Trans. Signal Process.*, 51(2):560–574, 2003.

[208] M. A. T. Figueiredo and R. D. Nowak. An EM algorithm for wavelet-based image restoration. *IEEE Trans. Image Process.*, 12(8):906–916, 2003.

[209] M. A. T. Figueiredo, R. D. Nowak, and S. J. Wright. Gradient projection for sparse reconstruction: application to compressed sensing and other inverse problems. *IEEE J. Sel. Topics Signal Process.*, 1(4):586–597, 2007.

[210] S. G. Finlayson, J. D. Bowers, J. Ito, J. L. Zittrain, A. L. Beam, and I. S. Kohane. Adversarial attacks on medical machine learning. *Science*, 363(6433):1287–1289, 2019.

[211] C. E. Floyd. An artificial neural network for SPECT image reconstruction. *IEEE Trans. Med. Imag.*, 10(3):485–487, 1991.

[212] M. Fornasier and H. Rauhut. Compressive sensing. In O. Scherzer, editor, *Handbook of Mathematical Methods in Imaging*, pages 205–256. Springer, New York, NY, 2nd edition, 2015.

[213] S. Foucart. Stability and robustness of ℓ_1-minimizations with Weibull matrices and redundant dictionaries. *Linear Algebra Appl.*, 441:4–21, 2014.

[214] S. Foucart and H. Rauhut. *A Mathematical Introduction to Compressive Sensing*. Applied and Numerical Harmonic Analysis. Birkhäuser, New York, NY, 2013.

[215] K. Fountoulakis, J. Gondzio, and P. Zhlobich. Matrix-free interior point method for compressed sensing problems. *Math. Program. Comput.*, 6(1):1–31, 2014.

[216] M. Friedlander, H. Mansour, R. Saab, and I. Yilmaz. Recovering compressively sampled signals using partial support information. *IEEE Trans. Inf. Theory*, 58(2):1122–1134, 2012.

[217] J. Frikel. Sparse regularization in limited angle tomography. *Appl. Comput. Harmon. Anal.*, 34(1):117–141, 2013.

[218] L. Fu, T.-C. Lee, S. M. Kim, A. M. Alessio, P. E. Kinahan, Z. Chang, K. Sauer, M. K. Kalra, and B. De Man. Comparison between pre-log and post-log statistical models in ultra-low-dose CT reconstruction. *IEEE Trans. Med. Imag.*, 36(3):707–720, 2017.

[219] J. J. Fuchs. On sparse representations in arbitrary redundant bases. *IEEE Trans. Inf. Theory*, 50(6):1341–1344, 2004.

[220] P. Gács and L. Lovász. Khachiyan's algorithm for linear programming. In *Mathematical Programming at Oberwolfach*, pages 61–68. Springer, 1981.

[221] X. Gao. *Penalized Methods for High-Dimensional Least Absolute Deviations Regression*. PhD thesis, The University of Iowa, 2008.

[222] X. Gao and J. Huang. Asymptotic analysis of high-dimensional LAD regression with LASSO. *Statist. Sinica*, 20(4):1485–1506, 2010.

[223] M. Gataric and C. Poon. A practical guide to the recovery of wavelet coefficients from Fourier measurements. *SIAM J. Sci. Comput.*, 38(2):A1075–A1099, 2016.

[224] E. Gauss. *Walsh Funktionen für Ingenieure und Naturwissenschaftler*. Springer, Wiesbaden, 1994.

[225] M. E. Gehm and D. J. Brady. Compressive sensing in the EO/IR. *Appl. Opt.*, 54(8):C14–C22, 2015.

[226] M. Genzel, G. Kutyniok, and M. März. ℓ^1-analysis minimization and generalized (co-)sparsity: when does recovery succeed? *Appl. Comput. Harmon. Anal. (in press)*, 2020.

[227] M. Genzel, M. März, and R. Seidel. Compressed sensing with 1D total variation: breaking sample complexity barriers via non-uniform recovery. *arXiv:2001.09952*, 2020.

[228] D. Gilton, G. Ongie, and R. Willett. Neumann networks for linear inverse problems in imaging. *IEEE Trans. Comput. Imag.*, 6:328–343, 2020.

[229] T. Goldstein and S. Osher. The split Bregman method for L1-regularized problems. *SIAM J. Imaging Sci.*, 2(2):323–343, 2009.

[230] T. Goldstein and C. Studer. Phasemax: convex phase retrieval via basis pursuit. *IEEE Trans. Inf. Theory*, 64(4):2675–2689, 2018.

[231] T. Goldstein, L. Xu, K. F. Kelly, and R. G. Baraniuk. The STOne transform: multi-resolution image enhancement and real-time compressive video. *IEEE Trans. Image Process.*, 24(12):5581–5593, 2015.

[232] B. Golubov, A. Efimov, and V. Skvortsov. *Walsh Series and Transforms: Theory and Applications*, volume 64 of *Mathematics and its Applications*. Springer, Netherlands, 1991.

[233] I. Goodfellow, Y. Bengio, and A. Courville. *Deep Learning*. The MIT Press, Cambridge, MA, 2016.

[234] I. Goodfellow, J. Pouget-Abadie, M. Mirza, B. Xu, D. Warde-Farley, S. Ozair, A. Courville, and Y. Bengio. Generative adversarial nets. In *Advances in Neural Information Processing Systems*, pages 2672–2680, 2014.

[235] I. Goodfellow, J. Shlens, and C. Szegedy. Explaining and harnessing adversarial examples. *arXiv:1412.6572*, 2014.

[236] N. M. Gottschling, V. Antun, B. Adcock, and A. C. Hansen. The troublesome kernel: why deep learning for inverse problems is typically unstable. *arXiv:2001.01258*, 2020.

[237] B. Gözcü, R. J. Mahabadi, Y.-H. Li, E. Ilcak, T. Çukur, J. Scarlett, and V. Cevher. Learning-based compressive MRI. *IEEE Trans. Med. Imag.*, 37(6):1394–1406, 2018.

[238] C. G. Graff and E. Y. Sidky. Compressive sensing in medical imaging. *Appl. Opt.*, 54(8):C23–C44, 2015.

[239] K. Gregor and Y. LeCun. Learning fast approximations of sparse coding. In *International Conference on Machine Learning*, pages 399–406, 2010.

[240] R. Gribonval, H. Rauhut, K. Schnass, and P. Vandergheynst. Atoms of all channels, unite! Average case analysis of multi-channel sparse recovery using greedy algorithms. *J. Fourier Anal. Appl.*, 13(5):655–687, 2008.

[241] K. Gröchenig, Z. Rzeszotnik, and T. Strohmer. Quantitative estimates for the finite section method and Banach algebras of matrices. *Integral Equations and Operator Theory*, 67(2):183–202, 2011.

[242] P. Grohs, F. Hornung, A. Jentzen, and P. Von Wurstemberger. A proof that artificial neural networks overcome the curse of dimensionality in the numerical approximation of Black-Scholes partial differential equations. *arXiv:1809.02362*, 2018.

[243] D. Gross. Recovering low-rank matrices from few coefficients in any basis. *IEEE Trans. Inf. Theory*, 57(3):1548–1566, 2011.

[244] M. Grötschel, L. Lovász, and A. Schrijver. *Geometric Algorithms and Combinatorial Optimization*, volume 2 of *Algorithms and Combinatorics*. Springer, Berlin, 2nd edition, 1993.

[245] M. Guerquin-Kern, L. Lejeune, K. P. Pruessmann, and M. Unser. Realistic analytical phantoms for parallel magnetic resonance imaging. *IEEE Trans. Med. Imag.*, 31(3):626–636, 2012.

[246] I. Gühring, G. Kutyniok, and P. Petersen. Error bounds for approximations with deep ReLU neural networks in $W^{s,p}$ norms. *Anal. Appl.*, 18(5):803–859, 2020.

[247] K. Guo, G. Kutyniok, and D. Labate. Sparse multidimensional representations using anisotropic dilation and shear operators. In G. Chen and M.-J. Lai, editors, *Wavelets and Splines: Athens 2005*, pages 189–201. Nashboro Press, Brentwood, TN, 2006.

[248] K. Guo and D. Labate. Optimally sparse multidimensional representation using shearlets. *SIAM J. Math. Anal.*, 39(1):298–318, 2007.

[249] H. Gupta, K. H. Jin, H. Q. Nguyen, M. T. McCann, and M. Unser. CNN-based projected gradient descent for consistent CT image reconstruction. *IEEE Trans. Med. Imag.*, 37(6):1440–1453, 2018.

[250] R. Hagen, S. Roch, and B. Silbermann. *C^*-Algebras and Numerical Analysis*, volume 236 of *Pure and Applied Mathematics*. CRC Press, New York, 2001.

[251] J. Haldar, D. Hernando, and Z. Liang. Compressed-sensing MRI with random encoding. *IEEE Trans. Med. Imag.*, 30(4):893–903, 2011.

[252] E. T. Hale, W. Yin, and Y. Zhang. Fixed-point continuation for ℓ_1-minimization: methodology and convergence. *SIAM J. Optim.*, 19(3):1107–1130, 2008.

[253] K. Hammernik, T. Klatzer, E. Kobler, M. P. Recht, D. K. Sodickson, T. Pock, and F. Knoll. Learning a variational network for reconstruction of accelerated MRI data. *Magn. Reson. Med.*, 79(6):3055–3071, 2018.

[254] A. C. Hansen. On the approximation of spectra of linear operators on Hilbert spaces. *J. Funct. Anal.*, 254(8):2092–2126, 2008.

[255] A. C. Hansen. On the solvability complexity index, the n-pseudospectrum and approximations of spectra of operators. *J. Amer. Math. Soc.*, 24(1):81–124, 2011.

[256] A. C. Hansen and B. Roman. On structure and optimisation in computational harmonic analysis - the key aspects in sparse regularisation. In *Harmonic Analysis and Applications (in press)*. Springer, Berlin, 2020.

[257] A. C. Hansen and L. Terhaar. On the stable sampling rate for binary measurements and wavelet reconstruction. *Appl. Comput. Harmon. Anal.*, 48(2):630–654, 2020.

[258] T. Hastie, R. Tibshirani, and M. Wainwright. *Statistical Learning with Sparsity: The Lasso and Generalizations*. Number 143 in Monographs on Statistics and Applied Probability. CRC Press, Boca Raton, FL, 2015.

[259] I. Haviv and O. Regev. The restricted isometry property of subsampled Fourier matrices. In *Proceedings of the 2016 Annual ACM-SIAM Symposium on Discrete Algorithms*, pages 288–297. SIAM, Philadelphia, PA, 2016.

[260] B. He, Y. You, and X. Yuan. On the convergence of primal-dual hybrid gradient algorithm. *SIAM J. Imaging Sci.*, 7(4):2526–2537, 2014.

[261] K. He, X. Zhang, S. Ren, and J. Sun. Deep residual learning for image recognition. In *2016 IEEE Conference on Computer Vision and Pattern Recognition (CVPR)*, pages 770–778, 2016.

[262] L. He and L. Carin. Exploiting structure in wavelet-based Bayesian compressive sensing. *IEEE Trans. Signal Process.*, 57(9):3488–3497, 2009.

[263] L. He, H. Chen, and L. Carin. Tree-structured compressive sensing with variational Bayesian analysis. *IEEE Signal Process. Lett.*, 17(3):233–236, 2010.

[264] E. Hernández and G. Weiss. *A First Course on Wavelets*. Studies in Advanced Mathematics. CRC Press, Boca Raton, FL, 1996.

[265] C. F. Higham and D. J. Higham. Deep learning: an introduction for applied mathematicians. *SIAM Rev.*, 61(4):860–891, 2019.

[266] J. A. Hogan and J. D. Lakey. *Duration and Bandwidth Limiting: Prolate Functions, Sampling, and Applications*. Applied and Numerical Harmonic Analysis. Birkhäuser, Basel, 2012.

[267] D. J. Holland, M. J. Bostock, L. F. Gladden, and D. Nietlispach. Fast multidimensional NMR spectroscopy using compressed sensing. *Angew. Chem. Int. Ed.*, 50(29):6548–6551, 2011.

[268] K. Hornik. Approximation capabilities of multilayer feedforward networks. *Neural Networks*, 4(2):251–257, 1991.

[269] G. Huang, H. Jiang, K. Matthews, and P. Wilford. Lensless imaging by compressive sensing. In *20th IEEE International Conference on Image Processing*, 2013.

[270] J. Huang and T. Zhang. The benefit of group sparsity. *Ann. Statist.*, 38(4):1978–2004, 2010.

[271] Y. Huang, T. Würfl, K. Breininger, L. Liu, G. Lauritsch, and A. Maier. Some investigations on robustness of deep learning in limited angle tomography. In *International Conference on Medical Image Computing and Computer-Assisted Intervention*, pages 145–153, 2018.

[272] J.-C. Hütter and P. Rigollet. Optimal rates for total variation denoising. In V. Feldman, A. Rakhlin, and O. Shamir, editors, *29th Annual Conference on Learning Theory*, volume 49 of *Proceedings of Machine Learning Research*, pages 1115–1146. PMLR, 2016.

[273] Q. Huynh-Thu and M. Ghanbari. Scope of validity of PSNR in image/video quality assessment. *Electron. Lett.*, 44(13):800–801, 2008.

[274] K. Jaganathan, Y. C. Eldar, and B. Hassibi. Phase retrieval: an overview of recent developments. In A. Stern, editor, *Optical Compressive Imaging*, Series in Optics and Optoelectronics, pages 263–296. CRC Press, Boca Raton, FL, 2017.

[275] Y. Jang, T. Zhao, S. Hong, and H. Lee. Adversarial defense via learning to generate diverse attacks. In *Proceedings of the IEEE International Conference on Computer Vision*, pages 2740–2749, 2019.

[276] O. R. Jaspan, R. Fleysher, and M. L. Lipton. Compressed sensing MRI: a review of the clinical literature. *Brit. J. Radiol.*, 88(1056):20150487, 2015.

[277] H. Jiang, Z. Chen, Y. Shi, B. Dai, and T. Zhao. Learning to defense by learning to attack. *arXiv:1811.01213*, 2018.

[278] K. H. Jin, M. T. McCann, E. Froustey, and M. Unser. Deep convolutional neural network for inverse problems in imaging. *IEEE Trans. Image Process.*, 26(9):4509–4522, 2017.

[279] A. Jones, A. Tamtögl, I. Calvo-Almazán, and A. C. Hansen. Continuous compressed sensing for surface dynamical processes with helium atom scattering. *Sci. Rep.*, 6(1):27776, 2016.

[280] J. S. Jørgensen, S. B. Coban, W. R. B. Lionheart, S. A. McDonald, and P. J. Withers. SparseBeads data: benchmarking sparsity-regularized computed tomography. *Meas. Sci. Technol.*, 28(12):124005, 2017.

[281] J. S. Jørgensen, C. Kruschel, and D. A. Lorenz. Testable uniqueness conditions for empirical assessment of undersampling levels in total variation-regularized X-ray CT. *Inverse Probl. Sci. Eng.*, 23(8):1283–1305, 2015.

[282] J. S. Jørgensen and E. Y. Sidky. How little data is enough? Phase-diagram analysis of sparsity-regularized X-ray CT. *Philos. Trans. Roy. Soc. A*, 373(2043):20140387, 2015.

[283] J. S. Jørgensen, E. Y. Sidky, and X. Pan. Quantifying admissible undersampling for sparsity-exploiting iterative image reconstruction in X-ray CT. *IEEE Trans. Med. Imag.*, 32(2):460–473, 2013.

[284] M. Kabanava and H. Rauhut. Analysis ℓ_1-recovery with frames and Gaussian measurements. *Acta Appl. Math.*, 140(1):173–195, 2015.

[285] M. Kabanava and H. Rauhut. Cosparsity in compressed sensing. In H. Boche, R. Calderbank, G. Kutyniok, and J. Vybíral, editors, *Compressed Sensing and its Applications: MATHEON Workshop 2013*, Applied and Numerical Harmonic Analysis, pages 315–339. Birkhäuser, Cham, 2015.

[286] H. Karimi, J. Nutini, and M. Schmidt. Linear convergence of gradient and proximal-gradient methods under the Polyak-Łojasiewicz condition. In P. Frasconi, N. Landwehr, G. Manco, and J. Vreeken, editors, *Machine Learning and Knowledge Discovery in Databases. ECML PKDD 2016*, volume 9851 of *Lecture Notes in Computer Science*, pages 795–811. Springer, Cham, 2016.

[287] N. Karmarkar. A new polynomial-time algorithm for linear programming. *Combinatorica*, 4(4):373–395, 1984.

[288] O. Katz, Y. Bromberg, and Y. Silberberg. Compressive ghost imaging. *Appl. Phys. Lett.*, 95(13):131110, 2009.

[289] K. Kazimierczuk and V. Y. Orekhov. Accelerated NMR spectroscopy by using compressed sensing. *Angew. Chem. Int. Ed.*, 50(24):5556–5559, 2011.

[290] L. G. Khachiyan. Polynomial algorithms in linear programming. *Zh. Vychisl. Mat. Mat. Fiz.*, 20(1):51–68, 1980.

[291] S. J. Kim, K. Koh, M. Lustig, S. Boyd, and D. Gorinevsky. An interior-point method for large-scale ℓ_1-regularized least squares. *IEEE J. Sel. Topics Signal Process.*, 1(4):606–617, 2007.

[292] F. Knoll, K. Bredies, T. Pock, and R. Stollberger. Second order total generalized variation (TGV) for MRI. *Magn. Reson. Med.*, 65(2):480–491, 2011.

[293] F. Knoll, C. Clason, C. Diwoky, and R. Stollberger. Adapted random sampling patterns for accelerated MRI. *Magn. Reson. Mater. Phy.*, 24(1):43–50, 2011.

[294] F. Knoll, K. Hammernik, C. Zhang, S. Moeller, T. Pock, D. K. Sodickson, and M. Akçakaya. Deep-learning methods for parallel magnetic resonance imaging reconstruction: a survey of the current approaches, trends, and issues. *IEEE Signal Process. Mag.*, 37(1):128–140, 2020.

[295] F. Knoll, T. Murrell, A. Sriram, N. Yakubova, J. Zbontar, M. Rabbat, A. Defazio, M. J. Muckley, D. K. Sodickson, C. L. Zitnick, and M. P. Recht. Advancing machine learning for MR image reconstruction with an open competition: overview of the 2019 fastMRI challenge. *Magn. Reson. Med.*, 84(6):3054–3070, 2020.

[296] T. Knopp, S. Kunis, and D. Potts. A note on the iterative MRI reconstruction from nonuniform k-space data. *Int. J. Biomed. Imaging*, 2007:024727, 2007.

[297] N. Komodakis and J.-C. Pesquet. Playing with duality: an overview of recent primal-dual approaches for solving large-scale optimization problems. *IEEE Signal Process. Mag.*, 32(6):31–54, 2015.

[298] F. Krahmer, C. Kruschel, and M. Sandbichler. Total variation minimization in compressed sensing. In H. Boche, G. Caire, R. Calderbank, M. März, G. Kutyniok, and R. Mathar, editors, *Compressed Sensing and its Applications: Second International MATHEON Conference 2015*, Applied and Numerical Harmonic Analysis, pages 333–358. Birkhäuser, Cham, 2017.

[299] F. Krahmer, S. Mendelson, and H. Rauhut. Suprema of chaos processes and the restricted isometry property. *Comm. Pure Appl. Math.*, 67(11):1877–1904, 2014.

[300] F. Krahmer, D. Needell, and R. Ward. Compressive sensing with redundant dictionaries and structured measurements. *SIAM J. Math. Anal.*, 47(6):4606–4629, 2015.

[301] F. Krahmer, H. Rauhut, and R. Ward. Local coherence sampling in compressed sensing. In *Proceedings of the 10th International Conference on Sampling Theory and Applications*, pages 476–480, 2013.

[302] F. Krahmer and R. Ward. Stable and robust sampling strategies for compressive imaging. *IEEE Trans. Image Process.*, 23(2):612–622, 2013.

[303] A. Krizhevsky, I. Sutskever, and G. E. Hinton. ImageNet classification with deep convolutional neural networks. *Advances in Neural Information Processing Systems*, pages 1097–1105, 2012.

[304] A. Krogh and J. A. Hertz. A simple weight decay can improve generalization. In *Advances in Neural Information Processing Systems*, pages 950–957, 1992.

[305] P. Kuchment. *The Radon Transform and Medical Imaging*. CBMS-NSF Regional Conference Series in Applied Mathematics. Society for Industrial and Applied Mathematics, Philadelphia, PA, 2013.

[306] R. Kueng and D. Gross. RIPless compressed sensing from anisotropic measurements. *Linear Algebra Appl.*, 441:110–123, 2014.

[307] A. Kurakin, I. J. Goodfellow, and S. Bengio. Adversarial machine learning at scale. *arXiv:1611.01236*, 2016.

[308] G. Kutyniok and D. Labate, editors. *Shearlets: Multiscale Analysis for Multivariate Data*. Applied and Numerical Harmonic Analysis. Birkhäuser, Basel, 2012.

[309] G. Kutyniok and W.-Q. Lim. Compactly supported shearlets are optimally sparse. *J. Approx. Theory*, 163(11):1564–1589, 2011.

[310] G. Kutyniok and W.-Q. Lim. Optimal compressive imaging of Fourier data. *SIAM J. Imaging Sci.*, 11(1):507–546, 2018.

[311] D. Labate, W.-Q. Lim, G. Kutyniok, and G. Weiss. Sparse multidimensional representation using shearlets. In M. Papadakis, A. F. Laine, and M. A. Unser, editors, *Wavelets XI*, volume 5914, pages 254–262. International Society for Optics and Photonics, SPIE, 2005.

[312] M.-J. Lai and Y. Liu. The null space property for sparse recovery from multiple measurement vectors. *Appl. Comput. Harmon. Anal.*, 30(3):402–406, 2011.

[313] D. J. Larkman and R. G. Nunes. Parallel magnetic resonance imaging. *Phys. Med. Biol.*, 52(7):R15, 2007.

[314] P. E. Z. Larson, S. Hu, M. Lustig, A. B. Kerr, S. J. Nelson, J. Kurhanewicz, J. M. Pauly, and D. B. Vigneron. Fast dynamic 3D MR spectroscopic imaging with compressed sensing and multiband excitation pulses for hyperpolarized 13C studies. *Magn. Reson. Med.*, 65(3):610–619, 2011.

[315] J. N. Laska, M. A. Davenport, and R. G. Baraniuk. Exact signal recovery from sparsely corrupted measurements through the pursuit of justice. In *2009 Conference Record of the Forty-Third Asilomar Conference on Signals, Systems and Computers*, pages 1556–1560, 2009.

[316] E. L. Lawler. The great mathematical Sputnik of 1979. *Math. Intelligencer*, 2(4):191–198, 1980.

[317] Y. Le Cun, Y. Bengio, and G. Hinton. Deep learning. *Nature*, 521(7553):436–444, 2015.

[318] E. Le Pennec and S. Mallat. Sparse geometric image representations with bandelets. *IEEE Trans. Image Process.*, 14(4):423–438, 2005.

[319] R. Leary, Z. Saghi, P. A. Midgley, and D. J. Holland. Compressed sensing electron tomography. *Ultramicroscopy*, 131:70–91, 2013.

[320] M. Ledoux. *The Concentration of Measure Phenomenon*. Number 89 in Mathematical Surveys and Monographs. American Mathematical Society, Providence, RI, 2001.

[321] K. Lee, Y. Bresler, and M. Junge. Oblique pursuits for compressed sensing. *IEEE Trans. Inf. Theory*, 59(9):6111–6141, 2013.

[322] C. Li and B. Adcock. Compressed sensing with local structure: uniform recovery guarantees for the sparsity in levels class. *Appl. Comput. Harmon. Anal.*, 46(3):453–477, 2019.

[323] X. Li. Compressed sensing and matrix completion with a constant proportion of corruptions. *Constr. Approx.*, 37(1):73–99, 2013.

[324] D. Liang, J. Cheng, Z. Ke, and L. Ying. Deep magnetic resonance image reconstruction: inverse problems meet neural networks. *IEEE Signal Process. Mag.*, 37(1):141–151, 2020.

[325] S. Liang and R. Srikant. Why deep neural networks for function approximation? *arXiv:1610.04161*, 2016.

[326] Z.-P. Liang and P. C. Lauterbur. *Principles of Magnetic Resonance Imaging: A Signal Processing Perspective*. IEEE Press Series on Biomedical Engineering. Wiley–IEEE Press, New York, 2000.

[327] D. J. Lin, P. M. Johnson, F. Knoll, and Y. W. Lui. Artificial intelligence for MR image reconstruction: an overview for clinicians. *J. Magn. Reson. Imaging (in press)*, 2020.

[328] M. Lindner. *Infinite Matrices and their Finite Sections: An Introduction to the Limit Operator Method*. Frontiers in Mathematics. Birkhäuser, Basel, 2006.

[329] S. Ling and T. Strohmer. Self-calibration and biconvex compressive sensing. *Inverse Problems*, 31(11):115002, 2015.

[330] B. Liu, Y. M. Zou, and L. Ying. SparseSENSE: application of compressed sensing in parallel MRI. In *2008 International Conference on Information Technology and Applications in Biomedicine*, pages 127–130, 2008.

[331] J. Long, E. Shelhamer, and T. Darrell. Fully convolutional networks for semantic segmentation. In *2015 IEEE Conference on Computer Vision and Pattern Recognition (CVPR)*, pages 3431–3440, 2015.

[332] Y. Lou, T. Zeng, S. Osher, and J. Xin. A weighted difference of anisotropic and isotropic total variation model for image processing. *SIAM J. Imaging Sci.*, 8(3):1798–1823, 2015.

[333] A. Lucas, M. Iliadis, R. Molina, and A. K. Katsaggelos. Using deep neural networks for inverse problems in imaging: beyond analytical methods. *IEEE Signal Process. Mag.*, 35(1):20–36, 2018.

[334] A. Lundervold and A. Lundervold. An overview of deep learning in medical imaging focusing on MRI. *Z. Med. Phys.*, 29(2):102–127, 2019.

[335] M. Lustig. *Sparse MRI*. PhD thesis, Stanford University, 2008.

[336] M. Lustig, D. L. Donoho, and J. M. Pauly. Sparse MRI: the application of compressed sensing for rapid MRI imaging. *Magn. Reson. Med.*, 58(6):1182–1195, 2007.

[337] M. Lustig, D. L. Donoho, J. M. Santos, and J. M. Pauly. Compressed sensing MRI. *IEEE Signal Process. Mag.*, 25(2):72–82, 2008.

[338] J. Ma and M. März. A multilevel based reweighting algorithm with joint regularizers for sparse recovery. *arXiv:1604.06941*, 2016.

[339] J. Ma and G. Plonka. The curvelet transform. *IEEE Signal Process. Mag.*, 27(2):118–133, 2010.

[340] A. Macovski. Noise in MRI. *Magn. Reson. Imaging*, 36(3):494–497, 1996.

[341] A. Madry, A. Makelov, L. Schmidt, D. Tsipras, and A. Vladu. Towards deep learning models resistant to adversarial attacks. *arXiv:1706.06083*, 2017.

[342] A. Majumdar. *Compressed Sensing for Magnetic Resonance Image Reconstruction*. Cambridge University Press, Cambridge, 2015.

[343] A. Majumdar and R. K. Ward. Calibration-less multi-coil MR image reconstruction. *Magn. Reson. Imaging*, 30(7):1032–1045, 2012.

[344] S. Mallat. *A Wavelet Tour of Signal Processing: The Sparse Way*. Academic Press, Amsterdam, 3rd edition, 2009.

[345] S. Mallat. Understanding deep convolutional networks. *Philos. Trans. Roy. Soc. A*, 374(2065):20150203, 2016.

[346] S. Mallat and G. Peyré. A review of bandlet methods for geometrical image representation. *Numer. Algorithms*, 44(3):205–234, 2007.

[347] R. F. Marcia, Z. T. Harmany, and R. M. Willett. Compressive coded aperture imaging. In C. A. Bouman, E. L. Miller, and I. Pollak, editors, *Computational Imaging VII*, volume 7246, pages 106–118. International Society for Optics and Photonics, SPIE, 2009.

[348] R. F. Marcia, R. M. Willett, and Z. T. Harmany. Compressive optical imaging: architectures and algorithms. In G. Cristobal, P. Schelken, and H. Thienpont, editors, *Optical and Digital Image Processing: Fundamentals and Applications*, pages 485–505. Wiley, New York, 2011.

[349] M. Mardani, Q. Sun, S. Vasawanala, V. Papyan, H. Monajemi, J. Pauly, and D. Donoho. Neural proximal gradient descent for compressive imaging. In *Advances in Neural Information Processing Systems*, pages 9596–9606, 2018.

[350] J. Markoff. Scientists see promise in deep-learning programs. `www.nytimes.com/2012/11/24/science/scientists-see-advances-in-deep-learning-a-part-of-artificial-intelligence.html`, November 2012.

[351] K. Marwah, G. Wetzstein, Y. Bando, and R. Raskar. Compressive light field photography using overcomplete dictionaries and optimized projections. *ACM Trans. Graph.*, 32(46), 2013.

[352] Y. V. Matiyasevich. *Hilbert's Tenth Problem*. The MIT Press, Cambridge, MA, 1993.

[353] M. T. McCann, K. H. Jin, and M. Unser. Convolutional neural networks for inverse problems in imaging: a review. *IEEE Signal Process. Mag.*, 34(6):85–95, 2017.

[354] D. W. McRobbie, E. A. Moore, M. J. Graves, and M. R. Prince. *MRI: From Picture to Proton*. Cambridge University Press, Cambridge, 2nd edition, 2006.

[355] C. A. Metzler, A. Mousavi, and R. G. Baraniuk. Learned D-AMP: principled neural network based compressive image recovery. In *Advances in Neural Information Processing Systems*, pages 1770–1781, 2017.

[356] M. Mishali and Y. C. Eldar. Xampling: analog to digital at sub-Nyquist rates. *IET Circuits, Devices, & Systems*, 5(1):8–20, 2011.

[357] M. Mishali, Y. C. Eldar, and A. J. Elron. Xampling: signal acquisition and processing in union of subspaces. *IEEE Trans. Signal Process.*, 59(10):4719–4734, 2011.

[358] V. Monga, Y. Li, and Y. C. Eldar. Algorithm unrolling: interpretable, efficient deep learning for signal and image processing. *arXiv:1912.10557*, 2019.

[359] S. Moosavi-Dezfooli, A. Fawzi, O. Fawzi, and P. Frossard. Universal adversarial perturbations. In *2017 IEEE Conference on Computer Vision and Pattern Recognition (CVPR)*, pages 86–94, 2017.

[360] S. M. Moosavi-Dezfooli, A. Fawzi, and P. Frossard. DeepFool: a simple and accurate method to fool deep neural networks. In *2016 IEEE Conference on Computer Vision and Pattern Recognition (CVPR)*, pages 2574–2582, 2016.

[361] A. Moshtaghpour. *Computational Interferometry for Hyperspectral Imaging*. PhD thesis, Université catholique de Louvain, 2019.

[362] A. Moshtaghpour, J. B. Dias, and L. Jacques. Close encounters of the binary kind: signal reconstruction guarantees for compressive Hadamard sampling with Haar wavelet basis. *IEEE Trans. Inf. Theory*, 66(11):7253–7273, 2020.

[363] J. F. C. Mota, N. Deligiannis, and M. R. D. Rodrigues. Compressed sensing with prior information: strategies, geometry, and bounds. *IEEE Trans. Inf. Theory*, 63(7):4472–4496, 2017.

[364] R. Motwani and P. Raghavan. *Randomized Algorithms*. Cambridge University Press, Cambridge, 1995.

[365] M. J. Muckley, B. Riemenschneider, A. Radmanesh, S. Kim, G. Jeong, J. Ko, Y. Jun, H. Shin, D. Hwang, M. Mostapha, S. Arberet, D. Nickel, Z. Ramzi, P. Ciuciu, J.-L. Starck, J. Teuwen, D. Karkalousos, C. Zhang, A. Sriram, Z. Huang, N. Yakubova, Y. Lui, and

F. Knoll. State-of-the-art machine learning MRI reconstruction in 2020: results of the second fastMRI challenge. *arXiv:2012.06318*, 2020.

[366] J. L. Mueller and S. Siltanen. *Linear and Nonlinear Inverse Problems with Practical Applications*. Computational Science & Engineering. Society for Industrial and Applied Mathematics, Philadelphia, PA, 2012.

[367] M. Murphy, M. Alley, J. Demmel, K. Keutzer, S. Vasanawala, and M. Lustig. Fast l_1-SPIRiT compressed sensing parallel imaging MRI: scalable parallel implementation and clinically feasible runtime. *IEEE Trans. Med. Imag.*, 31(6):1250–1262, Jun. 2012.

[368] S. Nam, M. E. Davies, M. Elad, and R. Gribonval. The cosparse analysis model and algorithms. *Appl. Comput. Harmon. Anal.*, 34(1):30–56, 2013.

[369] B. K. Natarajan. Sparse approximate solutions to linear systems. *SIAM J. Comput.*, 24(2):227–234, 1995.

[370] F. Natterer and F. Wübbeling. *Mathematical Methods in Image Reconstruction*. Mathematical Modeling and Computation. Society for Industrial and Applied Mathematics, Philadelphia, PA, 2001.

[371] D. Needell and J. A. Tropp. CoSaMP: Iterative signal recovery from incomplete and inaccurate samples. *Appl. Comput. Harmon. Anal.*, 26(3):301–321, 2008.

[372] D. Needell and R. Ward. Near-optimal compressed sensing guarantees for total variation minimization. *IEEE Trans. Image Process.*, 22(10):3941–3949, 2013.

[373] D. Needell and R. Ward. Stable image reconstruction using total variation minimization. *SIAM J. Imaging Sci.*, 6(2):1035–1058, 2013.

[374] A. Nemirovski. Polynomial time methods in convex programming. In J. Renegar, M. Shub, and S. Smale, editors, *The Mathematics of Numerical Analysis*, volume 32, pages 543–589. AMS-SIAM Summer Seminar on Applied Mathematics, 1995.

[375] A. S. Nemirovski and D. B. Yudin. *Problem Complexity and Method Efficiency in Optimization*. Wiley-Interscience, New York, 1983.

[376] Y. Nesterov. A method for solving the convex programming problem with convergence rate $O(1/k^2)$. *Soviet Math. Dokl.*, 27(2):372–376, 1983.

[377] Y. Nesterov. Smooth minimization of non-smooth functions. *Math. Program.*, 103(1):127–152, 2005.

[378] Y. Nesterov. *Lectures on Convex Optimization*, volume 137 of *Springer Optimization and Its Applications*. Springer, Cham, 2nd edition, 2018.

[379] Y. Nesterov and A. Nemirovskii. *Interior-Point Polynomial Algorithms in Convex Programming*. Studies in Applied and Numerical Mathematics. Society for Industrial and Applied Mathematics, Philadelphia, PA, 1994.

[380] A. Nguyen, J. Yosinki, and J. Clune. Deep neural networks are easily fooled: high confidence predictions for unrecognizable images. In *2015 IEEE Conference on Computer Vision and Pattern Recognition (CVPR)*, pages 427–436, 2015.

[381] T. Nguyen and T. D. Tran. Exact recoverability from dense corrupted observations via ℓ_1-minimization. *IEEE Trans. Inf. Theory*, 59(4):2017–2035, 2013.

[382] D. G. Nishimura. *Principles of Magnetic Resonance Imaging*. Lulu Press, Raleigh, NC, 2010.

[383] J. Nocedal and S. J. Wright. *Numerical Optimization*. Springer Series in Operations Research and Financial Engineering. Springer, New York, NY, 2nd edition, 2006.

[384] G. Ongie, A. Jalal, C. A. Metzler, R. G. Baraniuk, A. G. Dimakis, and R. Willett. Deep learning techniques for inverse problems in imaging. *IEEE J. Sel. Areas Inf. Theory*, 1(1):39–56, 2020.

[385] M. Osborne, B. Presnell, and B. Turlach. A new approach to variable selection in least squares problems. *IMA J. Numer. Anal.*, 20(3):389–403, 2000.

[386] X. Pan, E. Y. Sidky, and M. Vannier. Why do commercial CT scanners still employ traditional, filtered back-projection for image reconstruction? *Inverse Problems*, 25(12):1230009, 2009.

[387] P. Petersen and F. Voigtlaender. Optimal approximation of piecewise smooth functions using deep ReLU neural networks. *Neural Networks*, 108:296–330, 2018.

[388] S. Petra and C. Schnörr. Average case recovery analysis of tomographic compressive sensing. *Linear Algebra Appl.*, 441:168–198, 2014.

[389] G. Peyré, J. Fadili, and J.-L. Starck. Learning the morphological diversity. *SIAM J. Imaging Sci.*, 3(3):646–669, 2010.

[390] A. Pinkus. Approximation theory of the MLP model in neural networks. *Acta Numer.*, 8:143–195, 1999.

[391] Y. Plan. *Compressed Sensing, Sparse Approximation, and Low-Rank Matrix Estimation*. PhD thesis, California Institute of Technology, 2011.

[392] T. Pock, D. Cremers, H. Bischof, and A. Chambolle. An algorithm for minimizing the Mumford–Shah functional. In *2009 IEEE 12th International Conference on Computer Vision*, pages 1133–1140, 2009.

[393] C. Poon. On the role of total variation in compressed sensing. *SIAM J. Imaging Sci.*, 8(1):682–720, 2015.

[394] C. Poon. Structure dependent sampling in compressed sensing: theoretical guarantees for tight frames. *Appl. Comput. Harmon. Anal.*, 42(3):402–451, 2017.

[395] C. Poon, N. Keriven, and G. Peyré. The geometry of off-the-grid compressed sensing. *arXiv:1802.08464*, 2018.

[396] D. Potts, G. Steidl, and M. Tasche. Fast Fourier Transforms for nonequispaced data: a tutorial. In J. J. Benedetto and P. J. S. G. Ferreira, editors, *Modern Sampling Theory*, Applied and Numerical Harmonic Analysis, pages 247–270. Birkhäuser, Boston, MA, 2001.

[397] K. P. Pruessmann, M. Weiger, M. B. Scheidigger, and P. Boesiger. SENSE: Sensitivity encoding for fast MRI. *Magn. Reson. Med.*, 42(5):952–962, 1999.

[398] G. Puy, M. E. Davies, and R. Gribonval. Recipes for stable linear embeddings from Hilbert spaces to $\mathbb{R}^m$. *IEEE Trans. Inf. Theory*, 63(4):2171–2187, 2017.

[399] G. Puy, J. P. Marques, R. Gruetter, J. Thiran, D. Van De Ville, P. Vandergheynst, and Y. Wiaux. Spread spectrum magnetic resonance imaging. *IEEE Trans. Med. Imag.*, 31(3):586–598, 2012.

[400] G. Puy, P. Vandergheynst, and Y. Wiaux. On variable density compressive sampling. *IEEE Signal Process. Lett.*, 18(10):595–598, 2011.

[401] X. Qu, Y. Chen, X. Zhuang, Z. Yan, D. Guo, and Z. Chen. Spread spectrum compressed sensing MRI using chirp radio frequency pulses. In *2016 IEEE International Conference on Acoustics, Speech and Signal Processing (ICASSP)*, pages 689–693, 2016.

[402] A. Raj, Y. Bresler, and B. Li. Improving robustness of deep-learning-based image reconstruction. In H. Daumé III and A. Singh, editors, *Proceedings of the 37th International Conference on Machine Learning*, volume 119 of *Proceedings of Machine Learning Research*, pages 7932–7942. PMLR, 2020.

[403] S. Ramani, Z. Liu, J. Rosen, J.-F. Nielsen, and J. A. Fessler. Regularization parameter selection for nonlinear iterative image restoration and MRI reconstruction using GCV and SURE-based methods. *IEEE Trans. Image Process.*, 21(8):3659–3672, 2012.

[404] H. Rauhut. Random sampling of sparse trigonometric polynomials. *Appl. Comput. Harmon. Anal.*, 22(1):16–42, 2007.

[405] H. Rauhut. Compressive sensing and structured random matrices. In M. Fornasier, editor, *Theoretical Foundations and Numerical Methods for Sparse Recovery*, volume 9 of *Radon Series in Computational and Applied Mathematics*, pages 1–92. de Gruyter, Berlin, 2010.

[406] H. Rauhut and R. Ward. Sparse recovery for spherical harmonic expansions. In *Proceedings of the 9th International Conference on Sampling Theory and Applications*, 2011.

[407] H. Rauhut and R. Ward. Sparse Legendre expansions via ℓ_1-minimization. *J. Approx. Theory*, 164(5):517–533, 2012.

[408] H. Rauhut and R. Ward. Interpolation via weighted ℓ_1 minimization. *Appl. Comput. Harmon. Anal.*, 40(2):321–351, 2016.

[409] S. Ravishankar and Y. Bresler. Adaptive sampling design for compressed sensing MRI. In *2011 Annual International Conference of the IEEE Engineering in Medicine and Biology Society*, pages 3751–3755, 2011.

[410] S. Ravishankar and Y. Bresler. MR image reconstruction from highly undersampled k-space data by dictionary learning. *IEEE Trans. Med. Imag.*, 30(5):1028–1041, 2011.

[411] S. Ravishankar, J. C. Ye, and J. A. Fessler. Image reconstruction: from sparsity to data-adaptive methods and machine learning. *Proc. IEEE*, 108(1):86–109, 2020.

[412] B. Recht, M. Fazel, and P. A. Parrilo. Guaranteed minimum-rank solutions of linear matrix equations via nuclear norm minimization. *SIAM Rev.*, 52(3):471–501, 2010.

[413] R. Reed. Pruning algorithms-a survey. *IEEE Trans. Neural Netw.*, 4(5):740–747, 1993.

[414] R. T. Rockafeller. *Convex Analysis*. Princeton Mathematical Series. Princeton University Press, Princeton, NJ, 1970.

[415] B. Roman, A. Bastounis, B. Adcock, and A. C. Hansen. On fundamentals of models and sampling in compressed sensing. *Preprint*, 2015.

[416] B. Roman, A. C. Hansen, and B. Adcock. On asymptotic structure in compressed sensing. *arXiv:1406.4178*, 2014.

[417] Y. Romano, M. Elad, and P. Milanfar. The little engine that could: Regularization by Denoising (RED). *SIAM J. Imaging Sci.*, 10(4):1804–1844, 2017.

[418] J. Romberg. Imaging via compressive sampling. *IEEE Signal Process. Mag.*, 25(2):14–20, 2008.

[419] J. Romberg. Compressive sensing by random convolution. *SIAM J. Imaging Sci.*, 2(4):1098–1128, 2009.

[420] O. Ronneberger, P. Fischer, and T. Brox. U-net: convolutional networks for biomedical image segmentation. In *International Conference on Medical Image Computing and Computer Assisted Intervention*, pages 234–241, 2015.

[421] S. Roth and M. J. Black. Field of experts. *Int. J. Comput. Vis.*, 82(2):205, 2009.

[422] V. Roulet and A. Boumal, N. d'Aspremont. Computational complexity versus statistical performance on sparse recovery problems. *Inf. Inference*, 9(1):1–32, 2020.

[423] M. Rudelson and R. Vershynin. On sparse reconstruction from Fourier and Gaussian measurements. *Comm. Pure Appl. Math.*, 61(8):1025–1045, 2008.

[424] L. I. Rudin, S. Osher, and E. Fatemi. Nonlinear total variation based noise removal algorithms. *Physica D*, 60(1–4):259–268, 1992.

[425] O. Russakovsky, J. Deng, H. Su, J. Krause, S. Satheesh, S. Ma, Z. Huang, A. Karpathy, A. Khosla, M. Bernstein, A. C. Berg, and F.-F. Li. Imagenet large scale visual recognition challenge. *Int. J. Comput. Vis.*, 115(3):211–252, 2015.

[426] C. M. Sandino, J. Y. Cheng, F. Chen, M. Mardani, J. M. Pauly, and S. S. Vasanawala. Compressed sensing: from research to clinical practice with deep neural networks. *IEEE Signal Process. Mag.*, 31(1):117–127, 2020.

[427] J. Schlemper, J. Caballero, J. V. Hajnal, A. Price, and D. Rueckert. A deep cascade of convolutional neural networks for MR image reconstruction. In M. Niethammer, M. Styner, S. Aylward, H. Zhu, I. Oguz, P.-T. Yap, and D. Shen, editors, *Information Processing in Medical Imaging*, volume 10265 of *Lecture Notes in Computer Science*, pages 647–658. Springer, Cham, 2017.

[428] J. Schmidhuber. Deep learning in neural networks: an overview. *Neural Networks*, 61:85–117, 2015.

[429] L. Schmidt, S. Santurkar, D. Tsipras, K. Talwar, and A. Madry. Adversarially robust generalization requires more data. In *Advances in Neural Information Processing Systems*, pages 5014–5026, 2018.

[430] P. Schniter and S. Rangan. Compressive phase retrieval via generalized approximate message passing. *IEEE Trans. Signal Process.*, 63(4):1043–1055, 2015.

[431] C. Schwab and J. Zech. Deep learning in high dimension: neural network expression rates for generalized polynomial chaos expansions in UQ. *Anal. Appl.*, 17(1):19–55, 2019.

[432] I. W. Selesnick, R. G. Baraniuk, and N. C. Kingsbury. The dual-tree complex wavelet transform. *IEEE Signal Process. Mag.*, 22(6):123–151, 2005.

[433] I. W. Selesnick and M. A. T. Figueiredo. Signal restoration with overcomplete wavelet transforms: comparison of analysis and synthesis priors. In V. K. Goyal, M. Papadakis, and D. V. D. Ville, editors, *Wavelets XIII*, volume 7446, pages 107–121. International Society for Optics and Photonics, SPIE, 2009.

[434] S. Setzer. Operator splittings, Bregman methods and frame shrinkage in image processing. *Int. J. Comput. Vis.*, 92(3):265–280, 2011.

[435] M. Sharif, S. Bhagavatula, L. Bauer, and M. K. Reiter. Accessorize to a crime: real and stealthy attacks on state-of-the-art face recognition. In *Proceedings of the 2016 ACM SIGSAC Conference on Computer and Communications Security*, pages 1528–1540. Association for Computing Machinery, 2016.

[436] C. Shen, D. Nguyen, Z. Zhou, S. B. Jiang, B. Dong, and X. Jia. An introduction to deep learning in medical physics: advantages, potential, and challenges. *Phys. Med. Biol.*, 65(5):05TR01, 2020.

[437] L. A. Shepp and B. F. Logan. The Fourier reconstruction of a head section. *IEEE Trans. Nucl. Sci.*, 21(3):21–43, 1974.

[438] P. J. Shin, P. E. Z. Larson, M. A. Ohliger, M. Elad, J. M. Pauly, D. B. Vigneron, and M. Lustig. Calibrationless parallel imaging reconstruction based on structured low-rank matrix completion. *Magn. Reson. Med.*, 72(4):959–970, 2014.

[439] E. Y. Sidky, C. M. Kao, and X. Pan. Accurate image reconstruction from few-views and limited-angle data in divergent-beam CT. *J. X-Ray. Sci. Technol.*, 14(2):119–139, 2006.

[440] E. Y. Sidky and X. Pan. Image reconstruction in circular cone-beam computed tomography by constrained, total-variation minimization. *Phys. Med. Biol.*, 53(17):4777–4807, 2008.

[441] A. Sinha, H. Namkoong, and J. Duchi. Certifying some distributional robustness with principled adversarial training. *arXiv:1710.10571*, 2017.

[442] V. Sinha. Iterative reconstruction with ZEISS OptiRecon. `www.zeiss.com/microscopy/int/about-us/press-releases/2018/zeiss-optirecon.html`, April 2018.

[443] D. Slepian. Prolate spheroidal wave functions, Fourier analysis, and uncertainty — V: the discrete case. *Bell Syst. Tech. J.*, 57(5):1371–1430, 1978.

[444] S. Smale. Complexity theory and numerical analysis. *Acta Numer.*, 6:523–551, 1997.

[445] S. Smale. Mathematical problems for the next century. *Math. Intelligencer*, 20(2):7–15, 1998.

[446] S. Som and P. Schniter. Compressive imaging using approximate message passing and a Markov-tree prior. *IEEE Trans. Signal Process.*, 60(7):3439–3448, 2012.

[447] G. Song and A. Gelb. Approximating the inverse frame operator from localized frames. *Appl. Comput. Harmon. Anal.*, 35(1):94–110, 2013.

[448] J.-L. Starck, F. Murtagh, and J. Fadili. *Sparse Image and Signal Processing: Wavelets and Related Geometric Multiscale Analysis*. Cambridge University Press, Cambridge, 2nd edition, 2015.

[449] G. Strang and G. Fix. A Fourier analysis of the finite element variational method. In G. Geymonat, editor, *Constructive Aspect of Functional Analysis*, volume 57 of *C.I.M.E. Summer Schools*, pages 793–840. Springer, Berlin, 1971.

[450] G. Strang and T. Nguyen. *Wavelets and Filter Banks*. Wellesley–Cambridge Press, Wellesley, MA, 1996.

[451] T. Strohmer. Measure what should be measured: progress and challenges in compressive sensing. *IEEE Signal Process. Lett.*, 19(12):887–893, 2012.

[452] C. Studer, P. Kuppinger, G. Pope, and H. Bölcskei. Recovery of sparsely corrupted signals. *IEEE Trans. Inf. Theory*, 58(5):3115–3130, 2012.

[453] V. Studer, J. Bobin, M. Chahid, H. Moussavi, E. J. Candès, and M. Dahan. Compressive fluorescence microscopy for biological and hyperspectral imaging. *Proc. Natl. Acad. Sci. USA*, 109(26):1679–1687, 2011.

[454] C. Szegedy, W. Zaremba, I. Sutskever, J. Bruna, D. Erhan, I. J. Goodfellow, and R. Fergus. Intriguing properties of neural networks. *arXiv:1312.6199*, 2013.

[455] G. Tang, B. N. Bhaskar, P. Shah, and B. Recht. Compressed sensing off the grid. *IEEE Trans. Inf. Theory*, 59(11):7465–7490, 2013.

[456] K. C. Tezcan, C. F. Baumgartner, R. Luechinger, K. P. Pruessmann, and E. Konukoglu. MR image reconstruction using deep density priors. *IEEE Trans. Med. Imag.*, 38(7):1633–1642, 2019.

[457] L. Thesing, V. Antun, and A. C. Hansen. What do AI algorithms actually learn? – on false structures in deep learning. *arXiv:1906.01478*, 2019.

[458] L. Thesing and A. C. Hansen. Non-uniform recovery guarantees for binary measurements and infinite-dimensional compressed sensing. *arXiv:1909.01143*, 2019.

[459] S. Thys, W. Van Ranst, and T. Goedemé. Fooling automated surveillance cameras: adversarial patches to attack person detection. In *2019 IEEE/CVF Conference on Computer Vision and Pattern Recognition Workshops (CVPRW)*, pages 49–55, 2019.

[460] R. Tibshirani. Regression shrinkage and selection via the lasso. *J. R. Statist. Soc. B.*, 58(1):267–288, 1996.

[461] A. M. Tillmann and M. E. Pfetsch. The computational complexity of the restricted isometry property, the nullspace property, and related concepts in compressed sensing. *IEEE Trans. Inf. Theory*, 60(2):1248–1259, 2014.

[462] C. Trabelsi, O. Bilaniuk, D. Serdyuk, S. Subramanian, J. F. Santos, S. Mehri, N. Rostamzadeh, Y. Bengio, and C. J. Pal. Deep complex networks. *arXiv:1705.09792*, 2017.

[463] F. Tramèr, A. Kurakin, N. Papernot, I. Goodfellow, D. Boneh, and P. McDaniel. Ensemble adversarial training: attacks and defenses. *arXiv:1705.07204*, 2017.

[464] H. Tran and C. Webster. A class of null space conditions for sparse recovery via nonconvex, non-separable minimizations. *Results Appl. Math.*, 3:100011, 2019.

[465] Y. Traonmilin and R. Gribonval. Stable recovery of low-dimensional cones in Hilbert spaces: one RIP to rule them all. *Appl. Comput. Harmon. Anal.*, 45(1):170–205, 2018.

[466] Y. Traonmilin, G. Puy, R. Gribonval, and M. E. Davies. Compressed sensing in Hilbert spaces. In H. Boche, G. Caire, R. Calderbank, M. März, G. Kutyniok, and R. Mathar, editors, *Compressed Sensing and its Applications: Second International MATHEON Conference 2015*, Applied and Numerical Harmonic Analysis, pages 359–384. Birkhäuser, Cham, 2017.

[467] J. A. Tropp. Recovery of short, complex linear combinations via l_1 minimization. *IEEE Trans. Inf. Theory*, 51(4):1568–1570, 2005.

[468] J. A. Tropp. Just relax: convex programming methods for identifying sparse signals in noise. *IEEE Trans. Inf. Theory*, 52(3):1030–1051, 2006.

[469] J. A. Tropp, A. C. Gilbert, and M. J. Strauss. Algorithms for simultaneous sparse approximation. Part II: Convex relaxation. *Signal Process.*, 86(3):589–602, 2006.

[470] Y. Tsaig and D. L. Donoho. Extensions of compressed sensing. *Signal Process.*, 86(3):549–571, 2006.

[471] P. Tseng. On accelerated proximal gradient methods for convex-concave optimization. *Preprint*, 2008.

[472] A. M. Turing. On computable numbers, with an application to the Entscheidungsproblem. *Proc. Lond. Math. Soc.*, s2-42(1):230–265, 1937.

[473] M. Uecker. Parallel magnetic resonance imaging. *arXiv:1501.06209*, 2015.

[474] M. Unser. A representer theorem for deep neural networks. *J. Mach. Learn. Res.*, 20(110):1–30, 2019.

[475] S. van de Geer. *Estimation and Testing Under Sparsity: École d'Été de Probabilités de Saint-Flour XLV – 2015*, volume 2159 of *Lecture Notes in Mathematics*. Springer, Cham, 2016.

[476] S. A. van de Geer and P. Bühlmann. On the conditions used to prove oracle results for the Lasso. *Electron. J. Stat.*, 3:1360–1392, 2009.

[477] E. van den Berg and M. P. Friedlander. Probing the Pareto frontier for basis pursuit solutions. *SIAM J. Sci. Comput.*, 31(2):890–912, 2009.

[478] E. van den Berg and M. P. Friedlander. Theoretical and empirical results for recovery from multiple measurements. *IEEE Trans. Inf. Theory*, 56(5):2516–2527, 2010.

[479] S. S. Vasanwala, M. J. Murphy, M. T. Alley, P. Lai, K. Keutzer, J. M. Pauly, and M. Lustig. Practical parallel imaging compressed sensing MRI: summary of two years of experience in accelerating body MRI of pediatric patients. In *2011 IEEE International Symposium on Biomedical Imaging: From Nano to Macro*, pages 1039–1043, 2011.

[480] V. Velisavljevic, B. Beferull-Lozano, M. Vetterli, and P. L. Dragotti. Directionlets: anisotropic multidirectional representation with separable filtering. *IEEE Trans. Image Process.*, 15(7):1916–1933, 2006.

[481] S. V. Venkatakrishnan, C. A. Bouman, and B. Wohlberg. Plug-and-play priors for model based reconstruction. In *2013 IEEE Global Conference on Signal and Information Processing*, pages 945–948, 2013.

[482] R. Vidal, J. Bruna, R. Giryes, and S. Soatto. Mathematics of deep learning. *arXiv:1712.04721*, 2017.

[483] M. Vidyasagar. *An Introduction to Compressed Sensing*. Society for Industrial and Applied Mathematics, Philadelphia, PA, 2019.

[484] I. Waldspurger, A. d'Aspremont, and S. Mallat. Phase recovery, MaxCut and complex semidefinite programming. *Math. Program.*, 149(1):47–81, 2015.

[485] J. L. Walsh. A closed set of normal orthogonal functions. *Amer. J. Math.*, 45(1):5–24, 1923.

[486] G. Wang, J. C. Ye, K. Mueller, and J. A. Fessler. Image reconstruction is a new frontier of machine learning. *IEEE Trans. Med. Imag.*, 37(6):1289–1296, 2018.

[487] H. Wang, G. Li, and G. Jiang. Robust regression shrinkage and consistent variable selection through the LAD-Lasso. *J. Bus. Econom. Statist.*, 25(3):347–355, 2007.

[488] H. Wang and C.-N. Yu. A direct approach to robust deep learning using adversarial networks. *arXiv:1905.09591*, 2019.

[489] S. Wang, S. Fidler, and R. Urtasun. Proximal deep structured models. In *Advances in Neural Information Processing Systems*, pages 865–873, 2016.

[490] Z. Wang and G. R. Arce. Variable density compressed image sampling. *IEEE Trans. Image Process.*, 19(1):264–270, 2010.

[491] Z. Wang and A. C. Bovik. Mean squared error: love it or leave it? A new look at signal fidelity measures. *IEEE Signal Process. Mag.*, 26(1):98–117, 2009.

[492] D. S. Weller, J. R. Polimeni, L. Grady, L. L. Wald, E. Adalsteinsson, and V. K. Goyal. Sparsity-promoting calibration for GRAPPA accelerated parallel MRI reconstruction. *IEEE Trans. Med. Imag.*, 32(7):1325–1335, 2013.

[493] B. Wen, S. Ravishankar, L. Pfister, and Y. Bresler. Transform learning for magnetic resonance image reconstruction: from model-based learning to building neural networks. *IEEE Signal Process. Mag.*, 37(1):41–53, 2020.

[494] Z. Wen, W. Yin, D. Goldfarb, and Y. Zhang. A fast algorithm for sparse reconstruction based on shrinkage, subspace optimization, and continuation. *SIAM J. Sci. Comput.*, 32(4):1832–1857, 2010.

[495] Y. Wiaux, L. Jacques, G. Puy, A. M. M. Scaife, and P. Vandergheynst. Compressed sensing imaging techniques for radio interferometry. *Mon. Not. R. Astron. Soc.*, 395(3):1733–1742, 2009.

[496] R. M. Willett. The dark side of image reconstruction: emerging methods for photon-limited imaging. *SIAM News*, October 2014.

[497] R. M. Willett, R. F. Marcia, and J. M. Nichols. Compressed sensing for practical optical imaging systems: a tutorial. *Opt. Eng.*, 50(7):072601, 2011.

[498] R. M. Willett and R. D. Nowak. Platelets: a multiscale approach for recovering edges and surfaces in photon-limited medical imaging. *IEEE Trans. Med. Imag.*, 22(3):332–350, 2003.

[499] R. R. Wiyatno, A. Xu, O. Dia, and A. de Berker. Adversarial examples in modern machine learning: a review. *arXiv:1911.05268*, 2019.

[500] B. Wohlberg. Efficient algorithms for convolutional sparse representations. *IEEE Trans. Image Process.*, 25(1):301–315, 2016.

[501] P. Wojtaszczyk. *A Mathematical Introduction to Wavelets*. Cambridge University Press, Cambridge, 1997.

[502] P. Wojtaszczyk. Stability and instance optimality for Gaussian measurements in compressed sensing. *Found. Comput. Math.*, 10(1):1–13, 2010.

[503] E. Wong, F. Schmidt, J. H. Metzen, and J. Z. Kolter. Scaling provable adversarial defenses. In *Advances in Neural Information Processing Systems*, pages 8400–8409, 2018.

[504] J. Woodworth and R. Chartrand. Compressed sensing recovery via nonconvex shrinkage penalties. *Inverse Problems*, 32(7):075004, 2016.

[505] J. Wright and Y. Ma. Dense correction via ℓ_1-minimization. *IEEE Trans. Inf. Theory*, 56(7):3540–3560, 2010.

[506] S. J. Wright, R. D. Nowak, and M. A. T. Figueiredo. Sparse reconstruction by separable approximation. *IEEE Trans. Signal Process.*, 57(7):2479–2493, 2009.

[507] B. Wu, R. P. Millane, R. Watts, and P. Bones. Applying compressed sensing in parallel MRI. In *Proc. Intl. Soc. Mag. Reson. Med.*, 2008.

[508] C. Xiao, B. Li, J. yan Zhu, W. He, M. Liu, and D. Song. Generating adversarial examples with adversarial networks. In *Proceedings of the Twenty-Seventh International Joint Conference on Artificial Intelligence, IJCAI-18*, pages 3905–3911. International Joint Conferences on Artificial Intelligence Organization, 7 2018.

[509] J. Xu. *Parameter estimation, model selection and inferences in L1-based linear regression.* PhD thesis, Columbia University, 2005.

[510] J. Xu and Z. Ying. Simultaneous estimation and variable selection in median regression using Lasso-type penalty. *Ann. Inst. Statist. Math.*, 62(3):487–514, 2010.

[511] W. Xu, D. Evans, and Y. Qi. Feature squeezing: detecting adversarial examples in deep neural networks. *arXiv:1704.01155*, 2017.

[512] G. Yang, S. Yu, H. Dong, G. Slabaugh, P. L. Dragotti, X. Ye, F. Liu, S. Arridge, J. Keegan, Y. Guo, and D. Firmin. DAGAN: deep de-aliasing generative adversarial networks for fast compressed sensing MRI reconstruction. *IEEE Trans. Med. Imag.*, 37(6):1310–1321, 2018.

[513] J. Yang and J. Zhang. Alternating direction algorithms for ℓ_1-problems in compressive sensing. *SIAM J. Sci. Comput.*, 33(1):250–278, 2011.

[514] Y. Yang, J. Sun, H. Li, and Z. Xu. Deep ADMM-Net for compressive sensing MRI. In *Advances in Neural Information Processing Systems*, pages 10–18, 2016.

[515] Y. Yang, J. Sun, H. Li, and Z. Xu. ADMM-CSNet: a deep learning approach for image compressive sensing. *IEEE Trans. Pattern Anal. Machine Intell.*, 42(3):521–538, 2020.

[516] D. Yarotsky. Error bounds for approximations with deep ReLU networks. *Neural Networks*, 94:103–114, 2017.

[517] D. Yarotsky. Optimal approximation of continuous functions by very deep ReLU networks. In S. Bubeck, V. Perchet, and P. Rigollet, editors, *Proceedings of the 31st Conference On Learning Theory*, volume 75 of *Proceedings of Machine Learning Research*, pages 639–649. PMLR, 2018.

[518] P. Yin, Y. Lou, Q. He, and J. Xin. Minimization of ℓ_{1-2} for compressed sensing. *SIAM J. Sci. Comput.*, 37(1):A536–A563, 2015.

[519] L. Ying and J. Sheng. Joint image reconstruction and sensitivity estimation in SENSE (JSENSE). *Magn. Reson. Med.*, 57(6):1196–1202, 2007.

[520] H. Zhang and B. Dong. A review on deep learning in medical image reconstruction. *J. Oper. Res. Soc. China*, 8(2):311–340, 2020.

[521] J. Zhang and B. Ghanem. ISTA-Net: interpretable optimization-inspired deep network for image compressive sensing. In *2018 IEEE/CVF Conference on Computer Vision and Pattern Recognition*, pages 1828–1837, 2018.

[522] K. Zhang, W. Zuo, Y. Chen, D. Meng, and L. Zhang. Beyond a Gaussian denoiser: residual learning of deep CNN for image denoising. *IEEE Trans. Image Process.*, 26(7):3142–3155, 2017.

[523] R. Zhang and S. Li. Optimal D-RIP bounds in compressed sensing. *Acta Math. Sin. (Engl. Ser.)*, 31(5):755–766, 2015.

[524] X. Zhang, M. Burger, and S. Osher. A unified primal-dual algorithm framework based on Bregman iteration. *J. Sci. Comput.*, 46(1):20–46, 2011.

[525] Y. T. Zhou, R. Chellappa, A. Vaid, and B. K. Jenkin. Image restoration using a neural network. *IEEE Trans. Acoust., Speech, Signal Process.*, 36(7):1141–1151, 1988.

[526] Z. Zhou and A. M. So. A unified approach to error bounds for structured convex optimization problems. *Math. Program.*, 165(2):689–728, 2017.

[527] B. Zhu, J. Z. Liu, S. F. Cauley, B. R. Rosen, and M. S. Rosen. Image reconstruction by domain-transform manifold learning. *Nature*, 555(7697):487–492, 2018.

[528] L. Zhu, W. Zhang, D. Elnatan, and B. Huang. Faster STORM using compressed sensing. *Nat. Methods*, 9(7):721–723, 2012.

Index